BRITISH ATHLETICS 2002

Compiled by the
National Union of Track Statisticians

Editors: Rob Whittingham & Peter Matthews

Assistant Editors: Tony Miller, Ian Hodge and Martin Rix

Published by: Umbra Athletics Limited,
Unit 1 Bredbury Business Park,
Bredbury Park Way, Bredbury, Stockport, SK6 2SN
Tel: 0161 406 6320 Fax: 0161 406 6732

ISBN 0 9540390 1 7

Front Cover: Jonathan Edwards, gold medal winner in Edmonton and the four British women who have set records this year - Paula Radcliffe, Susan Jones, Janine Whitlock and Lorraine Shaw

Photos: All photographs provided by Mark Shearman,
22, Grovelands Road, Purley, Surrey, CR8 4LA
Tel: 020 8660 0156 Fax: 020 8660 3437
His help is greatly appreciated

Distributed by: Umbra Athletics Limited,
Unit 1 Bredbury Business Park,
Bredbury Park Way, Bredbury, Stockport, SK6 2SN
Tel: 0161 406 6320 Fax: 0161 406 6732

Printed in Great Britain by: Clowes Group,
Beccles, Suffolk, NR34 9QE

CONTENTS

National Union of Track Statisticians and Compilers 4
Abbreviations 4
Venues 5
Introduction (*by Rob Whittingham*) 6
Athletics Addresses 7
Major Outdoor Fixtures in 2002 8
Best Authentic Performances Men 9
Best Authentic Performances Women 16
National Records of the United Kingdom Men 23
National Records of the United Kingdom Women 27
UK Indoor Records 31
UK All Time Men 32
UK All Time Under 23 Men 50
UK All Time Under 20 Men 53
UK All Time Under 17 Men 58
UK All Time Under 15 Men 63
UK All Time Under 13 Men 66
UK All Time Women 68
UK All Time Under 23 Women 84
UK All Time Under 20 Women 87
UK All Time Under 17 Women 92
UK All Time Under 15 Women 96
UK All Time Under 13 Women 98
UK Club Relay Records 101
Major International Matches & Championships in 2001 102
Regional Championships 132
Area Championships 133
AAA Age Championships 134
UK Merit Rankings (*by Peter Matthews*) 135
2001 Men's Lists 158
2001 Women's Lists 260
Colour Plates 256/257
Men's Index 350
Women's Index 384
Obituaries 411
Amendments to 2001 Annual 413
World Youth Championships 414
Other Publications 415

NATIONAL UNION OF TRACK STATISTICIANS AND COMPILERS

Annual

General Editors - Rob Whittingham, Peter Matthews

Assistant Editors - Ian Hodge, Tony Miller, Martin Rix

Records - Bob Sparks All Time Lists and Index - Martin Rix, Tony Miller

Results - Brian Hatch, Brian Webster and Peter Matthews

Men's Lists - Ian Hodge (HJ, PV and overall), Joe Barrass (sprints), Tim Grose (800m to 10,000m), John Walsh (Marathon), Shirley Hitchcock (Hurdles), Bill Myers (LJ, TJ),Tony O'Neill (throws).

Under 20 & Under 17 Men - Ian Hodge with above compilers

Under 15 Men - Ian Hodge Under 13 Men - Liz Smart

Women's Lists - Tony Miller (including U17), Peter Martin (including U20), Bill Green (U15 & U13)

Walks - John Powell Relays - Keith Morbey Multi-Events - Alan Lindop

Also acknowledgements for specific help to Arnold Black (Scotland), John Glover and Alan Keys (Northern Ireland) and various other NUTS members.

ABBREVIATIONS & NOTES

A - mark set at altitude over 1000m
a - automatic timing only known to one tenth of a second
D - performance made in a Decathlon
dh - downhill
e - estimated time
et - extra trial
ex - exhibition
h - heat
H - performance made in a Heptathlon
hc - handicap race
i - indoor
jo - jump off
m - position in race when intermediate time taken
mx - performance in mixed race
O - performance made in an Octathlon
o - over age
P - performance made in a Pentathlon
Q - qualifying round
q - quarter final
r - race number
s - semi final
t - track
u - unofficial time
un - unconfirmed performance
w - wind assisted (> 2.0 m/sec)
W - wind assisted (over 4m/sec in decathlon/heptathlon)
x - relay team may include outside age-group members
+ - intermediate time
* - legal performance where best is wind assisted
" - photo electric cell time
- Unratified (may not be ratifiable)
& - as yet unratified
§ - now competes for another nation
¶ - drugs ban (as per IAAF)

AGE GROUP DESIGNATIONS

U13 - Under 13	(born 1.9.88 or later)	U15 - Under 15	(born 1.9.86 to 31.8.88)
U17 - Under 17	(born 1.9.84 to 31.8.86)	U20 - Under 20	(born 1.1.82 to 31.8.84)
Vxx - Veteran	(age 40 or over Men)	Vxx - Veteran	(age 35 or over Women)

Care must be taken with very young age groups for athletes with an unknown date of birth from Northern Ireland since their age groups differ slightly.

Italics indicates the athlete competes for a British club but is not eligible to represent Britain.

MULTI - EVENTS

Pentathlon, Heptathlon and Decathlon lists show the complete breakdown of individual performances in the following order:

Pentathlon (women) - 100mH, SP, HJ, LJ, 800m; Junior: LJ, SP, 75mH, HJ, 800m
Heptathlon (women) - 100mH, HJ, SP, 200m (1st day); LJ, JT, 800m (2nd day) (80mH - Inters)
Decathlon (men) - 100m, LJ, SP, HJ, 400m (1st day); 110mH, DT, PV, JT, 1500m (2nd day)

Totals which include performances made with following winds in excess of 4 m/s are denoted by W. The date shown is the second day of competition.

RANKING LISTS:

These show the best performances in each event recorded during the 2001 season. For each performance the following details are shown:

Performance; wind reading (where appropriate); name (with, where appropriate, age-group category); date of birth (DDMMYY); position in competition; venue; date.

The following numbers are used, although strength of performance or lack of information may vary the guidelines -

50 perfomances 100 athletes for each standard event

Age Groups - 40 Under 20, 30 Under 17, 20 Under 15, 10 Under 13

In the junior men, athletes are shown in older age groups if their performances merit this, e.g. an U15 can appear in the U17 list etc. For junior women, athletes are shown in their age group as per womens rules, although juniors of any age will be shown in the main list on merit.

INDEX

Club details and previous personal bests, where better than those recorded in 2001, are shown in the index for all athletes in the main lists.

VENUES

Tim Grose has done major research on all British Tracks and a full list was shown in the 2000 annual; this list will be repeated in some subsequent annuals - full details at www.runtrackdir.com

(London tracks for clarification)

LONDON (B)	Barn Elms Sports Ground, Rocks Lane, Barnes (6L, 8S)
LONDON (BP)	Battersea Park
LONDON (Cat)	Ladywell Arena, Silvermere Road, Catford (6L, 8S)
LONDON (Col)	Metropolitan Police (Hendon) Track, Hendon Police Training Coll, Colindale (6L, 6S)
LONDON (CP)	Crystal Palace National Sports Centre, Ledrington Road
LONDON (Cr)	Croydon Sports Arena, Albert Road
LONDON (DC)	Dulwich College, College Road, Dulwich (300m, 6L, 6S)
LONDON (Elt)	Sutcliffe Park, Eltham Road (6L, 8S)
LONDON (FP)	Finsbury Park, Endymion Road (6L, 10S)
LONDON (Ha)	New River Sports Centre, White Hart Lane, Wood Green, Haringey
LONDON (He)	Barnet Copthall Stadium, Great North Way, Hendon
LONDON (ME)	Mile End Stadium, Rhodeswell Road
LONDON (Nh)	Terence McMillan Stadium, Newham Leisure Centre, Plaistow
LONDON (Pa)	Paddington Recreation Ground, Randolph Avenue (6L, 6S)
LONDON (PH)	Parliament Hill Fields, Highgate Road, Hampstead
LONDON (SP)	Southwark Park, Hawkstone Road, Surrey Quays (7L, 7S)
LONDON (TB)	Tooting Bec Athletics Track, Tooting Bec Road
LONDON (WF)	Waltham Forest Track, Chingford Road, Walthamstow
LONDON (Wil)	Willesden Sports Stadium, Donnington Road (6L, 8S)
LONDON (WL)	Linford Christie Stadium, Du Cane Road, West London
LONDON (WP)	Wimbledon Park, Home Park Road (6L, 8S)

INTRODUCTION - by Rob Whittingham

This year has been one with varying success for athletics at the very top level. Only two medals in the World Championships in Edmonton brought the immediate tabloid headlines of the imminent decline of British athletics. The top junior athletes performed very well at international level and the potential for keeping Britain as a top athletic nation is still there. However, the top level is so competitive that a couple of injuries to key athletes can give the perception of athletics failing. I do not agree with this, but it is unfortunate that government funding often depends on the number of medals won at the last international competition. This year's European Championships and Commonwealth Games should give many athletes their chance to shine.

As ever, the annual is only possible through huge efforts from many people. Peter Matthews continues to dedicate a large amount of his time to ensure accuracy and completeness and Tony Miller has made an extraordinary contribution in the women's section. Again all the compilers for the junior age groups have done a great job in what can sometimes be difficult conditions. Brian Hatch has done such a good job on the results section I have had to expand this area.

The book would not be be possible without help from all the Umbra staff, Mary has done a great deal of input to the database and Julie Fletcher now plays a significant role in all areas of the book production. Marty still assists and encourages me with my time consuming 'hobby'.

I continue to receive support from UK Athletics and also work with them on www.ukathletics.net, the web site for British athletics.

I have made only minor changes to the format of the book. These include the adoption of the IOC/IAAF standard abbreviations for countries eg.

IRL Ireland NED Holland SUI Switzerland ESP Spain etc.

I have also added page headers to most sections to allow easier navigation. Peter Matthews has provided an obituaries section and I have included the IAAF world rankings in Peter's merit lists.

As usual any corrections are always welcome.

Rob Whittingham
March 2002

7 Birch Green Glossop SK13 8PR
e-mail rob@umbra.co.uk

UK ATHLETICS AND OTHER ADDRESSES

UK Athletics
Athletics House
10 Harborne Road
Edgbaston
Birmingham B15 3AA
Tel: 0121 456 5098

SCOTLAND

Scotland A.F.
Caledonia House
Reheughs Rigg, South Gyle
Edinburgh EH12 9DQ
Tel: 0131 317 7320

NORTHERN IRELAND

Northern Ireland A.A.F.
Honorary Secretary: J.Allen
Athletics House
Old Coach Road
Belfast BT9 5PR
Tel: 02890 602707

North of England A.A.
Studio 106, EMCO House
5/7 New York Road
Leeds LS2 7PJ
Tel: 01532 461835

Commonwealth Games Councils:
England
General Secretary: Miss A.Hogbin
Tavistock House South, Tavistock Square
London WC1H 9JZ
Tel: 0207 388 6643

Scotland
Honorary Secretary: G.A.Hunter OBE
139 Old Dalkeith Road
Little France
Edinburgh EH16 4SZ
Tel: 0131 664 1070

British Athletics League
Honorary Secretary: D. Jeacock
16 Church Street
Wotton Bassett
Wilts SN4 7BQ

Supporters Club - British Athletics Club
Honorary Secretary: Mrs M.Pieri
11 Railway Road
Newbury, Berks RG14 7PE
Tel: 01635 33400

Athletics Weekly
Editor: Nigel Walsh
Descartes Publishing Limited
83 Park Road, Peterborough PE1 2TN
Tel: 01733 898440

AAA of England
Edgbaston House
3 Duchess Place
Hagley Road
Birmingham B16 8NM
Tel: 0121 452 1500

WALES

A.A. of Wales
Catash Road
Catash
Newport NP18 1WA
Tel: 01633 423833

Midland Counties A.A.
11th Floor Edgbaston House
3 Duchess Place
Hagley Road
Birmingham
B16 8NM
Tel: 0121 456 1896

South of England A.A.
23 Mitcham Lane
Streatham
London SW16 6LQ
Tel: 0208 664 7244

Northern Ireland
Honorary Secretary: R.J.McColgan MBE
22 Mountcoole Park, Cave Hill
Belfast BT14 8JR
Tel: 01232 716558

Wales
Honorary Secretary: M.John MBE
Pennant
Blaenau, Ammanford
Dyfed SA18 3BZ
Tel: 0269 850390

National Young Athletes' League
Honorary Secretary: N. Bailey
15 Chaseley Avenue
Cannock
Staffs WS11 1JG
Tel: 01543 574624

Sports Council
The Sports Council
16 Upper Woburn Place
London WC1H OQP
Tel: 0171 388 1277

National Union of Track Statisticians
Secretary: Dr. S. Hitchcock
54 Woodbury Avenue
Petersfield GU32 2EB
Tel: 01730 260278

MAJOR OUTDOOR FIXTURES IN 2002

MAY

4-6	British Universities Championships	Bedford
11-12	County Championships	Various
11-12	Scottish District Championships	Various
18	Aqua-Pura International	Loughborough
25-26	CAU Inter Counties Championships	Bedford

JUNE

4	Bedford International Games	Bedford
8	Northern Ireland Championships	Belfast
8-9	Scottish Championships	Scotstoun, Glasgow
8-9	Welsh Championships	Newport
15	English County Schools Championships	Various
15-16	Aqua-Pura Commonwealth Games Trials	Manchester
22-23	SPAR European Cup Super League	Annecy, FRA
29-30	Norwich Union AAA U23 & U20 Champs	Bedford
29-30	European Cup Combined Events – Men, Women	Slovenia(M) Poland(W)
30	Norwich Union Classic GP II	Sheffield

JULY

6	Throws International	Verazdin, HUN
6	GBR v ITA v ESP U20	Gorizia, ITA
8	Welsh Games	Cardiff
12-13	English Schools Championships	Nottingham
12-14	Norwich Union European Trials & AAA Champs	Birmingham
16-21	World Junior Championships	Kingston, JAM
19	Dublin Games	Dublin, IRL
20	GBR v GER U23	Liverpool
26-31	Commonwealth Games (athletics)	Manchester

AUGUST

3	GBR v FRA v ESP U23	Albertville, FRA
3-4	GBR v SUI v SUI Combined Events	Rapperswil, SUI
6-11	European Championships	Munich, GER
10-11	AAA U17 & U15 Championships	Crystal Palace, London
18	Norwich Union Challenge GBR v USA v RUS	Scotstoun, Glasgow
23	Norwich Union British Grand Prix	Crystal Palace, London
24	Throws International	Nitra, SVK
31	U19 International	Namur, BEL

SEPTEMBER

8	AAA 10km Road Championships	Bradford
14	IAAF Grand Prix Final	Paris, FRA
20-21	IAAF World Cup	Madrid, ESP

OCTOBER

6	The Great North Run	Tyneside
12-13	IAAF World Walking Cup	Turin, ITA
26	AAAoE Road Relay Championships	Sutton Park, Birmingham

DECEMBER

8	European Cross Country Championships	Medulin, CRO

RECORDS - MEN

as at 31 December 2001

W = World, E = European, C = Commonwealth, A = UK All-Comers, N = UK, J = Junior

100m	W	9.79		Maurice Greene	USA	16	Jun	99	Athens
	E,N	9.87		Linford Christie		15	Aug	93	Stuttgart
	C	9.84		Donovan Bailey	CAN	27	Jul	96	Atlanta
		9.84		Bruny Surin	CAN	22	Aug	99	Seville
	A	9.97		Maurice Greene	USA	7	Aug	99	London (CP)
	WJ	10.05	#	Davidson Ezinwa	NGR	4	Jan	90	Bauchi
	WJ,EJ,NJ	10.06		Dwain Chambers		25	Jul	97	Ljubljana
200m	W	19.32		Michael Johnson	USA	1	Aug	96	Atlanta
	E	19.72	A	Pietro Mennea	ITA	12	Sep	79	Mexico City
	C	19.68		Frank Fredericks	NAM	1	Aug	96	Atlanta
	A	19.85		Michael Johnson	USA	6	Jul	90	Edinburgh
	N	19.87	A#	John Regis		31	Jul	94	Sestriere
		19.94		John Regis		20	Aug	93	Stuttgart
	WJ	20.07	#	Lorenzo Daniel	USA	18	May	85	Starkville
		20.13		Roy Martin	USA	16	Jun	85	Indianapolis
	EJ,NJ	20.29		Christian Malcolm		19	Sep	98	Kuala Lumpur
300m	W	30.85	A	Michael Johnson	USA	24	Mar	00	Pretoria
	E,C,A,N	31.56		Doug Walker	Sco	19	Jul	98	Gateshead
	WJ	32.08	+	Steve Lewis	USA	28	Sep	88	Seoul
	EJ,NJ	32.53		Mark Richardson		14	Jul	91	London (Ha)
400m	W	43.18		Michael Johnson	USA	26	Aug	99	Seville
	E	44.33		Thomas Schönlebe	GER	3	Sep	87	Rome
	C	44.17		Innocent Egbunike	NGR	19	Aug	87	Zürich
	A	43.98		Michael Johnson	USA	10	Jul	92	London (CP)
	N	44.36		Iwan Thomas		13	Jul	97	Birmingham
	WJ	43.87		Steve Lewis	USA	28	Sep	88	Seoul
	EJ	45.01		Thomas Schönlebe	GER	15	Jul	84	Berlin
	NJ	45.36		Roger Black		24	Aug	85	Cottbus
600m	W	1:12.81		Johnny Gray	USA	24	May	86	Santa Monica
	E	1:14.41		Andrea Longo	ITA	30	Aug	00	Roverto
	C	1:13.2		John Kipkurgat	KEN	23	Mar	74	Pointe-à-Pierre
	A,N	1:14.95		Steve Heard		14	Jul	91	London (Ha)
	WJ	1:14.8	A	Mark Winzenreid	USA	31	Aug	68	Echo Summit
	NJ	1:16.79		Andrew Lill		24	Jul	90	Mansfield
800m	W,E	1:41.11		Wilson Kipketer	DEN	24	Aug	97	Cologne
	C,N	1:41.73	"	Sebastian Coe	Eng	10	Jun	81	Florence
	A	1:43.22		Steve Cram		31	Jul	86	Edinburgh
	WJ	1:43.64		Japheth Kimutai	KEN	13	Aug	97	Zürich
	EJ	1:44.33		Yuriy Borzakovskiy	RUS	25	Sep	00	Sydney
	NJ	1:45.64		David Sharpe		5	Sep	86	Brussels
1000m	W,C	2:11.96		Noah Ngeny	KEN	17	Jul	99	Nice
	E,N	2:12.18		Sebastian Coe		11	Jul	81	Oslo
	A	2:12.88		Steve Cram		9	Aug	85	Gateshead
	WJ	2:15.00		Benjamin Kipkurui	KEN	17	Jul	99	Nice
	EJ	2:17.40		Yuriy Borzakovskiy	RUS	8	Jul	00	Nice
	NJ	2:18.98		David Sharpe		19	Aug	86	Birmingham
1500m	W	3:26.00		Hicham El Guerrouj	MAR	14	Jul	98	Rome
	E	3:28.95		Fermín Cacho	ESP	13	Aug	97	Zürich
	C	3:26.34		Bernard Lagat	KEN	24	Aug	01	Brussels
	A	3:30.2		Hicham El Guerrouj	MAR	5	Aug	00	London (CP)
	N	3:29.67		Steve Cram		16	Jul	85	Nice

1500m	WJ	3:32.91	#	Noah Ngeny	KEN	16 Aug 97	Monaco
		3:33.16		Benjamin Kipkurui	KEN	11 Aug 99	Zürich
	EJ	3:35.51		Reyes Estévez	ESP	16 Aug 95	Zürich
	NJ	3:36.6		Graham Williamson		17 Jul 79	Oslo
1 Mile	W	3:43.13		Hicham El Guerrouj	MAR	7 Jul 99	Rome
	E,N	3:46.32		Steve Cram	Eng	27 Jul 85	Oslo
	C	3:43.40		Noah Ngeny	KEN	7 Jul 99	Rome
	A	3:45.96		Hicham El Guerrouj	MAR	5 Aug 00	London (CP)
	WJ	3:50.41		Noah Ngeny	KEN	16 Jul 97	Nice
	EJ,NJ	3:53.15		Graham Williamson		17 Jul 79	Oslo
2000m	W	4:44.79		Hicham El Guerrouj	MAR	7 Sep 99	Berlin
	E,N	4:51.39		Steve Cram		4 Aug 85	Budapest
	C	4:48.74		John Kibowen	KEN	1 Aug 98	Hechtel
	A	4:48.36		Hicham El Guerrouj	MAR	19 Jul 98	Gateshead
	WJ	4:59.14		Ali Saïdi-Sief	ALG	29 Jun 97	Villeneuve d'Ascq
	EJ	5:04.4		Harald Hudak	GER	30 Jun 76	Oslo
	NJ	5:06.56		Jon Richards		7 Jul 82	Oslo
3000m	W,C	7:20.67		Daniel Komen	KEN	1 Sep 96	Rieti
	E	7:26.62		Mohammed Mourit	BEL	18 Aug 00	Monaco
	A	7:29.69		Haile Gebrselassie	ETH	7 Aug 99	London (CP)
	N	7:32.79		Dave Moorcroft		17 Jul 82	London (CP)
	WJ	7:30.67		Kenenisa Bekele	KEN	24 Aug 01	Brussels
	EJ	7:43.20		Ari Paunonen	FIN	22 Jun 77	Cologne
	NJ	7:48.28		Jon Richards		9 Jul 83	Oslo
2 Miles	W,C	7:58.61		Daniel Komen	KEN	19 Jul 97	Hechtel
	E	8:13.2	i#	Emiel Puttemans	BEL	18 Feb 73	Berlin
	E,N	8:13.51		Steve Ovett		15 Sep 78	London (CP)
	A	8:01.72		Haile Gebrselassie	ETH	7 Aug 99	London (CP)
	WJ	8:13.47		Richard Limo	KEN	30 May 99	Hengelo
	EJ,NJ	8:28.31		Steve Binns		31 Aug 79	London (CP)
5000m	W	12:39.36		Haile Gebreselassie	ETH	13 Jun 98	Helsinki
	E	12:49.71		Mohammed Mourit	BEL	25 Aug 00	Brussels
	C	12:39.74		Daniel Komen	KEN	22 Aug 97	Brussels
	A	12:50.38	i#	Haile Gebrselassie	ETH	14 Feb 99	Birmingham
		13:06.23		Haile Gebrselassie	ETH	5 Aug 00	London (CP)
	N	13:00.41		Dave Moorcroft		7 Jul 82	Oslo
	WJ	12:53.72		Philip Mosima	KEN	5 Jun 96	Rome
	EJ,NJ	13:27.04		Steve Binns		14 Sep 79	London (CP)
10000m	W	26:22.75		Haile Gebreselassie	ETH	1 Jun 98	Hengelo
	E	26:52.30		Mohammed Mourhit	BEL	3 Sep 99	Brussels
	C	26:27.85		Paul Tergat	KEN	22 Aug 97	Brussels
	A	27:20.38		Aloÿs Nizigama	BUR	7 Jul 95	London (CP)
	N	27:18.14	#	Jon Brown		28 Aug 98	Brussels
		27:23.06		Eamonn Martin		2 Jul 88	Oslo
	WJ	27:11.18		Richard Chelimo	KEN	25 Jun 91	Hengelo
	EJ	28:22.48		Christian Leuprecht	ITA	4 Sep 90	Koblenz
	NJ	29:21.9		Jon Brown		21 Apr 90	Walnut
20000m	W	56:55.6		Arturo Barrios	MEX	30 Mar 91	La Flèche
	E	57:18.4		Dionisio Castro	POR	31 Mar 90	La Flèche
	C,N	57:28.7		Carl Thackery	Eng	31 Mar 90	La Flèche
	A	58:39.0		Ron Hill		9 Nov 68	Leicester
1 Hour	W	21,101 m		Arturo Barrios	MEX	30 Mar 91	La Flèche
	E	20,944 m		Jos Hermens	HOL	1 May 76	Papendal
	C,N	20,855 m		Carl Thackery	Eng	31 Mar 90	La Flèche
	A	20,472 m		Ron Hill		9 Nov 68	Leicester
	NJ	18,221 m		Eddie Twohig		16 Jun 81	Leamington

25000m	W	1:13:55.8		Toshihiko Seko	JPN	22 Mar 81	Christchurch, NZL
	E	1:13:57.6		Stéphane Franke	GER	30 Mar 99	Walnut
	C,A,N	1:15:22.6		Ron Hill	Eng	21 Jul 65	Bolton
30000m	W	1:29:18.78		Toshihiko Seko	JPN	22 Mar 81	Christchurch, NZL
	E,C,A,N	1:31:30.4		Jim Alder	Sco	5 Sep 70	London (CP)
Half Marathon	W,C	59:06		Paul Tergat	KEN	26 Mar 00	Lisbon
	E	59:43		António Pinto	POR	15 Mar 98	Lisbon
	A	60:02		Benson Masya	KEN	18 Sep 94	South Shields
	N	60:09	#	Paul Evans		15 Jan 95	Marrakech
		60:59		Steve Jones		8 Jun 86	South Shields
	WJ	59:37		Faustin Baha	TAN	26 Mar 00	Lisbon
	NJ	66:41		Stuart Jones		12 Jun 88	Weaverham
Marathon	W	2:05:42		Khalid Khannouchi	MAR	24 Oct 99	Chicago
	E,A	2:06:36		António Pinto	POR	16 Apr 00	London
	C	2:06:16		Moses Tanui	KEN	24 Oct 99	Chicago
	N	2:07:13		Steve Jones		20 Oct 85	Chicago
	WJ	2:10:46		Li Zhuhong	CHN	14 Oct 01	Beijing
	NJ	2:23:28		Eddie Twohig		28 Mar 82	Wolverhampton
2000m SC	W,C	5:14.43		Julius Kariuki	KEN	21 Aug 90	Rovereto
	E	5:18.36		Alessandro Lambruschini	ITA	12 Sep 89	Verona
	A	5:19.68		Samson Obwocha	KEN	19 Jul 86	Birmingham
	N	5:19.86		Mark Rowland		28 Aug 88	London (CP)
	WJ,EJ	5:25.01		Arsenios Tsiminos	GRE	2 Oct 80	Athens
	NJ	5:29.61		Colin Reitz		18 Aug 79	Bydgoszcz
3000m SC	W	7:55.28		Brahim Boulami	MAR	24 Aug 01	Brussels
	W,C	7:55.72		Bernard Barmasai	KEN	24 Aug 97	Cologne
	E	8:07.62		Joseph Mahmoud	FRA	24 Aug 84	Brussels
	A	8:08.11		Patrick Sang	KEN	7 Jul 95	London (CP)
	N	8:07.96		Mark Rowland		30 Sep 88	Seoul
	WJ	7:58.66		Stephen Cherono	KEN	24 Aug 01	Brussels
	EJ	8:29.50		Ralf Pönitzsch	GER	19 Aug 76	Warsaw
	NJ	8:29.85		Paul Davies-Hale		31 Aug 81	London (CP)
110m H	W,E,C,N	12.91		Colin Jackson	Wal	20 Aug 93	Stuttgart
	A	13.03		Colin Jackson		4 Sep 94	Sheffield
	WJ	13.23		Renaldo Nehemiah	USA	16 Aug 78	Zürich
	EJ,NJ	13.44		Colin Jackson		19 Jul 86	Athens
200m H	W,E	22.55		Laurant Ottoz	ITA	31 May 95	Milan
	C	22.59		Darryl Wohlsen	AUS	14 Mar 96	Brisbane
	A,N	22.63		Colin Jackson		1 Jun 91	Cardiff
	NJ	24.02		Paul Gray		13 Sep 87	London (CP)
400m H	W	46.78		Kevin Young	USA	6 Aug 92	Barcelona
	E	47.37		Stéphane Diagana	FRA	5 Jul 95	Lausanne
	C	47.10		Samuel Matete	ZAM	7 Aug 91	Zürich
	A	47.67		Kevin Young	USA	14 Aug 92	Sheffield
	N	47.82		Kriss Akabusi		6 Aug 92	Barcelona
	WJ	48.02		Danny Harris	USA	17 Jun 84	Los Angeles
	EJ	48.74		Vladimir Budko	RUS	18 Aug 84	Moscow
	NJ	50.22		Martin Briggs		28 Aug 83	Schwechat
High Jump	W	2.45		Javier Sotomayor	CUB	27 Jul 93	Salamanca
	E	2.42		Patrik Sjöberg	SWE	30 Jun 87	Stockholm
		2.42	i#	Carlo Thränhardt	GER	26 Feb 88	Berlin
	C,N	2.38	i#	Steve Smith	Eng	4 Feb 94	Wuppertal
	C	2.38		Troy Kemp	BAH	12 Jul 95	Nice

High	A	2.41		Javier Sotomayor	CUB	15	Jul	94	London (CP)
	N,WJ,EJ,NJ	2.37		Steve Smith		20	Sep	92	Seoul
Jump	N	2.37		Steve Smith		22	Aug	93	Stuttgart
	WJ,EJ	2.37		Dragutin Topic	YUG	12	Aug	90	Plovdiv
Pole	W,E	6.15	i#	Sergey Bubka	UKR	21	Feb	93	Donetsk
Vault		6.14	A	Sergey Bubka	UKR	31	Jul	94	Sestriere
	C	6.05		Dmitriy Markov	AUS	9	Aug	01	Edmonton
	A	6.05		Sergey Bubka	UKR	10	Sep	93	London (CP)
	N	5.80		Nick Buckfield		27	May	98	Hania
	WJ,EJ	5.80		Maksim Tarasov	RUS	14	Jul	89	Bryansk
	NJ	5.50		Neil Winter		9	Aug	92	San GiulianoTerme
Long	W	8.95		Mike Powell	USA	30	Aug	91	Tokyo
Jump	E	8.86	A	Robert Emmiyan	ARM	22	May	87	Tsakhkadzor
	C	8.62		James Beckford	JAM	5	Apr	97	Orlando
	A	8.54		Mike Powell	USA	10	Sep	93	London (CP)
	N	8.23		Lynn Davies		30	Jun	68	Berne
	WJ	8.34		Randy Williams	USA	8	Sep	72	Munich
	EJ	8.24		Vladimir Ochkan	UKR	21	Jun	87	St. Petersburg
	NJ	7.98		Stewart Faulkner		6	Aug	88	Birmingham
		7.98		Jonathan Moore		29	Jul	01	Dole
Triple	W,E,C,N	18.29		Jonathan Edwards	Eng	7	Aug	95	Gothenburg
Jump	A	18.00		Jonathan Edwards		27	Aug	95	London (CP)
	WJ,EJ	17.50		Volker Mai	GER	23	Jun	85	Erfurt
	NJ	16.58		Tosi Fasinro		15	Jun	91	Espoo
Shot	W	23.12		Randy Barnes	USA	20	May	90	Los Angeles (Ww)
	E	23.06		Ulf Timmermann	GER	22	May	88	Hania
	C	21.97		Janus Robberts	RSA	2	Jun	01	Eugene
	N	21.68		Geoff Capes		18	May	80	Cwmbrân
	A	22.28	#	Brian Oldfield	USA	18	Jun	75	Edinburgh
		21.75		John Godina	USA	17	Aug	97	London (CP)
	WJ	21.05	i#	Terry Albritton	USA	22	Feb	74	New York
		20.65	#	Mike Carter	USA	4	Jul	79	Boston
		20.39	A	Janus Robberts	RSA	7	Mar	98	Germiston
	EJ	20.20		Udo Beyer	GER	6	Jul	74	Leipzig
	NJ	19.46		Carl Myerscough		6	Sep	98	Blackpool
Discus	W,E	74.08		Jürgen Schult	GER	6	Jun	86	Neubrandenburg
	C	69.96		Frantz Kruger	RSA	30	Mar	01	Stellenbosch
	A	68.32		John Powell	USA	30	Aug	82	London (CP)
	N	66.64		Perriss Wilkins		6	Jun	98	Birmingham (Un)
	WJ	65.62	#	Werner Reiterer	AUS	15	Dec	87	Melbourne
	WJ,EJ	63.64		Werner Hartmann	GER	25	Jun	78	Strasbourg
	NJ	60.97		Emeka Udechuku		5	Jul	98	Bedford
Hammer	W,E	86.74		Yuriy Sedykh	UKR/RUS	30	Aug	86	Stuttgart
	C	79.40		Chris Harmse	RSA	3	Nov	01	Pretoria
	A	85.60		Yuriy Sedykh	UKR/RUS	13	Jul	84	London (CP)
	N	77.54		Martin Girvan		12	May	84	Wolverhampton
	WJ,EJ	78.33		Olli-Pekka Karjalainen	FIN	5	Aug	99	Seinäjoki
	NJ	67.48		Paul Head		16	Sep	84	Karlovac
Javelin	W,E	98.48		Jan Zelezny	CZE	25	May	96	Jena
	C,N	91.46		Steve Backley	Eng	25	Jan	92	Auckland (NS)
	A	95.66		Jan Zelezny	CZE	29	Aug	93	Sheffield
	WJ,EJ	83.87		Andreas Thorkildsen	NOR	7	Jun	01	Fana
	NJ	79.50		Steve Backley		5	Jun	88	Derby
Pent.	W,A	4282		Bill Toomey	USA	16	Aug	69	London (CP)
	E	4273		Rein Aun	EST	18	Jul	68	Tartu
	C,N	3841		Barry King	Eng	20	May	70	Santa Barbara
	NJ	3112		Wayne Dubose		21	Jul	74	London (VP)

Dec.	W,E	9026		Roman Sebrle	CZE	27	May	01	Götzis
	C,N	8847		Daley Thompson	Eng	9	Aug	84	Los Angeles
	A	8663		Daley Thompson		28	Jul	86	Edinburgh
	WJ,EJ	8397		Torsten Voss	GER	7	Jul	82	Erfurt
	NJ	8082		Daley Thompson		31	Jul	77	Sittard
(with 1986 Javelin)									
	C,N	8811	#	Daley Thompson	Eng	28	Aug	86	Stuttgart
	WJ,EJ	8114	#	Michael Kohnle	GER	25	Aug	89	Varazdin
	NJ	7488	#	David Bigham		9	Aug	90	Plovdiv
4x100m	W	37.40		United States		8	Aug	92	Barcelona
		37.40		United States		21	Aug	93	Stuttgart
	E,N	37.73		UK National Team		29	Aug	99	Seville
	C	37.69		Canada		3	Aug	96	Atlanta
	A	37.95		United States		28	Aug	00	Gateshead
		37.93	#	Hudson Smith International	USA/TRI	22	Jul	01	London (CP)
	WJ	39.00	A	United States		18	Jul	83	Colorado Springs
	EJ,NJ	39.05		UK National Team		22	Oct	00	Santiago
4x200m	W	1:18.68		Santa Monica T.C.	USA	17	Apr	94	Walnut
	E	1:21.10		Italy		29	Sep	83	Cagliari
	C	1:20.79		Jamaica		24	Apr	88	Walnut
	A,N	1:21.29		UK National Team		23	Jun	89	Birmingham
	NJ	1:25.40	i#	UK National Team		2	Mar	96	Liévin
		1:27.6		Borough of Enfield Harriers		13	Jun	82	London (He)
4x400m	W	2:54.20		United States		22	Jul	98	Uniondale
	E,N	2:56.60		UK National Team		3	Aug	96	Atlanta
	C	2:56.75		Jamaica		10	Aug	97	Athens
	A	2:59.85		UK National Team		19	Aug	96	Gateshead
	WJ	3:01.90		United States		20	Jul	86	Athens
	(EJ),NJ	3:03.80		UK National Team		12	Aug	90	Plovdiv
	EJ	3:04.58		East Germany		23	Aug	81	Utrecht
4x800m	WECAN	7:03.89		UK National Team	Eng	30	Aug	82	London (CP)
	NJ	7:26.2		BMC Junior Squad		2	Sep	95	Oxford
4x1500m	W,E	14:38.8		West Germany		16	Aug	77	Cologne
	C	14:40.4		New Zealand		22	Aug	73	Oslo
	A	15:04.7		Italy		5	Jun	92	Sheffield
	N	14:56.8	a#	BMC National Squad		23	Jun	79	Bourges
		15:04.6		UK National Team		5	May	76	Athens (NF)
	NJ	15:52.0		BMC Junior Squad		30	Apr	97	Watford
4x1Mile	W,E	15:49.08		Irish Republic		17	Aug	85	Dublin (B)
	C	15:59.57		New Zealand		1	Mar	83	Auckland
	A	16:21.1		BMC National Squad		10	Jul	93	Oxford
	N	16:17.4		Bristol A.C./Western Kentucky U		25	Apr	75	Des Moines
	NJ	16:56.8		BMC Junior Squad		10	Jul	93	Oxford
Track Walking									
1500m	W,E	5:12.0		Algis Grigaliunas	LIT	12	May	90	Vilnius
	C	5:19.1		Dave Smith	AUS	7	Feb	83	Melbourne
	A,N	5:46.2	a	Roger Mills		29	Aug	75	London (CP)
	N	5:19.22	i#	Tim Berrett §		9	Feb	90	East Rutherford
1 Mile	W	5:33.53	i#	Tim Lewis	USA	5	Feb	88	New York
	W,E	5:36.9		Algis Grigaliunas	LIT	12	May	90	Vilnius
	C	5:54.6	i#	Marcel Jobin	CAN	16	Feb	80	Houston
	C,A,N	5:58.9	mx	Andy Penn	Eng	13	Aug	97	Rugby
	N	5:56.39	i#	Tim Berrett §		2	Feb	90	New York
	NJ	6:09.2		Phil Vesty		23	Jun	82	Leicester

3000m	W,E	10:47.11		Giovanni DeBenedictis	ITA	19	May	90	S. G. Valdarno
	C	10:56.22		Andrew Jachno	AUS	7	Feb	91	Melbourne
	A	11:19.00	i#	Axel Noack	GER	23	Feb	90	Glasgow
		11:19.9		Tim Berrett	CAN	20	Apr	92	Tonbridge
	N	11:24.4		Mark Easton		10	May	89	Tonbridge
	WJ,EJ	11:13.2		Jozef Pribilinec	SVK	28	Mar	79	Banská Bystrica
	NJ	11:54.23		Tim Berrett §		23	Jun	84	London (CP)
5000m	W	18:05.49		Hatem Ghoula	TUN	1	May	97	Tunis
	E	18:07.08	i#	Mikhail Shchennikov	RUS	14	Feb	95	Moscow
		18:17.22		Robert Korzeniowski	POL	3	Jul	92	Reims
	C	18:47.56	i#	Tim Berrett	CAN	20	Feb	93	Winnipeg
		18:51.39		Nick A'Hern	AUS	21	Feb	98	Auckland (NS)
	A	18:56.27	i#	Axel Noack	GER	23	Feb	90	Glasgow
	A,N	19:35.0		Darrell Stone		16	May	89	Brighton
	WJ,EJ	19:19.3		Mikhail Shchennikov	RUS	9	Aug	86	Chemnitz
	NJ	20:16.40		Philip King		26	Jun	93	Lübeck
10000m	W,E	38:02.60		Jozef Pribilinec	SVK	30	Aug	85	Banská Bystrica
	C	38:06.6		Dave Smith	AUS	25	Sep	86	Sydney
	A	39:26.02		Guillaume Leblanc	CAN	29	Jun	90	Gateshead
	N	40:06.65		Ian McCombie		4	Jun	89	Jarrow
	WJ,EJ	38:46.4		Viktor Burayev	RUS	20	May	00	Moscow
	NJ	41:52.13		Darrell Stone		7	Aug	87	Birmingham
(Road)	W,E	37:11		Roman Rasskazov	RUS	28	May	00	Saransk
	NJ	41:47		Darrell Stone		26	Sep	87	Paris
1 Hour	W	15,577 m		Bernardo Segura	MEX	7	May	94	Fana
	E	15,447 m		Jozef Pribilinec	SVK	6	Sep	86	Hildesheim
	C	15,300 m		Dave Smith	AUS	6	Sep	86	Hildesheim
	A	14,383 m		Anatoliy Solomin	UKR	26	Aug	77	Edinburgh
	N	14,324 m	#	Ian McCombie		7	Jul	85	London (SP)
		14,158 m		Mark Easton		12	Sep	87	Woodford
	NJ	13,487 m		Darrell Stone		12	Sep	87	Woodford
20000m	W	1:17:25.6		Bernardo Segura	MEX	7	May	94	Fana
	E	1:18:35.2		Stefan Johansson	SWE	15	May	92	Fana
	C	1:19:48.1		Nathan Deakes	AUS	4	Sep	01	Brisbane
	A	1:24:07.6	#	Phil Vesty		1	Dec	84	Leicester
		1:24:22.0		José Marín	ESP	28	Jun	81	Brighton
	N	1:23:26.5		Ian McCombie		26	May	90	Fana
	WJ,EJ	1:21:29.2	#	Viktor Burayev	RUS	4	Sep	01	Brisbane
	WJ	1:22:16.0		Li Mingcai	CHN	3	Mar	90	Donetsk
	EJ	1:22:42		Andrey Perlov	RUS	6	Sep	80	Hefei
	NJ	1:31:34.4		Gordon Vale		28	Jun	81	Brighton
2 Hours	W,E	29,572 m		Maurizio Damilano	ITA	4	Oct	92	Cuneo
	C	28,800 m	#	Guillaume Leblanc	CAN	16	Jun	90	Sept Îles
		27,720 m		Craig Barratt	NZL	19	Jul	98	Auckland
	A,N	27,262 m	#	Chris Maddocks		31	Dec	89	Plymouth
	A	26,265 m		Jorge Llopart	ESP	28	Jun	81	Brighton
	N	26,037 m		Ron Wallwork		31	Jul	71	Blackburn
30000m	W,E	2:01:44.1		Maurizio Damilano	ITA	4	Oct	92	Cuneo
	C	2:04:55.7		Guillaume Leblanc	CAN	16	Jun	90	Sept Îles
	A,N	2:11:54	#	Chris Maddocks		31	Dec	89	Plymouth
	A	2:17:26.4		Jorge Llopart	ESP	28	Jun	81	Brighton
	N	2:19:18		Chris Maddocks		22	Sep	84	Birmingham
50000m	W,E	3:40:57.9		Thierry Toutain	FRA	29	Sep	96	Héricourt
	C	3:43:50.0		Simon Baker	AUS	9	Sep	90	Melbourne
	A	4:03:52		Gerhard Weidner	GER	1	Jun	75	Woodford
	N	4:05:44.6		Paul Blagg		26	May	90	Fana

Race Walking - Fastest Recorded Times

20km	W	1:17:25.6 t	Bernardo Segura	MEX	7 May 94	Fana
	E	1:17:46	Roman Rasskazov	RUS	19 May 00	Moscow
	C	1:18:14	Nathan Deakes	AUS	16 Jun 01	Dublin
	A	1:20:18	Francisco Fernández	ESP	23 Apr 00	Leamington
	N	1:22:03	Ian McCombie		23 Sep 88	Seoul
	WJ,EJ	1:18:06	Viktor Burayev	RUS	4 Mar 01	Adler
	NJ	1:26:13	Tim Berrett §		25 Feb 84	Dartford
30km	W,E	2:01:44.1 t	Maurizio Damilano	ITA	4 Oct 92	Cuneo
	C	2:04:55.7 t	Guillaume Leblanc	CAN	16 Jun 90	Sept Îles
	A	2:07:47	Simon Baker	AUS	31 Jul 86	Edinburgh
	N	2:07:56	Ian McCombie		27 Apr 86	Edinburgh
	WJ,EJ	2:10:19.4 t	Ralf Kowalsky	GER	29 Mar 81	Berlin (E)
	NJ	2:30:46	Phil Vesty		31 Jul 82	London (VP)
50km	W,E	3:37:26	Valeriy Spitsyn	RUS	21 May 00	Moscow
	C	3:43:13	Simon Baker	AUS	28 May 89	L'Hospitalet
	A	3:47:31	Hartwig Gauder	GER	28 Sep 85	St. John's, IoM
	N	3:51:37	Chris Maddocks		28 Oct 90	Burrator
	WJ	4:00:04	Hao Huanquan	CHN	10 Apr 94	Beijing
	EJ	4:07:23	Aleksandr Volgin	RUS	27 Sep 86	Zhytomyr
	NJ	4:18:18	Gordon Vale		24 Oct 81	Lassing

RECORDS set in 2001

1500m	C	3:26.34	Bernard Lagat	KEN	24 Aug 01	Brussels
3000m	WJ	7:30.67	Kenenisa Bekele	KEN	24 Aug 01	Brussels
Marathon	WJ	2:10:46	Li Zhuhong	CHN	14 Oct 01	Beijing
3000SC	W	7:55.28	Brahim Boulami	MAR	24 Aug 01	Brussels
	WJ	7:58.66	Stephen Cherono	KEN	24 Aug 01	Brussels
PV	C	6.05	Dmitriy Markov	AUS	9 Aug 01	Edmonton
LJ	NJ=	7.98	Jonathan Moore		29 Jul 01	Dole
SP	C=	21.68	Janus Robberts	RSA	2 Jun 01	Eugene
	C	21.97	Janus Robberts	RSA	2 Jun 01	Eugene
DT	C	69.96	Frantz Kruger	RSA	30 Mar 01	Stellenbosch
HT	C	78.90	Stuart Rendell	AUS	3 Jul 01	Szombathely
	C	78.93	Stuart Rendell	AUS	15 Jul 01	Szombathely
	C	78.99 #	Stuart Rendell	AUS	30 Jul 01	Calgary
	C	79.40	Chris Harmse	RSA	3 Nov 01	Pretoria
JT	WJ,EJ	83.87	Andreas Thorkildsen	NOR	7 Jun 01	Fana
Dec	W,E	9026	Roman Sebrle	CZE	27 May 01	Götzis
4x100	A	37.93 #	Hudson Smith International	USA/TRI	22 Jul 01	London (CP)
20kWR	WJ,EJ	1:18:06	Viktor Burayev	RUS	4 Mar 01	Adler
	C	1:18:14	Nathan Deakes	AUS	16 Jun 01	Dublin

Track Walking

20000m	C	1:19:48.1	Nathan Deakes	AUS	4 Sep 01	Brisbane
	WJ,EJ	1:21:29.2 #	Viktor Burayev	RUS	4 Sep 01	Brisbane

Race Walking

20 km	WJ,EJ	1:18:06	Viktor Burayev	RUS	4 Mar 01	Adler
	C	1:18:14	Nathan Deakes	AUS	16 Jun 01	Dublin

Note	9.97 #	Mark Lewis-Francis		4 Aug 01	Edmonton

would qualify as WJ, EJ, NJ but cannot be ratified because wind guage was faulty, it is thought to be probably wind aided.

RECORDS - WOMEN

as at 31 December 2001

100m	W	10.49		Florence Griffith Joyner	USA	16	Jul	88	Indianapolis
	E	10.73		Christine Arron	FRA	19	Aug	98	Budapest
	C	10.74		Merlene Ottey	JAM	7	Sep	96	Milan
	A	10.78		Marion Jones	USA	5	Aug	00	London (CP)
	N	11.10		Kathy Smallwood/Cook		5	Sep	81	Rome
	WJ,EJ	10.88		Marlies Oelsner/Göhr	GER	1	Jul	77	Dresden
	NJ	11.27	A	Kathy Smallwood/Cook		9	Sep	79	Mexico City
200m	W	21.34		Florence Griffith Joyner	USA	29	Sep	88	Seoul
	E	21.71		Marita Koch	GER	10	Jun	79	Chemnitz
		21.71	#	Marita Koch	GER	21	Jul	84	Potsdam
		21.71		Heike Drechsler	GER	29	Jun	86	Jena
		21.71	#	Heike Drechsler	GER	29	Aug	86	Stuttgart
	C	21.64		Merlene Ottey	JAM	13	Sep	91	Brussels
	A	22.23		Merlene Ottey	JAM	9	Sep	94	London (CP)
	N	22.10		Kathy Cook		9	Aug	84	Los Angeles
	WJ,EJ	22.19		Natalya Bochina	RUS	30	Jul	80	Moscow
	NJ	22.70	A	Kathy Smallwood/Cook		12	Sep	79	Mexico City
300m	W,E	35.00	+	Marie-José Pérec	FRA	27	Aug	91	Tokyo
		34.1	+	Marita Koch	GER	6	Oct	85	Canberra
	C,A,N	35.46		Kathy Cook	Eng	18	Aug	84	London (CP)
	A	35.46		Chandra Cheeseborough	USA	18	Aug	84	London (CP)
	WJ,EJ	36.24	+	Grit Breuer	GER	29	Aug	90	Split
		35.4	+	Christina Brehmer/Lathan	GER	29	Jul	76	Montréal
	NJ	36.46		Linsey Macdonald		13	Jul	80	London (CP)
		36.2		Donna Murray/Hartley		7	Aug	74	London (CP)
400m	W,E	47.60		Marita Koch	GER	6	Oct	85	Canberra
	C	48.63		Cathy Freeman	AUS	29	Jul	96	Atlanta
	A	49.33		Tatána Kocembová	CZE	20	Aug	83	London (CP)
	N	49.43		Kathy Cook		6	Aug	84	Los Angeles
	WJ,EJ	49.42		Grit Breuer	GER	27	Aug	91	Tokyo
	NJ	51.16		Linsey Macdonald		15	Jun	80	London (CP)
600m	W	1:22.63		Ana Fidelia Quirot	CUB	25	Jul	97	Guadalajara
	E	1:23.5		Doina Melinte	ROM	27	Jul	86	Poiana Brasov
	C	1:25.37		Charmaine Howell	JAM	14	Sep	00	Sydney (OWT)
	A	1:25.90		Delisa Walton-Floyd	USA	28	Aug	88	London (CP)
	N	1:26.0		Kelly Holmes	Eng	13	Aug	95	Gothenburg
	WJ,EJ	1:25.2		Vera Nikolic	YUG		Jun	67	Belgrade
	NJ	1:27.33		Lorraine Baker		13	Jul	80	London (CP)
800m	W,E	1:53.28		Jarmila Kratochvílová	CZE	26	Jul	83	Munich
	C	1:55.29		Maria Lurdes Mutola	MOZ	24	Aug	97	Cologne
	A	1:57.14		Jarmila Kratochvílová	CZE	24	Jun	85	Belfast
	N	1:56.21		Kelly Holmes		9	Sep	95	Monaco
	WJ	1:57.18		Wang Yuan	CHN	8	Sep	93	Beijing
	EJ	1:57.45	#	Hildegard Ullrich	GER	31	Aug	78	Prague
		1:59.17		Birte Bruhns	GER	20	Jul	88	Berlin
	NJ	2:01.11		Lynne MacDougall		18	Aug	84	London (CP)
1000m	W,E	2:28.98		Svetlana Masterkova	RUS	23	Aug	96	Brussels
	C	2:29.66		Maria Lurdes Mutola	MOZ	23	Aug	96	Brussels
	A	2:32.08	i#	Maria Lurdes Mutola	MOZ	10	Feb	96	Birmingham
	A,N	2:32.55		Kelly Holmes		15	Jun	97	Leeds
	WJ,EJ	2:35.4	a	Irina Nikitina	RUS	5	Aug	79	Podolsk
		2:35.4		Kathrin Wühn	GER	12	Jul	84	Potsadam
	NJ	2:38.58		Jo White		9	Sep	77	London (CP)

1500m	W	3:50.46		Qu Yunxia	CHN	11	Sep	93	Beijing
	E	3:52.47		Tatyana Kazankina	RUS	13	Aug	80	Zürich
	C	3:57.41		Jackline Maranga	KEN	8	Aug	98	Monaco
	A,N	3:58.07		Kelly Holmes		29	Jun	97	Sheffield
	WJ	3:51.34		Lang Yinglai	CHN	18	Oct	97	Shanghai
	(EJ,)NJ	3:59.96		Zola Budd/Pieterse		30	Aug	85	Brussels
	EJ	4:03.45		Anita Weyermann	SUI	3	Jul	96	Lausanne
1 Mile	W,E	4:12.56		Svetlana Masterkova	RUS	14	Aug	96	Zürich
	C,N,WJ,EJ,NJ	4:17.57		Zola Budd/Pieterse	Eng	21	Aug	85	Zürich
	A	4:19.59		Mary Slaney	USA	2	Aug	85	London (CP)
2000m	W,E,A	5:25.36		Sonia O'Sullivan	IRL	8	Jul	94	Edinburgh
	C,N	5:26.93		Yvonne Murray	Sco	8	Jul	94	Edinburgh
	WJ,EJ,NJ	5:33.15		Zola Budd/Pieterse		13	Jul	84	London (CP)
3000m	W	8:06.11		Wang Junxia	CHN	13	Sep	93	Beijing
	E,A	8:21.64		Sonia O'Sullivan	IRL	15	Jul	94	London (CP)
	C,N	8:26.97		Paula Radcliffe	Eng	29	Jun	01	Rome
	WJ,EJ,NJ	8:28.83		Zola Budd/Pieterse		7	Sep	85	Rome
2 Miles	W	9:11.97	mx	Regina Jacobs	USA	12	Aug	99	Los Gatos
	W,E	9:19.56		Sonia O'Sullivan	IRL	27	Jun	98	Cork
	C	9:27.18		Kathy Butler	CAN	27	Jun	98	Cork
	A	9:27.6	+e	Paula Radcliffe		22	Jul	01	London (CP)
	A,N	9:32.07		Paula Radcliffe		23	May	99	Loughborough
	N	9:27.5	e	Paula Radcliffe		22	Aug	97	Brussels
	NJ	9:29.6		Zola Budd/Peiterse		26	Aug	85	London (CP)
		10:35.10		Jane Potter		23	May	99	Loughborough
5000m	W	14:28.09		Jiang Bo	CHN	23	Oct	97	Shanghai
	E	14:29.32		Olga Yegorova	RUS	31	Aug	01	Berlin
	C	14:39.83		Leah Malot	KEN	1	Sep	00	Berlin
	A	14:41.23		Ayelech Worku	ETH	5	Aug	00	London (CP)
	N	14:43.54		Paula Radcliffe		7	Aug	99	London (CP)
	WJ	14:39.96	#	Yin Lili	CHN	23	Oct	97	Shanghai
		14:45.90		Jiang Bo	CHN	24	Oct	95	Nanjing
	(EJ,)NJ	14:48.07		Zola Budd/Pieterse		26	Aug	85	London (CP)
	EJ	14:56.22		Annemari Sandell	FIN	8	Jul	96	Stockholm
10000m	W	29:31.78		Wang Junxia	CHN	8	Sep	93	Beijing
	E	30:13.74		Ingrid Kristiansen	NOR	5	Jul	86	Oslo
	C,N	30:26.97		Paula Radcliffe	Eng	30	Sep	00	Sydney
	A	30:52.51		Elana Meyer	RSA	10	Sep	94	London (CP)
	WJ	30:39.41		Lan Lixin	CHN	19	Oct	97	Shanghai
	EJ	31:40.42		Annemari Sandell	FIN	27	Jul	96	Atlanta
	NJ	34:31.41	#	Tanya Povey		3	Jun	98	Amherst
1 Hour	W,C	18,393 m	#	Tegla Loroupe	KEN	3	Sep	00	Borgholzhausen
	W,C	18,340 m		Tegla Loroupe	KEN	7	Aug	98	Borgholzhausen
	E	18,084 m		Silvana Cruciata	ITA	4	May	81	Rome
	A,N	16,460 m	i#	Bronwen Cardy-Wise		8	Mar	92	Birmingham
	N	16,495 m	#	Michaela McCallum		2	Apr	00	Asti
	A,N	16,364 m		Alison Fletcher		3	Sep	97	Bromley
	NJ	14,580 m		Paula Simpson		20	Oct	93	Bebington
20000m	W,C	1:05:26.6		Tegla Loroupe	KEN	3	Sep	00	Borgholzhausen
	W	1:06:48.8		Izumi Maki	JPN	19	Sep	93	Amagasaki
	E	1:06:55.5	#	Rosa Mota	POR	14	May	83	Lisbon
	A,N	1:15:46		Caroline Hunter-Rowe	Eng	6	Mar	94	Barry
25000m	W,E	1:29:29.2		Karolina Szabó	HUN	22	Apr	88	Budapest
	C,A,N	1:35:16		Caroline Hunter-Rowe	Eng	6	Mar	94	Barry
30000m	W,E	1:47:05.6		Karolina Szabó	HUN	22	Apr	88	Budapest
	C,A,N	1:55:03		Caroline Hunter-Rowe	Eng	6	Mar	94	Barry

Half Marathon	W,C	65:44	#	Susan Chepkemei	KEN	1 Apr 01	Lisbon
	W	66:43		Masako Chiba	JPN	19 Jan 97	Tokyo
	E	66:40	#	Ingrid Kristiansen	NOR	5 Apr 87	Sandnes
	E,A,N	66:47		Paula Radcliffe		7 Oct 01	Bristol
	C	66:44		Elana Meyer	RSA	15 Jan 99	Tokyo
	WJ	69:05		Delillah Asiago	KEN	5 May 91	Exeter
	NJ	77:52		Kathy Williams		28 Mar 82	Barry
Marathon	W,C	2:18:47		Catherine Ndereba	KEN	7 Oct 01	Chicago
	E,A	2:21:06		Ingrid Kristiansen	NOR	21 Apr 85	London
	N	2:25:56		Véronique Marot		23 Apr 89	London
	WJ	2:23:37		Liu Min	CHN	14 Oct 01	Beijing
	NJ	2:50:09		Siobhan Quenby		16 Oct 83	Milan
2000m SC	W,E	6:11.84		Marina Pluzhnikova	RUS	25 Jul 94	St. Petersburg
	C,A	6:19.00		Irene Limika	KEN	20 May 01	Loughborough
	N	6:29.79		Tara Krzywicki		20 May 01	Loughborough
	WJ	6:25.77		Melissa Rollison	AUS	1 May 00	Sydney
	EJ	6:31.31		Yelena Sayko	UKR	13 Jul 97	Kiev
	NJ	6:55.04		Jo Ankier		22 Jul 01	Grosseto
3000m SC	W,E	9:25.31		Justyna Bak	POL	9 Jul 01	Nice
	C,WJ	9:30.70		Melissa Rollison	AUS	4 Sep 01	Brisbane
	A	9:48.72		Elizabeth Jackson	USA	1 Jul 01	Glasgow (S)
	N	9:52.71		Tara Krzywicki	Eng	1 Jul 01	Glasgow (S)
	EJ	10:04.99	#	Ulla Tuimala	FIN	2 Sep 01	Gothenburg
	NJ	12:11.1		Lindsey Oliver		22 Aug 93	Horsham
100m H	W,E	12.21		Yordanka Donkova	BUL	20 Aug 88	Stara Zagora
	C	12.44		Glory Alozie	NGR	28 Aug 99	Seville
	A	12.51		Ginka Zagorcheva	BUL	12 Sep 86	London (CP)
	N	12.80		Angie Thorp		31 Jul 96	Atlanta
	WJ	12.76	#	Liu Jing	CHN	18 Oct 97	Shanghai
		12.84		Aliuska López	CUB	16 Jul 87	Zagreb
	EJ	12.88		Yelena Ovcharova	UKR	25 Jun 95	Villeneuve d'Ascq
	NJ	13.25		Diane Allahgreen		21 Jul 94	Lisbon
400m H	W	52.61		Kim Batten	USA	11 Aug 95	Gothenburg
	E,C,N	52.74		Sally Gunnell	Eng	19 Aug 93	Stuttgart
	A	53.69		Sandra Farmer-Patrick	USA	10 Sep 93	London (CP)
	WJ	55.15		Huang Xiaoxiao	CHN	22 Nov 01	Guangzhou
	EJ	55.26		Ionela Tîrlea	ROM	12 Jul 95	Nice
	NJ	57.27		Vicki Jamison		28 Jul 96	Bedford
High Jump	W,E	2.09		Stefka Kostadinova	BUL	30 Aug 87	Rome
	C	2.04		Hestrie Cloete	RSA	4 Aug 99	Monaco
	A	2.03		Ulrike Meyfarth	GER	21 Aug 83	London (CP)
		2.03		Tamara Bykova	RUS	21 Aug 83	London (CP)
	N	1.95		Diana Elliott/Davies		26 Jun 82	Oslo
		1.95	i#	Debbie Marti		23 Feb 97	Birmingham
		1.95		Susan Jones		24 Jun 01	Bremen
	WJ,EJ	2.01	#	Olga Turchak	KZK/UKR	7 Jul 86	Moscow
		2.01		Heike Balck	GER	18 Jun 89	Chemnitz
	NJ	1.91		Lea Haggett		2 Jun 91	Hania
		1.91		Susan Jones		31 Aug 97	Catania
Pole Vault	W	4.81		Stacy Dragila	USA	9 Jun 01	Palo Alto
	E	4.75		Svetlana Feofanova	RUS	6 Aug 01	Edmonton
	C	4.60		Emma George	AUS	20 Feb 99	Sydney
	A	4.72		Stacy Dragila	USA	22 Jul 01	London (CP)
	N	4.40		Janine Whitlock		14 Jul 01	Birmingham
	WJ,EJ	4.46	#	Yelena Isinbayeva	RUS	31 Aug 01	Berlin
		4.40		Yelena Isinbayeva	RUS	24 Jul 00	Tula
	NJ	3.90		Ellie Spain		6 May 00	Eton

Long Jump	W,E	7.52		Galina Chistyakova	RUS	11	Jun	88	St. Petersburg
	C,N,NJ	6.90		Beverly Kinch	Eng	14	Aug	83	Helsinki
	A	7.14		Galina Chistyakova	RUS	24	Jun	89	Birmingham
	WJ,EJ	7.14	#	Heike Daute/Drechsler	GER	4	Jun	83	Bratislava
Triple Jump	W,E	15.50		Inessa Kravets	UKR	10	Aug	95	Gothenburg
	C,N	15.16	i#	Ashia Hansen	Eng	28	Feb	98	Valencia
		15.15		Ashia Hansen	Eng	13	Sep	97	Fukuoka
	A	14.98		Tatyana Lebedyeva	RUS	16	Jul	00	Gateshead
	WJ,EJ	14.62		Tereza Marinova	BUL	25	Aug	96	Sydney
	NJ	13.05		Michelle Griffith		16	Jun	90	London (CP)
Shot	W,E	22.63		Natalya Lisovskaya	RUS	7	Jun	87	Moscow
	C	19.74		Gael Mulhall/Martin	AUS	14	Jul	84	Berkeley
	A	21.95		Natalya Lisovskaya	RUS	29	Jul	88	Edinburgh
	N	19.36		Judy Oakes		14	Aug	88	Gateshead
	WJ,EJ	20.54		Astrid Kumbernuss	GER	1	Jul	89	Orimattila
	NJ	17.10		Myrtle Augee		16	Jun	84	London (CP)
Discus	W,E	76.80		Gabriele Reinsch	GER	9	Jul	88	Neubrandenburg
	C	68.72		Daniela Costian	AUS	22	Jan	94	Auckland
	A	73.04		Ilke Wyludda	GER	5	Aug	89	Gateshead
	N	67.48		Meg Ritchie		26	Apr	81	Walnut
	WJ,EJ	74.40		Ilke Wyludda	GER	13	Sep	88	Berlin
	NJ	54.81		Claire Smithson		1	Jul	01	Bedford
Hammer	W,E	76.07		Mihaela Melinte	ROM	29	Aug	99	Rüdingen
	C	70.19	#	Bronwyn Eagles	AUS	30	Jul	01	Calgary
	C	68.87		Bronwyn Eagles	AUS	7	Aug	01	Edmonton
	A	70.20		Olga Kuzenkova	RUS	15	Jul	00	Gateshead
	N	68.15		Lorraine Shaw		17	Mar	01	Nice/Boulouris
	WJ,EJ	71.71		Kamila Skolimowska	POL	9	Sep	01	Melbourne
	NJ	57.97		Rachael Beverley		25	Jul	98	Birmingham
Javelin	W	71.54		Osleidys Menéndez	CUB	1	Jul	01	Rethymno
	E	69.48		Trine Hattestad	NOR	28	Jul	00	Oslo
	C	66.80		Louise Currey	AUS	5	Aug	00	Gold Coast (RB)
	A	63.23		Ana Mirela Termure	ROM	15	Jul	00	Gateshead
	N	59.50		Karen Martin		14	Jul	99	Cosford
	WJ	61.99		Wang Yaning	CHN	14	Oct	99	Huizhou
	EJ	61.79	#	Nikolett Szabó	HUN	23	May	99	Schwechat
	EJ	61.52		Nikolett Szabó	HUN	8	Aug	99	Riga
	NJ	54.61		Kelly Morgan		4	Sep	99	Exeter
Hept.	W	7291		Jackie Joyner-Kersee	USA	24	Sep	88	Seoul
	E	7007		Larisa Nikitina	RUS	11	Jun	89	Bryansk
	C,N	6831		Denise Lewis	Eng	30	Jul	00	Talence
	A	6419		Birgit Clarius	GER	21	Jul	91	Sheffield
	WJ,EJ	6465		Sybille Thiele	GER	28	Aug	83	Schwechat
	NJ	5833		Joanne Mulliner		11	Aug	85	Lons-le-Saunier
(with 1999 Javelin)									
	W,E	6861		Eunice Barber	FRA	22	Aug	99	Seville
	A	5719		Barbora Potáková	CZE	21	May	00	Hexham
	WJ,EJ	6056		Carolina Klüft	SWE	21	Oct	00	Santiago
	NJ	5283		Chloe Cozens		23	May	99	Alhama de Murcia
4x100m	W,E	41.37		East Germany		6	Oct	85	Canberra
	C	41.92		Bahamas		29	Aug	99	Seville
	A	41.87		East Germany		5	Aug	89	Gateshead
	N	42.43		UK National Team		1	Aug	80	Moscow
	WJ,EJ	43.33	#	East Germany		20	Jul	88	Berlin
	WJ	43.38		United States		11	Jul	99	Tampa
	EJ	43.48		East Germany		31	Jul	88	Sudbury
	NJ	44.16		UK National Team		12	Aug	90	Plovdiv

4x200m	W	1:27.46		United States		29 Apr 00	Philadelphia
	E	1:28.15		East Germany		9 Aug 80	Jena
	C	1:30.23		Jamaica		28 Apr 01	Philadelphia
	N	1:31.57		UK National Team		20 Aug 77	London (CP)
	A	1:31.49		Russia		5 Jun 93	Portsmouth
	NJ	1:38.34	i#	UK National Team		2 Mar 96	Liévin
		1:42.2		London Olympiades AC		19 Aug 72	Bracknell
4x400m	W,E	3:15.17		U.S.S.R.		1 Oct 88	Seoul
	C	3:20.65		Jamaica		12 Aug 01	Edmonton
	A	3:20.79		Czechoslovakia		21 Aug 83	London (CP)
	N	3:22.01		UK National Team		1 Sep 91	Tokyo
	WJ,EJ	3:28.39		East Germany		31 Jul 88	Sudbury
	NJ	3:33.82		UK National Team		22 Oct 00	Santiago
4x800m	W,E	7:50.17		U.S.S.R.		5 Aug 84	Moscow
	C	8:20.73		UK National Team	Eng	5 Jun 93	Portsmouth
	A	7:57.08		Russia		5 Jun 93	Portsmouth
	N	8:19.9		UK National Team		5 Jun 92	Sheffield
	NJ	8:39.6		BMC Junior Squad		17 Jul 96	Watford
4x1500m	W,C,A	17:09.75		Australia		25 Jun 00	London (BP)
	E	17:19.09		Irish Republic		25 Jun 00	London (BP)
	N	17:41.0		BMC National Squad	Eng	30 Apr 97	Watford
	NJ	18:38.0		BMC Junior Squad		30 Apr 97	Watford
4x1Mile	W	18:39.58		University of Oregon		3 May 85	Eugene
	ECAN	19:17.3		BMC National Squad	Eng	10 Jul 93	Oxford
	NJ	20:16.2		BMC Junior Squad		11 Jun 97	Watford
Track Walking							
1500m	W,C	5:50.41		Kerry Saxby-Junna	AUS	20 Jan 91	Sydney
	E	5:53.0		Sada Eidikyte	LIT	12 May 90	Vilnius
	A	6:04.5	i#	Beate Anders/Gummelt	GER	4 Mar 90	Glasgow
	A,NJ	6:58.5		Carol Tyson		5 Sep 76	Gateshead
	N	6:32.16		Niobe Menendez		13 Aug 00	Tullamore
1 Mile	W,E	6:16.45	#	Kjersti Plätzer	NOR	2 Sep 01	Knarvik
		6:19.31		Ileana Salvador	ITA	15 Jun 91	Siderno
	C	6:35.47	i#	Ann Peel	CAN	15 Feb 87	Fairfax
		6:47.9		Sue Cook	AUS	14 Mar 81	Canberra
	A	6:30.7	i#	Beate Anders/Gummelt	GER	4 Mar 90	Glasgow
	N	7:08.9	mx#	Catherine Charnock		22 Aug 00	Rugby
	A,N	7:14.3		Carol Tyson		17 Sep 77	London (PH)
	NJ	7:31.6		Kate Horwill		22 Aug 93	Solihull
3000m	W,E	11:40.33	i#	Claudia Iovan	ROM	30 Jan 99	Bucharest
		11:48.24		Ileana Salvador	ITA	29 Aug 93	Padua
	C	11:51.26		Kerry Saxby-Junna	AUS	7 Feb 91	Melbourne
	A	12:32.37		Yelena Nikolayeva	RUS	19 Jun 88	Portsmouth
	N	12:49.16		Betty Sworowski		28 Jul 90	Wrexham
	WJ,EJ	12:21.7	i#	Susana Feitór	POR	19 Feb 94	Braga
		12:24.47		Claudia Iovan	ROM	24 Jul 97	Ljubljana
	NJ	13:03.4		Vicky Lupton/White		18 May 91	Sheffield
5000m	W,C	20:03.0	#	Kerry Saxby-Junna	AUS	11 Feb 96	Sydney
		20:13.26		Kerry Saxby-Junna	AUS	25 Feb 96	Hobart
	E	20:07.52	#	Beate Anders/Gummelt	GER	23 Jun 90	Rostock
		20:21.69		Annarita Sidoti	ITA	1 Jul 95	Cesenatico
	A	21:08.65		Yelena Nikolayeva	RUS	19 Jun 88	Portsmouth
	N	21:52.4	#	Vicky Lupton/White		9 Aug 95	Sheffield (W)
		22:01.53		Lisa Kehler		26 Jul 98	Birmingham
	WJ,EJ	20:31.4		Irina Stankina	RUS	10 Feb 96	Adler
	NJ	22:36.81		Vicky Lupton/White		15 Jun 91	Espoo

5k(Road)	W,E	20:05		Olga Polyakova	RUS	28 May 00	Saransk
	WJ,EJ	20:24		Lyudmila Yefimkina	RUS	28 May 00	Saransk
	N	21:36		Vicky Lupton/White		18 Jul 92	Sheffield
10000m	W,E	41:56.23		Nadezhda Ryashkina	RUS	24 Jul 90	Seattle
	C	41:57.22		Kerry Saxby-Junna	AUS	24 Jul 90	Seattle
	A,N	45:09.57		Lisa Kehler		13 Aug 00	Birmingham
	WJ	42:49.7		Gao Hongmiao	CHN	15 Mar 92	Jinan
	EJ	43:35.2		Lyudmila Yefimkina	RUS	20 May 00	Moscow
	NJ	47:04		Vicky Lupton		30 Mar 91	Sheffield (W)
1 Hour	W	13,194 m		Victoria Herazo	USA	5 Dec 92	Santa Monica
	E	12,913 m		Valentina Sachuk	UKR	24 Jun 99	Belaya Tserkov
	C	12,805 m		Wendy Muldoon	AUS	25 Jun 94	Melbourne
	A,N,NJ	11,590 m		Lisa Langford/Kehler		13 Sep 86	Woodford
20000m	W,E	1:26:52.3		Olimpiada Ivanova	RUS	6 Sep 01	Brisbane
	C	1:33:40.2		Kerry Saxby-Junna	AUS	6 Sep 01	Brisbane
	A,N	1:56:59.7		Cath Reader		21 Oct 95	Loughborough
	WJ	1:37:33.9		Gao Kelian	CHN	18 Sep 99	Xian
	EJ	1:39:20.5		Vera Santos	POR	4 Aug 00	Almada
2 Hours	W,C	22,747 m		Carolyn Vanstan	AUS	20 Jun 92	Melbourne
	E	22,239 m		Jana Zárubová	CZE	12 Oct 85	Prague
	A,N	20,502 m		Cath Reader		21 Oct 95	Loughborough
30000m	W,E	2:56:36.0		Cinzia Chianda	ITA	18 Oct 86	Limbiate
50000m	W,E	4:55:19.4		Svetlana Bychenkova	RUS	27 Jun 98	St. Petersburg
	C,N	5:26:59		Sandra Brown	Eng	27 Oct 90	Étréchy
Road Walking - Fastest Recorded Times							
10km	W,E	41:04		Yelena Nikolayeva	RUS	20 Apr 96	Sochi
	C	41:30		Kerry Saxby-Junna	AUS	27 Aug 88	Canberra
	A	43:44	+	Kjersti Plätzer	NOR	21 Apr 01	Leamington
	N	45:03		Lisa Kehler		19 Sep 98	Kuala Lumpur
	WJ,EJ	41:55		Irina Stankina	RUS	11 Feb 95	Adler
	NJ	47:04	t	Vicky Lupton/White		30 Mar 91	Sheffield (W)
20km	W,E	1:24:50		Olimpiada Ivanova	RUS	4 Mar 01	Adler
	C	1:28:56		Jane Saville	AUS	6 May 00	Vallensbæk
	A	1:28:40		Liu Hongyu	CHN	23 Apr 00	Leamington
	N	1:33:57		Lisa Kehler		17 Jun 00	Eisenhüttenstadt
	WJ,EJ	1:27:35		Natalya Fedoskina	RUS	2 May 99	Mézidon-Canon
	NJ	1:52:03		Vicky Lupton/White		13 Oct 91	Sheffield
50km	W,E	4:34:16		Yelena Ginko	BLR	29 Oct 01	Scanzorosciate
	C,A,N	4:50:51		Sandra Brown	Eng	13 Jul 91	Basildon
	WJ,EJ	5:08:18		Yelena Michailova	RUS	8 Sep 01	St. Petersburg
RECORDS set in 2001							
3000m	C,N	8:26.97		Paula Radcliffe	Eng	29 Jun 01	Rome
2M	A	9:27.6	+e	Paula Radcliffe		22 Jul 01	London (CP)
5000m	E	14:29.32		Olga Yegorova	RUS	31 Aug 01	Berlin
	C,N	14:32.44		Paula Radcliffe	Eng	31 Aug 01	Berlin
HMar	W,C	1:05:44	#	Susan Chepkemei	KEN	1 Apr 01	Lisbon
	E,A,N	1:06:47		Paula Radcliffe		7 Oct 01	Bristol
Marathon	W	2:19:46		Naoko Takahashi	JPN	30 Sep 01	Berlin
	W,C	2:18:47		Catherine Ndereba	KEN	7 Oct 01	Chicago
	WJ	2:23:37		Liu Min	CHN	14 Oct 01	Beijing
400H	WJ	55.15		Huang Xiaoxiao	CHN	22 Nov 01	Guangzhou
2000SC	C,A	6:19.00		Irene Limika	KEN	20 May 01	Loughborough
	N	6:29.79		Tara Krzywicki		20 May 01	Loughborough
	NJ	7:06.0		Jo Ankier		14 Jun 01	Southampton
	NJ	7:01.2		Kathryn Frost		20 Jun 01	Woodford
	NJ	6:55.04		Jo Ankier		22 Jul 01	Grosseto
3000SC	A	9:48.72		Elizabeth Jackson	USA	1 Jul 01	Glasgow (S)

3000SC	C,N	9:52.71		Tara Krzywicki	Eng	1 Jul 01	Glasgow (S)
	W,E	9:25.31		Justyna Bak	POL	9 Jul 01	Nice
	C	9:39.51		Irene Limika	KEN	9 Jul 01	Nice
	WJ,EJ	10:04.99	#	Ulla Tuimala	FIN	2 Sep 01	Gothenburg
	C,WJ	9:30.70		Melissa Rollison	AUS	4 Sep 01	Brisbane
HJ	N=	1.95		Susan Jones		24 Jun 01	Bremen
PV	E	4.58 i		Svetlana Feofanova	RUS	27 Jan 01	Karlsruhe
	W=	4.63 i		Stacy Dragila	USA	2 Feb 01	New York
	W	4.66A i	#	Stacy Dragila	USA	9 Feb 01	Pocatello
	WJ,EJ	4.47 i		Yelena Isinbayeva	RUS	10 Feb 01	Budapest (OH)
	W,E	4.64 i		Svetlana Feofanova	RUS	11 Feb 01	Dortmund
	W=	4.66A i		Stacy Dragila	USA	17 Feb 01	Pocatello
	W	4.70A i		Stacy Dragila	USA	17 Feb 01	Pocatello
	E	4.65 i		Svetlana Feofanova	RUS	21 Feb 01	Piraeus
	A	4.44 i	#	Svetlana Feofanova	RUS	18 Mar 01	Glasgow
	A=	4.44 i	#	Doris Auer	AUT	18 Mar 01	Glasgow
	A	4.56 i	#	Svetlana Feofanova	RUS	18 Mar 01	Glasgow
	W	4.65A	#	Stacy Dragila	USA	27 Apr 01	Pocatello
	W	4.70A	#	Stacy Dragila	USA	27 Apr 01	Pocatello
	W	4.71		Stacy Dragila	USA	9 Jun 01	Palo Alto
	W	4.81		Stacy Dragila	USA	9 Jun 01	Palo Alto
	E	4.57	#	Svetlana Feofanova	RUS	11 Jun 01	Athens
	E	4.60	#	Svetlana Feofanova	RUS	23 Jun 01	Bremen
	WJ,EJ	4.42	#	Yelena Isinbayeva	RUS	29 Jun 01	Rome
	E	4.61	#	Monika Pyrek	POL	1 Jul 01	Bydgoszcz
	N	4.36		Janine Whitlock		1 Jul 01	Budapest
	E	4.62	#	Svetlana Feofanova	RUS	9 Jul 01	Nice
	E	4.65		Svetlana Feofanova	RUS	14 Jul 01	Tula
	E	4.70		Svetlana Feofanova	RUS	14 Jul 01	Tula
	A,N	4.40		Janine Whitlock		14 Jul 01	Birmingham
	A	4.45		Svetlana Feofanova	RUS	22 Jul 01	London (CP)
	A	4.45		Stacy Dragila	USA	22 Jul 01	London (CP)
	A	4.55		Svetlana Feofanova	RUS	22 Jul 01	London (CP)
	A	4.55		Stacy Dragila	USA	22 Jul 01	London (CP)
	A	4.65		Stacy Dragila	USA	22 Jul 01	London (CP)
	A	4.65		Svetlana Feofanova	RUS	22 Jul 01	London (CP)
	A	4.72		Stacy Dragila	USA	22 Jul 01	London (CP)
	E=	4.70		Svetlana Feofanova	RUS	6 Aug 01	Edmonton
	E	4.75		Svetlana Feofanova	RUS	6 Aug 01	Edmonton
	WJ,EJ	4.46	#	Yelena Isinbayeva	RUS	31 Aug 01	Berlin
DT	NJ	54.81		Claire Smithson		1 Jul 01	Bedford
HT	C	68.73		Bronwyn Eagles	AUS	18 Feb 01	Canberra
	C	68.83		Bronwyn Eagles	AUS	11 Mar 01	Hobart
	N	68.15		Lorraine Shaw		17 Mar 01	Nice/Boulouris
	C	69.24	#	Bronwyn Eagles	AUS	26 Jul 01	Calgary
	C	70.19	#	Bronwyn Eagles	AUS	30 Jul 01	Calgary
	C	68.87		Bronwyn Eagles	AUS	7 Aug 01	Edmonton
	WJ,EJ	71.71		Kamila Skolimowska	POL	9 Sep 01	Melbourne
JT	W	71.54		Osleidys Menéndez	CUB	1 Jul 01	Rethymno
	NJ	55.40		Goldie Sayers		22 Jul 01	Grosseto
4x200	C	1:30.23		Jamaica		28 Apr 01	Philadelphia
4x400	C	3:20.65		Jamaica		12 Aug 01	Edmonton
Track Walking							
1Mile	W,E	6:16.45	#	Kjersti Plätzer	NOR	2 Sep 01	Knarvik
20k	W,E	1:29:36.4	#	Susana Feitor	POR	21 Jul 01	Lisbon
	W,E	1:26:52.3		Olimpiada Ivanova	RUS	6 Sep 01	Brisbane
	C	1:33:40.2		Kerry Saxby-Junna	AUS	6 Sep 01	Brisbane
Road Walking							
10k	A	43:44+		Kjersti Plätzer	NOR	21 Apr 01	Leamington
20k	W,E	1:24:50		Olimpiada Ivanova	RUS	4 Mar 01	Adler
50k	WJ,EJ	5:08:18		Yelena Michailova	RUS	8 Sep 01	St. Petersburg
50k	W,E	4:34:16		Yelena Ginko	BLR	29 Oct 01	Scanzorosciate

NATIONAL RECORDS OF THE UK - MEN

as at 31 December 2001

These are the best authentic performances for the four home countries of the U.K.
E = England S = Scotland W = Wales NI = Northern Ireland

100m	E	9.87		Linford Christie	15 Aug 93	Stuttgart, GER
	S	10.11		Allan Wells	24 Jul 80	Moscow, RUS
	W	10.11		Christian Malcolm	5 Aug 01	Edmonton, CAN
	NI	10.46		Mark Forsythe	17 Jun 89	Tel Aviv, ISR
200m	E	19.87	A#	John Regis	31 Jul 94	Sestriere, ITA
		19.94		John Regis	20 Aug 93	Stuttgart, GER
	W	20.08		Christian Malcolm	8 Aug 01	Edmonton, CAN
	S	20.21		Allan Wells	28 Jul 80	Moscow, RUS
	NI	20.81		Paul McBurney	24 Aug 94	Victoria, CAN
300m	S	31.56		Dougie Walker	19 Jul 98	Gateshead
	E	31.67		John Regis	17 Jul 92	Gateshead
	W	32.06		Jamie Baulch	31 May 97	Cardiff
	NI	33.77		Simon Baird	24 Jun 85	Belfast
400m	W	44.36		Iwan Thomas	13 Jul 97	Birmingham
	E	44.37		Roger Black	3 Jul 96	Lausanne, SUI
		44.37		Mark Richardson	9 Jul 98	Oslo, NOR
		44.37		Mark Richardson	8 Aug 98	Monaco, MON
	S	44.93		David Jenkins	21 Jun 75	Eugene, USA
	NI	45.85		Paul McBurney	13 Jul 97	Birmingham
600m	E	1:14.95		Steve Heard	14 Jul 91	London (Ha)
	S	1:15.4		Tom McKean	21 Jul 91	Grangemouth
	W	1:17.8	i	Bob Adams	20 Dec 69	Cosford
		1:18.02		Glen Grant	2 Aug 78	Edmonton, CAN
	NI	1:18.3	i	Joe Chivers	14 Dec 74	Cosford
		1:20.1		Kenneth Thompson	24 May 80	Belfast
800m	E	1:41.73	"	Sebastian Coe	10 Jun 81	Florence, ITA
	S	1:43.88		Tom McKean	28 Jul 89	London (CP)
	W	1:45.44		Neil Horsfield	28 Jul 90	Wrexham
	NI	1:45.96		James McIlroy	5 Aug 00	London (CP)
		1:45.32		while representing IRL	16 Jul 98	Nice
1000m	E	2:12.18		Sebastian Coe	11 Jul 81	Oslo, NOR
	S	2:16.82		Graham Williamson	17 Jul 84	Edinburgh
	W	2:17.36		Neil Horsfield	9 Aug 91	Gateshead
	NI	2:19.05		Mark Kirk	5 Aug 87	Oslo, NOR
		2:15.57		James McIlroy (IRL perIAAF)	5 Sep 99	Rieti, ITA
1500m	E	3:29.67		Steve Cram	16 Jul 85	Nice, FRA
	S	3:33.83		John Robson	4 Sep 79	Brussels, BEL
	NI	3:34.76		Gary Lough	9 Sep 95	Monaco, MON
	W	3:35.08		Neil Horsfield	10 Aug 90	Brussels, BEL
1 Mile	E	3:46.32		Steve Cram	27 Jul 85	Oslo, NOR
	S	3:50.64		Graham Williamson	13 Jul 82	Cork, IRL
	W	3:54.39		Neil Horsfield	8 Jul 86	Cork, IRL
	NI	3:55.0		Jim McGuinness	11 Jul 77	Dublin (B), IRL
2000m	E	4:51.39		Steve Cram	4 Aug 85	Budapest, HUN
	S	4:58.38		Graham Williamson	29 Aug 83	London (CP)
	NI	5:02.61		Steve Martin	9 Jun 84	Belfast
	W	5:05.32		Tony Simmons	4 Jul 75	London (CP)

3000m	E	7:32.79	Dave Moorcroft	17 Jul 82	London (CP)
	S	7:45.81	John Robson	13 Jul 84	London (CP)
	W	7:46.40	Ian Hamer	20 Jan 90	Auckland, NZL
	NI	7:49.1	Paul Lawther	27 Jun 78	Oslo, NOR
2 Miles	E	8:13.51	Steve Ovett	15 Sep 78	London (CP)
	S	8:19.37	Nat Muir	27 Jun 80	London (CP)
	W	8:20.28	David James	27 Jun 80	London (CP)
	NI	8:30.6	Paul Lawther	28 May 77	Belfast
5000m	E	13:00.41	Dave Moorcroft	7 Jul 82	Oslo, NOR
	W	13:09.80	Ian Hamer	9 Jun 92	Rome, ITA
	S	13:17.9	Nat Muir	15 Jul 80	Oslo, NOR
	NI	13:27.63	Dermot Donnelly	1 Aug 98	Hechtel, BEL
10000m	E	27:18.14 #	Jon Brown	28 Aug 98	Brussels, BEL
		27:23.06	Eamonn Martin	2 Jul 88	Oslo, NOR
	W	27:39.14	Steve Jones	9 Jul 83	Oslo, NOR
	S	27:43.03	Ian Stewart	9 Sep 77	London (CP)
	NI	28:38.56	Dermot Donnelly	29 Jun 97	Sheffield
20000m	E	57:28.7	Carl Thackery	31 Mar 90	La Flèche, FRA
	S	59:24.0	Jim Alder	9 Nov 68	Leicester
	W	69:37.0	Mick McGeoch	4 Mar 90	Barry
	NI	77:16.0	Ian Anderson	5 Mar 00	Barry
1 Hour	E	20,855 m	Carl Thackery	31 Mar 90	La Flèche, FRA
	S	20,201 m	Jim Alder	9 Nov 68	Leicester
	W	18,898 m	Mike Rowland	7 Aug 73	Stockholm, SWE
	NI	18,354 m	Dave Smyth	19 Sep 65	Bristol (?)
25000m	E	1:15:22.6	Ron Hill	21 Jul 65	Bolton
	S	1:15:34.4	Jim Alder	5 Sep 70	London (CP)
	W	1:27:01.0 e	Mick McGeoch	4 Mar 90	Barry
	NI	1:37:18.0 e	Ian Anderson	5 Mar 00	Barry
30000m	S	1:31:30.4	Jim Alder	5 Sep 70	London (CP)
	E	1:31:56.4	Tim Johnston	5 Sep 70	London (CP)
	W	1:33:49.0	Bernie Plain	1 Dec 73	Bristol
	NI	1:57:30.0	Ian Anderson	5 Mar 00	Barry
Half Marathon	E	60:09 #	Paul Evans	15 Jan 95	Marrakesh, MAR
		61:03	Nick Rose	15 Sep 85	Philadelphia, USA
	W	60:59	Steve Jones	8 Jun 86	South Shields
	S	61:34 #	Paul Evans	15 Mar 92	Lisbon, POR
		62:28	Allister Hutton	21 Jun 87	South Shields
	NI	62:16	Jim Haughey	20 Sep 87	Philadelphia, USA
Marathon	W	2:07:13	Steve Jones	20 Oct 85	Chicago, USA
	E	2:08:33	Charlie Spedding	21 Apr 85	London
	S	2:09:16	Allister Hutton	21 Apr 85	London
	NI	2:13:06	Greg Hannon	13 May 79	Coventry
2000m SC	E	5:19.86	Mark Rowland	28 Aug 88	London (CP)
	S	5:21.77	Tom Hanlon	11 Jun 92	Caserta, ITA
	W	5:23.6	Roger Hackney	10 Jun 82	Birmingham
	NI	5:31.09	Peter McColgan	5 Aug 86	Gateshead
3000m SC	E	8:07.96	Mark Rowland	30 Sep 88	Seoul, SKO
	S	8:12.58	Tom Hanlon	3 Aug 91	Monaco, MON
	W	8:18.91	Roger Hackney	30 Jul 88	Hechtel, BEL
	NI	8:27.93	Peter McColgan	25 Jun 91	Hengelo, NED

110m H	W	12.91		Colin Jackson	20 Aug 93	Stuttgart, GER
	E	13.00		Tony Jarrett	20 Aug 93	Stuttgart, GER
	S	13.66		Ross Baillie	20 Feb 99	Sydney, AUS
	NI	14.19		C.J. Kirkpatrick	16 Jun 73	Edinburgh
200m H	W	22.63		Colin Jackson	1 Jun 91	Cardiff
	E	22.79		John Regis	1 Jun 91	Cardiff
	S	23.76		Angus McKenzie	22 Aug 81	Edinburgh
	NI	24.81		Terry Price	31 Aug 92	Belfast
400m H	E	47.82		Kriss Akabusi	6 Aug 92	Barcelona, ESP
	W	49.16		Paul Gray	18 Aug 98	Budapest, HUN
	NI	49.60		Phil Beattie	28 Jul 86	Edinburgh
	S	50.24		Charles Robertson-Adams	4 Jul 01	Loughborough
High Jump	E	2.38	i	Steve Smith	4 Feb 94	Wuppertal, GER
		2.37		Steve Smith	20 Sep 92	Seoul, SKO
		2.37		Steve Smith	22 Aug 93	Stuttgart, GER
	S	2.31		Geoff Parsons	26 Aug 94	Victoria, CAN
	W	2.25		Robert Mitchell	28 Jul 01	Bedford
	NI	2.20		Floyd Manderson	14 Jul 85	London (CP)
		2.20		Floyd Manderson	21 Jun 86	London (CP)
		2.20		Floyd Manderson	16 Aug 86	Leiden, NED
Pole Vault	E	5.80		Nick Buckfield	27 May 98	Hania, GRE
	W	5.60		Neil Winter	19 Aug 95	Enfield
	NI	5.25		Mike Bull	22 Sep 73	London (CP)
	S	5.21		Graham Eggleton	10 Jul 82	Grangemouth
Long Jump	W	8.23		Lynn Davies	30 Jun 68	Berne, SUI
	E	8.15		Stewart Faulkner	16 Jul 90	Belfast
	NI	8.14		Mark Forsythe	7 Jul 91	Rhede, GER
	S	7.88		Darren Ritchie	20 Aug 00	Bedford
Triple Jump	E	18.29		Jonathan Edwards	7 Aug 95	Gothenburg, SWE
	W	16.28		Steven Shalders	13 Jul 01	Amsterdam, NED
	S	16.17		John Mackenzie	17 Sep 94	Bedford
	NI	15.78		Michael McDonald	31 Jul 94	Corby
Shot	E	21.68		Geoff Capes	18 May 80	Cwmbrân
	W	20.45		Shaun Pickering	17 Aug 97	London (CP)
	S	18.93		Paul Buxton	13 May 77	Los Angeles(Ww), USA
	NI	16.56		Iain McMullan	28 Jul 01	Belfast
Discus	E	66.64		Perriss Wilkins	6 Jun 98	Birmingham (Un)
	W	60.43		Lee Newman	12 Aug 98	Enfield
	S	59.84	#	Colin Sutherland ¶	10 Jun 78	San Jose, USA
		58.58		Darrin Morris	22 Jun 91	Enfield
	NI	51.76		John Moreland	1 Jul 95	Antrim
Hammer	NI	77.54		Martin Girvan	12 May 84	Wolverhampton
	E	77.30		David Smith	13 Jul 85	London (CP)
	S	75.40		Chris Black	23 Jul 83	London (CP)
	W	68.64		Shaun Pickering	7 Apr 84	Stanford, USA
Javelin	E	91.46		Steve Backley	25 Jan 92	Auckland(NS), NZL
	W	81.70		Nigel Bevan	28 Jun 92	Birmingham
	NI	70.34	#	Damien Crawford	20 Jul 91	Hayes
		67.60		Dean Smahon	9 Jul 94	King's Lynn
	S	69.20		Roddy James	28 Apr 89	Des Moines, USA

Dec.	E	8847		Daley Thompson	9	Aug	84	Los Angeles, USA
	S	7885	#h	Brad McStravick	6	May	84	Birmingham
		7856	#	Brad McStravick	28	May	84	Cwmbrân
	NI	7874		Colin Boreham	23	May	82	Götzis, AUT
	W	7308	h	Clive Longe	29	Jun	69	Kassel, GER
		7268		Paul Edwards ¶	14	Aug	83	Bonn, GER
(with 1986 Javelin)								
	E	8811	#	Daley Thompson	28	Aug	86	Stuttgart, GER
	S	7739		Jamie Quarry	30	May	99	Arles, FRA
	W	7071	#	Paul Jones	4	Jun	00	Arles, FRA
	NI	6911		Brendan McConville	10	Jun	01	Arles, FRA
4x100m	E	37.73		J. Gardener, D.Campbell (UK)				
				M.Devonish, D.Chambers	29	Aug	99	Seville, ESP
	W	38.73		K. Williams, D. Turner,				
				C. Malcolm, J. Henthorn	21	Sep	98	Kuala Lumpur, MAS
	S	39.24		D. Jenkins, A. Wells,				
				C. Sharp, A. McMaster	12	Aug	78	Edmonton, CAN
	NI	40.71		J. McAdorey, I. Craig,				
				P. Brizzell, M. Allen	22	Jun	96	Belfast
4x400m	E	2:57.53		R. Black, D. Redmond, (UK)				
				J. Regis, K. Akabusi	1	Sep	91	Tokyo, JAP
	W	3:01.86		P. Gray, J. Baulch,				
				D. Turner, I. Thomas	21	Sep	98	Kuala Lumpur, MAS
	S	3:04.68		M. Davidson, T. McKean,				
				D. Strang, B. Whittle	3	Feb	90	Auckland, NZL
	NI	3:07.27		B. Forbes, M. Douglas,				
				E. King, P. McBurney	21	Sep	98	Kuala Lumpur, MAS
Track Walking								
3000m	E	11:24.4		Mark Easton	10	May	89	Tonbridge
	W	11:45.77		Steve Johnson	20	Jun	87	Cwmbrân
	S	11:53.3	#	Martin Bell	9	Aug	95	Birmingham
		11:59.47		Martin Bell	25	May	98	Bedford
	NI	13:15.0		David Smyth	5	Sep	70	Plymouth
5000m	E	19:22.29	i	Martin Rush	8	Feb	92	Birmingham
		19:35.0		Darrell Stone	16	May	89	Brighton
	W	20:08.04	i	Steve Barry	5	Mar	83	Budapest, HUN
		20:22.0		Steve Barry	20	Mar	82	London (WL)
	S	20:13.0		Martin Bell	2	May	92	Enfield
	NI	23:50.0		Jimmy Todd	28	Aug	68	Ballyclare
10000m	E	40:06.65		Ian McCombie	4	Jun	89	Jarrow
	W	41:13.62		Steve Barry	19	Jun	82	London (CP)
	S	41:13.65		Martin Bell	22	Jul	95	Cardiff
	NI	47:37.6		David Smyth	26	Apr	70	Bournemouth
1 Hour	E	14,324 m	#	Ian McCombie	7	Jul	85	London (SP)
		14,158 m		Mark Easton	12	Sep	87	Woodford
	W	13,987 m		Steve Barry	28	Jun	81	Brighton
	S	13,393 m		Bill Sutherland	27	Sep	69	London (He)
	NI	12,690 m	#	David Smyth	26	Apr	70	Bournemouth
		12,646 m		David Smyth	23	Sep	67	London (PH)
20000m	E	1:23:26.5		Ian McCombie	26	May	90	Fana, NOR
	W	1:26:22.0		Steve Barry	28	Jun	81	Brighton
	S	1:38:53.6		Alan Buchanan	6	Jul	75	Brighton
2 Hours	E	27,262 m	#	Chris Maddocks	31	Dec	89	Plymouth
		26,037 m		Ron Wallwork	31	Jul	71	Blackburn

Road Walking

10km	E	40:17		Chris Maddocks	30	Apr 89	Burrator
	W	40:35		Steve Barry	14	May 83	Southport
	S	41:28		Martin Bell	24	Apr 99	Sheffield
	NI	44:49	#	David Smyth	20	Jun 70	Clevedon
		51:53		Arthur Agnew	6	Aug 80	Helsinki, FIN
		51:53		G. Smyth	6	Aug 80	Helsinki, FIN
20km	E	1:22:03		Ian McCombie	23	Sep 88	Seoul, SKO
	W	1:22:51		Steve Barry	26	Feb 83	Douglas, I of M
	S	1:25:42		Martin Bell	9	May 92	Lancaster
	NI	1:39:01		David Smyth		Jul 67	Cardiff
30km	E	2:07:56		Ian McCombie	27	Apr 86	Edinburgh
	W	2:10:16		Steve Barry	7	Oct 82	Brisbane, AUS
	S	2:22:21		Martin Bell	8	May 94	Cardiff
	NI	2:41:15		David Smyth	26	Apr 69	Winterbourne
50km	E	3:51:37		Chris Maddocks	28	Oct 90	Burrator
	W	4:11:59		Bob Dobson	22	Oct 81	Lassing, AUT
	S	4:13:18		Graham White	27	Jun 98	Stockport
	NI	4:45:48		David Smyth	3	May 69	Bristol

NATIONAL RECORDS OF THE UK - WOMEN

as at 31 December 2001

100m	E	11.10		Kathy Smallwood/Cook	5	Sep 81	Rome, ITA
	W	11.39		Sallyanne Short	12	Jul 92	Cwmbrân
	S	11.40		Helen Golden/Hogarth	20	Jul 74	London (CP)
	NI	11.91	#	Joan Atkinson	1	Sep 61	Sofia, BUL
		11.93		Vicki Jamison	2	Aug 97	Belfast
200m	E	22.10		Kathy Cook	9	Aug 84	Los Angeles, USA
	W	22.80		Michelle Scutt	12	Jun 82	Antrim
	S	22.98		Sandra Whittaker	8	Aug 84	Los Angeles, USA
	NI	23.62		Linda McCurry	8	Aug 78	Edmonton, CAN
300m	E	35.46		Kathy Cook	18	Aug 84	London (CP)
	W	36.01		Michelle Probert/Scutt	13	Jul 80	London (CP)
	S	36.46		Linsey Macdonald	13	Jul 80	London (CP)
	NI	38.20		Linda McCurry	2	Aug 78	Edmonton, CAN
400m	E	49.43		Kathy Cook	6	Aug 84	Los Angeles, USA
	W	50.63		Michelle Scutt	31	May 82	Cwmbrân
	S	50.71		Allison Curbishley	18	Sep 98	Kuala Lumpur, MAS
	NI	52.54		Stephanie Llewellyn	9	Jul 95	Cwmbrân
		52.4		Stephanie Llewellyn	1	Jul 95	London (He)
600m	E	1:26.0		Kelly Holmes	13	Aug 95	Gothenburg, SWE
	W	1:26.5		Kirsty McDermott/Wade	21	Aug 85	Zürich, SWZ
	S	1:27.4	i	Linsey Macdonald	12	Dec 81	Cosford
		1:29.88		Anne Clarkson/Purvis	25	Sep 82	Brisbane, AUS
	NI	1:29.46		Jo Latimer	19	May 93	Birmingham
800m	E	1:56.21		Kelly Holmes	9	Sep 95	Monaco, MON
	W	1:57.42		Kirsty McDermott/Wade	24	Jun 85	Belfast
	S	2:00.15		Rosemary Stirling/Wright	3	Sep 72	Munich, GER
	NI	2:01.83		Amanda Crowe	18	Sep 98	Kuala Lumpur, MAS
1000m	E	2:32.55		Kelly Holmes	15	Jun 97	Leeds
	W	2:33.70		Kirsty McDermott/Wade	9	Aug 85	Gateshead
	S	2:37.05		Christine Whittingham	27	Jun 86	Gateshead
	NI	2:48.59		Jane Ewing	26	Jun 90	Antrim

1500m	E	3:58.07		Kelly Holmes	29	Jun	97	Sheffield
	W	4:00.73		Kirsty Wade	26	Jul	87	Gateshead
	S	4:01.20		Yvonne Murray	4	Jul	87	Oslo, NOR
	NI	4:10.68		Amanda Crowe	21	Sep	98	Kuala Lumpur, MAS
1 Mile	E	4:17.57		Zola Budd	21	Aug	85	Zürich, SUI
	W	4:19.41		Kirsty McDermott/Wade	27	Jul	85	Oslo, NOR
	S	4:22.64		Yvonne Murray	22	Jul	94	Oslo, NOR
	NI	4:32.99		Amanda Crowe	30	Aug	98	Glasgow (S)
2000m	S	5:26.93		Yvonne Murray	8	Jul	94	Edinburgh
	E	5:30.19		Zola Budd	11	Jul	86	London (CP)
	W	5:45.81	i	Kirsty Wade	13	Mar	87	Cosford
		5:50.17		Susan Tooby/Wightman	13	Jul	84	London (CP)
	NI	5:57.24		Ursula McKee/McGloin	25	Jun	90	Antrim
3000m	E	8:26.97		Paula Radcliffe	29	Jun	01	Rome, ITA
	S	8:29.02		Yvonne Murray	25	Sep	88	Seoul, SKO
	W	8:47.59		Hayley Tullett	15	Jul	00	Gateshead
	NI	9:16.25		Ursula McKee/McGloin	7	Jun	90	Helsinki, FIN
2 Miles	E	9:27.5	e	Paula Radcliffe	22	Aug	97	Brussels, BEL
		9:32.07		Paula Radcliffe	23	May	99	Loughborough
	S	9:36.85	i	Yvonne Murray	15	Mar	87	Cosford
		9:51.38		Hayley Haining	23	May	99	Loughborough
	W	9:49.73		Hayley Tullett	23	May	99	Loughborough
5000m	E	14:32.44		Paula Radcliffe	31	Aug	01	Berlin, GER
	S	14:56.94		Yvonne Murray	7	Jul	95	London (CP)
	W	15:13.22		Angela Tooby/Tooby-Smith	5	Aug	87	Oslo, NOR
	NI	16:50.22	#	Teresa Duffy	30	May	99	Bedford
		16:54.47		Ann Terek	23	Jul	95	Cardiff
10000m	E	30:26.97		Paula Radcliffe	30	Sep	00	Sydney, AUS
	S	30:57.07		Liz McColgan	25	Jun	91	Hengelo, NED
	W	31:55.30		Angela Tooby/Tooby-Smith	4	Sep	87	Rome, ITA
	NI	36:19.98	#	Teresa Kidd	25	Aug	85	Dublin (S), IRL
1 Hour	E	16,495 m	#	Michaela McCallum	2	Apr	00	Asti
		16,364 m		Alison Fletcher	3	Sep	97	Bromley
	W	16,460 m	i#	Bronwen Cardy-Wise	8	Mar	92	Birmingham
		14,400 m		Ann Franklin	5	Mar	89	Barry
	S	12,800 m		Leslie Watson	12	Mar	83	London (He)
20000m	E	1:15:46		Carolyn Hunter-Rowe	6	Mar	94	Barry
	W	1:23:56		Ann Franklin	9	Mar	86	Barry
25000m	E	1:35:16	e	Carolyn Hunter-Rowe	6	Mar	94	Barry
	W	1:44:58	e	Ann Franklin	9	Mar	86	Barry
	S	1:54:55		Leslie Watson	12	Mar	83	London (He)
30000m	E	1:55:03		Carolyn Hunter-Rowe	6	Mar	94	Barry
	W	2:05:59		Ann Franklin	9	Mar	86	Barry
	S	2:16:44		Leslie Watson	12	Mar	83	London (He)
Half	E	66:47		Paula Radcliffe	7	Oct	01	Bristol
Marathon	S	67:11		Liz McColgan	26	Jan	92	Tokyo, JPN
	W	69:56		Susan Tooby/Wightman	24	Jul	88	South Shields
	NI	75:57	#	Moira O'Boyle/O'Neill	23	Mar	86	Cavan, IRL
		76:23		Moira O'Neill	24	Sep	88	Londonderry
Marathon	E	2:25:56		Véronique Marot	23	Apr	89	London
	S	2:26:52		Liz McColgan	13	Apr	97	London
	W	2:31:33		Susan Tooby/Wightman	23	Sep	88	Seoul, SKO
	NI	2:37:06		Moira O'Neill	31	Oct	88	Dublin, IRL

2000mSC	E	6:29.79		Tara Krzywicki	20 May 01	Loughborough
	S	7:01.74		Allison Higgins	18 Jul 01	Glasgow (S)
	W	7:34.66		Claire Martin	2 May 98	Bath
	NI	8:01.8		Gemma Turley	30 Jun 01	Bangor (NI)
3000mSC	E	9:52.71		Tara Krzywicki	1 Jul 01	Glasgow (S)
	S	10:55.70		Allison Higgins	11 Aug 01	Glasgow (S)
	W	12:35.60		Sian Davies	5 Jul 01	Stretford
100m H	E	12.80		Angie Thorp	31 Jul 96	Atlanta, USA
	W	12.91		Kay Morley-Brown	2 Feb 90	Auckland, NZL
	NI	13.29		Mary Peters	2 Sep 72	Munich, GER
	S	13.35		Pat Rollo	30 Jul 83	London (CP)
400m H	E	52.74		Sally Gunnell	19 Aug 93	Stuttgart, GER
	S	55.24		Sinead Dudgeon	24 Jul 99	Birmingham
	NI	55.91		Elaine McLaughlin	26 Sep 88	Seoul, SKO
	W	56.43		Alyson Layzell	16 Jun 96	Birmingham
High Jump	E	1.95		Diana Elliott/Davies	26 Jun 82	Oslo, NOR
		1.95	i	Debbie Marti	23 Feb 97	Birmingham
		1.95		Susan Jones	24 Jun 01	Bremen, GER
	NI	1.92		Janet Boyle	29 Sep 88	Seoul, SKO
	S	1.91		Jayne Barnetson	7 Jul 89	Edinburgh
	W	1.85	i	Julie Crane	13 Feb 00	Cardiff
		1.84		Sarah Rowe	22 Aug 81	Utrecht, NED
		1.84		Sarah Rowe	31 May 82	Cwmbrân
Pole Vault	E	4.40		Janine Whitlock	14 Jul 01	Birmingham
	W	4.15		Rhian Clarke	7 Apr 00	Austin, USA
	S	3.95	A&	Alison Jessee	25 Jun 99	El Paso, USA
		3.95	A&	Alison Jessee	11 Jul 99	Albuquerque, USA
		3.60		Alison Jessee	4 Aug 98	Cardiff
		3.60		Alison Jessee	21 Apr 00	Tucson, USA
		3.60		Alison Jessee	8 Jul 00	Glasgow
		3.60		Alison Jessee	12 Aug 00	Birmingham
		3.60		Alison Jessee	24 Jun 01	Glasgow (S)
		3.60		Kirsty Maguire	18 Jul 01	Glasgow (S)
		3.60		Kirsty Maguire	4 Aug 01	Wigan
	NI	3.81		Zoe Brown	9 Sep 01	Derby
Long Jump	E	6.90		Bev Kinch	14 Aug 83	Helsinki, FIN
	W	6.52		Gillian Regan	28 Aug 82	Swansea
	S	6.43	#	Moira Walls/Maguire	18 Sep 70	Bucharest, ROM
		6.43		Myra Nimmo	27 May 73	Edinburgh
	NI	6.11		Thelma Hopkins	29 Sep 56	Budapest, HUN
		6.11		Michelle Rea	11 Aug 90	Maia, POR
Triple Jump	E	15.16	i	Ashia Hansen	28 Feb 98	Valencia, ESP
		15.15		Ashia Hansen	13 Sep 97	Fukuoka, JPN
	S	12.89		Karen Hambrook/Skeggs	17 May 92	London (CP)
	W	12.14		Jayne Ludlow	21 May 94	Istanbul, TUR
	NI	11.93		Sharon Oakes	13 Aug 00	Edinburgh
Shot	E	19.36		Judy Oakes	14 Aug 88	Gateshead
	S	18.99		Meg Ritchie	7 May 83	Tucson, USA
	W	19.06	i	Venissa Head	7 Apr 84	St. Athan
		18.93		Venissa Head	13 May 84	Haverfordwest
	NI	16.40	i	Mary Peters	28 Feb 70	Bucharest, ROM
		16.31		Mary Peters	1 Jun 66	Belfast (PP)
Discus	S	67.48		Meg Ritchie	26 Apr 81	Walnut, USA
	W	64.68		Venissa Head	18 Jul 83	Athens, GRE
	E	60.82		Shelley Drew	25 Jul 98	Birmingham
	NI	60.72		Jackie McKernan	18 Jul 93	Buffalo, USA

Hammer	E	68.15	Lorraine Shaw	17 Mar 01	Nice/Boulouris, FRA
	S	58.31	Mhairi Walters	25 Aug 01	Edinburgh
	W	57.40	Sarah Moore	29 Apr 01	London (Col)
	NI	48.90	Julie Kirkpatrick	15 Jun 96	Dublin (S), IRL
Javelin	E	59.50	Karen Martin	14 Jul 99	Cosford
	S	57.19	Lorna Jackson	9 Jul 00	Peterborough
	NI	47.72	Alison Moffitt	21 Aug 99	Belfast
	W	46.89	Caroline White	19 Jun 99	Colwyn Bay
Hept.	E	6831	Denise Lewis	30 Jul 00	Talence, FRA
	S	5803	Jayne Barnetson	20 Aug 89	Kiyev, UKR
	W	5642	Sarah Rowe	23 Aug 81	Utrecht, NED
	NI	5065 h	Catherine Scott	13 Sep 87	Tullamore, IRL
		4564	Wendy Phillips	18 Jul 82	Birmingham
(with 1999 Javelin)					
	S	5257	Chloe Cozens	24 Sep 00	Watford
	W	5186	Rebecca Jones	4 Jun 00	Arles, FRA
4x100m	E	42.43	H. Oakes, K. Cook, (UK) B. Callender, S. Lannaman	1 Aug 80	Moscow, RUS
	S	45.37	J. Booth, K. Hogg, J. Neilson, S. Whittaker	8 Jun 86	Lloret de Mar, ESP
		45.2	A. MacRitchie, S. Pringle, (ESH) H. Hogarth, E. Sutherland	27 Jun 70	London (CP)
	W	45.37	H. Miles, S. Lewis, S. Short, C. Smart	2 Aug 86	Edinburgh
	NI	46.36	K. Graham, H. Gourlay, J. Robinson, R. Gaylor	31 Aug 85	Tel Aviv, ISR
4x400m	E	3:22.01	L. Hanson, P. Smith, (UK) S. Gunnell, L. Staines	1 Sep 91	Tokyo, JPN
	S	3:32.92	S. Whittaker, A. Purvis, A. Baxter, L. Macdonald	9 Oct 82	Brisbane, AUS
	W	3:35.60	C. Smart, K. Wade, D. Fryar, M. Scutt	4 Jul 82	Dublin (S), IRL
	NI	3:40.12	Z. Arnold, V. Jamison, J. Latimer, S. Llewellyn	22 Jun 96	Belfast
Track Walking					
3000m	E	12:49.16	Betty Sworowski	28 Jul 90	Wrexham
	S	13:16.23	Verity Snook	27 May 96	Bedford
	W	14:28.2	Karen Dunster	18 May 91	Portsmouth
5000m	E	21:52.4 #	Vicky Lupton/White	9 Aug 95	Sheffield (W)
		22:01.53	Lisa Kehler	26 Jul 98	Birmingham
	S	23:22.52	Verity Snook	19 Jun 94	Horsham
	W	24:32.92	Karen Nipper	21 Jul 84	Lyngby, DEN
10000m	E	45:09.57	Lisa Kehler	13 Aug 00	Birmingham
	S	47:10.07	Verity Larby/Snook	19 Jun 93	Horsham
	W	50:25.0 mx	Lisa Simpson	1 Apr 87	Hornchurch
		51:00.0	Karen Nipper	21 Feb 81	Leicester
1 Hour	E	11,590 m	Lisa Langford/Kehler	13 Sep 86	Woodford
20000m	E	1:56:59.7	Cath Reader	21 Oct 95	Loughborough
2 Hours	E	20,502 m	Cath Reader	21 Oct 95	Loughborough
Road Walking					
5km	E	21:36	Vicky Lupton/White	18 Jul 92	Sheffield
	S	22:45	Verity Snook	25 Aug 94	Victoria, CAN
	W	23:35	Lisa Simpson	31 Oct 87	Cardiff
10km	E	45:03	Lisa Kehler	19 Sep 98	Kuala Lumpur, MAS
	S	46:06	Verity Snook	25 Aug 94	Victoria, CAN
	W	49:33	Lisa Simpson	14 Mar 87	Ham
20km	E	1:33:57	Lisa Kehler	17 Jun 00	Eisenhüttenstadt, GER
	S	1:36:40	Sara Cattermole	4 Mar 00	Perth, AUS
50km	E	4:50:51	Sandra Brown	13 Jul 91	Basildon

UK INDOOR RECORDS

as at 31 December 2001

MEN

50m	5.61	+	Jason Gardener	16 Feb 00	Madrid, ESP
60m	6.46		Jason Gardener	7 Mar 99	Maebashi, JPN
200m	20.25		Linford Christie	19 Feb 95	Liévin, FRA
300m	32.90		Ade Mafe	31 Jan 92	Karlsruhe, GER
400m	45.39		Jamie Baulch	9 Feb 97	Birmingham
800m	1:44.91		Sebastian Coe	12 Mar 83	Cosford
1000m	2:17.86		Matthew Yates	22 Feb 92	Birmingham
1500m	3:34.20		Peter Elliott	27 Feb 90	Seville, ESP
1 Mile	3:52.02		Peter Elliott	9 Feb 90	East Rutherford, USA
2000m	4:57.09		John Mayock	25 Feb 01	Liévin, FRA
3000m	7:43.31		John Mayock	23 Feb 97	Birmingham
5000m	13:21.27		Nick Rose	12 Feb 82	New York, USA
50m Hurdles	6.40		Colin Jackson	5 Feb 99	Budapest, HUN
60m Hurdles	7.30		Colin Jackson	6 Mar 94	Sindelfingen, GER
High Jump	2.38		Steve Smith	4 Feb 94	Wuppertal, GER
Pole Vault	5.61		Nick Buckfield	3 Feb 96	Birmingham
Long Jump	8.05		Barrington Williams	11 Feb 89	Cosford
	8.05	#	Stewart Faulkner	27 Feb 90	Seville, ESP
Triple Jump	17.64		Jonathan Edwards	15 Feb 98	Birmingham
Shot	20.98		Geoff Capes	16 Jan 76	Los Angeles, USA
	20.98	#	Geoff Capes	14 Feb 76	Winnipeg, CAN
Heptathlon	5978		Alex Kruger	12 Mar 95	Barcelona, ESP
			(7.16, 7.23, 14.79, 2.16, 8.36, 4.90, 2:48.66)		
5000m Walk	19:22.29		Martin Rush	8 Feb 92	Birmingham
4 x 200m Relay	1:22.11		UK National Team	3 Mar 91	Glasgow
			(Linford Christie, Darren Braithwaite, Ade Mafe, John Regis)		
4 x 400m Relay	3:03.20		UK National Team	7 Mar 99	Maebashi, JPN
			(Allyn Condon, Solomon Wariso, Adrian Patrick, Jamie Baulch)		

WOMEN

50m	6.21		Wendy Hoyte	22 Feb 81	Grenoble, FRA
60m	7.13		Bev Kinch	23 Feb 86	Madrid, ESP
200m	22.83		Katharine Merry	14 Feb 99	Birmingham
300m	37.46	A	Sharon Colyear/Danville	14 Mar 81	Pocatello, USA
400m	50.53		Katharine Merry	18 Feb 01	Birmingham
800m	2:01.12		Jane Colebrook/Finch	13 Mar 77	San Sebastián, ESP
1000m	2:38.95		Kirsty Wade	1 Feb 87	Stuttgart, GER
1500m	4:06.75		Hayley Tullett	19 Mar 01	Glasgow
1 Mile	4:23.86		Kirsty Wade	5 Feb 88	New York, USA
2000m	5:40.86		Yvonne Murray	20 Feb 93	Birmingham
3000m	8:34.80		Liz McColgan	4 Mar 89	Budapest, HUN
5000m	15:03.17		Liz McColgan	22 Feb 92	Birmingham
50m Hurdles	7.03		Yvette Wray/Luker	21 Feb 81	Grenoble, FRA
60m Hurdles	7.99		Diane Allahgreen	26 Feb 00	Ghent, BEL
High Jump	1.95		Debbie Marti	23 Feb 97	Birmingham
Pole Vault	4.31		Janine Whitlock	2 Feb 00	Birmingham
Long Jump	6.70		Sue Hearnshaw/Telfer	3 Mar 84	Gothenburg, SWE (r3)
	6.70		Sue Hearnshaw/Telfer	3 Mar 84	Gothenburg, SWE (r6)
	6.70		Jo Wise	9 Mar 97	Paris (B), FRA
Triple Jump	15.16		Ashia Hansen	28 Feb 98	Valencia, ESP
Shot	19.06		Venissa Head	7 Apr 84	St. Athan
Pentathlon	4392		Julie Hollman	28 Jan 01	Prague, CZE
			(8.78, 1.81, 12.98, 6.13, 2:19.57)		
3000m Walk	13:12.01		Julie Drake	12 Mar 93	Toronto, CAN
4 x 200m Relay	1:33.96		UK National Team	23 Feb 90	Glasgow
			(Paula Thomas, Jenni Stoute, Linda Staines, Sally Gunnell)		
4 x 400m Relay	3:32.25		UK National Team	9 Mar 97	Paris (B), FRA
			(Phylis Smith, Sally Gunnell, Michelle Thomas, Donna Fraser)		

UK ALL TIME LISTS - MEN
as at 31 December 2001

100 Metres

	9.87	Linford Christie ¶	15 Aug 93
	9.91	Christie	23 Aug 94
	9.92	Christie	25 Aug 91
	9.96	Christie	1 Aug 92
	9.97	Christie	24 Sep 88
	9.97	Christie	15 Aug 93
	9.97 A	Christie	23 Sep 95
	9.97	Dwain Chambers	22 Aug 99
	9.98	Christie	23 Aug 94
	9.98	Jason Gardener	2 Jul 99
	10.04	Darren Campbell	19 Aug 98
	10.09	Jason Livingston ¶	13 Jun 92
	10.10	Mark Lewis-Francis	5 Aug 00
	10.11	Allan Wells	24 Jul 80
	10.11	Christian Malcolm	5 Aug 01
	10.12	Darren Braithwaite	15 Jul 95
10	10.13	Marlon Devonish	17 Sep 98
	10.15	Michael Rosswess	15 Sep 91
	10.15	John Regis	29 May 93
	10.17	Ian Mackie	25 Aug 96
	10.20	Cameron Sharp	24 Aug 83
	10.20	Elliot Bunney	14 Jun 86
	10.21 A	Ainsley Bennett	8 Sep 79
	10.21	Jamie Henderson	6 Aug 87
	10.21	Allyn Condon	14 Aug 99
	10.22	Mike McFarlane	20 Jun 86
20	10.23	Marcus Adam	26 Jul 91
	10.23	Jason John	15 Jul 94
	10.23	Terry Williams	22 Aug 94
	10.24	Chris Lambert	14 Jul 01
	10.26	Daley Thompson	27 Aug 86
	10.26	Ernest Obeng	1 Aug 87
	10.28	Julian Golding	22 Jul 97
	10.28	Jon Barbour	17 Jun 00
	10.29	Peter Radford (10.31?)	13 Sep 58
	10.29	Colin Jackson	28 Jul 90
30	10.30	Clarence Callender	26 Jul 91
	10.30 A	Doug Bignall	6 Jul 00
		10.30	22 Apr 01
	10.31	Doug Walker ¶	11 Jun 97
	10.31	Owusu Dako	16 Apr 00
	10.32	Buster Watson	1 Jul 83
	10.32	Donovan Reid	4 Aug 84
	10.32	Lincoln Asquith	11 Aug 86
	10.32	Lenny Paul	29 May 93
	10.32	Toby Box	28 Jun 95
	10.32	Daniel Money	28 Aug 97
40	10.33	Brian Green	15 Jul 72
	10.33	Solomon Wariso	19 Jun 94
	10.34	Drew McMaster	9 Jul 83
	10.34	Barrington Williams	5 Aug 88
	10.34	Kevin Williams	11 Jun 97
	10.35 A	Barrie Kelly	13 Oct 68
	10.35	Brian Taylor	29 May 93
	10.35	Mark Richardson ¶	2 May 98
	10.35 A	Akinola Lashore	10 Apr 99
	10.35	Mark Findlay ¶	19 Jun 99
50	10.36	David Jenkins	24 Jun 72
	10.36	Uvie Ugono	1 Ju1 00

wind assisted

	9.90	Christie	24 Aug 91
	9.91	Christie	11 Jun 94
	9.93	Christie	28 Jan 90
	9.95	Christie	22 Jun 90
	9.97 †	Mark Lewis-Francis	4 Aug 01
	9.97 †	Chambers	4 Aug 01
	10.00	Ian Mackie	18 Jul 98
	10.01	Doug Walker ¶	18 Jul 98
	10.02	Allan Wells	4 Oct 82
	10.07	Cameron Sharp	4 Oct 82
	10.07	John Regis	28 Aug 90
	10.07	Toby Box	11 Jun 94
	10.07	Michael Rosswess	11 Jun 94
	10.08	Mike McFarlane	27 May 84
10	10.08	Jason John	11 Jun 94
	10.09 †	Christian Malcolm	4 Aug 01
	10.10	Donovan Reid	26 Jun 83
	10.11	Drew McMaster	26 Jun 83
	10.12	Buster Watson	27 May 84
	10.13	Jon Barbour	30 Jun 01
	10.14	Ernest Obeng	20 Jun 87
	10.14	Marcus Adam	28 Jan 90
	10.16	Daniel Money	21 Jun 97
	10.17	Terry Williams	23 Aug 94
20	10.17	Owusu Dako	5 Jul 98
	10.17	Tyrone Edgar	30 Jun 01
	10.20	Lincoln Asquith	6 Jul 85
	10.22	Jamie Henthorn	29 Aug 97
	10.22	Danny Joyce	30 Aug 97
	10.22	Dwayne Grant	30 Jun 01
	10.25	Lenny Paul	14 Jul 91
	10.26	Peter Little	21 May 80
	10.26	Doug Turner	13 Jul 96
	10.27	Barrington Williams	2 Jul 88
30	10.27	Clarence Callender	22 Jun 91
	10.27 A	Doug Bignall	4 Jul 00
		10.29	13 Jul 01
	10.28	Du'aine Ladejo	23 May 98
	10.29	Trevor Cameron	11 Jun 94
	10.30	Kevin Williams	27 Jul 97
	10.31	Jim Evans	22 Aug 81

† wind gauge faulty - probably windy

hand timing

10.1	David Jenkins	20 May 72
10.1	Brian Green	3 Jun 72

hand timing - wind assisted

10.0	Allan Wells	16 Jun 79
10.0	Drew McMaster	1 Jun 80
10.1	Dave Roberts	17 Jul 82

200 Metres

	19.87 A	John Regis	31 Jul 94
	19.94	Regis	20 Aug 93
	20.01	Regis	2 Aug 94
	20.08	Christian Malcolm	8 Aug 01
	20.09	Regis	5 Aug 92
	20.09	Linford Christie ¶	28 Sep 88
	20.09	Malcolm	24 Aug 01
	20.11	Regis	30 Aug 90
	20.11	Christie	25 Jun 95
	20.12	Regis	10 Jul 91
	20.13	Darren Campbell	27 Sep 00
	20.18	Julian Golding	19 Sep 98
	20.21	Allan Wells	28 Jul 80
	20.25	Marlon Devonish	25 Aug 99
	20.31	Dwain Chambers	22 Jul 01
	20.35	Doug Walker ¶	26 Jul 98
10	20.36	Todd Bennett	28 May 84
	20.41	Marcus Adam	13 Jun 92
	20.42 A	Ainsley Bennett	12 Sep 79
		20.84	31 Aug 80
	20.43	Mike McFarlane	7 Oct 82
	20.43	Doug Turner	9 Jun 96
	20.47	Cameron Sharp	9 Sep 82
	20.47	Darren Braithwaite	13 May 95
	20.50	Terry Williams	24 Aug 94
	20.50	Tony Jarrett	16 Jul 95
	20.50	Solomon Wariso	16 Jul 95
20	20.51	Michael Rosswess	28 Sep 88
	20.53 i	Allyn Condon	8 Feb 98
		20.63	19 Jul 97
	20.54	Ade Mafe	25 Aug 85
	20.56	Roger Black	4 May 96
	20.57	Owusu Dako	16 Jul 95
	20.62	Buster Watson	5 Jun 83
	20.62	Donovan Reid	28 May 84
	20.62	Mark Richardson ¶	24 Aug 97
	20.63	Chris Lambert	21 Aug 99
	20.64	Dwayne Grant	16 Jun 01
30	20.65	Jason Gardener	11 Jul 99
	20.66 A	Dick Steane	15 Oct 68
	20.66	David Jenkins	27 Aug 73
	20.67	Tim Benjamin	17 Jun 01
	20.70	Chris Monk	20 Aug 73
	20.72	Toby Box	24 Aug 94
	20.73 A	Ralph Banthorpe	15 Oct 68
	20.75	Dave Clark	20 Jan 90
	20.76	Andy Carrott	5 Jul 88
	20.76	Clarence Callender	24 Jun 91
40	20.77	Drew McMaster	9 Jul 83
	20.79	Phil Goedluck	6 Aug 94
	20.79	Paul White	27 May 96
	20.79	Jon Barbour	9 Sep 00
	20.81	Mike St. Louis	21 Jun 86
	20.81	Paul McBurney	24 Aug 94
	20.83	Martin Reynolds	22 Jul 70
	20.83	Claude Moseley	23 Aug 81
	20.83	John Stewart	9 Sep 00
	20.84	Brian Green	4 Sep 71
50	20.84	Earl Tulloch	25 May 81
	20.84	Jamie Baulch	24 Aug 94

wind assisted (* 220 yards time less 0.12)

	20.08	Regis	2 Jul 93
	20.10	Marcus Adam	1 Feb 90
	20.11	Allan Wells	20 Jun 80
	20.26	Ade Mafe	1 Feb 90
	20.36	Doug Turner	27 Jul 97
	20.48	Michael Rosswess	9 Sep 90
	20.51	Jason John	2 Jul 93
	20.55	Buster Watson	10 Aug 85
	20.59	Allyn Condon	25 Jul 99
	20.60	Tim Benjamin	7 Aug 99
10	20.61	Martin Reynolds	22 Jul 70
	20.61	Ed White	11 Jul 99
	20.62	Adrian Patrick	10 Jun 95
	20.64	Drew McMaster	23 Aug 80
	20.68	Ian Mackie	29 May 00
	20.70 *	Dave Jones	20 May 61
	20.70	Trevor Hoyte	14 Sep 79
	20.73	Phil Goedluck	23 Apr 95
	20.75	Daniel Money	26 May 97
	20.76	Paul McBurney	26 May 97
20	20.80	Ben Lewis	11 Jul 99
	20.83	Graham Beasley	18 Jul 01
	20.84	Nigel Stickings	9 Jul 93

hand timing (* 220 yards time less 0.1)

20.3	David Jenkins	19 Aug 72
20.4 *	Peter Radford	28 May 60
20.6	Donovan Reid	1 Jul 84
20.7 *	Menzies Campbell	10 Jun 67
20.7	Martin Reynolds	2 Aug 70
20.7	Brian Green	3 Jun 72
20.7	Drew McMaster	16 Aug 80
20.7	Claude Moseley	28 Aug 81

hand timing - wind assisted

20.4	Buster Watson	11 Aug 85
20.4	Dwayne Grant	1 Jul 01
20.5	Roger Black	6 Jul 96
20.6	Ainsley Bennett	22 Jun 74
20.6	Mark Richardson ¶	6 Jul 96

300 Metres

	31.56	Doug Walker ¶	19 Jul 98
	31.67	John Regis	17 Jul 92
	31.87	Mark Richardson ¶	19 Jul 98
	31.98	Regis	19 Jun 93
	31.99	Regis	21 Jun 91
	32.06	Jamie Baulch	31 May 97
	32.08	Roger Black	8 Aug 86
	32.14	Todd Bennett	18 Aug 84
	32.23	Solomon Wariso	19 Jul 98
	32.26	Mark Hylton	19 Jul 98
	32.32	Derek Redmond	16 Jul 88
10	32.36	Iwan Thomas	19 Jul 98
	32.44	David Jenkins	4 Jul 75
	32.45	David Grindley	19 Jun 93
	during 400m		
	32.06 +	Roger Black	29 Aug 91
	32.08 +	Iwan Thomas	5 Aug 97
	32.26 +	Derek Redmond	1 Sep 87
	32.35 +	David Grindley	26 Jun 93

400 Metres

	44.36	Iwan Thomas	13	Jul	97
	44.37	Roger Black	3	Jul	96
	44.37	Mark Richardson ¶	9	Jul	98
	44.37	Richardson	8	Aug	98
	44.38	Thomas	8	Aug	98
	44.39	Black	16	Jun	96
	44.41	Black	29	Jul	96
	44.46	Thomas	2	Jul	97
	44.47	David Grindley	3	Aug	92
	44.47	Richardson	5	Aug	97
	44.47	Richardson	24	Aug	99
	44.50	Derek Redmond	1	Sep	87
	44.57	Jamie Baulch	3	Jul	96
	44.66	Du'aine Ladejo	16	Jun	96
	44.68	Solomon Wariso	26	Jul	98
	44.93	David Jenkins	21	Jun	75
10	44.93	Kriss Akabusi	7	Aug	88
	45.20	Sean Baldock	12	Aug	00
	45.22	Brian Whittle	25	Sep	88
	45.24	Mark Hylton	12	Aug	98
	45.26	Phil Brown	26	May	85
	45.27	Todd Bennett	7	Aug	88
	45.30	Ade Mafe	23	Jul	93
	45.33	Paul Sanders	15	Jun	91
	45.37	Daniel Caines	23	Sep	00
	45.47	David McKenzie	12	Jun	94
20	45.48	John Regis	17	Apr	93
	45.49	Glen Cohen	21	May	78
	45.63	Adrian Patrick	5	Jul	95
	45.64	Paul Harmsworth	7	Aug	88
	45.65	Alan Bell	14	Jun	80
	45.67	Roger Hunter	19	May	85
	45.69	Jared Deacon	29	Jul	00
	45.74	Steve Heard	26	May	85
	45.75	Robbie Brightwell	19	Oct	64
	45.76	Guy Bullock	16	Jun	96
30	45.81	Terry Whitehead	14	Jun	80
	45.83	Geoff Dearman	29	Jul	00
	45.84	Richard Knowles	18	May	97
	45.85	Paul McBurney	13	Jul	97
	45.88	Wayne McDonald	17	Aug	91
	45.91 A	Martin Winbolt-Lewis	17	Oct	68
	45.92	Mark Thomas	27	Jun	87
	45.94	Paul Slythe	26	Jul	98
	45.97	Steve Scutt	14	Sep	79
	46.03	Peter Crampton	8	Aug	87
40	46.04	Alan Slack	27	Jun	85
	46.08	Tim Graham	19	Oct	64
	46.08	Rod Milne	15	Jun	80
	46.10	Peter Gabbett	7	Sep	72
	46.10	Tim Benjamin	25	Aug	01
	46.11	Martin Reynolds	4	Sep	72
	46.15	Ainsley Bennett	29	Aug	75
	46.16	Gary Armstrong	15	Jul	72
	46.16	Claude Moseley	1	Jul	83
	46.18	Garry Cook	14	Jun	80
50	46.19	Roy Dickens	28	May	84
	46.20	Dave Nolan	9	Jun	96
	46.22	Mark Sesay	25	May	97

hand timing (* 440 yards time less 0.3)

45.6 *	Robbie Brightwell	14	Jul	62
45.7	Adrian Metcalfe	2	Sep	61
45.9	Colin Campbell	2	Jul	68
46.0	Garry Cook	20	May	81

600 Metres

1:14.95	Steve Heard	14	Jul	91
1:15.0 +	Sebastian Coe	10	Jun	81
1:15.4	Garry Cook	30	Jul	84
1:15.4	Tom McKean	21	Jul	91
1:15.6	David Jenkins	3	Aug	74
1:15.94	Brian Whittle	28	Jul	92

800 Metres (* 880 yards time less 0.60)

1:41.73"	Sebastian Coe	10	Jun	81	
1:42.33	Coe	5	Jul	79	
1:42.88	Steve Cram	21	Aug	85	
1:42.97	Peter Elliott	30	May	90	
1:43.07	Coe	25	Aug	85	
1:43.19	Cram	7	Sep	86	
1:43.22	Cram	31	Jul	86	
1:43.38	Coe	29	Aug	89	
1:43.41	Elliott	1	Sep	87	
1:43.42	Cram	17	Aug	88	
1:43.84	Martin Steele	10	Jul	93	
1:43.88	Tom McKean	28	Jul	89	
1:43.98	David Sharpe	19	Aug	92	
1:44.09	Steve Ovett	31	Aug	78	
1:44.55	Garry Cook	29	Aug	84	
1:44.59	Tony Morrell	2	Jul	88	
1:44.65	Ikem Billy	21	Jul	84	10
1:44.65	Steve Heard	26	Aug	92	
1:44.92	Curtis Robb	15	Aug	93	
1:45.05	Matthew Yates	26	Aug	92	
1:45.12	Andy Carter	14	Jul	73	
1:45.14	Chris McGeorge	28	Jun	83	
1:45.14	John Gladwin	22	Jul	86	
1:45.31	Rob Harrison	21	Jul	84	
1:45.32	James McIlroy (IRE)	16	Jul	98	
1:45.35	Kevin McKay	16	Aug	92	
1:45.44	Neil Horsfield	28	Jul	90	20
1:45.47	Brian Whittle	20	Jul	90	
1:45.6	Graham Williamson	12	Jun	83	
1:45.64	Paul Herbert	5	Jun	88	
1:45.66	Paul Forbes	8	Jun	83	
1:45.68	Mark Sesay	7	Aug	99	
1:45.69	Steve Crabb	17	Aug	88	
1:45.69	Craig Winrow	21	Jun	96	
1:45.71	Andy Hart	19	Sep	98	
1:45.76	Frank Clement	10	Jul	76	
1:45.81	David Strang	12	Jul	96	30
1:45.81	Anthony Whiteman	5	Aug	00	
1:45.82	Jason Lobo	7	Aug	99	
1:46.10	Gary Marlow	10	Jul	87	
1:46.1	Colin Campbell	26	Jul	72	
1:46.16	Gareth Brown	2	Jul	84	
1:46.20	David Warren	29	Jun	80	
1:46.21	Pete Browne	14	Jul	73	
1:46.26	Phil Lewis	27	Jan	74	

	1:46.3 a	Chris Carter	4 Sep 66
40	1:46.37	Andrew Lill	28 Jun 92
	1:46.4	Paul Walker	22 Jul 97
	1:46.51	John Boulter	18 Jun 66
	1:46.6	Derek Johnson	9 Aug 57
	1:46.63	Peter Hoffmann	11 Jun 78
	1:46.64	Dave Moorcroft	25 Jul 82
	1:46.65	Steve Caldwell	31 May 82
	1:46.72	Mal Edwards	13 Sep 87
	1:46.80 *	John Davies I	3 Jun 68
	1:46.8	Bob Adams	9 Aug 69
50	1:46.8	Dave Cropper	1 Jul 73
	1:46.8	Dave McMeekin	6 Jun 74

1000 Metres

	2:12.18	Sebastian Coe	11 Jul 81
	2:12.88	Steve Cram	9 Aug 85
	2:13.40	Coe	1 Jul 80
	2:14.90	Coe	16 Jul 86
	2:15.57	James McIlroy	5 Sep 99
	2:15.91	Steve Ovett	6 Sep 79
	2:16.30	Peter Elliott	17 Jan 90
	2:16.34	Matthew Yates	6 Jul 90
	2:16.82	Graham Williamson	17 Jul 84
	2:16.99	Tony Morrell	28 Aug 88
	2:17.14	John Gladwin	6 Jul 90
10	2:17.20	Rob Harrison	18 Aug 84
	2:17.36	Neil Horsfield	9 Aug 91
	2:17.43	Gareth Brown	18 Aug 84
	2:17.45	Chris McGeorge	20 Aug 84
	2:17.63	Kevin McKay	14 Jul 89
	2:17.75	Steve Crabb	5 Aug 87
	2:17.79	David Sharpe	31 Aug 92
	2:17.95	Mark Scruton	17 Jul 84
	2:17.96	Ikem Billy	14 Jul 89
	2:18.18	Mal Edwards	11 Jul 86
20	2:18.2	John Boulter	6 Sep 69
	2:18.28	Garry Cook	23 Aug 81
	2:18.31 i	David Strang	30 Jan 93
	2:18.33	Gary Marlow	5 Aug 87
	2:18.35	Paul Larkins	27 Jun 86
	2:18.48	John Mayock	11 Aug 96

1500 Metres (+ during 1 mile)

	3:29.67	Steve Cram	16 Jul 85
	3:29.77	Sebastian Coe	7 Sep 86
	3:30.15	Cram	5 Sep 86
	3:30.77	Steve Ovett	4 Sep 83
	3:30.95	Cram	19 Aug 88
	3:31.34	Cram	27 Jun 85
	3:31.36	Ovett	27 Aug 80
	3:31.43	Cram	19 Aug 87
	3:31.57	Ovett	29 Jul 81
	3:31.66	Cram	26 Aug 83
	3:31.86	John Mayock	22 Aug 97
	3:31.95	Coe	7 Jul 81
	3:31.95	Ovett	8 Jul 81
	3:32.34	Anthony Whiteman	16 Aug 97
	3:32.69	Peter Elliott	16 Sep 90
	3:33.34	Steve Crabb	4 Jul 87
	3:33.79	Dave Moorcroft	27 Jul 82
	3:33.83	John Robson	4 Sep 79
10	3:34.00	Matthew Yates	13 Sep 91
	3:34.01	Graham Williamson	28 Jun 83
	3:34.1 +	Tony Morrell	14 Jul 90
	3:34.50	Adrian Passey	4 Jul 87
	3:34.53	Mark Rowland	27 Jul 88
	3:34.59	Kevin McKay	24 Aug 97
	3:34.76	Gary Lough	9 Sep 95
	3:35.08	Neil Horsfield	10 Aug 90
	3:35.26	John Gladwin	5 Sep 86
	3:35.28	Jack Buckner	1 Jul 86
20	3:35.66	Frank Clement	12 Aug 78
	3:35.74	Rob Harrison	26 May 86
	3:35.94	Paul Larkins	10 Jul 87
	3:35.97	Andrew Graffin	9 Jul 01
	3:36.53	David Strang	15 Jul 94
	3:36.81	Mike Kearns	26 Jul 77
	3:37.55	Colin Reitz	27 Jun 85
	3:37.64	Brendan Foster	2 Feb 74
	3:37.75	Jon McCallum	1 Aug 00
	3:37.88	Jason Dullforce	17 Jul 92
30	3:37.97	Rod Finch	30 Jul 93
	3:37.99	Rob Denmark	5 Jun 95
	3:38.05	Glen Grant	12 Aug 78
	3:38.06	Tim Hutchings	31 Aug 84
	3:38.08	Tom Hanlon	28 Jun 92
	3:38.1	Jim McGuinness	1 Aug 77
	3:38.2 a	James Espir	11 Jul 80
	3:38.22	Peter Stewart	15 Jul 72
	3:38.31	Matt Barnes	23 Jul 93
	3:38.33	Tom Mayo	22 Jul 01
	3:38.34		19 Aug 01
40	3:38.52	Ray Smedley	15 Jul 72
	3:38.56	Curtis Robb	26 Jun 93
	3:38.64	Simon Fairbrother	17 Jun 92
	3:38.65	Ian Stewart II	8 Aug 81
	3:38.66	Glen Stewart	26 May 96
	3:38.68	John Kirkbride	15 Jul 72
	3:38.7	Jim Douglas	27 Jun 72
	3:38.78	Mark Scruton	17 Jun 84
	3:38.8	Paul Lawther	12 Jun 77
	3:38.9	Ian Hamer	5 Aug 89
50	3:38.93	Brian Treacy	28 Aug 94
	3:38.94	Michael East	4 Jul 01
	3:39.0	David Lewis	9 Aug 83

1 Mile

3:46.32	Steve Cram	27 Jul 85
3:47.33	Sebastian Coe	28 Aug 81
3:48.31	Cram	5 Jul 86
3:48.40	Steve Ovett	26 Aug 81
3:48.53	Coe	19 Aug 81
3:48.8	Ovett	1 Jul 80
3:48.85	Cram	2 Jul 88
3:48.95	Coe	17 Jul 79
3:49.20	Peter Elliott	2 Jul 88
3:49.22	Coe	27 Jul 85
3:49.25	Ovett	11 Jul 81
3:49.34	Dave Moorcroft	26 Jun 82

	3:49.46	Elliott	6	Jul	91
	3:49.49	Cram	12	Sep	86
	3:49.57	Ovett	31	Aug	79
	3:49.65	Cram	29	Aug	84
	3:49.66	Ovett	14	Jul	81
	3:49.76	Elliott	14	Jul	90
	3:49.90	Cram	13	Jul	82
	3:49.95	Cram	19	Aug	81
	3:50.32	John Mayock	5	Jul	96
	3:50.64	Graham Williamson	13	Jul	82
	3:51.02	John Gladwin	19	Aug	87
	3:51.31	Tony Morrell	14	Jul	90
10	3:51.57	Jack Buckner	29	Aug	84
	3:51.76hc	Steve Crabb	14	Aug	87
		3:52.20	1	Jul	89
	3:51.90	Anthony Whiteman	16	Jul	98
	3:52.44	John Robson	11	Jul	81
	3:52.75	Matthew Yates	10	Jul	93
	3:52.99	Mark Rowland	10	Sep	86
	3:53.20	Ian Stewart II	25	Aug	82
	3:53.64	Kevin McKay	22	Jul	94
	3:53.82	Gary Staines	12	Aug	90
	3:53.85	Rob Harrison	15	Jul	86
20	3:54.2	Frank Clement	27	Jun	78
	3:54.30	David Strang	22	Jul	94
	3:54.39	Neil Horsfield	8	Jul	86
	3:54.53	Tim Hutchings	31	Jul	82
	3:54.9	Adrian Passey	20	Aug	89
	3:55.0	Jim McGuinness	11	Jul	77
	3:55.3	Peter Stewart	10	Jun	72
	3:55.38	Rob Denmark	12	Aug	90
	3:55.41	Colin Reitz	31	Jul	82
	3:55.42	Andrew Graffin	20	Aug	01
30	3:55.57	Tom Mayo	22	Jul	01
	3:55.68	Alan Simpson	30	Aug	65
	3:55.8	Geoff Smith	15	Aug	81
	3:55.84	Neil Caddy	25	Aug	96
	3:55.9	Brendan Foster	10	Jun	72
	3:55.91	Gary Lough	27	Aug	95
	3:55.96	David Lewis	23	Aug	83
	3:56.0	Jim Douglas	10	Jun	72
	3:56.04	Mike Downes	25	Aug	82
	3:56.1	Neill Duggan	11	Jun	66
40	3:56.19	Ian Hamer	5	Jul	91
	3:56.29 i	Andy Keith	22	Jan	94
	3:56.36	Steve Martin	5	Aug	86
	3:56.38	Mike McLeod	31	Aug	79
	3:56.5	John Kirkbride	10	Jun	72
	3:56.5	Paul Davies-Hale	20	Aug	89
	3:56.6	Walter Wilkinson	31	May	71
	3:56.65	Paul Larkins	17	Jul	87
	3:56.7	James Espir	15	Aug	81
	3:56.71	Chris McGeorge	5	Jul	88
50	3:56.8	Ian McCafferty	11	Jun	69
	3:56.83	Simon Fairbrother	17	Aug	90
	3:56.9 a	Ron Speirs	30	Apr	77
	3:56.95	Sean Cahill	31	Aug	79
	3:56.95	Dave Clarke	17	Jul	82
	3:56.90	Alan Salter	9	Jul	85
	3:57.07	Neil Ovington	11	Jul	86

2000 Metres

4:51.39	Steve Cram	4	Aug	85	
4:52.82	Peter Elliott	15	Sep	87	
4:53.06	Jack Buckner	15	Sep	87	
4:53.69	Gary Staines	15	Sep	87	
4:55.20	Cram	28	Aug	88	
4:55.72	Elliott	28	Aug	88	
4:56.75	John Mayock	30	Jul	99	
4:57.71	Steve Ovett	7	Jul	82	
4:57.82	Ovett	3	Jun	78	
4:58.38	Graham Williamson	29	Aug	83	
4:58.57	Mayock	7	Sep	99	
4:58.84	Sebastian Coe	5	Jun	82	
4:59.57	Nick Rose	3	Jun	78	
5:00.37	Tim Hutchings	29	Aug	83	10
5:01.09	Eamonn Martin	19	Jun	84	
5:01.28	Andrew Graffin	25	Jun	00	
5:01.48	Paul Larkins	5	Jun	88	
5:02.35	Sean Cahill	4	Aug	85	
5:02.61	Steve Martin	19	Jun	84	
5:02.8 a	Frank Clement	10	Sep	78	
5:02.86	David Moorcroft	19	Jul	86	
5:02.90	Allen Graffin	25	Jun	00	
5:02.93	Brendan Foster	4	Jul	75	
5:02.98	Ian Stewart I	4	Jul	75	20
5:02.98	Gary Lough	11	Aug	96	
5:02.99	Neil Caddy	11	Aug	96	
5:03.16	Dave Bedford	8	Jul	72	
5:03.8	Lawrie Spence	26	May	78	
5:04.11	Rob Denmark	11	Aug	96	

3000 Metres (+ during 2 Miles)

7:32.79	Dave Moorcroft	17	Jul	82	
7:35.1	Brendan Foster	3	Aug	74	
7:36.40	John Nuttall	10	Jul	96	
7:39.55	Rob Denmark	1	Aug	93	
7:39.72	Denmark	15	Jul	92	
7:40.4	Nick Rose	27	Jun	78	
7:40.43	Jack Buckner	5	Jul	86	
7:40.94	Eamonn Martin	9	Jul	83	
7:41.3	Steve Ovett	23	Sep	77	
7:41.79	Gary Staines	14	Jul	90	
7:42.26	Graeme Fell	9	Jul	83	10
7:42.47	David Lewis	9	Jul	83	
7:42.77	Billy Dee	18	Jul	92	
7:43.03	Tim Hutchings	14	Jul	89	
7:43.1 +	Steve Cram	29	Aug	83	
7:43.31 i	John Mayock	23	Feb	97	
	7:47.28	23	Jul	95	
7:43.61	Anthony Whiteman	27	Jun	98	
7:43.90	Ian Stewart II	26	Jun	82	
7:44.40	Colin Reitz	9	Jul	83	
7:44.76	Paul Davies-Hale	20	Jul	85	
7:45.2 +	Geoff Turnbull	12	Sep	86	20
7:45.29	Dennis Coates	9	Sep	77	
7:45.41	Jon Brown	1	Aug	98	
7:45.81	John Robson	13	Jul	84	
7:46.22 i	Mark Rowland	27	Feb	90	
	7:49.82	28	Jul	89	
7:46.39	Adrian Royle	28	Jun	83	

	7:46.40	Ian Hamer	20 Jan 90
	7:46.4	David Bedford	21 Jun 72
	7:46.6 +	Dave Black	14 Sep 73
	7:46.83	Ian Stewart I	26 May 76
30	7:46.85 i	Ricky Wilde	15 Mar 70
	7:46.95	David James	26 May 80
	7:47.12	Simon Mugglestone	27 Jun 88
	7:47.54	Paul Larkins	14 Jul 89
	7:47.56	Dick Callan	15 Jul 83
	7:47.6	Dick Taylor	6 Sep 69
	7:48.00	Richard Nerurkar	15 Jul 92
	7:48.09	Adrian Passey	28 Jul 89
	7:48.18	Mike McLeod	9 Jul 78
	7:48.28	Jon Richards	9 Jul 83
40	7:48.28	Ian Gillespie	25 May 97
	7:48.6 +	Nat Muir	27 Jun 80
	7:48.66	Julian Goater	26 May 80
	7:48.76	Neil Caddy	2 Aug 98
	7:48.81	Tim Redman	18 Aug 84
	7:49.1	Paul Lawther	27 Jun 78
	7:49.45	Gary Lough	30 May 95
	7:49.47	Roger Hackney	13 Jul 84
	7:49.64	Barry Smith	26 Jul 81
	7:49.72	Ray Smedley	9 Jul 78
50	7:49.80	Steve Jones	13 Jul 84
	7:49.83 i	Andy Keith	6 Feb 94
	7:50.04	Karl Keska	2 Aug 98
	7:50.20	Jon Solly	8 Aug 86

2 Miles

	8:13.51	Steve Ovett	15 Sep 78
	8:13.68	Brendan Foster	27 Aug 73
	8:14.93	Steve Cram	29 Aug 83
	8:15.53	Tim Hutchings	12 Sep 86
	8:15.98	Geoff Turnbull	12 Sep 86
	8:16.75	Dave Moorcroft	20 Aug 82
	8:16.94	Foster	17 Jul 79
	8:17.12	Jack Buckner	12 Sep 86
	8:17.79	Cram	16 Jul 88
	8:18.4 i	Nick Rose	17 Feb 78
		8:22.41	15 Sep 78
	8:18.57	Moorcroft	27 Jun 80
	8:18.98	Eamonn Martin	16 Jul 88
10	8:19.37	Nat Muir	27 Jun 80
	8:20.28	David James	27 Jun 80
	8:20.66	David Lewis	7 Sep 84
	8:21.09	Barry Smith	27 Jun 80
	8:21.86	David Black	14 Sep 73
	8:21.97	Rob Denmark	9 Aug 91
	8:22.0	Ian Stewart I	14 Aug 72
	8:22.65	Ian Hamer	17 Jul 92
	8:22.7 i	Graeme Fell	19 Feb 82
	8:22.98	Geoff Smith	27 Jun 80
20	8:23.16	Gary Staines	9 Aug 91
	8:23.80	Billy Dee	9 Aug 91
	8:23.92	Ray Smedley	6 Aug 76
	8:24.58	Adrian Royle	16 May 82
	8:24.82	Eddie Wedderburn	16 Jul 88
	8:25.02	Tony Simmons	6 Aug 76
	8:25.52	Colin Reitz	19 Aug 86

5000 Metres

13:00.41	Dave Moorcroft	7 Jul 82	
13:09.80	Ian Hamer	9 Jun 92	
13:10.15	Jack Buckner	31 Aug 86	
13:10.24	Rob Denmark	9 Jun 92	
13:10.47	Buckner	9 Jun 92	
13:10.48	Buckner	19 Aug 87	
13:11.50	Tim Hutchings	11 Aug 84	
13:12.88	Hutchings	31 Aug 86	
13:13.01	Denmark	17 Jul 91	
13:13.77	Denmark	15 Jun 95	
13:14.28	Gary Staines	15 Aug 90	
13:14.6 a	Brendan Foster	29 Jan 74	
13:15.59	Julian Goater	11 Sep 81	
13:16.70	John Nuttall	8 Jun 95	
13:17.21	Dave Bedford	14 Jul 72	10
13:17.21	Keith Cullen	19 Jul 97	
13:17.84	Eamonn Martin	14 Jul 89	
13:17.9	Nat Muir	15 Jul 80	
13:18.06	Ian Gillespie	19 Jul 97	
13:18.6	Steve Jones	10 Jun 82	
13:18.91	Nick Rose	28 Jun 84	
13:19.03	Jon Brown	5 Aug 98	
13:19.66	Ian McCafferty	14 Jul 72	
13:20.06	Steve Ovett	30 Jun 86	
13:20.09	Adrian Passey	19 Jul 97	20
13:21.13	David Lewis	4 Jul 85	
13:21.14	Barry Smith	7 Jun 81	
13:21.2	Tony Simmons	23 May 76	
13:21.60	Paul Davies-Hale	8 Jul 88	
13:21.73	Geoff Turnbull	5 Sep 86	
13:21.83	Mark Rowland	1 Jun 88	
13:22.17 i	Geoff Smith	12 Feb 82	
	13:26.33	8 Aug 81	
13:22.39	Jon Solly	7 Jul 86	
13:22.54	Dave Clarke	28 Jun 83	
13:22.8 a	Ian Stewart I	25 Jul 70	30
13:23.07	Karl Keska	7 Aug 99	
13:23.26	Mike McLeod	24 Jun 80	
13:23.36	Richard Nerurkar	10 Aug 90	
13:23.48	John Doherty	1 Jun 85	
13:23.52	Dave Black	29 Jan 74	
13:23.71	Steve Binns	1 Jun 88	
13:24.44	Mike Openshaw	14 Jul 01	
13:25.38	Paul Evans	28 Jun 95	
13:26.0	Bernie Ford	30 Jul 77	
13:26.19	Adrian Royle	4 Jul 83	40
13:26.2	Dick Taylor	13 Jun 70	
13:26.74	Craig Mochrie	25 Aug 89	
13:26.97	John Mayock	9 Jun 92	
13:27.14	Dick Callan	25 Aug 82	
13:27.41	Billy Dee	10 Jul 92	
13:27.63	Dermot Donnelly	1 Aug 98	
13:27.75	Rod Finch	1 Aug 98	
13:28.15	Malcolm Prince	14 Sep 79	
13:28.22	Kris Bowditch	25 Jun 00	
13:28.29	Simon Mugglestone	8 Jul 88	50
13:28.58	Steve Cram	3 Jun 89	
13:28.7 a	Charlie Spedding	13 Aug 78	
13:28.99	Steve Emson	4 Sep 79	

10000 Metres

	27:18.14	Jon Brown	28 Aug 98
	27:23.06	Eamonn Martin	2 Jul 88
	27:27.47	Brown	31 May 97
	27:30.3	Brendan Foster	23 Jun 78
	27:30.80	Dave Bedford	13 Jul 73
	27:31.19	Nick Rose	9 Jul 83
	27:32.65	Foster	29 Aug 78
	27:34.58	Julian Goater	26 Jun 82
	27:36.27	David Black	29 Aug 78
	27:36.62	Foster	9 Sep 77
	27:39.14	Steve Jones	9 Jul 83
	27:39.76	Mike McLeod	4 Sep 79
10	27:40.03	Richard Nerurkar	10 Jul 93
	27:43.03	Ian Stewart I	9 Sep 77
	27:43.59	Tony Simmons	30 Jun 77
	27:43.74	Bernie Ford	9 Sep 77
	27:43.76	Geoff Smith	13 Jun 81
	27:44.09	Karl Keska	25 Sep 00
	27:47.16	Adrian Royle	10 Apr 82
	27:47.79	Paul Evans	5 Jul 93
	27:48.73	Gary Staines	6 Jul 91
	27:50.33	Keith Cullen	10 Apr 99
20	27:51.76	Jon Solly	20 Jun 86
	27:55.66	Steve Binns	9 Jul 83
	27:55.77	Dave Clarke	25 May 82
	27:57.77	Ian Hamer	13 Sep 91
	27:59.12	Allister Hutton	30 May 86
	27:59.24	Carl Thackery	16 Jul 87
	27:59.33	Steve Harris	22 Jul 86
	28:00.50	Andres Jones	22 Jul 00
	28:00.62	Jim Brown	1 Aug 75
	28:00.64	Billy Dee	13 Sep 91
30	28:03.31	Rob Denmark	22 Jul 00
	28:04.04	Andy Bristow	17 Aug 90
	28:04.2	Ian Robinson	20 Apr 96
	28:04.48	Mark Steinle	22 Jul 00
	28:05.2	Dave Murphy	10 Apr 81
	28:06.13	Barry Smith	7 Aug 81
	28:06.6	Dick Taylor	22 Jun 69
	28:07.43	John Nuttall	25 Aug 95
	28:07.57	Tim Hutchings	7 Jul 90
	28:08.12	Charlie Spedding	23 Jul 83
40	28:08.44	David Lewis	5 Jun 88
	28:09.39	Mark Dalloway	5 Jun 88
	28:11.07	Karl Harrison	20 Jun 86
	28:11.71	Lachie Stewart	18 Jul 70
	28:11.85	Lawrie Spence	29 May 83
	28:13.04	Gerry Helme	29 May 83
	28:13.13	Colin Moore	29 Jun 90
	28:13.36	Jack Buckner	13 Sep 91
	28:14.08	Jon Richards	20 Jun 86
	28:14.65	Mike Tagg	10 Aug 71
50	28:14.89	Bernie Plain	1 Aug 75
	28:15.58	Martin McLoughlin	20 Jun 86
	28:16.0	Mike Baxter	23 May 74
	28:16.73	Neil Coupland	11 Jun 77
	28:17.00	Justin Hobbs	29 Jun 94
	28:18.6	John Davies II	11 Apr 79
	28:18.68	Terry Thornton	17 Aug 90

10 Kilometres Road

27:34	Nick Rose	1 Apr 84	
27:53	Mike O'Reilly	19 Oct 86	
27:55	Mark Scrutton	5 Mar 84	
27:56	John Doherty	4 Jul 86	
27:58	Steve Harris	5 Apr 86	
27:59	Steve Jones	28 Apr 84	
28:02	Steve Binns	15 Apr 89	
28:03	Jon Solly	5 Apr 86	
28:03	Jack Buckner	28 Feb 87	
28:05	Jon Brown	17 Oct 93	10
28:06	Geoff Smith	2 Mar 85	
28:07	Colin Reitz	28 Apr 84	
28:07	Peter Whitehead	4 Jul 96	
28:09	Dave Moorcroft	16 May 82	
28:10	Adrian Leek	10 Mar 84	
28:10	Dave Clarke	5 May 85	
28:11	Jon Richards	5 May 85	
28:12	Dave Murphy	19 May 85	
28:13	Allister Hutton	28 Apr 84	
28:13	Paul Evans	8 Jan 95	20
28:14	Karl Harrison	5 May 85	
28:14	David Lewis	5 Apr 86	
28:14	Eamonn Martin	30 Apr 89	
28:17	Paul Davies-Hale	21 Apr 85	
28:17	Colin Moore	5 May 85	
28:18	Steve Kenyon	15 Sep 85	
28:19	Peter Tootell	28 Apr 84	
28:19	Nigel Gates	5 May 85	
28:19	Terry Greene	4 Apr 87	

course measurement uncertain

27:56	Steve Harris	4 Dec 83
28:00	Roger Hackney	4 Dec 83
28:01	Barry Smith	4 Dec 83
28:01	Steve Kenyon	21 Sep 86
28:04	Dave Bedford	27 Mar 77
28:08	Kevin Forster	15 Jul 84
28:08	Dave Clarke	15 Jul 84
28:10	John McLaughlin	19 May 84

downhill

27:20	Jon Brown	24 Sep 95
27:57	Malcolm East	25 Sep 82

short (50m)

27:50	Mark Scrutton	6 Dec 81

10 Miles Road

46:02	Richard Nerurkar	17 Oct 93	
46:11	Gary Staines	10 Oct 93	
46:19	Nerurkar	23 Jul 95	
46:25	Carl Thackery	7 Apr 91	
46:35	Paul Evans	21 Sep 97	
46:41	Roger Hackney	6 Apr 86	
46:42	Dave Murphy	28 Apr 84	
46:43	Nick Rose	25 Apr 87	
46:48	Geoff Smith	2 May 82	
46:49	Steve Jones	2 Apr 89	
47:00	Paul Davies-Hale	10 Oct 93	10
47:02	Martin McLoughlin	10 Oct 93	
47:10	Colin Moore	6 Nov 88	
47:10	Jack Buckner	11 Oct 92	

intermediate times

46:10 +	Paul Evans	14 Sep 97	
46:21 +	Nigel Adams	15 Sep 91	
46:21 +	Carl Thackery	15 Sep 91	
46:23 +	Allister Hutton	1 Jan 85	

estimated times

46:02 +	Steve Jones	8 Jun 86	

course measurement uncertain

45:13	Ian Stewart I	8 May 77	
45:37	Barry Smith	22 Mar 81	
45:44	Mike McLeod	9 Apr 78	
46:03	Colin Moore	29 Aug 83	
46:08	Nick Rose	26 Apr 81	
46:11	Steve Kenyon	20 Jun 81	
46:14	Charlie Spedding	12 Oct 86	
46:17	Brendan Foster	9 Apr 78	

downhill

46:05	Allister Hutton	3 Apr 82	

Half Marathon

	1:00:59	Steve Jones	8 Jun 86
	1:01:03	Nick Rose	15 Sep 85
	1:01:04	Carl Thackery	12 Apr 87
	1:01:06	Richard Nerurkar	14 Apr 96
	1:01:13	Thackery	3 Oct 93
	1:01:14	Jones	11 Aug 85
	1:01:17	David Lewis	20 Sep 92
	1:01:18	Paul Evans	14 Sep 97
	1:01:28	Steve Brooks	23 Mar 97
	1:01:31	Steve Kenyon	8 Jun 86
	1:01:39	Geoff Smith	25 Sep 83
10	1:01:39	Paul Davies-Hale	15 Sep 91
	1:01:49	Jon Brown	14 Sep 97
	1:01:53	Nigel Adams	15 Sep 91
	1:01:56	Mark Flint	22 Aug 93
	1:01:57	Gary Staines	14 Sep 97
	1:02:07	Kevin Forster	5 Apr 87
	1:02:07	Martyn Brewer	20 Sep 87
	1:02:07	Andrew Pearson	14 Sep 97
	1:02:08	Steve Harris	20 Oct 85
	1:02:11	Dave Clarke	5 Apr 92
20	1:02:11	Keith Cullen	20 Aug 00
	1:02:15	Dave Murphy	16 Sep 84
	1:02:16	Jim Haughey	20 Sep 87
	1:02:19	Dave Long I	11 Dec 81
	1:02:22	Colin Moore	26 May 85
	1:02:23	Mark Steinle	10 Oct 99
	1:02:24	Jimmy Ashworth	8 Jun 86
	1:02:25	Barry Royden	18 Sep 94
	1:02:28	Terry Greene	12 Apr 86
	1:02:28	Allister Hutton	21 Jun 87
30	1:02:28	Andy Coleman	22 Oct 00

course measurement uncertain

1:00:09	Paul Evans	15 Jan 95
1:01:47	Dave Long II	17 Mar 91
1:02:08	Ray Smedly	28 Mar 82
1:02:09	Steve Anders	25 Sep 88
1:02:19	Mike Carroll	3 Jun 90
1:02:23	Charlie Spedding	15 Mar 87

Marathon

2:07:13	Steve Jones	20 Oct 85	
2:08:05	Jones	21 Oct 84	
2:08:16	Jones	21 Apr 85	
2:08:20	Jones	6 Nov 88	
2:08:33	Charlie Spedding	21 Apr 85	
2:08:36	Richard Nerurkar	13 Apr 97	
2:08:52	Paul Evans	20 Oct 96	
2:09:08	Geoff Smith	23 Oct 83	
2:09:12	Ian Thompson	31 Jan 74	
2:09:16	Allister Hutton	21 Apr 85	
2:09:24	Hugh Jones	9 May 82	
2:09:28	Ron Hill	23 Jul 70	
2:09:28	John Graham	23 May 81	10
2:09:43	Mike Gratton	17 Apr 83	
2:09:44	Jon Brown	18 Apr 99	
2:09:54	Tony Milovsorov	23 Apr 89	
2:10:12	Gerry Helme	17 Apr 83	
2:10:30	Dave Long II	21 Apr 91	
2:10:35	Steve Brace	21 Jan 96	
2:10:39	Mike O'Reilly	5 Dec 93	
2:10:46	Mark Steinle	22 Apr 01	
2:10:48	Bill Adcocks	8 Dec 68	
2:10:50	Eamonn Martin	18 Apr 93	20
2:10:51	Bernie Ford	2 Dec 79	
2:10:52	Kevin Forster	17 Apr 88	
2:10:55	Chris Bunyan	18 Apr 83	
2:11:06	Dave Buzza	31 Oct 93	
2:11:18	Dave Murphy	12 Jun 83	
2:11:22	Dave Cannon	6 Sep 80	
2:11:25	Paul Davies-Hale	29 Oct 89	
2:11:25	Gary Staines	20 Oct 96	
2:11:35	Malcolm East	20 Apr 81	
2:11:36	Kenny Stuart	15 Jan 89	30
2:11:40	Steve Kenyon	13 Jun 82	
2:11:43	Jimmy Ashworth	29 Sep 85	
2:11:44	Jim Dingwall	17 Apr 83	
2:11:50	Fraser Clyne	2 Dec 84	
2:11:54	Martin McCarthy	17 Apr 83	
2:11:58	Mark Hudspith	2 Apr 95	
2:12:04	Jim Alder	23 Jul 70	
2:12:07	Jon Solly	14 Oct 90	
2:12:07	Mark Flint	17 Apr 94	
2:12:12	Dennis Fowles	13 May 84	40
2:12:12	Andy Green	25 Apr 93	
2:12:13	John Wheway	17 Apr 88	
2:12:17	Dave Long I	16 Jan 82	
2:12:19	Don Faircloth	23 Jul 70	
2:12:23	Peter Whitehead	2 Apr 95	
2:12:32	Trevor Wright	3 Dec 78	
2:12:33	Tony Simmons	7 May 78	
2:12:37	Carl Thackery	25 Oct 92	
2:12:41	Derek Stevens	16 Jun 84	
2:12:50	Jeff Norman	7 May 78	50
2:13:06	Greg Hannon	13 May 79	
2:13:12	Chris Stewart	8 Dec 74	
2:13:15	Ray Crabb	17 Apr 83	
2:13:16	Norman Wilson	20 Apr 81	
2:13:17	Mike Hurd	26 Sep 82	
2:13:17	Geoff Wightman	29 Sep 91	

2000 Metres Steeplechase

	5:19.86	Mark Rowland	28 Aug 88
	5:20.56	Rowland	17 Aug 90
	5:21.77	Tom Hanlon	11 Jun 92
	5:22.37	Rowland	16 Sep 90
	5:22.96	Hanlon	16 Sep 90
	5:23.56	Tom Buckner	17 Jul 92
	5:23.6	Roger Hackney	10 Jun 82
	5:23.71	Colin Walker	28 Aug 88
	5:23.87	Colin Reitz	28 Jun 84
	5:24.91	Eddie Wedderburn	19 Aug 86
	5:26.24	Paul Davies-Hale	26 Aug 85
	5:26.64	Nick Peach	19 Aug 86
10	5:26.82 "	David Lewis	12 Jun 83
	5:30.6	Dennis Coates	23 Apr 78
	5:30.86	Tony Staynings	26 May 76
	5:31.04	John Hartigan	17 Aug 90
	5:31.09	Peter McColgan	5 Aug 86
	5:31.43	John Bicourt	26 May 76
	5:31.59	Mick Hawkins	20 Jan 90
	5:32.45	Neil Smart	17 Aug 90
	5:33.09	Spencer Duval	17 Jul 92
	5:33.59	Mark Sinclair	19 Aug 86
20	5:33.76	Graeme Fell	9 Sep 79

3000 Metres Steeplechase

	8:07.96	Mark Rowland	30 Sep 88
	8:12.11	Colin Reitz	5 Sep 86
	8:12.58	Tom Hanlon	3 Aug 91
	8:13.27	Rowland	30 Aug 90
	8:13.50	Reitz	4 Aug 85
	8:13.65	Hanlon	4 Jul 92
	8:13.78	Reitz	21 Jul 84
	8:14.73	Hanlon	15 Jul 92
	8:14.95	Reitz	27 Jul 85
	8:15.16	Graeme Fell	17 Aug 83
	8:18.32	Eddie Wedderburn	5 Jul 88
	8:18.91	Roger Hackney	30 Jul 88
	8:18.95	Dennis Coates	25 Jul 76
	8:20.83	Paul Davies-Hale	10 Jun 84
	8:22.48	John Davies II	13 Sep 74
10	8:22.82	John Bicourt	8 Jun 76
	8:23.90	Justin Chaston	18 Jul 94
	8:24.64	Spencer Duval	16 Jul 95
	8:25.15	Colin Walker	28 Jun 92
	8:25.37	Christian Stephenson	19 Aug 00
	8:25.50	Tom Buckner	28 Aug 92
	8:26.05	Keith Cullen	21 Aug 95
	8:26.33	Rob Hough	6 Jul 96
	8:26.4	Andy Holden	15 Sep 72
	8:26.6	Gordon Rimmer	4 Jun 80
20	8:27.21	Tony Staynings	15 Jun 80
	8:27.8	Steve Hollings	5 Aug 73
	8:27.93	Peter McColgan	25 Jun 91
	8:28.6	Dave Bedford	10 Sep 71
	8:29.46	Julian Marsay	14 Jul 79
	8:29.72	David Lewis	29 May 83
	8:30.6 a	Peter Griffiths	17 Jul 77
	8:30.8	Gerry Stevens	1 Sep 69
	8:31.09	Ian Gilmour	16 Jul 78
	8:31.22	Dave Lee	19 Jun 92
30	8:32.00	Steve Jones	8 Aug 80
	8:32.06	David Camp	10 Aug 74
	8:32.13	Barry Knight	25 Jul 82
	8:32.4 a	Maurice Herriott	17 Oct 64
	8:32.68	Ben Whitby	15 Jul 01
	8:33.0	John Jackson	13 Aug 69
	8:33.15	Stuart Stokes	15 Ju1 01
	8:33.8 a	Gareth Bryan-Jones	23 Jul 70
	8:33.8	Peter Morris	4 Aug 73
	8:33.83	Richard Charleston	24 May 80
40	8:33.89	Nick Peach	21 Jun 86
	8:33.97	John Hartigan	20 Jul 90
	8:34.67	Craig Wheeler	9 Jun 99
	8:34.77	Kevin Capper	18 Aug 85
	8:34.83	Ken Baker	1 Jul 84
	8:35.49	Micky Morris	14 Aug 76
	8:35.52	Neil Smart	28 Aug 89
	8:35.6	Ron McAndrew	9 Jul 71
	8:35.8	John Wild	3 Aug 77
	8:36.2 a	Bernie Hayward	26 Jan 74
50	8:36.55	Mick Hawkins	16 Jul 95

110 Metres Hurdles

	12.91	Colin Jackson	20 Aug 93
	12.97 A	Jackson	28 Jul 93
	12.98	Jackson	15 Sep 94
	12.99	Jackson	3 Sep 93
	12.99	Jackson	6 Sep 94
	13.00	Tony Jarrett	20 Aug 93
	13.02	Jackson	30 Aug 94
	13.02	Jackson	22 Aug 98
	13.03	Jackson	4 Sep 94
	13.04	Jackson	16 Aug 92
	13.04	Jackson	12 Aug 94
	13.04	Jarrett	12 Aug 95
	13.04	Jackson	25 Aug 99
	13.29	Jon Ridgeon	15 Jul 87
	13.42	David Nelson	27 Aug 91
	13.43	Mark Holtom	4 Oct 82
	13.44	Hugh Teape	14 Aug 92
	13.49	Andy Tulloch	30 Jun 99
	13.51	Nigel Walker	3 Aug 90
	13.53	Paul Gray	22 Aug 94
10	13.60	Wilbert Greaves	21 Aug 85
	13.60	Neil Owen	28 Jun 95
	13.62	Damien Greaves	30 Jul 00
	13.66	Ross Baillie	20 Feb 99
	13.69	Berwyn Price	18 Aug 73
	13.72	David Hemery	1 Aug 70
	13.75	Lloyd Cowan	17 Jul 94
	13.79	Alan Pascoe	17 Jun 72
	13.82	Mensah Elliott	30 Jul 00
	13.82	Chris Baillie	7 Jul 01
20	13.83	Dominic Bradley	14 Jul 01
	13.86	Ken Campbell	23 Aug 94
	13.95	Robert Newton	27 Aug 00
	13.96	Steve Buckeridge	31 May 86
	14.00	Matt Douglas	23 May 99
	14.02	Mark Lambeth	9 Jul 95

	14.03	Brett St Louis	27	Jun	87
	14.03	Brian Taylor	19	May	96
	14.04	Daley Thompson	28	Aug	86
	14.04	Mike Robbins	1	May	99
30	14.05	Liam Collins	4	Jun	00
	14.06	Natham Palmer	20	Jul	01
	14.08	Paul Brice	26	Aug	83
	14.09	Colin Hamplett	11	Aug	90
	14.10	Graham Gower	15	Jul	72
	14.10	Bob Danville	4	Jul	76
	14.10	Jamie Quarry	25	Jun	94
	14.10	Duncan Malins	1	Jul	00
	14.11	Neil Fraser	11	Jul	87
	14.11	Ererton Harrison	31	Jul	91
40	14.12	Matthew Clements	17	May	98
	14.13	Mark Stern	22	Jun	96
	14.14	Mike Hogan	5	Sep	63
	14.14	Max Robertson	7	Jun	86
	14.14	Martin Nicholson	12	Jun	94
	14.16 A	Mike Parker	16	Oct	68
	14.16	Martyn Hendry	25	Aug	97
	14.16	Dominic Girdler	21	Jul	01
	14.17	Colin Bovell	23	Jul	94
	14.18	Chris Breen	13	Jul	75
50	14.18	James Archampong	21	Jul	94
	14.19	C. J. Kirkpatrick	16	Jun	73
	14.20 A	Stuart Storey	16	Oct	68
	14.20	Kevin Lumsdon	16	Jul	94
	14.21	David Wilson	15	Jul	72
	14.21	Alan Cronin	13	Jul	75
	14.21	Mark Whitby	14	Jun	85
	14.23	Alan Tapp	14	Jun	86
	14.24	Kieran Moore	7	Jun	86

wind assisted

	12.94 A	Jackson	31	Jul	94
	12.95	Jackson	10	Sep	89
	12.99	Jackson	23	Jun	89
	13.01	Jackson	2	Jul	93
	13.49	Nigel Walker	3	Jun	89
	13.65	Berwyn Price	25	Aug	75
	13.66	David Hemery	18	Jul	70
	13.69	Mensah Elliott	19	Aug	00
	13.70	Chris Baillie	1	Jul	01
	13.93	Robert Newton	7	Aug	99
	13.96	Mike Robbins	28	Mar	98
	13.97	Brett St Louis	30	Jul	88
	13.99	Bob Danville	14	Aug	76
10	14.06	Tony James	22	Aug	81
	14.07	Dominic Girdler	20	Jul	01
	14.08	David Wilson	15	Jul	72
	14.08	Duncan Malins	18	Jun	00
	14.11	Mark Stern	20	Jun	93
	14.14	James Archampong	25	May	96
	14.16	Mark Hatton	14	Jul	79
	14.17	C. J. Kirkpatrick	13	Jul	74
	14.19	Alan Cronin	25	Aug	75
	14.19	Norman Ashman	15	Aug	92
20	14.22	Phil Barthropp	1	Jul	84
	14.22	Dave Sweetman	24	May	98
	14.22	Tony Gill	14	Aug	99
	14.22	Andy Turner	14	Jul	01
	14.23	Gus McKenzie	21	May	80
	14.23	John Wallace	26	Jul	86
	14.23	Greg Dunson	10	Jun	89
	14.24	Ben Warmington	5	Jul	98

hand timing

13.5	Berwyn Price	1	Jul	73	
13.6	David Hemery	5	Jul	69	
13.7	Alan Pascoe	5	Jul	69	
13.7	C. J. Kirkpatrick	29	Jun	74	
13.7	Mensah Elliott	2	Sep	00	
13.8	Martin Nicholson	25	Jun	94	
13.9	Mike Parker	2	Oct	63	
13.9	David Wilson	29	Jun	74	
13.9	Brian Taylor	8	May	93	
14.1	Stuart Storey	2	Aug	67	10
14.1	Colin Bovell	17	Jul	94	
14.1 y	Laurie Taitt	13	Jul	63	

hand timing - wind assisted

12.8	Colin Jackson	10	Jan	90
13.0	Jarrett	2	Jun	96
13.4	Berwyn Price	7	Jul	76
13.5	Neil Owen	2	Jun	96
13.7	Lloyd Cowan	27	Apr	95
14.0	Laurie Taitt	13	Sep	62
14.0 y	Bob Birrell	9	Sep	61

400 Metres Hurdles

47.82	Kriss Akabusi	6	Aug	92	
47.86	Akabusi	27	Aug	91	
47.91	Akabusi	26	Aug	91	
47.92	Akabusi	29	Aug	90	
48.01	Akabusi	5	Aug	92	
48.12 A	David Hemery	15	Oct	68	
	48.52	2	Sep	72	
48.14	Chris Rawlinson	11	Aug	99	
48.22	Rawlinson	7	Jun	00	
48.22	Rawlinson	5	Jul	00	
48.26	Akabusi	10	Jul	92	
48.59	Alan Pascoe	30	Jun	75	
48.73	Jon Ridgeon	6	Sep	92	
49.03 A	John Sherwood	15	Oct	68	
	49.88	13	Aug	69	
49.07	Gary Cadogan	22	Jul	94	
49.11	Gary Oakes	26	Jul	80	
49.16	Paul Gray	18	Aug	98	
49.25	Max Robertson	28	Aug	90	10
49.26	Peter Crampton	8	Aug	94	
49.26	Matt Douglas	30	Aug	00	
49.29	Du'aine Thorne-Ladejo	9	Jun	01	
49.30	Anthony Borsumato	29	Aug	01	
49.49	Mark Holtom	20	Jul	85	
49.57	Matt Elias	14	Jul	01	
49.60	Phil Beattie	28	Jul	86	
49.65	Bill Hartley	2	Aug	75	
49.82	Martin Gillingham	14	Aug	87	
49.82	Gary Jennings	27	Jun	95	20
49.86	Martin Briggs	6	Jun	84	
49.95	Steve Sole	24	Jul	83	

	49.96	Tony Williams	24 Jul 99
	50.01	Phil Harries	5 Jun 88
	50.05	Lawrence Lynch	15 Jun 96
	50.1 a	John Cooper	16 Oct 64
	50.16	Paul Thompson	17 May 96
	50.19	Steve Coupland	12 Jun 94
	50.24	Charles Robertson-Adams	4 Jul 01
30	50.37	Bob Danville	27 Jul 82
	50.38	Andy Todd	18 Sep 69
	50.40	James Hillier	1 Jul 01
	50.49	Eddie Betts	13 Jul 97
	50.52	Paul Hibbert	30 Jun 96
	50.58	Colin O'Neill	29 Jan 74
	50.58	Mike Whittingham	7 Aug 82
	50.68	Peter Warden	18 Jun 66
	50.70	Noel Levy	8 Jul 94
	50.70	Richard McDonald	17 Aug 01
40	50.71	Steve Hawkins	4 Jun 89
	50.79	Mark Davidson	17 Jun 89
	50.79	Lloyd Cowan	3 Jun 95
	50.82 "	Paul Atherton	12 Jun 83
		50.91	6 Jun 84
	50.84	Mark Whitby	6 Jun 84
	50.86	Wilbert Greaves	18 May 80
	50.88	Greg Dunson	7 Jun 92
	50.91	Brian Whittle	5 Jun 93
	50.94	Trevor Burton	17 Jul 87
	50.97	Dave Savage	15 Jun 96
50	50.98	Tom Farrell	15 Jun 60
	50.98	Stan Devine	14 Jul 82
	51.04	Peter Kelly	12 Jun 76
	51.08	Tim Gwynne	30 May 94
	51.09	Steve Black	14 Jul 73

hand timing

49.9	Andy Todd	9 Oct 69
50.5	Wilbert Greaves	12 Feb 80
50.7	Steve Black	20 Aug 74
50.7	Stewart McCallum	21 Mar 76
50.8	Dave Schärer	26 Jun 71
51.0	Chris Surety	2 Sep 61

High Jump

	2.38 i	Steve Smith	4 Feb 94
		2.37	20 Sep 92
	2.37 i	Smith	14 Mar 93
	2.37	Smith	22 Aug 93
	2.37 i	Dalton Grant	13 Mar 94
		2.36	1 Sep 91
	2.36 i	Smith	5 Feb 93
	2.36 i	Smith	24 Feb 94
	2.36 i	Smith	10 Feb 96
	2.36 i	Smith	8 Feb 98
	2.36	Smith	27 Jun 99
	2.32 i	Brendan Reilly	24 Feb 94
		2.31	17 Jul 92
	2.31	Geoff Parsons	26 Aug 94
	2.30	Ben Challenger	13 Jul 99
	2.28 i	John Holman	28 Jan 89
		2.24	27 May 89
	2.26	James Brierley	3 Aug 96
	2.25	Floyd Manderson	20 Aug 88
	2.25	Robert Mitchell	28 Jul 01
10	2.24	Mark Naylor	28 Jun 80
	2.24	John Hill	23 Aug 85
	2.24	Phil McDonnell	26 Aug 85
	2.23	Mark Lakey	29 Aug 82
	2.23 i	David Abrahams	12 Mar 83
		2.19	7 Oct 82
	2.22	Danny Graham	20 May 00
	2.21	Fayyaz Ahmed	29 Jun 86
	2.21	Steve Chapman	30 Jul 89
	2.20	Brian Burgess	11 Jun 78
	2.20	Trevor Llewelyn	15 Jul 83
20	2.20	Byron Morrison	14 Jul 84
	2.20 i	Henderson Pierre	10 Jan 87
		2.18	16 Aug 86
	2.20	Alex Kruger	18 Jun 88
	2.20	Ossie Cham	21 May 89
	2.20 i	Warren Caswell	10 Mar 90
		2.18	2 Sep 90
	2.20	Colin Bent	16 Jun 96
	2.20 i	Stuart Ohrland	1 Feb 97
		2.18	28 Aug 99
	2.20	Stuart Smith	13 Apr 97
	2.20	David Barnetson	3 Aug 97
	2.20 i	Samson Oni †	28 Jan 01
		2.18 †	30 Jun 01
		2.15	12 Jul 01
30	2.20	Dan Turner	28 May 01
	2.19 i	Mike Robbins	3 Feb 96
		2.17	5 Aug 95
	2.18	Tim Foulger	23 Sep 79
	2.18	Rupert Charles	25 Jul 82
	2.18	Steve Ritchie	15 Jul 89
	2.18	Hopeton Lindo	23 Jul 89
	2.18	Andrew Lynch	9 Jul 95
	2.18 i	Tony Gilhooly	9 Mar 97
		2.18	12 Sep 99
	2.18	Chuka Enih-Snell	21 Apr 01
	2.17 i	Richard Aspden	11 Feb 99
		2.16	7 Jul 95
40	2.16 i	Mike Butterfield	23 Jan 76
	2.16 i	Claude Moseley	13 Apr 80
		2.16	19 Jul 81
	2.16 i	David Watson	13 Mar 82
		2.15	19 Aug 84
	2.16	Andy Hutchinson	2 Sep 84
	2.16	Mike Powell	3 Sep 88
	2.16	John Wallace	29 Jul 90
	2.16	Rob Brocklebank	7 Jul 95
	2.16	Ian Holliday	8 Aug 98
	2.16 i	Jason McDade	24 Jan 99
		2.15	30 Aug 98
	2.16 i	Andrew Penk	20 Feb 00
		2.15	31 May 97

† Note Oni not eligible for Britain until July 2001

Pole Vault

	5.80	Nick Buckfield	27 May 98
	5.75	Buckfield	7 Sep 97
	5.75 A	Buckfield	14 Apr 01
	5.71	Buckfield	16 Jun 96
	5.70	Buckfield	23 Jul 95
	5.70	Buckfield	8 Aug 97
	5.70	Buckfield	10 Aug 97
	5.65	Keith Stock	7 Jul 81
	5.65	Buckfield	26 May 96
	5.62	Buckfield	29 May 97
	5.61	Kevin Hughes	28 Jul 99
	5.60	Neil Winter	19 Aug 95
	5.59	Brian Hooper	6 Sep 80
	5.55	Paul Williamson	13 May 00
	5.52	Mike Edwards	13 May 93
	5.45 i	Andy Ashurst	16 Feb 92
		5.40	19 Jun 88
	5.45	Mike Barber	27 Jul 97
10	5.40 A	Jeff Gutteridge ¶	23 Apr 80
		5.40	5 Jun 83
	5.40 i	Matt Belsham	10 Feb 96
		5.35	26 Jun 93
	5.40	Tim Thomas	2 Aug 97
	5.40	Ben Flint	25 Jul 99
	5.35	Ian Tullett	26 Jul 98
	5.30	Dean Mellor	17 Jun 95
	5.30	Christian North	25 Jul 99
	5.26	Mark Johnson	31 Aug 91
	5.25	Mike Bull	22 Sep 73
	5.25	Allan Williams	29 Aug 77
20	5.25	Daley Thompson	15 Jun 86
	5.25	Tom Richards	8 Aug 99
	5.21	Graham Eggleton	10 Jul 82
	5.21 i	Christian Linskey	20 Feb 99
		5.20	24 May 98
	5.20	Billy Davey	5 Jun 83
	5.20	Warren Siley	4 Aug 90
	5.20	Mark Hodgkinson	24 Aug 96
	5.20	Neil Young	2 Aug 97
	5.20	Mark Davis	25 Jul 99
	5.20	Scott Simpson	1 Jul 01
30	5.20	Ashley Swain	15 Jul 01
	5.18	Steve Chappell	15 Jun 78
	5.11	Andrew Gayle	10 Aug 91
	5.10	Darren Wright	12 Jun 88
	5.10	Paul Phelps	9 Jul 89
	5.10	Mark Grant	20 May 95
	5.02	Bob Kingman	29 Aug 94
	5.02 i	Craig Guite	11 Jan 97
	5.01	Paul Hoad	16 Aug 86
	5.01	Andrew Penk	31 Aug 01
40	5.00	Richard Gammage	19 Aug 84
	5.00	Brian Taylor	5 May 91
	5.00	Dan Gilby	20 Jul 91
	5.00	Paul Wray	26 Jul 91
	5.00	Alex Greig	31 May 92
	5.00	Barry Thomas	23 Aug 92
	5.00	Ian Wilding	1 Jun 96
	5.00	Andrew Weston	29 Jul 98
	5.00	Matt Weaver	25 Jul 99

Long Jump

8.23	Lynn Davies	30 Jun 68	
8.18 A	Davies	9 Apr 66	
8.15	Stewart Faulkner	16 Jul 90	
8.14	Davies	18 Jun 69	
8.14	Faulkner	25 Aug 89	
8.14	Mark Forsythe	7 Jul 91	
8.13 A	Davies	6 Apr 66	
8.13 A	Davies	19 Oct 67	
8.13	Faulkner	12 Aug 89	
8.11	Nathan Morgan	24 Jul 98	
8.10	Fred Salle	9 Sep 94	
8.08	Roy Mitchell	27 Sep 80	
8.05 i	Barrington Williams	11 Feb 89	
	8.01	17 Jun 89	
8.03	Steve Phillips	5 Aug 98	
8.01	Daley Thompson	8 Aug 84	
8.00	Derrick Brown	7 Aug 85	10
7.98	Alan Lerwill	29 Jun 74	
7.98	Jonathan Moore	29 Jul 01	
7.94 i	Paul Johnson	10 Mar 89	
	7.85	3 Jun 89	
7.91	John King	26 Sep 87	
7.90	Ian Simpson	3 Jun 89	
7.90	Chris Davidson	19 Jun 99	
7.90	Darren Ritchie	19 Aug 00	
7.89	George Audu	12 Aug 00	
7.87	Keith Fleming	7 Jun 87	
7.87	Chris Tomlinson	18 Aug 01	20
7.84	Wayne Griffith	25 Aug 89	
7.83	Phil Idowu	25 Jul 00	
7.79	John Morbey	11 Jul 64	
7.79	Geoff Hignett	31 May 71	
7.79	Don Porter	13 Jul 75	
7.77	Len Tyson	25 Jul 82	
7.77	Dean Macey	27 Sep 00	
7.76	Carl Howard	31 Jul 93	
7.75	Ken Cocks	2 Jul 78	
7.75	Trevor Hoyte	6 May 84	30
7.75	Michael Morgan	30 Jul 94	
7.74	Fred Alsop	6 Jun 64	
7.74 i	Phil Scott	17 Feb 73	
	7.68	27 May 73	
7.74 i	Aston Moore	10 Jan 81	
7.74	John Herbert	14 Jul 85	
7.74	David Burgess	4 Jul 87	
7.73	Jason Canning	20 Apr 88	
7.72	Femi Abejide	20 Jun 86	
7.71	Billie Kirkpatrick	2 Jun 78	
7.71 i	Keith Connor	20 Feb 81	40
7.70	Kevin Liddington	27 Aug 88	
7.70	Julian Flynn	19 Jun 99	
7.68	Garry Slade	1 Aug 92	
7.67	Dave Walker	14 Sep 68	
7.67	Oni Onuorah	15 Jun 96	
7.66	Tony Henry	12 Jun 77	
7.66	Barry Nevison	7 Jul 85	
7.66	John Shepherd	18 Jun 88	
7.65 i	John Munroe	11 Feb 95	
	7.64	24 Jun 95	

wind assisted

	8.19	Chris Tomlinson	11 Aug 01
	8.17	Mark Forsythe	11 Jun 89
	8.16	Roy Mitchell	26 Jun 76
	8.15	Alan Lerwill	29 May 72
	8.15	Lerwill	15 Jul 72
	8.14	Forsythe	23 Jun 89
	8.12	Derrick Brown	14 Jun 86
	8.11	Daley Thompson	7 Aug 78
	8.07	Steve Phillips	11 Jul 99
	8.04	Ian Simpson	3 Jun 89
	7.96	Colin Jackson	17 May 86
10	7.94	John Herbert	25 Jul 82
	7.94	John King	20 Jun 86
	7.94	Chris Davidson	21 Jun 97
	7.93	David Burgess	15 Jun 86
	7.92	Darren Ritchie	26 Jun 99
	7.91	Steve Ingram	18 Jun 94
	7.89	John Shepherd	20 Jun 86
	7.87	Paul Johnson	15 May 88
	7.84	Darren Thompson	16 Jun 01
	7.82	Peter Reed	20 Jul 68
20	7.82	Femi Abejide	20 Jun 86
	7.82	Kevin Liddington	25 Jun 89
	7.81	Enyinna Chukukere	9 Apr 94
	7.81	Oni Onuorah	21 Aug 95
	7.76	Aston Moore	7 Aug 77
	7.76	Julian Flynn	19 Jun 99
	7.72	Ken McKay	21 Jun 85
	7.72	Nick Riley	18 Jun 88
	7.70	Derek Cole	29 May 72

Triple Jump

	18.29	Jonathan Edwards	7 Aug 95
	18.01	Edwards	9 Jul 98
	18.00	Edwards	27 Aug 95
	17.99	Edwards	23 Aug 98
	17.98	Edwards	18 Jul 95
	17.92	Edwards	6 Aug 01
	17.88	Edwards	27 Jul 96
	17.82	Edwards	25 Jun 96
	17.79	Edwards	14 Aug 96
	17.75	Edwards	12 Aug 98
	17.57 A	Keith Connor	5 Jun 82
		17.31 i	13 Mar 81
		17.30	9 Jun 82
	17.41	John Herbert	2 Sep 85
	17.33	Phil Idowu	4 Jun 01
	17.30	Larry Achike	23 Sep 00
	17.21	Tosi Fasinro	27 Jul 93
	17.18	Francis Agyepong	7 Jul 95
	17.06	Julian Golley	10 Sep 94
	17.01	Eric McCalla	3 Aug 84
10	16.87	Mike Makin	2 Aug 86
	16.86	Aston Moore	16 Aug 81
	16.75	Vernon Samuels	7 Aug 88
	16.63 A	Femi Akinsanya	10 Apr 99
		16.58	15 Jun 96
	16.57	Tosin Oke	8 Aug 99
	16.46	Fred Alsop	16 Oct 64
	16.43	Jonathan Moore	22 Jul 01
	16.32	Tayo Erogbogbo	21 Aug 95
	16.30	Nick Thomas	22 Jul 00
	16.30	Femi Abejide	27 Jun 85
20	16.29 i	David Johnson	1 Mar 78
		16.18	22 Jun 75
	16.28	Steven Shalders	13 Jul 01
	16.26	Joe Sweeney	3 Aug 91
	16.22	Derek Boosey	15 Jun 68
	16.20	Rez Cameron	5 Jun 88
	16.18	Tony Wadhams	6 Jul 69
	16.17	John Mackenzie	17 Sep 94
	16.16	Conroy Brown	19 Sep 81
	16.15	Wayne Green	10 Jul 88
	16.15	Michael Brown	23 Jul 89
30	16.13	Steven Anderson	11 Jun 83
	16.10	Alan Lerwill	28 Aug 71
	16.09	Courtney Charles	17 Jun 90
	16.08	Craig Duncan	21 Jun 86
	16.02	Peter Akwaboah	15 Jun 89
	15.98	Frank Attoh	5 Sep 80
	15.97	Mike Ralph	23 Jul 64
	15.97	Carl Howard	6 May 95
	15.95	Derek Browne	12 Jun 93
	15.92	John Slaney	15 Oct 77
40	15.92	Lawrence Lynch	13 Jul 85
	15.91 i	Akin Oyediran	3 Mar 84
	15.91	Dave Emanuel	31 Aug 91
	15.90	David Wood	16 Sep 84
	15.88	John Phillips	14 May 78
	15.87	Chris Colman	15 Jul 78
	15.87	Stewart Faulkner	22 Aug 87
	15.86 i	Donovan Perkins	23 Jan 81
	15.86	Joe Allison	24 Aug 85
	15.82	Graham Hamlyn	12 Jul 68
50	15.82 i	Charles Madeira-Cole	15 Mar 98
	15.82	Jon Wallace	11 Jul 98

wind assisted

	18.43	Jonathan Edwards	25 Jun 95
	18.08	Edwards	23 Jul 95
	18.03	Edwards	2 Jul 95
	17.81	Keith Connor	9 Oct 82
	17.38	Phillips Idowu	1 Jul 01
	17.31	Larry Achike	15 Jul 00
	17.30	Tosi Fasinro	12 Jun 93
	17.29 A	Francis Agyepong	29 Jul 95
		17.24	2 Jul 95
	17.02	Aston Moore	14 Jun 81
	16.82	Vernon Samuels	24 Jun 89
	16.65	Fred Alsop	13 Aug 65
10	16.49	Tony Wadhams	16 Sep 69
	16.44	Tayo Erogbogbo	31 May 97
	16.38	Femi Abejide	10 Jun 89
	16.38	Courtney Charles	22 Jul 90
	16.33	David Johnson	28 May 78
	16.32	Craig Duncan	20 Jun 87
	16.32	Rez Cameron	21 May 89
	16.21	Alan Lerwill	28 Aug 71
	16.17	Chris Colman	15 Jul 78
	16.12	Donovan Perkins	21 Sep 80

Shot

	21.68	Geoff Capes	18 May 80
	21.55	Capes	28 May 76
	21.50	Capes	24 May 80
	21.37	Capes	10 Aug 74
	21.36	Capes	19 Jun 76
	21.35	Capes	5 Jun 80
	21.30	Capes	3 Jul 77
	21.20	Capes	22 Aug 76
	21.18	Capes	8 May 76
	21.15	Capes	23 May 76
	20.85 i	Mark Proctor	25 Jan 98
		20.40	7 Jul 99
	20.45	Shaun Pickering	17 Aug 97
	20.43	Mike Winch	22 May 74
	20.33	Paul Edwards ¶	9 Jul 91
	19.72	Mark Edwards	16 Aug 00
	19.56	Arthur Rowe	7 Aug 61
	19.49	Matt Simson	28 Aug 94
	19.46	Carl Myerscough ¶	6 Sep 98
10	19.44 i	Simon Williams	28 Jan 89
		19.17	18 May 91
	19.43	Bill Tancred	18 May 74
	19.18	Jeff Teale ¶	7 Aug 68
	19.01	Billy Cole	21 Jun 86
	18.94	Bob Dale	12 Jun 76
	18.93	Paul Buxton	13 May 77
	18.85	Lee Newman	2 Jun 96
	18.79	Steph Hayward	6 Sep 00
	18.62	Martyn Lucking	2 Oct 62
	18.59 i	Alan Carter	11 Apr 65
		18.26	1 May 65
20	18.50	Mike Lindsay	2 Jul 63
	18.46	Roger Kennedy	22 May 77
	18.46 i	Simon Rodhouse	20 Feb 82
		18.20	25 Jul 82
	18.35	Peter Tancred	9 Jul 74
	18.34	Richard Slaney	3 Jul 83
	18.29 i	Emeka Udechuku	14 Jan 01
		18.23	5 Jul 01
	18.14 i	Neal Brunning ¶	26 Jan 92
		17.45	17 Aug 91
	18.05	John Watts	19 Aug 72
	18.04	Andy Vince	30 Apr 83
	17.96	Nigel Spratley	28 Aug 94
30	17.95	Graham Savory	4 Jun 88
	17.92	Nick Tabor	9 Apr 83
	17.87	Bill Fuller	15 Jul 72
	17.87 i	Ian Lindley	15 Mar 81
		17.58	25 May 81
	17.87 i	Antony Zaidman	22 Jan 83
		17.22	4 Jul 81
	17.79	John Alderson	31 Jul 74
	17.78	Steve Whyte	11 Feb 89
	17.69 i	David Readle	24 Feb 01
		17.50	25 Mar 00
	17.62	Neil Gray	7 Jun 89
	17.55	David Callaway	1 Aug 93
40	17.54	Eric Irvine	16 Aug 86
	17.47	Carl Jennings	13 Sep 87
	17.45	Abi Ekoku	3 Feb 90
	17.44	Hamish Davidson	3 Jun 78
	17.41	Lee Wiltshire	1 May 94
	17.41	Jamie Cockburn	12 May 96
	17.40	Barry King	11 Apr 70
	17.40	Allan Seatory	27 Apr 75
	17.36 i	Chris Ellis	8 Dec 84

Discus

66.64	Perris Wilkins	6 Jun 98	
65.22	Wilkins	30 Aug 97	
65.16	Richard Slaney	1 Jul 85	
65.11	Glen Smith	18 Jul 99	
65.08	Robert Weir	19 Aug 00	
64.94	Bill Tancred	21 Jul 74	
64.87	Wilkins	12 Jun 99	
64.68	Slaney	6 Jul 84	
64.65	Wilkins	22 Jul 00	
64.64	Slaney	30 Apr 82	
62.36	Peter Tancred	8 May 80	
62.07	Emeka Udechuku	19 Aug 00	
61.86	Paul Mardle	13 Jun 84	
61.62	Peter Gordon	15 Jun 91	
61.14	Simon Williams	18 Apr 92	10
61.10	Kevin Brown	30 Aug 97	
61.00	Allan Seatory	6 Oct 74	
60.92	Graham Savory	10 May 86	
60.48	Lee Newman	10 May 97	
60.42	Mike Cushion	16 Aug 75	
60.19	Carl Myerscough ¶	8 Aug 98	
60.08	Abi Ekoku	16 May 90	
59.84	Colin Sutherland ¶	10 Jun 78	
59.76	John Hillier	27 Jul 74	
59.70	John Watts	14 Jul 72	20
58.64	Steve Casey	19 May 91	
58.58	Darrin Morris	22 Jun 91	
58.36	Paul Reed	11 Jul 99	
58.34	Geoff Capes	29 Sep 73	
58.08	Mike Winch	7 Sep 75	
57.58	Arthur McKenzie	17 Aug 69	
57.14	Mark Proctor	24 Jun 00	
57.12	Paul Edwards ¶	10 Aug 88	
57.10	Dennis Roscoe	3 May 80	
57.00	Gerry Carr	17 Jul 65	30
56.71	Roy Hollingsworth	14 Sep 63	
56.66	Gary Herrington	15 Jun 96	
56.42	Paul Buxton	6 Aug 76	
56.40	Guy Dirkin	1 Aug 75	
55.68	Neville Thompson	12 Jun 93	
55.68	Leith Marar	24 Jul 96	
55.60	Jeff Clare	25 Jul 88	
55.52	Jamie Murphy	29 Jul 95	
55.42	Geoff Tyler	3 May 80	
55.34	Nick Woolcott	27 Jul 88	40
55.32	Mike Lindsay	4 May 60	
55.04	Denzil McDonald	28 Aug 95	
54.78	Colin Bastien	29 Mar 87	
54.38	Shaun Pickering	26 Aug 89	
54.36	Matt Symonds	24 Jun 95	
54.27	Mark Pharoah	27 Nov 56	
54.25	Bruce Robb	17 Jun 01	
54.16	Scott Hayes	23 Mar 97	
54.01	Eric Cleaver	21 Oct 62	

Hammer

	77.54	Martin Girvan	12 May 84
	77.30	Dave Smith I	13 Jul 85
	77.16	Girvan	13 Jul 84
	77.04	Smith I	25 May 85
	77.02	Matt Mileham	11 May 84
	76.92	Girvan	5 May 84
	76.60	Smith I	6 Sep 86
	76.43	Mick Jones	2 Jun 01
	76.38	Girvan	25 Apr 84
	76.36	Smith I	5 May 85
	76.36	Smith I	29 Jun 85
	75.40	Chris Black	23 Jul 83
	75.10	Dave Smith II	27 May 96
	75.08	Robert Weir	3 Oct 82
	74.02	Paul Head	30 Aug 90
	73.86	Barry Williams	1 Jul 76
10	73.80	Jason Byrne	19 Sep 92
	73.20	Paul Dickenson	22 May 76
	72.63	Bill Beauchamp	25 Jul 99
	71.60	Shane Peacock	24 Jun 90
	71.28	Peter Vivian	25 Jun 95
	71.00	Ian Chipchase	17 Aug 74
	70.88	Howard Payne	29 Jun 74
	70.33	John Pearson	30 Jul 00
	70.30	Stewart Rogerson	14 Aug 88
	70.28	Paul Buxton	19 May 79
20	69.52	Jim Whitehead	23 Sep 79
	69.38	Mike Floyd	18 Jun 00
	68.64	Shaun Pickering	7 Apr 84
	68.18	Ron James	2 Jun 82
	67.82	Steve Whyte	15 Apr 89
	67.45	Steve Pearson	27 Jun 98
	67.32	Gareth Cook	1 Jun 91
	66.97	Chris Howe	6 Jun 98
	66.53	Russell Devine	15 Feb 01
	65.32	Simon Bown	20 Jun 99
30	65.30	Karl Andrews	2 Jul 94
	64.95	Mike Ellis	4 Jun 59
	64.80	Bruce Fraser	30 Sep 73
	64.64	Iain Park	22 Jul 98
	64.54	Michael Petra	30 May 79
	64.39	Craig Ellams	19 Aug 00
	64.36	Andrew Tolputt	27 Jun 87
	63.83	Matthew Bell	11 Sep 01
	63.74	Mark Sterling	18 Jul 84
	63.71	David Allen	26 Jun 99
40	63.20	Peter Gordon	17 Sep 82
	63.16	Graham Callow	29 May 89
	62.88	Anthony Swain	13 Apr 97
	62.70	Paul Barnard	19 Jul 95
	62.60	Peter Weir	2 Aug 87
	62.60	Rob Earle	1 Aug 95
	62.56	Adrian Palmer	6 Aug 94
	62.54	Tony Elvin	25 May 70
	62.42	Malcolm Fenton	16 May 82
	62.40	Lawrie Nisbet	5 Jul 86
50	62.32	Peter Aston	6 Sep 75
	62.28	Lawrie Bryce	13 Oct 73

Javelin

91.46	Steve Backley	25 Jan 92	
90.81	Backley	22 Jul 01	
89.89	Backley	19 Jul 98	
89.85	Backley	23 Sep 00	
89.72	Backley	23 Aug 98	
89.58	Backley	2 Jul 90	
89.22	Backley	11 Jun 98	
89.02	Backley	30 May 97	
88.80	Backley	2 Aug 98	
88.71 A	Backley	13 Sep 98	
86.94	Mick Hill	13 Jun 93	
85.67	Mark Roberson	19 Jul 98	
85.09	Nick Nieland	13 Aug 00	
83.84	Roald Bradstock	2 May 87	
82.38	Colin Mackenzie	7 Aug 93	
81.70	Nigel Bevan	28 Jun 92	
80.98	Dave Ottley	24 Sep 88	
78.54	Gary Jenson	17 Sep 89	
78.33 A	David Parker	24 Mar 01	10
77.84	Peter Yates	21 Feb 87	
76.66 i	Stuart Faben	3 Mar 96	
	75.37	22 Apr 00	
75.52	Marcus Humphries	25 Jul 87	
75.32	Steve Harrison	9 Jul 95	
75.28	Nigel Stainton	5 Aug 89	
74.90	Daryl Brand	27 Jun 86	
74.72	Chris Crutchley	13 Jul 86	
74.70	Myles Cottrell	16 May 92	
73.88	Keith Beard	12 May 90	
73.56	Dan Carter	16 Sep 00	20
73.26	David Messom	25 Apr 87	
72.92	Stefan Baldwin	8 May 93	
71.86	Tony Hatton	3 May 93	
71.79	Phill Sharpe	27 Aug 00	
70.90	Shane Lewis	6 Jun 98	
70.30	Tim Newenham	11 Jun 89	
70.12	Paul Morgan	12 Sep 87	
70.10	Richard Hooper	21 May 89	
70.00	Paul Bushnell	22 Jul 90	
70.00	Phil Parry	2 Jul 94	30
69.90	Ken Hayford	5 Jul 87	
69.90	Tony Smith	6 Jul 96	
69.20	Roddy James	28 Apr 89	
69.02	Kevin Murch	2 Sep 89	
68.91	Stuart Loughran	26 Jul 98	
68.84	James Hurrion	12 Jul 91	
68.78	Neil McLellan	23 Jun 01	
68.74	Jon Clarke	14 Jun 86	
68.74	Tony Norman	23 May 87	
68.70	Robert Mullen	2 Jul 96	40
68.38	James Drennen	12 Jul 91	
68.30	Mark Lawrence	31 Jul 88	
68.10	Paul Edgington	12 Oct 86	
68.08	Tim Kitney	13 Sep 98	
68.02	Mark Francis	12 Jul 97	
67.62	Alan Holloway	25 Jun 89	
67.60	Dean Smahon	9 Jul 94	
67.48	Rob Laing	31 May 87	
67.44	John Guthrie	17 May 89	
67.22	Richard Atkinson	14 Aug 93	50

Decathlon (1985 Tables)

	8847	Daley Thompson	9 Aug 84	
	8811	Thompson	28 Aug 86	
	8774	Thompson	8 Sep 82	
	8730	Thompson	23 May 82	
	8714	Thompson	13 Aug 83	
	8667	Thompson	18 May 86	
	8663	Thompson	28 Jul 86	
	8648	Thompson	18 May 80	
	8603	Dean Macey	7 Aug 01	
		8567	28 Sep 00	
	8131	Alex Kruger	2 Jul 95	
	7980	Simon Shirley	24 Aug 94	
	7922 w	Brad McStravick	28 May 84	
		7885	6 May 84	
	7904	David Bigham	28 Jun 92	
	7901	Peter Gabbett	22 May 72	
	7889	Eugene Gilkes	18 May 86	
	7874	Colin Boreham	23 May 82	
10	7861	Anthony Brannen	30 Apr 95	
	7787	Brian Taylor	30 May 93	
	7766	Barry Thomas	2 Sep 95	
	7748	Eric Hollingsworth	30 May 93	
	7740	Greg Richards	7 Jun 87	
	7739	Jamie Quarry	30 May 99	
	7713	James Stevenson	5 Jun 93	
	7708	Fidelis Obikwu	28 May 84	
	7663	Rafer Joseph	24 Aug 94	
	7643 w	Tom Leeson	8 Sep 85	
		7565	11 Aug 85	
20	7635 w	Du'aine Ladejo	24 May 98	
		7633	18 Sep 98	
	7596	Mike Corden	27 Jun 76	
	7594	Mark Bishop	3 Sep 89	
	7579	Mark Luscombe	8 May 88	
	7571	Alexis Sharp	17 Apr 98	
	7535	Duncan Mathieson	24 Jun 90	
	7515	Ken Hayford	9 Jun 85	
	7500	Barry King	22 May 72	
	7500	Pan Zeniou	2 Aug 81	
	7439	Kevan Lobb	19 Aug 84	
30	7431	Alan Drayton	8 Aug 78	
	7425	Anthony Southward	16 Jun 96	
	7425 w	Paul Field	21 May 95	
		7295	2 Jul 95	
	7367	John Garner	8 May 88	
	7363	Mike Bull	27 Jan 74	
	7363	Nick Phipps	27 Jun 76	
	7335	Stewart McCallum	19 Aug 73	
	7308	Clive Longe	29 Jun 69	
	7295	Stephen Rogers	4 Jun 95	
	7275	Buster Watson	18 Jun 78	
40	7268	Paul Edwards ¶	14 Aug 83	
	7240	Paul Allan	25 Aug 91	
	7221	Andy Lewis	19 Jun 94	
	7198	Robert Betts	7 Aug 83	
	7172	Dave Kidner	20 Aug 72	
	7159	Roger Hunter	20 Jul 97	
	7147	Justin Whitfield	12 May 85	
	7146	Steve Bonnett	30 May 99	
	7136	Billy Jewers	3 Sep 89	
	7129	John Heanley	15 Jul 01	
	7116	Fyn Corcoran	23 May 99	50

3000 Metres Track Walk

11:24.4	Mark Easton	10 May 89	
11:28.4	Phil Vesty	9 May 84	
11:29.6 i	Tim Berrett	21 Jan 90	
	11:54.23	23 Jun 84	
11:31.0	Andi Drake	22 Jul 90	
11:32.2	Ian McCombie	20 Jul 88	
11:33.4	Steve Partington	12 Jul 95	
11:35.5	Andy Penn	10 May 97	
11:39.0 i+	Martin Rush	8 Feb 92	
	11:49.48	1 Jul 84	
11:44.68	Roger Mills	7 Aug 81	
11:45.1	Chris Maddocks	9 Aug 87	10
11:45.77	Steve Johnson	20 Jun 87	
11:47.12 i	Philip King	26 Feb 95	
	11:49.64	29 May 95	
11:49.0	Darrell Stone	10 Jul 90	
11:51.1	Paul Nihill	5 Jun 71	
11:52.51	Sean Martindale	28 Jul 90	
11:53.3	Martin Bell	9 Aug 95	
11:53.46	Steve Barry	21 Aug 82	
11:54.7	Mike Parker	20 Apr 82	
11:55.0	Phil Embleton	24 May 71	

10000 Metres Track Walk

40:06.65	Ian McCombie	4 Jun 89	
40:39.77	McCombie	5 Jun 88	
40:42.53	McCombie	28 Aug 89	
40:45.87	McCombie	25 May 87	
40:47.5 +	McCombie	26 May 90	
40:53.60	Phil Vesty	28 May 84	
40:55.6	Martin Rush	14 Sep 91	
41:06.57	Chris Maddocks	20 Jun 87	
41:10.11	Darrell Stone	16 Jul 95	
41:13.62	Steve Barry	19 Jun 82	
41:13.65	Martin Bell	22 Jul 95	
41:14.3	Mark Easton	5 Feb 89	
41:14.61	Steve Partington	16 Jul 95	
41:18.64	Andi Drake	5 Jun 88	10
41:49.06	Sean Martindale	26 Jun 90	
41:55.5	Phil Embleton	14 Apr 71	
41:59.10	Andy Penn	27 Jul 91	
42:06.35	Gordon Vale	2 Aug 81	
42:08.57	Paul Blagg	28 Aug 89	
42:23.0	Mike Parker	2 Feb 86	
42:28.0	Philip King	17 May 95	
42:34.6	Paul Nihill	28 May 72	
42:35.6	Ken Matthews	1 Aug 60	
42:40.0	Brian Adams	29 Mar 75	20
42:41.6	Mick Greasley	25 May 80	
42:42.18	Steve Johnson	5 Jun 88	
42:44.0	George Nibre	2 Apr 80	
42:45.0	Tim Berrett	22 Jul 88	
42:54.6	Roger Mills	25 May 80	

track short

40:54.7	Steve Barry	19 Mar 83

20 Kilometres Road Walk

	1:22:03	Ian McCombie	23 Sep 88
	1:22:12	Chris Maddocks	3 May 92
	1:22:35	Maddocks	27 May 89
	1:22:37	McCombie	11 May 85
	1:22:51	Steve Barry	26 Feb 83
	1:22:58	McCombie	27 May 89
	1:23:15	Barry	14 May 83
	1:23:24	McCombie	24 May 86
	1:23:26	McCombie	28 Feb 87
	1:23:26.5t	McCombie	26 May 90
	1:23:34	Andy Penn	29 Feb 92
	1:23:34	Martin Rush	29 Feb 92
	1:23:58	Darrell Stone	24 Feb 96
	1:24:04	Mark Easton	25 Feb 89
	1:24:04.0t	Andi Drake	26 May 90
	1:24:07.6t	Phil Vesty	1 Dec 84
10	1:24:09	Steve Partington	24 Sep 94
	1:24:25	Tim Berrett	21 Apr 90
	1:24:50	Paul Nihill	30 Jul 72
	1:25:42	Martin Bell	9 May 92
	1:25:53.6t	Sean Martindale	28 Apr 89
	1:26:53	Chris Cheeseman	21 Mar 99
	1:27:00	Roger Mills	30 Jun 80
	1:27:04.0t	Steve Hollier	9 Jan 00
	1:27:16	Les Morton	25 Feb 89
	1:27:35	Olly Flynn	3 Oct 76
20	1:27:46	Brian Adams	11 Oct 75
	1:27:59	Phil Embleton	3 Apr 71
	1:28:02	Paul Blagg	27 Feb 82
	1:28:15	Ken Matthews	23 Jul 60
	1:28:26	Chris Harvey	29 Sep 79
	1:28:30	Allan King	11 May 85
	1:28:34	Chris Smith	11 May 85
	1:28:37	Dave Jarman	30 Jun 80
	1:28:40	Matt Hales	21 Apr 01
	1:28:46	Jimmy Ball	4 Apr 87
30	1:28:46	Steve Taylor	20 Dec 92
	1:28:46	Jamie O'Rawe	21 Mar 99
	1:28:50	Amos Seddon	3 Aug 74
	1:29:07	Philip King	20 Aug 95
	1:29:19	Stuart Phillips	31 May 92
	1:29:24	George Nibre	6 Apr 80
	1:29:27	Graham White	19 Apr 97
	1:29:29 +	Steve Johnson	16 Apr 89
	1:29:37	John Warhurst	28 Jul 73
	1:29:42	Dennis Jackson	10 May 86
40	1:29:48	Mike Parker	8 May 82
	1:29:48	Martin Young	31 Mar 96
	1:29:49	Peter Marlow	3 Aug 74
	1:29:56	Don Bearman	17 Feb 01
	1:30:00	John Webb	18 May 68
	1:30:02	Bob Dobson	3 Aug 74
	1:30:15	Gareth Brown	13 May 89
	1:30:16	Roy Thorpe	28 Jul 73
	1:30:22	Roy Sheppard	26 Apr 80
	1:30:27.38t	Steve Gower	10 Jun 78
50	1:30:30	Graham Morris	23 Feb 80
	1:30:35	Peter Fullager	4 Apr 70
	1:30:51	Mick Greasley	4 May 80

50 Kilometres Road Walk

3:51:37	Chris Maddocks	28 Oct 90	
3:53:14	Maddocks	25 Nov 95	
3:57:10	Maddocks	12 Mar 00	
3:57:48	Les Morton	30 Apr 89	
3:58:25	Morton	20 Mar 88	
3:58:36	Morton	11 Oct 92	
3:59:30	Morton	30 Sep 88	
3:59:55	Paul Blagg	5 Sep 87	
4:00:02	Maddocks	11 Oct 92	
4:00:07	Blagg	30 Sep 88	
4:03:08	Dennis Jackson	16 Mar 86	
4:03:53	Mark Easton	25 Apr 98	
4:06:14	Barry Graham	20 Apr 85	
4:07:18	Steve Hollier	18 Jun 00	
4:07:23	Bob Dobson	21 Oct 79	
4:07:49	Chris Cheesman	2 May 99	
4:07:57	Ian Richards	20 Apr 80	10
4:08:41	Adrian James	12 Apr 80	
4:09:15un	Don Thompson	10 Oct 65	
	4:12:19	20 Jun 59	
4:09:22	Mike Smith	27 Mar 89	
4:10:23	Darrell Stone	6 May 90	
4:10:42	Amos Seddon	9 Mar 80	
4:11:32	Paul Nihill	18 Oct 64	
4:12:00	Sean Martindale	16 Oct 93	
4:12:02	Martin Rush	28 Jul 91	
4:12:37	John Warhurst	27 May 72	
4:12:50	Darren Thorn	6 May 90	20
4:13:18	Graham White	27 Jun 98	
4:13:25	Allan King	16 Apr 83	
4:14:03	Tom Misson	20 Jun 59	
4:14:25	Dave Cotton	15 Jul 78	
4:15:14	Shaun Lightman	13 Oct 73	
4:15:22	Brian Adams	17 Sep 78	
4:15:52	Ray Middleton	27 May 72	
4:16:30	Karl Atton	20 Apr 97	
4:16:47	George Nibre	9 Mar 80	
4:17:24	Andi Drake	18 Oct 87	30
4:17:34	Gordon Vale	9 Oct 83	
4:17:52	Stuart Elms	17 Apr 76	
4:18:30	Peter Ryan	10 Apr 82	
4:19:00	Carl Lawton	17 Jul 71	
4:19:13	Bryan Eley	19 Jul 69	
4:19:26	Roger Mills	9 Apr 83	
4:19:55	Mick Holmes	4 Aug 73	
4:19:57	Barry Ingarfield	21 Oct 79	
4:20:05	George Chaplin	27 May 72	
4:20:43	Tim Watt	8 Oct 95	40
4:20:48	Andrew Trigg	1 May 88	
4:20:51	Murray Lambden	18 Jul 82	
4:21:02	Ron Wallwork	17 Jul 71	
4:22:05	Mel McCann	14 Sep 86	
4:22:41.0t	Charley Fogg	1 Jun 75	
4:23:12	Peter Hodkinson	21 Jul 79	
4:23:22	Chris Berwick	12 Jul 86	
4:23:32	John Lees	19 Mar 78	
4:23:43	Roy Thorpe	17 Jul 76	
4:23:50	Paul Jarman	18 Jul 81	50
4:24:02	Howard Timms	15 Jul 72	

4 x 100 Metres Relay

37.73 Great Britain & NI 29 Aug 99
Gardener, Campbell, Devonish,Chambers
37.77 Great Britain & NI 22 Aug 93
Jackson, Jarrett, Regis, Christie ¶
37.98 Great Britain & NI 1 Sep 90
Braithwaite, Regis, Adam, Christie ¶
38.05 Great Britain & NI 21 Aug 93
John, Jarrett, Braithwaite, Christie ¶
38.08 Great Britain & NI 8 Aug 92
Adam, Jarrett, Regis, Christie ¶
38.09 Great Britain & NI 1 Sep 91
Jarrett, Regis, Braithwaite, Christie ¶
38.09 A Great Britain & NI 12 Sep 98
Condon, Devonish, Golding, Chambers
38.14 Great Britain & NI 10 Aug 97
Braithwaite, Campbell, Walker, Golding
38.16 Great Britain & NI 19 Jun 99
Gardener, Campbell, Devonish, Golding
10 38.17 Great Britain & NI 'A' 7 Aug 99
Gardener, Campbell, Devonish,Golding
38.20 England 21 Sep 98
Chambers, Devonish, Golding, Campbell
38.25 Great Britain & NI 9 Aug 97
Chambers, Campbell, Braithwaite, Golding
38.28 Great Britain & NI 1 Oct 88
Bunney, Regis, McFarlane, Christie ¶
38.31 Great Britain & NI 28 Aug 99
Gardener, Campbell, Condon, Chambers
38.34 Great Britain & NI 9 Sep 89
Callender, Regis, Adam, Christie ¶
38.35 Great Britain & NI 28 Aug 00
Chambers, Campbell, Devonish, Gardener
38.36 Great Britain & NI 31 Aug 91
Jarrett, Regis, Braithwaite, Christie ¶
38.39 Great Britain & NI 5 Aug 89
Jarrett, Regis, Adam, Christie ¶
38.41 Great Britain & NI 15 Jul 00
Malcolm, Campbell, Devonish, Chambers
20 38.46 Great Britain & NI 10 Sep 94
Braithwaite, Jarrett, Regis, Christie ¶
38.47 Great Britain & NI 9 Aug 97
Campbell, Devonish, Braithwaite, Golding
38.47 Great Britain & NI 22 Aug 98
Condon, Campbell, Devonish, Chambers
38.52 Great Britain & NI 1 Oct 88
Bunney, Regis, McFarlane, Christie ¶
38.52 Great Britain & NI 22 Aug 98
Condon, Campbell, Walker, Golding
38.52 Great Britain & NI 22 Jul 01
Chambers, Devonish, Malcolm, Barbour
38.53 Great Britain & NI 26 Jun 93
John, Jarrett, Regis, Christie ¶
38.56 Great Britain & NI 27 Jun 98
Condon, Campbell, Walker, Golding
38.58 Great Britain & NI 'B' 7 Aug 99
Condon, Mackie, Regis, Chambers
38.62 Great Britain & NI 1 Aug 80
McFarlane, Wells, Sharp, McMaster
30 38.62 England 20 Sep 98
Gardener, Devonish, Chambers, Campbell

4 x 400 Metres Relay

2:56.60 Great Britain & NI 3 Aug 96
Thomas, Baulch, Richardson ¶, Black
2:56.65 Great Britain & NI 10 Aug 97
Thomas, Black, Baulch, Richardson ¶
2:57.53 Great Britain & NI 1 Sep 91
Black, Redmond, Regis, Akabusi
2:58.22 Great Britain & NI 1 Sep 90
Sanders, Akabusi, Regis, Black
2:58.68 Great Britain & NI 23 Aug 98
Hylton, Baulch, Thomas, Richardson ¶
2:58.86 Great Britain & NI 6 Sep 87
Redmond, Akabusi, Black, Brown
2:59.13 Great Britain & NI 11 Aug 84
Akabusi, Cook, Bennett, Brown
2:59.13 Great Britain & NI 14 Aug 94
McKenzie, Whittle, Black, Ladejo
2:59.46 Great Britain & NI 22 Jun 97
Black, Baulch, Thomas, Richardson ¶
2:59.49 Great Britain & NI 31 Aug 91 10
Mafe, Redmond, Richardson ¶, Akabusi
2:59.71 A Great Britain & NI 13 Sep 98
Hylton, Baulch, Baldock, Thomas
2:59.73 Great Britain & NI 8 Aug 92
Black, Grindley, Akabusi, Regis
2:59.84 Great Britain & NI 31 Aug 86
Redmond, Akabusi, Whittle, Black
2:59.85 Great Britain & NI 19 Aug 96
Baulch, Hylton, Richardson ¶, Black
3:00.19 Great Britain & NI 9 Aug 97
Hylton, Black, Baulch, Thomas
3:00.25 Great Britain & NI 27 Jun 93
Ladejo, Akabusi, Regis, Grindley
3:00.34 Great Britain & NI 25 Jun 95
Thomas, Patrick, Richardson ¶, Black
3:00.46 Great Britain & NI 10 Sep 72
Reynolds, Pascoe, Hemery, Jenkins
3:00.58 Great Britain & NI 30 Jun 91
Sanders, Akabusi, Whittle, Black
3:00.61 Great Britain & NI 20 Jun 99 20
Hylton, Baulch, Wariso, Richardson ¶
3:00.68 Great Britain & NI 11 Sep 82
Jenkins, Cook, Bennett, Brown
3:00.82 England 21 Sep 98
Slythe, Wariso, Hylton, Richardson ¶
3:00.93 Great Britain & NI 19 Jun 92
Redmond, Akabusi, Ladejo, Black
3:00.95 Great Britain & NI 28 Jun 98
Black, Baulch, Thomas, Richardson ¶
3:00.96 Great Britain & NI 11 Aug 01
Hylton, Thomas, Benjamin, Richardson ¶
3:01.03 Great Britain & NI U2319 Jul 92
McKenzie, Grindley, Richardson ¶, Ladejo
3:01.12 Great Britain & NI 28 Jun 87
Harmsworth, Whittle, Bennett, Black
3:01.20 Great Britain & NI 7 Aug 92
Richardson ¶, Akabusi, Black, Ladejo
3:01.21 A Great Britain & NI 20 Oct 68
Winbolt-Lewis, Campbell, Hemery, Sherwood

UNDER 23

100 Metres

9.97	Dwain Chambers	22	Aug	99
10.09	Jason Livingston ¶	13	Jun	92
10.11	Christian Malcolm	5	Aug	01
10.13	Marlon Devonish	17	Sep	98
10.17	Ian Mackie	25	Aug	96
10.20	Elliot Bunney	14	Jun	86
10.24	Chris Lambert	14	Jul	01
10.28	Marcus Adam	11	Aug	89
10.28	Darren Braithwaite	3	Aug	90
10.28	Julian Golding	22	Jul	97
10.28	Jon Barbour	17	Jun	00
wind assisted				
10.07	Toby Box	11	Jun	94
10.09 †	Christian Malcolm	5	Aug	01
10.10	Donovan Reid	26	Jun	83
10.11	Mike McFarlane	4	Oct	82
10.12	Jason John	29	Aug	93
10.13	Jon Barbour	30	Jun	01
10.14	Marcus Adam	28	Jan	90
10.16	Daniel Money	21	Jun	97
hand timing				
10.1	David Jenkins	20	May	72
10.2	Derek Redmond	2	May	87
wind assisted				
10.1	Drew McMaster	16	Jun	79

200 Metres

20.08	Christian Malcolm	8	Aug	01
20.18	John Regis	3	Sep	87
20.36	Todd Bennett	28	May	84
20.38	Julian Golding	24	Aug	97
20.43	Mike McFarlane	7	Oct	82
20.57	Owusu Dako	16	Jul	95
20.62	Donovan Reid	28	May	84
20.63	Roger Black	12	Sep	86
20.63	Marcus Adam	4	Aug	90
20.65	Marlon Devonish	25	Aug	97
wind assisted				
20.10	Marcus Adam	1	Feb	90
20.51	Jason John	2	Jul	93
20.53	Dougie Walker	8	May	95
20.55	Darren Campbell	2	Jul	93
hand timing				
20.3	David Jenkins	19	Aug	72

400 Metres

44.47	David Grindley	3	Aug	92
44.50	Derek Redmond	1	Sep	87
44.59	Roger Black	29	Aug	86
44.66 A	Iwan Thomas	14	Apr	96
	44.69	16	Jun	96
45.09	Mark Richardson ¶	10	Jul	92
45.14	Jamie Baulch	23	Aug	95
45.18	David Jenkins	16	Aug	74
45.24	Mark Hylton	12	Aug	98
45.25	Du'aine Ladejo	3	Jun	92
45.37	Daniel Caines	23	Sep	00

800 Metres

1:43.97	Sebastian Coe	15	Sep	78
1:43.98	Peter Elliott	23	Aug	83
1:44.45	Steve Cram	17	Jul	82
1:44.65	Ikem Billy	21	Jul	84
1:44.92	Curtis Robb	15	Aug	93
1:45.14	Chris McGeorge	28	Jun	83
1:45.32	James McIlroy (IRL)	16	Jul	98
1:45.44	Steve Ovett	25	Jul	76
1:45.64	Paul Herbert	5	Jun	88
1:45.70	David Sharpe	2	Jul	88

1000 Metres

2:15.12	Steve Cram	17	Sep	82
2:16.34	Matthew Yates	6	Jul	90

1500 Metres

3:33.66	Steve Cram	18	Aug	82
3:33.83	John Robson	4	Sep	79
3:34.00	Matthew Yates	13	Sep	91
3:34.45	Steve Ovett	3	Sep	77
3:35.16	Steve Crabb	28	Jun	84
3:35.72	Graham Williamson	15	Jul	80
3:36.70	Kevin McKay	20	Jul	90
3:36.97	Peter Elliott	1	Jul	84
3:37.25	Jack Buckner	31	Aug	83
3:37.38	Frank Clement	30	Jul	74

1 Mile

3:49.90	Steve Cram	13	Jul	82
3:50.64	Graham Williamson	13	Jul	82
3:52.74	John Robson	17	Jul	79
3:53.20	Ian Stewart II	25	Aug	82
3:53.44	Jack Buckner	13	Jul	82
3:54.36	Steve Crabb	21	Jul	84
3:54.39	Neil Horsfield	8	Jul	86
3:54.69	Steve Ovett	26	Jun	77
3:55.38	Rob Denmark	12	Aug	90
3:55.41	Colin Reitz	31	Jul	82

2000 Metres

5:01.90	Jack Buckner	29	Aug	83
5:02.67	Gary Staines	4	Aug	85
5:02.99	Neil Caddy	11	Aug	96

3000 Metres

7:41.3	Steve Ovett	23	Sep	77
7:42.47	David Lewis	9	Jul	83
7:43.90	Ian Stewart II	26	Jun	82
7:45.45	Paul Davies-Hale	13	Jul	84
7:46.6+	David Black	14	Sep	73
7:47.12	Simon Mugglestone	27	Jun	88
7:47.82	Steve Cram	26	Jul	81
7:48.6+	Nat Muir	27	Jun	80
7:48.47 i	John Mayock	1	Mar	92
7:49.45	Paul Lawther	9	Sep	77

2 Miles

8:19.37	Nat Muir	27	Jun	80
8:21.86	David Black	14	Sep	73

5000 Metres

13:17.9	Nat Muir	15 Jul 80
13:19.78	Jon Brown	2 Jul 93
13:22.2	Dave Bedford	12 Jun 71
13:22.85	Ian Stewart I	25 Jul 70
13:23.52	David Black	29 Jan 74
13:24.59	Paul Davies-Hale	1 Jun 84
13:25.0	Steve Ovett	30 Jul 77
13:26.97	John Mayock	9 Jun 92
13:28.29	Simon Mugglestone	8 Jul 88
13:29.28 i	Steve Binns	12 Feb 82

10000 Metres

27:47.0	Dave Bedford	10 Jul 71
27:48.49	David Black	25 Jan 74
28:09.95	Bernie Ford	6 Oct 73
28:12.42	Dave Murphy	13 Jul 79
28:14.08	Jon Richards	20 Jun 86
28:18.8	Nicky Lees	7 May 79
28:19.6	Jon Brown	17 Apr 92
28:20.71	Jim Brown	12 Jul 74
28:20.76	Steve Binns	27 Aug 82
28:24.01	Jack Lane	10 Aug 71

Marathon

2:12:19	Don Faircloth	23 Jul 70
2:16:04	Ian Ray	27 Oct 79
2:16:21	Norman Wilson	10 Sep 77
2:16:47	Ieuan Ellis	19 Sep 82
2:17:13	Brent Jones	13 May 84

3000 Metres Steeplechase

8:16.52	Tom Hanlon	23 Aug 89
8:18.80	Colin Reitz	6 Jul 82
8:20.83	Paul Davies-Hale	10 Jun 84
8:22.48	John Davies	13 Sep 74
8:28.6	Dave Bedford	10 Sep 71
8:29.72	David Lewis	29 May 83
8:29.86	Tony Staynings	2 Aug 75
8:30.64	Dennis Coates	2 Aug 75
8:31.72	Keith Cullen	28 Jun 92
8:31.80	Graeme Fell	8 Aug 81

110 Metres Hurdles

13.11 A	Colin Jackson	11 Aug 88
	13.11	14 Jul 89
13.21	Tony Jarrett	31 Aug 90
13.29	Jon Ridgeon	15 Jul 87
13.57	David Nelson	11 Aug 89
13.60	Neil Owen	28 Jun 95
13.66	Ross Baillie	20 Feb 99
13.69	Berwyn Price	18 Aug 73
13.71	Mark Holtom	6 Sep 80
13.78	Nigel Walker	24 Jun 84
13.82	Damien Greaves	21 Jun 97
13.82	Chris Baillie	7 Jul 01
wind assisted		
12.95	Colin Jackson	10 Sep 89
hand timing		
13.5	Berwyn Price	1 Jul 73

400 Metres Hurdles

49.11	Gary Oakes	26 Jul 80
49.57	Matt Elias	14 Jul 01
49.75	Max Robertson	30 Aug 85
49.86	Martin Briggs	6 Jun 84
50.01	Phil Harries	5 Jun 88
50.20	Matt Douglas	17 Sep 98
50.24	Martin Gillingham	24 Jun 84
50.38	Andy Todd	18 Sep 69
50.43	Philip Beattie	6 Jun 84
50.43	Charles Robertson-Adams	17 Aug 97
hand timing		
49.9	Andy Todd	9 Oct 69
50.2	John Sherwood	2 Sep 67

High Jump

2.38 i	Steve Smith	4 Feb 94
	2.37	22 Aug 93
2.32 i	Brendan Reilly	24 Feb 94
	2.31	17 Jul 92
2.31	Dalton Grant	25 Sep 88
2.30 i	Geoff Parsons	25 Jan 86
	2.28	18 May 86
2.30	Ben Challenger	13 Jul 99
2.28 i	John Holman	28 Jan 89
	2.24	27 May 89
2.25	Robert Mitchell	28 Jul 01
2.23	Phil McDonnell	29 Jul 84
2.22 i	Mark Naylor	3 Feb 79
2.22	Danny Graham	20 May 00

Pole Vault

5.70	Nick Buckfield	23 Jul 95
5.60	Neil Winter	19 Aug 95
5.50	Paul Williamson	6 Jul 96
5.42	Mike Barber	26 Aug 95
5.40	Ben Flint	25 Jul 99
5.35	Andy Ashurst	29 Jun 85
5.35	Matt Belsham	26 Jun 93
5.31	Mike Edwards	10 Jun 90
5.30 i	Kevin Hughes	25 Feb 95
	5.30	28 Aug 95

Long Jump

8.15	Stewart Faulkner	16 Jul 90
8.11	Nathan Morgan	24 Jul 98
8.07	Lynn Davies	18 Oct 64
8.04	Roy Mitchell	25 Jun 77
8.00	Daley Thompson	25 Jul 80
8.00	Derrick Brown	7 Aug 85
7.97	Fred Salle	13 Jul 86
7.94 i	Paul Johnson	10 Mar 89
7.89	John King	26 Jul 85
7.87	Keith Fleming	7 Jun 87
7.87	Chris Tomlinson	18 Aug 01
wind assisted		
8.16	Roy Mitchell	26 Jun 76
8.11	Daley Thompson	7 Aug 78
7.94	John Herbert	25 Jul 82
7.94	Chris Davidson	21 Jun 97

Triple Jump

17.21	Tosi Fasinro	27	Jul	93
17.12	Phil Idowu	23	Sep	00
17.05	John Herbert	8	Jul	83
16.95	Julian Golley	10	Jul	92
16.76	Keith Connor	12	Aug	78
16.74	Jonathan Edwards	23	Jul	88
16.71	Vernon Samuels	18	May	86
16.69	Aston Moore	12	Aug	78
16.54	Eric McCalla	17	Sep	82
16.47	Mike Makin	1	Jul	84
16.41	Francis Agyepong	2	Aug	87

wind assisted

17.30	Tosi Fasinro	12	Jun	93
17.21	Keith Connor	12	Aug	78
16.76	Aston Moore	25	Sep	78
16.44	Tayo Erogbogbo	31	May	97

Shot

19.48	Geoff Capes	21	Aug	71
19.44 i	Simon Williams	28	Jan	89
	18.93	23	Jul	89
19.23	Matt Simson	23	May	91
19.01	Billy Cole	21	Jun	86
18.97	Carl Myerscough ¶	25	Jul	99
18.93	Paul Buxton	13	May	77
18.59 i	Alan Carter	11	Apr	65
	18.26	1	May	65
18.46	Lee Newman	9	Jul	95
18.40	Steph Hayward	9	Jun	96
18.29 i	Emeka Udechuku	14	Jan	01
	18.23	5	Jul	01

Discus

62.07	Emeka Udechuku	19	Aug	00
61.86	Paul Mardle	13	Jun	84
60.48	Robert Weir	13	May	83
59.78	Glen Smith	5	Jun	94
58.99	Carl Myerscough ¶	2	Jul	99
58.52	Colin Sutherland ¶	1	May	77
58.34	Lee Newman	9	Jun	94
58.08	Simon Williams	11	Jun	89
57.04	Richard Slaney	23	Jul	77
56.42	Paul Buxton	6	Aug	76
55.90	Peter Tancred	13	Aug	69

downhill

57.56	Peter Tancred	26	Jul	69

Hammer

75.10	Dave Smith II	27	May	96
75.08	Robert Weir	3	Oct	82
74.62	David Smith I	15	Jul	84
74.18	Martin Girvan	31	May	82
73.80	Jason Byrne	19	Sep	92
71.08	Paul Head	1	Sep	85
71.00	Ian Chipchase	17	Aug	74
69.34	Paul Buxton	26	Aug	77
68.30	Mick Jones	1	Jul	84
67.60	Ron James	19	Sep	81
67.32	Gareth Cook	1	Jun	91

Javelin (1986 Model)

89.58	Steve Backley	2	Jul	90
80.92	Mark Roberson	12	Jun	88
79.70	Nigel Bevan	3	Feb	90
78.56	Mick Hill	2	Aug	86
78.54	Gary Jenson	17	Sep	89
78.33	David Parker	24	Mar	01
76.66 i	Stuart Faben	3	Mar	96
	74.24	29	Jul	95
76.28	Nick Nieland	9	Jul	94
74.70	Myles Cottrell	16	May	92
73.56	Dan Carter	16	Sep	00
71.94	Steve Harrison	9	Jul	94
71.86	Stefan Baldwin	17	May	92

Decathlon (1985 Tables)

8648	Daley Thompson	18	May	80
8556	Dean Macey	25	Aug	99
7904	David Bigham	28	Jun	92
7723 w	Eugene Gilkes	8	Jul	84
	7660	8	Jul	84
7713	Jim Stevenson	5	Jun	93
7668	Fidelis Obikwu	5	Oct	82
7643 w	Tom Leeson	8	Sep	85
	7565	11	Aug	85
7616	Barry Thomas	23	Aug	92
7610	Jamie Quarry	24	Aug	94
7594	Mark Bishop	3	Sep	89
7567	Brian Taylor	8	Jul	90
7535	Duncan Mathieson	24	Jun	90

3000 Metres Track Walk

11:28.4	Phil Vesty	9	May	84

10000 Metres Track Walk

40:53.60	Phil Vesty	28	May	84
41:24.7	Martin Rush	6	Jul	86
41:51.55	Andi Drake	25	May	87
41:55.6	Darrell Stone	7	Feb	88
42:24.61	Ian McCombie	29	May	83
42:28.0	Philip King	17	May	95
43:00.67	Sean Martindale	5	Jun	88
43:10.4	Gareth Holloway	2	May	92
43:12.85	Matt Hales	12	Aug	00
43:26.2	Gordon Vale	20	Mar	82

20 Kilometres Road Walk

1:24:07.6t	Phil Vesty	1	Dec	84
1:24:53	Andi Drake	27	Jun	87
1:26:14	Darrell Stone	27	Mar	89
1:26:21	Ian McCombie	8	Aug	82
1:26:32	Martin Rush	25	Feb	84
1:28:02	Paul Blagg	27	Feb	82
1:28:15	Mark Easton	11	May	85
1:28:17	Andy Penn	21	May	88
1:28:40	Matt Hales	21	Apr	01
1:29:01	Steve Partington	11	May	85

50 Kilometres Road Walk

4:10:23	Darrell Stone	6	May	90

UNDER 20

100 Metres

	10.06	Dwain Chambers	25	Jul	97
	10.10	Mark Lewis-Francis	21	Aug	99
	10.12	Christian Malcolm	29	Jul	98
	10.21	Jamie Henderson	6	Aug	87
	10.25	Jason Livingston ¶	9	Aug	90
	10.25	Jason Gardener	21	Jul	94
	10.29	Peter Radford (10.31?)	13	Sep	58
	10.31	Chris Lambert	21	Aug	99
	10.32	Mike McFarlane	6	Aug	78
10	10.34	Lincoln Asquith	25	Aug	83
	10.37	Darren Campbell	26	Jul	91
	10.38	Elliot Bunney	22	Aug	85
	10.39	Jason John	28	Jul	90
	10.39	Tyrone Edgar	7	Oct	00
	10.41	Jamie Henthorn	28	Jul	95
	10.43	Julian Golding	20	Jul	94
	10.44	Steve Gookey	3	Aug	90
	10.44	Jason Fergus	16	Sep	92
	10.45	Luke Davis	21	Jul	97
20	10.46	Marcus Adam	6	Aug	87

wind assisted

9.97 †	Mark Lewis-Francis	4	Aug	01
10.10	Christian Malcolm	18	Jul	98
10.17	Tyrone Edgar	30	Jun	01
10.22	Lincoln Asquith	26	Jun	83
10.22	Dwayne Grant	30	Jun	01
10.28	Darren Campbell	26	Jul	91
10.29	Mike McFarlane	7	Aug	78
10.29	Elliot Bunney	27	May	84
10.29	Trevor Cameron	11	Jun	94
10.31	Aidan Syers	30	Jun	01
10.34	Darren Braithwaite	25	Jun	88
10.34	Julian Golding	17	Sep	94

hand timing

10.3	Martin Reynolds	29	Jun	68

200 Metres

	20.29	Christian Malcolm	19	Sep	98
	20.54	Ade Mafe	25	Aug	85
	20.63	Chris Lambert	21	Aug	99
	20.64	Dwayne Grant	16	Jun	01
	20.67	David Jenkins	4	Sep	71
	20.67	Tim Benjamin	17	Jun	01
	20.73 A	Ralph Banthorpe	15	Oct	68
	20.78	John Regis	29	Sep	85
	20.80	Mike McFarlane	1	Jul	79
10	20.85	Richard Ashby	25	Aug	85
	20.86	Lincoln Asquith	28	Aug	83
	20.86	Roger Hunter	5	May	84
	20.87	Donovan Reid	7	Oct	82
	20.87	Mark Smith	28	Jul	90
	20.87	Darren Campbell	19	Sep	92
	20.91	Jamie Baulch	18	Sep	92
	20.91	Ian Mackie	23	Jul	94
	20.92	Marcus Adam	8	Aug	87
	20.94	Marlon Devonish	6	Aug	95
20	20.95	Allyn Condon	26	Jun	93

wind assisted

20.60	Tim Benjamin	7	Aug	99
20.61	Darren Campbell	11	Aug	91
20.73	Julian Golding	17	Sep	94
20.80	Ben Lewis	11	Jul	99
20.85	Mark Smith	1	Jul	90

hand timing

20.6	David Jenkins	19	Sep	71

hand timing - wind assisted

20.4	Dwayne Grant	1	Jul	01
20.7	Lincoln Asquith	2	Jul	83

300 Metres

32.53	Mark Richardson ¶	14	Jul	91

400 Metres

45.36	Roger Black	24	Aug	85	
45.41	David Grindley	10	Aug	91	
45.45	David Jenkins	13	Aug	71	
45.53	Mark Richardson ¶	10	Aug	91	
45.83	Mark Hylton	16	Jul	95	
46.03	Peter Crampton	8	Aug	87	
46.10	Tim Benjamin	25	Aug	01	
46.13	Guy Bullock	31	Jul	93	
46.22	Wayne McDonald	17	Jun	89	
46.32	Derek Redmond	9	Sep	84	10
46.46	Adrian Metcalfe	19	Sep	61	
46.48	Roger Hunter	20	May	84	
46.53	Mark Thomas	15	Sep	84	
46.54	Michael Parper	7	Jun	97	
46.56	Roy Dickens	6	Sep	80	
46.59	Carl Southam	17	Sep	92	
46.63	Melvin Fowell	18	Aug	79	
46.64	Alloy Wilson	31	Jul	98	
46.65	Darren Bernard	20	May	88	
46.66	Du'aine Ladejo	9	Aug	90	20

hand timing

45.7	Adrian Metcalfe	2	Sep	61

800 Metres (* 880 yards time less 0.60)

1:45.64	David Sharpe	5	Sep	86	
1:45.77	Steve Ovett	4	Sep	74	
1:46.46	John Gladwin	7	Jul	82	
1:46.63	Curtis Robb	6	Jul	91	
1:46.80*	John Davies I	3	Jun	68	
1:47.0	Ikem Billy	12	Jun	83	
1:47.02	Chris McGeorge	8	Aug	81	
1:47.22	Kevin McKay	5	Jun	88	
1:47.27	Tom Lerwill	22	Aug	96	
1:47.35	Peter Elliott	23	Aug	81	10
1:47.53	Graham Williamson	1	Aug	79	
1:47.6	Julian Spooner	24	Apr	79	
1:47.69	Simon Lees	5	Sep	98	
1:47.70	Darryl Taylor	13	Jul	84	
1:47.71	Dane Joseph	15	Sep	78	
1:47.73	Colin Szwed	9	Sep	77	
1:47.75	Garry Cook	3	Jul	77	
1:47.79	Craig Winrow	20	Jul	90	
1:47.85	Steve Crabb	17	Sep	82	
1:47.96*	Dave Wilcox	8	Jul	66	20

1000 Metres

2:18.98	David Sharpe	19	Aug	86
2:19.92	Graham Williamson	8	Jul	79
2:20.0	Steve Ovett	17	Aug	73
2:20.02	Darryl Taylor	18	Aug	84
2:20.37	Johan Boakes	17	Jun	84
2:21.17	Curtis Robb	16	Sep	90
2:21.41	Stuart Paton	17	Sep	82
2:21.7 A	David Strang (GBR?)	26	Jan	87
2:21.71	Kevin Glastonbury	18	Jun	77

1500 Metres

3:36.6 +	Graham Williamson	17	Jul	79
3:40.09	Steve Cram	27	Aug	78
3:40.68	Brian Treacy	24	Jul	90
3:40.72	Gary Taylor	8	Jul	81
3:40.90	David Robertson	28	Jul	92
3:41.59	Chris Sly	22	Jul	77
3:42.2	Paul Wynn	9	Aug	83
3:42.5	Colin Reitz	8	Aug	79
3:42.67	Matthew Hibberd	28	Jul	92
3:42.7	David Sharpe	17	Oct	85
3:42.86	Stuart Paton	29	Aug	82
3:42.89	Alistair Currie	17	Jul	84
3:43.1 a	Paul Lawther	31	Jan	74
3:43.24	Nick Hopkins	15	Jun	85
3:43.37	Davey Wilson	4	Jul	87
3:43.39	Johan Boakes	30	May	87
3:43.4	Tom Mayo	5	Jun	96
3:43.5	Matt Dixon	7	Aug	97
3:43.69	Jon Richards	1	Jul	83
3:43.8	John Nuttall	24	Jun	86

1 Mile

3:53.15	Graham Williamson	17	Jul	79
3:57.03	Steve Cram	14	Sep	79
3:58.68	Steve Flint	26	May	80
3:59.4	Steve Ovett	17	Jul	74
4:00.31	Johan Boakes	5	Aug	86
4:00.6	Simon Mugglestone	16	Sep	87
4:00.67	Brian Treacy	22	Aug	90
4:01.0	David Sharpe	3	May	86

2000 Metres

5:06.56	Jon Richards	7	Jul	82

3000 Metres

7:48.28	Jon Richards	9	Jul	83
7:51.84	Steve Binns	8	Sep	79
7:56.28	John Doherty	13	Jul	80
7:59.55	Paul Davies-Hale	8	Aug	81
8:00.1 a	Micky Morton	11	Jul	78
8:00.7	Graham Williamson	29	Jul	78
8:00.73	David Black	24	Jul	71
8:00.8	Steve Anders	1	Aug	78
8:00.88	Paul Taylor	12	Jun	85
8:01.2	Ian Stewart I	7	Sep	68
8:01.26	Darius Burrows	21	Aug	94
8:01.43	Nat Muir	28	Aug	77
8:01.44	Colin Reitz	16	May	79

5000 Metres

13:27.04	Steve Binns	14	Sep	79
13:35.95	Paul Davies-Hale	11	Sep	81
13:37.4	David Black	10	Sep	71
13:43.82	Simon Mugglestone	24	May	87
13:44.64	Julian Goater	14	Jul	72
13:48.74	Jon Richards	28	May	83
13:48.84	John Doherty	8	Aug	80
13:49.1 a	Nat Muir	21	Aug	77
13:53.30	Ian Stewart I	3	Aug	68
13:53.3 a	Nicky Lees	21	Aug	77
13:54.2	Mick Morton	1	Jul	78
13:54.52	Keith Cullen	8	Jun	91
13:56.31	Mohamed Farah	23	Jun	01
14:00.7	Peter Tootell	19	Jun	82
14:00.7	Mike Chorlton	19	Jun	82
14:00.85	Paul Taylor	15	Sep	84
14:03.0	Steve Anders	1	Jul	78
14:03.09	Jon Brown	11	Aug	90
14:03.4	Jim Brown	26	Jun	71
14:05.0	Paul Bannon	24	Jun	72

10000 Metres

29:21.9	Jon Brown	21	Apr	90
29:38.6	Ray Crabb	18	Apr	73
29:44.0	Richard Green	27	Sep	75
29:44.8	Jack Lane	23	Sep	69
29:45.8	Dave Murphy	17	Jul	76

2000 Metres Steeplechase

5:29.61	Colin Reitz	18	Aug	79
5:31.12	Paul Davies-Hale	22	Aug	81
5:32.84	Tom Hanlon	20	Jul	86
5:34.8 a	Micky Morris	24	Aug	75
5:38.01	Ken Baker	1	Aug	82
5:38.2	Spencer Duval	8	Jul	89
5:39.3 a	Graeme Fell	11	Jul	78
5:39.93	Eddie Wedderburn	9	Sep	79
5:40.2	Paul Campbell	31	Jul	77
5:40.2	John Hartigan	27	Jun	84

3000 Metres Steeplechase

8:29.85	Paul Davies-Hale	31	Aug	81
8:42.75	Colin Reitz	6	Jun	79
8:43.21	Kevin Nash	2	Jun	96
8:44.68	Alastair O'Connor	12	Aug	90
8:44.91	Ken Baker	30	May	82
8:45.65	Spencer Duval	17	Jun	89
8:47.49	Tom Hanlon	8	Jun	86
8:48.43	Graeme Fell	16	Jul	78
8:50.14	Dave Long I	13	Jul	73
8:51.02	Tony Staynings	14	Jul	72
8:54.15	Stuart Kefford	18	Sep	92
8:54.6	Micky Morris	7	Sep	75
8:54.92	Mark Wortley	4	Jun	88
8:56.0	John Davies	13	Jun	71
8:56.0	Eddie Wedderburn	3	Jun	79
8:56.36	Dave Robertson	15	Jun	91
8:57.4	Keith Cullen	8	May	91
8:57.83	Iain Murdoch	3	May	99
8:59.09	Ben Whitby	27	Jul	96
8:59.2	Maurice Herriott	3	Sep	58

110 Metres Hurdles (3'3")

13.57	Chris Baillie	21 Aug 99	
13.77	Kevin Lumsdon	8 Aug 92	
13.90	Robert Newton	10 Jul 99	
13.97	Dominic Girdler	2 Sep 01	
14.01	Jamie Quarry	13 Jul 91	
14.06	Neil Owen	4 Jul 92	
14.07	Leo Barker	12 Jul 97	
14.08	Liam Collins	12 Jul 97	
14.11	Nathan Palmer	22 Aug 99	
14.13	Derek Wilson	25 Jun 83	10

wind assisted

13.92	Matthew Clements	27 Aug 94	
13.96	Dominic Girdler	8 Jul 00	

hand timing

13.8	Jon Ridgeon	13 Jul 84	
13.8	Paul Gray	16 Jul 88	

hand timing - wind assisted

13.6	Mark Holtom	9 Jul 77	
13.8	Paul Brice	9 Jul 83	
13.8	Colin Jackson	15 Jul 84	
13.8	Brett St Louis	11 Jul 87	

110 Metres Hurdles (3'6")

13.44	Colin Jackson	19 Jul 86	
13.46	Jon Ridgeon	23 Aug 85	
13.72	Tony Jarrett	24 May 87	
13.84	Chris Baillie	27 Aug 00	
13.91	David Nelson	21 Jun 86	
13.95	Robert Newton	4 Sep 00	
13.97	Paul Gray	30 Jul 88	
14.01	Ross Baillie	25 Aug 96	
14.03	Brett St Louis	27 Jun 87	
14.04	Damien Greaves	25 Aug 96	10
14.06	Mark Holtom	7 Aug 77	
14.06	Nathan Palmer	20 Jul 01	
14.08	Paul Brice	26 Aug 83	
14.14	Neil Owen	17 Sep 92	
14.16	Dominic Girdler	21 Jul 01	
14.18	James Archampong	21 Jul 94	
14.21	Berwyn Price	12 Sep 70	
14.24	Nigel Walker	17 Sep 82	
14.25	Ben Warmington	31 Jul 98	
14.26	Alan Scott	24 Jun 01	

wind assisted

13.42	Colin Jackson	27 Jul 86	
13.82	David Nelson	5 Jul 86	
13.92	Chris Baillie	7 Aug 99	
13.93	Robert Newton	7 Aug 99	
14.07	Dominic Girdler	20 Jul 01	

400 Metres Hurdles

50.22	Martin Briggs	28 Aug 83	
50.70	Noel Levy	8 Jul 94	
51.07	Philip Beattie	20 Aug 82	
51.15 A	Andy Todd	18 Oct 67	
	51.70	23 Sep 67	
51.31	Gary Oakes	9 Sep 77	
51.39	Richard McDonald	19 Jun 99	
51.48	Bob Brown	19 Jun 88	
51.51	Max Robertson	24 Jul 82	
51.55	Mark Whitby	26 Aug 83	
51.63	Mark Rowlands	21 Jun 97	10
51.66	Paul Goacher	2 Aug 80	
51.71	Matthew Elias	7 Jun 97	
51.73	Matt Douglas	29 Jul 95	
51.91	Peter Campbell	19 Jun 88	
51.97	Bel Blik	17 Aug 85	
52.24	Andrew Abrahams	11 Aug 84	
52.25	Jeffrey Christie	16 Jun 01	
52.26	Gary Jennings	30 Jun 91	
52.26	Charles Robertson-Adams	15 Jun 96	
52.29	Steven Green	7 Jul 01	20

hand timing

51.0	Richard McDonald	24 Jul 99	
51.5	Max Robertson	10 Jul 82	
51.5	Matthew Elias	6 Jun 98	
51.8	Jeffrey Christie	1 Jul 01	

High Jump

2.37	Steve Smith	20 Sep 92	
2.27	Brendan Reilly	27 May 90	
2.26	James Brierley	3 Aug 96	
2.25	Geoff Parsons	9 Jul 83	
2.24	John Hill	23 Aug 85	
2.23	Mark Lakey (U17)	29 Aug 82	
2.23 i	Ben Challenger	1 Mar 97	
	2.21	24 Aug 96	
2.22	Dalton Grant	3 Jul 85	
2.20	Byron Morrison	14 Jul 84	
2.18	Ossie Cham	14 Jun 80	10
2.18	Alex Kruger	26 Jun 82	
2.18	Steve Ritchie	15 Jul 89	
2.18	Hopeton Lindo	23 Jul 89	
2.18	Chuka Enih-Snell	21 Apr 01	
2.17	Stuart Ohrland	27 Aug 94	
2.17	Mike Robbins	5 Aug 95	
2.16 i	Claude Moseley	13 Apr 80	
2.16	Andy Hutchison	2 Sep 84	
2.16	John Holman	4 Jul 87	
2.16	Andrew Lynch	18 Sep 93	20
2.16	Richard Aspden	7 Jul 95	
2.16	Rob Brocklebank	7 Jul 95	
2.16 i	Jason McDade	24 Jan 99	

Pole Vault

5.50	Neil Winter	9 Aug 92	
5.30	Matt Belsham	16 Sep 90	
5.21	Andy Ashurst	2 Sep 84	
5.21 i	Christian Linskey	20 Feb 99	
	5.20	24 May 98	
5.20	Billy Davey	5 Jun 83	
5.20	Warren Siley	4 Aug 90	
5.20	Nick Buckfield	31 May 92	
5.20	Ben Flint	2 Aug 97	
5.10	Brian Hooper	1 Oct 72	
5.10	Mike Edwards	20 Jun 87	10
5.10	Mark Davis	9 Jun 96	
5.05	Ian Tullett	22 Aug 87	
5.05	Dean Mellor	7 Jul 90	
5.02	Paul Williamson	29 May 93	

	5.00	Keith Stock	3	Jul	76
	5.00	Bob Kingman	2	May	92
	5.00	Tim Thomas	17	Jun	92
	5.00	Mike Barber	1	Jul	92
	5.00 sq	Ian Wilding	16	Jul	94
20	5.00	Neil Young	18	May	96

Long Jump

	7.98	Stewart Faulkner	6	Aug	88
	7.98	Jonathan Moore	29	Jul	01
	7.91	Steve Phillips	10	Aug	91
	7.90	Nathan Morgan	25	Jul	97
	7.84	Wayne Griffith	25	Aug	89
	7.76	Carl Howard	31	Jul	93
	7.73	Jason Canning	20	Apr	88
	7.72	Daley Thompson	21	May	77
	7.70	Kevin Liddington	27	Aug	88
10	7.66	Barry Nevison	7	Jul	85
	7.62	Colin Mitchell	11	Jul	78
	7.62	Chris Tomlinson	21	Oct	00
	7.61	Darren Gomersall	19	Jul	87
	7.58	Fred Salle	11	Jun	83
	7.56	John Herbert	11	Jul	81
	7.56	Colin Jackson	31	Aug	85
	7.56	Stuart Wells	12	Jul	97
	7.56	Darren Thompson	30	May	98
	7.54	Derrick Brown	26	Jun	82

wind assisted

8.04	Stewart Faulkner	20	Aug	88
7.97	Nathan Morgan	13	Jul	96
7.96	Colin Jackson	17	May	86
7.82	Kevin Liddington	25	Jun	89
7.72	John Herbert	15	Jun	80
7.66	Mark Awanah	30	Jun	01
7.60	Brian Robinson (U17)	21	Jul	97
7.58	Gus Udo	8	Jul	78
7.58	Garry Slade	6	Jun	87
7.56	Eddie Starrs	22	Jul	79

Triple Jump

	16.58	Tosi Fasinro	15	Jun	91
	16.57	Tosin Oke	8	Aug	99
	16.53	Larry Achike	24	Jul	94
	16.43	Jonathan Moore	22	Jul	01
	16.24	Aston Moore	11	Jun	75
	16.22	Mike Makin	17	May	81
	16.13	Steven Anderson	11	Jun	83
	16.03	John Herbert	23	Jun	81
	15.99	Steven Shalders	20	Oct	00
10	15.95	Keith Connor	30	Aug	76
	15.94	Vernon Samuels	27	Jun	82
	15.93	Tayo Erogbogbo	17	Sep	94
	15.92	Lawrence Lynch	13	Jul	85
	15.88	Julian Golley	28	Jul	90
	15.87	Stewart Faulkner	22	Aug	87
	15.86	Phillips Idowu	5	Jul	97
	15.84	Francis Agyepong	29	Sep	84
	15.82	Jon Wallace	11	Jul	98
	15.80	David Johnson	14	Jul	72
20	15.79	Paul Johnson	27	Jun	87

wind assisted

16.81	Tosi Fasinro	15	Jun	91
16.67	Larry Achike	24	Jul	94
16.43	Mike Makin	14	Jun	81
16.34	Phillips Idowu	27	Jul	97
16.31	Aston Moore	9	Aug	75
16.07	Vernon Samuels	14	Aug	82
16.01	Julian Golley	22	Jul	90
15.96	Paul Johnson	27	Jun	87
15.95	Lawrence Lynch	26	May	86
15.81	Junior Campbell	28	May	89

Shot (7.26kg)

19.46	Carl Myerscough ¶	6	Sep	98	
18.21 i	Matt Simson	3	Feb	89	
	18.11	27	Aug	89	
17.78 i	Billy Cole	10	Mar	84	
	17.72	2	Jun	84	
17.36 i	Chris Ellis	8	Dec	84	
	17.10	7	Jul	85	
17.26 i	Geoff Capes	16	Nov	68	
	16.80	30	Jul	68	
17.25	Emeka Udechuku	20	Sep	97	
17.22	Antony Zaidman	4	Jul	81	
16.69	Gregg Beard	30	Sep	00	
16.61	Simon Williams	10	Aug	86	
16.60	Alan Carter	11	May	63	10
16.48	Martyn Lucking	24	Aug	57	
16.47	Paul Buxton	25	May	75	
16.23 i	David Readle	30	Jan	99	
	16.15	3	Jul	99	
16.21	Mike Lindsay	29	Jul	57	
16.20 i	Nigel Spratley	19	Mar	89	
	16.04	20	May	89	
16.18	Tony Satchwell	23	Apr	72	
16.10	Martin Fletcher	19	Jun	88	
16.03	Jon Wood	26	Sep	70	
15.94	Andy Vince	5	May	78	
15.94	Mitchell Smith	23	Mar	85	20

Shot (6.25kg)

21.03	Carl Myerscough ¶	13	May	98	
19.47	Matt Simson	20	May	89	
19.15	Billy Cole	19	May	84	
18.66 i	Simon Williams	15	Nov	86	
	18.52	11	Jul	86	
18.20 i	Chris Ellis	16	Feb	85	
	18.13	14	Jul	84	
18.06	Greg Beard	2	Sep	01	
17.81	Antony Zaidman	16	May	81	
17.74	Emeka Udechuku	9	Aug	98	
17.67	David Readle	22	Aug	99	
17.58	Nigel Spratley	28	May	89	10
17.32	Andy Vince	15	May	77	
17.31	Mitchell Smith	11	Jun	85	
17.31	Lyndon Woodward	10	Jul	99	
17.30	Jamie Cockburn	20	Sep	92	
17.26	Neil Gray	19	May	84	
17.26 i	Neal Brunning ¶	9	Dec	89	
17.22	Richard Slaney	22	Jul	75	

Discus (2kg)

60.97	Emeka Udechuku	5 Jul 98	
60.19	Carl Myerscough ¶	8 Aug 98	
55.10	Glen Smith	31 Aug 91	
53.42	Paul Mardle	25 Jul 81	
53.40	Robert Weir	10 Aug 80	
53.32	Paul Buxton	9 Aug 75	
53.02	Simon Williams	16 Aug 86	
52.94	Lee Newman	29 Aug 92	
52.84	Jamie Murphy	14 Jun 92	
52.14	Robert Russell	4 Jul 93	10
51.70	Richard Slaney	27 Jul 75	
51.66	Neal Brunning ¶	30 Jul 89	
51.28	Adam Major	10 Sep 00	
51.10	Mike Lindsay	29 May 57	
51.08	Peter Weir	1 Aug 82	
51.05	Luke Rosenberg	4 Jul 99	
50.74	Tony Satchwell	21 Aug 72	
50.64	Colin Bastien	9 Jun 85	
50.46	Neil Boyton	16 Jul 83	
50.07	Scot Thompson	27 Aug 00	20

Discus (1.75kg)

64.35	Emeka Udechuku	21 Jun 98	
61.81	Carl Myerscough ¶	18 Aug 98	
60.76	Glen Smith	26 May 91	
56.64	Jamie Murphy	19 May 90	
56.10	Lee Newman	4 Jul 92	
56.00	Simon Williams	17 May 86	
55.94	Mark Davies	19 Aug 90	
55.44	Neal Brunning ¶	8 Jul 89	
55.16	Adam Major	10 Sep 00	
55.00	Robert Russell	16 May 93	10

Hammer (7.26kg)

67.48	Paul Head	16 Sep 84	
67.10	Jason Byrne	6 Aug 89	
66.14	Martin Girvan	21 Jul 79	
65.86	Robert Weir	6 Sep 80	
65.30	Karl Andrews	2 Jul 94	
64.14	Ian Chipchase	25 Sep 71	
63.84	Andrew Tolputt	7 Sep 86	
63.72	Gareth Cook	10 Jul 88	
62.82	Mick Jones	29 Aug 82	
62.02	Peter Vivian	1 Jul 89	10
61.34	Ron James	22 Apr 78	
61.22	Malcolm Croad	25 Aug 92	
61.10	Vaughan Cooper	5 May 84	
60.86	David Smith I	2 Aug 81	
60.34	Tony Kenneally	1 Aug 82	
60.24	Paul Buxton	17 Jun 75	
60.04	Eric Berry	16 Jun 73	
59.98	David Smith II	3 Jul 93	
59.80	Matthew Bell	7 Jun 97	
59.12	Andrew Grierson	18 Jul 98	20

Hammer (6.25kg)

74.92	Jason Byrne	17 Dec 89	
73.28	Robert Weir	14 Sep 80	
72.66	Paul Head	2 Sep 84	
71.84	Gareth Cook	28 May 88	
70.36	Andrew Tolputt	21 Sep 86	
69.10	Karl Andrews	3 Aug 94	
67.80	Martin Girvan	7 Jul 79	
67.52	Vaughan Cooper	19 May 84	
67.48	Mick Jones	2 Jun 82	
66.38	Tony Kenneally	10 Jul 82	10

Javelin

79.50	Steve Backley	5 Jun 88	
77.48	David Parker	14 Aug 99	
74.54	Gary Jenson	19 Sep 86	
74.24	Mark Roberson	18 Jul 86	
73.76	Nigel Bevan	29 Aug 87	
71.79	Phill Sharpe	27 Aug 00	
71.74	Myles Cottrell	29 Jul 89	
71.14	Dan Carter	11 Jul 98	
69.62	Stefan Baldwin	8 Jul 89	
68.84	James Hurrion	12 Jul 91	10
68.74	Jon Clarke	14 Jun 86	
68.38	James Drennen	12 Jul 91	
68.30	Mark Lawrence	31 Jul 88	
68.08	Tim Kitney	13 Sep 98	
67.22	Richard Atkinson	14 Aug 93	
66.74	Stuart Faben	22 Jul 94	
66.62	Mark Francis	13 Jul 96	
66.21	Clifton Green	4 May 98	
65.70	Duncan MacDonald	17 Jul 93	
65.34	Paul Cooper	11 Jun 95	20

Decathlon (1985 Tables)

8082	Daley Thompson	31 Jul 77	
7488	David Bigham	9 Aug 90	
7480	Dean Macey	22 Aug 96	
7299	Eugene Gilkes	24 May 81	
7274	Jim Stevenson	24 Jun 90	
7247	Brian Taylor	7 May 89	
7169	Barry Thomas	5 Aug 90	
7126	Fidelis Obikwu	16 Sep 79	
7112	Gavin Sunshine	30 Jul 93	
7018	Jamie Quarry	30 Jun 91	10
6958	Roy Mitchell	29 Sep 74	
6936	Anthony Brannen	24 May 87	
6925	Roger Hunter	4 Jun 95	
6843	Ed Coats	30 May 99	
6839	Mark Bushell	30 Apr 95	
6812	Nigel Skinner	19 Aug 84	
6809	Rafer Joseph	26 Jul 87	
6801 w	Kevan Lobb	18 Jun 78	
6774	Jason McDade	30 May 99	
6788	Adrian Hemery	10 Jun 01	20

Junior Implements

7134	Dean Macey	17 Sep 95	
6958 w	Roger Hunter	18 Sep 94	
6789	Jamie Quarry	16 Sep 90	
6762	Fyn Corcoran	22 Sep 96	
6678	Darren Hatton	21 Sep 97	
6674	John Heanley	19 Sep 99	
6672	Martin Troy	17 Sep 95	
6636	Jason McDade	19 Sep 99	

3000 Metres Track Walk

11:54.23	Tim Berrett	23	Jun	84
12:01.89 i	Philip King	21	Feb	93
	12:02.0	12	May	92
12:02.04	Phil Vesty	24	Jul	82
12:16.5	David Hucks	5	Aug	84
12:19.8	Gordon Vale	11	Mar	81

5000 Metres Track Walk

20:16.40	Philip King	26	Jun	93
20:33.4 +	Darrell Stone	7	Aug	87
20:47.23	Lloyd Finch	14	Jul	01
20:55.4	Tim Berrett	9	Jun	84
21:00.5 +	Phil Vesty	19	Jun	82

10000 Metres Track Walk

	41:52.13	Darrell Stone	7	Aug	87
	42:06.35	Gordon Vale	2	Aug	81
	42:46.3	Phil Vesty	20	Mar	82
	42:47.7	Philip King	2	May	92
	43:04.09	Tim Berrett	25	Aug	83
	43:42.75	Martin Rush	29	May	83
	43:54.25	Gareth Brown	7	Aug	87
	44:22.12	Gareth Holloway	5	Jun	88
	44:22.4	Jon Vincent	1	Apr	89
10	44:29.4	Lloyd Finch	1	Jul	01
	44:30.0	Andy Penn	15	Mar	86
	44:38.0	Ian McCombie	29	Mar	80
	44:53.0	Michael Kemp	4	Apr	98
	45:04.28	Andi Drake	1	Jul	84
	45:04.37	Ian Ashforth	3	Aug	85
	45:06.19	Jon Bott	25	May	87
	45:13.50	Kirk Taylor	23	Aug	87
	45:17.0	Bob Chaplain	28	Jun	75
	45:20.0	Jacky Lord	3	Aug	74
20	45:20.42	Steve Hollier	2	Jul	95

10k Road - where superior to track time

41:47	Darrell Stone	26	Sep	87
42:29	Steve Hollier	10	Dec	95
42:39	Martin Rush	7	May	83
42:40	Tim Berrett	18	Feb	84
43:18	Richard Dorman	18	Oct	80
43:35	Gareth Brown	12	Apr	87
43:38 hc	Lloyd Finch (U17)	20	Nov	99
43:50	Kirk Taylor	12	Apr	87
43:53	Michael Kemp	25	Apr	98
44:06	Dom King	21	Apr	01
44:08	Nathan Kavanagh	5	May	85
44:08	Gareth Holloway	8	Jul	89
44:09	Jimmy Ball	16	Oct	82

20 Kilometres Road Walk

1:26:13	Tim Berrett	25	Feb	84
1:29:10	Phil Vesty	18	Jul	82
1:31:34.4t	Gordon Vale	28	Jun	81
1:32:46	Graham Morris	26	Feb	77
1:33:03	Darrell Stone	10	May	86

50 Kilometres Road Walk

4:18:18	Gordon Vale	24	Oct	81

UNDER 17

100 Metres

10.31	Mark Lewis-Francis	21	Aug	99	
10.56	Rikki Fifton	29	Jul	01	
10.60	Tyrone Edgar	16	Aug	98	
10.64	Jon Barbour	12	Jul	97	
10.66	Ben Lewis	7	Sep	97	
10.67	Michael Nartey	28	Sep	91	
10.69	Mike McFarlane	13	Aug	76	
10.70	Steve Green	15	Jul	72	
10.70	Karl Forde	3	Jul	99	
10.71	Luke Davis	12	Jul	96	10
10.71	Tim Benjamin	16	Aug	98	
10.72	Peter Little	6	Aug	77	
10.72	Trevor Cameron	7	Aug	93	
10.73	Danny Joyce	17	Aug	91	
wind assisted					
10.26	Mark Lewis-Francis	5	Aug	99	
10.38	Kevin Mark	3	Jul	93	
10.44	Luke Davis	13	Jul	96	
10.51	Tim Benjamin	4	Jul	98	
10.56	Dwain Chambers	8	Jul	94	
10.57	Trevor Cameron	3	Jul	93	
10.58	Tyrone Edgar	16	Aug	98	
10.60	Matthew Ouche	7	Jul	01	
10.62	Elliot Bunney	25	Jun	83	
10.62	Jamie Nixon	7	Jul	85	10
10.65	Mike Williams	20	Jun	87	
hand timing					
10.5	Michael Powell	17	Sep	78	

200 Metres

20.92	Ade Mafe	27	Aug	83	
21.19	Tim Benjamin	31	Jul	98	
21.24	Peter Little	21	Aug	77	
21.25	Mark Richardson ¶	24	Jul	88	
21.44	Roger Hunter	2	Aug	81	
21.45	Monu Miah	29	Jul	00	
21.46	Simon Farenden	7	Jul	01	
21.51	Darren Campbell	15	Sep	90	
21.51	Ben Lewis	19	Jul	97	
21.53	Steve Eden	2	Aug	81	10
21.56	Trevor Cameron	8	Aug	93	
21.58	Christian Malcolm	9	Jul	95	
21.62	Tyrone Edgar	24	May	98	
21.63	Richard Ashby	7	Aug	83	
21.64	Elliot Bunney	7	Aug	83	
21.64	Adam Rogers	14	Aug	99	
wind assisted					
20.98	Tim Benjamin	18	Jul	98	
21.17	Mark Richardson	20	Aug	88	
21.25	Trevor Cameron	25	Sep	93	
21.31	Monu Miah	15	Jul	00	
21.32	Graham Beasley	9	Jul	94	
21.38	Elliot Bunney	13	Aug	83	
21.38	Ben Lewis	12	Jul	97	
21.39	Laurence Oboh	15	Jul	00	
hand timing - wind assisted					
21.0	Peter Little	30	Jul	77	

400 Metres

	46.43	Mark Richardson ¶	28 Jul 88
	46.74	Guy Bullock	17 Sep 92
	47.81	Mark Hylton	17 Jul 93
	47.86	Kris Stewart	13 Jul 96
	48.05	David Naismith	10 Aug 96
	48.11	Gary Thomas	18 Sep 82
	48.22	Robert Tobin	8 Jul 00
	48.25	Adrian Patrick	2 Sep 89
	48.34	Richard McNabb	27 Aug 95
10	48.35	James Hilston	6 Aug 95
	48.36	David Simpson	29 May 89
	48.41	Mark Tyler	11 Aug 84
	48.46	Phil Harvey	24 Jun 79
	48.46	Simon Tunnicliffe	29 May 99
	48.50	Russell Nicholls	10 Jul 99

hand timing

47.6	Kris Stewart	3 Aug 96
48.2	David Simpson	8 Jul 89
48.3	David McKenzie	21 Sep 86
48.4	Steve Ovett	20 Aug 72
48.4	Chris Thompson	1 Aug 81
48.4	Martin Bradbury	31 Jul 99

800 Metres

	1:49.9	Mark Sesay	18 Jul 89
	1:50.7	Peter Elliott	16 Sep 79
	1:50.90	Craig Winrow	21 Aug 88
	1:51.0	Chris McGeorge	1 Jul 78
	1:51.05	Mal Edwards	20 Sep 74
	1:51.3	Julian Spooner	3 Aug 77
	1:51.4	Kevin McKay	19 Aug 85
	1:51.6	Neil Horsfield	31 Aug 83
	1:51.6	David Gerard	21 Jul 84
10	1:51.8	Paul Burgess	14 Jul 87
	1:51.9 +	Johan Boakes	17 Jun 84
	1:52.0	Paul Causey	21 Jul 84
	1:52.21	Malcolm Hassan	21 Aug 99
	1:52.29	Simon Young	7 Aug 90
	1:52.36	Michael Rimmer	19 Jun 01

1000 Metres

2:20.37	Johan Boakes	17 Jun 84

1500 Metres

	3:47.7	Steve Cram	14 May 77
	3:48.49	Johan Boakes	28 Jun 84
	3:49.9	Kelvin Newton	20 Jun 79
	3:51.1	Jason Lobo	30 Aug 86
	3:51.4	Darren Mead	26 Jul 85
	3:51.7	Martin Forder	19 Sep 86
	3:51.8	Mark Sesay	22 Aug 89
	3:52.0	Stuart Poore	6 Sep 89
	3:52.47	Simon Young	4 Aug 90
10	3:52.6	Glen Stewart	19 Sep 87
	3:52.78	Clifton Bradeley	2 Aug 81
	3:52.9	Steve Johnson	8 Jul 89
	3:53.0	Mark Bateman	31 Aug 74
	3:53.16	Robert Farish	2 Aug 81
	3:53.3	Richard Bunn	8 Jul 89

1 Mile

4:06.7	Barrie Williams	22 Apr 72

2000 Metres

5:28.2 +	Kevin Steere	10 Jul 71

3000 Metres

8:13.42	Barrie Moss	15 Jul 72	
8:15.34	Kevin Steere	30 Aug 71	
8:16.18	Mohammed Farah	21 Aug 99	
8:19.08	Darren Mead	26 Aug 85	
8:19.38	Johan Boakes	24 Jun 84	
8:24.2	Simon Goodwin	16 Jul 80	
8:24.2	Jason Lobo	13 Aug 86	
8:25.2	Colin Clarkson	3 Aug 77	
8:26.3	Paul Williams	10 Aug 83	
8:26.6	Jon Dennis	23 Apr 86	10
8:26.92	Jon Richards	5 Sep 80	
8:29.09	Steve Fury	18 Aug 84	
8:29.4	Darrell Smith	16 Jul 83	
8:30.4	Nicky Lees	15 Jul 74	
8:30.4	David Lewis	13 Aug 78	
8:30.4	David Thompson	8 Jul 89	

5000 Metres

14:41.8	Nicky Lees	24 Aug 74

1500 Metres Steeplechase

4:11.2	Steve Evans	15 Jul 74	
4:12.3	Chris Sly	15 Jul 74	
4:13.1	John Crowley	15 Jul 74	
4:13.2	David Lewis	1 Jul 78	
4:13.7	Danny Fleming	31 Jul 77	
4:13.9	Eddie Wedderburn	31 Jul 77	
4:14.0	Dave Robertson	8 Jul 89	
4:14.4	Stephen Arnold	7 Sep 85	
4:15.0	David Caton	9 Jun 84	
4:15.0	Spencer Duval	12 Jul 86	10
4:15.2	Garrie Richardson	8 Jul 89	
4:15.3	John Wilson	26 Jul 75	
4:16.6	Adrian Green	9 Jun 84	
4:17.4	Spencer Newport	9 Jul 83	
4:17.7	Kevin Capper	8 Aug 76	
4:17.7	Stuart Kefford	8 Jul 89	

2000 Metres Steeplechase

5:55.0	David Lewis	20 Aug 78

3000 Metres Steeplechase

9:16.6	Colin Reitz	19 Sep 76

100 Metres Hurdles (3'0")

12.60	Tristan Anthony	14 Aug 99
12.68	Matthew Clements	8 Aug 93
12.90	Steve Markham	17 Aug 91
12.91	Allan Scott	14 Aug 99
12.97	Jon Snade	8 Aug 93
12.97	Andy Turner	16 Aug 97
12.98	Robert Newton	16 Aug 97
12.99	Dominic Girdler	11 Jul 98

13.01 Hugh Teape 3 Aug 80
10 13.05 Brett St Louis 4 Aug 85
13.07 Jon Ridgeon 7 Aug 83
13.07 David O'Leary 3 Aug 96
13.09 Damien Greaves 8 Jul 94
13.09 Chris Baillie 16 Aug 97
13.10 Ricky Glover 17 Aug 91

wind assisted

12.47 Matthew Clements 9 Jul 94
12.70 Damien Greaves 9 Jul 94
12.88 Nick Csemiczky 13 Jul 91
12.90 Ricky Glover 13 Jul 91
12.90 Ben Warmington 8 Jul 95
12.96 Nathan Palmer 15 Aug 98
12.96 Dominic Girdler 15 Aug 98
12.99 Neil Owen 1 Jul 90

hand timing

12.8 Brett St Louis 28 Jul 85
12.8 Richard Dunn 29 Jun 91
12.9 Hugh Teape 31 Aug 80

hand timing - wind assisted

12.6 Brett St Louis 20 Jul 85
12.9 Jon Ridgeon 9 Jul 83
12.9 Dominic Girdler 13 Sep 98

110 Metres Hurdles (3'0")

13.71 Matthew Clements 19 May 94
14.16 Ben Warmington 12 Jul 95
14.19 Ross Baillie 19 May 94

hand timing

13.6 Jon Ridgeon 16 Jul 83

110 Metres Hurdles (3'3")

15.07 Edward Dunford 10 Sep 00

wind assisted

13.92 Matthew Clements 27 Aug 94

hand timing

14.5 Kieran Moore 30 Aug 80

110 Metres Hurdles (3'6")

14.89 Tristan Anthony 4 Jul 99

400 Metres Hurdles (2'9")

52.20 Tristan Anthony 18 Jul 99
52.69 Jeffrey Christie 18 Jul 99
52.81 Richard McDonald 10 Aug 96
53.14 Martin Briggs 2 Aug 80
53.26 Nange Ursell 11 Jul 98
53.30 Mark Rowlands 31 Jul 94
53.55 Charles Robertson-Adams 31 Jul 94
53.58 Noel Levy 13 Jul 91
53.64 Dean Park 17 May 94
10 53.69 Max Robertson 2 Aug 80
53.69 Bob Brown 9 Aug 86
53.71 Andrew Bargh 11 Jul 92
53.82 Robert Taylor 9 Aug 86
53.84 Rhys Williams 5 Aug 00

hand timing

53.2 Phil Beattie 24 May 80
53.8 Carl McMullen 20 Jul 96

400 Metres Hurdles (3'0")

53.06 Phil Beattie 2 Aug 80
53.31 Richard McDonald 28 Jul 96

High Jump

2.23 Mark Lakey 29 Aug 82
2.15 Ossie Cham 14 Jul 79
2.15 Brendan Reilly 7 May 89
2.15 Stanley Osuide 1 Sep 91
2.15 Chuka Enih-Snell 10 Sep 00
2.12 Femi Abejide 11 Jul 81
2.11 Leroy Lucas 6 Aug 83
2.11 i Ken McKeown 12 Jul 98
2.11 18 Jul 98
2.10 Dalton Grant 18 Sep 82
2.10 Tim Blakeway 29 Aug 87 10
2.10 James Brierley 16 May 93
2.10 Martin Lloyd 28 Sep 96
2.10 Martin Aram 23 Jul 00
2.09 Steve Smith 10 Sep 89
2.09 Sam Hood 27 Aug 00

Pole Vault

5.20 Neil Winter 2 Sep 90
5.15 Christian Linskey 23 Aug 96
4.90 Warren Siley 8 Sep 89
4.80 Billy Davey 14 Sep 80
4.76 Nick Buckfield 11 Jun 89
4.72 Ian Lewis 24 Aug 85
4.71 Chris Tremayne 27 Aug 01
4.70 Richard Smith 7 Jun 97
4.70 Mark Christie 25 Aug 01
4.66 Mike Edwards 24 Aug 85 10
4.60 Ben Flint 10 Jun 95
4.53 Keith Stock 5 Sep 73
4.50 Christian North 26 Aug 90
4.50 Mike Barber 15 Sep 90
4.50 Neil Young 5 Jun 93
4.50 Chris Type 4 Jul 98
4.50 Cameron Johnston 15 Aug 99
4.50 Paul Stevens 8 Jul 00

Long Jump

7.53 Brian Robinson 21 Jul 97
7.46 Jonathan Moore 30 Jul 00
7.33 Onen Eyong 6 Jul 01
7.32 Kevin Liddington 16 May 87
7.25 Alan Slack 12 Jun 76
7.21 Hugh Teape 17 May 80
7.21 Jordan Lau 8 Jul 00
7.20 Hugh Davidson 21 Jun 80
7.19 Oni Onuorah 8 Jul 89
7.19 Jermaine Bernard 21 Jul 01 10
7.18 Barry Nevison 1 May 83
7.17 Hugh Whyte 15 Jul 79
7.17 Mark Awanah 4 Jul 99
7.15 Matthew John 29 Jun 86
7.14 Stewart Faulkner 17 Aug 85

wind assisted

7.60 Brian Robinson 21 Jul 97

7.47	Onen Eyong	2 Sep 01
7.40	Matthew John	10 May 86
7.27	David Mountford	25 Jul 98
7.25	Nathan Morgan	27 Aug 94
7.25	Mark Awanah	25 Jul 98
7.23	Oni Onuorah	26 May 90
7.23	Andy Turner	20 Sep 97
7.22	Paul Hanson	7 Jul 78

Triple Jump

16.02	Jonathan Moore	13 Aug 00
15.65	Vernon Samuels	18 Jul 81
15.50	Junior Campbell	18 May 86
15.45	Steven Anderson	2 Aug 81
15.28	Larry Achike	22 Jun 91
note resident but not British citizen at this time		
15.14	Marvin Bramble	8 Aug 93
15.14	Steven Shalders	18 Jul 98
14.94	Hugh Teape	17 May 80
10 14.93	Mark Whitehead	26 Aug 85
14.90	Lawrence Lynch	21 Jul 84
14.84	Peter Vaughan	2 May 83
14.83	Malwyn Gordon	10 Jul 98
14.82	Philip Ferdinand	5 Sep 99
14.77	Carl Howard	13 Jul 90
14.76	Delroy Ricketts	13 Jul 90
14.76	Jon Wallace	3 Sep 95
wind assisted		
15.40	Steven Shalders	18 Jul 98
15.25	Marvin Bramble	3 Jul 93
15.08	Lawrence Lynch	29 Apr 84
15.06	Craig Duncan	7 Aug 82
15.01	Malwyn Gordon	15 Aug 98
14.93	Chris Tomlinson	18 Jul 98
14.88	Carl Howard	13 Jul 90
14.87	Darren Gomersall	3 Aug 85
14.84	Nick Leech	8 Jul 78

Shot (7.26kg)

17.30	Carl Myerscough ¶	3 Aug 96

Shot (6.25kg)

16.88	Gregg Beard	29 Aug 99

Shot (5kg)

21.20	Carl Myerscough ¶	22 Sep 96
19.22	Chris Ellis	4 Jun 82
18.91	Gregg Beard	19 Sep 99
18.90	Neal Brunning ¶	6 Sep 87
18.44	Matt Simson	27 Jul 86
18.43	Emeka Udechuku	28 May 95
18.25	Billy Cole	1 Aug 81
17.91	Antony Zaidman	28 May 78
17.76	George Brocklebank	22 Jul 79
10 17.61	Derrick Squire	15 Jul 00
17.40	Osita Iwenjiora	20 Sep 89
17.36	Piers Selby	10 Jul 92
17.34	Carl Saggers	30 Jul 00
17.30	Jason Mulcahy	7 Jul 89
17.24	Mark Edwards	20 Aug 91

Discus (2kg)

50.60	Carl Myerscough ¶	28 Jul 96
48.96	Emeka Udechuku	19 Aug 95

Discus (1.75kg)

54.70	Emeka Udechuku	18 Jun 95
52.50	Paul Mardle	7 Jul 79

Discus (1.5kg)

62.22	Emeka Udechuku	10 Jul 95
58.14	Carl Myerscough ¶	12 May 96
56.14	Chris Symonds	6 Sep 87
55.94	Simon Williams I	9 Sep 84
55.90	Guy Litherland	14 Sep 85
55.72	Keith Homer	27 Jun 82
55.52	Glen Smith	14 May 88
55.36	Neal Brunning ¶	7 Jun 87
55.17	Gregg Beard	30 May 99
54.18	Matt Symonds	21 Jul 84 10
53.98	Felice Miele	10 Jul 98
53.80	Paul Mardle	19 May 79
53.69	Carl Saggers	17 Sep 00
52.84	Simon Williams II	31 Aug 97
52.76	Julian Willett	17 Jun 89
52.76	James South	1 Sep 91
52.62	Ashley Knott	22 Sep 91
52.44	Garry Hagan	4 Aug 01

Hammer (7.26kg)

59.94	Andrew Tolputt	30 Sep 84
57.04	Peter Vivian	27 Jun 87

Hammer (6.25kg)

66.70	Andrew Tolputt	2 Sep 84
64.00	Matthew Sutton	22 Aug 98

Hammer (5kg)

76.28	Andrew Tolputt	11 Aug 84
73.90	Paul Head	29 Aug 81
73.76	Matthew Sutton	14 Jun 98
73.00	Nick Steinmetz	17 Jul 93
71.34	Tony Kenneally	7 Sep 80
70.82	Jason Byrne	20 Jun 87
68.62	Peter Vivian	16 May 87
68.27	Carl Saggers	17 Jun 00
67.64	Gareth Cook	22 Sep 85
67.48	Chris Howe	24 Jun 84 10
67.21	Ross Thompson	22 Aug 98
66.92	Paul Murden	8 May 85
66.30	Malcolm Croad	21 Jul 90
65.70	Ross Kidner	26 May 97
64.82	Vaughan Cooper	13 May 82
64.40	Jonathan Bond	14 May 89
64.32	Neil Homer	18 Aug 84
64.18	Charles Beresford	1 May 89
63.64	Graeme Allan	19 Jul 97

Javelin (800g -1986 model)

68.26	David Parker	19 May 96
61.00	Phill Sharpe	6 Jul 97

Javelin (800g Original model)

72.78	Gary Jenson	10 Sep 83
69.84	Colin Mackenzie	12 May 79
66.14	David Messom	14 May 81
65.32	Marcus Humphries	26 Aug 78
64.80	Paul Bushnell	1 Sep 85
64.34	Steve Backley	1 Sep 85
63.44	Michael Williams	16 Sep 79

Javelin (700g)

	73.56	David Parker	20 Jul 96
	72.48	Gary Jenson	3 Jul 83
	70.30	Colin Mackenzie	6 Jul 79
	68.88	Phill Sharpe	19 Jul 97
	68.26	Ian Marsh	30 Jul 77
	68.18	James Hurrion	3 Jun 90
	67.31	Lee Doran	21 Jul 01
	66.88	David Messom	4 Jul 81
	66.86	Michael Williams	16 Jul 79
10	66.52	Marcus Humphries	17 Sep 78
	66.00	Dan Carter	1 Sep 96
	65.92	Tim Kitney	10 Aug 96
	65.68	Tim Eldridge	18 Aug 91
	65.16	Mark Wells	31 May 77
	64.92	Jason Beaumont	11 Jun 83
	64.92	Paul Bushnell	20 Sep 85
	64.80	Justin Rubio	1 Sep 85
	64.68	Paul Godwin	19 May 90

Decathlon (Senior Implements)

6484	David Bigham	27 Sep 87
6299	Tom Leeson	21 Sep 80

Decathlon (Junior Implements)

6554	Jim Stevenson	25 Sep 88
6093	Robert Hughes	28 May 89

Decathlon (U17 Implements)

6712	Edward Dunford	3 Sep 00
6706	David Bigham	28 Jun 87
6047	Jeremy Lay	30 Jun 85

with 100m

5531	Jim Stevenson	18 Sep 88
5304	Tom Leeson	28 Sep 80
5194	Bryan Long	26 Sep 76
5106	Jeremy Lay	29 Sep 85
5096	Onochie Onuorah	17 Sep 89
5090	David Vidgen	22 Sep 91

Octathlon

	5741	Edward Dunford	17 Jun 01
	5550	Dominic Girdler	20 Sep 98
	5426	John Holtby	20 Sep 98
	5423	Leo Barker	17 Sep 95
	5378	Matthew Lewis	20 Sep 92
	5311	Dean Macey	18 Sep 94
	5279	Andrae Davis	21 Sep 97
	5238	Neil Scrivener	21 Sep 97
	5208	Fyn Corcoran	18 Sep 94
10	5158	Ed Coats	25 Aug 96
	5149	Paul Hourihan	19 Sep 93
	5144	Marc Newton	17 Sep 95
	5136	Jamie Russell	20 Sep 98
	5121	Chris Hindley	20 Sep 92
	5102	Matt Douglas	22 Aug 93
	5093	Robert Hollinger	21 Sep 97
	5059	Mark Bushell	19 Sep 93

3000 Metres Track Walk

12:04.9	Philip King	18 May 91
12:29.90	Andy Parker	2 Jul 00
12:34.98	Lloyd Finch	17 Jul 99
12:35.94	David Hucks	30 Aug 82
12:50.9	Jon Vincent	8 Jul 87
12:50.67 i	Stuart Monk	18 Feb 95
	12:52.9	12 Jul 95
13:03.5	Ian Ashforth	16 Sep 84
13:05.18	Cameron Smith	3 Sep 00
13:05.8	Sean Maxwell	8 Aug 76

5000 Metres Track Walk

20:46.5	Philip King	29 Sep 91	
21:52.7	Stuart Monk	22 Jul 95	
21:58.8	Luke Finch	22 Sep 01	
22:17.5	Russell Hutchings	27 Sep 86	
22:19.11	Lloyd Finch	18 Sep 99	
22:32.5	Gareth Holloway	27 Sep 86	
22:35.0	Ian Ashforth	6 Jun 84	
22:37.0	Jon Bott	27 Sep 86	
22:42.0	Martin Young	20 Aug 88	
22:42.19	Jon Vincent	6 Jun 86	10
22:48.91	Andy Parker	30 Jul 00	
22:50.51	Dom King	18 Sep 99	
22:53.7	Tim Berrett	28 Jun 81	
22:53.8	David Hucks	10 Mar 82	
22:57.7	Michael Kemp	31 Aug 96	
23:01.0	Karl Atton	19 Apr 88	
23:16.1	Thomas Taylor	31 May 97	

5k Road - where superior to track time

21:33	Jon Vincent	1 Nov 86
21:47	Lloyd Finch	20 Jun 99
22:04	Gareth Holloway	14 Sep 86
22:05	Karl Atton	19 Mar 88
22:30	Gordon Vale	15 Oct 77
22:31	Jon Bott	3 May 86
22:39	Matthew Hales	23 Jun 96
22:41	Thomas Taylor	26 Apr 97

10000 Metres Track Walk

43:56.5	Philip King	2 Feb 91
45:47.0	Ian Ashforth	12 Sep 84
45:52.39	Lloyd Finch	4 Jul 99
46:11.0	Jon Vincent	20 May 87

10k Road - where superior to track time

43:38 hc	Lloyd Finch	20 Nov 99
44:21		13 Nov 99
43:49	Philip King	29 Jun 91
45:43	Jon Vincent	7 Mar 87

UNDER 15

100 Metres

10.93	Mark Lewis-Francis	12	Jul	97
11.05	Jamie Nixon	21	Jul	84
11.11	Tristan Anthony	17	Aug	97
11.20	Jamie McNiel	29	May	99
11.21	Kevin Mark	13	Jul	91
11.22	Chris Blake	7	Aug	93
11.23	Ray Burke	11	Aug	84
11.23	Charles Gordon	12	Aug	90
11.23	Julian Thomas	27	May	01
11.24	Mike Williams II	19	Jul	86
11.24	Jamie Gill	30	Jul	00
wind assisted				
11.00	Steve Wiggans	9	Jul	94
11.00	Craig Pickering	11	Aug	01
11.04	Joe Brown	13	Jul	96
11.05	Ray Burke	11	Aug	84
11.06	Duncan Game	5	Jul	86
11.06	Paul Chantler	9	Jul	94
11.07	Wade Bennett-Jackson	7	Jul	01
11.09	Nedum Onuoha	7	Jul	01
11.09	Frank N'Goran	7	Jul	01
11.09	Julian Thomas	7	Jul	01
hand timing				
11.0	Norman Ellis	23	Jul	89
hand timing - wind assisted				
11.0	Malcolm James	24	Jun	77
11.0	Ian Strange	24	Jun	77
11.0	John Burt	6	Sep	80
11.0	Hilton Thompson	6	Aug	89
11.0	Jeffrey Anderson	6	Aug	89
11.0	Matthew Clements	15	Sep	91

200 Metres

22.30	Jamie Nixon	29	Sep	84
22.31	Mike Williams II	10	Aug	86
22.35	Tristan Anthony	12	Jul	97
22.40	Ben Lewis	8	Jul	95
22.54	Matthew Clements	16	Aug	92
22.58	Jamahl Alert-Khan	12	Aug	01
22.64	Martin Blencowe	8	Jul	00
22.65	Daniel Angus	12	Jul	96
22.65	Simon Farenden	25	Jun	00
22.68	Andrew Watkins	4	Aug	01
22.69	Chris Blake	8	Aug	93
22.74	Laurence Oboh	11	Jul	98
22.76	Julian Thomas	12	Aug	01
wind assisted				
22.03	Julian Thomas	7	Jul	01
22.26	Steven Daly	9	Jul	94
22.26	Simon Farenden	8	Jul	00
22.28	Jamahl Alert-Khan	7	Jul	01
22.39	André Duffus	9	Jul	94
22.40	Tom Hyde	15	Aug	98
22.43	Martin Blencoe	8	Jul	00
hand timing				
22.2	Mike Williams II	12	Jul	86
22.3	Tony Cairns	12	Jul	86
hand timing - wind assisted				
21.9	Tony Cairns	21	Jun	86

300 Metres

37.45	Matthew Petty	5	Jul	97
hand timing				
35.9	Richard Davenport	26	Jul	00
during 400m				
35.7 +	Richard Davenport	23	Aug	00

400 Metres

49.74	Richard Davenport	23	Aug	00
49.96	Craig Erskine	18	Jul	98
49.97	David McKenzie	23	Jun	85
49.98	Ryan Preddy	11	Jul	98
50.65	Ian Lowthian	29	Jul	95
50.67	Fola Onibije	10	Jul	99
50.72	Craig Glanville	7	Jul	01
50.78	Mike Snow	12	Jul	97
50.88	Aaron Evans	17	Aug	96
50.99	Cephas Howard	13	Jul	91
51.00	Paul Roberts	22	Jul	84
51.09	David Vass	8	Jul	00
hand timing				
49.8	Mark Tyler	25	Aug	82
49.9	David McKenzie	11	Aug	85
50.0	Simon Heaton	7	Jul	79
50.1	Ade Mafe	6	Sep	81
50.3	Malcolm James	29	Aug	77
50.7	Cephas Howard	19	May	91
50.9	Alan Leonard	30	Aug	78
50.9	Noel Goode	7	Jul	79

600 Metres

1:23.6	Chris Davies	26	Jul	00

800 Metres

1:55.56	Michael Rimmer	25	Jul	00
1:56.1	Craig Winrow	12	Jul	86
1:56.6	Paul Burgess	13	Jul	85
1:57.1	Delroy Smith	12	Jul	86
1:57.12	Michael Combe	14	Aug	93
1:57.24	Tony Jarman	15	Sep	78
1:57.5	Noel Goode	11	Jul	79
1:57.5	Ryan Preddy	7	Jun	98
1:57.7	Eric Kimani	15	Sep	81
1:57.7	Mark Sesay	11	Aug	87
1:57.87	Austin Finn	7	Jul	91
1:58.1	Piers Counsell	12	Jul	86

1000 Metres

2:35.4	Alex Felce	25	Jul	01

1500 Metres

4:03.0	Glen Stewart	28	Aug	85
4:03.0	Scott West	28	Aug	90
4:03.52	Mike Isherwood	17	Sep	82
4:03.56	Richard Youngs	17	Sep	82
4:03.6	Doug Stones	7	Jul	79
4:03.7	David Gerard	31	Jul	83

4:04.52	Chris Reynolds	10 Jul 99
4:04.63	Lee Bowron	29 Jul 00
4:05.26	Alex Felce	31 Jul 01
4:05.7	Ben Mabon	1 Sep 85
4:05.8	Graham Green	19 Jun 79
4:05.9	Glen Coppin	25 Jun 97

1 Mile

4:21.9	Glen Stewart	11 Sep 85

2000 Metres

5:45.8	Richard Slater	16 Jun 74

3000 Metres

8:47.0	Ben Mabon	16 Jul 85
8:47.48	Mohammed Farah	5 Jul 97
8:48.8	Dale Smith	14 Aug 85
8:51.1	Mark Slowikowski	4 Jun 80
8:53.66	Tom Snow	7 Jun 00
8:54.6	Gary Taylor	14 Sep 77
8:54.6	David Bean	22 Jul 79
8:56.0	Paul Ryder	29 Aug 79
8:56.4	Stuart Bond	10 Sep 91
8:57.0	Philip Hennessy	28 Jul 82
8:57.6	Chris Taylor	16 Jul 69
8:58.4	James Clarke	30 Sep 81

80 Metres Hurdles (2'9")

10.71	Matthew Clements	15 Aug 92
10.82	Richard Alexis-Smith	12 Aug 01
10.95	Chris Musa	7 Jul 01
10.99	Edward Dunford	14 Aug 99
11.04	Leon McRae	8 Jul 95
11.07	Robert Hollinger	8 Jul 95
11.10	Seb Bastow	13 Jul 96
11.10	Chris Tye-Walker	12 Jul 97
11.15	Matthew Hansford	16 Sep 00
11.20	Tony Lashley	13 Jul 91

wind assisted

10.68	Richard Alexis-Smith	12 Aug 01
10.73	Chris Musa	7 Jul 01
10.99	Tom Stimson	7 Jul 01
11.00	Tom Benn	9 Jul 94
11.02	Nick Dowsett	10 Jul 93

hand timing

11.0	Austin Drysdale	22 Jun 75

hand timing - wind assisted

11.0	Tim Greenwood	29 Jun 97

100 Metres Hurdles (3'0")

13.3	Matthew Clements	23 Aug 92

400 Metres Hurdles (2'6")

60.1	Jonathan Gorrie	17 Jun 78

High Jump

2.04	Ross Hepburn	22 Aug 76
2.01	Ken McKeown	10 Aug 96
1.97	Andrew Lynch	29 Aug 88
1.97	Wayne Gray	3 Sep 95
1.96	Chuka Enih-Snell	29 Aug 98
1.95	Mark Lakey	14 Sep 80
1.95	Mark Bidwell	26 Sep 99
1.94	Brian Hall	16 Aug 97
1.93	Ewan Gittins	21 Jul 84
1.91	Mark Smith	15 Jul 89
1.91	Ed Willers	9 Jul 94
1.91	Matthew Brereton	9 Jul 94
1.91	Jamie Russell	21 Sep 96

Pole Vault

4.31	Richard Smith	28 Aug 95
4.30	Neil Winter	2 Jul 88
4.30	Christian Linskey	18 Jun 94
4.18	Ian Lewis	24 May 83
4.00	Jimmy Lewis	9 Sep 79
3.90	Peter Eyre	2 Jul 89
3.90	Martin Parley	6 Jun 92
3.90	Steve Francis	12 Sep 93
3.90	Andrew Corey	17 Aug 96
3.85	Steven Brown	2 Jun 96

Long Jump

6.79	Oni Onuorah	17 Sep 88
6.77	Barry Nevison	30 Aug 81
6.74	Kevin Hibbins	17 Jun 95
6.71	Mark Awanah	17 Aug 97
6.68	Onew Eyong	9 Jul 99
6.67	Gary Wilson	27 Aug 00
6.65	Edward Dunford	25 Sep 99
6.65	Bernard Yeboah	27 Aug 00
6.62	Martin Giraud	25 May 92
6.59	Danny Smith	29 Aug 87
6.58	Tony Allen	8 Aug 82
6.55	Jonathan Moore	17 May 98
6.54	Jordon Lau	11 Jul 98

wind assisted

7.12	Oni Onuorah	17 Sep 88
6.72	David Gilkes	6 Apr 92
6.72	Onew Eyong	15 Aug 99
6.68	Jordon Lau	16 Aug 98
6.63	Ian Strange	77

downhill

6.77	Eric Wood	25 Aug 58

Triple Jump

13.86	Jamie Quarry	10 Jul 87
13.79	Paul Dundas	11 Jun 88
13.77	Eugene Hechevarria	16 Sep 78
13.71	Larry Achike	10 Jun 89

note resident but not British citizen at this time

13.69	Vernon Samuels	25 Aug 79
13.60	Steven Anderson	9 Jun 79
13.60	Steve Folkard	11 Jul 80
13.57	Errol Burrows	11 Jul 80
13.56	Delroy Ricketts	18 Jun 88
13.55	Darren Yeo	15 Jul 89
13.55	Michael Duberry	14 Jul 90
13.43	Michael Powell	12 Sep 76
13.43	Marvin Bramble	8 Sep 91

wind assisted

13.92	Eugene Hechevarria	7	Jul	78
13.87	Vernon Samuels	20	Sep	79
13.83	Chris Tomlinson	12	Jul	96
13.73	Donovan Fraser	6	Jul	79
13.69	Kevin O'Shaughnessy	7	Jul	78
13.60	Dean Taylor	12	Jul	96
13.58	Daniel Puddick	26	May	93

Shot (5kg)

15.62	Chris Ellis	18	Jun	80

Shot (4kg)

18.71	Chris Ellis	14	Jun	80
16.54	Geoff Hodgson	7	Jul	72
16.50	Carl Saggers	14	Jul	98
16.39	Pete Waterman	2	Jul	94
16.39	Gregg Beard	25	Aug	97
16.29	Neal Brunning ¶	11	Sep	85
16.14	Chris Gearing	12	May	01
16.12	Daniel Hepplewhite	26	Aug	01
16.11	Billy Cole	6	Jul	79
16.11	Andrae Davis	29	Jul	00
16.05	John Nicholls	29	Jun	80
16.01	Ian McLaughlin	18	Sep	91

Discus (1.5kg)

44.20	Matt Symonds	18	Sep	82

Discus (1.25kg)

53.08	Emeka Udechuku	5	Sep	93
52.43	Sam Herrington	1	Sep	01
50.80	Paul Mardle	3	Sep	77
50.32	Chris Symonds	23	Jul	85
50.04	Keith Homer	11	Jul	80
49.36	James Muirhead	12	May	85
49.32	Lucan Douglas	16	Sep	79
49.22	Spencer English	1	Jun	86
49.10	Simon Bissell	27	Aug	00
48.84	Witold Leonowicz	23	Aug	80
48.78	Neville Lynch	7	Sep	80

Hammer (5kg)

60.10	Andrew Tolputt	5	Sep	82

Hammer (4kg)

70.78	Andrew Tolputt	9	Jul	82
67.24	Peter Vivian	22	Sep	85
65.42	Matthew Sutton	29	Sep	96
64.28	Jason Byrne	22	Sep	85
63.68	Paul Binley	29	Sep	85
63.60	Richard Fedder	26	Aug	79
63.16	Tony Kenneally	29	May	78
62.06	Nick Steinmetz	4	Aug	91
61.32	John Barnes	8	Jun	96
61.08	Neil Curtis	11	Sep	88
60.52	Ian McLaughlin	21	Aug	91

Javelin (700g)

58.76	Dan Carter	29	Aug	94

Javelin (600g 1999 Model)

58.27	Mark Lindsay	30	Aug	99
54.11	Thomas Rees	5	Aug	00
53.93	Farron Paul	9	Apr	00

Javelin (600g pre 1999 Model)

62.70	Paul Godwin	21	May	89
60.56	David Messom	6	Jul	79
60.56	Clifton Green	3	Jul	94
60.34	Richard Lainson	18	Aug	96
59.88	James Hurrion	17	Sep	88
59.52	Paul Brice	19	Aug	79
58.94	Dan Carter	7	Aug	94
58.74	Philips Olweny	6	Aug	95
58.58	Justin Rubio	11	Jun	83
58.58	Rhys Williams	10	Aug	96

Decathlon (Under 15 implements)

5341	Jamie Quarry	28	Jun	87

Octathlon (Under 15 implements)

3933	Aidan Turnbull	1	Oct	95

Pentathlon (80H,SP,LJ,HJ,800)

3403	Edward Dunford	22	Aug	99
3281	Andrae Davis	16	Sep	00
3272	Chris Dack	20	Sep	97
3187	Marc Newton	27	Aug	94
3163	Kevin Drury	27	Aug	94
3129	Mark Awanah	24	Aug	97
3039	Chuka Enih-Snell	23	Aug	98
3024	Tom Benn	17	Sep	94
3014	Chris Jenkins	21	Sep	96
3001	Louis Moore	16	Sep	00
2995	Marcellas Peters	18	Sep	93
2993	Sam Allen	18	Sep	93

(100,SP,LJ,HJ,800)

3199	Onochie Onuorah	17	Sep	88
3085 w	Cephas Howard	21	Sep	91

3000 Metres Track Walk

12:44.64	Lloyd Finch	24	May	98
13:19.57	Philip King	29	May	89
13:35.0	Russell Hutchings	7	Sep	85
13:45.0	John Murphy	14	May	95
13:51.0	Robert Mecham	12	May	92
13:57.06	James Davis	29	Aug	99
13:58.0	Jon Vincent	7	Sep	85
14:03.0	Neil Simpson	1	Apr	89
14:03.5	Nathan Kavanagh	20	Sep	81
14:09.93	Luke Finch	30	Jul	00

3k Road - where superior to track time

13:20	Jonathan Deakin	18	Sep	88
13:29	Robert Mecham	20	Apr	92
13:32	Russell Hutchings	10	Nov	84
13:39	Neil Simpson	6	May	89
13:43	Nathan Kavanagh	21	Feb	81

5000 Metres Track Walk

22:54.0	Lloyd Finch	15	Jul	98

UNDER 13

75 Metres

9.6	Josh Baxter	11 Jul 01

80 Metres

10.17	Ricky Jasper	12 Aug 95
hand timing		
10.0	Adam Rogers	15 Jul 95

100 Metres

11.86	Chris Julien	3 Sep 00
12.14	Mark Lewis-Francis	3 Sep 95
12.29	Paul Moore	28 Aug 99
wind assisted		
12.25	Leon Cameron	8 Sep 96
hand timing		
11.8	Cephas Howard	2 Jul 89
11.9	Stephen Buttler	26 Sep 87
12.0	Michael Tietz	22 Jul 90
12.0	Paul Twidale	11 Sep 99
hand timing - wind assisted		
11.6	Tristan Anthony	28 Aug 95
11.9	Michael Tietz	3 Jun 90

150 Metres

18.5	Tom Rayner	5 Jul 00

200 Metres

24.79	Leon Cameron	8 Sep 96
25.36	Mark Lewis-Francis	3 Sep 95
wind assisted		
24.28	Chris Julien	3 Sep 00
24.86	Tom Rayner	3 Sep 00
hand timing		
24.0	Stephen Buttler	26 Jul 87
24.1	Tristan Anthony	30 Jul 95
24.4	Cephas Howard	3 Sep 89
24.8	Michael Brown	8 Sep 85
24.8	Paul Twidale	16 May 99
24.9	Joelle Powell	4 Jun 00
25.0	Tyrone Keating	4 Sep 94
25.0	Jamaal Dixon	16 Aug 98
25.0	Chris Julien	2 Jul 00

300 Metres

41.8	Dominic Jones	5 Jul 97

400 Metres

58.06	Sam Allen	25 May 91
hand timing		
55.1	Cephas Howard	2 Jul 89
56.5	Craig Erskine	22 Sep 96
57.1	Wayne McDonald	17 Aug 83
57.3	E. Francis	18 May 74
57.4	David Tucker	78
57.6	Frank Adesoyan	27 Aug 90

600 Metres

1:34.7+	Eric Kimani	9 Sep 79

800 Metres

2:04.1	Ben Mabon	8 Jul 83
2:06.4	Eric Kimani	11 Aug 79
2:11.0	Brendan Waters	17 Jun 89
2:11.2	Chris Perrington	6 Aug 78
2:11.2	Gerry Maley	7 Jul 82
2:11.3	Ahmed Ali	10 May 98

1000 Metres

2:54.1	Stephen Holmes	1 Aug 93

1500 Metres

4:18.4	Eric Kimani	26 Sep 79
4:20.5	Ben Mabon	18 Jun 83
4:22.3	David Gerard	12 Aug 81
4:23.9	Mark Slowikowski	12 Jul 78
4:28.0	Ciaran Murphy	16 Jun 84
4:29.3	Dylan Gregory	21 Aug 83
4:29.7	Adam Hickey	28 Aug 00

1 Mile

4:52.0	Tom Quinn	20 Jul 69

3000 Metres

9:31.4	Ben Mabon	24 Jul 83
9:41.4	Mark Slowikowski	21 May 78
9:47.99	Robert Pickering	25 Jun 00
9:49.5	John Tilley	9 Jul 86
9:50.45	Adam Hickey	30 Aug 00
9:50.7	Jacob McCulloch	31 May 00
9:51.1	Sam Hall	23 Sep 98

70 Metres Hurdles (2'3")

11.2	Brendan Kennedy	12 Jun 99
11.2	Elliot Donaldson	17 Jun 99

75 Metres Hurdles (2'3")

11.7	Stephen Cotterill	16 Jul 78
11.7	Sean Ashton	12 Sep 98
11.8	Edward Dunford	28 Sep 97

75 Metres Hurdles (2'6")

wind assisted		
11.98	Chris Douglas	2 Sep 00

80 Metres Hurdles (2'6")

12.74	Jermaine Bernard	14 Sep 97
hand timing		
11.9	Matthew Clements	27 Aug 90
12.1	Sean Ashton	27 May 98
12.4	Jon Crawshaw	14 Aug 94
12.5	Leo Cotterell	26 Sep 87
12.5	Tristan Anthony	9 Jul 95
12.6	James Dunford	2 Aug 98

80 Metres Hurdles (2'9")

12.92	Sam Allen	18 Aug 91
hand timing		
12.6	James Dunford	27 Sep 98
12.7	James Shipp	9 Jun 90

High Jump

1.70	Adrian Pettigrew	22 Jun 99
1.68	Sam Allen	22 Sep 91
1.68	James Dunford	29 Sep 98
1.67	Glen Carpenter	3 Jul 83
1.67	Jamie Dalton	28 Jun 92
1.66	Shane Smith	11 May 86
1.66	Tim Greenwood	95

Pole Vault

3.40	Neil Winter	27 Jul 86
3.20	Ian Lewis	8 Sep 81
3.00	Luke Cutts	14 May 00

Long Jump

5.65	Sam Allen	14 Sep 91
5.64	Kevin Hibbins	18 Jul 93
5.62	Paul Twidale	31 Jul 99
5.61	Robert Creese	23 Jun 90
5.58	Edward Dunford	27 Sep 97
5.58	Matthew Hislop	5 Sep 99
5.55	Jason Davis	9 Jul 95
5.53	Jermaine Bernard	21 Sep 97

wind assisted

5.76	Seamas Cassidy	5 Sep 99
5.74	Edward Dunford	21 Sep 97

Triple Jump

12.57	Rigsby Agoreyo	9 Aug 69
11.78	Edward Dunford	27 Sep 97
11.75	A. Kacon	15 Sep 01

Shot (4kg)

12.65	Matthew Evans	12 Aug 01

Shot (3.25kg)

14.47	Matthew Evans	22 Jul 01
13.36	Chris Hughes	21 Aug 91
13.11	Tony Quinn	28 Aug 93
12.60	Carl Saggers	7 Jul 96
12.58	Daniel Hepplewhite	15 Aug 99
12.58	Sam Herrington	5 Sep 99
12.46	Paul Beard	31 Aug 86
12.42	Edward Dunford	28 Sep 97

Shot (2.72kg)

13.49	Martin Wilson	13 Sep 92

Discus (1.25kg)

36.98	Sam Herrington	5 Sep 99

Discus (1kg)

42.50	Sam Herrington	12 Sep 99
42.38	Ben Barnes	1 Sep 91
38.92	Chris Hughes	28 Jul 91
38.58	Carl Saggers	15 Sep 96
38.30	Liam Walsh	13 Aug 94
35.50	Edward Dunford	20 Sep 97
35.35	Matthew Evans	28 Jul 01
34.46	Simon Bulley	6 Sep 97

Discus (750g)

43.70	Sam Herrington	8 Jul 99

Hammer (4kg)

38.72	Adrian Johnson	30 Sep 84
38.64	Ross Thompson	14 Aug 94

Hammer (3.25kg)

44.38	Ross Thompson	4 Sep 94
36.96	Edward Dunford	24 Sep 97
35.22	Sean Lewis	30 Sep 00

Javelin (600g Pre 1999 Model)

39.62	P. Shearing	23 May 76

Javelin (400g)

43.02	Max Shale	8 Aug 93
42.29	Edward Dunford	27 Sep 97
41.86	James Dunford	29 Sep 98
41.32	A. Westergren	5 Jul 80
41.20	S. Ahma	2 Jul 92
40.91	Adam Akehurst	30 Jul 00
40.60	Philip Mann	13 Sep 98

Pentathlon (80H,SP,LJ,HJ,800 U15)

2444	James Dunford	27 Sep 98

Pentathlon (75H,SP,LJ,HJ,800)

2562	Edward Dunford	28 Sep 97

1000 Metres Track Walk

4:46.0	Luke Finch	15 Jul 98
4:48.0	Dan King	21 Sep 95
4:48.0	Dom King	21 Sep 95

1k Road - where superior to track time

4:34	Luke Finch	27 Sep 97
4:42	Dom King	23 Sep 95
4:44	Nick Ball	16 Jul 00

2000 Metres Track Walk

9:40.0	Luke Finch	12 Nov 97
9:40.3	Thomas Taylor	19 Jun 93
9:51.0	Lloyd Finch	11 Aug 96
9:57.0	Jamie Nunn	7 Feb 88
10:06.0	Grant Ringshaw	23 Jul 78
10:10.0hc	Dom King	23 Mar 95
10:11.0	John Griffiths	1 Jul 84
10:11.0	Philip King	30 Jun 87

2k Road - where superior to track time

9:16	Lloyd Finch	28 Sep 96
9:38	Luke Finch	12 Sep 98
9:55 hc	Nick Ball	5 Sep 00
9:56	Grant Ringshaw	27 Oct 79
10:01	Gareth Brown	27 Oct 79
10:01	Paul Miles	28 Sep 96

3000 Metres Track Walk

15:02.62	Lloyd Finch	21 Sep 96

3k Road - where superior to track time

14:44	Martin Young	22 Sep 84

UK ALL TIME LISTS - WOMEN

100 Metres

	11.10	Kathy Cook	5 Sep 81
	11.13	Cook	29 Aug 83
	11.15	Paula Thomas	23 Aug 94
	11.16	Andrea Lynch	11 Jun 75
	11.20	Sonia Lannaman	25 Jul 80
	11.20	Heather Oakes	26 Sep 80
	11.22	Lynch	21 Aug 76
	11.22	Lannaman	13 Aug 77
	11.22	Lynch	20 Aug 77
	11.22 A	Bev Callender	8 Sep 79
		11.35	22 Jul 81
	11.22	Oakes	27 Jul 86
	11.24	Joice Maduaka	19 Jun 99
	11.27	Stephi Douglas	26 Jul 91
	11.29	Bev Kinch	6 Jul 90
10	11.29	Abi Oyepitan	1 Jul 01
	11.31	Wendy Hoyte	4 Oct 82
	11.31	Shirley Thomas	3 Jul 83
	11.31	Simmone Jacobs	24 Sep 88
	11.32	Joan Baptiste	24 Aug 83
	11.32	Christine Bloomfield	3 Jul 99
	11.34	Katharine Merry	25 Jun 94
	11.34	Shani Anderson	26 Aug 00
	11.35	Sharon Danville	20 Aug 77
	11.35	Marcia Richardson	4 Jun 00
20	11.36 A	Della Pascoe	14 Oct 68
	11.37	Amanda Forrester	1 Jul 01
	11.39 A	Val Peat	14 Oct 68
	11.39	Sallyanne Short	12 Jul 92
	11.40	Helen Hogarth	20 Jul 74
	11.41	Jayne Andrews	27 May 84
	11.43	Donita Benjamin	11 Aug 00
	11.44	Sam Davies	11 Aug 00
	11.44	Sarah Wilhelmy	6 May 01
	11.45	Helen Burkart	26 Aug 83
30	11.46 A	Donna Hartley	22 Mar 75
	11.46	Eleanor Cohen	30 Jul 82
	11.47	Mary Agyepong	20 Jun 87
	11.48	Carmen Smart	26 Aug 89
	11.48	Geraldine McLeod	26 May 96
	11.48	Andrea Coore	1 Jun 97
	11.48	Catherine Murphy	22 Apr 01
	11.49	Sophia Smith	25 Aug 96
	11.50	Sandra Whittaker	14 Jun 86
	11.50	Helen Miles	5 Aug 88
40	11.50	Diana Allahgreen	28 May 01
	11.51	Kaye Scott	28 May 83
	11.51	Sarah Reilly	21 Jun 97
	11.52	Pippa Windle	6 Jun 86
	11.53	Sharon Williams	31 Aug 95
	11.54	Dorothy Hyman	15 Oct 64
	11.54	Janis Neilson	24 May 87
	11.54	Aileen McGillivary	27 Jun 92
	11.55	Anita Neil	1 Sep 72
	11.56	Janine Whitlock	14 Aug 99
50	11.57	Michelle Scutt	2 Sep 84
	11.57	Donna Fraser	29 May 00

wind assisted

Time	Name	Date	Rank
10.93	Sonia Lannaman	17 Jul 77	
11.01	Heather Oakes	21 May 80	
11.06	Lannaman	21 May 80	
11.08	Oakes	27 May 84	
11.08	Kathy Cook	24 Aug 83	
11.10	Cook	13 Sep 80	
11.11	Lannaman	5 Jun 80	
11.11	Cook	26 Jun 83	
11.13	Bev Kinch	6 Jul 83	
11.13	Shirley Thomas	27 May 84	
11.13	Paula Thomas	20 Aug 88	
11.17	Abi Oyepitan	30 Jun 01	
11.18	Wendy Hoyte	4 Oct 82	
11.18	Simmone Jacobs	11 Jun 97	
11.19	Bev Callender	21 May 80	10
11.23	Joan Baptiste	24 Aug 83	
11.23	Jayne Andrews	17 Jul 84	
11.24	Sarah Wilhelmy	9 Jun 01	
11.27	Katharine Merry	11 Jun 94	
11.29	Marcia Richardson	29 May 00	
11.32	Donna Fraser	25 Apr 97	
11.34	Sandra Whittaker	22 May 83	
11.36	Sallyanne Short	26 Aug 89	
11.37	Val Peat	17 Jul 70	
11.37	Kaye Scott	22 May 83	20
11.37	Helen Burkart	11 Sep 83	
11.38	Diana Allahgreen	28 May 01	
11.39	Pippa Windle	24 Jul 87	
11.40	Phylis Smith	3 Jun 90	
11.41	Helen Miles	20 Aug 88	
11.43	Dorothy Hyman	2 Sep 60	
11.43	Aileen McGillivary	10 Jul 93	
11.43	Clova Court	26 May 97	
11.43	Vernicha James	14 Apr 01	
11.45	Michelle Scutt	12 Jun 82	30
11.45	Rebecca White	4 Jul 98	
11.46	Geraldine McLeod	9 Jul 93	
11.48	Jakki Harman	23 Jul 88	
11.48	Angie Thorp	7 Jul 96	
11.49	Ellena Ruddock	29 May 00	
11.50	Margot Wells	15 Jul 78	
11.50	Rebecca Drummond	9 Jul 94	
11.50	Sabrina Scott	30 Jun 01	

hand timing

10.9	Andrea Lynch	28 May 77
11.1	Sonia Lannaman	29 Jun 80
11.1	Heather Oakes	29 Jun 80
11.1	Joan Baptiste	16 Jul 85
11.2	Helen Golden	29 Jun 74
11.2	Sharon Danville	25 Jun 77
11.2	Bev Kinch	14 Jul 84
11.2	Geraldine McLeod	21 May 94

hand timing - wind assisted

10.8	Sonia Lannaman	22 May 76
11.1	Sharon Danville	22 May 76
11.1	Bev Kinch	9 May 87
11.2	Margaret Williams	15 May 76
11.2	Donna Fraser	31 Jan 98

200 Metres

	22.10	Kathy Cook	9 Aug 84
	22.13	Cook	9 Sep 82
	22.21	Cook	20 Aug 84
	22.25	Cook	22 Aug 84
	22.26	Cook	24 Aug 83
	22.31	Cook	8 Aug 80
	22.37	Cook	14 Aug 83
	22.38	Cook	9 Aug 84
	22.53	Cook	25 Aug 82
	22.57	Cook	13 Aug 83
	22.58	Sonia Lannaman	18 May 80
	22.69	Paula Thomas	26 Aug 94
	22.72	Bev Callender	30 Jul 80
	22.73	Jenni Stoute	3 Aug 92
	22.75	Donna Hartley	17 Jun 78
	22.76	Katharine Merry	25 Jul 00
	22.80	Michelle Scutt	12 Jun 82
	22.83	Joice Maduaka	25 Jul 99
10	22.85	Christine Bloomfield	25 Jul 99
	22.86	Joan Baptiste	9 Aug 84
	22.92	Heather Oakes	28 Aug 86
	22.93	Vernicha James	21 Jul 01
	22.95	Simmone Jacobs	25 Apr 96
	22.96 i	Donna Fraser	23 Feb 97
		23.08	22 Jul 00
	22.98	Sandra Whittaker	8 Aug 84
	23.06	Sam Davies	28 Aug 00
	23.10	Diane Smith	11 Aug 90
	23.14	Helen Hogarth	7 Sep 73
20	23.14	Helen Burkart	17 Jul 82
	23.15	Andrea Lynch	25 Aug 75
	23.17	Stephi Douglas	12 Jun 94
	23.18	Joslyn Hoyte-Smith	9 Jun 82
	23.20	Sarah Reilly	21 Jun 97
	23.20	Shani Anderson	10 Sep 00
	23.23	Sarah Wilhelmy	13 Jun 98
	23.24	Sallyanne Short	28 Jun 92
	23.28	Catherine Murphy	25 Jul 99
	23.29	Verona Elder	17 Jun 78
30	23.29	Aileen McGillivary	25 Jul 93
	23.30	Sally Gunnell	13 Jun 93
	23.30	Janine Whitlock	25 Jul 99
	23.33	Linsey Macdonald	9 Jun 82
	23.33	Allison Curbishley	8 Jun 98
	23.34	Val Peat	19 Sep 69
	23.35	Melanie Neef	2 Jul 95
	23.36	Shirley Thomas	10 Jun 84
	23.36	Louise Stuart	4 Aug 90
	23.40	Dorothy Hyman	18 Aug 62
40	23.40	Sharon Danville	9 Sep 77
	23.40	Phylis Smith	6 Jun 92
	23.42 A	Lillian Board	17 Oct 68
	23.42	Debbie Bunn	17 Jun 78
	23.43	Sue Hearnshaw	16 Jun 84
	23.45	Amy Spencer	15 Jul 01
	23.46	Janine MacGregor	22 Aug 81
	23.47 A	Angela Baxter	10 May 86
	23.47	Geraldine McLeod	24 Aug 94
	23.48	Wendy Hoyte	7 Jun 75
	23.48	Denise Ramsden	21 Aug 76 50
	23.48	Margaret Williams	21 Aug 76

wind assisted

22.21	Cook	7 Oct 82	
22.48	Michelle Scutt	4 Jul 82	
22.69	Bev Callender	24 Jun 81	
22.84	Sarah Wilhelmy	10 Jun 01	
22.90	Andrea Lynch	11 Jun 75	
22.90	Donna Fraser	25 Apr 97	
22.90	Allison Curbishley	17 Jul 98	
22.97	Helen Golden	26 Jul 74	
23.00	Joslyn Hoyte-Smith	13 Jun 82	
23.11	Linsey Macdonald	5 Jul 80	
23.12	Shani Anderson	16 Jun 01	10
23.14	Shirley Thomas	28 May 84	
23.15	Margaret Williams	22 Jul 70	
23.19	Sallyanne Short	29 Jan 90	
23.23	Sinead Dudgeon	29 Jul 00	
23.32	Louise Stuart	4 Jun 89	
23.36	Lorna Boothe	30 Mar 80	
23.39 A	Angela Baxter	12 Apr 86	
23.41	Louise Fraser	16 Jun 91	
23.46	Maureen Tranter	21 Jul 70	

hand timing

22.9	Heather Oakes	3 May 80
22.9	Helen Barnett	6 Aug 83
23.0	Helen Golden	30 Jun 74
23.1	Andrea Lynch	21 May 77
23.1	Linda Keough	5 Jul 89
23.2	Dorothy Hyman	3 Oct 63
23.2	Margaret Williams	2 Aug 70
23.3	Sharon Danville	30 Jun 74
23.3	Linsey Macdonald	8 May 82
23.3	Louise Stuart	25 Aug 91

hand timing - wind assisted

23.1	Margaret Williams	14 Jul 74
23.1	Sharon Danville	17 Sep 77
23.1	Linda McCurry	2 Jul 78
23.2	Debbie Bunn	2 Jul 78
23.2	Sybil Joseph	1 Jun 85

300 Metres

35.46	Kathy Cook	18 Aug 84	
35.51	Cook	9 Sep 83	
35.71	Donna Fraser	28 Aug 00	
36.00	Katharine Merry	28 Aug 00	
36.01	Michelle Scutt	13 Jul 80	
36.44	Sally Gunnell	30 Jul 93	
36.45	Joslyn Hoyte-Smith	5 Jul 80	
36.46	Linsey Macdonald	13 Jul 80	
36.65	Joan Baptiste	18 Aug 84	
36.69	Helen Burkart	9 Sep 83	
36.92	Phylis Smith	11 Aug 96	10
36.95	Jenni Stoute	21 Jul 91	
36.97	Donna Hartley	4 Jul 75	
37.30	Verona Elder	26 May 76	
37.33	Melanie Neef	8 Jul 94	

hand timing

36.2	Donna Hartley	7 Aug 74
37.0	Linda Keough	22 Jul 89

400 Metres

	49.43	Kathy Cook	6 Aug 84
	49.59	Katharine Merry	11 Jun 01
	49.72	Merry	25 Sep 00
	49.79	Donna Fraser	25 Sep 00
	50.05	Merry	8 Jul 00
	50.21	Merry	24 Aug 99
	50.21	Fraser	24 Sep 00
	50.28	Merry	25 Jun 00
	50.32	Merry	24 Sep 00
	50.40	Phylis Smith	3 Aug 92
	50.63	Michelle Scutt	31 May 82
	50.71	Allison Curbishley	18 Sep 98
	50.75	Joslyn Hoyte-Smith	18 Jun 82
	50.93	Lorraine Hanson	26 Aug 91
	50.98	Linda Staines	26 Aug 91
10	51.04	Sally Gunnell	20 Jul 94
	51.16	Linsey Macdonald	15 Jun 80
	51.18	Melanie Neef	6 Aug 95
	51.28	Donna Hartley	12 Jul 75
	51.41	Sandra Douglas	2 Aug 92
	51.53	Jenni Stoute	12 Aug 89
	51.70	Verona Elder	10 Jun 78
	51.84	Catherine Murphy	8 Jun 01
	51.93	Janine MacGregor	28 Aug 81
	51.97	Linda Forsyth	31 May 82
20	52.05	Sinead Dudgeon	3 Jul 99
	52.05	Lee McConnell	28 Aug 01
	52.12 A	Lillian Board	16 Oct 68
		53.00	2 Sep 68
	52.13	Helen Burkart	28 Jun 84
	52.15 i	Lesley Owusu	9 Mar 01
		52.27	15 Jul 01
	52.20	Ann Packer	17 Oct 64
	52.26	Pat Beckford	14 Aug 88
	52.40	Helen Frost	17 Sep 00
	52.43	Gladys Taylor	2 Sep 84
	52.47	Michelle Thomas	3 Jul 99
30	52.48	Georgina Oladapo	16 Jun 96
	52.52	Sybil Joseph	14 Sep 85
	52.54	Stephanie Llewellyn	9 Jul 95
	52.57 A	Janet Simpson	16 Oct 68
	52.65	Jane Parry	11 Jun 83
	52.67	Tracey Lawton	8 Jul 84
	52.71	Loreen Hall	18 Jun 88
	52.75	Sandra Leigh	12 Jul 91
	52.75	Helen Thieme	13 Jul 01
	52.77	Michelle Pierre	29 Jul 97
40	52.79	Angela Piggford	2 Jul 89
	52.80	Sian Lewis	18 Jun 83
	52.83	Ruth Patten	10 Jul 79
	52.85	Jannette Roscoe	3 Sep 74
	52.89	Janet Smith	6 Aug 88
	52.97	Vicki Jamison	1 Aug 98
	52.98	Karen Ford	6 Aug 78
	52.98	Dyanna Clarke	28 Jul 79
	52.99	Angela Baxter	24 Jul 82
	53.01 i	Marilyn Neufville	14 Mar 70
50	53.08	Bev Callender	21 Aug 76
	53.16	Joy Grieveson	14 Sep 63

hand timing

51.2	Donna Hartley	28 Jul 78
51.4	Verona Elder	22 May 76
52.2	Liz Barnes	22 May 76
52.4	Stephanie Llewellyn	1 Jul 95
52.6	Marilyn Neufville	20 Jun 70

600 Metres

1:26.0 +	Kelly Holmes	13 Aug 95
1:26.18	Diane Modahl	22 Aug 87
1:26.5 +	Kirsty Wade	21 Aug 85

800 Metres

1:56.21	Kelly Holmes	9 Sep 95	
1:56.80	Holmes	25 Sep 00	
1:56.95	Holmes	13 Aug 95	
1:57.14	Holmes	7 Jul 97	
1:57.42	Kirsty Wade	24 Jun 85	
1:57.45	Wade	21 Aug 85	
1:57.48	Wade	17 Aug 85	
1:57.56	Holmes	16 Jul 95	
1:57.84	Holmes	15 Jun 96	
1:57.88	Wade	9 Jul 85	
1:57.88	Holmes	17 Aug 01	
1:58.65	Diane Modahl	14 Jul 90	
1:58.97	Shireen Bailey	15 Sep 87	
1:59.05	Christina Cahill	4 Aug 79	
1:59.67	Lorraine Baker	15 Aug 86	
1:59.76	Paula Fryer	17 Jul 91	
1:59.81	Ann Griffiths	10 Aug 94	
2:00.10	Tanya Blake	31 May 98	
2:00.15	Rosemary Wright	3 Sep 72	10
2:00.20	Anne Purvis	7 Jul 82	
2:00.30	Cherry Hanson	25 Jul 81	
2:00.39	Bev Nicholson	28 Aug 88	
2:00.55mx	Zola Budd	21 Jun 86	
2:00.6 a	Jane Finch	9 Jul 77	
2:00.80	Yvonne Murray	10 Jul 87	
2:01.1 a	Ann Packer	20 Oct 64	
2:01.11	Lynne MacDougall	18 Aug 84	
2:01.2	Joan Allison	1 Jul 73	
2:01.2	Christine Whittingham	26 Aug 78	20
2:01.24	Chris Benning	28 Jul 79	
2:01.25	Hayley Tullett	22 Jul 00	
2:01.35	Liz Barnes	10 Jul 76	
2:01.36	Gillian Dainty	31 Aug 83	
2:01.40	Janet Bell	10 Jul 87	
2:01.48	Lesley Kiernan	11 Jun 77	
2:01.50	Lillian Board	18 Sep 69	
2:01.65	Teena Colebrook	21 Jul 84	
2:01.66	Pat Cropper	12 Aug 71	
2:01.67	Sonya Bowyer	24 Jun 95	30
2:01.7	Ann Middle	28 Aug 91	
2:01.82	Linda Keough	1 Aug 93	
2:01.83	Amanda Crowe	18 Sep 98	
2:01.86	Helen Daniel	10 Jul 87	
2:01.87	Dawn Gandy	19 Jun 88	
2:01.93	Sue Bevan	19 Jul 91	
2:02.0	Margaret Coomber	1 Jul 73	
2:02.0	Jo White	13 Aug 77	

	2:02.0	Lynne Robinson	26 Jul 89
40	2:02.34	Lynn Gibson	14 Aug 92
	2:02.39	Emma Davies	17 Sep 98
	2:02.47	Abigail Hunte	16 Jul 95
	2:02.6	Evelyn McMeekin	20 Aug 78
	2:02.69	Natalie Tait	16 Jul 95
	2:02.70	Janet Marlow	15 Jun 80
	2:02.79	Sue Morley	27 Jul 85
	2:02.81	Jo Fenn	9 Jun 01
	2:02.83	Mary Kitson	21 Jul 91
	2:02.89	Wendy Sly	30 Jul 83
50	2:02.9	Sheila Carey	10 Sep 71

1000 Metres

	2:32.55	Kelly Holmes	15 Jun 97
	2:32.82	Holmes	23 Jul 95
	2:33.18	Holmes	25 Aug 95
	2:33.70	Kirsty Wade	9 Aug 85
	2:34.92	Christina Cahill	9 Aug 85
	2:35.32	Shireen Bailey	19 Jul 86
	2:35.51	Lorraine Baker	19 Jul 86
	2:35.86	Diane Modahl	29 Aug 93
	2:37.05	Christine Whittingham	27 Jun 86
	2:37.29	Yvonne Murray	14 Jul 89
	2:37.61	Bev Hartigan	14 Jul 89
10	2:37.82	Gillian Dainty	11 Sep 81
	2:38.44	Evelyn McMeekin	23 Aug 78
	2:38.58	Jo White	9 Sep 77
	2:38.67	Lynne MacDougall	19 Jul 86
	2:38.83	Lynn Gibson	29 Aug 93
	2:39.23	Teena Colebrook	24 Jul 90
	2:39.29	Ann Griffiths	16 Sep 90
	2:39.42	Mary Cotton	26 May 76
	2:39.78	Liz Barnes	26 May 76

1500 Metres

	3:58.07	Kelly Holmes	29 Jun 97
	3:59.96	Zola Budd	30 Aug 85
	4:00.57	Christina Cahill	6 Jul 84
	4:00.64	Cahill	1 Oct 88
	4:00.73	Kirsty Wade	26 Jul 87
	4:01.13	Holmes	5 Jul 96
	4:01.20	Yvonne Murray	4 Jul 87
	4:01.23	Hayley Tullett	28 Jul 00
	4:01.38	Liz McColgan	4 Jul 87
	4:01.41	Wade	5 Sep 87
	4:01.53	Chris Benning	15 Aug 79
	4:02.32	Shireen Bailey	1 Oct 88
10	4:03.17	Alison Wyeth	7 Aug 93
	4:04.14	Wendy Sly	14 Aug 83
	4:04.81	Sheila Carey	9 Sep 72
	4:04.82	Helen Pattinson	25 Jul 00
	4:05.37	Paula Radcliffe	1 Ju1 01
	4:05.66	Bev Hartigan	20 Jul 90
	4:05.75	Lynn Gibson	20 Jul 94
	4:05.96	Lynne MacDougall	20 Aug 84
	4:06.0	Mary Cotton	24 Jun 78
	4:06.24	Christine Whittingham	5 Jul 86
20	4:07.11	Janet Marlow	18 Aug 82
	4:07.28	Joanne Pavey	29 Jun 97
	4:07.59	Ann Griffiths	9 Jun 92
	4:07.69	Teena Colebrook	19 Aug 90
	4:07.90	Gillian Dainty	16 Jun 84
	4:09.26	Lisa York	13 Jun 92
	4:09.29	Angela Newport	20 Jul 94
	4:09.37	Joyce Smith	7 Sep 72
	4:09.46	Karen Hargrave	4 Sep 89
	4:09.5	Penny Forse	6 Aug 80
30	4:10.07	Maxine Baker	28 Jun 92
	4:10.10	Cherry Hanson	30 Aug 81
	4:10.21	Kathy Carter	31 Jul 82
	4:10.22	Kelly Caffel	20 Aug 00
	4:10.32	Lynne Robinson	30 Jul 94
	4:10.41	Jo White	10 Jun 84
	4:10.66	Joan Allison	2 Feb 74
	4:10.68	Amanda Crowe	21 Sep 98
	4:10.7 mx	Sonya Bowyer	16 Jul 96
	4:10.75	Sonia McGeorge	20 Jul 90
40	4:10.76	Ruth Partridge	16 Jun 84
	4:11.00	Sue Morley	6 Jul 85
	4:11.12	Bridget Smyth	26 May 85
	4:11.23	Paula Fudge	31 Jul 81
	4:11.24 i	Nicky Morris	7 Jan 89
	4:11.46	Ursula McGloin	20 Jan 90
	4:11.51	Jane Shields	4 Sep 83
	4:11.57	Sue Lamb	18 Jun 96
	4:11.75	Debbie Peel	31 Jul 82
	4:11.82	Una English	28 Jun 92
50	4:11.85	Jo Dering	28 Jul 90
	4:11.94	Lorraine Baker	5 Jul 90

1 Mile

	4:17.57	Zola Budd	21 Aug 85
	4:19.41	Kirsty Wade	27 Jul 85
	4:21.61	Wade	5 Sep 86
	4:22.64	Christina Cahill	7 Sep 84
	4:22.64	Yvonne Murray	22 Jul 94
	4:24.57	Chris Benning	7 Sep 84
	4:24.87	Alison Wyeth	6 Jul 91
	4:24.94	Paula Radcliffe	14 Aug 96
	4:26.11	Liz McColgan	10 Jul 87
	4:26.16	Teena Colebrook	14 Jul 90
10	4:26.50 i	Hayley Tullett	6 Feb 00
	4:26.52	Bev Hartigan	14 Aug 92
	4:27.80	Lisa York	14 Aug 92
	4:28.04	Kelly Holmes	30 Aug 98
	4:28.07	Wendy Sly	18 Aug 84
	4:28.8	Karen Hargrave	20 Aug 89
	4:29.15	Sue Morley	18 Aug 84
	4:30.08	Lynne MacDougall	7 Sep 84
	4:30.29	Jane Shields	9 Sep 83
	4:30.77	Joanne Pavey	30 Aug 97
20	4:30.89	Ruth Partridge	18 Aug 84
	4:31.17	Lynn Gibson	1 Jul 94
	4:31.24 i	Jo White	5 Feb 83
	4:31.45	Shireen Bailey	17 Sep 89
	4:31.65	Gillian Dainty	26 Jun 82
	4:31.83	Angela Davies	1 Jul 94
	4:32.00	Carole Bradford	18 Aug 84
	4:32.32	Debbie Gunning	5 Jul 91

2000 Metres

	5:26.93	Yvonne Murray	8 Jul 94
	5:29.58	Murray	11 Jul 86
	5:30.19	Zola Budd	11 Jul 86
	5:33.85	Christina Cahill	13 Jul 84
	5:37.00	Chris Benning	13 Jul 84
	5:38.50	Alison Wyeth	29 Aug 93
	5:39.20	Paula Radcliffe	29 Aug 93
	5:40.24	Liz McColgan	22 Aug 87
	5:42.15	Wendy Sly	17 Sep 82
	5:43.24	Sue Morley	13 Jul 84
10	5:45.0 i	Bev Hartigan	20 Feb 93
	estimated		
	5:44.0 +	Joanne Pavey	28 Aug 00

3000 Metres

	8:26.97	Paula Radcliffe	29 Jun 01
	8:27.40	Radcliffe	11 Aug 99
	8:28.07	Radcliffe	17 Aug 01
	8:28.83	Zola Budd	7 Sep 85
	8:28.85	Radcliffe	11 Aug 00
	8:29.02	Yvonne Murray	25 Sep 88
	8:29.60	Murray	15 Jul 94
	8:30.30	Murray	10 Jul 93
	8:31.61	Radcliffe	7 Jul 99
	8:32.02	Radcliffe	24 Aug 01
	8:34.80 i	Liz McColgan	4 Mar 89
		8:38.23	15 Jul 91
	8:36.58	Joanne Pavey	24 Aug 01
	8:37.06	Wendy Sly	10 Aug 83
	8:38.42	Alison Wyeth	16 Aug 93
	8:40.97	Kathy Butler	24 Aug 01
	8:44.46	Chris Benning	22 Aug 84
10	8:45.39	Hayley Tullett	15 Jul 00
	8:45.69	Jane Shields	10 Aug 83
	8:47.36	Jill Boltz	17 Aug 88
	8:47.59	Angela Tooby-Smith	5 Jul 88
	8:47.7	Kirsty Wade	5 Aug 87
	8:47.71	Lisa York	31 Jul 92
	8:48.72	Karen Hargrave	28 Jan 90
	8:48.74	Paula Fudge	29 Aug 78
	8:49.89	Christina Cahill	20 Jul 85
	8:50.52	Debbie Peel	7 Aug 82
20	8:51.33	Sonia McGeorge	29 Aug 90
	8:51.40	Ruth Partridge	7 Aug 82
	8:52.79	Ann Ford	28 Aug 77
	8:53.52 i	Nicky Morris	4 Mar 89
		8:59.46	24 Jun 89
	8:55.53	Joyce Smith	19 Jul 74
	8:56.09	Andrea Wallace	10 Jul 92
	8:56.39	Sue Morley	21 Jul 84
	8:57.17	Susan Wightman	6 Jun 84
	8:57.2	Kathy Carter	7 Apr 84
	8:57.75 mx	Sarah Wilkinson	27 Jun 00
30	8:58.44	Kath Binns	26 May 80
	8:58.59	Andrea Whitcombe	26 Jul 91
	8:59.39	Regina Joyce	8 May 81
	8:59.45	Jo Dering	11 Aug 90
	8:59.65	Gillian Dainty	20 Jul 83
	9:00.21	Carole Bradford	9 Jul 85
	9:00.3	Bridget Smyth	20 Apr 91
	9:00.68	Alison Wright	23 Jun 81
	9:01.67	Melissa Watson	27 Jun 88
	9:02.25	Julie Holland	11 Aug 90
40	9:02.47	Laura Adam	4 Jun 94

5000 Metres

	14:32.44	Paula Radcliffe	31 Aug 01
	14:43.54	Radcliffe	7 Aug 99
	14:44.21	Radcliffe	22 Jul 01
	14:44.36	Radcliffe	5 Aug 00
	14:45.51	Radcliffe	22 Aug 97
	14:46.76	Radcliffe	16 Aug 96
	14:48.07	Zola Budd	26 Aug 85
	14:48.79	Radcliffe	20 Jun 99
	14:49.27	Radcliffe	7 Jul 95
	14:49.84	Radcliffe	24 Jun 01
	14:56.94	Yvonne Murray	7 Jul 95
	14:58.27	Joanne Pavey	25 Sep 00
	14:59.56	Liz McColgan	22 Jul 95
	15:00.37	Alison Wyeth	7 Jul 95
	15:09.98	Jill Boltz	18 Jul 92
	15:13.22	Angela Tooby-Smith	5 Aug 87
	15:14.51	Paula Fudge	13 Sep 81
10	15:14.62	Kathy Butler	12 May 01
	15:19.12	Hayley Yelling	22 Jul 01
	15:21.45	Wendy Sly	5 Aug 87
	15:28.63	Andrea Wallace	2 Jul 92
	15:29.04	Sonia McGeorge	27 May 96
	15:31.78	Julie Holland	18 Jul 90
	15:32.19	Susan Wightman	26 May 85
	15:32.34	Jane Shields	5 Jun 88
	15:32.62	Andrea Whitcombe	25 Jun 00
	15:34.16	Jill Harrison	26 May 85
20	15:34.40	Lucy Elliott	2 Jun 97
	15:36.35	Birhan Dagne	5 Aug 00
	15:38.84	Ann Ford	5 Jun 82
	15:40.14	Helen Titterington	17 Jul 89
	15:40.85	Sarah Wilkinson	11 Jul 00
	15:41.11	Angie Hulley	18 Jul 90
	15:41.68	Debbie Peel	27 Jun 85
	15:43.99	Angela Newport	9 Jun 99
	15:45.03	Lynne MacDougall	29 Jun 97
	15:46.05	Hayley Haining	7 Aug 99
30	15:48.1 mx	Tara Krzywicki	5 Aug 98
		15:53.28	25 Jul 98
	15:49.6	Kath Binns	5 Apr 80
	15:50.85	Liz Yelling	1 Aug 98
	15:51.62	Carol Greenwood	26 May 85
	15:52.2	Ruth Partridge	23 Aug 89
	15:53.84	Heather Knight	6 Jul 96
	15:53.86	Sarah Bentley	22 Jul 95
	15:54.9	Amanda Parkinson	23 Jun 01
	15:55.64	Katie Skorupska	9 Jun 99
	15:56.0	Lucy Taylor	15 May 90
40	15:56.04	Vikki McPherson	25 Jul 98
	15:56.4+	Sue Crehan	4 Jul 87
	15:56.58	Gillian Palmer	13 Aug 00
	15:56.83	Suzanne Rigg	30 Jul 94
	15:57.06	Louise Watson	24 Jun 95

10000 Metres

Rank	Time	Name	Date
	30:26.97	Paula Radcliffe	30 Sep 00
	30:27.13	Radcliffe	26 Aug 99
	30:40.70	Radcliffe	10 Apr 99
	30:48.58	Radcliffe	4 Apr 98
	30:55.80	Radcliffe	7 Apr 01
	30:57.07	Liz McColgan	25 Jun 91
	31:06.99	McColgan	2 Jul 88
	31:07.88	Jill Hunter	30 Jun 91
	31:08.44	McColgan	30 Sep 88
	31:14.31	McColgan	30 Aug 91
	31:53.36	Wendy Sly	8 Oct 88
	31:55.30	Angela Tooby-Smith	4 Sep 87
	31:56.97	Yvonne Murray	24 Aug 94
	31:59.27	Kathy Butler	20 Apr 01
	32:20.95	Susan Wightman	2 Jul 88
	32:21.61	Andrea Wallace	6 Jun 92
10	32:24.63	Sue Crehan	4 Jul 87
	32:30.4	Birhan Dagne	22 Jul 00
	32:32.42	Vikki McPherson	15 Jul 93
	32:34.7	Sarah Wilkinson	22 Jul 00
	32:36.09	Helen Titterington	29 Aug 89
	32:41.29	Jenny Clague	20 Jun 93
	32:42.0	Jane Shields	24 Aug 88
	32:42.84	Angie Hulley	6 Aug 89
	32:44.06	Suzanne Rigg	27 Jun 93
	32:47.78	Julie Holland	31 Aug 90
20	32:52.5	Hayley Yelling	22 Jul 00
	32:57.17	Kath Binns	15 Aug 80
	32:58.2	Claire Lavers	20 Apr 91
	33:04.55	Tara Krzywicki	10 Apr 99
	33:05.43	Elspeth Turner	1 Jun 88
	33:07.9	Liz Yelling	22 Jul 00
	33:10.25	Shireen Barbour	5 Jul 86
	33:10.94	Marina Stedman	28 Jul 86
	33:12.8	Lucy Elliott	5 Jun 99
	33:17.88	Karen Macleod	1 Jul 89
30	33:19.19	Bernadette Madigan	27 Apr 85
	33:19.48	Heather Knight	6 Jun 92
	33:21.46	Louise Watson	14 Jun 96
	33:23.25	Zahara Hyde-Peters	12 Jun 94
	33:25.74	Penny Thackery	9 Jun 01
	33:26.79	Amanda Allen	6 Jun 92
	33:27.69	Jill Harrison	22 Jun 86
	33:29.27	Bev Jenkins	9 Jun 01
	33:30.0	Annette Bell	10 Aug 91
	33:30.27	Angie Joiner	4 Apr 98
40	33:34.03	Lynn Everington	26 May 86
	33:34.7	Priscilla Welch	2 Jun 84
	33:34.77	Debbie Peel	22 Jun 86
	33:34.96	Carol Greenwood	12 Jun 94
	33:38.36	Jo Thompson	29 Jun 97
	33:39.0	Veronique Marot	5 Apr 86
	33:40.3	Sandra Branney	3 Sep 89
	33:40.6	Andrea Paolillo	5 Apr 86
	33:41.16	Lucy Wright	29 Jun 97
	33:46.1	Vicki Vaughan	15 May 91
50	33:47.47	Cathy Newman	22 Jun 90
	33:53.4 mx	Nicky McCracken	19 Sep 89
	33:57.86	Alison Rose	12 Jun 94

10 Kilometres Road

Rank	Time	Name	Date
	30:39	Liz McColgan	11 Mar 89
	30:47	Paula Radcliffe	9 Jun 01
	30:59	McColgan	6 Feb 88
	31:07	McColgan	21 Feb 87
	31:13	McColgan	10 Oct 87
	31:29	Wendy Sly	27 Mar 83
	31:42	Jill Hunter	21 Jan 89
	31:56	Andrea Wallace	4 Aug 91
	32:14	Priscilla Welch	23 Mar 85
	32:15	Angela Tooby-Smith	31 Mar 84
	32:20	Zola Budd	2 Mar 85
	32:24	Yvonne Murray	2 Nov 97
10	32:27	Ruth Partridge	11 Mar 89
	32:31	Heather Knight	6 Nov 94
	32:35	Suzanne Rigg	15 Aug 92
	32:38	Jane Shields	23 Mar 85
	32:38	Marian Sutton	28 Sep 97
	32:41	Jill Harrison	21 Feb 87
	32:43	Teresa Dyer	1 Jan 93
	32:44	Carole Bradford	14 Oct 85
	32:44	Paula Fudge	13 Mar 88
	32:45	Sarah Wilkinson	4 Dec 99
20	32:46	Kirsty Wade	28 Feb 87
	32:47	Chris Benning	15 Mar 87
	32:52	Susan Wightman	29 Oct 89
	32:55	Hayley Yelling	4 Jun 00
	32:56	Alison Wyeth	20 Mar 94
	33:00	Sheila Catford	24 Aug 88
	33:02	Bev Hartigan	8 Apr 95
	33:02	Lucy Elliott	19 Apr 98
	33:03	Cathy Newman	6 Feb 88
	33:04	Glynis Penny	1 Jan 86
30	33:04	Gillian Stacey	24 Jan 93

course measurement uncertain

31:43	Zola Budd	6 May 84
31:58	Sandra Branney	10 May 89
32:03	Paula Fudge	29 Aug 82
32:29	Yvonne Danson	13 Nov 94
32:36	Mary Cotton	5 Aug 84
32:41	Susan Wightman	4 Mar 84
32:42	Veronique Marot	30 Sep 84
32:46	Amanda Allen	25 Feb 96
32:47	Debbie Peel	15 Apr 84
32:54	Shireen Barbour	3 Aug 86
32:59	Sharon Astley	20 Sep 87

10 Miles Road

Rank	Time	Name	Date
	51:41	Jill Hunter	20 Apr 91
	51:56	Hunter	7 Apr 91
	51:51	Angie Hulley	18 Nov 89
	52:00	Liz McColgan	5 Oct 97
	52:15	Marian Sutton	5 Oct 97
	53:42	Suzanne Rigg	10 Oct 93
	53:44	Paula Fudge	21 Sep 85
	53:44	Andrea Wallace	7 Mar 93
	53:49	Véronique Marot	25 Aug 85
	53:50	Yvonne Murray	6 Oct 96
10	53:51	Priscilla Welch	5 Apr 87
	54:12	Alison Gooderham	6 Nov 88

intermediate times

	51:41 +	Paula Radcliffe	22 Oct 00
	53:00 +	Andrea Wallace	5 May 91

course measurement uncertain

	53:17	Joyce Smith	12 Oct 80
	53:44	Sarah Rowell	10 Mar 84

downhill

	53:42	Karen Macleod	11 Apr 93

Half Marathon

	1:07:07	Paula Radcliffe	22 Oct 00
	1:07:07	Radcliffe	22 Oct 00
	1:07:11	Liz McColgan	26 Jan 92
	1:08:42	McColgan	11 Oct 92
	1:08:53	McColgan	20 Sep 92
	1:09:39	Andrea Wallace	21 Mar 93
	1:09:41	Marian Sutton	14 Sep 97
	1:09:56	Susan Wightman	24 Jul 88
	1:10:54	Alison Wyeth	29 Mar 98
	1:11:17	Veronique Marot	21 Jun 87
	1:11:29	Liz Yelling	22 Oct 00
	1:11:33	Vikki McPherson	14 Sep 97
10	1:11:36	Ann Ford	30 Jun 85
	1:11:37	Paula Fudge	24 Jul 88
	1:11:38	Sally Ellis	20 Mar 88
	1:11:44	Jill Harrison	29 Mar 87
	1:11:44	Lorna Irving	6 Sep 87
	1:12:06	Sarah Rowell	11 Nov 84
	1:12:07	Suzanne Rigg	3 Oct 93
	1:12:22	Sandra Branney	4 May 86
	1:12:24	Jill Boltz	15 Sep 91
	1:12:25	Angie Hulley	1 Apr 90
20	1:12:25	Yvonne Murray	15 Sep 96
	1:12:29	Cathy Newman	25 Aug 90
	1:12:43	Amanda Allen	16 Sep 01
	1:12:49	Sheila Catford	11 Sep 88
	1:12:53	Birhan Dagne	22 Aug 99

intermediate times

	1:11:44 +	Sally-Ann Hales	21 Apr 85
	1:11:59 +	Angie Hulley	1 Jan 89
	1:12:17 +	Priscilla Welch	1 Nov 87

estimated time

	1:11:57 +	Priscilla Welch	10 May 87

course measurement uncertain

	1:11:44	Karen Macleod	15 Jan 95
	1:12:23	Lynn Everington	6 Sep 87
	1:12:32	Yvonne Danson	31 Jul 94

Marathon

	2:25:56	Véronique Marot	23 Apr 89
	2:26:51	Priscilla Welch	10 May 87
	2:26:52	Liz McColgan	13 Apr 97
	2:26:54	McColgan	26 Apr 98
	2:27:32	McColgan	3 Nov 91
	2:27:38	McColgan	15 Nov 92
	2:27:54	McColgan	21 Apr 96
	2:28:04	Marot	20 Oct 85
	2:28:06	Sarah Rowell	21 Apr 85
	2:28:38	Sally-Ann Hales	21 Apr 85
	2:28:42	Marian Sutton	24 Oct 99
	2:29:29	Sally Eastall	8 Dec 91
	2:29:43	Joyce Smith	9 May 82
	2:29:47	Paula Fudge	30 Oct 88
10	2:30:38	Ann Ford	17 Apr 88
	2:30:51	Angie Hulley	23 Sep 88
	2:30:53	Yvonne Danson	17 Apr 95
	2:31:33	Susan Wightman	23 Sep 88
	2:31:33	Andrea Wallace	12 Apr 92
	2:31:45	Lynn Harding	23 Apr 89
	2:32:53	Gillian Castka	2 Dec 84
	2:33:04	Sheila Catford	23 Apr 89
	2:33:07	Nicky McCracken	22 Apr 90
	2:33:16	Karen Macleod	27 Aug 94
20	2:33:22	Carolyn Naisby	6 Dec 87
	2:33:24	Sally Ellis	23 Apr 89
	2:33:38	Lynda Bain	21 Apr 85
	2:33:41	Sue Reinsford	16 Apr 00
	2:34:11	Sally Goldsmith	3 Mar 96
	2:34:19	Jill Harrison	23 Apr 89
	2:34:21	Suzanne Rigg	24 Sep 95
	2:34:26	Heather MacDuff	16 Oct 88
	2:35:03	Sandra Branney	23 Apr 89
	2:35:10	Sue Crehan	17 Apr 88
30	2:35:18	Karen Holdsworth	29 Sep 85
	2:35:18	Debbie Noy	13 Oct 91
	2:35:32	Rose Ellis	23 Apr 89
	2:35:39	Hayley Nash	27 Aug 94
	2:35:40	Debbie Robinson	29 Oct 01
	2:35:53	Julie Coleby	13 May 84
	2:36:02	Bev Hartigan	30 Sep 01
	2:36:06	Margaret Lockley	13 May 84
	2:36:12	Kath Binns	12 Jun 82
	2:36:21	Glynis Penny	17 Apr 83
40	2:36:29	Danielle Sanderson	7 Aug 94
	2:36:31	Julia Cornford	20 Apr 86
	2:36:32	Marina Stedman	23 Apr 89
	2:36:34	Lorna Irving	1 Aug 86
	2:36:40	Teresa Dyer	17 Apr 94
	2:36:52	Gillian Horovitz	20 Jun 92
	2:37:06	Moira O'Neill	31 Oct 88
	2:37:14	Cath Mijovic	22 Oct 95
	2:37:20	Lynne MacDougall	22 Apr 01
	2:37:26	Caroline Horne	21 Apr 85
50	2:37:36	Sandra Mewett	17 Jan 88

course measurement uncertain

	2:35:05	Carol Gould	26 Oct 80

100 Kilometres Road

7:27:19	Carolyn Hunter-Rowe	8 Aug 93
7:42:17	Trudi Thomson	26 Jun 94
7:48:33	Eleanor Robinson	7 Oct 89

2000 Metres Steeplechase (2'6")

6:29.79	Tara Krzywicki	20 May 01
6:36.02	Jayne Spark	8 Aug 00
6:53.02	Clare Martin	20 May 01

3000 Metres Steeplechase (2'6")

9:52.71	Tara Krzywicki	1 Jul 01
10:21.21	Lois Joslin	20 Apr 01
10:44.69	Clare Martin	5 Jun 01

100 Metres Hurdles

	12.80	Angie Thorp	31	Jul	96
	12.82	Sally Gunnell	17	Aug	88
	12.87	Shirley Strong	24	Aug	83
	12.88	Strong	10	Aug	84
	12.90	Jacqui Agyepong	25	Jun	95
	12.91	Strong	12	Aug	83
	12.91	Kay Morley-Brown	2	Feb	90
	12.93	Agyepong	6	Jul	94
	12.93	Agyepong	8	Jul	94
	12.93	Thorp	29	Jul	96
	12.95	Keri Maddox	25	Aug	99
	12.99	Diane Allahgreen	26	Aug	99
	13.03	Lesley-Ann Skeete	3	Aug	90
	13.04	Clova Court	9	Aug	94
10	13.05	Judy Simpson	29	Aug	86
	13.07	Lorna Boothe	7	Oct	82
	13.08	Sam Farquharson	4	Jul	94
	13.11	Sharon Danville	22	Jun	76
	13.13	Denise Lewis	29	Jul	00
	13.16	Wendy Jeal	27	Aug	86
	13.17	Melanie Wilkins	18	Jun	00
	13.20	Natasha Danvers	2	May	98
	13.24	Kim Hagger	31	Aug	87
	13.26	Michelle Campbell	3	Aug	90
20	13.29	Mary Peters	2	Sep	72
	13.32	Sam Baker	29	Aug	93
	13.34	Judy Vernon	7	Sep	73
	13.35	Pat Rollo	30	Jul	83
	13.36	Louise Fraser	17	Aug	91
	13.36	Sarah Claxton	27	May	01
	13.40	Julie Pratt	1	Aug	99
	13.44	Judith Robinson	1	Jul	89
	13.45	Lorna Drysdale	20	Jul	74
	13.46	Tessa Sanderson	25	Jul	81
30	13.46	Nathalie Byer	26	Aug	83
	13.46	Rachel King	3	Jul	99
	13.47	Heather Ross	16	Jun	84
	13.49	Blondelle Caines	17	Jul	77
	13.49	Liz Fairs	30	Jul	00
	13.50 A	Yvette Wray-Luker	8	Sep	79
		13.57	15	Jul	79
	13.52	Bianca Liston	30	Jul	00
	13.53	Ann Simmonds	4	Sep	72
	13.53	Lynne Green	27	Jun	88
	13.54	Debbie Brennan	7	Aug	88
40	13.57	Bethan Edwards	29	Aug	92
	13.58	Lauraine Cameron	19	Jun	90
	13.59	Jane Hale	19	May	96
	13.60	Elaine McMaster	7	Oct	82
	13.60	Joanne Mulliner	25	Jul	87
	13.62	Gillian Evans	1	Jul	83
	13.62	Jill Kirk	3	Jul	83
	13.62	Danielle Freeman	3	Jun	00
	13.66	Helen Worsey	20	Jul	01
	13.68	Heather Platt	7	Jul	85
50	13.70	Yinka Idowu	14	Jun	92
	13.71	Margot Wells	4	Aug	82
	13.71	Kerry Jury	30	Jun	01
	13.73	Ann Girvan	7	Aug	82

wind assisted

12.78	Shirley Strong	8	Oct	82	
12.78	Strong	13	Aug	83	
12.80	Sally Gunnell	29	Jul	88	
12.83	Strong	13	Sep	81	
12.84 A	Kay Morley-Brown	8	Aug	90	
12.86	Strong	9	Aug	84	
12.86	Gunnell	5	Jun	88	
12.90	Lorna Boothe	8	Oct	82	
12.98	Diane Allahgreen	1	Jul	01	
13.01	Lesley-Ann Skeete	1	Feb	90	
13.06	Sharon Danville	14	Jul	84	
13.08	Michelle Campbell	26	May	95	
13.08	Melani Wilkins	26	May	95	
13.12	Pat Rollo	27	May	84	10
13.19	Natasha Danvers	22	Apr	00	
13.22	Heather Ross	27	May	84	
13.28	Sarah Claxton	5	Jul	98	
13.28	Julie Pratt	23	May	99	
13.36	Judith Robinson	11	Jul	87	
13.39	Debbie Brennan	29	Jul	88	
13.39	Lauraine Cameron	1	Jul	90	
13.44	Yvette Wray-Luker	21	May	80	
13.44	Kerry Robin-Millerchip	27	May	84	
13.44	Rachel King	28	May	98	20
13.48	Elaine McMaster	12	Jun	82	
13.48	Joanne Mulliner	25	Jul	87	
13.54	Jill Kirk	7	Jun	86	
13.56	Ann Girvan	15	Jul	84	
13.57	Katy Sketchley	14	Jun	98	
13.61	Clare Milborrow	28	May	00	
13.62	Yinka Idowu	17	Sep	94	
13.63	Heather Platt	1	Jul	84	
13.66	Maureen Prendergast	14	Apr	84	
13.71	Sue Longden	21	May	80	30
13.71	Manndy Laing	12	Jun	82	
13.71	Kerry Jury	22	May	99	

hand timing

13.0	Judy Vernon	29	Jun	74
13.0	Blondelle Caines	29	Jun	74
13.1	Melanie Wilkins	2	Jul	95
13.2	Pat Rollo	11	Jun	83
13.3	Ann Simmonds	29	Jul	72
13.3	Debbie Brennan	16	Jul	89
13.4	Christine Bell	2	Aug	70
13.4	Bianca Liston	15	Jul	00
13.5	Pat Pryce	26	Jul	72
13.5	Liz Sutherland	29	Mar	76
13.5	Sue Longden	26	Jun	76
13.5	Yvette Wray-Luker	7	Jun	80
13.5	Jill Kirk	7	Aug	83

hand timing - wind assisted

12.7	Kay Morley-Brown	10	Jan	90
12.8	Natasha Danvers	3	Apr	99
12.9	Judy Vernon	18	May	74
13.1	Mary Peters	19	Aug	72
13.2	Ann Simmonds	19	Aug	72
13.2	Liz Sutherland	8	May	76
13.3	Kerry Robin-Millerchip	9	May	87
13.5	Myra Nimmo	24	Jul	74

400 Metres Hurdles

	52.74	Sally Gunnell	19 Aug 93
	53.16	Gunnell	29 Aug 91
	53.23	Gunnell	5 Aug 92
	53.33	Gunnell	12 Aug 94
	53.51	Gunnell	24 Jul 94
	53.52	Gunnell	4 Aug 93
	53.62	Gunnell	7 Aug 91
	53.73	Gunnell	26 Jun 93
	53.78	Gunnell	3 Aug 91
	53.78	Gunnell	3 Aug 92
	54.63	Gowry Retchakan	3 Aug 92
	54.94	Natasha Danvers	31 Aug 01
	55.22	Keri Maddox	12 Aug 00
	55.24	Sinead Dudgeon	24 Jul 99
	55.91	Elaine McLaughlin	26 Sep 88
	56.04	Sue Chick	10 Aug 83
	56.05	Wendy Cearns	13 Aug 89
	56.06	Christine Warden	28 Jul 79
10	56.15	Jacqui Parker	27 Jul 91
	56.26	Louise Fraser	7 Jun 92
	56.42	Vicki Jamison	20 Jun 98
	56.43	Alyson Layzell	16 Jun 96
	56.46	Yvette Wray-Luker	11 Jul 81
	56.61	Louise Brunning	16 Jun 96
	56.70	Lorraine Hanson	13 Aug 89
	56.72	Gladys Taylor	6 Aug 84
	57.00	Simone Gandy	6 Aug 88
	57.07	Verona Elder	15 Jul 83
20	57.38	Sarah Dean	27 Jul 91
	57.41	Jennie Matthews	6 Aug 88
	57.43	Liz Sutherland	6 Jul 78
	57.49	Maureen Prendergast	16 Jun 84
	57.52	Clare Sugden	3 Jun 90
	57.55	Sharon Danville	8 May 81
	57.76	Aileen Mills	5 Aug 86
	57.79	Susan Cluney	15 Jun 80
	57.81	Margaret Southerden	10 Jul 82
	57.86	Teresa Hoyle	29 Jul 83
30	57.92	Tracey Duncan	29 Jul 00
	58.02	Vyv Rhodes	28 Jun 92
	58.04	Clare Bleasdale	16 Jul 94
	58.09	Stephanie McCann	12 Jun 94
	58.16	Diane Fryar	9 Jul 83
	58.19	Sara Elson	4 Jul 92
	58.28	Carol Dawkins	14 Sep 85
	58.31	Jannette Roscoe	19 Jul 75
	58.31	Fiona Laing	18 Sep 81
	58.35	Debbie Skerritt	11 Jul 81
40	58.41	Lynn Edwards	19 Jun 88
	58.43	Jane Low	24 Aug 94
	58.44	Maggie Still	19 Jun 88
	58.50	Nicola Sutton	23 May 99
	58.51	Julie Vine	17 Jun 90
	58.55	Jackie Stokoe	19 Jul 75
	58.62	Sharon Allen	3 May 97
	58.68	Kay Simpson	15 Jul 83
	58.68	Vicky Lee	5 Aug 86
	58.75	Katie Jones	29 Jul 00
50	58.79	Sheila Peak	25 Jul 87

hand timing

57.5	Vicky Lee	28 Jun 86
57.8	Teresa Hoyle	26 Jul 86
58.0	Fiona Laing	28 Aug 81
58.2	Debbie Skerritt	6 Jun 81
58.6	Jane Finch	21 Sep 80

High Jump

1.95	Diana Davies	26 Jun 82	
1.95 i	Debbie Marti	23 Feb 97	
	1.94	9 Jun 96	
1.95	Susan Jones	24 Jun 01	
1.94	Louise Gittens	25 May 80	
1.94 i	Davies	7 Mar 82	
1.94 i	Marti	3 Feb 91	
1.94 i	Jo Jennings	13 Mar 93	
	1.91	20 Sep 98	
1.94	Marti	9 Jun 96	
1.94	Marti	15 Jun 96	
1.93	Michelle Dunkley	2 Sep 00	
1.92	Barbara Simmonds	31 Jul 82	
1.92	Judy Simpson	8 Aug 83	
1.92	Janet Boyle	29 Sep 88	
1.92 i	Julia Bennett	10 Mar 90	10
	1.89	11 Jun 94	
1.92	Lea Goodman	15 Jun 96	
1.91	Ann-Marie Cording	19 Sep 81	
1.91	Gillian Evans	30 Apr 83	
1.91	Jayne Barnetson	7 Jul 89	
1.90	Kim Hagger	17 May 86	
1.90	Sharon Hutchings	1 Aug 86	
1.88 i	Debbie McDowell	17 Jan 88	
	1.82	7 May 88	
1.88 i	Kerry Roberts	16 Feb 92	
	1.86	6 Jun 92	
1.88 i	Kelly Thirkle	16 Feb 92	
	1.85	10 Aug 91	
1.88	Lee McConnell	19 Aug 00	20
1.87	Barbara Lawton	22 Sep 73	
1.87	Moira Maguire	11 May 80	
1.87	Louise Manning	6 May 84	
1.87	Rachael Forrest	7 Jul 95	
1.87	Denise Lewis	21 Aug 99	
1.87	Aileen Wilson	15 Jul 01	
1.86	Claire Summerfield	7 Aug 82	
1.86	Jennifer Farrell	11 May 86	
1.86	Catherine Scott	8 May 87	
1.86	Michele Marsella	31 May 87	30
1.85	Brenda Flowers	20 Aug 77	
1.85	Gillian Cadman	3 Jun 78	
1.85	Julie Peacock	8 Jul 94	
1.85	Hazel Melvin	3 Aug 97	
1.85 i	Julie Crane	13 Feb 00	
	1.83	30 May 98	
1.84	Sarah Rowe	22 Aug 81	
1.84	Ursula Fay	6 Aug 83	
1.84	Tonia Schofield	20 Aug 83	
1.83	Linda Hedmark	4 Jul 71	
1.83	Val Rutter	19 Jun 74	40
1.83 i	Ros Few	25 Feb 75	

	1.83	Denise Hinton	8 Aug 80
	1.83	Joanne Brand	4 Jun 83
	1.83	Rhona Scobie	4 Aug 85
	1.83	Marion Hughes	19 Jul 86
	1.83	Tracey Clarke	2 Aug 87
	1.83	Kay Fletcher	17 Jun 89
	1.83	Gillian Black	25 Jul 99
	1.83 i	Rebecca Jones	4 Mar 00
		1.83	3 Jun 00
50	1.83	Julie Hollman	9 Jun 01
	1.83	Stephanie Higham	20 Jul 01

Pole Vault

	4.40	Janine Whitlock	14 Jul 01
	4.36	Whitlock	1 Jul 01
	4.35	Whitlock	5 Jun 00
	4.35	Whitlock	27 Jul 01
	4.35	Whitlock	4 Aug 01
	4.35	Whitlock	6 Aug 01
	4.34	Whitlock	23 Jun 01
	4.31	Whitlock	30 May 98
	4.31 i	Whitlock	20 Feb 00
	4.31	Whitlock	7 Jul 01
	4.20	Irie Hill	6 Aug 00
	4.20 i	Rhian Clarke	10 Mar 01
		4.15	7 Apr 00
	4.04	Lucy Webber	15 Jul 00
	4.00	Alison Davies	12 Aug 00
	3.95 A	Allie Jessee	25 Jun 99
		3.60	4 Aug 98
	3.91	Emma Hornby	27 Jun 98
	3.90	Kate Staples	26 May 96
	3.90	Ellie Spain	6 May 00
10	3.90	Tracey Bloomfield	4 Jun 00
	3.90	Sonia Lawrence	14 Jul 01
	3.83	Hilary Smith	10 Jun 01
	3.81	Zoe Brown	9 Sep 01
	3.80	Paula Wilson	25 Jul 98
	3.80	Kate Dennison	26 Aug 01
	3.76 A	Krissy Owen	1 May 99
		3.55	16 Apr 99
	3.75	Louise Schramm	19 Jul 98
	3.75	Liz Hughes	20 May 01
	3.75	Gael Davies	4 Jul 01
20	3.72	Linda Stanton	11 Jun 95
	3.66 i	Lindsay Hodges	24 Feb 01
		3.55	14 Aug 99
	3.60	Fiona Harrison	25 May 98
	3.60	Clare Ridgley	25 May 98
	3.60 i	Larissa Lowe	4 Feb 01
		3.60	21 Jul 01
	3.60 i	Laura Patterson	18 Feb 01
		3.60	12 May 01
	3.60 i	Rebecca Lumb	7 Jul 01
		3.60	4 Aug 01
	3.60	Kirsty Maguire	18 Jul 01
	3.60	Catherine MacRae	11 Aug 01
	3.55	Kim Rothman	17 Jun 98
30	3.53	Rebekah Telford	10 Jun 01
	3.51	Hannah Olson	19 Aug 01
	3.50	Noelle Bradshaw	25 Jul 98
	3.50	Becky Ridgley	23 May 99
	3.50	Helen Roscoe	9 Sep 00
	3.50 i	Louise Gauld	27 Jan 01
		3.41	2 Aug 00
	3.50	Natalie Olson	23 Jun 01
	3.50	Caroline Nutt	19 Aug 01
	3.45	Ruth Anness	24 Jun 01
	3.40 i	Claire Adams	26 Feb 95
		3.30	18 Jun 95
40	3.40	Maria Newton	10 May 98
	3.40	Danielle Codd	4 Jul 98
	3.40	Nicole Green	24 Jun 00
	3.40 i	Anna Leyshon	18 Feb 01
		3.30	20 May 01
	3.40	Gillian Cooke	5 May 01
	3.40	Kath Callaghan	19 May 01
	3.40	Kim Skinner	11 Aug 01
	3.35	Kathryn Dowsett	24 Apr 99
	3.30	Kate Alexander	20 Jul 96
	3.30	Stacey Dicker	7 Sep 96
50	3.30	Kate Rowe	14 Aug 99
	3.30	Eugenie Lewis	29 Apr 00
	3.30 i	Janet Vousden	7 Jan 01
	3.30	James Harding	16 Sep 01

Long Jump

	6.90	Bev Kinch	14 Aug 83
	6.88	Fiona May	18 Jul 90
	6.86	May	6 Jul 90
	6.86 A	May	28 Jul 93
	6.85	May	12 Jul 90
	6.83	Sue Hearnshaw	6 May 84
	6.82	May	30 Jul 88
	6.82	May	29 Jun 90
	6.80	May	6 Aug 89
	6.80	Hearnshaw	26 Jun 84
	6.76	Mary Rand	14 Oct 64
	6.76	Jo Wise	2 Aug 99
	6.75	Joyce Hepher	14 Sep 85
	6.73	Sheila Sherwood	23 Jul 70
	6.73	Yinka Idowu	7 Aug 93
	6.70	Kim Hagger	30 Aug 86
10	6.69	Sue Reeve	10 Jun 79
	6.69	Denise Lewis	30 Jul 00
	6.63	Mary Agyepong	17 Jun 89
	6.59	Jade Johnson	11 Aug 01
	6.56	Sarah Claxton	23 May 99
	6.55	Ann Simmonds	22 Jul 70
	6.52	Gill Regan	29 Aug 82
	6.52	Georgina Oladapo	16 Jun 84
	6.51 i	Ruth Howell	23 Feb 74
		6.49	16 Jun 72
	6.51	Julie Hollman	3 Sep 00
20	6.47 A	Ashia Hansen	26 Jan 96
		6.27	26 Jun 94
	6.45	Carol Zeniou	12 May 82
	6.45	Margaret Cheetham	18 Aug 84
	6.44	Sharon Danville	15 Jun 77
	6.44	Barbara Clarke	13 Sep 81

	6.43	Myra Nimmo	27 May 73
	6.40	Judy Simpson	26 Aug 84
	6.40	Sharon Bowie	28 Jun 86
	6.39	Moira Maguire	22 Jul 70
	6.39	Maureen Chitty	28 Jun 72
30	6.39	Sue Longden	12 Sep 76
	6.39	Tracy Joseph	27 Jun 98
	6.37	Kelly Wenlock	24 Apr 82
	6.36	Andrea Coore	19 Jul 98
	6.34 i	Barbara-Anne Barrett	20 Feb 71
		6.31	14 Aug 71
	6.33 i	Barbara Lawton	21 Nov 70
	6.33	Glenys Morton	19 Jul 81
	6.33	Joanne Mulliner	13 Sep 86
	6.33	Jo Dear	19 May 93
	6.33	Ruth Irving	2 Jun 01
40	6.32	Helen Garrett	7 Jun 87
	6.32	Jo Willoughby	28 May 89
	6.31	Lorraine Campbell	19 May 85
	6.28	Janet Robson	4 May 77
	6.28	Vikki Schofield	16 Jul 95
	6.27	Alix Stevenson	13 Jun 70
	6.27	Anita Neil	29 Aug 70
	6.27	Sandra Green	14 Jun 80
	6.27	Allison Manley	16 Aug 80
	6.27	Liz Ghojefa	23 Jul 95
50	6.26	Maria Smallwood	14 Jun 80
	6.26	Donita Benjamin	19 Aug 00

wind unconfirmed

	6.43	Moira Maguire	18 Sep 70

wind assisted

	7.00	Sue Hearnshaw	27 May 84
	6.98	Fiona May	4 Jun 89
	6.93	Bev Kinch	14 Aug 83
	6.84	Sue Reeve	25 Jun 77
	6.80	Joyce Hepher	22 Jun 85
	6.77	Denise Lewis	1 Jun 97
	6.68	Jade Johnson	28 May 01
	6.65	Mary Agyepong	4 Jun 89
	6.57	Ann Simmonds	22 Aug 70
10	6.56	Judy Simpson	30 Aug 86
	6.54	Ruth Howell	16 Jun 72
	6.54	Myra Nimmo	19 Jun 76
	6.49	Margaret Cheetham	4 Sep 83
	6.48	Moira Maguire	17 May 70
	6.45	Donita Benjamin	23 Jul 00
	6.44	Tracy Joseph	21 Jun 97
	6.41	Allison Manley	28 Jul 79
	6.40	Barbara-Anne Barrett	17 Jul 71
	6.39	Alix Stevenson	6 Jun 70
20	6.39	Carolyn Ross	19 Apr 87
	6.38	Joanne Mulliner	1 Jun 85
	6.38	Jo Willoughby	6 Aug 89
	6.38	Ann Danson	7 Aug 94
	6.36	Karen Murray	9 Jul 77
	6.34	Janet Frank-Lynch	8 Jul 78
	6.34	Jill Moreton	8 Jul 78
	6.32	Diana Davies	22 May 88
	6.32	Liz Ghojefa	16 Jul 94
	6.29	Evette Finikin	1 May 89
30	6.29	Karen Skeggs	17 Jun 89

Triple Jump

15.16 i	Ashia Hansen	28 Feb 98	
	15.15	13 Sep 97	
15.02 i	Hansen	7 Mar 99	
14.96	Hansen	11 Sep 99	
14.94	Hansen	29 Jun 97	
14.85 i	Hansen	15 Feb 98	
14.81 i	Hansen	21 Feb 99	
14.78	Hansen	25 Aug 96	
14.77	Hansen	2 Aug 97	
14.76 i	Hansen	14 Feb 99	
14.08	Michelle Griffith	11 Jun 94	
13.95	Connie Henry	27 Jun 98	
13.64	Rachel Kirby	7 Aug 94	
13.56	Mary Agyepong	5 Jun 92	
13.46	Evette Finikin	26 Jul 91	
13.11	Jade Johnson	19 Aug 01	
13.03	Shani Anderson	4 May 96	
13.03	Kate Evans	26 Apr 97	
12.97	Debbie Rowe	22 Jul 00	10
12.94	Lorna Turner	9 Jul 94	
12.92	Liz Patrick	5 Aug 00	
12.89	Karen Skeggs	17 May 92	
12.85	Rebecca White	14 Jul 01	
12.84	Anna-Maria Thorpe	23 May 99	
12.67	Caroline Stead	1 Jun 96	
12.64	Liz Ghojefa	4 Sep 93	
12.64	Jodie Hurst	23 Jul 00	
12.61	Kerensa Denham	14 Jun 98	
12.55	Pamela Anderson	29 Jun 96	20
12.52	Leandra Polius	1 Jul 00	
12.50	Julia Johnson	21 Jun 98	
12.45	Lea Goodman	11 Nov 95	
12.42	Liz Gibbens	2 Jul 95	
12.41 i	Judy Kotey	28 Feb 98	
	12.33	17 May 98	
12.35	Angela Williams	19 May 01	
12.22	Mary Rand	18 Jun 59	
12.22	Allison Forbes	9 Sep 89	
12.22	Nikki Barr	16 Aug 92	
12.18	Justina Cruickshank	26 May 96	30
12.17	Katherine Streatfield	26 May 01	
12.15 i	Fiona Davidson	22 Jan 95	
	11.91	29 Jun 96	
12.14	Jayne Ludlow	21 May 94	
12.13 i	Maggie Still	21 Jan 96	
	12.03	2 Jun 96	
12.11 i	Caroline Warden	21 Jan 96	
	12.06	1 May 94	
12.11	Marcia Walker	11 Aug 96	
12.10	Jane Falconer	30 Aug 93	
12.10	Rachel Brenton	21 Jul 01	
12.10	Hazel Carwardine	19 Aug 01	
12.05	Charmaine Turner	19 Aug 01	40
12.04	Rachel Peacock	19 Aug 01	
12.03	Stephanie Aneto	17 May 97	
12.01 i	Emily Parker	25 Feb 01	
	11.98	14 Jul 01	
11.97	Jo Morris	24 Jun 00	
11.96	Linsi Robinson	30 Jun 01	

	11.93	Sharon Oakes	13 Aug 00
	11.91	Lisa Brown	30 Jul 95
	11.90 i	Joanne Stanley	12 Dec 99
	11.88	Rachel Atkinson	9 May 98
50	11.88	Emily Parker	7 Jul 00

wind assisted

	14.78 A	Hansen	1 Feb 97
	14.14	Michelle Griffith	25 Jul 00
	13.14	Debbie Rowe	22 Jul 00
	13.09	Rebecca White	30 Jun 01
	13.04	Kate Evans	23 Jul 00
	12.93	Karen Skeggs	13 Jun 92
	12.61	Judy Kotey	5 Jul 98
	12.55	Lauraine Cameron	30 Aug 93
	12.42	Nikki Barr	28 Jun 97
	12.37	Jane Falconer	30 Aug 93
10	12.31	Caroline Warden	23 Jul 94
	12.27	Rachel Brenton	21 Jul 01
	12.21	Justina Cruickshank	19 May 96
	12.20	Rachel Atkinson	28 Jul 96
	12.18	Michelle Rea	29 Jun 91
	12.10	Rachel Peacock	30 Jun 01
	12.07	Jo Morris	13 Jul 96
	12.07	Rachel Peacock	18 Jul 98
	12.07	Susan Furlonger	28 May 00
	12.06	Fiona Davidson	2 Jun 96
20	12.06	Stephanie Aneto	7 Jun 97

Shot

	19.36	Judy Oakes	14 Aug 88
	19.33	Oakes	3 Sep 88
	19.26	Oakes	29 Jul 88
	19.13	Oakes	20 Aug 88
	19.06 i	Venissa Head	7 Apr 84
		18.93	13 May 84
	19.05	Oakes	16 Jul 88
	19.03	Myrtle Augee	2 Jun 90
	19.01	Oakes	17 Sep 88
	19.01	Oakes	11 Jun 89
	19.01	Oakes	11 May 96
	18.99	Meg Ritchie	7 May 83
	17.53	Angela Littlewood	24 Jul 80
	17.45	Yvonne Hanson-Nortey	28 Jul 89
	17.08	Jo Duncan	19 Aug 01
	16.57	Maggie Lynes	20 Jul 94
	16.40 i	Mary Peters	28 Feb 70
		16.31	1 Jun 66
10	16.40	Julie Dunkley	12 Aug 00
	16.29	Brenda Bedford	26 May 76
	16.12	Denise Lewis	21 Aug 99
	16.05	Janis Kerr	15 May 76
	15.95 i	Philippa Roles	6 Feb 99
		15.19	5 Jul 01
	15.85 i	Alison Grey	12 Feb 94
		15.69	11 Jun 94
	15.81	Tracy Axten	19 Jul 98
	15.80	Sharon Andrews	30 Jul 93
	15.75 i	Caroline Savory	23 Feb 83
		15.50	19 Jun 83
	15.60 i	Justine Buttle	27 Feb 88
		15.45	25 Aug 88
20	15.55	Christina Bennett	13 Jun 99
	15.48	Mary Anderson	8 Sep 85
	15.46	Vanessa Redford	14 Jun 80
	15.45	Susan King	27 Mar 83
	15.44	Vickie Foster	14 May 00
	15.41	Fatima Whitbread	29 Apr 84
	15.32 i	Helen Hounsell	13 Feb 82
		14.91	22 May 82
	15.32	Eva Massey	14 Jul 01
	15.23	Judy Simpson	18 Jun 88
	15.21	Uju Efobi	23 Apr 94
30	15.18	Suzanne Allday	18 May 64
	15.18 i	Lana Newton	Jan 79
		15.09	6 Sep 78
	15.09	Jayne Berry	22 Jul 93
	15.09	Nicola Gautier	1 Jul 00
	15.08	Janet Kane	3 Jun 79
	15.08	Susan Tudor	30 May 82
	14.98 i	Sandra Smith	21 Dec 85
		14.95	18 Aug 85
	14.88 i	Jenny Kelly	10 Mar 90
		14.73	18 May 91
	14.88	Debbie Callaway	15 May 93
	14.77	Gay Porter	11 Apr 70
40	14.76 i	Carol Parker	14 Dec 91
		14.71	1 Sep 90
	14.75 i	Cynthia Gregory	12 Dec 81
		14.70	29 Aug 81
	14.68	Eleanor Gatrell	18 Jul 98
	14.68	Claire Smithson	26 May 01
	14.67	Rosemary Payne	23 Apr 74
	14.66 i	Terri Salt	7 Jan 84
	14.62	Kathryn Farr	7 Jun 92
	14.59	Dawn Grazette	19 May 91
	14.53	Emma Beales	12 Sep 92
	14.51	Pauline Richards	4 Jul 98
50	14.46 i	Heather Yule	3 Feb 73

Discus

	67.48	Meg Ritchie	26 Apr 81
	67.44	Ritchie	14 Jul 83
	66.04	Ritchie	15 May 82
	65.96	Ritchie	19 Jul 80
	65.78	Ritchie	17 Jul 81
	65.34	Ritchie	24 Apr 83
	65.18	Ritchie	17 May 81
	65.08	Ritchie	26 Apr 80
	65.02	Ritchie	5 May 84
	65.00	Ritchie	24 Apr 82
	64.68	Venissa Head	18 Jul 83
	60.82	Shelley Drew	25 Jul 98
	60.72	Jackie McKernan	18 Jul 93
	60.00	Philippa Roles	9 May 99
	58.56	Debbie Callaway	19 May 96
	58.18	Tracy Axten	31 May 97
	58.02	Rosemary Payne	3 Jun 72
	57.75	Emma Merry	9 Aug 99
10	57.32	Lynda Wright	16 Jun 84
	56.24	Sharon Andrews	12 Jun 94
	56.06	Kathryn Farr	27 Jun 87

	55.52	Jane Aucott	17 Jan 90
	55.42	Lesley Bryant	12 Sep 80
	55.06	Janet Kane	17 Jun 78
	55.04	Lorraine Shaw	14 May 94
	54.81	Claire Smithson	1 Jul 01
	54.72	Karen Pugh	27 Jul 86
	54.68	Emma Beales	10 Jun 95
20	54.46	Ellen Mulvihill	14 May 86
	54.46	Janette Picton	17 Aug 90
	54.24	Nicola Talbot	15 May 93
	53.96	Julia Avis	27 Apr 86
	53.66	Rosanne Lister	22 Jun 91
	53.44	Judy Oakes	20 Aug 88
	53.16	Sarah Winckless	18 Jun 94
	53.12	Emma Carpenter	1 Sep 01
	52.52	Alison Grey	18 Jun 94
	52.46	Vanessa Redford	4 Jul 82
30	52.31	Lauren Keightley	18 Jul 98
	51.82	Catherine Bradley	20 Jul 85
	51.79	Rebecca Roles	31 May 99
	51.60	Dorothy Chipchase	20 Jul 73
	51.18	Angela Sellars	12 Aug 90
	51.12	Joanne Brand	26 May 86
	50.98	Sarah Henton	30 Aug 97
	50.57	Brenda Bedford	24 Aug 68
	50.06	Joanne Jackson	7 May 89
	50.04	Morag Bremner	27 Apr 86
40	49.92	Fiona Condon	10 Apr 82
	49.84	Janis Kerr	15 May 77
	49.84	Denise Sturman	12 Apr 81
	49.66	Gay Porter	19 Aug 70
	49.58	Jackie Wright	2 Aug 75
	49.48	Gwen Bird	20 Jul 91
	49.44	Myrtle Augee	14 May 95
	49.30	Amanda Barnes	18 Jun 88
	49.25	Vickie Foster	20 May 00
	49.20	Jane Tabor	5 Apr 86
50	49.12	Jean Robertson	14 Jul 74

downhill

51.04	Fiona Condon	7 Jul 79

Hammer

	68.15	Lorraine Shaw	17 Mar 01
	67.98	Shaw	24 Jun 01
	67.94	Shaw	2 Jun 01
	67.68	Shaw	3 Jul 01
	67.62	Shaw	27 Feb 01
	67.44	Shaw	15 Jul 00
	67.43	Shaw	19 May 01
	67.14	Shaw	15 Jun 01
	67.10	Shaw	9 Aug 99
	66.97	Shaw	15 Jul 01
	63.96	Lyn Sprules	20 Aug 00
	63.61	Liz Pidgeon	27 May 00
	60.88	Rachael Beverley	23 May 99
	60.35	Zoe Derham	10 Jun 01
	58.83	Suzanne Roberts	9 Sep 00
	58.31	Mhairi Walters	25 Aug 01
	57.95	Diana Holden	18 Jul 98
	57.40	Sarah Moore	29 Apr 01
10	56.76	Esther Augee	15 May 93
	56.62	Lesley Brannan	13 May 01
	55.60	Ann Gardner	9 May 98
	55.42	Vicci Scott	23 Jul 01
	55.09	Philippa Roles	9 May 99
	54.72	Helen Arnold	26 Jul 97
	54.54	Nicola Dudman	29 Jul 01
	54.15	Sarah Harrison	4 Jul 99
	54.12	Carys Parry	29 Apr 01
	54.03	Catherine Garden	25 Apr 99
20	53.74	Christina Bennett	20 Aug 00
	53.13	Katy Lamb	14 Jul 01
	52.28	Samantha Burns-Salmond	3 May 97
	52.10	Shirley Webb	2 Sep 01
	52.00	Laura Douglas	9 Sep 01
	51.94	Lucy Marshall	4 May 01
	51.62	Fiona Whitehead	24 Apr 93
	51.62	Julie Lavender	15 May 94
	51.34	Helen Taylor	12 Aug 01
	51.04	Jo Holloway	4 Aug 01
30	50.73	Andrea Jenkins	10 Jun 01
	50.62	Janet Smith	16 Aug 97
	50.38	Irene Duffin	31 May 97
	50.34	Jean Clark	27 Jul 97
	50.27	Helen Wilding	17 Jun 01
	49.68	Sue Last	12 Aug 00
	49.10	Lindsey Jones	25 Aug 97
	48.94	Francis Miller	12 Jul 01
	48.90	Julie Kirkpatrick	15 Jun 96
	48.66	Karen Chambers	8 Apr 00
40	48.32	Helen McCreadie	9 Jun 96
	47.70	Angela Bonner	11 May 96
	47.63	Joanne John	16 Jun 01
	47.52	Vicki Clark	1 Aug 98
	47.38	Belinda Heil	2 Jul 00
	47.06	Caroline Manning	22 Jul 95
	46.86	Leanne Taylor	12 Jun 97
	46.64	Myrtle Augee	5 Jul 95
	46.39	Karen Bell	25 Jun 00
	46.10	Diane Smith	17 Jun 01
50	46.01	Janette Brown	15 Jul 00

Javelin (1999 Model)

	59.50	Karen Martin	14 Jul 99
	58.45	Martin	12 Aug 00
	58.07	Martin	4 Jun 00
	57.99	Martin	5 Aug 00
	57.75	Martin	12 Aug 00
	57.31	Martin	6 Aug 00
	58.45	Kelly Morgan	12 Aug 00
	57.19	Lorna Jackson	9 Jul 00
	55.91	Kirsty Morrison	23 May 99
	55.40	Goldie Sayers	22 Jul 01
	53.06	Shelley Holroyd	7 May 00
	52.86	Linda Gray	10 Jun 01
	52.76	Jenny Kemp	23 Jun 01
	51.79	Chloe Cozens	3 Sep 00
10	51.13	Denise Lewis	19 Aug 00
	50.85	Sharon Gibson	18 Jul 99
	49.25	Nicola Gautier	1 Jul 01

	48.24	Tammie Francis	29 Apr 00
	47.72	Alison Moffitt	21 Aug 99
	47.57	Amy Harvey	7 Oct 00
	47.55	Katie Amos	16 Jun 01
	47.26	Joanne Bruce	18 Jul 99
	47.13	Samantha Redd	30 Jun 01
	46.89	Caroline White	19 Jun 99
20	46.81	Noelle Bradshaw	19 Aug 00
	46.29	Katy Watts	23 Jun 01
	46.02	Clova Court	12 Aug 00
	45.84	Suzanne Finnis	24 Jun 00
	45.81	Jennifer West	27 May 01
	45.65	Louise Matthews	2 Sep 01
	45.37	Katherine Evans	3 Jul 99
	45.29	Lucy Stevenson	30 Aug 99
	44.31	Melanie Burrows	16 Jun 01
	44.11	Rachel Dunn	7 Jul 01
30	43.75	Paula Collis	28 Jul 01
	43.74	Sylveen Monaghan	27 May 01
	43.70	Chrissie Head	13 Aug 00
	43.70	Jenny Grimstone	11 Aug 01

Javelin (pre 1999)

	77.44	Fatima Whitbread	28 Aug 86
	76.64	Whitbread	6 Sep 87
	76.34	Whitbread	4 Jul 87
	76.32	Whitbread	29 Aug 86
	75.62	Whitbread	25 May 87
	74.74	Whitbread	26 Aug 87
	73.58	Tessa Sanderson	26 Jun 83
	73.32	Whitbread	20 Jun 87
	62.32	Sharon Gibson	16 May 87
	62.22	Diane Royle	18 May 85
	60.12	Shelley Holroyd	16 Jun 96
	60.00	Julie Abel	24 May 87
	59.40	Karen Hough	28 Aug 86
	59.36	Kirsty Morrison	4 Sep 93
	58.60	Jeanette Rose	30 May 82
10	58.39	Lorna Jackson	6 Jun 98
	57.90	Anna Heaver	1 Jul 87
	57.84	Mandy Liverton	3 Jun 90
	57.82	Karen Martin	19 Sep 98
	56.96	Nicky Emblem	1 Feb 90
	56.50	Caroline White	8 Jun 91
	56.50	Denise Lewis	11 Aug 96
	55.70	Lynn Hayhoe	31 May 92
	55.60	Sue Platt	15 Jun 68
	55.38	Catherine Garside	19 May 84
20	55.36	Jackie Zaslona	30 Aug 80
	55.30	Clova Court	27 Aug 91
	55.04	Joanne Harding	24 May 87
	54.50	Karen Costello	11 Jun 94
	54.19	Rosemary Morgan	25 Apr 64
	54.02	Janeen Williams	29 Mar 80
	53.88	Sharon Avann	21 Jul 73
	53.32	Maxine Jervis	27 Aug 78
	53.04	Kelly Morgan	17 May 98
	52.58	Shona Urquhart	17 Jun 83
30	52.48	Gail Hornby	22 Jun 90
	52.40	Noelle Bradshaw	30 Jun 93

Heptathlon (1985 Tables)

6831	Denise Lewis	30 Jul 00	
6736	Lewis	1 Jun 97	
6724	Lewis	22 Aug 99	
6654	Lewis	4 Aug 97	
6645	Lewis	26 May 96	
6623	Judy Simpson	30 Aug 86	
6584	Lewis	24 Sep 00	
6559	Lewis	22 Aug 98	
6513	Lewis	17 Sep 98	
6347	Simpson	11 Sep 83	
6259	Kim Hagger	18 May 86	
6125	Tessa Sanderson	12 Jul 81	
6094	Joanne Mulliner	7 Jun 87	
6022	Clova Court	27 Aug 91	
6005 w	Kerry Jury	24 May 98	
	5908	1 Aug 99	
5933	Julie Hollman	1 Jul 01	
5826	Jenny Kelly	3 Jul 94	
5803	Jayne Barnetson	20 Aug 89	10
5784	Nicola Gautier	1 Jul 01	
5776	Kathy Warren	12 Jul 81	
5747 w	Julia Bennett	5 May 96	
	5538	4 Jun 00	
5702	Yinka Idowu	21 May 95	
5700	Vikki Schofield	5 May 96	
5691 w	Pauline Richards	24 May 98	
	5563	5 Jul 98	
5644	Danielle Freeman	4 Jun 00	
5642	Sarah Rowe	23 Aug 81	
5633	Marcia Marriott	18 May 86	
5632	Emma Beales	1 Aug 93	20
5618 w	Sarah Damm	5 May 96	
	5392	30 Apr 95	
5594	Gillian Evans	22 May 83	
5585	Kelly Sotherton	13 Jul 97	
5555 w	Diana Bennett	24 May 98	
	5550	1 Jun 97	
5554	Katherine Livesey	17 May 01	
5548	Val Walsh	18 May 86	
5517	Shona Urquhart	21 Aug 88	
5495	Charmaine Johnson	24 May 92	
5493	Sally Gunnell	28 May 84	
5455	Claire Phythian	19 May 95	30
5446	Manndy Laing	7 Aug 83	
5434 w	Debbie Woolgar	8 Jul 90	
	5380	18 Jun 89	
5424	Lisa Gibbs	1 Aug 93	
5409	Uju Efobi	19 Jun 94	
5391 w	Jackie Kinsella	22 Jun 86	
	5331	19 Jul 86	
5389	Sarah Owen	15 Aug 82	
5384	Sue Longden	8 May 82	
5358 w	Chloe Cozens	24 May 98	
	5283	23 May 99	
5353	Emma Lindsay	23 Aug 94	
5351	Wendy Laing	1 Aug 93	40
5339	Tracy Joseph	4 Aug 96	
5297	Kim Crowther	24 Aug 86	
5279	Fiona Harrison	21 Oct 00	

	5273 w	Debbie Marti	11 Aug 85
		5216	7 Jul 85
	5259 w	Anne Hollman	8 Aug 99
		5258	26 May 96
	5244	Val Lemoignan	19 Apr 84
	5242	Allison Manley	28 Mar 81
	5208	Michelle Stone	30 Sep 84
	5208	Mary Anderson	24 Aug 86
50	5190	Wendy Jeal	2 Jun 91

3000 Metres Track Walk

	12:49.16	Betty Sworowski	28 Jul 90
	12:50.61	Lisa Kehler	29 Jul 00
	12:59.3	Vicky Lupton	13 May 95
	13:12.01 i	Julie Drake	12 Mar 93
		13:16.0	11 Dec 90
	13:13.3	Cal Partington	12 Jul 95
	13:14.73	Niobe Menendez	11 Aug 01
	13:16.23	Verity Snook	27 May 96
	13:21.5	Catherine Charnock	8 May 99
	13:25.2	Carol Tyson	6 Jul 79
10	13:28.0	Helen Elleker	22 Jul 90

5000 Metres Track Walk

	21:52.4	Vicky Lupton	9 Aug 95
	21:57.68	Lisa Kehler	25 Jun 90
	22:01.53	Kehler	26 Jul 98
	22:02.06	Betty Sworowski	28 Aug 89
	22:08.69	Kehler	30 May 98
	22:37.47	Julie Drake	17 Jul 93
	22:41.19	Cal Partington	16 Jul 95
	22:51.23	Helen Elleker	25 Jun 90
	23:11.2	Carol Tyson	30 Jun 79
	23:11.7	Catherine Charnock	19 Jun 99
	23:15.04	Bev Allen	25 May 87
10	23:19.2	Marion Fawkes	30 Jun 79
	23:20.00	Ginney Birch	25 May 85
	23:22.52	Verity Snook	19 Jun 94
	23:34.43	Sylvia Black	5 Jul 92
	23:35.54	Nicky Jackson	25 May 87
	23:38.3	Irene Bateman	28 Jun 81
	23:46.30	Niobe Menendez	14 Jul 01
	23:46.7	Lillian Millen	28 Jun 81
	23:47.6	Melanie Wright	29 May 94
	23:51.1	Jill Barrett	5 May 84
20	23:55.27	Susan Ashforth	25 May 85

5k Road - where superior to track time

	21:36	Vicky Lupton	18 Jul 92
	21:50	Betty Sworowski	6 May 90
	21:55 hc	Lisa Kehler	13 Jul 98
	22:45 +	Verity Snook	25 Aug 94
	22:51	Marion Fawkes	29 Sep 79
	22:59	Carol Tyson	29 Sep 79
	23:00 +	Bev Allen	1 Sep 87
	23:09	Catherine Charnock	5 Jun 99
	23:13	Sylvia Black	13 Feb 93
10	23:24	Melanie Wright	9 Apr 95
	23:25	Irene Bateman	29 Sep 79
	23:32 +	Sara-Jane Cattermole	23 Jul 00

10000 Metres Track Walk

45:09.57	Lisa Kehler	13 Aug 00	
45:18.8	Vicky Lupton	2 Sep 95	
45:53.9	Julie Drake	26 May 90	
46:23.08	Betty Sworowski	4 Aug 91	
46:25.2	Helen Elleker	26 May 90	
47:10.07	Verity Snook	19 Jun 93	
47:56.3	Ginney Birch	15 Jun 85	
47:58.3	Bev Allen	21 Jun 86	
48:11.4	Marion Fawkes	8 Jul 79	
48:20.0	Cal Partington	7 May 94	10
48:34.5	Carol Tyson	22 Aug 81	
48:35.8	Melanie Wright	2 Sep 95	
48:56.5	Sarah Brown	18 Apr 91	
48:57.6	Irene Bateman	20 Mar 82	
49:27.0	Sylvia Black	22 Apr 95	
49:39.0	Karen Ratcliffe	22 May 91	
49:41.0	Elaine Callanin	22 Apr 95	
49:51.6	Sara-Jane Cattermole	7 Feb 01	
49:52.1	Niobe Menendez	29 Sep 01	
50:10.2	Brenda Lupton	17 Mar 84	20

track short

48:52.5	Irene Bateman	19 Mar 83	

10k Road - where superior to track time

45:03	Lisa Kehler	19 Sep 98	
45:59	Betty Sworowski	24 Aug 91	
46:06	Verity Snook	25 Aug 94	
46:26	Cal Partington	1 Jul 95	
47:05	Sara-Jane Cattermole	15 Jul 01	
47:51	Catherine Charnock	5 Sep 99	
47:58	Nicky Jackson	27 Jun 87	
47:59	Sylvia Black	29 Mar 92	
48:18	Melanie Wright	9 May 92	
48:30	Karen Ratcliffe	16 Apr 94	10
48:36	Kim Braznell	25 Apr 98	
48:47	Irene Bateman	20 Jun 81	

20 Kilometres Road Walk

1:33:57	Lisa Kehler	17 Jun 00	
1:36:40	Sara Cattermole	4 Mar 00	
1:37:44	Vicky Lupton	27 Jun 99	
1:38:29	Catherine Charnock	11 Sep 99	
1:40:12	Niobe Menendez	21 Mar 99	
1:40:45	Irene Bateman	9 Apr 83	
1:42:02 hc	Lillian Millen	9 Apr 83	
	1:44:42	2 Apr 83	
1:43:50	Betty Sworowski	22 Feb 88	
1:43:52	Sylvia Black	14 Jun 97	
1:44:29	Kim Braznell	21 Mar 99	10
1:45:11	Elaine Callanin	16 Oct 93	
1:46:15	Sharon Tonks	21 Apr 01	
1:46:48	Lisa Crump	27 Jun 99	
1:47:10	Liz Corran	29 Jun 96	
1:47:21	Debbie Wallen	17 Apr 99	
1:47:39	Jane Gibson	16 Jun 01	
1:47:46	Wendy Bennett	16 Jun 01	

50 Kilometres Road Walk

4:50:51	Sandra Brown	13 Jul 91	
5:01:52	Lillian Millen	16 Apr 83	

4 x 100 Metres Relay

42.43 Great Britain & NI 1 Aug 80
Oakes, Cook, Callender, Lannaman
42.60 Great Britain & NI 11 Aug 01
Richardson, Wilhelmy, James, Oyepitan
42.66 Great Britain & NI 11 Sep 82
Hoyte, Cook, Callender, S.Thomas
42.71 Great Britain & NI 10 Aug 83
Baptiste, Cook, Callender, S.Thomas
42.72 Great Britain & NI 3 Sep 78
Callender, Cook, Danville, Lannaman
43.02 Great Britain & NI 26 Sep 80
Oakes, Cook, Callender, Scutt
43.03 Great Britain & NI 15 Aug 81
Hoyte, Cook, Callender, S.Thomas
43.06 Great Britain & NI 10 Aug 83
Baptiste, Cook, Callender, S.Thomas
43.08 Great Britain & NI 11 Aug 01
Richardson, Wilhelmy, James, Oyepitan
10 43.11 Great Britain & NI 11 Aug 84
Jacobs, Cook, Callender, Oakes
43.15 England 9 Oct 82
Hoyte, Cook, Callender, Lannaman
43.18 Great Britain & NI 4 Aug 79
Barnett, Hoyte, Cook, Oakes
43.18 Great Britain & NI 20 Aug 83
Baptiste, Cook, Callender, S.Thomas
43.19 Great Britain & NI 20 Sep 80
Oakes, Cook, Callender, Scutt
43.19 Great Britain & N.I. 29 Sep 00
Maduaka, Richardson, Davies, Anderson
43.21 Great Britain & NI 18 Aug 82
Hoyte, Cook, Callender, S.Thomas
43.26 A Great Britain & NI Students 13 Sep 79
Wray, Cook, Patten, Callender
43.26 Great Britain & N.I. 29 Sep 00
Maduaka, Richardson, Wilhelmy, Anderson
43.30 Great Britain & NI 30 Aug 86
P.Thomas, Cook, Baptiste, Hoyte
20 43.3 Great Britain & NI 1 Jul 80
Oakes, Cook, Callender, Lannaman
43.31 Great Britain & NI 28 Aug 99
Richardson, Anderson, Bloomfield, Maduaka
43.32 Great Britain & NI 5 Jun 80
Oakes, Cook, Callender, Lannaman
43.32 Great Britain & NI 1 Sep 90
Douglas, Kinch, Jacobs, P.Thomas
43.35 Great Britain & NI 17 Aug 85
Andrews, Baptiste, Joseph, Oakes
43.36 Great Britain & NI'A' 13 Jul 80
Oakes, Cook, Callender, Lannaman
43.36 Great Britain & NI 23 Jun 81
Hoyte, Cook, Callender, S.Thomas
43.37 Great Britain & NI'A' 30 Aug 82
Hoyte, Cook, Callender, S.Thomas
43.38 Great Britain & NI 8 Aug 86
P.Thomas, Cook, Baptiste, Oakes
43.39 England 2 Aug 86
P.Thomas, Cook, Baptiste, Oakes
30 43.43 Great Britain & NI 31 Aug 91
Douglas, Kinch, Jacobs, P.Thomas

4 x 400 Metres Relay

3:22.01 Great Britain & NI 1 Sep 91
Hanson, Smith, Gunnell, Keough
3:23.41 Great Britain & NI 22 Aug 93
Keough, Smith, Joseph, Gunnell
3:23.89 Great Britain & NI 31 Aug 91
Smith, Hanson, Keough, Gunnell
3:24.14 Great Britain & NI 14 Aug 94
Neef, Keough, Smith, Gunnell
3:24.23 Great Britain & NI 8 Aug 92
Smith, Douglas, Stoute, Gunnell
3:24.25 Great Britain & NI 30 Jun 91
Gunnell, Hanson, Stoute, Keough
3:24.36 Great Britain & NI 5 Jun 93
Smith, Joseph, Stoute, Gunnell
3:24.78 Great Britain & NI 1 Sep 90
Gunnell, Stoute, Beckford, Keough
3:25.20 Great Britain & NI 7 Aug 92
Douglas, Smith, Stoute, Gunnell
3:25.28 Great Britain & N.I. 29 Sep 00 10
Frost, D.Fraser, Curbishley, Merry
3:25.50 Great Britain & NI 12 Aug 95
Neef, Llewellyn, Hanson, Oladapo
3:25.51 Great Britain & NI 11 Aug 84
Scutt, Barnett, Taylor, Hoyte-Smith
3:25.66 Great Britain & NI 23 Aug 98
Fraser, Jamison, Merry, Curbishley
3:25.67 Great Britain & N.I. 30 Sep 00
(Danvers, D.Fraser, Curbishley, Merry)
3:25.78 Great Britain & NI 9 Aug 97
Curbishley, Pierre, Thomas, Fraser
3:25.82 Great Britain & NI 11 Sep 82
Cook, Macdonald, Taylor, Hoyte-Smith
3:25.87 Great Britain & NI 19 Jun 82
Forsyth, Hoyte-Smith, Elder, Scutt
3:26.27 Great Britain & NI 10 Aug 97
Curbishley, Pierre, Thomas, Fraser
3:26.48 Great Britain & NI 22 Jun 97
Curbishley, Fraser, Thomas, Gunnell
3:26.54 Great Britain & NI 6 Aug 89 20
Keough, Stoute, Piggford, Gunnell
3:26.6 a Great Britain & NI 17 Aug 75
Roscoe, Taylor, Elder, Hartley
3:26.89 Great Britain & NI 1 Oct 88
Keough, Stoute, Piggford, Gunnell
3:26.89 Great Britain & NI 13 Aug 95
Neef, Llewellyn, Hanson, Oladapo
3:26.94 Great Britain & NI 12 Aug 01
McConnell, Frost, Danvers, Murphy
3:27.04 Great Britain & NI 21 Aug 93
Keough, Smith, Joseph, Gunnell
3:27.06 England 28 Aug 94
Smith, Joseph, Keough, Gunnell
3:27.09 Great Britain & NI 30 Jul 76
Barnes, Taylor, Elder, Hartley
3:27.17 Great Britain & NI 3 Sep 78
Williams, Hoyte-Smith, Elder, Hartley
3:27.19 England 12 Aug 78
Patten, Hoyte-Smith, Elder, Hartley
3:27.25 Great Britain & NI 13 Aug 94 30
Neef, Keough, Smith, Gunnell

UNDER 23

100 Metres

11.10	Kathy Smallwood	5 Sep 81
11.20	Heather Hunte	26 Sep 80
11.22	Sonia Lannaman	13 Aug 77
11.25	Paula Dunn	27 Aug 86
11.27	Andrea Lynch	20 Jul 74
11.27	Stephi Douglas	26 Jul 91
11.27	Abi Oyepitan	1 Jul 01
11.31	Shirley Thomas	3 Jul 83
11.31	Simmone Jacobs	24 Sep 88
11.34	Katharine Merry	25 Jun 94
wind assisted		
10.93	Sonia Lannaman	17 Jul 77
11.01	Heather Hunte	21 May 80
11.13	Shirley Thomas	27 May 84
11.14	Paula Dunn	27 Jul 86
11.17	Abi Oyepitan	30 Jun 01
11.23	Jayne Andrews	17 Jul 84
11.24	Sarah Wilhelmy	9 Jun 01
11.25	Andrea Lynch	27 Jul 74
11.27	Katharine Merry	11 Jun 94
11.30	Bev Goddard	15 Jul 78
hand timing		
11.1	Andrea Lynch	29 Jun 74
11.1	Heather Hunte	29 Jun 80
hand timing - wind assisted		
10.8	Sonia Lannaman	22 May 76
10.9	Andrea Lynch	18 May 74
11.1	Sharon Colyear	22 May 76

200 Metres

22.13	Kathy Smallwood	9 Sep 82
22.80	Michelle Scutt	12 Jun 82
22.81	Sonia Lannaman	2 May 76
22.85	Katharine Merry	12 Jun 94
22.98	Sandra Whittaker	8 Aug 84
23.06	Heather Hunte	15 Jun 80
23.06	Sam Davies	28 Aug 00
23.11	Bev Goddard	17 Jun 78
23.14	Helen Golden	7 Sep 73
23.18	Andrea Lynch	26 May 74
wind assisted		
22.48	Michelle Scutt	4 Jul 82
22.69	Sonia Lannaman	10 Jul 77
22.84	Sarah Wilhelmy	10 Jun 01
22.90	Allison Curbishley	17 Jul 98
22.95	Bev Goddard	10 Aug 78
22.97	Helen Golden	26 Jul 74
23.14	Shirley Thomas	28 May 84
hand timing		
22.9	Heather Hunte	3 May 80
hand timing - wind assisted		
22.6	Sonia Lannaman	23 May 76

300 Metres

36.01	Michelle Probert	13 Jul 80
during 400m		
35.8+	Kathy Smallwood	17 Sep 82

400 Metres

50.46	Kathy Smallwood	17 Sep 82
50.63	Michelle Scutt	31 May 82
50.71	Allison Curbishley	18 Sep 98
51.28	Donna Murray	12 Jul 75
51.77 i	Sally Gunnell	6 Mar 88
51.93	Janine MacGregor	28 Aug 81
51.94	Verona Bernard	26 Jan 74
51.97	Linda Forsyth	31 May 82
52.12A	Lillian Board	16 Oct 68
52.20	Ann Packer	17 Oct 64

600 Metres

1:26.18	Diane Edwards	22 Aug 87

800 Metres

1:59.05	Christina Boxer	4 Aug 79
1:59.30	Diane Edwards	4 Jul 87
1:59.67	Lorraine Baker	15 Aug 86
1:59.76	Paula Fryer	17 Jul 91
2:00.39	Bev Nicholson	28 Aug 88
2:00.55 mx	Zola Budd	21 Jun 86
2:00.56	Kirsty McDermott	17 Sep 82
2:00.6a	Jane Colebrook	9 Jul 77
2:01.1a	Ann Packer	20 Oct 64
2:01.2	Christine McMeekin	26 Aug 78

1000 Metres

2:35.51	Lorraine Baker	19 Jul 86

1500 Metres

4:01.93	Zola Budd	7 Jun 86
4:05.76	Yvonne Murray	5 Jul 86
4:06.0	Mary Stewart	24 Jun 78
4:06.84	Paula Radcliffe	2 Jul 95
4:07.06	Christina Boxer	15 Aug 79
4:07.98	Bev Nicholson	7 Jul 89
4:08.92	Janet Marlow	12 Jul 80
4:09.26	Lisa York	13 Jun 92
4:09.7a	Chris Benning	23 Aug 77
4:10.07	Maxine Newman	28 Jun 92

1 Mile

4:23.08	Yvonne Murray	5 Sep 86

2000 Metres

5:29.58	Yvonne Murray	11 Jul 86
5:30.19	Zola Budd	11 Jul 86

3000 Metres

8:34.43	Zola Budd	30 Jun 86
8:37.15	Yvonne Murray	28 Aug 86
8:40.40	Paula Radcliffe	16 Aug 93
8:46.53	Liz Lynch	18 Jul 86
8:47.36	Jill Hunter	17 Aug 88
8:47.71	Lisa York	31 Jul 92
8:51.40	Ruth Smeeth	7 Aug 82
8:53.78	Wendy Smith	26 May 80
8:53.98	Jane Furniss	30 May 82
8:58.44	Kath Binns	26 May 80

5000 Metres

14:49.27	Paula Radcliffe	7 Jul 95
15:17.77	Jill Hunter	26 Aug 88
15:34.92	Jane Furniss	26 Jun 82
15:36.35	Birhan Dagne	5 Aug 00
15:40.14	Helen Titterington	17 Jul 89
15:41.58+	Liz Lynch	30 Aug 86
15:49.6	Kath Binns	5 Apr 80
15:50.54	Yvonne Murray	28 May 84
15:55.64	Katie Skorupska	9 Jun 99
15:56.58	Gillian Palmer	13 Aug 00

10000 Metres

31:41.42	Liz Lynch	28 Jul 86
32:30.4	Birhan Dagne	22 Jul 00
32:32.42	Vikki McPherson	15 Jul 93
32:36.09	Helen Titterington	29 Aug 89
32:41.29	Jenny Clague	20 Jun 93
32:57.17	Kath Binns	15 Aug 80
33:40.6	Andrea Everett	5 Apr 86
33:43.80	Yvonne Murray	27 Jul 85
34:11.2	Lisa Hollick	15 May 91
34:15.52	Elspeth Turner	1 Apr 87

2000 Metres Steeplechase

7:04.20	Lois Joslin	8 Aug 99

3000 Metres Steeplechase

10:21.21	Lois Juslin	20 Apr 01

100 Metres Hurdles

12.82	Sally Gunnell	17 Aug 88
13.03	Diane Allahgreen	11 Jul 97
13.06	Shirley Strong	11 Jul 80
13.07	Lesley-Ann Skeete	14 Aug 87
13.11	Sharon Colyear	22 Jun 76
13.17	Jacqui Agyepong	3 Aug 90
13.20	Natasha Danvers	2 May 98
13.22	Judy Livermore	3 Oct 82
13.24	Keri Maddox	12 Jun 93
13.26	Michelle Edwards	3 Aug 90
wind assisted		
12.80	Sally Gunnell	29 Jul 88
13.20	Keri Maddox	2 Jul 93
13.22	Heather Ross	27 May 84
hand timing		
13.0	Blondelle Thompson	29 Jun 74
hand timing - wind assisted		
12.8	Natasha Danvers	3 Apr 99

400 Metres Hurdles

54.03	Sally Gunnell	28 Sep 88
55.69	Natasha Danvers	19 Jul 98
56.26	Louise Fraser	7 Jun 92
56.42	Vicki Jamison	20 Jun 98
57.03	Sue Morley	12 Jun 82
57.45	Jacqui Parker	5 Aug 88
57.56	Simone Gandy	14 Jun 86
57.79	Susan Dalgoutte	15 Jun 80
57.81	Wendy Griffiths	7 Aug 82
57.86	Teresa Hoyle	29 Jul 83
hand timing		
57.5	Vicky Lee	28 Jun 86
57.5	Simone Gandy	28 Jun 86

High Jump

1.95	Diana Elliott	26 Jun 82
1.94	Louise Miller	25 May 80
1.93	Susan Jones	2 Sep 00
1.93	Michelle Dunkley	2 Sep 00
1.92	Barbara Simmonds	31 Jul 82
1.92 i	Julia Bennett	10 Mar 90
1.91	Ann-Marie Cording	19 Sep 81
1.91	Jayne Barnetson	7 Jul 89
1.90 i	Lea Haggett	3 Jan 92
	1.89	6 May 92
1.89	Judy Livermore	9 Sep 82

Pole Vault

3.90 i	Rhian Clarke	8 Mar 97
	3.90	31 May 97
3.90	Tracey Bloomfield	4 Jun 00
3.90	Sonia Lawrence	14 Jul 01
3.75	Gael Davies	4 Jul 01
3.72	Linda Stanton	11 Jun 95
3.60 i	Janine Whitlock	30 Dec 95
3.60	Clare Ridgley	25 May 98
3.60 i	Laura Patterson	18 Feb 01
	3.60	12 May 01
3.60	Catherine MacRae	11 Aug 01
3.50	Helen Roscoe	9 Sep 00
3.50 i	Louise Gauld	27 Jan 01

Long Jump

6.88	Fiona May	18 Jul 90
6.79	Bev Kinch	7 Jul 84
6.75	Joyce Oladapo	14 Sep 85
6.73	Yinka Idowu	7 Aug 93
6.59	Jade Johnson	11 Aug 01
6.58	Mary Berkeley	14 Sep 85
6.57	Jo Wise	25 May 92
6.56	Denise Lewis	12 Jun 94
6.56	Sarah Claxton	23 May 99
6.55	Ann Wilson	22 Jul 70
wind assisted		
6.98	Fiona May	4 Jun 89
6.80	Joyce Oladapo	22 Jun 85
6.68	Jade Johnson	28 May 01
6.59	Jo Wise	2 Jul 93

Triple Jump

13.75	Michelle Griffith	18 Jul 93
13.48 i	Ashia Hansen	13 Feb 93
	13.31	18 Jul 92
13.31	Connie Henry	9 Jul 94
13.16	Rachel Kirby	26 Jul 91
13.11	Jade Johnson	19 Aug 01
13.03	Shani Anderson	4 May 96
12.94	Lorna Turner	9 Jul 94
12.85	Rebecca White	14 Jul 01
12.81	Karen Hambrook	15 Jun 91
12.61	Liz Patrick	28 Aug 99

wind assisted

13.93	Michelle Griffith	2 Jul 93
13.55	Ashia Hansen	2 Jul 93
13.09	Rebecca White	30 Jun 01
12.69	Liz Patrick	18 Jul 99

Shot

18.19	Myrtle Augee	14 Aug 87
17.20	Judy Oakes	8 Aug 80
16.55	Yvonne Hanson-Nortey	15 Jun 86
16.40	Julie Dunkley	12 Aug 00
15.95 i	Philippa Roles	6 Feb 99
15.85 i	Alison Grey	12 Feb 94
	15.69	11 Jun 94
15.72	Venissa Head	12 Jun 77
15.55	Christina Bennett	13 Jun 99
15.32 i	Helen Hounsell	13 Feb 82
15.32	Eva Massey	14 Jul 01

Discus

60.00	Philippa Roles	9 May 99
57.32	Lynda Whiteley	16 Jun 84
56.06	Kathryn Farr	27 Jun 87
55.70	Shelley Drew	25 Jun 95
55.52	Jane Aucott	17 Jan 90
54.72	Karen Pugh	27 Jul 86
54.46	Ellen Mulvihill	14 May 86
54.24	Nicola Talbot	15 May 93
54.16	Janet Thompson	15 May 76
53.78	Emma Beales	30 Aug 93

Hammer

61.70	Lyn Sprules	12 Jul 97
60.88	Rachael Beverley	23 May 99
60.37	Liz Pidgeon	31 Jul 99
60.35	Zoe Derham	10 Jun 01
58.83	Suzanne Roberts	9 Sep 00
58.31	Mhairi Walters	25 Aug 01
55.86	Diana Holden	21 Jun 97
55.42	Vicci Scott	23 Jun 01
55.09	Philippa Roles	9 May 99
54.15	Sarah Harrison	4 Jul 99

Javelin (1999 Model)

58.45	Kelly Morgan	12 Aug 00
52.76	Jenny Kemp	23 Jun 01
51.79	Chloe Cozens	3 Sep 00
48.24	Tammie Francis	29 Apr 00
47.26	Joanne Bruce	18 Jul 99
46.75	Katie Amos	19 Jun 99
46.29	Katy Watts	23 Jun 01
45.81	Jennifer West	27 May 01
45.37	Katherine Evans	3 Jul 99
44.67	Nicola Gautier	2 May 99

Javelin (pre 1999 Model)

69.54	Fatima Whitbread	3 Jul 83
67.20	Tessa Sanderson	17 Jul 77
60.10	Shelley Holroyd	16 Jul 93
60.00	Julie Abel	24 May 87
59.88	Sharon Gibson	3 Jul 83
58.20	Lorna Jackson	16 Jun 96
57.82	Mandy Liverton	21 Jun 92
56.28	Anna Lockton	20 Jul 85
55.42	Kirsty Morrison	14 Jun 97
55.34	Caroline White	20 Jan 90

Heptathlon (1985 Tables)

6325	Denise Lewis	23 Aug 94
6259	Judy Livermore	10 Sep 82
6094	Joanne Mulliner	7 Jun 87
5816 w	Julie Hollman	24 May 98
5803	Jayne Barnetson	20 Aug 89
5765	Kim Hagger	17 Jul 83
5765	Jenny Kelly	5 Aug 90
5760	Nicola Gautier	23 May 99
5671	Vikki Schofield	3 Jul 94
5644	Danielle Freeman	4 Jun 00

3000 Metres Track Walk

13:15.16+	Vicky Lupton	28 Jun 92

5000 Metres Track Walk

22:12.21	Vicky Lupton	28 Jun 92
22:19.04	Lisa Langford	25 May 87
22:40.0	Julie Drake	21 May 91

5k Road - where superior to track time

21:36	Vicky Lupton	18 Jul 92
22:09	Lisa Langford	8 Apr 89

10000 Metres Track Walk

45:53.9	Julie Drake	26 May 90
46:30.0	Vicky Lupton	14 Sep 94
49:59.0	Carol Tyson	25 Mar 78

10k Road - where superior to track time

45:42	Lisa Langford	3 May 87
45:48	Vicky Lupton	25 Aug 94

20 Kilometres Road Walk

1:38:25	Sara Cattermole	31 Oct 99
1:44:48	Vicky Lupton	3 Sep 94
1:47:21	Debbie Wallen	17 Apr 99
1:49:12	Nikki Huckerby	26 Sep 99
1:49:18	Helen Sharratt	16 Oct 93
1:52:37	Sally Warren	23 Apr 00
1:59:33	Melanie Brookes	9 Aug 86
2:00:26	Elaine Allen	4 Sep 83
2:08:23	Suzanne Ford-Dunn	16 Oct 93
2:09:23	Diane Wood	4 Sep 83

UNDER 20

100 Metres

11.27A Kathy Smallwood 9 Sep 79
 11.42 11 Aug 79
11.30 Bev Kinch 5 Jul 83
11.36A Della James 14 Oct 68
11.43 Shirley Thomas 7 Aug 82
11.45 Sonia Lannaman (U17) 1 Sep 72
11.45 Simmone Jacobs 6 Jul 84
11.52 Katharine Merry 16 Sep 92
11.53 Marcia Richardson 21 Jul 91
11.54 Wendy Clarke 8 Jun 75
10 11.59 Heather Hunte 9 Sep 77
11.59 Stephi Douglas 23 Jul 88
11.59 Rebecca Drummond 8 Jul 95
11.61 Diane Smith (U17) 9 Aug 90
11.61 Donna Hoggarth 16 Sep 92
11.62 Helen Miles 22 Aug 85
11.63 Jane Parry 29 May 82
11.63 Sallyanne Short 23 Aug 87
11.63 Tatum Nelson 25 Jul 97
11.64 Helen Barnett 21 Aug 76
20 11.64 Georgina Oladapo 22 Aug 85

wind assisted

11.13 Bev Kinch 6 Jul 83
11.25 Shirley Thomas 20 Aug 81
11.26 Simmone Jacobs 27 May 84
11.40 Katharine Merry 3 Jul 93
11.43 Dorothy Hyman 2 Sep 60
11.43 Vernicha James 14 Apr 01
11.45 Stephi Douglas 25 Jun 88
11.45 Rebecca White 4 Jul 98
11.45 Abi Oyepitan 4 Jul 98
10 11.47 Helen Golden 17 Jul 70
11.50 Rebecca Drummond (U17) 9 Jul 94
11.50 Sam Davies 18 Jul 98
11.53 Wendy Clarke 22 Aug 75
11.53 Sharon Dolby 16 Aug 86
11.55 Donna Hoggarth 29 Aug 92

hand timing

11.3 Sonia Lannaman 9 Jun 74
11.3 Heather Hunte 15 Jul 78
11.4 Della James 2 Aug 67

hand timing - wind assisted

11.2 Wendy Clarke 22 May 76
11.3 Helen Golden 30 May 70
11.3 Linsey Macdonald (U17) 3 May 80
11.4 Anita Neil 30 Jun 68
11.4 Helen Barnett 16 May 76
11.4 Jane Parry (U17) 5 Jul 80

downhill

11.3 w Denise Ramsden 28 Jun 69

200 Metres

22.70 A Kathy Smallwood 12 Sep 79
 22.84 5 Aug 79
22.93 Vernicha James 21 Jul 01
23.10 Diane Smith (U17) 11 Aug 90
23.20 Katharine Merry 13 Jun 93
23.23 Sonia Lannaman 25 Aug 75
23.23 Sarah Wilhelmy 13 Jun 98
23.24 Sandra Whittaker 12 Jun 82
23.28 Simmone Jacobs (U17) 28 Aug 83
23.33 Linsey Macdonald 9 Jun 82
23.35 Donna Murray 26 May 74 10
23.42 Debbie Bunn (U17) 17 Jun 78
23.45 Amy Spencer (U17) 15 Jul 01
23.46 Shirley Thomas 31 May 82
23.48 Wendy Clarke 7 Jun 75
23.51 Sharon Colyear 26 May 74
23.54 Jane Parry 30 Jul 83
23.57 Sophia Smith 30 Jul 93
23.59 Eleanor Thomas 17 Jul 77
23.60 Michelle Probert (U17) 12 Sep 76
23.61 Danielle Norville 16 Jun 01 20

wind assisted

23.01 Simmone Jacobs 28 May 84
23.11 Linsey Macdonald (U17) 5 Jul 80
23.16 Donna Murray 27 Jul 74
23.20 Sarah Wilhelmy 18 Jul 98
23.42 Helen Golden 22 Jul 70
23.54 Janine MacGregor 17 Jun 78
23.55 Sallyanne Short 25 Jul 87

hand timing

23.1 Sonia Lannaman 7 Jun 75
23.3 Donna Murray 9 Jun 74
23.3 Sharon Colyear 30 Jun 74
23.3 Linsey Macdonald 8 May 82
23.4 Helen Barnett 17 Jul 76

hand timing - wind assisted

22.9 Donna Murray 14 Jul 74
23.2 Debbie Bunn (U17) 2 Jul 78
23.3 Angela Bridgeman 15 Aug 82

300 Metres

36.46 Linsey Macdonald (U17) 13 Jul 80

400 Metres

51.16 Linsey Macdonald (U17) 15 Jun 80
51.77 Donna Murray 30 Jul 74
52.54 Donna Fraser 10 Aug 91
52.65 Jane Parry 11 Jun 83
52.80 Sian Morris 18 Jun 83
52.98 Karen Williams 6 Aug 78
52.99 Angela Bridgeman 24 Jul 82
53.01 i Marilyn Neufville 14 Mar 70
53.08 Loreen Hall 29 Jul 84
53.14 Michelle Probert 28 Jul 79 10
53.20 Verona Bernard 8 Jul 72
53.29 Lisa Miller 20 Jul 01
53.48 Lillian Board 22 Sep 67
53.52 Ruth Kennedy 25 Sep 74
53.52 Kim Wall 20 Jul 01
53.59 Janine MacGregor 11 Jul 78
53.73 Paulette McLean 24 Aug 89
53.75 Linda Keough (U17) 8 Aug 80
53.84 Jenny Meadows 12 Aug 00
53.92 Alison Reid 25 Jul 81 20
54.00 Heather Brookes 12 Aug 00

hand timing

	52.6	Marilyn Neufville	20 Jun 70
	52.8	Lillian Board	9 Jul 67
	52.9	Verona Bernard	15 Sep 72
	53.3	Tracey Burges	5 Sep 81
	53.5	Ruth Kennedy	30 Jun 74
	53.7	Linda Keough (U17)	2 Aug 80
	53.8	Alison Reid	28 May 81

600 Metres

	1:27.33	Lorraine Baker (U17)	13 Jul 80

800 Metres (*880yds less 0.7)

	2:01.11	Lynne MacDougall	18 Aug 84
	2:01.66	Lorraine Baker	26 Jun 82
	2:02.00	Diane Edwards	14 Sep 85
	2:02.0	Jo White (U17)	13 Aug 77
	2:02.18	Lynne Robinson	18 Jul 86
	2:02.8 a	Lesley Kiernan	2 Sep 74
	2:02.88 i	Kirsty McDermott	22 Feb 81
		2:04.01	29 Jul 81
	2:03.11	Janet Prictoe	19 Aug 78
	2:03.18	Paula Newnham	17 Jun 78
10	2:03.53	Christine McMeekin	25 Aug 75
	2:04.30	Bridget Smyth	19 Aug 86
	2:04.6	Janet Lawrence	26 Jul 77
	2:04.7*	Rosemary Stirling	13 Aug 66
	2:04.85	Louise Parker	28 Jul 79
	2:04.95	Denise Kiernan	3 Jun 78
	2:05.0 i	Jane Colebrook	11 Dec 76
	2:05.05	Rebecca Lyne	31 Jul 01
	2:05.07	Bev Nicholson	25 May 86
	2:05.1	Paula Fryer	14 Jun 88
20	2:05.1	Natalie Tait	22 Jul 89

1000 Metres

	2:38.58	Jo White (U17)	9 Sep 77

1500 Metres

	3:59.96	Zola Budd	30 Aug 85
	4:05.96	Lynne MacDougall	20 Aug 84
	4:11.12	Bridget Smyth	26 May 85
	4:13.38	Emma Ward	7 May 01
	4:13.40	Wendy Smith	19 Aug 78
	4:14.40	Janet Lawrence	20 Aug 77
	4:14.50	Wendy Wright	20 Jun 87
	4:14.56	Andrea Whitcombe	22 Aug 90
	4:14.58	Ruth Smeeth	16 Jul 78
10	4:14.73	Mary Stewart	2 Feb 74
	4:15.1	Yvonne Murray	18 Jul 82
	4:15.39	Lisa York	26 Aug 89
	4:15.55	Sandra Arthurton (U17)	29 Jul 78
	4:16.10	Katie Fairbrass	29 May 83
	4:16.12	Elise Lyon	3 Jul 83
	4:16.13	Bernadette Madigan	12 Aug 79
	4:16.2 i	Jo White	28 Jan 78
		4:16.8 (U17)	30 Jul 77
	4:16.4	Julie Holland	15 May 84
	4:16.51	Maxine Newman	26 Aug 89
20	4:16.8	Norine Braithwaite	20 Jun 70

1 Mile

4:17.57	Zola Budd	21 Aug 85	

2000 Metres

5:33.15	Zola Budd	13 Jul 84	

3000 Metres

8:28.83	Zola Budd	7 Sep 85	
8:51.78	Paula Radcliffe	20 Sep 92	
9:03.35	Philippa Mason	19 Jul 86	
9:04.14	Yvonne Murray	28 May 83	
9:06.16	Helen Titterington	19 Jun 88	
9:07.02	Carol Haigh	24 Jun 85	
9:09.14	Lisa York	19 Jul 89	
9:10.9	Julie Holland	7 Apr 84	
9:12.28	Hayley Haining	20 Jul 91	
9:12.97	Bernadette Madigan	30 Jun 79	10
9:13.4 mx	Caroline Walsh	30 Jun 99	
	9:20.38	7 Aug 99	
9:13.81	Andrea Whitcombe	12 Aug 90	
9:14.10	Maxine Newman	19 Jul 89	
9:15.82	Ruth Smeeth	17 Jun 78	
9:17.70 i	Alice Braham	3 Dec 94	
9:18.07	Heidi Moulder	1 Aug 93	
9:20.0	Judith Shepherd	13 Aug 77	
9:20.9	Wendy Wright	26 Apr 86	
9:21.20	Nikki Slater	3 Jul 94	
9:21.8	Wendy Smith	12 Aug 78	20

5000 Metres

14:48.07	Zola Budd	26 Aug 85	
15:51.62	Carol Haigh	26 May 85	
15:52.55	Yvonne Murray	29 May 83	
16:11.61 i	Jenny Clague	22 Feb 92	
16:15.36	Louise Kelly	31 Jul 98	
16:16.39	Collette Fagan	20 Jul 01	
16:16.77 i	Paula Radcliffe	22 Feb 92	
16:35.56	Gillian Stacey	22 Aug 90	
16:37.18	Henrietta Freeman	19 Aug 00	
16:41.9	Katie Skorupska	22 Jun 96	10
16:47.4	Sally James	7 Sep 83	
16:48.44	Claire Forbes	21 Apr 90	
16:49.2	Sam Baines	6 Jun 87	
16:50.4	Amanda Tremble	9 Aug 95	
16:50.84	Fiona Truman	30 Apr 88	
16:55.99	Louise Damen	16 Jun 01	
16:58.87	Tanya Povey	23 Apr 98	
17:09.8	Karen Fletcher	23 Aug 98	
17:09.97	Alison Hollington	30 Jul 82	
17:10.92	Donna Rutherford	3 May 92	20

10000 Metres

34:31.41	Tanya Povey	3 Jun 98	

2000 Metres Steeplechase

6:55.04	Jo Ankier	22 Jul 01	
7:01.2	Kathryn Frost	20 Jun 01	
7:11.2	Bryony Frost	20 Jun 01	

3000 Metres Steeplechase

12:11.1	Lindsey Oliver	22 Aug 93	

100 Metres Hurdles

	13.25	Diane Allahgreen	21 Jul 94
	13.30	Sally Gunnell	16 Jun 84
	13.32	Keri Maddox	21 Jul 91
	13.45	Natasha Danvers	6 Aug 95
	13.46	Nathalie Byer	26 Aug 83
	13.47	Sam Baker	30 Jun 91
	13.49	Angie Thorp	30 Jun 91
	13.50	Lesley-Ann Skeete	6 Jun 86
	13.52	Julie Pratt	5 Jul 98
10	13.56	Wendy McDonnell	3 Jun 79
	13.57	Bethan Edwards	29 Aug 92
	13.58	Lauraine Cameron	19 Jun 90
	13.62	Sarah Claxton	18 Jul 98
	13.66	Helen Worsey	20 Jul 01
	13.68	Jacqui Agyepong	7 Aug 87
	13.72	Judy Livermore	15 Jul 79
	13.73	Ann Girvan (U17)	7 Aug 82
	13.73	Yinka Idowu	10 Aug 91
	13.75	Sue Scott	21 Jul 70
20	13.76	Shirley Strong	20 Aug 77

wind assisted

	13.24	Lesley-Ann Skeete	7 Jun 86
	13.28	Sarah Claxton	5 Jul 98
	13.39	Lauraine Cameron	1 Jul 90
	13.45	Louise Fraser	30 Jul 89
	13.45	Sam Baker	30 Jun 91
	13.46	Wendy McDonnell	30 Jun 79
	13.48	Julie Pratt	5 Jul 98
	13.55	Shirley Strong	10 Jul 77
	13.56	Ann Girvan	15 Jul 84
10	13.72	Kate Forsyth	6 Jul 97

hand timing

13.5	Christine Perera	19 Jul 68

hand timing - wind assisted

13.1	Sally Gunnell	7 Jul 84
13.3	Keri Maddox	14 Jul 90
13.4	Judy Livermore	27 May 79
13.4	Sam Baker	14 Jul 90

400 Metres Hurdles

	57.27	Vicki Jamison	28 Jul 96
	58.02	Vyv Rhodes	28 Jun 92
	58.37	Alyson Evans	1 Sep 85
	58.68	Kay Simpson	15 Jul 83
	58.76	Simone Gandy	28 May 84
	58.91	Rachael Kay	6 Aug 99
	58.96	Nicola Sanders	17 Jul 99
	59.00	Diane Heath	19 Jul 75
	59.01	Sara Elson	24 Aug 89
10	59.04	Allison Curbishley	31 Jul 93
	59.12	Tracy Allen	29 Jul 89
	59.13	Sue Morley	12 Aug 79
	59.39	Tracey Duncan	29 Jul 98
	59.52	Debbie Church	25 Jul 81
	59.56	Lucy Elliott	26 Jul 85
	59.65	Debbie Duncan	7 Aug 87
	60.06	Faye Harding (U17)	13 Jul 01
	60.07	Michelle Cooney	6 Jul 85
	60.07	Gemma Dooney	18 Aug 01
20	60.15	Kate Norman	2 Jul 95

hand timing

58.3	Simone Gandy	14 Jul 84
58.7	Sara Elson	18 Jun 89
59.0	Tracy Allen	9 Jul 88
59.3	Michelle Cooney	13 Jul 85
59.4	Diane Wade	21 Jul 79
59.5	Samantha Flynn	12 Jul 86
59.7	Keri Maddox (U17)	9 Jul 88
59.9	Denise Kiernan	6 Sep 78
60.0	Jacqui Parker	13 Jul 85

High Jump

1.91	Lea Haggett	2 Jun 91	
1.91	Susan Jones	31 Aug 97	
1.90	Jo Jennings	29 Sep 88	
1.89	Debbie Marti (U17)	2 Jun 84	
1.89 i	Michelle Dunkley	16 Feb 97	
	1.87	7 Jul 95	
1.88	Jayne Barnetson	3 Aug 85	
1.87	Louise Manning	6 May 84	
1.87	Rachael Forrest	7 Jul 95	
1.87	Aileen Wilson	15 Jul 01	
1.86	Barbara Simmonds	9 Sep 79	10
1.86	Claire Summerfield	7 Aug 82	
1.86	Michele Wheeler	31 May 87	
1.85	Gillian Hitchen	3 Jun 78	
1.85	Sharon McPeake	22 Sep 81	
1.85	Julia Bennett	15 Apr 89	
1.84	Louise Miller	12 May 79	
1.84	Sarah Rowe	22 Aug 81	
1.84	Ursula Fay (U17)	6 Aug 83	
1.83	Diana Elliott	15 Jun 80	
1.83	Jennifer Little	30 Jun 84	20
1.83	Kerry Roberts	22 Jun 86	
1.83	Tracey Clarke (U17)	2 Aug 87	
1.83 i	Rebecca Jones	4 Mar 00	
	1.83	3 Jun 00	
1.83	Stephanie Higham	20 Jul 01	

Pole Vault

3.90	Ellie Spain	6 May 00	
3.81	Zoe Brown	9 Sep 01	
3.80	Kate Dennison	26 Aug 01	
3.75	Tracey Bloomfield	9 Aug 98	
3.70	Rhian Clarke	10 Aug 96	
3.65 i	Lindsay Hodges	6 Feb 00	
	3.55 (U17)	14 Aug 99	
3.60	Fiona Harrison (U17)	25 May 98	
3.60	Kirsty Maguire	18 Jul 01	
3.51 i	Clare Ridgley	17 Feb 96	
	3.50	6 May 96	
3.51	Hannah Olson (U15)	19 Aug 01	10
3.50	Becky Ridgley	23 May 99	
3.50	Natalie Olson (U17)	9 Sep 00	
3.50	Caroline Nutt	19 Aug 01	
3.45	Laura Patterson	4 Sep 99	
3.40	Danielle Codd	4 Jul 98	
3.40	Gillian Cooke	5 May 01	
3.40	Kim Skinner	11 Aug 01	
3.30	Louise Gauld	23 May 99	
	6 athletes at 3.20		

Long Jump

	6.90	Bev Kinch	14 Aug 83
	6.82	Fiona May	30 Jul 88
	6.68	Sue Hearnshaw	22 Sep 79
	6.63	Yinka Idowu	21 May 89
	6.55	Joyce Oladapo	30 Jul 83
	6.52	Georgina Oladapo	16 Jun 84
	6.52	Sarah Claxton	31 Jul 98
	6.52	Jade Johnson	23 May 99
	6.47	Jo Wise	30 Jul 88
10	6.45	Margaret Cheetham (U17)	18 Aug 84
	6.43	Myra Nimmo	27 May 73
	6.39	Moira Walls	22 Jul 70
	6.35	Sharon Bowie	1 Jun 85
	6.34	Ann Wilson	3 Aug 68
	6.33	Jo Dear	19 May 93
	6.31	Joanne Mulliner	1 Jun 85
	6.27	Sheila Parkin	3 Aug 64
	6.26	Maria Smallwood	14 Jun 80
	6.25	Lisa Armstrong	15 Jul 92
20	6.24	Karen Murray	16 Jul 77

wind unconfirmed

6.43	Moira Walls	18 Sep 70

wind assisted

6.93	Bev Kinch	14 Aug 83
6.88	Fiona May	30 Jul 88
6.71	Yinka Idowu	15 Jun 91
6.69	Jo Wise	30 Jul 88
6.53	Sarah Claxton	12 Jul 97
6.49	Margaret Cheetham (U17)	4 Sep 83
6.48	Moira Walls	17 May 70
6.41	Ann Wilson	30 Jun 68

Triple Jump

	13.05	Michelle Griffith	16 Jun 90
	12.50	Julia Johnson	21 Jun 98
	12.43	Shani Anderson	26 Jun 93
	12.42	Liz Gibbens	2 Jul 95
	12.41 i	Judy Kotey	28 Feb 98
		12.33	17 May 98
	12.27	Lorna Turner	26 May 91
	12.22	Mary Bignal	18 Jun 59
	12.22	Angela Williams	16 Sep 00
	12.20	Jodie Hurst	8 Jun 96
10	12.18	Justina Cruickshank	26 May 96
	12.17	Katharine Streatfield	26 May 01
	12.14	Jayne Ludlow (U17)	21 May 94
	12.10	Jane Falconer	30 Aug 93
	12.10	Pamela Anderson	2 Jul 95
	12.10	Rachel Brenton (U17)	21 Jul 01
	12.04	Rachel Peacock	26 Aug 01
	12.01 i	Emily Parker (U17)	25 Feb 01
		11.98	14 Jul 01
	11.96	Linsi Robinson	30 Jun 01
	11.93	Sharon Oakes	13 Aug 00
20	11.91	Lisa Brown	30 Jul 95

wind assisted

12.61	Judy Kotey	5 Jul 98
12.48	Lorna Turner	30 Jun 91
12.44	Shani Anderson	9 Jul 94
12.37	Jane Falconer	30 Aug 93

Shot

17.10	Myrtle Augee	16 Jun 84	
16.24 i	Judy Oakes	26 Feb 77	
	16.05	26 Aug 77	
15.72 i	Alison Grey	29 Feb 92	
	15.26	13 Jul 91	
15.60 i	Justine Buttle	27 Feb 88	
	15.45	25 Aug 88	
15.48	Mary Anderson	8 Sep 85	
15.45	Susan King	27 Mar 83	
15.27	Julie Dunkley	21 Jun 98	
14.75 i	Cynthia Gregory	12 Dec 81	
	14.70	29 Aug 81	
14.71 i	Nicola Gautier	26 Jan 97	
	14.37	12 Jul 97	
14.68	Claire Smithson	26 May 01	10
14.66 i	Terri Salt	7 Jan 84	
14.60	Philippa Roles	4 Sep 96	
14.59	Dawn Grazette	19 May 91	
14.59 i	Christina Bennett	16 Mar 97	
14.54	Carol Cooksley	9 Jul 88	
14.54 i	Jayne Berry	18 Mar 89	
	14.45	17 Jun 88	
14.49	Eva Massey	9 Aug 99	
14.36	Venissa Head	4 Jul 75	
14.34	Rebecca Peake	18 Aug 89	
14.33	Jenny Kelly	27 May 01	20

Discus

54.81	Claire Smithson	1 Jul 01	
54.78	Lynda Whiteley	4 Oct 82	
53.12	Emma Carpenter	1 Sep 01	
53.10	Kathryn Farr	19 Jul 86	
52.58	Emma Merry	22 Aug 93	
52.31	Lauren Keightley	18 Jul 98	
51.82	Catherine Bradley	20 Jul 85	
51.60	Philippa Roles	24 Jul 97	
51.24	Jane Aucott	11 Jun 86	
51.12	Janette Picton	6 Jun 82	10
50.44	Karen Pugh	8 Jul 83	
50.34	Angela Sellars	27 Jul 86	
50.30	Julia Avis	19 Sep 82	
49.74	Shelley Drew	10 May 92	
49.60	Fiona Condon	3 Jun 79	
49.56	Sarah Winckless	2 May 92	
49.42	Rosanne Lister	29 Aug 88	
49.30	Amanda Barnes	18 Jun 88	
49.24	Lesley Mallin	31 May 75	
49.00	Tracey Whincup	26 Jun 84	20

Hammer

57.97	Rachael Beverley	25 Jul 98	
55.10	Mhairi Walters	27 May 00	
54.72	Helen Arnold	26 Jul 97	
54.54	Nicola Dudman	29 Jul 01	
54.48	Lyn Sprules	2 Jul 94	
53.80	Carys Parry	17 Oct 00	
53.34	Diana Holden	13 Aug 94	
53.13	Katy Lamb	14 Jul 01	
52.33	Zoe Derham	13 Jun 99	
52.00	Laura Douglas	9 Sep 01	10

	51.62	Julie Lavender	15	May	94
	51.54	Lucy Marshall	3	Sep	00
	51.34	Helen Taylor	12	Aug	01
	50.66	Vicci Scott	12	Sep	99
	50.52	Catherine Garden	3	Aug	97
	50.50	Sarah Harrison	2	Aug	97
	49.48	Samantha Burns-Salmond	13	Aug	95
	48.98	Liz Pidgeon	21	Sep	96
	48.98	Francis Miller (U17)	21	Sep	96
20	48.18	Suzanne Roberts	1	Jun	97

Javelin (1999 Model)

	55.40	Goldie Sayers	22	Jul	01
	54.61	Kelly Morgan	4	Sep	99
	52.54	Jenny Kemp	3	Jul	99
	48.15	Chloe Cozens	19	Jun	99
	47.57	Amy Harvey	7	Oct	00
	47.13	Samantha Redd	30	Jun	01
	45.84	Suzanne Finnis	24	Jun	00
	45.65	Louise Matthews	2	Sep	01
	45.24	Katy Watts	10	Jul	99
10	44.11	Rachel Dunn	7	Jul	01

Javelin (pre 1999 Model)

	60.14	Fatima Whitbread	7	May	80
	59.40	Karen Hough	28	Aug	86
	59.36	Kirsty Morrison	4	Sep	93
	57.84	Mandy Liverton	3	Jun	90
	57.82	Shelley Holroyd	9	Aug	92
	57.80	Julie Abel	5	Jun	83
	56.96	Nicky Emblem	1	Feb	90
	55.72	Karen Martin	25	Jul	92
	55.38	Catherine Garside	19	May	84
10	55.04	Tessa Sanderson	26	Sep	74

Heptathlon (1985 Tables)

	5833	Joanne Mulliner	11	Aug	85
	5642	Sarah Rowe	23	Aug	81
	5496	Yinka Idowu	3	Sep	89
	5493	Sally Gunnell	28	May	84
	5484	Denise Lewis	30	Jun	91
	5459	Jenny Kelly	30	Jul	88
	5391 w	Jackie Kinsella	22	Jun	86
		5331	19	Jul	86
	5377	Uju Efobi	18	Jul	93
	5358 w	Chloe Cozens	24	May	98
		5283	23	May	99
10	5311	Nicola Gautier	21	Sep	97
	5299	Emma Beales	26	Aug	90
	5279	Fiona Harrison	21	Oct	00
	5273 w	Debbie Marti	11	Aug	85
		5216	7	Jul	85
	5258 w	Danielle Freeman	23	May	99
		5237	19	Jul	98
	5246	Val Walsh	7	Aug	83
	5215	Katherine Livesey	1	Jun	97
	5208	Michelle Stone (U17)	30	Sep	84
	5208	Mary Anderson	24	Aug	86
	5187 w	Anne Hollman	2	May	93
20	5186	Rebecca Jones	4	Jun	00

3000 Metres Track Walk

13:03.4	Vicky Lupton	18	May	91	
13:47.0	Julie Drake	5	Jul	88	
13:53.0 e+	Lisa Langford	23	Aug	85	
	14:01.0	17	Aug	85	
14:04.1	Susan Ashforth (U17)	19	May	85	
14:09.81	Amy Hales (U17)	19	Sep	98	

5000 Metres Track Walk

22:36.81	Vicky Lupton	15	Jun	91	
23:31.67	Lisa Langford	23	Aug	85	
23:55.27	Susan Ashforth (U17)	25	May	85	
23:56.9	Julie Drake	24	May	88	
24:02.15	Nicky Jackson	27	May	84	
24:08.4	Jill Barrett	28	May	83	
24:19.0	Vicky Lawrence	13	Jun	87	
24:24.31	Andrea Crofts	4	Jun	89	
24:27.73	Carolyn Brown	29	Aug	92	
24:28.60	Debbie Wallen	26	Jul	98	10
24:34.6	Tracy Devlin	17	Sep	89	
24:35.0	Joanne Pope	16	Dec	90	

5k Road - where superior to track time

23:05	Lisa Langford	2	Nov	85	
23:18	Julie Drake	27	Feb	88	
23:35	Lisa Simpson	31	Oct	87	
23:44	Nicky Jackson	12	May	84	
23:46	Jill Barrett	14	May	83	
23:54	Vicky Lawrence	26	Sep	87	

10000 Metres Track Walk

47:04.0	Vicky Lupton	30	Mar	91	
48:34.0mx	Lisa Langford	15	Mar	86	
	49:07.8	21	Jun	86	
49:48.7	Julie Drake	7	Feb	88	
50:25.0mx	Lisa Simpson	1	Apr	87	
	51:54.5	27	Sep	86	
51:00.0	Karen Nipper (U17)	21	Feb	81	
51:31.2	Helen Ringshaw	17	Mar	84	
52:09.0	Elaine Cox	8	Apr	78	
52:10.4	Sarah Brown	20	Mar	82	
52:48.5	Kate Horwill	22	Aug	92	
53:11.4	Jill Barrett	28	Mar	81	10
53:36.0mx	Suzie Pratt	15	Mar	86	
53:39.0	Karen Eden	22	Mar	80	

short

50:11.2	Jill Barrett	19	Mar	83

10k Road - where superior to track time

49:10	Vicky Lawrence	14	Mar	87
49:14	Carolyn Brown	29	Mar	92
49:26	Julie Drake	21	May	88
49:33	Lisa Simpson	14	Mar	87
49:47	Jill Barrett	24	Sep	83
51:15	Nicky Jackson	18	Nov	84
51:36	Nicola Phillips	23	Apr	00
51:51	Elaine Cox	2	Sep	79
52:00	Theresa Ashman	9	May	92

Note: LJ, Hep. Although Idowu competed for UK Juniors, she was a Nigerian citizen at the time.

UNDER 17

100 Metres

11.45	Sonia Lannaman	1 Sep 72
11.59	Simmone Jacobs	25 Aug 83
11.60	Katharine Merry	28 Jul 90
11.61	Diane Smith	9 Aug 90
11.66	Amy Spencer	16 Jun 01
11.69	Jane Parry	6 Jun 81
11.70	Linsey Macdonald	24 May 80
11.73	Etta Kessebeh	20 Aug 81
11.77	Hayley Clements	26 Jul 85
10 11.78	Tatum Nelson	16 May 94
11.79	Janet Smith	26 Jul 85
11.80	Sharon Dolby	26 Jul 85
11.81	Lisa Goreeph	6 Jun 82
11.83"	Sarah Wilhelmy	13 May 95
wind assisted		
11.47	Katharine Merry (U15)	17 Jun 89
11.50	Rebecca Drummond	9 Jul 94
11.61	Linsey Macdonald	16 Jun 79
11.62	Kathleen Lithgow	25 Jun 88
11.62	Donna Maylor	4 Jul 98
11.63	Sharon Dolby	10 Aug 85
11.67	Tatum Nelson (U15)	10 Jul 93
hand timing		
11.6	Denise Ramsden	19 Jul 68
11.6	Linsey Macdonald	25 May 80
11.6	Jane Parry	2 Aug 80
hand timing - wind assisted		
11.3	Linsey Macdonald	3 May 80
11.4	Sonia Lannaman	3 Jun 72
11.4	Jane Parry	5 Jul 80
11.5	Sharon Dolby	20 Jul 85

200 Metres

23.10	Diane Smith	11 Aug 90
23.28	Simmone Jacobs	28 Aug 83
23.42	Debbie Bunn	17 Jun 78
23.43	Linsey Macdonald	20 Aug 80
23.45	Amy Spencer	15 Jul 01
23.49 i	Vernicha James	30 Jan 00
	23.62	8 Jul 00
23.50	Katharine Merry	20 Jul 91
23.60	Michelle Probert	12 Sep 76
23.66	Jane Parry	15 Jun 80
10 23.69	Donna Fraser	1 Jul 89
23.79	Sharon Colyear	5 Sep 71
23.90	Angela Bridgeman	20 Aug 80
23.95	Helen Golden	30 Aug 69
23.97	Lisa Goreeph	31 Jul 82
24.06	Fay Nixon	4 Jun 76
wind assisted		
23.11	Linsey Macdonald	5 Jul 80
23.41	Katharine Merry	15 Jun 91
23.48	Vernicha James	21 Aug 99
23.64	Jane Parry	5 Jul 80
23.70	Sonia Lannaman	16 Jun 72
23.85	Helen Golden	1 Sep 69
23.99	Sarah Wilhelmy	13 Jul 96
hand timing (* 220 yards less 0.1)		
23.8 *	Marilyn Neufville	27 Jul 68
23.8	Janis Walsh (U15)	23 Jun 74
23.8	Janet Smith	1 Jun 85
23.9	Fay Nixon	24 Jul 76
23.9	Hayley Clements	1 Jun 85
hand timing - wind assisted		
23.2	Debbie Bunn	2 Jul 78
23.3	Amy Spencer	1 Jul 01

300 Metres

36.46	Linsey Macdonald	13 Jul 80
38.19	Eleanor Caney	22 Jul 00
38.21	Lesley Owusu	27 Aug 95
38.49	Kim Wall	24 May 98
38.60	Karlene Palmer	12 Jul 97
38.75	Gabi Howell	24 May 98
38.90	Liza Parry	15 Jul 00
38.95	Maria Bolsover	8 Jul 95
39.04	Heather McKay	19 Jun 98
39.07	Nicola Sanders	24 May 98 10
39.21	Lisa Miller	10 Jul 99
39.22	Jenny Meadows	11 Jul 97
39.25	Rebecca White	17 Aug 96
39.34	Ruth Watson	12 Jul 96
39.36	Olivia Hines	29 Jul 00
hand timing		
38.2	Marilyn Neufville	6 Sep 69
38.4	Kim Wall	10 May 98
38.6	Fay Nixon	10 Sep 77
38.7	Katharine Merry	1 Sep 91

400 Metres

51.16	Linsey Macdonald	15 Jun 80
53.08	Loreen Hall	29 Jul 84
53.75	Linda Keough	8 Aug 80
54.01	Angela Bridgeman	16 Aug 80
54.25	Emma Langston	19 Jun 88
54.57	Lesley Owusu	9 Sep 95
hand timing		
53.7	Linda Keough	2 Aug 80

600 Metres

1:27.33	Lorraine Baker	13 Jul 80

800 Metres

2:02.0	Jo White	13 Aug 77
2:03.66	Lesley Kiernan	26 Aug 73
2:03.72	Lorraine Baker	15 Jun 80
2:04.85	Louise Parker	28 Jul 79
2:05.86	Charlotte Moore	31 Jul 01
2:06.5	Rachel Hughes (U15)	19 Jul 82
2:06.5	Emma Langston	10 Aug 88
2:06.51	Danielle Barnes	15 Jul 01
2:06.53	Lynne Robinson	6 Jul 85
2:06.72	Jemma Simpson	19 Aug 00 10
2:06.8	Jayne Heathcote	31 May 87
2:07.0	Bridget Smyth	27 Jun 84
2:07.25	Morag MacLarty	21 Jul 01
2:07.3	Amanda Alford	7 May 80
2:07.32	Amanda Pritchard	22 Jun 96

1000 Metres

	2:38.58	Jo White	9 Sep 77

1500 Metres

	4:15.20	Bridget Smyth	29 Jul 84
	4:15.55	Sandra Arthurton	29 Jul 78
	4:16.8	Jo White	30 Jul 77
	4:21.88	Jeina Mitchell	20 Jul 91
	4:22.25	Karen Hughes	24 May 81
	4:22.25	Clare Keller	7 Jul 85
	4:22.51	Elise Lyon	31 Jul 82
	4:23.07	Charlotte Moore	22 Aug 01
	4:23.11	Gillian Stacey	2 Sep 89
10	4:23.25	Denise Kiernan	20 Aug 77
	4:23.37	Dawn Hargan	14 Jun 87
	4:23.45	Isabel Linaker (U15)	7 Jul 90
	4:23.6	Janette Howes	5 Sep 81
	4:23.75	Lynne MacDougall	24 May 81
	4:23.96	Zoe Jelbert	19 Aug 00

1 Mile

	4:46.0	Sandra Arthurton	13 May 78

3000 Metres

	9:28.9	Bridget Smyth	21 Apr 84
	9:30.0	Yvonne Murray	4 Jul 81
	9:31.69	Rachel Nathan	18 Aug 01
	9:32.20	Nikki Slater	28 Aug 93
	9:33.1	Alison Hollington	6 Jun 81
	9:34.5	Louise Watson	28 Aug 88
	9:34.79	Helen Titterington	28 Jun 86
	9:34.9 mx	Charlotte Dale	16 Jul 00
		9:35.25	19 Aug 00
	9:35.46+	Danielle Barnes	23 May 01
10	9:35.52	Courtney Birch	15 Jul 00
	9:36.8	Karen Hughes	4 Jun 80
	9:37.54 i	Zoe Jelbert	5 Feb 00
	9:38.1	Elise Lyon	12 Sep 81
	9:38.2	Amanda Alford	7 Mar 79
	9:39.9	Sharon Willicombe	8 Jul 88

5000 Metres

	17:45.2	Kathy Williams	10 May 80

80 Metres Hurdles (2'6")

	11.02	Helen Worsey	15 Aug 98
	11.07	Amanda Parker	7 Jun 86
	11.12	Sam Farquharson	7 Jun 86
	11.13	Claire St. John	2 Jun 79
	11.16	Ann Girvan	4 Jul 81
	11.16	Stephi Douglas	27 Jul 85
	11.17	Sara McGreavy	14 Aug 99
	11.20	Ann Wilson	11 Aug 66
	11.20	Louise Brunning	25 Jul 87
10	11.20	Symone Belle	30 Jul 00
	11.22	Sharon Davidge	18 Jul 98
	11.23	Rachel Rigby	25 Jul 87
	11.25	Louise Fraser	25 Jul 87
	11.26	Liz Fairs	17 Jul 93
	11.29	Nina Thompson	7 Aug 88

wind assisted

	10.96	Helen Worsey	11 Jul 98
	11.00	Sharon Davidge	11 Jul 98
	11.03	Wendy McDonnell	20 Aug 77

hand timing

	11.0	Wendy McDonnell	2 Jul 77

hand timing - wind assisted

	10.9	Ann Wilson	16 Jul 66
	10.9	Wendy McDonnell	9 Jul 77
	10.9	Sam Farquharson	20 Jul 85

100 Metres Hurdles (2'6")

	13.66	Ann Girvan	25 Jul 81

100 Metres Hurdles (2'9")

	13.73	Ann Girvan	7 Aug 82
	13.88	Natasha Danvers	28 Aug 93
	13.98	Claire St. John	11 Aug 79
	14.04	Lauraine Cameron	7 Aug 88
	14.24	Pam St. Ange	2 Oct 82
	14.24	Angie Thorp	9 Jul 89
	14.39	Michelle Stone	18 Aug 84
	14.40	Vicki Jamison	22 Jun 93

wind assisted

	13.67	Ann Girvan	4 Jul 82
	13.76	Natasha Danvers	27 Aug 94
	14.10	Sue Mapstone	25 Aug 73
	14.27	Heather Ross	27 Aug 78

hand timing

	13.7	Ann Girvan	29 Aug 81
	14.1	Pam St Ange	7 Aug 83

hand timing - wind assisted

	13.7	Nathalie Byer	4 Sep 82
	13.9	Angie Thorp	9 Sep 89

300 Metres Hurdles

	41.98	Rachael Kay	3 Aug 97
	41.99	Natasha Danvers	10 Jul 93
	42.50	Justine Roach	21 Jul 01
	42.58	Syreeta Williams	12 Jul 97
	42.67	Vicki Jamison	17 Jul 93
	42.68	Gemma Dooney	15 Jul 00
	42.87	Nusrat Ceesay	12 Jul 97
	42.91	Allison Curbishley	18 Aug 91
	43.03	Val Theobalds	13 Aug 89
10	43.03	Wendy Davidson	15 Aug 99
	43.06	Claire Griffiths	18 Aug 91
	43.08	Yewande Ige	13 Jul 96
	43.12	Keri Maddox	6 Aug 88
	43.12	Sian Scott	30 Jul 00
	43.20	Faye Harding	22 Jul 01

hand timing

	41.8	Rachael Kay	17 Aug 97
	42.4	Keri Maddox	8 May 88
	42.4	Syreeta Williams	17 Aug 97
	42.5	Louise Brunning	8 May 88
	42.6	Sian Scott	10 Jun 00
	42.8	Rachel Stafford	8 Jul 89
	42.8	Vyv Rhodes	8 Jul 89
	42.9	Val Theobalds	17 Jun 89

400 Metres Hurdles

	60.06	Faye Harding	13 Jul 01
	60.87	Karin Hendrickse	31 Jul 82
	60.93	Rachael Kay	21 Jul 97
	61.02	Claire Edwards	8 Sep 91
	61.04	Allison Curbishley	26 Jul 92

hand timing

	59.7	Keri Maddox	9 Jul 88
	60.8	Jayne Puckeridge	9 Jul 88

High Jump

	1.89	Debbie Marti	2 Jun 84
	1.85	Louise Manning	11 Sep 82
	1.85	Jayne Barnetson	21 Jul 84
	1.84	Ursula Fay	6 Aug 83
	1.83	Jo Jennings	26 Jul 85
	1.83	Tracey Clarke	2 Aug 87
	1.83	Aileen Wilson	8 Jul 00
	1.82	Elaine Hickey	9 Aug 80
	1.82	Kerry Roberts	16 Jul 83
10	1.82	Susan Jones	20 May 94
	1.81	Barbara Simmonds	22 Jul 78
	1.81	Lea Haggett (U15)	6 Jun 86
		1.80	3 Sep 88
	1.80	Carol Mathers	10 Jun 73
	1.80	Susan Brown	28 Jul 79

Pole Vault

	3.60	Fiona Harrison	25 May 98
	3.55	Lindsay Hodges	14 Aug 99
	3.51	Hannah Olson (U15)	19 Aug 01
	3.50	Natalie Olson	23 Jun 01
	3.44	Clare Ridgley	10 Sep 94
	3.40	Kim Skinner (U15)	12 Aug 01
	3.30	Rhian Clarke	4 Jul 93
	3.20	Rebecca Roles	31 Aug 96
	3.20	Ellie Spain	13 Sep 98
10	3.20 i	Kirsty Maguire	20 Feb 99
	3.20	Kate Dennison	15 Jul 00
	3.20 i	Sunny Brar	4 Feb 01
	3.20	Rachel Gibbens	12 May 01
	3.20	Claire Holmes	23 Sep 01

Long Jump

	6.45	Margaret Cheetham	18 Aug 84
	6.32	Georgina Oladapo	23 Jul 83
	6.30	Fiona May (U15)	7 Jul 84
		6.27	14 Jun 86
	6.26	Jo Wise	31 May 87
	6.25	Sue Hearnshaw	9 Jul 77
	6.24	Sarah Claxton	15 Jun 96
	6.23	Sue Scott	27 Jul 68
	6.22	Ann Wilson	18 Sep 66
	6.22	Michelle Stone	28 Apr 84
	6.18	Sheila Parkin	4 Aug 62
	6.15	Zainab Ceesay	20 Aug 00
	6.14	Bev Kinch	26 Jul 80
	6.13	Sonya Henry	7 Jul 85
	6.13	Jade Johnson	28 May 95
	6.12	Karen Glen	10 Aug 80

wind assisted

	6.49	Margaret Cheetham (U15)	4 Sep 83
		6.49	23 Sep 84
	6.47	Fiona May	28 Jun 86
	6.41	Sue Hearnshaw	9 Jul 77
	6.34	Sarah Claxton	12 Jul 96
	6.33	Sue Scott	27 Aug 68
	6.28	Bev Kinch	6 Sep 80
	6.24	Jade Johnson	28 May 95
	6.15	Sue Mapstone	27 May 72
	6.15	Karen Glen	5 Jul 80

Triple Jump

	12.14	Jayne Ludlow	21 May 94
	12.10	Rachel Brenton	21 Jul 01
	12.01 i	Emily Parker	25 Feb 01
		11.98	14 Jul 01
	11.87	Angela Barratt	21 Jul 01
	11.83	Carly Robson	7 Jul 00
	11.82	Julia Johnson	30 Jun 96
	11.76	Allison McAllister	26 May 01
	11.76	Kosnatu Abdulai	27 May 01
	11.71	Hayley Warrilow	30 Jun 96
10	11.68 i	Syreeta Williams	16 Feb 97
	11.64	Rachel Peacock	19 Jul 97
	11.61	Aisha Myton	30 Jul 00
	11.59	Tolu Jegede	30 Jun 96
	11.58 i	Linsi Robinson	6 Feb 00
	11.50	Michelle Johansen	20 Aug 00

wind assisted

	12.27	Rachel Brenton	21 Jul 01
	12.07	Rachel Peacock	18 Jul 98
	12.05	Emily Parker	2 Sep 01
	12.03	Angela Barratt	17 Jun 01
	11.75	Michelle Doherty	21 Jul 01
	11.69	Claire Quigg	18 Jul 98
	11.68	Rachel Hogg	18 Jul 98
	11.60	Lara Richards	15 Aug 99
	11.58	Natalie Brant	17 Jul 99

Shot

	15.08	Justine Buttle	16 Aug 86
	14.40	Susan King	17 May 81
	14.04	Mary Anderson	6 May 84
	14.03 i	Terri Salt	19 Mar 83
		13.77	17 Sep 83
	13.94	Jenny Bloss	13 May 67
	13.89 i	Alison Grey	11 Feb 89
		13.83	20 May 89
	13.68 i	Philippa Roles	26 Feb 94
		13.65	6 Aug 94
	13.64	Cynthia Gregory	20 Aug 80
	13.58 i	Natalie Hart	19 Mar 88
		13.32	28 Aug 88
	13.49	Lana Newton	11 Jul 75
	13.46	Julie Dunkley	22 Jun 96
	13.35	Carol Cooksley	6 Sep 86
	13.35	Claire Smithson	4 Jul 99
	13.24	Myrtle Augee	2 Aug 81
	13.20	Jayne Thornton	9 Jul 86

Discus

	51.60	Emma Merry	27 Jun 90
	49.56	Jane Aucott	3 Aug 85
	49.36	Claire Smithson	10 Jul 99
	48.88	Philippa Roles	13 Aug 94
	48.84	Karen Pugh	7 Aug 82
	47.58	Catherine Bradley	14 Jul 84
	47.54	Lauren Keightley	12 Jul 95
	47.50	Sarah Symonds	16 May 90
	47.24	Amanda Barnes	3 Aug 85
10	46.76	Fiona Condon	6 Aug 77
	46.55	Emma Carpenter	5 Sep 98
	46.34	Janette Picton	25 Mar 79
	45.93	Joanne Street	3 Jul 99
	45.72	Sarah Winckless	1 Jul 90
	45.52	Jayne Thornton	12 May 86

Hammer

	48.94	Frances Miller	12 Jul 01
	48.66	Zoe Derham	16 Aug 97
	47.68	Diana Holden	31 Jul 91
	47.62	Nicola Dudman	11 Jun 00
	46.98	Helen Arnold	29 Jul 95
	46.82	Carys Parry	30 Aug 97
	45.58	Julie Lavender	13 Sep 92
	45.54	Laura Douglas	26 Jun 99
	45.15	Angela Lockley	12 Aug 01
10	44.86	Laura Chalmers	10 Jun 01
	44.70	Rachael Beverley	15 Jul 95
	43.64	Catherine Garden	30 Apr 95
	43.36	Vicki Clark	16 Aug 97
	43.10	Lucy Marshall	15 Aug 98
	42.29	Sarah Dobriskey	9 Sep 01

Javelin (1999 Model)

	45.24	Samantha Redd	27 May 00
	43.11	Charlotte Rees	28 Aug 00
	42.82	Becky Bartlett	8 Sep 01
	42.37	Jo Chapman	26 May 01
	41.99	Sarah Ellis	27 May 00
	41.44	Louise Watton (U15)	8 Sep 01
	41.35	Lauren Therin	6 Jul 00
	41.11	Alison Siggery	5 Aug 00
	41.05	Debbie Collinson	17 Jun 01
10	40.98	Lisa Fryer	20 Jun 00
	40.78	Hayley Thomas (U15)	11 Aug 01
	40.70	Helen Mounteney	9 Jun 01

Javelin (pre 1999 Model)

	56.02	Mandy Liverton	11 Jun 89
	53.42	Karen Hough	15 Jul 84
	53.22	Kirsty Morrison	15 Aug 92
	51.92	Goldie Sayers	17 May 98
	51.50	Shelley Holroyd	22 Jul 89
	50.82	Nicky Emblem	19 Jun 87
	50.04	Kim Lisbon	19 Feb 84
	50.02	Angelique Pullen	31 Aug 85
	49.24	Jacqui Barclay	7 Aug 82
10	49.00	Kelly Morgan	27 Apr 96
	48.34	Fatima Whitbread	29 Aug 77

Heptathlon (1985 Tables) Senior

	5208	Michelle Stone	30 Sep 84
	5184	Claire Phythian	20 Aug 89
	4815 w	Julie Hollman	2 May 93
		4807	30 May 93
	4801	Jessica Ennis	5 Aug 01
	4784	Jackie Kinsella	12 May 85

Heptathlon (1985 Tables) with 80mH

	5037	Michelle Stone	1 Jul 84
	5031	Yinka Idowu	18 Sep 88
	4945	Phyllis Agbo	24 Jun 01
	4915	Denise Lewis	24 Jul 88
	4861	Clover Wynter-Pink	26 Jun 94
	4841	Rebecca Lewis	18 Sep 94
	4839	Jackie Kinsella	21 Jul 85
	4830 w	Katherine Livesey	22 Sep 96
		4790	28 Jul 96
	4794	Claire Phythian	22 May 88
10	4780	Danielle Freeman	23 Jun 96
	4746	Chloe Cozens	22 Sep 96
	4742	Julie Hollman	26 Sep 93
	4673	Denise Bolton	19 Sep 93
	4666	Tina Thirwell	20 Sep 98
	4657	Rebecca Jones	4 Jul 99

with 100mH

	5071	Debbie Marti	5 Jun 83
	4661	Suzanne Sherratt	23 Aug 81

3000 Metres Track Walk

	14:04.1	Susan Ashforth	19 May 85
	14:09.81	Amy Hales	19 Sep 98
	14:17.96 i	Katie Ford	28 Feb 98
	14:20.70	Sophie Hales	15 Sep 01
	14:21.0	Julie Drake	25 Jun 85
	14:21.90	Katie Stones	15 Sep 01

5000 Metres Track Walk

	23:55.27	Susan Ashforth	25 May 85
	24:22.3	Vicky Lawrence	21 Jun 86
	24:34.6	Tracy Devlin	17 Sep 89
	24:45.4	Karen Eden	9 Jul 78
	24:57.5	Angela Hodd	24 Jun 86
	25:11.46	Nicola Phillips	21 Aug 99
	25:13.8	Carla Jarvis	2 Jun 91
	25:15.3	Vicky Lupton	3 Sep 88
	25:18.5	Jill Barrett	16 Aug 80
10	25:20.0	Katie Ford	10 Sep 97
	25:25.02	Nina Howley	31 Jul 94
	25:25.80	Kim Macadam	25 May 85
	25:26.41	Becky Tisshaw	6 Jul 97
	25:31.14	Zena Lindley	4 Jun 89
	25:31.5	Sophie Hales	29 Sep 01

5k Road - where superior to track time

	23:57	Sarah Brown	6 Dec 80
	24:20	Karen Eden	3 Dec 78

10000 Metres Track Walk

	51:00.0	Karen Nipper	21 Feb 81
	53:34.1	Vicky Lupton	5 Sep 87

UNDER 15

100 Metres

11.67	Katharine Merry	13	May	89
11.86	Hayley Clements	2	Jul	83
11.89	Joanne Gardner	20	Aug	77
11.92	Jane Parry (U13)	20	Aug	77
11.95	Tatum Nelson	7	Aug	93
12.00	Diane Smith	15	Sep	89
12.02	Renate Chinyou	28	Aug	88
12.02	Sarah Wilhelmy	28	May	94
12.02	Amy Spencer	29	Jul	00
12.07	Margaret Cheetham	29	Jul	83
12.09	Libby Alder	8	Jul	95
12.10 A	Helen Seery	25	Jul	91
12.10	Lesley Owusu	7	Aug	93

wind assisted

11.47	Katharine Merry	17	Jun	89
11.67	Tatum Nelson	10	Jul	93
11.78	Jane Parry	8	Aug	78
11.84	Janis Walsh	26	May	74
11.88	Sarah Claxton	9	Jul	94
11.92	Sinead Johnson	11	Aug	01

hand timing

11.8	Janis Walsh	7	Jul	74
11.8	Joanne Gardner	2	Jul	77
11.9	Sonia Lannaman	9	Aug	69
11.9	Linsey Macdonald	26	Aug	78
11.9	Jane Perry	22	Apr	79
11.9	Etta Kessebeh	11	Jul	80

hand timing - wind assisted

11.7	Diane Smith	30	Jul	89
11.8	Sonia Lannaman	30	May	70
11.8	Debbie Bunn (U13)	28	Jun	75
11.8	Delmena Doyley	6	Jul	79

200 Metres

23.72	Katharine Merry	17	Jun	89
23.90	Diane Smith	3	Sep	89
24.05	Jane Parry	16	Jul	78
24.31	Amy Spencer	8	Jul	00
24.39	Hayley Clements	3	Jul	83
24.44	Rachael Kay	8	Jul	95
24.51	Tatum Nelson	8	Aug	93
24.54	Sarah Wilhelmy	31	Jul	94
24.58	Simmone Jacobs	25	Jul	81
24.58	Donna Fraser	22	Aug	87
24.59	Janet Smith	30	Jul	83

wind assisted

23.54	Katharine Merry	30	Jul	89
23.99	Sarah Wilhelmy	9	Jul	94
24.24	Amy Spencer	8	Jul	00
24.25	Vernicha James	11	Jul	98
24.35	Tatum Nelson	27	Jun	93

hand timing

23.8	Janis Walsh	23	Jun	74
24.1	Sonia Lannaman	29	Aug	70

hand timing - wind assisted

23.6	Jane Parry (U13)	9	Jul	77
23.8	Diane Smith	9	Sep	89

300 Metres

41.1	Maria Bolsover	10	Apr	94

400 Metres

56.7	Jane Colebrook	25	Jun	72

800 Metres

2:06.5	Rachel Hughes	19	Jul	82
2:08.7	Emma Langston	12	Jul	86
2:09.58	Sally Ludlam	8	Jun	75
2:09.6	Isabel Linaker	1	Aug	90
2:09.77	Lorraine Baker	19	Aug	78
2:09.80	Hannah Curnock	15	Aug	92
2:10.1	Lesley Kiernan	9	Jul	71
2:10.3	Carol Pannell	9	Jul	71
2:10.6	Christina Boxer	10	Jul	71
2:10.6	Natalie Tait	12	Jul	86
2:10.66	Amanda Pritchard	15	Jul	94
2:10.76	Carolyn Wells	19	Aug	78

1000 Metres

2:51.4	Hayley Haining	20	Aug	86

1500 Metres

4:23.45	Isabel Linaker	7	Jul	90
4:27.9	Joanne Davis	9	Jul	88
4:29.0	Claire Allen	8	Jul	89
4:29.6	Lynne MacDougall	16	Jul	79
4:29.9	Heidi Hosking	9	Jul	88
4:30.4	Claire Nicholson	18	Jun	87
4:31.12	Karen Hughes	31	Aug	79
4:31.45	Amanda Alford	22	Jul	78
4:31.6	Michelle Lavercombe	13	Jun	81
4:31.70	Jennifer Mockler	4	Aug	96
4:32.0	Elise Lyon	2	Apr	80
4:32.0	Jojo Tulloh	13	Jul	85
4:32.0	Julie Adkin	13	Aug	86
4:32.0	Katrina Wootton	15	Jul	00

1 Mile

4:54.7	Hannah Curnock	9	Sep	92

75 Metres Hurdles (2'6")

10.86	Heather Jones	17	Jun	01
10.93	Rachel Halstead-Peel	27	Jul	85
11.00	Louise Fraser	27	Jul	85
11.00	Danielle Selley	20	Jun	98
11.01	Nathalie Byer	16	Aug	80
11.06	Jessica Ennis	30	Jul	00
11.06	Phyllis Agbo	17	Sep	00
11.07	Symone Belle	10	Jul	99
11.08	Nicola Hall	29	May	94
11.08	Sara McGreavy	12	Jul	97
11.09	Catherine Murphy	6	Aug	88
11.09	Orla Bermingham	25	Aug	90

wind assisted

10.95	Symone Belle	9	Jul	99
11.00	Leah McGuire	7	Jul	01
11.01	Naomi Hodge-Dallaway	8	Jul	95
11.05	Helen Worsey	13	Jul	96

hand timing

10.8	Symone Belle	29 Aug 99

hand timing - wind assisted

10.7	Orla Bermingham	14 Jul 90
10.8	Nathalie Byer	12 Jul 80
10.8	Ann Girvan	12 Jul 80

80 Metres Hurdles (2'6") U17

11.44	Catherine Crawford	4 Jul 99

High Jump

1.83	Ursula Fay	5 Jun 82
1.81	Debbie Marti	18 Sep 82
1.81	Lea Haggett	6 Jun 86
1.80	Jo Jennings	12 Aug 84
1.79 i	Julia Charlton	24 Feb 80
	1.78	13 Jul 80
1.79	Aileen Wilson	4 Jul 98
1.78	Claire Summerfield	28 Jul 79
1.75	Anne Gilson	2 Jun 73
1.75	Claire Smith	8 Aug 82
1.75	Jane Falconer	10 Jun 89
1.75	Stephanie Pywell	6 Jul 01

Pole Vault

3.51	Hannah Olson	19 Aug 01
3.50	Fiona Harrison	24 Aug 96
3.40	Kim Skinner	12 Aug 01
3.20	Natalie Olson	9 Sep 00
3.10	Cariann Cutts	14 Aug 99
2.85	Zoe Holland	25 Jul 99

Long Jump

6.34	Margaret Cheetham	14 Aug 83
6.30	Fiona May	7 Jul 84
6.07	Georgina Oladapo	21 Jun 81
5.98	Sandy French	22 Jul 78
5.93	Jackie Harris	10 Jul 87
5.91	Symone Belle	29 Aug 99
5.88	Sue Scott	11 Aug 66
5.86	Tammy McCammon	18 Aug 91
5.86	Rebekah Passley	12 Aug 01
5.85	Kim Hagger	20 Aug 76
5.81	Yvonne Hallett	24 Aug 86
5.80	Monique Parris	23 May 98
5.78	Pam St. Ange	15 Aug 81
5.76	Debbie Marti	31 Jul 82

wind assisted

6.49	Margaret Cheetham	4 Sep 83
6.05	Katharine Merry	18 Sep 88
6.02	Michelle Stone	10 Jul 82
5.99	Sandy French	8 Jul 78
5.86	Donna Maylor	13 Jul 96
5.85	Karen Glen	8 Jul 78
5.80	Sue Mapstone	26 Jun 71

Triple Jump

11.47	Ruth Hatch	23 Sep 01

wind assisted

11.48	Ruth Hatch	23 Sep 01

Shot (4kg)

12.16	Susan King	8 Sep 79

Shot (3.25kg)

14.27	Susan King	19 May 79
13.88 i	Chloe Edwards	21 Apr 01
13.69	Gloria Achille	21 Jun 80
13.61	Justine Buttle	4 Aug 84
13.22	Emily Steele	23 Jul 89
13.11	Amy Wilson	2 Sep 95
13.08	Ashley Morris	11 Aug 84
13.05	Tracy Page	21 Jun 86
13.04	Navdeep Dhaliwal	17 May 92
12.97	Alison Grey	23 Aug 87
12.96	April Kalu	23 Jun 96
12.95	Cynthia Gregory	7 Jul 78

Discus

44.12	Philippa Roles	30 Aug 92
41.92	Catherine Garden	12 Sep 93
40.92	Sandra McDonald	24 Jun 78
40.84	Natalie Kerr	24 Jul 94
40.54	Claire Smithson	25 May 97
40.44	Catherine MacIntyre	12 Sep 82
40.34	Natalie Hart	23 Mar 86
40.22	Emma Merry	27 Aug 88
40.18	Kelly Mellis	17 Sep 94
40.14	Clare Tank	29 Aug 88
39.76	Alix Gallagher	6 Jun 87
39.38	Charladee Clarke	1 Sep 85
39.38	Alex Hajipavlis	13 Aug 95

Hammer (4kg)

38.00	Catherine Garden	14 Mar 93

Hammer (3.25kg)

42.18	Laura Chalmers	22 Aug 00
40.70	Catherine Marvin	9 Sep 01
40.54	Laura Chalmers	9 Jul 00
39.75	Shaeleen Bruce	9 Jul 00
39.35	Kirsty Walters	8 May 99
38.32	Sarah Holt	15 Jul 00

Javelin (1999 Model)

41.44	Louise Watton	8 Sep 01
40.78	Hayley Thomas	11 Aug 01
38.01	Lauren Therin	15 Aug 99
37.40	Rebecca Pyne	20 Jun 99
36.37	Melissa O'Neill	1 Sep 01
36.03	Kelly-Jane Berry	28 Aug 00
35.98	Debbie Collinson	24 Jun 00
35.10	Cara Moseley	16 Jun 01

Javelin (pre 1999 Model)

48.40	Mandy Liverton	31 Aug 87
46.98	Kirsty Morrison	30 Jun 90
43.16	Shelley Holroyd	27 Jun 87
43.08	Karen Hough	4 Sep 82
42.70	Emily Steele	23 Sep 89
41.56	Goldie Sayers	12 Jul 96

Pentathlon (with 800m & 75m hdls)

3518	Katharine Merry	18 Sep 88
3509	Aileen Wilson	20 Sep 98
3333	Jackie Harris	27 Jun 87
3296	Claire Everett	19 Sep 93
3236	Emma Perkins	10 Sep 00
3225	Amy Nuttell	26 Jun 94
3216	Sally Gunnell	23 Aug 80
3213	Julie Hollman	22 Sep 91
3207	Louise Hazel	17 Sep 00
3195	Julia Charlton	10 May 80
3193	Sam Foster	26 Jun 94
3186	Lauraine Cameron	16 Aug 86
with 80mH		
3444	Jane Shepherd	16 Jul 83
3350	Claire Smith	3 Jul 82
3295	Paula Khouri	16 Jul 83
3283	Jackie Kinsella	16 Jul 83
3260	Debbie Marti	14 Aug 82
3186	Michelle Stone	3 Jul 82

2000 Metres Track Walk

9:35.0	Karen Eden	17 Jun 77

2500 Metres Track Walk

11:50.0	Susan Ashforth	12 Sep 84

3000 Metres Track Walk

14:56.4	Sarah Bennett	26 Sep 93
15:00.0	Susan Ashforth	19 Jun 84
15:00.6	Sally Wish	16 Sep 72
15:06.69	Kelly Mann	30 May 98
15:14.6	Amy Hales	31 Aug 96
15:16.4	Natalie Watson	31 Aug 96
15:18.3	Vicky Lawrence	17 Jul 83
15:19.0	Tracy Devlin	28 Mar 87
15:25.06	Sophie Hales	18 Sep 99
15:26.63	Nicola Phillips	20 Sep 97
15:28.0	Kim Macadam	3 Sep 83
15:30.0	Nikola Ellis	1 Sep 84
15:31.0	Philippa Savage	3 Sep 88
short track		
15:18.7	Sharon Tonks	19 Mar 83
3k Road - where superior to track time		
14:47	Amy Hales	23 Jun 96
14:48	Nikola Ellis	16 Sep 84
14:55	Lisa Langford	6 Dec 80
14:58	Carolyn Brown	19 Aug 87
14:59	Julie Snead	16 Sep 84
15:07	Stephanie Cooper	10 Dec 83
15:09	Angela Hodd	29 Jul 84
15:10	Vicky Lawrence	15 Apr 84
15:13	Jill Barrett	28 Jan 78

5000 Metres Track Walk

26:47.0hc	Amy Hales	15 Dec 96
26:52.0	Nina Howley	14 Sep 92
5k Road - where superior to track time		
26:20	Tracy Devlin	14 Feb 87

UNDER 13

75 Metres

9.83	Amy Spencer	6 Sep 98
9.98	Jenny Igbokwe	3 Sep 00
10.01	Jane Chadwick	3 Sep 00
10.02	Charlene Lashley	6 Sep 98
10.05	Michaela McCalla	1 Sep 01
wind assisted		
9.96	Joanne Wainwright	8 Sep 96
hand timing		
9.7	Carley Wenham	12 Jul 00
9.8	Amy Spencer	19 Jul 98
9.8	Rachel Follos	18 Jul 99
9.9	Cherie Pierre	21 Jul 96
9.9	Charlene Lashley	17 May 98
9.9	Nicola Gossman	2 May 99
9.9	Sinead Johnson	18 Jul 99
9.9	Leah McGuire	30 Aug 99
wind unconfirmed		
9.8	Felicity James	1 Jul 01
9.9	Hannah Frankson	1 Jul 01

80 Metres

10.2	Jane Riley	1 Jun 85
10.2	Helen Seery	20 May 89

100 Metres

11.92	Jane Parry	20 Aug 77
12.32	Katharine Merry	24 Jul 87
12.65	Sarah Claxton	4 Jul 92
hand timing		
12.1	Katharine Merry	26 Sep 87
12.3	Joanne Gardner	24 Aug 75
12.3	Debbie Bunn	30 Aug 75
hand timing - wind assisted		
11.8	Debbie Bunn	28 Jun 75

150 Metres

19.47	Amy Spencer	6 Sep 98
19.69	Louise Dickson	4 Sep 99
19.78	Rebecca Smith	3 Sep 95
19.78	Jane Chadwick	3 Sep 00
hand timing		
19.1	Emma Ania	7 Sep 91
19.1	Emma Heath	18 Jul 99
19.2	Helen Seery	19 Feb 89
19.2	Amy Spencer	28 Jun 98
19.2	Rachel Follos	18 Jul 99
19.2	Stacey Simpson	21 May 00
19.2	Laura Cox	21 May 00
19.3	Alanna Wain	29 Jun 97
19.3	Natalie Pearson	21 May 00
19.4	Vernicha James	1 Sep 96
19.4	Emma Burrows	18 Jul 99
19.4	Sinead Johnson	18 Jul 99

200 Metres

24.49	Jane Parry	20 Aug 77
25.87	Amy Spencer	2 Aug 98
25.88	Myra McShannon	4 Sep 88

hand timing

24.2	Jane Parry	28 May 77
25.4	Katharine Merry	21 Jun 87
25.4	Myra McShannon	8 May 88
25.6	Debbie Bunn	5 Jul 75
25.6	Joanne Gardner	24 Aug 75
25.6	Jane Riley	30 Jun 85

wind assisted

23.6	Jane Parry	9 Jul 77

600 Metres

1:37.3	Lisa Lanini	19 Mar 00
1:37.5	Hannah Wood	17 Jul 94
1:38.5	Jenny Meadows	4 Apr 93

800 Metres

2:14.8	Janet Lawrence	10 Jul 71
2:15.05	Rachel Hughes	11 Sep 81
2:16.1	Lisa Lanini	5 Aug 00
2:16.8	Angela Davies	25 Jul 83
2:17.20	Emma Langston	7 Sep 84
2:17.6	Michelle Wilkinson	22 Jun 85
2:17.9	Melissa Rooney	20 Jun 81
2:18.1	Lileath Rose	19 Jun 76

1000 Metres

3:00.1	Charlotte Moore	25 Aug 97
3:05.9	Natalie Yates	27 May 01
3:06.4	Charlotte Browning	6 Aug 00
3:08.1	Cheryl Hammond	4 Jul 99
3:08.2	Kelly Deacon	14 May 95
3:08.2	Rhea Fallows	27 Aug 01

1200 Metres

3:46.4	Lisa Lanini	18 Jul 99
3:49.1	Megan Foley	2 Jul 00
3:50.4	Lynsey Jepson	1 Aug 99
3:50.9	Charlotte Browning	4 Jul 00
3:51.1	Natalie Yates	1 Jul 01
3:51.3	Stephanie Bloor	2 Jul 00
3:52.5	Emily Pidgeon	20 May 01
3:52.9	Emma Hunt	17 May 98
3:53.1	Sara Luck	11 Jul 99
3:53.3	Ellie McLoughlin	22 Jul 01

1500 Metres

4:36.9	Rachel Hughes	20 Jul 81
4:39.3	Charlotte Moore	2 Aug 97
4:42.1	Stacey Washington	18 Jul 84

1 Mile

5:22.2	Emily Pidgeon	26 Aug 01

70 Metres Hurdles (2'3")

11.17	Anne-Marie Massey	3 Sep 95
11.24	Alana Watson	8 Sep 96
11.35	Nafalya Francis	27 Aug 01
11.46	Sandra Gunn	13 Aug 88
11.51	Kelly Marshall	11 Jul 98
11.55	Anna Salter	14 Sep 97

wind assisted

11.02	Nafalya Francis	27 Aug 01
11.21	Sandra Gunn	4 Sep 88
11.26	Catriona Burr	4 Sep 88
11.32	Joanne Baker	3 Sep 00

hand timing

11.0	Katharine Merry	20 Sep 87
11.0	Justine Roach	13 Sep 97
11.1	Sarah Claxton	14 Jun 92
11.1	Emma Makin	26 May 98
11.1	Leah McGuire	9 May 99
11.2	Clare Stuart	19 Jun 88

wind unconfirmed

11.1	Nafalya Francis	1 Jul 01

75 Metres Hurdles (2'6")

11.78	Caroline Pearce	7 Aug 93

hand timing

11.3	Katharine Merry	26 Sep 87

High Jump

1.69	Katharine Merry	26 Sep 87
1.68	Julia Charlton	6 Aug 78
1.65	Debbie Marti	20 Sep 80
1.65	Jane Falconer	20 Sep 87
1.63	Lindsey Marriott	11 Aug 79
1.63	Paula Davidge	13 Sep 81
1.60	Denise Wilkinson	17 Jul 76
1.59	Julie O'Dell	28 Jul 74
1.59	Julia Cockram	18 May 80
1.59	Bev Green	30 Aug 86

Pole Vault

3.10	Hannah Olson	9 Sep 00
2.80	Kim Skinner	24 May 00
2.30	Lauren Stoney	5 Aug 96

Long Jump

5.71	Sandy French	20 Aug 76
5.45	Sarah Wilhelmy	31 Aug 92
5.43	Margaret Cheetham	19 Sep 81
5.42	Katharine Merry	7 Jun 87
5.40	Kerry Gray	1 Sep 84
5.38	Toyin Campbell	6 Aug 77
5.35	Debbie Bunn	7 Sep 75
5.34	Fiona May	12 Jun 82
5.33	Kathryn Dowsett	7 Sep 91
5.32	Ann Flannery	18 Sep 82

wind assisted

5.55	Katharine Merry	10 Jul 87

Triple Jump

9.55	Fiona Ferbrache	14 Jul 94

Shot (3.25kg)

12.20	Susan King	3 Sep 77
10.84	Eden Francis	16 Sep 01
10.77	Michele Morgan	19 Jun 82
10.54	Claire Burnett	1 Sep 85
10.49	Alison Grey	3 Aug 85

Shot (2.72kg)

12.07	Becki Hall	14 Aug 01
11.59	Eden Francis	8 Sep 01
11.50	Nimi Iniekio	5 Sep 99
11.42	Candee Rhule	29 Jul 00
11.04	Amy Wilson	12 Sep 93
10.91	Catherine Garden	8 Sep 91
10.83	Nicola Stevenson	27 Aug 01
10.72	Kayleigh Southgate	3 Sep 00
10.60	Lucy Rann	29 Aug 93
10.56	Candace Schofield	17 Aug 97

Discus (1kg)

34.22	Catherine Garden	25 Aug 91
31.34	Sandra Biddlecombe	9 Sep 90
30.54	Fiona Condon	15 Sep 73
30.02	Alison Moffitt	6 Jul 82

Discus (750g)

39.44	Catherine Garden	8 Sep 91
37.64	Sandra Biddlecombe	4 Jul 90
34.80	Rebecca Saunders	28 Aug 00
34.61	Becki Hall	27 Aug 01
32.70	Claire Smithson	26 Aug 95
32.52	Candace Schofield	7 Sep 97
32.16	Christina Carding	25 Jul 99
31.46	Sian Howe	21 Sep 96
30.54	Eleanor Garden	10 Sep 89
30.48	F. Thompson	2 Sep 01

Hammer (3.25kg)

22.76	Ruth Hay	7 Sep 00

Javelin (600g 1999 model)

31.16	Laura Carr	1 Sep 01

Javelin (600g original model)

32.02	Claire Lacey	20 Sep 87
31.60	Emma Langston	2 Sep 84
31.44	Alison Moffitt	6 Jul 82
31.28	Eve Russell	2 Sep 95

Javelin (400g)

38.07	Louise Watton	12 Sep 99
36.06	Samantha Redd	1 Sep 96
34.27	Laura Carr	29 Jul 01
33.90	Lauren Therin	6 Sep 98
33.46	Emma Claydon	26 Jul 92
33.32	Melanie Vaggers	27 Sep 94
32.60	Candace Schofield	10 Aug 97
32.38	Eve Russell	30 Jul 95
31.87	Georgina Field	31 Aug 98
31.74	Josie Jamieson	28 Aug 99

Pentathlon (Under 15 implements)

2607	Jane Shepherd	6 Jun 81
2604	Alison Kerboas	19 Sep 93
2541 ?	Jane Falconer	23 Aug 87

Pentathlon

2811	Katharine Merry	20 Sep 87
2551	Sarah Wilhelmy	2 Aug 92
2519	Naida Bromley	30 Aug 99
2505	Caroline Pearce	26 Sep 93
2451	Seonaid Ferry	17 Jul 94
2419	Donna Medlock	7 Aug 94

1000 Metres Track Walk

4:53.4	Fiona McGorum	9 Sep 01
5:11.1	Amy Hales	4 Sep 94
5:14.6	Natasha Fox	31 Aug 98
5:17.0	Elizabeth Ryan	10 Jun 79
5:18.0	Margaret O'Rawe	28 Sep 80
5:19.3	Jemma Black	15 Oct 95
5:21.0	Sarah Bennett	30 Sep 90
5:22.6	Carley Tomlin	29 May 00
5:23.0	Hayley Dyke	15 Jul 98
5:27.0	Katrina Todd	27 Nov 77

1k Road - where superior to track time

4:42	Kelly Mann	23 Sep 95
4:43	Natalie Watson	23 Sep 95
4:50	Sarah Bennett	23 Sep 90

2000 Metres Track Walk

10:09.0	Kelly Mann	10 Sep 95
10:17.0	Sarah Bennett	27 Sep 92
10:19.0	Joanne Ashforth	7 Sep 85
10:19.8	Fiona McGorum	29 Sep 01
10:31.0	Claire Walker	7 Sep 85
10:31.0	Jo Pickett	25 Apr 92
10:32.0	Karen Eden	25 Aug 75
10:37.0	Karen Bowers	29 Sep 79
10:38.1	Rebecca Mersh	29 Sep 01
10:41.0	Amy Hales	7 May 94

2k Road - where superior to track time

10:03	Kelly Mann	23 Jun 96
10:36	Yvette Eden	24 Jan 76
10:38	Hayley Hutchings	28 Sep 96
10:39	Laura Fryer	23 Jun 96
10:42	Natalie Evans	28 Sep 96

2500 Metres Track Walk

12:48.9	Claire Walker	20 Jul 85
12:50.5	Vicky Lawrence	4 Jul 82

2.5k Road - where superior to track time

12:39	Amy Hales	16 Oct 93
12:41	Stephanie Cooper	1 May 82

3000 Metres Track Walk

15:41.0	Kelly Mann	30 Jul 95

3k Road - where superior to track time

15:25	Nicola Greenfield	21 Mar 87
15:44	Sarah Bennett	1 Mar 92

UK CLUB RECORDS

MEN

Seniors

4 x 100m	39.49	Haringey	1 Jun 91
4 x 200m	1:23.5	Team Solent	19 Jul 87
4 x 400m	3:04.48	Team Solent	29 Jun 90
1600m Medley	3:20.8	Wolverhampton & Bilston	1 Jun 75
4 x 800m	7:24.4*	North Staffs and Stone	27 Jul 65
4 x 1500m	15:12.6	Bristol	5 Aug 75

* = 4 x 880y time less 2.8sec

Under 20

4 x 100m	41.30	Victoria Park	14 Aug 76
4 x 200m	1:27.6	Enfield	13 Jun 82
4 x 400m	3:15.3	Enfield	5 Sep 82
1600m Medley	3:31.6	Cardiff	14 Aug 71
4 x 800m	7:35.3	Liverpool H	14 Aug 90
4 x 1500m	16:04.3	Blackburn	15 Sep 79
4 x 110H	1:04.8	Oundle Sch	19 May 79

Under 17

4 x 100m	42.22	Thames V H	24 Jun 89
4 x 200m	1:31.2	Herc Wimb	12 Jul 78
4 x 400m	3:23.1 o	Enfield	1 Oct 80
	3:23.2	Haringey	26 Jul 88
1600m Medley	3:36.1	Thurrock	13 Jun 84
4 x 800m	7:52.1	Clydebank	29 Aug 87
4 x 1500m	16:27.0	Liverpool H	14 Sep 88

Under 15

4 x 100m	44.62	Sale	29 Aug 93
4 x 200m	1:36.9	Belgrave	19 Sep 93
4 x 400m	3:31.5o?	Ayr Seaforth	5 Sep 82
	3:31.6	Shaftesbury B	26 Jul 88
1600m Medley	3:48.4	Blackheath	28 Sep 86
4 x 800m	8:13.28o?	Clydebank	2 Sep 89
	8:16.8	Shaftesbury B	14Sep 88
4 x 1500m	17:52.4 o	Stretford	22 Oct 85
	18:18.4	Tonbridge	6 Jul 80

Under 13

4 x 100m	50.32	Shaftesbury B	5 Sep 99
4 x 200m	1:49.7	Braintree	29 Aug 94
4 x 400m	4:04.5	Blackheath	12 Sep 93
1600m Medley	4:13.7	Blackheath	28 Sep 86
4 x 800m	9:29.8	Sale	28 Jun 88

WOMEN

Seniors

4 x 100m	43.79	Hounslow	18 Sep 82
4 x 200m	1:35.15	Stretford	14 Jul 91
4 x 400m	3:31.62	Essex Ladies	31 May 92
1600m Medley	3:50.6	Coventry Godiva	5 May 84
3 x 800m	6:32.4	Cambridge H	29 Jun 74
4 x 800m	8:41.0	Cambridge H	26 May 75

Under 20

4 x 100m	46.80	Birchfield	26 Sep 98
4 x 200m	1:46.4	Millfield School	11 May 00
4 x 400m	3:51.6	Birchfield	23 Aug 98
	3:51.67	Sale Harriers	23 Sep 89
3 x 800m	7:33.2	Essex Ladies	12 Jun 94

Under 17

4 x 100m	47.52o	Hounslow	2 Oct 82
	47.8	B of Enfield	20 Jul 75
	47.8	Croydon	15 Sep 82
	48.08	Wigan & D	6 Sep 92
4 x 200m	1:42.2	London Oly.	19 Aug 72
4 x 400m	3:52.1	City of Hull	3 Jul 82
1600m Medley	4:07.8	Warrington	14 Aug 75
3 x 800m	6:46.5	Haslemere	15 Sep 79
	6:46.5	Bromley L	1 Jul 84
4 x 800m	8:53.1	Havering	24 May 80

Under 15

4 x 100m	48.5	Haringey	15 Sep 79
	49.08	Radley L	16 Jul 83
4 x 200m	1:44.0	Bristol	15 Sep 79
3 x 800m	6:39.8	Havering	13 Sep 78
4 x 800m	9:21.4	Sale	5 Aug 78

Under 13

4 x 100m	53.09	Wigan	5 Sep 99
4 x 200m	1:52.5	Mitcham	24 Jul 82
3 x 800m	7:18.0	Mid Hants	14 Sep 83
4 x 800m	10:02.4	Warrington	16 Sep 75

o overage by current rules

AAA INDOOR CHAMPIONSHIPS & NORWICH UNION WORLD INDOOR TRIALS

Birmingham 27 - 28 January 2001

Daniel Caines' win in the 400m in 45.75 was the leading performance and instantly installed him as favourite for the World Indoor Championships. The other notable performance in the men's events, John Skeete's win in the 60m was nullified by a positive drugs test. Catherine Murphy scored a fine double with two Welsh records in the 200 and 400.

MEN

60 Metres (27 Jan)
1. Christian Malcolm 6.72
2. Jason Livingston 6.72
3. Daniel Money 6.74
4. Jonathan Oparka 6.78
5. Tim Benjamin 6.78

(1) John Skeete dsq drg (6.59)

200 Metres (28 Jan)
1. Allyn Condon 20.60
2. Doug Turner 20.93
3. Tim Benjamin 21.11
4. Jamie Baulch 21.26

dns Christian Malcolm

400 Metres (28 Jan)
1. Daniel Caines 45.75
2. Mark Hylton 46.24
3. Matthew Elias 46.91
4. Mark Brown 47.21
5. Paul Slythe 47.65
6. Adam Buckley 48.63

800 Metres (28 Jan)
1. Eddie King 1:49.98
2. Andy Hart 1:50.10
3. Neil Speaight 1:50.19
4. Matthew Shone 1:50.49
5. Tom Lerwill 1:51.11
6. Noel Edwards 2:01.86

1500 Metres (27 Jan)
1. Angus MacLean 3:48.02
2. Michael Skinner 3:48.03
3. Simon Lees 3:48.68
4. Steve Sharp 3:49.18
5. James Bowler 3:49.35
6. Richard Ward 3:50.77

3000 Metres (28 Jan)
1. Mark Miles 8:19.89
2. Rob Whalley 8:20.36
3. Andrew Graffin 8:20.94
4. Ian Grime 8:21.23
5. Steven Body 8:22.99
6. Martin Yelling 8:23.21

60 Metres Hurdles (28 Jan)
1. Dominic Bradley 7.84

2= Chris Baillie 7.94

2= Dominic Girdler 7.94

4. Neil Owen 7.97
5. Duncan Malins 8.02
6. Nathan Palmer 8.03

High Jump (28 Jan)
1. Samson Oni 2.20
2. Robert Mitchell 2.15
3. Stuart Ohrland 2.05
4. Luke Crawley 2.05

Pole Vault (27 Jan)
1. Tim Thomas 5.35
2. Mark Davis 5.10
3. Ian Tullett 5.00
4. Christian North 5.00

5= Christian Linskey 4.80

5= Scott Simpson 4.80

Long Jump (28 Jan)
1. Chris Tomlinson 7.41
2. Julian Flynn 7.14
3. Mark Awanah 7.03
4. Leigh Smith 7.04
5. Essop Merrick 6.90
6. Levi Edwards 6.89

Triple Jump (27 Jan)
1. Julian Golley 16.22
2. Tosin Oke 16.08
3. Gable Garenamotse BOT 15.92
4. Nicholas Thomas 15.87
5. John Hilton 14.97
6. Martin Rossiter 14.91

Shot (27 Jan)
1. Emeka Udechuku 18.19
2. Lee Newman 17.58
3. Erik van Vreumingen NED 17.23
4. Steve Whyte 16.71
5. Gary Sollitt 16.40
6. David Condon 16.22

3000 Metres Walk (27 Jan)
1. Robert Heffernan IRL 11:19.27
2. Andi Drake 12:02.24
3. Jamie Costin IRL 12:07:05
4. Colin Griffin IRL 12:07.94
5. Matthew Hales 12:08.57
6. Patrick Ryan IRL 12:36.79

Heptathlon (Birmingham 20 Jan)
1. John Heanley 5148
2. Dominic Shepherd 5116
3. Ben Roberts 5036
4. Anthony Sawyer 5023
5. Gavin Fordham 4829
6. Paul Gilding 4631

WOMEN

60 Metres (27 Jan)
1. Marcia Richardson 7.28
2. Diane Allahgreen 7.32
3. Christine Bloomfield 7.38
4. Abiodun Oyepitan 7.40
5. Donita Benjamin 7.46
6. Amanda Forrester 7.48

200 Metres (28 Jan)
1. Catherine Murphy 23.35
2. Emily Freeman 23.77
3. Ciara Sheehy IRL 23.95
4. Sam Davies 24.19

dns Donna Fraser

400 Metres (27 Jan)
1. Catherine Murphy 52.31
2. Sinead Dudgeon 52.47
3. Karen Gear 53.71
4. Heather Brookes 55.61
5. Kathryn Sage 55.64
6. Tracey Duncan 55.74

800 Metres (28 Jan)
1. Kelly Holmes 2:05.26
2. Jo Fenn 2:06:02
3. Jeina Mitchell 2:06.86
4. Sarah Knights 2:08.22
5. Alex Carter 2:08.85
6. Celia Brown 2:10.82

1500 Metres (27 Jan)
1. Freda Davoren IRL 4:19.85
2. Zoe Jelbert 4:23.16
3. Hayley Parkinson-Ovens 4:24.06
4. Maria Sharp 4:25.60
5. Pauline Thom 4:25.94
6. Danielle Thornal 4:26.00

3000 Metres (27 Jan)
1. Maria Lynch IRL 9:35.92
2. Emma Ford 9:42.42
3. Jilly Ingman 9:44.36
4. Sarah Bull 9:54.74

60 Metres Hurdles (28 Jan)

1.	Melanie Wilkins		8.20
2.	Sarah Claxton		8.28
3.	Bianca Liston		8.38
4.	Julie Pratt		8.44
5.	Derval O`Rourke	IRL	8.53
6.	Clova Court		8.55

High Jump (27 Jan)

1.	Susan Jones		1.85
2.	Wanita May	CAN	1.85
3.	Gillian Black		1.70
4=	Stephanie Higham		1.65
4=	Gayle O`Connor		1.65
6.	Antonia Bemrose		1.65

Pole Vault (28 Jan)

1.	Janine Whitlock		4.05
2.	Clare Ridgley		3.50
3.	Hilary Smith		3.50
4=	Irie Hill		3.50
4=	Lindsay Hodges		3.50
4=	Larissa Lowe		3.50

Long Jump (28 Jan)

1.	Ann Danson		5.97
2.	Kelly Sotherton		5.94
3.	Kimberley Rothman		5.82
4.	Debbie Harrison		5.80
5.	Ruth Irving		5.79
6.	Sarah Wellstead		5.74

Triple Jump (27 Jan)

1.	Michelle Griffith		13.25
2.	Liz Patrick		12.57
3.	T. Robinson-Scanlon	JAM	12.42
4.	Rebecca White		12.39
5.	Anna-Maria Thorpe		12.23
6.	Jodie Hurst		12.10

Shot (28 Jan)

1.	Lieja Koeman	NED	17.26
2.	Julie Dunkley		15.47
3.	Philippa Roles		15.18
4.	Joanne Duncan		15.17
5.	Maggie Lynes		15.08
6.	Eleanor Gatrell		14.24

3000 Metres Walk (27 Jan)

1.	Gillian O`Sullivan	IRL	12:23.45
2.	Sharon Tonks		14:02.55
3.	Niobe Menendez		14:04.49
4.	Kath Horwill		14:47.59

Pentathlon (Birmingham 20 Jan)

1.	Kelly Sotherton		4116
2.	Kerry Jury		4063
3.	Nicola Gautier		3989
4.	Fiona Harrison		3827
5.	Laura Curtis		3587
6.	Hannah Stares		3475

NORWICH UNION AAA INDOOR JUNIOR CHAMPIONSHIPS

Birmingham 24 - 25 February 2001

There were a host of excellent performances at these championships - Tim Benjamin 20.78 for 200m, Edward Dunford after winning the pentathlon in January, won the U17 hurdles together with two seconds and a third. Julian Thomas won both U15 sprints with a tremendous time in 200m. For the women, Amy Spencer won both U17 sprints, she won both U15 titles last year. Heather Jones broke Katherine Merry's record in the heats of the U15 60 Hurdles.

MEN	Under 20		Under 17			Under 15		
60	Mark Lewis-Francis	6.67	Matthew Ouche		6.99	Julian Thomas		7.37
200	Tim Benjamin	20.78	Rikki Fifton		22.21	Julian Thomas		22.74
400	Adam Rogers	48.11	Richard Davenport		49.49	Craig Glanville		51.38
800	Andy Fulford	1:55.52	Richard Dowse		1:58.59	Alex Felce		2:03.88
1500	Richard Ward	4:01.07	David Ward	IRL	4:13.54			
3000	Richard Ward	8:27.53	Ahmed Ali		8:58.74			
60H	Dominic Girdler	7.99	Edward Dunford		8.07	Richard Alexis-Smith		8.28
HJ	Chuka Enih-Snell	2.14	Martyn Bernard		1.95	Alan Hassall		1.79
PV	Daniel Broadhead	4.50	Chris Tremayne		4.40	Nathan Lawton		3.20
LJ	Thomas Roe	6.88	Onen Eyong		6.78	Paul Twidale		6.00
TJ	Kevin Thompson	14.36	Gary White		13.72			
SP	Greg Beard	16.10	Eoin Leen	IRL	18.25	Chris Gearing		14.73
3kW	Lloyd Finch	12:30.97						
Hept	Alex Zulewski	4700	Edward Dunford (Pent)		3710	Ryan Shaw (Pent)		2815

WOMEN	Under 20			Under 17		Under 15		
60	Danielle Norville		7.54	Amy Spencer	7.54	Sinead Johnson		7.74
200	Vernicha James		23.80	Amy Spencer	24.14	Nicola Gossman		24.81
400	Lesley Clarkson		56.39	Gemma Nicol (300)	39.97			
800	Rebecca Lyne		2:10.67	Rachael Thompson	2:12.53	Clara Durkan	IRL	2:17.66
1500	Jo Ankier		4:31.79	Dani Barnes	4:33.73			
3000	Zoe Jelbert		9:48.55					
60H	Lauren McLoughlin		8.61	Symone Belle	8.52	Heather Jones		8.85
HJ	Deidre Ryan	IRL	1.81	Rebecka Bell	1.70	Steph Pywell		1.67
PV	Lindsay Hodges		3.66	Natalie Olson	3.25			
LJ	Danielle Humphreys		5.78	Symone Belle	5.71	Stephanie Madgett		5.17
TJ	Rachel Peacock		12.01	Emily Parker	12.01			
SP	Charlotte Spelzini		13.10	Frances Miller	12.80	Chloe Edwards		12.45
3kW	Nicola Phillips		14:49.40					
Pent	Rebecca Jones		3592	Hollie Lundgren	3101	Caroline Smith		2556

Hept & Pent Birmingham 20/21 Jan

CZE v ESP v FRA v GB & NI v NED Combined Indoors

Prague, CZE 27 - 28 January 2001

MEN – Heptathlon

1.	Lionel Marceny	CZE	5763
6.	**Jamie Quarry**		**5602**
9.	**Barry Thomas**		**5472**
15.	**Paul Jones**		**5360**
16.	**Dominic Shepherd**		**5027**

Team Score

1.	France	17170
2.	Spain	16789
3.	**Great Britain & NI**	**16434**

WOMEN – Pentathlon

1.	**Julie Hollman**	**4392**
7.	**Nicola Gautier**	**4010**
13.	**Kerry Jury**	**3772**

Team Score

1.	**Great Britain & NI**	**12174**
2.	Netherlands	12127
3.	Czech Republic	12113

FRA v GB & NI v GER U23 & U20 Combined Indoors

Nogent-sur-Oise, FRA 24 - 25 February 2001

MEN U23 – Heptathlon

1.	Romain Barras	FRA	5560
4.	**John Heanley**		**5311**
6.	**Anthony Sawyer**		**4871**
	Ben Roberts		**dnf**

MEN U20 – Heptathlon

1.	Nadir El Fassi	FRA	5567
4.	**Alex Zulewski**		**4614**
6.	**Paul Tohill**		**4475**
7.	**Louis Evling-Jones**		**4317**

WOMEN U23 – Pentathlon

1.	Katja Keller	GER	4208
5.	**Fiona Harrison**		**3967**
8.	**Laura Curtis**		**3654**
10.	**Kate Brewington**		**3441**

WOMEN U20 – Pentathlon

1.	Antonia Schulze-Borges	GER	4210
3.	**Rebecca Jones**		**3714**
9.	**Hannah Barnes**		**3198**
10.	**Natalie Hulse**		**3163**

FRA v GB & NI v GER v ITA U20 Indoors

Vittel, FRA 3 March 2001

MEN

60 Metres A Race 1

1.	Ronald Pognon	FRA	6.73
2.	**Dwayne Grant**		**6.83**

60 Metres A Race 2

1.	**Dwayne Grant**		**6.79**

60 Metres B Race 1

1.	Martial Kanga	FRA	6.92
3.	**Laurence Oboh**		**6.98**

60 Metres B Race 2

1.	Michael Pfaff	GER	6.91
2.	**Laurence Oboh**		**6.92**

200 Metres A

1.	Sebastien Ernst	GER	21.99
3.	**Tyrone Edgar**		**22.94**

200 Metres B

1.	**Tim Benjamin**		**21.52**

400 Metres A

1.	Cesar Boileau	FRA	49.62
3.	**Adam Rogers**		**51.42**

400 Metres B

1.	Steffen Sattelmaier	GER	49.32
2.	**Robert Tobin**		**49.52**

800 Metres

1.	Rene Herms	GER	1:56.08
2.	**Andrew Fulford**		**1:56.80**
4.	**James Nusrat**		**1:56.97**

1500 Metres

1.	Martin Uhlich	GER	4:00.17
2.	**Richard Ward**		**4:01.04**
4.	**Ricky Soos**		**4:03.20**

60 Metres Hurdles A Race 1

1.	**Nathan Palmer**		**8.19**

60 Metres Hurdles B Race 1

1.	**Dominic Girdler**		**8.02**

60 Metres Hurdles Race 2

1.	**Nathan Palmer**		**8.06**
2.	**Dominic Girdler**		**8.07**

High Jump

1.	Mathias Cianci	FRA	2.15
5.	**Chuka Enih-Snell**		**2.08**
7.	**Darryl Stone**		**2.04**

Pole Vault

1.	Dennis Leyckes	GER	5.20
6.	**Alan Jervis**		**4.40**
7.	**Daniel Broadhead**		**4.40**

Long Jump

1.	Mickael Hanany	FRA	7.42
6.	**Thomas Roe**		**7.03**
8.	**Onen Eyong**		**6.65**

Triple Jump

1.	Davy Manga	FRA	15.50
7.	**Lewis Cheung**		**14.60**
8.	**Kevin Thompson**		**14.59**

Shot

1.	Martin Geske	GER	16.40
2.	**Greg Beard**		**16.38**
7.	**Derrick Squire**		**13.72**

5000 Metres Walk
1. Paul Gassebner ITA 21:05.31
6. Cameron Smith 23:31.82
dsqLloyd Finch

WOMEN
60 Metres A Race 1
1. Katchi Habel GER 7.38
3. Danielle Norville 7.59

60 Metres A Race 2
1. Katchi Hable GER 7.33
3. Danielle Norville 7.59

60 Metres B Race 1
1. Karen Oughton 7.71

60 Metres B Race 2
1. Cecile Sellier FRA 7.68
2. Karen Oughton 7.71

200 Metres A
1. Amy Spencer 24.30

200 Metres B
1. Lisa Miller 24.87

400 Metres A
1. Ursula Ellecosta ITA 55.77
4. Lesley Clarkson 58.86

400 Metres B
1. Eileen Muller GER 56.62
3. Gaby Howell 58.00

800 Metres
1. Janina Goldfuss GER 2:09.62
2. Rebecca Lyne 2:10.92
3. Jemma Simpson 2:11.46

4 x 400 Metres
1. Germany 3:18.40
3. Great Britain & NI 3:20.57
Tobin, Aplin, Brackstone, Rogers

1500 Metres
1. Kerstin Werner GER 4:29.03
3. Zoe Jelbert 4:34.34
4. Jo Ankier 4:34.54

60 Metres Hurdles A Race 1
1. Nadine Hentschke GER 8.28
2. Lauren McLoughlin 8.58

60 Metres Hurdles A Race 2
1. Nadine Hentschke GER 8.36
3. Lauren McLoughlin 8.60

60 Metres Hurdles B Race 1
1. Micol Cattaneo ITA 8.52
4. Gemma Ferguson 9.00

60 Metres Hurdles B Race 2
1. Marie Dia FRA 8.55
3. Gemma Ferguson 8.82

High Jump
1. Kathryn Holinski GER 1.88
6. Rebecca Jones 1.72
7= Stephanie Higham 1.72

Pole Vault
1. Floe Kuhnert GER 4.10
5= Lindsay Hodges 3.60
8. Kate Dennison 3.30

Match Result Men
1. Germany 154
2. France 135
3. Great Britain & NI 128
4. Italy 103

Long Jump
1. Valeria Canella ITA 6.08
4. Symone Belle 6.01
8. Danielle Humphries 5.51

Triple Jump
1. Simona La Mantia ITA 13.30
7. Rachel Peacock 11.59
8. Emily Parker 10.98

Shot
1. Claudia Villeneuve FRA 15.53
6. Charlotte Spelzini 12.97
7. Rebecca Peake 12.96

3000 Metres Walk
1. Melissa Rodriguez FRA 13:44.42
5. Sophie Hales 14:38.18
7. Nicola Phillips 14:49.40

4 x 400 Metres
1. Germany 3:46.18
3. Great Britain & NI 3:51.82
Howell, Smellie, Singer, Clarkson

Match Result Women
1. Germany 166
2. France 135
3. Italy 112.5
4. Great Britain & NI 108.5

GB & NI v FRA U23 Indoors
Cardiff 10 March 2001

MEN
60 Metres
1. Darren Chinn 6.80
4. John Oparka 6.82

200 Metres
1. Daniel Abdenzoar-Foule FRA 21.5
3. Luke Davies 22.3
4. Henry Richards 22.7

400 Metres
1. Adam Buckley 48.08
3. Steve Surety 49.39

800 Metres
1. Simon Lees 1:52.9
3. Dave Moulton 1:55.0

1500 Metres
1. Sebastian Cosson FRA 3:44.40
2. James Bowler 3:45.24
4. Michael Skinner 3:53.78

60 Metres Hurdles
1. Cedric Lavanne FRA 7.80
2. Chris Baillie 8.00
dnf Robert Newton

High Jump
1. Gregory Cabella FRA 2.20
3. Samson Oni 2.20
4. Robert Mitchell 2.17

Pole Vault
1. Charles Peuf-Pierre FRA 5.20
3. Scott Simpson 5.10
4. Ashley Swain 4.80

Long Jump
1. Yann Domenech FRA 7.82
2. Chris Tomlinson 7.37
4. John Heanley 6.94

Triple Jump
1. Tosin Oke 15.76
3. Steven Shalders 15.11

Shot
1. Emeka Udechuku 17.69
3. Lyndon Woodward 16.25

3000 Metres Walk
1. Mickael Rousseau FRA 12:16.3
2. Lloyd Finch 12:26.0
dnf Dominic King

4 x 400 Metres
1. Great Britain & NI 3:14.50
(Buckley, ?, ?, ?)

WOMEN

60 Metres

1.	Celine Thelamon	FRA	7.50
2.	**Katherine Endacott**		**7.52**
3.	**Susan Burnside**		**7.55**

200 Metres

1.	Fanny Gerance	FRA	24.27
2.	**Emma Whitter**		**24.34**
3.	**Helen Roscoe**		**25.20**

400 Metres

1.	**Helen Thieme**		**54.20**
3.	**Heather Brookes**		**56.85**

800 Metres

1.	**Amanda Pritchard**		**2:08.72**
4.	**Karen Johns**		**2:13.06**

1500 Metres

1.	Karine Senejoux	FRA	4:29.59
3.	**Sonia Thomas**		**4:35.59**
4.	**Karen Montador**		**4:35.83**

60 Metres Hurdles

1.	Joanna Bujak	FRA	8.39
3.	**Fiona Harrison**		**8.68**
4.	**Tamsin Stephens**		**8.75**

High Jump

1.	Christelle Preau	FRA	1.78
2.	**Gillian Black**		**1.72**
4.	**Judith Payne**		**1.69**

Pole Vault

1.	Emile Becot	FRA	3.80
3.	**Sonia Lawrence**		**3.70**
4.	**Laura Patterson**		**3.60**

Long Jump

1.	**Sarah Wellstead**		**5.84**
3.	**Joanna Trotman**		**5.63**

Triple Jump

1.	Amy Zingo	FRA	13.44
2.	**Rebecca White**		**12.70**
4.	**Charmaine Turner**		**11.64**

Shot

1.	**Eva Massey**		**14.47**
4.	**Kara Nwidobe**		**12.67**

4 x 400 Metres

1. Great Britain & NI 3:43.56
(Brooks, Pritchard, Meadows,Thieme)

Match Result

1.	France	135
2.	**Great Britain & NI**	**113**

8th IAAF WORLD INDOOR CHAMPIONSHIPS

Lisbon, POR 9 - 11 March 2001

Jonathan Edwards started the championships with a silver medal before the opening ceremony in an exciting triple jump which showed that the attempt to downgrade the field events was badly thought out. Christian Malcolm ran a good race for 2nd from the outside lane and Mark Lewis-Francis showed great form for his bronze. The star for Britain was Daniel Caines - he took control of every race and was a worthy world champion, it was a great pity his season effectively ended here.

MEN

60 Metres (11 Mar)

1.	Tim Harden	USA	6.44
2.	Tim Montgomery	USA	6.46
3.	**Mark Lewis-Francis**		**6.51**
	(1h8 6.61, 2s1 6.56)		
4.	Freddy Mayola	CUB	6.55
5.	Matthew Shirvington	AUS	6.55
6.	Tim Goebel	GER	6.59
3h2	**Christian Malcolm**		**6.77**

200 Metres (10 Mar)

1.	Shawn Crawford	USA	20.63
2.	**Christian Malcolm**		**20.76**
	(1h6 21.05, 1s1 20.76)		
3.	Patrick van Balkom	NED	20.96
4.	Christopher Williams	JAM	21.12
5.	**Allyn Condon**		**21.69**
	(2h1 20.93, 2s2 21.12)		
dns	Kevin Little	USA	

400 Metres (11 Mar)

1.	**Daniel Caines**		**46.40**
	(1h2 46.65, 1s1 46.43)		
2.	Milton Campbell	USA	46.45
3.	Danny McFarlane	JAM	46.74
4.	David Canal	ESP	46.99
5.	**Mark Hylton**		**47.03**
	(1h1 46.79, 2s2 46.87)		
dnf	James Davis	USA	

800 Metres (11 Mar)

1.	Yuriy Borzakovskiy	RUS	1:44.49
2.	Johan Botha	RSA	1:46.42
3.	Andre Bucher	SUI	1:46.46
4.	David Lelei	KEN	1:46.88
5.	Glode Duby	BOT	1:46.90
6.	Pawel Czapiewski	POL	1:50.51

1500 Metres (10 Mar)

1.	Rui Silva	POR	3:51.06
2.	Reyes Estevez	ESP	3:51.24
3.	Noah Ngeny	KEN	3:51.63
4.	Laban Rotich	KEN	3:51.71
5.	Adil Kaouch	MAR	3:51.91
6.	Seneca Lassiter	USA	3:52.39

3000 Metres (11 Mar)

1.	Hicham El Guerrouj	MAR	7:37.74
2.	Mohammed Mourhit	BEL	7:38.94
3.	Alberto Garcia	ESP	7:39.96
4.	**John Mayock**		**7:44.08**
	(6h2 7:51.10)		
5.	Million Wolde	ETH	7:44.54
6.	Bernard Lagat	KEN	7:45.52

60 Metres Hurdles (9 Mar)

1.	Terrence Trammell	USA	7.51
2.	Anier Garcia	CUB	7.54
3.	Shaun Bownes	RSA	7.55
4.	Robert Kronberg	SWE	7.57
5.	Yoel Hernandez	CUB	7.58
6.	Elmar Lichtenegger	AUT	7.65

High Jump (11 Mar)

1.	Stefan Holm	SWE	2.32
2.	Andrey Sokolovskiy	UKR	2.29
3.	Staffan Strand	SWE	2.29
4.	Nathan Leeper	USA	2.29
5=	Javier Sotomayor	CUB	2.25
5=	Martin Buss	GER	2.25

Pole Vault (10 Mar)

1.	Lawrence Johnson	USA	5.95
2.	Tye Harvey	USA	5.90
3.	Romain Mesnil	FRA	5.85
4.	Aleksandr Averbukh	ISR	5.70
5.	Pavel Gerasimov	RUS	5.70
6.	Okkert Brits	RSA	5.60

Long Jump (11 Mar)

1.	Ivan Pedroso	CUB	8.43
2.	Kareen Streete-Thompson	CAY	8.16
3.	Carlos Calado	POR	8.16
4.	Peter Burge	AUS	8.11
5.	Melvin Lister	USA	8.10
6.	Kevin Dilworth	USA	7.97

Triple Jump (9 Mar)

1.	Paolo Camossi	ITA	17.32
2.	**Jonathan Edwards**		**17.26**
3.	Andrew Murphy	AUS	17.20
4.	Charles Friedek	GER	17.13
5.	Rostislav Dimitrov	BUL	16.91
6.	Fabrizio Donato	ITA	16.77

Shot (9 Mar)

1.	John Godina	USA	20.82
2.	Adam Nelson	USA	20.72
3.	Manuel Martinez	ESP	20.67
4.	Timo Aaltonen	FIN	20.24
5.	Paolo Dal Soglio	ITA	20.17
6.	Miroslav Menc	CZE	20.08

WOMEN

60 Metres (11 Mar)

1.	Chandra Sturrup	BAH	7.05
2.	Angela Williams	USA	7.09
3.	Chryste Gaines	USA	7.12
4.	Sevatheda Fynes	BAH	7.15
5.	Mercy Nku	NGR	7.15
6.	Petya Pendareva	BUL	7.16

200 Metres (10 Mar)

1.	Juliet Campbell	JAM	22.64
2.	LaTasha Jenkins	USA	22.96
3.	Natalya Safronnikova	BLR	23.17
4.	Susanthika Jayasinghe	SRI	23.24
5.	Muriel Hurtis	FRA	23.63
6.	Alenka Bikar	SLO	23.74

400 Metres (11 Mar)

1.	Sandie Richards	JAM	51.04
2.	Olga Kotlyarova	RUS	51.56
3.	Olesya Zykina	RUS	51.71
4.	Nadjina Kaltouma	CHA	52.49
5.	Monique Hennagan	USA	52.83
6.	Suziann Reid	USA	71.50
4s1	**Catherine Murphy (1h3 52.61)**		**52.45**

800 Metres (11 Mar)

1.	Maria Mutola	MOZ	1:59.74
2.	Stephanie Graf	AUT	1:59.78
3.	Helena Fuchsova	CZE	2:01.18
4.	Lwiza John	TAN	2:01.76
5.	Yelena Afanasyeva	RUS	2:02.17
6.	Jolanda Ceplak	SLO	2:02.67
4h2	**Joanne Fenn**		**2:05.16**

Heptathlon (10/11 Mar)

1.	Roman Sebrle	CZE	6420
2.	Jon Arnar Magnusson	ISL	6233
3.	Lev Lobodin	RUS	6202
4.	Stephen Moore	USA	6132
5.	Erki Nool	EST	6074
6.	Aleksandr Yurkov	UKR	6059

1500 Metres (11 Mar)

1.	Hasna Benhassi	MAR	4:10.83
2.	Violeta Szekely	ROM	4:11.17
3.	Natalya Gorelova	RUS	4:11.74
4.	Carla Sacramento	POR	4:11.76
5.	Daniela Yordanova	BUL	4:12.79
6.	Alesya Turova	BLR	4:13.67

3000 Metres (10 Mar)

1.	Olga Yegorova	RUS	8:37.48
2.	Gabriela Szabo	ROM	8:39.65
3.	Yelena Zadorozhnaya	RUS	8:40.15
4.	Marta Dominguez	ESP	8:40.98
5.	Dong Yanmei	CHN	8:41.34
6.	Benita Willis	AUS	8:42.75
8.	**Hayley Parry-Tullett (5h1 9:02.33)**		**8:45.36**
11.	**Kathy Butler (6h2 8:58.60)**		**9:04.81**

60 Metres Hurdles (9 Mar)

1.	Anjanette Kirkland	USA	7.85
2.	Michelle Freeman	JAM	7.92
3.	Nicole Ramalalanirina	FRA	7.96
4.	Olga Shishigina	KAZ	7.96
5.	Svetlana Laukhova	RUS	7.99
6.	Linda Ferga	FRA	8.06
8s2	**Melanie Wilkins (4h2 8.19)**		**8.30**

High Jump (9 Mar)

1.	Kajsa Berqvist	SWE	2.00
2.	Inga Babakova	UKR	2.00
3.	Venelina Veneva	BUL	1.96
4.	Amy Acuff	USA	1.96
5=	Dora Gyorffy	HUN	1.93
5=	Viktoriya Palamar	UKR	1.93

Pole Vault (10 Mar)

1.	Pavla Hamackova	CZE	4.56
2=	Svetlana Feofanova	RUS	4.51
2=	Kellie Suttle	USA	4.51
4.	Stacy Dragila	USA	4.51
5.	Tanya Koleva	BUL	4.35
6.	Yvonne Buschbaum	GER	4.25

4 x 400 Metres (11 Mar)

1.	Poland	3:04.47
2.	United States	3:04.64
3.	Russia	3:04.82
4.	Jamaica	3:05.45
5.	Great Britain & NI (Hylton, Thorne-Ladejo, Elias, Caines)	3:09.21
3h1	**(Elias, Slythe, Brown, Thorne-Ladejo)**	**3:07.57**
6.	Nigeria	3:16.53

Long Jump (11 Mar)

1.	Dawn Burrell	USA	7.03
2.	Tatyana Kotova	RUS	6.98
3.	Niurka Montalvo	ESP	6.88
4.	Fiona May	ITA	6.87
5.	Heike Drechsler	GER	6.75
6.	Lyudmila Galkina	RUS	6.71

Triple Jump (9 Mar)

1.	Tereza Marinova	BUL	14.91
2.	Tatyana Lebedeva	RUS	14.85
3.	Tiombe Hurd	USA	14.19
4.	Olga Bolshova	MDA	14.17
5.	Oksana Rogova	RUS	14.17
6.	Cristina Nicolau	ROM	14.05

Shot (9 Mar)

1.	Larisa Peleshenko	RUS	19.84
2.	Nadezhda Ostapchuk	BLR	19.24
3.	Svetlana Krivelyova	RUS	19.18
4.	Nadine Kleinert-Schmitt	GER	18.87
5.	Yumileidi Cumba	CUB	18.61
6.	Katarzyna Zakowicz	POL	18.59

Pentathlon (9 Mar)

1.	Natalya Sazanovich	BLR	4850
2.	Yelena Prokhorova	RUS	4711
3.	Karin Specht-Ertl	GER	4678
4.	Natalya Roshchupkina	RUS	4664
5.	Sabine Braun	GER	4646
6.	Anzhela Kinet	TUR	4558

4 x 400 Metres (11 Mar)

1.	Russia	3:30.00
2.	Jamaica	3:30.79
3.	Germany	3:31.00
4.	United States	3:32.76

Regional Cross Country Championships

Scotland

Irvine 24 February 2001

MEN

1. Chris Robison 38:49

WOMEN

1. Ellen Leggate 30:30

Wales

Heath Park, Cardiff 25 February 2001

MEN

1. Christian Stephenson 38:06

WOMEN

1. Catherine Dugdale 22:49

Northern Ireland

Cancelled due to foot and mouth

Norwich Union International
GB & NI v RUS v Scandinavia v All Stars v GB Lions Indoors
Glasgow 18 March 2001

This was very much an 'end of season' meeting with one exception - Hayley Tullett broke Zola Budd's long standing record in the 1500 metres, finishing second to Gorelova in 4:06.75. The medallists from the World Championships all performed well.

MEN

60 Metres
1. Greg Saddler AS/USA 6.60
2. Mark Lewis-Francis GBL 6.62
3. Christian Malcolm 6.65

200 Metres
1. Christian Malcolm 20.99
2. Tim Benjamin AS 21.06
3. Allyn Condon GBL 21.40

400 Metres
1. Daniel Caines 46.21
4. Paul Slythe GBL 47.60

800 Metres
1. Yuriy Borzakovskiy RUS 1:47.50
4. Neil Speaight 1:49.70
5. Simon Lees GBL 1:49.80

1500 Metres
1. John Mayock 3:44.84
5. Jon McCallum GBL 3:51.53

60 Metres Hurdles
1. Yuriy Pechonkin RUS 7.53
4. Dominic Bradley 7.95
5. Neil Owen GBL 8.16

Triple Jump
1. Jonathan Edwards 17.19
5. Julian Golley GBL 15.60

Shot
1. Adam Nelson AS/USA 20.20
4. Lee Newman GBL 17.08
5. Emeka Udechuku 16.66

4 x 400 Metres
1. Russia 3:06.02
3. Great Britain & NI 3:10.04
(Condon, Slythe, Jennings, Caines)
5. Great Britain Lions 3:16.27
(Middleton, Baird, Martin, Buckley)

WOMEN

60 Metres
1. Marina Kislova RUS 7.17
3. Marcia Richardson 7.36
4. Donita Benjamin GBL 7.56

200 Metres
1. Juliet Campbell AS/JAM 23.12
2. Donna Fraser 24.11
3. Ellena Ruddock GBL 24.33

400 Metres
1. Olga Kotlyarova RUS 51.54
3. Catherine Murphy 52.49
4. Helen Thieme GBL 54.42

800 Metres
1. Stephanie Graf AS/AUT 2:01.09
3. Jo Fenn 2:04.44
4. Jeina Mitchell GBL 2:07.31

1500 Metres
1. Natalya Gorelova RUS 4:05.48
2. Hayley Tullett 4:06.75
4. Hayley Parkinson-Ovens GBL 4:24.82

60 Metres Hurdles
1. Svetlana Laukhova RUS 8.00
2. Melanie Wilkins 8.15
4. Rachel King GBL 8.48

High Jump
1. Kajsa Bergqvist SCA/SWE 1.97
4. Aileen Wilson 1.75
5. Gillian Black GBL 1.70

Pole Vault
1. Svetlana Feofanova RUS 4.56
3. Janine Whitlock 4.05
5. Lindsay Hodges GBL 3.50

Long Jump
1. Lyudmila Galkina RUS 6.81
3. Julie Hollman 6.18
4. Ann Danson GBL 6.11

4 x 400 Metres
1. Russia 3:30.32
3. Great Britain & NI 3:40.51
(Thieme, Dudgeon, Murphy, Fraser)
4. Great Britain Lions 3:41.51
(Symonds, Mitchell, Sage, Meadows)

Match Result
1. Russia 76
2. All Stars 75
3. Great Britain & NI 62
4. Scandinavia 36
5. Great Britain Lions 36

REEBOK CAU INTER-COUNTIES CHAMPIONSHIPS & WORLD TRIALS
Nottingham 10 February 2001

Most of the favourites performed well with Mohamed Farah adding the Under 20 title to the Under 17 and Under 15 titles he had won in previous years despite being hampered by illness.

MEN 12k
1. Glynn Tromans 38:11
2. Keith Cullen 38:24
3. Dominic Bannister 38:25
4. Matt Smith 38:32
5. Alan Buckley 38:43
6. Nick Comerford 38:50

MEN 4k
1. Spencer Barden 12:25
2. Glen Stewart 12:29
3. Rob Whalley 12:32
4. Angus Maclean 12:34
5. Christian Stephenson 12:36
6. Chris Thompson 12:38

WOMEN 8k
1. Liz Yelling 28:28
2. Hayley Yelling 28:41
3. Tara Krzywicki 29:02
4. Angela Newport 29:16
5. Ellen Leggate 29:23
6. Debbie Sullivan 29:25

WOMEN 4k
1. Helen Pattinson 14:11
2. Jenny Brown 14:27
3. Juliet Potter 14:36
4. Amanda Parkinson 14:40
5. Lucy Wright 14:42
6. Catherine Berry 14:48

JUNIOR MEN 8k
1. Mohamed Farah 26:21
2. Steven Ablitt 26:23
3. Ed Jackson 26:24
4. Paul Shaw 26:28
5. Andrew Baddeley 26:30
6. Adam Bowden 26:37

JUNIOR WOMEN 6k
1. Louise Damen 22:45
2. Emma Ward 22:59
3. Collette Fagan 23:17
4. Faye Fullerton 23:50
5. Henrietta Freeman 24:07
6. Catherine Hare 24:22

ENGLISH NATIONAL CROSS COUNTRY CHAMPIONSHIPS

Durham 24 February 2001

MEN 12k

1.	Mike Openshaw	36:52
2.	Sam Haughian	36:54
3.	Bill Farquharson	37:30

WOMEN 8k

1.	Liz Yelling	28:08
2.	Angela Newport	28:35
3.	Hayley Yelling	29:01

U20 MEN 10k

1.	Chris Thompson	31:17
2.	Chris Bolt	31:27
3.	Lee McCash	31:28

U20 WOMEN 5k

1.	Juliet Potter	18:02
3.	Emma Ward	18:17
3.	Gemma Phillips	18:58

U17 MEN 6k

1.	Steve Ablitt	20:19
2.	Daniel Lewis	20:41
3.	Mark Draper	20:43

U17 WOMEN 5k

1.	Faye Fullerton	18:46

U15 WOMEN 3.6k

1.	Rachael Nathan	14:07

U13 WOMEN 3k

1.	Charlotte Browning	11:14

IAAF WORLD CROSS COUNTRY CHAMPIONSHIPS

Ostend, BEL 24 - 25 March 2001

These championships were very much a one woman show for Brtiain, but what a show. Paula Radcliffe *outsprinted* Wami on the first day to win the long course championship and came back on the second day and failed by just one second to win a second gold medal. Her performances meant Britain finished fourth in both team competitions. Other British performances were a little disappointing with only Kathy Butler and Liz Yelling managing top twenty postions although Emma Ward's run was encouraging.

MEN 4.1k (24 Mar)

1.	Enock Koech	KEN	12:40
2.	Kenenisa Bekele	ETH	12:42
3.	Benjamin Limo	KEN	12:43
4.	Sammy Kipketer	KEN	12:44
5.	Cyrus Kataron	KEN	12:45
6.	Albert Chepkurui	KEN	12:46
27.	**Spencer Barden**		**13:25**
38.	**Christian Stephenson**		**13:30**
56.	**Glenn Stewart**		**13:38**
75.	**Rob Whalley**		**13:55**
77.	**Angus Maclean**		**13:57**
130.	**Mark Miles**		**14:58**

Team

1.	Kenya	13
2.	Morocco	48
3.	Ethiopia	51
10.	**Great Britain & NI**	**196**

MEN 12.3k (25 Mar)

1.	Mohammed Mourhit	BEL	39:53
2.	Sergey Lebed	UKR	40:03
3.	Charles Kamathi	KEN	40:05
4.	Paulo Guerra	POR	40:06
5.	Paul Kosgei	KEN	40:09
6.	Driss El Himer	FRA	40:13
38.	**Karl Keska**		**41:38**
48.	**Dominic Bannister**		**42:02**
61.	**Glynn Tromans**		**42:33**
65.	**Matt O`Dowd**		**42:37**
94.	**Matthew Smith**		**43:58**
dnf	**Keith Cullen**		

Team

1.	Kenya	33
2.	France	72
3.	United States	87
13.	**Great Britain & NI**	**212**

JUNIOR MEN 7.7k (25 Mar)

1.	Kenenisa Bekele	ETH	25:04
2.	Duncan Lebo	KEN	25:37
3.	Dathan Ritzenhein	USA	25:46
4.	Nicholas Kemboi	KEN	25:52
5.	Matt Tegenkamp	USA	25:55
6.	Robert Kipchumba	KEN	26:00
59.	**Mohammed Farah**		**28:06**
80.	**Andrew Baddeley**		**28:27**
95.	**Adam Bowden**		**28:45**
98.	**Paul Shaw**		**28:49**
118.	**Steven Ablitt**		**29:24**
124.	**Edward Jackson**		**29:54**

Team

1.	Kenya	24
2.	Ethiopia	25
3.	Uganda	68
15.	**Great Britain & NI**	**332**

WOMEN 7.7k (24 Mar)

1.	**Paula Radcliffe**		**27.49**
2.	Gete Wami	ETH	27:52
3.	Lydia Cheromei	KEN	28:07
4.	Susan Chepkemei	KEN	28:13
5.	Pamela Chepchumba	KEN	28:20
6.	Leah Malot	KEN	28:36
17.	Liz Yelling		29:44
32.	Hayley Yelling		30:18
33.	Tara Krzywicki		30:25
51.	Angela Newport		31:04
74.	Ellen Leggate		32:41

Team

1.	Kenya	18
2.	Ethiopia	70
3.	France	77
4.	**Great Britain & NI**	**83**

WOMEN 4.1k (25 Mar)

1.	Gete Wami	ETH	14:46
2.	**Paula Radcliffe**		**14:47**
3.	Edith Masai	KEN	14:57
4.	Merima Denboba	ETH	15:04
5.	Werknesh Kidane	ETH	15:06
6.	Benita Willis	AUS	15:06
12.	Kathy Butler		15:25
32.	Amanda Parkinson		15:56
35.	Helen Pattinson		15:59
71.	Juliet Potter		16:43
78.	Jenny Brown		16:59

Team

1.	Ethiopia	26
2.	Kenya	32
3.	Romania	78
4.	**Great Britain & NI**	**81**

JUNIOR WOMEN 5.9k (24 Mar)

1.	Viola Kibiwot	KEN	22:05
2.	Abebech Negussie	ETH	22:05
3.	Aster Bacha	ETH	22:05
4.	Vivian Cheruiyot	KEN	22:06
5.	Tirunesh Dibaba	ETH	22:08
6.	Tereza Yohannes	ETH	22:10
23.	**Emma Ward**		**23:31**
32.	**Louise Damen**		**23:48**
38.	**Collette Fagan**		**24:02**
48.	**Faye Fullerton**		**24:18**
62.	**Elizabeth Lilley**		**24:41**
66.	**Henrietta Freeman**		**24:45**

Team

1.	Ethiopia	16
2.	Kenya	20
3.	Japan	59
6.	**Great Britain & NI**	**141**

EAA EUROPEAN CHALLENGE 10000 Metres

Barakaldo, ESP 7 April 2001

The windy conditions meant no very fast times. Paula Radcliffe was unhappy with her time, little did she realise this was to be the world's fastest time for 2001. Karl Keska ran a sensible race and achieved a qualifying time for the World Championships.

MEN (Race A)

1.	Jose Rios	ESP	27:49.35
2.	Helder Ornelas	POR	28:01.94
3.	Kamiel Maase	NED	28:02.37
4.	**Karl Keska**		**28:06.29**

MEN (Race B)

1.	Mohamed Serbouti	FRA	28:46.62
2.	Eliseo Martin	ESP	28:47.62
3.	**Matt O`Dowd**		**28:52.97**
7.	**Matt Smith**		**29:28.35**
11.	**Mark Miles**		**30:03.82**

Team

1.	Spain	1:24:32.03
2.	Portugal	1:26:16.19
3.	**Great Britain & NI**	**1:26:27.61**

WOMEN

1.	**Paula Radcliffe**		**30:55.80**
2.	Irina Mikitenko	GER	31:29.55
3.	Monica Rosa	POR	32:22.25
17.	**Liz Yelling**		**33:45.58**
20.	**Tara Krzywicki**		**33:59.79**

Team

1.	Spain	1:37:41.97
2.	**Great Britain & NI**	**1:38:41.17**
3.	Portugal	1:39:00.62

LONDON MARATHON 22 April 2001

(including AAA Championships)

Magnificent performances by El Mouaziz, Tergat and all the top women, but little to cheer for Britain except a PB for Mark Steinle in sixth place.

MEN

1.	Abdelkader El Mouaziz	MAR	2:07:11
2.	Paul Tergat	KEN	2:08:15
3.	Antonio Pinto	POR	2:09:36
4.	Tesfaye Jifar	ETH	2:09:45
5.	Japhet Kosgei	KEN	2:10:45
6.	**Mark Steinle (1-AAA)**		**2:10:46**
7.	Takayuki Inubushi	JPN	2:11:42
8.	Abel Anton	ESP	2:11:57
9.	Hendrick Ramaala	RSA	2:12:02
10.	Gert Thys	RSA	2:12:11
11.	**Mark Hudspith (2-AAA)**		**2:13:12**
17.	**Simon Pride**		**2:16:27**
19.	**Billy Burns (3-AAA)**		**2:18:29**
20.	**Robert Holladay**		**2:19:26**
21.	**Rhodri Jones**		**2:19:27**
22.	**Barry Royden**		**2:19:31**
23.	**Nick Francis**		**2:20:00**

UK Team Champions

1.	Morpeth Harriers	9:44.25

WOMEN

1.	Derartu Tulu	ETH	2:23:57
2.	Svetlana Zakharova	RUS	2:24:04
3.	Joyce Chepchumba	KEN	2:24:12
4.	Lidia Simon	ROM	2:24:15
5.	Elfenesh Alemu	ETH	2:24:29
6.	Nuta Olaru	ROM	2:25:18
7.	Alina Ivanova	RUS	2:25:34
8.	Tegla Loroupe	KEN	2:26:10
9.	Adriana Fernandez	MEX	2:26:22
10.	Madina Biktagirova	RUS	2:27:14
16.	**Lynne MacDougall**		**2:37:20**
17.	**Bev Hartigan (1-AAA)**		**2:37:45**
22.	**Debbie Robinson (2-AAA)**		**2:42:19**
23.	**Louise Watson (3-AAA)**		**2:43:49**
25.	**Vicky Pincombe**		**2:43:52**
26.	**Clare Pauzers**		**2:44:35**
27.	**Ruth Pickvance**		**2:46:14**
28.	**Sharon Dixon**		**2:46:32**

UK Team Champions

1.	Sutton in Ashfield	8:42:19

AAA 100k CHAMPIONSHIPS

Moreton-in-Marsh 20 May 2001

MEN

1.	Alan Reid	7:13:30
2.	Ian Anderson	7:17:18
3.	Chris Finill	7:24:20

WOMEN

1.	Danielle Sanderson	8:17:37
2.	Victoria Musgrove	9:07:19
3.	Cecelia Petersson	10:04:12

EAA EUROPEAN CUP OF RACE WALKING

Dudince, SVK 19 May 2001

MEN (20k)

1.	Viktor Burayev	RUS	1:19:30
2.	Yevgeniy Misyulya	BLR	1:19:45
3.	Andreas Erm	GER	1:19:51
45.	**Matt Hales**		**1:30:08**

Team 1. Russia 13

MEN (50k)

1.	Jesus Angel Garcia	ESP	3:44:26
2.	Nikolay Matyukhin	RUS	3:45:48
3.	Vladimir Potemin	RUS	3:46:12
33.	**Steve Hollier**		**4:20:50**
37.	**Chris Cheeseman**		**4:24:48**

Team 1. Russia 11

JUNIOR MEN (10k)

1.	Yevgeniy Demkov	RUS	41:16
2.	Sergey Lystsov	RUS	41:18
3.	Mikalai Seradovich	BLR	41:30
29.	**Lloyd Finch**		**45:35**
36.	**Andrew Parker**		**46:17**
43.	**Cameron Smith**		**50:33**

Team

1.	Russia	3
14.	**Great Britain & NI**	**65**

WOMEN (20k)

1.	Olimpiada Ivanova	RUS	1:26:48
2.	Natalya Fedoskina	RUS	1:26:50
3.	Elisabetta Perrone	ITA	1:27:09

Team 1. Russia 8

JUNIOR WOMEN (10k)

1.	Tatyana Kozlova	RUS	46:08
2.	Maryna Tikhanava	BLR	46:31
3.	Yekaterina Izmaylova	RUS	46:42

Team 1. Russia 4

GB & NI v ESP (U23) Liverpool 23 June 2001

Strong winds in the finishing straight kept down the times as Britain secured a good victory thanks to a very impressive performance by the women. The men won every sprint and hurdle event and performed well in the vertical jumps and throws with a double win by Udechuku.

MEN

100 Metres wind –1.0
1. **Jonathan Barbour** **10.66**
2. **Jon Oparka** **10.81**

200 Metres wind –1.5
1. **Jonathan Barbour** **21.56**
3. **Ben Lewis** **22.14**

400 Metres
1. **David Naismith** **47.82**
4. **Simon Plaskitt** **48.30**

800 Metres
1. Manuel Olmedo ESP 1:51.55
3. **Jon Stewart** **1:52.13**
4. **Alasdair McLean-Foreman** **1:52.91**

1500 Metres
1. Xavier Areny ESP 4:00.37
3. **James Bowler** **4:00.96**
4. **Michael Skinner** **4:01.20**

3000 Metres Steeplechase
1. Raul Moya ESP 9:03.62
3. **Gary Blackman** **9:19.74**
dnf Bruce Raeside

110 Metres Hurdles wind –1.5
1. **Chris Baillie** **14.12**
dsq Rob Newton

400 Metres Hurdles
1. **Matt Elias** **50.69**
4. **Leon McCrae** **52.40**

High Jump
1. Miguel de Lucas ESP 2.10
2. **Danny Graham** **2.10**
3. **Colin McMaster** **2.10**

Pole Vault
1. Robert Villa ESP 5.40
3. **Scott Simpson** **5.00**
4. **Chris Type** **4.50**

Long Jump
1. **Darren Thompson** **7.50w**
3. **Andre Fernandez** **7.34w**

Triple Jump
1. **Steven Shalders** **16.06**
3. **Tosin Oke** **15.55**

Shot
1. **Emeka Udechuku** **17.88**
4. **Nick Owen** **15.15**

Discus
1. **Emeka Udechuku** **59.43**
4. **Luke Rosenberg** **48.89**

Hammer
1. Joan Bea ESP 60.65
2. **Andrew Frost** **59.48**
4. **David Little** **55.14**

Javelin
1. **David Parker** **75.62**
4. **Phil Sharpe** **62.17**

4 x 100 Metres
1. **Great Britain & NI** **40.30**
(Oparka, Barbour, Chin, Lewis)
dnf Spain

4 x 400 Metres
1. **Great Britain & NI** **3:10.70**
(Buckley, Bayley, Lowthian, Lewis)
2. Spain 3:10.81

WOMEN

100 Metres wind –3.2
1. **Abi Oyepitan** **12.08**
2. **Sabrina Scott** **12.22**

200 Metres wind –3.1
1. **Abi Oyepitan** **24.24**
2. **Susan Burnside** **24.60**

400 Metres
1. **Helen Thieme** **53.25**
2. **Jenny Meadows** **53.70**

800 Metres
1. Natalia Rodriguez ESP 2:04.20
2. **Kelly Caffell** **2:04.59**
3. **Alex Carter** **2:05.33**

1500 Metres
1. Iris Fuentes Pila ESP 4:20.4
2. **Rachael Felton** **4:22.4**
3. **Karen Montador** **4:25.6**

100 Metres Hurdles wind –4.0
1. **Tamsin Stephens** **14.55**
4. **Sarah Claxton** **14.85**

400 Metres Hurdles
1. **Tracey Duncan** **59.29**
2. **Hannah Wood** **60.20**

High Jump
1. **Lindsay McDonnell** **1.75**
2. **Gillian Black** **1.70**

Pole Vault
1. Maria Sanchez ESP 4.10
2. Sonya Lawrence 3.70
nh Tracey Bloomfield

Long Jump
1. **Sarah Wellstead** **6.10w**
3. **Sarah Claxton** **5.98w**

Triple Jump
1. Patricia Sarrapio ESP 12.65w
3. **Leandra Polius** **12.35w**
4. **Charmaine Turner** **11.87w**

Shot
1. **Julie Dunkley** **15.88**
3. **Eva Massey** **15.09**

Discus
1. **Rebecca Roles** **47.60**
3. **Eva Massey** **45.98**

Hammer
1. **Zoe Derham** **59.27**
2. **Mhairi Walters** **56.86**

Javelin
1. Mercedes Chilla ESP 54.46
2. **Jenny Kemp** **52.76**
3. **Chloe Cozens** **48.73**

4 x 100 Metres
Great Britain & NI (U20) gst **45.42**
(Norville, Caney, Spencer, James)
1. **Great Britain & NI** **45.54**
(Oyepitan, Burnside, Scott, Roscoe)
2. Spain 46.89

4 x 400 Metres
1. **Great Britain & NI** **3:38.70**
(Gear, Meadows, Duncan, Thieme)
2. Spain 3:49.03

Match Result
1. **Great Britain & NI** **177**
2. Spain 150

SPAR EUROPEAN CUP SUPER LEAGUE

Bremen, GER 23 - 24 June 2001

After a fantastic win last year the men proved that history does not repeat itself, as, with a depleted team, they fell back to fifth, on equal points with Germany in sixth. The women performed much better with fourth place and quite close to third. Performance of the meet was Susan Jones who equalled Diane Davies high jump record almost nineteen years to the day when it was set.

MEN

100 Metres wind +1.4 (23 Jun)

1.	**Mark Lewis-Francis**		**10.13**
2.	Kostas Kederis	GRE	10.15
3.	Frederic Krantz	FRA	10.27
4.	Marco Torrieri	ITA	10.29
5.	Tim Goebel	GER	10.35
6.	Marcin Krzywanski	POL	10.42
7.	Sergey Bychkov	RUS	10.46
8.	Pedro Nolet	ESP	10.48

200 Metres wind –0.7 (24 Jun)

1.	Kostas Kederis	GRE	20.31
2.	**Marlon Devonish**		**20.59**
3.	Martin Urbas	POL	20.69
4.	Alessandro Cavallaro	ITA	20.84
5.	Marc Blume	GER	21.14
6.	Aleksandr Ryabov	RUS	21.41
dsq	Alberto Dorrego	ESP	
dsq	Christophe Cheval	FRA	(20.82)

400 Metres (23 Jun)

1.	Marc Raquil	FRA	44.95
2.	Robert Mackowiak	POL	45.48
3.	David Canal	ESP	45.52
4.	Ingo Schultz	GER	45.53
5.	Alessandro Attene	ITA	45.92
6.	Dmitriy Golovastov	RUS	46.11
7.	**Iwan Thomas**		**46.14**
8.	Anastasios Goussis	GRE	47.05

800 Metres (24 Jun)

1.	Pawel Czapiewski	POL	1:48.28
2.	Andrea Longo	ITA	1:48.54
3.	**Simon Lees**		**1:48.80**
4.	Dmitriy Bogdanov	RUS	1:48.97
5.	Jimmy Lomba	FRA	1:49.13
6.	Tarik Bourrouag	GER	1:49.36
7.	Israel Dominguez	ESP	1:49.65
8.	Pavlos Farouggias	GRE	1:50.05

1500 Metres (23 Jun)

1.	Jose Redolat	ESP	3:45.81
2.	Mehdi Baala	FRA	3:46.29
3.	Leszek Zblewski	POL	3:47.06
4.	Christian Obrist	ITA	3:47.69
5.	Panayiotis Stroubakos	GRE	3:48.11
6.	**Tom Mayo**		**3:48.69**
7.	Andrey Zadorozhniy	RUS	3:48.81
8.	Benjamin Hetzler	GER	3:50.08

3000 Metres (24 Jun)

1.	Driss Maazouzi	FRA	7:52.26
2.	Andres Diaz	ESP	7:52.59
3.	**John Mayock**		**7:56.06**
4.	Wolfram Muller	GER	7:56.16
5.	Sergey Drygin	RUS	7:57.09
6.	Leszek Zblewski	POL	7:57.47
7.	Ferdinando Vicari	ITA	7:58.49
8.	Ioannis Neanidis	GRE	8:10.84

5000 Metres (23 Jun)

1.	Smail Sghir	FRA	13:50.47
2.	Alberto Garcia	ESP	13:50.96
3.	Marco Mazza	ITA	13:55.85
4.	**Mike Openshaw**		**13:58.15**
5.	Jan Fitschen	GER	13:58.68
6.	Mikhail Yeginov	RUS	14:00.24
7.	Dariusz Kruczkowski	POL	14:08.83
8.	Anastasios Fragos	GRE	14:33.38

3000 Metres Steeplechase (24 Jun)

1.	Bouabdallah Tahri	FRA	8:38.02
2.	Antonio Jimenez	ESP	8:38.09
3.	Ralf Assmus	GER	8:39.34
4.	Roman Usov	RUS	8:41.08
5.	Luciano Di Pardo	ITA	8:42.72
6.	Jan Zakrzewski	POL	8:44.79
7.	Georgios Kobogiannis	GRE	8:47.81
8.	**Ben Whitby**		**8:50.13**

110 Metres Hurdles wind +1.3 (24 Jun)

1.	Yevgeniy Pechonkin	RUS	13.38
2.	Florian Schwarthoff	GER	13.57
3.	**Tony Jarrett**		**13.58**
4.	Emiliano Pizzoli	ITA	13.71
5.	Krzysztof Mehlich	POL	13.86
6.	Hipolito Montesinos	ESP	13.88
7.	Ladji Doucoure	FRA	14.02
8.	Dimitrios Pietris	GRE	14.04

400 Metres Hurdles (23 Jun)

1.	Fabrizio Mori	ITA	48.39
2.	Marek Plawgo	POL	48.98
3.	Stephane Diagana	FRA	49.07
4.	Ruslan Mashchenko	RUS	49.53
5.	**Chris Rawlinson**		**50.11**
6.	Periklis Iakovakis	GRE	50.28
7.	Ivan Rodriguez	ESP	50.44
8.	Jan Reinberg	GER	51.66

High Jump (23 Jun)

1.	Yaroslav Rybakov	RUS	2.28
2.	Grzegorz Sposob	POL	2.23
3.	Martin Buss	GER	2.19
4.	**Robert Mitchell**		**2.19**
5.	David Antona	ESP	2.19
6.	Dimitrios Syrakos	GRE	2.19
7.	Gregory Gabella	FRA	2.15
8.	Giulio Ciotti	ITA	2.15

Pole Vault (24 Jun)

1.	Michael Stolle	GER	5.75
2.	Adam Kolasa	POL	5.68
3.	Vasiliy Gorshkov	RUS	5.68
4.	Khalid Lachheb	FRA	5.68
5.	Montxu Miranda	ESP	5.50
6.	Marios Evangelou	GRE	5.10
nh	**Nick Buckfield**		**(5.40)**
dns	Massimo Allevi	ITA	

Long Jump (23 Jun)

1.	Danila Burkenya	RUS	7.89
2.	**Chris Tomlinson**		**7.67**
3.	Grzegorz Marciniszyn	POL	7.64
4.	Alessio Rimoldi	ITA	7.63
5.	Konstantin Krause	GER	7.60
6.	Konstadinos Koukodimos	GRE	7.55
7.	Yann Domenech	FRA	7.49
8.	Yago Lamela	ESP	7.48

Triple Jump (24 Jun)

1.	**Jonathan Edwards**		**17.26**
2.	Christos Metetoglou	GRE	17.19
3.	Paolo Camossi	ITA	16.97
4.	Andrey Kurennoy	RUS	16.63
5.	Karl Taillepierre	FRA	16.63
6.	Jacek Kazmierowski	POL	16.30
7.	Julio Lopez	ESP	16.19
8.	Charles Friedek	GER	16.14

Shot (23 Jun)

1.	Manuel Martinez	ESP	21.03
2.	Pavel Chumachenko	RUS	20.54
3.	Paolo Dal Soglio	ITA	20.02
4.	Ralf Bartels	GER	19.50
5.	Leszek Sliwa	POL	18.85
6.	Yves Niare	FRA	18.64
7.	Vaios Tigas	GRE	18.48
8.	**Mark Proctor**		**18.10**

Discus (24 Jun)

1.	Lars Riedel	GER	66.63
2.	Mario Pestano	ESP	65.60
3.	Dmitriy Shevchenko	RUS	65.26
4.	Olgierd Stanski	POL	61.11
5.	Diego Fortuna	ITA	59.81
6.	Jean-C.Retel	FRA	58.64
7.	**Bob Weir**		**58.23**
8.	Sawas Panavoglou	GRE	58.14

Hammer (23 Jun)

1.	Szymon Ziolkowski	POL	80.87
2.	Nicola Vizzoni	ITA	80.13
3.	Hristos Polyhroniou	GRE	78.34
4.	Nicolas Figere	FRA	76.90

5.	Karsten Kobs	GER	75.59
6.	**Mick Jones**		**73.67**
7.	Moises Campeny	ESP	70.44
8.	Andrey Yevgenyev	RUS	70.20

Javelin (24 Jun)

1.	Kostas Gatsioudis	GRE	88.33
2.	Sergey Makarov	RUS	83.24
3.	Raymond Hecht	GER	83.05
4.	**Nick Nieland**		**80.84**
5.	Rajmund Kolko	POL	79.20
6.	Alberto Desiderio	ITA	75.34
7.	David Brisseault	FRA	73.48
8.	Gustavo Dacal	ESP	71.26

4 x 100 Metres (23 Jun)

1.	Italy	38.89
2.	**Great Britain & NI**	**38.99**
	(Condon, Devonish, Malcolm, Lewis-Francis)	
3.	Poland	39.00
4.	Germany	39.48
5.	Spain	39.58
6.	Greece	39.62
7.	Russia	40.27
dsq	France	(39.34)

4 x 400 Metres (24 Jun)

1.	Poland	3:01.79
2.	Russia	3:02.09
3.	Germany	3:02.71
4.	**Great Britain & NI**	**3:02.79**
	(Deacon, Thomas, Thorne-Ladejo, Richardson)	
5.	France	3:02.92
6.	Italy	3:05.38
7.	Greece	3:05.64
8.	Spain	3:07.87

Match Result

1.	Poland	107
2.	Russia	97
3.	Italy	94
4.	Germany	93
5.	**Great Britain & NI**	**91**
6.	France	87
7.	Spain	77
8.	Greece	67

Note Cheval FRA dsq for drugs in 200 and 4 x 100.

WOMEN

100 Metres wind +2.8 (23 Jun)

1.	Marina Kislova	RUS	11.23w
2.	Natalya Safronnikova	BLR	11.26w
3.	Katia Benth	FRA	11.38w
4.	Gaby Rockmeier	GER	11.38w
5.	**Joice Maduaka**		**11.45w**
6.	Manuela Levorato	ITA	11.47w
7.	Pavla Andryskova	CZE	11.73w
8.	Evelina Lisenco	ROM	11.83w

200 Metres wind –0.7 (24 Jun)

1.	Natalya Safronnikova	BLR	22.68
2.	Ionela Tirlea	ROM	22.85
3.	Svetlana Goncharenko	RUS	22.87
4.	Birgit Rockmeier	GER	23.04
5.	Manuela Levorato	ITA	23.18
6.	**Katharine Merry**		**23.21**
7.	Fabe Dia	FRA	23.29
8.	Erika Suchovska	CZE	23.79

400 Metres (23 Jun)

1.	Grit Breuer	GER	50.49
2.	Francine Landre	FRA	51.21
3.	Natalya Antyukh	RUS	51.37
4.	Otilia Ruicu	ROM	51.65
5.	**Alison Curbishley**		**51.99**
6.	Anna Kozak	BLR	52.08
7.	Danielle Perpoli	ITA	52.13
8.	Tereza Zizalova	CZE	54.06

800 Metres (23 Jun)

1.	Irina Mistyukevich	RUS	1:59.09
2.	Yvonne Teichmann	GER	1:59.39
3.	Natalya Dukhnova	BLR	1:59.95
4.	Virginie Fouquet	FRA	2:01.82
5.	**Tanya Blake**		**2:02.30**
6.	Petra Sedlakova	CZE	2:02.67
7.	Sara Palmas	ITA	2:04.86
8.	Elena Iagar	ROM	2:05.68

1500 Metres (24 Jun)

1.	Violeta Szekely	ROM	4:06.43
2.	Olga Yegorova	RUS	4:06.59
3.	**Hayley Tullett**		**4:07.83**
4.	Alesya Turova	BLR	4:08.80
5.	Kathleen Friedrich	GER	4:09.79
6.	Andrea Suldesova	CZE	4:10.28
7.	Hanane Sabri	FRA	4:11.73
8.	Sara Palmas	ITA	4:14.97

3000 Metres (23 June)

1.	**Kathy Butler**		**9:03.71**
2.	Cristina Grosu	ROM	9:04.91
3.	Fatima Yvelain	FRA	9:05.30
4.	Liliya Volkova	RUS	9:06.78
5.	Elisa Rea	ITA	9:06.95
6.	Sabrina Mockenhaupt	GER	9:07.96
7.	Renata Hoppova	CZE	9:16.04
8.	Svetlana Klimkovich	BLR	9:23.73

5000 Metres (23 Jun)

1.	Yelena Zadorozhnaya	RUS	14:40.47
2.	**Paula Radcliffe**		**14:49.84**
3.	Mihaela Botezan	ROM	15:08.78
4.	Yamna Belkacem	FRA	15:23.66
5.	Elisa Rea	ITA	15:33.40
6.	Luminita Zaituc	GER	15:41.39
7.	Lyudmila Volchik	BLR	16:17.76
8.	Maria Volna	CZE	16:34.77

100 Metres Hurdles wind +0.6 (24 Jun)

1.	Irina Korotya	RUS	13.06
2.	Linda Ferga	FRA	13.10
3.	Kirsten Bolm	GER	13.15
4.	**Diane Allahgreen**		**13.23**
5.	Margaret Macchiut	ITA	13.23
6.	Eva Miklos	ROM	13.53
7.	Lucie Skrobakova	CZE	13.70
dsq	Yevgeniya Likhuta	BLR	

400 Metres Hurdles (23 Jun)

1.	Yuliya Nosova	RUS	53.84
2.	Ionela Tirlea	ROM	55.08
3.	Heike Meissner	GER	55.33
4.	Sylvanie Morandais	FRA	55.50
5.	Tatyana Kurochkina	BLR	56.17
6.	Monika Niederstatter	ITA	56.85
7.	Alena Rucklova	CZE	57.60
8.	**Natasha Danvers**		**62.97 (fell)**

High Jump (24 Jun)

1.	**Susan Jones**		**1.95**
2.	Alina Astafei	GER	1.89
3=	Olga Kaliturina	RUS	1.89
3=	Antonietta Di Martino	ITA	1.89
5.	Oana Pantelimon	ROM	1.89
6.	Olga Shedova	BLR	1.83
7.	Christelle Preau	FRA	1.80
8.	Eva Strakova	CZE	1.80

Pole Vault (23 Jun)

1.	Svetlana Feofanova	RUS	4.60
2.	**Janine Whitlock**		**4.34**
3.	Pavia Hamackova	CZE	4.34
4.	Christine Adams	GER	4.20
5.	Vanessa Boslak	FRA	4.20
6.	Arianna Farfaletti	ITA	4.10
7.	Yuliya Taratynova	BLR	3.60
dns	Silvia Ristea	ROM	

Long Jump (24 Jun)

1.	Heike Drechsler	GER	6.79
2.	Eunice Barber	FRA	6.71
3.	Fiona May	ITA	6.57
4.	Olga Rublyova	RUS	6.51
5.	**Jade Johnson**		**6.49**
6.	Eva Miklos	ROM	6.44
7.	Lucie Komrskova	CZE	6.34
8.	Natalya Safronova	BLR	6.34

Triple Jump (23 Jun)

1.	Tatyana Lebedeva	RUS	14.89
2.	Natalya Safronova	BLR	14.10w
3.	Cristina Nicolau	ROM	13.83
4.	Barbara Lah	ITA	13.69
5.	Nicole Herschmann	GER	13.69
6.	Amy Zongo	FRA	13.45w
7.	**Rebecca White**		**12.82**
8.	Martina Darmovzalova	CZE	12.77

Shot (24 Jun)

1.	Nadine Kleinert-Schmitt	GER	19.30
2.	Irina Korzhanenko	RUS	19.27
3.	Assunta Legnante	ITA	17.51
4.	Elena Hila	ROM	17.38
5.	Yelena Ivanenko	BLR	17.22
6.	Laurence Manfredi	FRA	16.73
7.	Vera Pospisilova	CZE	15.53
8.	**Joanne Duncan**		**15.26**

Discus (23 Jun)

1.	Franka Dietzsch	GER	64.64
2.	Natalya Sadova	RUS	63.77
3.	Nicoleta Grasu	ROM	62.33
4.	Vera Pospisilova	CZE	58.96
5.	Agnese Maffeis	ITA	58.17
6.	Melina Robert-Michon	FRA	58.07
7.	Lyudmila Starovoytova	BLR	56.98
8.	**Philippa Roles**		**54.18**

Hammer (24 Jun)

1.	Olga Tsander	BLR	68.40
2.	Kirsten Munchow	GER	68.09
3.	**Lorraine Shaw**		**67.98**
4.	Manuella Montebrun	FRA	66.58
5.	Esther Balassini	ITA	65.49
6.	Alla Davydova	RUS	62.13
7.	Cristina Buzau	ROM	61.80
8.	Marketa Hajdu	CZE	58.30

Javelin (23 Jun)

1.	Nikola Tomeckova	CZE	64.77
2.	Steffi Nerius	GER	63.12
3.	Claudia Coslovich	ITA	63.07
4.	Tatyana Shikolenko	RUS	61.85
5.	Ana Mirela Termure	ROM	61.61
6.	Oksana Velichko	BLR	56.11
7.	Sarah Walter	FRA	55.27
8.	**Karen Martin**		**52.63**

4 x 100 Metres (23 Jun)

1.	Germany	43.02
2.	Russia	43.15
3.	France	43.45
4.	**Great Britain & NI**	**43.53**
	(Allahgreen, Richardson, Maduaka, Anderson)	
5.	Italy	44.66
6.	Czech Republic	45.50
dsq	Romania	
dsq	Belarus	

4 x 400 Metres (24 Jun)

1.	Germany	3:23.81
2.	Russia	3:24.58
3.	France	3:26.23
4.	**Great Britain & NI**	**3:28.15**
	(Murphy, Frost, Blake, Owusu)	
5.	Belarus	3:28.17
6.	Romania	3:29.04
7.	Italy	3:31.96
8.	Czech Republic	3:36.35

Match Result

1.	Russia	126.5
2.	Germany	111
3.	France	86
4.	**Great Britain & NI**	**82**
5.	Romania	78
6.	Italy	72.5
7.	Belarus	70
8.	Czech Republic	47

EUROPEAN CUP FOR COMBINED EVENTS

Kaunas, LTU
30 June - 1 July 2001

MEN (League 2)

1.	Mario Anibal	POR	8213
2.	Krzystof Andrzjek	POL	7860
3.	Michal Modelski	POL	7483
4.	**Barry Thomas**		**7385**
9.	**Anthony Southward**		**7133**
12.	**Fyn Corcoran**		**7020**
16.	**Brendan McConville**		**6862**

Team Result

1.	Poland	22596
2.	Belarus	21820
3.	**Great Britain & NI**	**21538**

Ried, AUT
30 June - 1 July 2001

WOMEN (League 1)

1.	Yuliya Akulenko	UKR	6001
2.	**Julie Hollman**		**5933**
3.	Athina Papasotiriou	GRE	5862
8.	**Nicola Gautier**		**5784**
10.	**Kerry Jury**		**5687**
14.	**Julia Bennett**		**5534**

Team Result

1.	Ukraine	17670
2.	**Great Britain & NI**	**17404**

NORWICH UNION CHALLENGE GB & NI v USA v RUS

Glasgow 1 July 2001

A prize fund of $250,000 kept the big names at this meeting but the overall level of performance was a little disappointing. However, Jonathan Edwards did not disappoint with a world leading 17.66 in the triple jump. For the women Tara Krzywicki set a new British record in the 3000 Metres steeplechase and Paula Radcliffe improved her PB in the 1500.

MEN

100 Metres wind +2.2

1.	Jon Drummond	USA	10.10w
2.	**Dwain Chambers**		**10.13w**
3.	**Mark Lewis-Francis**		**10.25w**

200 Metres wind +2.4

1.	Kevin Little	USA	20.31w
2.	**Christian Malcolm**		**20.47w**
3.	**Marlon Devonish**		**20.50w**

400 Metres

1.	**Mark Richardson**	**46.20**
5.	**Iwan Thomas**	**46.68**

800 Metres
1. Yuriy Borzakovskiy RUS 1:48.50
2. Neil Speaight 1:48.88
4. Simon Lees 1:49.12

1500 Metres
1. Seneca Lassiter USA 3:50.78
4. John Mayock 3:51.32
5. Tom Mayo 3:51.96

110 Metres Hurdles wind +2.1
1. Allen Johnson USA 13.31w
2. Colin Jackson 13.37w
5. Tony Jarrett 13.47w

400 Metres Hurdles
1. Angelo Taylor USA 49.01
2. Chris Rawlinson 49.22
5. Du'aine Thorne-Ladejo 49.70

High Jump
1. Charles Austin USA 2.25
5. Rob Mitchell 2.14
6. Dalton Grant 2.14

Triple Jump
1. Jonathan Edwards 17.66
2. Phillips Idowu 17.38w

Discus
1. John Godina USA 65.54
4. Bob Weir 61.79
6. Glen Smith 59.00

Javelin
1. Breaux Greer USA 85.74
2. Steve Backley 84.26
3. Mick Hill 83.42

4 x 100 Metres
1. Great Britain & NI 38.69
(Chambers, Devonish, Macolm, Lewis-Francis)

WOMEN

100 Metres wind +1.6
1. Chryste Gaines USA 11.19
2. Abi Oyepitan 11.29
4. Marcia Richardson 11.52

400 Metres
1. Katharine Merry 51.03
4. Donna Fraser 53.02

1500 Metres
1. Olga Yegorova RUS 4:02.76
3. Paula Radcliffe 4:05.37
6. Helen Pattinson 4:09.22

100 Metres Hurdles wind +2.1
1. Svetlana Laukhova RUS 12.76w
4. Diane Allahgreen 12.98w
6. Melanie Wilkins 13.08w

3000 Metres Steeplechase
1. Liz Jackson USA 9:48.72
2. Tara Krzywicki 9:52.71
6. Clare Martin 10:46.01

Long Jump
1. Olga Rublyova RUS 6.80w
2. Jade Johnson 6.67w
3. Denise Lewis 6.53w

4 x 100 Metres
1. Russia 43.84
2. Great Britain & NI 44.18
(Allahgreen, Richardson, Maduaka, Anderson)

Match Result
1. United States 135
2. Great Britain & NI 131
3. Russia 111

EUROPEAN U23 CHAMPIONSHIPS
Amsterdam, NED 12 - 15 July 2001

A great championship for Britain with six gold medals. Indeed the young athletes showed the seniors the way with their dominance at the relays - the 4 x 100 men only managed a silver, all the other teams won gold. Pick of the individual golds was Matt Elias going under 50 seconds in both heats and finals at 400 hurdles - but both John Barbour and Jade Johnson won hard earned victories. Four more individual medals and a host of good performances gives high hopes for Britain on the European stage.

MEN

100 Metres wind +2.2 (13 Jul)
1. Jonathan Barbour 10.26w
(1h3 10.43)
2. Fabrice Calligny FRA 10.40w
3. Przemyslaw Rogowski POL 10.45w

200 Metres wind +0.1 (14 Jul)
1. Marcin Jedrusinski POL 20.94
2. Lukasz Chyla POL 20.99
3. Mark Howard IRL 21.00
6. Jonathan Barbour 21.10
(4h2 21.24)

400 Metres (13 Jul)
1. Yuriy Borzakovskiy RUS 46.06
2. Marc-Alexander Scheer GER 46.43
3. Rafal Wieruszewski POL 46.57
6. David Naismith 46.84
(2h1 46.82)

800 Metres (15 Jul)
1. Antonio Reina ESP 1:47.74
2. Joeri Jansen BEL 1:47.80
3. Nicolas Aissat FRA 1:47.81
4. Simon Lees 1:47.82
(2h1 1:49.26)
6h2 Chris Moss 1:49.71

1500 Metres (14 Jul)
1. Wolfram Muller GER 3:38.94
2. Ivan Geshko UKR 3:39.37
3. Sergio Gallardo ESP 3:39.50
5. Angus MacLean 3:41.36
(3h1 3:46.45)
10. James Bowler 3:44.39
(7h2 3:44.88)

5000 Metres (15 Jul)
1. Yusef El Nasri ESP 14:02.97
2. Dmitriy Baranovskiy UKR 14:03.67
3. Balazs Csillag HUN 14:04.84
5. Chris Thompson 14:06.00
6. Sam Haughian 14:06.03

10000 Metres (12 Jul)
1. Dmitriy Baranovskiy UKR 29:13.36
2. Koen Raymaekers NED 29:15.24
3. Mattia Maccagnan ITA 29:15.32
9. Adam Sutton 29:28.32

3000 Metres Steeplechase (14 Jul)
1. Pavel Potapovich RUS 8:35.85
2. Vadim Slobodenyuk UKR 8:37.09
3. Henrik Skoog SWE 8:38.27
9h2 Adam Franklin 8:54.39
10h1 Iain Murdoch 9:01.00

110 Metres Hurdles wind +0.4 (15 Jul)
1. Artur Budzillo POL 13.76
2. Felipe Vivancos ESP 13.79
3. Chris Baillie 13.85
(2h2 14.03)
3h3 Robert Newton 14.09

400 Metres Hurdles (14 Jul)
1. Matt Elias 49.57
(1h1 49.90)
2. Periklis Iakovakis GRE 49.63
3. Mikael Jakobsson SWE 50.86
3h3Richard McDonald 51.08

High Jump (14 Jul)
1. Rozle Prezelj SLO 2.21
2. Aleksandr Veryutin BLR 2.18
3. Fabrice Saint Jean FRA 2.18
6= Robert Mitchell 2.12
10=Danny Graham 2.12
nm Samson Oni
(2.15Q)

Pole Vault (15 Jul)
1. Lars Borgeling GER 5.60
2. Mikko Latvala FIN 5.50
3. Giuseppe Gibilisco ITA 5.50

Long Jump (15 Jul)
1. Yann Domenech FRA 8.00
2. Vladimir Zyuskov UKR 7.90
3. Shahriar Bigdeli GER 7.81
6. Chris Tomlinson 7.70
(7.73Q)

Triple Jump (13 Jul)
1. Christian Olsson SWE 17.24
2. Igor Spasovkhodskiy RUS 17.08
3. Ionut Punga ROM 16.81
7. Steve Shalders 16.28

Shot (15 Jul)
1. Mikulas Konopka SVK 19.79
2. Yuriy Belov BLR 19.38
3. Leszek Sliwa POL 19.08

Discus (14 Jul)
1. Zoltan Kovago HUN 63.85
2. Heinrich Seitz GER 59.50
3. Gabor Mate HUN 59.45
7. Emeka Udechuku 57.25

Hammer (15 Jul)
1. Nicolas Figere FRA 80.88
2. Olli-Pekka Karjalainen FIN 80.54
3. Miloslav Konopka SVK 76.28

Javelin (14 Jul)
1. Bjorn Lange GER 80.85
2. Aleksandr Baranovskiy RUS 76.74
3. Janis Liepa LAT 74.26

9. David Parker 69.78
(75.16Q)
18Q Dan Carter 65.47

Decathlon (12/13 Jul)
1. Andre Niklaus GER 8042
2. Jaakko Oja iemi FIN 7907
3. William Frullani ITA 7871

20k Walk (15 Jul)
1. Juan Manuel Molina ESP 1:23:03
2. Stepan Yudin RUS 1:23:10
3. Jose Dominguez ESP 1:23:16
dsqMatt Hales

4 x 100 Metres (15 Jul)
1. Poland 39.41
2. Great Britain & NI 39.45
(Oparka, Barbour, Chinn, Lewis)
(2h2 Chatt for Barbour 39.90)
3. Slovenia 39.95

4 x 400 Metres (15 Jul)
1. Great Britain & NI 3:05.24
(Naismith, Potter, Chatt, Elias)
(1h1 McDonald for Chatt 3:07.33)
2. Germany 3:05.39
3. Russia 3:06.41

WOMEN

100 Metres wind –1.2 (13 Jul)
1. Sina Schielke GER 11.52
2. Abiodun Oyepitan 11.58
(1h3 11.43)
3. Johanna Manninen FIN 11.61
4h2Susan Burnside 11.94
8h3Sabrina Scott 11.94

200 Metres wind –0.3 (14 Jul)
1. Johanna Manninen FIN 23.30
2. Sina Schielke GER 23.45
3. Ciara Sheehy IRL 23.54
7. Helen Roscoe 23.96
(4h2 24.01)
8. Emily Freeman 24.03
(5h2 24.12)
6h1Melanie Purkiss 26.98

400 Metres (13 Jul)
1. Antonina Yefremova UKR 52.29
2. Helen Thieme 52.75
(2h2 52.88)
3. Aneta Lemiesz POL 53.25
5. Karen Gear 53.91
(3h1 53.31)
6. Jenny Meadows 54.05
(4h1 53.32)

800 Metres (15 Jul)
1. Anna Zagorska POL 2:07.27
2. Irina Somesan ROM 2:07.27
3. Tatyana Rodionova RUS 2:07.60
5h1Alex Carter 2:05.24

1500 Metres (14 Jul)
1. Alesya Turova BLR 4:09.71
2. Natalia Rodriguez ESP 4:11.20
3. Kelly Caffel 4:12.30
(2h2 4:17.39)
7h1Rachel Felton 4:20.81

5000 Metres (14 Jul)
1. Katalin Szentgyorgyi HUN 15:40.55
2. Anastasiya Zubova RUS 15:40.78
3. Tatyana Khmelyova RUS 15:51.88
7. Juliet Potter 16:02.99
12. Gillian Palmer 16:18.68
15. Karen Hind 16:47.11

10000 Metres (13 Jul)
1. Olga Romanova RUS 33:36.03
2. Sonja Stolic YUG 33:37.02
3. Sabrina Mockenhaupt GER 33:38.38

3000 Metres Steeplechase (13 Jul)
1. Melanie Schulz GER 10:03.34
2. Livia Toth HUN 10:04.99
3. Sigrid Bempt BEL 10:08.46

100 Metres Hurdles wind+1.2 (15 Jul)
1. Susanna Kallur SWE 12.96
2. Jenny Kallur SWE 13.19
3. Tessy Prediger GER 13.31
5. Julie Pratt 13.46
(2h2 13.71)

400 Metres Hurdles (14 Jul)
1. Sylvanie Morandais FRA 56.30
2. Aleksandra Pieluzek POL 56.51
3. Irena Zauna LAT 57.03
h1 Tracey Duncan dnf

High Jump (15 Jul)
1. Ruth Beitia ESP 1.87
2= Candeger Kilincer TUR 1.87
2= Marina Kuptsova RUS 1.87

Pole Vault (14 Jul)
1. Monika Pyrek POL 4.40
2. Annika Becker GER 4.40
3. Carolin Hingst GER 4.30

Long Jump (13 Jul)
1. Jade Johnson 6.52
2. Concepcion Montaner ESP 6.46
3. Aurelie Felix FRA 6.41

Triple Jump (15 Jul)
1. Irina Vasilyeva RUS 13.80
2. Marija Martinovic YUG 13.72
3. Amy Zongo FRA 13.68

Shot (12 Jul)
1. Nadezhda Ostapchuk BLR 19.73
2. Lucica Ciobanu ROM 17.59
3. Kathleen Kluge GER 17.06
10. Julie Dunkley 15.79

Discus (15 Jul)

1.	Melina Robert-Michon	FRA	58.52
2.	Ileana Brindusoiu	ROM	58.25
3.	Olga Goncharenko	BLR	57.71
14Q	**Rebecca Roles**		**48.52**

Hammer (13 Jul)

1.	Manuealla Montebrun	FRA	66.73
2.	Sini Poyry	FIN	64.71
3.	Cecilia Nilsson	SWE	64.06
22Q	**Zoe Derham**		**55.53**

Javelin (12 Jul)

1.	Nikolett Szabo	HUN	60.69
2.	Mercedes Chilla	ESP	57.78
3.	Moonika Aava	EST	56.12
17Q	**Jennifer Kemp**		**48.95**

Heptathlon (14-15 Jul)

1.	Liga Klavina	LAT	6279
2.	Svetlana Sokolova	RUS	6179
3.	Austra Skujyte	LTU	6087

20k Walk (15 Jul)

1.	Elisa Rigaudo	ITA	1:29:54
2.	Rita Turava	BLR	1:30:15
3.	Larissa Safronova	RUS	1:32:06

4 x 100 Metres (15 Jul)

1.	**Great Britain & NI**	**44.31**
	(Burnside, Roscoe, Scott, Oyepitan)	
2.	Belarus	44.64
3.	Finland	44.76

4 x 400 Metres (15 Jul)

1.	**Great Britain & NI**	**3:31.74**
	(Gear, Meadows, Duncan, Thieme)	
2.	Poland	3:32.38
3.	Ukraine	3:34.16

AAA CHAMPIONSHIPS Birmingham 13 - 15 July 2001
Including Norwich Union World Trials

A handful of top class performances, a 35th pole vault record for Janine Whitlock and a seventeen year old winner in Lloyd Finch, but somehow these championships failed to come alive. Perhaps it was an insight into the performances in the World Championships. There were the normal number of athletes missing through injury, but the most worrying aspect was the number of athletes in some events - the men's and women's high jump totalled nine between them.

MEN

100 Metres wind +1.7 (14 Jul)

1.	Dwain Chambers	10.01
2.	Mark Lewis-Francis	10.12
3.	Christian Malcolm	10.21
4.	Chris Lambert	10.24
5.	Doug Bignall	10.31
6.	Darren Campbell	10.38
7.	Curtis Browne	10.50
8.	Akinola Lashore	10.62

200 Metres wind+0.6 (15 Jul)

1.	Marlon Devonish	20.52
2.	Christian Malcolm	20.63
3.	Dwain Chambers	20.65
4.	Doug Turner	20.75
5.	Julian Golding	21.00
6.	Tim Benjamin	21.05
7.	Graham Beasley	21.48
dns	Chris Lambert	

400 Metres (15 Jul)

1.	Mark Richardson	45.79
2.	Iwan Thomas	46.00
3.	Mark Hylton	46.36
4.	Jamie Baulch	46.56
5.	Sean Baldock	46.61
6.	Jared Deacon	46.67
7.	Peter Brend	47.03
8.	Cori Henry	47.69

800 Metres (15 Jul)

1.	Neil Speaight	1:49.63
2.	James McIlroy	1:49.95
3.	Grant Cuddy	1:50.47
4.	Alasdair Donaldson	1:50.80
5.	Matthew Shone	1:50.81
6.	Neil Dougal	1:51.19
7.	Andy Young	1:51.72
8.	John Stewart	1:52.20

1500 Metres (15 Jul)

1.	John Mayock	3:44.05
2.	Tony Whiteman	3:44.40
3.	Tom Mayo	3:44.52
4.	Michael East	3:44.68
5.	James Thie	3:45.50
6.	Richard Ashe	3:45.87
7.	Andrew Graffin	3:46.34
8.	Vince Wilson	3:47.39

5000 Metres (15 Jul)

1.	Jon Wild	13:52.72
2.	Matt O'Dowd	13:53.53
3.	Mark Miles	13:53.74
4.	Spencer Barden	13:54.26
5.	Christian Nicolson	13:54.50
6.	Julian Moorhouse	13:55.37
7.	Steffan White	13:56.56
8.	Glen Stewart	14:00.08

10000 Metres (Watford 9 June)

	Seamus Power	IRL	28:18.38
1.	Glynn Tromans		28:31.33
2.	Jon Wild		28:39.33
3.	Glen Stewart		28:40.14
4.	Ian Hudspith		28:40.63
	Jean-Philippe Vindex	FRA	28:40.82
	Christian Nemeth	BEL	28:42.73
5.	Matt Smith		28:43.45

3000 Metres Steeplechase (15 Jul)

1.	Ben Whitby	8:32.68
2.	Stuart Stokes	8:33.15
3.	Christian Stephenson	8:39.33
4.	Charles Low	8:40.85
5.	Donald Naylor	8:45.93
6.	David Mitchinson	8:52.34
7.	Andrew Hennessy	8:53.59
8.	Rob Hough	9:03.57

110 Metres Hurdles wind+0.8 (14 Jul)

1.	Tony Jarrett	13.66
2.	Damien Greaves	13.68
3.	Dominic Bradley	13.83
4.	Neil Owen	13.87
5.	Paul Gray	13.88
6.	Mensah Elliott	13.88
7.	Duncan Malins	14.19
8.	Andrew Turner	14.29

400 Metres Hurdles (15 Jul)

1.	Chris Rawlinson	48.68
2.	Du'aine Thorne-Ladejo	49.44
3.	Anthony Borsumato	49.53
4.	Matthew Douglas	50.39
5.	James Hillier	51.37
6.	Steve Surety	51.82
7.	Richard Scott	53.33
8.	Robert Lewis	54.26

High Jump (14 Jul)

1.	Ben Challenger	2.17
2.	Dalton Grant	2.12
3.	Ian Holliday	2.07
4.	Colin McMaster	2.02

Pole Vault (15 Jul)

1.	Paul Williamson	5.30
2.	Tim Thomas	5.30
3.	Ashley Swain	5.20
4.	Ian Tullett	5.20
5.	Kevin Hughes	5.20
6=	Dean Mellor	4.80
6=	Scott Simpson	4.80
8=	Christian Linksey	4.80
8=	Matthew Weaver	4.80

Long Jump (14 Jul)
1. Nathan Morgan 7.80
2. Darren Thompson 7.52
3. Chris Davidson 7.37w
4. Steve Phillips 7.33
5. Paul Ralph 7.02
6. Stuart Wells 6.98
7. Gareth Brown 6.85
8. Anthony Malcolm 6.59

Triple Jump (15 Jul)
1. Jonathan Edwards 17.59
2. Larry Achike 16.99
3. Phillips Idowu 16.88
4. Julian Golley 16.30
5. Mike McKernan 15.49
6. Femi Akinsaya 15.48
7. Charles Madeira-Cole 15.10
8. Nicholas Thomas 14.97

Shot (15 Jul)
1. Mark Proctor 18.38
2. Emeka Udechuku 18.01
3. Scott Rider 16.86
4. David Condon 16.47

5. Lee Newman 16.41
6. Bruce Robb 16.34
7. Iain McMullan 15.99
8. Lyndon Woodward 15.97

Discus (15 Jul)
1. Glen Smith 59.99
2. Bob Weir 59.92
3. Perriss Wilkins 56.89
4. Emeka Udechuku 53.36
5. Bruce Robb 50.95
6. Matthew Twigg 50.51
7. Scott Rider 50.06
8. Neil Elliott 48.83

Hammer (14 Jul)
1. Mick Jones 74.40
2. Paul Head 70.33
3. Simon Bown 64.76
4. Shane Peacock 63.55
5. Chris Howe 61.95
6. Craig Ellams 61.11
7. Graham Holder 60.93
8. Chris Black 57.36

Javelin (15 Jul)
1. Mark Roberson 80.80
2. Mick Hill 79.98
3. Nick Nieland 77.91
4. Terry McHugh IRL 77.45
5. Neil McLellan 66.68
6. Tom Dobbing 62.06

5k Walk (14 Jul)
1. Lloyd Finch 20:47.23
2. Steve Hollier 21:04.36
3. Chris Cheeseman 21:05.29
4. Andrew Penn 21:18.02
5. Andrew Goudie 21:49.63
6. Dominic King 21:50.48
7. Mark Easton 22:10.65
8. Andrew Parker 22:36.98

Decathlon (Bedford 14-15 Jul)
1. John Heanley 7129
2. Darren Hatton 7019
3. James Holder CAN 6999
4. Anthony Sawyer 6983
5. Scott Exley 6594
6. Gavin Fordham 6590

WOMEN

100 Metres wind +2.3 (14 Jul)
1. Sarah Wilhelmy 11.41w
2. Amanda Forrester 11.42w
3. Joice Maduaka 11.42w
4. Marcia Richardson 11.45w
5. Shani Anderson 11.52w
6. Donita Benjamin 11.66w
7. Susan Williams 11.89w

dns Sam Davies

200 Metres wind +1.2 (15 Jul)
1. Sarah Reilly IRL 23.42
2. Shani Anderson 23.43
3. Susan Williams 23.79
4. Nathalie Beattie 24.51
5. Kelly Sotherton 24.53
6. Tatum Nelson 24.58
7. Nicole Bowring 24.64

Joice Maduaka dns

400 Metres (15 Jul)
1. Lesley Owusu 52.27
2. Donna Fraser 52.57
3. Lee McConnell 52.93
4. Helen Frost 53.19
5. Catherine Murphy 53.50
6. Dawn Higgins 54.97
7. Kim Goodwin 55.54
8. Michelle Thomas 55.57

800 Metres (14 Jul)
1. Kelly Holmes 2:02.61
2. Tanya Blake 2:04.08
3. Hayley Tullett 2:04.67
4. Alison Curbishley 2:05.22
5. Jo Fenn 2:05.58
6. Susan Scott 2:06.01
7. Rachel Newcombe 2:07.53
8. Mary McClung 2:11.10

1500 Metres (14 Jul)
1. Helen Pattinson 4:14.49
2. Liz Yelling 4:15.01
3. Ellen Leggate 4:16.13
4. Sarah Bull 4:19.30
5. Jo Wilkinson 4:22.34
6. Kerry Smithson 4:22.74
7. Hayley Parkinson-Ovens 4:23.20
8. Ann-Marie Hutchinson 4:29.62

5000 Metres (15 Jul)
1. Joanne Pavey 15:15.98
2. Hayley Yelling 15:23.28
3. Kathy Butler 15:34.12
4. Catherine Berry 15:57.61
5. Birhan Dagne 16:16.24
6. Deborah Sullivan 16:18.62

10000 Metres (Watford 9 Jun)

Irene Limika KEN 32:42.79
1. Penny Thackray 33:25.74
2. Beverley Jenkins 33:29.27
3. Sheila Fairweather 34:23.55
4. Debra Robinson 34:52.41
5. Louise Watson 35:41.99

100 Metres Hurdles wind +0.8 (15 Jul)
1. Diane Allahgreen 13.11
2. Melanie Wilkins 13.24
3. Keri Maddox 13.35
4. Denise Lewis 13.42
5. Rachel King 13.52
6. Clova Court 13.71
7. Helen Worsey 13.90

dnf Kerry Jury

400 Metres Hurdles (14 Jul)
1. Sinead Dudgeon 56.37
2. Keri Maddox 58.00
3. Hannah Wood 60.24
4. Hannah Stares 61.11
5. Celia Brown 61.26
6. Sian Scott 62.29
7. Nusrat Ceesay 62.75
8. Kim Heffernan 71.99

High Jump (15 Jul)

1. Susan Jones 1.91
2. Michelle Dunkley 1.86

3= Julie Hollman 1.68
3= Kerry Jury 1.68
5. Denise Lewis 1.68

Pole Vault (14 Jul)
1. Janine Whitlock 4.40
2. Lucy Webber 4.00
3. Irie Hill 4.00
4. Tracey Bloomfield 3.90
5. Sonia Lawrence 3.90
6. Laura Ballotta 3.80
7. Hilary Smith 3.60
8. Emma Hornby 3.60

Long Jump (15 Jul)
1. Ann Danson 6.15
2. Julie Hollman 6.09
3. Kelly Sotherton 5.99

4. Donita Benjamin 5.98
5. Ruth Irving 5.93
6. Kimberley Rothman 5.74
7. Debbie Harrison 5.64
8. Margaret Veldman NED 5.51

Triple Jump (14 Jul)
1. Ashia Hansen 14.09
2. Deborah Rowe 12.96w +2.3
3. Rebecca White 12.85
4. Caroline Stead 12.43w +2.5
5. Liz Patrick 12.27
6. Katie Evans 12.26
7. Marcia Walker 12.09
8. Anna-Maria Thorpe 12.08

Shot (14 Jul)
1. Jo Duncan 16.84
2. Julie Dunkley 16.31
3. Eva Massey 15.32
4. Maggie Lynes 14.87
5. Vicki Foster 14.23
6. Natasha Smith 13.13

Discus (14 Jul)
1. Shelley Drew 57.22
2. Philippa Roles 53.45
3. Vicki Foster 46.94
4. Debbie Callaway 44.20
5. Elaine Cank 43.07
6. Joanna Bradley 42.13

Hammer (15 Jul)
1. Lorraine Shaw 66.97
2. Lyn Sprules 59.38
3. Zoe Derham 59.30
4. Liz Pidgeon 58.97
5. Diana Holden 55.71
6. Sarah Moore 55.33
7. Suzanne Roberts 55.28
8. Lesley Brannan 54.97

Javelin (14 Jul)
1. Karen Martin 54.82
2. Kelly Morgan 54.49
3. Lorna Jackson 52.74
4. Linda Gray 50.01

5. Kirsty Morrison 49.42
6. Sharon Gibson 45.90
7. Denise Lewis 45.89
8. Katy Watts 43.01

5k Walk (14 Jul)
1. Niobe Menendez 23:46.30
2. Sharon Tonks 24:20.46
3. Wendy Bennett 24:35.85
4. Estle Viljoen 24:53.02
5. Miranda Heathcote 25:36.56
6. Karen Radcliffe 25:59.47

Heptathlon (Bedford 14-15 Jul)
1. Laura Redmond 5068
2. Katherine Brewington 4969
3. Charmaine Johnson 4908
4. Sarah Still 4825
5. Caroline Pearce 4795
6. Danielle Parkinson 4688
7. Claire Everett 4616
8. Victoria Consterdine
4372

EUROPEAN JUNIOR CHAMPIONSHIPS
Grosseto, ITA 19 - 22 July 2001

As with the U23 Championships, the Juniors showed their enormous potential and came home with seventeen medals. Mark Lewis-Francis won gold in both 100 and 4 x 100 relay as expected but most of the other medals were breakthroughs. Tim Benjamin's transfer to the 400 metres brought not only an individual gold but a silver in the 4 x 400 relay and also gold in the 4 x 100 relay. Vernicha James was one of the youngest winners and helped the sprint relay team to a medal. Two medals in the women's 400 m and gold in the 4 x 400 relay matched the U23 with medals in all the relays.

MEN

100 Metres wind +2.4 (20 Jul)
1. Mark Lewis-Francis 10.09w
(1h1 10.64)
2. Tim Goebel GER 10.18w
3. Igor Blazevic CRO 10.31w
4. Tyrone Edgar 10.35w
(2h3 10.77)

200 Metres wind +0.8 (21 Jul)
1. Ronald Pognon FRA 20.80
2. Kevin Ranse BEL 20.89
3. Dwayne Grant 20.92
(1h1 21.22)
5h2 Tim Abeyie 21.59

400 Metres (20 Jul)
1. Tim Benjamin 46.43
(1h1 47.33)
2. Johan Wissman SWE 46.81
3. Bastian Swillims GER 46.88
6. Robert Tobin 47.62
(2h2 47.42)

800 Metres (22 Jul)
1. Rene Herms GER 1:46.98
2. Arnoud Okken NED 1:48.02
3. Ricky Soos 1:48.43
(2h2 1:51.95)
7h1 James Nasrat 1:55.66

1500 Metres (22 Jul)
1. Cosimo Caliandro ITA 3:48.49
2. Tomasz Babiskiewicz POL 3:48.66
3. Arturo Casado ESP 3:48.76
8. Richard Ward 3:50.43
13. Matthew Jones 3:59.21

5000 Metres (22 Jul)
1. Mohamed Farah 14:09.91
2. Bruno Saramago POR 14:11.65
3. Noel Cutillas ESP 14:12.43

10000 Metres (19 Jul)
1. Vasiliy Matvichuk UKR 30:43.19
2. Aleksandr Nikalayuk BLR 30:46.37
3. Abdulrahman Kara TUR 31:00.36

3000 Metres Steeplechase (22 Jul)
1. Radoslaw Poplawski POL 8:46.36
2. Mircea Bogdan ROM 8:49.76
3. Hristoforos Meroussis GRE 8:51.87

110 Metres Hurdles wind +1.2 (21 Jul)
1. Philip Nossmy SWE 13.81
2. Sebastian Siebert GER 13.83
3. Dominic Girdler 14.16
(2h2 14.07w)
6. Nathan Palmer 14.28
(2h1 14.06)

400 Metres Hurdles (21 Jul)
1. Christian Duma GER 50.26
2. Henning Hackelbusch GER 50.76
3. Mikhail Lipskiy RUS 51.00
4h1 Jeffrey Christie 52.80
4h2 Steve Green 53.27

High Jump (21 Jul)
1. Andrey Chubsa BLR 2.23
2. Jiri Krehula CZE 2.21
3. Mickael Hanany FRA 2.19
12. Chuka Enih-Snell 1.95
(2.12Q)
18Q Darryl Stone 2.00

Pole Vault (22 Jul)
1. Dmitriy Kuptsov RUS 5.55
2. Kevin Rans BEL 5.50
3. Stavros Kouroupakis GRE 5.35

Long Jump (20 Jul)
1. Louis Tsatoumas GRE 7.98w
2. Jan Zumer SLO 7.72w
3. Dmitriy Sapinski RUS 7.72

Triple Jump (22 Jul)
1. Marian Oprea ROM 16.65
2. Jonathan Moore 16.43
3. Viktor Yastrebov UKR 16.43

Shot (20 Jul)
1. Michal Hodun POL 18.23
2. Robert Haggblom FIN 17.96
3. Marco Fortes POR 17.86
17Q Greg Beard 15.18

Discus (21 Jul)
1. Michal Hodun POL 57.95
2. Arnost Holovsky CZE 54.46
3. Dmitry Sivakov BLR 54.23

Hammer (22 Jul)
1. Krisztian Pars HUN 69.42
2. Aleksey Yeliseyev RUS 68.32
3. Esref Apak TUR 67.56

Javelin (21 Jul)
1. Aleksandr Ivanov RUS 80.18
2. Andreas Thorkildsen NOR 76.98
3. Saki Kuusisto FIN 76.98

Decathlon (19/20 Jul)
1. Ladji Doucoure FRA 7747
2. Lars Albert GER 7683
3. Atis Vaisjuns LAT 7497

10k Walk (21 Jul)
1. Yevgeniy Demkov RUS 43:34.12
2. Sergey Lystov RUS 43:39.46
3. Benjamin Kucinski POL 43:44.87
17. Dominic King 47:08.54
dsqLloyd Finch

4 x 100 Metres (22 Jul)
1. Great Britain & NI 39.24
(Edgar, Grant, Benjamin, Lewis-Francis)
(1h1 39.68)
2. France 39.76
3. Poland 39.96

4 x 400 Metres (22 Jul)
1. Poland 3:06.12
2. Great Britain & NI 3:06.21
(Tobin, Nicholls, Ellis, Benjamin)
(2h2 3:09.95 Christie for Benjamin)
3. Spain 3:07.47

WOMEN

100 Metres wind +2.1 (20 Jul)
1. Katchi Habel GER 11.24w
2. Gwlays Belliard FRA 11.50w
3. Amelie Huyghes FRA 11.59w
5. Danielle Norville 11.75w
(3h1 11.96)

200 Metres wind +1.4 (21 Jul)
1. Vernicha James 22.93
(1h3 23.44)
2. Katchi Habel GER 23.38
3. Maja Nose SLO 23.60

400 Metres (20 Jul)
1. Tatyana Firova RUS 52.94
2. Lisa Miller 53.29
(2h2 54.04)
3. Kim Wall 53.52
(1h1 54.21)

800 Metres (21 Jul)
1. Lucia Klocova SVK 2:03.76
2. Kirsten Werner GER 2:03.99
3. Tatyana Petlyuk UKR 2:04.15
4. Rebecca Lyne 2:05.44
(2h3 2:05.96)
6. Olivia Hines 2:06.01
(2h1 2:06.09)

1500 Metres (22 Jul)
1. Ljiljana Culibrk CRO 4:13.13
2. Emma Ward 4:13.51
(2h2 4:19.97)
3. Riina Tolonen FIN 4:14.48

3000 Metres (21 Jul)
1. Elvan Abeylegesse TUR 8:53.42
2. Tatyana Chulak RUS 9:02.65
3. Ulla Tuimala FIN 9:07.35
12. Louise Damen 9:38.02

5000 Metres (20 Jul)
1. Elvan Abeylegesse TUR 15:21.12
2. Elina Lindgren FIN 16:11.55
3. Collette Fagan 16:16.39

2000 Metres Steeplechase (22 Jul)
1. Cartalina Oprea ROM 6:34.89
2. Gwendoline Despres FRA 6:36.06
3. Antje Hoffmann GER 6:36.47
8. Jo Ankier 6:55.04
11. Kathryn Frost 7:04.34

100 Metres Hurdles wind +2.1 (20 Jul)
1. Gergana Stoyanova BUL 13.04w
2. Adrianna Lamalle FRA 13.08w
3. Lucie Skrobakova CZE 13.30w
4h2Helen Worsey 13.66
6h1Sarah McGreavy 13.88w

400 Metres Hurdles (21 Jul)
1. Zofia Malachowska POL 57.78
2. Patricia Lopes POR 57.93
3. Mariya Menshikova RUS 58.83

High Jump (22 Jul)
1. Ramona Pop ROM 1.88
2. Anna Chicherova RUS 1.88
3. Anna Ksok POL 1.88
8. Aileen Wilson 1.86
12. Stephanie Higham 1.79
(1.83Q)

Pole Vault (21 Jul)
1. Yelena Isinbayeva RUS 4.40
2. Natalya Kushtsh UKR 4.15
3. Vanessa Boslak FRA 4.15

Long Jump (22 Jul)
1. Anastasia Ilyina RUS 6.38
2. Alina Militaru ROM 6.32
3. Katarzyna Klisowska POL 6.26

Triple Jump (20 Jul)
1. Anastasia Ilyina RUS 13.86
2. Athanassia Perra GRE 13.73w
3. Viktoriya Gurova RUS 13.41

Shot (19 Jul)
1. Natalya Kharaneka BLR 16.92
2. Kristin Marten GER 16.02
3. Claudia Villeneuve FRA 15.82

Discus (20 Jul)
1. Natalya Fokina UKR 56.69
2. Vera Begic CRO 55.02
3. Olga Chernogorova BLR 54.49
6. Emma Carpenter 53.00
8. Claire Smithson 49.61

Hammer (21 Jul)
1. Ivana Brkljacic CRO 64.18
2. Martina Danisova SVK 61.97
3. Berta Castells ESP 61.04

Javelin (22 Jul)
1. Galina Kahova BLR 55.40
2. Goldie Sayers 55.40
3. Marion Bonaudo FRA 53.71

Heptathlon (21/22 Jul)
1. Carolina Kluft SWE 6022
2. Maren Freisen GER 5956
3. Olga Karas RUS 5745

10k Walk (19 Jul)
1. Tatyana Kozlova RUS 46:22.67
2. Athanassia Tzoumeleka GRE 46:29.20
3. Beatriz Pascual ESP 46:49.81

4 x 100 Metres (22 Jul)
1. Germany 44.16
2. France 44.37
3. Great Britain & NI 44.66
(Norville, Caney, Spencer, James)

4 x 400 Metres (22 Jul)
1. Great Britain & NI 3:34.63
(Wall, Hines, James, Miller)
2. Germany 3:36.20
3. Romania 3:41.12

FRA v GB & NI (U19) Dole, FRA 29 July 2001

A very close fought international match with only two points separating the overall team results. Danielle Norville was a double winner taking both the women's sprints.

MEN

100 Metres wind –0.3
1. **Aidan Syers** **10.52**
2. **Rikki Fifton** **10.56**
4. **Laurence Oboh** **10.70**

200 Metres wind –0.1
1. Xavier Guillaume FRA 21.13
2. **Laurence Oboh** **21.30**
3. **Simon Farenden** **21.63**
4. **David Ripley** **21.81**

400 Metres
1. **Robert Tobin** **47.10**
3. **Russell Nicholls** **47.80**
5. **Ryan Palmer** **48.55**

800 Metres
1. Mathias Castingo FRA 1:50.99
3. **Chris Watson** **1:53.47**
dsq **James Nasrat**

1500 Metres
1. **Chris Stoves** **3:54.0**
2. **Derek Watson** **3:55.7**

3000 Metres
1. **Edward Prickett** **8:35.41**
3. **Tom Sharland** **8:41.49**

110 Metres Hurdles wind –1.5
1. Eddy Delepine FRA 14.50
3. **Ross Tressider** **15.54**
4. **David Hughes** **15.65**

400 Metres Hurdles
1. **Steven Green** **52.62**
3. **Mark Winship** **54.83**

2000 Metres Steeplechase
1. Mounir Yemmouni FRA 5:51.23
2. **Stephen Murphy** **5:55.26**
4. **Daniel Lewis** **6:09.06**

High Jump
1. Herve Paris FRA 2.10
2= **Darryl Stone** **2.03**
2= **Martin Aram** **2.03**

Pole Vault
1. Vincent Favretto FRA 5.15
3. **Paul Stevens** **4.70**
4. **Richard Hurren** **4.10**

Long Jump
1. **Jonathan Moore** **7.98**
3. **Onen Eyong** **7.26**

Triple jump
1. Daniel Mayaud FRA 15.12
3. **Kevin Thompson** **14.67**
4. **Lewis Cheung** **13.66**

Shot
1. Bertrand Vili FRA 16.82
3. **David Dawson** **14.26**
4. **Derrick Squire** **14.17**

Discus
1. Bertrand Vili FRA 51.97
3. **Chris Orr** **41.84**
4. **Carl Saggers** **40.93**

Hammer
1. Frederic Pouzy FRA 64.12
2. **Carl Saggers** **55.56**
3. **Tom Dempsey** **55.48**

Javelin
1. **Andrew Gallagher** **63.92**
4. **Sam Goddard** **56.77**

5k Walk
1. **Lloyd Finch** **21:47.8**
2. **Dominic King** **22:24.6**

4 x 100 Metres
1. **France** **40.97**
dnf **Great Britain & NI**
(Syers, Oboh, Fifton, Ripley)

4 x 400 Metres
1. France 3:11.02
2. **Great Britain & NI** **3:11.83**
(Nicholls, Green, Palmer, Tobin)

Match result – Men
1. France 178
2. **Great Britain & NI** **167**

WOMEN

100 Metres wind –0.3
1. **Danielle Norville** **11.83**
2. **Anyika Onuora** **11.86**
4. **Amala Onuora** **12.01**

200 Metres wind –1.2
1. **Danielle Norville** **24.07**
3. **Lisa Miller** **24.41**
6. **Karen Oughton** **25.09**

400 Metres
1. **Kim Wall** **54.43**
2. **Olivia Hines** **54.97**
3. **Christine Ohurugu** **55.29**

800 Metres
1. **Jemma Simpson** **2:08.33**
2. **Ellie Childs** **2:09.20**

1500 Metres
1. **Zoe Jelbert** **4:30.9**
3. **Danielle Barnes** **4:33.0**

3000 Metres
1. **Rachael Nathan** **9:35.26**
2. **Charlotte Dale** **9:41.31**

100 Metres Hurdles wind –0.1
1. **Stefanie Pullinger** **13.9**
4. **Leyna Hird** **14.5**

400 Metres Hurdles
1. Christelle Charles FRA 60.05
2. **Gemma Dooney** **61.09**
3. **Faye Harding** **61.09**

High Jump
1. **Stephanie Higham** **1.80**
4. **Claire Wright** **1.68**

Pole Vault
1. Leatitia Feneon FRA 3.81
3. **Zoe Brown** **3.60**
4. **Kirsty Maguire** **3.35**

Long Jump
1. Celine Laporte FRA 6.03
2. **Elaine Smith** **5.97**
4. **Sarah Humphreys** **5.54**

Triple Jump
1. Zelica Montout FRA 12.57
3. **Katherine Streatfield** **12.15**
4. **Angela Barratt** **11.76**

Shot
1. Claudia Villeneive FRA 15.54
3. **Rebecca Peake** **13.68**
4. **Claire Smithson** **13.41**

Discus
1. **Claire Smithson** **50.68**
3. **Ellisha Dee** **40.45**

Hammer
1. **Nicola Dudman** **54.54**
4. **Frances Miller** **48.10**

Javelin
1. Doriane Gilibert FRA 46.87
3. **Louise Matthews** **44.46**
4. **Samantha Redd** **40.43**

3k Walk
1. Julie Goubault FRA 13:58.36
2. **Katie Stones** **14:25.91**
4. **Clare Reeves** **16:31.41**

4 x 100 Metres
1. France 45.92
2. **Great Britain & NI** **45.94**
(Am. Onuora, Norville, Caney, An.Onuora)

4 x 400 Metres
1. **Great Britain & NI** **3:39.04**
(Hines, Ohurugu, Miller, Wall)
2. France 3:44.99

Match Result – Women
1. **Great Britain & NI** **171**
2. France 162

Match Result – Combined
1. France 340
2. **Great Britain & NI** **338**

8th IAAF WORLD CHAMPIONSHIPS
Edmonton, CAN 3 - 12 August 2001

By every criteria this was a poor championship for Britain - only two medals and a smaller number of finallists than in any previous World Championship. Certainly injury did play a part - no Merry, Lewis or Campbell, but at this level there is no room for the slightest error and some of Britain's stars did not shine. Indeed Jonathan Edwards only qualified on his last jump and Dean Macey battled injury for two days, it could have been much worse.

MEN

100 Metres wind –0.2 (5 Aug)
1. Maurice Greene USA 9.82
2. Tim Montgomery USA 9.85
3. Bernard Williams USA 9.94
4. Ato Boldon TRI 9.98
5. **Dwain Chambers** **9.99**
(2h9 10.27, 1q4 9.97w?, 3s2 10.10)
6. Kim Collins SKN 10.07
7. **Christian Malcolm** **10.11**
(2h4 10.24, 2q5 10.09w?, 4s2 10.24)
8. Abdul Aziz Zakari GHA 10.24
5s1 Mark Lewis-Francis **10.26**
(1h8 10.21, 1q3 9.97w?)

200 Metres wind +0.1 (9 Aug)
1. Konstadinos Kederis GRE 20.04
2. Christopher Williams USA 20.20
3= Shawn Crawford USA 20.20
3= Kim Collins SKN 20.20
5. **Christian Malcolm** **20.22**
(1h5 20.37, 1q1 20.13, 1s1 20.08)
6. Stephane Buckland MRI 20.24
7. Kevin Little USA 20.25
8. **Marlon Devonish** **20.38**
(2h3 20.58, 3q2 20.44, 4s2 20.29)
5q4 Dwain Chambers **20.60**
(4h2 20.80)

400 Metres (6 Aug)
1. Avard Moncur BAH 44.64
2. Ingo Schulz GER 44.87
3. Greg Haughton JAM 44.98
4. Antonio Pettigrew USA 44.99
5. Eric Milazar MRI 45.13
6. Hamdam Al-Bishi KSA 45.23
7. Alleyne Francique GRN 46.23
dnf Robert Mackowiak POL
4s1 Mark Richardson **45.14**
(2h2 45.66)
8s2 Iwan Thomas **46.72**
(3h5 45.92)
5h7 Jamie Baulch **46.15**

800 Metres (7 Aug)
1. Andre Bucher SUI 1:43.70
2. Wilfred Bungei KEN 1:44.55
3. Pawel Czapiewski POL 1:44.63
4. William Yiampoy KEN 1:44.96
5. Nils Schumann GER 1:45.00
6. Mbulaeni Mulaudzi RSA 1:45.01
7. Khalid Tighazouine MAR 1:45.58
8. Hezekiel Sepeng RSA 1:46.68

1500 Metres (12 Aug)
1. Hicham El Guerrouj MAR 3:30.68
2. Bernard Lagat KEN 3:31.10
3. Driss Maazouzi FRA 3:31.54
4. William Chirchir KEN 3:31.91
5. Reyes Esyevez ESP 3:32.34
6. Jose Redolat ESP 3:34.29
7. Rui Silva POR 3:35.74
8. Abdelkader Hachlaf MAR 3:36.54
7s1 Anthony Whiteman **3:36.77**
(6h2 3:37.75)
10s2 John Mayock **3:42.63**
(8h1 3:39.24)

5000 Metres (10 Aug)
1. Richard Limo KEN 13:00.77
2. Million Wolde ETH 13:03.47
3. John Kibowen KEN 13:05.20
4. Alberto Garcia ESP 13:05.60
5. Ismail Sghir FRA 13:07.71
6. Sammy Kipketer KEN 13:08.46
7. Abiyote Abate ETH 13:14.07
8. Hailu Mekonnen ETH 13:20.24
dsq Ali Saidi-Sief (drugs)
13s2 Mike Openshaw **14:00.84**

10000 Metres (8 Aug)
1. Charles Kamathi KEN 27:53.25
2. Assefa Mezgebu ETH 27:53.97
3. Haile Gebrselassie ETH 27:54.41
4. Yibeltal Admassu ETH 27:55.24
5. Fabian Roncero ESP 27:56.07
6. Jose Rios ESP 27:56.68
7. Paul Kosgei KEN 27:57.56
8. John Ch. Korir KEN 27:58.06

Marathon (3 Aug)
1. Gezahegne Abera ETH 2:12:42
2. Simon Biwott KEN 2:12:43
3. Stefano Baldini ITA 2:13:18
4. Tesfaye Tolla ETH 2:13:58
5. Shigeru Aburaya JPN 2:14:07
6. Abdelkader El Mouaziz MAR 2:15:41
7. Tesfaye Jifar ETH 2:16:52
8. Yoshiteru Morishita JPN 2:17:05

World Cup – Team Result
1. Ethiopia 6:43:32
2. Japan 6:48:36
3. Italy 6:51:56

3000 Metres Steeplechase (8 Aug)
1. Reuben Kosgei KEN 8:15.16
2. Ali Ezzine MAR 8:16.21
3. Bernard Barmasai KEN 8:16.59
4. Luis Miguel Martin ESP 8:18.87
5. Bouabdallah Tahri FRA 8:19.56
6. Antonio Jimenez ESP 8:19.82
7. Khamis Abdullah QAT 8:20.01
8. Raymond Yator KEN 8:20.87

110 Metres Hurdles wind –0.3 (9 Aug)
1. Allen Johnson USA 13.04
2. Anier Garcia CUB 13.07
3. Dudley Dorival HAI 13.25
4. Yoel Hernandez CUB 13.30
5. Robert Kronberg SWE 13.51
6. Yevgeniy Pechonkin RUS 13.52
7. Dawane Wallace USA 13.76
8. Shaun Bownes RSA 13.84
s2 Tony Jarrett **dsq**
(3h1 13.64)
6h2 Paul Gray **13.96**
h3 Damien Greaves **dsq**

400 Metres Hurdles (10 Aug)
1. Felix Sanchez DOM 47.49
2. Fabrizio Mori ITA 47.54
3. Dai Tamesue JPN 47.89
4. Hadi Al-Somaily KSA 47.99
5. **Chris Rawlinson** **48.54**
(1h5 49.38, 1s2 48.27)
6. Pawel Januszewski POL 48.57
7. Jiri Muzik CZE 49.07
Boris Gorban RUS dq
6s1 Anthony Borsumato **49.48**
(4h4 49.65)

High Jump (8 Aug)
1. Martin Buss GER 2.36
2= Yaroslav Rybakov RUS 2.33
2= Vyacheslav Voronin RUS 2.33
4. Javier Sotomayor CUB 2.33
5= Stefan Holm SWE 2.30
5= Sergey Klyugin RUS 2.30

7= Mark Boswell CAN 2.25
7= Staffan Strand SWE 2.25
18=QBen Challenger 2.20

Pole Vault (9 Aug)
1. Dmitriy Markov AUS 6.05
2. Aleksandr Averbukh ISR 5.85
3. Nick Hysong USA 5.85
4. Michael Stolle GER 5.85
5. Romain Mesnil FRA 5.85
6= Richard Spiegelburg GER 5.75
6= Christian Tamminga NED 5.75
8. Adam Kolasa POL 5.75
22=QNick Buckfield 5.30

Long Jump (11 Aug)
1. Ivan Pedroso CUB 8.40
2. Savante Stringfellow USA 8.24
3. Carlos Calado POR 8.21
4. Miguel Pate USA 8.21w
5. Kareem Streete-Thompson CAY 8.10
6. Aleksey Lukashevich UKR 8.10
7. James Beckford JAM 8.08
8. Dwight Phillips USA 7.92

Triple Jump (6 Aug)
1. Jonathan Edwards 17.92 (17.46Q)
2. Christian Olsson SWE 17.47
3. Igor Spasovhodskiy RUS 17.44
4. Yoel Garcia CUB 17.40
5. Walter Davis USA 17.20
6. Brian Wellman BER 16.81
7. Larry Achike 17.69 (17.15Q)
8. Rostislav Dimitrov BUL 16.72w
9. Phillips Idowu 16.60 (16.74Q)

Shot (4 Aug)
1. John Godina USA 21.87
2. Adam Nelson USA 21.24
3. Arsi Harju FIN 20.93
4. Manuel Martinez ESP 20.91
5. Dragan Peric YUG 20.91
6. Yuriy Belonog UKR 20.83
7. Conny Karlsson FIN 20.78
8. Brad Snyder CAN 20.63
30Q Mark Proctor 17.75

Discus (8 Aug)
1. Lars Riedel GER 69.72
2. Virgilijus Alekna LTU 69.40
3. Michael Mollenbeck GER 67.61
4. Dmitriy Shevchenko RUS 67.57
5. Adam Setliff USA 66.55
6. Vasiliy Kaptyukh BLR 66.25
7. Roland Varga HUN 65.86
8. Frantz Kruger RSA 65.27
15Q Robert Weir 61.05

Hammer (5 Aug)
1. Szymon Ziolkowski POL 83.38
2. Koji Murofushi JPN 82.92
3. Ilya Konovalov RUS 80.27
4. Nicola Vizzoni ITA 80.13
5. Andrey Skvaruk UKR 79.93
6. Balazs Kiss HUN 79.75
7. Igor Astapkovich BLR 79.72
8. Tibor Gecsek HUN 79.34
27Q Mick Jones 73.31

Javelin (12 Aug)
1. Jan Zelezny CZE 92.80
2. Aki Parviainen FIN 91.31
3. Kostas Gatsioudis GRE 89.95
4. Breaux Greer USA 87.00
5. Raymond Hecht GER 86.46
6. Boris Henry GER 85.52
7. Sergey Makarov RUS 83.64
8. Eriks Rags LAT 82.62
12. Mick Hill 77.81 (84.88Q)
14QSteve Backley 81.50
21QNick Nieland 78.02

Decathlon (6/7 Aug)
1. Tomas Dvorak CZE 8902
2. Erki Nool EST 8815
3. Dean Macey 8603
4. Attila Zsivoczky HUN 8371
5. Lev Lobodin RUS 8352
6. Jiri Ryba CZE 8332
7. Stefan Schmid GER 8307
8. Laurent Hernu FRA 8280

20k Walk (4 Aug)
1. Roman Rasskazov RUS 1:20:31
2. Ilya Markov RUS 1:20:33
3. Viktor Burayev RUS 1:20:36
4. Nathan Deakes AUS 1:20:55
5. David Marquez ESP 1:21:09
6. Joel Sanchez MEX 1:22:05
7. Satoshi Yanagisawa JPN 1:22:11
8. Jefferson Perez ECU 1:22:20

50k Walk (10 Aug)
1. Robert Korzeniowski POL 3:42:08
2. Jesus Garcia ESP 3:43:07
3. Edgar Hernandez MEX 3:46:13
4. Aigars Fadejevs LAT 3:46:20
5. Vladimir Potemin RUS 3:46:53
6. Valenti Massana ESP 3:48:28
7. Curt Clausen USA 3:50.46
8. Marco Giungi ITA 3:51:09

4 x 100 Metres (12 Aug)
1. United Sates 37.92
2. South Africa 38.47
3. Trinidad & Tobago 38.58
4. Australia 38.83
5. Japan 38.96
6. Ivory Coast 39.18
7. Poland 39.71

Brazil dnf

h4 Great Britain & NI dnf (Chambers, Devonish, Malcolm, Barbour)

4 x 400 Metres (12 Aug)
1. United States 2:57.54
2. Bahamas 2:58.19
3. Jamaica 2:58.39
4. Poland 2:59.71
5. Brazil 3:01.09
6. **Great Britain & NI 3:01.26 (Thomas, Baulch, Benjamin, Richardson) (2h1 3:00.96 Hylton for Baulch)**
7. Spain 3:02.24
8. Germany 3:03.52

WOMEN

100 Metres wind –0.3 (6 Aug)
1. Zhanna Pintusevich UKR 10.82
2. Marion Jones USA 10.85
3. Ekaterini Thanou GRE 10.91
4. Chandra Sturrup BAH 11.02
5. Chryste Gaines USA 11.06
6. Debbie Ferguson BAH 11.13
7. Kelli White USA 11.15
8. Mercy Nku NGR 11.17

7q2Abiodun Oyepitan 11.61 (3h8 11.45)
8q4Marcia Richardson 11.59 (4h3 11.52)
5h6Shani Anderson 11.54

200 Metres wind –0.8 (10 Aug)
1. Marion Jones USA 22.39
2. Debbie Ferguson BAH 22.52
3. Kelli White USA 22.56
4. LaTasha Jenkins USA 22.85
5. Cydonie Mothersill CAY 22.88
6. Juliet Campbell JAM 22.99
7. Alenka Bikar SLO 23.00
8. Myriam Mani CMR 23.15

400 Metres (7 Aug)
1. Amy Mbacke Thiam SEN 49.86
2. Lorraine Fenton JAM 49.88
3. Ana Guevara MEX 49.97
4. Grit Breuer GER 50.49
5. Nadjina Kaltouma CHA 50.80
6. Olesya Zykina RUS 50.93
7. Mireille Nguimbo CMR 51.97

dnf Falilat Ogunkoya NGR

6s3Donna Fraser 51.77 (4h5 52.02)
4h5Catherine Murphy 52.40

800 Metres (12 Aug)
1. Maria Mutola MOZ 1:57.17
2. Stephanie Graf AUT 1:57.20
3. Letitia Vriesde SUR 1:57.35
4. Faith Macharia KEN 1:58.98
5. Diane Cummins CAN 1:59.49
6. Kelly Holmes 1:59.76
(2h1 2:00.08, 2s1 2:01.90)
7. Mayte Martinez ESP 2:00.09
8. Ivonne Teichmann GER 2:04.33

1500 Metres (7 Aug)
1. Gabriela Szabo ROM 4:00.57
2. Violeta Szekely ROM 4:01.70
3. Natalya Gorelova RUS 4:02.40
4. Carla Sacramento POR 4:03.96
5. Lidia Chojecka POL 4:06.70
6. Natalia Rodriguez ESP 4:07.10
7. Alesya Turova BLR 4:07.25
8. Sureyya Ayhan TUR 4:08.17
9s2 Hayley Tullett 4:13.95
(2h3 4:13.60)
9s1 Helen Pattinson 4:16.39
(9h2 4:13.06)

5000 Metres (11 Aug)
1. Olga Yegorova RUS 15:03.39
2. Marta Dominguez ESP 15:06.59
3. Ayelech Worku ETH 15:10.17
4. Dong Yanmei CHN 15:10.73
5. Irina Mikitenko GER 15:13.93
6. Yelena Zadorozhnaya RUS 15:16.15
7. Edith Masai KEN 15:17.67
8. Gabriela Szabo ROM 15:19.55
11. Joanne Pavey 15:28.41
(2h2 15:10.62)
7h1 Kathy Butler 15:20.78
16h1 Hayley Yelling 15:59.39

10000 Metres (7 Aug)
1. Derartu Tulu ETH 31:48.81
2. Berhane Adere ETH 31:48.85
3. Gete Wami ETH 31:49.98
4. Paula Radcliffe 31:50.06
5. Mihaela Botezan ROM 32:03.46
6. Lyudmila Petrova RUS 32:04.94
7. Asmae Leghzaoui MAR 32:06.35
8. Yamna Belkacem FRA 32:09.21

Marathon (12 Aug)
1. Lidia Simon ROM 2:26:01
2. Reiko Toas JPN 2:26:06
3. Svetlana Zakharova RUS 2:26:18
4. Yoku Shibui JPN 2:26:33
5. Sonja Krolik GER 2:28:17
6. Florence Barsosio KEN 2:28:36
7. Shitaye Gemeche ETH 2:28:40
8. Lyubov Morgunova RUS 2:28:54

World Cup – Team Result
1. Japan 7:22:36
2. Russia 7:26.00
3. Romania 7:29.44

100 Metres Hurdles wind +2.0 (11 Aug)
1. Anjanette Kirkland USA 12.42
2. Gail Devers USA 12.54
3. Olga Shishigina KAZ 12.58
4. Svetla Dimitrova BUL 12.58
5. Jenny Adams USA 12.63
6. Dianne Rose-Henley JAM 12.79
7. Linda Ferga FRA 12.80
8. Vonette Dixon JAM 13.02

400 Metres Hurdles (8 Aug)
1. Nezha Bidouane MAR 53.34
2. Yuliya Nosova RUS 54.27
3. Daimi Pernia CUB 54.51
4. Tonja Buford-Bailey USA 54.55
5. Debbie-Ann Parris JAM 54.68
6. Ionela Tirlea ROM 55.36
7. Deon Hemmings JAM 55.83
8. Sandra Glover USA 57.42
8s2 Sinead Dudgeon 56.92
(2h4 56.07)
4h3 Natasha Danvers 56.36
7h2 Keri Maddox 57.55

High Jump (12 Aug)
1. Hestrie Cloete RSA 2.00
2. Inga Babakova UKR 2.00
3. Kajsa Bergqvist SWE 1.97
4. Venelina Veneva BUL 1.97
5. Vita Palamar UKR 1.94
6. Blanka Vlasic CRO 1.94
7= Monica Dinescu ROM 1.90
7= Dora Gyorffy HUN 1.90
13=Q Susan Jones 1.88

Pole Vault (6 Aug)
1. Stacy Dragila USA 4.75
2. Svetlana Feofanova RUS 4.75
3. Monika Pyrek POL 4.55
4. Tatiana Grigorieva AUS 4.55
5. Gao Shuying CHN 4.50
6. Thorey Elisdottir ISL 4.45
7. Yvonne Buschbaum GER 4.45
8. Pavla Hamackova CZE 4.45
9. Janine Whitlock 4.35
(4.35Q)

Long Jump (7 Aug)
1. Fiona May ITA 7.02w
2. Tatyana Kotova RUS 7.01w
3. Niurka Montalvo ESP 6.88w
4. Tunde Vaszi HUN 6.86
5. Valentina Gotovska LAT 6.84w
6. Niki Xanthou GRE 6.76w
7. Maurren Maggi BRA 6.73
8. Lyudmila Galkina RUS 6.70

Triple Jump (10 Aug)
1. Tatyana Lebedeva RUS 15.25
2. Francoise Mbango CMR 14.60
3. Tereza Marinova BUL 14.58
4. Magdelin Martinez ITA 14.52
5. Heli Koivula FIN 14.28
6. Cristina Nicolau ROM 14.17
7. Ashia Hansen 14.10
(14.51Q)
8. Trecia Smith JAM 13.92

Shot (5 Aug)
1. Yanina Korolchik BLR 20.61
2. Nadine Kleinert-Schmitt GER 19.86
3. Vita Pavlysh UKR 19.41
4. Larisa Peleshenko RUS 19.37
5. Irina Korzhanenko RUS 19.35
6. Astrid Kumbernuss GER 19.25
7. Nadezhda Ostapchuk BLR 18.98
8. Yumileida Cumba CUB 18.73

Discus (11 Aug)
1. Natalya Sadova RUS 68.57
2. Ellina Zvereva BLR 67.10
3. Nicoleta Grasu ROM 66.24
4. Anastasia Kelesidou GRE 65.50
5. Franka Dietzsch GER 65.38
6. Seilala Sua USA 63.74
7. Vera Pospisilova CZE 61.47
8. Kristin Kuehl USA 61.04

Hammer (7 Aug)
1. Yipsi Moreno CUB 70.65
2. Olga Kuzenkova RUS 70.61
3. Bronwyn Eagles AUS 68.87
4. Kamila Skolimowska POL 68.05
5. Manuela Montebrun FRA 67.78
6. Lorraine Shaw 65.89
7. Florence Ezeh FRA 65.88
8. Ivana Brkljacic CRO 65.43

Javelin (6 Aug)
1. Osleidys Menendez CUB 69.53
2. Mirela Tzelili GRE 65.78
3. Sonia Bisset CUB 64.69
4. Nikola Tomeckova CZE 63.11
5. Steffi Nerius GER 62.08
6. Mikaela Ingberg FIN 61.94
7. Xiomara Rivero CUB 61.60
8. Aggeliki Tsiolakoudi GRE 61.01

Heptathlon (4/5 Aug)
1. Yelena Prokhorova RUS 6694
2. Natalya Sazanovich BLR 6539
3. Shelia Burrell USA 6472
4. Natalya Roshchupkina RUS 6294
5. Karin Ertl GER 6283
6. Austra Skujyte LTU 6112
7. DeDee Nathan USA 6073
8. Irina Belova RUS 6061

20k Walk (9 Aug)
1. Olimpiada Ivanova RUS 1:27:48
2. Valentina Tsbulskaya BLR 1:28:49
3. Elisabetta Perrone ITA 1:28:56
4. Erica Alfridi ITA 1:29:48
5. Maria Vasco ESP 1:30:19
6. Norica Cimpean ROM 1:30:39
7. Melanie Seeger GER 1:30:41
8. Annarita Sidoti ITA 1:31:40

4 x 100 Metres (11 Aug)

1. United States 41.71
2. Germany 42.32
3. France 42.39
4. Jamaica 42.40
5. Nigeria 42.52
6. **Great Britain & NI 42.60**

(Richardson, Wilhelmy, James, Oyepitan)
(3h1 43.08)

7. Greece 43.25
8. Russia 43.58

4 x 400 Metres (12 Aug)

1. Jamaica 3:20.65
2. Germany 3:21.97
3. Russia 3:24.92
4. United States 3:26.88
5. **Great Britain & NI 3:26.94**

(McConnell, Frost, Danvers, Murphy)
(2h2 3:27.25)
(McConnell, Owusu, Murphy, Fraser)

6. France 3:27.54
7. Poland 3:27.78
8. Canada 3:27.93

GB & NI v FRA v GER v ITA v SUI Combined Events
Bedford 4 - 5 August 2001

MEN Decathlon

1. David Botrel FRA 7306
3. **Fyn Corcoran 7039**
5. **Darren Hatton 7020**
7. **Scott Exley 6759**
8. **John Heanley 6753**

MEN U23 Decathlon

1. Matthias Spahn GER 7600
12. **Brendan McConville 6702**
13. **Adrian Hemery 6573**
16. **Gavin Fordham 5993**

dnf Jason McDade

MEN U20 Decathlon

1. Nadir El Fassi FRA 7007
13. **James Wright 6177**
15. **Steven Hughes 6114**
16. **Carl Marchment 6048**
17. **John Dickinson 5976**

WOMEN Heptathlon

1. **Julie Hollman 5537**
2. **Kerry Jury 5476**
3. **Julia Bennett 5406**

dnf Nicola Gautier

WOMEN U23 Heptathlon

1. Annellie Schrader GER 5513
5. **Laura Redmond 5039**
9. **Kate Brewington 4711**

dnf Caroline Pearce
dnf Fiona Harrison

WOMEN U20 Heptathlon

1. Jennifer Oesner GER 5500
4. **Rosalyn Gonse 5053**
9. **Jessica Ennis 4801**
16. **Wendy Davidson 4441**
17. **Natalie Hulse 4386**

GB & NI v FRA v 'A' INTERNATIONAL
Ashford 11 August 2001

MEN

100 Metres wind –2.9

1. **Chris Lambert 10.74**
3. **Jason Gardener 10.92**
5. **Darren Chin** U23 **10.96**

200 Metres wind –2.0

1. **Doug Turner 21.55**
2. **Daniel Money 21.78**
6. **James Chatt** U23 **22.04**

400 Metres

1. **Jared Deacon 47.24**
3. **Adam Potter** U23 **48.06**
6. **Neil Jennings 50.41**

800 Metres

1. Florent Lacasse FRA 1:47.76
4. **Neil Dougal** U23 **1:50.65**
5. **Gary Vickers 1:50.84**
6. **Alasdair Donaldson 1:51.34**

1500 Metres

1. Siahka Bamba FRA 3:57.85
4. **James Thie 3:59.11**
5. **Neil Bangs** U23 **3:59.45**
6. **Richard Ashe 3:59.51**

3000 Metres

1. Mustapha Essaid FRA 8:03.99
2. **Jon Wild 8:04.95**
4. **Spencer Barden 8:11.36**
5. **Chris Thompson** U23 **8:35.56**

3000 Metres Steeplechase

1. **Stuart Stokes 8:59.10**
3. **Don Naylor 9:02.31**
6. **Andy Franklin** U23 **9:20.85**

110 Metres Hurdles wind –3.4

1. Vincent Clarico FRA 14.14
3. **Mensah Elliott 14.29**
4. **Neil Owen 14.86**

dnf Andrew Turner U23

400 Metres Hurdles

1. Oliver Jean-Theodore FRA 50.73
2. **Richard McDonald** U23 **52.53**
5. **Matt Douglas 52.99**
6. **Charles Robertson-Adams 53.89**

High Jump

1. **Dalton Grant 2.21**

3= **Rob Mitchell** U23 **2.18**

6. **Ian Holliday 2.10**

Pole Vault

1. **Tim Thomas 5.40**
3. **Paul Williamson 5.20**
6. **Scott Simpson** U23 **4.80**

Long Jump

Gable Garenamotse gst/BOT 8.26w

1. **Chris Tomlinson** U23 **8.19w**
5. **Darren Thompson 7.58w**
6. **Steve Shalders 7.28w**

Triple Jump

1. **Julian Golley 16.93w**
4. **Femi Akinsaya 16.28w**
6. **Steve Shalders** U23 **15.88**

Shot

1. **Lee Newman 17.59**
4. **Emeka Udechuku 16.71**
6. **Nicholas Owen** U23 **14.16**

Discus

1. **Glen Smith 61.29**
2. **Emeka Udechuku 59.53**
6. **Luke Rosenberg** U23 **49.35**

Hammer
1. Raphael Piolanti FRA 72.28
4. **Paul Head 64.69**
5. **Andy Frost U23 60.39**

Javelin
1. **Mark Roberson 78.60**
3. **David Parker 70.06**
6. **Dan Carter U23 63.46**

WOMEN

100 Metres wind –2.5
1. Celine Thelamon FRA 12.07
4. **Kelly Thomas U23 12.39**
5. **Susan Williams 12.47**
6. **Simone Jacobs 12.65**

200 Metres wind –2.1
1. **Emily Freeman U23 24.22**
2. **Helen Roscoe 24.52**
3. **Susan Williams 24.59**

400 Metres
1. **Karen Gear 54.28**
2. **Jenny Meadows 54.41**
5. **Lois Cresswell U23 56.28**

800 Metres
Susan Scott gst 2:05.64
1. **Tanya Blake 2:05.99**
2. **Kelly Caffel U23 2:06.37**
5. **Jo Fenn 2:07.62**

1500 Metres
1. Latifa Essarokh FRA 4:25.77
3. **Sarah Bull 4:26.27**
4. **Alex Carter U23 4:27.40**
5. **Kerry Smithson 4:27.65**

3000 Metres
1. **Liz Yelling 9:20.23**
3. **Amanda Parkinson 9:27.59**
4. **Juliet Potter U23 9:28.77**

5k Walk – non scoring
1. Herve Davaux FRA 21:32.97
4. **Andrew Goudie 22:10.13**

4 x 100 Metres
1. France 40.10
2. **Great Britain & NI 40.74**
(Gardner, Turner, Owen, Lambert)

100 Metres Hurdles wind –2.5
1. Haydy Aron FRA 13.74
2. **Melanie Wilkins 13.88**
5. **Julie Pratt U23 14.42**
6. **Rachel King 14.49**

400 Metres Hurdles
1. **Tracey Duncan 58.15**
4. **Hannah Wood 61.05**
6. **Hannah Stares 62.26**

High Jump
1. **Michelle Dunkley 1.86**
3. **Lindsay McDonnell U23 1.80**
6. **Jo Steele 1.75**

Pole Vault
1. Emilie Becot FRA 4.25
2= **Irie Hill 3.80**
5. **Sonia Lawrence U23 3.70**
6. **Lucy Webber 3.60**

Long Jump
1. **Jade Johnson U23 6.60w**
2. **Ann Danson 6.36w**
3. **Julie Hollman 6.31w**

Triple Jump
1. Stephanie Luzieux FRA 13.74w
4. **Debbie Rowe 12.81w**
5. **Rebecca White U23 12.66w**
6. **Liz Patrick 12.57w**

4 x 400 Metres
1. **Great Britain & NI 3:11.47**
(Jennings, Hillier, Brend, Deacon)
2. France 3:11.70

Match Result – Men
1. France 205.5
2. **Great Britain & NI 179.5**

Shot
1. Natalya Lisovskaya FRA 16.48
2. **Joanne Duncan 15.84**
3. **Julie Dunkley 15.50**
4. **Eva Massey U23 15.06**

Discus
1. **Shelley Drew 59.10**
3. **Philippa Roles 54.95**
6. **Rebecca Roles U23 48.77**

Hammer
1. **Lynn Sprules 59.61**
2. **Zoe Derham U23 59.08**
3. **Liz Pidgeon 58.84**

Javelin
1. **Karen Martin 51.14**
5. **Katy Watts U23 42.52**

3k Walk
1. **Niobe Menendez 13:14.73**
5. **Wendy Bennett 14:37.53**
6. **Sophie Hales U23 14:48.50**

4 x 100 Metres
1. France 45.09
2. **Great Britain & NI 46.08**
(Thomas, Williams, Roscoe, Freeman)

4 x 400 Metres
1. **Great Britain & NI 3:40.27**
(Gear, Cresswell, Duncan, Meadows)
2. France 3:43.43

Match Result – Women
1. **Great Britain & NI 189.5**
2. France 173.5

Match Result - Combined
1. France 379
2. **Great Britain & NI 369**

GB & NI v USA (U20) Stoke-on-Trent 18 August 2001

MEN

100 Metres wind –3.1
1. **Tyrone Edgar 10.78**
2. **Aidan Syers 10.87**

200 Metres wind –0.9
1. **Dwayne Grant 21.00**
3. **Tim Abeyie 21.55**

400 Metres
1. Brandon Matlock USA 47.01
3. **Robert Tobin 47.94**
dnf Russell Nicholls

800 Metres
1. Jesse O`Connell USA 1:49.53
2. **Chris Stoves 1:50.23**
3. **Andrew Fulford 1:50.82**

1500 Metres
1. **Ricky Soos 4:00.91**
4. **Ed Prickett 4:04.10**

3000 Metres
1. **Mohamed Farah 8:20.35**
4. **Tom Sharland 8:35.05**

2000 Metres Steeplechase
1. **Adam Bowden 5:45.00**
2. **Jermaine Mays 5:47.29**

110 Metres Hurdles wind –1.5
1. Joshua Walker USA 14.28
2. **Nathan Palmer 14.39**
4. **Dominic Girdler 14.54**

400 Metres Hurdles
1. Dwight Ruff USA 51.29
3. **Jeff Christie 52.38**
4. **Richard Smith 52.48**

High Jump
1. Jason Hill USA 2.14
3. Martin Aram 2.05
4. Darryl Stone 2.00

Pole Vault
1= Matt Campbell USA 4.70
1= Ian Dare USA 4.70
3. Paul Stevens 4.60
4. Chris Tremayne 4.50

Long Jump
1. Jonathan Moore 7.93
3. Mark Awanah 7.25

Triple Jump
1. Daniel Harris USA 15.69
2. Nathan Douglas 15.50
4. Phillip Ferdinand 14.68

Shot
1. Jeff Chakouian USA 19.21
3. Greg Beard 16.28
4. David Dawson 14.09

Discus
1. Sean Shields USA 46.36
2. Greg Beard 46.16
4. Daniel Greaves 43.20

Hammer
1. Joshua McCaughey USA 61.44
2. Carl Saggers 58.12
3. Peter Field 55.44

Javelin
1. Andrew Gallagher 66.95
4. Alex van der Merwe 47.57

4 x 100 Metres
1. Great Britain & NI 40.79
(Syers, Edgar, Abeyie, Grant)
2. United States 41.15

4 x 400 Metres
1. United States 3:10.92
2. Great Britain & NI 3:14.31
(Christie, Green, Smith, Tobin)

Match Score – Men
1. United States 106
2. Great Britain & NI 88

WOMEN

100 Metres wind ?
1. Anyika Onuora 11.96
4. Jade Lucas-Read 12.10

200 Metres wind -0.7
1. Lashauntea Moore USA 23.99
2. Danielle Norville 24.37
4. Phyllis Agbo 25.50

400 Metres
1. Stephanie Smith USA 53.99
2. Kim Wall 54.32
3. Lesley Clarkson 55.20

800 Metres
1. Rebecca Lyne 2:06.10
2. Olivia Hines 2:07.75

1500 Metres
1. Emma Ward 4:19.75
2. Natalie Lewis 4:31.08

3000 Metres
1. Rachael Nathan 9:31.69
dnf Louise Damen

100 Metres Hurdles wind -0.7
1. Ashlee Williams USA 13.75
2. Helen Worsey 13.98
4. Stefanie Pullinger 14.44

400 Metres Hurdles
1. Sheena Johnson USA 58.56
3. Sian Scott 61.02
4. Faye Harding 61.10

High Jump
1. Stephanie Higham 1.76
2. Emma Perkins 1.76

Pole Vault
1. Samantha Shepard USA 3.85
3. Zoe Brown 3.70
4. Kate Dennison 3.55

Long Jump
1. Ychlindria Spears USA 6.05
2. Phyllis Agbo 5.91
3. Elaine Smith 5.89

Triple Jump
1. Nicole Toney USA 12.87
3. Rachel Brenton 11.82
4. Katherine Streatfield 11.79

Shot
1. Jillian Camarena USA 16.20
3. Rebecca Peake 14.34
4. Charlotte Spelzini 13.99

Discus
1. Melissa Bickett USA 51.23
2. Claire Smithson 50.93
3. Emma Carpenter 50.51

Hammer
1. Nicola Dudman 52.37
2. Katy Lamb 51.97

Javelin
1. Goldie Sayers 52.74
4. Louise Matthews 41.35

4 x 100 Metres
1. United States 45.28
2. Great Britain & NI 45.73
(Onuora, Norville, Spencer, Lucas-Read)

4 x 400 Metres
1. Great Britain & NI 3:36.39
(Hines, Clarkson, Miller, Wall)
2. United States 3:36.90

Match Score- Women
1. United States 95
2. Great Britain & NI 88

UK HALF MARATHON Glasgow, 19 August 2001
(Incorporating World Championship Trials)

MEN
1. Abner Chipu RSA 63:23
2. Kassa Tadessa 1-AAA 64:04
3. Tomoo Tsubota JPN 64:06
5. Daniel Robinson 2-AAA 64:27
6. Nick Jones 3-AAA 64:29

WOMEN
1. Joyce Chepchumba KEN 69:15
2. Esther Kiplagat KEN 72:08
3. Takako Kotorida JPN 72:18
4. Liz Yelling 1-AAA 72:54
7. Liz Allott 2-AAA 73:38
8. Birhan Dagne 3-AAA 73:52

IAU WORLD 100km CHALLENGE
Cleder FRA, 26 August 2001

MEN
1. Yasufumi Mikami JPN 6:33:28
2. Rich Hanna USA 6:43:09
3. Pascal Fetizon FRA 6:44:48

WOMEN
1. Elvira Kolpakova RUS 7:31:12
2. Marina Bychkova RUS 7:38:21
3. Monica Casiraghi ITA 7:39:42
7. Danielle Sanderson 7:58:16

WORLD STUDENT GAMES

Beijing, CHN 27 August - 1 September 2001

Two gold medals, one silver and one bronze at these high quality championships. Natasha Danvers came back from injury to win an unexpected title, Abi Oyepitan ran at her best and deserved to win. The women's 4 x 400 relay continued their run of medals and Chris Lambert won a sprint medal. The biggest disappointment was Susan Jones who would have won a medal on her best form.

MEN

100 Metres wind –0.8 (28 Aug)

1.	Markus Brunson	USA	10.15
2.	Gennadiy Chernovol	KAZ	10.29
3.	**Chris Lambert**		**10.38**
(1h10 10.32, 1q1 10.37, 1s2 10.32)			

200 Metres wind –0.8 (31 Aug)

1.	Marcin Urbas	POL	20.56
2.	Gennadiy Chernovol	KAZ	20.57
3.	Corne du Plessis	RSA	20.58
5s1	**Chris Lambert**		**20.86w**
	(1h4 20.84, 2q2 20.87)		

400 Metres (29 Aug)

1.	Andrew Pierce	USA	45.34
2.	Clinton Hill	AUS	45.63
3.	Andrey Tverdostup	UKR	45.78

800 Metres (1 Sep)

1.	Khalid Tighazouine	MAR	1:45.27
2.	Derrick Peterson	USA	1:45.49
3.	Otukile Lekote	BOT	1:45.63
7s2	**Neil Speaight**		**1:48.87**
	(2h3 1:49.43)		
s1	**Simon Lees**	**dnf**	
	(2h6 1:49.89)		

1500 Metres (29 Aug)

1.	Pedro Esteso	ESP	3:43.98
2.	Gareth Turnbull	IRL	3:44.48
3.	Alexis Abraham	FRA	3:44.48
8.	**Angus Mclean**		**3:46.24**
	(2h1 3:48.86)		

5000 Metres (1 Sep)

1.	Sergey Lebed	UKR	13:44.24
2.	Mikhail Yeginov	RUS	13:46.63
3.	Christian Belz	SUI	13:48.21
8.	**Chris Thompson**		**13:56.55**
	(9s1 14:16.45)		

10000 Metres (27 Aug)

1.	John Kanyi	KEN	28:27.42
2.	Ignacio Caceres	ESP	28:43.63
3.	Kazuyoshi Tokumoto	JPN	28:47.34

Half Marathon (1 Sep)

1.	Masakazu Fujiwara	JPN	64:12
2.	Wodage Zvadya	ISR	64:30
3.	Ryohki Matsushita	JPN	64:53

3000 Metres Steeplechase (29 Aug)

1.	Anthony Famiglietti	USA	8:21.97
2.	Jakub Czaja	POL	8:23.00
3.	Christian Belz	SUI	8:24.46

110 Metres Hurdles wind +1.6(28 Aug)

1.	Liu Xiang	CHN	13.33
2.	Elmar Lichtenegger	AUT	13.36
3.	Robert Kronberg	SWE	13.40

400 Metres Hurdles (31 Aug)

1.	Alwyn Myburgh	RSA	48.09
2.	Yevheniy Meleshenko	KAZ	48.46
3.	Chen Tien-Wen	TPE	48.63
6h1	**Charles Robertson-Adams**		**52.88**

High Jump (29 Aug)

1.	Aleksandr Kravtsov	RUS	2.28
2.	Gennadiy Moroz	BLR	2.28
3.	Tora Harris	USA	2.26

Pole Vault (30 Aug)

1.	Aleksandr Averbukh	ISR	5.80
2.	Stepan Janacek	CZE	5.70
3.	Laurens Looije	NED	5.60

Long Jump (29 Aug)

1.	Miguel Pate	USA	8.07
2.	Stepan Louw	NAM	8.04
3.	Gable Garenamotse	BOT	7.99

Triple Jump (31 Aug)

1.	Kenta Bell	USA	17.22
2.	Marian Oprea	ROM	17.11
3.	Jadel Gregorio	BRA	16.92

Shot (30 Aug)

1.	Manuel Martinez	ESP	20.97
2.	Yuriy Belonog	UKR	20.16
3.	Milan Haborak	SVK	19.80
20Q	**Emeka Udechuku**		**16.77**
Q	**Mark Edwards**		**nm**

Discus (29 Aug)

1.	Aleksander Tammert	EST	65.19
2.	Leonid Cherevko	BLR	63.15
3.	Aleksandr Malashevich	BLR	62.81
12.	**Emeka Udechuku**		**55.58**
	(58.67Q)		

Hammer (28 Aug)

1.	Nicola Vizzoni	ITA	78.41
2.	Vladislav Piskunov	UKR	77.99
3.	Adrian Annus	HUN	77.73

Javelin (1 Sep)

1.	Eriks Rags	LAT	82.72
2.	Isbel Luaces	CUB	81.68
3.	Gergely Horvath	HUN	80.03
11.	**David Parker**		**69.03**
	(73.89Q)		

Decathlon (30/31 Aug)

1.	Raul Duany	CUB	8069
2.	Vladimir Mikhaylenko	UKR	8019
3.	Qi Haifeng	CHN	8019

20k Walk (29 Aug)

1.	Lorenzo Civallero	ITA	1:24:42
2.	Juan Molina	ESP	1:25:07
3.	He Xiaodong	CHN	1:25:17

4 x 100 Metres (1 Sep)

1.	Japan	38.77
2.	United States	39.14
3.	Italy	39.35

4 x 400 Metres (1 Sep)

1.	United States	3:02.83
2.	Ukraine	3:02.87
3.	Japan	3:03.63

WOMEN

100 Metres wind +1.1 (28 Aug)

1.	**Abiodun Oyepitan**		**11.42**
	(1h4 11.31, 1q3 11.47, 1s2 11.29)		
2.	Zeng Xiujun	CHN	11.58
3.	Mireille Donders	SUI	11.59
8.	**Amanda Forrester**		**11.77**
	(2h5 11.40, 4q2 11.65, 4s1 11.61)		

200 Metres wind +0.5 (31 Aug)

1.	Li Xumei	CHN	22.86
2.	Kim Gevaert	BEL	22.94
3.	Natalya Safronnikova	BLR	23.16
8q3	**Susan Burnside**		**24.42**
	(5h2 24.15w +2.2)		
7q2	**Helen Roscoe**		**24.55**
	(5h3 24.30)		

400 Metres (29 Aug)

1.	Demetria Washington	USA	51.22
2.	Otilia Ruicu	ROM	51.82
3.	Mukele Barber	USA	51.92
6.	**Lee McConnell**		**52.44**
	(2h4 52.99, 3s2 52.05)		
5s1	**Lesley Owusu**		**53.20**
	(2h3 53.02)		

800 Metres (1 Sep)
1. Brigita Langerholc SLO 2:00.96
2. Nedia Semedo POR 2:01.64
3. Tatyana Rodionova RUS 2:01.68

3h2Alex Carter 2:06.50

1500 Metres (29 Aug)
1. Sureyya Ayhan TUR 4:06.91
2. Cristina Grosu ROM 4:08.84
3. Sabine Fischer SUI 4:08.93

5h3Kelly Caffel 4:18.36

5000 Metres (1 Sep)
1. Dong Yanmei CHN 15:30.28
2. Tatyana Khmeleva RUS 15:43.18
3. Yoshiko Fujinaga JPN 15:43.94

10000 Metres (28 Aug)
1. Dong Yanmei CHN 32:45.14
2. Yoshiko Fujinaga JPN 32:53.55
3. Yukiko Akaba JPN 32:57.35

Half Marathon (1 Sep)
1. Ham Pong-sil PRK 75:24
2. Miki Oyama JPN 75:31
3. Kim Chang-ok PRK 75:36

100 Metres Hurdles wind –0.1(28 Aug)
1. Su Yiping CHN 12.95
2. Maurren Maggi BRA 13.13
3. Jacquie Munro AUS 13.17
4. **Diane Allahgreen 13.18**
   (2h4 13.29, 3s2 13.32)

400 Metres Hurdles (31 Aug)
1. **Natasha Danvers 54.94**
   (1h3 57.26, 1s2 55.70)
2. Malgorzata Pskit POL 55.27
3. Sonia Brito AUS 55.72

4h4Tracey Duncan 59.30

High Jump (31 Aug)
1. Vita Palamar UKR 1.96
2. Nicole Forrester CAN 1.94
3. Nevena Lendjel CRO 1.91

4= Susan Jones 1.88
14Q Michelle Dunkley 1.85

Pole Vault (29 Aug)
1. Gao Shuying CHN 4.52
2. Sabine Schulte GER 4.35
3. Sarka Mladkova CZE 4.20

9. Rhian Clarke 4.00

Long Jump (28 Aug)
1. Maurren Maggi BRA 6.83
2. Guan Yingnan CHN 6.56
3. Kumiko Ikeda JPN 6.52

Triple Jump (1 Sep)
1. Tatyana Lebedeva RUS 14.81
2. Natalya Safronova BLR 14.57
3. Yelena Oleynikova RUS 14.39w

Shot (27 Aug)
1. Yumileidi Cumba CUB 18.90
2. Lee Myung-sun KOR 18.79
3. Katarzyna Zakowicz POL 18.31

Discus (30 Aug)
1. Li Qiumei CHN 61.66
2. Li Yanfeng CHN 60.50
3. Melina Robert-Michon FRA 58.04

6. Philippa Roles 55.02
(56.28Q)

Hammer (30 Aug)
1. Manuela Montebrun FRA 69.78
2. Yipsi Moreno CUB 68.39
3. Lyudmila Gubkina BLR 67.97

23Q Liz Pidgeon 54.29

Javelin (29 Aug)
1. Osleidis Menendez CUB 69.82
2. Nikola Tomeckova CZE 62.20
3. Wei Jianhua CHN 57.84

Heptathlon (28/29 Aug)
1. Jane Jamieson AUS 6041
2. Svetlana Sokolova RUS 5985
3. Sonja Kesselschlager GER 5973

16. Nicola Gautier 4596

10k Walk (29 Aug)
1. Gao Hongmiao CHN 43:20
2. Susana Feitor POR 43:40
3. Wang Liping CHN 44:01

4 x 100 Metres (1 Sep)
1. China 43.72
2. Brasil 44.13
3. France 44.24

s2 Great Britian & NI dnf
(Allahgreen, Forrester, Oyepitan, Burnside)

4 x 400 Metres (1 Sep)
1. United States 3:28.04
2. **Great Britain & NI 3:30.40**
   (Danvers, Meadows, McConnell, Duncan)
3. Belarus 3:30.65

Ist UK CHAMPIONSHIP
Glasgow (Scotstoun)
11 August 2001

WOMEN

3000 Metres Steeplechase
1. Tara Krzywicki 9:55.01
2. Allison Higgins 10:55.70
3. Paula Gowing 11:26.15
4. Fiona Lampkin 12:03.79
5. Susan McGrenagan 12:15.79
6. Alison White 12:17.98

HUN v GB & NI v SVK v UKR v YUG (U20) Walks
Budapest, HUN 9 September 2001

MEN 10k
1. **Lloyd Finch 43:49**

7. Dominic King 45:45
11. Andrew Parker 47:44

Team Result
1. Ukraine 15
2. Slovakia 16
3. **Great Britain & NI 18**

WOMEN 5k
1. Edina Fusti HUN 23:12

4. Sophie Hales 25:10
6. Katie Stones 25:47
15. Bryna Chrismas 27:58

Team Result
1. Slovakia 15
2. Hungary 18
3. **Great Britain & NI 23**

RWA NATIONAL WALK CHAMPIONSHIPS

London (Victoria Park) 25 March 2001

MEN 50k

1.	Michael Smith	4:33:17
2.	Chris Cheeseman	4:41:44
3.	Peter Kaneen	4:43:14
4.	Peter Ryan	4:52:22
5.	Colin Bradley	4:54:38
6.	Chris Berwick	4:54:54

Team

1. Surrey WC 285

WOMEN 5k

1.	Sharon Tonks		24:51
2.	Estle Viljoen	RSA	25:10
3.	Sophie Hales		25:46
4.	Jo Hesketh		26:07
5.	Nicola Phillips		27:18
6.	Claire Reeves		28:26

Team

1. Dartford A 281

Birmingham (Perry Park) 5 May 2001

MEN 35k

1.	Mark Easton	2:55:00
2.	Darrell Stone	2:58:19
3.	Michael Smith	2:58:35
4.	Gareth Brown	3:04:15
5.	Peter Ryan	3:14:08
6.	Chris Berwick	3:14:54

Team

1. Coventry 281

WOMEN 10k

1.	Olive Loughnane	IRL	46:35
2.	Niobe Menendez		49:19
3.	Sarah Cattermole		50:42
4.	Wendy Bennett		50:45
5.	Estle Viljoen	RSA	51:41
6.	Catherine Charnock		52:48

Team

1. Steyning 285

Sheffield 7 July 2001

MEN 20k

1.	Andrew Penn	1:31:09
2.	Steven Hollier	1:32:56
3.	Steven Partington	1:33:30
4.	Mark Easton	1:33:54
5.	Chris Cheeseman	1:34:11
6.	Andrew O`Rawe	1:39:48

Team

1. Road Hoggs 273

WOMEN 20k

	Linda Betto	ITA/gst	1:54:27
1.	Sheila Bull		2:18:53

IAAF WORLD HALF MARATHON CHAMPIONSHIPS

Bristol 7 October 2001

Paula Radcliffe defended her world title in an awesome way winning by just under a minute in a very fast time and a certain Haile Gebreselassie added the men's title to his list of honours. With both runners planning their marathon debut in London in 2002, it should be an event to look forward to. PBs by Liz Yelling and Annie Emmerson just failed to bring the women's team into the medals.

MEN

1.	Haile Gebrselassie	ETH	60:03
2.	Tesfaye Jifar	ETH	60:04
3.	John Yuda	TAN	60:12
4.	Hendrick Ramaala	RSA	60:15
5.	Tesfaye Tola	ETH	60:24
6.	Evans Rutto	KEN	60:43
7.	Peter Chebet	KEN	60:56
8.	Christopher Cheboiboch	KEN	61:14
9.	Jaouad Gharib	MAR	61:41
10.	Khalid Shah	MAR	61:41
21.	**Matt O`Dowd**		**62:40**
51.	**Nick Jones**		**64:00**
57.	**Dan Robinson**		**64:23**
75.	**Kassa Tadesse**		**65:39**
80.	**Andrew Morgan-Lee**		**65:51**

Team Result

1.	Ethiopia	3:00:31
2.	Kenya	3:02:53
3.	Tanzania	3:05:08
11.	**Great Britain & NI**	**3:11:03**

WOMEN

1.	**Paula Radcliffe**		**66:47**
2.	Susan Chepkemei	KEN	67:36
3.	Berhane Adere	ETH	68:17
4.	Mizuki Noguchi	JPN	68:23
5.	Jelena Prokopchuka	LAT	68:43
6.	Elana Meyer	RSA	68:56
7.	Olivera Jevtic	YUG	69:51
8.	Isabellah Ochichi	KEN	70:01
9.	Yasuyo Iwamoto	JPN	70:06
10.	Mihaela Botezan	ROM	70:11
23.	**Liz Yelling**		**71:29**
31.	**Annie Emmerson**		**73:00**
dnf	**Elizabeth Allott**		
dnf	**Birhan Dagne**		

Team Result

1.	Kenya	3:28:04
2.	Japan	3:30:08
3.	Ethiopia	3:30:20
4.	**Great Britain & NI**	**3:31:16**

EKIDEN RELAY

Chiba, JPN

23 November 2001

MEN (10k, 5k, 10k, 5k, 12.195k)

1.	South Africa	2:01:56
2.	Japan	2:02:08
3.	Brasil	2:02:14
10.	**Great Britain & NI**	**2:06:12**
	Rod Finch	**29:36**
	John Mayock	**14:00**
	Ian Hudspith	**29:51**
	Mark Morgan	**14:35**
	Paul Evans	**38:10**

WOMEN (10k, 5k, 10k, 5k, 4.767k, 7.428k)

1.	Japan	2:13:33
2.	Ethiopia	2:14:26
3.	Russia	2:17:00
9.	**Great Britain & NI**	**2:24:35**
	Birhan Dagne	**34:29**
	Hayley Tullett	**16:21**
	Andrea Whitcombe	**35:07**
	Caroline Hoyte	**17:07**
	Lucy Wright	**16:16**
	Andrea Green	**25:15**

SPAR EUROPEAN CROSS COUNTRY CHAMPIONSHIPS

Thun, SUI 9 December 2001

Last year's medals were exactly duplicated with one gold and three silvers, although this year it was the junior men who won the top prize. Mohamed Farah gained a well earned individual silver and even the senior men had something to cheer about with Sam Haughian's sixth place. This was the final Championship of 2001 and the constant success of the junior teams throughout the year gives hope for the future.

MEN (9150m)

1.	Sergey Lebed	UKR	27:52
2.	Kamiel Maase	NED	28:05
3.	Antonio Jimenez	ESP	28:10
4.	Gabriele De Nard	ITA	28:11
5.	Christian Belz	SUI	28:12
6.	**Sam Haughian**		**28:12**
23.	**Glynn Tromans**		**28:38**
28.	**Karl Keska**		**28:45**
35.	**Chris Thompson**		**28:55**
42.	**Andres Jones**		**29:07**
dnf	**Ben Noad**		

Team

1.	Spain	40
2.	France	50
3.	Portugal	72
5.	**Great Britain & NI**	**92**

JUNIOR MEN (6150m)

1.	Vasyl Matviychuk	UKR	19:29
2.	**Mohamed Farah**		**19:38**
3.	Stefano Scaini	ITA	19:39
6.	**Adam Bowden**		**19:43**
13.	**Matthew Bowser**		**19:58**
33.	**Andrew Lemoncello**		**20:13**
53.	**Nick Goodliffe**		**20:38**
	Tom Sharland		**dnf**

Team

1.	**Great Britain & NI**	**54**
2.	Portugal	67
3.	France	68

JUNIOR WOMEN (3150m)

1.	Elvan Abeylegesse	TUR	10:35
2.	Tatyana Chulakh	RUS	10:53
3.	Snezana Kostic	YUG	10:54
5.	**Charlotte Dale**		**11:07**
15.	**Louise Damen**		**11:19**
16.	**Kate Reed**		**11:21**
18.	**Freya Murray**		**11:22**
28.	**Sally Oldfield**		**11:36**
36.	**Lisa Dobriskey**		**11:40**

Team

1.	Russia	35
2.	**Great Britain & NI**	**54**
3.	Turkey	79

SENIOR WOMEN (4650m)

1.	Yamna Belkacem	FRA	15:48
2.	Olga Romanova	RUS	15:49
3.	Justyna Bak	POL	15:51
4.	Olivera Jevtic	YUG	15:54
5.	**Liz Yelling**		**15:55**
6.	Helena Sampaio	POR	15:55
8.	**Hayley Yelling**		**15:58**
12.	**Kathy Butler**		**16:08**
24.	**Sharon Morris**		**16:19**
30.	**Helen Pattinson**		**16:27**
34.	**Tara Krzywicki**		**16:29**

Team

1.	Portugal	41
2.	**Great Britain & NI**	**49**
3.	France	66

IAU EUROPEAN 100k CHAMPIONSHIPS

Winschoten, NED
29 September 2001

MEN

1.	Vladimr Netreba	RUS	6:45:43
2.	Attila Vozar	HUN	6:47:57
3.	Miroslav Windis	SLO	6:52:57
14.	**Ian Anderson**		**7:29:29**

WOMEN

1.	Ricarda Botzon	GER	7:31:55
2.	Marina Bytchkova	RUS	7:37:02
3.	Karine Herry	FRA	7:42:36
13.	**Hilary Walker**		**8:50:19**
18.	**Victoria Musgrove**		**9:54:49**

EKIDEN RELAY

Yokohama, JPN
25 February 2001

WOMEN (5k, 10k, 6k, 6.195k, 10k, 5k)

1.	Russia	2:12:50
10.	**Great Britain & NI**	**2:23:05**
	Catherine Berry	**15:59**
	Debbie Robinson	**34:56**
	Vicky Gill	**19:52**
	Claire Naylor	**21:42**
	Penny Thackray	**34:54**
	Sharon Morris	**16:42**

EKIDEN RELAY

Seoul, KOR
8 April 2001

WOMEN

1.	Russia	2:17:37
10.	**Great Britain & NI**	**2:28:18**
	Debbie Sullivan	
	Catherine Dugdale	
	Jodie Swallow	
	Gemma Phillips	
	Bev Jenkins	
	Vicky Gil	
	Marian Sutton	

REGIONAL CHAMPIONSHIPS

	SCOTLAND Scotstoun, Glasgow 23 – 24 June			WALES Cardiff 16 – 17 June			NORTHERN IRELAND Belfast 28 July	
MEN				**MEN**			**MEN**	
100	Ian Mackie	10.30		Christian Malcolm	10.40		John McAdorey IRL	10.54
200	Ian Mackie	20.85		Doug Turner	20.54		Jonathan McGee	22.74
400	Kris Stewart	47.53		Matt Elias	46.9		Paul McKee	47.34
800	Thomas Nimmo	1:51.34		Thomas Cordy	1:55.1		Raymond Adams	1:53.94
1500	Andrew Renfree	3:58.56		Christian Stephenson	4:00.31		Noel Pollock	3:59.47
5000	Andy Caine	14:36.02		Richard Szade	15:02.2		Kevin Seward	15:26.1
10000	Neil Wilkinson	30:33.0		Andres Jones	30:20.7		Kenny Butler	32:03.59
3kSt	Steven Cairns	9:03.08		Phil Cook	9:44.69		Ian Barrett	10:11.59
110H	Chris Baillie	13.99		Paul Gray	13.78		Paul Conroy IRL	14.56
400H	Charles Robertson-Adams	50.45		James Hillier	51.23		Ian Neely	54.98
HJ	James Wild	2.00		not contested			Paul Tohill	1.90
PV	Jamie Quarry	4.50		Tim Thomas	5.20		Brendan McConville	4.20
LJ	Darren Ritchie	6.88		Gareth Brown	6.99w		Simon Sawhney	6.78
TJ	Stuart Benson	13.46		Steven Shalders	16.26w		Paul Curran	14.13
SP	Bruce Robb	16.67		Lee Newman	17.23		Iain McMullen	16.56
DT	Kevin Brown JAM	52.03		Lee Newman	56.17		Richard Murphy	33.52
HT	David Allan	62.25		Graham Holder	61.50		Andrew Lee	35.43
JT	David Sketchley	61.00		Derek Hermann	57.37		Damien Crawford IRL	56.47
Dec	Kenneth Pearson	4239		Ben Roberts	6475		Brendan McConville	6699
			3kW	Cameron Smith	13:23.5			
Dec	Edinburgh 7/8 Jul		10000	Barry 8 August		10k	Antrim 21 July	
			Dec	Aberdare 23/24 June		Dec	Antrim 21/22 July	
WOMEN				**WOMEN**			**WOMEN**	
100	Susan Burnside	11.74		Rachel King	12.04		Vicki Jamison	12.20
200	Natalie Beattie	24.74		Catherine Murphy	23.35w		Vicki Jamison	25.07
400	Lee McConnell	52.41		Dawn Higgins	55.14		Vicki Jamison	54.70
800	Susan Scott	2:06.61		Hayley Tullett	2:04.97		Christine Long	2:25.18
1500	Hayley Parkinson-Ovens	4:19.87		Ann-M.Hutchinson	4:30.45		Jill Shannon	4:47.07
5000	Allison Higgins	16:47.10		Ceri Thomas	19:04.89	3000	Sharon Hatch	9:48.01
100H	Alyssa Fullelove	14.19		Rachel King	13.58w		Geraldine Finnegan IRL	19.00
400H	Sinead Dudgeon	57.1		Donna-M. Porazinski	60.42		Lesley O`Connor IRL	68.81
HJ	Aileen Wilson	1.80		Alisa Wallace	1.60		Sharon Foley IRL	1.76
PV	Gael Davies	3.65		Rhian Clarke	3.60		Erin Kinnear	3.35
LJ	Ruth Irving	6.10w		Gemma Jones	5.56		Mary Devlin	5.62
TJ	Sharon Foley IRL	11.97		Leanne Rowlands	10.68		Sharon Foley IRL	12.41
SP	Mhairi Walters	13.30		Philippa Roles	15.12		Eva Massey	15.30
DT	Navdeep Dhaliwal	44.58		Philippa Roles	55.06		Eva Massey	44.20
HT	Vicci Scott	55.42		Sarah Moore	56.77		Eva Massey	38.71
JT	Lorna Jackson	49.97		Charlotte Rees	38.21		Paula Collis	43.75
Hept	Abigail Ashby	3801		Stephanie Little	4214		not contested	
			3kW	Keirina Rowland	18:37.3			
Hept	Edinburgh 7/8 Jul		Hept	Aberdare 23/24 June				

AREA CHAMPIONSHIPS

SOUTH — London (Ha) 16 – 17 June
MIDLAND — Birmingham 17 June
NORTH — Liverpool 17 June

MEN

Event	South		Event	Midland		Event	North	
100	Graham Beasley	10.82		Brendon Ghent	10.53		Daniel Money	10.45w
200	Julian Golding	21.18		Ben Lewis	21.13w		Daniel Money	21.11w
400	Mark Hylton	46.8		Cori Henry	47.41		Jared Deacon	47.47
800	Richard Ashe	1:52.26		Gary Vickers	1:52.47		Rob Watkinson	1:53.42
1500	Chris Thompson	3:47.43		Gregg Taylor	3:54.86		Phillip Tedd	3:53.9
5000	Guy Amos	14:19.57	3000	Kevin Hayes	8:40.9	5000	Gareth Raven	14:40.96
10k	Sam Haughian	29:10.5	5000	Julian Wilkie	15:24.87	10k	Mick Hill	30:35.16
3kSt	Patrick Davoren	9:01.93		Billy Farquharson	9:12.23		Robert Berry	9:08.43
110H	Mensah Elliott	14.10		Robert Newton	14.42w		Dominic Bradley	14.01w
400H	Steven Surety	52.68		Paul Hibbert	53.34		David Brackstone	53.5
HJ	Dan Turner	2.15		Mark Mandy IRL	2.00		Danny Graham	2.10
PV	Ian Tullett	5.00		Christian North	4.90		Dean Mellor	4.60
LJ	Darren Thompson	7.84w		not contested			Jamie Quarry	6.90w
TJ	Julian Golley	16.13		Mike McKernan	15.46		not contested	
SP	Dave Condon	16.62		Morris Fox	15.79		Paul Reed	16.43
DT	Luke Rosenberg	50.59		Kevin Brown JAM	50.04		Peter Gordon	50.33
HT	Paul Head	65.36		Matthew Bell	60.28		David Smith	72.89
JT	Neil McLellan	67.32		Leon Karagiounis GRE	57.77		Phill Sharpe	63.84
Dec	Alex Gibson	6330		Roger Hunter	6749		Anthony Southward	7022
10kW	Mark Easton	47:52.86		Andi Drake	43:21			

South		Midland		North	
10k	Brighton 22 Aug	Dec	Birmingham 16/17 June	10k	Stretford 8 May
Dec	London (He) 11/12 Aug	10kW	Tamworth 22 September	Dec	Hexham 19/20 May
10kW	London (He) 12 Aug				

WOMEN

Event	South		Event	Midland		Event	North	
100	Marcia Richardson	11.64		Amanda Forrester	11.50		Emily Freeman	11.67w
200	Joice Maduaka	23.62		Helen Roscoe	23.92w		Jennifer Meadows	23.90w
400	Karen Gear	53.59		Michelle Thomas	55.06		Kim Goodwin	56.1
800	Sarah Knights	2:08.57		Sally Evans	2:12.76		Bev Blakeman	2:08.9
1500	Jeina Mitchell	4:20.7		Juliet Potter	4:29.15		Julie Mitchell	4:36.4
5000	Jo Lodge	16:43.69		Clare Martin	17:41.87		Penny Thackray	16:18.32
						10k	Pauline Powell	34:52.46
						3kSt	Jayne Knowles	10:49.39
100H	Melani Wilkins	13.33		Keri Maddox	13.56w		Diane Allahgreen	13.42w
400H	Tracey Duncan	59.67		Keri Maddox	59.55		Rachael Kay	62.03
HJ	Debora Marti	1.65		Aneska Binks	1.63		Gayle O`Connor	1.75
PV	Tracey Bloomfield	3.80		Emma Hornby	3.65		Rebekah Telford	3.50
LJ	Donita Benjamin	6.03		Kelly Sotherton	6.07		Ann Danson	6.19w
TJ	Liz Patrick	12.15		Jodie Hurst	11.60		Hazel Carwardine	12.03w
SP	Jo Duncan	15.83		Lynette Bristow	9.91		Helen Wilding	12.76
DT	Shelley Drew	52.85		Nicola Talbot	45.91		Kara Nwidobie	44.32
HT	Lyn Sprules	62.99		Zoe Derham	53.81		Victoria Scott	53.14
JT	Katie Amos	47.55		Sharon Gibson	44.33		Linda Gray	50.25
Hept	Judith Butler	3936		Vicky Williams	4194		Sarah Todd	4280
10kW	Estle Viljoen	52:18.23	5kW	Wendy Bennett	24:24			

South		Midland		North	
PV	London (He) 26 Aug	Hept	Birmingham 16/17 June	10k	Stretford 8 May
Hept	London (He) 11/12 Aug	5kW	Tamworth 22 September	3kSt	Stretford 3 Jul
10kW	London (He) 12 Aug			Hept	Hexham 19/20 May

AGE CHAMPIONSHIPS

	U23			U20			U17	
	Bedford 30 June - 1 July			Bedford 30 June - 1 July			Sheffield 11 - 12 August	
MEN				**MEN**			**MEN**	
100	Jonathan Barbour	10.13w		Tyrone Edgar	10.17w		Rikki Fifton	10.60w
200	Jonathan Barbour	20.8w		Dwayne Grant	20.4w		Rikki Fifton	21.48w
400	David Naismith	47.13		Robert Tobin	47.3		Richard Davenport	49.74
800	Chris Moss	1:53.0		Ricky Soos	1:56.97		Michael Rimmer	1:55.67
1500	Angus Maclean	3:47.6		Derek Watson	3:50.1		Mark Shankey	3:57.10
5000	Adam Sutton	14:25.84		Ed Prickett	15:01.03	3000	Luke Northall	8:43.20
3kSt	Andrew Franklin	8:51.4		Jermaine Mays	9:10.8	1500St	William Docherty	4:27.51
110H	Robert Newton	14.0w		Dominic Girdler	14.2	100H	Edward Dunford	13.16
400H	Matt Elias	50.1		Jeff Christie	51.8		Rupert Gardner	54.98
HJ	Samson Oni	2.18		Chuka Enih-Snell	2.14		Martyn Bernard	1.99
PV	Scott Simpson	5.20		Richard Hurren	4.60		Chris Tremayne	4.50
LJ	Chris Tomlinson	7.61		Jonathan Moore	7.98w		Onen Eyong	7.28w
TJ	Nicholas Thomas	15.54		Nathan Douglas	15.06		Enyioma Anomelechi	14.15w
SP	Emeka Udechuku	17.90		Greg Beard	16.23		Eoin Leen IRL	18.33
DT	Emeka Udechuku	59.84		Greg Beard	47.20		Garry Hagan	50.01
HT	Andy Frost	61.30		Thomas Dempsey	56.33		Paul Farley	56.94
JT	David Parker	75.53		Alex van der Merwe	64.04		Lee Doran	58.32
			Dec	Steven Hughes	6151	Oct	Edward Dunford	5636
			10kW	Lloyd Finch	44:29.4	5kW	Luke Finch	23:50.61
			Dec	Bedford 14/15 Jul		Oct	Birmingham 29/30 September	
WOMEN				**WOMEN**			**WOMEN**	
100	Abiodun Oyepitan	11.17w		Vernicha James	11.44w		Amalachukwe Onuora	12.02
200	Helen Roscoe	23.4w		Amy Spencer	23.3w		Jemma Sims	24.86
400	Helen Thieme	53.27		Lisa Miller	54.02	300	Faye Harding	40.01
800	Alex Carter	2:07.10		Rebecca Lyne	2:09.64		Morag McLarty	2:08.42
1500	Alex Carter	4:23.0		Emma Ward	4:26.1		Rosie Smith	4:40.10
3000	Gillian Palmer	9:39.4		Collette Fagan	9:36.1		Emma Hunt	10:00.65
100H	Julie Pratt	13.5w		Helen Worsey	13.8w	80H	Channelle Garnett	11.31
400H	Hannah Wood	60.5		Gemma Dooney	60.6	300H	Joanne Erskine	43.71
HJ	Gayle O`Connor	1.75		Aileen Wilson	1.82		Emma Perkins	1.74
PV	Gael Davies	3.70		Kate Dennison	3.65		Erin Kinnear IRL	3.50
LJ	Sarah Wellstead	6.02w		Elaine Smith	5.92w		Phyllis Agbo	5.77w
TJ	Rebecca White	13.09w		Rachel Peacock	12.10w		Rachel Brenton	11.86
SP	Julie Dunkley	16.31		Rebecca Peake	14.13		Frances Miller	12.31
DT	Rebecca Roles	49.06		Claire Smithson	54.81		Danielle Hall	41.28
HT	Zoe Derham	57.05		Katy Lamb	52.17		Frances Miller	48.18
JT	Jennifer Kemp	48.97		Goldie Sayers	53.74		Jo Chapman	41.78
			Hept	Rosalyne Gonse	4875		Emily Parker	4436
			5kW	Sophie Hales	26:29.35		Bryna Chrismas	27:42.35
			Hept	Bedford 14/15 Jul		Hept	Birmingham 29/30 September	

U15 Sheffield 11 - 12 August

MEN			80H	Richard Alexis-Smith	10.68w	DT	Sam Herrington	49.10
100	Craig Pickering	11.00w	HJ	Alan Hassall	1.86	HT	Gavin Hill	51.03
200	Jahmal Alert-Khan	22.58	PV	Carl Titman	3.35	JT	Ben Lee	48.18
400	Craig Glanville	51.93	LJ	Ryan Thomas	6.34w	Pent	Pepi Nanci	2974
800	Matthew Wood	2:00.97	TJ	William Harwood	12.86w	3kW	Luke Davis	15:47.32
1500	Ross Toole	4:15.61	SP	Daniel Hepplewhite	15.61	Pent	Birmingham 29/30 September	
WOMEN			75H	Heather Jones	10.95	JT	Louise Watton	38.29
100	Sinead Johnson	11.92w	HJ	Shani Rainford	1.64	Pent	Cherri Morrison	2861
200	Nicola Gossman	24.85	LJ	Rebekah Passley	5.86	3kW	Rebecca Mersh	16:03.25
800	Elizabeth McWilliams	2:16.26	SP	Chloe Edwards	11.70			
1500	Charlotte Browning	4:35.85	DT	Christina Carding	36.70	Pent	Birmingham 29/30 September	

UK MERIT RANKINGS 2001 by Peter Matthews

This is the 34th successive year that I have compiled annual merit rankings of British athletes – an assessment of form during the outdoor season. The major factors by which the rankings are determined are win-loss record, performances in the major meetings, and sequence of marks. While indoor marks are excluded from the main rankings, for the first time this year I have also assessed overall form including these, and have appended any changes at the end of appropriate events.

I endeavour to be as objective as possible, but form can often provide conflicting evidence, or perhaps an athlete may not have shown good enough results against leading rivals, or in very important competition, to justify a ranking which his or her ability might otherwise warrant. I can only rank athletes on what they have actually achieved. Much depends on having appropriate opportunities and perhaps getting invitations for the prestige meetings. Difficulties also arise when athletes reach peak form at different parts of the season or, through injury, miss significant competition. Also, increasingly, many of our top athletes are competing overseas instead of in domestic meetings, which makes comparisons of form difficult. It is often difficult to compare juniors with seniors and in 2001 many top U23 and U20 athletes missed the AAAs through clashes of fixtures.

Once again it should be pointed out that the rankings are by no means necessarily the order in which I think the athletes would have finished in an idealised contest, but simply my attempt to assess what has actually happened in 2001.

I hope that I have not missed many performances, but I would be very pleased to receive any missing results at 10 Madgeways Close, Great Amwell, Herts SG12 9RU.

For each event the top 12 are ranked. On the first line is shown the athlete's name, then their date of birth followed, in brackets, by the number of years ranked in the top 12 (including 2001) and their ranking last year (2000), in italics their IAAF world ranking, their best mark prior to 2001, and their best performances of the year (generally six), followed for completeness, by significant indoor marks indicated by 'i'. Then follow placings at major meetings, providing a summary of the athlete's year at the event. *(Note: IAAF rankings include indoor performances)*

Abbreviations include

AAA-23	AAA Under-23 Championships
AAA-J	AAA Under-20 Championships
Bedl	Bedford International
BGP	British Grand Prix at Crystal Palace
BL	British League
B.Univs	British Universities at Glasgow
CAU	Inter-Counties at Bedford
Cup	BAL Cup Final at Bedford (also major clashes in semis – sf)
Derby	U20/U23 Inter-Regional 29/7
E.Clubs	European Clubs Cup
ECp	European Cup
EdIG	Edinburgh International Games
EJ	European Junior Championships at Grosseto
E.Sch	English Schools
Eur23	European U23 Championships at Amsterdam
GhCl	NU Gateshead Classic
GPF	Grand Prix Final
GWG	Goodwill Games at Brisbane
IR	Inter-Regional at Birmingham
IS	Inter-Services
JLF	Junior League Final
Jnr IA	Junior Inter-Area at Ipswich
LI	Loughborough International
Lough	Loughborough Development Meeting (4 Jul)
U23L	Under 23 International v France and Germany at Liverpool
v FRA	ENG v France 'B' at Ashford
v USA	UK v USA and Russia at Glasgow
World	World Championships at Edmonton
WUG	World University Championships at Beijing
WY	World Youth Championships at Debrecen

100 METRES

1. **Dwain Chambers** 5.4.78 (6y, 1) *IAAF 5* 9.97 '99 9.97w?, 9.99, 10.00, 10.01, 10.01, 10.06, 10.09, 10.10
1 E.Clubs, 1 Kalamata, 1 Seville, 1 Nuremberg, 2 v USA, 3 Lausanne, 1 AAA, 2 BGP, 5 World, 2 Zurich, 2 GhCl, 4 Brussels, 1 GWG
2. **Mark Lewis-Francis** 4.9.82 (3y, 3) *IAAF 13* 10.10 '00 9.97w?, 10.09w, 10.12, 10.12, 10.13, 10.13
1 Tallahassee, 2 Philadelphia, 1 BL1 (2), 1 Cup sf Wigan, 1 Mannheim, 1 ECp, 4 v USA, 2 AAA, 1 EJ, 5sf World, 6 GhCl, 6 Brussels
3. **Christian Malcolm** 3.6.79 (5y, 7) *IAAF 15* 10.12/10.10w '98 10.09w?, 10.11, 10.17, 10.19w, 10.20, 10.21
1 LI, 1 BL2 (2), 1 Arles, 1 Helsinki, 2 Lille, 1 Welsh, 4B Rome, 3 AAA, 2B BGP, 7 World, 8 Brussels
4. **Jonathan Barbour** 3.11.80 (2y, 6) *IAAF 63* 10.28 '00 10.13w, 10.24w, 10.26w, 10.27w, 10.28, 10.29w, 10.30
1r6 Irvine, 2 LI, 1 CAU, 4 Arles, 1 vSPA-23, 1 AAA-23, 5 Cottbus, 1 Eur23, 4B BGP, 5 GhCl, 3 T'saloniki, 1 Nitra, 7 GWG
5. **Chris Lambert** 6.4.81 (2y, -) *IAAF 75* 10.31 '99 10.24, 10.24, 10.28, 10.30w, 10.32, 10.32
2B BL1 (2), 2 South, 2 AAA-23, 1 Cork, 4 AAA, 3B BGP, 1 v FRA, 3 WUG
6. **Doug Bignall** 20.10.74 (2y, 10) *IAAF 57* 10.30A, 10.43, 10.27Aw '00 10.29w, 10.30, 10.30, 10.31, 10.33, 10.39
1B1 Walnut, 1 BL2 (3), 5 AAA, 1B BGP, 4 GhCl
7. **Darren Campbell** 12.9.73 (10y, 2) *IAAF 43* 10.04 '98 10.16, 10.37, 10.38, 10.38, 10.44w, 10.46
1 Austin, 1 Madrid, 6 Nice, 6 AAA, 7 BGP
8. **Marlon Devonish** 1.6.76 (5y, 8) *IAAF 94* 10.13 '98 10.29w, 10.30, 10.31, 10.32, 10.36, 10.38
2B1 Walnut, 1r1 Fullerton, 3 LI, 2 CAU, 3 Poznan, 5 Lille, 7h Z¸rich, 4 T'saloniki

9= **Ian Mackie** 27.2.75 (6y, 5) 10.17 '96, 10.00w '98 10.19w, 10.30, 10.39, 10.54, 10.55w; 10.4
1 Scot, 3g vUSA, 3 Cork, dns sf AAA, 6B BGP, 1= EdIG

9= **Doug Turner** 2.12.66 (2y, -) 10.40 '97, 10.26w '96 10.26w, 10.32w, 10.37, 10.39, 10.45, 10.46
2 Bangor, 2 Welsh, 1 Budapest, 2 Byrkjelo, 1= EdIG, 2 Avezzano

11. **Tyrone Edgar** 29.3.82 (1y, -) 10.39 '00 10.17w, 10.24w, 10.35w, 10.57, 10.58, 10.59
6r1 Fullerton, 2 BL1 (1), 5 LI, 2 Sth-J, 1 AAA-J, 4 EJ, 1 v USA-J, 4 EdIG
12. **Jason Gardener** 18.9.75 (7y, 4) 9.98 '99 10.23, 10.28, 10.38, 10.92; 10.5
2 Ingolstadt, 8 Seville, 3 v FRA

– **Daniel Money** 17.10.76 (2y, -) 10.32, 10.16w '97 10.33w, 10.45w, 10.45w, 10.46, 10.46w, 10.50
4 LI, 4 CAU, 1 North, 2 Cork, 2B Glasgow, BL1: 1,-,-,1B

– **Dwayne Grant** 17.7.82 (0y, -) 10.61, 10.57w '00 10.22w, 10.26w, 10.45w, 10.47, 10.47, 10.50; 10.4
1B LI, 1 Sth-J, 2 BL1 (2), 1B Mannheim, 2 AAA-J, 1 Jnr AA

Chambers takes his third successive top ranking, with a fine year including runnimng 9.99 for 5th in the World Champs and ending the year with a big win at the Goodwill Games. Lewis-Francis ran that wonderful 9.97 in the quarter-finals at the World Champs and was denied a chance of that being a World Junior record by the failure to take a wind reading; he then slipped to only 5th in his semi. Malcolm achieves his best 100m ranking; he excelled to make the World final, but was beaten 2-0 by Lewis-Francis, who also ran the faster set of times. Lewis-Francis won at the European Cup and took the European Junior gold and Barbour took the European Under-23 gold. Lambert, who had ranked 11th in 1999, made an outstanding return from injury to take 4th at the AAAs and then the World University Games bronze. Campbell ran an exciting 10.16 in his first race, but his season was then dashed in injury. Similarly Gardener was restricted to just four meetings. Money just misses a ranking. After four years at 10.31 each year, the 10th best performer is a record 10.30.

200 METRES

1. **Christian Malcolm** 3.6.79 (5y, 2) *IAAF 3* 20.19 '00 20.08, 20.09, 20.13, 20.22, 20.24, 20.37
1 LI, 1 Helsinki, 2 Lille, 2 v USA, 2 AAA, 2 BGP, 5 World, 2 Z¸rich, 2 GhCl, 3 Brussels, 5 GWG, 4 GPF
2. **Marlon Devonish** 1.6.76 (6y, 3) *IAAF 15* 20.25 '99 20.29, 20.38, 20.40, 20.44, 20.47, 20.50
2B MSR, 1r1 Fullerton, 1A LI, 2 Kalamata, 1 Hengelo, 1 Poznan, 3 Lille, 2 ECp, 3 v USA, 1 AAA, 4 BGP, 8 World, 4 GhCl, 2 T'saloniki, 8 Brussels, 4 GWG
3. **Dwain Chambers** 5.4.78 (3y, 12) *IAAF 41* 20.68 '99 20.31, 20.60, 20.65, 20.79, 20.80, 20.90
2A LI, 3 AAA, 1 BGP, 5qf World
4. **Doug Turner** 2.12.66 (7y, 9) *IAAF 51* 20.43 '96, 20.36w '97 20.54, 20.57w, 20.75, 20.87, 20.87w, 20.90w
8 Roodepoort, 3 F-de-France, 2 Bangor, 1 Welsh, 2 Budapest, 1 BL2 (3), 4 AAA, 1 Byrkjelo, 1 EdIG
5. **Dwayne Grant** 17.7.82 (1y, -) 20.88 '00 20.64, 20.90, 20.90w, 20.92, 20.96; 20.4w, 20.9
1 Sth-J, 1 BL1 (2), 1r2 Mannheim, 1 AAA-J, 3 EJ, 1 v USA-J, 3 EdIG, 1 Jnr AA
6. **Julian Golding** 17.2.75 (8y,7) *IAAF 76* 20.18 '98 20.81, 20.85, 21.00, 21.04, 21.11, 21.17
2r1 Fullerton, 3 LI, 1 South, 2 Funchal, 2 Braga, 5 AAA, 2 Patra
7. **Jonathan Barbour** 3.11.80 (2y, 10) 20.79 '00 20.78, 20.95, 21.08, 21.10, 21.24; 20.8w
6r1 Fullerton, 1B LI, 4 CAU, 1 vSPA-23, 1 AAA-23, 6 Eur23, 1 Nitra
8. **Tim Benjamin** 2.5.82 (3y, 5) *IAAF 51* 20.72/20.60w '99 20.67, 20.85w, 20.87w, 20.88w, 20.98; 20.6w; 20.78i, 20.86i 4 LI, 1 Bangor, 2 Arles, 2 Welsh, 2 AAA-J, 1B BL2 (3), 6 AAA
9. **Chris Lambert** 6.4.81 (2y, -) 20.63 '99 20.84, 20.86w, 20.87, 21.08, 21.29, 21.38w
2B BL1 (2), 1 Cup sf Rugby, dns sf South, 3 Cork, dns AAA, 5sf WUG

10. **Daniel Money** 17.10.76 (2y, -) 20.92, 20.75w '97 20.92w, 20.99, 21.06, 21.11w, 21.12, 21.21
2 LI, 3 CAU, 1 North, 2 Cork, 3h2 AAA, 1 Cup, BL1: 1,-,-,1
11. **Tyrone Edgar** 29.3.82 (1y, -) 21.62, 21.55w '98 20.96, 21.07w, 21.61, 21.63; 20.8w, 21.0w
1r2 Fullerton, 2 Sth-J, 2r3 Mannheim, 3 AAA-J, BL1: 2,-,1B,-
12. **Darren Campbell** 12.9.73 (7y, 1) 20.13 '0 20.41, 21.21
1 Austin, 8 BGP
Allyn Condon 24.8.74 (6y, 8) *IAAF 32* 20.63 '97, 20.53i '98
20.99, 21.55, 21.60, 21.66; 21.4w; 20.60i, 20.63i, 20.72i, 20.85i, 20.93i 1 CAU, 3 Hengelo, 4h3 AAA
Ian Mackie 27.2.75 (3y, 4) 20.90, 20.68w '00 20.85, 21.0 1 Scot

Including Indoors: 6. Condon, 7. Golding, 8. Benjamin, 9. Barbour, 10. Lambert, 11. Money, 12. Edgar

After 5th in 1997, 3rd in 1998 and 1999 and 2nd in 2000, Malcolm progressed smoothly to top ranking; the only disappointment in a great season being that, in his eighth race at the Worlds, he was not quite able to match his semi-final form and just missed a medal. Devonish also made the World final and ranked 2nd (as in 1999) and Chambers made an exciting breakthrough at the British Grand Prix. Turner was a clear fourth and he is followed by the European Junior bronze medallist, Dwayne Grant. The Olympic silver medallist Campbell managed only two races.

400 METRES

1. **Mark Richardson** 26.7.72 (12y, 1) *IAAF 26* 44.37 '98 45.14, 45.22, 45.66, 45.79, 45.84, 46.20
1 v USA, 1 AAA, 1 BGP, 4s1 World, 5 GhCl
2. **Iwan Thomas** 5.1.74 (7y, 6) *IAAF 37* 44.36 '97 45.70, 45.77, 45.82, 45.82, 45.92, 45.93
7 Roodepoort, 3 Tula, 3 Helsinki, 7 ECp, 1 Dublin, 5 v USA, 1 BL1 (3), 2 AAA, 5 BGP, 8s2 World, 4 GhCl, 3r2 T'saloniki, 4 Rovereto
3. **Daniel Caines** 15.5.79 (2y, 3) *IAAF 6* 45.37 '00 45.58, 45.87; 45.61i, 45.75i, 46.21i, 46.29i
6 Seville, 6 BGP
4. **Mark Hylton** 24.9.76 (8y, 10) *IAAF 23* 45.24 '98 46.09, 46.36, 46.67, 46.71, 46.8, 46.91; 46.24i, 46.42i, 46.63i
2 LI, 1 South, 1 Cork, 3 AAA, 7 BGP
5. **Jamie Baulch** 3.5.73 (8y, 2) *IAAF 21* 44.57 '96 46.15, 46.32, 46.33, 46.44, 46.56, 46.72; 46.52i
dnf Welsh, 5 Funchal, 4 Luzern, 4 AAA, 8 BGP, 5h World, 6 GhCl
6. **Tim Benjamin** 2.5.82 (1y, -) 48.5 '98 46.10, 46.43, 46.45, 46.50, 47.33
1 Lough 4/7, 1 EJ, 7 GhCl, 1 EdIG
7. **Sean Baldock** 3.12.76 (5y, 4) 45.20 '00 46.35, 46.61, 46.67, 46.86, 47.40, 47.66
2 E.Clubs, 2 BL1 (2), 3 Dublin, 5 AAA
8. **Jared Deacon** 15.10.75 (7y, 5) 45.69 '00 46.56, 46.6, 46.67, 46.76, 46.9, 47.01
4B Walnut, 2 N.East, 1 North, 2 Cork, 6 AAA, 1 v FRA, BL1: -,1,-,1
9. **David Naismith** 15.12.79 (3y, 12) 46.27 '99 46.82, 46.82, 46.84, 46.94, 47.12, 47.13
1 LI, 3 Geneva, 7 Helsinki, 1 vSPA-23, 1 AAA-23, 6 Eur23, 2 Cup, 2 Derby
10. **Peter Brend** 2.2.77 (1y, -) 47.08 '00 46.8, 47.03, 47.1, 47.20, 47.20, 47.34
2 CAU, 1 Cup sf Ha, 2 South, 1 IR, 7 AAA, 4g v FRA, BL2: 1,-,1,1
11. **Dean Macey** 12.12.77 (1y, -) 46.41 '00 46.21; 1D World Dec
12. **Robert Tobin** 20.12.83 (1y, -) 48.22 '00 47.10, 47.3, 47.42, 47.62, 47.69, 47.73
4 LI, 1 AAA-J, 1 E.Sch, 6 EJ, 1 v FRA-J, 3 v USA-J, 1 Jnr IA

\- **Adam Potter** 12.4.80 (0y, -) 49.0 '00 46.75, 47.5, 47.61, 47.78, 48.0, 48.06
2 AAA-23, 3 Lough 4/7, 1 Derby, 3 v FRA
\- **Matt Elias** 25.4.79 (0y, -) 47.25 '00 46.9, 47.4, 48.65; 46.88i, 46.91i, 47.16i, 47.31i 1 BL2 (2), 1 Welsh
\- **Du'aine Thorne-Ladejo** 14.2.71 (8y, -) 44.66 '96 no outdoor; 46.31i, 46.83i, 46.89i
nr **Paul McKee** IRE 15.10.77 45.92 '00 46.42, 46.88, 46.98, 47.10, 47.13, 47.21
1C F-de-France, 4 Gosier, 1 Bangor, 3 Budapest, 4 Dublin, 1 Irish, 1 NI, 5sf WUG

Including Indoors: 2. Caines, 3. Thomas,Ö10. Elias, 11. Brend, 12. Thorne-Ladejo

It was a disappointing year for British 400m running. Richardson, at last clear of the Nandrolene suspension, ranked top for the fourth time, but Caines, after winning the World Indoor title, could race only twice outdoors, and Thomas and Baulch struggled to capture their accustomed form. On the plus side, Benjamin moved up most successfully. Just as in 2000, Dean Macey raced but once, but this time his outstanding run in the decathlon at Edmonton gets him a ranking. 17 year-old Robert Tobin had a fine year to take the final rankings place. The 10th best mark outdoors of 46.75 was the worst since 1984 and compared to 46.19 in 2000 and the record 46.06 in 1996.

800 METRES

1. **Simon Lees** 19.11.79 (2y, -) *IAAF 63* 1:47.69 '98 1:47.35, 1:47.39, 1:47.78, 1:47.82, 1:48.80, 1:49.12
1 B.Univs, 1 LI, 3 ECp, 4 v USA, 4 Eur-23, 4 BGP, dns sf WUG
2. **Neil Speaight** 9.9.78 (3y, 6) *IAAF 76* 1:48.1 '99 1:47.16, 1:47.59, 1:47.67, 1:47.79, 1:48.10, 1:48.22
2 E.Clubs, 2 LI, 1 Watford, 2 Dublin, 2 Tartu, 2 v USA, 1 AAA, 7 BGP, 7sf WUG, BL1: 2,1,-,-
3. **James McIlroy** 30.12.76 (3y, 1) 1:45.32 '98 1:47.42, 1:47.95, 1:49.47, 1:49.95, 1:51.15, 1:51.35
2 Victoria, 9 Stanford, 2 AAA, 6 BGP
4. **Grant Cuddy** 6.1.77 (2y, 1) 1:47.2 '97 1:48.27, 1:48.41, 1:48.90, 1:50.05, 1:50.41, 1:50.47
1A Wyth, 2 Watford, 4 Solihull, 2 Glasgow, 6 Cork, 3 AAA, BL1: 4B,3,-,-

5. **Matthew Shone** 10.7.75 (3y, -) 1:47.99 '99 1:48.67, 1:48.88, 1:48.90, 1:48.97, 1:49.31, 1:49.8
3 LI, 3 Watford, 4 Budapest, 5 AAA, 1 BMC-F, 4 EdIG, BL1: 1,2,-,1
6. **Ricky Soos** 28.6.83 (1y, -) 1:51.22 '00 1:48.43, 1:48.5, 1:51.84, 1:51.95, 1:52.14
1 Mid-J, 1 Bangor, 1 Lough 13/6, 1 AAA-J, 3 Eur-J, 1 Derby-J
7. **Andrew Graffin** 20.12.77 (2y, 9) 1:49.1 '00 1:47.5, 1:49.09, 1:49.67
8 Solihull, 6 Glasgow, 1 Watford 29/8
8. **Chris Moss** 17.6.79 (3y, 5) 1:47.75 '00 1:48.94, 1:49.07, 1:49.2, 1:49.71, 1:50.04, 1:51.0
4 LI, 2 Lough 13/6, 4 Watford, 10 Solihull, 1 AAA-23, 6h Eur-23
9. **Alasdair Donaldson** 21.6.77 (4y, 4) 1:47.32 '00 1:49.41, 1:49.47, 1:49.59, 1:49.61, 1:49.77, 1:50.70
5 LI, 2 Riga, 6 Bratislava, 5 Watford, 6 Budapest, 1 Cup, 4 AAA, 4 Watford 25/7, 1 Stretford 31/7, 6 v FRA
10. **Neil Dougal** 7.3.80 (1y, -) 1:51.01 '00 1:48.71, 1:50.23, 1:50.65, 1:50.84, 1:51.19, 1:52.19
6 AAA, 2 Watford 25/7, 4 v FRA, 2 EdIG
11. **Rob Watkinson** 10.3.74 (1y, -) 1:49.62, 1:49.80, 1:49.8, 1:49.90, 1:50.11, 1:50.48
4 B.Univs, 2 Yorks, 7 LI, 1B Wyth, 3 CAU, 1 North, 4B Solihull, 8 Glasgow, 6s2 AAA, 2 Stretford 31/7, 3 BMC-F
12. **Gary Vickers** 26.2.71 (1y, -) 1:50.51 '00 1:48.85, 1:49.60, 1:49.7, 1:50.1, 1:50.27, 1:50.83
5 CAU, 2B Wyth, 4B Watford, 3 Lough 13/6, 1 Mid, 3B Solihull, 2 IR, 3 Cardiff, 5s1 AAA, 3 Watford 25/7, 5 v FRA, 9 GhCl

Angus Maclean 20.9.80 (1y, -) 1:49.82 '00 1:49.39, 1:49.74, 1:49.76 2 B.Univs, 4 Cardiff
Michael East 20.1.78 (0y, -) 1:48.95 '00 1:48.66, 1:51.73; 1 BL1 (3), 3 Solihull
Anthony Whiteman 13.11.71 (4y, 2) 1:45.81 '00 1:49.00, 1:50.79, 1:51.97 2 BL1 (3), 8 Watford, 5 Solihull

New lows, unfortunately, as not only is the tenth best of 1:48.85 the worst since 1976, but a best of 1:47.16 is the worst season's lead since 1970, and a very far cry from the 1980s, when the 10th best record was set at 1:46.16 in 1984 (that year there were 25 men under 1:48.85). But our top two, Speaight and Lees made encouraging progress. Lees (whose only previous ranking was 10th in 1998) took the top spot with a 2-1 record over Speaight and good runs in the European races. Cuddy returned, having previoulsy ranked in 1997. 18 year-old Soos showed rich promise and took the European Junior bronze. Overall the 12 ranked are a most inexperienced bunch, with Donaldson's 4 years being the most.

1500 METRES – 1 MILE

1. **John Mayock** 26.10.70 (10y, 1) *IAAF 17* 3:31.86 '97, 3:50.32M '96 3:34.43, 3:34.80, 3:35.73, 3:54.05M (3:37.6), 3:39.24, 3:58.49M 7 Prague, 4 v USA, 6 Nice, 1 AAA, 4 BGP, 10s2 World, 9 Zurich, 13 Brussels, 2 And'jar, 7 GWG
2. **Anthony Whiteman** 13.11.71 (6y, 2) *IAAF 41* 3:32.34 '97, 3:51.90M '98 3:34.88, 3:36.77, 3:37.60, 3:37.75, 3:55.16M (3:38.5), 3:40.86 12 Nuremberg, 5g v USA, 2 AAA, 8 BGP, 7s1 World, 4B Zurich, 4 GhCl, dnf Rieti
3. **Tom Mayo** 2.5.77 (3y, -) *IAAF 72* 3:41.2/4:00.02M '98 3:55.57M (3:38.3), 3:38.34, 3:39.27, 3:41.28, 3:44.52, 3:48.69 1 Watford, 6 ECp, 6 v USA, 3 AAA, 9 BGP, 5 GhCl, 9 Rieti
4. **Andrew Graffin** 20.12.77 (3y, 3) *IAAF 43* 3:36.18/3:56.13M '00 3:35.97, 3:36.41, 3:37.77, 3:55.42M, 3:39.80, 3:40.44 7 Hengelo, 3 Watford, 14 Lausanne, 7 Nice, 7 AAA, 10ht World, 5 Linz, 6 Rieti
5. **Michael East** 20.1.78 (2y, 8) *IAAF 94* 3:40.13/4:04.65M '00 3:38.94, 3:39.47, 3:59.61M (3:42.9), 3:43.94, 3:44.68 2 Watford, 1 Dublin, 2 Arnhem, 4 AAA, 13 BGP
6. **Angus Maclean** 20.9.80 (2y, 11) 3:41.19 '00 3:39.88, 3:41.00, 3:41.36, 3:41.66, 3:46.24, 3:46.45
3 LI, 1 BL2 (2), 4 Watford, 1 AAA-23, 5 Eur-23, 1 Watford 25/7, 9 Zurich-23, 8 WUG
7. **Richard Ashe** 5.10.74 (3y, 9) 3:41.2/3:59.98M '96 3:42.58, 3:43.20, 3:45.87, 3:51.0
2 Cup sf H'gey, 1 Solihull, 6 AAA, 3 Watford 25/7, 6 v FRA
8. **James Thie** 27.6.78 (2y, 12) 3:42.85/4:01.7M '00 3:44.51, 3:45.27, 3:45.50, 3:46.06, 3:49.18
3 B.Univs, 3 Solihull, 3 Cardiff, 5 AAA, 14 Watford 25/7, 5 v FRA, 1 BL2 (4)
9. **James Bowler** 2.9.79 (1y, -) 3:49.55 '00 3:41.75, 3:44.39, 3:44.88, 3:44.93, 3:47.06, 3:47.33
5 B.Univs, 4 Wyth, 1B LI, 5 Watford, 3 vSPA-23, 3 AAA-23, 10 Eur-23
10. **Vince Wilson** 1.4.73 (1y, -) 3:43.38 '96 3:42.81, 3:44.41, 3:44.79, 3:45.82, 3:47.39
8 Watford, 3 Wyth, 7 Solihull, 17 Cork, 8 AAA, 6 Watford 25/7
11. **Christian Stephenson** 22.7.74 (2y, -) 3:43.85 '98, 4:00.4M '00 3:41.94, 3:51.46, 3:54.6
6 Watford, 1 Welsh. BL2: 1,2,1,5B
12. **Gregg Taylor** 1.8.77 (1y, -) 3:44.79 '00 3:42.73, 3:45.47, 3:46.16, 3:47.00, 3:47.50
6 B.Univs, 11 Wyth, 1 Mid, 5 Solihull, 1 IR, 5h1 AAA, 4 Watford 25/7, 1 Stretford 31/7; BL2: -,3,2,2

– **Jonathan McCallum** 19.11.75 (3y, 5) 3:37.75 '00 3:42.16, 3:43.66; 3:46.95i 4 LI, 6 Hani·
– **Adam Zawadski** 19.12.74 (0y, -) 3:44.2 '97 3:42.90, 3:43.29, 3:45.98, 3:48.21
5 LI, 9 Watford, 13 Cork, 6h1 AAA
nr **Gareth Turnbull IRE** 14.5.79 3:39.08 '00 3:38.28, 3:39.93, 3:42.18, 3:42.78, 3:44.21
1 B.Univs, 2 LI 4 Cork, 9 Eur-23, 2 WUG

M = 1 mile time (1500m times in brackets).

Mayock was top for the seventh successive year (a new record for the event) and Whiteman second for the sixth successive year. Whiteman was much the best of the UK trio at the Worlds. Mayo (10th in 1998 and 11th in 1999) had by far his best season and ran for Britain in the European Cup; he beat Graffin 2-1, although he was a long way behind in Rieti and Graffin had the faster times. Maclean ran well to make two major championship finals. There was quite a gap after the top six, and standards fell back, so that the 10th best of 3:42.58 compared to 3:41.19 in 2000 and 3:42.37 in 1999, and is the worst since 1974 (peak 3:38.02 in 1986, when there were 25 men under 3:42.58).

3000 METRES (Not ranked)

John Mayock 26.10.70 7:43.31i '97, 7:47.28 '95 7:56.06, 7:57.11; 7:44.08i, 7:51.10i; 3 ECp, 1 GhCl
Michael Openshaw 8.4.72 7:55.12 '00 7:54.10; 1 LI
Matt O'Dowd 15.4.76 7:55.9 '97
7:55.75, 8:05.5e+; 2 LI
Rob Denmark 23.11.68 7:39.55 '93
7:59.57, 8:05.5e+; 5 LI

5000 METRES

1. **Michael Openshaw** 8.4.72 (3y, 2) *IAAF 83* 13:37.97 '00 13:24.44, 13:33.26, 13:37.86, 13:58.15, 14:00.84
   6 Milan, 4 ECp, 2 Cork 14 Heusden, 13ht World
2. **Matt O'Dowd** 15.4.76 (2y, -) 13:37.00 '99 13:30.56, 13:49.99, 13:50.67, 13:53.53
   4 Wyth, 3 Solihull, 6 Cork, 2 AAA
3. **Karl Keska** 7.5.72 (5y, 10) 13:23.07 '99 13:24.63; 16 Heusden
4. **Rob Denmark** 23.11.68 (10y, -) 13:10.24 '92 13:36.30, 13:42.70, 14:02.05, 14:05e+
   1 Wyth, 4 Solihull, 4 Dublin
5. **Glen Stewart** 7.12.70 (2y, 4) 13:38.37 '00 13:37.17, 13:43.72, 13:57.65, 14:00.08, 14:15.19
   3 Wyth, 5 Solihull, 14 Cork, 8 AAA, 1 EdIG
6. **Allen Graffin** 20.12.77 (2y, 8) 13:41.42 '00 13:40.07, 13:41.09, 13:42.15, 13:52.08
   7 Stellenbosch, 13 Milan, 3 Bratislava, 6 Solihull
7. **Jon Wild** 30.8.73 (1y, -) 13:45.1 '96 13:52.72; 1 AAA
8. **Chris Thompson** 17.4.81 (1y, -) 14:06.52 '00 13:45.27, 13:56.55, 14:06.00, 14:16.45. 14:26.67
   1 B.Univs, 7 Solihull, 5 Eur-23, 8 WUG
9. **Sam Haughian** 9.7.79 (1y, -) 13:55.81 '99 13:46.35, 13:49.55, 14:06.03, 14:27.6
   1 Cup sf Eton, 8 Solihull, 6 Eur-23, 2 Watford 1/8
10. **Glynn Tromans** 17.3.69 (4y, -) 13:44.27 '99 13:43.40, 14:04.9+, 14:11.6 2 Wyth
11. **Julian Moorhouse** 13.11.71 (3y, 7) 13:42.35 '00 13:51.75, 13:52.88, 13:55.37, 14:02.97
    5 Wyth, 9 Solihull, 6 AAA, 3 Watford 1/8
12. **Mark Miles** 24.3.77 (1y, -) 13:56.55 '99 13:53.74; 3 AAA

Top ranking is taken by Openshaw, who reduced his pb by over 13 seconds, just as he had done in 2000, and qualified for the Worlds. Kark Keska was unable to run there through injury and he only ran one 5000m race. O'Dowd (5th in 1999) returns with a solid season. Wild is difficult to rank – he won the AAAs but it was in a slow time and it his only race at the event. He and the youngsters Thompson and Haughian are the top newcomers. Tromans, who had three times placed 11th to 12th, came into the top 10 for the first time at this event. The 18 year-old Mohamed Farah ran 13:56.31 at Solihull for 17th on the British list and went on to win the European Junior title. The 10th best standard of 13:51.75 compared to 13:45.26 in 2000 and was the worste since 1970; the record level was 13:28.44 in 1984 (when there were 37 men under 13:51.75). 10th best was under 13:40 every year from 1977 to 1992, but not since; we are now in a different age, but of course it might yet get much worse.

10,000 METRES

1. **Karl Keska** 7.5.72 (3y, 1) 27:44.09 '00 4 Eur Challenge 28:06.29
2. **Glynn Tromans** 17.3.69 (5y, 9) 28:21.07 '99 2 (1) AAA 28:31.33
3. **Jon Wild** 30.8.73 (1y, -) 0 3 (2) AAA 28:39.33
4. **Glen Stewart** 7.12.70 (1y, -) 0 4 (3) AAA 28:40.14
5. **Ian Hudspith** 23.9.70 (3y, 8) 28:35.11 '97 5 AAA 28:40.63
6. **Matt Smith** 26.12.74 (1y, -) 0 8 AAA 28:43.45, 7B E.Chall 29:28.35
7. **Rob Denmark** 23.11.68 (6y, 3) 28:03.31 '00 9 AAA 28:46.70
8. **Matt O'Dowd** 15.4.76 (1y, -) 29:45.16 '99 3B E.Chall 28:52.97
9. **Adam Sutton** 22.3.81 (1y, -) 0 11 Walnut 29:10.98, 9 Eur-23 29:28.32
10. **Sam Haughian** 9.7.79 (1y, -) 0 1 South 29:10.5
11. **David Taylor** 9.1.64 (4y, -) 29:00.04 '99 11 AAA 29:22.22
12. **Tony O'Brien** 14.11.70 (1y, -) 29:51.0 '96 12 AAA 29:28.70

Keska retains his top ranking with his good run in the European Challenge. The AAA medallists follow, but all ran just one 10,000m track race, and several of our top distance runners rank after running their first 10,000m track race – but we desperately need more track racing from them. Seven men were new to the rankings at this event,

HALF MARATHON (First ranked 1999)

1. **Matt O'Dowd** 15.4.76 (2y, -) 62:38 99 21 World 62:40
2. **Paul Evans** 13.4.61 (2y, 3) 60:09? '95, 61:18 ;97 2 Hastings 64:29, 5 GNR 63:15
3. **Nick Jones** 10.7.74 (3y, 4) 63:12 '00 6 Gt.Scot (3 UK) 64:29, 51 World 64:00
4. **Daniel Robinson** 13.1.75 (1y, -) 66:52 '00 4 Enschede 64:43, 5 Gt Scot (2 UK) 64:27, 57 World 64:23
5. **Kassa Tadesse** 21.8.74 (1y, -) 62:51 '97 2 Gt Scot (1 UK) 64:04, 75 World 65:39
6 **Nick Wetheridge** 11.10.72 (2y, 8) 64:09 '00 1 Enschede 64:03

7. **Rob Denmark** 23.11.68 (2y, -) 62:37 '94 11 GNR 64:13
8. **Rob Birchall** 14.6.70 (1y, -) 65:46 '98 25 Lisbon 65:03, 2 Enschede 64:30, 8 Gt.Scot 65:23
9. **Andy Morgan-Lee** 1.3.69 (1y, -) 0 7 Gt.Scot 64:51, 16 GNR 65:41, 80 World 65:51
10. **Paul Green** 7.4.72 (1y, -) 66:43 '00 1 Bath 64:57

nr **John Mutai** KEN 26.5.66 60:52 '99 3 GNR 62:49

MARATHON

1. **Mark Steinle** 22.11.74 (2y, 3) 2:11:18 '00 6 London (1 AAA) 2:10:46
2. **Jon Brown** 27.2.71 (4y, 1) 2:09:44 '99 dnf London, 1 Victoria 2:20:28, 6 New York 2:11:24
3. **Mark Hudspith** 19.1.69 (7y, 5) 2:11:58 '95 11 London (2 AAA) 2:13:13
4. **Simon Pride** 20.7.67 (2y, 8) 2:18:49 '00 14 Dubai 2:20:03, 17 London 2:16:27, 1 Scot 2:28:34, 8 Dublin 2:17:37
5. **Daniel Robinson** 13.1.75 (1y, -) 0 9 Frankfurt 2:16:51
6. **Carl Warren** 28.9.69 (2y, -) 2:20:58 '99 13 Dubai 2:20:01, 32 Berlin 2:18:38
7. **Billy Burns** 13.12.69 (2y, -) 2:15:42 '00 19 London (3 AAA) 2:18:29
8. **Paul Evans** 13.4.61 (8y, -) 2:08:52 '96 dnf London, 23 Chicago 2:18:35
9. **Stuart Hall** 21.12.64 (1y, -) 2:21:48 '99 25 Chicago 2:18:46
10. **Robert Holladay** 10.1.75 (1y, -) 0 20 London 2:19:26
11. **Rhodri Jones** 14.8.66 (3y, 10) 2:18:34 '00 21 London 2:19:27
12. **Barry Royden** 15.12.66 (2y, 11) 2:18:54 '00 22 London 2:19:32

nr **John Mutai** KEN 26.5.662:13:20 '00 5 Dubai 2:14:49, 4 Dublin 2:14:133

Steinle was unable to run at the Worlds or in New York through injury, but his London run gave him top ranking ahead of Brown, who came back from injury to run well in New York. Just as in 2000, Pride's four marathons compared to one or two for all the other men. 12 men under 2:20 is better than our worst year of 1999, but otherwise one has to go back into the 1960s for lower levels.

3000 METRES STEEPLECHASE

1. **Ben Whitby** 6.1.77 (4y, 11) *IAAF 89* 8:41.79 '98 8:32.68, 8:33.25, 8:50.13, 8:56.4, 8:59.12
   1 BL2 (1), 1 Wyth, 8 E.Cp, 1 AAA
2. **Stuart Stokes** 15.12.76 (5y, 3) *IAAF 61* 8:33.61 '00 8:33.15, 8:35.37, 8:35.57, 8:37.76, 8:46.01, 8:47.02
   4 Wyth, 5 Hani-, 10 Athens, 2 AAA, 2 Cup, 1 v FRA, 7 Linz
3. **Christian Stephenson** 22.7.74 *IAAF 87* (4y, 1) 8:25.37 '01 8:38.46, 8:39.33, 8:54.48, 8:56.86, 9:03.3
   2 Wyth, 7 Luzern, 3 AAA, 1 BL2 (4)
4. **Charlie Low** 9.10.74 (4y, 5) *IAAF 92* 8:37.63 '00 8:40.85, 8:42.89, 8:49.59, 8:54.22, 8:55.94, 9:01.45
   2 LI, 8 Wyth, 3 Tula, 4 AAA, 3 Cup, BL1: -,-,2,2
5. **Donald Naylor** 5.9.71 (3y, 9) 8:44.03 '00 8:39.2, 8:45.93, 8:47.5, 8:54.67, 8:58.0, 9:01.76
   2 Solihull, 5 Dublin, 5 AAA, 3 v FRA, 1 EdIG, BL3: -,1,-,1
6. **Andrew Franklin** 13.9.80 (1y, -) 9:04.77 '00 8:42.82, 8:45.41, 8:51.4, 8:54.39, 9:15.98, 9:20.85
   1 B.Univs, 3 Wyth, 1 AAA-23, 9h2 Eur-23, 1 Derby, 6 v FRA
7. **David Mitchinson** 4.9.78 (3y, 7) 8:45.06 '00 8:45.9, 8:50.80, 8:52.34, 8:52.73, 8:59.25, 9:10.26
   2 BL1 (1), 4 LI, 5 Wyth, 4 Solihull, 6 AAA
8. **Andrew Hennessy** 24.8.77 (2y, -) 8:39.71 '99 8:45.4, 8:53.59, 8:53.60, 8:59.66, 9:07.97
   5 B.Univs, 5 LI, 3 Solihull, 7 AAA
9. **Justin Chaston** 4.11.68 (11y, 2) 8:23.90 '94 8:46.29, 8:47.53 5 E.Clubs, 1 BL1 (4)
10. **Iain Murdoch** 10.7.80 (2y, 10) 8:42.79 '00 8:49.55, 8:49.91, 8:57.0, 9:01.00, 9:03.8, 9:04.4
    2 B.Univs, 3 LI, 6 Solihull, 2 AAA-23, 10h1 Eur-23
11. **Rob Hough** 3.6.72 (6y, -) 8:26.36 '96 8:56.64, 8:58.14, 9:01.2, 9:03.57, 9:11.7 7 Wyth, 3 CAU, 8 AAA
12. **Rob Berry** 29.7.69 (1y, -) 8:59.52 '99 8:51.2, 8:59.29, 9:08.43, 9:26.30 1 North, 5 Solihull, 11 AAA

– **Steve Cairns** 3.11.67 (0y, -) 8:55.92 '99 8:56.16, 8:58.72, 9:02.12, 9:02.64, 9:03.08, 9:15.26
  1 Scot, 2 EdIG, BL1: 1,2,3,3

Whitby was second in 1998 in his first year in the rankings, and after 9th and 11th in 1999-2000, takes over at the top. He made an exciting breakthrough at Wythenshawe and later ran a little quicker at the AAAs, Stokes, with the best depth of performances, maintained his progress: 11-8-5-3-2 in his five years in the rankings. Stephenson top for the last three years, slipped. Franklin improved his best by 22 seconds and was the top newcomer. Chaston maintained his place, as he was twice flown back from the USA by Belgrave Harriers.

110 METRES HURDLES

1. **Colin Jackson** 18.2.67 (18y, 1) *IAAF 7* 12.91 '93, 12.8w '90 13.32, 13.36, 13.37, 13.37, 13.37w, 13.38
   2 Ingolstadt, 3 Ostrava, 3 Jena, 1 Dortmund, 2= Athens, 3= Prague, 1 Rome, 2 v USA, 4 Paris, 5 Monaco, 5 BGP, 4 Zurich, 4 GhCl, 5 Brussels, 5 GWG, 5 GPF, 3 Yokohama
2. **Anthony Jarrett** 13.8.68 *IAAF 17* (16y, 2) 13.00 '93 13.45, 13.47w, 13.51, 13.57, 13.58, 13.62
   1 LI, 6 Hani-, 1 Tula, 2 Helsinki, 3 ECp, 5 Oslo, 5 v USA, 1 AAA, 6 BGP, fs sf World
3. **Damien Greaves** 19.9.77 (7y, 3) *IAAF 70* 13.22 '00 13.68, 13.69w, 13.70, 13.81, 13.85, 13.89
   3 LI, 1/4 Geneva, 1 Scot, 1 Dublin, 1A Lough, 2 AAA, 1 Cup, 2fs World, BL1: 1B,2,-,-

4. **Paul Gray** 25.5.69 (12y, 8) *IAAF 81* 13.53 '94 13.63, 13.67w, 13.73w, 13.78, 13.80, 13.88
4 LI, 2 CAU, 7 Poznan, 1 Welsh, 2 Budapest, 4 Dublin, 5 AAA, 1 Bedl, 6h2 World, BL2: -,1,1,1
5. **Chris Baillie** 21.4.81 (3y, 6) 13.84 '00 13.70w, 13.82, 13.85, 13.86w, 13.95, 13.95w
2 LI, 1 CAU, 1 vSPA-23, 2 Scot, 6g v USA, 3 Eur-23, 3 Bedl, 4 Cup, 1 EdIG, BL1: -,5,2,2
6. **Mensah Elliott** 29.8.76 (3y, 4) 13.82/13.69w '00 13.88, 13.89, 13.92, 13.94, 13.96, 13.97
5 LI, 3 CAU, 1 Cup sf Eton, 1 South, 1 IR, 2A Lough, 6 AAA, 1B Bedl, 3 Cup, 3 v FRA, BL1: 2,3,3,1
7. **Dominic Bradley** 22.12.76 (3y, 12) 14.26, 14.07w '98 13.83, 13.96w, 14.01w, 14.02, 14.04w, 14.05; 14.0w
1B LI, 4 CAU, 1 Cup sf Wigan, 1 North, 2 IR, dnfA Lough, 3 AAA, 4 Bedl, BL1: 4,1B,1B,-
8. **Neil Owen** 18.10.73 (8y, 5) 13.60 '95, 13.5w '96 13.87, 13.94, 13.97, 14.00, 14.02, 14.03
2B LI, 2 E.Clubs, 2 South, 3g vSPA-23, 3 IR, 1B Lough, 4 AAA, 2 Bedl, 2 Cup, 4 v FRA, BL1: 3,4,4,3
9. **Robert Newton** 10.5.81 (3y, 7) 13.95 '00, 13.93w '99 14.09, 14.20w, 14.24, 14.27, 14.36; 14.0w, 14.0w
2 B.Univs, 8 LI, 5 CAU, 2 Cup sf Wigan, 1 Mid, dq (2fs) vSPA-23, 1 AAA-23, 4A Lough, 3h Eur-23, 5 Cup, 1 Derby, BL1: -,6,5,-
10. **Dominic Girdler** 6.3.82 (1y, -) 14.30 '99 14.07w, 14.16, 14.24, 14.29w, 14.30, , 14.42; 14.2, 14.3w
6 LI, 7 CAU, 4 Mannheim, 1 AAA-J, 5h1 AAA, 3 Eur-J, 4 v USA-J
11. **Duncan Malins** 12.6.78 (2y, 9) 14.10, 14.08w '00 14.19, 14.24, 14.32w, 14.33, 14.34, 14.48; 14.4
7 LI, 6 CAU, 2 Cup sf Eton, 3 South, 3B Lough, 7 AAA, 5 Bedl, BL1: 5,2B,-,5
12. **Mohammed Sillah-Freckleton** 11.9.80 (1y, -) 14.65, 14.6 '99 14.34w, 14.42, 14.58w, 14.61w; 14.2, 14.2w, 14.4 4 South, 2 AAA-23, 2B Lough, 3B Bedl, BL1: -,4B,2B,1B
– **Nathan Palmer** 16.6.82 (1y, -) 14.45, 14.34w '00 14.06, 14.25, 14.28, 14.39, 14.54; 14.2, 14.2w
3h2 CAU, 2 Welsh, 2 AAA-J, 5B Lough, 1B BL2 (3), 6 Eur-J, 3 Derby-J, 2 v USA-J

Jackson is UK No. 1 for a record 14th time and tenth year in succession; he has now ranked in the world's top ten for 16 successive seasons. He slipped a little in world terms as shown by the fact that he won only three of his 18 competitions, but he was always in the top five. Jarrett, who won his first AAA title, is number two for the 13th time (and he was top in 1991). Greaves stays in third place as he beat Gray 3-0. Elliott beat Owen 8-2 and is 3-3 with Baillie, who added to his championships successes with European U23 bronze. Bradley joined this group and beat Owen 3-2, but was 1-4 down to Elliott. Girdler and Palmer, European Junior 3rd and 6th, were the highest newcomers. Standards remain good at this event, as although the 10th best of 14.09 was below the 14.05 of 1999 and 2000, it is the third best ever.

400 METRES HURDLES

1. **Chris Rawlinson** 19.5.72 (7y, 1) *IAAF 7* 48.14 '99 48.27, 48.54, 48.68, 48.91, 48.96, 49.11
4 E.Clubs, 1 LI, 1 BL1 (2), 4 Milan, 2 Seville, 5 ECp, 4 Rome, 2 v USA, 2r2 Lausanne, 1 AAA, 5 BGP, 5 World, 6 Zurich, 7 Linz, 6 T'saloniki, 5 Rovereto
2. **Anthony Borsumato** 13.12.73 (5y, 2) *IAAF 21* 49.68 '99 49.30, 49.38, 49.40, 49.48, 49.53, 49.65
4 Ostrava, 3 Jena, 5 Milan, 2 Dortmund, 6 Rome, 5 Zagreb, 3 AAA, 6 BGP, 6s1 World, 1 BL1 (4), 6 Linz, 3 Rovereto, 6 Rieti
3. **Du'aine Thorne-Ladejo** 14.2.71 (2y, 6) *IAAF 20* 50.09 '00 49.29, 49.37, 49.44, 49.44, 49.56A, 49.70
4/3 in SA, 6 Ostrava, 6 Hani-, 1 Tula, 1 Dublin, 5 v USA, 1 BL1 (3), 2 AAA, 4 BGP, 5 T'saloniki, 6 Rovereto, 5 Rieti
4. **Matt Elias** 25.4.79 (4y, 9) *IAAF 63* 50.84 '99 49.57, 49.90, 50.1, 50.37, 50.51, 50.68
3 Austin, 1A LI, 4 Meilen, 1 vSPA-23, 1 AAA-23, 1 Eur-23, 8 BGP
5. **Matthew Douglas** 26.11.76 (7y, 2) *IAAF 54* 49.26 '00 49.68, 49.70, 49.9, 50.25, 50.39, 50.59
2 B.Univs, 5 LI, 1 CAU, 5 Rethimno, 1A Lough, 2 BL1 (3), 4 AAA, 1 Bedl, 7 v FRA, 5h WUG
6. **James Hillier** 3.4.78 (3y, 10) *IAAF 96* 51.30 '99 50.40, 50.49, 50.63, 50.77, 50.79, 51.00
1 B.Univs, 2 LI, 1r2 Tarare, 1 Welsh, 3 Budapest, 4A Lough, 5 AAA, 1 Cup, 2g v FRA, BL1: -,2,-,2
7. **Charles Robertson-Adams** 5.12.77 (2y, -) 50.43 '97 50.24, 50.45, 50.95, 51.36, 51.48, 51.7
2 BL1 (1), 4 LI, 1 Cup sf Eton, 1 Riga, 2 Istanbul, 1 Scot, 8 Budapest, 3A Lough, 8 v FRA, 6h WUG
8. **Richard McDonald** 11.1.80 (3y, 8) 51.0 '99, 51.09 '00 50.70, 51.06, 51.07, 51.08, 51.36, 51.4
3 B.Univs, 2A LI, 3 Istanbul, 2 Scot, 2 AAA-23, 1B Lough, 3h Eur-23, 2 Cup, 4 v FRA, 4 Namur, BL1: -,4,-,3
9. **Steve Surety** 18.2.80 (1y, -) 52.39 '00 51.8, 51.82, 51.91, 51.99, 52.13, 52.40
4 B.Univs, 3A LI, 7 CAU, 1 South, 3= AAA-23, 6 AAA, 1 Derby, 3g v FRA
10. **Robert Lewis** 2.9.78 (2y, 11) 51.29 '00 51.69, 52.21, 52.32, 52.33, 52.5, 52.5
3 Andorra, 2 CAU, 2 South, 2B Lough, 8 AAA, BL3: 1,1,1,1
11. **Paul Hibbert** 31.3.65 (7y, 4) 50.52 '96 51.31, 52.53, 53.14, 53.19, 53.34, 53.5
3 LI, 1 Mid, 3 Dublin, 3h3 AAA, BL1: 1,1B,-,-
12. **Leon McRae** 3.11.80 (1y, -) 53.23 '00 51.8, 51.8, 51.96, 52.09, 52.3, 52.40
5 B.Univs, 3 BL1 (2), 1 Cup sf H'gey, 4 vSPA-23, 3= AAA-23
- **Jeffrey Christie** 24.9.82 (1y, -) 52.5 '00 51.8, 52.25, 52.38, 52.47, 52.76, 52.80
1 Mid-J, 6 LI, 3 CAU, 2r2 Mannheim, 1 AAA-J, 4h EJ, 3 v USA-J, 1 Jnr IA

Rawlinson is top for the fourth time and was a fine fifth in the World Championships. There Borsumato also ran well, but Ladejo (who beat Borsumato 3-2 overall) was unable to contest his heat due to a hamstring niggle in warm-up. Rawlinson ran 14 times under 50 seconds, Borsumato 11 and Ladejo 9. Elias made notable progress with four pbs: 50.51 in May, then 50.1 to win the AAA-U23s and 49.90 and 49.57 at the European U23s. Hillier ran seven times under his pre-season best, and it was good to see the 1997 AAA champion Robertson-Adams in the rankings for the first time since then.

HIGH JUMP

1. **Ben Challenger** 7.3.78 (5y, 1) *IAAF 47* 2.30 '99 2.26, 2.21, 2.20, 2.20, 2.17, 2.15
   5 LI, 8 Tula, 1 Funchal, 1 BL1 (3), 1 AAA, 11= Stockholm, 1 Cup, dnq 18= World, 5= Leverkusen
2. **Dalton Grant** 10.4.66 (17y, 6) *IAAF 57* 2.37i '94, 2.36 '91 2.23, 2.21, 2.20, 2.20, 2.20, 2.19; 2.26i, 2.21i
   1 LI, 1 CAU, 5 Tula, 8 Helsinki, 6 v USA, 2 AAA, 3 Cup, 1 Plate, 1 v FRA, BL1: -,2,2,-
3. **Robert Mitchell** 14.9.80 (3y, 2) *IAAF 50* 2.20 '00 2.25, 2.24, 2.23, 2.20, 2.20, 2.20; 2.21i
   2 LI, 2 CAU, 1 Arles, 4 ECp, 5 v USA, 6= Eur-23, 1 Bedl, 2 Cup, 2 Plate, 3= v FRA, 7= Jumpsl, BL1: 2,1,3,1
4. **Danny Graham** 3.8.79 (5y, 5) 2.22 '00 2.21, 2.16, 2.15, 2.15, 2.14, 2.12; 2.14i
   2 BL3 (2), 1 Cup sf Wigan, 1 North, 2 vSPA-23, 2 AAA-23, 10 Eur-23, 1 Derby
5. **Samson Oni** 25.6.81 (1y, nr) 2.16 '99 2.18, 2.16, 2.15, 2.15, 2.10; 2.20i, 2.20i
   10 BL1 (1), 3 LI, 1 AAA-23, nh Eur-23, 5-6g v FRA
6. **Dan Turner** 27.11.78 (4y, 8) 2.15 '97 2.20, 2.15, 2.15, 2.14, 2.11, 2.05
   3 CAU, 1 South, 2 Dublin, 3 Cork, BL2: 1,1,-,-
7. **Chuka Enih-Snell** 2.3.84 (2y, 10) 2.15 '00 2.18, 2.14, 2.14, 2.12, 2.11, 2.10; 2.14i
   1 BL3 (2), 4 LI, 1 Welsh-J, 1 Welsh Sch, 1 AAA-J, 12 WY, 12 EJ
8. **Jamie Russell** 1.10.81 (2y, 11) 2.12/2.14i '00 2.15, 2.11, 2.10, 2.10, 2.10, 2.05; 2.16i
   2 BL2 (1), 6 CAU, 2 Cup sf Wigan, 5 Cork
9. **Ian Holliday** 9.12.73 (5y, 9) 2.16 '98 2.10, 2.10, 2.10, 2.07, 2.05, 2.05
   4 CAU, 1 IR, 3 AAA, 5 Cup, 7 v FRA, BL1: -,-,4,3
10. **Colin McMaster** 15.1.80 (1y, -) 2.15 '97 2.10, 2.10, 2.05, 2.05, 2.05, 2.02; 2.13i
    5 CAU, 1 Cup sf Rugby, 3 vSPA-23, 3 AAA-23, 4 AAA, BL1: 7=,4=,-,-
11. **Martin Aram** 2.12.83 (1y, -) 2.10 '00 2.10, 2.10, 2.08, 2.05, 2.05, 2.05; 2.08i
    1 Nth-J, 5 North, 1 Island G, 2 AAA-J, 2= v FRA-J, 4 v USA-J
12. **Rob Brocklebank** 12.10.76 (5y, -) 2.16 '95 2.12, 2.10, 2.05, 2.05, 2.00
    4 Cup sf Wigan, 3 IR, BL1: 3=,-,7,2

– **Dean Macey** 12.12.77 (0y, -) 2.13 '95 2.15; 2D World Dec; only HJ competition

Including Indoors: 4. Oni, 5. Graham.

Challenger, although not back to his best, retains top ranking. There was little between the marks set by the top three, but Grant just had the edge on Mitchell 5-3 on win-loss, and Challenger was ahead of both: 3-2 v Grant, 2-1 v Mitchell. Grant beats Geoff Parsons's record of 16 years in the rankings and set UK age bests for 34 and 35 year olds. Mitchell, Graham and Oni all competed at the European Under-23s, but sadly all were below par in the final. 10th best of 2.13 was the lowest since 1987.

POLE VAULT

1. **Nick Buckfield** 5.6.73 (10y, 9) 5.80 '98 5.75A, 5.60, 5.40, 5.30
   1 El Paso, nh ECp, 1g Cup, dnq 22= World, 4= GhCl
2. **Tim Thomas** 18.11.73 (7y, 3) *IAAF 80* 5.40 '97 5.40, 5.40, 5.30, 5.30, 5.30, 5.20; 5.40i, 5.35i, 5.33i
   4= Dessau, 8 Arles, 1 Welsh, 1 Cork, 2 AAA, 1 Plate, 1 v FRA
3. **Paul Williamson** 16.6.74 (9y, 2) *IAAF 93* 5.55 '00 5.30A, 5.30, 5.30, 5.30, 5.25. 5.20
   2 El Paso, 5 Modesto, 2 Arles, 2 South, 2 Cork, 1 AAA, 2g Cup, 3 v FRA, BL2: -,1,-,1
4. **Ian Tullett** 15.8.69 (13y, 6) 5.35 '98 5.20, 5.07, 5.05, 5.00, 5.00, 5.00
   5 Azusa, 5= Long Beach, 2 LI, 8 E.Clubs, 9 Arles, 1 South, 4 AAA, 4 Cup, BL1: -,2,2,2
5. **Ashley Swain** 3.10.80 (2y, 12) 4.90 '99 5.20, 5.10, 5.10, 5.00, 5.00, 4.90
   2 B.Univs, 4= CAU, 1 Cup sf H'gey, 3 South, 2 AAA-23, 3 AAA, 1 Derby, 2 BL2 (4), 6g v FRA
6. **Kevin Hughes** 30.4.73 (9y, 1) 5.61 '99 5.20, 4.90 1 BL1 (3), 5 AAA
7. **Scott Simpson** 21.7.79 (2y, -) 5.10i '00, 5.00 '99 5.20, 5.10, 5.05, 5.00, 5.00, 5.00; 5.10i
   1 B.Univs, 1 West, 1 LI, nh CAU, 10 Arles, 3 vSPA-23, 1 AAA-23, 6= AAA, 2 Derby, 7 v FRA
8. **Christian Linskey** 14.6.80 (4y, -) 5.21i '99, 5.20 "98 5.20, 5.00, 4.80, 4.80, 4.80, 4.80
   2 Azusa, 3 LI, 3 AAA-23, 3= Cork, 8= AAA, 5= Cup, 1 BL1 (4)
9. **Tom Richards** 13.11.78 (3y, 8) 5.25 '99 5.00, 4.95, 4.90, 4.90, 4.80, 4.70; 4.80i
   1 Cam v Ox, 1 Cup sf Eton, nh AAA, BL1: 1,-,4,3
10. **Ben Flint** 16.9.78 (5y, 4) 5.40 '99 5.05A, 5.00, 4.80, 4.80
    7= El Paso, nh AAA, 2 Plate, BL1: -,-,3,4/5
11. **Mark Grant** 17.5.71 (6y, -) 5.10 '95 5.11, 5.00, 4.85, 4.80, 4.80, 4.80
    2 CAU, 2 Cup sf Eton, BL4: 1,1,-,1
12. **Christian North** 2.2.74 (2y, -) 5.30 '99 5.00, 4.90, 4.85, 4.80, 4.60, 4.55; 5.15i, 5.00i, 4.90i
    1 Mid, 1 IR, 10 AAA

– **Dean Mellor** 25.11.71 (11y, -) 5.30 '95 5.00, 4.80, 4.80, 4.80, 4.80, 4.70
  8= CAU, 1 Cup sf Wigan, 1 North, 3 IR, 6= AAA, 3 Cup, BL1: 4,3,5,4/5

– **Mark Davis** 1.3.77 (3y, 7) 5.20 '99 4.60; 5.10, 5.00i, 4.80i, 4.60i

Including Indoors: 6. Simpson, 7. Swain, 8. North, 9. Linskey, 10. Davis, 11. Richards, 12. Grant

Buckfield returned to the top ranking he held each year 1995-8. Williamson and Thomas were 1-2 in 2000, but swap places this year; they were 2-2 outdoors on win-loss but Thomas had better marks. There were no newcomers to the rankings, but Swain made the most progress.

LONG JUMP

1. **Nathan Morgan** 30.6.78 (7y, 1) *IAAF 41* 8.11 '98 7.97, 7.86, 7.81w, 7.80, 7.71, 7.71w; 7.83, 7.78i
   1 LI, 4 Kalamata, 4 Athens, 1 Braga, 1 BL1 (3), 1 AAA, 2 Bedl, 1 Cup
2. **Chris Tomlinson** 15.9.81 (3y, 10) *IAAF 74* 7.62 '00 8.19w, 7.87, 7.75, 7.73, 7.70, 7.69
   1 T'hassee, 2 LI, 3 CAU, 2 ECp, 1 AAA-23, 6 Eur-23, 3 Bedl, 1 Derby, 2 v FRA, 1g BL1 (4)
3. **Jonathan Moore** 31.5.84 (2y, 12) *IAAF 98* 7.46 '00 7.98, 7.98w, 7.93, 7.79w, 7.68, 7.42
   1 Bangor, 1 E.Sch, 1 AAA-J, 1 v FRA-J, 1 v USA-J, nj JLF
4. **Darren Thompson** 6.11.79 (4y, 9) 7.56 '98 7.84w, 7.65w, 7.58w, 7.53, 7.52, 7.50w
   8 E.Clubs, 2 Bangor, 2 Arles, 1 South, 2 vSPA-23, 2 AAA-23, 2 AAA, 4 Bedl, 3 Cup, 6 v FRA, BL1: 1,-,-,4
5. **Steve Phillips** 17.3.72 (11y, 4) 8.03 '98, 8.07w '99 7.60, 7.55, 7.50, 7.43, 7.35, 7.33
   1 Cup sf Rugby, 1 IR, 4 AAA, BL4: 1,1,1,2
6. **Chris Davidson** 4.12.75 (6y, 7) 7.90 '99, 7.94w '97 7.62, 7.37w/7.16, 7.29w/7.14, 7.18
   4 LI, 2 BL1 (3), 3 AAA, 2 Cup
7. **Onen Eyong** 18.2.85 (1y, -) 7.21 '00 7.47w, 7.46w, 7.43w, 7.33, 7.33, 7.30
   1 E.Sch-I, 3 AAA-J, 1 Sch.Int, 3 v FRA-J, 1 AAA-17, 6g v USA-J, 1 Jnr IA, 1 JLF
8. **Darren Ritchie** 14.2.75 (5y, 2) 7.90 '00, 7.92w '99 7.69w, 7.56w, 7.00, 6.88, 6.80
   6 LI, dns CAU, 9 Arles, 1 Scot
9. **Dean Macey** 12.12.77 (3y, 5) 7.77 '00 7.59; 4 Dec Worlds
10. **Julian Flynn** 3.7.72 (6y, 8) 7.70/7.76w '99 7.51w, 7.25, 7.25, 7.13w, 6.99w; 7.14i
    6 CAU, 11 Arles, 3 Dublin, nj AAA, BL1: 7,2,7,-
11. **Femi Akinsanya** 29.11.69 (1y, -) 7.37 '96 7.31, 7.29, 7.25, 7.22; BL3: 1,-,-,1
12. **Mark Awanah** 23.9.82 (1y, -) 7.37 '00 7.66w, 7.25, 6.98; 7.03i 2 AAA-J, 3 v USA-J; BL1: 12,11,6,-

– **David Mountford** 23.6.82 (0y, -) 7.33 '00 7.32w, 7.29w?, 7.21w, 7.21w, 7.18, 7.16
  3 LI, 5 Cup sf Rugby, 4 AAA-J, 1 Lough, 4g v USA-J, BL3: 3,2,1,-

nr **Gable Garenamtose BOT** 28.2.77 7.65 '00 8.26w, 7.99, 7.84w, 7.83, 7.73w/7.72, 7.70w; 7.80i
  1 B.Univs, 1 CAU, 1 BL2 (2), 1g vSPA-23, 1 Bedl, 1 Ashford, 3 WUG

Top ranking is tricky, with Moore (still a junior for 2002 and 2003) producing three 7.90m plus performances, and Tomlinson competing well in the European Cup and U23 Champs, and ending with a great 8.19w against France. But although he disappointed in not exceeding the 7.97 with which he started the outdoor season, Morgan was the best in domestic competition, and crucially beat Tomlinson 2-0, so is top for the fourth time. Thompson progressed well to rank fourth and 16 year-old Eyong showed great potential. Last year's number two, Ritchie, had his season cut short by injury, the no. 3, George Audu, did not compete and the no. 6, Idowu, only long jumped once (7.23). So the number of national class jumpers was diminished and the rankings are completed by some men with exceedingly thin seasons. The legal tenth best of 7.29 is the worst since 1970 (and over 10cm worse than in any of the last 20 years).

TRIPLE JUMP

1. **Jonathan Edwards** 10.5.66 (15y, 1) *IAAF 1* 18.29/18.43w '95
   17.92, 17.66, 17.59, 17.56, 17.53w, 17.46; 17.60i; 16 out + 6 in over 17m
   1 Bangor, 1 Milan, 2 Helsinki, 1 Nuremberg, 1 ECp, 1 v USA, 1 Madrid, 1 AAA, 1 Stockholm, 1 BGP, 1 World, 1 GhCl, 1 Malm^, 1 Lahti, 1 Rovereto, 1 GWG. 2 Yokohama
2. **Larry Achike** 31.1.75 (10y, 2) *IAAF 4* 17.30/17.31w '00 17.21, 17.15, 17.10, 16.99, 16.97, 16.97w 1 Sydney, 3 Helsinki, 2 Nuremberg, 1 Budapest, 2 AAA, 2 BGP, 7 World, 2 GhCl, 7 Malm^, 2 Rovereto, 5 GWG, BL1: -,-,1,1
3. **Phillips Idowu** 30.12.78 (5y, 3) *IAAF 10* 17.12 '00 17.38w, 17.33, 17.23, 17.05, 16.89, 16.88
   1 BL1 (1), 1 LI, 1 E.Clubs, 1 Hanìa, 1 Cup sf Rugby, 5 Helsinki, 2 v USA, 3 AAA, 3 BGP, 9 World
4. **Jonathan Moore** 31.5.84 (2y, 9) *IAAF 78* 16.02 '00 16.43, 16.36, 16.32, 16.03, 15.80
   2 LI, 2 Mannheim, 1 WY, 2 EJ
5. **Julian Golley** 12.9.71 (12y, 4) *IAAF 32* 17.06 '94 16.93w, 16.30, 16.21, 16.13, 16.10, 16.08; 16.40i, 16.22i
   3 LI, 1 South, 5 Budapest, 2 Cork, 4 AAA, 8 BGP, 8 GhCl, 1 v FRA, 7 Rovereto
6. **Steven Shalders** 24.12.81 (3y, 10) *IAAF 93* 15.99 '00 16.28, 16.26w, 16.06, 15.89w, 15.88, 15.88
   5 LI, 1 Welsh, 1 vSPA-23, 7 Eur-23, 1 Derby, 7 v FRA, BL2: 1,1,-,-
7. **Femi Akinsanya** 29.11.69 (9y, 6) 16.63A '99, 16.58 '96 16.28w, 15.96, 15.93, 15.87, 15.76, 15.62
   1 CAU, 4 Cork, 6 AAA, 4 v FRA, BL3: 1,-,-,1
8. **Charles Madeira-Cole** 29.11.77 (4y, -) 15.79, 15.81w '98 15.86w/15.59, 15.58w/15.05, 15.20, 15.10, 15.02w/14.92, 14.81 2 Welsh, 8 Budapest, 7 AAA, 2 Cup, BL1: -,3,2,-
9. **Tosin Oke** 1.10.80 (3y, 7) *IAAF 93* 16.57 '99 15.72, 15.55, 14.99w; 16.08i, 15.76i, 14.86i 4 LI, 2 Bangor, 3 vSPA-23
10. **Michael McKernan** 28.11.78 (1y, -) 15.22 '99, 15.31w '00 15.49, 15.46, 14.92, 14.81, 14.79, 14.72
    1 Mid, 1 IR, 5 AAA
11. **Nathan Douglas** 4.12.82 (1y, -) 15.18 '00 15.50, 15.23, 15.13w, 15.10, 15.06, 14.63
    1 AAA-J, 1 E.Sch, 1 Derby-J, 4 v USA-J

12 **Nicholas Thomas** 4.4.79 (4y, 8) 16.31 '00 15.54, 15.08w, 14.97, 14.78w; 15.87i, 15.38i, 15.03i
   2 Cup sf Eton, 1 AAA-23, 8 AAA, BL1: 2,4,12,-

– **Tosi Fasinro** 28.3.72 (11y, 12) 17.21, 17.31w '93 15.50, 15.45, 15.28, 14.63, 14.22; 14.70i
  1 Cup sf H'gey, 2 South, BL2: 2,2,-,-

Including Indoors: 8. Oke, 9. Thomas, 10. Madeira-Cole, 11. McKernan, 12. Douglas
The peerless Edwards is UK no.1 for the 12th time and 11th year in succession (tying the record for any event set by Linford Christie at 100m 1986-96). He won 15 of his 17 competitions outdoors and 5 of 7 indoors. Outdoors he was over 16.98 every time and dropped below 17m just once indoors (16.78 in Karlsruhe). Just as in 2000 he was world number one and is accompanied by both Achike (runner-up for the fourth successive year) and Idowu in the world top eight. The precocious Moore beat Golley easily on the one occasion they met. Oke beat Thomas 4-1. Francis Agyepong drops out after 17 years in the rankings. Sadly standards in depth do not match those at the top and the 10th best of 15.59 is the worst since 1982.

SHOT

1. **Mark Proctor** 15.1.63 (11y, 1) *IAAF 65* 20.40 '99, 20.85i '98 19.30, 18.98, 18.89, 18.75, 18.64, 18.38
   8 Halle, 1 Lough 13/6, 8 ECp, 1 IS, 1 Bedl, 2 BL1 (3), 1 AAA, 1 Cup, dnq 30 World
2. **Emeka Udechuku** 10.7.79 (5y, 4) 18.10 '00 18.23, 18.02, 18.01, 17.90, 17.88, 17.82; 18.29i, 18.19i
   1 B.Univs, 1 CAU, 2 Lough 13/6, 1 vSPA-23, 1 AAA-23, 3 Varazdin, 2 AAA, 2 Cup, 1 Derby, 4 v FRA, dnq 20 WUG, BL2: 2,3,3,-
3. **Lee Newman** 1.5.73 (9y, 5) 18.85 '96 18.37, 18.28, 17.59, 17.46, 17.39, 17.25; 17.73i, 17.58i, 17.56i
   1 Cup sf Rugby, 1 Welsh, 2 Dublin, 5 AAA, 3 Cup, 1 v FRA, BL1: 1,1,5,2
4. **Mark Edwards** 2.12.74 (6y, 3) *IAAF 82* 19.72 '00 19.64, 18.99, 18.10, 18.02, 17.41, 17.30
   10 Halle, 1 LI, dnq nt WUG
5. **David Condon** 11.4.72 (5y, 6) 17.16 '00 16.92, 16.69, 16.63, 16.62, 16.47, 16.41
   2 LI, 2 CAU, 4 Tula, 1 South, 3 Dublin, 4 AAA, BL1: 3,4,6,3
6. **Scott Rider** 22.9.77 (2y, 7) 17.04 '00 16.86, 16.59, 16.58, 16.36, 16.30, 16.26
   4 LI, 2 Cup sf H'gey, 3 South, 1 IR, 3 AAA, BL2: 1,3,-,1
7. **Bruce Robb** 27.7.77 (2y, 8) 16.55 '00 16.67, 16.35, 16.34, 16.34, 16.16, 16.11
   11B Walnut, 5 LI, 3 CAU, 1 Scot, 7 Budapest, 6 AAA
8. **Steve Whyte** 13.1.72 (11y, -) 17.78 '89 16.45, 16.35, 16.11, 16.01, 16.00, 15.92; 16.71i
   3 LI, 4 CAU, 1 Cup sf Eton, 2 Scot, 2 South, BL4: 1,1,1,-
9. **Iain McMullen** 15.6.78 (2y, 12) 16.20 '00 16.56, 16.38, 16.30, 16.18, 16.11, 16.11
   2 B.Univs, 6 LI, 7 CAU, 2 Cup sf Wigan, 3 Scot, 1 Irish, 7 AAA, 1 NI, BL2: 4,2,1,2
10. **Lyndon Woodward** 25.11.80 (1y, -) 16.30 '00 16.48, 16.24, 16.21, 16.21, 15.97, 15.94; 16.45i, 16.25i
    2 Cup sf Rugby, 3 Lough 13/6, 2 Mid, 2 AAA-23, 8 AAA, 1 Plate, 2 Derby
11. **Gary Sollitt** 13.1.72 (8y, 10) 17.14 '97 16.58, 16.44, 15.98, 15.85, 15.82, 15.76; 16.40i, 16.33i
    5 CAU, 1 Cup sf H'gey, 4 South, BL2: 2,1,2,3
12. **Greg Beard** 10.9.82 (2y, 11) 16.69 '00 16.32, 16.28, 16.23, 15.92, 15.91, 15.81; 16.38i, 16.10i, 16.01i
    7 LI, 6 CAU, 1 Bangor, 7 Mannheim, 1 AAA-J, 17 EJ, 3 v USA-J

\- **David Readle** 10.2.80 (2y, 9) 16.23i/16.15 '99 15.47, 17.69i, 16.33i, 15.81i, 15.75i, 15.75i, 15.59i 4 North
nr **Stephan Hayward** 30.7.74 (6y, 2) 18.79 '00 16.58, 14.44 1 ECp-1A, 10 BL1 (3)

Including Indoors: 9. Sollitt, 10. Beard, 11. McMullen, 12. Woodward
Proctor was number one for the fifth time, although well below his best. Edwards had a big 19.64 in May, but 17.41 was his best against major opposition. Udechuku and Newman were 3-3 (3-2 to Newman indoors), but Udechuku was much better at the AAAs (over 18m indoors and out). Hayward, number two in 2000 was missed and he competed just twice, including for Ireland in the European Cup.

DISCUS

1. **Robert Weir** 4.2.61 (14y, 1) *IAAF 45* 65.08 '00 63.03, 61.79, 61.35, 61.05, 60.67, 60.48
   6 Salinas, 9 Stanford, 7 ECp, 4 v USA, 1 Lough, 1 BL1 (3), 2 AAA, 1g Cup, dnq 15 World
2. **Glen Smith** 21.5.72 (11y, 2) *IAAF 48* 65.11 '99 61.29, 60.55, 60.38, 59.99, 59.27, 59.11 3 Irvine,
   7 Modesto, 9 Halle, 1 CAU, 3 Tula, 2 Dublin, 6 v USA, 1 Varazdin, 1 AAA, 3 Cup, 1 v FRA, BL1: -,1,2,1
3. **Emeka Udechuku** 10.7.79 (5y, 3) *IAAF 66* 62.07 '00 59.97, 59.84, 59.53, 59.43, 58.67, 58.58
   1 B.Univs, 3B Halle, 1 LI, 1 Lough 23/5 & 13/6, 5 CAU, 1 vSPA-23, 1 AAA-23, 3 Varazdin, 7 Eur-23, 4 AAA, 2 Cup, 1 Derby, 2 v FRA, 12 WUG, BL1: 3,2,3,-
4. **Perriss Wilkins** 12.12.69 (6y, 4) *IAAF 73* 66.64 '98 61.68, 58.17, 58.08, 56.89, 55.92, 55.86
   2 LI, 2 CAU, 1 Cup sf Wigan, 3 AAA, 4 Cup, BL1: 1,3,4,2
5. **Lee Newman** 1.5.73 (9y, 6) 60.48 '97 57.38, 56.47, 56.17, 54.20, 53.23, 52.21
   1 Welsh, 3 Dublin, 2 Lough, BL1: 2,-,5,4
6. **Bruce Robb** 27.7.77 (2y, 7) 53.31 '00 54.25, 53.09, 53.06, 52.84, 52.47, 52.40
   9 Walnut, 3 LI, 4 CAU, 3 Scot, 8 Budapest, 5 AAA, 1 EdIG, 1 BLQ
7. **Kevin Brown UK/JAM** 10.9.64 (17y, 5) 61.10 '97 54.33, 53.78, 52.03, 51.80, 51.76, 51.71
   6 E.Clubs, 1 Cup sf Rugby, 1 Mid, 1 Scot, 5 Cup, BL1: 6,5,-,3
8. **Scott Rider** 22.9.77 (3y, 10) 52.81 '00 51.17, 50.65, 50.59, 50.06, 49.93, 49.87
   1 Cup sf H'gey, 4 South, 2 IR, 7 AAA, 2 WF, 2 EdIG, BL2: 1,1,-,1
9. **Peter Gordon** 2.7.51 (19y, 11) 61.62 '91 54.68, 51.05, 50.57, 50.33, 49.55
   1 Yorks, 1 North, 2 Scot

10. **Paul Reed** 2.6.62 (9y, 8) 58.36 '99 53.24, 51.97, 51.69, 50.79, 50.38, 50.20
2 Lough 23/5, 2 Cup sf Wigan, 2 North, 1 Police, 9 AAA, BL1: 4,4,6,7
11. **Luke Rosenberg** 29.6.80 (1y, -) 51.05 '99 52.81, 52.64, 52.47, 51.12, 50.59, 49.45 4 LI, 4 Lough 23/5, 3 CAU, 3 Lough 13/6, 4 vSPA-23, 1 South, 2 AAA-23, 3 Lough, 12 AAA, 6 Cup, 6 v FRA, 1 WF, BL2: -,4,1,2
12. **Abi Ekoku** 13.4.66 (7y, -) 60.08 '90 54.47, 53.46, 52.82, 50.93

Now a veteran, Weir is top for the 11th time, an event record, with the last nine in succession. Smith is 2nd for the sixth successive year and Udechuku beat Wilkins 4-3 as they remain third and fourth. 50 year-old Gordon has a record 24-year span in the rankings. There is a lower turnover in this event than any other and Rosenberg was the one newcomer this year.

HAMMER

1. **Michael Jones** 23.7.63 (20y, 1) *IAAF 34* 75.94 '00 76.43, 74.40, 73.91, 73.78, 73.68, 73.67
6B EAA-Nice, 1/1 Colindale, 5 E.Clubs, 4 Tula, 6 ECp, 1 AAA, 1 Cup, dnq 27 World, BL1: 1,1,1,-
2. **David Smith** 2.11.74 (8y, 6) *IAAF 60* 75.10 '96 73.30, 72.89, 72.44, 71.84, 70.86, 69.01
1 LI, 1 CAU, 1 Cup sf Rugby, 1 North, 1 Dublin, BL1: 2,2,3,1
3. **Paul Head** 1.7.65 (19y, 2) *IAAF 85* 74.02 '90 70.33, 69.91, 69.21, 68.17, 67.90, 67.59
1 Essex, 2 LI, 2 CAU, 1 South, 1 IR, 2 AAA, 2 Cup, BL1: 3,3,2,2
4. **Bill Beauchamp** 9.9.70 (7y, 5) *IAAF 89* 72.63 '99 72.60, 69.54, 67.55, 67.46, 67.22, 67.13
2/2 Colindale, 10 Halle, 3 CAU. 1 Cup sf H'gey, BL2; 1,1,1,1
5. **Michael Floyd** 26.9.76 (4y, 4) 69.38 '00 66.49, 66.24, 64.74, 64.71, 64.25, 62.74
3 LI, 4 CAU, 1 Cup sf Wigan, 2 North, 6 Cup, BL1: 4,4,5,-
6. **Simon Bown** 21.11.74 (4y, 7) 65.32 '99 65.19, 64.79, 64.76, 64.75, 64.74, 64.16
3/3 Colindale, 2 Essex, 9 CAU, 1 Cup sf Eton, 2 South, 2 IR, 3 AAA, BL1: 5,5,4,3
7. **Shane Peacock** 5.3.63 (16y, 8) 71.60 '90 63.98, 63.55, 62.37, 62.14, 61.09, 61.01
2 Cup sf Wigan, 4 AAA, 3 Cup, BL1: 6,6,6,5
8. **Russell Devine** 24.4.68 (7y, 11) 66.00 '99 66.53, 65.11, 63.56, 63.12, 62.52; 3 AUS Ch
9. **John Pearson** 30.4.66 (13y, 3) 70.33 '00 65.90, 64.83, 63.72, 62.78, 62.68, 62.09 4 LI
10. **Chris Howe** 17.11.67 (12y, 12) 66.97 '98 63.40, 62.22, 61.95, 61.31, 60.31, 60.15
2 Cup sf H'gey, 3 South, 5 AAA, 4 Cup, BL1: 7,13,8,4
11. **Matthew Bell** 2.6.78 (1y, -) 63.59 '99 63.83, 61.66, 61.55, 60.48, 60.34, 60.28 15 CAU, 1 Mid, 3 IR, 10 AAA
12. **Craig Ellams** 24.11.72 (5y, 10) 64.39 '00 62.69, 62.24, 61.11, 61.02, 59.59, 59.46
4/5 Colindale, 2 Cup sf Rugby, 2 Mid, 4 IR, 6 AAA, BL3: 2,2,3,1
– **Graham Holder** 16.1.72 (0y, -) 61.91 '99 61.50, 60.93, 60.53, 60.32, 60.27, 60.20
5/4 Colindale, 7 LI, 6 CAU, 3 Cup sf Rugby, 1 Welsh, 9 Budapest, 7 AAA, 5 Cup

Jones was top for the fourth successive year – and by a wide margin. In each of those four years he has improved his personal best and this was his 20th successive year in the top ten with the last 16 in the top four. Smith came back to second place and Head produced his one 70m competition of the year at his last AAAs. He ranks third and has been in the top five for 15 years in succession.

JAVELIN

1. **Steve Backley** 12.2.69 (15y, 1) *IAAF 4* 91.46 '92 90.81, 87.84, 86.74, 85.38, 84.40, 84.26
2 Ostrava, 4 Athens, 2 v USA, 1 Nice, 3 Oslo, 1 BGP, dnq 14 World, 1 GhCl, 3 Brussels, 4 GWG, 4 GPF
2. **Mick Hill** 22.10.64 (18y, 3) *IAAF 21* 86.94 '93 84.88, 83.42, 83.04, 81.90, 81.59, 80.58A
1/5/2 in RSA, 1 LI, 3 Ostrava, 1 Bangor, 10 Athens, 6 Helsinki, 9 Rome, 3 v USA, 2 AAA, nt BGP, 12 World
3. **Nick Nieland** 31.1.72 (10y, 2) *IAAF 18* 85.09 '00 82.93, 82.22, 80.84, 78.97, 78.02, 77.91
1 Halle, 5 Helsinki, 4 ECp, 1 Dublin, 9 Nice, 3 AAA, 8 Stockholm, 8 BGP, dnq 21 World, 1 BL1 (4), 8 GhCl
4. **Mark Roberson** 13.3.67 (16y, 4) *IAAF 35* 85.67 '98 80.80, 79.61, 79.03A, 78.60, 78.17A, 77.60
2/2/3/2/3 in RSA, 1 Alfaz, 2 LI, 2 CAU, 2 Bangor, 1 AAA, 9 BGP, 1 v FRA, 7 GhCl, BL1: 1,-,1,2
5. **David Parker** 28.2.80 (6y, 5) *IAAF 69* 78.24 '00 78.33A, 76.24, 75.62, 75.53, 75.16, 74.56 4 P'stroom, 1 B.Univs, 3 LI, 1 CAU, 1 BL1 (2), 1 Cup sf Rugby, 1 vSPA-23, 1 AAA-23, 9 Eur-23, 1 Cup, 1 Derby, 3 v FRA, 11 WUG
6. **Dan Carter** 15.4.80 (4y, 7) 73.56 '00 73.00, 71.29, 70.00, 69.55, 68.51, 68.44
2 B.Univs, 4 LI, 3 CAU, nt AAA-23, dnq 18 Eur-23, 6 v FRA, BL1: 2,2,-,6
7. **Stuart Faben** 28.2.75 (7y, 6) 75.37 '00, 76.66i '96 73.15, 72.25, 69.27, 64.94 3 Alfaz, 8 E.Clubs
8. **Neil McLellan** 10.9.78 (2y, 9) 68.27 '00 68.78, 68.05, 67,32, 66.90, 66.68, 66.66 1 South, 3 Cork, 5 AAA
9. **Phill Sharpe** 6.3.81 (3y, 8) 71.79 '00 68.49, 66.61, 64.72, 64.35, 63.84, 63.69
8 Halle-U23, 4 CAU, 1 Cup sf Wigan, 1 North, 4 vSPA-23, 2 AAA-23, BL1: -,4,-,5
10. **Andrew Gallagher** 15.2.83 (1y, -) 56.84 '00 66.95, 64.39, 63.92, 62.91, 60.77
2 AAA-J, 1 v FRA-J, 1 v USA-J, BL1: 3,-,3,-
11. **Tom Dobbing** 5.2.73 (1y, -) 65.22 '93 65.01, 63.04, 62.96, 62.06, 59.49
5 CAU, 1 Lough 13/6, 2 Scot, 1 IS, 6 AAA, BL3: -,1,2,-
12. **Clifton Green** 10.10.79 (1y, -) 66.21 '98 66.73, 66.43, 64.83, 61.62 12 CAU, 2 Cup, BL1: -,-,5,3
– **Keith Beard** 8.11.61 (11y, 10) 76.10 '91 68.08, 65.27, 63.01, 61.69 3th Dutch Champs
– **Stuart Loughran** 19.2.76 (2y, -) 68.91 '98 66.29, 63.52; BL3: -,-,1,2

Backley is number one for a record 12th time and his 90.81 at Crystal Palace was his best throw for nine years, but otherwise he was a little below his usual exemplary standards and won only three of his 12 competitions. Hill was the only one of the British trio to make the World final, his 17th in a major championship, and he ranks in the top three for the 16th consecutive year and as No.2 for the 11th time. Nieland and Roberson were 2-2. Parker was 5th for the fourth successive year and then, as usual, there was a big gap. Carter and Faben (who did not compete after May and who completes seven years always ranked between 6th and 8th) were on their own, with another 4-5 metres to the rest. Top junior, Gallagher, improved ten metres. Tenth best at 68.08 is the worst ever with the current javelin specification (introduced in 1986).

DECATHLON

1. **Dean Macey** 12.12.77 (4y, 1) 8567 '00   3 WCh 8603
2. **Jamie Quarry** 15.11.72 (9y, 2) 7739 '99   7 Arles 7625, dnf Azusa,
3. **Barry Thomas** 28.4.72 (11y, 3) *IAAF 96* 7766 '95   11 Arles 7410, 4 ECp2 7385
4. **Anthony Southward** (6y, -) 7425 '96   9 ECp2 7133, 17 Arles 7107, 1 North 7022
5. **Fyn Corcoran** 17.3.78 (3y, 9) 7116 '99   18 Arles 7050, 3 NU Int 7039, 12 ECp2 7020
6. **John Heanley** 25.9.80 (1y, -) 6563 '00   1 AAA 7129, 24 Arles 6869, 8 NU Int 6753
7. **Darren Hatton** 21.3.79 (2y, -) 6508w, 6471 '98   5 NU Int 7020, 2 AAA 7019, 1 Kent 6820, 26 Arles 6759, 2 Woodford 6496
8. **Anthony Sawyer** 29.4.80 (2y, 12) 6680 '00   4 AAA 6983, 1 HCI 6953, 1 Woodford 6820, dnf Mid
9. **Brendan McConville** 3.1.79 (2y, 10) 6720w/6561 '00   23 Arles 6905, 16 ECp2 6862, 2 HCI 6818, 12 NU Int 6702, 1 NI 6699
10. **Scott Exley** 9.2.78 (1y, -) 6221 '98   7 NU Int 6759, 5 AAA 6594
11. **Adrian Hemery** 6.8.82 (1y, -) 6302 '00   25 Arles 6788, 13 NU23 6573, 3 Woodford 6421, dnf Scot
12. **Roger Hunter** 10.3.76 (4y, -) 7159 '97   1 Mid 6749, dnf AAA

HCI – Home Countries International at Sheffield   NU Int – v France, Italy, Switzerland and Germany at Bedford

Macey takes his third top ranking and was superb in (medical) adversity in Edmonton. Quarry is second for the fourth time in five years (he was first equal in 1998) and Thomas retained third place. None of those ranked 4-8 in last year's rankings completed a decathlon this year, but there were good improvements by those ranked 6th to 11th. Adrian Hemery's father David ranked 3rd at this event in 1969 (with 6760 points on current tables).

20 KILOMETRES WALK

1. **Andrew Penn** 31.3.67 (11y, 2) 1:23:34 '92
   1 B'ham 1:31:56, 7 Dublin 1:28:18, 1 RWA 1:31:09, 4 Swiss 1:29:33
2. **Steve Hollier** 27.2.76 (4y, 6) 1:28:34 '99, 1:27:04ut '00   4 Manx 1:29:26, 9 Dublin 1:29:27, 2 RWA 1:32:56
3. **Matthew Hales** 6.10.79 (3y, 5) 1:30:38 '99   8 Leamington (1 UK) 1:28:40, 45 ECp 1:30:08, dq Eur-23
4. **Steve Partington** 17.9.65 (15y, 9) 1:24:19 '90   12 Leamington 1:33:00, 10 Dublin 1:29:52, 3 RWA 1:33:30
5. **Mark Easton** 24.5.63 (12y, 7) 1:24:04 '89
   1 Surrey 1:32:39, 9 Leamington 1:29:40, 11 Dublin 1:31:31, 4 RWA 1:33:54
6. **Chris Cheeseman** 11.12.58 (7y, -) 1:26:53 '99
   6 Manx 1:30:26, 2 Surrey 1:33:33, 10 Leamington 1:30:32, 5 RWA 1:34:11
7. **Darrell Stone** 2.2.68 (13y, 3) 1:23:58 '96, 1:23:27sh '93   1 Sussex 1:28:51, dq Leamington
8. **Don Bearman** 16.4.66 (2y, 10) 1:32:33 '00
   5 Manx 1:29:56, 2 Sussex 1:33:48, 13 Leamington 1:34:05, 13 Dublin 1:34:37
9. **Andrew Goudie** 4.10.78 (1y, -)   3 Surrey 1:37:36, 14 Leamington 1:34:40, 14 Dublin 1:35:33
10. **Karl Atton** 14.9.71 (3y, -) 1:33:41 '99   1 North 1:35:10, 15 Leamington 1:35:03
11. **Andy O'Rawe** 8.9.63 (3y, 10) 1:34:05 '96   16 Leamington 1:35:45, 6 RWA 1:39:48

Penn returns to the top ranking he had in 1997. Hales was the only selection for the European Cup. The 10th best time of 1:35:10 is the worst since 1967.

50 KILOMETRES WALK

1. **Steve Hollier** 27.2.76 (4y, 2) 4:07:18 '00   7 Dudince 4:09:27, 23 ECp 4:20:50, 1 Dutch 4:26:35
2. **Chris Cheeseman** 11.12.58 (6y, 3) 4:07:49 '99   2 RWA 4:41:44, 37 ECp 4:24:48, 4 Dublin 4:18:00
3. **Karl Atton** 14.9.71 (4y, -) 4:16:30 '97   10 Dudince 4:18:59
4. **Darrell Stone** 2.2.68 (3y, 5) 4:10:23 '90   5 Dublin 4:21:55
5. **Mike Smith** 20.4.63 (9y, 10) 4:09:22 '89   1 RWA 4:33:17, 6 Dublin 4:32:55
6. **Peter Kaneen** 12.7.61 (2y, 9) 4:50:47 '00   3 RWA 4:43:14, 7 Dublin 4:40:00

After three years in the top three, Hollier takes over top ranking for the first time. The number ranked (after 10 in 2000) once again drops.

WOMEN

100 METRES

1. **Abi Oyepitan** 30.12.79 (4y, 8) *IAAF 45* 11.52 '00, 11.45w '98 11.17w, 11.20w, 11.24w, 11.29, 11.29, 11.31
1 B.Univs, 1 LI, 1 CAU, 1r2 Lille, 1 vSPA-23, 2 v USA, 1 AAA-23, 2 Eur-23, 5h1 BGP, 7q2 World, 1 WUG
2. **Sarah Wilhelmy** 2.2.80 (1y, -) *IAAF 72* 11.49 '00 11.24w, 11.41w, 11.44, 11.45, 11.47, 11.48
5 Bridgetown, 1r2 Arles, 1 AAA, 1A Bedl, 7 BGP, 6 GhCl
3. **Amanda Forrester** 29.9.78 (2y, 9) *IAAF 92* 11.55 '00 11.37, 11.40, 11.40w, 11.41w, 11.42w. 11.44
3 CAU, 1 BL3 (1), 1 Cup sf Rugby, 1 Mid, 1 Glasgow, 2 AAA, 6 BGP, 8 WUG
4. **Joice Maduaka** 30.9.73 (5y, 2) *IAAF 56* 11.24 '99 11.38w, 11.42, 11.42, 11.42w, 11.43, 11.43 2/7/2 in RSA,
3r1 Fullerton, 2 LI, 1 Bergen, 3r1 Arles, 2 South, 5 ECp, 2 Glasgow, 1 Dublin, 5 Zagreb, 3 AAA, 2A Bedl, 5 BGP, 6 Rieti
5. **Marcia Richardson** 10.2.72 (11y, 1) *IAAF 48* 11.35/11.29w '00 11.42w, 11.43, 11.44, 11.44w, 11.45w, 11.46
1C2 Walnut, 2r1 Fullerton, 4 LI, 4 CAU, 6r1 Arles, 1 South, 2B1 Bremen, 4 v USA, 4 Dublin, 4 AAA, 1 Cup,
4h1 BGP, 8q4 World, 7 GhCl
6. **Shani Anderson** 7.8.75 (5y, 3) *IAAF 89* 11.34/11.3w '00 11.40, 11.45w, 11.46, 11.46, 11.47, 11.48
2B2 Walnut, 3 LI, 7 Kiev, 4 Hengelo, 5r1 Arles, 3B1 Bremen, 3 Glasgow, 1 BL2 (2), 5 AAA, 4A Bedl, 5h6 World
7. **Diane Allahgreen** 21.2.75 (2y, -) *IAAF 79* 11.66/11.6 '99 11.38w, 11.50, 11.59, 11.63, 11.65, 11.68; 11,5w
1C3 Walnut, 2 B.Univs, 1B LI, 2 CAU, 1 Cork, 3A Bedl
8. **Donita Benjamin** 7.3.72 (2y, 5) 11.43 '00 11.63, 11.65w, 11.66w, 11.68, 11.76, 11.76
7 CAU, 2 Cup sf Eton, 6 South, 4 Glasgow, 1 IS, 6 AAA, 6A Bedl, 1 IR, BL1; 3,2,4
9. **Christine Bloomfield** 12.2.68 (5y, 6) 11.32 '99 11.50w, 11.67, 11.68, 11.73, 11.75, 11.77
2B LI, 1 Basel, 2r2 Arles, 3 South, 3h1 Budapest, dns AAA
10. **Sabrina Scott** 2.6.79 (1y, -) 11.81 '00 11.50w, 11.60w, 11.68, 11.70, 11.73w, 11.81; 11.7
3B LI, 5 CAU, 7 Tula, 4 South, 2 vSPA-23, 2 AAA-23, 8h3 Eur-23, 3 Derby
11. **Catherine Murphy** 21.9.75 (5y, 10) 11.67 '99, 11.6 '96, 11.63w '94 11.48, 11.63w, 11.67, 11.81w; 11.9w
3B2 Walnut, 6 CAU
12. **Vernicha James** 6.6.84 (1y, -) 11.85 '00 11.43w, 11.44w, 11.61w, 12.05 3r1 Azusa, 4 Sth-J, 1 AAA-J
– **Susan Burnside** 3.2.80 (1y, -) 11.88 '00 11.61w, 11.74, 11.81, 11.83, 11.86, 11.89; 11.6w, 11.7w
3 B.Univs, 6 LI, 1 Cup sf Wigan, 1 Scot, 3 AAA-23, 4h2 Eur-23, 1 BL1 (3)
– **Amy Spencer** 19.9.85 (0y, -) 12.02 '00 11.66, 11.68, 11.68; 11.9, 12.1 5 LI, 3 Mannheim

There was a considerable change in this event, with none of the top three having ever previously been in the top five. Oyepitan took a big leap forward, so that after ranking 6th, 8th and 8th 1998-2000, she took over top ranking, with World Universities' gold and European U23 silver and unbeaten by a British athlete. The AAA champion Wilhelmy is second in her first year ranked at this event, and is followed by Forrester, who was second at the AAAs and reached the WUG final; they beat Maduaka 3-1 and 2-1 respectively. Maduaka beat Richardson 5-2 and Anderson v Richardson was 2-2. Allahgreen could have been higher with more competitions.

200 METRES

1. **Vernicha James** 6.6.84 (2y, 8) *IAAF 75* 23.59 '00, 23.48w '99 22.93, 23.24w, 23.30, 23.41w, 23.44,
23.61w; 23.6 1r2 Azusa, 3 LI, 1 Sth-J, 3 Bangor, 2 Mannheim, 1 E.Sch, 1 EJ
2. **Joice Maduaka** 30.9.73 (6y, 6) *IAAF 35* 22.83 '99 23.04w, 23.14A, 23.31, 23.33, 23.41w, 23.42
3/1/1 in RSA, 1r1 Fullerton, 1B LI, 4 Ingolstadt, 2 Bangor, 1 South, 2 Dublin, dns AAA, 1 Bedl
3. **Sarah Wilhelmy** 2.2.80 (4y, 4) 23.23/23.20w '98 22.84w, 23.27, 23.37 3 Bridgetown, 1 Arles, 4 Nuremberg
4. **Katharine Merry** 21.9.74 (11y, 1) 22.76 '00 23.12, 23.21 1 Austin, 6 ECp
5. **Shani Anderson** 7.8.75 (3y, 5) *IAAF 69* 23.20 '00 23.12w, 23.35w, 23.42w, 23.43, 23.44, 23.46w; 23.2
2r1 Azusa, 1 LI, 2 Arles, 1 Istanbul, 1B BL1 (2), 2 AAA, 4 Bedl, 1 Nitra
6. **Amy Spencer** 19.9.85 (1y, -) 24.31/24.24w '00 23.45, 23.54w, 23.63, 24.03; 23.3w, 23.7, 24.0
1B Bangor, 1 AAA-J, 2 WY
7. **Catherine Murphy** 21.9.75 (8y, 7) *IAAF 59* 23.28 '99 23.35w, 23.65w, 23.74, 23.82, 23.85; 23.8, 23.8;
23.35i, 23.36i, 23.70i, 23.73i 6rA Walnut, 1r1 Irvine, 1 CAU, 1 Welsh, 1 BL1 (2), 7 Linz
8. **Helen Roscoe** 4.12.79 (1y,-) 24.41 '00, 24.31w '96 23.80, 23.92w, 23.96, 24.01, 24.02, 24.09; 23.4w, 23.8
1 B.Univs, 8 E.Clubs, 2 Cup sf Wigan, 1 Mid, 1 vSPA-23, 1 AAA-23, 2 BL1 (2), 7 Eur-23, 2 v FRA, 7q2 WUG
9. **Lee McConnell** 9.10.78 (1y, -) 24.2 '99, 24.0w '94 23.66, 23.85; 23.9, 24.0 2 CAU, 1 G'mouth
10. **Lesley Owusu** 21.12.78 (1y, -) 24.13 '00 23.75w, 23.76w, 23.86, 23.89, 23.92, 23.93;
23.73i, 23.80i, 23.86i 1 IR, 3 BL1 (2), 5 Bedl
11. **Abi Oyepitan** 30.12.79 (1y, -) 23.98/23.82w '99 23.71, 24.24; 1 BL1 (1), 2 v SPA-23
12. **Emily Freeman** 24.11.80 (1y,-) *IAAF 97* 24.19i '97, 24.34 '99 23.72, 23.93w, 24.03, 24.12, 24.13; 23.9w, 24.0w;
23.67i, 23.77i, 23.83i 5 LI, 5 CAU, 2 North, 3g v SPA-23, 3 AAA-23, 8 Eur-23, 1 Derby, 1 v FRA, 1 Nth IC, BL1: 3,4,2
– **Susan Williams** 2.6.77 (2y, 12) 23.59 '99 23.76w, 23.79, 23.94w, 24.01, 24.18, 24.46; 24.4
2 Surrey, 7 CAU, 1 Cup sf H'gey, 2 South, 2 IR, 3 AAA, 6 Bedl, 1 Plate, 3 v FRA
– **Danielle Norville** 18.1.83 (0y, -) 24.9/24.92w/24.6w '00, 24.96 '99 23.61, 23.75, 23.90, 24.05, 24.07, 24.37
4 Mannheim, 1 v FRA-J, 2 v USA-J
– **Donna Fraser** 7.11.72 (9y, 2) 22.96i/22.90w '97, 23.08 '00 23.97; 24.1; 23.61i, 23.74i, 24.08i, 24.11i 3 Braga
nr **Sarah Reilly** IRE 3.7.73 (2y, -) 23.12 '00 23.02, 23.06w, 23.22, 23.24, 23.42, 23.44w
3 CAU, 1 Bangor, 1 ECp1A, 1 Budapest, 1 AAA, 1 Irish, 6s3 World

Including indoors: 6. Murphy, 7. Spencer, 8. Owusu, 9. Freeman, 10. Roscoe, 11. McConnell, 12. Fraser
A very confused picture here, with few confrontations by our leading runners, some of whom ran the event very infrequently. Nobody really stood out for top ranking, which goes to James, who won the European U20 title and still has two years to go as a junior. 15 year-old Spencer bursts into the top ten with silver at the World Youth Championships and is one of six newcomers to the rankings at this event. Last year's 2nd and 3rd, Donna Fraser and Samantha Davies drop out.

400 METRES

1. **Katharine Merry** 21.9.74 (3y, 1) *IAAF 3* 49.72 '00 49.59, 50.44, 50.67, 51.03; 50.53i, 51.54i
1 Milan, 1 Athens, 1 v USA, 1 BGP
2. **Donna Fraser** 7.11.72 (9y, 2) *IAAF 37* 49.79 '00 51.77, 52.02, 52.57, 52.77, 53.02, 54.46
4 v USA, 2 AAA, 8 BGP, 6s3 World
3. **Lee McConnell** 9.10.78 (1y, -) *IAAF 51* 53.81 '99 52.05, 52.31, 52.41, 52.44, 52.93, 52.99
1 LI, 1 Riga, 1 Scot, 1 Budapest, 3 AAA, 6 WUG
4. **Catherine Murphy** 21.9.75 (2y, 6) *IAAF 20* 52.72 '00 51.84, 52.27, 52.37, 52.40, 52.65, 52.74; 51.99i, 52.31i 2 BL1 (1), 4 Seville, 4 Helsinki, 5 Funchal, 5 AAA, 5 BGP, 4h3 World
5. **Allison Curbishley** 3.6.76 (6y, 3) 50.71 '98 51.99, 52.48 1 BL1 (1), 5 ECp
6. **Lesley Owusu** 21.12.78 (3y, 7) *IAAF 35* 53.02 '00 52.27, 52.49, 52.66, 52.88, 52.93, 52.93A; 52.15i, 52.37i, 52.49i 2 DrakeR, 1 BL1 (2), 1 AAA, 6 BGP, 5s1 WUG
7. **Helen Frost** 12.3.74 (5y, 4) *IAAF 75* 52.40 '00 52.68, 52.79, 52.89, 52.91A, 52.99, 53.08
1/1 in RSA, 2 Riga, 5r1 Tula, 1 Dublin, 4 Budapest, 5 Cork, 4 AAA, 2 Bedl, 1 Cup
8. **Helen Thieme** 28.9.81 (1y, -) *IAAF 91* 54.32 '99 52.75, 52.88, 53.25, 53.27, 54.1, 54.8
1 CAU, 1 vSPA-23, 1 AAA-23, 2 Eur-23
9. **Karen Gear** 30.9.79 (2y, 11) 54.03 '00 53.31, 53.59, 53.67, 53.91, 53.99, 54.28
2 CAU, 1 South, 2 AAA-23, 8 Cork, 5 Eur-23, 1 Derby, 1 v FRA
10. **Lisa Miller** 13.1.83 (1y, -) 53.86 '00 53.29, 53.46, 54.02, 54.04, 54.66, 55.0
1r3 Mannheim, 2 E.Sch, 1 AAA-J, 2 EJ
11. **Jennifer Meadows** 17.4.81 (2y, 12) 53.84 '00 53.32, 53.65, 53.70, 53.83, 54.05, 54.41
2 LI, 2 vSPA-23, 3 AAA-23, 6 Eur-23, 1 BL3 (3), 2 v FRA
12. **Kim Wall** 21.4.83 (1y, -) 54.41 '00 53.52, 54.04, 54.12, 54.21, 54.32, 54.43
3 LI, 2 AAA-J, 1 E.Sch, 3 EJ, 1 v FRA-J, 2 v USA-J

– **Sinead Dudgeon** 9.7.76 (2y, 5) 52.05 '99 52.47i, 53.72i, 54.10i, 56.17i

Including indoors: 9. Dudgeon, rest move down one place.
Merry is top for the third time, she was unbeaten, twice indoors and four outdoors; and was probably the best in the world when fit, but, sadly, had to miss the World Championships. Fraser started late but improved with almost every race, to run season's bests in heat and semi at the Worlds. She just heads a strong and closely matched group to rank second for the fifth successive year. McConnell had a splendid first major season at the event, ending by running a personal best in the semis of the World University Games before 6th in the final. Curbishley only ran the event twice, but secured a high ranking with 51.99 in the European Cup. The quartet that won the World Junior 4x400m in 2000, Wall, Meadows, Thieme and Miller, all made encouraging progress, with Miller and Wall taking silver and bronze at the European U20s (and both remain juniors for 2002). Thieme and Meadows were 2nd and 6th at the European U23s with Gear 5th in that event, for a splendid three in the top six. The tenth best of 53.31 has been bettered only once before (53.0 way back in 1982).

800 METRES

1. **Kelly Holmes** 19.4.70 (9y, 1) *IAAF 3* 1:56.21 '95 1:57.88, 1:57.90, 1:58.10, 1:58.85, 1:59.27, 1:59.41
1 Madrid, 1 AAA, 5 Monaco, 2 BGP, 6 World, 2 Zurich, 1 GhCl, 2 Brussels, 4 Berlin, 2 GWG, 2 GPF
2. **Tanya Blake** 16.1.71 (5y, 4) *IAAF 40* 2:00.10 '98 2:01.87, 2:02.30, 2:02.74, 2:04.08, 2:05.43, 2:05.97
2 Hengelo, 1 Eur.Small States G, 5 ECp, 2 Dublin, 2 AAA, 9 BGP, 2 v FRA, 11 GhCl, 7 Mediterranean G
3. **Allison Curbishley** 3.6.76 (1y, -) *IAAF 96* 2:17.7 '90 2:03.30, 2:04.40, 2:04.51, 2:04.94, 2:05.22, 2:07.0mx 1 Watford, 2 Budapest, 4 AAA, 11 BGP
4. **Joanne Fenn** 19.10.74 (4y, 6) *IAAF 46* 2:04.19 '00 2:02.81, 2:03.40, 2:04.28, 2:04.32, 2:04.59, 2:04.60
1 LI, 4 Rehlingen, 6 Tula, 7 Nuremberg, 4 Dublin, 2 Braga, 1 BL1 (2), 5 AAA, 1 Bedl, 13 BGP, 6 v FRA
5. **Hayley Tullett** 17.2.73 (6y, 2) 2:01.25 '00 2:04.67, 2:04.97, 2:05.59, 2:05.98 1 Welsh, 3 AAA
6. **Susan Scott** 26.9.77 (1y, -) 2:07.1mx, 2:07.77 '98 2:03.96, 2:04.25, 2:04.88, 2:05.64, 2:06.01, 2:06.61
3 Wyth, 1 Scot, 6 AAA, 1g v FRA, 1 EdIG
7. **Alex Carter** 1.4.80 (2y, 10) 2:03.78mp '00 2:04.9, 2:04.94, 2:04.94mx, 2:05.24, 2:05.33, 2:06.20
2 LI, 2 Wyth, 1 Lough 13/6, 3 vSPA-23, 1 AAA-23, 5h Eur-23, 3h WUG
8. **Emma Davies** 9.10.78 (4y, 5) 2:02.39 '98 2:04.70, 2:05.01, 2:05.60, 2:05.99, 2:06.61, 2:07.27
3 Watford, 2 Welsh, 1 Solihull, 6 Budapest, 4 Braga, dnf ht AAA, 3 Cup
9. **Rachel Newcombe** 25.2.67 (4y, 8) 2:03.28 '98 2:04.98, 2:05.11, 2:06.4, 2:07.06, 2:07.07, 2:07.53
3 LI, 3 Welsh, 3 Budapest, 7 AAA, BL2: 1,-,2
10. **Mary McClung** 19.12.71 (3y, 11) 2:03.92 '00 2:05.02, 2:06.29, 2:06.5, 2:06.85, 2:07.20, 2:07.53
8 Budapest, 8 AAA, 1 Cup, 2 EdIG, BL1: -,2,1

11. **Rebecca Lyne** 4.7.82 (1y, -) 2:05.27 '00 2:05.05, 2:05.44, 2:05.96, 2:06.05, 2:06.10, 2:06.87
1 Nth-J, 6 Bangor, 2 Mannheim, 1 AAA-J, 4 EJ, 1 Stretford 31/7, 1 v USA-J
12. **Lucy Vaughan** 20.4.69 (1y, -) 2:08.8mx, 2:09.22 '00 2:03.9, 2:05.6, 2:07.1, 2:07.12, 2:08.9 1 BL2 (3)
– **Jeina Mitchell** 21.1.75 (4y, 9) 2:03.36 '97 2:04.04, 2:05.35, 2:09.24; 2:06.86i, 2:07.31i, 2:08.80i
2 Irvine, 2 CAU, 2B Tula
– **Kelly Caffel** 10.2.79 (1y, 12=) 2:03.48mp '00 2:04.59, 2:06.37; 2 vSPA-23, 3 v FRA
– **Sally Evans** 14.5.75 (1y, -) 2:07.07 '00 2:04.97, 2:05.91, 2:06.09, 2:06.77, 2:07.33, 2:07.49
6 E.Clubs, 1 Mid, 3 Solihull, 1 IR, 1 Cardiff, 3h3 AAA, 2 Cup, 2 BL1 (3)

mp = male pacemaker, mx = mixed race

Holmes is top ranked for the seventh time at 800m and by the end of the year was third best in the world; she ran eight sub 2 minute times and 11 better than any other British runner. The AAA top six take the top six placings, but Tullett is fifth rather than third as she only contested two events at 800m. Curbishley had a good first season concentrating on this event.

1500 METRES

1. **Hayley Tullett** 17.2.73 (5y, 1) *IAAF 8* 4:01.23 '00 4:03.54, 4:04.23, 4:07.83, 4:09.31, 4:13.60, 4:13.95; 4:06.75i 4 Hengelo, 3 ECp, 5 Rome, 6 Monaco, 9s2 World
2. **Helen Pattinson** 2.1.74 (4y, 3) *IAAF 33* 4:04.82 '00 4:07.56, 4:09.22, 4:10.86, 4:11.01, 4:13.06, 4:13.40
7 Hengelo, 11 Rome, 6 v USA, 8 Nice, 1 AAA, 9s1 World
3. **Paula Radcliffe** 17.12.73 (8y, 5) 4:05.81 '98, 4:24.94M '96 4:05.37; 3 v USA
4. **Kelly Caffell** 10.2.79 (3y, 4) *IAAF 53* 4:10.22 '00 4:11.99, 4:12.30, 4:12.34, 4:13.29, 4:13.53, 4:13.78
1 LI, 3 Kiev, 3 Luzern, 4 Funchal, 3 Eur-23, 1 Watford 25/7, 5ht WUG
5. **Emma Ward** 2.1.82 (1y, -) *IAAF 84* 4:19.70 '00 4:13.38, 4:13.51, 4:15.22, 4:19.75, 4:19.97, 4:26.1
1 B.Univs, 3 LI, 1 Cup sf Rugby, 1 AAA-J, 2 EJ, 1 v USA-J
6. **Kerry Smithson** 13.9.76 (2y, -) *IAAF 99* 4:17.6 '98 4:13.02, 4:16.56, 4:19.08, 4:20.8, 4:22.74, 4:22.85
5 E.Clubs, 3 Wyth, 1 Watford, 2 Solihull, 3 Dublin, 6 AAA, 1 BL1 (3), 5 v FRA
7. **Rachel Newcombe** 25.2.67 (1y, -) *IAAF 93* 4:24.18 '00 4:14.01, 4:15.16, 4:17.83, 4:18.16, 4:18.60, 4:33.0
1 BL2 (1), 2 Wyth, 6 Watford, 4 Solihull, 2 Cardiff, 1 BMC-F
8. **Ellen Leggate** 4.2.78 (1y, -) 4:20.17 '97 4:14.46, 4:16.13, 4:18.95, 4:19.29, 4:21.4
3 B.Univs, 1 Varsity, 7 Cork, 8 Watford, 3 AAA
9. **Sarah Bull** 4.6.75 (1y, -) 4:21.02 '98 4:13.68, 4:17.10, 4:18.32, 4:19.30, 4:26.27; 4:30.7i
4 Watford, 3 Solihull, 4 AAA, 1 Stretford 31/7, 3 v FRA
10. **Jeina Mitchell** 21.1.75 (1y, -) 4:19.09 '92 4:14.14, 4:20.7, 4:23.09, 4:24.46, 4:27.69
2 LI, 1 South, 12 Cork, 5 Dublin, dnf AAA
11. **Alex Carter** 1.4.80 (3y, 9) 4:17.98 '00 4:14.44, 4:21.76, 4:23.0, 4:27.40
2 B.Univs, 10 Watford, 1 AAA-23, 4 v FRA
12. **Liz Yelling** 5.12.74 (2y, 12) 4:16.75 '00 4:15.01, 4:23.10, 4:24.30 11 Watford, 2 AAA
– **Kathy Butler** 22.10.73 (2y, 6) 4:07.68 '97 4:12.08; 8 Stanford
– **Susan Scott** 26.9.77 (3y, 11) 4:16.16 '99 4:16.29, 4:18.37 3 Budapest, 9 Tula

Tullett retains her top ranking and Pattinson moves up a place to second. While neither was able to advance from the World Champs semis and did not have as good a season as in 2000, they are up in world class, with Paula Radcliffe, who had just one race at this distance. The consistent Caffel retained her fourth ranking. Ward is the highest newcomer, and the European Junior silver medallist already has an extraordinary collection of titles at track and cross-country. Smithson returned successful after two years out and is in a very closely matched group ranked 5-12. In 2000 the tenth best of 4:17.45 was the second worst in 23 years, but encouragingly 12 women bettered 4:15 in 2001 and tenth of 4:14.14 was the best since 1994.

3000 METRES (not ranked)

Paula Radcliffe 17.12.73 8:27.40 '99 8:26.97, 8:28.07, 8:32.02, 8:42.47, 8:44.7+, 8:48.74+
5 Rome, 5 Zurich, 1 GhCl, 6 Brussels
Jo Pavey 20.9.73 8:36.70 '00 8:36.58, 8:44.05, 8:50.0+, 8:51.14, 8:58.97, 9:13.6+
7 Lausanne, 2 GhCl, 9 Brussels, 2 Rieti
Kathy Butler 22.10.73 8:48.37 '99 8:40.97, 8:43.23 8:46.01, 8:52.05, 8:53.63, 9:03.71; 8:54.96i
2 Eugene, 1 ECp, 13 Rome, 10 Paris, 3 GhCl, 10 Brussels
Hayley Tullett 17.2.73 8:45.39 '00 8:51.73; 8:45.36i, 8:48.25i, 8:52.18i, 9:02.23i 7 Seville
Liz Yelling 5.12.74 9:11.4mx '00, 9:15.25 '98 8:57.3mx, 9:08.13mx, 9:20.23; 1 v FRA
Hayley Yelling 3.1.74 9:02.88mp '00 8:58.98mx, 9:03.5+, 9:12.80+
Helen Pattinson 2.1.74 9:09.18 '00 9:03.71, 9:05.70; 1 LI, 6 GhCl
Amanda Parkinson 21.7.71 9:02.67mx '00, 9:19.6 '96 9:04.26mx, 9:25.9e+, 9:27.59; 3 v FRA
Angela Newport 21.10.70 9:05.86mx/9:08.46 '00 9:08.12, 9:08.91mx; 2 LI
Ellen Leggate 4.2.78 9:45.2 '98 9:08.7mx, 9:46.2mx
Bev Jenkins 6.2.70 9:16.02 '00 9:08.90mx, 9:41.63; 1 IR
Catherine Berry 8.10.75 9:25.38 '00 9:09.61mx, 9:21.89, 9:29.4+; 9:33.90i

+ during longer race

Radcliffe broke her British and Commonwealth record at Rome. Pavey and Butler also improved and are now 5th and 8th on the UK all-time list. Tenth at 9:08.7 was the best since 1992.

5000 METRES (Previously ranked 1982-90, 1992, 1995-2000)

1. **Paula Radcliffe** 17.12.73 (6y, 1) *IAAF 3* 14:43.54 '99 14:32.44, 14:44.21, 14:49.84, 15:22.62+
   2 ECp, 1 BGP, 3 Berlin
2. **Jo Pavey** 20.9.73 (2y, 2) *IAAF 24* 14:58.27 '00 15:00.56, 15:10.62, 15:15.98, 15:16.47, 15:28.41
   1 AAA, 7 BGP, 11 World, 6 Berlin
3. **Kathy Butler** (ex CAN) 22.10.73 (2y, 7) *IAAF 21* 15:10.69 '98 15:14.62, 15:17.96, 15:20.78, 15:34.12, 16:29.38 2/1 Madison, 3 AAA, 7h1 World, 3 GWG
4. **Hayley Yelling** 3.1.74 (2y, 3) *IAAF 85* 15:36.27 '00 15:19.12, 15:23.28, 15:50.36, 15:59.39
   1 Wyth, 2 AAA, 10 BGP, 16h1 World
5. **Juliet Potter** 24.10.81 (1y, -) 0 15:57.4, 15:59.88, 16:02.99, 16:15.6
   3 Wyth, 1 CAU, 2 Solihull, 7 Eur-23
6. **Catherine Berry** 8.10.75 (2y, 10) 16:00.97 '00 15:57.61, 16:05.88; 2 Penn R, 4 AAA
7. **Amanda Parkinson** 21.7.71 (2y, 11) 15:56.64 '00 15:54.9; 1 Solihull, dnf BGP
8. **Gillian Palmer** 30.12.80 (2y, 9) 15:56.58 '00 16:10.94, 16:18.68, 16:22.4, 16:22.91, 16:25.13
   2B Walnut, 1 Drake R, 8 Eugene, 5 Solihull, 12 Eur-23
9. **Angela Newport** 21.10.70 (4y, 8) 15:43.99 '99 15:57.32, 16:23.79, 16:33.2
   2 Wyth, 8 Solihull, 7 Cork
10. **Bev Jenkins** 6.2.70 (2y, -) 16:08.96 '99 16:10.26, 16:18.55, 16:37.13, 16:37.6+
    4 Wyth, 2 North, 10 Cork
11. **Karen Hind** 31.7.79 (1y, -) 16:05.80 '00 16:04.1, 16:47.11; 3 Solihull, 15 Eur-23
12. **Jodie Swallow** 23.6.81 (1y, -) 0 16:11.78, 16:29.59; 1 B.Univs, 6 Wyth

– **Birhan Dagne** 8.4.78 (3y, 6) 15:36.35 '00 16:16.24; 5 AAA

Radcliffe took 11 seconds off her Commonwealth record at Berlin, and is top for the seventh time. Pavey is again runner-up, excelling to make the World final after similarly making the Olympic final in 2000, and Butler is third, followed by the redoubtable Hayley Yelling who fought so well to make the World Champs qualifying standard. Potter is the highest newcomer.

10,000 METRES

1 **Paula Radcliffe** 17.12.73 (4y, 1) *IAAF 3* 30:26.97 '00 1 E.Chall 30:55.80, 4 World 31:50.06
2 **Kathy Butler** (ex CAN) 22.10.73 (1y, -) *IAAF 21* 0 1 Walnut 31:59.27, 5 GWG 32:18.36
3 **Penny Thackray** 18.8.74 (1y, -) 34:48.57 '98 2 (1) AAA 33:25.74
4 **Bev Jenkins** 6.2.70 (3y, 7) 33:49.8 '00 3 (2) AAA 33:29.27
5 **Liz Yelling** 5.12.74 (2y, 5) 33:07.9 '00 17 Eur Challenge 33:45.48
6 **Tara Krzywicki** 9.3.74 (4y, 6) 33:04.55 '99 20 Eur Challenge 33:59.79
7 **Sheila Fairweather** 24.11.77 (4y, 11) 34:32.70 '99 4 (3) AAA 34:23.55
8 **Charlotte Sanderson** 18.3.79 (1y, -) 0 4 Stanford 34:25.78
9 **Allison Higgins** 8.4.72 (1y, -) 0 1 Poole 34:29.3mx
10= **Pauline Powell** 17.5.73 (1y, -) 0 1 North 34:52.46
10= **Debbie Robinson** 31.1.68 (1y, -) 0 5 (4) AAA 34:52.41

Radcliffe is top for the fourth year at this event. She has a closer rival this year, but Butler was still over a minute slower and then there was another minute and a half gap.

HALF MARATHON (First ranked 1999)

1. **Paula Radcliffe** 17.12.73 (3y, 1) 67:07 '00 1 World 66:47
2. **Liz Yelling** 5.12.74 (2y, 2) 72:31 '00 4 Gt.Scot (1 UK) 72:26, 23 World 71:29, 3 Stroud 75:12
3. **Annie Emmerson** 10.5.70 (1y, -) 75:52 '00 1 Bath 73:01, 31 World 73:00
4. **Amanda Wright/Allen** 14.7.68 (1y, -) 74:00 '97 1 Lake Vyrnwy 72:43
5. **Beth Allott** 9.2.77 (3y, 7) 73:40 '00 7 Gt.Scot (2 UK) 73:39, dnf World
6. **Andrea Green** 14.12.68 (2y, 5) 73:28 '00
   1 Tun.Wells 75:36, 1 Hastings 77:08, 9 Berlin 74:58, 1 Dartford 75:51, 1 Bristol 74:56, 1 Stroud 73:56
7. **Birhan Dagne** 8.4.78 (3y, 4) 72:53 '99 8 Gt.Scot (3 UK) 73:53, dnf World
8. **Sharon Morris** 5.7.68 (1y, -) 0 14 GNR 74:04
9. **Bev Hartigan** 10.6.67 (1y, -) 0 2 Bath 74:06, 10 Gt.Scot 74:45
10. **Lynne MacDougall** 18.2.65 (2y, 8) 74:50 '00 1 Alloa 74:37, 12 Gt.Scot 75:27, 15 GNR 74:24
11. **Vicky Pincombe** 19.6.73 (2y, 10) 75:14 '98 4 Bath 76:13, 1 Gt.West 77:10, 11 Gt.Scot 74:59, 4 Stroud 75:33
12. **Jo Wilkinson** 2.5.73 (1y, -) 13 Gt.Scot 75:51, 16 GNR 75:01

nr **Teresa Duffy** IRE 6.7.69 74:51 '00 7 Berlin 72:57

Radcliffe retained her World title in a European record time and is again top ranked at three different events for the third successive year. Yelling stays in 2nd place and is followed by triathlete Emmerson.

MARATHON

1. **Bev Hartigan** 10.6.67 (1y, -) 0 17 London (1 AAA/UK) 2:37:45, 7 Berlin 2:36:02
2. **Debbie Robinson** 31.1.68 (1y, -) 2:52:26 '00 22 London (2 AAA) 2:42:19, 1 Dublin 2:35:40
3. **Beth Allott** 9.2.77 (1y, -) 2:55:19 '98 2 Lisbon 2:34:43
4. **Lynne MacDougall** 18.2.65 (2y, 3) 2:38:32 '00 16 London 2:37:20
5. **Trudi Thomson** 18.1.59 (6y, 6) 2:38:23 '95
   6 Dubai 2:46:32, 16 Pyongyang 2:41:49, 1 Scot 2:49:33, 5 Dublin 2:50:28
6. **Louise Watson** 13.12.71 (1y, -) 2:49:19 '00 23 London (3 AAA) 2:43:49, 4 Carpi 2:44:23
7. **Amy Stiles** 6.2.75 (1y, -) 2:47:48 '00 17 Rotterdam 2:45:02, 7 Amsterdam 2:45:16
8. **Vicky Pincombe** 19.6.73 (1y, 0) 0 25 London 2:43:52
9. **Clare Pauzers** 2.8.62 (2y, -) 2:43:27 '97 26 London 2:44:35
10. **Ruth Pickvance** 29.9.61 (1y, -) 2:59:14 '90 27 London 2:46:14, 25 New York 2:45:23
11. **Shona Crombie-Hicks** 1.6.71 (2y, 8) 2:42:44 '00 1 Copenhagen 2:45:23
12. **Sharon Dixon** 22.4.68 (2y, 12) 2:46:30 '00 28 London 2:46:32

nr **Teresa Duffy** 6.7.69 IRE 2:37:36 '00 15 London 2:35:27, 39 World 2:43:33, 3 Dublin 2:43:36

Neither of the top two in 2000 – Sue Reinsford and Marian Sutton – competed this year. They are replaced by Hartigan, who starred in the middle distances a decade ago with a best of 2nd at 1500m in 1989, and by the fast-improving Robinson. MacDougall beat them both in London, but did not race again at the distance and Allott ended the year with the fastest time, but only contested one marathon There are, in all, seven newcomers to the rankings.

3000 METRES STEEPLECHASE

1. **Tara Krzywicki** 9.3.74 (1y, -) 10:08.11 '00 2 v USA 9:52.71, 1 UK 9:55.01. 2000m: 2 LI 6:29.79
2. **Clare Martin** 14.9.74 (1y, -) 0 1 Stretford 10:44.69, 6 v USA 10:46.01, 1 UK 2000m: 3 LI 6:53.02
3. **Lois Joslin** 1.3.79 (1y, -) 0 5 Walnut 10:21.21, 6 Stanford 10:50.53, 10:54.34, 10h NCAA 11:12.20
4. **Jayne Knowles (Spark)** 16.9.70 (1y, -) 0 1 North 10:49.39

Rankings included for the first time. Krzywicki smashed the UK records for both 2000m and 3000m steeple and was on the edge of the world top ten.

100 METRES HURDLES

1. **Diane Allahgreen** 21.2.75 (8y, 2) *IAAF 33* 12.99 '99 12.98w, 13.08, 13.11, 13.14, 13.15w, 13.16
   1B Walnut, 1 B.Univs, 1 LI, 2 CAU, 3 Lisbon, 1 North, 4 ECp, 4 v USA, 3 Vasteras, 2 Cork, 1 AAA, 1 Bedl, 4 WUG
2. **Melani Wilkins** 18.1.73 (8y, 3) *IAAF 56* 13.17 '00, 13.1 '95 13.08w, 13.22w, 13.24, 13.27, 13.27, 13.28
   2 LI, 1 CAU, 1 Basel, 4 Tula, 1 South, 6 v USA, 2 AAA, 2 Bedl, 2 Cup, 2 v FRA, 1 GhCl, 2 Konigs W, BL1: 1,2, -
3. **Keri Maddox** 4.7.72 (12y, 1) *IAAF 84* 12.95 '99 13.24, 13.35, 13.38, 13.44, 13.47, 13.52
   4 E.Clubs, 1 Mid, 1 IR, 1 Lough, 1 BL1 (2), 3 AAA, 1 Cup
4. **Denise Lewis** 27.8.72 (10y, 6) 13.13 '00 13.29w, 13.41w, 13.42, 13.52, 13.56, 13.62
   2 BL1 (1), 2 Seville, 7 Luzern, 7g v USA, 4 AAA
5. **Julie Pratt** 20.3.79 (5y, 5) 13.40/13.28w '99 & 00 13.43w, 13.46, 13.47, 13.50, 13.50, 13.50; 13.4w
   3 Alfaz, 3 LI, 4 CAU, 1 Geneva, 2 South, 1 AAA-23, 4 Braga, 5 Cork, 5 Eur-23, 3 Bedl, 2 Derby, 5 v FRA, 2 GhCl, 3 Konigs W, BL1: 3.-,2
6. **Rachel King** 11.5.76 (5y, 7) 13.46 '99, 13.44w '98 13.51, 13.52, 13.52, 13.54, 13.58w, 13.59
   4 LI, 5 CAU, 3 Basel, 1 Cup sf H'gey, 1 Welsh, 1 Budapest, 3 Lough, 6 Cork, 5 AAA, 3 Cup, 6 v FRA
7. **Sarah Claxton** 23.9.79 (5y, 11) 13.59 '99, 13.28w '98 13.36, 13.55, 13.60, 14.50; 13.8, 13.8
   3 CAU, dnf South, 4 vSPA-23
8. **Clova Court** 10.2.60 (11y, 10) 13.04 '94 13.60, 13.70, 13.71, 13.77, 13.82, 13.90
   6 CAU, 3 Dublin, 4 Lough, 6 AAA, BL1: 1B,1B,3
9. **Liz Fairs** 1.12.77 (3y, 9) 13.49 '00 13.73w, 13.81, 13.87, 13.90, 13.91, 13.91w; 13.6w
   7 CAU, 1 Cup sf Wigan, 2 North, 2 IR, 3h3 AAA, BL1: 4,3,5
10. **Helen Worsey** 29.8.82 (2y, 12) 13.89/13.76w '00 13.66, 13.80, 13.90, 13.92, 13.98, 14.00w; 13.8w
    8s1 CAU, 2 Mid, 1 AAA-J, 5 Lough, 7 AAA, 4h2 EJ, 2 v USA-J, BL1: -,5,4
11. **Kerry Jury** 19.11.68 (1y, -) 13.92 '00, 13.71w '99 13.71, 13.82, 13.93, 13.98w, 14.00, 14.04
    7s1 CAU, dnf AAA, 3 GhCl, BL1: 5,4,-
12. **Sara McGreavy** 13.12.82 (1y, -) 14.01, 13.88w '00 13.77w, 13.88w, 13.93w, 13.94, 13.95, 14.07; 13.9w
    8 CAU, 3 Mid, 2 AAA-J, 1 E.Sch, 6h1 EJ, 2 Derby-J, 3 v USA-J, 4 GhCl

After two years ranked second Allahgreen returned to the top ranking she held in 1997. She just missed the A standard for the World Championships of 13.05, but was close to it many times and had run 12.98 with a +2.1 wind. As it transpired, however, she was injured and could not have run at the Worlds. Wilkins had her best ever season for second, followed by Maddox, who has now announced her retirement. Lewis competed enough at this event for 4th and Pratt is fifth for the fourth successive year. Court, aged 31 when she first ranked at the event, continues to set age records in her 11th year in the rankings.

400 METRES HURDLES

1. **Natasha Danvers** 19.9.77 (5y, 1) *IAAF 12* 54.95 '00 54.94, 55.37, 55.70, 55.95, 56.08, 56.36
   1 Walnut, 2 F-de-France, 1 Pac-10, 1 Stanford, 8 ECp (fell), 4h3 World, 3 GhCl, 1 WUG
2. **Sinead Dudgeon** 9.7.76 (5y, 3) *IAAF 23* 55.24 '99 56.07, 56.37, 56.46, 56.53, 56.83, 56.92
   1 BL1 (1), 1 Dortmund, 1 Scot, 2 Budapest, 1A Lough, 1 AAA, 5 BGP, 8s2 World
3. **Keri Maddox** 4.7.72 (6y, 2) *IAAF 46* 55.22 '00 57.18, 57.2, 57.48, 57.55, 58.00, 58.07
   4 E.Clubs, 1 Mid, 5 Luzern, 1 IR, 1 BL1 (2), 2 AAA, 7 BGP, 1 Cup, 7h2 World
4. **Tracey Duncan** 16.5.79 (3y, 4) 57.92 '00 58.15, 58.4, 58.48, 59.29, 59.30, 59.49
   1 CAU, 2r2 Tarare, 1 South, 1 vSPA-23, 2B Lough, dnf ht Eur-23, 1 BL1 (3), 1 v FRA, 4h4 WUG
5. **Hannah Wood** 17.11.81 (2y, 12) 60.86 '00 59.55, 59.80, 60.0, 60.05, 60.08, 60.20
   3 B.Univs, 4B LI, 1 Lough 13/6, 2 vSPA-23, 1 AAA-23, 3B Lough, 3 AAA, 4A Bedl, 2 Derby, 5 v FRA, 1 Antwerp
6. **Celia Brown** 22.1.77 (2y, 9) 60.08 '00 59.49, 60.53, 60.96, 61.0, 61.23, 61.26
   2 B.Univs, 2 LI, 2 Mid, 3 Dublin, 3 BL1 (2), 5 AAA, 3 Cup
7. **Hannah Stares** 13.11.78 (1y, -) 62.9 '00 60.28, 60.29, 60.5, 60.78, 60.9, 61.11
   1B LI, 5 CAU, 1 Cup sf H'gey, 5B Lough, 4 AAA, 5A Bedl, 7 v FRA
8. **Gemma Dooney** 12.5.84 (1y, -) 63.1 '00 60.07, 60.6, 60.70, 61.09, 62.4, 62.5
   1B BL3 (1), 1 AAA-J, 1 E.Sch, 2 v FRA-J, 2g v USA-J
9. **Faye Harding** 7.9.85 (1y, -) 0 60.06, 60.21, 60.45, 61.09, 61.10, 61.8
   3 Lough 13/6, 2 Welsh, 5 WY, 3 v FRA-J, 5 v USA-J
10. **Sian Scott** 20.3.84 (1y, -) 63.15 '00 60.50, 60.8, 61.02, 61.3, 61.32, 61.5
    2 Cup sf H'gey, 3 AAA-J, 2 E.Sch, 6 AAA, 2 Yth Oly, 4 v USA-J, BL4: -1,1,
11. **Nusrat Ceesay** 18.3.81 (1y, -) 60.53 '98 60.6, 60.79, 60.99, 61.1, 61.12, 61.3
    3B LI, dns CAU, 3r4 Tarare, dnf South, 3g v SPA-23, 3 AAA-23, 2C Lough, 7 AAA, 2 Plate, 3 Derby
12. **Jennie Mathews** (Pearson) 3.7.62 (15y, 4) 57.41 '88 61.0, 61.1, 61.1, 61.3, 61.35, 61.73
    3 CAU, 1 W.Vets, 1 BL3 (3)

– **Gowry Hodge** 21.6.60 (11y, 8) 54.63 '92 59.5

nr **Maiteland Marks** USA 19.9.76 60.31 '00 57.81, 57.82, 57.97, 58.16, 58.25, 58.6
1 B.Univs, 1 LI, 1r2 Tarare, 4A Lough, 3A Bedl, 2 Cup, 4g v FRA

nr **Michelle Carey** IRE 20.2.81 61.07 '00 59.64, 59.99, 60.54, 60.58, 60.78, 60.8
4 B.Univs, 2B LI, 2 CAU, 2 AAA-23, 4B Lough, 1 Irish, 1 Derby

Whereas in 2000 Danvers won a close call for top ranking, this year she achieved it with ease although she missed the peak of the season through injury; her best result coming at the end when she won the World Universities title. Dudgeon, Maddox and Duncan followed 2-3-4, as the top four were separated by about a second apiece, with an even bigger gap to the rest. The top newcomers are Dooney, Harding and Scott still juniors until 2003, 2004 and 2003 respectively. In contrast 41 year-old Hodge was sixth fastest in Britain in her one race of the year and Mathews just makes the rankings for the 15th time with better depth of times than some youngsters who ran faster than her once. Tenth best at 60.28 was just better than 2000 but otherwise the worst since 1978.

HIGH JUMP

1. **Susan Jones** 8.6.78 (8y, 1) *IAAF 14* 1.93 '00 1.95, 1.94, 1.91, 1.90, 1.89, 1.89
   1 LI, 1 CAU, 1 Lisbon, 1 ECp, 1 Budapest, 1 AAA, 4= BGP, dnq 13= World, 4= WUG, BL1: 1,2,-
2. **Michelle Dunkley** 26.1.78 (6y, 2) *IAAF 37* 1.93 '00 1.90, 1.89, 1.89, 1.88, 1.86, 1.86
   2 LI, 4 Tula, 1g Scot, 4 Budapest, 2 AAA, 8 BGP, 1 v FRA, dnq 14 WUG, BL1: -,1,1
3. **Aileen Wilson** 30.3.84 (4y, 7) *IAAF 77* 1.83 '00 1.87, 1.86, 1.84, 1.83, 1.82, 1.82
   1 Walnut, 1 Corinth, 1 BL2 (1), 2 Scot, 1 AAA-J, 1 E.Sch, 1 WY, 8 EJ
4. **Stephanie Higham** 26.12.83 (1y, -) 1.78 '00 1.83, 1.82, 1.81, 1.80, 1.79, 1.77
   1 Nth-J, 1 Scot-J, 3 Scot, 2 North, 2 AAA-J, 2 E.Sch, 12 EJ, 1 v FRA-J, 1 v USA-J, 2 EdIG
5. **Julia Bennett** 26.3.70 (14y, 11) 1.89 '94, 1.92i '90 1.84, 1.83, 1.80, 1.80, 1.80, 1.78
   1 Cork, 1 Plate, 4 Jumpsl
6. **Lindsey-Ann McDonnell** 13.8.79 (1y, -) 1.75 '99 1.80, 1.80, 1.79, 1.78, 1.78, 1.75
   1 vSPA-23, 2 Derby, 3 v FRA, 5= Jumps I
7. **Julie Hollman** 16.2.77 (2y, -) 1.81 '97 1.83, 1.81, 1.78, 1.75, 1.70, 1.68; 1.81i 4 BL2 (1), 3= AAA
8. **Rebecca Jones** 17.1.83 (3y, 10) 1.83 '00 1.80, 1.80, 1.76, 1.76, 1.76, 1.70; 1.79i, 1.77i
   6 LI, 1 Welsh-J, 3 AAA-J, 4 Cork, 1 EdIG
9. **Jo Jennings-Steele** 20.9.69 (13y, 3) 1.94i '93, 1.91 '98 1.80, 1.78, 1.75, 1.75, 1.75, 1.75
   1 Yorks, 2 CAU, 1 sf Rugby, 1 Cup, 6 v FRA, BL2: 2,1,1
10. **Debbie Marti** 14.5.68 (16y,6) 1.94 '96, 1.95i '97 1.78, 1.76, 1.75, 1.75, 1.75, 1.75 3 LI, 1 South, 3 Dublin
11. **Lea Haggett** 9.5.72 (9y, 8) 1.92 '96 1.80, 1.76, 1.75, 1.75 1 IR, 3 Cork
12. **Emma Perkins** 4.9.85 (1y, -) 1.68 '00 1.78, 1.76, 1.74, 1.74, 1.73, 1.72
    1 Sth-17, 1 E.Sch-I, 1 Sch.Int, 1 AAA-17, 2 v USA-J

– **Kerry Jury** 19.11.68 (5y, -) 1.81 '97 1.78, 1.77, 1.75, 1.70, 1.70, 1.68; 1.76i 3 Yorks, 3= AAA

Jones equalled the 19 year-old British record when achieving a splendid European Cup victory; she could not match that later but was on the edge of the world top ten. Dunkley kept her second ranking and Wilson maintained her progress with a rise to third place (her fourth year ranked yet still only 17). Another junior, Higham, made her debut in the rankings at fourth. In 2000 I wrote that eleven women over 1.83 returns us to the standards of 1982-9, but sadly that number dropped to six in 2001 and only ten at 1.80 or more. Third place at the AAAs going at 1.68 was a most depressing low. Three of the 2000 rankings: McConnell (4th), Mikneviciute (5th) and Crane (9th) did not compete in 2001.

POLE VAULT

1. **Janine Whitlock** 11.8.73 (6y, 1) *IAAF 18* 4.35 '00
   4.40, 4.36, 4.35, 4.35, 4.35, 4.34; all 13 outdoors and 8 indoor competitions at 4.00 or better
   1 LI, 1 CAU, 1 BL1 (1), 1 Tula, 7 Prague, 2 ECp, 1 Budapest, 1 AAA, 5 BGP, 9 World
2. **Irie Hill** 16.1.69 (3y, 2) *IAAF 87* 4.20 '00 4.00, 4.00, 3.95, 3.90, 3.90, 3.90
   5 AUS Ch, 12= Modesto, 1 Cup sf Eton, 1g IR, 2 Lough, 2 BL1 (2), 3 AAA, 2= v FRA
3. **Rhian Clarke** 19.4.77 (9y, 3) *IAAF 72* 4.15 '00 4.10, 4.00, 4.00, 3.85, 3.80, 3.80; 4.20i 4.05i, 4.03i
   4/1 Austin, nh Walnut, 15= NCAA, 6= Arles, 1 Welsh, 9 WUG
4. **Lucy Webber** 5.2.72 (4y, 5) 4.04 '00 4.00A, 4.00, 3.96, 3.85, 3.85, 3.80
   21= Walnut, 2 CAU, 2 IR, 1 Lough, 2 AAA, 3= Cup, 7 v FRA, 3 Jumps I
5. **Tracey Bloomfield** 13.9.79 (4y, 4) 3.90 '00 3.90, 3.80, 3.80, 3.80, 3.70, 3.70
   3 CAU, 13 Arles, nh vSPA-23, 3= AAA-23, 4 AAA, 1 BL2 (3), 5 v FRA, 1 South
6. **Sonia Lawrence** 19.1.80 (1y, -) 0 3.90, 3.85, 3.70, 3.70, 3.65, 3.40; 3.90i, 3.70i
   1 B.Univs, 15 Arles, 2 Welsh, 2 vSPA-23, 3= AAA-23, 5 AAA, 1 Derby, 6 v FRA
7. **Emma Hornby** 12.12.73 (5y, 8) 3.91 '98 3.75, 3.70, 3.65, 3.65, 3.65, 3.61
   3 LI, 4 CAU, 2 Lough 13/6, 1 Cup sf H'gey, 1 Mid, 3 IR, 4 Lough, 8 AAA, 2 Cup, BL1: 3,4,-
8. **Hilary Smith** 28.2.76 (1y, -) 3.50 '00 3.83, 3.75, 3.70, 3.70, 3.60, 3.60
   6 CAU, 1 Lough 13/6, 2 Mid, 1/1 Wrexham, 4 IR, 5 Lough, 7 AAA, 4 JumpsI
9. **Kate Dennison** 7.5.84 (1y, -) 3.20 '00 3.80, 3.80, 3.75, 3.65, 3.60, 3.60
   2 Staffs, 1 Mid-J, 2 Cup sf Rugby, 1 AAA-J, 1 E.Sch, 3 Yth Oly, 4 v USA-J, 1 BL3 (3), 1 Jnr IA
10. **Zoe Brown** 15.9.83 (1y, -) 3.00 '00 3.81, 3.70, 3.60, 3.60, 3.60, 3.60
    4= LI, 1 Irish Sch, 1 Cup sf Rugby, 2 AAA-J, 1 Irish, 3 v FRA-J, 2= BL1 (3), 3 v USA-J, 1 JLF
11. **Gael Davies** 5.2.79 (1y, -) 3.55 '00 3.75, 3.70, 3.65, 3.30, 3.30
    4 B.Univs, 1 Scot, 1 AAA-23, 3 Lough
12. **Laura Patterson** 31.1.81 (1y, -) 3.45 '99 3.60, 3.60, 3.60, 3.50, 3.50, 3.50; 3.60i, 3.60i
    2 B.Univs, 1 Staffs, 4= LI, 5 CAU, 4 South, 3g vSPA-23, 2 AAA-23, 6 Lough, 9= AAA, 2 Derby

– **Elizabeth Hughes** 9.6.77 (1y, 10) 3.70 '00 3.75; 3.70i; 2 LI

Including indoors: 2. Clarke, 3. Hill
Whitlock was top ranked for the fifth time and set British records at 4.36 and 4.40. The next three are very closely matched and Hill-Webber was 2-2. Hill is second for the third successive year and Clarke has uniquely ranked every year since this event was first included in 1993. Lawrence, former Commonwealth Games gymnastics silver medallist, made a great start to a pole vaulting career. Hornby beat Smith 5-2. Twelve women over 3.75 is easily a record.

LONG JUMP

1. **Jade Johnson** 7.6.80 (5y, 3) *IAAF 17* 6.58 '00 6.68w, 6.67w/6.58, 6.60w/6.59, 6.58, 6.55w, 6.52
   1 Surrey, 2 LI, 1 CAU, 1 Arles, 4 Helsinki, 5 ECp, 2 v USA, 1 Eur-23, 1 BedI, 1 v FRA, 6 T'saloniki
2. **Denise Lewis** 27.8.72 (10y, 1) 6.69 '00, 6.77w '97 6.53w/6.34, 6.46, 6.16
   3 Seville, 4 Luzern, 3 v USA
3. **Ann Danson** 4.5.71 (8y, 6) *IAAF 100* 6.21 '00, 6.38w '94 6.36w, 6.21, 6.19w, 6.15, 6.15, 6.11
   4 LI, 6 E.Clubs, 6 Arles, 1 North, 2 IR, 1 AAA, 1 Cup, 2 v FRA, 1 Nth IC, BL1: 1,3,1
4. **Julie Hollman** 16.2.77 (5y, 7) *IAAF 97* 6.51 '00 6.37w/6.35, 6.31w, 6.27, 6.17, 6.12w, 6.11; 6.18i, 6.13i
   5 CAU, 2H Arles, 4 Cork, 2 AAA, 3 v FRA, 2 K^nigs W
5. **Joanne Wise** 15.3.71 (12y, 2) 6.76 '99 6.46w, 6.35A; 6.34i 1/1 in RSA
6. **Kelly Sotherton** 13.11.76 (3y, 10) 6.10 '97, 6.24w '00 6.28w, 6.23, 6.19, 6.15w, 6.07, 5.99
   2 CAU, 2 BL1 (1), 4H Arles, 1 Mid, 2 Dublin, 3 AAA, 3 Cup
7. **Donita Benjamin** 7.3.72 (3y, 5) 6.26/6.45w '00 6.22w, 6.13w, 6.07, 6.06, 6.03, 5.98
   3 CAU, 1 South, 1 IR, 1 IS, 4 AAA, 2 Cup, BL1: 4,2,2
8. **Ruth Irving** 20.7.74 (8y, -) 6.28 '98 6.33, 6.27, 6.12w/6.08, 6.12w, 6.10w, 6.08
   3 LI, 4 CAU, 1 Riga, 2 North, 1 Scot, 4 BL1 (2), 5 AAA, 3 EdIG
9. **Sarah Wellstead** 22.10.79 (1y, -) 5.86 '98 6.14w, 6.10, 6.10w, 6.08w, 6.04w, 6.03w
   2 Surrey, 6 CAU, 5 South, 1 vSPA-23, 1 AAA-23, 4 BedI, 1 Plate, 2 Derby, 1 WF
10. **Sarah Claxton** 23.9.79 (6y, 4) 6.56 '99 6.27, 6.12, 5.98w/5.89, 5.91, 5.73, 5.72
    8 CAU, 4 Arles, 3 South, 3 vSPA-23, 1 Biella
11. **Joyce Hepher** 11.2.64 (14y, 8) 6.75, 6.80w '85 6.24, 6.02w, 5.87 7 CAU, 6 Cork
12. **Julia Bennett** 26.3.70 (2y, -) 6.13i '98, 6.12 '94 6.05, 6.05w, 6.00, 5.99, 5.95, 5.914 Surrey, 6H Arles, 2 Plate

Johnson takes the top ranking for the first time, won the European U23 gold medal, and found a new consistency, unfortunately just below the excessively-high IAAF World Championships standard. Lewis had just three competitions as did Wise, one indoors and two in South Africa in February. The consistent Danson won her first AAA title. Hepher had a consistent set of marks and ranks for an event record 13th time over a 20-year span. The tenth best of 6.16 is the best since 1987, although well short of the record 6.30 set in 1984.

TRIPLE JUMP

1. **Ashia Hansen** 5.12.71 (10y, 1) *IAAF 12* 15.15 '97, 15.16i '98 14.51, 14.18w, 14.10, 14.09, 14.07, 13.94
1 AAA, 1 Visby, 4 BGP, 7 World, 5 GhCl, 3 Viareggio, 5 Rieti
2. **Debbie Rowe** 8.9.72 (8y, 5) 12.97/13.14w '00 12.97w, 12.96w/12.90, 12.88, 12.81w, 12.70w, 12.64w
1 CAU, 4 Tula, 1 IR, 2 AAA, 1 Cup, 4 v FRA, BL1: 1,1,1
3. **Rebecca White** 5.6.80 (2y, 11) 12.24 '00 13.09w, 12.85, 12.84, 12.84, 12.82, 12.68; 12.70i
1 B.Univs, 1 LI, 6 E.Clubs, 1 Cup sf Wigan, 7 ECp, 1 AAA-23, 3 AAA, 2 Cup, 1 Derby, 5 v FRA, BL1: -,2,3
4. **Jade Johnson** 7.6.80 (1y, -) 0 13.11, 13.02 1 Eton, 8 GhCl
5. **Elizabeth Patrick** 29.8.77 (3y, 4) 12.92 '00 12.57w, 12.38, 12.38, 12.38w/12.37, 12.33, 12.27; 12.82i, 12.57i, 12.55i 2 LI, 2 CAU, 1 Cup sf H'gey, 1 South, 2 IR, 5 AAA, 2g Irish, 2 Rugby, 6 v FRA, BL1; 2,3,2
6. **Katie Evans** 4.2.74 (7y, 6) 13.03 '97 12.63, 12.52, 12.51, 12.30, 12.26, 11.66; 12.25i
6 AAA, 3 Cup, 1 Rugby, BL2: 1,1,1
7. **Caroline Stead** 14.9.71 (8y, 9) 12.67 '96 12.43w/11.95, 12.11, 12.10, 12.10w, 11.96, 11.93; 12.08i
4 LI, 4 CAU, 2 Cup sf H'gey, 4 South, 4 AAA, 1 WF
8. **Anna-Maria Thorpe** 15.7.71 (4y, 8) 12.84 '99 12.18w?, 12.17, 12.08, 11.91; 12.23i, 12.14i
3 Cup sf Eton, 8 AAA, 1 Plate, 2 WF
9. **Leandra Polius** 14.5.80 (2y, 10) 12.52 '00 12.35w/12.19, 12.23, 12.18, 12.03, 11.96, 11.94
1 Cup sf Eton, 2 South, 3 vSPA-23, 2 AAA-23, 9 AAA, 2 Plate, 3 Derby, 4 WF
10. **Katharine Streatfield** 28.7.83 (1y, -) 11.61 '00 12.17, 12.15, 12.15, 12.07, 12.05, 11.79
3 LI, 2 Corinth, 2 AAA-J, 1 E.Sch, 4 v FRA-J, 6 v USA-J, 5 Sth IC-J
11. **Marcia Walker** 27.5.70 (1y, -) 11.78 '97 12.11, 12.09, 12.02, 11.84, 11.84, 11.80w
2 Cup sf Eton, 7 South, 7 AAA, 4 Cup, BL1: 4,4,4
12. **Rachel Peacock** 18.5.82 (1y, -) 11.79 '00, 12.07w '98 12.10w, 12.04, 12.01, 11.67w, 11.63, 11.62; 12.01i. 11.70i 2 B.Univs, 5 LI, 1 Sth-J, 1 AAA-J, 1 BL4 (2), 3g v USA-J, 1 Sth IC-J

– **Angela Williams** 13.5.81 (0y, -) 12.22 '00 12.35, 12.22, 12.10, 12.00, 11.95, 11.93; 12.05i 1 BL3 (3)
– **Michelle Griffith** 6.10.71 (11y, 2) 14.08 '94, 14.14w '00 13.39i, 13.25i
– **Jodie Hurst** 21.6.77 (4y, 7) 12.64 '00 11.98, 11.92, 11.60; 12.32i, 12.11i, 12.10i 3 CAU, 1 Mid, BL1: 3,-,5

Including Indoors: 2. Griffiths, rest down a place, to 10. Hurst, 11. Polius, 12. Streatfield
Hansen again missed much of the year but was far ahead of any other UK athlete and ranks top for the seventh time. Griffith competed twice indoors, but missed the whole outdoor season through injury. Rowe beat White, who made a big advance, 5-0, to take second ranking, while Johnson made a promising debut at the event but in just two competitions did not meet them. Overall standards were down and 10th best of 12.23 was the worst since 1991.

SHOT

1. **Joanne Duncan** 27.12.66 (8y, 3) *IAAF 54* 16.12 '99 17.08, 16.99, 16.84, 16.59, 16.56, 16.46; 16.81i
1 LI, 1 CAU, 1 South, 8 ECp, 1 IR, 1 AAA, 1 Varazdin, 2 v FRA, 1 WF, BL1: 1,1,3
2. **Julie Dunkley** 11.9.79 (5y, 2) *IAAF 83* 16.40 '00 16.31, 16.31, 15.97, 15.88, 15.86, 15.84
1 B.Univs, 8 Halle, 1 vSPA-23, 1 AAA-23, 2 BL1 (2), 2 AAA, 1 Cup, 10 Eur-23, 3 v FRA, 2 WF
3. **Eva Massey** 22.12.80 (3y, 8) 14.90 '00 15.32, 15.30, 15.27, 15.09, 15.06, 15.06
3 CAU, 1 Bangor, 1 Cup sf Eton, 3 vSPA-23, 2 AAA-23, 3 AAA, 1 Irish, 1 NI, 4 v FRA, BL1: -,5,1
4. **Maggie Lynes** 19.2.63 (14y, 7) 16.57 '94 15.09, 15.05, 15.04, 14.98, 14.98, 14.98; 15.31i, 15.10i, 15.08i
1 Cup sf H'gey, 2 South, 2 IR, 4 AAA, 5g v FRA, 3 WF, BL1: 4,3,2
5. **Philippa Roles** 1.3.78 (6y, 9) 15.95i '99, 14.84 '00 15.19, 15.12, 14.96, 14.82, 14.80, 14.66; 15.79i, 15.23i, 15.18i, 15.13i 2 LI, 6 E.Clubs, 1 Cup sf Wigan, 1 Welsh, 2 Varazdin, 2 Cup, BL1: 5,4,4
6. **Vickie Foster** 1.4.71 (6y, 6) 15.44 '00 14.66, 14.61, 14.47, 14.46, 14.39, 14.25
1 West, 2 CAU, 2 Cup sf H'gey, 3 South, 5 AAA, BL2: 1,1,1
7. **Christina Bennett** 27.2.78 (5y, 5) 15.55 '99 15.00, 14.96, 14.81, 14.72, 14.54, 14.12
1 Surrey, 3 Cup sf H'gey, 1 Plate, 4 WF
8. **Denise Lewis** 27.8.72 (5y, 4) 16.12 '99 15.45; 2 BL1 (1)
9. **Nicola Gautier** 21.3.78 (2y, -) 15.09 '00 14.64, 14.53, 14.42, 13.75, 13.62, 13.52 4 LI, 5 CAU, BL1: 7,8,-
10. **Natasha Smith** 6.6.77 (1y, -) 14.12 '97 14.00, 13.81, 13.78, 13.63, 13.58, 13.38
4 CAU, 6 AAA, 4 Cup, BL1: 8,6,5
11. **Myrtle Augee** 4.2.65 (19y, -) 19.03 '90 14.50, 14.25, 14.10, 13.78, 12.89
12. **Rebecca Peake** 22.6.83 (1y, -) 12.90 '00 14.34, 14.13, 13.85, 13.68, 13.25, 13.24
1 Nth-J, 3 Cup sf Wigan, 4 IR, 1 AAA-J, 1 BL4 (2), 2 E.Sch, 3 v FRA-J, 3 v USA-J

Including Indoors: 12. Eleanor Gatrell (14.24i/13.95)
Duncan made a substantial improvement and clearly took the first top ranking of the 'post-Oakes' era. Dunkley is second and then there was a metre gap to Massey, who was re-classified as British and ranked 8th for 2000. Lewis only competed once, but that was still enough for a top ten ranking. Augee, competing mainly in the Southern League, returned for a 19th year in the rankings.

DISCUS

1. **Shelley Drew/Newman** 8.8.73 (10y, 1) *IAAF 40* 60.82 '98 59.10, 58.75, 58.44, 58.35, 57.69, 57.22
6 Halle, 1 CAU, 1 Cup sf H'gey, 1 South, 2 Dublin, 1 IR, 1 Lough, 1g BL1 (2), 1 AAA, 1 Cup, 1 Plate, 1 v FRA

2. **Philippa Roles** 1.3.78 (7y, 2) *IAAF 53* 60.00 '99 58.98, 56.86, 56.51, 56.28, 55.06, 55.02
3B Nice, 5 Halle, 1 LI, 7 E.Clubs, 1 Cup sf Wigan, 1 Welsh, 8 ECp, 4 Budapest, 3 Varazdin, 2 AAA, 3 Cup, 3 v FRA, 6 WUG, BL1: 1,2,2
3. **Claire Smithson** 3.8.83 (3y, 6) 52.19 '00 54.81, 53.65, 53.13, 52.80, 52.74, 51.77
4 LI, 1 Sth-J, 4 Mannheim, 1 AAA-J, 1 E.Sch, 8 EJ, 1 v FRA-J, 2 v USA-J, 1 Jnr IA
4. **Emma Carpenter** 16.5.82 (2y, 7) 52.21 '00 53.12, 53.00, 52.38, 50.93, 50.51, 50.35
2 Sth-J, 5 LI, 6 Mannheim, 2 AAA-J, 6 Varazdin, 6 EJ, 3 v USA-J, 2 Jnr IA
5. **Emma Merry** 2.7.74 (12y, 3) 57.75 '99 51.25, 49.97, 49.73, 49.53, 49.16, 47.97 3 LI, BL2: 1,1,1
6. **Rebecca Roles** 14.12.79 (2y, -) 51.79 '99 51.79, 51.40, 50.43, 50.10, 49.25, 49.06 2 LI, 11 CAU, 1 Cup sf Rugby, 2 Welsh, 1 vSPA-23, 1 AAA-23, 3 Dublin, dnq 14 Eur-23, 4 Cup, 6 v FRA, BL2: 2,3,2
7. **Nicola Talbot** 17.2.72 (9y, 10) 54.24 '93 47.79, 47.40, 46.95, 46.87, 46.30, 45.97
2 CAU, 1 Mid, 3 IR, BL1: 4,3,-
8. **Vickie Foster** 1.4.71 (4y, 12) 49.25 '00 46.94, 46.82, 46.11, 46.09, 45.85, 45.81
1 West, 3 CAU, 3 Cup sf H'gey, 3 South, 3 AAA, BL2: 3,4,3
9. **Debbie Callaway** 15.7.64 (18y, 4) 58.56 '96 46.97, 45.93, 45.79, 45.47, 45.34, 44.55
2 South, 2 IR, 4 AAA, BL2: 4,2,4
10. **Tracy Axten** 20.7.63 (13y, 5) 58.18 '97 47.93, 46.90, 45.81, 45.47, 45.13, 43.11
2 Cup sf Rugby, 5 Cup, BL1: 5,4,5
11. **Emma Beales** 7.12.71 (7y, -) 54.68 '95 46.57, 46.49, 46.46, 45.64, 45.54, 45.50 4 CAU, 1 Cup sf Eton, 10 South
12. **Eva Massey** 22.12.80 (1y, -) 47.72 '00 47.23, 46.56, 45.98, 44.20, 43.73, 43.61
2 Cup sf Eton, 3 vSPA-23, 5 AAA-23, 1 Irish, 1 NI, BL1: -,6,4
– **Jackie McKernan** 1.7.65 (15y, -) 60.72 '93 50.33; 3 Bangor
– **Lorraine Shaw** 2.4.68 (8y, 9) 55.04 '94 47.26, 44.57; BL1: 3,5,-

Drew ranks first for the fifth successive year and was 4-1 against P Roles, her closest challenger and second for the third successive year. The juniors Smithson and Carpenter continued to progress, with Smithson still a junior in 2002. Merry did not compete much, but beat Roles 3-1. Callaway's 18 years in the rankings sets an event record and Beales returns after four years out. 10th best of 47.26 was the worst since 1983.

HAMMER

1. **Lorraine Shaw** 2.4.68 (8y, 1) *IAAF 8* 67.44 '00 68.15, 67.98, 67.94, 67.68, 67.62, 67.43
1/1/1 in SA, 3 EAA-Nice, 1/1 Colindale, 1 Halle, 2 E.Clubs, 1 Batt.Pk, 1 Tula, 3 C-Ferrand, 3 ECp, 2 Budapest, 1 Szom, 1 AAA, 1 Cup, 6 World, 3 GhCl, BL1: 1,1,-
2. **Lyn Sprules** 11.9.75 (9y, 2) *IAAF 57* 63.96 '00 62.99, 62.26, 60.92, 60.41, 60.32, 59.61
1 CAU, 1 Cup sf Rugby, 1 South, 2 Dublin, 2 AAA, 1 Bedl, 1 v FRA, 1 Plate, BL1: 3,2,-
3. **Elizabeth Pidgeon** 27.4.77 (6y, 3) *IAAF 70* 63.61 '00 62.00, 61.48, 60.28, 60.22, 59.75, 59.60
9 Halle, 2 CAU, 2 Cup sf H'gey, 2 South, 4 Budapest, 4 Szom, 1 Varazdin, 4 AAA, 2 Bedl, 3 v FRA, dnq 23 WUG, BL1: 2,-,1
4. **Zoe Derham** 24.11.80 (4y, 6) *IAAF 90* 55.57 '00 60.35, 59.57, 59.30, 59.27, 59.08, 58.53
1C Colindale, 1 West, 8 U23 Halle, 2 Batt.Pk, 1 Cup sf H'gey, 1 Mid, 1 vSPA-23, 1 AAA-23, dnq 22 Eur-23, 3 AAA, 2 Cup, 1 Derby, 2 v FRA, 1 Rugby, BL1: 4,3,2
5. **Sarah Moore** 15.3.73 (10y, 7) 56.60 '97 57.40, 56.77, 56.43, 56.12, 55.48, 55.33
2/3 Colindale, 2 West, 5 LI, 1 Welsh, 10 Budapest, 8 Szom, 6 Varazdin, 6 AAA, 2 Rugby, 3 EdIG, BL3: 1,-,1
6. **Suzanne Roberts** 19.12.78 (2y, 4) 58.83 '00 57.62, 57.51, 55.28, 55.28, 54.64, 54.58
1 B.Univs, 1 Yorks, 1 LI, 7 AAA, 3 Cup, 1 Nth IC, BL1: -,4,5
7. **Mhairi Walters** 19.6.81 (2y, 11) 55.10 '00 58.31, 56.86, 56.14, 53.61, 53.60, 53.38
2 LI, 2 vSPA-23, 2 AAA-23, 1 BL2 (2), 9 AAA, 1 EdIG
8. **Diana Holden** 12.2.75 (11y, 9) 57.95 '98 56.21, 55.71, 54.12, 53.98, 53.94, 53.42
3/2 Colindale, 3 Batt.Pk, 3 Cup sf H'gey, 3 South, 1 IR, 5 AAA, 4 Cup
9. **Lesley Brannan** 13.9.76 (1y, -) 51.86 '00 56.62, 54.97, 52.94, 52.57, 52.54, 52.47
2 Welsh, 3 Dublin, 8 AAA, 3 Rugby, BL1: 6,7,3
10. **Vicci Scott** 21.9.80 (1y, -) 53.19 '00 55.42, 54.70, 54.63, 54.58, 54.12, 53.33
3 B.Univs, 4 LI, 7 CAU, 2 sf Rugby, 1 North, 1 Scot, 3 AAA-23, 13 AAA, 3 Derby, 2 Nth IC, BL2: 1,3, -
11. **Rachael Beverley** 23.7.79 (6y, 5) 60.88 '99 56.06, 54.60, 53.13, 51.79 3 LI, BL1: 5.5,-
12. **Nicola Dudman** 5.10.83 (1y, -) 47.62 '00 54.54, 52.74, 52.71, 52.63, 52.37, 51.57
2J/4/4 Colindale, 2 Sth-J, 6 Batt.Pk, 6 South, 2 AAA-J, 1 E.Sch, 10 AAA, 4 Bedl, 1 v FRA-J, 1 v USA-J, 1 Jnr IA
– **Carys Parry** 24.7.81 (3y, 10) 53.80 '00 54.12, 52.72, 52.34, 51.94, 51.69, 50.59
2 B.Univs, 2C Colindale, 6 LI, 6 CAU, 3 Welsh, 4 AAA-23, 14 AAA, 2 Derby

Shaw set her 14th and 15th British records and ranks top for the seventh time and sixth in the world. She had all 22 competitions over 63m. Sprules is second for the seventh time in the last eight years (she was 1st in 1997), Pidgeon is again third and Derham became the fifth British woman ever to exceed 60m. Derham was 3-2 v Pidgeon, but the latter just had the edge overall. 5th to 8th were closely matched. English (Shaw), Scottish (Walters) and Welsh (Moore) records were all broken. Scott-Parry was 3-3, but Scott had the better marks, and several others just miss rankings in what is now by far the highest standard and most popular throwing event for British women. The tenth best at 56.06 again improved the record level (1999 – 53.60, 2000 – 54.68).

JAVELIN

1. **Karen Martin** 24.11.74 (10y, 2) *IAAF 46* 59.50 '00 55.85, 55.59, 55.30, 54.82, 53.03, 52.63
   4 Halle, 8 ECp, 1 IS, 1 Bedl, 1 AAA, 1 v FRA, BL4: -,1,1
2. **Goldie Sayers** 16.7.82 (4y, 4) *IAAF 77* 54.58 '00 55.40, 53.97, 53.74, 52.74, 51.20, 49.51
   1 AAA-J, 2 EJ, 1 v USA-J, 6 Tampere, 5 Lahti, BL2: -,1,2
3. **Kelly Morgan** 17.6.80 (4y, 1) 58.45 '00 54.49, 53.75, 53.14, 51.90 2 AAA, 2 Cup, 1 BL1 (3)
4. **Kirsty Morrison** 28.10.75 (9y, 8) *IAAF 99* 55.91 '99, 59.36# '93 53.10, 51.92, 51.60, 51.43, 51.25, 50.94
   2 LI, 1 CAU, 2 Bangor, 5 AAA, BL3: -,1,1
5. **Linda Gray** 23.3.71 (2y, 11) *IAAF 100* 48.77 '00 52.86, 51.74, 51.39, 50.25, 50.01, 49.98
   2 CAU, 4 Bangor, 1 Cup sf Eton, 1 North, 2 IR, 2 Varazdin, 4 AAA, BL2: 1,-,1
6. **Lorna Jackson** 9.1.74 (9y, 3) 57.19 '00, 58.39# '98 52.74, 49.97, 46.01 1 Scot, 6 Budapest, 3 AAA
7. **Jennifer Kemp** 18.2.80 (3y, 6) 52.54 '99 52.76, 48.97, 48.95, 48.59, 47.91
   3 LI, 3 CAU, 2 vSPA-23, 1 AAA-23, dnq 17 Eur-23
8. **Chloe Cozens** 9.4.80 (3y, 7) 51.79 '00 51.65, 48.73, 48.24, 47.88, 43.90
   1 LI, 3 Bangor, 3 vSPA-23, 3 AAA-23
9. **Sharon Gibson** 31.12.61 (22y, 10) 50.85 '99, 62.32# '87 49.36, 46.68, 46.21, 45.90, 44.33, 44.27
   1 Mid, 1 IR, 6 AAA
10. **Kate Amos** 13.11.78 (3y, -) 46.75 '99, 50.34# '98 47.55, 46.96, 46.00, 45.70, 45.02 (45.10?), 44.63
    5 CAU, 1 South, 3 IR, 9 AAA
11. **Katy Watts** 25.3.81 (1y, -) 45.24 '99 46.29, 45.31, 44.80, 44.38, 43.95, 43.41
    1 B.Univs, 2 AAA-23, 8 AAA, 2 Derby, 5 v FRA, BL4: 1,2,2
12. **Samantha Redd** 16.2.84 (1y, -) 45.24 '00 47.13, 46.36, 45.63, 44.59, 42.31, 41.36
    4 LI, 3 E.Sch, 2 AAA-J, dnq 20 Yth Oly, 4 v FRA-J

= old specification

Martin takes over top ranking after four years at number two, and although Morgan beat Sayers at their only meeting, the latter takes second place due principally to her splendid British junior record in taking the European Junior silver medal. Gibson is ranked for the 22nd successive year (just one behind Tessa Sanderson's record), but there is little depth in this event.

HEPTATHLON

1. **Julie Hollman** 16.2.77 (5y, 3) *IAAF 22* 5816w '98, 5685 '00 2 ECp1 5933, 3 Arles 5840, 1 NU Int 5537
2. **Nicola Gautier** 21.3.78 (6y, 5) *IAAF 62* 5760 '99 8 ECp1 5784, 12 Arles 5666, dnf NU Int, dnf WUG
3. **Kerry Jury** 19.11.68 (12y, 2) *IAAF 59* 6005w '98, 5908 '99 10 ECp1 5687, 15 Arles 5635, 1 HCI 5589, 2 NU Int 5476
4. **Julia Bennett** 26.3.70 (10y, 6) *IAAF 92* 5747w '96, 5538 '00 14 ECp1 5534, 18 Arles 5508, 3 NU Int 5406/5452a
5. **Katherine Livesey** 15.12.79 (5y, 12) 5239w '99, 5215 '97 3 Big 12 5554, 1 Lawrence 5385, 10 NCAA 5375
6. **Kelly Sotherton** 13.11.76 (3y, 7) 5585 '97 20 Arles 5410, dnf Dutch
7. **Laura Redmond** 19.4.81 (1y, -) 4954 '00 31 Arles 5114, 2 HCI 5107, 1 AAA 5068, 5 NU23 5039
8. **Fiona Harrison** 30.11.81 (3y, 10) 5279 '00 26 Arles 5208, dnf Welsh 4245, dnf NU23
9. **Rosalyn Gonse** 1.3.82 (1y, -) 4557 '00 4 NU Int-J 5053, 1 Hexham 4900, 1 AAA-J 4875, 1 Mid-J 4529
10. **Kate Brewington** 15.10.81 (1y, -) 4736 '00 2 AAA 4969, 9 NU Int-23 4711
11. **Rebecca Jones** 17.1.83 (1y, -) 5186 '00 32 Arles 4959, 1 Welsh-J 4814, dnf AAA-J
12. **Charmaine Johnson** 4.6.63 (11y, -) 5495 '92 3 AAA 4908, 1 Welsh 4716, 4 HCI 4690

HCI – Home Countries International at Sheffield
NU Int – v France, Italy, Switzerland and Germany at Bedford

Sadly Denise Lewis, top for the last seven years, did not contest a heptathlon in 2001 and Hollman, who also set a British indoor record at pentathlon (4392) takes over the top ranking. Johnson returns to the rankings after six years out. Overall standards were down and tenth best of 4969 is the worst since 1992, the only other year below 5000 in the 20 years of the event.

WALKS

Priority is given to form at the standard international distance of 20 kilometres, although performances at other distances are also taken into account. 3000m and 5000m performances are on the track, unless indicated by R for road marks (+ indicates intermediate time). All distances from 10k up are on the road unless shown by t. Previous bests are shown for track 5000m and road or track 10km and 20km.

1. **Niobe Menendez** 1.9.66 (4y, 2) 24:22.84 '00, 49:10 '99, 1:40:12 '99
   3000m: 13:14.73, 14:08.70+; 14:04.49i; 1 v FRA 5km: 23:46.30; 24:53R: 1 CAU, 1 AAA
   10km: 48:08, 49:19, 49:37+. 49:52.1t, 50:52; 10 E.Clubs, 2 RWA, 1 IA, 1 B'ham
   20km: 4 Leamington 1:45:19, 8 Dublin 1:41:37, 3 Swiss 1:42:08
2. **Sharon Tonks** 18.4.70 (4y, 4) 25:35.15 '89, 49:46 '00, 1:49:19 '00
   3000m: 14:11.6, 14:19.51, 15:00.0; 14:02.55i; 1 IR, 1 Coventry
   5km: 24:20.46; 23:54R, 24:30R, 24:51R, 24:58R; 1 Mid, 1 RWA, 2 AAA 10km: 53:04 1 Mid, dnf RWA
   20km: 2 Manx 1:50:27, 5 Leamington 1:46:15, 16 Dublin 1:53:22, 6 Swiss 1:46:53

3. **Sara-Jane Cattermole** 29.1.77 (3y, 3) 24:59.0 '99, 47:47 '00, 1:36:40 '00
3000m: 14:05.6, 14:12.4, 14:16.02mx, 14:57.3
5000m: 24:43.9mx, 25:05.3; 24:23R; 1 Steyning
10km: 47:05, 48:28, 49:51.6t; 50:42, 51:06; 3 RWA
20km: 1 Murdoch 1:39:10/1:40:42, 6 Leamington 1:47:35, 1 Essex 1:49:50, dq Dublin, 1 Perth 1:39:41

4 **Jane Gibson (Kennaugh)** 26.1.73 (3y, 6) 51:34 '99, 1:48:24 '99
3000m: 14:21.01; 2 IR 5km: 25:16.2; 25:11R 10km: 53:37, 53:58.1t; 1 Manx
20km: 7 Leamington 1:48:55, 1 Manx Ch 1:51:19, 14 Dublin 1:47:39, dq RWA

5. **Wendy Bennett** 21.12.65 (1y, -) 24:58R '00
3000m: 14:22.42, 14:33.0, 14:37.53; 3 IR, 5 v FRA 5km: 24:24.0, 24:35.85; 24:36R; 3 AAA
10km: 48:58, 49:36, 50:18, 50:45, 51:13.4t; 4 RWA, 2 IA, 1 Worcester, 2 B'ham 20km: 15 Dublin 1:47:46

6. **Lisa Kehler** 15.3.67 (16y, 1) 21:57.68 '90, 45:03 '98, 1:33:57 '00 10km: 48:16; 1 Birmimgham

7. **Joanne Hesketh** 16.6.69 (1y, -) 54:59 '00. 1:55:33 '00
3000m: 15:13.41; 2 Sussex 5km: 25:35R, 25:59R, 26:07R, 26:11R; 4 RWA, 4 Steyning
10km: 53:08, 54:08, 54:27.9t, 55:21; 15 E.Clubs, 8 RWA, 3 Mid
20km: 3 Manx 1:51:43, 1 Sussex 1:52:25, 8 Leamington 1:50:35

8. **Karen Ratcliffe** 1.6.61 (6y, -) 24:12.11 '93, 48:30 '94, 1:59:45 '89
3000m: 15:17.0; 2 Coventry 5000m: 25:21.0, 25:59.47; 6 AAA, 2 Mid
10km: 51:45, 52:28.2t 54:37; 3 IA, 2 Mid, 2 Worcester

9. **Catherine Charnock** 3.5.75 (5y, 10) 23:11.7 '99, 47:51 '99, 1:38:29 '99
10km: 52:48; 6 RWA

10. **Elizabeth Corran** 23.9.55 (3y, -) 24:40.91 '96, 51:03.0t '95, 1:47:10 '96
5km: 25:52R 20km: 4 Manx 1:52:54

nr **Estle Viljoen** RSA 8.7.70
3000m: 14:25.4, 14:52.7; 1 CAU, 1 Sth IC
5km: 24:53.02; 24:13R, 24:54R, 25:03R, 25:10R; 2 RWA. 4 AAA
10km: 51:41, 52:18.23; 5 RWA, 1 South 20km: 1 Surrey 1:52:40, 13 Dublin 1:47:18

Ranked 10-3-2-1 from 1998, Menendez was clearly top with Kehler not competing this year until a good 10km right at the end of the year ensured her of a ranking. Cattermole was again much faster on her own in Perth than elsewhere, and Tonks beat her at Leamington. Bennett made notable progress; she had better marks at the shorter distances, but was beaten by Gibson in her one 20km race.

With thanks to Tony Miller, Alan Lindop, Ian Hodge, Ian Tempest, Matthew Fraser Moat, John Powell, Julie Fletcher and Rob Whittingham for their comments.

UK Merit Rankings 1968-2001

Summary of achievements at standard events (not including occasional rankings for such events as men's 3000m, women's 200mh, 5000m (until it replaced 3000m in 1995) or half marathon).
Leading points scorers all events - 12 points for a first place to 1 for 12th

Men

1	Daley Thompson	417.5
2	Chris Maddocks	303.5
3	Linford Christie	300
4	Steve Ovett	288
5	Mike Winch	281.5
6	David Jenkins	276
7	Sebastian Coe	262
8	Steve Cram	252.5
9	Brendan Foster	244.5
10	John Regis	237.5
11	Colin Jackson	229
12	Alan Pascoe	225
13	Peter Tancred	218
14	Bob Dobson	
216		
15	John Herbert	211

Women

1	Denise Lewis	385
2	Judy Simpson	379
3	Sally Gunnell	346.5
4	Judy Oakes	344.5
5	Yvonne Murray	329.5
6	Tessa Sanderson	323
7	Liz McColgan	311.5
8	Christina Boxer/Cahill	302
9	Ann Simmonds +	281
10	Kathy Cook	272.5
11	Kim Hagger	264.5
12	Simmone Jacobs	260.5
13	Venissa Head	243.5
14	Paula Radcliffe	237
15	Sonia Lannaman	234.5
16	Margaret Ritchie	234
17	Sharon Colyear	232

+ indicates would have added to score from rankings pre 1968

2001 LISTS - MEN

50 Metres - Indoors

5.71	Doug Bignall		20.10.74	1r3	Los Angeles CA, USA	20 Jan
5.83 +	Christian Malcolm	U23	3.06.79	4h1m	Lievin, FRA	25 Feb

55 Metres - Indoors

6.0	Chris Lambert	U23	6.04.81	1	Boston, USA	18 Feb

60 Metres - Indoors

6.51	Mark Lewis-Francis	U20	4.09.82	3	Lisbon, POR	11 Mar
	6.56			2s1	Lisbon, POR	11 Mar
	6.61			1h8	Lisbon, POR	11 Mar
	6.62			2	Glasgow	18 Mar
	6.65			5	Birmingham	18 Feb
	6.67			1	Birmingham	25 Feb
	6.68			1	Birmingham	10 Feb
	6.68			2h2	Birmingham	18 Feb
	6.69			1s1	Birmingham	25 Feb
	6.71			1r1	Birmingham	3 Feb
	6.72			2h2	Stockholm, SWE	15 Feb
	6.73			6	Stockholm, SWE	15 Feb
6.64	Christian Malcolm	U23	3.06.79	1	Cardiff	11 Feb
	6.64			6	Ghent, BEL	23 Feb
	6.65			2h1	Birmingham	18 Feb
	6.65			4h2	Ghent, BEL	23 Feb
	6.65			3	Glasgow	18 Mar
	6.67			6	Birmingham	18 Feb
	6.68			1	Cardiff	4 Feb
	6.71			1s2	Birmingham	27 Jan
	6.71			5	Stockholm, SWE	15 Feb
	6.72			2	Birmingham	27 Jan
	6.73			3h1	Stockholm, SWE	15 Feb
	6.75			4s1	Lievin, FRA	25 Feb
6.65	Jason Livingston ¶		17.03.71	1	Glasgow	21 Jan
	6.66			1s3	Birmingham	27 Jan
	6.67			1	Birmingham	25 Feb
	6.68			1h3	Birmingham	27 Jan
	6.69			1s1	Birmingham	25 Feb
	6.70			2	Cardiff	11 Feb
	6.72			3	Birmingham	27 Jan
6.65	Chris Lambert	U23	6.04.81	2h1	Lexington, USA	24 Feb
	6.67			3	Lexington, USA	25 Feb
6.72 !	John Skeete ¶		8.09.78	1h2	Glasgow	21 Jan
	6.73			1s2	Birmingham	13 Jan
	6.74			1	Birmingham	13 Jan
6.73	Daniel Money		17.10.76	2h3	Birmingham	27 Jan
	6.73			2s3	Birmingham	27 Jan
	6.73			4h1	Birmingham	18 Feb
	6.73			8	Birmingham	18 Feb
	6.74			4	Birmingham	27 Jan
6.74	Jonathon Oparka	U23	27.01.80	1	Glasgow	17 Feb
6.74	Allyn Condon		24.08.74	6h1	Birmingham	18 Feb
6.75	Tim Benjamin	U20	2.05.82	3s3	Birmingham	27 Jan
	44 performances to 6.75 by 9 athletes					
6.76	Doug Turner		2.12.66	1	Cardiff	21 Jan
(10)						
6.77	Brendon Ghent		7.09.76	3s2	Birmingham	27 Jan
6.79	Kevin Williams		15.12.71	7	Birmingham	27 Jan

6.79		Nathan Morgan		30.06.78	1	Cardiff	18 Feb
6.79		Dwayne Grant	U20	17.07.82	1A2	Vittel, FRA	3 Mar
6.80		Darren Chin	U23	30.06.81	4s2	Birmingham	27 Jan
6.81		Curtis Browne		11.09.75	3s1	Birmingham	27 Jan
6.82		Brian Doyle		12.03.77	2	Glasgow	13 Jan
6.82		John Stewart	U23	30.12.79	4s1	Birmingham	27 Jan
6.82		Aiah Yambasu		10.11.73	5s2	Birmingham	27 Jan
6.82		Akinola Lashore		28.03.73	3	Cardiff	4 Feb
	(20)						
6.84		Nick Thomas	U23	4.04.79	4s3	Birmingham	27 Jan
6.85		Terence Stamp		18.02.70	2r1	Birmingham	7 Jan
6.85		Dominic Shepherd		11.12.76	1H	Birmingham	20 Jan
6.85		Kevin Ellis		18.06.76	1h4	Birmingham	27 Jan
6.86		Daniel Caines	U23	15.05.79	1s3	Birmingham	13 Jan
6.86		Tyrone Edgar	U20	29.03.82	2s3	Birmingham	25 Feb
6.88		Dominic Bradley		22.12.76	1r2	Birmingham	7 Jan
6.88		Tyrone Swaray		7.11.77	3h3	Birmingham	27 Jan
6.90		Henry Richards	U23	15.05.81	2h7	Birmingham	27 Jan
6.90		Mark Hanson	U23	13.05.81	3	Glasgow	17 Feb
	(30)						
6.90		James Chatt	U23	11.02.80	2s2	Glasgow	17 Feb
6.91		Richard Rubenis		10.11.73	2h7	Birmingham	13 Jan
6.91		Colin Wilson		30.10.77	2	Bedford	13 Jan
6.91		Laurence Oboh	U20	14.05.84	2s1	Birmingham	25 Feb
6.92		Jamie Henthorn		20.02.77	6s3	Birmingham	27 Jan
6.93		Luke Davis	U23	1.01.80	4h1	Birmingham	27 Jan
6.93		Mark McIntyre		14.10.70	5	Cardiff	4 Feb
6.94		Tim Barton		3.10.70	4r1	Birmingham	3 Feb
6.95		Gavin Eastman	U23	28.06.80	8s2	Birmingham	27 Jan
6.97		Karl Forde	U20	15.04.83	1	Birmingham	10 Feb
	(40)						
6.98		Steven Shalders	U23	24.12.81	3	Cardiff	20 Jan
6.99		Mark Brown		3.11.76	5s1	Birmingham	13 Jan
6.99		Joshua Wood		19.04.74	5h3	Birmingham	27 Jan
6.99		Matthew Ouche	U17	6.03.85	1	Birmingham	25 Feb

Suspended for drug offence

6.59	John Skeete ¶		8.09.78	(1)	Birmingham	27 Jan
	6.60			(1s1)	Birmingham	27 Jan
	6.67			(1h2)	Birmingham	27 Jan

hand timing

6.7	John Skeete ¶		(6.72)	2	Glasgow	21 Jan
6.8	Colin Wilson		(6.91)	1	Eton	7 Jan
6.8	Kevin Ellis		(6.85)	4	Glasgow	21 Jan
6.9	Leon McRae	U23	3.11.80	2	Eton	7 Jan
6.9	Alloy Wilson	U23	25.01.80	1r2A	London (CP)	17 Jan
6.9	Marlon Dickson		17.11.78	1h	London (Ha)	4 Feb

Foreign

6.89	*John McAdorey (IRL)*	*16.09.74*	*1h*	*Nenagh, IRL*	*3 Feb*

Note

The following main list for the 100 metres does not show the performances of Chambers, Lewis-Francis and Malcolm set in the quarter finals at Edmonton. These performances, all personal bests, are thought to be probably wind assisted and are shown in that list with a *. The wind guage readings for these races were false and there is evidence of wind on that afternoon. This, together with the large number of personal/seasonal bests set in these quarterfinals, have led the editors to classify the performances in this way.

100 Metres

9.99	-0.2	Dwain Chambers		5.04.78	5	Edmonton, CAN	5	Aug
		10.00 1.1			3	Lausanne, SUI	4	Jul
		10.01 0.6			1	Seville, ESP	8	Jun
		10.01 1.7			1	Birmingham	14	Jul
		10.06 0.0			4	Brussels, BEL	24	Aug
		10.09 0.2			2	Zurich, SUI	17	Aug
		10.10 -1.7			3s2	Edmonton, CAN	5	Aug
		10.11 -0.8			2	London (CP)	22	Jul
		10.11 -0.3			1	Brisbane, AUS	5	Sep
		10.12 0.0			1	Madrid, ESP	26	May
		10.12 1.1			1h2	Seville, ESP	8	Jun
		10.14 -0.2			1	Nuremberg, GER	17	Jun
		10.20 0.5			1s1	Birmingham	14	Jul
		10.27 0.0			2h9	Edmonton, CAN	4	Aug
		10.29 -1.6			1h2	Zurich, SUI	17	Aug
		10.31			2	Gateshead	19	Aug
		10.36 1.8			1h4	Birmingham	13	Jul
10.11	-0.2	Christian Malcolm	U23	3.06.79	7	Edmonton, CAN	5	Aug
		10.17 0.6			1	Helsinki, FIN	14	Jun
		10.20 0.0			8	Brussels, BEL	24	Aug
		10.21 1.7			3	Birmingham	14	Jul
		10.24 0.2			4rB	Rome, ITA	29	Jun
		10.24 0.3			2h4	Edmonton, CAN	4	Aug
		10.24 -1.7			4s2	Edmonton, CAN	5	Aug
		10.27 0.5			2s1	Birmingham	14	Jul
		10.28 0.6			2	Villeneuve d'Ascq, FRA	17	Jun
		10.29 1.9			1	Loughborough	20	May
		10.35 -0.1			2rB	London (CP)	22	Jul
		10.40 -0.8			1	Cardiff	16	Jun
10.12	-1.3	Mark Lewis-Francis	U20	4.09.82	1	Tallahassee FL, USA	14	Apr
		10.12 1.7			2	Birmingham	14	Jul
		10.13 1.1			2	Philadelphia PA, USA	28	Apr
		10.13 1.4			1	Bremen, GER	23	Jun
		10.14 1.6			1s2	Birmingham	14	Jul
		10.18 1.8			1	Mannheim, GER	16	Jun
		10.20 2.0			1h2	Birmingham	13	Jul
		10.20 0.0			6	Brussels, BEL	24	Aug
		10.21 0.7			1h8	Edmonton, CAN	4	Aug
		10.26 -1.2			5s1	Edmonton, CAN	5	Aug
		10.31 0.9			1h5	Mannheim, GER	16	Jun
10.16	1.3	Darren Campbell		12.09.73	1r1	Austin TX, USA	5	May
		10.37 0.0			1rB	Madrid, ESP	26	May
		10.38 1.6			3s2	Birmingham	14	Jul
		10.38 1.7			6	Birmingham	14	Jul
10.23	0.9	Jason Gardener		18.09.75	2h1	Seville, ESP	8	Jun
		10.28 0.0			2	Ingolstadt, GER	27	May
		10.38 0.9			1h2	Ingolstadt, GER	27	May
10.24	1.6	Chris Lambert	U23	6.04.81	2s2	Birmingham	14	Jul
		10.24 1.7			4	Birmingham	14	Jul
		10.28 2.0			2h2	Birmingham	13	Jul
		10.32 0.0			1h10	Beijing, CHN	27	Aug
		10.32 -0.7			1s2	Beijing, CHN	28	Aug
		10.35 -0.1			3rB	London (CP)	22	Jul
		10.37 -1.0			1q1	Beijing, CHN	27	Aug
		10.38 -0.8			3	Beijing, CHN	28	Aug
10.28	0.3	Jon Barbour	U23	3.11.80	3	Thessaloniki, GRE	22	Aug
		10.30 1.6			1	Konigs Wusterhausen, GER	28	Aug
		10.36 1.9			2	Loughborough	20	May
		10.38 -0.3			1r6	Irvine CA, USA	5	May
		10.39 -0.1			4rB	London (CP)	22	Jul

10.30	0.6	Doug Bignall		20.10.74	1rB1	Walnut CA, USA	22 Apr
		10.30 -0.1			1rB	London (CP)	22 Jul
		10.31 1.7			5	Birmingham	14 Jul
		10.33 0.5			3s1	Birmingham	14 Jul
		10.39 0.0			1	Eagle Rock, USA	12 May
		10.39			4	Gateshead	19 Aug
10.30	0.6	Marlon Devonish		1.06.76	3	Poznan, POL	8 Jun
		10.31 0.3			4	Thessaloniki, GRE	22 Aug
		10.32 0.6			2rB1	Walnut CA, USA	22 Apr
		10.36 0.6			5	Villeneuve d'Ascq, FRA	17 Jun
		10.38 0.8			1r1	Fullerton CA, USA	26 Apr
10.30	1.5	Ian Mackie		27.02.75	1	Glasgow (S)	23 Jun
		10.39 0.5			1=	Edinburgh	25 Aug
	(10)						
10.37	1.1	Doug Turner		2.12.66	2	Avezzano, ITA	19 Aug
		10.39 -0.5			1=	Edinburgh	25 Aug
10.38	1.5	Nathan Morgan		30.06.78	1rB	London (He)	5 May
		76 performances to 10.40 by 12 athletes					
10.42	-0.2	Allyn Condon		24.08.74	5	Nuremberg, GER	17 Jun
10.46	1.1	Daniel Money		17.10.76	1	London (He)	5 May
10.47	1.7	Dwayne Grant	U20	17.07.82	1rB	Mannheim, GER	16 Jun
10.49	1.1	Tyrone Edgar	U20	29.03.82	2	London (He)	5 May
10.50	1.7	Curtis Browne		11.09.75	7	Birmingham	14 Jul
10.52	1.8	Darren Chin	U23	30.06.81	2	Bedford	21 Jul
10.52	-0.1	Aidan Syers	U20	29.06.83	1	Dole, FRA	29 Jul
10.53	1.6	Brendon Ghent		7.09.76	1	Birmingham	16 Jun
	(20)						
10.54	1.4	Akinola Lashore		28.03.73	2	Eton	7 Jul
10.54	1.4	Dominic Bradley		22.12.76	3	Eton	7 Jul
10.56	-0.1	Rikki Fifton	U17	17.06.85	2	Dole, FRA	29 Jul
10.57	1.7	Tim Benjamin	U20	2.05.82	1h3	Cardiff	16 Jun
10.58	1.6	Ben Lewis	U23	6.03.81	2	Birmingham	16 Jun
10.60	-1.9	Mark Richardson ¶		26.07.72	2	Cardiff	8 Jul
10.61	1.4	Jonathon Oparka	U23	27.01.80	4	Eton	7 Jul
10.63	2.0	Akeem Ogunyemi		4.06.74	3h2	Birmingham	13 Jul
10.64	1.1	Dan Donovan		8.10.70	4	London (He)	5 May
10.65	1.5	Nick Smith	U20	6.12.82	2	Glasgow	23 Jun
	(30)						
10.65	1.4	Graham Beasley		24.10.77	5	Eton	7 Jul
10.65	0.8	Kevin Ellis		18.06.76	3	Bedford	18 Jul
10.68	0.8	Mark Hylton		24.09.76	6r1	Fullerton CA, USA	26 Apr
10.68	0.0	Jamie Henthorn		20.02.77	1	Glasgow (S)	6 May
10.69	1.1	Tim Abeyie	U20	7.11.82	2h3	Bedford	30 Jun
10.69	1.8	Nick Thomas	U23	4.04.79	4h4	Birmingham	13 Jul
10.70	-1.0	Brian Doyle		12.03.77	8	Tula, RUS	8 Jun
10.70		David Samuyiwa		4.08.72	1	Lyngby, DEN	9 Jun
10.70	2.0	Kevin Williams		15.12.71	4h2	Birmingham	13 Jul
10.70	-0.1	Laurence Oboh	U20	14.05.84	4	Dole, FRA	29 Jul
	(40)						
10.71		J. Joseph			1	Aldershot	26 Jul
10.72	2.0	Terence Stamp		18.02.70	5h2	Birmingham	13 Jul
10.72	-0.7	Dean Macey		12.12.77	1D1	Edmonton, CAN	6 Aug
10.74	1.6	Richard Knowles		12.11.75	3	Birmingham	16 Jun
10.74	1.7	Daniel Plummer	U23	4.01.81	1rC	Bedford	18 Jul
10.76		Mark Hanson	U23	13.05.81	2h1	London (Ha)	16 Jun
10.76	0.7	Uvie Ugono		8.03.78	2rB	Eton	7 Jul
10.77	-1.0	Julian Golding		17.02.75	7	Braga, POR	4 Jul
10.77	1.1	Gary Jones		6.01.72	4rC	Bedford	18 Jul
10.78	1.6	Clive Turner	U17	24.11.84	1s3	Sheffield	11 Aug
	(50)						

10.79	-0.7	Jamie Baulch		3.05.73	5r3	Austin TX, USA	5 May
10.79		James Chatt	U23	11.02.80	3h1	London (Ha)	16 Jun
10.79	1.4	John Stewart	U23	30.12.79	8	Eton	7 Jul
10.81	1.5	Phillips Idowu		30.12.78	2rB	London (He)	5 May
10.81		Aiah Yambasu		10.11.73	3h2	London (Ha)	16 Jun
10.81	1.6	Steve Buttler		20.02.75	5	Birmingham	16 Jun
10.81	0.7	Gavin Eastman	U23	28.06.80	1	Derby	29 Jul
10.81	1.7	Matthew Ouche	U17	6.03.85	2s1	Sheffield	11 Aug
10.82	1.7	Steven Fowles	U17	16.05.85	3s1	Sheffield	11 Aug
10.83	1.1	Tim Ward	U20	27.05.82	3h3	Bedford	30 Jun
	(60)						
10.83	0.4	Jamie McNiel	U17	23.11.84	1	Tullamore, IRL	21 Jul
10.83	1.5	Chris Tomlinson	U23	15.09.81	2	Cudworth	26 Aug
10.84	1.8	Tim Barton		3.10.70	6h4	Birmingham	13 Jul
10.85	1.6	Henry Richards	U23	15.05.81	6	Birmingham	16 Jun
10.85		Graham Hedman	U23	6.02.79	1	Watford	25 Jul
10.85	1.6	James Ellington	U17	6.09.85	2s3	Sheffield	11 Aug
10.87	2.0	Nathan Honour		15.11.77	6h2	Birmingham	13 Jul
10.87	1.9	Scott Exley		9.02.78	1D	Bedford	4 Aug
10.87	1.6	Leon Baptiste	U17	23.05.85	3s3	Sheffield	11 Aug
10.87	0.7	Matthew Thomas		27.04.76	5rB	Jarrow	18 Aug
	(70)						
10.87	1.5	Darren Scott		7.03.69	3	Cudworth	26 Aug
10.88		Essop Merrick		24.05.74	2	Watford	27 Jun
10.88	0.3	Michael Smith	U23	3.06.79	2	Derby	29 Jul
10.89		Anthony Noel		8.09.63	2	Watford	25 Jul
10.90	0.0	John Jordan	U23	18.01.81	4	Glasgow	6 May
10.90	0.2	Marlon Dickson		17.11.78	1h4	London (Ha)	16 Jun
10.90	0.8	Adebowale Ademuyewo	U20	14.05.83	3h2	Exeter	6 Jul
10.90	0.6	Lawrence Baird		14.12.77	1	Stretford	28 Aug
10.91		Ricky Alfred		20.12.77	1rB	Bedford	28 Jul
10.92	1.3	Alastair Gordon		16.04.78	1	Birmingham	30 Jun
	(80)						
10.93	1.1	Darren Thompson	U23	6.11.79	8	London (He)	5 May
10.93	1.7	Andrew Matthews	U17	26.10.84	2s2	Sheffield	11 Aug
10.94		William Pobie		6.12.78	4h2	London (Ha)	16 Jun
10.95	0.9	Christopher Hamilton		4.11.78	1	Scunthorpe	18 Aug
10.95		Dominic Girdler	U20	6.03.82	1	Tamworth	27 Aug
10.96	0.7	Monu Miah	U20	10.01.84	1h3	Watford	27 May
10.96	-0.2	Dominique Richards	U23	12.09.79	4s2	London (Ha)	16 Jun
10.97	1.6	Lewis Kite	U23	23.11.79	7	Birmingham	17 Jun
10.97	1.3	Mensah Elliott		29.08.76	3	Birmingham	30 Jun
10.97	2.0	Gavin Neblett	U23	27.12.79	7h2	Birmingham	13 Jul
	(90)						
10.97	0.3	Leroy Slue	U23	11.12.81	1	London (BP)	22 Aug
10.97		Richard Rubenis		10.11.73	1	Tamworth	27 Aug
10.98	1.6	Jared Deacon		15.10.75	5r2	Fullerton CA, USA	26 Apr
10.98	0.7	Ugochi Anomelechi	U20	29.10.83	2	Watford	27 May
10.98		David Pratt		23.11.75	2	Bedford	11 Jul
10.98	0.3	Dominic Papura	U23	12.02.81	3	Derby	29 Jul
10.99	1.4	Philip Ellershaw		9.02.76	4rB	Birmingham	30 Jun
10.99	1.7	Lloyd Rice	U17	13.02.85	3s2	Sheffield	11 Aug
10.99	1.8	Andrew Whitmore	U17	8.02.85	1h2	London (He)	26 Aug

wind assisted

9.97 *		Mark Lewis-Francis	U20	(10.12)	1q3	Edmonton, CAN	4 Aug
		10.09 2.4			1	Grosseto, ITA	20 Jul
		10.25 2.2			4	Glasgow (S)	1 Jul
		10.28 2.1			1	Birmingham	2 Jun

9.97 *		Dwain Chambers		(9.99)	1q4	Edmonton, CAN	4 Aug
		10.13 2.2			2	Glasgow (S)	1 Jul
		10.14 2.8			1	Kalamata, GRE	2 Jun
10.09 *		Christian Malcolm	U23	(10.11)	2q5	Edmonton, CAN	4 Aug
		10.19 2.3			1r1	Arles, FRA	9 Jun
		10.21 2.2			1h1	Birmingham	13 Jul
10.13	3.8	Jon Barbour	U23	(10.28)	1	Bedford	30 Jun
		10.24 2.6			1	Bedford	27 May
		10.26 2.2			1	Amsterdam, NED	13 Jul
		10.27 2.8			1	Nitra, SVK	25 Aug
		10.29 4.5			1h2	Bedford	30 Jun
10.17	4.3	Tyrone Edgar	U20	(10.49)	1	Bedford	30 Jun
		10.24 5.9			1	Bangor, NI	2 Jun
		10.35 2.4			4	Grosseto, ITA	20 Jul
10.19	2.2	Ian Mackie		(10.30)	3	Glasgow (S)	1 Jul
10.22	4.3	Dwayne Grant	U20	(10.47)	2	Bedford	30 Jun
		10.26 4.2			1	Ipswich	2 Sep
10.26	2.5	Doug Turner		(10.37)	1	Budapest, HUN	1 Jul
		10.32 5.9			2	Bangor, NI	2 Jun
10.29	2.6	Marlon Devonish		(10.30)	2	Bedford	27 May
		10.39 2.2			1s2	Bedford	27 May
10.29	2.2	Doug Bignall		(10.30)	2h1	Birmingham	13 Jul
10.30	3.8	Lambert	U23	(10.24)	2	Bedford	30 Jun
		10.35 2.8			1h1	Bedford	30 Jun
10.31	4.3	Aidan Syers	U20	(10.52)	3	Bedford	30 Jun
10.33	2.7	Daniel Money		(10.46)	2rB	Glasgow (S)	1 Jul
10.36	5.9	Tim Benjamin	U20	(10.57)	4	Bangor, NI	2 Jun
		10.36 4.3			4	Bedford	30 Jun
		32 performances to 10.40 by 14 athletes					
10.42	4.2	Tim Abeyie	U20	(10.69)	2	Ipswich	2 Sep
10.43	2.6	Jason Fergus		11.10.73	3	Bedford	27 May
10.43	4.5	Gavin Eastman	U23	(10.81)	2h2	Bedford	30 Jun
10.43	3.8	Jonathon Oparka	U23	(10.61)	3	Bedford	30 Jun
10.50	2.8	Jamie Henthorn		(10.68)	2r3	Arles, FRA	9 Jun
10.50	4.5	Michael Smith	U23	(10.88)	3h2	Bedford	30 Jun
10.51	4.3	Nick Smith	U20	(10.65)	5	Bedford	30 Jun
10.58	3.8	James Chatt	U23	(10.79)	6	Bedford	30 Jun
10.60	2.6	Gary Jones		(10.77)	8	Bedford	27 May
10.60	2.6	Mark Hanson	U23	(10.76)	3s2	Bedford	30 Jun
10.60	5.0	Matthew Ouche	U17	(10.81)	1	Exeter	7 Jul
10.61	2.3	Kevin Williams		(10.70)	4r2	Arles, FRA	9 Jun
10.61	3.4	Chris Tomlinson	U23	(10.83)	2h3	Bedford	30 Jun
10.63	2.1	Dan Donovan		(10.64)	4	Birmingham	2 Jun
10.63	4.3	Tim Ward	U20	(10.83)	7	Bedford	30 Jun
10.64	5.9	Monu Miah	U20	(10.96)	2	Bangor, NI	2 Jun
10.64	2.2	Graham Beasley		(10.65)	4h1	Birmingham	13 Jul
10.66	2.7	Laurence Oboh	U20	(10.70)	2	Exeter	7 Jul
10.67	2.2	Dominique Richards	U23	(10.96)	5s2	Bedford	27 May
10.67	4.5	Iwan Thomas		5.01.74	2rB	Bangor, NI	2 Jun
10.68	2.1	Uvie Ugono		(10.76)	4h3	Birmingham	13 Jul
10.69	5.0	Clive Turner	U17	(10.78)	2	Exeter	7 Jul
10.70	4.5	Dominic Papura	U23	(10.98)	5h2	Bedford	30 Jun
10.70	4.5	William Pobie		(10.94)	4h2	Bedford	30 Jun
10.70	3.9	Henry Richards	U23	(10.85)	2h4	Bedford	30 Jun
10.71	4.2	Karl Forde	U20	15.04.83	3	Ipswich	2 Sep
10.76	5.0	Jamie McNiel	U17	(10.83)	3	Exeter	7 Jul
10.77	2.2	Colin Wilson		30.10.77	6h1	Birmingham	13 Jul

10.78	2.7	Adebowale Ademuyewo	U20	(10.90)	3	Exeter	7 Jul
10.78	2.9	Scott Exley		(10.87)	1D	Bedford	14 Jul
10.78	2.2	Steven Fowles	U17	(10.82)	2	Sheffield	11 Aug
10.81	3.6	Luke Davis	U23	1.01.80	4B	Birmingham	2 Jun
10.82	2.1	Leon McRae	U23	3.11.80	6	Birmingham	2 Jun
10.82	2.2	Andrew Whitmore	U17	(10.99)	2	London (He)	26 Aug
10.84 w?		Finlay Wright	U23	7.02.81	1	New Haven, USA	14 Apr
10.84	2.4	John Jordan	U23	(10.90)	1s3	Glasgow	6 May
10.84	3.9	Craig Telford	U23	1.06.79	4h4	Bedford	30 Jun
10.87	5.0	Ross O'Donovan	U17	12.03.86	4	Exeter	7 Jul
10.88	4.3	James Moore	U20	18.11.83	8	Bedford	30 Jun
10.88	2.9	Andrew Lewis		9.03.68	2D	Bedford	14 Jul
10.89	3.3	Philip Ellershaw		(10.99)	4	Liverpool	17 Jun
10.89	3.4	Michael Bourne	U23	18.09.79	4h3	Bedford	30 Jun
10.90	2.7	Jason Harding	U20	24.09.82	4	Exeter	6 Jul
10.92		Rob Harle	U23	1.06.79	2	New Haven, USA	14 Apr
10.93	2.4	Ken Campbell		30.09.72	3h1	Glasgow (S)	23 Jun
10.94	2.1	Andrew Walcott		11.01.75	7	Birmingham	2 Jun
10.94	2.8	Ben Ellis	U23	16.11.81	5h1	Bedford	30 Jun
10.94	3.9	Edwin Grey	U23	23.03.81	5h4	Bedford	30 Jun
10.95	3.3	Phil Kerry	U20	19.03.83	4h2	Bedford	30 Jun
10.95	4.2	Peter Vickers	U20	11.06.84	5	Ipswich	2 Sep
10.96	3.3	Ugochi Anomelechi	U20	(10.98)	5h2	Bedford	30 Jun
10.96	2.2	Nathan Douglas	U20	4.12.82	3	London (He)	26 Aug
10.97	3.4	Lloyd Rice	U17	(10.99)	2s3	Exeter	7 Jul
10.98	3.3	Martin Roberts	U20	20.09.83	6h2	Bedford	30 Jun

hand timing

10.3 w	4.7	Barbour	U23	(10.28)	1h2	Bedford	27 May
		10.3 w 2.4			1s1	Bedford	30 Jun
10.3 w	4.9	Dwayne Grant	U20	(10.47)	1s1	Bedford	30 Jun
		10.4			2	London (BP)	20 Jun
10.4	1.2	Mackie		(10.30)	1	Grangemouth	17 Jun
10.4	1.9	Tyrone Edgar	U20	(10.49)	1s2	Bedford	30 Jun
10.4 w	2.6	Jason Fergus		(10.43w)	1h1	Southend	12 May
		10.7 1.2			1h4	Bedford	27 May
		7 performances to 10.4 by 5 athletes including 4 wind assisted					
10.5		Darren Chin	U23	(10.52)	1	London (B)	9 Sep
10.5 w	2.6	Mark Brown		3.11.76	2h1	Southend	12 May
10.6		David Samuyiwa		(10.70)	1	Bournemouth	12 May
10.6	1.2	Jonathon Oparka	U23	(10.61)	2	Grangemouth	17 Jun
10.6		Tim Abeyie	U20	(10.69)	1	Guildford	29 Jul
10.6 w		Chris Tomlinson	U23	(10.83)	1	Grimsby	5 May
10.6 w	2.9	Kevin Ellis		(10.65)	1	Liverpool	5 May
10.6 w		Terence Stamp		(10.72)	1h2	Southend	12 May
10.6 w		Nick Thomas	U23	(10.69)	2h2	Southend	12 May
10.6 w		Ben Ellis	U23	(10.94w)	1	Basildon	2 Jun
10.6 w		Lewis Kite	U23	(10.97)	2	Gloucester	9 Jun
10.6 w?		J. Joseph		(10.71)	1h	Portsmouth (RN)	27 Jun
10.7		Nathan Honour		(10.87)	1	Ashford	5 May
10.7		James Chatt	U23	(10.79)	1	Ashford	12 May
10.7	1.0	Dominique Richards	U23	(10.96)	1	Kingston	12 May
10.7	0.6	Gary Jones		(10.77)	3h3	Bedford	27 May
10.7		Adam Potter	U23	12.04.80	1	St. Peter Port GUE	2 Jun
10.7	-0.9	Marlon Dickson		(10.90)	2	London (BP)	6 Jun
10.7		Uvie Ugono		(10.76)	6	London (BP)	20 Jun
10.7		Adam Charlton	U20	11.05.84	1	London (Col)	21 Jul

10.7		Daniel Plummer	U23	(10.74)	1	Guildford	21 Jul
10.7	1.9	Anthony Noel		(10.89)	1	Eton	15 Aug
10.7 w	2.9	Ricky Alfred		(10.91)	3	Liverpool	5 May
10.7 w	4.4	Paul Slythe		5.09.74	1h1	Ashford	12 May
		10.8			2	Ashford	12 May
10.7 w		Mark Hanson	U23	(10.76)	1	Loughborough	16 May
10.7 w		Howard Frost	U23	9.12.81	1	London (Cat)	29 May
10.8		Ian Clarke		6.11.72	1	Watford	25 Apr
10.8		Rob Harle	U23	(10.92w)	1	St. Ives	12 May
10.8	-0.5	Gavin Eastman	U23	(10.81)	1	London (He)	12 May
10.8		Cori Henry		9.12.76	1	Nottingham	13 May
10.8		Michael Smith	U23	(10.88)	1	Bolton	20 May
10.8	1.1	Matthew Ouche	U17	(10.81)	3	Watford	26 May
10.8		Andrew Morey		16.01.72	1	Stevenage	2 Jun
10.8	-0.2	Aiah Yambasu		(10.81)	4	London (Ha)	10 Jun
10.8	1.3	Will MacGee		9.06.68	1	London (FP)	11 Jun
10.8		William Pobie		(10.94)	1rB	London (TB)	24 Jun
10.8	1.9	Tim Ward	U20	(10.83)	4s2	Bedford	30 Jun
10.8	1.8	Philip Ellershaw		(10.99)	1	Jarrow	7 Jul
10.8		Colin Wilson		(10.77w)	1	London (PH)	7 Jul
10.8		Sam Omonua		16.06.76	2	Guildford	21 Jul
10.8		Brian Darby		14.10.72	1rB	Yate	21 Jul
10.8		Alastair Gordon		(10.92)	1rB	Woodford	21 Jul
10.8		Tim Barton		(10.84)	1	Yate	21 Jul
10.8		Dominic Papura	U23	(10.98)	1	Gloucester	4 Aug
10.8		Leroy Slue	U23	(10.97)	1	London (TB)	14 Aug
10.8		Stuart Benson	U23	12.02.81	1	Glasgow (S)	9 Sep
10.8 w		Ugochi Anomelechi	U20	(10.98)	2	Ashford	5 May
10.8 w	5.5	Ray Salami		11.04.75	3h1	Kingston	12 May
10.8 w		Andy Turner	U23	19.09.80	2	Loughborough	16 May
10.8 w		Steve Surety	U23	18.02.80	3	Loughborough	16 May
10.8 w	4.7	Jonathan Carleton	U23	4.11.79	2h2	Bedford	27 May
10.8 w	2.9	Andrew Parker	U23	1.08.80	2	Cardiff	2 Jun
10.8 w		Phil Kerry	U20	(10.95w)	1	Leamington	9 Jun
10.8 w	3.4	Christopher Hamilton		(10.95)	2h2	Liverpool	17 Jun
10.8 w	2.4	Finlay Wright	U23	(10.84w)	6s1	Bedford	30 Jun
10.8 w		Russell Frost	U23	23.06.80	2	London (Cat)	29 May

unknown athlete/wrong name

10.7		G. Mbirh			1rB	Portsmouth	21 Jul

doubtful timing

10.5		Ken Campbell		(10.93w)	1h3	Melbourne, AUS	3 Feb
10.6 w		Andrew Parker	U23	(10.8w)	1	Gloucester	9 Jun
10.7 w		Anthony Mayo		8.07.74	3	Gloucester	9 Jun

Additional Juniors

10.9		Stephen Gordon		14.02.83	1	Dundee	20 Jun
10.9		Lloyd Rice	U17	(10.99)	2	Yate	21 Jul
10.9		Gary Carr		24.09.82	1	Bournemouth	4 Aug
10.9		Robert Tobin		20.12.83	2	Worthing	4 Aug
10.9		Paul Whitehouse		10.03.83		Nuneaton	5 Aug
10.9 w		David Riley	U17	25.10.84	1	Gateshead	9 Jun
10.9 w	4.9	Alex Riley		17.09.83	6	Bedford	30 Jun

Additional Under 17 (1 - 12 above)

11.0		Jamie Gill		29.10.85	1	Halesowen	6 May
		11.11 w 2.2			2h8	Sheffield	11 Aug
		11.19 1.7			5s2	Sheffield	11 Aug
11.0		Fabian Collymore		19.10.84	2	Southend	12 May
11.0		Stuart Haley		9.12.84	1	Gateshead	20 May
11.0	1.1	Matt Barclay		1.11.84	4	Watford	26 May
11.0		Richard Davenport		12.09.85	2	Gloucester	4 Aug
11.0		Ryan de Haaff		9.11.84	1	Guernsey	31 Aug
11.0		Simon Farenden		6.10.85	1	Cleckheaton	16 Sep
11.00 w	2.4	Craig Pickering	U15	16.10.86	1	Sheffield	11 Aug
		11.12 1.3			1s1	Sheffield	11 Aug
	(20)						
11.0 w		Paul Newark		3.10.84	1h1	Ashford	12 May
		11.1			2	Ashford	12 May
11.0 w		Tom Carroll		3.05.85	1	Jarrow	18 Jul
11.0 w		Warren Prince		18.03.85	1	Rugby	18 Aug
11.01	1.7	Ross O'Donovan		(10.87w)	4s2	Sheffield	11 Aug
11.01 w	5.0	Justin Hoyte		20.11.84	8	Exeter	7 Jul
11.02	0.0	David Grieves		17.11.84	1	Sunderland	6 May
11.06 w	3.0	Peter Harpham		2.11.84	2h3	Sheffield	11 Aug
		11.18 1.6			4s3	Sheffield	11 Aug
11.07 w	4.4	Wade Bennett-Jackson	U15	27.02.87	1	Exeter	7 Jul
		11.50 1.2			2h2	Exeter	6 Jul
11.08		D. Whittaker			1	Warrington	1 Apr
11.08		Ryan James		10.05.85	1	Tamworth	27 Aug
	(30)						
11.09 w	4.4	Frank N'Goran	U15	22.07.87	3	Exeter	7 Jul
		11.33 1.3			1h4	Exeter	6 Jul
11.09 w	4.4	Chinedum Onuoha	U15	12.11.86	2	Exeter	7 Jul
		11.3 -0.8			1	Stoke-on-Trent	16 Jun
		11.35 0.0			1h1	Exeter	6 Jul
11.09 w	3.0	Julian Thomas	U15	28.12.86	1s2	Sheffield	11 Aug
		11.1			1	Yate	1 Jul
		11.23 -0.8			1	Birmingham	27 May
11.10	-0.7	Alex Stones		17.09.84	2	Birmingham	26 May
11.1		Adam Robson		6.11.85	2	Jarrow	5 May
11.1		U. Trocey			1rB	London (Nh)	6 May
11.1		Alex Animashaun		23.07.85	1	Harrow	22 May
		11.17 w 3.3			5h2	Exeter	6 Jul
11.1		Edward Dunford		15.09.84	1	Leamington	16 Jun
11.1		Steven Harvey		24.01.85	1	Bingham	1 Jul
11.1		Joseph Samuel		27.12.84	1	Linwood	6 Sep
	(40)						
11.1		Daniel Gould		9.11.84	1	Bury St. Edmunds	16 Sep
11.11 w	4.4	Sosthene Yao	U15	7.08.87	4	Exeter	7 Jul
		11.4			1	London (BP)	9 Jun
		11.43 1.2			1h2	Exeter	6 Jul
11.11 w	3.0	Jamahl Alert-Khan	U15	12.09.86	2s2	Sheffield	11 Aug
		11.17 1.1			1h6	Sheffield	11 Aug
11.12 w	2.4	Alex Coley		8.02.86	2h5	Sheffield	11 Aug
		11.13 1.7			4s1	Sheffield	11 Aug
11.16 w	4.4	Alex Nelson	U15	21.03.88	6	Exeter	7 Jul
		11.4			2	Yate	1 Jul
11.16 w	4.2	David Aguirreburualde		29.11.85	2h7	Sheffield	11 Aug
11.17 w	4.4	Theo Wedderburn	U15	1.01.88	1	St. Ives	12 May
		11.29 1.9			1	London (He)	26 Aug
11.18 w	3.0	Paul Judson		20.06.86	3h3	Sheffield	11 Aug
11.18 w	2.4	Danny Holland		7.11.84	3h5	Sheffield	11 Aug
11.18 w	2.4	Chris Musa	U15	5.12.86	3	Sheffield	11 Aug
		11.26 1.3			2s1	Sheffield	11 Aug

Additional Under 15 (1 - 13 above)

11.19 w 2.2	Andrew Watkins	8.12.87	1	Cardiff	17	Jun
	11.29 1.4		1	Connah's Quay	4	Aug
11.19 w 4.4	James Davies	29.09.86	8	Exeter	7	Jul
	11.49 0.0		2s2	Exeter	7	Jul
11.2 w	Ryan Scott	20.02.87	1	Yate	2	Sep
	11.35 w 3.0		5s2	Sheffield	11	Aug
	11.5		2	Stoke-on-Trent	16	Jun
11.24 w 3.0	Steve Hunter	22.12.86	4s2	Sheffield	11	Aug
	11.40 1.5		1h5	Sheffield	11	Aug
11.27 w 2.2	James Boreham	27.11.86	2	Cardiff	17	Jun
	11.58 -2.3		2	Cardiff	6	Jul
11.30 w	Andrew Bartlett	17.02.87	2	Bedford	9	Sep
	11.36 1.1		2h6	Sheffield	11	Aug
11.38 1.5	Marimba Odundo-Mendez	30.09.86	1h3	Sheffield	11	Aug
(20)						
11.4	Scott Masters	29.11.86	1	Telford	22	Jul
11.4 w	Rikki Storey	25.09.86	1	Yate	1	Jul
11.43 w	Stephen Thompson	5.09.86	2	Antrim	9	Jun
	11.48 1.5		2h3	Sheffield	11	Aug
11.5	Gary Atkinson	7.01.87	1	Cudworth	6	May
11.5	Uche Odouza		1	Exeter	16	Jun
11.5 0.8	Jonathan Sherratt	18.10.86	3	Stoke-on-Trent	16	Jun
11.5	Set Osho	28.09.86	1	Enfield	22	Jul
11.5	Alan Wilson	12.10.86	1	Glasgow (S)	9	Sep
11.5 w	Ben Lavender	25.12.86	1	Jarrow	18	Jul
11.51 w 4.4	Ryan Thomas	21.03.87	3h2	Sheffield	11	Aug
(30)						
11.52 -0.6	Chris Julien	14.09.87	2	Birmingham	2	Sep
11.57 w 3.9	Harold Buchanan	13.10.86	1h2	Cudworth	26	May

Under 13

12.2	David Pitt	1.09.88	1	Stourport	10	Jun
12.3	Josh Baxter	15.09.88	1	Reading	3	Jun
12.5	Ricardo Francis	26.11.88	1	Middlesbrough	20	May
12.5	Ani Zamani	17.09.88	1	Harrow	1	Jul
12.6	Daniel Edwards-Palmer	19.09.88	1	London (Col)	3	Jun
12.6	Richard Batten	12.10.88	1	Enfield	22	Jul

Foreign

10.36 w 5.9	*John McAdorey (IRL)*	*16.09.74*	*3*	*Bangor, NI*	*2*	*Jun*
	10.46 0.9		*1r2*	*Geneva, SUI*	*9*	*Jun*
10.5 w 4.7	*Nicholas Hogan (IRL) U23*	*15.10.80*	*3s2*	*Bedford*	*27*	*May*
	10.55 w 2.2		*3s2*	*Bedford*	*7*	*May*
	10.7		*1*	*Reading*	*12*	*May*
10.59 0.5	*Paul Brizzel (IRL)*	*3.10.76*	*8*	*Vaasa, FIN*	*23*	*Jun*
10.76	*Joselyn Thomas (SLE)*	*11.07.71*	*2*	*Aldershot*	*26*	*Aug*
11.55 1.5	*Takayuki Homma (JPN)U15*	*19.02.87*	*2h5*	*Sheffield*	*11*	*Aug*

200 Metres

20.08	1.0	Christian Malcolm	U23	3.06.79	1s1	Edmonton, CAN	8 Aug
		20.09 0.1			3	Brussels, BEL	24 Aug
		20.13 1.2			1q1	Edmonton, CAN	7 Aug
		20.22 0.1			5	Edmonton, CAN	9 Aug
		20.24 -1.1			2	Zurich, SUI	17 Aug
		20.37 -0.6			1h5	Edmonton, CAN	7 Aug
		20.40 0.1			1	Helsinki, FIN	14 Jun
		20.45 -0.6			2	London (CP)	22 Jul
		20.47 0.0			2	Gateshead	19 Aug
		20.55 1.0			4	Melbourne, AUS	9 Sep
		20.58 i			1	Birmingham	18 Feb
		20.60 0.7			2	Villeneuve d'Ascq, FRA	17 Jun
		20.63 -1.0			1	Loughborough	20 May
		20.63 0.6			2	Birmingham	15 Jul
		20.76 i			1s1	Lisbon, POR	9 Mar
		20.76 i			2	Lisbon, POR	10 Mar
		20.77 1.4			1h3	Birmingham	14 Jul
		20.77 -0.2			5	Brisbane, AUS	6 Sep
		20.99 i			1	Glasgow	18 Mar
		(20.46 i dsq			(1)	Lievin, FRA	25 Feb)
20.29	0.7	Marlon Devonish		1.06.76	4s2	Edmonton, CAN	8 Aug
		20.38 0.1			8	Edmonton, CAN	9 Aug
		20.40 0.0			1	Poznan, POL	8 Jun
		20.44 1.1			3q2	Edmonton, CAN	7 Aug
		20.47 0.3			2	Thessaloniki, GRE	22 Aug
		20.50 0.1			8	Brussels, BEL	24 Aug
		20.52 1.8			1	Hengelo, NED	4 Jun
		20.52 0.6			1	Birmingham	15 Jul
		20.55 1.1			1h1	Birmingham	14 Jul
		20.55 -0.6			4	London (CP)	22 Jul
		20.58 -1.6			2h3	Edmonton, CAN	7 Aug
		20.59 -0.7			2	Bremen, GER	24 Jun
		20.61 0.7			3	Villeneuve d'Ascq, FRA	17 Jun
		20.74 -0.2			4	Brisbane, AUS	6 Sep
		20.75 0.0			4	Gateshead	19 Aug
		20.82 -0.3			1rB	Loughborough	20 May
		20.89 0.1			2	Kalamata, GRE	2 Jun
20.31	-0.6	Dwain Chambers		5.04.78	1	London (CP)	22 Jul
		20.60 -1.4			5q4	Edmonton, CAN	7 Aug
		20.65 0.6			3	Birmingham	15 Jul
		20.79 1.1			1h2	Birmingham	14 Jul
		20.80 1.0			4h2	Edmonton, CAN	7 Aug
		20.90 -0.3			2rB	Loughborough	20 May
20.41	1.7	Darren Campbell		12.09.73	1r1	Austin TX, USA	5 May
20.54	1.3	Doug Turner		2.12.66	1	Cardiff	17 Jun
		20.75 0.6			4	Birmingham	15 Jul
		20.87 0.1			1	Byrkjelo, NOR	22 Jul
		20.91 0.9			1	Edinburgh	25 Aug
		20.93 i			2	Birmingham	28 Jan
		20.94 i			1s1	Birmingham	28 Jan
20.60 i		Allyn Condon		24.08.74	1	Birmingham	28 Jan
		20.63 i			2	Birmingham	18 Feb
		20.72 i			2rB	Lievin, FRA	25 Feb
		20.85 i			1s3	Birmingham	28 Jan
		20.93 i			2h1	Lisbon, POR	9 Mar
		20.99 1.8			3	Hengelo, NED	4 Jun

20.64	0.6	Dwayne Grant	U20	17.07.82	1r2	Mannheim, GER	16 Jun
		20.90 0.9			1	Birmingham	2 Jun
		20.92 0.8			3	Grosseto, ITA	21 Jul
		20.96 2.0			1h2	Bedford	1 Jul
20.67	1.3	Tim Benjamin	U20	2.05.82	2	Cardiff	17 Jun
		20.78 i			1	Birmingham	24 Feb
		20.86 i			1s2	Birmingham	24 Feb
		20.98 1.1			3h1	Birmingham	14 Jul
		20.99 i			2	Glasgow	18 Mar
20.78	1.8	Jon Barbour	U23	3.11.80	1	Nitra, SVK	25 Aug
		20.95 2.0			1s2	Bedford	28 May
20.81	1.1	Julian Golding		17.02.75	2h1	Birmingham	14 Jul
		20.85 -0.6			2	Funchal, POR	30 Jun
20.84	0.0	Chris Lambert	U23	6.04.81	1h4	Beijing, CHN	30 Aug
		20.87 1.4			2q2	Beijing, CHN	30 Aug
20.85	1.2	Ian Mackie		27.02.75	1	Glasgow (S)	24 Jun
20.96	0.4	Tyrone Edgar	U20	29.03.82	2r3	Mannheim, GER	16 Jun
20.99	-1.0	Daniel Money		17.10.76	2	Loughborough	20 May

73 performances to 21.00 by 14 athletes including 14 indoors and 1 dsq

21.02 i		Jamie Baulch		3.05.73	2s3	Birmingham	28 Jan
21.05	1.8	Daniel Caines	U23	15.05.79	4	Hengelo, NED	4 Jun
21.09	2.0	Doug Walker ¶		28.07.73	3s2	Bedford	28 May
21.10	0.9	Mark Hylton		24.09.76	4r1	Fullerton CA, USA	26 Apr
21.14 A	0.0	Iwan Thomas		5.01.74	7	Potchefstroom, RSA	12 Feb
21.18	1.1	Graham Beasley		24.10.77	4h1	Birmingham	14 Jul
	(20)						
21.20	1.4	Brian Doyle		12.03.77	3h3	Birmingham	14 Jul
21.26	1.8	Richard Knowles		12.11.75	1rB	Jarrow	18 Aug
21.29	1.2	Kris Stewart	U23	11.04.80	3	Glasgow (S)	24 Jun
21.30	2.0	Brendon Ghent		7.09.76	5s2	Bedford	28 May
21.30	-0.1	Laurence Oboh	U20	14.05.84	2	Dole, FRA	29 Jul
21.30	1.8	Jared Deacon		15.10.75	2rB	Jarrow	18 Aug
21.31	-0.7	Mark Richardson ¶		26.07.72	2	Cardiff	8 Jul
21.37 i		Jamie Henthorn		20.02.77	2s1	Birmingham	28 Jan
		21.51 1.3			3	Cardiff	17 Jun
21.40	0.9	Dan Donovan		8.10.70	5	Birmingham	2 Jun
21.40	1.1	Doug Bignall		20.10.74	4h2	Birmingham	14 Jul
	(30)						
21.46	2.0	Simon Farenden	U17	6.10.85	1	Exeter	7 Jul
21.48 i		John Stewart	U23	30.12.79	1r1	Birmingham	11 Feb
		21.60 1.8			4rB	Jarrow	18 Aug
21.48	0.9	Ben Lewis	U23	6.03.81	6	Birmingham	2 Jun
21.53	-1.3	James Chatt	U23	11.02.80	1	Derby	29 Jul
21.55	-0.9	Tim Abeyie	U20	7.11.82	3	Stoke-on-Trent	18 Aug
21.56		Graham Hedman	U23	6.02.79	1	Watford	25 Jul
21.57	2.0	Darren Scott		7.03.69	6s2	Bedford	28 May
21.58 i+		Du'aine Thorne-Ladejo		14.02.71	1m	Birmingham	18 Feb
21.58	1.8	Nick Smith	U20	6.12.82	3rB	Jarrow	18 Aug
21.59	1.1	Cori Henry		9.12.76	2s1	Bedford	28 May
	(40)						
21.63	2.0	Paul Campbell	U23	26.03.80	7s2	Bedford	28 May
21.64	1.1	Dominique Richards	U23	12.09.79	3s1	Bedford	28 May
21.64	-1.3	David Naismith	U23	15.12.79	3	Eton	7 Jul
21.67	-0.3	Jason Fergus		11.10.73	4rB	Loughborough	20 May
21.67	1.3	Dominic Papura	U23	12.02.81	4	Cardiff	17 Jun
21.67	2.0	David Riley	U17	25.10.84	2	Exeter	7 Jul
21.67	2.0	Rikki Fifton	U17	17.06.85	3	Exeter	7 Jul
21.72 i		Luke Davis	U23	1.01.80	1h1	Birmingham	11 Feb
21.72	0.8	Cypren Edmunds		20.06.70	4B	Izegem, BEL	9 Jun
21.72	1.4	Leon Baptiste	U17	23.05.85	1	Tullamore, IRL	22 Jul
	(50)						

21.73	1.1	Alastair Gordon		16.04.78	1	Crawley	13 May
21.73		Kevin Ellis		18.06.76	2	Bedford	28 Jul
21.76	1.4	Gary Jones		6.01.72	5h3	Birmingham	14 Jul
21.76	1.0	Matthew Ouche	U17	6.03.85	2	Murcia, ESP	26 Jul
21.81	1.1	Tim Bayley	U23	4.10.81	2	Crawley	13 May
21.82	1.6	Michael Champion		3.01.75	6rB	Jarrow	18 Aug
21.84	1.1	Nathan Honour		15.11.77	6h1	Birmingham	14 Jul
21.86		Jonathan Carleton	U23	4.11.79	3	Dublin, IRL	13 May
21.88	0.3	Robert Clay		11.05.80	1s3	Glasgow (S)	6 May
21.89 i		Mark Brown		3.11.76	2s3	Birmingham	14 Jan
	(60)						
21.89	-2.4	Finlay Wright	U23	7.02.81	5	London (Ha)	17 Jun
21.90	1.3	Mike Groves	U20	21.03.84	5	Cardiff	17 Jun
21.90		Ben Ellis	U23	16.11.81	3h1	London (Ha)	17 Jun
21.90	1.0	Kevin Williams		15.12.71	3r2	Budapest, HUN	1 Jul
21.91	2.0	Tim Ward	U20	27.05.82	3h2	Bedford	1 Jul
21.92 i		Henry Richards	U23	15.05.81	2	Birmingham	11 Feb
		22.04 0.1			3	Derby	29 Jul
21.92		Ricky Alfred		20.12.77	1	Bedford	20 May
21.92	1.5	James Bridge	U20	28.11.83	1	London (BP)	6 Jun
21.92	2.0	Paul Slythe		5.09.74	4	Bedford	21 Jul
21.94	-0.8	Peter Brend		2.02.77	3rB	Cardiff	8 Jul
	(70)						
21.94		Akinola Lashore		28.03.73	1	London (BP)	22 Aug
21.95	1.1	Marlon Dickson		17.11.78	5s1	Bedford	28 May
21.95	0.0	Ian Deeth	U23	25.06.79	4	London (BP)	20 Jun
21.95	1.5	Adam Potter	U23	12.04.80	1	Beveren, BEL	8 Sep
21.97 i		Karl Forde	U20	15.04.83	1h2	Birmingham	11 Feb
21.99		Stuart Connolly	U20	9.02.83	2	Gateshead	25 Aug
22.02	0.9	Michael Afilaka		16.11.71	7	Birmingham	2 Jun
22.02		Mark Campbell	U20	6.07.82	2	Antrim	6 Jun
22.02	1.4	Adam Charlton	U20	11.05.84	2h1	Exeter	6 Jul
22.03	1.4	Daniel Plummer	U23	4.01.81	6	Jarrow	18 Aug
	(80)						
22.05		J. Joseph			1	Aldershot	26 Jul
22.06	1.4	Martin Roberts	U20	20.09.83	3h1	Exeter	6 Jul
22.07 i		James Marshall	U23	6.02.81	1h1	Birmingham	4 Feb
22.07		Anthony Noel		8.09.63	3	Watford	25 Jul
22.08 i		Aaron Aplin	U20	25.11.83	2	Birmingham	11 Feb
		22.24 -1.3			1	Birmingham	26 May
22.08		Ryan Preddy	U20	30.01.84	1	Sutton Coldfield	21 Jul
22.09	1.9	Chris Rawlinson		19.05.72	4r2	Fullerton CA, USA	26 Apr
22.09	-0.3	Nicholas Dawson		11.05.78	5rB	Loughborough	20 May
22.09	0.0	Fola Onibije	U17	25.09.84	1h4	Exeter	6 Jul
22.09	1.6	Nick Thomas	U23	4.04.79	7=	Jarrow	18 Aug
	(90)						
22.09	0.7	Matthew Thomas		27.04.76		Jarrow	21 Aug
22.10	-1.3	Michael Smith	U23	3.06.79	4	Derby	29 Jul
22.10	0.0	Lawrence Baird		14.12.77	1	Stretford	28 Aug
22.12	2.0	Leon McRae	U23	3.11.80	6	Bedford	21 Jul
22.13	-2.4	Gavin Eastman	U23	28.06.80	7	London (Ha)	17 Jun
22.14 i		Monu Miah	U20	10.01.84	2s1	Birmingham	24 Feb
22.14	1.8	Clive Turner	U17	24.11.84	2	Maribor, SLO	22 Sep
22.15	0.7	Nange Ursell	U23	1.10.81	1rB	London (BP)	20 Jun
22.15	2.0	Mark Awanah	U20	23.09.82	4h2	Bedford	1 Jul
22.15	2.0	Daniel Cossins	U17	22.12.84	5	Exeter	7 Jul
	(100)						
22.16		Roddy Pitt	U23	4.03.81	1	Grangemouth	1 Aug
22.18	-1.6	Gavin Stephens		12.09.77	4	Glasgow (S)	6 May
22.21	-2.6	Sam Ellis	U20	23.06.82	1	Sheffield	12 May
22.21	1.6	Andrew Steele	U17	19.09.84	2	Cudworth	26 May

wind assisted

20.47	2.4	Malcolm	U23	(20.08)	2	Glasgow (S)	1 Jul
20.50	2.4	Devonish		(20.29)	3	Glasgow (S)	1 Jul
		20.67 3.2			2rB4	Walnut CA, USA	22 Apr
20.57	2.6	Turner		(20.54)	1h1	Cardiff	17 Jun
		20.87 2.7			2	Budapest, HUN	1 Jul
		20.90 4.7			2	Bangor, NI	2 Jun
20.83	3.0	Graham Beasley		(21.18)	1	Bedford	18 Jul
20.85	2.5	Benjamin	U20	(20.67)	1h2	Cardiff	17 Jun
		20.87 3.4			2	Arles, FRA	10 Jun
		20.88 4.7			1	Bangor, NI	2 Jun
20.86	2.7	Lambert	U23	(20.84)	5s1	Beijing, CHN	31 Aug
20.90	3.8	Grant	U20	(20.64)	1	Ipswich	2 Sep
20.92	2.1	Daniel Money		(20.99)	1	London (He)	5 May
20.93	2.6	Jamie Baulch		3.05.73	2r2	Austin TX, USA	5 May
		14 performances to 21.00 by 9 athletes					
21.13	3.1	Ben Lewis	U23	(21.48)	1	Birmingham	17 Jun
21.14	3.1	Brendon Ghent		(21.30)	2	Birmingham	17 Jun
21.25	4.7	Iwan Thomas		(21.14A)	4	Bangor, NI	2 Jun
21.31	3.8	Tim Abeyie	U20	(21.55)	2	Ipswich	2 Sep
21.43	3.3	Sean Baldock		3.12.76	1r2	London (He)	5 May
21.48	3.4	Rikki Fifton	U17	(21.67)	1	Sheffield	12 Aug
21.53	2.3	Nick Thomas	U23	(22.09)	1rB	Bedford	18 Jul
21.59	4.1	Leon McRae	U23	(22.12)	3rB	Birmingham	2 Jun
21.59	2.3	Gary Jones		(21.76)	1rC	Bedford	18 Jul
21.61	2.6	Dominic Papura	U23	(21.67)	2h1	Cardiff	17 Jun
21.66	3.3	Akinola Lashore		(21.94)	3r2	London (He)	5 May
21.66	2.6	Martin Roberts	U20	(22.06)	2	Exeter	7 Jul
21.66	2.6	Adam Charlton	U20	(22.02)	3	Exeter	7 Jul
21.66	2.3	Daniel Plummer	U23	(22.03)	2rB	Bedford	18 Jul
21.67	2.4	Chris Rawlinson		(22.09)	2r2	Azusa, USA	14 Apr
21.68	4.1	Michael Champion		(21.82)	4rB	Birmingham	2 Jun
21.73	2.3	Brian Darby		14.10.72	3rB	Bedford	18 Jul
21.74	2.1	Alex Fugallo		28.01.70	7r1	London (He)	5 May
21.74	2.6	Daniel Brandwood	U20	1.10.82	4	Exeter	7 Jul
21.76	3.3	Dominic Bradley		22.12.76	4r2	London (He)	5 May
21.77	2.1	Nicholas Dawson		(22.09)	8r1	London (He)	5 May
21.80	3.3	Ryan Palmer	U20	21.06.83	5rB	London (He)	5 May
21.82	4.4	Steve Webb		17.07.78	2	Liverpool	17 Jun
21.85	2.3	Geoff Dearman		4.08.77	6rB	Bedford	18 Jul
21.89	2.6	John Kelley	U20	6.08.84	5	Exeter	7 Jul
21.90	2.6	James Bridge	U20	(21.92)	6	Exeter	7 Jul
21.94	3.4	James Ellington	U17	6.09.85	2	Sheffield	12 Aug
21.97	3.1	Steve Buttler		20.02.75	3	Birmingham	17 Jun
21.99	4.4	Philip Ellershaw		9.02.76	3	Liverpool	17 Jun
22.03	2.9	Julian Thomas	U15	28.12.86	1	Exeter	7 Jul
22.05	3.8	Alex Riley	U20	17.09.83	3	Ipswich	2 Sep
22.08	3.8	Dominic Girdler	U20	6.03.82	4	Ipswich	2 Sep
22.11	4.1	Luke Davis	U23	1.01.80	6rB	Birmingham	2 Jun
22.13	3.1	Jim Tipper		16.05.72	4	Birmingham	17 Jun
22.13	2.1	Neil Jennings		18.09.77	3	London (He)	26 Aug
22.20		Rob Harle	U23	1.06.79	1	New Haven, USA	14 Apr

hand timing

20.4 w	3.7	Dwayne Grant	U20	(20.64)	1	Bedford	1 Jul
		20.9 0.9			1	Watford	26 May
20.6 w	3.7	Tim Benjamin	U20	(20.67)	2	Bedford	1 Jul
20.8 w	3.7	Tyrone Edgar	U20	(20.96)	3	Bedford	1 Jul
		21.0 0.9			2	Watford	26 May

5 performances to 21.0 by 3 athletes including 3 wind assisted

21.1 w	3.8	Ben Lewis	U23	(21.48)	1	Cannock	12 May
21.2 w	2.5	Jason Fergus		(21.67)	1	Southend	13 May
21.2 w	3.2	James Chatt	U23	(21.53)	2	Bedford	1 Jul
21.3 w	3.2	Graham Hedman	U23	(21.56)	4	Bedford	1 Jul
21.4		Cori Henry		(21.59)	1	Nottingham	12 May
21.4	0.9	Tim Abeyie	U20	(21.55)	3	Watford	26 May
21.4		Adam Potter	U23	(21.95)	1	Hemel Hempstead	21 Jul
21.4 w	4.8	Rikki Fifton	U17	(21.67)	1	London (Ha)	27 Jun
		21.5 0.0			1	Watford	27 May
21.4 w	3.2	Gavin Eastman	U23	(22.13)	5	Bedford	1 Jul
		21.7 0.8			1	London (He)	12 May
21.5	-1.0	Jamie Henthorn		(21.51)	2	Watford	2 Jun
21.5	-1.0	Jamie Baulch		(21.02i)	3	Watford	2 Jun
21.5 w	2.5	Mark Brown		(21.89i)	2	Southend	13 May
21.5 w	3.2	Dominic Papura	U23	(21.67)	6	Bedford	1 Jul
		21.6			2	Loughborough	28 Apr
21.5 w	3.7	Nick Smith	U20	(21.58)	5	Bedford	1 Jul
21.5 w	4.4	Ben Ellis	U23	(21.90)	1rB	Watford	8 Sep
		21.7			1	Basingstoke	5 May
21.6		Adam Charlton	U20	(22.02)	1	London (Col)	21 Jul
21.6		Jason Gardener		18.09.75	1	Oxford	4 Aug
21.6 w	2.4	Dominique Richards	U23	(21.64)	2h1	Bedford	28 May
21.7		Robert Tobin	U20	20.12.83	1	Harrow	29 Apr
21.7	0.2	Matthew Ouche	U17	(21.76)	1	Colchester	7 May
21.7	-1.4	James Bridge	U20	(21.92)	1	Ashford	13 May
21.7		Nathan Honour		(21.84)	1	London (Elt)	2 Jun
21.7		Brian Darby		(21.73w)	1	Yate	21 Jul
21.7 w	4.2	Kevin Ellis		(21.73)	2	Cardiff	2 Jun
21.7 w	3.2	Mark Hanson	U23	13.05.81	7	Bedford	1 Jul
		22.0 1.1			3h3	Bedford	1 Jul
21.8		Ricky Alfred		(21.92)	2	Liverpool	5 May
21.8	-1.0	David Samuyiwa		4.08.72	7	Watford	2 Jun
21.8	-0.6	Finlay Wright	U23	(21.89)	1rB	Watford	2 Jun
21.8	-0.6	Michael Champion		(21.82)	1	Eton	10 Jun
21.8	-0.7	Luke Davis	U23	(22.11w)	2	Rugby	10 Jun
21.8		Tim Ward	U20	(21.91)	1	Stoke-on-Trent	17 Jun
21.8	-0.3	Daniel Cossins	U17	(22.15)	1	Stoke-on-Trent	17 Jun
21.8		Geoff Dearman		(21.85w)	1	Watford	15 Aug
21.8 w	3.8	Steve Buttler		(21.97w)	2	Cannock	12 May
		22.0			1	Birmingham	11 Jul
21.8 w	2.5	John Jordan	U23	18.01.81	3	Southend	13 May
21.8 w	4.4	Robert Lewis		2.09.78	1rB	Cardiff	2 Jun
		22.0 0.3			3	Peterborough	7 Jul
21.8 w		John Kelley	U20	(21.89w)	2	Rotherham	17 Jun
21.9	0.2	Fabian Collymore	U17	19.10.84	2	Colchester	7 May
21.9		Dominic Bradley		(21.76w)	1	Warrington	12 May
21.9		Gareth Jones	U20	1.07.82	1	Stretford	13 May
21.9		Geoffrey Djan	U20	21.07.82	2	Stoke-on-Trent	17 Jun
21.9		Jim Tipper		(22.13w)	1	Corby	18 Aug
21.9	-0.5	Peter Brend		(21.94)	1rB	Eton	18 Aug

21.9 w	2.8	Marlon Dickson		(21.95)	2	Kingston	13 May
21.9 w	4.2	Ian Leaman		14.10.78	1	Exeter	13 May
21.9 w	4.4	Aaron Aplin	U20	25.11.83	2rB	Cardiff	2 Jun
21.9 w	4.2	Ben Watkins		12.11.78	3	Cardiff	2 Jun
21.9 w	4.4	Michael Smith	U23	(22.10)	3	Watford	8 Sep
		22.0			1	Grimsby	5 May
21.9 w	4.4	Roddy Pitt	U23	(22.16)	2	Watford	8 Sep
22.0		Scott Herbert		12.02.74	1	Bedford	5 May
22.0		Daniel Brandwood	U20	(21.74w)	1	Hull	9 May
22.0		Rob Harle	U23	(22.20w)	2	Cambridge	19 May
22.0		Stuart Marshall	U23	2.12.80	1	Stafford	20 May
22.0		Philip Ellershaw		(21.99w)	1	Blackpool	2 Jun
22.0		Anthony Noel		(22.07)	2	London (Elt)	2 Jun
22.0		Derek Morgan		4.04.69	2	Stafford	2 Jun
22.0	-0.6	Michael Afilaka		(22.02)	3	Eton	10 Jun
22.0		Ryan Palmer	U20	(21.80w)	3	Stoke-on-Trent	17 Jun
22.0		Aidan Syers	U20	29.06.83	1	London (Cr)	23 Jun
22.0		Nathan Martin	U17	16.11.84	1rB	London (TB)	23 Jun
22.0		Wayne Martin		12.08.76	1rB	London (TB)	24 Jun
22.0		Gavin Stephens		(22.18)	1	Woodford	21 Jul
22.0 w	4.4	David Brackstone	U20	13.03.82	3rB	Cardiff	2 Jun
22.0 w	3.6	Adam Buckley	U23	6.12.80	3	Wigan	10 Jun
22.0 w	4.8	Andre Fernandez	U23	2.03.80	3	London (Ha)	27 Jun
22.0 w	4.8	Sam Omonua		16.06.76	2	London (Ha)	27 Jun
22.0 w	3.2	Shane King		8.02.74	1rB	Watford	8 Sep
22.0 w	4.4	William Pobie		6.12.78	4	Watford	8 Sep

unknown athlete/wrong name

21.7		G. Mbirh			1	Portsmouth	21 Jul

Additional Under 17 (1 - 13 above)

22.1		Richard Davenport		12.09.85	1	Cheltenham	11 Jul
22.1		Steele		(22.21)	1	Stretford	17 Jul
22.2		Alex Stones		17.09.84	1	Mansfield	18 Aug
22.28 w	2.9	Jamahl Alert-Khan	U15	12.09.86	2	Exeter	7 Jul
		22.58 1.9			1	Sheffield	12 Aug
22.3		Neil Mitchell			1	Leamington	12 May
22.3		Thomas	U15	(22.03w)	1	Yate	1 Jul
		22.74 i			1	Birmingham	24 Feb
		22.76 1.9			2	Sheffield	12 Aug
22.3		Jamie Gill		29.10.85	2	Corby	18 Aug
		22.35 w 3.4			4	Sheffield	12 Aug
		22.65 1.9			4s2	Sheffield	12 Aug
22.33		Warren Prince		18.03.85	1	Bedford	28 Jul
22.35	1.6	Stuart Haley		9.12.84	3	Cudworth	26 May
	(20)						
22.40 w	2.9	Matt Barclay		1.11.84	1	Crawley	12 May
		22.4			1	Hoo	3 Jun
22.4		Peter Warke		22.05.86	3	Dublin, IRL	23 Jun
		22.69 1.4			6	Tullamore, IRL	21 Jul
22.4		Jamie McNiel		23.11.84	1	Tamworth	18 Aug
22.4		Iain Hunt		24.11.84	1	Newport	8 Sep
		22.41 w 2.5			4h2	Cardiff	17 Jun
		22.67 1.4			4	Tullamore, IRL	21 Jul
22.48 i		Kamil Tejan Cole		21.01.85	2	Birmingham	24 Feb
22.49	0.0	Collymore		(21.9)	3h3	Watford	27 May
22.50 w	2.9	Marimba Odundo-Mendez	U15	30.09.86	3	Exeter	7 Jul
		22.79 i			2	Birmingham	24 Feb
		22.80 1.9			3	Sheffield	12 Aug

22.60	1.9	Alex Coley		8.02.86	3s2	Sheffield	12 Aug
22.6	0.0	Ellington		(21.94w)	4	Watford	27 May
		22.61 -1.2			1h4	Sheffield	12 Aug
22.6		Robert Smith		3.03.85	3	Colchester	7 May
22.61 w	2.8	Andrew Watkins	U15	8.12.87	1	Cardiff	16 Jun
		22.68 1.4			1	Connah's Quay	4 Aug
22.68		Grant Burnett		21.03.85	2	Grangemouth	10 Jun

Additional Under 15 (1 - 4 above)

22.8 w		Gary Atkinson	7.01.87	1	Bebington	3 Jun
		23.00 0.4		1h2	Exeter	6 Jul
22.8 w		Keiran Turner	8.02.87	2	Bebington	3 Jun
		23.6		1	Wigan	1 Jul
22.82 w	2.8	James Boreham	27.11.86	2	Cardiff	16 Jun
		23.40 -2.3		2	Cardiff	7 Jul
22.89 ?		Wade Bennett-Jackson	27.02.87			
		23.03 0.8		1h	London (He)	26 Aug
22.91 w	2.1	Ryan Scott	20.02.87	2s1	Exeter	7 Jul
		23.0 1.5		2	Stoke-on-Trent	17 Jun
		23.11 0.4		2h2	Exeter	6 Jul
22.94 w	2.8	Andrew Bartlett	17.02.87	2s2	Exeter	7 Jul
		23.04 0.9		2h5	Exeter	6 Jul
	(10)					
22.99 w		Stephen Thompson	5.09.86	1	Antrim	16 Jun
		23.42 1.9		6	Sheffield	12 Aug
23.0		Chris Musa	5.12.86	1	Colchester	28 Aug
23.04 w	2.1	Set Osho	28.09.86	5	Exeter	7 Jul
		23.10 0.9		3h5	Exeter	6 Jul
23.09 w	2.9	Steve Hunter	22.12.86	3s2	Exeter	7 Jul
		23.47 -0.1		3h3	Exeter	6 Jul
23.10 w	2.8	Glen Kaighan	14.11.86	2s2	Exeter	7 Jul
		23.45 0.2		2h1	Exeter	6 Jul
23.1		Sosthene Yao	7.08.87	3	London (Cat)	11 Aug
23.11	0.4	Thomas Gore	15.01.87	3h2	Exeter	6 Jul
23.2		Bradley Stimson	1.09.86	1	Bury St. Edmunds	
		23.44 w 2.1		4s2	Exeter	6 Jul
		23.52 0.0		1h4	Exeter	6 Jul
23.23 w	2.2	Craig Pickering	16.10.86	3s2	Sheffield	12 Aug
		23.29 1.1		2h4	Sheffield	12 Aug
23.30 w	2.8	Ben Lavender	25.12.86	3s3	Exeter	7 Jul
		23.33 0.1		2h3	Exeter	7 Jul
	(20)					
23.3		Alex Nelson	21.03.88	2	Yate	1 Jul
23.3 w		Harold Buchanan	13.10.86	2	Bebington	3 Jun
		23.55 1.2		3	Cudworth	26 May
23.3 w	6.0	Michael Johnson	28.09.86	1	Exeter	16 Jun
23.34	0.1	Carlton Farnham		6h3	Exeter	7 Jul
23.4		Craig Glanville	21.09.86	1	Cudworth	6 May
23.4 w	6.0	Martin Cranie	26.09.86	2	Exeter	16 Jun
23.4 w	6.0	Will Pedley	22.09.86	3	Exeter	16 Jun
23.43 w	2.8	Matthew Hislop	31.01.87	4s2	Exeter	7 Jul
23.49	0.2	Joseph Wright	16.12.86	3h1	Exeter	6 Jul
23.5		Ben Higgins	27.09.86	1	Ipswich	29 Apr
	(30)					
23.5		Chris Julien	14.09.87	1	Hoo	3 Jun
23.6		Ian Miller	9.01.87	h	Leamington	9 Jun
23.6		Scott Masters	29.11.86	1	Telford	22 Jul

Under 13

25.4		David Pitt		1.09.88	1	Yate	1 Jul
25.6	1.0	Ani Zamani		17.09.88	1	Kingston	29 Jul
25.7		Ricardo Francis		26.11.88	1	Sheffield	3 Jun
25.7		Alain Kacou		25.10.88	1	Battersea Park	4 Aug
25.80		Josh Baxter		15.09.88	1	Reading	3 Jun
25.9	1.0	Garai Wekwete		9.10.88	2	Kingston	29 Jul
26.0		Danny Doyley		28.12.88	1	Harrow	1 Jul
26.0		Nathan Williams		12.05.89	1	Peterborough	22 Jul
26.0		Michael Hinton		22.02.89	1	Telford	22 Jul
26.0		Eddie Kamoga		25.12.88	2	Peterborough	22 Jul

Foreign

20.86	*0.4*	*Paul Brizzel (IRL)*		*3.10.76*	*1=r5*	*Irvine CA, USA*	*6 May*
21.42	*-0.3*	*Paul McKee (IRL)*		*15.10.77*	*6q4*	*Beijing, CHN*	*30 Aug*
21.73	*1.6*	*Lee Okoroafu (NGR)*		*12.09.76*	*5rB*	*Jarrow*	*18 Aug*
21.87	*0.6*	*Liam McDermid (IRL)*	*U17*	*23.11.84*	*4s2*	*Debrecen, HUN*	*14 Jul*

300 Metres

34.06	Jonathan Edwards		6.11.78	1rB	Loughborough	4 Jul
34.14	Simon Plaskett	U23	9.04.79	3	Brasschaat, BEL	15 Aug
34.2	Mark Brown		3.11.76	1	Barking	18 Mar
	34.33			4	Loughborough	4 Jul
34.7	Adam Potter	U23	12.04.80	1	Bath	24 Jun
34.8	Andre Fernandez	U23	2.03.80	1	Watford	11 Apr
34.84 i	Ian Deeth	U23	25.06.79	1	Birmingham	13 Feb
35.0	Kevin Ellis		18.06.76	1	Peterborough	1 Apr
35.2	James Chatt	U23	11.02.80	1	Tonbridge	16 Apr
35.29 i	Steve Surety	U23	18.02.80	2rC	Birmingham	13 Feb
35.29	Peter Lloyd-Jones		28.09.76	4rB	Loughborough	4 Jul
	(10)					
35.40	Ian Lowthian	U23	10.10.80	5rB	Loughborough	4 Jul
35.47 i	Tony Gill		19.09.77	1rB	Birmingham	13 Feb
35.60 i	Sandy Scott		1.09.76	1	Glasgow	7 Feb
35.6	Howard Frost	U23	9.12.81	1	Crawley	24 Mar
35.6	Russell Frost	U23	23.06.80	2	Crawley	24 Mar
35.8	Nathan Honour		15.11.77	2	Kingston	18 Mar

intermediate time

32.8 i+	Daniel Caines	U23	15.05.79	1m	Birmingham	18 Feb

Foreign

34.83	*Rob Fanning (IRL)*		*31.10.78*	*3rB*	*Loughborough*	*4 Jul*

400 Metres

45.14	Mark Richardson ¶		26.07.72	4s1	Edmonton, CAN	5 Aug
	45.22			1	London (CP)	22 Jul
	45.66			2h2	Edmonton, CAN	4 Aug
	45.79			1	Birmingham	15 Jul
	45.84			5	Gateshead	19 Aug
	46.20			1	Glasgow (S)	1 Jul
	46.46			2s2	Birmingham	14 Jul
45.58	Daniel Caines	U23	15.05.79	6	Seville, ESP	8 Jun
	45.61 i			1	Birmingham	18 Feb
	45.75 i			1	Birmingham	28 Jan
	45.87			6	London (CP)	22 Jul
	46.21 i			1	Glasgow	18 Mar
	46.29 i			1s1	Birmingham	27 Jan
	46.34 i			1r2	Stockholm, SWE	15 Feb
	46.40 i			1	Lisbon, POR	11 Mar
	46.43 i			1s1	Lisbon, POR	10 Mar

45.70	Iwan Thomas		5.01.74	1	Watford	25 Jul
	45.77			1	Eton	7 Jul
	45.82			5	London (CP)	22 Jul
	45.82			4	Gateshead	19 Aug
	45.92			3h5	Edmonton, CAN	4 Aug
	45.93			3r2	Thessaloniki, GRE	22 Aug
	45.95			1	Dublin, IRL	29 Jun
	46.00			2	Birmingham	15 Jul
	46.12 A			7	Roodepoort, RSA	16 Mar
	46.14			7	Bremen, GER	23 Jun
	46.16			3	Tula, RUS	9 Jun
	46.33			1s2	Birmingham	14 Jul
	46.35			4	Rovereto, ITA	29 Aug
46.09	Mark Hylton		24.09.76	7	London (CP)	22 Jul
	46.24 i			2	Birmingham	28 Jan
	46.36			3	Birmingham	15 Jul
	46.42 i			2	Birmingham	18 Feb
46.10	Tim Benjamin	U20	2.05.82	1	Edinburgh	25 Aug
	46.43			1	Grosseto, ITA	20 Jul
	46.45			1	Loughborough	4 Jul
	46.50			7	Gateshead	19 Aug
46.15	Jamie Baulch		3.05.73	5h7	Edmonton, CAN	4 Aug
	46.32			8	London (CP)	22 Jul
	46.33			6	Gateshead	19 Aug
	46.44			5	Funchal, POR	30 Jun
46.21	Dean Macey		12.12.77	1D3	Edmonton, CAN	6 Aug
46.31 i	Du'aine Thorne-Ladejo		14.02.71	1rB	Birmingham	18 Feb
46.35	Sean Baldock		3.12.76	2	Madrid, ESP	26 May
	44 performances to 46.5 by 9 athletes including 10 indoors					
46.56	Jared Deacon		15.10.75	4rB	Walnut CA, USA	22 Apr
(10)						
46.75	Adam Potter	U23	12.04.80	1	Derby	29 Jul
46.8	Peter Brend		2.02.77	1	Eton	18 Aug
	47.03			7	Birmingham	15 Jul
46.82	David Naismith	U23	15.12.79	1	Loughborough	20 May
46.88 i	Matt Elias	U23	25.04.79	2s1	Birmingham	27 Jan
	46.9			1	Cardiff	16 Jun
46.91	Neil Jennings		18.09.77	1	Gateshead	12 May
47.10	Robert Tobin	U20	20.12.83	1	Dole, FRA	29 Jul
47.1	James Chatt	U23	11.02.80	1	Chelmsford	4 Aug
47.14	Paul Slythe		5.09.74	2	Watford	25 Jul
47.18	Simon Plaskett	U23	9.04.79	3	Derby	29 Jul
47.2	Cori Henry		9.12.76	1	Cardiff	2 Jun
	47.41			1	Birmingham	17 Jun
(20)						
47.21 i	Mark Brown		3.11.76	4	Birmingham	28 Jan
	47.67			1rB	Eton	7 Jul
47.3	Richard Knowles		12.11.75	2	Jarrow	18 Aug
	47.82			6s2	Birmingham	14 Jul
47.37 i	Adam Buckley	U23	6.12.80	3	Birmingham	14 Jan
	47.55			3	Glasgow	7 May
47.40	Brian Darby		14.10.72	2h2	Birmingham	13 Jul
47.46	Jonathan Edwards		6.11.78	2	Glasgow (S)	7 May
47.51	Mark Sesay		13.12.72	1rB	Cardiff	8 Jul
47.52	Tim Bayley	U23	4.10.81	3	Watford	25 Jul
47.53	Kris Stewart	U23	11.04.80	1	Glasgow (S)	23 Jun
47.55	Andrew Mitchell		30.07.76	2	Glasgow (S)	23 Jun
47.61	Nick Budden		17.11.75	2B	Loughborough	20 May
(30)						
47.63	Graham Hedman	U23	6.02.79	3	Eton	7 Jul
47.64	Geoff Dearman		4.08.77	4	Eton	7 Jul

47.67	Richard McDonald	U23	11.01.80	5	Derby	29 Jul
47.7	Matt Douglas		26.11.76	1	Watford	23 May
	48.86 i			4h4	Birmingham	27 Jan
47.7	Sam Ellis	U20	23.06.82	2	Bedford	1 Jul
	47.92			4	Loughborough	4 Jul
47.80	Ryan Preddy	U20	30.01.84	4s1	Debrecen, HUN	13 Jul
47.80	Russell Nicholls	U20	8.03.83	3	Dole, FRA	29 Jul
47.9	Adam Charlton	U20	11.05.84	1	Bedford	22 Aug
	48.01			2h1	London (He)	26 Aug
47.92	Ian Lowthian	U23	10.10.80	4	Terre Haute, USA	19 May
47.93 i	Allyn Condon		24.08.74	1r2	Cardiff	11 Feb
	(40)					
47.97	Lawrence Baird		14.12.77	1	Stretford	3 Jul
48.03	Andre Fernandez	U23	2.03.80	2	Cardiff	8 Jul
48.06	Bradley Yiend	U23	25.10.80	3rB	Eton	7 Jul
48.08	Geoffrey Djan	U20	21.07.82	7	Eton	7 Jul
48.09	Jonathan Simpson	U20	27.05.82	1	Corinth, GRE	26 May
48.10	Ian Deeth	U23	25.06.79	2h4	London (Ha)	16 Jun
48.1	Russell Frost	U23	23.06.80	3	London (Ha)	17 Jun
48.1	James Davies	U20	5.12.82	4	Bedford	30 Jun
	48.25			3s1	Bedford	30 Jun
48.1	Eddie Williams		1.10.70	3	Eton	18 Aug
48.11 i	Adam Rogers	U20	10.04.83	1	Birmingham	25 Feb
	(50)					
48.20	Robert Lewis		2.09.78	4	Watford	25 Jul
48.3	Ryan Palmer	U20	21.06.83	5	Bedford	30 Jun
	48.55			5	Dole, FRA	29 Jul
48.32 i	Wayne Martin		12.08.76	4	Birmingham	14 Jan
48.32	David Pratt		23.11.75	1	Bedford	28 Jul
48.36 i	Steve Surety	U23	18.02.80	2	Birmingham	7 Jan
	48.7			1	Ware	7 Jul
48.38	Leon McRae	U23	3.11.80	3s1	Bedford	27 May
48.4	Graham Beasley		24.10.77	5	Eton	7 Jul
48.45	Keiron Murray		18.06.75	1	Douglas IOM	12 Jul
48.48	Alastair Gordon		16.04.78	2	Birmingham	30 Jun
48.49 i	Alloy Wilson	U23	25.01.80	3h7	Birmingham	27 Jan
	48.5			3h1	Bedford	30 Jun
	(60)					
48.5	Chris Sleeman	U23	20.03.80	2	Loughborough	13 Jun
48.5	Dominique Richards	U23	12.09.79	1	London (TB)	28 Jul
48.52 i	Colin Philip	U23	8.06.79	4	Glasgow	18 Feb
	48.98			3	Glasgow (S)	23 Jun
48.54 i	Barry Middleton		10.03.75	1h2	Birmingham	27 Jan
48.54	Martin Bradbury	U20	20.10.82	2h1	Exeter	6 Jul
48.57	Lee Notman		14.10.75	2	Edinburgh	12 May
48.59	Richard Davenport	U17	12.09.85	2	Murcia, ESP	23 Jul
48.6	Stuart Marshall	U23	2.12.80	1	Leamington	12 May
	48.98			4	Birmingham	17 Jun
48.6	Peter Lloyd-Jones		28.09.76	2	Stafford	18 Aug
48.62	Andrew Steele	U17	19.09.84	1	Exeter	7 Jul
	(70)					
48.63	Gavin Stephens		12.09.77	6s1	Bedford	27 May
48.70	Tom Nimmo		9.05.71	3	Edinburgh	12 May
48.7	Steve Webb		17.07.78	2	Cardiff	2 Jun
	48.94			4	Birmingham	30 Jun
48.7	Richard Workman		31.05.71	4	Wigan	10 Jun
	48.93			2	Stretford	31 Jul
48.75	Alasdair Donaldson		21.06.77	2h1	Glasgow (S)	23 Jun
48.82 i	Michael Parper		20.05.78	4s1	Birmingham	13 Jan
48.82	Scott Keenan	U23	31.07.81	3h1	Glasgow (S)	23 Jun
48.82	Vernon Small	U20	1.01.82	1	Maribor, SLO	23 Sep

48.87 i	Simon Lees	U23	19.11.79	1	Birmingham	10 Feb
48.89	Chris Bennett	U23	18.10.80	1h1	Portsmouth	13 May
(80)						
48.90	Chris Smith	U23	26.04.79	2	Stretford	19 Jun
48.9	Hugh Kerr		4.01.76	1	Ayr	22 Apr
48.9	Paul Laslett	U23	12.05.80	1	Guildford	23 Jun
48.9	Darren Edlin	U20	10.04.82	3h3	Bedford	30 Jun
	48.96			2	Stretford	14 Aug
48.92	Andrew Delafield	U23	19.03.80	1	Sheffield	12 May
48.93	Noel Levy		22.06.75	4s2	Bedford	27 May
48.93	James McIlroy		30.12.76	1h1	Belfast	28 Jul
48.94 i	Chris Page	U23	13.11.80	2h7	Birmingham	13 Jan
48.96 i	Philip Octave		12.06.78	3h1	Birmingham	27 Jan
	49.1			2	London (He)	13 May
49.02	Barry O'Brien		3.07.76	3	Gateshead	12 May
(90)						
49.04	Paul Curtis	U23	29.05.80	6h2	Birmingham	13 Jul
49.07 i	Wayne Ellwood		26.09.74	4	Birmingham	4 Feb
49.10	Neil Dougal	U23	7.03.80	1	Grangemouth	4 Jul
49.1	Paul Hibbert		31.03.65	6	Wigan	10 Jun
49.1	Jeffrey Christie	U20	24.09.82	1	Leamington	16 Jun
49.1	Nathan Honour		15.11.77	1	London (He)	23 Jun
49.1	Andrew Bennett	U20	30.09.82	1	Bedford	24 Jun
	49.26			2	Derby	9 Sep
Additional Under 20 (1 - 18 above)						
49.14	Jimmy Watkins		30.10.82	3h1	Exeter	6 Jul
49.17	Ben Caldwell		3.03.82	1s2	Glasgow (S)	6 May
(20)						
49.19	Robert Smith	U17	3.03.85	2	Tullamore, IRL	21 Jul
49.2	David Creak		30.08.83	1	Norwich	12 May
	49.33			4h1	Exeter	6 Jul
49.21	John Dunlop			2s2	Glasgow (S)	6 May
49.24	Gavin Dublin		5.10.83	2h2	Exeter	6 Jul
49.33 i	Mike Snow		5.09.82	1	Birmingham	10 Feb
49.33 i	David Brackstone		13.03.82	3s1	Birmingham	24 Feb
	49.4			2	Peterborough	7 Jul
49.33	Lee Mason		23.01.83	2	Watford	27 May
49.38	Daniel Bray		6.09.83	4h2	Exeter	6 Jul
49.45	Rhys Williams		27.02.84	1	Connah's Quay	4 Aug
49.5	Neil Wynne		14.04.82	1	Cardiff	16 Jun
(30)						
49.5	Daniel Brandwood		1.10.82	1D	Bedford	14 Jul
Additional Under 17 (1 - 3 above)						
49.6	Stephen Gill		25.09.84	1	Sheffield (W)	3 Jun
	50.00			3s1	Exeter	6 Jul
49.6	Daniel Cossins		22.12.84	1B	Watford	29 Aug
49.7	Michael Rimmer		3.02.86	1	Bury	20 May
49.73	Richard Sheeran		27.11.85	1	Cudworth	27 May
49.89	Philip Taylor		20.03.85	2	Cudworth	27 May
50.12	Shane Smith		13.05.85	1	Gateshead	12 May
50.18	Simon Toye		24.09.85	5	Exeter	7 Jul
(10)						
50.3	Peter Warke		22.05.86	1	Antrim	16 Jun
50.33 i	Graham Blackman		25.03.85	2	Birmingham	24 Feb
	50.64			4h3	Exeter	6 Jul
50.39 i	Rupert Gardner		9.10.84	3	Birmingham	24 Feb
	50.6			1O	Abingdon	23 Jun
50.4	Darren St.Clair		6.04.85	2	Crawley	5 Aug
50.5	Oliver Barrett		25.12.84	1	Bury St. Edmunds	12 May
50.5	Simon Farenden		6.10.85	1	Sheffield (W)	1 Jul

50.6 i	Daniel Lambert		2.07.85	1rE	Boston, USA	18 Feb
	51.0			2rB	Crawley	5 Aug
50.67	Daniel Petros		8.08.85	2	Watford	27 May
50.70	Ian Allerton		18.04.85	3	Watford	27 May
50.71	Richard Turner		23.09.84	3	Cudworth	27 May
	(20)					
50.72	Craig Glanville	U15	21.09.86	1	Exeter	7 Jul
50.80	Grant Burnett		21.03.85	3	Tullamore, IRL	21 Jul
50.91	Alex Budd		6.12.84	1	Portsmouth	12 May
50.91	David Vass		31.12.85	3h2	Exeter	6 Jul
51.0	Matthew Peel		7.01.85	3	Crawley	5 Aug
Additional Under 15 (1 above)						
51.34	Jonathan Hiorns		2.10.86	2	Exeter	7 Jul
51.77	Harold Buchanan		13.10.86	3	Exeter	7 Jul
52.1	Adam Parker		25.09.86	1	Watford	8 Jul
52.15	Stephen Wibberley		4.01.87	2	Scunthorpe	18 Aug
52.23 i	Paul Twidale		30.09.86	2	Birmingham	24 Feb
	52.59			6	Exeter	7 Jul
52.29	John Billingham		16.10.86	2	Sheffield	12 Aug
52.32	Richard Buck		14.11.86	3	Scunthorpe	18 Aug
52.57	Keiran Turner		8.02.87	5	Exeter	7 Jul
52.78	Tyrone Crow		14.09.86	4	Sheffield	12 Aug
	(10)					
52.93	Ben Walpole		1.11.86	4s1	Exeter	6 Jul
52.94	Tom Stanley		11.04.87	5s1	Exeter	6 Jul
52.96	Richard Strachan		18.11.86	1	Sheffield	13 May
53.0	Moyo Sankofa		12.12.86	1	London (TB)	28 Jul
53.15	Lewis Robson		9.01.88	1	Gateshead	25 Aug
53.2	Jon Baty		1.02.87	1	Nottingham	1 Sep
53.27 ?	Andrew Watkins		8.12.87			
	53.3			1	Neath	27 Aug
53.3	Andrew Bartlett		17.02.87	1	Bromley	1 Jul
53.4	Joseph Wayman		18.02.87	3	Nottingham	8 Sep
53.5	James Ash		1.09.86	1	Tipton	11 Jun
	(20)					
53.5	Michael Montague		30.05.87	1	Glasgow (S)	19 Aug
53.58	Jon Witty		1.10.86	1	Birmingham	27 May
Under 13						
58.3	James Phillips		13.12.88	11	Birmingham	1 Jul
59.6	James Mee		1.07.89	1	Nottingham	1 Apr
59.9	Luke Greenwood		31.10.88	1	Exeter	29 May
60.2	Matthew Young		6.07.89	1	Bedford	22 Aug
61.9	Luke Smallwood		11.09.88	1	Erith	8 Jul
62.9	Jermaine Conteh		12.05.89	1	Tooting	29 Jul
Foreign						
46.42	*Paul McKee (IRL)*		*15.10.77*	*3*	*Dublin, IRL*	*22 Jul*
48.3	*Rob Fanning (IRL)*		*31.10.78*	*1*	*Bolton*	*20 May*
	48.46 i			*2*	*Birmingham*	*4 Feb*
	48.93			*4h1*	*Bedford*	*27 May*
48.77	*Paul McBurney (IRL)*		*14.03.72*	*1*	*Belfast*	*25 Aug*
48.78	*Liam McDermid (IRL)*	*U17*	*23.11.84*	*1*	*Tullamore, IRL*	*24 Jun*

800 Metres

1:47.16	Neil Speaight		9.09.78	2	Tartu, EST	19 Jun
	1:47.59			2	Loughborough	20 May
	1:47.67			1	Watford	9 Jun
	1:47.79			2	Dublin, IRL	29 Jun
	1:48.10			7	London (CP)	22 Jul
	1:48.22			2	Madrid, ESP	27 May
	1:48.87			7s2	Beijing, CHN	31 Aug
	1:48.88			2	Glasgow (S)	1 Jul

1:47.35	Simon Lees	U23	19.11.79	4	London (CP)	22	Jul
	1:47.39			1	Loughborough	20	May
	1:47.78			1	Glasgow (S)	7	May
	1:47.82			4	Amsterdam, NED	15	Jul
	1:48.80			3	Bremen, GER	24	Jun
1:47.42	James McIlroy		30.12.76	2	Victoria, CAN	25	May
	1:47.95			6	London (CP)	22	Jul
1:47.5	Andrew Graffin		20.12.77	1	Watford	29	Aug
1:48.27	Grant Cuddy		6.01.77	2	Watford	9	Jun
	1:48.41			2rB	Glasgow (S)	1	Jul
	1:48.90			4	Solihull	23	Jun
1:48.43	Ricky Soos	U20	28.06.83	3	Grosseto, ITA	21	Jul
	1:48.5			1	Loughborough	13	Jun
1:48.66	Michael East		20.01.78	3	Solihull	23	Jun
1:48.67	Matt Shone		10.07.75	3	Loughborough	20	May
	1:48.88			1h1	Cardiff	17	Jun
	1:48.90			3	Watford	9	Jun
	1:48.97			1	Glasgow (S)	11	Aug
1:48.71	Neil Dougal	U23	7.03.80	2	Watford	25	Jul
1:48.85	Gary Vickers		26.02.71	3	Watford	25	Jul
(10)							
1:48.95	Chris Moss	U23	17.06.79	4	Watford	9	Jun
1:49.00	Anthony Whiteman		13.11.71	5	Solihull	23	Jun
	30 performances to 1:49.00 by 12 athletes						
1:49.03	Vince Wilson		1.04.73	5rB	Glasgow (S)	1	Jul
1:49.39	Angus Maclean	U23	20.09.80	2	Glasgow (S)	7	May
1:49.4	Justin Swift-Smith		28.08.74	2rB	Solihull	23	Jun
1:49.41	Alasdair Donaldson		21.06.77	4	Watford	25	Jul
1:49.47	Tom Mayo		2.05.77	2	Glasgow (S)	11	Aug
1:49.62	Rob Watkinson		10.03.74	3	Glasgow (S)	11	Aug
1:49.69 i	Chris Mulvaney	U23	25.05.81	3	Fayetteville, USA	9	Feb
1:49.74	Andrew Brown		17.06.77	4	Glasgow (S)	11	Aug
(20)							
1:49.78	Richard Girvan		26.07.76	3	Dublin, IRL	22	Jul
1:49.84	Alasdair Mclean-Foreman	U23	10.11.81	1rC	Princeton, USA	12	May
1:49.85	Chris Bolt	U23	21.09.80	5	Watford	25	Jul
1:49.85	Gregg Taylor		1.08.77	1	Bedford	22	Aug
1:49.90	Mark Sesay		13.12.72	2	Stretford	19	Jun
1:49.94	Jon Stewart	U23	22.05.80	3	Stretford	31	Jul
1:49.98 i	Eddie King		26.11.75	1	Birmingham	28	Jan
	1:50.87			2rB	Eton	7	Jul
1:50.00	Andy Young		20.06.77	1rB	Watford	9	Jun
1:50.01	Peter Walsh	U23	5.05.80	1	Stretford	28	Aug
1:50.05	James Nasrat	U20	10.01.83	7	Watford	9	Jun
(30)							
1:50.10 i	Andy Hart		13.09.69	2	Birmingham	28	Jan
1:50.10	James Mayo		24.02.75	7	Tula, RUS	9	Jun
1:50.13	Chris Stoves	U20	20.02.84	8	Loughborough	20	May
1:50.31	Phillip Tulba		20.09.73	4	Stretford	31	Jul
1:50.32	Tom Nimmo		9.05.71	9rB	Glasgow (S)	1	Jul
1:50.32	Terry Feasey		5.08.77	2	Bedford	22	Aug
1:50.5	Richard Ashe		5.10.74	2	Watford	15	Aug
1:50.56	Raymond Adams	U23	5.11.81	9	Loughborough	20	May
1:50.62	Brad Donkin		6.12.71	2	Manchester	23	May
1:50.70	Stuart Bailey		6.08.78	2rB	Watford	9	Jun
(40)							
1:50.7	Malcolm Hassan	U20	27.11.82	1	Gateshead	1	Aug
1:50.8	David Moulton	U23	7.09.81	3	London (TB)	22	Aug
1:50.82	Andrew Fulford	U20	23.06.82	3	Stoke-on-Trent	18	Aug
1:50.83	Jason Lobo		18.09.69	7	Melbourne, AUS	1	Mar
1:50.89	Chris Watson	U20	22.05.83	7	Cardiff	4	Jul

1:50.9		Richard Ward	U20	5.05.82	1	London (TB)	4 Jul
1:50.9		Tim Alexander	U23	6.09.79	1rB	Watford	15 Aug
1:50.9		Joe Kidger	U23	16.03.80	3	Watford	29 Aug
1:51.02		Roger Morley		20.09.77	7	Watford	25 Jul
1:51.03		Steve Rees-Jones		24.12.74	1	Watford	27 Jun
	(50)						
1:51.11 i		Tom Lerwill		17.05.77	5	Birmingham	28 Jan
1:51.16		Phil Tedd		7.11.76	3rC	Solihull	23 Jun
1:51.2		Tom Ranger		20.11.77	2	Gateshead	1 Aug
1:51.2		Michael Skinner	U23	21.11.79	4	Watford	29 Aug
1:51.29		Noel Edwards		16.12.72	4rC	Solihull	23 Jun
1:51.4		Graeme Walker	U23	20.02.79	4	Basauri, ESP	27 May
1:51.51		Mark Goodger		17.12.78	6	Glasgow (S)	7 May
1:51.6		Royston Green	U20	4.01.82	1	Exeter	26 Jun
1:51.62		Matthew Clarke		15.11.76	9	Watford	25 Jul
1:51.64		Eddie Williams		1.10.70	4h5	Birmingham	13 Jul
	(60)						
1:51.7		Greg McEwan	U23	9.04.81	1rC	Glasgow (S)	11 Aug
1:51.7		Rob Hooton		5.05.73	6	Watford	29 Aug
1:51.76		James Thie		27.06.78	7rB	Watford	9 Jun
1:51.78		David Gow	U23	9.02.79	2h2	Arlington TX, USA	13 May
1:51.78		Stewart Reid		15.11.73	4rB	Eton	7 Jul
1:51.8		Andi Knight		26.10.68	4	London (TB)	22 Aug
1:51.81		Nigel Carlisle		30.12.75	7	Dublin, IRL	22 Jul
1:51.84		Ben Cooke	U23	10.04.81	7	Glasgow (S)	7 May
1:51.86		Carl Tipton		4.02.77	1rD	Manchester	23 May
1:51.87		Dan Hermann	U23	3.03.81	4	Stretford	14 Aug
	(70)						
1:51.90		Chris Livesey	U23	8.08.80	5	Stretford	14 Aug
1:52.0		Paul Laslett	U23	12.05.80	7	Watford	29 Aug
1:52.02		Paul Morby	U23	15.01.79	1rC	Manchester	23 May
1:52.03		Garth Watson		20.04.73	7rC	Solihull	23 Jun
1:52.08		Simon Deakin		5.10.77	5	Stretford	5 Jun
1:52.09		Robert Whittle	U23	14.06.81	1rD	Solihull	23 Jun
1:52.10		Alister Moses		5.07.78	10	Watford	25 Jul
1:52.10		Ryan Davoile		29.09.78	5	Bedford	22 Aug
1:52.1		Ian Davey	U20	25.10.82	4	Jarrow	6 Jun
1:52.1		Ian Munro	U20	5.09.83	2rC	Glasgow (S)	11 Aug
	(80)						
1:52.11		Neil Kirk		14.09.78	2h3	Oxford, USA	18 May
1:52.14		Gavin Thompson	U23	9.04.80	1rB	Loughborough	20 May
1:52.2		Hugh Kerr		4.01.76	1	Ayr	6 Jun
1:52.2		Jermaine Mays	U20	23.12.82	1	London (He)	23 Jun
1:52.2		Gavin Massingham	U20	4.10.82	4	Gateshead	1 Aug
1:52.2		Neil Bangs	U23	28.03.80	2rB	Watford	15 Aug
1:52.2		Andrew Brown		20.12.77	3rB	Watford	15 Aug
1:52.2		Louis Wells		6.02.78	5	Eton	18 Aug
1:52.21 i		Andy Kett		1.09.77	3	Cardiff	18 Feb
1:52.24		Lee Cadwallader		17.01.69	4rB	Manchester	23 May
	(90)						
1:52.25		Denis Murphy	U23	14.09.79	1rD	Watford	9 Jun
1:52.28		Marcus Bridges		18.03.71	2rD	Watford	9 Jun
1:52.3		Adam Zawadski		19.12.74	4	Loughborough	13 Jun
1:52.33		Najib Hliouat		28.08.77	2rC	Manchester	23 May
1:52.36		Michael Rimmer	U17	3.02.86	2rB	Stretford	19 Jun
1:52.37		Dominic Hall		21.02.71	3rB	Watford	25 Jul
1:52.38		Matt Davies		23.07.71	5rB	Eton	7 Jul
1:52.4		James Bowler	U23	2.09.79	1	Solihull	13 Jun
1:52.4		Nic Andrews	U23	3.10.81	3	Salisbury	22 Jul
1:52.46		Mark Turner		9.11.72	1rF	Solihull	23 Jun
	(100)						

1:52.47	Stephen Davies	U20	16.02.84	3rD	Watford	9 Jun
1:52.48	Paul Cooper		30.01.75	3rC	Manchester	23 May
1:52.56	Nathan Dosanjh	U23	13.02.79	5rE	Knoxville TN, USA	13 Apr
1:52.6	Andrew Baddeley	U20	20.06.82	1	Cambridge	19 May
1:52.6	Andrew Sherman	U23	28.09.81	2	Exeter	26 Jun
1:52.63	Gavin Maley		19.05.78	2	London (Ha)	17 Jun
1:52.69	Kevin Sheppard	U23	21.01.79	2rF	Solihull	23 Jun
1:52.7	David Anderson		2.10.77	5	Gateshead	1 Aug
1:52.7	Jonathan Burrell		24.11.75	6rB	Watford	15 Aug
1:52.7	Sean Kelly		8.11.72	5rB	Watford	15 Aug
	(110)					
1:52.81	Jason Dupuy		31.01.71	5h1	Birmingham	13 Jul
1:52.89	Gary Richards	U20	22.04.82	1	Stretford	8 May
1:52.97	Steve Green		18.02.71	5	Stretford	19 Jun
Additional Under 20 (1 - 16 above)						
1:53.01	Mark Glennie		19.02.82	1rE	Watford	9 Jun
1:53.04	Adam Davies		27.07.84	3rE	Solihull	23 Jun
1:53.1	Mohamed Farah		23.03.83	1	Watford	2 Jun
1:53.1	Paul Richardson		11.02.82	1rB	Loughborough	13 Jun
	(20)					
1:53.13	Damien Moss		2.09.82	7rB	Watford	25 Jul
1:53.21	Paul Ard		14.10.82	1rG	Solihull	23 Jun
1:53.3	Edward Jackson		4.01.82	8rB	Watford	15 Aug
1:53.35	Adam Bowden		5.08.82	1	Watford	12 May
1:53.4	Simon Rusbridge		13.05.82	3	Solihull	13 Jun
1:53.53	Michael Coltherd		28.12.82	1rC	Stretford	31 Jul
1:53.6	Robert Tobin		20.12.83	5rB	Watford	29 Aug
1:53.64	Chris Reynolds	U17	23.01.85	3rG	Solihull	23 Jun
1:53.7	Adam Vandenberg		2.06.84	10rB	Watford	15 Aug
1:53.84	Chris Iddon		8.10.82	1	Bedford	22 Jul
	(30)					
1:53.89	Scott Overall		9.02.83	3	Watford	1 Aug
1:53.95	Richard Dowse	U17	3.01.85	4rG	Solihull	23 Jun
1:54.01	Russell Slade		25.04.83	3rC	Watford	25 Jul
1:54.13	Robert Smith		3.12.82	2	Watford	25 Jul
1:54.22	Richard Weir		7.08.84	3rF	Watford	9 Jun
1:54.24	Ben Rees		25.03.82	1	Watford	27 May
1:54.24	Richard Davenport	U17	12.09.85	1rB	Watford	30 May
1:54.29	Ahmed Ali	U17	31.03.86	5	Watford	1 Aug
1:54.32	Matthew Jones		10.10.82	4	Stretford	8 May
1:54.32	Matt Simpkins		9.05.82	4rF	Solihull	23 Jun
	(40)					
1:54.5	Dave Ragan		26.03.83	1	Portsmouth	9 Jun
1:54.5	Tom Holden		2.02.84	5	Solihull	13 Jun
1:54.54	Ryan Preddy		30.01.84	5rB	Stretford	19 Jun
1:54.60	Chris Clements		19.07.83	3	Watford	25 Jul
1:54.6	Darren St.Clair	U17	6.04.85	2	Bedford	24 Jun
Additional Under 17 (1 - 6 above)						
1:54.84	Tom Snow		7.09.85	8	Watford	1 Aug
1:55.50	Oliver Barrett		25.12.84	7rC	Watford	25 Jul
1:55.68	Chris Parr		13.11.84	1	Gateshead	25 Aug
1:55.8	Shugri Omar		20.12.84	10rB	Watford	29 Aug
	(10)					
1:55.9	Kris Berry		13.11.84	1	Livingston	29 Aug
1:56.19	Graeme Oudney		11.04.85	4	Stretford	11 Sep
1:56.2	Dan Foley		11.09.84	1	Stourport	18 Aug
1:56.26	Rory Smith		12.12.84	3rE	Stretford	31 Jul
1:56.4	Adam Watt		29.10.84	1	Aberdeen	5 Aug
1:56.60	Chris Hillier		23.02.85	1rC	Watford	27 Jun
1:56.6	Richard Sheeran		27.11.85	1	Stretford	17 Jul

1:56.7	Robin MacIntosh		2.03.85	3rD	Stretford	17 Jul
1:56.7	Alan Wales		7.08.85	2	Aberdeen	5 Aug
1:56.71	Darren Malin		19.06.85	3rC	Stretford	14 Aug
	(20)					
1:57.0	Mark Johnston		18.10.84	3	Livingston	29 Aug
1:57.34	Chris Saville		9.10.84	1	Watford	12 May
1:57.36	Andy Teate		6.09.84	1	Birmingham	1 Sep
1:57.44	Jason Atkinson		28.10.85	3rD	Cardiff	4 Jul
1:57.5	Kelly Cox		21.01.85	2	London (TB)	24 Jun
1:57.6	Ben Wiffen		30.10.84	2rB	London (TB)	18 Jul
1:57.7	Matt Warley		1.08.85	4	Cheltenham	18 Jul
1:57.8	Alistair Hay		7.09.85	2	Inverness	26 Aug
1:57.86	Mark Shankey		19.12.84	1	Duffel, BEL	19 May
1:57.92	Alex Budd		6.12.84	1	Portsmouth	12 May
	(30)					
1:58.02	Graham Powell		7.03.85	2h1	Exeter	6 Jul
1:58.10	David Proctor		22.10.85	1rB	Stretford	11 Sep
1:58.20	Tom Lancashire		2.07.85	5	Cudworth	26 Aug
1:58.2	Russell Shute		21.05.85	6rB	Solihull	13 Jun
1:58.21	Michael Smart		18.11.85	2	Birmingham	2 Sep
1:58.40	Stuart Morland		16.05.86	3	Birmingham	2 Sep
1:58.4	Matt Furber		28.10.84	3	Crawley	5 Aug
1:58.48	Andrew Graham		14.11.84	1s1	Exeter	6 Jul
Under 15						
1:59.21	Craig Bravington		9.12.86	6rB	Watford	25 Jul
2:00.1	Alex Felce		11.09.86	1	Gloucester	4 Aug
	1:58.79 i	U17		2rC	Cardiff	9 Dec
2:00.49	Matt Wood		14.12.86	3rC	Stretford	31 Jul
2:01.38	Ben Harding		12.12.86	2	Sheffield	12 Aug
2:02.4	Matthew Reeves		9.10.86	1	Blackpool	22 Jul
2:02.41	Udobi Nzelu		11.10.86	1	Birmingham	2 Sep
2:02.62	Tom Michaelson		3.01.87	4	Stretford	27 May
2:03.0	Jonathan Long		4.10.86	6rB	Watford	5 Sep
2:03.1	Anthony Welford		5.10.87		Jarrow	20 May
2:03.20	Nathan Shrubb		11.10.86	5	Sheffield	12 Aug
	(10)					
2:03.6	Craig Glanville		21.09.86	1P	Jarrow	23 Jun
2:04.3	Stephen Wibberley		4.01.87	1	Colwyn Bay	1 Sep
2:04.46	John Mannion		7.07.87	6	Sheffield	12 Aug
2:04.48	Jesse Barker		7.03.87	2	Birmingham	2 Sep
2:04.8	Steven Gregg		27.06.87	1	Derby	27 May
2:04.91	David Bowker		27.11.86	2h5	Exeter	6 Jul
2:04.96	Abdi Igi		12.12.87	2	Watford	27 May
2:05.04	Ed Pisano		22.11.86	4	Birmingham	2 Sep
2:05.1	Michael Morgan		22.11.86	1	Belfast	23 Aug
2:05.25	Michael Makasi		6.12.86	3s1	Exeter	6 Jul
	(20)					
2:05.25	Hamish Robertson		1.11.86	6rE	Watford	25 Jul
2:05.26	Eddie Brown		6.10.86	1h2	Exeter	6 Jul
2:05.27	Danny Malone		4.11.86	4s2	Exeter	6 Jul
2:05.43	Owen Vale		1.06.87	2h4	Exeter	6 Jul
Under 13						
2:16.0	Stephen Feasey		12.09.88	1	Hull	1 Jul
2:16.1	Andrew Lagan		15.12.88	1	Blackpool	9 Sep
2:17.7 mx	Darren Tremble		6.04.89	4rC	Crawley	18 Jul
2:17.8	James Phillips		13.12.88	1	Tonbridge	3 Jul
2:18.5	Nathan Woodward		17.10.89	1	Nottingham	9 Sep
Foreign						
1:49.35	*Conor Sweeney (IRL)*	*U23*	*28.12.81*	*2*	*Dublin, IRL*	*21 Jul*

1000 Metres

2:24.88 i	Andy Hart		13.09.69	7	Boston, USA	4	Feb

1500 Metres

3:34.43	John Mayock		26.10.70	13	Brussels, BEL	24	Aug
	3:34.80			9	Zurich, SUI	17	Aug
	3:35.73			6	Nice, FRA	9	Jul
	3:36.25 i			2	Birmingham	18	Feb
	3:37.6 +			3m	London (CP)	22	Jul
	3:39.09 i+			4m	Stockholm, SWE	15	Feb
	3:39.24			8h1	Edmonton, CAN	9	Aug
	3:41.37			7	Prague, CZE	18	Jun
	3:42.28			2	Andujar, ESP	5	Sep
	3:42.63			10s2	Edmonton, CAN	10	Aug
3:34.88	Anthony Whiteman		13.11.71	4rB	Zurich, SUI	17	Aug
	3:36.77			7s1	Edmonton, CAN	10	Aug
	3:37.60			4	Gateshead	19	Aug
	3:37.75			6h2	Edmonton, CAN	9	Aug
	3:38.5 +			6m	London (CP)	22	Jul
	3:40.86			12	Nuremberg, GER	17	Jun
3:35.97	Andrew Graffin		20.12.77	7	Nice, FRA	9	Jul
	3:36.41			6	Rieti, ITA	2	Sep
	3:37.77			14	Lausanne, SUI	4	Jul
	3:39.80			3	Watford	9	Jun
	3:40.44			10h3	Edmonton, CAN	9	Aug
	3:42.67			7	Hengelo, NED	4	Jun
3:38.3 +	Tom Mayo		2.05.77	5m	London (CP)	22	Jul
	3:38.34			5	Gateshead	19	Aug
	3:39.27			1	Watford	9	Jun
	3:41.28			9	Rieti, ITA	2	Sep
3:38.94	Michael East		20.01.78	2	Arnhem, NED	4	Jul
	3:39.47			2	Watford	9	Jun
	3:42.9 +			13m	London (CP)	22	Jul
3:39.88	Angus Maclean	U23	20.09.80	4	Watford	9	Jun
	3:41.00			1	Watford	25	Jul
	3:41.36			5	Amsterdam, NED	14	Jul
	3:41.66			3	Loughborough	20	May
3:41.75	James Bowler	U23	2.09.79	5	Watford	9	Jun
3:41.94	Chris Stephenson		22.07.74	6	Watford	9	Jun
3:42.16	Jon McCallum		19.11.75	4	Loughborough	20	May
3:42.58	Richard Ashe		5.10.74	3	Watford	25	Jul
(10)							
3:42.73	Gregg Taylor		1.08.77	4	Watford	25	Jul
3:42.77	Simon Lees	U23	19.11.79	7	Watford	9	Jun
3:42.81	Vince Wilson		1.04.73	8	Watford	9	Jun
3:42.90	Adam Zawadski		19.12.74	5	Loughborough	20	May
	41 performances to 3:43.00 by 14 athletes including 2 indoors						
3:43.55	Chris Thompson	U23	17.04.81	10	Watford	9	Jun
3:43.79	Glen Stewart		7.12.70	7	Loughborough	20	May
3:44.09	Steve Rees-Jones		24.12.74	2	Solihull	23	Jun
3:44.33	Chris Moss	U23	17.06.79	2	Glasgow (S)	7	May
3:44.51	James Thie		27.06.78	3	Solihull	23	Jun
3:44.55	Simon Deakin		5.10.77	2	Manchester	23	May
(20)							
3:44.62	Alister Moses		5.07.78	2	Watford	15	Aug
3:44.82	Phil Tedd		7.11.76	12	Watford	9	Jun
3:44.96	Richard Ward	U20	5.05.82	4	Solihull	23	Jun
3:45.28	Michael Skinner	U23	21.11.79	4	Glasgow (S)	7	May
3:45.30	Tom Ranger		20.11.77	7	Watford	25	Jul
3:45.33	Steve Sharp		31.12.75	6	Manchester	23	May

3:45.67	Chris Bolt	U23	21.09.80	6	Solihull	23 Jun
3:45.70	Iain Murdoch	U23	10.07.80	1	Heusden, BEL	14 Jul
3:45.82	Chris Livesey	U23	8.08.80	1	Stretford	28 Aug
3:45.92	Rod Finch		5.08.67	10	Watford	25 Jul
	(30)					
3:45.98	James Tonner		3.06.75	1	Eton	7 Jul
3:46.04	Julian Moorhouse		13.11.71	2	Stretford	28 Aug
3:46.10	Ben Whitby		6.01.77	2rB	Watford	9 Jun
3:46.10	Matt Smith		26.12.74	11	Watford	25 Jul
3:46.1	Mohamed Farah	U20	23.03.83	1	Watford	29 Aug
3:46.13	Pat Davoren		13.03.72	1	Watford	27 Jun
3:46.19	Matt Shone		10.07.75	2	Eton	7 Jul
3:46.24	Justin Swift-Smith		28.08.74	4	Cardiff	4 Jul
3:46.32	Stuart Stokes		15.12.76	2	Watford	27 Jun
3:46.44	Richard Girvan		26.07.76	8	Manchester	23 May
	(40)					
3:46.46	Mark Miles		24.03.77	3rB	Watford	9 Jun
3:46.49	Ian Grime		29.09.70	12	Watford	25 Jul
3:46.55	Phillip Tulba		20.09.73	5	Cardiff	4 Jul
3:46.70	Ricky Soos	U20	28.06.83	8	Solihull	23 Jun
3:46.77	David Anderson		2.10.77	1	Stretford	3 Jul
3:46.84	Nick McCormick	U23	11.09.81	9	Manchester	23 May
3:46.89	Neil Kirk		14.09.78	2	Ann Arbor, USA	11 May
3:46.90	Don Naylor		5.09.71	14	Cork, IRL	7 Jul
3:47.13	Sam Haughian	U23	9.07.79	13	Watford	25 Jul
3:47.21	Matt O'Dowd		15.04.76	5rB	Watford	9 Jun
	(50)					
3:47.27	Gareth Price	U23	27.11.79	6rB	Watford	9 Jun
3:47.29	Rob Scanlon		13.04.74	2	Stretford	19 Jun
3:47.65	Steve Green		18.02.71	4	Stretford	28 Aug
3:47.70	Jon Wild		30.08.73	3	Stretford	31 Jul
3:47.71	Tim Don		14.01.78	8	Stellenbosch, RSA	30 Mar
3:47.91	Mick Morris		16.07.74	8rB	Watford	9 Jun
3:47.94	James Fewtrell	U23	22.12.80	2rB	Manchester	23 May
3:47.97	Matthew Jones	U20	10.10.82	11	Solihull	23 Jun
3:48.06	Steve Body		6.01.75	1rC	Watford	9 Jun
3:48.15	Ed Prickett	U20	28.01.83	1rB	Watford	25 Jul
	(60)					
3:48.27	Adam Bowden	U20	5.08.82	2rC	Watford	9 Jun
3:48.29	Nick Goodliffe	U20	12.05.82	5	Stretford	28 Aug
3:48.31	Andrew Sherman	U23	28.09.81	2rB	Watford	25 Jul
3:48.35	Rob Watkinson		10.03.74	6	Stretford	28 Aug
3:48.37	Jason Lobo		18.09.69	10	Stellenbosch, RSA	30 Mar
3:48.54	Neil Bangs	U23	28.03.80	12	Solihull	23 Jun
3:48.56	Gavin Thompson	U23	9.04.80	3rC	Watford	9 Jun
3:48.79	Ben Cooke	U23	10.04.81	3rB	Manchester	23 May
3:48.89	Ivan Hollingsworth		20.05.75	1rB	Solihull	23 Jun
3:48.91	Kevin Sheppard	U23	21.01.79	8	Watford	15 Aug
	(70)					
3:48.97	Mike Gregory		5.11.76	9	Watford	15 Aug
3:49.01	Chris Mulvaney	U23	25.05.81	4	Des Moines, USA	28 Apr
3:49.12	Andrew Franklin	U23	13.09.80	3rB	Watford	25 Jul
3:49.21	Stuart Bailey		6.08.78	5	Stretford	31 Jul
3:49.22	Ben Tickner	U23	13.07.81	4rB	Manchester	23 May
3:49.27	Michael Green		12.10.76	3rB	Atlanta GA, USA	18 May
3:49.50	Robert Whittle	U23	14.06.81	4rB	Loughborough	20 May
3:49.55	Martin Airey		28.10.70	7rC	Watford	9 Jun
3:49.70	Nick Wetheridge		11.10.72	9rC	Watford	9 Jun
3:49.71	Steve Neill		11.08.66	10	Watford	15 Aug
	(80)					
3:49.79	Robert Smith	U20	3.12.82	10rC	Watford	9 Jun

3:49.87	Mark Sanford		19.04.78	5rB	Watford	25 Jul
3:49.90	Kojo Kyereme		23.12.74	1rB	Cardiff	4 Jul
3:50.01	Steven Vernon	U23	17.10.80	6rB	Loughborough	20 May
3:50.01	Chris Stoves	U20	20.02.84	1	Stretford	5 Jun
3:50.1	Derek Watson	U20	22.05.83	1	Bedford	1 Jul
3:50.12	Rob Berry		29.07.69	3	Stretford	3 Jul
3:50.2	Chris Davies		19.10.76	1	Telford	12 May
3:50.38	Tony O'Brien		14.11.70	2	Stretford	5 Jun
3:50.53	Ray Ward		22.08.75	7	Stretford	31 Jul
(90)						
3:50.59	Kevin Farrow		8.09.75	3	Stretford	5 Jun
3:50.6	Kevin Hayes		10.11.70	6	Watford	29 Aug
3:50.74	Dave Mitchinson		4.09.78	6rB	Watford	25 Jul
3:50.79	Matt Davies		23.07.71	1rB	Eton	7 Jul
3:50.86	Andy Renfree		18.05.75	6	Cardiff	4 Jul
3:50.91	Ewen North		13.07.78	7rB	Watford	25 Jul
3:51.00	Paul Freary		3.04.68	4	Stretford	5 Jun
3:51.05	Carl Tipton		4.02.77	6	Stretford	3 Jul
3:51.09	Matthew Bowser	U20	3.07.83	8	Stretford	31 Jul
3:51.11	Jonathan Burrell		24.11.75	8rB	Watford	25 Jul
(100)						
3:51.18	Bradley Yewer	U23	10.02.79	3rD	Watford	9 Jun
3:51.23	David Cowlishaw		17.09.67	4rD	Watford	9 Jun
3:51.3	Ian Hudspith		23.09.70	1	Jarrow	7 Jul
3:51.37	Steve Murphy	U20	6.01.83	3	Bedford	22 Aug
3:51.4	Scott Sterling		6.12.78	1	Loughborough	13 Jun
3:51.4	Mark McIntosh	U20	8.08.82	8	Watford	29 Aug
3:51.42	Martin Hilton		9.05.75	1	Stretford	14 Aug
3:51.43	Martyn Cryer	U23	16.10.81	3	Stretford	19 Jun
3:51.48	Scott Overall	U20	9.02.83	4	Watford	27 May
3:51.60	Jonathan Earnshaw		24.08.77	13	Watford	15 Aug
(110)						
3:51.77	Andrew Hennessy		24.08.77	9	London (Ha)	17 Jun
3:51.80	Nathan Dosanjh	U23	13.02.79	10	Stanford, USA	4 May
3:51.83	Brad Donkin		6.12.71	9	Stretford	31 Jul

Additional Under 20 (1 - 15 above)

3:52.15	Andrew Baddeley	20.06.82	1	Philadelphia PA, USA	8 Apr
3:52.58	Royston Green	4.01.82	7rD	Watford	9 Jun
3:52.7	Jermaine Mays	23.12.82	1	Perivale	7 Jul
3:53.0	Andrew Fulford	23.06.82	2	Exeter	31 Jul
3:53.5	Tom Carter	20.08.82	5	Bedford	1 Jul
(20)					
3:53.99	Malcolm Hassan	27.11.82	1	Gateshead	12 May
3:54.0	Matt Simpkins	9.05.82	4	Loughborough	13 Jun
3:54.4	Mark Draper	28.06.84	7	Bedford	1 Jul
3:54.4	Edward Jackson	4.01.82	13	Watford	29 Aug
3:54.46	Lee Turner	30.06.82	1rB	Stretford	31 Jul

Under 17

3:54.54	Colin McCourt	11.12.84	1rC	Watford	25 Jul
3:55.77	Tom Lancashire	2.07.85	1	Tullamore, IRL	21 Jul
3:56.6	Ahmed Ali	31.03.86	3rB	Watford	29 Aug
3:56.94	Mark Shankey	19.12.84	3	Vilvoorde, BEL	23 Jun
3:57.04	Ben Wiffen	30.10.84	5rC	Watford	25 Jul
3:57.62	Chris Reynolds	23.01.85	12rB	Watford	15 Aug
3:58.7	Michael Smart	18.11.85	1	Watford	19 Sep
3:59.79	Mark Johnston	18.10.84	2	Stretford	11 Sep
4:00.20	Lee Emanuel	24.01.85	3	Sheffield	12 Aug
4:00.3	Michael Rimmer	3.02.86	1	Sheffield (W)	3 Jun
(10)					

4:00.59	Anthony Moran	8.01.86	10rB	Stretford	31 Jul
4:00.83	Lee Bowron	2.10.85	1	Watford	27 May
4:00.91	Darren Malin	19.06.85	3	Tullamore, IRL	21 Jul
4:01.21	Chris Parr	13.11.84	9	Stretford	28 Aug
4:01.28	Shugri Omar	20.12.84	5	Sheffield	12 Aug
4:01.46	Daniel Robinson	23.10.84	4rC	Watford	15 Aug
4:01.75	Luke Gunn	22.03.85	5rE	Solihull	23 Jun
4:02.26	Russell Shute	21.05.85	6rD	Solihull	23 Jun
4:02.4	Tom Snow	7.09.85	11rB	Watford	29 Aug
4:02.41	Rory Smith	12.12.84	6	Sheffield	12 Aug
	(20)				
4:02.49	Alex Hodgkinson	1.12.84	3	Watford	27 May
4:02.49	Lewis Cadman	6.07.85	11rF	Watford	9 Jun
4:02.78	Darren Doyle-Howson	23.05.85	4	Tullamore, IRL	21 Jul
4:03.16	Phil Williams	28.09.84	3	Stretford	11 Sep
4:03.76	Ryan McLeod	7.06.85	2	Cudworth	27 May
4:03.80	Tom Humphries	24.09.84	7	Sheffield	12 Aug
	4:03.8		1	Tipton	1 Jul
4:04.11	Alan Wales	7.08.85	5rC	Cardiff	4 Jul
4:04.3	Adam Watt	29.10.84	2	Grangemouth	17 Jun
4:04.7	Rob Hayward	22.09.84	4h1	Watford	26 May
4:04.73	Sean Dirrane	17.10.85	4	Scunthorpe	18 Aug
	(30)				
4:04.8	Stephen Enright	5.09.84	3	Stretford	17 Jul
4:04.92	Robin MacIntosh	2.03.85	5	Tullamore, IRL	21 Jul

Under 15

4:05.48	Alex Felce	11.09.86	10rC	Stretford	31 Jul
4:09.4	James Mitchell	11.10.86	9rC	Watford	29 Aug
4:13.2	Tom Michaelson	3.01.87	1	Stoke-on-Trent	17 Jun
4:15.43	Paul McHugh	5.06.87	1h2	Exeter	6 Jul
4:15.61	Ross Toole	8.10.86	1	Sheffield	12 Aug
4:15.67	Nick Zissler	12.09.86	2h2	Exeter	6 Jul
4:15.8	Ben Harding	12.12.86	4	Crawley	18 Jul
4:16.41	Hamish Robertson	1.11.86	3	Exeter	7 Jul
4:16.59	Richard Newton	10.02.87	1	Scunthorpe	18 Aug
4:16.75	Tim Haughian	29.11.86	2	Sheffield	12 Aug
	(10)				
4:17.8	Adrian Holliday	17.01.87	2	Carlisle	17 Jun
4:17.88	Carl Shubotham	10.04.87	11rB	Stretford	19 Jun
4:17.99	Laurence Cox	15.03.88	5h2	Exeter	6 Jul
4:18.3	Matthew Lomax	19.09.86	1	Jarrow	9 Jun
4:19.2	Craig Bravington	9.12.86	1	Bournemouth	12 May
4:19.2 ?	Anthony Welford	5.10.87		Tynedale	3 Jun
4:19.65	Steven Bruce	19.10.86	5h1	Exeter	6 Jul
4:20.29	Nathan Shrubb	11.10.86	6h1	Exeter	6 Jul
4:20.32	Robert Morter	25.10.86	1	Neath	26 Aug
4:20.34	James Bulman	7.11.86	7h1	Exeter	6 Jul
	(20)				
4:20.50	Ben McDonald	9.11.86	1	Birmingham	27 May
4:20.71	Abdi Igi	12.12.87	5	Watford	30 May
4:20.9	Matt Wood	14.12.86	1	Blackpool	12 May
4:20.9	Martin Paterson		1	Solihull	22 Jul

Under 13

4:40.1	Richard Mattock	1.10.88	1	Gloucester	4 Aug
4:44.7	Ashley Reece	8.09.88	1	Milton Keynes	8 Jul
4:46.2	Matthew Young	6.07.89	5rB	Watford	19 Sep
4:47.3	Christopher Dodds	30.01.89	1	Birmingham	1 Jul
4:47.4	Robert Heaney	10.02.89	1	Bedford	17 Jun
4:47.9	Stuart Huntingdon	2.12.88	1	Birmingham	1 Jul

Foreign

3:38.28	*Gareth Turnbull (IRL)*	*U23*	*14.05.79*	*2*	*Loughborough*	*20 May*
3:43.85	*Conor Sweeney (IRL)*	*U23*	*28.12.81*	*1rB*	*Watford*	*9 Jun*
3:44.26	*Colm McLean (IRL)*	*U23*	*7.06.80*	*1*	*Manchester*	*23 May*
3:47.57	*Gary Murray IRL)*	*U23*	*31.01.80*	*6*	*Watford*	*15 Aug*

1 Mile

3:54.05	John Mayock		26.10.70	4	London (CP)	22 Jul
	3:55.07 i			4	Stockholm, SWE	15 Feb
	3:58.49			7	Brisbane, AUS	6 Sep
3:55.16	Anthony Whiteman		13.11.71	8	London (CP)	22 Jul
3:55.42	Andrew Graffin		20.12.77	5	Linz, AUT	20 Aug
3:55.57	Tom Mayo		2.05.77	9	London (CP)	22 Jul
3:59.61	Michael East		20.01.78	13	London (CP)	22 Jul
4:02.83 i#	Neil Kirk		14.09.78	2	Notre Dame, USA	3 Mar
4:02.95 i#	Chris Mulvaney	U23	25.05.81	7	Ames, USA	2 Mar
4:05.4	Iain Murdoch	U23	10.07.80	3	Dumfries	4 Aug
4:06.74	Andy Renfree		18.05.75	1	Glasgow (S)	18 Jul
4:07.45	Nick McCormick	U23	11.09.81	4	Glasgow (S)	11 Aug
	(10)					
4:07.7	David Anderson		2.10.77	4	Dumfries	29 Jul
4:09.2	Vince Wilson		1.04.73	5	Dumfries	29 Jul
4:09.23	James Fewtrell	U23	22.12.80	5	Glasgow (S)	11 Aug
4:09.24	Gregg Taylor		1.08.77	6	Glasgow (S)	11 Aug
4:09.9	Steve Body		6.01.75	1	Bedford	28 May
4:09.9	Chris Bolt	U23	21.09.80	2	Bedford	28 May
4:10.12	Andy Young		20.06.77	7	Glasgow (S)	11 Aug
4:10.8	Pat Davoren		13.03.72	3	Bedford	28 May
4:11.27 i#	Nathan Dosanjh	U23	13.02.79	11	Notre Dame, USA	3 Feb

Under 17

4:27.0	Chris Lamb		11.05.85	2	Jarrow	8 Aug
4:30.3	Ryan McLeod		7.06.85	3	Jarrow	8 Aug

Foreign

4:06.70	*Gary Murray (IRL)*	*U23*	*31.01.80*	*2*	*Glasgow (S)*	*11 Aug*

2000 Metres

4:57.09 i	John Mayock		26.10.70	2	Lievin, FRA	25 Feb

3000 Metres

7:44.08 i	John Mayock		26.10.70	4	Lisbon, POR	11 Mar
	7:51.10 i			6h2	Lisbon, POR	9 Mar
	7:56.06			3	Bremen, GER	24 Jun
	7:57.11			1	Gateshead	19 Aug
7:54.10	Michael Openshaw		8.04.72	1	Loughborough	20 May
7:55.75	Matt O'Dowd		15.04.76	2	Loughborough	20 May
7:58.30 i	Rob Whalley		11.02.68	1	Cardiff	4 Feb
	7:59.12 i			1	Cardiff	9 Dec
7:59.57	Rob Denmark		23.11.68	5	Loughborough	20 May
7:59.58 i	Ian Gillespie		18.05.70	2	Cardiff	9 Dec
	10 performances to 8:00.00 by 6 athletes including 5 indoors					
8:00.62	Tom Mayo		2.05.77	1	Watford	30 May
8:00.92	Spencer Barden		31.03.73	6	Loughborough	20 May
8:02.78	Jon Wild		30.08.73	1	Cardiff	4 Jul
8:03.94	Sam Haughian	U23	9.07.79	8	Gateshead	19 Aug
(10)						
8:04.01	Chris Thompson	U23	17.04.81	2	Cardiff	4 Jul

8:04.57	Christian Nicolson		19.09.73	4	Cardiff	4 Jul
8:04.82 i	Glen Stewart		7.12.70	1	Glasgow	21 Jan
	8:05.8 e+			m	Solihull	23 Jun
8:05.08	Steffan White		21.12.72	5	Cardiff	4 Jul
8:05.16 A	Allen Graffin		20.12.77	4	Pretoria, RSA	23 Mar
8:05.64	Matt Smith		26.12.74	6	Cardiff	4 Jul
8:05.90	Mark Miles		24.03.77	7	Cardiff	4 Jul
8:07.11	Phil Mowbray		19.03.73	1	Grangemouth	1 Aug
8:07.27 i#	Jon McCallum		19.11.75	5	Tampere, FIN	12 Feb
8:07.57	Julian Moorhouse		13.11.71	1	Stretford	3 Jul
	(20)					
8:07.60	Glynn Tromans		17.03.69	8	Cardiff	4 Jul
8:08.04	James Fewtrell	U23	22.12.80	9	Cardiff	4 Jul
8:09.11 i	Phillip Tulba		20.09.73	1	Birmingham	14 Jan
8:09.19	James Bowler	U23	2.09.79	4	Merksem, BEL	4 Aug
8:09.24	Mohamed Farah	U20	23.03.83	7	Loughborough	20 May
8:10.06	Michael Green		12.10.76	1	Troy, USA	7 Apr
8:10.45	Ben Noad		6.05.76	10	Cardiff	4 Jul
8:10.53	Stephen Hepples	U23	6.01.80	9	Loughborough	20 May
8:10.68	Gregg Taylor		1.08.77	2	Stretford	3 Jul
8:11.32 i	Steve Body		6.01.75	4	Birmingham	14 Jan
	8:14.53			2	Watford	30 May
	(30)					
8:11.79	Ian Hudspith		23.09.70	3	Stretford	3 Jul
8:11.88	Simon Deakin		5.10.77	11	Cardiff	4 Jul
8:11.92	Don Naylor		5.09.71	2	Grangemouth	1 Aug
8:12.77 i	Adam Sutton	U23	22.03.81	3	Boston, USA	19 Jan
8:12.77	Michael East		20.01.78	10	Loughborough	20 May
8:13.29	Chris Livesey	U23	8.08.80	4	Stretford	3 Jul
8:14.03 i	Rod Finch		5.08.67	2	Cardiff	4 Feb
	8:15.39			5	Glasgow (S)	11 Aug
8:14.04 i	Angus Maclean	U23	20.09.80	3	Cardiff	9 Dec
	8:14.54			4	Glasgow (S)	11 Aug
8:14.19 i	James Thie		27.06.78	4	Cardiff	9 Dec
8:14.46 i	Robert Gould		16.01.76	5	Birmingham	14 Jan
	8:21.76			8	Stretford	3 Jul
	(40)					
8:14.62 A	Jason Lobo		18.09.69	6	Pretoria, RSA	23 Mar
8:15.01	Chris Stephenson		22.07.74	12	Cardiff	4 Jul
8:15.90	Lee McCash	U23	22.10.81	5	Stretford	3 Jul
8:15.90	Neil Bangs	U23	28.03.80	1rB	Cardiff	4 Jul
8:16.17	Martin Hilton		9.05.75	2rB	Cardiff	4 Jul
8:17.3	Alister Moses		5.07.78	1	Watford	29 Aug
8:17.46 i	Ian Grime		29.09.70	2h1	Birmingham	27 Jan
8:17.83	Andy Caine		17.06.77	11	Loughborough	20 May
8:18.44 i	Kevin Nash		6.02.77	7	Birmingham	14 Jan
8:18.61	Justin Swift-Smith		28.08.74	1	Street	7 May
	(50)					
8:18.82 i	Andrew Hennessy		24.08.77	3h1	Birmingham	27 Jan
8:19.43 i	Graeme Reid	U23	14.04.79	4	Boston, USA	26 Jan
8:19.53 i	Paul Howarth		30.10.77	4	Indianapolis, USA	10 Feb
8:19.86	Rob Berry		29.07.69	4	Stretford	8 May
8:19.9	Ed Prickett	U20	28.01.83	2	Watford	29 Aug
8:20.06 i	Iain Murdoch	U23	10.07.80	1	Glasgow	14 Jan
8:20.12	Jerome Brooks		9.08.73	3rB	Cardiff	4 Jul
8:20.18	Tony O'Brien		14.11.70	6	Stretford	3 Jul
8:20.24	Martyn Cryer	U23	16.10.81	7	Stretford	3 Jul
8:20.80	Ewen North		13.07.78	4rB	Cardiff	4 Jul
	(60)					
8:20.94 i	Andrew Graffin		20.12.77	3	Birmingham	28 Jan

8:20.98 i	Chris Bolt	U23	21.09.80	5	Cardiff	9 Dec
8:21.13 i	Matthew Plano		8.10.76	2	Milwaukee, USA	19 Jan
8:21.16 i	Kevin Farrow		8.09.75	3h2	Birmingham	27 Jan
8:21.27	Gareth Raven		9.05.74	2	Stretford	31 Jul
8:21.3	Neil Wilkinson		12.03.69	2	Stretford	17 Jul
8:23.04	Guy Amos		15.06.63	1	Birmingham	30 Jun
8:23.21 i	Martin Yelling		7.02.72	6	Birmingham	28 Jan
8:23.25	Nick Goodliffe	U20	12.05.82	3	Stoke-on-Trent	18 Aug
8:24.24	Paul Green		7.04.72	3	Stretford	31 Jul
(70)						
8:24.5	David Taylor		9.01.64	1	London (TB)	22 Aug
8:24.81 i	Steve Rees-Jones		24.12.74	8	Birmingham	14 Jan
8:24.85	Tom Sharland	U20	5.10.83	2	Exeter	7 Jul
Additional Under 20 (1 - 4 above)						
8:25.0	Antony Ford		26.05.83	4	Stretford	17 Jul
8:26.53	Benjamin Fish		21.05.82	1	Stretford	28 Aug
8:26.7	Adam Bowden		5.08.82	1	Watford	19 Sep
8:27.07 i	Richard Ward		5.05.82	6	Cardiff	9 Dec
	8:39.1			1	Kingston	12 May
8:28.0	Scott Overall		9.02.83	2	Brighton	22 Aug
8:28.4	Mark McIntosh		8.08.82	2	Watford	19 Sep
(10)						
8:29.15	Steve Murphy		6.01.83	4	Watford	30 May
8:29.53	Mark Draper		28.06.84	5	Watford	30 May
8:29.53	Matthew Bowser		3.07.83	1	Stretford	14 Aug
8:30.7 i	James Williams		17.07.82	2	Cardiff	7 Feb
8:30.9	Peter Kellie		2.01.84	7	Watford	29 Aug
8:31.22	Mark Shankey	U17	19.12.84	12	Duffel, BEL	2 May
8:31.74	Phil Nicholls		29.09.83	5	Exeter	7 Jul
8:32.5	Philip Banks		8.03.83	10	Watford	29 Aug
8:35.25	Steven Ablitt		16.11.83	3	Stretford	14 Aug
8:35.39	Ian Boneham		30.09.82	6	Exeter	7 Jul
(20)						
8:35.83 i	Andrew Rayner		16.01.82	9	Cardiff	9 Dec
8:37.3	Chris Parr	U17	13.11.84	2	Gateshead	1 Aug
8:37.5	Andrew Pickett		11.05.82	2	Watford	15 Aug
8:38.94	Colin McCourt	U17	11.12.84	1	Tullamore, IRL	21 Jul
8:39.00	Luke Northall	U17	30.11.84	5	Stretford	14 Aug
Additional Under 17 (1 - 4 above)						
8:41.13	Richard Parker		22.02.85	13	Stretford	3 Jul
8:42.11	Anthony Moran		8.01.86	3	Tullamore, IRL	21 Jul
8:44.4	Lewis Cadman		6.07.85	6	Watford	25 Jul
8:44.82	Ahmed Ali		31.03.86	3	Exeter	7 Jul
8:46.0	Matthew Barnes-Smith		5.10.85	9	Watford	25 Jul
8:46.12	Shugri Omar		20.12.84	10	Watford	30 May
(10)						
8:47.08	Chris Lamb		11.05.85	1	Scunthorpe	18 Aug
8:48.36	Jem Scragg		30.12.84	6	Street	7 May
8:50.82	Tom Fahey		27.09.84	5	Exeter	7 Jul
8:50.87	Craig Ivemy		28.03.86	4	Sheffield	11 Aug
8:51.00 i	Tommy Davies	U20	3.08.85	2rB	Cardiff	9 Dec
8:51.92	Rory Smith		12.12.84	2	Scunthorpe	18 Aug
8:52.02	Stephen Enright		5.09.84	9	Stretford	31 Jul
8:52.51	Ben Jones		14.01.86	6h1	Exeter	6 Jul
8:53.27	Darren Malin		19.06.85	1	Edinburgh	13 May
8:53.59	Jonathan Blackledge		15.09.84	7h1	Exeter	6 Jul
(20)						
8:53.6	Tom Snow		7.09.85	1	Basildon	22 Sep
8:53.61	Tom Humphries		24.09.84	6	Exeter	7 Jul

8:54.90	Matthew Ashton	13.12.84	3	London (Ha)	17 Jun
8:54.9	Ryan McLeod	7.06.85	5	Gateshead	1 Aug
8:55.31	Adam Watt	29.10.84	2	Edinburgh	13 May
8:55.49	James Lockley	25.06.85	9h1	Exeter	6 Jul
8:55.74	Shaun Pickering	3.02.85	7	Stretford	5 Jun
8:55.8	Sam Jacobs	19.09.84	1rB	Watford	25 Jul
8:56.09	Alan Wales	7.08.85	1	Grangemouth	10 Jun
8:56.36	Oliver Holden	20.05.86	4h2	Exeter	6 Jul
	(30)				
8:56.37	James Hogan	2.12.84	5h2	Exeter	6 Jul
8:56.58	Peter Emmett	24.04.85	2	Cardiff	16 Jun
8:56.7	Gavin Smith	15.02.85	2rB	Watford	25 Jul
8:57.39	Alan Stewart	9.12.84	10	Stretford	19 Jun
8:58.34	Phil Williams	28.09.84	14	Stretford	28 Aug
8:58.42	Sean Dirrane	17.10.85	5	Stretford	11 Sep
8:58.43	Mark Buckingham	4.05.85	11	Stretford	19 Jun
8:58.9	Steve Ames	2.07.85	4rB	Watford	25 Jul
8:59.5	Chris Knights	17.10.85	1	Peterborough	27 Aug

Under 15

8:59.6	James Mitchell	11.10.86	2	Peterborough	27 Aug
9:09.3	Alex Felce	11.09.86	5	Solihull	16 May
9:13.7	Andrew Friend	2.08.87	12rB	Watford	25 Jul
9:14.8	Tom Michaelson	3.01.87	4	Stretford	6 Mar
9:19.4	Ben Harding	12.12.86	1	Southampton	8 Sep
9:24.5	Daniel Russell	2.04.87	16rB	Watford	25 Jul
9:24.61	Abdi Igi	12.12.87	2	London (Ha)	17 Jun
9:24.78	David Bottjer	24.11.86	3	London (Ha)	17 Jun
9:26.2	Tim Haughian	29.11.86	1rB	Watford	1 Aug
9:26.3	Hamish Robertson	1.11.86	1	Sheffield	28 Apr
	(10)				
9:26.70	Dominik Morton	13.12.86	1	Birmingham	1 Sep
9:27.5	Adrian Holliday	17.01.87	1	Warrington	3 Jun
9:28.2	Ross Toole	8.10.86	1	Linwood	6 Sep
9:28.89	Matthew Lomax	19.09.86	1	Cudworth	27 May
9:29.17	Carl Shubotham	10.04.87	8rB	Stretford	31 Jul
9:30.9	Andrew Livingstone	3.05.88	1	Basildon	22 Sep
9:32.6	Paul McHugh	5.06.87	1	Wigan	1 Jul
9:34.01	James Philipson	18.03.87	2	Cudworth	27 May
9:34.42	Laurence Cox	15.03.88	5	London (Ha)	17 Jun
9:36.9	Jack Taylor	5.06.87	1	Hoo	22 Jul
	(20)				
9:37.08	Robert Pickering	3.11.87	3	Cudworth	27 May
9:38.4	Jonathan Davies	2.03.87	1	Tipton	1 Jul
9:38.5	Matthew Howes	6.01.87	11	Watford	15 Aug
9:39.3	Ashleigh Pain	16.10.87	2	Tipton	1 Jul

5000 Metres

13:24.44	Michael Openshaw	8.04.72	15	Heusden, BEL	14 Jul
	13:33.26		6	Milan, ITA	6 Jun
	13:37.86		2	Cork, IRL	7 Jul
	13:58.15		4	Bremen, GER	23 Jun
13:24.63	Karl Keska	7.05.72	16	Heusden, BEL	14 Jul
13:30.56	Matt O'Dowd	15.04.76	3	Solihull	23 Jun
	13:49.99		4	Manchester	23 May
	13:50.67		6	Cork, IRL	7 Jul
	13:53.53		2	Birmingham	15 Jul
13:36.30	Rob Denmark	23.11.68	4	Solihull	23 Jun
	13:42.70		1	Manchester	23 May

13:37.17	Glen Stewart		7.12.70	5	Solihull	23 Jun
	13:43.72			3	Manchester	23 May
	13:57.65			1	Edinburgh	25 Aug
13:40.07	Allen Graffin		20.12.77	3	Bratislava, SVK	12 Jun
	13:41.09			13	Milan, ITA	6 Jun
	13:42.15			6	Solihull	23 Jun
	13:52.08			7	Stellenbosch, RSA	30 Mar
13:43.40	Glynn Tromans		17.03.69	2	Manchester	23 May
13:45.27	Chris Thompson	U23	17.04.81	7	Solihull	23 Jun
	13:56.55			8	Beijing, CHN	1 Sep
13:46.35	Sam Haughian	U23	9.07.79	2	Watford	1 Aug
	13:49.55			8	Solihull	23 Jun
13:51.75	Julian Moorhouse		13.11.71	3	Watford	1 Aug
	13:52.88			9	Solihull	23 Jun
	13:55.37			6	Birmingham	15 Jul
(10)						
13:52.72	Jon Wild		30.08.73	1	Birmingham	15 Jul
13:53.4	Keith Cullen		13.06.72	1	London (BP)	20 May
	13:56.7 +			2m	Watford	9 Jun
13:53.74	Mark Miles		24.03.77	3	Birmingham	15 Jul
13:53.77	Nick Wetheridge		11.10.72	10	Solihull	23 Jun
13:54.26	Spencer Barden		31.03.73	4	Birmingham	15 Jul
13:54.50	Christian Nicolson		19.09.73	5	Birmingham	15 Jul
13:56.31	Mohamed Farah	U20	23.03.83	12	Solihull	23 Jun
13:56.44	Guy Amos		15.06.63	13	Solihull	23 Jun
13:56.56	Steffan White		21.12.72	7	Birmingham	15 Jul
13:58.48	Phil Mowbray		19.03.73	2	Edinburgh	25 Aug
	37 performances to 14:00.00 by 20 athletes					
14:01.86	Tony O'Brien		14.11.70	15	Solihull	23 Jun
14:03.16	Matt Smith		26.12.74	9	Birmingham	15 Jul
14:03.20	Tom Mayo		2.05.77	12	Melbourne, AUS	1 Mar
14:03.23 i	Ben Noad		6.05.76	1rB	Boston, USA	18 Feb
	14:11.40			2	Waltham, MA, USA	2 Jun
14:03.50	Ian Hudspith		23.09.70	6	Manchester	23 May
14:03.61	Adam Sutton	U23	22.03.81	7	Princeton, USA	18 May
14:04.46	Graeme Reid	U23	14.04.79	9	Philadelphia PA, USA	26 Apr
14:08.14	David Taylor		9.01.64	7	Manchester	23 May
14:09.41	Stephen Hepples	U23	6.01.80	9	Manchester	23 May
14:11.42	Andy Caine		17.06.77	10	Manchester	23 May
(30)						
14:12.50	Mark Hudspith		19.01.69	11	Manchester	23 May
14:12.56	Robert Gould		16.01.76	12	Manchester	23 May
14:13.29	Alan Buckley		25.10.74	13	Manchester	23 May
14:13.30	Malcolm Campbell		3.01.71	7	Raleigh NC, USA	30 Mar
14:14.38	Michael Green		12.10.76	2	Knoxville TN, USA	12 Apr
14:16.24	Gareth Raven		9.05.74	14	Manchester	23 May
14:18.53	Steve Sharp		31.12.75	6	Watford	1 Aug
14:19.14	Dave Mitchinson		4.09.78	7	Watford	1 Aug
14:19.90	Don Naylor		5.09.71	1	Grangemouth	7 Jun
14:20.12	Paul Green		7.04.72	3	Eton	7 Jul
(40)						
14:20.44	Rob Birchall		14.06.70	2	Bedford	21 Jul
14:23.14	Steve Brooks		8.06.70	2	Arnhem, NED	13 Jun
14:23.42	Lee McCash	U23	22.10.81	5	Eton	7 Jul
14:24.39	Ian Gillespie		18.05.70	3	Jarrow	18 Aug
14:25.8	Simon Deakin		5.10.77	3rB	Solihull	23 Jun
14:26.84	Pat Davoren		13.03.72	8	Watford	1 Aug
14:27.06	Chris Davies		19.10.76	2	Glasgow (S)	7 May
14:27.7	Oliver Laws	U23	18.03.80	4rB	Solihull	23 Jun
14:28.81	Ian Grime		29.09.70	4	Jarrow	18 Aug
14:29.96	Kairn Stone		21.10.76	6	Eton	7 Jul

14:30.10	Andy Morgan-Lee		1.03.69	14	Birmingham	15 Jul
14:31.21	Richard Gardiner		11.06.73	2rB	Manchester	23 May
14:31.72	Peter Grime		8.11.69	3rB	Manchester	23 May
14:31.74	Martyn Cryer	U23	16.10.81	2	Bedford	30 Jun
14:31.8	Neil Wilkinson		12.03.69	1	Oldham	4 Aug
14:32.22 i	Matthew Plano		8.10.76	2	Houston, USA	23 Feb
14:33.99	Ed Prickett	U20	28.01.83	10	Watford	1 Aug
14:34.5	Danny Robinson		4.08.73	6rB	Solihull	23 Jun
14:34.52	Ben Tickner	U23	13.07.81	6	Glasgow (S)	5 May
14:35.0	Bobby Quinn		10.12.65	1	Grangemouth	15 Jul
(60)						
14:35.26	Tom Hart		7.12.77	11	Watford	1 Aug
14:35.78	Dominic Bannister		1.04.68	6	Jarrow	18 Aug
14:37.2	Mark Morgan		19.08.72	1	Peterborough	7 Jul
14:38.15	Benjamin Fish	U20	21.05.82	5rB	Manchester	23 May
14:38.15	Stuart Major		5.05.70	12	Watford	1 Aug
14:38.4	Andrew Franklin	U23	13.09.80	1	Eton	18 Aug
14:38.96	Michael East		20.01.78	3	London (He)	5 May
14:39.42 i#	Paul Howarth		30.10.77	18rB	Notre Dame, USA	2 Feb
14:39.80	Dan Leggate		5.10.74	2	Glasgow (S)	23 Jun
14:40.01	Paul Freary		3.04.68	1	Birmingham	2 Jun
(70)						
14:40.80	Andrew Swearman		1.02.74	6rB	Manchester	23 May
14:41.42	Nick Goodliffe	U20	12.05.82	7	Glasgow (S)	7 May
14:42.4	Jason Simpson			1	London (TB)	28 Jul
14:42.66	Jerome Brooks		9.08.73	20	Solihull	23 Jun
14:43.3	Steve Cairns		3.11.67	1	Solihull	27 Jun
14:43.50	Mick Hill		2.09.75	16	Manchester	23 May
14:43.73	Jonathan Phillips	U23	8.05.80	8	Glasgow (S)	7 May
14:43.92	Daniel Dalmedo	U23	14.03.80	9	Glasgow (S)	7 May
14:45.0	Alaister Russell		17.06.68	2	Grangemouth	15 Jul
14:45.3	Huw Lobb		29.08.76	1	Rugby	10 Jun
(80)						
14:45.76	Alaster Stewart		5.10.72	7	Eton	7 Jul
14:46.51	Nick Talbot		14.12.77	6	Philadelphia PA, USA	8 Apr
14:46.6	Paul Farmer		23.11.77	3	Eton	10 Jun

Additional Under 20 (1 - 4 above)

14:54.5	Phil Nicholls		29.09.83	11rB	Solihull	23 Jun
14:54.98	Matthew Jones		10.10.82	10rB	Manchester	23 May
14:58.6	Andrew Lemoncello		12.10.82	1	Greenock	17 Jun
15:00.21	Tom Sharland		5.10.83	15	Watford	1 Aug
15:01.20	Antony Ford		26.05.83	2	Bedford	30 Jun
15:04.51	Steven Ablitt		16.11.83	3	Bedford	30 Jun
(10)						
15:15.58	Andrew Pickett		11.05.82	2	London (BP)	8 Aug
15:18.0	Robert Russell		13.07.82	6	Eton	18 Aug
15:18.0	Jermaine Mays		23.12.82	1	London (Cat)	18 Sep
15:18.69	Philip McGlory		2.09.83	3	Cudworth	26 May
15:23.51	David Webb		17.03.82	12	Glasgow (S)	5 May
15:28.2	Matthew Jones		12.02.82	20rB	Solihull	23 Jun
15:29.2	Tom Fahey	U17	27.09.84	1	London (B)	23 Jun

Foreign

13:58.88	*Craig Kirkwood (NZL)*		*8.10.74*	*14*	*Solihull*	*23 Jun*
14:04.28	*Emil de Jonge (RSA)*		*2.09.72*	*1*	*Jarrow*	*18 Aug*
14:05.27	*Gareth Turnbull (IRL)*	*U23*	*14.05.79*	*1*	*Tullamore, IRL*	*3 Jul*
14:19.31	*Joe McAllister (IRL)*	*U23*	*23.12.80*	*15*	*Manchester*	*23 May*
14:49.2	*Anton van Zyl (RSA)*		*20.01.75*	*1*	*London (He)*	*23 Jun*

5 Kilometres Road

14:12	Keith Cullen		13.06.72	2	Stevenage	27 May
14:13	Chris Thompson	U23	17.04.81	1	Bath	25 Mar
14:13	Ben Noad		6.05.76	1	Lincoln, USA	27 May
14:15	Rob Denmark		23.11.68	2	Bath	25 Mar
14:15	Jon Wild		30.08.73	3	Stevenage	27 May
14:16	Tony O'Brien		14.11.70	3	Bath	25 Mar
14:16	David Taylor		9.01.64	4	Bath	25 Mar
14:19	Kevin Farrow		8.09.75	5	Bath	25 Mar
14:22	Ben Whitby		6.01.77	6	Bath	25 Mar
14:23	James Bowler	U23	2.09.79	7	Bath	25 Mar
(10)						
14:25	Angus Maclean	U23	20.09.80	1	Poole	30 Mar
14:25	Glynn Tromans		17.03.69	4	Stevenage	27 May

5 Miles Road

22:59	Karl Keska	7.05.72	5	Balmoral	14 Apr
23:08	Matt O'Dowd	15.04.76	8	Balmoral	14 Apr
23:18	Rob Denmark	23.11.68	1	Portsmouth	2 Dec
23:20	Ben Noad	6.05.76	2	Loughrea, IRL	21 Oct
23:22	Rob Whalley	11.02.68	2	Portsmouth	2 Dec
23:26	Andres Jones	3.02.77	3	Portsmouth	2 Dec
23:28	Rod Finch	5.08.67	4	Portsmouth	2 Dec
23:31	Andy Coleman	29.09.74	1	Alsager	4 Feb
23:32	John Mayock	26.10.70	4	Loughrea, IRL	21 Oct
23:32	Matt Smith	26.12.74	5	Portsmouth	2 Dec
(10)					
23:33	Mark Morgan	19.08.72	5	Loughrea, IRL	21 Oct
23:34	Mark Hudspith	19.01.69	3	Alsager	4 Feb
23:34	Allen Graffin	20.12.77	10	Balmoral	14 Apr
23:40	Glynn Tromans	17.03.69	1	Coventry	27 Jun
23:40	Steve Sharp	31.12.75	6	Portsmouth	2 Dec
23:42	David Taylor	9.01.64	7	Portsmouth	2 Dec
23:48	Alister Moses	5.07.78	8	Portsmouth	2 Dec
23:49	Kris Bowditch	14.01.75	9	Portsmouth	2 Dec
23:50	Steve Body	6.01.75	1	Wolverton	24 Nov
23:50	Ian Gillespie	18.05.70	10	Portsmouth	2 Dec
(20)					
23:50	Michael East	20.01.78	11	Portsmouth	2 Dec

10000 Metres

28:06.29	Karl Keska		7.05.72	4	Barakaldo, ESP	7 Apr
28:31.33	Glynn Tromans		17.03.69	2	Watford	9 Jun
28:39.33	Jon Wild		30.08.73	3	Watford	9 Jun
28:40.14	Glen Stewart		7.12.70	4	Watford	9 Jun
28:40.63	Ian Hudspith		23.09.70	5	Watford	9 Jun
28:43.45	Matt Smith		26.12.74	8	Watford	9 Jun
	29:28.35			7rB	Barakaldo, ESP	7 Apr
28:46.70	Rob Denmark		23.11.68	9	Watford	9 Jun
28:52.97	Matt O'Dowd		15.04.76	3rB	Barakaldo, ESP	7 Apr
29:10.5	Sam Haughian	U23	9.07.79	1	Brighton	22 Aug
29:10.98	Adam Sutton	U23	22.03.81	11	Walnut CA, USA	20 Apr
	29:28.32			9	Amsterdam, NED	12 Jul
(10)						
29:22.22	David Taylor		9.01.64	11	Watford	9 Jun
29:28.70	Tony O'Brien		14.11.70	12	Watford	9 Jun
29:31.98	Danny Robinson		4.08.73	13	Watford	9 Jun
29:33.94	Andy Caine		17.06.77	14	Watford	9 Jun
29:34.10	Robert Gould		16.01.76	15	Watford	9 Jun
29:45.31	Alan Buckley		25.10.74	16	Watford	9 Jun

29:53.66	Malcolm Campbell		3.01.71	3	Waltham, MA, USA	2	Jun
30:00.4	Dave Mitchinson		4.09.78	2	Brighton	22	Aug
30:03.82	Mark Miles		24.03.77	11rB	Barakaldo, ESP	7	Apr
30:04.5	Neil Wilkinson		12.03.69	3	Brighton	22	Aug
(20)							
30:20.7	Andres Jones		3.02.77	1	Barry	8	Aug
30:28.67	Chris Birchall	U23	8.03.79	17	Philadelphia PA, USA	26	Apr
30:35.16	Mick Hill		2.09.75	1	Stretford	8	May
30:39.00	Dan Leggate		5.10.74	1	London (Ha)	10	Jun
30:40.52	Simon Cotton		26.07.67	18	Watford	9	Jun
30:40.93	Paul Green		7.04.72	1	Bedford	21	Jul
30:41.9	Barry Royden		15.12.66	4	Brighton	22	Aug
30:43.54	Colin Moore	V40	25.11.60	1	Douglas IOM	13	Jul
30:48.8	Michael Coleman		14.05.78	5	Brighton	22	Aug
30:51.12	Stuart Major		5.05.70	19	Watford	9	Jun
(30)							
30:52.69	Peter Grime		8.11.69	2	Glasgow (S)	5	May
30:54.32	Brad Poore		24.07.78	2	San Francisco, USA	11	May
30:54.39	David Ricketts	U23	2.12.79	3	Glasgow (S)	5	May
30:55.5	Richard Gardiner		11.06.73	2	Barry	8	Aug
30:57.96	Kassa Tadesse		21.08.74	2	Bedford	21	Jul
31:01.35	James Fitzsimmons		20.04.74	1	Bedford	27	May
31:02.15	Carl Morris	U23	5.05.80	4	Glasgow (S)	7	May
31:03.76	Kairn Stone		21.10.76	3	Bedford	21	Jul
31:04.8	Rod Leach		29.05.72	2	Glasgow (S)	23	Jun
31:06.3	Tom Hart		7.12.77	1	Eton	10	Jun
(40)							
31:09.3	Benjamin Fish	U20	21.05.82	1	Bolton	20	May
31:10.6	Bill Foster	V40	9.08.58	2	Eton	10	Jun
31:16.11	Craig McBurney		8.09.68	2	Bedford	27	May
31:16.80	Will Levett		6.09.75	21	Watford	9	Jun
31:16.8	Tony Duffy	V45	26.06.56	2	Bolton	20	May
31:17.5	Shaun Tobin		13.10.62	3	Barry	8	Aug
31:20.4	Phil Cook		7.05.69	4	Barry	8	Aug
31:22.5	Jamie Jones		8.12.71	6	Brighton	22	Aug
31:23.18	Andrew Muir		20.06.73	5	Glasgow (S)	5	May
31:30.91	Oliver Laws	U23	18.03.80	6	Glasgow (S)	5	May
(50)							
31:32.84	Stephen Platts		12.03.66	3	Bedford	27	May
31:34.7	Kevin Blake		29.05.67	1	Newport	20	May
31:36.55	Mike Boyle	V40	29.12.60	1	Eton	24	Jun
31:38.0	Arthur Deane	V45	22.05.54	3	Bolton	20	May
31:39.23	Andrew Norman	U23	19.08.80	22	Watford	9	Jun
31:40.80	Dave Norman		4.11.78	2	Stretford	8	May
31:45.1	Martin Ferguson		17.09.64	3	Glasgow (S)	23	Jun
31:48	Steve Murdoch	V40	16.04.61	1	St. Helens	9	Sep
31:48.69	Gavin Tomlinson	U23	2.02.80	7	Glasgow (S)	5	May
31:52.18	Barry Stephenson			8	Glasgow (S)	5	May
(60)							
31:53.89	Andrew Weir		22.08.67	4	Bedford	27	May
31:55.0	Keith Newton		14.03.63	7	Brighton	22	Aug
31:55.6	Alan Stimpson		25.04.68	1		24	Jun
31:58.5	Steve Edmonds		15.05.69	2	Wigan	10	Jun
31:58.9	Sullivan Smith		23.10.74	5	Barry	8	Aug
31:59.6	George Kirk		15.10.70	4	Bolton	20	May

Foreign

30:05.34	*John Downes (IRL)*		*21.07.67*	*17*	*Watford*	*9*	*Jun*

10000 Metres Road

28:48	Matt O'Dowd		15.04.76	2	Swansea	23 Sep
28:53	Rob Denmark		23.11.68	2	Cheltenham	9 Sep
28:56	Karl Keska		7.05.72	4	Houilles, FRA	30 Dec
28:59	John Mayock		26.10.70	1	Sheffield	2 Dec

Where better than track bests

29:10	Ben Noad		6.05.76	5	Cheltenham	9 Sep
29:16	Kassa Tadesse		21.08.74	3	Paris, FRA	19 May
29:17	Martin Palmer		5.04.77	6	Cheltenham	9 Sep
29:25	Paul Evans	V40	13.04.61	8	Cheltenham	9 Sep
29:26	Rod Finch		5.08.67	9	Cheltenham	9 Sep
29:29	Rob Birchall		14.06.70	2	Manchester	24 Jun
(10)						
29:39	Nick Jones		10.07.74	11	Cheltenham	9 Sep
29:42	Danny Robinson		4.08.73	12	Cheltenham	9 Sep
29:44	Malcolm Campbell		3.01.71	21	Atlanta GA, USA	4 Jul
29:46	Ian Grime		29.09.70	9	Basel, SUI	24 Nov
29:48	Steve Body		6.01.75	1	Eastleigh	18 Mar
29:48	Dominic Bannister		1.04.68	2	Chester-Le-Street	8 Aug
29:51	Martin Yelling		7.02.72	2	Eastleigh	18 Mar
29:51	Tommy Murray	V40	18.05.61	1	Clydebank	31 May
29:52	Andy Morgan-Lee		1.03.69	13	Cheltenham	9 Sep
29:52	Michael Openshaw		8.04.72	1	Bradford	21 Oct

Foreign

29:08	*Emil de Jonge (NED)*		*2.09.72*	*4*	*Cheltenham*	*9 Sep*
29:41	*John Mutai (KEN)*		*26.05.66*	*6*	*Swansea*	*23 Sep*

10 Miles Road

48:25 +	Jon Brown		27.02.71	m	New York, USA	4 Nov
48:32	Kassa Tadesse		21.08.74	8	Portsmouth	14 Oct
48:49	Ben Noad		6.05.76	9	Portsmouth	14 Oct
48:51	Carl Warren		28.09.69	1	Sale	5 Aug
49:02 +	Mark Steinle		22.11.74	m	London	22 Apr
49:08	Stuart Hall		21.12.64	2	Manchester	5 Aug
49:13	Nick Jones		10.07.74	1	Leyland	8 Jul
49:14	Nick Comerford		23.04.66	1	Walsall	9 Dec
49:17	Steve Brooks		8.06.70	16	Tilburg, NED	3 Jun
49:30	Sam Haughian	U23	9.07.79	1	Twickenham	23 Sep
	(10)					
49:34	Matthew Vaux-Harvey		30.03.76	10	Portsmouth	14 Oct
49:44	Rob Denmark		23.11.68	11	Portsmouth	14 Oct
49:48	Carl Thackery		14.10.62	1	Pocklington	25 Feb
49:51	Allan Adams		11.09.72	12	Portsmouth	14 Oct

Foreign

48:17	*John Mutai (KEN)*		*26.05.66*	*7*	*Portsmouth*	*14 Oct*

Half Marathon

62:40	Matt O'Dowd		15.04.76	21	Bristol	7 Oct
63:15	Paul Evans	V40	13.04.61	5	South Shields	16 Sep
63:52 +	Jon Brown		27.02.71	m	New York, USA	4 Nov
64:00	Nick Jones		10.07.74	51	Bristol	7 Oct
64:03	Nick Wetheridge		11.10.72	1	Enschede, NED	27 May
64:04	Kassa Tadesse		21.08.74	2	Glasgow	19 Aug
64:05 +	Mark Steinle		22.11.74	m	London	22 Apr
64:13	Rob Denmark		23.11.68	11	South Shields	16 Sep
64:19 +	Billy Burns		13.12.69	m	London	22 Apr
64:23	Danny Robinson		4.08.73	57	Bristol	7 Oct

64:30	Rob Birchall		14.06.70	2	Enschede, NED	27 May
64:46	Robert Gould		16.01.76	5	Enschede, NED	27 May
64:50	Guy Amos		15.06.63	6	Enschede, NED	27 May
64:51	Andy Morgan-Lee		1.03.69	7	Glasgow	19 Aug
64:53	Peter Fleming	V40	5.01.61	3	Austin TX, USA	4 Feb
64:57	Paul Green		7.04.72	1	Bath	18 Mar
65:08	Larry Matthews		11.08.65	1	Lake Vyrnwy	16 Sep
65:13	Malcolm Campbell		3.01.71	3		28 Jan
65:25	John Brown		2.02.69	13	South Shields	16 Sep
65:34	Glen Stewart		7.12.70	9	Glasgow	19 Aug
	(20)					
65:39	Allan Adams		11.09.72	15	South Shields	16 Sep
65:39	Glynn Tromans		17.03.69	3	Stroud	28 Oct
65:40 +	Tony O'Brien		14.11.70	m	London	22 Apr
65:40 +	Mark Hudspith		19.01.69	m	London	22 Apr
65:42	Ian Hudspith		23.09.70	11	Glasgow	19 Aug
65:42	Stuart Hall		21.12.64	17	South Shields	16 Sep
66:00	Tony Graham		15.10.63	3	Bath	18 Mar
66:01	Darren Hiscox		21.03.72	4	Bath	18 Mar
66:02	Steve Brooks		8.06.70	17	The Hague, NED	25 Mar
66:04	Duncan Mason		8.12.68	5	Bath	18 Mar
	(30)					
66:05	Gareth Raven		9.05.74	19	South Shields	16 Sep
66:29	Martin Rees	V45	28.02.53	1	Cheddar	10 Nov
66:45	Mike Simpson		6.01.70	6	Bath	18 Mar
66:46	Tommy Murray	V40	18.05.61	1	East Kilbride	17 Jun
66:48	Robert Deakin		21.10.66	3	Lake Vyrnwy	16 Sep
66:48	Mark Dalkins		9.09.71	4	Lake Vyrnwy	16 Sep
66:48	Martin Yelling		7.02.72	7	Stroud	28 Oct

Foreign

62:49	*John Mutai (KEN)*		*26.05.66*	*3*	*South Shields*	*16 Sep*
64:57	*Craig Kirkwood (NZL)*		*8.10.74*	*12*	*South Shields*	*16 Sep*

Marathon

2:10:46	Mark Steinle		22.11.74	6	London	22 Apr
2:11:24	Jon Brown		27.02.71	6	New York, USA	4 Nov
	2:20:28			1	Victoria, CAN	7 Oct
2:13:13	Mark Hudspith		19.01.69	11	London	22 Apr
2:16:27	Simon Pride		20.07.67	17	London	22 Apr
	2:17:37			8	Dublin, IRL	29 Oct
	2:20:03			14	Dubai, UAE	12 Jan
2:16:51	Danny Robinson		13.01.75	9	Frankfurt, GER	28 Oct
2:18:29	Billy Burns		13.12.69	19	London	22 Apr
2:18:35	Paul Evans	V40	13.04.61	23	Chicago, USA	7 Oct
2:18:38	Carl Warren		28.09.69	32	Berlin, GER	30 Sep
	2:20:01			13	Dubai, UAE	12 Jan
2:18:46	Stuart Hall		21.12.64	25	Chicago, USA	7 Oct
2:19:26	Rob Holladay		10.01.75	20	London	22 Apr
	(10)					
2:19:27	Rhodri Jones		14.08.66	21	London	22 Apr
2:19:32	Barry Royden		15.12.66	22	London	22 Apr
2:20:00	Nick Francis		29.08.71	23	London	22 Apr
2:20:32	Nick Jones		10.07.74	17	Frankfurt, GER	28 Oct
2:20:36	Malcolm Campbell		3.01.71	2	Columbus, USA	21 Oct
2:21:47	Michael Coleman		14.05.78	26	London	22 Apr
2:21:52	Ian Fisher		15.09.70	27	London	22 Apr
2:22:22	Allan Adams		11.09.72	12	Dublin, IRL	29 Oct
2:22:32	Richard Mason		25.09.69	28	London	22 Apr
2:23:08	Duncan Mason		8.12.68	30	London	22 Apr
	(20)					

2:23:17	Mike Proudlove		26.01.70	31	London	22	Apr
2:23:29	Robert Deakin		21.10.66	15	Dublin, IRL	29	Oct
2:23:46	Nathan Vengdasalam		11.03.64	33	London	22	Apr
2:24:24	James Fitzsimmons		20.04.74	35	London	22	Apr
2:24:45	Kenny Butler		17.09.63	36	London	22	Apr
2:25:23	Chris Cariss		1.03.75	1	Manchester	23	Sep
2:25:47	Darren Bilton		9.03.72	16	Amsterdam, NED	21	Oct
2:26:05	Michael Green		12.10.76	5	Huntsville, USA	8	Dec
2:26:38	Chris Teague		11.03.69	1	Lake Buena Vista, USA	7	Jan
2:27:22	Ian Malone		17.03.64	39	London	22	Apr
(30)							
2:27:36	Larry Matthews		11.08.65	17	Amsterdam, NED	21	Oct
2:27:37	Joe Loader		21.07.73	40	London	22	Apr
2:27:40	John Heap		8.11.70	41	London	22	Apr
2:27:44	Ray Plant		13.05.68	17	Dubai, UAE	12	Jan
2:27:50	Bill Speake		24.01.71	42	London	22	Apr
2:27:52	Ieuan Ellis	V40	11.05.60	43	London	22	Apr
2:28:24	Stewart MacDonald		10.12.65	48	London	22	Apr
2:28:24	Dennis Walmsley		5.09.62	1	Stratford	29	Apr
2:28:42	Andy Wetherill	V40	6.12.57	3	Manchester	23	Sep
2:28:52	Tony Duffy	V40	26.06.56	49	London	22	Apr
(40)							
2:29:02	Gareth Williams		16.08.66	50	London	22	Apr
2:29:02	Jamie Reid		1.01.75	57	Berlin, GER	30	Sep
2:29:33	Dave Symons	V40	21.10.58	52	London	22	Apr
2:29:49	John Redmond	V40	15.10.57	53	London	22	Apr
2:29:54	Nick Janvier		9.08.70	54	London	22	Apr
2:30:14	John McFarlane		9.06.72	55	London	22	Apr
2:30:17	Darren Hale	V40	2.10.59	1	Sheffield	29	Apr
2:30:22	Simon Edney	V40		4	Manchester	23	Sep
2:30:34	Paul Richards		13.02.65	57	London	22	Apr
2:30:41	Andrew Rees		1.02.71	58	London	22	Apr
(50)							
2:30:45	Paul Harwood		19.07.71	59	London	22	Apr
2:30:54	Stephen Littler		20.09.73	5	Manchester	23	Sep
2:30:59	Mark Roberts	V40	12.02.59	1	Stoke-on-Trent	17	Jun
2:31:05	Alan McCullough		9.08.63	4	Belfast	7	May
2:31:22	David Brady		5.07.62	5	Belfast	7	May
2:31:27	Steve Payne	V45	1.12.55	3	Washington	28	Oct
2:31:40	Seb Shepley		23.11.67	26	Dublin, IRL	29	Oct
2:32:20	David Rodgers		16.06.67	1	Fort William	29	Apr
2:32:27	William Cockerell		74	60	London	22	Apr
2:32:31	Jamie Jones		8.12.71	61	London	22	Apr
(60)							
2:32:35	Hugh Jones	V45	1.11.55	2	Bridgetown, BAR	2	Dec
2:32:40	Martin Ferguson		17.09.64	63	London	22	Apr
2:32:44	Brian Cole			64	London	22	Apr
2:32:51	Mike Waine	V45	17.02.56	65	London	22	Apr
2:32:54	Nick Berrill		63	25	Amsterdam, NED	21	Oct
2:33:07	Phil Cook		7.05.69	69	Berlin, GER	30	Sep
2:33:30	Terry Wall		12.06.70	66	London	22	Apr
2:33:31	Mark Healy		4.04.70	67	London	22	Apr
2:33:53	Toby Tanser		21.07.68	79	New York, USA	4	Nov
2:33:56	Peter Roper		66	68	London	22	Apr
(70)							
2:34:03	Stephen Keywood	V40	28.09.61	69	London	22	Apr
2:34:07	Alan Reid		19.04.66	2	Fort William	29	Apr
2:34:08	Alex Rowe	V40	10.04.57	70	London	22	Apr
2:34:12	Mike McGeoch	V45	15.08.55	81	Berlin, GER	30	Sep
2:34:15	Stephen Ross		65	71	London	22	Apr
2:34:18	Dave Neill	V45	56	72	London	22	Apr

2:34:20	Ian Crampton		28.01.62	73	London	22 Apr
2:34:23	Peter Johnson	V45	54	74	London	22 Apr
2:34:28	Terry Mitchell	V40	23.08.59	6	Belfast	7 May
2:34:31	Alan Ruben	V40	9.03.57	62	Boston, USA	16 Apr
(80)						
2:34:32	Martin Riley	V40	6.04.60	75	London	22 Apr
2:34:33	Simon Lund		22.12.65	1	Luton	2 Dec
2:34:38	James Arnold		26.02.66	76	London	22 Apr
2:34:40	Vincent Schmitt			1	Leicester	18 Sep
2:34:44	Andrew Clements	V40	59	77	London	22 Apr
2:34:48	John Castle		68	78	London	22 Apr
2:34:55	Harry Day	V40	2.04.59	1	Lake Vyrnwy	1 Jul
2:35:14	John Hartley	V40	21.11.56	2	Lake Vyrnwy	1 Jul
2:35:15	Chris Booth			6	Manchester	23 Sep
2:35:23	Alasdair Kean	V50	5.11.47	80	London	22 Apr
(90)						
2:35:25	Simon Bell		26.12.66	81	London	22 Apr
2:35:31	Dave Mansbridge		4.06.64	82	London	22 Apr
2:35:36	Kevin Tilley		67	84	London	22 Apr
2:35:38	Simon Pritchard		10.09.68	85	London	22 Apr
2:35:41	Andrew Hussey		17.05.73	3	Lake Vyrnwy	1 Jul
2:35:44	Mike Holmes	V45	13.03.53	86	London	22 Apr
2:35:51	Dermot McGonigle		62	87	London	22 Apr
2:35:52	Anthony Webb		75	88	London	22 Apr
2:35:58	Robin Bentley		17.02.65	89	London	22 Apr
2:36:03	Nicholas Kinsey	V40	10.11.59	91	London	22 Apr

Foreign

2:13:18	*Craig Kirkwood (NZL)*		*8.10.74*	*13*	*Chicago, USA*	*7 Oct*
2:14:13	*John Mutai (KEN)*		*26.05.66*	*4*	*Dublin, IRL*	*29 Oct*

100 Kilometres Road

7:13:30	Alan Reid		19.04.66		Moreton-in-Marsh	20 May
	7:58:34				Cleder, FRA	26 Aug
7:17:18	Ian Anderson		23.03.71		Moreton-in-Marsh	20 May
	7:29:29				Winschoten, NED	29 Sep
7:24:20	Chris Finill	V40	31.12.58		Moreton-in-Marsh	20 May
7:39:45	Peter Morrison				Moreton-in-Marsh	20 May
7:43:14	Mike Feighan		5.11.65		Moreton-in-Marsh	20 May
7:46:37	Dennis Walmsley		5.09.62		Moreton-in-Marsh	20 May
7:54:20	Mikk Bradley	V40	27.05.57		Moreton-in-Marsh	20 May
8:06:30	Colin Paton				Moreton-in-Marsh	20 May
8:15:18	Peter Gledhill				Moreton-in-Marsh	20 May

24 Hours Road

200.599 km	William Sichel	V45	1.10.53		Apeldoorn, NED	26 May
	188.600 km				Taipei, TAI	4 Mar
194.731 km	Ian Doherty		12.03.65	1	Doncaster	26 May
188.529 km	David Findel-Hawkins			2	Doncaster	26 May
185.250 km	Peter Crossman			3	Doncaster	26 May

1500 Metres Steeplechase - Under 17

4:20.43	Luke Gunn	22.03.85	1	Tullamore, IRL	21 Jul
4:27.51	William Docherty	2.04.85	1	Sheffield	12 Aug
4:27.90	Adam Watt	29.10.84	2	Sheffield	12 Aug
4:28.30	James Nickless	27.10.84	2	Exeter	7 Jul
4:29.65	Mark Buckingham	4.05.85	1	Cudworth	26 May
4:29.9	Ben Cox	19.03.85	1	Cheltenham	3 Jun
4:29.92	John Walker	4.03.85	3	Sheffield	12 Aug
4:30.04	Sam Hall	15.10.85	3	Exeter	7 Jul

4:31.13	Ryan Armstrong		11.07.85	2	Scunthorpe	18 Aug
4:32.4	Steven Webb			1	Watford	26 May
	(10)					
4:33.10	Chris Ramsey		2.11.84	4	Exeter	7 Jul
4:34.77	Jason Hall			7	Sheffield	12 Aug
4:35.33	Alex Haynes		6.09.84	8	Sheffield	12 Aug
4:35.5	Kirk Wilson		21.12.85	1		13 Jun
4:37.0	Paul White			1	Middlesbrough	9 Jun
4:37.36	Paul McCloskey		9.05.85	10	Sheffield	12 Aug
4:37.4	Gavin Smith		15.02.85	1	Crawley	5 Aug
4:38.2	Dean Lacy		29.12.84	1m1	Enfield	22 Jul
4:40.2	D. Singh			1m2	Enfield	22 Jul
4:40.38	Charles Lloyd-Harvey		21.10.84	1	Cardiff	7 Jul
	(20)					
4:40.8	Luke Northall		30.11.84	1	Stretford	22 Jul
4:41.6	Sean Dirrane		17.10.85	2	Stretford	22 Jul

2000 Metres Steeplechase

5:37.32	Iain Murdoch	U23	10.07.80	1	Watford	9 Jun
5:39.13	Stuart Stokes		15.12.76	1	Stretford	8 May
5:41.12	Andrew Franklin	U23	13.09.80	2	Watford	9 Jun
5:42.95	Craig Wheeler		14.06.76	2	Stretford	8 May
5:43.23	Ricky Soos	U20	28.06.83	1	Birmingham	27 May
5:45.00	Adam Bowden	U20	5.08.82	1	Stoke-on-Trent	18 Aug
5:45.65	Dave Mitchinson		4.09.78	3	Watford	9 Jun
5:47.29	Jermaine Mays	U20	23.12.82	2	Stoke-on-Trent	18 Aug

Additional Under 20 (1 - 3 above)

5:51.61	Peter Kellie	2.01.84	3	Stoke-on-Trent	18 Aug
5:55.26	Steve Murphy	6.01.83	2	Dole, FRA	29 Jul
5:58.12	James Bailey	1.10.82	2	Exeter	7 Jul
5:59.19	Paul Moores	3.08.84	2	Birmingham	27 May
5:59.78	Daniel Lewis	16.10.83	1	London (He)	26 Aug
6:00.26	Chris Warburton	23.08.83		Birmingham	27 May
6:02.5	Tom Bedford	12.12.83	3	Watford	26 May
	(10)				
6:02.6	Frank Tickner	12.10.83	1	Exeter	16 Jun
6:04.51	Ian Bowles	6.01.84	5	Exeter	7 Jul
6:05.75	Matthew Lole	23.01.83	6	Exeter	7 Jul
6:06.52	Chris Norris	8.10.82	7	Exeter	7 Jul
6:06.8	Phil Nicholls	29.09.83	2	Nuneaton	12 Aug
6:07.85	David Jones	19.02.84	1	Neath	27 Aug
6:09.5	Abdi Ali	26.12.82	1	Eton	12 Aug
6:10.83	Mark Donoghue	27.09.83	2	Cudworth	27 May
6:13.02	James Henry	31.07.84	3	Cudworth	27 May
6:14.9	William Bolton	7.10.82	1	Ashford	13 May

3000 Metres Steeplechase

8:32.68	Ben Whitby	6.01.77	1	Birmingham	15 Jul
	8:33.25		1	Manchester	23 May
	8:50.13		8	Bremen, GER	24 Jun
8:33.15	Stuart Stokes	15.12.76	2	Birmingham	15 Jul
	8:35.37		2	Bedford	21 Jul
	8:35.57		7	Linz, AUT	20 Aug
	8:37.76		10	Athens, GRE	11 Jun
	8:46.01		5	Hania, GRE	4 Jun
	8:47.02		4	Manchester	23 May
8:38.46	Chris Stephenson	22.07.74	2	Manchester	23 May
	8:39.33		3	Birmingham	15 Jul
	8:54.48		7	Lucerne, SUI	27 Jun

8:39.2	Don Naylor		5.09.71	1	Solihull	23	Jun
	8:45.93			5	Birmingham	15	Jul
	8:47.5			1	Stafford	18	Aug
	8:54.67			1	Edinburgh	25	Aug
8:40.85	Charlie Low		9.10.74	4	Birmingham	15	Jul
	8:42.89			3	Tula, RUS	8	Jun
	8:49.59			2	Loughborough	20	May
	8:54.22			2	Jarrow	18	Aug
8:42.82	Andrew Franklin	U23	13.09.80	3	Manchester	23	May
	8:45.41			1	Glasgow (S)	7	May
	8:51.4			1	Bedford	1	Jul
	8:54.39			9h2	Amsterdam, NED	12	Jul
8:45.4	Andrew Hennessy		24.08.77	3	Solihull	23	Jun
	8:53.59			7	Birmingham	15	Jul
	8:53.60			5	Loughborough	20	May
8:45.9	Dave Mitchinson		4.09.78	4	Solihull	23	Jun
	8:50.80			5	Manchester	23	May
	8:52.34			6	Birmingham	15	Jul
	8:52.73			4	Loughborough	20	May
8:46.29	Justin Chaston		4.11.68	1	Jarrow	18	Aug
	8:47.53			5	Madrid, ESP	26	May
8:49.55	Iain Murdoch	U23	10.07.80	2	Glasgow (S)	7	May
	8:49.91			3	Loughborough	20	May
	(10)						
8:51.2	Rob Berry		29.07.69	5	Solihull	23	Jun
	36 performances to 8:55.00 by 11 athletes						
8:55.38	Craig Wheeler		14.06.76	6	Manchester	23	May
8:56.11	Gary Blackman	U23	24.09.80	3	Glasgow (S)	7	May
8:56.16	Steve Cairns		3.11.67	3	Eton	7	Jul
8:56.64	Rob Hough		3.06.72	7	Manchester	23	May
8:57.63	Kevin Nash		6.02.77	6	Loughborough	20	May
8:57.63	Pat Davoren		13.03.72	3h2	Birmingham	13	Jul
8:57.93	James Fitzsimmons		20.04.74	4	Eton	7	Jul
8:59.27	Nick Talbot		14.12.77	6h2	Birmingham	13	Jul
9:01.28	Andrew Mitchell	U23	30.07.80	4	Glasgow (S)	7	May
	(20)						
9:04.3	Andy Morgan-Lee		1.03.69	1	Bedford	27	May
9:04.41	Andrew Lemoncello	U20	12.10.82	2	Corinth, GRE	27	May
9:05.77	Huw Lobb		29.08.76	3	London (Ha)	16	Jun
9:07.38	Lee Hurst		29.07.72	1	Stretford	11	Sep
9:08.48	Adam Bowden	U20	5.08.82	5	Mannheim, GER	15	Jun
9:08.6	Delroy Simon		27.11.78	2	Bedford	27	May
9:09.05	Paul Farmer		23.11.77	4	London (Ha)	16	Jun
9:10.8	Jermaine Mays	U20	23.12.82	1	Bedford	1	Jul
9:12.23	Billy Farquharson		14.04.75	1	Birmingham	16	Jun
9:13.0	Andy Fooks		26.04.75	4	Eton	18	Aug
	(30)						
9:13.14	Alan Wray		6.01.71	6	London (Ha)	16	Jun
9:14.6	Bruce Raeside	U23	2.12.81	3	Bedford	1	Jul
9:15.5	Chris Sampson		30.09.75	1	Rugby	18	Aug
9:16.8	Tony Forrest		22.12.76	4	Bedford	27	May
9:19.6	Simon Cotton		26.07.67	8	Solihull	23	Jun
9:20.4	Rod Leach		29.05.72	1	Cosford	4	Jul
9:20.78	Paul Howarth		30.10.77	5	Indianapolis, USA	5	May
9:21.4	Mike Hutchinson		5.10.65	5	Eton	18	Aug
9:21.56	Kevin Murphy		6.04.74	6	Eton	7	Jul
9:21.73	Richard Harris		16.08.71	1	Sheffield	13	May
	(40)						
9:21.92	Matthew Plano		8.10.76	5	Tampa, USA	11	May
9:22.0	Michael Noyce		31.10.77	1	Watford	8	Sep

9:22.7	Peter Kellie	U20	2.01.84	3	Bedford	1	Jul
9:23.01	Matthew Bell		14.07.76	6	Glasgow (S)	7	May
9:23.36	Glen Cornish	U23	27.10.79	3	Birmingham	2	Jun
9:23.84	Mark Griffith	U23	25.11.81	7	Eton	7	Jul
9:24.18	Keith Hood		13.09.72	3	Glasgow (S)	23	Jun
9:25.6	Sullivan Smith		16.09.76	3	Peterborough	7	Jul
9:26.80	Wayne Dashper		19.10.74	10	Manchester	23	May
9:26.9	James Williams	U20	17.07.82	6	Eton	18	Aug
(50)							
9:27.6	Andrew Thomas	U23	29.01.81	4	Bedford	1	Jul
9:27.87	Ron McWilliams		20.08.68	4	Glasgow (S)	23	Jun
9:28.0	Daniel Lewis	U20	16.10.83	4	Bedford	1	Jul
9:28.4	Chris Symonds		21.11.73	7	Eton	18	Aug
9:28.58	Ewan Malloch		4.08.76	8	London (Ha)	16	Jun
9:28.6	Stephen Norris		21.06.68		Salisbury	22	Jul
9:29.04	Lee Garland		18.12.74	1	Douglas IOM	12	Jul
9:30.67	Scott Olsen	U23	19.12.79	8	Glasgow (S)	7	May
9:30.75	Steve Millward	U23	29.06.79	9	Glasgow (S)	5	May
9:32.06	Daniel Yates	U23	7.06.81	2	Derby	29	Jul
(60)							
9:34.53	John Halligan	U20	4.05.83	2	Douglas IOM	12	Jul
9:35.9	Richard Williams	U23	22.10.81	1	Ware	7	Jul

Additional Under 20 (1 - 7 above)

9:36.4	Abdi Ali		26.12.82	9	Eton	18	Aug
9:41.5	Matthew Lole		23.01.83	1	Stafford	20	May
(10)							
9:42.32	Ian Bowles		6.01.84	2	Scunthorpe	18	Aug
9:45.56	James Bailey		1.10.82	8	London (He)	5	May
9:49.8	Andrew Sims		9.09.82	6	Bedford	1	Jul
9:52.3	William Docherty	U17	2.04.85	2	Inverness	26	Aug
9:53.1	Paul Moores		3.08.84	3	Corby	18	Aug
9:56.1	Alistair Smith		22.02.84	1	Guildford	23	Jun

Foreign

9:13.8	*Emil de Jonge (RSA)*		*2.09.72*	*1*	*London (He)*	*23*	*Jun*

60 Metres Hurdles - Indoors

7.84	Dominic Bradley		22.12.76	1	Birmingham	28	Jan
	7.89			1	Birmingham	14	Jan
	7.90			1	Cardiff	11	Feb
	7.91			1h2	Birmingham	28	Jan
	7.94			4	Glasgow	18	Mar
7.91	Chris Baillie	U23	21.04.81	1	Glasgow	21	Jan
	7.94			2h3	Birmingham	28	Jan
	7.94			2=	Birmingham	28	Jan
7.91	Mensah Elliott		29.08.76	2	Cardiff	11	Feb
7.92	Dominic Girdler	U20	6.03.82	2	Birmingham	14	Jan
	7.94			2=	Birmingham	28	Jan
7.93	Duncan Malins		12.06.78	1h3	Birmingham	28	Jan
7.97	Neil Owen		18.10.73	4	Birmingham	28	Jan
7.97	Paul Gray		25.05.69	3	Cardiff	11	Feb
7.98 rs?	Robert Newton	U23	10.05.81	2h1	Birmingham	28	Jan
	8.07			7	Birmingham	28	Jan
	15 performances to 8.00 by 8 athletes						
8.03	Nathan Palmer	U20	16.06.82	2h2	Birmingham	28	Jan
8.03	Allan Scott	U20	27.12.82	1h1	Glasgow	18	Feb
(10)							
8.07	Jamie Quarry		15.11.72	2	Glasgow	21	Jan
8.09	Liam Collins		23.10.78	1	Birmingham	13	Feb

8.10	Mohammed Sillah-Freckleton	U23	11.09.80	1	Bedford	13 Jan
8.12	Paul Crossley	U23	30.03.79	4h1	Birmingham	28 Jan
8.22	Andy Turner	U23	19.09.80	4h3	Birmingham	28 Jan
8.23	Martyn Hendry		10.04.75	4	Glasgow	21 Jan
8.23	Perry Batchelor		11.12.75	2	Birmingham	11 Feb
8.24	Tony Gill		19.09.77	2h1	Glasgow	18 Feb
8.25	Richard Sear	U23	21.08.79	2h5	Glasgow	18 Feb
8.28	Andrew Lewis		9.03.68	2B	Birmingham	13 Feb
	(20)					
8.29	Ian Cawley		21.11.78	2h2	Glasgow	18 Feb
8.36	Ashley Swain	U23	3.10.80	2h3	Glasgow	18 Feb
8.36	James Hillier		3.04.78	2rB	Ames, USA	7 Dec
8.39	Dominic Shepherd		11.12.76	3Hi	Prague, CZE	28 Jan
8.39	Matthew Butler	U23	4.04.80	3h5	Glasgow	18 Feb
8.41	Chris Tye-Walker	U20	20.09.82	4	Birmingham	25 Feb
8.42	Ben Roberts	U23	15.01.80	1H1	Birmingham	21 Jan
8.49	Anthony Sawyer	U23	29.04.80	H	Birmingham	21 Jan

hand timing

8.3	Richard Sear	U23	(8.25i)	1A1	London (CP)	13 Jan
8.4	Lee Tindal	U23	19.02.80	2A2	London (CP)	13 Jan
8.4	Paul Gilding		2.10.75	3A2	London (CP)	13 Jan
8.4	Andrew David		9.09.69	2	London (Ha)	4 Feb
8.4	Dwayne Stoddart	U23	29.12.80	1	Eton	10 Feb

60 Metres Hurdles - Men Under 20 (3'3") - Indoors

7.90	Dominic Girdler	U20	6.03.82	1	Cardiff	11 Feb
7.93	Robert Newton	U23	10.05.81	2	Cardiff	11 Feb

75 Metres Hurdles - Under 13

12.4	Carl Hamilton	30.06.89	1	Basildon	9 Jun
12.6	Mark Paprell	25.11.88	2	Basildon	9 Jun
12.6	Charles Dickson	25.11.88	3	Basildon	9 Jun
12.7	Michael Baker	6.04.90	1	Erith	8 Jul
12.9	Thomas Griffiths	18.09.88	1	Brecon	19 Aug
12.94 w 2.5	Greg Taylor	5.01.89	1	Grangemouth	12 Aug
12.99 w 2.5	Adam Henderson	18.02.89	2	Grangemouth	12 Aug

80 Metres Hurdles - Under 13

13.3	Gary Lam	24.02.89	1	Tamworth	15 Jul
13.5	Paul Dingle	4.09.88	1	Bournemouth	24 Jun
13.6	Richard Fox	20.09.88	1rA2	Kingston	29 Jul
13.7	Billy Marchant	27.08.89	2rA2	Kingston	29 Jul
13.7	Alex Al-Ameen	2.03.89	3rA2	Kingston	29 Jul
13.8	Liam Bradshaw	4.07.89	1rB2	Kingston	29 Jul

80 Metres Hurdles - Under 15

10.68 w 2.8	Richard Alexis-Smith	13.02.87	1	Sheffield	12 Aug
	10.82 1.4		1h2	Sheffield	12 Aug
10.73 w 5.5	Chris Musa	5.12.86	1	Exeter	7 Jul
	10.95 2.0		1s1	Exeter	7 Jul
10.99 w 5.5	Tom Stimson	2.09.86	3	Exeter	7 Jul
	11.27 0.1		1h3	Exeter	6 Jul
11.3 0.5	Edward Harrison	10.12.86	1P	Erith	16 Sep
	11.31 w 2.8		3	Sheffield	12 Aug
	11.46 1.4		2h2	Sheffield	12 Aug
11.35 w 2.5	Ogadina Duma	5.09.86	3s2	Exeter	7 Jul
	11.5		1	Enfield	22 Jul
	11.56 0.0		2h4	Exeter	6 Jul

11.37	2.0	Daniel Maynard	4.12.87	2s1	Exeter	7 Jul
11.4 w		Mardeep Shoker	9.02.87	1	Erith	9 Jun
		11.47 0.0		1h4	Exeter	6 Jul
11.44 w	2.8	Robert James	1.04.87	4	Sheffield	12 Aug
		11.62 0.7		1h3	Sheffield	12 Aug
11.45	1.5	Richard Hansard	5.11.86	2	Watford	27 May
11.47	0.6	Daniel Davis	12.12.87	3h2	Exeter	6 Jul
	(10)					
11.49	2.0	George Beeken	4.09.86	4s1	Exeter	7 Jul
11.50	1.1	Jordan Roye	3.11.87	1	Birmingham	1 Sep
11.5		G. Etherington		1	Exeter	16 Jun
		11.57 w 2.4		2h2	London (He)	26 Aug
		11.61 -0.4		3	London (He)	26 Aug
11.5		Uche Uduoza	15.10.86	1	Exeter	16 Jun
11.5 w		Blake Smith	16.02.87	1	Jersey	30 Jun
11.5 w		Jon Baty	1.02.87	1	Tamworth	13 Jul
		11.77		P	Hull	15 Sep
11.56	2.0	Adrian Pettigrew	12.11.86	5s1	Exeter	7 Jul
11.57 w	2.5	Joe Tenny	9.06.87	5s2	Exeter	7 Jul
		11.61 1.0		3h1	Sheffield	12 Aug
11.59	1.0	Peter Hutcheson	18.11.86	2h1	Sheffield	12 Aug
11.60		Paul Mudd	6.09.86	1P	Hull	16 Sep
	(20)					
11.6		Michael Johnson	28.09.86	1	Basingstoke	10 Jun
		11.78 1.5		3	Watford	27 May
11.63 w		Pepi Nanci	7.10.86	1	Bedford	9 Sep
		11.7		2	Peterborough	22 Jul
11.7		Ryan Shaw	30.12.86	1	Peterborough	22 Jul
		11.76		P	London (He)	12 Aug
11.78	0.7	Craig Glanville	21.09.86	2	Birmingham	2 Sep
11.79	1.0	Matthew Maloney	16.10.86	4h1	Sheffield	12 Aug
11.79	1.4	Joe Dickenson	7.12.86	4h2	Sheffield	12 Aug
11.8		Lewis Wright		1	Cardiff	13 Jul
		11.95 -1.8		3	Cardiff	7 Jul
11.8		Mark Hicks	12.07.87	1	Newport	9 Sep
		11.84 w 2.4		1	Cardiff	17 Jun
		11.92 -1.8		2	Cardiff	7 Jul
11.83	1.0	David Lucas	11.01.87	2h2	Watford	27 May
11.87	-0.7	Craig France	11.01.87	P	Birmingham	30 Sep
	(30)					
11.88	-1.8	Steven Boyles	19.01.87	1	Cardiff	7 Jul
11.89 w	2.5	Nick Pritchard	19.01.87	8s2	Exeter	7 Jul
11.90		Luke Reynolds	4.09.86	1	Antrim	16 Jun
11.9		Wayne Taylor	17.10.87	1	Jarrow	13 Jun
11.9		Tom Forster	27.09.86	4	Exeter	16 Jun
11.9		Daniel Harris	1.10.86	3	Exeter	16 Jun
		11.91		3P	Hull	16 Sep
11.9		Sosthene Aubyn-Yao	7.08.87	2P	Erith	16 Sep
11.96	1.0	Phil Jarrett	18.03.87	6h1	Sheffield	12 Aug

100 Metres Hurdles - Under 17 (3'0")

13.15 w	3.0	Edward Dunford	15.09.84	1	Exeter	7 Jul
		13.16 1.4		1	Sheffield	12 Aug
13.23	-0.2	Stephen Alexander	6.10.84	1O	Birmingham	29 Sep
13.45	1.4	Suote Nyamanyo	3.10.84	2	Sheffield	12 Aug
13.49 w	3.0	Anthony Bibby	12.03.85	2	Exeter	7 Jul
		13.83 1.6		2h2	Exeter	6 Jul
13.50 w	3.0	Richard Aidoo	15.02.85	3	Exeter	7 Jul
		13.60 1.5		2h1	Exeter	6 Jul
13.51 w	3.0	Chris Walters	23.09.84	4	Exeter	7 Jul
		13.86 1.6		3h2	Exeter	6 Jul

13.56	1.4	Duncan Rogers		10.10.84	3	Sheffield	12 Aug
13.60		Robert Henry		22.10.84	O	Hull	16 Sep
13.68	0.4	Nicholas Gayle		4.01.85	1	Birmingham	2 Sep
13.7	1.4	Matthew Hansford		20.02.86	1	Exeter	16 Jun
		14.01 0.4			3h3	Exeter	6 Jul
	(10)						
13.7	1.4	Edward Walsh		21.10.85	2	Exeter	16 Jun
13.7		Adam Draycott		7.11.84	1	Yate	1 Jul
		13.90 1.6			4h2	Exeter	6 Jul
13.72 w	2.1	Matthew Thompson		29.12.84	3	Tullamore, IRL	21 Jul
		13.9			2	Glasgow (S)	19 Aug
13.78 w	2.8	Fola Orlonishe		14.07.86	2h3	Sheffield	12 Aug
		14.0			1	Crawley	5 Aug
13.80 w	2.1	Darren Ho		20.03.85	4	Tullamore, IRL	21 Jul
		13.8			1	Glasgow (S)	19 Aug
		14.01 1.4			7	Sheffield	12 Aug
13.8	1.4	Callum McKay		17.02.85	2	Watford	27 May
13.82	1.5	Daniel Armstrong		16.11.84	3h1	Exeter	6 Jul
13.88	1.4	William Sharman		12.09.84	6	Sheffield	12 Aug
13.9		David Robertson		17.12.84	1O	Hexham	20 May
		13.96			1	Gateshead	13 May
13.97	-0.7	Andrew Johnson		13.05.86	2	Birmingham	1 Sep
	(20)						
14.0		Tom Reynolds		20.12.84	1	Antrim	26 May
		14.19 w 2.8			3	Deeside	4 Aug
14.0		Sean Ashton		20.09.85	1	Leicester	9 Jun
14.0		Chris Awde		14.02.85	1	Basildon	9 Jun
14.0		David Collard		25.01.85	1	Coatbridge	30 Jun
14.0		Richard Alexis-Smith	U15	13.02.87	1	London (TB)	5 Sep
14.10	-0.2	Rupert Gardner		9.10.84	4O	Birmingham	29 Sep
14.10	0.9	Michael Dyer		27.09.84	1O	Birmingham	29 Sep
14.1	1.4	Matthew Love		28.12.84	3	Watford	27 May
		14.13 0.4			5h3	Exeter	6 Jul
14.1		R. Smith			1	Cannock	9 Jun
14.12	1.0	Euron Roberts		18.11.85	1	Cardiff	16 Jun
	(30)						
14.14 w	2.2	Darren Lewis		12.04.86	4h2	Sheffield	11 Aug

Foreign

13.4		*Liam McDermid (IRL)*	*23.11.84*	*1*	*Glasgow (S)*	*3 Jun*
		13.68 1.8		*1*	*Grangemouth*	*10 Jun*

110 Metres Hurdles - Under 17 (3'0")

14.58	1.4	Edward Dunford	15.09.84	D	Debrecen, HUN	13 Jul

110 Metres Hurdles - Under 20 (3'3")

13.97	2.0	Dominic Girdler	6.03.82	1	Ipswich	2 Sep
14.16	1.1	Tristan Anthony	16.12.82	1	Watford	26 May
14.44	1.1	Kenneth Frempong	17.07.84	2	Watford	26 May
14.49 w	5.0	Chris Tye-Walker	20.09.82	2	Exeter	7 Jul
		14.64 1.1		4	Watford	26 May
14.60	1.1	Alex Zulewski	6.06.82	3	Watford	26 May
14.65	1.1	Isaac McCalla	28.03.82	5	Watford	26 May
14.69 w	5.0	Matthew Colton	5.11.82	3	Exeter	7 Jul
		14.77 2.0		3	Ipswich	2 Sep
14.71	0.9	Steve Green	15.01.83	2	London (He)	26 Aug
14.81 w	5.0	Ross Tressider	8.11.83	4	Exeter	7 Jul
		14.88 0.9		4	London (He)	26 Aug
14.82 w	5.0	James Peet	2.12.82	5	Exeter	7 Jul
		14.85 0.7		2h1	Exeter	6 Jul
14.83	-4.1	Allan Scott	27.12.82	1	Derby	9 Sep

14.85 w 5.0	David Hughes		31.05.84	6	Exeter	7 Jul
	15.06 0.7			5h1	Exeter	6 Jul
14.89 w 5.0	Robin Smith		11.09.83	7	Exeter	7 Jul
	14.99 0.7			3h1	Exeter	6 Jul
14.93 w 5.0	Liam Lucas		15.12.82	8	Exeter	7 Jul
	14.94 1.1			7	Watford	26 May
15.17 -0.2	John Holtby		27.03.82	1	Cudworth	26 May
15.17 0.7	Andrew Hopkinson		20.09.83	4h2	Exeter	6 Jul
15.25 0.2	Greg Smith		29.01.84	6h1	Watford	26 May
15.25 w 3.3	Andy Clements		28.11.82	1	Portsmouth	13 May
15.26	Paul Tohill		9.10.82	1D	Aberdare	24 Jun
15.29 -0.2	Richard Baderin		25.03.83	2	Cudworth	26 May
(20)						
15.37	Louis Evling-Jones		20.06.83	D	Hull	16 Sep
15.40 0.7	Richard Myers		21.12.83	7h2	Exeter	6 Jul
15.40	Tim Howell		6.12.82	D	Hull	16 Sep
15.44 w 2.2	Kris Jones		7.03.83	1	Neath	27 Aug
15.49 -4.1	Edward Dunford	U17	15.09.84	3	Derby	9 Sep

hand timing

13.9	Allan Scott		(14.83)	1	Guildford	29 Jul
14.4 w 2.8	Alex Zulewski		(14.60)	1	Southend	13 May
14.6	Chris Tye-Walker		(14.64)	1	Portsmouth	10 Jun
14.7	Mark Lishman	U17	24.11.84	1	Crawley	15 Apr
14.7	Steve Green		(14.71)	1	Exeter	2 Sep
14.7 w	Robin Smith		(14.99)	1	Stoke-on-Trent	17 Jun
14.7 w	David Hughes		(15.06)	2	Stoke-on-Trent	17 Jun
14.9	R. Alleyne	U17		1		29 Jul
14.9 w	Andrew Hopkinson		(15.17)	3	Stoke-on-Trent	17 Jun
15.0	Greg Smith		(15.25)	1	Brighton	12 Aug
(10)						
15.1 -4.8	Edward Dunford	U17	(15.49)	1	Wigan	29 Apr
15.1 0.7	Kris Jones		(15.44w)	1	Brecon	18 Jul
15.2	David Brackstone		13.03.82	1	Liverpool	12 Aug
15.3	Louis Evling-Jones		(15.37)	1	Grantham	10 Jun
15.5	Mark Winship		29.09.83	2	London (He)	13 May
15.5	Andy Clements		(15.25w)	D	Woking	10 Jun
15.5	A. McDonald			2	Exeter	16 Jun
15.5	Daniel Brandwood		1.10.82	1	Rotherham	17 Jun

110 Metres Hurdles

13.32 0.8	Colin Jackson	18.02.67	1	Dortmund, GER	9 Jun
	13.36 -0.8		2=	Athens, GRE	11 Jun
	13.37 -0.2		1	Rome, ITA	29 Jun
	13.37 0.2		5	Brussels, BEL	24 Aug
	13.38 -0.2		1	Kassel, GER	13 Jun
	13.42 0.1		4	Saint-Denis, FRA	6 Jul
	13.43 -0.4		1h1	Kassel, GER	13 Jun
	13.46 0.0		5r1	Zurich, SUI	17 Aug
	13.51 -0.7		5	Monaco, MON	20 Jul
	13.53 -1.3		3=	Prague, CZE	18 Jun
	13.56 0.0		2	Ingolstadt, GER	27 May
	13.57 -0.1		3	Ostrava, CZE	31 May
	13.61 0.8		3	Yokohama, JPN	15 Sep
	13.63 -0.4		5	Brisbane, AUS	5 Sep
	13.64 0.0		2h1	Ingolstadt, GER	27 May
	13.65 -0.9		5	London (CP)	22 Jul
	13.68 -0.8		1h3	Jena, GER	2 Jun
	13.68 -1.6		4	Gateshead	19 Aug
	13.68 -1.7		5	Melbourne, AUS	9 Sep
	13.73 -1.7		3	Jena, GER	2 Jun

13.45	0.2	Tony Jarrett		13.08.68	2	Helsinki, FIN	14 Jun
		13.51 0.9			5	Oslo, NOR	13 Jul
		13.57 1.3			1	Tula, RUS	8 Jun
		13.58 1.3			3	Bremen, GER	24 Jun
		13.62 -1.0			1h2	Birmingham	14 Jul
		13.64 0.1			3h1	Edmonton, CAN	7 Aug
		13.66 0.8			1	Birmingham	14 Jul
		13.72 1.0			1r2	Irvine CA, USA	6 May
		13.76 -1.5			1	Loughborough	20 May
		13.83 -0.9			6	London (CP)	22 Jul
13.63	1.4	Paul Gray		25.05.69	1	Bedford	18 Jul
		13.78 1.4			1	Cardiff	17 Jun
		13.80 1.0			3h2	Poznan, POL	8 Jun
		13.88 0.8			5	Birmingham	14 Jul
		13.89 0.0			7	Poznan, POL	8 Jun
		13.93 1.0			1	Cardiff	8 Jul
		13.96 -0.6			6h2	Edmonton, CAN	7 Aug
13.68	0.8	Damien Greaves		19.09.77	2	Birmingham	14 Jul
		13.70 1.8			1	Glasgow (S)	24 Jun
		13.81 1.3			2	Birmingham	2 Jun
		13.85 1.4			1	Bedford	21 Jul
		13.89 0.3			1r1	Geneva, SUI	9 Jun
		13.90 0.3			4r2	Geneva, SUI	9 Jun
		13.98 -2.3			1	Loughborough	4 Jul
13.82	0.8	Chris Baillie	U23	21.04.81	2	Eton	7 Jul
		13.85 0.4			3	Amsterdam, NED	15 Jul
		13.95 1.4			3	Bedford	18 Jul
		13.99 1.8			2	Glasgow (S)	24 Jun
13.83	0.8	Dominic Bradley		22.12.76	3	Birmingham	14 Jul
13.87	0.8	Neil Owen		18.10.73	4	Birmingham	14 Jul
		13.94 1.4			2	Bedford	18 Jul
		13.97 0.8			4	Eton	7 Jul
		14.00 -1.0			3h2	Birmingham	14 Jul
13.88	0.8	Mensah Elliott		29.08.76	6	Birmingham	14 Jul
		13.89 -1.0			2h2	Birmingham	14 Jul
		13.92 1.6			1	Jarrow	18 Aug
		13.94 1.7			1	Birmingham	30 Jun
		13.96 1.3			3	Birmingham	2 Jun
		13.97 0.8			3	Eton	7 Jul
		59 performances to 14.00 by 8 athletes					
14.06	1.7	Nathan Palmer	U20	16.06.82	2h1	Grosseto, ITA	20 Jul
14.09	0.4	Robert Newton	U23	10.05.81	3h3	Amsterdam, NED	14 Jul
	(10)						
14.16	1.2	Dominic Girdler	U20	6.03.82	3	Grosseto, ITA	21 Jul
14.19	0.8	Duncan Malins		12.06.78	7	Birmingham	14 Jul
14.26	1.8	Allan Scott	U20	27.12.82	3	Glasgow (S)	24 Jun
14.29	0.8	Andy Turner	U23	19.09.80	8	Birmingham	14 Jul
14.34	0.0	Dean Macey		12.12.77	2D2	Edmonton, CAN	7 Aug
14.42	1.8	Jamie Quarry		15.11.72	4	Glasgow (S)	24 Jun
14.42	-2.3	Mohammed Sillah-Freckleton	U23	11.09.80	2r2	Loughborough	4 Jul
14.42	-1.0	Paul Crossley	U23	30.03.79	5h2	Birmingham	14 Jul
14.51	0.4	Richard Sear	U23	21.08.79	3	Loughborough	20 May
14.54	-1.0	Perry Batchelor		11.12.75	6h2	Birmingham	14 Jul
	(20)						
14.63	-1.1	Matt Douglas		26.11.76	1h2	Glasgow (S)	6 May
14.66	-1.0	Dwayne Stoddart	U23	29.12.80	7h2	Birmingham	14 Jul
14.81	-2.8	Tristan Anthony	U20	16.12.82	1r3	Loughborough	4 Jun
14.82	-0.2	Lee Tindal	U23	19.02.80	5	London (Ha)	17 Jun
14.86	1.0	Ian Cawley		21.11.78	3	Cardiff	8 Jul
14.87	1.4	Luke Gittens	U23	4.01.81	3	Cardiff	17 Jun

14.87	1.1	Andrew Lewis		9.03.68	2rB	Cardiff	8 Jul
14.95	-2.8	Colin Roberts	U23	20.01.81	4h1	Loughborough	4 Jul
14.96	1.0	Anthony Southward		31.01.71	1D5	Arles, FRA	10 Jun
15.01	0.5	Jason McDade	U23	3.04.80	2r2	London (He)	5 May
	(30)						
15.02	-2.3	Tony Gill		19.09.77	2h3	Glasgow (S)	6 May
15.03	2.0	Anthony Sawyer	U23	29.04.80	2D	Birmingham	17 Jun
15.04	1.8	Barry Thomas		28.04.72	2D4	Arles, FRA	10 Jun
15.05	1.8	Francis Smith	U23	2.10.81	5	Glasgow (S)	24 Jun
15.13		Martyn Hendry		10.04.75	1	Edinburgh	12 May
15.14	2.0	Roger Hunter		10.03.76	D	Jarrow	17 Jun
15.15	0.5	James Parker	U23	29.09.80	5h2	Bedford	27 May
15.19	-1.6	Liam Collins		23.10.78	5	Glasgow (S)	7 May
15.21	1.8	Fyn Corcoran		17.03.78	4D4	Arles, FRA	10 Jun
15.25	1.1	Kirk Harries		7.08.74	3rB	Cardiff	8 Jul
	(40)						
15.28	1.5	John Heanley	U23	25.09.80	2D	Bedford	5 Aug
15.29	1.9	James Wright	U20	2.04.82	1D	Bedford	5 Aug
15.31	-0.5	Oke Odudu		24.10.76	3h1	Glasgow (S)	7 May
15.31	0.3	Peter Irving	U20	28.01.83	2h1	Douglas IOM	12 Jul
15.32	1.8	Gary McCracken		23.01.78	6	Glasgow (S)	24 Jun
15.37		Paul Tohill	U20	9.10.82	2	Belfast	28 Jul
15.41	-2.6	Paul Gilding		2.10.75	2h1	London (Ha)	17 Jun
15.47	0.9	Brendan McConville	U23	3.01.79	1D7	Arles, FRA	10 Jun
15.47	1.0	Alex Zulewski	U20	6.06.82	6	Cardiff	8 Jul
15.50	1.6	Dave Savage		13.11.72	7	Jarrow	18 Aug
	(50)						
15.53	0.5	Paul Hibbert		31.03.65	3rB	London (He)	5 May
15.53	1.9	Paul Jones		11.04.78	3D6	Arles, FRA	10 Jun
15.54		Gareth Evans		28.05.77	1	Cosford	4 Jul
15.56	0.9	Adrian Hemery	U20	6.08.82	2D7	Arles, FRA	10 Jun
15.56		Ben Roberts	U23	15.01.80	5D4	Arles, FRA	10 Jun
15.58	-2.6	Manuel Bello-Cano		3.01.70	6h1	London (Ha)	17 Jun

wind assisted

13.37	2.1	Jackson		(13.32)	2	Glasgow (S)	1 Jul
13.47	2.1	Jarrett		(13.45)	2	Helsinki, FIN	14 Jun
		13.47 2.1			5	Glasgow (S)	1 Jul
		13.62 2.8			1	Fullerton CA, USA	26 Apr
13.67	4.3	Gray		(13.63)	2	Budapest, HUN	1 Jul
		13.73 2.2			2h1	Birmingham	14 Jul
		13.90 2.1			2	Bedford	27 May
13.69	2.2	Greaves		(13.68)	1h1	Birmingham	14 Jul
13.70	2.1	Chris Baillie	U23	(13.82)	6	Glasgow (S)	1 Jul
		13.86 2.1			1	Bedford	27 May
		13.95 3.2			1h3	Bedford	27 May
13.96	2.2	Bradley		(13.83)	3h1	Birmingham	14 Jul
13.98	2.1	Elliott		(13.88)	3	Bedford	27 May
		13 performances to 14.00 by 7 athletes					
14.07	4.4	Dominic Girdler	U20	(14.16)	2h2	Grosseto, ITA	20 Jul
14.22	2.2	Andy Turner	U23	(14.29)	4h1	Birmingham	14 Jul
14.34	2.2	Richard Sear	U23	(14.51)	6h1	Birmingham	14 Jul
14.34	3.3	Mohammed Sillah-Freckleton	U23	(14.42)	1r2	Jarrow	18 Aug
14.37	2.4	Paul Crossley	U23	(14.42)	1	Bedford	28 Jul
14.50	2.5	Perry Batchelor		(14.54)	2	Birmingham	17 Jun
14.54	3.2	Dwayne Stoddart	U23	(14.66)	3h3	Bedford	27 May
14.58	2.4	Colin Roberts	U23	(14.95)	2	Bedford	28 Jul
14.64	2.4	Tristan Anthony	U20	(14.81)	3	Bedford	28 Jul
14.73	4.0	Liam Collins		(15.19)	5r2	Birmingham	2 Jun
14.73	2.2	Ian Cawley		(14.86)	5rB	Bedford	18 Jul

14.77	3.2	Lee Tindal	U23	(14.82)	5h3	Bedford	27	May
14.80	2.8	Anthony Sawyer	U23	(15.03)	1D	Bedford	15	Jul
14.90	2.8	Jason McDade	U23	(15.01)	2D	Bedford	15	Jul
14.93	2.8	John Heanley	U23	(15.28)	D	Bedford	15	Jul
15.03	3.3	Richard Scott		14.09.73	2rB	Jarrow	18	Aug
15.15	2.3	Paul Gilding		(15.41)	1D	Bedford	15	Jul
15.16	3.3	Paul Tohill	U20	(15.37)	3rB	Jarrow	18	Aug
15.26	2.5	Edwin Grey	U23	23.03.81	3	Birmingham	17	Jun
15.53	3.8	Richard Hunter		12.01.71	5	Liverpool	17	Jun
15.57 w?		Jonathon Crawshaw	U23	28.09.81	3	New Haven, USA	14	Apr
15.60	3.3	Richard McDonald	U23	11.01.80	4rB	Jarrow	18	Aug
hand timing								
14.0 w	3.0	Robert Newton	U23	(14.09)	1h1	Bedford	1	Jul
14.2	2.0	Mohammed Sillah-Freckleton	U23	(14.42)	1h3	Bedford	1	Jul
14.3 w	2.1	Paul Crossley	U23	(14.42)	1h2	Bedford	1	Jul
		14.4			1	Blackpool	2	Jun
14.3 w	3.0	Richard Sear	U23	(14.51)	4	Bedford	1	Jul
		14.4 1.7			1	Rugby	10	Jun
14.5	1.2	Dwayne Stoddart	U23	(14.66)	2	Eton	18	Aug
14.7	2.0	Lee Tindal	U23	(14.82)	3h3	Bedford	1	Jul
14.7	0.5	Colin Roberts	U23	(14.95)	2	Peterborough	7	Jul
14.8	1.3	Tristan Anthony	U20	(14.81)	4	Eton	10	Jun
14.8 w	3.0	Jason McDade	U23	(15.01)	3h1	Bedford	1	Jul
14.9	0.5	Liam Collins		(15.19)	2	Loughborough	13	Jun
15.0	1.6	John Heanley	U23	(15.28)	1	Kingston	12	May
15.0	-1.0	Tony Gill		(15.02)	1	Sheffield	12	May
15.0	1.4	Martyn Hendry		(15.13)	5h1	Bedford	27	May
15.0	2.0	Roger Hunter		10.03.76	D	Jarrow	17	Jun
15.0		Paul Beaumont		27.03.63	1	Portsmouth (RN)	27	Jun
15.0	1.5	Chris Tye-Walker	U20	20.09.82	3	Bedford	1	Jul
15.0		Paul Gilding		(15.41)	1	Woodford	21	Jul
15.1		James Parker	U23	(15.15)	1	Kingston	23	Jun
15.1		Fyn Corcoran		(15.21)	2	Kingston	23	Jun
15.2		Oke Odudu		(15.31)	1	Cambridge	19	May
15.2	1.9	Richard Scott		(15.03w)	5rB	Eton	7	Jul
15.2		Charles Edsall		2.05.74	1	Guildford	21	Jul
15.2		Alex Zulewski	U20	(15.47)	1	Ipswich	12	Aug
15.2 w	2.3	Isaac McCalla	U20	28.03.82	1	London (Ha)	27	Jun
15.3		Nigel Hayman		25.09.74	1	Ashford	5	May
15.3		Matthew Colton	U20	5.11.82	1	Basildon	2	Jun
15.3	1.5	Liam Lucas	U20	15.12.82	4	Bedford	1	Jul
15.4		Andy Gill		19.02.70	2	Liverpool	5	May
15.4		Alex Beech		17.04.77	2	Peterborough	2	Jun
15.4		Manuel Bello-Cano		(15.58)	1	London (BP)	2	Jun
15.4		Anthony Bliss		7.03.70	1r2	Blackpool	2	Jun
15.4		Andrew David		9.09.69	2	London (TB)	23	Jun
15.4	0.5	Ben Roberts	U23	(15.56)	4	Peterborough	7	Jul
15.5		Chin Nwokoro		13.03.77	1	St. Ives	13	May
15.5	1.7	Mark Roberts		1.09.69	3	Kingston	13	May
15.5		Kevin Furlong		19.05.70	1	Bebington	2	Jun
15.5		Charles Akpabio			3	London (TB)	23	Jun
15.5	-2.4	Dave Sweetman		27.01.71	1	Solihull	27	Jun
15.5	1.9	Adrian Hemery	U20	(15.56)	3h1	Bedford	1	Jul
15.6		James Tattershall	U23	25.11.81	1	Grimsby	5	May

15.6	1.6	Darren Dods		26.12.74	4	Kingston	13 May
15.6		Nick Edwards	U23	22.03.81	1m2	Bournemouth	20 May
15.6	1.7	Gary Myles		3.02.63	4	Rugby	10 Jun
15.6	0.3	Edwin Grey	U23	(15.26w)	2r2	Loughborough	13 Jun
15.6	0.5	James Peet	U20	2.12.82	5	Loughborough	13 Jun
15.6		Paul Lynas		15.09.76	1	Bangor	30 Jun
15.6		Andrew Hopkinson	U20	20.09.83	1	Stretford	27 Aug
15.6 w	2.6	Louis Evling-Jones	U20	20.06.83	3	Cardiff	2 Jun
Foreign							
15.1		*Lee Okoroafu (NGR)*		*12.09.76*	*1r2*	*Woodford*	*21 Jul*
15.12 w	*2.8*	*James Holder (CAN)*		*12.10.76*	*5D*	*Bedford*	*15 Jul*
15.3 w	*2.9*	*Joe Naughton (IRL)*		*17.10.74*	*2*	*Crawley*	*5 May*
15.3 w	*2.6*	*Franck Desailly (FRA)*		*20.01.73*	*2*	*Cardiff*	*2 Jun*
15.39	*-2.3*	*Ivan van Cleef*			*4h3*	*Glasgow (S)*	*7 May*

400 Metres Hurdles

48.27	Chris Rawlinson		19.05.72	1s2	Edmonton, CAN	8 Aug
	48.54			5	Edmonton, CAN	10 Aug
	48.68			1	Birmingham	15 Jul
	48.91			2	Seville, ESP	8 Jun
	48.96			4	Rome, ITA	29 Jun
	49.11			2r2	Lausanne, SUI	4 Jul
	49.22			2	Glasgow (S)	1 Jul
	49.38			1h5	Edmonton, CAN	7 Aug
	49.54			4	Milan, ITA	6 Jun
	49.56			5	London (CP)	22 Jul
	49.67			1	Loughborough	20 May
	49.80			4	Madrid, ESP	26 May
	49.86			6	Zurich, SUI	17 Aug
	49.86			7	Linz, AUT	20 Aug
	50.07			6	Thessaloniki, GRE	22 Aug
	50.11			5	Bremen, GER	23 Jun
	50.26			5	Rovereto, ITA	29 Aug
	50.57			1	Birmingham	2 Jun
	51.20			1h2	Birmingham	14 Jul
49.29	Du'aine Thorne-Ladejo		14.02.71	1	Tula, RUS	9 Jun
	49.37			4	London (CP)	22 Jul
	49.44			3	Stellenbosch, RSA	30 Mar
	49.44			2	Birmingham	15 Jul
	49.56 A			4	Pretoria, RSA	23 Mar
	49.70			5	Glasgow (S)	1 Jul
	49.77			1	Eton	7 Jul
	49.94			1	Dublin, IRL	30 Jun
	49.96			5	Rieti, ITA	2 Sep
	50.11			7	Thessaloniki, GRE	22 Aug
	50.51			6	Hania, GRE	4 Jun
	51.19			6	Ostrava, CZE	31 May
	51.48			6	Rovereto, ITA	29 Aug
49.30	Tony Borsumato		13.12.73	3	Rovereto, ITA	29 Aug
	49.38			6	Rome, ITA	29 Jun
	49.40			5	Zagreb, CRO	2 Jul
	49.48			6s1	Edmonton, CAN	8 Aug
	49.53			3	Birmingham	15 Jul
	49.65			4h4	Edmonton, CAN	7 Aug
	49.71			6	London (CP)	22 Jul
	49.72			6	Linz, AUT	20 Aug
	49.74			3	Jena, GER	2 Jun
	49.82			5	Milan, ITA	6 Jun
	49.86			4	Ostrava, CZE	31 May

(Borsumato)	50.20			6	Rieti, ITA	2	Sep
	50.22			1	Jarrow	18	Aug
	50.28			2	Dortmund, GER	9	Jun
	50.69			5	Prague, CZE	18	Jun
	51.19			2h3	Birmingham	14	Jul
49.57	Matt Elias	U23	25.04.79	1	Amsterdam, NED	14	Jul
	49.90			1h1	Amsterdam, NED	13	Jul
	50.1			1	Bedford	1	Jul
	50.37			8	London (CP)	22	Jul
	50.51			3	Austin TX, USA	5	May
	50.68			4	Meilen, SUI	17	Jun
	50.69			1	Liverpool	23	Jun
	51.22			1r2	Loughborough	20	May
49.68	Matt Douglas		26.11.76	4	Rethymnon, GRE	1	Jul
	49.70			1rA	Loughborough	4	Jul
	49.9			2	Eton	7	Jul
	50.25			2	Clusone, ITA	22	Jul
	50.39			4	Birmingham	15	Jul
	50.59			5h2	Beijing, CHN	30	Aug
	51.01			1h3	Birmingham	14	Jul
	51.09			1	Bedford	28	May
	51.29			3	Lignano, ITA	21	Jul
	51.37			5	Loughborough	20	May
	51.42			1	Bedford	18	Jul
50.24	Charles Robertson-Adams		5.12.77	3rA	Loughborough	4	Jul
	50.45			1	Glasgow (S)	24	Jun
	50.95			2	Istanbul, TUR	16	Jun
	51.36			4	Loughborough	20	May
	51.48			8	Budapest, HUN	1	Jul
50.40	James Hillier		3.04.78	3	Budapest, HUN	1	Jul
	50.49			1r2	Tarare, FRA	9	Jun
	50.63			2r5	Ambilly, FRA	10	Jun
	50.77			2	Loughborough	20	May
	50.79			2	Birmingham	2	Jun
	51.00			1	Glasgow (S)	6	May
	51.23			1	Cardiff	17	Jun
	51.37			5	Birmingham	15	Jul
50.70	Richard McDonald	U23	11.01.80	4	Namur, BEL	17	Aug
	51.06			3	Istanbul, TUR	16	Jun
	51.07			2	Glasgow (S)	24	Jun
	51.08			3h3	Amsterdam, NED	13	Jul
	51.36			1r2	Brasschaat, BEL	15	Aug
	51.4			2	Bedford	1	Jul
51.31	Paul Hibbert		31.03.65	3	Loughborough	20	May
	87 performances to 51.50 by 9 athletes						
51.69	Robert Lewis		2.09.78	3	Andorra, AND	12	May
(10)							
51.8	Leon McRae	U23	3.11.80	1	London (He)	9	Jun
	51.96			3	Birmingham	2	Jun
51.8	Steve Surety	U23	18.02.80	3=	Bedford	1	Jul
	51.82			6	Birmingham	15	Jul
51.8	Jeffrey Christie	U20	24.09.82	1	Bedford	1	Jul
	52.25			2r2	Mannheim, GER	16	Jun
52.29	Steve Green	U20	15.01.83	1	Exeter	7	Jul
52.3	Richard Smith	U20	12.10.82	2	Bedford	1	Jul
	52.36			2	Exeter	7	Jul
52.60	David Brackstone	U20	13.03.82	5	Stoke-on-Trent	18	Aug
52.6	Chris Sleeman	U23	20.03.80	5	Bedford	1	Jul
	52.97			2s1	Glasgow (S)	5	May
52.62	Bradley Yiend	U23	25.10.80	1r2	Ambilly, FRA	10	Jun

52.64	Andrew Bargh		21.08.76	1	Portsmouth	12 May
52.7	Richard Scott		14.09.73	3	Eton	7 Jul
(20)						
	53.27			3h1	Birmingham	14 Jul
52.9	Howard Frost	U23	9.12.81	6	Bedford	1 Jul
	54.13			5	Bedford	28 May
52.9	Dave Savage		13.11.72	4	Eton	7 Jul
	53.34			1r2	Jarrow	18 Aug
53.0	Rhys Williams	U20	27.02.84	5	Bedford	1 Jul
	53.42			1	Murcia, ESP	24 Jul
53.1	Jon Cuff	U23	30.03.80	3	Loughborough	13 Jun
	54.95			3h2	Bedford	30 Jun
53.22	Dale Garland	U23	13.10.80	3s1	Glasgow (S)	5 May
53.3	Nange Ursell	U23	1.10.81	7	Bedford	1 Jul
	54.31			6	Birmingham	2 Jun
53.3	Ian Neely		29.12.74	5	Eton	7 Jul
	53.86			3	Glasgow (S)	24 Jun
53.3	David O'Leary	U23	3.08.80	3	Peterborough	7 Jul
	54.40			2	Liverpool	17 Jun
53.46	Derek Paisley		1.12.73	5s1	Glasgow (S)	6 May
53.67	Jared Deacon		15.10.75	1	Gateshead	13 May
(30)						
53.68	Lee Wiscombe	U23	12.07.80	2	Gateshead	13 May
53.7	John McIlwham		29.02.72	1	Blackpool	2 Jun
	54.50			3	Liverpool	17 Jun
53.8	Lawrence Lynch		1.11.67	3	Eton	18 Aug
53.88	Andrew Bennett	U20	30.09.82	2	Derby	9 Sep
53.94	Gary Jennings		21.02.72	5	Birmingham	2 Jun
54.0	Joel Hopkins		24.11.77	1	Watford	2 Jun
	54.83			5h1	Birmingham	14 Jul
54.0	Alex Zulewski	U20	6.06.82	6	Bedford	1 Jul
	54.45			2	Cardiff	8 Jul
54.1	Joe Lloyd		9.04.73	2	Cheltenham	13 May
	54.68			3	Cardiff	17 Jun
54.1	Mark Winship	U20	29.09.83	7	Bedford	1 Jul
54.1	Howard Moscrop	V40	16.12.57	1	Rugby	18 Aug
(40)						
54.2	Ian Monaghan	U23	6.11.81	4	Eton	18 Aug
	55.74			6	Bedford	21 Jul
54.3	Ian Palmer	U23	22.11.81	2	Salisbury	22 Jul
54.37	Mensah Elliott		29.08.76	5	Jarrow	18 Aug
54.41	Peter Irving	U20	28.01.83	4	Exeter	7 Jul
54.5	Ben Caldwell	U20	3.03.82	1	Watford	8 Sep
	54.77			4r3	Loughborough	20 May
54.51	John Bell		10.09.73	3	Birmingham	16 Jun
54.52	Andrew Dean		30.06.78	4r3	Loughborough	4 Jul
54.6	Andy Clements	U20	28.11.82	2	Bournemouth	20 May
	55.11			1	Portsmouth	12 May
54.71	Gavin Hodgson		1.02.78	4	Bordeaux, FRA	8 Jul
54.97	Tony Gill		19.09.77	2h3	Glasgow (S)	5 May
(50)						
55.0	Simon Wilson		30.04.74	2	London (BP)	20 May
55.03	Andrew Hopkinson	U20	20.09.83	3	Ipswich	2 Sep
55.1	James Parker	U23	29.09.80	1	Kingston	23 Jun
55.1	Alastair Clay		12.09.78	3rB	Eton	7 Jul
	55.95			2	Sheffield	13 May
55.11	James Lee	U23	6.02.79	4h1	London (Ha)	16 Jun
55.18	Rupert Gardner	U17	9.10.84	3	London (He)	26 Aug
55.2	Gareth Rees	U20	15.01.82	1	Stoke-on-Trent	17 Jun
	55.83			5r2	Loughborough	20 May

55.21	John Squirrell		16.12.75	5	London (He)	5	May
55.3	Richard Gawthorpe	U23	28.01.81	2	Cambridge	19	May
	(60)						
55.3	Paul Crossley	U23	30.03.79	1	Jarrow	7	Jul
	55.64			1r2	Bedford	28	Jul
55.3	Mark Nitsch		3.03.78	3	Stafford	18	Aug
55.43	Lee Garland		18.12.74	3	Douglas IOM	10	Jul
55.46	Andy Gill		19.02.70	1	Bedford	13	May
55.5	Jon Goodwin		22.09.76	1	Kingston	21	Apr
55.5	Martin Holgate		2.11.65	2	London (TB)	23	Jun
55.60	Chris Herring	U23	3.03.81	4h4	Glasgow (S)	5	May
55.6	Alistair Burgess			3	Cambridge	19	May
	55.86			2h2	Glasgow	5	May
55.73	Matthew Williams	U20	31.01.84	7	Exeter	7	Jul
55.85	Robert Gascoigne		5.10.74	2	Scunthorpe	18	Aug
	(70)						
55.9	Jon Parker		1.05.76	6h2	Bedford	28	May
56.0	Rob Trezona		6.03.75	1m1	Bedford	20	May

Additional Under 20 (1 - 15 above)

56.2	Matthew Roberts		8.07.84	2	Crawley	9	Jun
	56.94			2	Crawley	13	May
56.36	Stephen Murphy		10.02.82	1	Grangemouth	10	Jun
56.4	Malcolm Hawkins		17.12.83	1	Cudworth	16	Jun
56.46	Ben Sumner		16.08.83	1r2	Derby	9	Sep
56.5	Tom Carey		26.02.84	4h2	Watford	26	May
	56.75			5	London (He)	26	Aug
	(20)						
56.68	Scott McKinlay		11.04.83	2	Grangemouth	10	Jun
56.7	Greg Smith		29.01.84	1rB	Salisbury	22	Jul
56.8	Kenny Elliott		5.07.83	1	Brecon	18	Jul
56.8	Michael Dyer	U17	27.09.84	1	Eton	12	Aug
57.0	Matthew Colton		5.11.82	1		29	Jul
57.0	Andrew Watson		9.03.83	1	Oxford	29	Jul
57.0	Ross Tressider		8.01.83	1		12	Aug

Foreign

51.97	*Stephen McDonnell (IRL)*	*U23*	*24.07.80*	*1*	*Dublin, IRL*	*22*	*Jun*
53.35	*Olau Thomassen (DEN)*	*U23*	*19.02.80*	*2*	*Aarhus, DEN*	*25*	*Aug*
54.67	*Lee Okoroafu (NGR)*		*12.09.76*	*2r2*	*Jarrow*	*18*	*Aug*

400 Metres Hurdles - Under 17

54.53	Rupert Gardner	9.10.84	1	Exeter	7	Jul
55.24	Callum McKay	17.02.85	2	Exeter	7	Jul
56.38	Andy Broadbent	2.09.84	1h1	Exeter	6	Jul
56.42	Ben Hazell	1.10.84	2h1	Exeter	6	Jul
56.55	Ben Manchester	1.04.85	1	Cudworth	26	May
56.62	Ryan Dinham	19.08.85	3h1	Exeter	6	Jul
56.70	Adam Fell	20.04.85	1	Sheffield	13	May
56.76	Charles de Nobrigga	22.11.84	4h1	Exeter	6	Jul
57.2	Michael Dyer	27.09.84	1	Oxford	22	Jul
57.51	Philip Thomas	21.10.84	2h1	Sheffield	11	Aug
	(10)					
57.63	Ian Purcell	20.12.84	3	Connah's Quay	4	Aug
57.68	Kevin Deighton	1.01.85	3h1	Sheffield	11	Aug
57.69	Darren Lewis	12.04.86	4h1	Sheffield	11	Aug
57.7	Graham Powell	7.03.85	2	Stretford	22	Jul
57.75	Joseph Maynard	25.07.85	1	Brecon	7	Jul
57.87	Craig MacKay	30.10.84	4	Connah's Quay	4	Aug
58.3	Andy Watts		1m2	Derby	22	Jul
58.4	Robert Smith	3.03.85	1	Southend	13	May

58.41	Peter Warke		22.05.86	1	Birmingham	1	Sep
58.5	Tom Robinson			2	Tonbridge	6	May
(20)							
58.5	Robert Sutton			1	Hayes	20	May
58.6	Robert Radzius		26.02.85	1	London (BP)	9	Jun
58.6	Daniel Lambert		2.07.85	1	Southend	22	Jul
58.61	Chris Jones		17.07.85	5h1	Exeter	6	Jul
58.9	Alex Sidoli		29.05.85	1	London (He)	9	Jun
58.9	Tom Crowe		9.03.85	3	Crawley	5	Aug
Foreign							
55.11	*Liam McDermid (IRL)*		*23.11.84*	*1*	*Connah's Quay*	*4*	*Aug*

High Jump

2.26 i	Dalton Grant		18.04.66	4	Banska Bystrica, SVK	14	Feb
	2.23			1	Bedford	28	May
	2.21 i			5	Siegen, GER	9	Feb
	2.21			1	Ashford	11	Aug
	2.20 i			7	Brno, SUI	16	Feb
	2.20			1	Southend	12	May
	2.20			3	Bedford	21	Jul
	2.20			2	Bedford	22	Jul
	2.19			1	Loughborough	20	May
	2.19			5	Buhl, GER	27	Jul
	2.18			5	Tula, RUS	8	Jun
	2.15			2	Eton	7	Jul
2.26	Ben Challenger		7.03.78	1	Bedford	21	Jul
	2.21			1	Funchal, POR	30	Jun
	2.20			1	Eton	7	Jul
	2.20			18Q=	Edmonton, CAN	5	Aug
	2.17			1	Birmingham	14	Jul
	2.15			11=	Stockholm, SWE	17	Jul
	2.15			5=	Leverkusen, GER	26	Aug
2.25	Robert Mitchell	U23	14.09.80	1	Bedford	28	Jul
	2.24			1	Alfaz del Pi, ESP	21	Apr
	2.23			2	Bedford	28	May
	2.21 i			1	Birmingham	7	Jan
	2.20			1	Birmingham	2	Jun
	2.20			2	Bedford	21	Jul
	2.20			1	Bedford	22	Jul
	2.20			1	Jarrow	18	Aug
	2.19			4	Bremen, GER	23	Jun
	2.18			3=	Ashford	11	Aug
	2.17 i			1	Cardiff	11	Feb
	2.17 i			4	Cardiff	10	Mar
	2.16			2	Loughborough	16	May
	2.15 i			1	Birmingham	14	Jan
	2.15 i			2	Birmingham	28	Jan
	2.15			2	London (He)	5	May
	2.15			1	Watford	13	May
	2.15			1	Arles, FRA	10	Jun
2.21	Danny Graham	U23	3.08.79	1	Stretford	19	Jun
	2.16			1	Wigan	10	Jun
	2.15			1	Bolton	20	May
	2.15			1	Derby	29	Jul
2.20 i	Samson Oni	U23	25.06.81	1	Birmingham	28	Jan
	2.20 i			3	Cardiff	10	Mar
	2.18			1	Bedford	30	Jun
	2.16			3	Loughborough	20	May
	2.15			Q	Amsterdam, NED	12	Jul
	2.15			5=	Ashford	11	Aug

2.20	Dan Turner		27.11.78	3	Bedford	28 May
	2.15			1	London (Ha)	17 Jun
	2.15			2	Dublin, IRL	29 Jun
2.18	Chuka Enih-Snell	U20	2.03.84	1	Walnut CA, USA	21 Apr
2.16 i	Jamie Russell	U23	1.10.81	1	Normal, USA	7 Dec
	2.15			1	Cleckheaton	24 Jun
2.15	Dean Macey		12.12.77	2D	Edmonton, CAN	6 Aug
	54 performances to 2.15 by 9 athletes including 11 indoors					
2.13 i	Colin McMaster	U23	15.01.80	1	Glasgow	21 Jan
	2.10			5	Bedford	28 May
	(10)					
2.12	Rob Brocklebank		12.10.76	2	Jarrow	18 Aug
2.11	Brian Hall	U20	17.11.82	1	Watford	8 Sep
2.10 i	Luke Crawley	U23	5.09.81	2	Birmingham	14 Jan
2.10 i	Robert Paul	U23	12.11.80	1	London (CP)	20 Jan
	2.06			6	Loughborough	20 May
2.10	Martin Aram	U20	2.12.83	1	Wigan	29 Apr
2.10	Darryl Stone	U20	6.06.83	1	Watford	26 May
2.10	Matthew Ostridge	U20	23.02.83	1	Birmingham	26 May
2.10	Ian Holliday		9.12.73	4	Bedford	28 May
2.10	Chris Giblin	U23	20.06.81	1	Stretford	28 May
2.10	Stanley Osuide		30.11.74	1	Eton	15 Aug
	(20)					
2.07	Theo Casey	U20	3.06.84	1	London (Elt)	29 Jul
2.06 i	James Hardie	U20	16.04.82	1P	Bedford	7 Jan
	2.02			1	St. Ives	12 May
2.06	Martyn Bernard	U17	15.12.84	1	Stretford	28 Aug
2.05 i	Stuart Ohrland		6.09.75	4=	Birmingham	14 Jan
	2.00			2	Southend	12 May
2.05 i	Darran Cronshaw		1.02.78	3	Birmingham	14 Jan
	2.00			2	Glasgow (S)	6 May
2.05 i	Mark Crowley	U20	15.11.83	1	Bedford	17 Feb
	2.05			1	Derby	24 Jun
2.05	James Wild	U20	1.10.82	2	Cudworth	27 May
2.05	Richard Aspden		15.10.76	2	London (Ha)	17 Jun
2.05	Julian Harrison		4.08.76	2	Stretford	19 Jun
2.05	Martin Lloyd	U23	18.06.80	4	Bedford	30 Jun
	(30)					
2.05	Colin Bent		12.04.70	1	Cosford	4 Jul
2.03	Kevin Wilson	U20	28.09.82	1	Bournemouth	29 Jul
2.01	Calvin Hall	U20	15.11.83	1	Leamington	9 Jun
2.01	Tom Parsons	U20	5.05.84	6	Exeter	6 Jul
2.01	Jamie Creighton	U20	15.09.83	1=	Stretford	17 Jul
2.01	Andrew McFarlane	U20	28.02.83	1=	Stretford	17 Jul
2.01	Adam Gallie	U17	5.11.84	1	Tullamore, IRL	21 Jul
2.00 i	Duncan McInnes		1.05.78	2	Glasgow	13 Jan
2.00 i	Gavin Fordham	U23	1.02.79	7	Birmingham	14 Jan
	1.96			2D	Bedford	14 Jul
2.00 i	Stuart Livingstone	U23	29.08.79	4	Glasgow	21 Jan
	2.00			1	Edinburgh	13 May
	(40)					
2.00 i	Mark Sweeney		26.02.77	5	Glasgow	18 Feb
2.00 i	Simon Thomas	U23	4.03.81	4	Glasgow	18 Feb
2.00 i	Robert Toms	U23	7.08.80	6=	Glasgow	18 Feb
2.00	James Alix	U23	24.12.81	1	Birmingham (Un)	16 Apr
2.00	Jason McDade	U23	3.04.80	6	London (He)	5 May
2.00	Greg Goodrem	U20	14.09.83	2	Southend	12 May
2.00	Brendan McConville	U23	3.01.79	1	Belfast	12 May
2.00	Brett Mason	U20	21.03.82	2	Sheffield	12 May
2.00	Mark Smith		14.09.74	1	London (TB)	20 May
2.00	Andrew Lowe		6.03.76	3	Watford	2 Jun

2.00	Ben Smith	U20	12.06.82	3	Bedford	24 Jun
2.00	Matt Little	U20	22.07.83	5=	Bedford	30 Jun
1.99 i	Anthony Sawyer	U23	29.04.80	1H	Birmingham	21 Jan
1.98	Gareth Moir	U23	17.12.80	1	Salisbury	13 May
1.98	Chris France	U20	29.01.84	2	Birmingham	26 May
1.98	Jon Breeze	U20	8.04.83	1	Street	9 Jun
1.98	Tom Salter	U20	7.01.83	1	Cannock	9 Jun
1.98	Paul Tohill	U20	9.10.82	1	Antrim	21 Jul
1.98	Kim Harland	U20	21.02.82	1	Neath	27 Aug
1.98	Edward Dunford	U17	15.09.84	1D	Sheffield	1 Sep
(60)						
1.96	Steve Bonnett		13.07.78	D	Arles, FRA	9 Jun
1.96	Barry Thomas		28.04.72	D	Arles, FRA	9 Jun
1.96	Ryan Westaway	U20	2.03.83	1D	Exeter	23 Jun
1.96	Stephen Alexander	U17	6.10.84	1O	Preston	24 Jun
1.96	Paul Curran		3.04.77	1	Bangor	30 Jun
1.96	Martin Ohrland	U23	19.11.79	1	Chelmsford	12 Aug
1.95 i	Paul Gilding		2.10.75	2	Birmingham	7 Jan
	1.95			1	Portsmouth	23 Jun
1.95 i	Khaled El Sheikh		26.07.78	2	Cardiff	4 Feb
	1.95			2	Eton	10 May
1.95 i	Camara Stewart	U20	11.09.83	2	Birmingham	11 Feb
1.95 i	Mark Elliott	U23	12.08.80	9	Glasgow	19 Feb
(70)						
1.95	James Brierley		31.07.77	2	Kingston	21 Apr
1.95	Tony Gilhooly		26.03.76	7=	London (He)	5 May
1.95	James Hilston	U23	25.02.79	1	London (BP)	5 May
1.95	Simon Hunt	U23	27.08.79	1	Worcester	5 May
1.95	Christopher Sutcliffe	U23	9.01.79	1	Crawley	5 May
1.95	Andrew Shepherd		9.11.78	3	Glasgow (S)	6 May
1.95	Mark Bidwell	U17	4.09.84	2	Derby	12 May
1.95	Gavin Fisher		18.11.77	1	Bury St. Edmunds	12 May
1.95	Greg Beacom		26.02.78	1	Bournemouth	20 May
1.95	Steve Linsell		13.10.63	2	Stretford	28 May
(80)						
1.95	Chris Binns	U20	7.05.82	1	Blackpool	2 Jun
1.95	Simon Whittingham		18.09.78	1	Bromley	2 Jun
1.95	Richard Sear	U23	21.08.79	3	London (TB)	6 Jun
1.95	William Sharman	U17	12.09.84	1	Corby	9 Jun
1.95	David Collard	U17	25.01.85	1	Grangemouth	10 Jun
1.95	Daniel Burns	U17	6.09.84	1	Carlisle	17 Jun
1.95	Andrew Palmer		13.04.77	4=	London (Ha)	17 Jun
1.95	Nick Dance	U20	27.09.83	1	Guildford	23 Jun
1.95	Gareth Dyball	U23	16.03.81	3	London (TB)	23 Jun
1.95	Zico Benjamin	U17	4.12.84	2O	Abingdon	24 Jun
(90)						
1.95	Mark Latham	U17	13.05.85	1	Wigan	1 Jul
1.95	Marc Ladrowski	U23	13.07.79	2	Cosford	4 Jul
1.95	Tom Vanhinsbergh		28.12.78	1	Crawley	18 Jul
1.95	Emeka Maddy	U17	19.12.84	2	Ashford	21 Jul
1.95	Chris Petts	U23	22.01.80	1	Ashford	21 Jul
1.95	J. Rutterford		1.09.78	1	Aldershot	26 Jul
1.95	Ian Leitch	U20	12.07.84	1	York	29 Jul
1.95	Stuart Rance			1	Portsmouth	4 Aug
1.95	Mark Latham		13.01.76	2	Stafford	18 Aug
1.95	Wanny Mkandwire	U23	4.10.80	2	Rugby	18 Aug
(100)						
1.95	Steven Prady	U17	19.02.85	1	Rugby	18 Aug
1.95	William Wyllie		12.07.73	3	Eton	18 Aug
1.95 i	Daniel Leonard	U20	3.01.84	2	Cardiff	9 Dec

Additional Under 17 (1 - 12 above)

1.91	Kevin Lutton		26.11.84	1	Aberdeen	9 May
1.90 i	Oliver Bournat		4.12.84	1	Bedford	14 Jan
1.90 i	Louis Moore		8.09.85	1P	Glasgow	24 Feb
1.90	Chris Knox		27.03.85	1	Bury St. Edmunds	13 May
1.90	Gareth Haines		21.11.84	1	Carmarthen	20 May
1.90	Matthew Burrows		27.11.84	1	Exeter	9 Jun
1.90	Alan Hassell	U15	24.06.87	1	Cannock	9 Jun
1.90	Graham Lumsden		7.05.85	1	Darlington	24 Jun
	(20)					
1.90	Karl Orford		28.12.84	1	Erith	1 Jul
1.90	Ricardo Prevost		31.10.85	1	Harrow	1 Jul
1.90	Matthew Haslett		16.09.84	1	Carlisle	22 Jul
1.90	H. Butt			1	Bedford	28 Jul
1.90	James Gilbert		19.11.85	1	Grantham	29 Jul
1.90	Thomas Mill		21.12.85	6=	Sheffield	11 Aug
1.90	Daniel Campbell		24.02.86	2	London (Cr)	12 Aug
1.90	Calvin Stewart		17.02.85	1	Salisbury	9 Sep

Additional Under 15 (1 above)

1.85	Darren Steadman	26.01.87	1	Bedford	29 Jul
1.84	Lee Pursglove	14.10.87	2	Exeter	6 Jul
1.83	Stephen Gardiner	21.09.86	1	Antrim	26 Jun
1.81	Uche Oduoza	15.10.86	1	Exeter	6 Jun
1.81	Adrian Pettigrew	12.11.86	1	London (BP)	9 Jun
1.81	Tim Maitland	5.12.86	3	Exeter	7 Jul
1.80	Pepi Nanci	7.10.86	1	Harrow	1 Jul
1.80	Thomas King	3.04.87	1	Perivale	1 Jul
1.80	Tim Payne	23.09.86	1	Solihull	22 Jul
	(10)				
1.80	Scott Keating	24.10.86	2	Bedford	9 Sep
1.79	Steve Hunter	22.12.86	1	Wakefield	6 May
1.75	Hamish Robertson	1.11.86	1	Grantham	12 May
1.75	Daniel Pope	24.12.86	1	Middlesbrough	20 May
1.75	Julian Thomas	28.12.86	1	Cannock	3 Jun
1.75	Kyle Hargreaves	11.07.87	1	Cudworth	9 Jun
1.75	Ben Smith	6.06.87	1	Crawley	9 Jun
1.75	Jonathan Bernstein	7.03.87	1	Basildon	9 Jun
1.75	Iain Wray	13.09.86	1	Carmarthen	13 Jun
1.75	Ian Newbury	17.09.86	1	Cardiff	17 Jun
	(20)				
1.75	Iain Mcdonald		1	Tipton	1 Jul
1.75	George Beeken	4.09.86	1	Bury St. Edmunds	1 Jul
1.75	Ben Wood		2	Perivale	1 Jul
1.75	Luke Ankers	23.10.86	6	Exeter	6 Jul
1.75	David Shields	18.02.88		Tullamore, IRL	20 Jul
1.75	A. Butler		1		22 Jul
1.75	Sean Salmon	29.11.86	1	London (TB)	28 Jul
1.75	Ryan Thomas	21.03.87		Crawley	8 Sep
1.75 i	Andrew Allan	9.04.88	1	Glasgow	9 Dec

Under 13

1.57	Joseph Green	1.11.88	1	Erith	16 Sep
1.55	Nicholas Fitzpatrick	29.10.88	1	Corby	23 Aug
1.52	Russell Bowers	21.03.89	P	Rotherham	16 Sep
1.50	Jimmy Dunne	21.10.88	1	Newport	17 Jun
1.50	Peter Rhodes	20.09.88	1	Carlisle	15 Jul
1.50	Alain Kacou	25.10.88	1	Battersea Park	4 Aug
1.50	Paul Smyth		1	Belfast	23 Aug
1.50	Christian Speight	2.12.88			

Foreign

2.10	*Mark Mandy (IRL)*	*19.11.72*	*3*	*Birmingham*	*2 Jun*
2.05	*Olu Robbin-Cocker (SLE)*	*27.11.75*	*2*	*Watford*	*2 Jun*
2.00 i	*Brendan Reilly (IRL)*	*23.12.72*	*3*	*Cardiff*	*11 Feb*
2.00	*Reg Stasaitis (LTU)*	*6.04.67*	*1*	*London (Col)*	*21 Jul*

Pole Vault

5.75 A	Nick Buckfield		5.06.73	1	El Paso TX, USA	14 Apr
	5.60			4=	Gateshead	19 Aug
	5.40			1	Bedford	21 Jul
	5.30			22Q=	Edmonton, CAN	7 Aug
5.40 i	Tim Thomas		18.11.73	1	Cardiff	11 Feb
	5.40			4=	Dessau, GER	30 May
	5.40			1	Ashford	11 Aug
	5.35 i			1	Birmingham	27 Jan
	5.33 i			1	Birmingham	13 Jan
	5.30			1	Cork, IRL	7 Jul
	5.30			2	Birmingham	15 Jul
	5.30			1	Bedford	22 Jul
	5.20 i			1	Cardiff	4 Feb
	5.20			1	Cardiff	17 Jun
	5.20			8=	Prague, CZE	18 Jun
	5.15			8	Arles, FRA	9 Jun
5.30 A	Paul Williamson		16.06.74	2	El Paso TX, USA	14 Apr
	5.30			5	Modesto CA, USA	12 May
	5.30			2=	Arles, FRA	9 Jun
	5.30			1	Birmingham	15 Jul
	5.25			1	Watford	2 Jun
	5.20			2	Bedford	21 Jul
	5.20			3	Ashford	11 Aug
	5.10			2	Cork, IRL	7 Jul
	5.10			1	Eton	18 Aug
5.20	Christian Linskey	U23	14.06.80	2	Azusa, USA	14 Apr
5.20	Scott Simpson	U23	21.07.79	1	Bedford	1 Jul
	5.10 i			3	Cardiff	10 Mar
	5.10			1	Glasgow (S)	6 May
	5.05			1	Loughborough	20 May
5.20	Ashley Swain	U23	3.10.80	3	Birmingham	15 Jul
	5.10			2	Bedford	1 Jul
	5.10			2	Eton	18 Aug
5.20	Ian Tullett		15.08.69	4	Birmingham	15 Jul
	5.07			5=	Long Beach, USA	21 Apr
	5.05			5	Azusa, USA	14 Apr
5.20	Kevin Hughes		30.04.73	5	Birmingham	15 Jul
5.15 i	Christian North		2.02.74	1	Cardiff	7 Feb
	5.00			1	Cheltenham	4 Jul
5.11	Mark Grant		17.05.71	1	Chelmsford	2 Sep
(10)						
5.10 i	Mark Davis		1.03.77	2	Birmingham	27 Jan
	4.60			1	Bedford	22 Aug
5.05 A	Ben Flint		16.09.78	7=	El Paso TX, USA	14 Apr
	5.00			2	Bedford	22 Jul
5.01	Andrew Penk		19.09.78	1	Colwyn Bay	31 Aug
5.00	Tom Richards		13.11.78	1	Eton	10 Jun
5.00	Dean Mellor		25.11.71	3	Bedford	21 Jul
	56 performances to 5.00 by 15 athletes including 7 indoors					
4.90	Mike Edwards		19.10.68	10	Waco, USA	21 Apr
4.90	Matt Weaver		14.11.73	1	Sheffield (W)	5 May
4.90	Bob Kingman		21.02.73	1	Birmingham	2 Jun
4.85	Barry Thomas		28.04.72	2D	Arles, FRA	10 Jun

4.85	Martin Densley	U23	1.05.81	1	Portsmouth	23	Jun
	(20)						
4.80	Leigh Walker		17.08.77	3=	Cork, IRL	7	Jul
4.76 i	Paul Jones		11.04.78	6H	Prague, CZE	28	Jan
	4.55			D	Arles, FRA	10	Jun
4.75	Chris Type	U23	5.10.81	5	Loughborough	20	May
4.72 i	Dominic Shepherd		11.12.76	1H	Birmingham	21	Jan
4.71	Chris Tremayne	U17	11.11.84	1	Tamworth	27	Aug
4.70	Egryn Jones		1.11.71	1	Kingston	13	May
4.70	Richard Smith	U23	17.01.81	4=	Bedford	27	May
4.70	Alan Richardson	U23	15.01.81	2	Wigan	10	Jun
4.70	Paul Stevens	U20	15.11.83	3	Dole, FRA	29	Jul
4.70	Dean Macey		12.12.77	14D	Edmonton, CAN	7	Aug
	(30)						
4.70	Mark Christie	U17	11.09.84	1	Gateshead	25	Aug
4.66 i	Andrew Wake		14.09.68	1	Gateshead	14	Mar
	4.60			1	Gateshead	12	May
	4.85 et			1	Gateshead	26	Aug
4.62	John Heanley	U23	25.09.80	1D	Bedford	15	Jul
4.60 i	Warren Jousiffe		27.05.77	2	Birmingham	7	Jan
	4.60			2	Sheffield (W)	5	May
4.60 i	Mark Beharrell	U23	10.01.81	1	Wakefield	13	Jan
	4.40			4	Birmingham	2	Jun
4.60	Matthew Buck		5.04.74	2=	London (He)	5	May
4.60	Chris Boundy	U23	25.12.79	2	Gateshead	12	May
4.60	Paul Thomas	U23	1.10.80	1	Portsmouth	12	May
4.60	Jamie Quarry		15.11.72	6	Loughborough	20	May
4.60	Richard Hurren	U20	24.09.83	1	Bedford	1	Jul
	(40)						
4.60	Adam Walker	U23	16.11.79	1	Jarrow	7	Jul
4.60	Cameron Johnston	U20	22.10.82	1	Woodford	21	Jul
4.60	Chris Mills		12.11.75	1	Southampton	4	Aug
4.55	Adam Davis		19.11.72	1	Corby	18	Aug
4.50 i	Rufus Cooper	U23	24.02.79	4	Glasgow	17	Feb
	4.50			1	Eton	22	Aug
4.50 i	Daniel Broadhead	U20	19.04.82	1	Birmingham	25	Feb
	4.30			1	Grimsby	5	May
4.50 i	Alan Jervis	U20	27.07.84	2	Birmingham	25	Feb
	4.20			1	Stoke-on-Trent	17	Jun
4.50	Brendan McConville	U23	3.01.79	1D	Antrim	22	Jul
4.50	Ian Noble		2.04.77	3	Gateshead	25	Aug
4.45	Anthony Southward		31.01.71	D	Arles, FRA	10	Jun
	(50)						
4.45	Jason Fry	U20	6.01.83	2	Exeter	7	Jul
4.45	Olly Mahoney	U20	21.10.83	3	Exeter	7	Jul
4.41	Ian McKenzie	U23	3.07.81	1	Greenock	17	Jun
4.40 i	Tim Holsgrove	U20	11.12.82	2	Wakefield	13	Jan
	4.40			6	Bedford	1	Jul
4.40	Jason O'Hara		28.10.76	6	Eton	7	Jul
4.40	Paul Walker	U17	15.08.85	2	Tullamore, IRL	21	Jul
4.40	Steve McLennan		17.11.78	1	Portsmouth	4	Aug
4.40	Stephen Day	U20	10.02.82	2	Watford	12	Aug
4.40	Gavin Showell		29.09.72	3	Corby	18	Aug
4.40	Matthew Dorrian	U20	24.03.84	1	Grangemouth	3	Sep
	(60)						
4.40 i	Keith Higham	U17	7.11.85	2	Glasgow	22	Dec
	4.10			1	Carlisle	22	Jul
4.33 i	Allan Williams	V45	30.05.53	1	Cardiff	17	Feb
	4.20			1	London (He)	12	Aug
4.32	Brian Hughes		6.01.70	2D	Bedford	15	Jul
4.30 i	Simon Lewis	U20	14.01.83	2	Birmingham	10	Feb
	4.20			3	Stafford	18	Aug

4.30	Paul Miles	U23	14.09.80	1	Tamworth	27 Aug
4.30	Darren Hatton	U23	21.03.79	1D	Erith	16 Sep
4.21	Simon Eastwood		18.04.65	2	Watford	16 Sep
4.20 i	Iain Black		18.09.70	1	Glasgow	14 Jan
4.20 i	Douglas Graham		1.01.77	2=	Glasgow	21 Jan
4.20 i	Gareth Lease		14.11.77	3	Cardiff	21 Jan
	(70)					
4.20 i	Stuart Caudery		19.11.66	4	Cardiff	18 Feb
4.20	Steve Leader		24.11.66	8=	Sheffield (W)	6 May
4.20	David McFall	U23	15.10.80	8	Glasgow (S)	6 May
4.20	Chris Wills		18.05.76	1	Leamington	12 May
4.20	Tom Benn	U23	20.04.80	1	Eton	2 Jun
4.20	Glyn Price		12.09.65	3	Cardiff	2 Jun
4.20	Steve Rogers		1.09.71	3	Jarrow	2 Jun
4.20	Andy Buchanan		12.09.70	1	Guildford	23 Jun
4.20	Steven Lewis	U17	20.05.86	4	Sheffield	12 Aug
4.20	Rob Thickpenny		17.07.76	3	Stafford	18 Aug
	(80)					
4.20	Nick Pritchard		5.12.72	1	Newport	22 Aug
4.15	Gerald Manville		21.12.78	2	Cosford	4 Jul
4.15	Zico Benjamin	U17	4.12.84	3	Exeter	7 Jul
4.13	Ed Coats	U23	14.06.80	2D	Bedford	2 Sep
4.13	Gavin Fordham	U23	1.02.79	2D	Bedford	2 Sep
4.12 i	Ben Roberts	U23	15.01.80	2=H	Birmingham	21 Jan
4.12 i	James Robinson		27.08.76	2=H	Birmingham	21 Jan
4.12	Anthony Sawyer	U23	29.04.80	D	Bedford	15 Jul
4.10 i	Matthew Peerless	U20	3.12.82	2	Glasgow	4 Feb
4.10	Alasdair Strange	U20	5.04.83	2	Edinburgh	12 May
	(90)					
4.10	Ian Parkinson	U23	17.02.79	1	Loughborough	16 May
4.10	Ian Bowley	U23	14.11.81	2	Watford	4 Aug
4.10	Shaun Taylor		19.01.76	1	Tamworth	18 Aug
4.10	Mark Harvey	U20	2.07.84	1	Neath	27 Aug
Additional Under 17 (1 - 6 above)						
4.05	Tom McDowell		11.02.85	2	Stoke-on-Trent	17 Jul
3.90	Kit Branch		5.06.85	1	Basildon	9 Jun
3.90	Ian Dodsworth		16.12.84	2	Gateshead	25 Aug
3.80	Martin Vincent		12.04.86	1	Sutton Coldfield	17 Jun
	(10)					
3.80	Tom Robinson		14.06.85	2	London (TB)	15 Sep
3.70	Steven Campbell		10.11.84	2	Grangemouth	17 Jun
3.70	Michael Cox		15.01.86	5	Derby	9 Sep
3.65	Ben Jackson		22.11.84	1	Perivale	1 Jul
3.60	Mark Laws		29.09.85	1	Gateshead	9 Jun
3.60	Jason Rees			1	Yate	1 Jul
3.60	Andrew Jones		13.02.85	6=	Sheffield	12 Aug
3.60	Mark Allen			8	Sheffield	12 Aug
3.60	Steven Carpenter		30.12.85	2	Eton	12 Aug
3.60	Brendan Burkinshaw		5.04.85	1	Scunthorpe	28 Aug
Under 15						
3.50	Nathan Lawton		3.11.86	1	Birmingham	2 Sep
3.45	Tom Davies		9.11.86	1	Tamworth	27 Aug
3.35	Carl Titman		9.09.86	1	Sheffield	11 Aug
3.30	Kyle Corrigan		27.09.86	3	Antrim	16 Jun
3.30	Luke Cutts		13.02.88	1	Cudworth	2 Sep
3.20	Gareth Lapsins		5.07.87	1	Burnley	20 May
3.10 i	Scott Costello		9.06.87	3	Birmingham	25 Feb
	3.10			5	Exeter	6 Jul
3.10	Joe Ive		12.05.87	1	London (He)	12 Aug

3.10		Nathan Bull		3.06.87	2	Telford	9 Sep
3.05		David Boylan		16.12.86		Tullamore, IRL	2 Jun
		(10)					
3.05		Ryan Sweetman		4.11.86	2	Birmingham	2 Sep
3.00		James Forbes		1.11.86	1	Edinburgh	12 May
3.00		James Hoad		1.02.88	2	Harrow	1 Jul
3.00		William Hibbard		24.03.87	7	Exeter	6 Jul
3.00		Max Hall		29.12.86	1	Dartford	22 Sep
2.90		Michael Garden		27.10.86	1	Basildon	9 Jun
2.90		J. Briody			1	Oxford	22 Jul
2.90		Ryan Cornell		10.07.87	1	Southampton	8 Sep
2.85		William Dunford		21.04.87	1	Halesowen	6 May

Foreign

4.75		*Alessandro Cambon*			*1*	*Connah's Quáy*	*26 May*
4.40 i		*Matt Pilborough (USA)*	*U23*	*10.07.79*	*2*	*Birmingham*	*10 Feb*
4.30 i		*Dirk Feil (GER)*		*9.03.65*	*1*	*Gateshead*	*11 Jan*
4.20		*Joe Naughton (IRL)*		*17.10.74*	*4*	*Crawley*	*5 May*

Long Jump

8.19 w	4.5	Chris Tomlinson	U23	15.09.81	2	Ashford	11 Aug
		7.87 0.8			1	Jarrow	18 Aug
		7.75 -0.7			1	Tallahassee FL, USA	14 Apr
		7.73 0.5			Q	Amsterdam, NED	15 Jul
		7.70 -0.2			6	Amsterdam, NED	15 Jul
		7.69 0.4			2	Loughborough	20 May
		7.67 1.1			2	Bremen, GER	23 Jun
		7.61 1.5			1	Bedford	29 Jun
		7.54 1.9			2	Argentan, FRA	15 Jun
		7.51 -0.3			3	Tula, RUS	9 Jun
		7.47 w 3.2			Q	Bedford	28 May
		7.45 0.5			3	Bedford	18 Jul
		7.42 i			1	Cardiff	11 Feb
		7.41 i			1	Birmingham	28 Feb
7.98	2.0	Jonathan Moore	U20	31.05.84	1	Dole, FRA	29 Jul
		7.98 w 3.1			1	Bedford	30 Jun
		7.93 0.7			1	Stoke-on-Trent	18 Aug
		7.79 w 4.0			1	Bangor	2 Jun
		7.68 0.0			1	Exeter	6 Jul
		7.42			1	Liverpool	12 Aug
7.97	1.0	Nathan Morgan		30.06.78	1	Loughborough	20 May
		7.86			4	Kalamata, GRE	2 Jun
		7.83 i			1	Budapest, HUN	10 Feb
		7.81 w 5.3			4	Arles, FRA	10 Jun
		7.80			1	Birmingham	14 Jul
		7.78 i			1	Cardiff	18 Feb
		7.71 0.2			1	Bedford	21 Jul
		7.71 w 2.2			1	Braga, POR	4 Jul
		7.56 0.7			2	Bedford	18 Jul
		7.44 2.0			1	Eton	7 Jul
7.84 w	2.9	Darren Thompson	U23	6.11.79	1	London (Ha)	16 Jun
		7.65 w 4.8			2	Bangor	2 Jun
		7.58 w 2.8			6	Ashford	11 Aug
		7.53 0.4			2	Bedford	29 Jun
		7.52 1.6			2	Birmingham	14 Jul
		7.50 w 4.1			2	Liverpool	23 Jun
		7.48 1.6			1	London (He)	5 May
		7.43 w 3.8			12	Arles, FRA	10 Jun
		7.41 0.0			4	Bedford	18 Jul
		7.40			8	Madrid, ESP	27 May

7.69 w	4.6	Darren Ritchie		14.02.75	9	Arles, FRA	10 Jun
		7.56 w 3.7			Q	Bedford	28 May
		7.00 -0.4			6	Loughborough	20 May
7.66 w	3.7	Mark Awanah	U20	23.09.82	2	Bedford	30 Jun
		7.25 1.7			3	Stoke-on-Trent	18 Aug
7.62	-0.2	Chris Davidson		4.12.75	2	Bedford	21 Jul
7.60		Steve Phillips		17.03.72	1	Loughborough	28 Apr
		7.55			1	Blackpool	2 Jun
		7.50 1.5			1	Crawley	5 May
		7.43			1	Jarrow	7 Jul
7.59	0.4	Dean Macey		12.12.77	4D	Edmonton, CAN	13 Aug
7.51 w	4.7	Julian Flynn		3.07.72	11	Arles, FRA	10 Jun
		7.25			3	Dublin, IRL	29 Jun
	(10)						
7.47 w	4.8	Onen Eyong	U17	18.02.85	1	Ipswich	2 Sep
		7.46			1	Derby	9 Sep
		7.43 w 2.4			3	Bedford	30 Jun
52 performances to 7.40 by 11 athletes including 16 wind assisted and 4 indoors							
7.39 w?		Adam Potter	U23	12.04.80	1	Bath	26 Aug
		7.07 0.3			2	Glasgow (S)	7 May
7.35 i		Andrew Lewis		9.03.68	1P	Gateshead	10 Mar
		7.21 w 2.6			D	Bedford	1 Sep
		7.00 1.4			4	London (Ha)	16 Jun
7.34 w	2.9	Julian Golley		12.09.71	2	Bedford	28 May
		7.18 1.9			*	Bedford	28 May
7.34 w	2.2	Andre Fernandez	U23	2.03.80	4	Liverpool	23 Jun
		7.18 1.7			4	Bedford	28 May
7.32 w	2.4	David Mountford	U20	23.06.82	4	Bedford	29 Jun
		7.29			1	Stoke-on-Trent	17 Jun
7.31		Femi Akinsanya		29.11.69	1	Liverpool	5 May
7.29		Jamie Quarry		15.11.72	1	Eton	18 Aug
7.29 w?		Paul Ralph		16.12.67	1	Sheffield	5 May
7.28 w	6.4	Kris Davies	U23	30.10.81	8	Budapest, HUN	1 Jul
		7.09 0.8			4	Loughborough	20 May
	(20)						
7.28 w	3.0	Steven Shalders	U23	24.12.81	7	Ashford	11 Aug
		7.20 i			2	Cardiff	27 Mar
7.27	1.2	Dominique Richards	U23	12.09.79	4	Bedford	21 Jul
7.25 w		Mark Lawrence		26.01.71	1	Cardiff	2 Jun
		6.91			1	Hull	20 May
7.25	1.1	Dale Garland	U23	13.10.80	2	Douglas IOM	7 Jul
7.25 w	2.6	Barry Thomas		28.04.72	11D	Arles, FRA	9 Jun
		6.98 1.1			4D	Kaunas, LIT	30 Jun
7.23 i		John Heanley	U23	25.09.80	1	Glasgow	17 Feb
		7.04			2	Sheffield	5 May
7.23	0.3	Phillips Idowu		30.12.78	2	Rugby	10 Jun
7.22		Alex Hall	U20	2.02.82	1	London (Cat)	5 May
7.22 w		Ioan Hughes		8.10.78	1	Connah's Quay	13 May
		7.14			1	Connah's Quay	10 Jun
7.21	0.0	Leigh Smith	U20	24.09.82	2	Exeter	7 Jul
	(30)						
7.20		Nathan Douglas	U20	4.12.82	1	Abingdon	13 May
7.20	1.5	Levi Edwards	U23	23.11.80	3	Bedford	29 Jun
7.20 w		Jon French		11.12.75	3	Cardiff	2 Jun
		6.88			4	Peterborough	7 Jul
7.19		Tom Roe	U20	25.06.82	2	Liverpool	5 May
7.19	2.0	Jermaine Bernard	U17	1.12.84	2	Tullamore, IRL	21 Jul
7.18		Stuart Wells	U23	26.07.79	1	Exeter	13 May
7.18		Jordon Lau	U20	23.09.83	1	Southend	13 May
7.15	0.3	Essop Merrick		24.05.74	3	Eton	7 Jul
7.14 w		Dave Butler		9.12.78	1	Stafford	2 Jun

7.14		Gareth Brown		2.09.73	1	Rugby	18	Aug
7.14 w	2.9	Stewart Faulkner		19.02.69	1	Wigan	10	Jun
		7.12			1	Gloucester	4	Aug
7.10		Adrian Phillips		29.07.75	1	London (TB)	4	Aug
7.10 w		Philip Greenland	U17	10.10.84	2	Kingston	10	Jun
		6.96 1.8			5	Sheffield	12	Aug
7.10 w		Bernard Yeboah	U17	7.01.86	1	Kingston	10	Jun
		7.03 1.2			Q	Sheffield	12	Aug
7.09 w	2.5	Gary Wilson	U17	18.09.85	4	Sheffield	12	Aug
		6.87 0.2			Q	Exeter	7	Jul
7.03		Barrington Williams	V45	11.09.55	1	Banbury	5	May
7.03		Paul Jones		11.04.78	D	Arles, FRA	9	Jun
7.00		Sam Nash		22.10.71	5	Watford	2	Jun
7.00	1.6	Fyn Corcoran		17.03.78	D	Arles, FRA	9	Jun
6.99 i		Olu Baptiste		19.10.78	2	London (CP)	10	Feb
	(50)							
6.96		Michael Nesbeth	U23	1.03.79	2	Kingston	12	May
6.96	1.8	Richard Burslem	U20	4.01.84	1	Cudworth	27	May
6.96		Ashley Swain	U23	3.10.80	7	Watford	2	Jun
6.96		James Morris	U23	2.12.79	3	Peterborough	7	Jul
6.95		Alan Saulters	U20	29.01.83	1	Antrim	26	May
6.95 w		Matt Barclay	U17	1.11.84	1	Crawley	13	May
		6.79			1	Crawley	9	Jun
6.94		Marlon Lewis	U20	7.09.83	1	Yate	21	Jul
6.94	1.4	Allan Scott	U20	27.12.82	2	Derby	9	Sep
6.93	1.8	Andy Turner	U23	19.09.80	3	Merksem, BEL	4	Aug
6.92		Neil Barton	U23	18.07.80	1	Luton	10	Jun
	(60)							
6.91		Simon Sawhney	U20	10.06.83	1	Tullamore, IRL	2	Jun
6.90 i		Nick Dowsett		24.11.78	2	Bedford	14	Jan
		6.88 w 3.6			6	Birmingham	2	Jun
6.90 i		Michael Allen	U23	7.03.80	2	Glasgow	21	Jan
6.90		Shane Williams	U17	13.08.85	3	Wakefield	29	Jul
6.90 w		Lewis Cheung	U20	12.12.83	1	Liverpool	22	Apr
6.89 w	3.8	Stephen Alexander	U17	6.10.84	2O	Birmingham	29	Sep
		6.73 0.8			1	Cudworth	27	May
6.88 i		Wayne Hay	U23	25.09.80	3	Glasgow	21	Jan
6.88 i		John Donnelly	U23	11.09.79	3	Glasgow	18	Feb
		6.85 1.2			5	Bangor	2	Jun
6.88		Jon Ramos	U23	29.06.80	2	Portsmouth	23	Jun
6.88		Darren Dods		26.12.74	2	London (BP)	21	Jul
	(70)							
6.88		Stephen Lake		10.03.73	1	Ashford	21	Jul
6.88		Geoff Ingram		31.01.68	1D	Cosford	31	Jul
6.88		Richardo Childs	U17	9.10.84	1	Brecon	19	Aug
6.87 i		Bob Berriman		29.03.73	1	Sheffield	22	Jan
		6.77 w 3.2			2	Liverpool	17	Jun
6.87		Suote Nyamanyo	U17	3.10.84	1	Middlesbrough	22	Jul
6.86		Jan Irving		4.03.77	3	Salisbury	12	May
6.86		Gary Smith		20.02.71	1	London (B)	9	Sep
6.85 i		Matthew Clay	U20	9.06.84	1P	Gateshead	10	Mar
		6.83 1.9			2	Cudworth	27	May
6.85		Andrew Patton	U23	23.01.81	1	Middlesbrough	14	Apr
6.85		Jamie Russell	U23	1.10.81	2	Hull	20	May
	(80)							
6.85		Louis Burgess	U20		1	Portsmouth	21	Jul
6.85		Adam Page		17.10.78	1	Harrow	21	Jul
6.85		Simon Roper	U23	20.09.79	1	Oldham	8	Sep
6.84	2.0	Darren Hatton	U23	21.03.79	5D	Bedford	4	Aug
6.83		Mitchell Wilkin	U17	6.12.85	1	Basildon	10	Jun
6.83		M. Marsh	U20		1	Exeter	16	Jun

6.83		Tony Malcolm		15.02.76	6	Cardiff	8 Jul
6.82	-1.8	Craig Elder	U20	22.05.82	5	Glasgow (S)	7 May
6.81		D. Williams			1	Stourport	18 Aug
6.81 w	3.1	Stuart Benson	U23	12.02.81	3	Wigan	10 Jun
	(90)						
6.80		Richard Hunter		12.01.71	1	Cleckheaton	8 Jul

Additional Under 17 (1 - 11 above)

6.79 w	4.4	Edward Dunford	15.09.84	1	Carshalton	23 Sep
		6.60 i		3	Birmingham	24 Feb
		6.55		1	Birmingham (Un)	16 Apr
6.77 w	2.4	Ryan James	10.05.85	5	Sheffield	12 Aug
		6.51		Q	Sheffield	12 Aug
6.74	1.5	Gandolph Muschamp	6.12.84	Q	Exeter	6 Jul
6.72 w		Alistair Hinze	25.09.85	1	Kingston	12 May
6.69 w	4.3	Richard Blair	15.09.84	4	Tullamore, IRL	21 Jul
6.68		Chris Kirk	6.09.85	1	Cleckheaton	9 Jun
6.67	0.7	Tom Connor	30.03.85	Q	Exeter	6 Jul
6.65		Ezekiel Ewulo	29.01.86	1	Ipswich	1 Jul
6.63	0.0	Louis Moore	8.09.85	Q	Exeter	6 Jul
	(20)					
6.59		Iain Hunt	24.11.84	2	Brecon	19 Aug
6.57 w	3.3	Calvin Stewart	17.02.85	1	Exeter	16 Jun
6.56		Chris Alexis	29.12.84	1	Woodford	28 Apr

Under 15

6.46	1.5	Daniel Harris	1.10.86	1	Exeter	6 Jul
6.46		Ryan Thomas	21.03.87	1	Crawley	8 Sep
6.33		Ryan Shaw	30.12.86	1	Basildon	9 Jun
6.28		Seamas Cassidy	12.11.86	1	London (Ha)	6 May
6.25 w		Chinedum Onuoha	12.11.86	1O	Preston	23 Jun
		6.01		1	Stretford	12 May
6.16 i		Craig Glanville	21.09.86	1	Gateshead	15 Mar
6.16	0.8	Greg Rutherford	17.11.86	5	Exeter	6 Jul
6.14		James Taylor		1	Crawley	12 May
6.11		Jamie Pearce	23.09.86	1	Kingston	9 Jun
6.11		Scott Keating	24.10.86	1	Milton Keynes	8 Jul
	(10)					
6.09	0.8	Kyle Griffiths	10.10.86	6	Exeter	6 Jul
6.08		Joshua Findlater		1	London (BP)	7 Jul
6.08	1.8	Mark Fletcher	4.11.86	3	Sheffield	11 Aug
6.07		Darren Steadman	26.01.87	1	Colchester	27 Aug
6.07		Phil Jarrett	18.03.87	1P	Rotherham	16 Sep
6.04		Andrew Holmes	20.04.87	1	Bury St. Edmunds	17 Jun
6.03		Sean Salmon	29.11.86	1	London (TB)	18 Aug
6.01		J. Jegede		1	London (Nh)	26 Aug
6.00 i		Paul Twidale	30.09.86	1	Birmingham	24 Feb
6.00		Chris Stanyard		3	Kingston	17 Jun

Under 13

5.26	Paul Dingle	4.09.88	1	Poole	8 Jul
5.19	Josh Baxter	15.09.88	1	Kingston	6 May
5.19	Steven Knox				14 Jun
5.16	Alain Kacou	25.10.88	2	Kingston	29 Jul
5.15	Bradley Pickup	4.04.89	2	Bournemouth	24 Jun
5.15	Luke Thomas	27.03.89	3	Kingston	29 Jul
5.13	Ashley Harris	18.03.89	1	Peterborough	22 Jul
5.11	Ben Hartland	14.06.89	P	Cardiff	15 May
5.00	Daniel Blackett	4.10.88	1	Carlisle	9 Sep

Foreign

8.26 w	*4.9*	*Gable Garenamotse (BOT)*	*U23*	*30.06.79*	*1*	*Ashford*	*11*	*Aug*
		7.99 0.3			*3*	*Beijing, CHN*	*29*	*Aug*
7.20	*-0.4*	*Lee Okoroafu (NGR)*		*12.09.76*	*1*	*Jarrow*	*18*	*Aug*
7.16 w	*2.1*	*Gareth Devlin (IRL)*		*2.06.76*	*Q*	*Bedford*	*28*	*May*
		6.93 0.2			*7*	*Loughborough*	*20*	*May*
7.09 w	*2.6*	*Gary Munroe (CAN)*		*12.04.69*	*3*	*Birmingham*	*2*	*Jun*
		6.98 1.1			*6*	*Bedford*	*21*	*Jul*
7.07		*Keston Thomas (GRN)*	*U23*	*17.04.81*	*1*	*London (BP)*	*21*	*Jul*
6.28		*Takayuki Homma (JPN)*	*U15*	*19.02.87*	*2*	*Southend*	*22*	*Jul*

Triple Jump

17.92	0.7	Jonathan Edwards	10.05.66	1	Edmonton, CAN	6	Aug
		17.66 0.7		1	Glasgow (S)	1	Jul
		17.60 i		1	Samara, RUS	1	Feb
		17.59 0.8		1	Birmingham	15	Jul
		17.56 0.5		1	Milan, ITA	6	Jun
		17.53 w 4.9		1	Bangor	2	Jun
		17.46 -0.2		Q	Edmonton, CAN	4	Aug
		17.40 0.4		1	Stockholm, SWE	17	Jul
		17.33 0.9		1	Malmo, SWE	20	Aug
		17.29 0.5		1	London (CP)	22	Jul
		17.27 0.0		1	Rovereto, ITA	29	Aug
		17.26 i		2	Lisbon, POR	9	Mar
		17.26 -0.1		1	Bremen, GER	24	Jun
		17.26 1.1		1	Brisbane, AUS	4	Sep
		17.22 1.2		1	Madrid, ESP	7	Jul
		17.20 0.9		1	Nuremberg, GER	17	Jun
		17.19 i		1	Glasgow	18	Mar
		17.14 0.9		1	Gateshead	19	Aug
		17.14 1.4		2	Yokohama, JPN	15	Sep
		17.13 i		1	Dortmund, GER	11	Feb
		17.13 i		1	Birmingham	18	Feb
		17.11 i		1	Stockholm, SWE	15	Feb
		16.99 0.2		2	Helsinki, FIN	14	Jun
		16.98 0.1		1	Lahti, FIN	26	Aug
		16.78 i		2	Karlsruhe, GER	27	Jan
17.38 w	2.6	Phillips Idowu	30.12.78	2	Glasgow (S)	1	Jul
		17.33 1.2		1	Hania, GRE	4	Jun
		17.23 0.0		1	Madrid, ESP	26	May
		17.05 1.4		3	London (CP)	22	Jul
		16.89 -0.5		1	Loughborough	20	May
		16.88 1.2		3	Birmingham	15	Jul
		16.74 0.2		Q	Edmonton, CAN	4	Aug
		16.60 0.3		9	Edmonton, CAN	6	Aug
		16.41 0.5		5	Helsinki, FIN	14	Jun
		16.32 w 2.7		1	London (He)	5	May
		16.20 1.9		*	London (He)	5	May
17.21	0.6	Larry Achike	31.01.75	2	London (CP)	22	Jul
		17.15 0.7		Q	Edmonton, CAN	4	Aug
		17.10 0.0		2	Rovereto, ITA	29	Aug
		16.99 0.5		2	Birmingham	15	Jul
		16.97 0.8		3	Helsinki, FIN	14	Jun
		16.97 w 3.2		1	Budapest, HUN	1	Jul
		16.96 1.3		2	Gateshead	19	Aug
		16.92 1.9		2	Nuremberg, GER	17	Jun
		16.86 1.7		1	Sydney, AUS	11	Feb
		16.80 -0.5		*	Budapest, HUN	1	Jul
		16.79 0.8		7	Edmonton, CAN	6	Aug
		16.36 1.3		5	Brisbane, AUS	4	Sep

16.93 w 3.1	Julian Golley		12.09.71	1	Ashford	11	Aug
	16.40 i			5	Birmingham	18	Feb
	16.30 0.5			4	Birmingham	15	Jul
	16.22 i			1	Birmingham	27	Jan
	16.21 0.7			2	Cork, IRL	7	Jul
16.43 1.1	Jonathan Moore	U20	31.05.84	2	Grosseto, ITA	22	Jul
	16.36 0.0			1	Debrecen, HUN	15	Jul
	16.32 1.4			2	Loughborough	20	May
16.28 -0.7	Steven Shalders	U23	24.12.81	7	Amsterdam, NED	13	Jul
	16.26 w 2.7			1	Cardiff	17	Jun
16.28 w 4.4	Femi Akinsanya		29.11.69	4	Ashford	11	Aug
	15.96 1.7			1	Bedford	27	May
59 performances to 16.20 by 7 athletes including 7 wind assisted and 9 indoors							
16.08 i	Tosin Oke	U23	1.10.80	2	Birmingham	27	Jan
	15.72 1.3			4	Loughborough	20	May
15.87 i	Nick Thomas	U23	4.04.79	4	Birmingham	27	Jan
	15.54 1.0			1	Bedford	1	Jul
15.86 w 3.0	Charles Madeira-Cole		29.11.77	2	Cardiff	17	Jun
	15.59 1.0			Q	Cardiff	17	Jun
(10)							
15.56 w 3.1	Tayo Erogbogbo		8.03.75	1	Birmingham	2	Jun
15.50 1.2	Tosi Fasinro		28.03.72	2	Watford	2	Jun
15.50 0.7	Nathan Douglas	U20	4.12.82	2	Stoke-on-Trent	18	Aug
15.49 0.4	Mike McKernan		28.11.78	5	Birmingham	15	Jul
15.47 w?	Michael Nesbeth	U23	1.03.79	1	Kingston	12	May
	15.34 1.7			2	Bedford	1	Jul
15.35	Chris Tomlinson	U23	15.09.81	2	Derby	29	Jul
15.34 w	Philip Ferdinand	U20	18.11.82	1	Derby	9	Sep
	14.72			1	Stoke-on-Trent	19	Jun
15.23 w 4.4	Jon Hilton		11.01.74	9	Budapest, HUN	1	Jul
	14.97 i			5	Birmingham	27	Jan
	14.82 0.7			2	Wigan	10	Jun
15.13	Paul Ralph		16.12.67	1	Cardiff	8	Jul
15.11 1.2	Martin Rossiter		4.09.69	2	Bedford	27	May
(20)							
15.01	Dave Sanderson		6.05.71	1	Sandown IOW	9	Sep
14.85	Michael Keeton		14.12.76	1	Peterborough	7	Jul
14.83 w 2.4	Keith Newton		12.12.68	1	Bedford	21	Jul
	14.79			1	Southend	12	May
14.80 w	Kevin Thompson	U20	24.10.83	2	Liverpool	5	May
	14.68 0.4			4	Stoke-on-Trent	18	Aug
14.76 w	Mark Lawrence		26.01.71	2	Cardiff	2	Jun
	14.67			3	Peterborough	7	Jul
14.72 w 2.9	Francis Agyepong		16.06.65	2	Jarrow	18	Aug
	14.19 0.0			5	Eton	7	Jul
14.71 w 2.8	Paul Weston		6.10.67	2	Birmingham	17	Jun
	14.65			3	Sheffield (W)	5	May
14.60 i	Lewis Cheung	U20	12.12.83	7	Vittel, FRA	3	Mar
	14.47 w 2.5			4	Exeter	7	Jul
	14.16			3	Derby	9	Sep
14.56 w	Alan Saulters	U20	29.01.83	1	Tullamore, IRL	2	Jun
	14.22			1	Antrim	16	Jun
14.55 w 5.0	Paul Revell	U23	18.11.80	1	Scunthorpe	18	Aug
(30)							
	14.08 0.0			*	Glasgow (S)	7	May
14.53	Ruddy Farquharson	V40	26.03.61	2	Brisbane, AUS	15	Jul
14.52 0.3	Semi Majekodunmi	U20	29.06.83	1	Exeter	16	Jun
14.48 w 3.7	Dale Garland	U23	13.10.80	2	Douglas IOM	13	Jul
	13.92 i			1	Cardiff	7	Feb
14.45 w 2.1	Sayo Ojo	U23	9.05.80	3	Bedford	1	Jul
	14.26			1	London (Ha)	27	Jun

14.42		John Heanley	U23	25.09.80	3	Cardiff	8 Jul
14.41	-0.5	Gary White	U17	16.06.85	1	Exeter	6 Jul
14.39 i		Rez Cameron	V40	18.05.60	2	Bordeaux, FRA	11 Mar
		14.35 0.2			1	Brisbane, AUS	11 Jul
14.38		Matt Randall		28.04.70	1	Norwich	13 May
14.37 i		Dan Adejuwon		27.11.76	2	Glasgow	21 Jan
		14.34			4	Watford	2 Jun
14.32 w		David Mountford	U20	23.06.82	2	Derby	9 Sep
	(40)						
14.30		Jason Comissiong	U20	7.09.83	4	Cardiff	8 Jul
14.30 w	3.1	John Donnelly	U23	11.09.79	5	Bangor	2 Jun
		14.12			1	Dublin, IRL	21 Apr
14.27 w	3.1	Mark Awanah	U20	23.09.82	8	Birmingham	2 Jun
14.26 w		Simon Sawhney	U20	10.06.83	2	Tullamore, IRL	2 Jun
		14.15			1	Brecon	18 Jul
14.25 w	3.1	Marvin Bramble		10.06.77	7	London (He)	5 May
14.25 w	3.5	Curtis May	U20	28.01.84	6	Exeter	7 Jul
		13.79 0.0			2	Watford	8 Sep
14.22	0.9	Dave Emanuel		27.12.66	4	Bedford	21 Jul
14.17 w	2.3	Julian Flynn		3.07.72	9	Birmingham	2 Jun
		14.00 1.7			*	Birmingham	2 Jun
14.16		David Wellstead	U20	17.12.82	1	Kingston	10 Jun
14.15	0.0	Ademola Oyediran	V40	27.11.59	1	Watford	8 Sep
	(50)						
14.15 w	3.0	Enyioma Anomelechi	U17	10.03.85	1	Sheffield	11 Aug
		13.70 i			1	London (CP)	10 Feb
		13.64 1.8			*	Sheffield	12 Aug
14.13		Matt Barton	U23	22.05.81	5	Douglas IOM	13 Jul
14.13		Adam Potter	U23	12.04.80	1	Hemel Hempstead	21 Jul
14.13		Paul Curran		3.04.77	1	Belfast	28 Jul
14.12		D. Wooler			1	Cosford	4 Jul
14.12 w	3.6	Anthony Nelson	U17	14.09.84	2	Sheffield	11 Aug
		13.94 1.9			*	Sheffield	12 Aug
14.12 w		Andy Bell	U17	2.09.84	1	Bedford	9 Sep
		13.70			1	Peterborough	29 Aug
14.10 w	5.2	Daniel Jillons	U20	3.04.83	7	Exeter	7 Jul
		13.94			1	Bury St. Edmunds	17 Jun
14.08		Matthew Thurgood	U20	29.12.83	1	Peterborough	29 Apr
14.08		Ezra Clarke		9.12.74	1	London (TB)	23 Jun
	(60)						
13.99		Adam Ireland		5.10.78	1	New Haven, USA	14 Apr
13.98		Robert Heaton	U23	6.05.81	2	New Haven, USA	14 Apr
13.98		Oladipo Senbanjo	U20	20.03.82	1	Cambridge	19 May
13.97		Lawrence Harvey	U23	26.08.81	1	London (Cr)	23 Jun
13.96 w	2.6	David Watson	U20	29.06.83	1	Grangemouth	16 Jun
13.95 w	4.1	Jonathon Oparka	U23	27.01.80	8	Jarrow	18 Jul
13.93		Christopher Spurling		27.11.75	1	Blackburn	8 Jul
13.93		David Budd	U23	8.12.79	4	Cudworth	26 Aug
13.92	0.5	Chris Alexis	U17	29.12.84	1	Birmingham	2 Sep
13.91 i		Jonathan Best	U20	9.11.82	2	Glasgow	4 Feb
	(70)						
13.90		Michael Brown		6.05.62	1	London (Ha)	5 May
13.90		Naved Childs	U23	12.05.81	2	Cambridge	19 May
13.87		Jon French		11.12.75	4	Cardiff	2 Jun
13.86		David Brown	U20	11.02.83	1	Barry	10 May
13.86		Dennis Fennemore	U20	19.06.84	1	Watford	12 May
13.84		Daniel Bray	U20	6.09.83	1	London (BP)	21 Jul
13.81		Ricky Brown		24.05.74	2	London (BP)	20 May
13.81		Peter Durham	U20	13.04.84	1	Jarrow	2 Jun

Additional Under 17 (1 - 5 above)

13.70	0.3	Graham Jackson		12.11.85	2	Birmingham	2 Sep
13.68	1.5	Richard Blair		15.09.84	3	Tullamore, IRL	21 Jul
13.63 w	3.1	Craig Phillips		29.09.85	4	Tullamore, IRL	21 Jul
13.63 w	2.3	Matthew Jacobs		28.02.85	5	Tullamore, IRL	21 Jul
		13.46			1	Brecon	7 Jul
13.50		Gary Wilson		18.09.85	1	Southend	22 Jul
	(10)						
13.49 w	3.6	Christian Campbell		10.06.85	6	Sheffield	12 Aug
13.41		David Taylor		21.11.84	1	Exeter	16 Jun
13.38	1.0	Ryan Chattington		2.09.84	3	Birmingham	2 Sep
13.36		Anthony Bibby		12.03.85	1	Middlesbrough	20 May
13.24		Andrew Nicholson		25.03.86	1	Crawley	9 Jun
13.24		Jermaine Bernard		1.12.84	2	Exeter	6 Jul

Under 15

13.20		William Harwood		25.09.86	1	Scunthorpe	13 May
12.81	1.7	Ian Miller		9.01.87	2	Sheffield	12 Aug
12.76 w	2.5	Aiden Collins		18.10.86	3	Sheffield	12 Aug
		12.44			1	Basildon	11 Jun
12.69 w	2.8	Jeavon Nicely		27.11.86	4	Sheffield	12 Aug
		12.60			2	Leamington	9 Jun
12.63	-0.9	Curtis Osano		8.03.87	2	Exeter	6 Jul
12.46 w	2.8	Joseph Evling-White		3.12.86	5	Sheffield	12 Aug
		12.43 -0.3			3	Exeter	6 Jul
12.33	0.0	Chris Jefferson			4	Exeter	6 Jul
12.28		Wayne Barrett		9.12.86	1	Exeter	16 Jun
12.22	-1.2	Mike Okoigun		1.02.87	5	Exeter	6 Jul
12.07		Robert Wallace		5.01.87	1	Kingston	16 Jul
12.06		Dexter Nicholls		28.05.87	1	London (BP)	9 Jun
12.03		Darren Bates		22.04.87	1	Liverpool	9 Jun
12.01		Grant Batten		11.12.86	2	Exeter	16 Jun

Under 13

11.75		Alain Kacou		25.10.88	1	Tooting	15 Sep
11.33		Joe Gibbins		12.11.88	1	Barry	26 Jun
10.52		Matthew Field		13.12.88	1	Kingston	27 Jun

Foreign

15.92 i		*Gable Garenamotse (BOT)*	*U23*	*30.06.79*	*3*	*Birmingham*	*27 Jan*
15.26	*0.7*	*Farel Meepandy (CGO)*	*U23*	*27.12.79*	*1*	*Glasgow*	*7 May*
14.88		*Reg Stasaitis (LTU)*		*6.04.67*	*1*	*London (Col)*	*21 Jul*
14.74 w	*2.1*	*Francois Tessen (FRA)*	*U23*	*80*	*2*	*Glasgow (S)*	*7 May*
		14.44 i			*3*	*Glasgow*	*18 Feb*
		14.31 0.2			***	*Glasgow (S)*	*7 May*
14.33	*1.7*	*Michael Corrigan (IRL)*		*1.12.77*	*4*	*Glasgow (S)*	*7 May*
14.29 i		*Michael McDonald (IRL)*		*24.08.65*	*3*	*Nenagh, IRL*	*4 Feb*
14.29		*Olu Robbin-Cocker (SLE)*		*27.11.75*	*6*	*Watford*	*2 Jun*
14.15 w	*2.9*	*Sakchai Makao*	*U20*	*10.12.82*	*4*	*Douglas IOM*	*13 Jul*
14.01		*Keston Thomas (GRN)*	*U23*	*17.04.81*	*1*	*Bromley*	*23 Jun*

Shot

19.64	Mark Edwards	2.12.74	1	Stretford	8 May
	18.99		1	Loughborough	12 May
	18.10		1	Loughborough	23 May
	18.02		1	Tamworth	5 May
	17.41		10	Halle, GER	19 May
	17.30		1	Worcester	31 Jul
	17.29		1	Loughborough	20 May

19.30	Mark Proctor		15.01.63	1	Bedford	18 Jul
	18.98 un				-, GER	Jun
	18.89			8	Halle, GER	19 May
	18.75			1	Cosford	4 Jul
	18.64			1	Loughborough	13 Jun
	18.38			1	Birmingham	15 Jul
	18.24			1	Cosford	20 Jun
	18.10			8	Bremen, GER	23 Jun
	18.03			2	Eton	7 Jul
	17.81			1	Bedford	21 Jul
	17.75			30Q	Edmonton, CAN	4 Aug
18.37	Lee Newman		1.05.73	1	Watford	13 Jun
	18.28			1	Birmingham (Un)	7 May
	17.73 i			1	Birmingham	4 Feb
	17.59			1	Ashford	11 Aug
	17.58 i			2	Birmingham	27 Jan
	17.56 i			1	Cardiff	11 Feb
	17.51 i			2	Birmingham	14 Jan
	17.46			1	Rugby	10 Jun
	17.39			1	Birmingham	2 Jun
	17.25			1	London (He)	5 May
	17.23			1	Cardiff	17 Jun
	17.20			2	Dublin, IRL	29 Jun
	17.08 i			4	Cardiff	18 Mar
18.29 i	Emeka Udechuku	U23	10.07.79	1	Birmingham	14 Jan
	18.23			3	Varazdin, CRO	5 Jul
	18.19 i			1	Birmingham	27 Jan
	18.02			2	Loughborough	13 Jun
	18.01			2	Birmingham	15 Jul
	17.90			1	Bedford	30 Jun
	17.89 i			1	London (CP)	20 Jan
	17.88			1	Liverpool	23 Jun
	17.84 i			1	Birmingham	Feb
	17.82			3	Eton	7 Jul
	17.71			1	Derby	29 Jul
	17.69 i			1	Cardiff	10 Mar
	17.59			1	Ashford	28 Aug
	17.46			1	Rugby	10 Jun
	17.43			2	Bedford	21 Jul
	17.23			1	Cardiff	16 Jul
	17.20 i			2	Cardiff	11 Feb
	17.04 i			1	Birmingham	13 Feb
	17.02 i			3	Stange, NOR	5 Feb
17.69 i	David Readle	U23	10.02.80	1	Carbondale, USA	24 Feb
	15.47			4	Liverpool	17 Jun
	50 performances to 17.00 by 5 athletes including 14 indoors					
16.92	David Condon		11.04.72	3	Dublin, IRL	29 Jun
16.86	Scott Rider		22.09.77	3	Birmingham	15 Jul
16.71 i	Steve Whyte		14.03.64	4	Birmingham	27 Jan
	16.45			2	London (Ha)	16 Jun
16.67	Bruce Robb		27.07.77	1	Glasgow (S)	23 Jun
16.58	Gary Sollitt		13.01.72	1	London (Ha)	10 Jun
(10)						
16.56	Iain McMullan		15.06.78	1	Belfast	28 Jul
16.48	Lyndon Woodward	U23	22.11.80	1	Cannock	13 May
16.43	Paul Reed		2.06.62	1	Liverpool	17 Jun
16.38 i	Greg Beard	U20	10.09.82	2	Vittel, FRA	3 Mar
	16.32			1	Bangor	2 Jun
16.18	Bryan Kelly		29.12.73	2	Liverpool	17 Jun
16.10	Morris Fox		30.04.63	1	Macclesfield	21 Apr

16.01	Shaun Pickering		14.11.61	1	Vught, NED	17	Jun
15.95	Guy %Marshall		24.09.71	3	Liverpool	17	Jun
15.86	Neil Elliott		10.04.71	2	Glasgow	18	Jul
15.77	Dean Macey		12.12.77	1	Harrow	21	Jul
(20)							
15.70	Bill Fuller		19.10.76	1	London (TB)	22	Aug
15.65	Mark Wiseman		9.02.69	2	Cosford	4	Jul
15.49	Nick Owen	U23	17.07.80	1	Kingston	4	Jul
15.47	Iain Styles		2.10.75	1	Birmingham (Un)	11	Jul
15.42	Scott Hayes		4.01.73	3	Sheffield (W)	5	May
15.38 i	Adam Major	U23	2.11.81	2	Glasgow	17	Feb
	15.00			9	Bedford	27	May
15.34	Simon Fricker		14.07.75	3	Cardiff	7	Jul
15.32 i	John Nicholls		1.09.65	2	Wakefield	13	Jan
	15.12			5	Wigan	10	Jun
15.16	Perriss Wilkins		12.12.69	2	Cudworth	26	Aug
15.09	Craig Rogers		14.02.76	3	Cannock	13	May
(30)							
15.05	Jason Young		18.07.69	1	Shotts	2	Jun
15.02 i	David Lovett		13.09.78	2	London (CP)	10	Feb
	14.85			1	Sandown IOW	9	Sep
14.87	Adam Davis		19.11.72	4	Loughborough	13	Jun
14.81	Willie Falconer		20.12.78	5	Glasgow (S)	23	Jun
14.78	Matthew Twigg		18.07.69	1	Rugby	18	Aug
14.77	Scot Thompson	U23	10.08.81	5	Glasgow (S)	6	May
14.71	Denzil McDonald		11.10.65	1	London (BP)	21	Jul
14.64	Mark Davies		10.01.71	1	Tonbridge	4	Aug
14.57	Marcus Gouldbourne	U23	12.06.81	1	Cleckheaton	7	Jul
14.56	Derrick Squire	U20	7.12.83	3	Cannock	5	May
(40)							
14.52	Andy Turner		29.08.63	2	Cardiff	17	Jun
14.42	James South		4.01.75	1	Perivale	5	May
14.42	David Dowson	U23	11.01.81	1	Scunthorpe	19	Aug
14.41	Graeme Allan	U23	24.09.80	3	Rugby	10	Jun
14.40 i	Mark Leitch		17.11.68	13	Birmingham	27	Jan
	13.85			4	Cosford	4	Jul
14.37	Gregor Edmunds		25.04.77	2	Shotts	2	Jun
14.29	Colin Smith	V40	11.09.57	1	Eton	23	Jun
14.26	Luke Rosenberg	U23	29.06.80	5	Loughborough	13	Jun
14.26	David Dawson	U20	3.02.84	4	Dole, FRA	29	Jul
14.25	Jamie Quarry		15.11.72	D	Arles, FRA	9	Jun
(50)							
14.21 i	Andrew Lewis		9.03.68	3	London (Ha)	4	Feb
14.20	Peter Maitland		21.01.73	17	Bedford	27	May
14.15 i	Barry Thomas		28.04.72	3H	Prague, CZE	28	Jan
	13.77			D	Kaunas, LIT	30	Jun
14.15	Justin Bryan		16.08.69	3	Cardiff	17	Jun
14.13	Andrew Rollins		20.03.78	8	Eton	18	Aug
14.13	Andrew Wain		2.06.65	1	Peterborough	27	Aug
14.12	Tony Zaidman		18.03.62	2	London (BP)	20	May
14.10	Tom Dobbing		5.02.73	2	Bedford	28	Jul
14.07	George Baker		14.08.76	3	Eton	10	Jun
14.07	Carl Saggers	U20	20.09.83	2	Colchester	28	Aug
(60)							
14.05 i	Ben Roberts	U23	15.01.80	2H	Nogent-sur-Oise, FRA	24	Feb
	13.98			1	Connah's Quay	2	May
14.05	Paul Corrigan		19.01.66	2	Loughborough	23	May
14.02	Daniel Brunt		23.04.76	6	Liverpool	17	Jun
	13.59			18	Bedford	27	May
13.99	David Abernethy	V45	5.09.55	1	Lancaster	2	Jun
13.94	Peter Cranfield	U17	26.09.84	1	Warrington	15	Jul

13.92	Gareth Cook		20.02.69	1	Sutton	23 Jun
13.92	Phil Adams		3.11.71	1	Nuneaton	5 Aug
13.89 i	Darren Hatton	U23	21.03.79	1H	Birmingham	20 Jan
	13.50			1D	Bedford	4 Aug
13.83	Andy Frost	U23	17.04.81	1	Abingdon	4 Aug
13.81 i	Ian Lindley	V45	3.12.55	1	Cardiff	17 Feb
	13.47			2V45	Eton	24 Jun
	(70)					
13.81	Guy Perryman	V40	2.11.58	2V40	Eton	24 Jun
13.81	Alistair Gunn	U23		1	Nethybridge	11 Aug
13.81	Glen Smith		21.05.72	11	Jarrow	18 Aug
13.76	Mike Small	V45	31.03.54	1	London (TB)	15 Sep
13.73	Simon Armstrong		29.05.62	3	Bournemouth	13 May
13.70	James Coombes	U23	4.10.81	4	Cardiff	17 Jun
13.68	Steven Lloyd		20.03.74	2	Chester	4 Aug
13.67	Gary Herrington	V40	31.03.61	3	Loughborough	23 May
13.67	John Cameron	U23	27.02.81	2	Nethybridge	11 Aug
13.66 i	Malcolm Fenton	V45	12.02.56	2	Cardiff	17 Feb
	(80)					
13.60	Fyn Corcoran		17.03.78	1	London (TB)	20 May
13.59 i	Andy Vince	V40	9.05.59	3	Grangemouth	27 Jan
13.59 i	Rob Earle	V40	15.09.60	1	Cardiff	17 Feb
	13.51			3	Eton	24 Jun
13.58	Richard Oparka	U20	28.07.82	4	Bedford	1 Jul
13.55	Brett Marsh		20.01.76	1	Par	13 May
13.53	Alex Gibson		3.11.77	1	Hayes	23 Jun
13.52	Simon Williams	U23	5.10.80	1	Basingstoke	5 May
13.51	Neil Griffin	V50	28.05.48	2	Eton	2 Jun
13.50	Manjit Singh Randhawa	U23	19.10.80	4	Tamworth	5 May
13.38	Steve Head	V40	21.10.58	3	Kingston	4 Aug
	(90)					
13.37	Anthony Southward		31.01.71	D	Arles, FRA	10 Jun
13.37	Paul Stronach		18.05.68	1	Worcester	18 Aug
13.36 i	Nick Vince	U20	29.01.82	4	Birmingham	24 Feb
13.36	George Cameron			3	Nethybridge	11 Aug
13.35	Tony Norman		5.07.63	2	Woking	21 Jul
13.34	Geoff Tyler	V50	30.09.48		Maison Alfort, FRA	20 Oct
13.32	Kyle Stevens	U17	3.06.85	1	Carshalton	23 Sep
13.31	Garry Hagan	U17	21.11.84	10	Glasgow (S)	23 Jun
13.31	Sam Westlake	U20	14.09.83	6	Beveren, BEL	8 Sep
13.28	Jason Crawford	U20	20.07.83	2	Hull	20 May

Additional Under 20 (1 - 11 above)

13.00	Martin Aram		2.12.83	5	Bedford	1 Jul

unconfirmed

15.85	Gregor Edmunds		25.04.77	3	Knebworth	28 May

Foreign

16.58	*Steph Hayward (IRL)*	*30.07.74*	*8*	*Vaasa, FIN*	*23 Jun*
15.39 i	*Tony Soalla-Bell (SLE)*	*3.10.76*	*1*	*Cardiff*	*24 Nov*
	14.77		*1*	*London (He)*	*23 Jun*
14.62	*Michael Hann*		*1*	*Windsor*	*10 May*
13.69	*Jeroen Westmeijer (NED)*	*5.07.70*	*3*	*Kingston*	*5 May*
13.57	*Kevin Brown (JAM)*	*10.09.64*	*8*	*Madrid, ESP*	*27 May*

Shot - Under 20 - 6.25kg

18.06	Greg Beard	10.09.82	1	Ipswich	2 Sep
15.73	Derrick Squire	7.12.83	1	Cannock	9 Jun
15.46	Carl Saggers	20.09.83	1	Watford	9 Jun
15.42	David Dawson	3.02.84	1	Exeter	9 Jun

14.82	Sam Westlake		14.09.83	2	Exeter	16 Jun
14.78	Nsa Harrison		27.11.83	1	Worcester	9 Jun
14.54	Peter Cranfield	U17	26.09.84	2	Derby	9 Sep
14.27	John Holtby		27.03.82	1	Cudworth	26 May
14.19	N. Kilko			2	Stoke-on-Trent	17 Jun
14.17 i	Nick Vince		29.01.82	1	Glasgow	4 Feb
	13.66			2	Grangemouth	10 Jun
(10)						
14.16	Stuart Millar		9.03.83	3	Exeter	16 Jun
14.14	Chris Orr		20.06.83	1	Carlisle	12 May
14.14	Grant Springings		26.02.82	4	Derby	9 Sep
14.12	Richard Oparka		28.07.82	1	Edinburgh	12 May
14.01	Martin Aram		2.12.83	2	Cudworth	26 May
13.99	Edward Dunford	U17	15.09.84	5	Derby	9 Sep
13.82	Paul Scott		3.01.82	3	Watford	26 May
13.76	Chris Wade		22.09.82	3	Cudworth	26 May
13.75	Garry Hagan	U17	21.11.84	2	Edinburgh	12 May
13.61 i	Brian Doherty		2.06.83	2	Glasgow	4 Feb
(20)						
13.59	Mark Thompson		7.07.82	1	Antrim	16 Jun
	(this may be senior implement)					
13.51	Tim Pritchard		7.10.82	4	Exeter	7 Jul

Shot - Under 17 - 5kg

16.43	Peter Cranfield	26.09.84	2	Tullamore, IRL	21 Jul
15.98	Edward Dunford	15.09.84	1O	Birmingham	17 Jun
15.97	Ndubuisi Monye	10.05.85	3	Tullamore, IRL	21 Jul
15.60	Garry Hagan	21.11.84	1	Glasgow	18 Apr
15.51	Glenn Williams	24.03.85	3	Sheffield	12 Aug
15.46	Dale Hewitson	11.09.84	1	Gateshead	25 Aug
15.41	Kyle Stevens	3.06.85	1	Kingston	9 Jun
15.31	Andrae Davis	27.09.85	3	Exeter	6 Jul
15.25	Bill Walter	11.10.85	4	Exeter	6 Jul
14.91	Jake Babb	7.12.85	1	Bath	29 Jul
(10)					
14.78	Alex Shorrock	28.09.84	1	Blackpool	12 May
14.64	Simon Cooke	3.10.85	2	Watford	27 May
14.60	Samuel Clague	26.02.86	1	Oxford	22 Jul
14.48	Oliver Bournat	4.12.84	1	Erith	9 Jun
14.43	Ben Lawrence	13.04.86	1	Cannock	3 Jun
14.36	James Holland	1.04.85	1	London (BP)	3 Jun
14.25	James Bergl	23.02.85	8	Exeter	6 Jul
14.17	Bobby Lockwood	1.02.86	2	London (TB)	15 Sep
14.17 i	Alistair McDiarmid	16.10.85	1	Glasgow	22 Dec
	14.05		2	Glasgow	18 Apr
14.14	Gareth Bull	3.03.85	1	Barry	10 May
(20)					
14.10	Ross Zeraffa	2.11.85	2	Basildon	9 Jun
14.04	Jake Evans	26.07.86	1	Carmarthen	12 Aug
13.97	David Bulley	4.06.86	2	Scunthorpe	18 Aug
13.93	Simon Bissell	25.12.85	2	Bebington	3 Jun
13.89	Roberts Jolley	26.04.85	3	Southend	12 May
13.86 i	Craig Sturrock	7.01.85	2	Glasgow	4 Feb
13.84	Tony Gallagher	16.10.84	2	Liverpool	12 May

Shot - Under 15 - 4kg

16.14	Chris Gearing	30.09.86	1	Ashford	12 May
16.12	Daniel Hepplewhite	2.09.86	1	London (He)	26 Aug
15.32	Sam Herrington	2.10.86	1	Birmingham	27 May
15.05	Pepi Nanci	7.10.86	1	Bedford	9 Sep

14.90	William Lowndes		10.10.86	1	Scunthorpe	18 Aug
14.79	Richard Parker		21.11.86	1	Birmingham	1 Sep
14.30	Barry Roberts		24.09.86	1	Neath	27 Aug
14.26	David Price		12.01.87	2	Connah's Quay	4 Aug
14.06	Shane Birch		22.10.87	2	Watford	16 Sep
13.89	Toby Hunt		28.12.86	1	Oxford	22 Jul
	(10)					
13.75	James Murphy			1P	Cardiff	15 May
13.64	Brendan Hall		5.09.87	5	Exeter	7 Jul
13.63	Michael Mertins		31.01.87	1	Tullamore, IRL	2 Jun
13.50	Jamie Towers			1	London (He)	3 Jun
13.41	Jacob Salt Berryman		27.10.86	1	London (TB)	6 May
13.21	Michael Howes		6.11.86	1	Cleckheaton	9 Jun
13.13	Bradley Williams		22.06.87	4	London (He)	26 Aug
13.09	Kyle Spiller		17.01.87	1	Newport	22 Aug
13.06	Thomas Edmunds		12.12.86	7	Exeter	7 Jul
13.05	Steven Parker		6.10.86	8	Exeter	7 Jul

Shot - Under 13 - 3.25kg

14.47	Matthew Evans		9.09.88	1	Cardiff	22 Jul
12.11	Marcus Higgins		3.11.88	1	Gloucester	17 Sep
11.97	Alain Kacou		25.10.88	1	Battersea Park	4 Aug
11.51	James Chapman		23.11.88	1	Birmingham	2 Sep
11.39	Ross Hayhurst		15.10.88	1	Blackpool	22 Jul
11.35	Eddie Kamoga		25.12.88	1	Peterborough	22 Jul
11.26	Sam Allan		16.09.88	1	Wakefield	23 Sep

Discus

63.03	Bob Weir	V40	4.02.61	1	Bedford	21 Jul
	61.79			4	Glasgow (S)	1 Jul
	61.35			6	Salinas, USA	22 May
	61.05			15Q	Edmonton, CAN	6 Aug
	60.67			9	Palo Alto, USA	9 Jun
	60.48			1	Loughborough	4 Jul
	59.92			2	Birmingham	15 Jul
	59.81			1	Eton	7 Jul
	58.23			7	Bremen, GER	24 Jun
	56.94			4	Palo Alto, USA	13 May
61.68	Perriss Wilkins		12.12.69	1	Cudworth	26 Aug
	58.17			1	Abingdon	12 May
	58.08			1	London (He)	5 May
	56.89			3	Birmingham	15 Jul
61.29	Glen Smith		21.05.72	1	Ashford	11 Aug
	60.55			2	Dublin, IRL	29 Jun
	60.38			1	Palo Alto, USA	4 May
	59.99			1	Birmingham	15 Jul
	59.27			1	Bedford	27 May
	59.11			2	Eton	7 Jul
	59.00			6	Glasgow (S)	1 Jul
	58.76			3	Irvine CA, USA	6 May
	58.69			3	Bedford	21 Jul
	58.58			1	Varazdin, CRO	5 Jul
	58.37			7	Modesto CA, USA	12 May
	58.16			1	Jarrow	18 Aug
	57.61			1	Birmingham	2 Jun
	57.33			3	Tula, RUS	9 Jun
	57.03			1	Bedford	22 Jul
	56.30			9	Halle, GER	19 May

59.97	Emeka Udechuku	U23	10.07.79	2	Bedford	21	Jul
	59.84			1	Bedford	30	Jun
	59.53			2	Ashford	11	Aug
	59.43			1	Liverpool	23	Jun
	58.67			Q	Beijing, CHN	28	Aug
	58.58			1	Loughborough	16	May
	58.40			3	Eton	7	Jul
	57.32			1	Watford	15	Aug
	57.30			1	Loughborough	13	Jun
	57.25			7	Amsterdam, NED	14	Jul
	57.04			3	London (He)	5	May
	56.90			3B	Halle, GER	19	May
	56.44			1	Derby	29	Jul
	56.31			3	Varazdin, CRO	5	Jul
	56.24			1	Loughborough	20	May
	56.15			1	Loughborough	23	May
57.38	Lee Newman		1.05.73	2	London (He)	5	May
	56.47			3	Dublin, IRL	29	Jun
	56.17			1	Cardiff	17	Jun
	49 performances to 56.00 by 5 athletes						
54.68	Peter Gordon	V45	2.07.51	1	Jarrow	30	Jun
54.47	Abi Ekoku		13.04.66	1	Stretford	8	Jul
54.25	Bruce Robb		27.07.77	1	Grangemouth	17	Jun
53.24	Paul Reed		2.06.62	1	Gateshead	12	May
52.97	David Lovett		13.09.78	1	Sandown IOW	9	Sep
	(10)						
52.81	Luke Rosenberg	U23	29.06.80	1	London (WF)	19	Aug
51.97	Neil Elliott		10.04.71	6	Bedford	27	May
51.84	Neville Thompson	V45	28.03.55	5	London (He)	5	May
51.63	Matthew Twigg		18.07.69	2	Rugby	10	Jun
51.61	Adam Major	U23	2.11.81	1	Inverness	15	Apr
51.42	Scot Thompson	U23	10.08.81	1	Gloucester	9	Jun
51.17	Scott Rider		22.09.77	1	London (Ha)	10	Jun
51.09	Gary Herrington	V40	31.03.61	1	Corby	13	May
51.07	Mark Wiseman		9.02.69	1	Carshalton	23	Sep
50.95	Bryan Kelly		29.12.73	1	Bolton	20	May
	(20)						
50.48	Mark Proctor		15.01.63	7	Bedford	21	Jul
50.24	Scott Hayes		4.01.73	2	Sheffield (W)	5	May
49.94	Simon Fricker		14.07.75	2	Beveren, BEL	8	Sep
49.57	Andrew Brittan		17.01.67	1	Nuneaton	5	Aug
48.49	Andrew Rollins		20.03.78	1	Stretford	6	Jun
48.46	James South		4.01.75	1	London (BP)	20	May
48.41	Nick Woolcott	V40	7.04.61	2	Cardiff	7	Jul
48.03	Marcus Gouldbourne	U23	12.06.81	2	Derby	29	Jul
47.47	Denzil McDonald		11.10.65	1	London (BP)	21	Jul
47.41	Dean Macey		12.12.77	3	Watford	2	Jun
	(30)						
47.20	Greg Beard	U20	10.09.82	1	Bedford	1	Jul
47.08	Rafer Joseph		21.07.68	2	Woking	21	Jul
46.97	Mark Edwards		2.12.74	1	Stretford	8	May
46.97	Leith Marar		7.11.68	1	Bromley	2	Jun
46.97	Michael Jemi-Alade		13.10.64	1	Cardiff	2	Jun
46.57	Andy Kruszewski	V40	7.04.59	1	Ashford	12	May
46.50	Steve Whyte		14.03.64	2	Eton	10	Jun
46.49	John Moreland	V40	13.09.58	2	Nuneaton	6	Jun
46.20	Mark Davies		10.01.71	4	London (WF)	19	Aug
46.10	Simon Williams	U23	5.10.80	1	London (BP)	20	May
	(40)						
46.01	Andy Turner		29.08.63	1	Exeter	22	Apr
45.93	Edward Reid	U23	22.07.81	2	Tamworth	5	May

45.33	Geoff Tyler	V50	30.09.48		Chelles, FRA	3 Oct
45.25	Morris Fox		30.04.63	2	Liverpool	5 May
45.12	Jeff Clare		21.03.65	3	Stretford	8 May
45.08	Andrew Flint		9.11.76	5	Sheffield (W)	5 May
44.92	David Abernethy	V45	5.09.55	1	Wigan	1 Jul
44.27	Daniel Brunt		23.04.76	1	Hull	20 May
44.08	Niklas Iliffe	U23	6.03.81	6	Cardiff	7 Jul
44.04	Justin Bryan		16.08.69	2	Cardiff	17 Jun
	(50)					
43.70	Carl Saggers	U20	20.09.83	1	Enfield	23 Jun
43.66	Daniel Greaves	U20	4.10.82	2	Bedford	30 Jun
	42.61			2	Derby	29 Jul
43.54	Gareth Cook		20.02.69	1	Kingston	12 May
43.34	Mike Small	V45	31.03.54	1	Ewell	29 Jun
43.25	Mikael Bottger		24.09.75	1	Oxford	4 Aug
43.24	Neil Sougrin		14.05.71	7	Sheffield (W)	5 May
43.07	Steven Lloyd		20.03.74	1	Shildon	2 Jun
43.01	David Readle	U23	10.02.80	2	Stretford	19 Jun
42.99	Neil Griffin	V50	28.05.48	3	Eton	2 Jun
42.92	Barry Thomas		28.04.72	3	Ashford	12 May
	(60)					
42.89	Chris Orr	U20	20.06.83	4	Bedford	30 Jun
42.86	Ian Taylor		2.07.67	3	Crawley	5 May
42.73	Paul Head		1.07.65	9	London (He)	5 May
42.51	John Little	V45	14.04.53	1	Carlisle	13 May
42.45	Richard Healey	V45	17.11.54	3	Woking	21 Jul
42.30	Darren Hatton	U23	21.03.79	2	London (Elt)	2 Jun
42.26	Garry Hagan	U17	21.11.84	4	Corinth, GRE	27 May
42.25	James Rumbold	U23	4.11.81	2	Portsmouth	23 Jun
42.03	Ali Morganella		28.05.77	8	Glasgow (S)	24 Jun
42.03	Adam Tear		12.08.75	1	Blackburn	7 Jul
	(70)					
42.02	Scott Jenns	U23	13.12.80	1	Mansfield	18 Aug
41.94	Greg Richards	V45	25.04.56	2	London (Col)	21 Jul
41.93	Brett Heath		6.01.75	1	Thurrock	4 Aug
41.80	Nick Owen	U23	17.07.80	1	Enfield	7 Jul
41.77	Ashley Ward		1.08.64	4	Rugby	18 Aug
41.65	Graeme Allan	U23	24.09.80	2	Stretford	19 Jun
41.62	Steven Hale		20.04.77	7	Birmingham	16 Jun
41.57	Jamie Quarry		15.11.72	10	Sheffield	5 May
41.57	Adam Davis		19.11.72	3	London (Ha)	27 Jun
41.47	Alan Rudkin		5.11.78	2	Peterborough	7 Jul
	(80)					
41.43	Chris Marland	U23	9.11.80	1	Neath	27 Aug
41.36	Willie Falconer		20.12.78	10	Glasgow (S)	24 Jun
41.31	Roger Hunter		10.03.76	1	Cleckheaton	1 Jul
41.22	Craig Burrows		8.08.74	1	Ilford	2 Jun
41.18	Sam Westlake	U20	14.09.83	1	Yeovil	27 Aug
41.17	Chris Howe		17.11.67	13	Eton	7 Jul
41.09	Brian Doherty	U20	2.06.83	6	Bedford	30 Jun
41.07	Jonathan Ward		25.11.65	4	Ashford	12 May
41.05	Rob Earle	V40	15.09.60	2	London (BP)	20 May
40.88	Gillen Carruthers	U20	24.09.82	1	Antrim	16 Jun
	(90)					
40.82	Andrew Wain		2.06.65	1	Peterborough	2 Jun
40.76	Simon Armstrong		29.05.62	3	Bournemouth	13 May
40.74	Damon Cripps		9.10.70		Liverpool	24 Jun
40.65	David Bauer		25.03.66	1	London (WF)	4 Aug
40.60	Alex Kruger		18.11.63	10	Eton	18 Aug
40.57	Simon Achurch		27.12.74	1	Watford	4 Aug
40.46	Roger Bate	U20	16.01.83	1	Warrington	5 May

40.40	Daniel Lethbridge	U23	1.04.81	5	Crawley	5 May
40.40	Graham Holder		16.01.72	4	Cardiff	17 Jun
40.37	James Taylor	U20	24.04.82	1	Sheffield	2 Jun
40.32	Nigel Winchcombe	V40	10.12.59	2	Eton	15 Aug
	(100)					
40.28	Anthony Southward		31.01.71	1D	Hexham	20 May
40.28	Gary Parsons		17.05.71	2	Cambridge	2 Jun
40.21	Peter Hughes	U20	12.12.83	2	Brecon	18 Jul
40.21	Iain Park		16.07.74	2	Coatbridge	26 Aug
40.12	Ben Roberts	U23	15.01.80	1	Connah's Quay	13 May
40.06	Alun Williams		22.06.62	5	Rugby	10 Jun
40.06	Leslie Richards	U17	29.03.85	2	York	4 Aug
40.06	Peter Roberts		19.09.71	4	Stafford	18 Aug

Foreign

54.33	*Kevin Brown (JAM)*		*10.09.64*	*5*	*Bedford*	*21 Jul*
48.43	*Garry Power (IRL)*		*1.09.62*	*1*	*Ashford*	*21 Jul*
44.23	*Heri Ziska (DEN)*		*12.10.67*	*1*	*London (TB)*	*23 Jun*
42.11	*Tony Soalla-Bell (SLE)*		*3.10.76*	*2*	*London (TB)*	*28 Jul*
40.21	*Michael Hann*			*8*	*Cardiff*	*7 Jul*

Discus - Under 20 - 1.75kg

52.20	Greg Beard		10.09.82	1	Ipswich	2 Sep
50.94	David Onwubalili		5.12.82	1	Exeter	6 Jul
49.61	Carl Saggers		20.09.83	2	Exeter	6 Jul
47.16	Daniel Greaves		4.10.82	3	Ipswich	2 Sep
46.07	Leslie Richards	U17	29.03.85	4	Ipswich	2 Sep
45.82	Garry Hagan	U17	21.11.84	2	Hayes	29 Apr
45.44	Roger Bate		16.01.83	1	Stretford	19 Jun
45.06	Chris Orr		20.06.83	1		
44.21	Sam Westlake		14.09.83	5	Exeter	6 Jul
43.90	Edward Dunford	U17	15.09.84	4	Derby	9 Sep
	(10)					
43.27	Tony Smith		11.01.83	6	Exeter	6 Jul
43.22	Brian Doherty		2.06.83	1	York	29 Jul
42.58	James Taylor		24.04.82	1	Sheffield	12 May
42.29	James Frimpong		17.09.82	1	Worcester	9 Jun
42.19	Tom Bivins		18.11.83	5	Ipswich	2 Sep
41.84	Stuart Semple		3.11.83	3	Watford	26 May
41.83	Robert Jukes		18.09.83	1	London (He)	16 Sep
41.55	Peter Favell		16.03.82	1	Cleckheaton	16 Sep
41.50	Peter Hughes		12.12.83	1	Aberdare	18 Aug
41.30	Nick Vince		29.01.82	2	Grangemouth	10 Jun
	(20)					
41.24	David Dawson		3.02.84	1	Exeter	30 Jan
41.21	Nsa Harrison		27.11.83	2	Worcester	9 Jun

Discus - Under 17 - 1.5kg

52.44	Garry Hagan		21.11.84	1	Connah's Quay	4 Aug
50.61	Leslie Richards		29.03.85	1	Gateshead	25 Aug
48.93	Gareth Bull		3.03.85	1	Cardiff	3 May
48.60	Alistair McDiarmid		16.10.85	1	Glasgow	14 Jun
48.38	Glenn Williams		24.03.85	1	Aberdare	10 Jun
48.07	Edward Dunford		15.09.84	1D	Sheffield	2 Sep
46.60	Simon Bissell		25.12.85	1	Stretford	31 Jul
46.26	Daniel Brew		20.11.84	1	Liverpool	9 Jun
46.23	Bobby Lockwood		1.02.86	1	Enfield	22 Jul
45.40	Peter Cranfield		26.09.84	2	Birmingham	2 Sep
	(10)					
45.26	Simon Cooke		3.10.85	1	Crawley	12 May
44.39	Kieran O'Keefe		19.03.86	3	Exeter	7 Jul

44.20	Simon Bulley	19.09.84	2	Liverpool	9 Jun
44.14	Lewis Williamson	7.09.85	1	Stretford	22 Jul
44.13	Paris Norriss	27.02.85	2O	Hull	15 Sep
43.75	Ben Kelsey	23.09.84	1	Bedford	6 May
43.64	Richard Greene	11.10.84	1	Crawley	5 Aug
43.27	Tony Gallagher	16.10.84	1	Bury	20 May
43.10	Mark Wyss	12.07.85	1	Nottingham	20 May
42.75	David Quinn	7.09.84	1	Antrim	18 Aug
	(20)				
42.51	James Holland	1.04.85	4	Watford	27 May
42.51	Andrew Thomas	14.06.86	6	Exeter	7 Jul
42.25	Michael McConkey	5.12.84	1	Antrim	9 Jun
41.90	Jamie McGough	20.05.85	2	Street	9 Jun
41.84	Kyle Stevens	3.06.85	1	London (TB)	28 Jul
41.69	James Bergl	23.02.85	1	Leamington	16 Jun
41.60	Ruan Smith	6.03.86	1	Basildon	20 May
41.24	Samuel Clague	26.02.86	3	Street	9 Jun
41.16	Andrae Davis	27.09.85	3O	Hull	15 Sep
41.09	Paul Farley	1.12.84	4	Crawley	5 Aug
	(30)				
41.03	Chris Awde	14.02.85	4O	Hull	15 Sep
40.67	James Sacha	10.02.86	2	Kingston	17 Jun

Discus - Under 15 - 1.25kg

52.43	Sam Herrington	2.10.86	1	Colwyn Bay	1 Sep
46.15	Nnamdi Efobi	14.09.86	1	Harrow	1 Jul
44.58	David Price	12.01.87	2	Sheffield	11 Aug
42.43	Chris Gearing	30.09.86	1	Hoo	22 Jul
41.35	Shane Birch	22.10.87	1	Erith	8 Mar
40.87	Barry Roberts	24.09.86	2	Neath	27 Aug
40.42	Alex Hitchens	12.12.86	1	Carn Brea	3 Jun
40.23	Gavin Hill	22.12.86	1	Scunthorpe	18 Aug
39.84	Daniel Hepplewhite	2.09.86	1	Sandown IOW	9 Sep
39.29	Adam Harris	7.09.86	1	Neath	24 Jun
	(10)				
39.15	Adam Melia	26.10.86	5	Sheffield	11 Aug
38.49	William Lowndes	10.10.86	2	Scunthorpe	18 Aug
38.48	Joe Connor	17.12.86	1	Liverpool	12 May
38.16	David Attwood	5.04.87	1	Abingdon	9 Sep
38.06	Simon Barrett	23.04.87	1	London (Cr)	20 May
38.00	Kyle Spiller	17.01.87	2	Cardiff	17 Jun
37.97	Toby Hunt	28.12.86	1	Eton	26 Aug
37.76	Chuma Mbanefo	25.02.87	2	London (He)	9 Jun
37.15	James McMeeken	25.09.86	7	Exeter	6 Jul

Discus - Under 13 - 1kg

35.35	Matthew Evans	9.09.88	1	Neath	28 Jul
31.42	Daniel Chapman	14.09.88	1	Southend	17 Jun
29.98	Tristan Davison	4.04.89	1	Ware	8 Jul
29.62	Oliver Forrest	11.09.88	1	Bedford	9 Sep
28.99	Alex Dawkings		1	Horsham	19 Aug
28.04	Alex Al-Ameen	2.03.89	1	Rochester	5 Aug
27.22	Jonathan Bennett	20.09.88	1	Horsham	17 Jun
26.69	Adam Thompson	8.11.88	1	Grantham	8 Sep
26.35	Christopher Allen	24.03.89	1	Ilford	29 Jul
26.16	Matthew Townsend		1	Kingston	29 Jul
	(10)				
25.01	Stephen Aarons	25.10.88	2	Rochester	5 Aug

Hammer

76.43	Mick Jones		23.07.63	1	Birmingham	2 Jun
	74.40			1	Birmingham	14 Jul
	73.91			4	Tula, RUS	9 Jun
	73.78			1	Crawley	12 May
	73.69			1	Bedford	21 Jul
	73.67			6	Bremen, GER	23 Jun
	73.53			1	Eton	7 Jul
	73.43			5	Madrid, ESP	26 May
	73.31			27Q	Edmonton, CAN	4 Aug
	72.88			1	London (Col)	29 Apr
	72.28			1	Crawley	24 Mar
	71.71			1	London (He)	5 May
	71.33			1B	London (Col)	29 Apr
	71.32			1	Sandown IOW	19 Aug
	68.39			6B	Nice, FRA	18 Mar
73.30	David Smith		2.11.74	1	Rugby	10 Jun
	72.89			1	Liverpool	17 Jun
	72.44			1	Grimsby	12 May
	71.84			1	Dublin, IRL	29 Jun
	70.86			2	Birmingham	2 Jun
	69.01			1	Loughborough	20 May
	68.70			1	Jarrow	18 Aug
	68.45			1	Bedford	28 May
	68.38			2	London (He)	5 May
72.60	William Beauchamp		9.09.70	2	London (Col)	29 Apr
	69.54			1	London (He)	12 May
	67.55			2B	London (Col)	29 Apr
	67.46			10	Halle, GER	19 May
	67.22			1	London (Ha)	10 Jun
	67.13			1	Watford	2 Jun
	66.41			3	Bedford	28 May
70.33	Paul Head		1.07.65	2	Birmingham	14 Jul
	69.91			3	Birmingham	2 Jun
	69.21			2	Eton	7 Jul
	68.17			3	London (He)	5 May
	67.90			2	Jarrow	18 Aug
	67.59			2	Loughborough	20 May
	67.39			2	Bedford	28 May
66.53	Russell Devine		24.04.68	1	Melbourne, AUS	15 Feb
66.49	Mike Floyd		26.09.76	4	Birmingham	2 Jun
	40 performances to 66.00 by 6 athletes					
65.90	John Pearson		30.04.66	1	Tamworth	5 May
65.19	Simon Bown		21.11.74	2	London (Ha)	17 Jun
63.98	Shane Peacock		5.03.63	3	Bedford	21 Jul
63.83	Matthew Bell		2.06.78	1	Corby	11 Sep
(10)						
63.54	Iain Park		16.07.74	1	Grendon Hall	6 Oct
63.40	Chris Howe		17.11.67	1	Portsmouth	4 Aug
62.69	Craig Ellams		24.11.72	4	London (Col)	29 Apr
62.25	David Allan		17.10.70	1	Glasgow (S)	24 Jun
61.50	Graham Holder		16.01.72	1	Cardiff	17 Jun
61.48	Glen Kerr		27.10.74	1C	London (Col)	29 Apr
61.30	Andy Frost	U23	17.04.81	1	Bedford	29 Jun
61.04	Graeme Allan	U23	24.09.80	7	Jarrow	18 Aug
60.78	Wayne Clarke		24.12.75	1	Peterborough	7 Jul
60.65	Rob Careless		7.09.74	1	Nottingham	1 Apr
(20)						
60.61	Steve Whyte		14.03.64	1	Jarrow	7 Jul
60.56	Adrian Palmer		10.08.69	2	Cardiff	17 Jun

60.43	Gareth Cook		20.02.69	1	Cambridge	2 Jun
59.90	Malcolm Fenton	V45	12.02.56	1	Ipswich	10 Jun
59.58	Steve Sammut		3.05.67	2	Cardiff	7 Jul
59.15	David Little	U23	28.02.81	4	Liverpool	17 Jun
59.05	Chris Black	V50	1.01.50	1	Wakefield	16 Sep
59.02	Paul Barnard		27.07.72	2	London (He)	12 May
58.76	Steve Minnikin		4.01.72	1	Hull	19 May
58.74	Chris Walsh		1.10.78	1	Gateshead	13 May
	(30)					
58.37	Kevin Davies		11.01.78	1	Cosford	4 Jul
58.29	Rob Earle	V40	15.09.60	8	Birmingham	2 Jun
58.12	Carl Saggers	U20	20.09.83	2	Stoke-on-Trent	18 Aug
57.34	Andrew Grierson	U23	23.11.79	4	Bedford	29 Jun
57.26	Tom Dempsey	U20	15.12.83	1	Tullamore, IRL	24 Jul
57.16	Peter Field	U20	21.05.82	4	Birmingham	17 Jun
56.91	Ross Thompson	U23	7.12.81	1	Jarrow	2 Jun
56.31	Mark Miller		10.11.71	1	Watford	13 May
55.64	Tim Wurr	U23	1.03.79	3	Glasgow (S)	6 May
55.46	Anthony Swain		17.01.75	1	Scunthorpe	18 Aug
	(40)					
55.37	Nick Williams	U20	2.02.82	4	Glasgow (S)	6 May
54.87	Stuart Thurgood		17.05.76	1	Ipswich	5 May
54.33	Calum Bruce		28.02.75	2	Edinburgh	29 Apr
54.20	Matthew Sutton	U23	8.09.81	7C	London (Col)	29 Apr
54.00	Bill Fuller		19.10.76	1	Kingston	23 Jun
53.77	Adam Beauford	U23	24.10.81	1	Bournemouth	20 May
53.23	Peter Fuller		30.04.78	1	Erith	7 Jul
53.20	David Nicholl		16.09.69	4	Liverpool	5 May
52.52 ?	John Owen		28.10.64	5	Peterborough	7 Jul
	47.53			5	Cardiff	2 Jun
52.50	Damon Cripps		9.10.70	1	Bolton	20 May
	(50)					
52.32	Maurice Hicks		1.01.70	5	London (Ha)	10 Jun
52.19	Nigel Winchcombe	V40	10.12.59	2	Cleckheaton	24 Jun
51.94	Graeme Mackay	U23	4.10.80	1	Cambridge	19 May
51.89	Chris Adams	U23	18.07.81	3	Stafford	18 Aug
51.67	Derrick Squire	U20	7.12.83	1	Bedford	22 Jul
51.43	Gavin Cook		30.03.70	1	London (Ha)	25 May
51.37	Matt Spicer		18.05.71	4	Tamworth	5 May
51.20	Kamran Khan	U20	2.10.83	2	Stretford	12 May
51.06	Russell Payne	V40	11.09.60	2	Nuneaton	5 Aug
50.87	Alan James		26.03.62	1	Peterborough	21 Jul
	(60)					
50.12	Nick Fogg		24.03.78	1	London (He)	23 Jun
50.10	John Parkin	U23	23.02.79	3	Cardiff	17 Jun
50.09	Mark Sheridan		17.06.70	2	Crawley	5 May
49.58	Marvin Edwards		28.04.69	2	Kingston	4 Aug
49.11	Steve McEvoy		23.05.63	1	Horsham	7 Jul
49.09	Paul Dickenson	V50	4.12.49	1	London (BP)	21 Jul
48.70	Dave Smith		21.06.62	5	Grendon Hall	6 Oct
48.63	Michael Madden		13.09.65	1	Par	7 Jul
48.61	Andy Turner		29.08.63	1	London (PH)	7 Jul
48.58	Darren Kerr		6.10.69	6	Liverpool	5 May
	(70)					
48.29 wt?	Chris Melluish	V55	15.07.44	3	Watford	29 Aug
47.95	Brett Marsh		20.01.76	1	Par	16 Sep
47.92	Ewart Hulse		21.01.62	1	Wrexham	11 Aug
47.81	Eric Kerr		9.12.64	1	Luton	23 Jun
47.79	Bruce Shepherd		20.03.67	1	Aberdeen	17 Nov
47.66	Matthew Frampton	U20	10.04.84	1	Eton	2 Jun
47.54	Jason Kingwell		8.10.70	4	Eton	10 Jun

47.53	Malcolm Croad		27.10.73	8	Watford	2 Jun
47.46	Mike Small	V45	31.03.54	2	Southampton	4 Aug
47.19	Neil Bulman		7.09.77	5	Tamworth	5 May
(80)						
47.07	Peter Cranfield	U17	26.09.84	1	Liverpool	4 Aug
46.99	Colin Smith	V40	11.09.57	2	Woking	21 Jul
46.98	Mark Proctor		15.01.63	2	Cosford	4 Jul
46.96	Alan Woods	V50	27.03.51	2	Corby	18 Aug
46.82	James Nunan	U20	16.09.83	1	Banbury	5 May
46.71	Ross Blight		28.05.77	9	Watford	2 Jun
46.61	Robert Taylor	U23	9.06.80	2	Wakefield	2 Jun
46.50	Keith Robinson	V45	9.02.52	3	Crawley	5 May
46.39	Roger Bate	U20	16.01.83	1	Stoke-on-Trent	28 Jul
46.29	Leslie McIntosh	U23	25.02.81	3	Cudworth	26 Aug
(90)						
46.27	Simon Gate	U20	21.09.82	3	Wakefield	2 Jun
46.03	Martin Hayes	U23	31.08.79	1	Derby	13 May
46.02	Jimmy Summers		7.10.65	3	Cosford	4 Jul
46.00	Michael Reiss		17.06.63	2	London (PH)	7 Jul
45.91	Gary Herrington	V40	31.03.61	6	Brisbane, AUS	Jul
45.75	Kirk Capeling	U23	27.02.80	1	Hoo	4 Aug
45.67	Scott Rider		22.09.77	8	Eton	18 Aug
45.62	Daniel Gamester		29.04.78	2	Sutton	23 Jun
45.59	Martin Roberts	V40	1.03.60	1	Derby	
45.09	Paul Derrien		5.08.71	1	Southampton	1 Jul

Foreign

61.94	*John Osazuwa (NGR)*	*U23*	*4.05.81*	*1*	*Perivale*	*7 Jul*
58.57	*Luke Greenfield (NZL)*	*U23*	*6.05.81*		*-, NZL*	
49.61	*Eduardo Reina (HON)*		*9.12.68*	*1*	*Cambridge*	*19 May*

Hammer - Under 20 - 6.25kg

65.75	Carl Saggers		20.09.83	1	Ipswich	2 Sep
62.53	Peter Field		21.05.82	1	Birmingham	26 May
61.25	Tom Dempsey		15.12.83	2	London (Col)	28 Apr
56.88	Nick Williams		2.02.82	1	Bebington	29 Apr
55.82	Roger Bate		16.01.83	1	Stretford	14 Aug
54.73	Timmon Whitehead		20.04.82	1	Sandown IOW	8 Apr
54.20	Matthew Frampton		10.04.84	1	Bournemouth	9 Jun
52.98	Derrick Squire		7.12.83	2	Ipswich	2 Sep
52.73	James Nunan		16.09.83	3	Birmingham	27 May
52.59	Karim Chester	U17	6.11.84	2	Bedford	24 Jun
(10)						
52.59	Chris James		9.12.82	2	Exeter	6 Jul
52.46	Kamran Khan		2.10.83	1	Cudworth	26 May
52.18	Greg Beard		10.09.82	1	Carshalton	23 Sep
51.55	Peter Cranfield	U17	26.09.84	1	Stoke-on-Trent	17 Jun
50.95	Simon Gate		21.09.82	1	Middlesbrough	14 Apr
50.86	John Hay		4.06.83	1	Corby	9 Jun
50.36	Ben Jones		6.11.82	6	Exeter	6 Jul
49.91	Simon Bissell	U17	25.12.85	3	Wakefield	29 Jul
49.21	Daniel Martin		9.03.82	2	Portsmouth	29 Apr
49.13	Paul Farley	U17	1.12.84	1	Sandown IOW	25 Jul
(20)						
49.08	Richard Greene	U17	11.10.84	1	Guildford	29 Jul
48.02	Ben Harper		7.09.82	2	Derby	22 Apr

Hammer - Under 17- 5kg

60.52	Karim Chester	6.11.84	1	Peterborough	22 Jul
59.50	Paul Farley	1.12.84	1	Exeter	6 Jul
58.53	James Forde	10.04.85	1	Birmingham	27 May
58.05	Simon Bissell	25.12.85	1	Stretford	31 Jul
57.55	Peter Cranfield	26.09.84	1	Liverpool	9 Jun
57.31	Laurence Harwood	9.03.85	2	Watford	26 May
56.70	Jason Joseph	27.11.85	5	Exeter	6 Jul
56.55	Richard Greene	11.10.84	2	Sheffield (W)	11 Aug
56.43	Glenn Williams	24.03.85	1	Carmarthen	28 Apr
56.17	Andrew Smith	2.10.84	6	Exeter	6 Jul
	(10)				
53.83	Fraser Campbell	30.05.86	4	Tullamore, IRL	21 Jul
53.70	Alistair McDiarmid	16.10.85	5	Tullamore, IRL	21 Jul
53.65	Gordon Grierson	12.10.85	7	Sheffield (W)	11 Aug
53.08	Robert Mungham	1.12.84	6	London (Col)	28 Apr
50.48	David Procter	11.11.84	1	Aberdare	15 Jul
50.15	Stephen Bates	9.09.84	1	Kingston	9 Jun
48.68	Patrick Russell	17.03.85	1	Exeter	16 Jun
48.61	David Steventon	6.12.84	1	Yate	1 Jul
48.17	Chris Baker	30.09.84	1	Crawley	9 Jun
48.15	Philip Collings	15.02.85	2	Exeter	16 Jun
	(20)				
48.12	Michael Jones	12.12.84	10	Exeter	6 Jul
47.84	Simon Bulley	19.09.84	3	Birmingham	1 Sep
47.76	Kieran O'Keefe	19.03.86	2	Yate	1 Jul
47.56	Ryan Holmes	31.10.84	1	Basildon	9 Jun
47.47	Gareth Bull	3.03.85	2	Cardiff	6 Jul

Hammer - Under 15 - 4kg

53.87	Chris Gearing	30.09.86	1	Watford	16 Sep
53.76	Nnamdi Efobi	14.09.86	1	Birmingham	2 Sep
51.03	Gavin Hill	22.12.86	1	Sheffield	11 Aug
50.92	Matthew Lambley	18.09.87	1	Grimsby	30 Sep
46.84	Jack Pallister	22.02.87		Blackpool	9 Sep
46.76	Michael Bomba	10.10.86	3	Stretford	14 Aug
46.68	Joe Connor	17.12.86	1	Blackpool	22 Jul
46.64	Sean Lewis	10.09.87	3	Stretford	9 Sep
46.27	Nick Harding	15.12.86	4	Sheffield	11 Aug
45.64	Michael Barton Smith	2.05.87	2	London (He)	26 Aug
	(10)				
44.53	Luke Shortman	14.10.87	1	Bury St. Edmunds	15 Sep
43.08	Pepi Nanci	7.10.86	1	Woodford	6 May
42.32	Stewart Arbuthnot	9.09.86	1	London (Col)	16 Sep

Javelin

90.81	Steve Backley	12.02.69	1	London (CP)	22 Jul
	87.84		2	Ostrava, CZE	31 May
	86.74		1	Gateshead	19 Aug
	85.38		4	Melbourne, AUS	9 Sep
	84.40		1	Nice, FRA	9 Jul
	84.26		2	Glasgow (S)	1 Jul
	83.34		4	Brisbane, AUS	6 Sep
	83.03		4	Athens, GRE	11 Jun
	82.85		3	Brussels, BEL	24 Aug
	82.51		3	Oslo, NOR	13 Jul
	81.95		7	Zurich, SUI	17 Aug
	81.50		14Q	Edmonton, CAN	10 Aug

84.88	Mick Hill		22.10.64	Q	Edmonton, CAN	10	Aug
	83.42			3	Glasgow (S)	1	Jul
	83.04			2	Stellenbosch, RSA	30	Mar
	81.90			2	Ventspils, LAT	15	Jun
	81.59			1	Loughborough	20	May
	80.58 A			1	Roodepoort, RSA	16	Mar
	79.98			2	Birmingham	15	Jul
	78.71			3	Ostrava, CZE	31	May
	77.81			12	Edmonton, CAN	12	Aug
	77.62			10	Athens, GRE	11	Jun
	77.36			1	Bangor	2	Jun
	76.66			6	Helsinki, FIN	14	Jun
	76.10 A			5	Pretoria, RSA	23	Mar
82.93	Nick Nieland		31.01.72	1	Dublin, IRL	29	Jun
	82.22			1	Halle, GER	19	May
	80.84			4	Bremen, GER	24	Jun
	78.97			5	Helsinki, FIN	14	Jun
	78.23			5	Nuremberg, GER	17	Jun
	78.02			21Q	Edmonton, CAN	10	Aug
	77.91			3	Birmingham	15	Jul
	77.41			8	Stockholm, SWE	17	Jul
	76.92			8	London (CP)	22	Jul
	75.31			8	Gateshead	19	Aug
80.80	Mark Roberson		13.03.67	1	Birmingham	15	Jul
	79.61			3	Stellenbosch, RSA	30	Mar
	79.03 A			2	Potchefstroom, RSA	24	Mar
	78.60			1	Ashford	11	Aug
	78.17 A			2	Potchefstroom, RSA	12	Feb
	77.60			2	Loughborough	20	May
	77.08 A			3	Pretoria, RSA	23	Mar
	76.78			7	Gateshead	19	Aug
	76.61			2	Port Elizabeth, RSA	16	Feb
	76.50			1	Alfaz del Pi, ESP	21	Apr
	76.08			9	London (CP)	22	Jul
	75.16			2	Bangor	2	Jun
78.33 A	David Parker	U23	28.02.80	4	Potchefstroom, RSA	24	Mar
	76.24			1	Bedford	28	May
	75.62			1	Liverpool	23	Jun
	75.53			1	Bedford	1	Jul
	75.16			Q	Amsterdam, NED	13	Jul
	52 performances to 75.00 by 5 athletes						
73.15	Stuart Faben		28.02.75	2	Alicante, ESP	18	Apr
73.00	Dan Carter	U23	15.04.80	3	Bedford	28	May
68.78	Neil McLellan		10.09.78	1	Caraquefon, FRA	23	Jun
68.49	Phill Sharpe	U23	6.03.81	4	Bedford	28	May
68.08	Keith Beard	V40	8.11.61	3	Tilburg, NED	7	Jul
(10)							
66.95	Andrew Gallagher	U20	15.02.83	1	Stoke-on-Trent	18	Aug
66.86	Peter Yates	V40	15.06.57	1	London (BP)	21	Jul
66.73	Clifton Green	U23	10.10.79	3	Jarrow	18	Aug
66.29	Stuart Loughran		19.02.76	1	Peterborough	7	Jul
65.89	Robert Charlesworth	U23	25.03.79	1	Liverpool	5	May
65.01	Tom Dobbing		5.02.73	5	Bedford	28	May
64.40	Stefan Baldwin		26.04.70	1	Stafford	18	Aug
64.20	Gerard Plunkett	U23	30.06.80	1	Grimsby	30	Sep
64.04	Alex van der Merwe	U20	5.01.84	1	Bedford	1	Jul
63.95	Jonathan Lundman	U23	7.12.81	1	Southend	12	May
(20)							
63.81	Simon Carter		5.03.75	2	Ashford	13	May
63.29	Nigel Bevan		3.01.68	3	Bedford	21	Jul

63.12	Matthew Allison		26.02.73	1	Leeds	4 Aug
62.27	Paul Cooper		4.12.76	3	London (Ha)	17 Jun
62.16	Phil Parry		4.10.65	1	Cardiff	7 Jul
61.91	Ian Burns		20.09.77	1	Blackburn	7 Jul
61.86	Darren Hatton	U23	21.03.79	1D	Bedford	15 Jul
61.77	David Sketchley		25.02.76	1	Ipswich	8 Apr
61.42	Trevor Ratcliffe		9.03.64	2	Hemel Hempstead	5 May
61.41	Paul Howard		19.10.66	4	London (Ha)	17 Jun
	(30)					
61.36	Jonathan Clarke		20.11.67	2	Cardiff	2 Jun
61.23	Kevin Murch	V40	11.11.58	1	Eton	23 Jun
61.05	Livon Houslin	V40	2.11.60	2	Watford	2 Jun
60.87	Tony Smith	V40	17.05.58	5	Birmingham	2 Jun
60.76	Tim Kitney	U23	26.04.80	4	Cork, IRL	7 Jul
60.45	Sam Armstrong		17.02.74	1	Grangemouth	17 Jun
60.15	Jason Hallett	U20	29.03.82	1	Derby	29 Jul
60.09	Andy Hayward		26.10.74	1	Wakefield	2 Jun
59.81	Anthony Lovett	U20	20.09.82	2	Eton	18 Aug
59.77	Michael Allen	U23	7.03.80	5	Bangor	2 Jun
	(40)					
59.64	Simon Bennett		16.10.72	2	Sheffield (W)	5 May
59.37	Sam Goddard	U20	4.01.83	2	Exeter	6 Jul
59.34	Stephen Melber	U23	26.02.79	3	Philadelphia PA, USA	8 Apr
59.20	Chris Smith		27.11.75	1	Edinburgh	12 May
59.02	Wesley Smith	U23	26.02.79	5	Bedford	1 Jul
58.98	Sean Carson	U20	13.04.84	1	Bedford	22 Jul
58.98	Jeremy Smyth		11.08.78	2	Douglas IOM	13 Aug
58.72	Rhys Williams	U23	4.10.81	1	Neath	15 May
58.68	Jim McFarlane	U23	16.06.79	1	Cambridge	19 May
58.64	Glyn Amos	V40	30.03.58	1	Middlesbrough	5 May
	(50)					
58.37	James Turner	U20	12.08.83	5	Bedford	1 Jul
58.35	Patrick Boundy	U23	19.02.79	3	Glasgow (S)	7 May
58.17	Livio Salvador-Aylott		18.07.73	6	Bedford	21 Jul
58.10	Steven Cotton	U23	8.02.79	2	Salisbury	22 Jul
58.05	Stuart Millar	U20	9.03.83	1	Tamworth	12 Aug
57.90	Ben Lloyd	U23	1.04.79	4	Douglas IOM	13 Jul
57.77	Derek Hermann	U23	7.04.79	7	Bedford	1 Jul
57.61	Jon Wilkinson		17.02.62	1	Telford	12 May
57.52	Ben Saville		10.11.77	1	Leeds	4 Aug
57.28	Alex Gibson		3.11.77	1	Ilford	2 Jun
	(60)					
56.90	David Evans		23.01.76	1	Worcester	18 Aug
56.75	Barry Thomas		28.04.72	D	Kaunas, LIT	1 Jul
56.59	James Deacon-Brown	U20	26.05.84	4	Exeter	6 Jul
56.54	Greg Markham		28.11.78	1	Blackburn	7 Jul
56.14	Peter Fraser		28.01.78	2	Aberdeen	15 Jul
56.12	Thomas Barcis	U20	30.05.83	1	Grantham	9 Jun
56.09	Matthew Dingley	U20	12.01.83	1	Wigan	29 Apr
56.06	Alex Kruger		18.11.63	1	Hayes	21 Jul
55.84	Lee Doran	U17	5.03.85	1	Cleckheaton	17 Jun
55.75	Richard Woodhall	U23	9.07.80	2	Birmingham	17 Jun
	(70)					
55.36	John Mitchell	U23	13.05.81	8	Bedford	1 Jul
55.29	Tony Norman		5.07.63	1	London (He)	23 Jun
55.06	Matthew Davies		16.09.78	4	Glasgow (S)	5 May
55.00	Craig Guest	U20	25.10.82	4	Derby	29 Jul

Foreign

66.80	*Petri Matakainen (FIN)*		*3.04.75*	*3*	*Birmingham*	*2 Jun*
63.75	*Ben Houghton (IRL)*	*U23*	*6.08.80*	*2*	*Derby*	*29 Jul*

61.75	*Leon Karagiounis (GRE)*	*15.10.75*	*2*	*Merksem, BEL*	*4 Aug*
56.63	*Damien Crawford (IRL)*	*22.08.68*	*5*	*Dublin, IRL*	*21 Jul*

Javelin - Under 17 - 700gm

67.31	Lee Doran	5.03.85	1	Tullamore, IRL	21 Jul
63.89	Mark Lindsay	5.11.84	1	Sheffield	12 May
61.02	Lewis Wallace	27.01.85	1	Hoo	3 Jun
58.32	Felix Hatton	9.10.84	1	Crawley	29 Aug
54.93	Edward Dunford	15.09.84	1	Yate	1 Jul
54.75	Thomas Rees	9.03.86	3	Tullamore, IRL	21 Jul
54.59	Martin Travis	10.07.85	1	Yate	2 Sep
54.32	Michael McConkey	5.12.84	1	Tullamore, IRL	2 Jun
53.82	James Curtis		2	Peterborough	22 Jul
53.39	Sam Kelvey	12.07.86	1	Birmingham	2 Sep
	(10)				
53.38	Matthew Huntley	29.10.84	1	Ipswich	1 Jul
53.18	Andrew Ormesher	29.05.85	2	Exeter	6 Jul
52.67	Andrew Harland	23.08.85	1	Great Yarmouth	5 Aug
52.63	Jonathan Smith	26.10.84	1	Bury St. Edmunds	17 Jun
52.48	James Heanley	1.04.85	1	Bracknell	9 Jun
52.22	Adam Broome	5.08.85	1	Bebington	3 Jun

Javelin - Under 15 - 600gm

51.77	Pepi Nanci	7.10.86	1	Harrow	1 Jul
51.34	Peter Hutcheson	18.11.86	1	Crawley	29 Aug
49.95	James Docking	19.11.86	1	Exeter	22 Apr
49.93	Chris Record	12.09.86	1	Perivale	1 Jul
49.04	Tyson Johnson	24.06.87	1	Telford	9 Sep
48.28	James Evans	7.11.86	1	Barry	26 Jun
48.18	Ben Lee	22.10.86	1	Sheffield	11 Aug
46.53	Tim Gardiner	20.11.86	2	Exeter	6 Jul
45.92	James Anderson	11.05.87	1	Woking	2 Sep
45.78	Matthew Bruton	18.10.86	3	Sheffield	11 Aug
	(10)				
45.70	Robert Smith	6.12.86	1	Brecon	19 Aug
45.43	William Dunford	21.04.87	4	Exeter	6 Jul
45.39	James Hopley	28.01.87	1	Connah's Quay	10 Jun
45.05	Tim Riddelsdell	26.01.87	1	Sandown IOW	9 Sep
44.99	Yiber Neziraj		1	London (BP)	4 Aug
44.87	Terry O'Leary	23.01.87	1	Hoo	3 Jun
44.73	Ben Martin	1.05.87	6	Exeter	6 Jul
44.32	Nick Childs	17.09.86	1	Peterborough	22 Jul
44.19	Martyn Massey		1	Cannock	12 May
44.04	Adam Akehurst	13.09.87	3	Woking	2 Sep
	(20)				
43.85	Thomas Toal	23.12.86	1	Derby	22 Jul
43.41	Ken Robertson	6.04.88	1	Edinburgh	30 Sep
43.37	Paul McKown	12.06.87	1	Scunthorpe	18 Aug
43.31	James Campbell	1.04.88	1	Cheltenham	25 Jul

Javelin - Under 13 - 400gm

40.05	Joe Seaward	22.10.88	1	Birmingham	1 Jul
38.70	Richard Marvin	29.01.89	1	Oxford	5 Aug
38.62	Jan Paul Capewell	10.01.89	1	Tamworth	15 Jul
37.07	George McCorkell	16.01.89	1	Edinburgh	1 Apr
36.00	Thomas Sloman		1	Cardiff	11 Jul
35.46	David Harrison	17.10.88	1	Bournemouth	24 Jun
35.43	Ross Nichol		1	London (He)	9 Jun
35.03	Ross Batten	1.03.89	1	Exeter	31 Jul
34.05	Garth Loughran	16.04.89	1	Carmarthen	9 Jun

Decathlon

8603	Dean Macey		12.12.77	3	Edmonton, CAN	7 Aug				
	10.72/-0.7	7.59/0.4	15.41	2.15	46.21	14.34/0.0	46.96	4.70	54.61	4:29.05
7625	Jamie Quarry		15.11.72	7	Arles, FRA	10 Jun				
	11.09/-1.0	7.24/0.9	14.25	1.90	49.38	14.52/1.6	39.04	4.55	46.50	4:29.62
7410	Barry Thomas		28.04.72	11	Arles, FRA	10 Jun				
	11.46/-1.7	7.25w/2.6	13.20	1.96	51.81	15.04/1.8	38.07	4.85	52.62	4:47.45
	7385			4	Kaunas, LIT	1 Jul				
	11.44/-0.4	6.98/1.1	13.77	1.92	52.11	15.37/-2.2	41.56	4.60	56.75	4:42.25
7133	Anthony Southward		31.01.71	9	Kaunas, LIT	1 Jul				
	11.45w/2.5	6.71/0.8	12.79	1.92	49.96	15.28/-2.0	39.22	4.20	51.59	4:41.12
	7107			17	Arles, FRA	10 Jun				
	11.35/-1.1	6.57/2.0	13.37	1.87	50.68	14.96/1.0	40.39	4.45	48.20	4:50.57
	7022			1	Hexham	20 May				
	11.3/1.9	6.55w/2.9	12.79	1.89	51.6	15.4/-1.2	40.28	4.30	52.83	4:37.3
7129	John Heanley	U23	25.09.80	1	Bedford	15 Jul				
	11.28w/3.7	6.95/0.4	10.08	1.90	50.02	14.93w/2.8	31.99	4.62	48.05	4:22.95
	6869			24	Arles, FRA	10 Jun				
	11.57/-2.1	6.83/1.8	9.44	1.90	50.50	15.31/1.9	33.93	4.45	44.96	4:23.91
	6753			8	Bedford	5 Aug				
	11.40/1.5	6.97w/2.2	9.94	1.87	50.35	15.28/1.5	30.20	4.40	38.56	4:26.53
7050	Fyn Corcoran		17.03.78	18	Arles, FRA	10 Jun				
	11.34/-1.7	7.00/1.6	13.22	1.78	50.28	15.21/1.8	38.07	4.05	48.10	4:34.32
	7039			3	Bedford	5 Aug				
	11.35/1.9	6.94/1.5	13.09	1.84	50.87	15.58/1.5	38.55	3.90	53.23	4:36.34
	7020			12	Kaunas, LIT	1 Jul				
	11.42/1.5	7.00/0.2	13.15	1.83	50.59	15.62/-1.6	39.95	3.60	53.23	4:31.63
7020	Darren Hatton	U23	21.03.79	5	Bedford	5 Aug				
	11.30/1.9	6.84/2.0	13.50	1.90	51.46	16.01/1.6	36.61	4.20	57.53	4:55.53
	7019			2	Bedford	15 Jul				
	11.39w/3.2	6.52/0.2	12.61	1.90	51.23	15.82/1.8	38.58	4.12	61.86	4:49.95
	6820			1	Erith	16 Sep				
	11.5	6.52	13.20	1.92	51.0	15.7	34.54	4.30	54.64	4:55.2
	6759			26	Arles, FRA	10 Jun				
	11.52/-1.1	6.67/0.3	12.70	1.87	50.82	16.11/0.9	39.28	3.95	49.98	4:52.92
	6496			2	Woodford	29 Apr				
	11.36/1.5	6.65	12.21	1.81	52.21	36.35	3.54	55.94	5:03.33	
6983	Anthony Sawyer	U23	29.04.80	4	Bedford	15 Jul				
	11.00w/2.9	6.65/0.2	12.46	1.87	50.46	14.80w/2.8	34.46	4.12	48.08	4:47.04
	6953			1	Sheffield	2 Sep				
	11.20/2.0	6.61/0.7	11.64	1.92	50.83	15.05w/3.3	35.74	4.03	50.25	4:40.03
	6820			1	Woodford	29 Apr				
	11.11/1.5	6.58	12.34	1.87	50.76	15.20	33.25	4.04	47.21	4:45.73
6911	Brendan McConville	U23	3.01.79	22	Arles, FRA	10 Jun				
	11.94/-2.1	6.77/-0.1	11.56	1.99	50.43	15.47/0.9	33.23	4.25	46.93	4:26.83
	6862			16	Kaunas, LIT	1 Jul				
	11.62/0.6	6.58/1.3	11.64	1.92	50.62	15.89/-0.5	34.71	4.20	48.81	4:26.38
	6818			3	Sheffield	2 Sep				
	11.60/2.0	6.74/2.0	11.35	1.92	50.68	15.85w/3.3	34.14	4.23	48.15	4:34.95
	6702			12	Bedford	5 Aug				
	11.62/0.8	6.63/1.6	11.45	1.84	50.35	15.55/1.6	31.26	4.20	47.06	4:33.25
	6699			1	Antrim	22 Jul				
	12.06	6.48	11.63	1.89	51.13	15.76	33.45	4.50	46.12	4:32.08
6788	Adrian Hemery	U20	6.08.82	25	Arles, FRA	10 Jun				
	11.56/-2.1	6.67/-0.4	12.14	1.81	50.37	15.56/0.9	36.33	3.95	47.25	4:30.93
	6573			13	Bedford	5 Aug				
	11.51/0.8	6.56/1.1	10.97	1.84	52.31	15.73/1.4	35.03	3.90	49.20	4:36.58
	6421			3	Woodford	29 Apr				
	11.52/1.5	6.26	11.46	1.75	52.64	16.08	37.42	3.84	46.69	4:33.13

(10)

6759 Scott Exley 9.02.78 7 Bedford 5 Aug
10.87/1.9 6.55/1.3 12.08 1.84 50.01 15.74/1.6 36.46 3.80 42.08 4:39.19
6594 5 Bedford 15 Jul
10.78w/2.9 6.34/0.4 12.18 1.81 49.97 15.82w/2.8 35.73 3.72 37.79 4:41.26
6749 Roger Hunter 10.03.76 1 Birmingham 17 Jun
11.27/1.9 6.63/1.7 12.34 1.87 50.86 15.14/2.0 36.66 3.50 48.73 4:44.86
6590 Gavin Fordham U23 1.02.79 6 Bedford 15 Jul
11.23w/3.2 6.46/1.2 10.20 1.96 50.87 16.15w/2.3 32.21 4.02 51.70 4:54.64
6499 2 Birmingham 17 Jun
11.30/1.9 6.20/0.2 10.04 1.87 49.97 16.09/2.0 31.30 4.10 48.97 4:44.53
6547 Jason McDade U23 3.04.80 7 Bedford 15 Jul
11.19w/3.2 6.42/1.9 12.05 1.99 52.58 14.90w/2.8 35.86 3.82 45.20 5:26.53
6511 Gerard Plunkett U23 30.06.80 1 Rotherham 16 Sep
11.4 6.12 12.68 1.84 53.4 16.1 34.93 38.5 60.61 4:48.7
6497 Ed Coats U23 14.06.80 4 Sheffield 2 Sep
11.34/2.0 6.52/1.9 12.03 1.77 51.63 16.63w/3.3 38.58 4.13 42.79 4:49.50
6476 Andrew Lewis 9.03.68 8 Bedford 15 Jul
10.88w/2.9 6.80/1.3 12.71 1.81 52.57 14.94w/2.8 31.30 4.02 39.00 5:22.54
6475 Ben Roberts U23 15.01.80 1 Aberdare 24 Jun
11.46w/2.1 6.26/1.7 13.68 1.86 53.12 15.73/1.5 38.05 4.00 49.08 5:24.65
6360 Alex Gibson 3.11.77 9 Bedford 15 Jul
11.11w/2.9 6.23/1.0 12.07 1.81 50.49 17.06/1.8 34.17 3.02 54.96 4:43.41
6294 Dale Garland U23 13.10.80 1 Watford 23 Sep
11.64/-1.3 6.76/1.7 9.60 1.92 49.77 16.2/-2.1 27.58 3.00 47.05 4:22.70
(20)
6250 Paul Tohill U20 9.10.82 5 Sheffield 2 Sep
11.71/1.9 6.66/1.5 10.31 1.98 52.37 15.47/1.7 31.40 3.73 34.22 4:49.66
6176 James Wright U20 2.04.82 13 Bedford 5 Aug
11.23w/2.4 6.45/-0.3 8.43 1.72 52.24 15.29/1.9 26.82 4.00 46.32 4:45.48
6151 Steve Hughes U20 25.02.82 1 Bedford 15 Jul
11.64/1.8 6.39/1.5 10.67 1.81 53.3 15.88w/2.5 33.11 3.92 42.44 4:55.58
6070 James Lowery U23 17.10.80 4 Woodford 29 Apr
11.52/1.5 6.37 10.37 1.84 53.46 15.90 32.73 3.74 43.06 5:05.60
6048 Carl Marchment U20 30.12.82 16 Bedford 5 Aug
11.58/0.4 6.45w/2.2 9.97 1.78 52.04 16.18/0.9 30.24 3.60 41.12 4:43.22
6030 Martin Lloyd U23 18.06.80 2 Erith 16 Sep
11.6 6.25 9.90 2.04 53.3 15.9 35.76 3.40 43.43 5:14.8
6025 Brian Hughes 6.01.70 10 Bedford 15 Jul
11.85w/3.4 6.05/1.0 9.94 1.78 53.96 16.49w/2.3 33.80 4.32 47.73 5:04.91
6005 Nick Owen U23 17.07.80 1 Crawley 9 Sep
11.5 6.14 15.48 1.66 54.3 17.3 40.28 3.60 42.21 5:08.9
5997 Robin Smith U20 11.09.83 7 Sheffield 2 Sep
11.49/1.9 6.31/1.9 9.59 1.80 51.59 15.84/1.7 31.21 3.53 39.10 4:53.38
5986 w John Dickinson U20 27.01.83 4 Bedford 15 Jul
11.62w/3.5 6.39/0.9 9.96 1.78 51.76 16.61W/4.1 31.62 3.52 38.07 4:38.02
5976 17 Bedford 5 Aug
11.56/2.0 6.59/1.5 8.99 1.78 52.06 17.31/0.9 31.14 3.80 37.20 4:34.08
(30)
5906 Mike Bull 6.06.70 12 Bedford 15 Jul
11.24w/3.7 6.09/-0.1 11.46 1.66 52.05 16.33/1.8 31.77 3.22 40.63 4:48.85
5866 Mark Roberts 1.09.69 2 Crawley 9 Sep
12.1 6.26 10.82 1.72 55.8 15.7 37.36 3.40 49.15 4:54.0
5797 Suna Bull 25.01.75 2 London (He) 12 Aug
11.56/-2.7 6.04w/3.2 11.61 1.56 50.96 17.35/-1.936.79 2.80 49.06 4:52.75
5738 Ryan Westaway U20 2.03.83 1 London (He) 12 Aug
12.08/-0.6 6.06/-0.4 9.68 1.92 53.10 16.77/-1.7 30.38 3.40 41.74 4:55.74
5723 Daniel Brandwood U20 1.10.82 6 Bedford 15 Jul
10.92w/3.5 5.68/0.9 10.29 1.63 49.47 16.48w/2.8 25.79 3.82 26.51 4:50.37
5689 Richard Hunter 12.01.71 2 Aberdare 24 Jun
11.85w/2.1 6.18w/3.0 11.16 1.65 53.69 15.97/1.5 30.24 3.60 32.96 4:50.56

5686	Geoff Ingram				31.01.68	1	Cosford			31 Jul
	12.1	6.33	10.78	1.70	54.9	16.8	35.45	3.22	49.71	4:56.6
5649	Chris Oakes				19.10.70	2	Cosford			31 Jul
	11.9	6.54	10.47	1.85	54.0	16.4	30.88	3.12	34.02	4:50.7
5639	Frank Chapman				17.01.70	3	Cosford			31 Jul
	12.1	58.9	11.61	1.64	53.3	16.2	35.07	3.62	35.98	4:53.0
5623	David Hughes			U20	31.05.84	2	Hexham			20 May
	11.2/1.4	5.90/0.8	10.42	1.74	51.1	16.1/-0.1	32.30	2.60	42.17	5:10.0
	(40)									
5620	Ashley Pritchard			U23	14.07.79	13	Bedford			15 Jul
	11.89w/3.4	5.82/0.3	8.58	1.75	53.30	16.38w/2.3	27.75	3.62	40.89	4:42.66
5568	Neil Fairlamb				13.03.76	6	Woodford			29 Apr
	11.91w/3.4	6.18	10.92	1.69	55.41	17.85	30.53	3.44	46.23	4:53.20
5562	Neil Rutterford				3.06.68	4	Cosford			31 Jul
	11.6	6.03	9.62	1.76	51.4	16.3	30.10	3.22	36.71	5:07.1
5545	Michael Bottger				24.09.75	14	Bedford			15 Jul
	11.92w/3.4	6.14/0.6	10.74	1.81	56.25	18.67/1.8	38.57	3.12	43.73	4:59.13
5495	James Parker			U23	29.09.80	3	Crawley			9 Sep
	11.8	6.13	8.25	1.87	52.6	15.7	24.63	2.60	41.58	4:45.3
5462	Tim Howell			U20	6.12.82	7	Woodford			29 Apr
	11.81w/3.4	5.61	10.51	1.72	54.50	15.89	28.79	3.24	38.82	5:02.19
5461	Chris Gunn			U20	13.09.82	9	Bedford			15 Jul
	11.95/1.8	5.70/1.0	10.74	1.72	56.32	16.80w/2.5	25.79	3.82	45.46	5:06.46
5405	Paul Torry			U20	17.10.82	10	Bedford			15 Jul
	11.68w/3.5	5.82/0.5	9.04	1.72	53.05	17.57w/4.7	30.62	3.12	35.39	4:41.66
5402	Simon Wilson				30.04.74	3	Erith			16 Sep
	12.1	6.26	9.69	1.71	52.0	16.1	25.79	2.90	37.74	4:50.6
5387	Paul Gilding				2.10.75	15	Bedford			15 Jul
	11.43w/3.2	6.34/1.2	10.68	1.90	54.42	15.15w/2.3	30.20	3.32	34.35	dnf
	(50)									
5376	Clint Barrett				21.11.77	4	Watford			23 Sep
	12.61/-1.3	5.63/0.0	9.27	1.71	54.53	17.2/-2.1	30.78	2.80	49.40	4:25.89
5369	Gerald Manville				21.12.78	5	Cosford			31 Jul
	12.3	5.94	8.59	1.79	53.9	18.4	29.91	3.72	38.30	4:36.5
5356	Gareth Moir			U23	17.12.80	16	Bedford			15 Jul
	11.12w/2.9	5.37/1.3	9.05	1.96	52.89	16.52w/2.3	27.24	2.52	37.21	5:19.65
5333	Lee Manvell			U23	11.12.80	17	Bedford			15 Jul
	12.06w/3.7	5.77/0.9	10.45	1.75	55.93	20.92/1.8	32.81	3.52	40.88	4:39.12
5316	Benjamin McIlroy			U20	2.09.83	12	Sheffield			2 Sep
	11.78/1.9	6.14/1.3	8.19	1.71	52.56	16.28w/1.7	22.84	3.43	29.45	4:54.63
5298 w	Simon Bull			U20	29.09.82	11	Bedford			15 Jul
	11.74/1.8	5.69/0.2	10.82	1.78	58.89	17.48W/4.7	35.93	3.02	46.60	5:22.18
	5106					17	Sheffield			2 Sep
	12.15/1.9	5.86w/2.2	11.04	1.74	57.50	18.80/1.7	33.30	2.93	47.56	5:24.37
5275	Robert Miller			U20	20.01.84	12	Bedford			15 Jul
	11.53/1.8	6.22/1.2	8.05	1.63	53.9	17.47w/2.5	25.23	2.82	48.91	4:59.10
5231	Gareth Evans				28.05.77	6	Cosford			31 Jul
	11.9	6.14	9.20	1.76	53.0	15.7	18.61	2.42	39.80	4:47.6
5229	Matt Tribble			U23	17.10.79	1	Crawley			9 Sep
	11.4	6.38	10.23	1.66	54.8	18.8	31.95	2.80	53.17	5:41.0
5160	Martin Ohrland			U23	19.11.79	6	Watford			23 Sep
	12.04	6.02	9.59	1.89	55.68	16.5	26.08	2.90	32.30	5:13.79
	(60)									
5121	Peter Coates				21.03.68	4	Hexham			23 Sep
	12.29/-0.1	6.03/0.2	8.93	1.62	53.28	17.74/-0.3	28.76	3.20	35.89	4:57.56
5116	Paul Slythe				5.09.74	4	Erith			16 Sep
	10.9	5.92	9.46	1.65	49.0	18.8	19.62	2.60	31.25	4:48.1
5076	Rob Weston				16.03.77	7	Cosford			31 Jul
	11.8	6.55	10.90	1.85	51.7	21.5	30.98	2.72	38.33	5:38.9
5063	James Roden			U23	24.11.81	7	Hexham			20 May
	12.0	5.44	9.42	1.71	58.4	17.1	29.92	2.30	55.52	4:53.2

5028 Chris Hunter U23 3.03.81 2 Hexham 23 Sep
12.13/-0.4 6.21/0.0 9.04 1.80 55.75 16.37/0.0 20.11 3.10 28.94 5:07.96
5015 Joe Appiah 26.10.70 5 Erith 16 Sep
11.3 6.20 8.21 1.77 54.5 15.7 22.24 2.20 33.54 5:17.1
5011 Rudi Moore U23 25.03.81 3 Antrim 22 Jul
11.94 6.27 9.13 1.74 54.23 18.72 26.00 2.70 37.20 5:05.29
4998 Sam Bishop U23 17.08.79 6 Birmingham 17 Jun
11.74/1.0 5.53/1.2 10.00 1.84 54.66 20.56w/3.0 29.91 3.00 34.18 5:05.53
4973 Neil Edwards U23 28.06.79 18 Bedford 15 Jul
12.39w/3.4 5.70/0.6 9.08 1.66 57.23 16.69/1.8 29.21 2.82 40.43 5:02.93
4910 Matthew Peerless U20 3.12.82 20 Sheffield 2 Sep
12.32/1.0 5.63w/2.1 10.41 1.65 59.64 16.95w/2.7 30.94 3.63 38.07 5:44.63
(70)
4902 Kenneth Pearson 9.07.72 21 Sheffield 2 Sep
12.79/1.0 5.49/1.0 9.66 1.77 59.06 18.25w/2.7 25.52 3.73 46.68 5:20.72

Foreign

6999 James Holder (CAN) 12.10.76 3 Bedford 15 Jul
11.30w/3.2 6.29/0.2 12.55 1.84 50.51 15.12w/2.8 34.49 4.22 53.25 4:27.99
6148 Cathal McGinley (IRL) U23 16.08.79 1 Tullamore, IRL 10 Jun
12.08 6.40 12.35 1.83 54.22 16.12 36.20 3.70 37.40 4:40.14

Decathlon - Under 20 with Under 20 implements

6308 David Hughes 31.05.84 1 Hull 16 Sep
11.29 6.74 10.79 1.78 51.45 15.38 36.76 3.50 42.47 5:10.12
6264 Robin Smith 11.09.83 2 Hull 16 Sep
11.56 6.18 11.25 1.87 52.17 15.52 34.56 3.50 45.08 4:54.53
6247 Louis Evling-Jones 20.06.83 1 Rugby 24 Jun
11.5 6.31 12.01 1.94 50.7 15.3 36.13 2.50 41.51 4:40.1
6218 w Andy Clements 28.11.82 1 Woking 24 Jun
11.8W/5.0 6.35/1.4 10.88 1.72 51.1 15.5/1.2 39.37 2.90 48.03 4:29.5
5796 8 Hull 16 Sep
12.09 6.05 10.68 1.66 51.08 16.50 34.46 3.00 47.54 4:49.36
6114 Paul Tohill 9.10.82 1 Aberdare 24 Jun
11.71w/2.1 6.71w/3.1 12.01 1.95 52.96 15.26/1.5 23.23 3.60 38.45 5:05.13
6058 Carl Marchment 30.12.82 3 Hull 16 Sep
11.86 6.51 11.26 1.84 52.56 15.97 33.34 3.50 41.73 5:03.38
5994 Ryan Westaway 2.03.83 1 Exeter 24 Jun
12.2 6.58 11.44 1.96 52.9 15.9 29.93 3.50 40.99 4:57.5
5953 Daniel Brandwood 1.10.82 5 Hull 16 Sep
11.22 5.98 10.65 1.60 50.22 15.85 34.28 3.90 30.39 4:57.89
5881 Chris Dack 28.11.82 6 Hull 16 Sep
11.83 6.13 13.06 1.72 54.16 15.92 36.44 3.10 48.10 5:21.92
5798 Matthew Walden 30.11.83 7 Hull 16 Sep
11.99 6.53 10.74 1.81 52.93 15.92 34.84 2.80 36.94 4:56.42
(10)
5452 Stephen Stapely 19.05.84 1 Erith 16 Sep
11.6 6.31 11.06 1.74 53.8 16.2 28.66 2.40 43.06 5:07.5
5413 Simon Bull 29.09.82 2 Aberdare 24 Jun
11.72w/2.1 5.78w/2.3 11.97 1.77 58.87 17.00/1.5 40.29 2.50 45.54 5:20.36
5398 Tim Howell 6.12.82 2 Preston 24 Jun
11.7 5.91 10.94 1.69 54.7 15.5 31.91 2.80 37.27 5:09.0
5375 Scott McKinlay 11.04.83 1 Grangemouth 8 Jul
11.96/-0.4 5.71 9.37 1.71 52.17 15.69/2.0 27.24 2.90 28.51 4:39.30
5372 Ross Tressider 8.01.83 9 Hull 16 Sep
11.99 6.03 9.77 1.75 53.33 15.02 30.91 2.30 33.71 5:06.91
5340 Matthew Thurgood 29.12.83 1 Watford 23 Sep
11.89/-1.0 6.23w/2.7 9.61 1.92 52.55 16.70/-1.8 21.23 2.10 37.66 4:50.04
5326 Tony Higbee 21.09.83 2 Exeter 24 Jun
11.8 6.42 10.27 1.84 55.3 16.4 30.27 2.70 33.40 5:11.5
5325 Matthew Clay 9.06.84 4 Hexham 20 May
11.7/1.4 6.66/1.7 10.66 1.80 53.7 20.8/0.2 31.59 2.50 43.55 4:48.8

5314	Benjamin McIlroy				2.09.83	1	Antrim			22 Jul
	12.28	6.04	9.42	1.74	53.05	16.15	23.54	3.40	32.89	4:59.47
5257	Robert Miller				20.01.84	3	Aberdare			24 Jun
	11.59w/2.1	6.33/1.2	9.23	1.71	52.74	19.00/1.5	25.62	2.70	45.19	4:59.47
	(20)									
5183	Mark Garner				2.11.83	10	Hull			16 Sep
	12.16	6.04	8.87	1.72	53.20	16.80	21.85	3.10	34.22	4:49.03
5119	Jake Elsworthy				9.03.83	1	Crawley			9 Sep
	11.8	5.04	10.51	1.60	52.5	17.2	29.01	3.00	35.52	4:44.9
5108	Wayne Balsdon				14.01.83	3	Exeter			24 Jun
	11.9	6.09	10.52	1.84	54.2	18.2	26.29	2.50	32.79	4:50.1
5098	Nicholas Foxworthy				20.05.83	1	Exeter			20 May
	12.4	5.84	9.46	1.83	56.8	16.7	32.30	2.90	46.12	5:33.7

Decathlon - Under 17 with Under 17 implements

6858	Edward Dunford				15.09.84	2	Sheffield			2 Sep
	11.55/1.0	6.52/1.0	15.50	1.98	53.71	13.39w/2.2	48.07	2.83	51.04	5:04.20
5569	Joe Lees				12.09.84	10	Sheffield			2 Sep
	11.67/1.0	6.14w/2.3	10.69	1.65	53.25	15.73w/2.2	28.98	2.83	49.19	4:34.96
5359	Tom Reynolds				20.12.84	11	Sheffield			2 Sep
	11.85/1.0	6.15w/2.9	10.42	1.65	14.42w/2.2		32.00	3.03	34.04	5:11.87
5208	Gareth Bull				3.03.85	15	Sheffield			2 Sep
	12.02/1.0	5.63w/3.9	13.56	1.65	59.05	17.01w/2.2	44.19	2.73	43.11	5:34.30
5070	Michael McConkey				5.12.84	18	Sheffield			2 Sep
	12.53/1.0	5.51/0.9	12.38	1.65	57.69	16.37w/2.2	37.00	2.73	37.86	5:02.25
5054	David Robertson				17.12.84	1	Hexham			23 Sep
	11.92/-0.4	6.00/-0.1	9.66	1.68	55.35	14.52/0.2	35.22	2.30	24.36	5:12.28

Octathlon - Under 17

5741	Edward Dunford				15.09.84	1	Birmingham			17 Jun
	13.32/0.5	6.39	51.80	53.27	1.90	47.71	15.98	5:07.58		(a)
5279	Andrae Davis				27.09.85	2	Hull			16 Sep
	5.96	41.16	42.55	52.31	14.56	1.77	14.29	4:31.18		(b)
4923	Chris Awde				14.02.85	3	Hull			16 Sep
	5.80	41.03	39.07	53.07	14.64	1.74	12.24	4:43.77		(b)
4896	Michael Dyer				27.09.84	4	Hull			16 Sep
	5.74	36.42	47.71	53.32	14.32	1.68	11.90	4:43.78		(b)
4775	Joe Lees				12.09.84	1	Hexham			20 May
	6.18	30.26	45.50	52.7	15.6/0.2	1.75	10.23	4:24.7		(b)
4771	Oliver Bournat				4.12.84	2	London (He)			12 Aug
	5.65/-3.6	15.23/-0.2	40.42	55.09	1.65	13.71	38.27	4:36.10		(c)
4760	Louis Moore				8.09.85	2	Birmingham			17 Jun
	14.59/0.5	6.41	42.53	53.73	1.84	31.80	11.25	5:11.34		(a)
4757	Stephen Alexander				6.10.84	2	Birmingham			30 Sep
	13.23/-0.2	6.89w/3.8	32.22	54.66	1.89	25.22	10.63	5:04.31		(a)
4728	Rupert Gardner				9.10.84	3	Birmingham			30 Sep
	14.10/-0.2	5.75/-1.2	39.29	51.06	1.77	24.59	10.38	4:30.91		(a)
4701	Daniel Armstrong				16.11.84	5	Hull			16 Sep
	5.16	36.92	41.73	53.52	13.99	1.80	11.36	4:59.68		(b)
	(10)									
4615	Robert Henry				22.10.84	7	Hull			16 Sep
	5.52	34.61	37.37	51.27	13.60	1.50	11.96	4:47.51		(b)
4543	Matthew Hansford				20.02.86	8	Hull			16 Sep
	5.89	32.83	35.26	54.83	14.31	1.74	11.51	5:00.02		(b)
4533	Ben Hazell				1.10.84	10	Hull			16 Sep
	5.98	24.32	40.61	52.84	15.21	1.62	11.70	4:33.60		(b)
4502	Zico Benjamin				4.12.84	3	Abingdon			24 Jun
	5.96	26.77	35.62	55.1	15.0	19.5	9.17	4:37.6		(b)
4480	Barrie Prowse				2.03.85	11	Hull			16 Sep
	5.30	28.66	38.35	53.54	15.48	1.74	10.32	4:21.55		(b)
4478	Paris Norriss				27.02.85	12	Hull			16 Sep
	5.08	44.13	51.49	57.80	16.33	1.62	12.69	5:02.68		(b)

4444 William Sharman 12.09.84 9 Birmingham 30 Sep
13.97/-0.2 5.94/-0.1 38.64 58.55 1.95 28.58 10.36 5:14.69 (a)
4436 Gareth Bull 3.03.85 2 Aberdare 24 Jun
5.73w/3.2 13.40 1.65 58.42 17.00/-1.6 47.00 42.25 5:17.23 (d)
4393 Ndubuisi Monye 10.05.85 3 Woking 24 Jun
5.53 41.08 23.73 55.6 16.7 1.90 15.10 5:24.3 (b)
4353 Kevin Sempers 24.11.85 1 Rotherham 16 Sep
14.5 5.84 10.90 56.4 30.14 1.87 31.09 5:04.1 (e)
(20)
4351 Daniel Thompson 27.12.84 3 Birmingham 17 Jun
14.43/0.5 5.76 32.67 52.94 1.72 25.05 10.24 4:50.75 (a)
4319 Thomas Jennings 27.01.85 15 Hull 16 Sep
5.23 33.26 44.61 55.52 14.98 1.77 11.87 5:33.59 (b)
4316 Robert Smith 3.03.85 16 Hull 16 Sep
5.19 23.76 33.57 49.93 14.96 1.68 8.69 4:28.32 (b)
4300 Christopher George 27.09.84 11 Birmingham 30 Sep
15.79/-0.4 5.51/-0.1 46.41 55.05 1.56 25.15 10.69 4:30.23 (a)
4253 Matthew Thompson 29.12.84 1 Grangemouth 8 Jul
5.32 39.79 29.49 57.1 14.48/0.9 1.50 12.96 5:02.86 (b)
4235 David Robertson 17.12.84 17 Hull 16 Sep
5.76 34.42 24.53 54.37 14.05 1.65 9.71 5:04.46 (b)
4227 Philip Thomas 21.10.84 3 Aberdare 24 Jun
5.45w/3.7 9.31 1.71 54.42 15.56/-1.6 24.72 37.78 4:31.83 (d)
4226 James Dunford 14.01.86 4 Abingdon 24 Jun
5.50 36.54 43.68 59.0 15.5 1.68 12.10 5:18.8 (b)
4217 Callum McKay 17.02.85 4 Woking 24 Jun
5.73 23.86 27.18 51.8 14.2 1.60 9.44 4:38.7 (b)

Order of Events
a) 100mH, LJ, JT, 400m, HJ, DT, SP, 1500m
b) LJ, DT, JT, 400m, 100mH, HJ, SP, 1500m
c) LJ, 100mH, JT, 400m, HJ, SP, DT, 1500m
d) LJ, SP, HJ, 400m, 100mH, DT, JT, 1500m
e) 100mH, LJ, SP, 400m, DT, HJ, JT, 1500m

Pentathlon - Under 15

2974 Pepi Nanci 7.10.86 1 Birmingham 29 Sep
11.87/-0.7 13.36 53.7/0.3 1.74 2:14.42 (a)
2962 Craig Glanville 21.09.86 1 Jarrow 23 Jun
12.4 11.57 5.71 1.66 2:03.6 (a)
2866 Ryan Thomas 21.03.87 1 Crawley 8 Sep
12.7 6.46 9.97 1.75 2:16.5 (b)
2786 Ryan Shaw 30.12.86 2 Birmingham 29 Sep
11.82/-0.7 11.93 5.71/-1.6 1.56 2:16.65 (a)
2778 Lewis Robson 9.01.88 1 Hexham 26 Aug
12.46 5.80 10.61 1.62 2:11.68 (b)
2768 Adrian Pettigrew 12.11.86 1 Woking 23 Jun
11.9 11.14 5.46 1.75 2:19.1 (a)
2764 Paul Mudd 6.09.86 3 Hull 15 Sep
11.60 10.82 5.47 1.61 2:14.43 (a)
2719 Darren Steadman 26.01.87 2 Rugby 23 Jun
12.3 8.95 5.71 1.79 2:16.4 (a)
2718 Phil Jarrett 18.03.87 1 Rotherham 16 Sep
11.8 6.07 11.99 1.70 2:35.1 (b)
2687 Scott Harwood 1.10.86 2 Rotherham 16 Sep
12.0 5.70 9.74 16.7 2:17.1 (b)
(10)
2682 Toby Hunt 28.12.86 2 London (He) 12 Aug
13.12/-2.4 12.74 5.60/0.9 1.54 2:15.21 (a)
2669 Paul Twidale 30.09.86 3 Rugby 23 Jun
13.0 10.90 6.07 1.46 2:10.7 (a)
2658 George Beeken 4.09.86 3 Birmingham 29 Sep
11.66/-0.7 10.57 5.36/0.5 1.68 2:22.84 (a)

2641	Sosthene Yao		7.08.87	1	Erith	16 Sep
	11.9 10.37 5.82 1.58 2:20.5				(a)	
2633	Jonathan Long		4.10.86	4	Birmingham	29 Sep
	12.48/0.9 9.72 5.10/0.2 1.59 2:07.03				(a)	
2614	Jon Baty		1.02.87	5	Hull	15 Sep
	11.77 10.20 4.93 1.67 2:16.97				(a)	
2611	Gary Sweeney		31.01.87	1	Glasgow	9 Jun
	13.7 5.60 25.6 11.13 2:16.1				(c)	
2608	Daniel Harris		1.10.86	1	Exeter	20 May
	12.4 9.89 6.17 1.69 2:29.3				(a)	
2606	Chinedum Onuoha		12.11.86	1	Preston	24 Jun
	12.2 10.19 6.25 1.52 2:23.5				(a)	
2601	Andrew Staniland		21.01.87	3	Rotherham	16 Sep
	12.1 5.74 11.91 1.64 2:31.6				(b)	
	(20)					
2592	Craig France		11.01.87	6	Birmingham	29 Sep
	11.87 10.52 5.30 1.62 2:21.33				(a)	
2585	Joseph Evling-White		3.12.86	4	Rugby	23 Jun
	12.9 11.73 5.78 1.64 2:26.0				(a)	
2569	Michael Emezie			1	Aberdare	23 Jun
	12.93w/2.4 10.79 5.25w/2.4 1.63 2:16.02				(a)	

Order of Events a) 80mH, SP, LJ, HJ, 800m
b) 80mH, LJ, SP, HJ, 800m
c) 80mH, LJ, 200, SP, 800m

2000 Metres Walk - Under 13 - Track

10:11.6	Derry Brown		12.03.89	1	Birmingham	29 Sep
10:14.7	Lewis Hayden		10.08.89	2	Birmingham	29 Sep
11:01.6	Andrew Graham		19.12.89	1	Dudley	14 Oct
overage						
10:00.0	Lewis Hayden	U15	10.08.89	1	Leicester	18 Oct
11:15.2	Mark Hambridge	U15	18.02.89	2	Dudley	14 Oct

3000 Metres Walk - Track

12:02.24 i	Andi Drake		6.02.65	2	Birmingham	27 Jan
12:08.57 i	Matthew Hales	U23	6.10.79	5	Birmingham	27 Jan
	12:51.96			1	Derby	29 Jul
12:09.8	Steve Partington		17.09.65	1	Douglas IOM	8 Aug
12:16.0	Andy Penn		31.03.67	1	Coventry	21 Jun
	12:28.14			1	Birmingham	30 Jun
	12:39.3			2	Bedford	28 May
12:26.0 i	Lloyd Finch	U20	26.10.83	2	Cardiff	10 Mar
	12:30.97 i			1	Birmingham	25 Feb
	12:32.07 +			1m	Birmingham	14 Jul
	12:33.9			1	Bedford	28 May
	12:41.1			1	Loughborough	13 May
12:37.64	Dom King	U20	30.05.83	1	Stoke-on-Trent	18 Aug
12:37.8	Andrew Goudie		4.10.78	1	Bromley	11 Jul
12:40.8	Dan King	U20	30.05.83	1	London (WF)	19 Aug
12:41.0	Steve Hollier		27.02.76	2	Coventry	21 Jul
12:46.13 i	Cameron Smith	U20	17.01.84	2	Birmingham	25 Feb
	13:07.0			3	Coventry	21 Jul
	(10)					
12:47.86	Andrew Parker	U20	10.12.83	2	Stoke-on-Trent	18 Aug
12:56.52	Luke Finch	U17	21.09.85	1	Ipswich	2 Sep
12:59.7	Mark Easton		24.05.63	1	Woodford	20 Jun
13:06.84	Mark Stewart		15.05.71	2	Birmingham	30 Jun
13:12.0	Mark Williams		7.09.64	3	Coventry	9 Aug
13:16.9	Peter Kaneen	V40	12.07.61	2	Douglas IOM	8 Aug

13:25.30	James Davis	U17	10.10.84	2	Tullamore, IRL	21 Jul
13:37.40	Noel Carmody	V40	24.12.56	1	Eton	23 Jun
13:41.85 i	Colin Bradley	V45	2.02.56	3	Bordeaux, FRA	10 Mar

5000 Metres Walk - Track

20:47.23	Lloyd Finch	U20	26.10.83	1	Birmingham	14 Jul
21:04.36	Steve Hollier		27.02.76	2	Birmingham	14 Jul
21:05.29	Chris Cheeseman	V40	11.12.58	3	Birmingham	14 Jul
21:07.5	Steve Partington		17.09.65	1	Douglas IOM	26 Sep
21:18.02	Andy Penn		31.03.67	4	Birmingham	14 Jul
21:42.4	Mark Easton		24.05.63	1	Woodford	22 Aug
21:49.63	Andrew Goudie		4.10.78	5	Birmingham	14 Jul
21:50.48	Dom King	U20	30.05.83	6	Birmingham	14 Jul
21:58.8	Luke Finch	U17	21.09.85	1	Tamworth	22 Sep
22:36.98	Andrew Parker	U20	10.12.83	8	Birmingham	14 Jul
(10)						
22:49.4	Dan King	U20	30.05.83	2	Hull	15 Sep
22:51.1	Peter Kaneen	V40	12.07.61	2	Douglas IOM	22 Sep
23:13.4	Mark Williams		7.09.64	2	Dudley	14 Oct
23:31.82 i	Cameron Smith	U20	17.01.84	6	Vittel, FRA	3 Mar
23:34.10	Tim Watt		19.09.66	10	Birmingham	14 Jul

Additional Juniors

23:44.5	Nathan Adams	U20	14.04.82	3	Birmingham	29 Sep
24:15.1	Neil Bates	U20	5.04.84	3	Douglas IOM	22 Aug
24:21.52	James Davis	U17	10.10.84	2	Sheffield	12 Aug

10000 Metres Walk - Track

43:21.0	Andi Drake		6.02.65	1	Tamworth	22 Sep
44:29.4	Lloyd Finch	U20	26.10.83	1	Bedford	1 Jul
44:30.3	Chris Cheeseman	V40	11.12.58	1	Crawley	16 Sep
45:25.9	Gareth Brown		10.05.68	2	Crawley	16 Sep
47:08.54	Dom King	U20	30.05.83	17	Grosseto, ITA	21 Jul
47:10.4	Luke Finch	U17	21.09.85	1	Leicester	15 Mar
47:24.5	Andrew Parker	U20	10.12.83	2	Bedford	1 Jul
47:42.76	Cameron Smith	U20	17.01.84	23	Debrecen, HUN	14 Jul
47:53.0	Jamie O'Rawe		3.02.73	1	Basildon	22 Sep
48:01.1	Martin Young		11.07.72	3	Birmingham	29 Sep

10 Kilometres Walk - Road

42:49	Andi Drake		6.02.65	1	Leamington	4 Mar
43:05 +	Darrell Stone		2.02.68	m	Leamington	21 Apr
	43:44			1	Bexley	8 Dec
43:21	Chris Cheeseman	V40	11.12.58	1	East Molesey	7 Jan
43:23	Don Bearman		16.04.66	2	East Molesey	7 Jan
43:23	Andy Penn		31.03.67	1	Leicester	2 Sep
43:38	Steve Partington		17.09.65	1	Douglas IOM	1 Apr
43:49	Lloyd Finch	U20	26.10.83	1	Budapest, HUN	9 Sep
44:00 +	Matthew Hales	U23	6.10.79	m	Leamington	21 Apr
44:00 +	Steve Hollier		27.02.76	8	Dublin, IRL	16 Jun
44:06	Dom King	U20	30.05.83	2	Leamington	21 Apr
(10)						
44:11	Jamie O'Rawe		3.02.73	3	East Molesey	7 Jan
44:38	Mark Easton		24.05.63	4	Bexley	8 Dec
44:57	Andrew Goudie		4.10.78	5	Bexley	8 Dec
46:00	Luke Finch	U17	21.09.85	1	Worcester	20 Oct
46:01	Kevin Walmsley		6.09.67	1	Isle of Man	21 Jan
46:17	Andrew Parker	U20	10.12.83	36	Dudince, SVK	19 May
46:21	Cameron Smith	U20	17.01.84	2	Birmingham	5 May
47:12	Peter Kaneen	V40	12.07.61	1	Castletown IOM	15 Aug
47:15	Karl Atton		14.09.71	2	Birmingham	17 Feb

20 Kilometres Walk - Road

1:28:18	Andy Penn		31.03.67	7	Dublin, IRL	16 Jun
	1:29:33			9	Mohlin, SUI	9 Sep
	1:31:09			1	Sheffield	7 Jul
	1:31:56			1	Birmingham	19 May
1:28:40	Matthew Hales	U23	6.10.79	8	Leamington	21 Apr
	1:30:08			38	Dudince, SVK	19 May
1:28:51	Darrell Stone		2.02.68	1	Steyning	24 Feb
1:29:26	Steve Hollier		27.02.76	4	Douglas IOM	17 Feb
	1:29:27			9	Dublin, IRL	16 Jun
	1:32:56			2	Sheffield	7 Jul
1:29:40	Mark Easton		24.05.63	9	Leamington	21 Apr
	1:31:31			11	Dublin, IRL	16 Jun
	1:32:39			1	South Croydon	24 Feb
1:29:52	Steve Partington		17.09.65	10	Dublin, IRL	16 Jun
	1:33:00			12	Leamington	21 Apr
1:29:56	Don Bearman		16.04.66	5	Douglas IOM	17 Feb
1:30:26	Chris Cheeseman	V40	11.12.58	8	Douglas IOM	17 Feb
	1:30:32			10	Leamington	21 Apr
1:34:40	Andrew Goudie		4.10.78	14	Leamington	21 Apr
1:35:03	Karl Atton		14.09.71	15	Leamington	21 Apr
	(10)					
1:35:45	Andy O'Rawe		8.09.63	16	Leamington	21 Apr
1:38:25	Jamie O'Rawe		3.02.73	6	Lugano, SUI	13 Oct
1:38:48	Mark Williams		7.09.64	17	Leamington	21 Apr
1:38:51	Mike Smith		20.04.63	9	Douglas IOM	17 Feb

30 Kilometres Walk - Road

2:18:31	Steve Hollier		27.02.76	1	Leek Wootton	18 Aug
2:28:00 +	Darrell Stone		2.02.68	2	Birmingham	5 May
	2:28:28 +			4	Dublin, IRL	16 Jun
2:35:16 +	Chris Cheeseman	V40	11.12.58	6	Dublin, IRL	16 Jun
2:37:11	Mike Smith		20.04.63	2	Leek Wootton	18 Aug

35 Kilometres Walk - Road

2:55:00	Mark Easton		24.05.63	1	Birmingham	5 May
2:58:19	Darrell Stone		2.02.68	2	Birmingham	5 May
2:58:35	Mike Smith		20.04.63	3	Birmingham	5 May

50 Kilometres Walk - Road

4:09:27	Steve Hollier		27.02.76	7	Dudince, SVK	24 Mar
	4:20:50			33	Dudince, SVK	19 May
	4:26:35			1	Tilburg, NED	14 Oct
4:18:00	Chris Cheeseman	V40	11.12.58	4	Dublin, IRL	16 Jun
	4:24:48			37	Dudince, SVK	19 May
4:18:59	Karl Atton		14.09.71	10	Dudince, SVK	24 Mar
4:21:55	Darrell Stone		2.02.68	5	Dublin, IRL	16 Jun
4:32:55	Mike Smith		20.04.63	6	Dublin, IRL	16 Jun
4:40:00	Peter Kaneen		12.07.61	7	Dublin, IRL	16 Jun
4:52:22	Peter Ryan	V45	9.04.54	4	London (VP)	25 Mar
4:54:38	Colin Bradley	V45	2.02.56	5	London (VP)	25 Mar
4:54:54	Chris Berwick	V50	1.05.46	6	London (VP)	25 Mar
4:55:53	Dave Turner	V40	20.10.57	1	Bradford	28 May

100 Miles Walk - Road

19:46:11	Bob Dobson	V55	4.11.42	1	Colchester	5 Aug
19:50:39	Richard Brown	V50	18.11.46	2	Colchester	5 Aug
21:32:39	Chris Flint	V55	6.12.44	5	Colchester	5 Aug

4 x 100 METRES

38.52	National Team (D.Chambers, M.Devonish, C.Malcolm, J.Barbour)		3	London (CP)	22 Jul
38.63	England (A.Condon, D.Campbell, M.Devonish, D.Chambers)		1	Loughborough	20 May
38.69	National Team (D.Chambers, M.Devonish, C.Malcolm, M.Lewis-Francis)		1	Glasgow (S)	1 Jul
38.71	National Team (J.Barbour, C.Malcolm, M.Devonish, D.Chambers)		1	Brisbane, AUS	7 Sep
38.99	National Team (A.Condon, M.Devonish, C.Malcolm, M.Lewis-Francis)		2	Bremen, GER	23 Jun
39.24	National Junior Team (T.Edgar, D.Grant, T.Benjamin, M.Lewis-Francis)	U20	1	Grosseto, ITA	22 Jul
39.45	National Under 23 Team (J.Oparka, J.Barbour, D.Chin, B.Lewis)		2	Amsterdam, NED	15 Jul
39.53	Belgrave Harriers (D.Chambers, D.Chin, D.Campbell, G.Beasley)		3	Madrid, ESP	26 May
39.54	National Team		2	Arles, FRA	10 Jun
39.55	National Junior Team (T.Edgar, D.Grant, T.Benjamin, M.Lewis-Francis)	U20	2	Loughborough	20 May
39.68	National Junior Team (T.Edgar, D.Grant, T.Benjamin, M.Lewis-Francis)	U20	1h1	Grosseto, ITA	22 Jul
39.90	National Under 23 Team (J.Oparka, J.Chatt, D.Chin, B.Lewis)		1h2	Amsterdam, NED	14 Jul
39.90	England (T.Edgar, B.Lewis, T.Abeyie, D.Grant)		1	Edinburgh	25 Aug
39.95	Scotland (J.Oparka, B.Doyle, I.Mackie, N.Smith)		2	Edinburgh	25 Aug
40.30	National Under 23 Team (J.Oparka, J.Barbour, D.Chin, B.Lewis)		1	Liverpool	23 Jun
40.31	National Junior Team (T.Edgar, D.Grant, T.Abeyie, M.Lewis-Francis)	U20	1	Mannheim, GER	16 Jun
40.37	Cardiff AAC		2	Cardiff	8 Jul
40.55	Wales/Cardiff AAC (K.Williams, C.Malcolm, J.Baulch, P.Gray)		3	Loughborough	20 May
40.67	Birchfield Harriers (D.Bradley, C.Browne, B.Lewis, M.Lewis-Francis)		1	Birmingham	2 Jun
40.74	UK 'B' team (J.Gardener, D.Turner, N.Owen, C.Lambert)		2	Ashford	11 Aug
40.79	National Junior Team (A.Syers, T.Edgar, T.Abeyie, D.Grant)	U20	1	Stoke-on-Trent	18 Aug
40.95	Scotland (I.Deeth, D.Walker, B.Doyle, C.Bailey)		4	Loughborough	20 May

Additional National Teams

42.92	Jersey	1	Douglas, IOM	13 Jul
43.41	Northern Ireland	5	Edinburgh	25 Aug

Additional Club Teams (1 - 3 above)

41.02	Woodford Green & Essex Ladies	1	Eton	7 Jul
41.12	Sale Harriers Manchester	1	Bedford	21 Jul
41.3	Windsor Slough E & H AC	2	Watford	2 Jun
41.47	Blackheath Harriers	3	Bedford	21 Jul
41.60	Enfield & Haringey AC	2	Cardiff	8 Jul
41.67	Loughborough Students	6	Loughborough	20 May
41.9	Newham & Essex Beagles	1	Eton	10 Jun
41.93	Border Harriers	2	Jarrow	18 Aug
42.03	Shaftesbury Barnet Harriers	3	Birmingham	2 Jun

42.13	Bath University		1	Glasgow (S)	7 May
42.29	Thames Valley Harriers		4	Cardiff	8 Jul
42.4	Team Solent		4	Watford	2 Jun
42.4	Harrow AC		1	London (Ha)	10 Jun
42.4	City of Edinburgh AC		1	Grangemouth	17 Jun
42.71	Oxford University		3	Glasgow (S)	7 May
42.8	City of Stoke AC		2	Stafford	18 Aug
42.9	Arbroath		2	Grangemouth	17 Jun
42.9	Notts AC		1	Cardiff	2 Jun
43.0	Luton United AC		1	Rugby	18 Aug
43.0	Peterborough AC		3	Stafford	18 Aug

Additional Under 20 Teams (1 - 5 above)

41.87	Wales		1	Derby	29 Jul
41.96	Belgrave Harriers		1	Derby	9 Sep
41.99	Midlands		2	Derby	29 Jul
42.02	National Team	U18	1h2	Murcia, ESP	25 Jul
42.02	South		3	Derby	29 Jul

Additional Under 20 Club Teams (1 above)

42.13	Shaftesbury Barnet Harriers		2	Derby	9 Sep
43.09	Birchfield Harriers		3	Derby	9 Sep
43.16	Sale Harriers Manchester		4	Derby	9 Sep
43.89	Enfield & Haringey AC	U17	1	Birmingham	2 Sep
43.9	Stewart's Melville	U19	1	Glasgow (S)	9 Jun
44.0	Blackheath Harriers		2	Bedford	24 Jun
44.0	Liverpool Pembroke & Sefton AC		1	Connah's Quay	29 Jul
44.4	Liverpool Harriers AC		2	Stoke-on-Trent	17 Jun
44.4	Notts AC	U17	1	Yate	1 Jul

Additional Under 17 Teams (1 - 2 above)

42.9	England Schools		2	Tullamore, IRL	21 Jul
43.23	Essex Schools		1h1	Exeter	7 Jul
43.4	West Midlands Schools		1	Stoke-on-Trent	16 Jun
43.44	London Schools		1h2	Exeter	7 Jul
43.80	Nottinghamshire Schools		3h1	Exeter	7 Jul
43.8	Middlesex AA		1	Crawley	5 Aug
43.83	Kent Schools		2	Exeter	7 Jul
43.9	Humberside Schools		1	York	15 Jun
43.9	Scotland Schools		3	Tullamore, IRL	21 Jul
44.0	Wales Schools		4	Tullamore, IRL	21 Jul

Additional Under 17 Club Teams (1 - 2 above)

44.5	Liverpool Pembroke & Sefton		1	Bury	20 May
44.8	Peterborough AC		1	Peterborough	22 Jul
44.9	Blackheath Harriers		1	Tonbridge	9 Sep
45.0	Harrow AC		1	Harrow	1 Jul
45.1	Cambridge Harriers		2	Tonbridge	9 Sep
45.2	Belgrave Harriers		1	London (Nh)	6 May
45.2	Shaftesbury Barnet Harriers		2	Peterborough	22 Jul
45.3	Clydesdale Harriers		1	Glasgow (S)	19 Aug

Under 15 Teams

44.56	West Midlands Schools		1	Exeter	7 Jul
45.20	Staffordshire Schools		2	Stoke-on-Trent	16 Jun
45.28	Essex Schools		1h2	Exeter	7 Jul
45.8	Lincolnshire Schools		1	Bury St Edmunds	16 Jun
45.89	Buckinghamshire Schools		3	Exeter	7 Jul
45.90	Greater Manchester Schools		3	Stoke-on-Trent	16 Jun
45.9	Birchfield Harriers		1	Yate	1 Jul

46.09	North East AA	1	Scunthorpe	18 Aug
46.1	Shaftesbury Barnet Harriers	1	Peterborough	22 Jul
46.15	Devon Schools	2h2	Exeter	7 Jul

Additional Under 15 Club Teams (1-2 above)

46.4	Gateshead Harriers	1	Middlesbrough	24 Jul
46.40	Enfield & Haringey AC	1	Birmingham	2 Sep
46.43	Croydon Harriers	1	Birmingham	1 Sep
46.9	Woodford Green & Essex Ladies	2	Peterborough	22 Jul
47.04	City of Stoke AC	2	Birmingham	2 Sep
47.1	Harrow AC	1	Harrow	1 Jul
47.2	Chelmsford AC	1	Basildon	22 Sep
47.3	Morpeth Harriers	2	Middlesbrough	24 Jul

Under 13 Teams

51.05	Shaftesbury Barnet Harriers	1	Birmingham	2 Sep
51.2	Enfield & Haringey AC	1	Peterborough	22 Jul
52.6	Middlesex AA	1	Kingston	29 Jul
53.02	Ayr Seaforth AAC	1	Glasgow (S)	24 Jun
53.3	Medway & Maidstone AC	1	Tonbridge	9 Sep
53.4	Ballymena Academy	1s	Antrim	26 May
53.6	Surrey AA	2	Kingston	29 Jul
53.67	Wirral AC	1	Birmingham	1 Sep
53.7	Croydon Harriers	1	Harrow	1 Jul

4 x 200 METRES

1:27.26 i	Loughborough University	1	Glasgow	Feb
1:27.60 i	Bath University	2	Glasgow	Feb
1:28.38 i	University College in Cardiff	3	Glasgow	Feb
1:29.45 i	Brunel University	2r1	Birmingham	13 Feb
1:30.59 i	Birmingham University	3r1	Birmingham	13 Feb
1:30.9	Oxford University	1	Oxford	4 Mar

Under 20 Teams

1:33.38 i	Ayr Seaforth AAC	1	Glasgow	11 Mar
1:33.5	Trinity School	1	Oxford	10 May
1:33.6	Millfield School	2	Oxford	10 May
1:35.01 i	Central AC	2	Glasgow	11 Mar

Under 17 Teams

1:35.30 i	Clydesdale Harriers	1	Glasgow	11 Mar
1:36.0	Aberdeen AAC	1	Dundee	8 Jul
1:37.3	Trinity School	1	Oxford	10 May
1:38.47 i	City of Edinburgh AC	2	Glasgow	21 Jan
1:38.5	Harrow School	2	Oxford	10 May
1:39.6	Croydon Harriers	1	Wimbledon	11 Jul

Under 15 Teams

1:41.0	Croydon Harriers	1	Croydon	24 Jun
1:42.0	Haberdashers' Aske's School	1	Oxford	10 May
1:42.2	Harrow School	2	Oxford	10 May
1:43.27 i	Giffnock North AC	1h2	Glasgow	11 Mar
1:43.7	Millfield School	1h1	Oxford	10 May
1:44.6	Bedford School	4	Oxford	10 May

Under 13 Teams

1:55.7	Croydon Harriers	1	Croydon	24 Jun
1:57.32 i	Ayr Seaforth AAC	1h2	Glasgow	11 Mar
2:01.00 i	Giffnock North AC	1h1	Glasgow	11 Mar
2:02.51 i	Harmeny AC	1h2	Glasgow	21 Jan

MARK LEWIS-FRANCIS. The top junior sprinter in the world.

TIM BENJAMIN. Great Gold medal, shame about the plate.

DANIEL CAINES. Running scared to become World Indoor Champion.

MATT ELIAS. Took 2 Gold medals in the European U23 Championships.

RICKY SOOS. Up and coming middle distance runner.

MOHAMED FARAH. Gold medal winner in the European U20 Championships & Silver in the team at the European Cross Country Championships.

JONATHAN MOORE. Britain's sensational new Long and Triple Jumper.

DEAN MACEY. Dean launches his medal winning assault at the World Championships.

VERNICHA JAMES. Vernicha celebrates her Gold medal at the European U20 Championships.

KIM WALL. Double medal winner at the European U20 Championships.

PAULA RADCLIFFE. When the going gets tough...

COLLETTE FAGAN. Gold medal winner in the team at the European Cross Country Championships.

SUSAN JONES. Susan celebrates equalling the 18 year-old British High Jump record.

JANINE WHITLOCK. On her way to setting her new British record.

JADE JOHNSON. Gold medal winner at the European U23 Championships.

LORRAINE SHAW. In the World's top 10 of Hammer Throwers.

4 x 400 METRES

3:00.96	National Team		2h1	Edmonton, CAN	11 Aug
	(M.Hylton 46.2 I.Thomas 44.8 T.Benjamin 45.46 M.Richardson 44.52)				
3:01.26	National Team		6	Edmonton, CAN	12 Aug
	(I.Thomas 45.8 J.Baulch 44.4 T.Benjamin 45.85 M.Richardson 45.17)				
3:02.79	National Team		4	Bremen, GER	24 Jun
	(J.Deacon 47.0 I.Thomas 44.8 D.Thorne-Ladejo 45.76 M.Richardson 45.26)				
3:05.24	National Under 23 Team	U23	1	Amsterdam, NED	15 Jul
	(D.Naismith, A.Potter, J.Chatt, M.Elias)				
3:05.53	Belgrave Harriers		3	Madrid, ESP	27 May
	(G.Dearman, T.Bayley 46.38 C.Rawlinson, S.Baldock)				
3:06.21	National Junior Team	U20	2	Grosseto, ITA	22 Jul
	(R.Tobin, R.Nicholls, S.Ellis, T.Benjamin)				
3:07.33	National Under 23 Team	U23	1h1	Amsterdam, NED	14 Jul
	(D.Naismith, A.Potter, R.McDonald, M.Elias)				
3:07.57 i	National Team		3h1	Lisbon, POR	10 Mar
	(M.Elias 47.33 P.Slythe 46.74 M.Brown 47.25 D.Thorne-Ladejo 46.25)				
3:08.18	Belgrave Harriers		1	Eton	7 Jul
	(T. Bayley, C. Rawlinson, G.Dearman, S.Baldock)				
3:08.73	Loughborough Students		1	Loughborough	20 May
	(N.Budden 49.3 D.Naismith 45.8 C.Rawlinson 46.7 J.Edwards 47.0)				
3:09.21 i	National Team		5	Lisbon, POR	11 Mar
	(M.Hylton 48.21 D.Thorne-Ladejo 46.75 M.Elias 46.62 D.Caines 47.63)				
3:09.95	National Junior Team	U20	2h2	Grosseto, ITA	21 Jul
	(R.Tobin, R.Nicholls, S.Ellis, J.Christie)				
3:10.04 i	National Team		3	Glasgow	18 Mar
	(A.Condon 48.40 P.Slythe 47.51 N.Jennings 47.46 D.Caines 46.67)				
3:10.21	British Universities		2	Loughborough	20 May
	(G.Dearman, S.Ellis, N.Jennings, A.Buckley)				
3:10.70	National U23 Team		1	Liverpool	23 Jun
	(A.Buckley, T.Bayley, I.Lowthian, M.Elias)				
3:11.47	National Under 23 Team		1	Ashford	11 Aug
	(N.Jennings, J.Hillier, P.Brend, J.Deacon)				
3:11.49	Loughborough Students		1	Glasgow (S)	7 May
3:11.83	National Team	U19	2	Dole, FRA	29 Jul
	(R.Nicholls, S.Green, R.Palmer, R.Tobin)				
3:11.95	Border Harriers		2	Eton	7 Jul
	(A.Mitchell, N.Carlisle, S.Reid, P.McKee)				
3:12.02	Belgrave Harriers		1	Birmingham	2 Jun

Additional National Teams

3:12.36	Wales	3	Loughborough	20 May
	(J.Hillier, J.Nasrat, C.Page, M.Elias)			
3:13.33	Scotland	5	Loughborough	20 May
	(C.Robertson-Adams, C.Phillips, G.Deeth, K.Stewart)			
3:19.28	Jersey	1	Douglas, IOM	13 Jul
3:23.00	Guernsey	3	Douglas, IOM	13 Jul

Additional Club Teams (1 - 3 above)

3:12.49	Bath University	2	Glasgow (S)	7 May
3:13.10	Birchfield Harriers	2	Birmingham	2 Jun
3:13.79	Woodford Green & Essex Ladies	3	Eton	7 Jul
3:14.0	Newham & Essex Beagles	2	Bedford	21 Jul
3:14.24	Sale Harriers Manchester	1	Jarrow	18 Aug
3:15.09	Shaftesbury Barnet Harriers	4	Jarrow	18 Aug
3:15.2	Thames Valley Harriers	1	Eton	18 Aug
3:16.1	Harrow AC	1	Watford	2 Jun
3:16.2	Team Solent	2	Watford	2 Jun
3:16.2	Cardiff AAC	3	Watford	2 Jun
3:17.0	Trafford AC	2	Eton	18 Aug

3:18.6	Blackheath Harriers	5	Bedford	21 Jul
3:18.8	City of Edinburgh AC	1	Cardiff	2 Jun
3:19.28	Brunel University	3	Glasgow (S)	7 May
3:19.3	Bolton United Harriers	1	Watford	8 Sep
3:19.6	Worthing & District Harriers	1	Southend	1 Jul
3:19.8	Pitreavie AAC	1	Grangemouth	17 Jun

Additional Under 20 Teams (1 - 3 above)

3:12.65	National Junior Team	4	Loughborough	20 May
	(J.Simpson, R.Nicholls, J.Christie, R.Tobin)			
3:14.31	National Junior Team	2	Stoke-on-Trent	18 Aug
	(J.Christie, S.Green, R.Smith, R.Tobin)			
3:17.60	South	1	Ipswich	2 Sep
3:17.74	North	2	Ipswich	2 Sep
3:18.25	Scotland	2	Corinth, GRE	27 May
	(M.Cullen, J.Simpson, S.Murphy, C.Watson)			
3:18.6	Enfield & Haringey AC	1	Bedford	24 Jun

Additional Under 20 National Teams

3:24.7	Welsh Schools	1	Brecon	18 Jul
3:25.7	AA of Wales	2	Brecon	18 Jul
3:28.5	Northern Ireland	3	Brecon	18 Jul

Additional Under 20 Club Teams (1 above)

3:22.01	Shaftesbury Barnet Harriers	2	Derby	9 Sep
3:22.3	Belgrave Harriers	1	Watford	12 Aug
3:23.4	Basingstoke & Mid Hants AC	1		17 Jun
3:26.6	Bolton United Harriers	1	Wakefield	29 Jul
3:26.8	City of Stoke AC	2	Wakefield	29 Jul
3:28.1	Blackheath Harriers	2	Hayes	29 Apr
3:28.6	Sale Harriers Manchester	1	Wigan	29 Apr
3:29.1	Trafford AC	1	Bebington	29 Apr
3:29.8	Notts AC	2	Wigan	29 Apr

Under 17 Teams

3:20.8	England Schools	1	Tullamore, IRL	21 Jul
3:27.6	Essex AA	1	Crawley	5 Aug
3:28.1	Scotland Schools	2	Tullamore, IRL	21 Jul
3:29.8	Liverpool Pembroke Sefton H & AC	1rB	Sheffield (W)	3 Jun
3:30.4	Wales Schools	4	Tullamore, IRL	21 Jul

Additional Under 17 Club Teams (1 above)

3:30.57	Enfield & Haringey AC	1	Birmingham	2 Sep
3:31.32	Aberdeen AAC	1	Glasgow (S)	24 Jun
3:31.5	Blackheath Harriers	1	Tonbridge	9 Sep
3:31.5	Tonbridge AC	2	Tonbridge	9 Sep
3:31.8	Cwmbran AC	1rB	Tipton	1 Jul
3:32.0	Bristol AC	1	Yate	1 Jul
3:32.2	Bexley AC	3	Tonbridge	9 Sep
3:32.6	Derby & County AC	1	Tipton	1 Jul
3:33.8	Woodford Green & Essex Ladies	1		20 May

Under 15 Teams

3:38.0	Liverpool Pembroke Sefton H & AC	1	Bury	20 May
3:38.5	Gateshead Harriers & AC	3	Middlesbrough	24 Jul
3:44.58	Mandale Harriers & AC	1	Birmingham	1 Sep
3:44.7	Kent AC	1	Tonbridge	9 Sep
3:46.2	Liverpool Harriers AC	1	Wigan	1 Jul
3:47.1	Ealing Southall & Middlesex AC	1	Perivale	1 Jul
3:47.15	Sale Harriers Manchester	1	Birmingham	2 Sep

3:47.9	Medway & Maidstone AC		2	Tonbridge	9 Sep
3:48.1	Enfield & Haringey AC		1	Harrow	1 Jul
3:50.1	Notts AC		1	Nottingham	20 May

Under 13 Team

4:45.3	Blackheath Harriers		1	Hoo	5 Aug

4 x 800 METRES

7:49.7	Cambridge University		1	Oxford	4 Mar
7:56.7	Sunderland H		1	Middlesbrough	24 Jul
7:57.9	Oxford University		2	Oxford	4 Mar
7:59.2	Chester le Street AC		2	Middlesbrough	24 Jul

Under 17 Teams

8:47.1	Millfield School		1	Oxford	10 May
8:52.6	Radley College		2	Oxford	10 May
9:01.3	Haberdashers' Aske's School		3	Oxford	10 May
9:03.5	Altrincham & District AC		1	Macclesfield	10 Jul

Under 15 Teams

9:47.7	Uppingham School		1	Oxford	10 May
9:47.9	Bedford School		2	Oxford	10 May
9:51.0	Millfield School		3	Oxford	10 May
9:53.6	Shrewsbury School		4	Oxford	10 May

Under 13 Team

10:27.6	Macclesfield Harriers		1	Macclesfield	19 Jun

3 x 800 METRES

Under 17 Teams

6:31.7	Chelmsford AC		1	Basildon	22 Sep
6:39.95	Cambuslang		1	Glasgow (S)	24 Jun
6:42.09	Harmeny AC		2	Glasgow (S)	24 Jun
6:45.35	Kilbarchan		3	Glasgow (S)	24 Jun
6:45.6	Southend-on-Sea AC		2	Basildon	22 Sep

Under 13 Teams

7:22.1	Ashford AC		1	Tonbridge	9 Sep
7:28.5	Chelmsford AC		1	Basildon	22 Sep
7:33.21	City of Edinburgh AC		1	Glasgow (S)	24 Jun
7:35.9	Newham & Essex Beagles		2	Basildon	22 Sep

1600 METRES MEDLEY

3:26.61 i	England		1	Cardiff	11 Feb
	(B.Ghent, A.Condon, A.Buckley, Edwards)				
3:27.3	Blackheath Harriers		1	Tonbridge	9 Sep
	(J.Wilkie, M.Champion, S.Jarred, A.Draper)				
3:28.14 i	Wales		2	Cardiff	11 Feb
	(J.Henthorn, C.Malcolm, J.Hillier, M.Shone)				
3:30.08 i	Midland Counties		2	Cardiff	17 Feb
	(Marshall, B.Ghent, Castillo, Vickers)				
3:31.54 i	England	U20	1	Cardiff	11 Feb
	(D.Grant, D.Girdler, M.Bradbury, R.Soos)				
3:32.1	Kent AC	U20	2	Tonbridge	9 Sep
	(C.Johnson, S.Wenden, C.Williams, J.Mays)				
3:32.44 i	Wales	U20	2	Cardiff	11 Feb
	(G.Llewellyn, T.Benjamin, G.Bevan, J.Nasrat)				

2001 LISTS - WOMEN

60 Metres - Indoors

7.27	Diane Allahgreen		21.02.75	1s2	Birmingham	27 Jan
	7.32			2	Birmingham	27 Jan
	7.38			8	Birmingham	18 Feb
	7.41			1h2	Birmingham	27 Jan
	7.42			1	Birmingham	13 Jan
	7.44			2s2	Birmingham	13 Jan
	7.47			1h4	Birmingham	13 Jan
7.28	Marcia Richardson		10.02.72	1	Birmingham	27 Jan
	7.34			6	Birmingham	18 Feb
	7.36			1h3	Birmingham	27 Jan
	7.36			1s1	Birmingham	27 Jan
	7.36			3	Glasgow	18 Mar
7.38	Christine Harrison-Bloomfield		12.02.68	3	Birmingham	27 Jan
	7.41			2s1	Birmingham	27 Jan
	7.45			1h1	Birmingham	27 Jan
	7.46			1r1	Birmingham	3 Feb
	7.49			2s1	Birmingham	13 Jan
	7.49			3	Birmingham	13 Jan
7.40	Donita Benjamin		7.03.72	2s2	Birmingham	27 Jan
	7.43			1s2	Birmingham	13 Jan
	7.46			1h4	Birmingham	27 Jan
	7.46			5	Birmingham	27 Jan
	7.49			2	Birmingham	13 Jan
7.40	Abi Oyepitan	U23	30.12.79	4	Birmingham	27 Jan
	7.44			3s2	Birmingham	27 Jan
7.44	Sam Davies	U23	20.09.79	1h2	Birmingham	13 Jan
	7.47			1s1	Birmingham	13 Jan
7.45	Susan Burnside	U23	3.02.80	3s1	Birmingham	27 Jan
	7.46			1s1	Glasgow	17 Feb
	7.47 !			1h1	Glasgow	21 Jan
	7.47			2h2	Birmingham	27 Jan
7.45	Amanda Forrester		29.09.78	4s2	Birmingham	27 Jan
	7.48			6	Birmingham	27 Jan
	7.49			1	Cardiff	11 Feb
	34 performances to 7.49 by 8 athletes					
7.52	Danielle Norville	U20	18.01.83	1s2	Birmingham	25 Feb
7.52	Katherine Endacott	U23	29.01.80	2	Cardiff	10 Mar
(10)						
7.54	Amy Spencer	U17	19.09.85	1	Birmingham	25 Feb
7.55	Lesley Owusu		21.12.78	4	Ames, USA	20 Jan
7.57	Tatum Nelson		17.12.78	3h4	Birmingham	27 Jan
7.59	Helen Roscoe	U23	4.12.79	4h3	Birmingham	27 Jan
7.60	Melanie Roberts		2.03.78	1r2	Birmingham	7 Jan
7.60	Vernicha James	U20	6.06.84	1h1	Birmingham	25 Feb
7.62	Emma Whitter	U23	20.07.80	3h2	Birmingham	27 Jan
7.63	Sinead Dudgeon		9.07.76	2	Glasgow	13 Jan
7.64	Emily Freeman	U23	24.11.80	2h4	Birmingham	13 Jan
7.64	Rebecca White	U23	5.06.80	1s3	Glasgow	17 Feb
(20)						
7.64	Karen Oughton	U20	26.01.83	1s1	Birmingham	25 Feb
7.65	Kathryn Evans	U20	1.03.84	1	Glasgow	4 Feb
7.66	Jeanette Kwakye	U20	20.03.83	2s2	Birmingham	25 Feb
7.67	Felicia Louisy		17.05.74	5s1	Birmingham	13 Jan
7.67	Ellena Ruddock		23.02.76	4h4	Birmingham	27 Jan
7.67	Angharad James	U23	7.04.79	8s2	Birmingham	27 Jan
7.72	Sharon Williams		20.05.70	2h1	Birmingham	27 Jan

7.73	Emma Bailey	U20	25.07.84	3s1	Birmingham	25 Feb
7.74	Nicola Gossman	U15	4.11.86	1	Glasgow	25 Jan
7.74	Xanine Powell	U23	21.05.79	5h4	Birmingham	27 Jan
	(30)					
7.74	Sinead Johnson	U15	24.12.86	1	Birmingham	25 Feb
7.75	Pamela Paterson	U17	26.10.85	2	Glasgow	25 Jan
7.75	Kelly Sotherton		13.11.76	3h1	Birmingham	3 Feb

Additional Under 17 (1 - 2 above)

7.83	Jemma Sims	2.05.85	1	Birmingham	3 Feb
7.85	Kimberley Velvick	3.01.85	1	Bedford	13 Jan
7.89	Kara Dunn	12.10.84	2	Birmingham	25 Feb
7.90	Laura Cunningham	14.02.85	1	Glasgow	4 Feb
7.90	Shereen Charles	27.10.84	3s2	Birmingham	25 Feb
7.91	Charlene Lashley	1.09.85	1h6	Birmingham	25 Feb
7.93	Yasmine Meite	6.09.84	4	Glasgow	4 Feb
7.94	Cara Roberts	24.05.85	2h2	Birmingham	25 Feb
	(10)				
7.94	Charli Croll	25.10.84	6s2	Birmingham	25 Feb
7.95	Tamara Doherty	15.11.85	1	Glasgow	28 Jan
7.95	Lauren Dickson	2.04.86	7s2	Birmingham	25 Feb

Additional Under 15 (1 - 2 above)

7.80	Louise Dickson	4.09.86	1	Glasgow	11 Feb
7.87	Lia Tappin	9.01.87	2	Birmingham	25 Feb
7.88	Louise Dickinson	5.11.86	2	Birmingham	4 Feb
7.97	Jemma Buttler	17.06.87	1rC	Birmingham	4 Feb
8.00	Carley Wenham	14.03.88	2h1	Birmingham	25 Feb
8.00	Michelle Nash	19.03.87	2h2	Birmingham	25 Feb
8.05	Jessica Tucker	3.06.87	1	Cardiff	4 Feb
8.05	Emma Heath	1.10.86	3	Birmingham	11 Feb
	(10)				
8.06	Natasha Date	18.11.86	4h3	Birmingham	25 Feb
8.08	Stacey Simpson	25.01.88	3	Glasgow	11 Feb
8.09	Danielle Barker	19.01.87	2	Cardiff	4 Feb

hand timing

7.5mx	Catherine Murphy		21.09.75	1	London (Ha)	4 Feb
7.5	Shani Anderson		7.08.75	1A1	London (CP)	7 Feb
7.7	Xanine Powell	U23	(7.74)	1r2	London (CP)	17 Jan
7.7	Lisa Miller	U20	13.01.83	1rB2	London (CP)	7 Feb
7.8	Kimberley Velvick	U17	(7.85)	2r1	London (CP)	7 Feb
7.9	Titi Ameobi	U17	20.11.84	1	Jarrow	7 Jan
7.9	Charli Croll	U17	(7.94)	1	London (CP)	17 Feb
8.0	Carly Jones	U15	(8.20)	1	Jarrow	25 Jan

Foreign

7.54	*Maiteland Marks (USA)*	*19.09.76*	*1s2*	*Glasgow*	*17 Feb*
7.58	*Sarah Reilly (IRL)*	*3.07.73*	*3s1*	*Birmingham*	*13 Jan*
7.69	*Leanne O'Callaghan (IRL)*	*15.07.74*	*6h3*	*Birmingham*	*27 Jan*

hand timing

7.5	*Maiteland Marks (USA)*	*(7.54i)*	*2*	*Glasgow*	*17 Feb*

75 Metres - Under 13

9.8		Felicity James	2.02.89	1	Cardiff	1 Jul
9.9		Hannah Frankson	11.01.89	1	Hayes	1 Jul
10.0		Joey Duck	14.04.89	1	London (CP)	20 May
10.0		Amy Gibbs	30.03.89	1	Enfield	1 Jul
10.05	0.6	Michaela McCalla		1r1	Birmingham	1 Sep
10.1		Natalie Doyle	5.01.89	1	Grangemouth	30 Jun
10.1		Stefanie Knight	4.02.89	1	Eton	1 Jul
10.1	-0.9	Lorraine Hoskins		1	Newport	22 Jul
10.1		Susan Roberts	22.11.88	1r1	Bournemouth	22 Jul

100 Metres

11.29	1.6	Abi Oyepitan	U23	30.12.79	2	Glasgow (S)	1	Jul
		11.29 0.0			1s2	Beijing, CHN	28	Aug
		11.31 1.3			1h4	Beijing, CHN	27	Aug
		11.42 -1.1			1	Beijing, CHN	28	Aug
		11.43 0.2			1h3	Amsterdam, NED	12	Jul
		11.45 -0.2			3h8	Edmonton, CAN	5	Aug
		11.46 0.0			1r2	Villeneuve d'Ascq, FRA	17	Jun
		11.47 -1.4			1q3	Beijing, CHN	27	Aug
		11.48 0.6			1	Glasgow (S)	6	May
		11.48 -0.9			1	Loughborough	20	May
		11.57 -0.8			1h3	Glasgow (S)	6	May
		11.58 -1.2			2	Amsterdam, NED	12	Jul
		11.61 -3.4			7q2	Edmonton, CAN	5	Aug
11.37	1.9	Amanda Forrester		29.09.78	1rB	Glasgow (S)	1	Jul
		11.40 1.7			2h5	Beijing, CHN	27	Aug
		11.44 1.0			2s1	Birmingham	14	Jul
		11.50 0.0			1	Birmingham	16	Jun
		11.54 -0.3			6	London (CP)	22	Jul
		11.56 -1.3			4h2	London (CP)	22	Jul
		11.58 1.7			2s1	Bedford	28	May
		11.61 -0.3			4s1	Beijing, CHN	28	Aug
		11.65 -1.5			4q2	Beijing, CHN	27	Aug
11.40	1.7	Shani Anderson		7.08.75	2B2	Walnut CA, USA	22	Apr
		11.46 1.8			3rB1	Bremen, GER	23	Jun
		11.46 0.6			1	Eton	7	Jul
		11.47 1.1			1h3	Birmingham	13	Jul
		11.48 0.3			4	Hengelo, NED	4	Jun
		11.48 -1.4			5r1	Arles, FRA	9	Jun
		11.50 1.9			3rB	Glasgow (S)	1	Jul
		11.54 -0.2			5h6	Edmonton, CAN	5	Aug
		11.58 1.6			2s2	Birmingham	14	Jul
		11.61 -0.9			3	Loughborough	20	May
		11.61 1.9			4	Bedford	18	Jul
11.42	-1.4	Joice Maduaka		30.09.73	3r1	Arles, FRA	9	Jun
		11.42 1.9			2rB	Glasgow (S)	1	Jul
		11.43 -0.3			1h2	Birmingham	13	Jul
		11.43 1.6			1s2	Birmingham	14	Jul
		11.47 1.7			3r1	Fullerton CA, USA	26	Apr
		11.51 -0.1			3h1	London (CP)	22	Jul
		11.52 -0.9			2	Loughborough	20	May
		11.54 -0.3			5	London (CP)	22	Jul
		11.55 1.9			2	Bedford	18	Jul
		11.61 -2.8			2	Stellenbosch, RSA	30	Mar
		11.63 A 0.3			7	Pretoria, RSA	23	Mar
		11.64 0.0			5	Zagreb, CRO	2	Jul
11.43	1.7	Marcia Richardson		10.02.72	2r1	Fullerton CA, USA	26	Apr
		11.44 1.0			1s1	Birmingham	14	Jul
		11.46 1.8			2rB1	Bremen, GER	23	Jun
		11.48 1.4			2h4	Birmingham	13	Jul
		11.52 1.6			4	Glasgow (S)	1	Jul
		11.52 -0.5			4h3	Edmonton, CAN	5	Aug
		11.57 -1.4			6r1	Arles, FRA	9	Jun
		11.59 -1.3			8q4	Edmonton, CAN	5	Aug
		11.60 -0.1			4h1	London (CP)	22	Jul
		11.62 -0.8			1h2	London (Ha)	16	Jun
		11.64 -0.9			1	London (Ha)	16	Jun
11.44	1.0	Sarah Wilhelmy	U23	2.02.80	1r4	Irvine CA, USA	6	May
		11.45 1.0			3s1	Birmingham	14	Jul
		11.47 1.4			1h4	Birmingham	13	Jul

(Wilhelmy)		11.48 1.9			1	Bedford	18 Jul
		11.52 -1.3			3h2	London (CP)	22 Jul
		11.54 -0.3			7	London (CP)	22 Jul
		11.55			5	Bridgetown, BAR	19 May
11.48	1.7	Catherine Murphy		21.09.75	3B2	Walnut CA, USA	22 Apr
11.50	1.7	Diane Allahgreen		21.02.75	1s1	Bedford	28 May
		11.59 1.9			3	Bedford	18 Jul
		11.63 0.6			2	Glasgow (S)	6 May
		11.65 -0.9			1rB	Loughborough	20 May
11.63	1.1	Donita Benjamin		7.03.72	2h3	Birmingham	13 Jul
		69 performances to 11.65 by 9 athletes					
11.66	1.6	Amy Spencer	U17	19.09.85	3	Mannheim, GER	16 Jun
	(10)						
11.67	1.0	Christine Harrison-Bloomfield		12.02.68	3r4	Irvine CA, USA	6 May
11.68	1.9	Sabrina Scott	U23	2.06.79	4h1	Tula, RUS	9 Jun
11.73	1.5	Helen Roscoe	U23	4.12.79	1rB	Eton	7 Jul
11.74	1.4	Susan Burnside	U23	3.02.80	1	Glasgow (S)	24 Jun
11.75		Danielle Norville	U20	18.01.83	1	Bridgetown, BAR	27 Mar
11.77	-0.2	Sam Davies	U23	20.09.79	6r2	Bremen, GER	24 Jun
11.82	-2.5	Jade Lucas-Read	U20	17.01.84	1	Murcia, ESP	24 Jul
11.83	1.0	Susie Williams		2.06.77	4s1	Birmingham	14 Jul
11.85	1.5	Simmone Jacobs		5.09.66	2rB	Eton	7 Jul
11.86	-0.3	Anyika Onuora	U17	28.10.84	2	Dole, FRA	29 Jul
	(20)						
11.87	0.6	Kelly Thomas	U23	9.01.81	3	Eton	7 Jul
11.90	1.8	Montell Douglas	U17	24.01.86	1	Birmingham	1 Sep
11.91	1.4	Natalie Beattie		30.01.78	2	Glasgow (S)	24 Jun
11.92	1.7	Emily Freeman	U23	24.11.80	4s1	Bedford	28 May
11.92	-0.3	Melanie Roberts		2.03.78	3h2	Birmingham	13 Jul
11.94	1.1	Jenny Meadows	U23	17.04.81	1r2	Gainesville FL, USA	21 Apr
11.94	1.1	Katherine Endacott	U23	29.01.80	4h3	Birmingham	13 Jul
11.96	0.0	Sinead Dudgeon		9.07.76	2	Edinburgh	12 May
11.96	1.4	Sharon Wilson		27.10.74	3	Glasgow (S)	24 Jun
11.98	1.7	Zoe Wilson		28.08.76	7r1	Fullerton CA, USA	26 Apr
	(30)						
11.98	0.6	Rebecca White	U23	5.06.80	4	Glasgow (S)	6 May
11.99	1.8	Lesley Owusu		21.12.78	3	Birmingham	30 Jun
12.00	1.4	Sian Robinson	U20	31.03.82	2h2	Bedford	30 Jun
12.00	0.6	Kelly Sotherton		13.11.76	4	Eton	7 Jul
12.01	-0.3	Amala Onuora	U17	16.03.86	4	Dole, FRA	29 Jul
12.02	2.0	Claire Rooney	U20	23.08.83	1	Grangemouth	10 Jun
12.03	0.1	Jeanette Kwakye	U20	20.03.83	1h1	Exeter	6 Jul
12.04	0.4	Rachel King		11.05.76	1	Cardiff	16 Jun
12.05	-0.9	Melanie Purkiss	U23	11.03.79	7	Loughborough	20 May
12.05	0.0	Vernicha James	U20	6.06.84	1h1	Watford	27 May
	(40)						
12.05	1.4	Karen Oughton	U20	26.01.83	3h2	Bedford	30 Jun
12.05	0.4	Donna Fraser		7.11.72	5	Braga, POR	4 Jul
12.06	-0.3	Angharad James	U23	7.04.79	5h2	Birmingham	13 Jul
12.09	-0.3	Eleanor Caney	U20	28.05.84	1	Birmingham	26 May
12.09	1.4	Sara Whigham	U20	7.10.83	4	Glasgow (S)	24 Jun
12.10	1.4	Helen Williams		2.06.77	3h4	Birmingham	13 Jul
12.11	1.9	Kadi-Ann Thomas	U17	10.02.86	2	Sheffield	11 Aug
12.12		Sinead Johnson	U15	24.12.86	1	Birmingham	26 May
12.12	1.1	Ellena Ruddock		23.02.76	5h3	Birmingham	13 Jul
12.13	0.8	Nicola Gossman	U15	4.11.86	2	Tullamore, IRL	21 Jul
	(50)						
12.14	0.8	Ann Danson		4.05.71	2rC	Eton	7 Jul
12.14	0.5	Amina Ceesay	U23	19.11.79	1	Bedford	22 Jul
12.14	0.8	Janine Whitlock		11.08.73	1	Cudworth	26 Aug
12.15		Kathryn Evans	U20	1.03.84	1	Inverness	22 Apr

12.15	0.8	Kirsteen McDiarmid	U17	28.04.86	3	Tullamore, IRL	21 Jul
12.15	1.9	Jemma Sims	U17	2.05.85	3	Sheffield	11 Aug
12.16	1.1	Felicia Louisy		17.05.74	6h3	Birmingham	13 Jul
12.18	1.8	Clare Milborrow		10.01.77	1	Crawley	12 May
12.18		Keeley Butler		24.03.75	2	Grangemouth	26 Aug
12.19	1.1	Julie Pratt	U23	20.03.79	2h3	Torrevieja, ESP	14 Apr
	(60)						
12.19	1.4	Emma Bryson	U23	5.04.81	6	Glasgow (S)	24 Jun
12.20	1.4	Karen Gear	U23	30.09.79	3h4	London (Ha)	16 Jun
12.20	1.7	Louise Hazel	U17	6.10.85	2s1	Exeter	6 Jul
12.20		Vicki Jamison		19.05.77	1	Belfast	28 Jul
12.21	1.7	Katherine Livesey	U23	15.12.79	1r1	Lincoln, USA	12 May
12.21	1.4	Lowri Jones	U20	22.07.83	5h2	Bedford	30 Jun
12.21	1.4	Lucy Stockbridge	U23	1.07.79	4h4	Birmingham	13 Jul
12.25	1.8	Nicole Crosby		23.10.76	6	Birmingham	30 Jun
12.25	0.0	Lanre Atijosan	U15	17.10.86	1h1	Exeter	6 Jul
12.25	1.1	Lisa Allen		7.04.78	7h3	Birmingham	13 Jul
	(70)						
12.25	0.8	Christina Clubley	U17	4.11.85	2	Cudworth	26 Aug
12.27	-0.8	Kate Denham	U23	18.03.80	3h2	London (Ha)	16 Jun
12.27	1.5	Titi Ameobi	U17	20.11.84	1h3	Exeter	6 Jul
12.28	1.7	Amy Dowsett	U17	30.12.84	3s1	Exeter	6 Jul
12.29	1.4	Carolyn McKenna	U20	4.05.84	6h2	Bedford	30 Jun
12.29	1.5	Clova Court	V40	10.02.60	3rB	Eton	7 Jul
12.29	1.9	Carley Wenham	(U15)	14.03.88	1	London (He)	26 Aug

Additional Under 17 (1 - 11 above)

12.30	1.2	Shereen Charles	27.10.84	3	Watford	27 May
12.30	1.5	Molly Russell	3.08.86	2h3	Exeter	6 Jul
12.31	1.3	Sarah Blackwell	1.10.84	2h4	Exeter	6 Jul
12.35	1.7	Nichola Nutting	14.09.84	5s1	Exeter	6 Jul
12.40	1.4	Louisa Wells	30.12.84	1h2	Watford	27 May
12.41	1.9	Nicole MacDermott	15.08.86	7	Sheffield	11 Aug
12.43	0.8	Kelly Massey	11.01.86	4h2	Exeter	6 Jul
12.49	1.2	Katie Flaherty	1.10.85	6	Watford	27 May
12.49	0.8	Kelly Birkin	27.04.86	6	Tullamore, IRL	21 Jul
	(20)					
12.49	-1.5	Michelle Webster	18.04.85	2	Bamburg, GER	15 Sep
12.50	1.2	Kimberley Velvick	3.01.85	7	Watford	27 May
12.52		Gemma Thompson	17.01.86	1	Antrim	9 Jun
12.54	1.3	Amanda Shaw	28.09.84	6s2	Sheffield	11 Aug
12.55		Pamela Paterson	26.10.85	1	Aberdeen	27 May
12.56	1.3	Kara Dunn	12.10.84	5h4	Exeter	6 Jul
12.57	1.9	Charli Croll	25.10.84	2h1	Watford	27 May
12.57		Jackie Scott	31.01.85	1rB	Grangemouth	26 Aug
12.58		Eleanor Richardson	1.07.86	1	Inverness	19 Aug
12.59	1.5	Sarah Holmes	21.11.85	3h3	Exeter	6 Jul
	(30)					
12.59	0.8	Sophie Newington	15.09.85	8	Tullamore, IRL	21 Jul

Additional Under 15 (1 - 4 above)

12.31		Denae Matthew	3.04.87	2	Birmingham	26 May
12.47	-0.8	Louise Dickson	4.09.86	1r1	Birmingham	2 Sep
12.49	1.9	Deandra Smith	3.12.86	2	London (He)	26 Aug
12.50	0.1	Emma Strachan	10.04.87	2h3	Exeter	6 Jul
12.52	0.7	Jemma Buttler	17.06.87	1r1	Birmingham	1 Sep
12.60	0.1	Tanya Hinds	19.05.88	3h3	Exeter	6 Jul
	(10)					
12.62	1.9	Lauren Duncan	21.03.88	3	London (He)	26 Aug
12.62		Kim Skinner	21.09.87	2	Grangemouth	26 Aug

wind assisted

11.17	3.7	Abi Oyepitan	U23	(11.29)	1	Bedford	30 Jun
		11.20 2.9			1	Bedford	28 May
		11.24 2.7			1h1	Bedford	30 Jun
		11.43 3.0			1s1	Bedford	28 May
11.24	2.5	Sarah Wilhelmy	U23	(11.44)	1r2	Arles, FRA	9 Jun
		11.41 2.3			1	Birmingham	14 Jul
11.38	2.9	Diane Allahgreen		(11.50)	2	Bedford	28 May
11.38	5.6	Joice Maduaka		(11.42)	1	Bangor	2 Jun
		11.42 2.3			3	Birmingham	14 Jul
		11.45 2.8			5	Bremen, GER	23 Jun
11.40	2.9	Forrester		(11.37)	3	Bedford	28 May
		11.41 2.2			1h1	Birmingham	13 Jul
		11.42 2.3			2	Birmingham	14 Jul
11.42	2.9	Marcia Richardson		(11.43)	4	Bedford	28 May
		11.44 5.6			1	Bedford	21 Jul
		11.45 2.3			4	Birmingham	14 Jul
		11.59 3.0			2s2	Bedford	28 May
11.43	3.4	Vernicha James	U20	(12.05)	3r1	Azusa, USA	14 Apr
		11.44 3.5			1	Bedford	30 Jun
		11.61 2.9			1h1	Bedford	30 Jun
11.45	3.2	Anderson		(11.40)	2	Claremont, USA	20 Apr
		11.52 2.3			5	Birmingham	14 Jul
		11.58 3.4			5	Azusa, USA	14 Apr
11.50	2.5	Christine Bloomfield	(11.67)	2r2	Arles, FRA		9 Jun
11.50	3.7	Sabrina Scott	U23	(11.68)	2	Bedford	30 Jun
		11.60 2.9			5	Bedford	28 May
11.59	2.5	Sam Davies	U23	(11.77)	3rB	Arles, FRA	9 Jun
11.61	3.7	Susan Burnside	U23	(11.74)	3	Bedford	30 Jun
11.63	2.9	Murphy		(11.48)	6	Bedford	28 May
11.64	3.5	Jade Lucas-Read	U20	(11.82)	2J	Bedford	30 Jun
11.65	2.9	Benjamin		(11.63)	7	Bedford	28 May
		31 performances to 11.65 by 15 athletes					
11.66	3.7	Emily Freeman	U23	(11.92)	4	Bedford	30 Jun
11.69	4.2	Danielle Norville	U20	(11.75)	1	Exeter	7 Jul
11.71	4.4	Kelly Thomas	U23	(11.87)	5	Bedford	30 Jun
11.74	5.3	Melanie Roberts		(11.92)	2	Liverpool	17 Jun
11.74	3.7	Melanie Purkiss	U23	(12.05)	6	Bedford	30 Jun
11.75	4.4	Janine Whitlock		(12.14)	1	Birmingham	2 Jun
11.76		Claire Lomas	U23	18.04.80	1	Edinburgh	1 Apr
11.76	3.7	Katherine Endacott	U23	(11.94)	7	Bedford	30 Jun
11.81	4.0	Tatum Nelson		17.12.78	1rB	Birmingham	2 Jun
11.82	2.7	Rebecca White	U23	(11.98)	3h1	Bedford	30 Jun
11.83	2.8	Sian Robinson	U20	(12.00)	1	Tamworth	27 Aug
11.86	5.3	Ann Danson		(12.14)	3	Liverpool	17 Jun
11.86	3.6	Amina Ceesay	U23	(12.14)	4h2	Bedford	30 Jun
11.87	2.9	Montell Douglas	U17	(11.90)	1	London (He)	26 Aug
11.88	4.2	Jeanette Kwakye	U20	(12.03)	3	Exeter	7 Jul
11.90	5.6	Ellena Ruddock		(12.12)	3	Bedford	21 Jul
11.92	2.9	Eleanor Caney	U20	(12.09)	1h3	Bedford	30 Jun
11.92	2.4	Sinead Johnson	U15	(12.12)	1	Sheffield	11 Aug
11.93	2.7	Lesley Owusu		(11.99)	2r2	Lincoln, USA	12 May
11.94	2.2	Lisa Miller	U20	13.01.83	1	Watford	27 May
11.96	5.5	Karen Oughton	U20	(12.05)	4	Bangor	2 Jun
11.96	2.2	Xanine Powell	U23	21.05.79	5h1	Birmingham	13 Jul
11.97	2.3	Amala Onuora	U17	(12.01)	1s1	Sheffield	11 Aug
12.01	3.3	Louise Hazel	U17	(12.20)	3	Exeter	7 Jul
12.03	2.9	Carley Wenham	U15	(12.29)	2	Exeter	7 Jul

12.04	3.0	Sara Whigham	U20	(12.09)	1h1	Glasgow (S)	24 Jun
12.04	2.8	Jemma Sims	U17	(12.15)	1h2	Sheffield	11 Aug
12.05	3.3	Kadi-Ann Thomas	U17	(12.11)	4	Exeter	7 Jul
12.06	5.3	Nicole Crosby		(12.25)	4	Liverpool	17 Jun
12.07	2.9	Kathryn Evans	U20	(12.15)	3h3	Bedford	30 Jun
12.07	3.3	Titi Ameobi	U17	(12.27)	5	Exeter	7 Jul
12.08	3.6	Lucy Stockbridge	U23	(12.21)	5h2	Bedford	30 Jun
12.09	2.4	Nicola Gossman	U15	(12.13)	2	Sheffield	11 Aug
12.13	4.0	Clova Court	V40	(12.29)	2rB	Birmingham	2 Jun
12.14	3.2	Anna Boyle	U20	29.03.83	1	Antrim	16 Jun
12.17	3.0	Sharon Williams		20.05.70	6s2	Bedford	28 May
12.18	2.7	Fiona Westwood	U23	27.02.81	4h1	Bedford	30 Jun
12.18	2.9	Lanre Atijosan	U15	(12.25)	3	Exeter	7 Jul
12.19	2.8	Christina Clubley	U17	(12.25)	2h2	Sheffield	11 Aug
12.20	5.6	Janette Niccolls		7.09.76	3	Bedford	22 Jul
12.21	4.2	Jemma Buttler	U15	(12.52)	2s1	Sheffield	11 Aug
12.22	4.4	Helen Thieme	U23	28.09.81	5	Birmingham	2 Jun
12.23	4.0	Melanie Pickersgill		20.04.73	4rB	Birmingham	2 Jun
12.23	3.3	Shereen Charles	U17	(12.30)	7	Exeter	7 Jul
12.24	4.0	Syreena Pinel	U23	13.01.79	5rB	Birmingham	2 Jun
12.26	4.2	Tamsin Lees	U20	24.04.84	5	Exeter	7 Jul
12.26	2.8	Rachel Harris	U20	17.07.82	2	Tamworth	27 Aug
12.28	5.3	Maria Morganella	U23	2.10.79	7	Liverpool	17 Jun
12.28	4.2	Stephanie Squires	U20	3.11.82	6	Exeter	7 Jul
12.28	5.6	Lisa Vannet		8.11.74	7	Bedford	21 Jul
12.29	2.9	Denae Matthew	U15	(12.31)	4	Exeter	7 Jul

Additional Under 17 (1 - 8 above)

12.33	3.0	Nichola Nutting	(12.35)	2h4	Sheffield	11 Aug
12.34	2.3	Nicole MacDermott	(12.41)	4s1	Sheffield	11 Aug
12.45	2.3	Tamara Doherty	15.11.85	6s1	Sheffield	11 Aug
12.46		Pamela Paterson	(12.55)	1	Edinburgh	1 Apr
12.46	3.0	Kelly Birkin	(12.49)	1h2	Cardiff	16 Jun
12.49	3.0	Lauren Dickson	2.04.86	4h1	Glasgow (S)	24 Jun
12.57	2.6	Katy Benneworth	5.10.84	4h3	Sheffield	11 Aug
12.58	2.3	Katie-Jane Mather	7.01.86	5h1	Sheffield	11 Aug
12.59	2.3	Katherine Jones	21.01.85	8s1	Sheffield	11 Aug

Additional Under 15 (1 - 6 above)

12.37		Louise Dickson	(12.47)	1r2	Edinburgh	1 Apr
12.43	2.9	Emma Strachan	(12.50)	5	Exeter	7 Jul
12.47	2.8	Danielle Barker	19.01.87	1	Cardiff	17 Jun
12.49	2.8	Jessica Tucker	3.06.87	2	Cardiff	17 Jun
12.49	4.2	Natalie Jowett	18.09.86	4s1	Sheffield	11 Aug
12.57	2.9	Tanya Hinds	(12.60)	7	Exeter	7 Jul
12.58	2.2	Joanna Birch	21.04.87	3h4	Sheffield	11 Aug
12.58	4.2	Anastasia Morrison	4.09.86	6s1	Sheffield	11 Aug
12.59	2.8	Danielle Price	8.11.86	3	Cardiff	17 Jun

hand timing

11.5	2.0	Oyepitan	U23	(11.29)	1h2	Bedford	28 May
11.5 w	3.1	Allahgreen		(11.50)	1h3	Bedford	28 May
11.6 mx		Forrester		(11.37)	1	Cannock	12 May
		11.6 1.5			1h4	Bedford	28 May
		11.6 0.7			1	Rugby	10 Jun
		11.6 w 3.2			1	London (Cr)	3 Jun
11.6 w	2.1	Richardson		(11.43)	1h1	Bedford	28 May
11.6 w	5.8	Susan Burnside	U23	(11.74)	1	Wigan	10 Jun

8 performances to 11.6 by 5 athletes including 4 wind assisted

11.8	-0.4	Emily Freeman	U23	(11.92)	2	Wigan	4	Aug
11.8 w	3.2	Jenny Meadows	U23	(11.94)	2	London (Cr)	3	Jun
11.9		Katherine Endacott	U23	(11.94)	1	Portsmouth	28	Apr
11.9		Rebecca White	U23	(11.98)	1	Guernsey	2	Jun
11.9	0.7	Ellena Ruddock		(12.12)	1	Coventry	5	Aug
11.9		Kim Wall	U20	21.04.83	1	Eton	11	Aug
11.9 w		Janette Niccolls		(12.20w)	1	Bournemouth	11	Aug
12.0		Karen Oughton	U20	(12.05)	1	Leamington	12	May
12.0		Eleanor Caney	U20	(12.09)	1	Stourport	12	May
12.0	1.1	Jade Johnson	U23	7.06.80	2	Kingston	12	May
12.0		Jemma Sims	U17	(12.15)	1	Nottingham	13	May
12.0		Helen Williams		(12.10)	1	Brighton	23	Jun
12.0		Melanie Purkiss	U23	(12.05)	2	Liverpool	8	Jul
12.0 w		Nicola Gossman	U15	(12.13)	1	Glasgow (S)	3	Jun
12.0 w		Kirsteen McDiarmid	U17	(12.15)	1	Glasgow (S)	3	Jun
12.0 w	3.1	Ellie Mardle		27.07.78	1	Stafford	7	Jul
12.0 w	2.7	Angharad James	U23	(12.06)	2	Wigan	8	Jul
12.1		Kay Reynolds		15.09.67	1	Abingdon	28	Apr
12.1		Sarah Zawada	U20	9.04.82	2	Abingdon	28	Apr
12.1		Kate Denham	U23	(12.27)	1	Braunton	19	May
12.1	1.5	Xanine Powell	U23	(11.96w)	4h4	Bedford	28	May
12.1	1.5	Sharon Williams		(12.17w)	5h4	Bedford	28	May
12.1		Lanre Atijosan	U15	(12.25)	1	Brighton	23	Jun
12.1		Michelle Turner		25.12.77	1	Kingston	23	Jun
12.1		Carley Wenham	U15	(12.29)	1	Eton	1	Jul
12.1		Shereen Charles	U17	(12.30)	1rB	Hayes	1	Jul
12.1		Sarah Blackwell	U17	(12.31)	2	Bebington	1	Jul
12.1		Ann Danson		(12.14)	1rB	Wigan	4	Aug
12.1	0.9	Keeley Butler		(12.18)	1rB	Coventry	5	Aug
12.1 w	3.1	Lisa Allen		(12.25)	5h2	Bedford	28	May
12.1 w	3.1	Kim Goodwin		16.05.70	2	Stafford	7	Jul
12.1 w	2.8	Kate Brewington	U23	15.10.81	1	Stafford	8	Sep

Additional Under 17 (1 - 4 above)

12.2		Gemma Thompson	(12.52)	1	Derry	5	May
12.2		Titi Ameobi	(12.27)	1	Gateshead	9	Jun
12.2		Louisa Wells	(12.40)	1	Bury St. Edmunds	1	Jul
12.2		Kelly Massey	(12.43)	2	Telford	1	Jul
12.2		Nichola Nutting	(12.35)	1	Nuneaton	22	Jul
12.2		Laura Ridley	20.03.86	1	Bury	22	Jul
12.2		Amanda Shaw	(12.54)	1	Cudworth	5	Aug
12.2		Nicola Robinson	16.04.86	2	Nuneaton	5	Aug
12.2 w		Tamara Doherty	(12.45w)	2	Glasgow (S)	3	Jun
12.3		Jessica Ennis	28.01.86	2	Sheffield	28	Apr
12.3	1.9	Katherine Jones	(12.59w)	1	Cannock	12	May
12.3		Kara Dunn	(12.56)	1	Hayes	1	Jul
12.3		Katie-Jane Mather	(12.58w)	2	Nuneaton	22	Jul
12.3 w	2.7	Katie Flaherty	(12.49)	1	Southend	12	May
		12.4		3	Stafford	20	May
12.3 w	5.3	Kimberley Velvick	(12.50)	1h1	Ashford	12	May
		12.4		1	Erith	9	Jun
12.3 w		Lucy Davidson	19.11.85	1	Yate	22	Jul
12.4		Joy Danby	5.09.84	1	Hull	9	Apr
12.4		Kiri Burbidge	2.10.85	1	Bournemouth	12	May
12.4	0.4	Symone Belle	12.11.84	1	London (He)	12	May
12.4	0.9	Natasha Cross	13.11.84	1	Exeter	16	Jun

12.4		Hannah Elwiss	8.12.84	1	Warrington	24 Jun
12.4		Leah Caddick	1.06.86	3	Bebington	1 Jul
12.4		Claire Warmington	7.06.85	4	Bebington	1 Jul
12.4 w	3.3	Katy Benneworth	(12.57w)	1h2	Ashford	12 May
12.4 w		Lauren Dickson	(12.49w)	3	Glasgow (S)	3 Jun
12.4 w		Amy Woodman	1.11.84	2	Yate	22 Jul

Additional Under 15 (1 - 3 above)

12.2		Victoria Burgess	4.10.86	2	Southampton	20 May
12.3		Louise Dickson	(12.47)	1	Coatbridge	30 Jun
12.3		Jemma Buttler	(12.52)	1r1	Telford	1 Jul
12.4		Lia Tappin	9.01.87	1	Enfield	1 Jul
12.4		Claire Jones	8.11.86	1	Aberdare	18 Aug
12.4		Deandra Smith	(12.49)	1	St. Albans	19 Aug
12.4		Natalie Jowett	(12.49w)	2	St. Albans	19 Aug
12.5		Tanya Hinds	(12.60)	2	Leicester	9 Jun
12.5		Venita Akpofure	1.01.87	1	Hayes	1 Jul
12.5		Kim Skinner	(12.62)	1	Grangemouth	9 Sep
12.5		Louise Dickinson	5.11.86	1	Blackpool	9 Sep
12.5 w	2.7	Camilla Harkness	10.01.87	3	Watford	26 May
		12.6 -0.9		1	Kingston	12 May
12.5 w	3.6	Hollie Buckingham	3.12.86	1	Exeter	16 Jun
12.5 w	3.6	Natasha Date	18.11.86	2	Exeter	16 Jun
12.6	1.4	Chloe Walcott	29.01.88	h	Kingston	12 May
12.6		Sabina Astarita	15.10.86	1h2	Glasgow (S)	7 Jun
12.6		Rachel Follos	15.10.86	2	Birmingham	9 Jun
12.6		Laura Willey	22.10.86	1	Bebington	1 Jul
12.6		Lucy Ellis	5.02.88	1	Newport	9 Sep
12.6 w		Sola Odunsi	22.08.87	1	Bedford	9 Sep

Under 13

12.9		Cherelle Norriston	29.11.88	2r1	London (TB)	14 Jul
		13.06 1.1		1r3	London (Ha)	7 Apr
12.93	1.4	Felicity James	2.02.89	1	Cardiff	17 Jun
13.0		Joey Duck	14.04.89	2	Crawley	28 Apr
		13.04 w 3.5		1	London (Ha)	
13.0		Stefanie Knight	4.02.89	1	London (TB)	17 Jun
13.0		Emma Baker	22.09.88	1	Carn Brea	8 Jul
13.0		Annabelle Lewis	20.03.89	1	London (TB)	28 Jul
13.1		Laura Hitchman	14.10.88	3r1	Brighton	23 Jun
13.1		Lorraine Hoskins		1	Birmingham	11 Jul
13.1		Joanne Smith	23.09.88	1	Glasgow	9 Sep
13.1		Sarah Roney	27.03.89	2	Glasgow	9 Sep
	(10)					
13.1		Rebecca Williams	18.03.89	1r2	Newport	9 Sep
13.1		Kayleigh Hill	12.12.88	1	Rotherham	15 Sep
13.2		Amy Gibbs	30.03.89	1	Bromley	16 Jun
13.2		Teresa Andrews		1	Swindon	23 Jun
13.2		Louise Hamilton	19.09.88	3	Glasgow	9 Sep
13.2		Zoe Llewelyn	5.10.88	1	Newport	9 Sep
		13.28 1.4		3	Cardiff	17 Jun
13.2 w	3.3	Charlotte Owen	27.12.88	1h1	Cardiff	17 Jun
		13.24 1.4		2	Cardiff	17 Jun
13.21		Hannah Frankson	11.01.89	1	London (Nh)	26 Aug

Doubtful

12.7		Felicity James	(12.93)	1	Cardiff	11 Jul

Foreign

11.53 w	*5.6*	*Sarah Reilly (IRL)*		*3.07.73*	*2*	*Bangor*	*2 Jun*
		11.63 2.0			*1*	*Palafrugell, ESP*	*19 May*
11.60	*0.8*	*Chioma Ajunwa ¶ (NGR)*		*25.12.71*	*1rC*	*Eton*	*7 Jul*
11.88 w	*5.6*	*Leanne O'Callaghan (IRL)*		*15.07.74*	*3*	*Bangor*	*2 Jun*
		12.1 2.0			*3h2*	*Bedford*	*28 May*
		12.26 -1.7			*6*	*Cork, IRL*	*7 Jul*
12.0		*Maiteland Marks (USA)*		*19.09.76*	*1*	*Loughborough*	*23 May*
12.09 w	*5.3*	*Margaret Veldman (NED)*		*7.06.74*	*5*	*Liverpool*	*17 Jun*

150 Metres - Under 13

19.2		Joey Duck		14.04.89	1	London (CP)	20 May
19.4		Felicity James		2.02.89	1	Yate	22 Jul
19.6		Lorraine Hoskins			1	Sutton Coldfield	1 Jul
19.7		Stefanie Knight		4.02.89	1	Eton	1 Jul
19.9		Sharifa Logan			1	Telford	1 Jul
19.9		Emma Baker		22.09.88	1	Portsmouth	1 Jul
20.0		Helen McDonnell		19.02.89	2	London (CP)	20 May
20.0		Annabelle Lewis		20.03.89	1	Wakefield	1 Jul
20.0		Sarah Schofield		8.10.88	1	Bebington	1 Jul
20.1		Shaliena Mars			3	London (CP)	20 May
	(10)						
20.1		Carling Meadows		26.09.88	1	Bebington	1 Jul
20.1		Charlotte O'Halloran			2	Yate	22 Jul
20.16	1.1	Michaela McCalla			1r1	Birmingham	1 Sep
20.2		Amy Gibbs		30.03.89	1	Erith	7 May
20.2		Susan Roberts		22.11.88	1	Portsmouth	1 Jul

200 Metres

22.93	1.4	Vernicha James	U20	6.06.84	1	Grosseto, ITA	21 Jul
		23.30 1.8			2	Mannheim, GER	16 Jun
		23.44 -0.1			1h3	Grosseto, ITA	21 Jul
23.12	0.0	Katharine Merry		21.09.74	1	Austin TX, USA	5 May
		23.21 0.3			6	Bremen, GER	24 Jun
23.14 A	1.0	Joice Maduaka		30.09.73	1	Pretoria, RSA	23 Mar
		23.31 -1.3			1	Stellenbosch, RSA	30 Mar
		23.33 0.9			1r1	Fullerton CA, USA	26 Apr
		23.42 -0.1			1rB	Loughborough	20 May
		23.52 -1.2			1h1	London (Ha)	17 Jun
		23.62 -1.7			1	London (Ha)	17 Jun
		23.71 A 0.0			3	Roodepoort, RSA	16 Mar
		23.73 -1.4			5	Cuxhaven, GER	21 May
		23.73 0.0			4	Ingolstadt, GER	27 May
23.27	-0.1	Sarah Wilhelmy	U23	2.02.80	3	Bridgetown, BAR	19 May
		23.37 0.5			4	Nuremberg, GER	17 Jun
23.35 i		Catherine Murphy		21.09.75	1	Birmingham	28 Jan
		23.36 i			1s1	Birmingham	28 Jan
		23.70 i			1	Birmingham	7 Jan
		23.73 i			1	Birmingham	14 Jan
		23.73 i			1h2	Birmingham	14 Jan
		23.73 i			1h3	Birmingham	28 Jan
		23.74			1	Eton	7 Jul
		23.75 i			1s1	Birmingham	14 Jan
23.43	1.2	Shani Anderson		7.08.75	2	Birmingham	15 Jul
		23.44 -0.6			1	Loughborough	20 May
		23.59 -0.3			1rB	Eton	7 Jul
23.45	0.0	Amy Spencer	U17	19.09.85	2	Debrecen, HUN	15 Jul
		23.63 0.4			1s3	Debrecen, HUN	14 Jul
23.61 i		Donna Fraser		7.11.72	4	Birmingham	18 Feb
		23.74 i			2s1	Birmingham	28 Jan
		23.97 0.9			3	Braga, POR	4 Jul

23.61	1.8	Danielle Norville	U20	18.01.83	4	Mannheim, GER	16 Jun
		23.75 -1.6			2	Bridgetown, BAR	16 Apr
23.66	-0.4	Lee McConnell		9.10.78	1	Grangemouth	7 Jul
	(10)						
23.67 i		Emily Freeman	U23	24.11.80	1s2	Birmingham	28 Jan
		23.72 -0.8			1	Derby	29 Jul
23.71	1.1	Abi Oyepitan	U23	30.12.79	1	Birmingham	2 Jun
23.73 i		Lesley Owusu		21.12.78	1	Lincoln, USA	24 Feb
		23.86 0.6			1	Lincoln, USA	12 May
23.77	1.2	Christine Bloomfield		12.02.68	1r3	Irvine CA, USA	6 May
23.79	1.2	Susie Williams		2.06.77	3	Birmingham	15 Jul
		40 performances to 23.79 by 15 athletes including 11 indoors					
23.80		Helen Roscoe	U23	4.12.79	2	Eton	7 Jul
23.81 i		Sam Davies	U23	20.09.79	2s2	Birmingham	28 Jan
		24.57 -3.3			3	Meilen, SUI	17 Jun
23.88	-0.4	Susan Burnside	U23	3.02.80	1h2	Edinburgh	13 May
23.99	-0.1	Marcia Richardson		10.02.72	3rB	Loughborough	20 May
24.06	-0.7	Melanie Purkiss	U23	11.03.79	5r1	Tula, RUS	9 Jun
	(20)						
24.07	1.1	Tatum Nelson		17.12.78	2	Birmingham	2 Jun
24.09 i		Lisa Miller	U20	13.01.83	2	Birmingham	24 Feb
		24.21 -0.1			4rB	Loughborough	20 May
24.11 i		Ellena Ruddock		23.02.76	2h1	Birmingham	28 Jan
		25.07 1.1			6	Bedford	21 Jul
24.17	1.3	Kelly Sotherton		13.11.76	1H1	Arles, FRA	9 Jun
24.18	-2.1	Sinead Dudgeon		9.07.76	2	Edinburgh	13 May
24.22 i		Emma Whitter	U23	20.07.80	2r1	Birmingham	3 Feb
24.32	0.9	Kerry Jury		19.11.68	1H	Ried, AUT	30 Jun
24.33	-1.0	Kim Wall	U20	21.04.83	2h2	London (Ha)	17 Jun
24.36	-3.0	Helen Frost		12.03.74	1	Stellenbosch, RSA	23 Feb
24.37	1.1	Helen Thieme	U23	28.09.81	4	Birmingham	2 Jun
	(30)						
24.37	-0.8	Angharad James	U23	7.04.79	3	Derby	29 Jul
24.40	-1.2	Sabrina Scott	U23	2.06.79	2h1	London (Ha)	17 Jun
24.42	-0.1	Eleanor Caney	U20	28.05.84	5rB	Loughborough	20 May
24.51	1.2	Natalie Beattie		30.01.78	4	Birmingham	15 Jul
24.58	-1.0	Kate Denham	U23	18.03.80	3h2	London (Ha)	17 Jun
24.58	1.1	Kelly Thomas	U23	9.01.81	2	Bedford	21 Jul
24.60	0.1	Denise Lewis		27.08.72	5	Tilburg, NED	8 Jul
24.60	1.1	Nicole Bowring		27.01.74	3	Bedford	21 Jul
24.62	1.2	Anyika Onuora	U17	28.10.84	1	Birmingham	2 Sep
24.68	-0.1	Jemma Sims	U17	2.05.85	1	Tullamore, IRL	21 Jul
	(40)						
24.70	0.2	Vicki Jamison		19.05.77	3	Edinburgh	25 Aug
24.72	1.4	Rachel Harris	U20	17.07.82	1	Tamworth	27 Aug
24.74 i		Xanine Powell	U23	21.05.79	4h2	Birmingham	28 Jan
		24.76 -1.0			4h2	London (Ha)	17 Jun
24.74	-0.8	Katherine Endacott	U23	29.01.80	4	Derby	29 Jul
24.75	0.6	Julie Hollman		16.02.77	2H2	Arles, FRA	9 Jun
24.78 i		Felicia Louisy		17.05.74	2h5	Birmingham	28 Jan
		24.81 1.0			5h1	Birmingham	14 Jul
24.78	1.0	Liz Williams		2.06.77	4h1	Birmingham	14 Jul
24.78	-0.8	Sonia Rice	U23	8.01.81	5	Derby	29 Jul
24.79 i		Melinda Cooksey	U20	19.05.84	1	Birmingham	11 Feb
24.80	-1.0	Emma Bryson	U23	5.04.81	2	Glasgow (S)	23 Jun
	(50)						
24.81 i		Nicola Gossman	U15	4.11.86	1	Birmingham	24 Feb
		24.85 1.2			1	Sheffield	12 Aug
24.81	0.6	Roseline Addo	U23	7.06.80	2h3	Lexington, USA	20 Apr
24.81		Kathryn Evans	U20	1.03.84	1	Glasgow (S)	29 Apr
24.87 i		Melanie Roberts		2.03.78	1r3	Birmingham	7 Jan

24.88	-0.4	Carey Easton	U23	16.11.79	2h2	Edinburgh	13 May
24.88	-1.0	Karlene Palmer	U23	23.10.80	5h2	London (Ha)	17 Jun
24.88	1.1	Lisa Vannet		8.11.74	4	Bedford	21 Jul
24.90	1.1	Liz Fairs		1.12.77	5	Birmingham	2 Jun
24.95	-1.7	Sian Robinson	U20	31.03.82	2	Derby	29 Jul
24.96	-0.5	Lesley Clarkson	U20	18.07.82	1	Inverness	8 Jul
	(60)						
24.96	2.0	Amala Onuora	U17	16.03.86	2	Sheffield	12 Aug
24.99	0.7	Nicole Crosby		23.10.76	3	Birmingham	30 Jun
25.00	1.6	Victoria Barr	U20	14.04.82	1	Cudworth	26 Aug
25.02		Keeley Butler		24.03.75	3	Grangemouth	26 Aug
25.03		Sharon Allen		23.10.68	3	New Jersey, USA	9 Jun
25.03	1.9	Montell Douglas	U17	24.01.86	1	Birmingham	1 Sep
25.04	1.2	Lia Tappin	U15	9.01.87	2	Sheffield	12 Aug
25.05	-0.3	Katie Flaherty	U17	1.10.85	7	Murcia, ESP	26 Jul
25.06 i		Sharon Williams		20.05.70	4h5	Birmingham	28 Jan
25.07		Sara Whigham	U20	7.10.83	1rB	Glasgow (S)	29 Apr
	(70)						
25.08	0.0	Lisa Trotman	U20	6.12.82	2h2	Exeter	6 Jul
25.09	-1.2	Karen Oughton	U20	26.01.83	6	Dole, FRA	29 Jul
25.11	1.1	Jennifer Culley		4.03.75	7	Bedford	21 Jul
25.12	-1.7	Maria Morganella	U23	2.10.79	3	Derby	29 Jul
25.13 i		Kim Goodwin		16.05.70	3r1	Birmingham	7 Jan
25.13	1.1	Nicola Gautier		21.03.78	6H5	Ried, AUT	30 Jun
25.13	1.2	Sinead Johnson	U15	24.12.86	3	Sheffield	12 Aug
25.13	1.5	Sarah Still		24.09.75	2H1	Sheffield	1 Sep
25.14	1.1	Julie Pratt	U23	20.03.79	6	Birmingham	2 Jun
25.15 i		Vicky Ward		19.06.72	2h4	Birmingham	14 Jan
	(80)						
25.16 i		Rachael Kay	U23	8.09.80	3h4	Birmingham	28 Jan
25.16		Melanie Pickersgill		20.04.73	8	Eton	7 Jul
25.16	-0.1	Kirsteen McDiarmid	U17	28.04.86	3	Tullamore, IRL	21 Jul
25.18	0.7	Katherine Jones	U17	21.01.85	2h3	Exeter	6 Jul
25.19 i		Heather Brookes	U23	17.07.81	5r1	Birmingham	3 Feb
25.19 i		Charli Croll	U17	25.10.84	3s1	Birmingham	24 Feb
25.20 i		Tamara Doherty	U17	15.11.85	2s2	Birmingham	24 Feb
		25.55			2	Grangemouth	1 Aug
25.24 i		Amina Ceesay	U23	19.11.79	5h3	Birmingham	28 Jan
25.24		Suzanne McGowan		13.04.78	1	Grangemouth	1 Aug
25.25	0.1	Jessica Ennis	U17	28.01.86	1H2	Bedford	14 Jul
	(90)						
25.26	-1.7	Helen Williams		2.06.77	4h3	London (Ha)	17 Jun
25.26	-1.0	Louise Whitehead		26.03.75	4r2	Budapest, HUN	1 Jul
25.27	0.8	Kessia Sherliker	U17	9.11.85	1h2	Exeter	6 Jul
25.27	1.0	Danielle Fawkes	U17	11.08.85	1	Nyiregyhaza, HUN	25 Jul
25.28		Jackie Scott	U17	31.01.85	1	Grangemouth	26 Aug

Additional Under 17 (1 - 14 above)

25.32 i		Kimberley Velvick	3.01.85	3s2	Birmingham	24 Feb
		25.57 0.8		4h2	Exeter	6 Jul
25.33	1.8	Amanda Shaw	28.09.84	3s1	Sheffield	12 Aug
25.34	1.9	Christina Clubley	4.11.85	2	Birmingham	1 Sep
25.36	1.9	Nicola Robinson	16.04.86	1	Tamworth	27 Aug
25.39	0.8	Emily Parker	7.11.84	1H1	Birmingham	29 Sep
25.41	0.8	Leah Caddick	1.06.86	2h2	Exeter	6 Jul
	(20)					
25.47	-0.1	Kelly Birkin	27.04.86	5	Tullamore, IRL	21 Jul
25.50	-0.7	Phyllis Agbo	16.12.85	4	Stoke-on-Trent	18 Aug
25.57		Gemma Nicol	27.07.86	2	Grangemouth	26 Aug
25.59 i		Rebecca Sweeney	9.02.85	1	Birmingham	7 Jan

Additional Under 15 (1 - 3 above)

25.30	0.2	Louise Dickson		4.09.86	1r1	Birmingham	2 Sep
25.50		Denae Matthew		3.04.87	1h	Tamworth	27 Aug
25.51	1.2	Lianne George		25.11.86	4	Sheffield	12 Aug
25.64 i		Louise Dickinson		5.11.86	1	Birmingham	4 Feb
		25.81 -2.1			1	Cudworth	27 May
25.64	1.2	Deandra Smith		3.12.86	5	Sheffield	12 Aug
25.66 i		Michelle Nash		19.03.87	2s1	Birmingham	24 Feb
		26.00 0.0			2h3	Exeter	6 Jul
25.67	1.0	Victoria Burgess		4.10.86	2	London (He)	26 Aug
	(10)						
25.81		Kim Skinner		21.09.87	1	Grangemouth	26 Aug
25.95	-0.6	Carley Wenham		14.03.88	1h2	Crawley	13 May
25.95	1.5	Camilla Harkness		10.01.87	1h3	Watford	27 May
25.98 i		Laura Cox		21.01.88	2	Birmingham	11 Feb
25.98	0.6	Heather Jones		10.09.86	2	Connah's Quay	4 Aug

wind assisted

22.84	4.2	Sarah Wilhelmy	U23	(23.27)	1	Arles, FRA	10 Jun
23.04	2.7	Joice Maduaka		(23.31)	1	Bedford	18 Jul
		23.41 7.8			2	Bangor	2 Jun
23.12	2.6	Shani Anderson		(23.43)	1	Istanbul, TUR	16 Jun
		23.35 4.2			2	Arles, FRA	10 Jun
		23.42 3.6			2r1	Azusa, USA	14 Apr
		23.46 3.2			2h2	Birmingham	14 Jul
		23.73 2.7			4	Bedford	18 Jul
23.24	4.6	James	U20	(22.93)	1	Exeter	7 Jul
		23.41 7.8			3	Bangor	2 Jun
		23.61 3.1			1r2	Azusa, USA	14 Apr
23.35	3.6	Catherine Murphy		(23.74)	1	Cardiff	17 Jun
		23.65 2.2			6	Walnut CA, USA	22 Apr
23.54	4.7	Spencer	U17	(23.45)	1rB	Bangor	2 Jun
23.75	2.7	Lesley Owusu		(23.86)	5	Bedford	18 Jul
23.76	3.2	Susie Williams		(23.79)	3h2	Birmingham	14 Jul
		16 performances to 23.79 by 8 athletes					
23.90	5.2	Jenny Meadows	U23	17.04.81	1	Liverpool	17 Jun
24.01	3.6	Kelly Sotherton		(24.17)	1rB	Birmingham	2 Jun
24.15	7.8	Eleanor Caney	U20	(24.42)	4	Bangor	2 Jun
24.19	2.7	Liz Williams		(24.78)	7	Bedford	18 Jul
24.28	4.1	Kim Wall	U20	(24.33)	1	Ipswich	2 Sep
24.32	2.6	Helen Thieme	U23	(24.37)	2	Birmingham	16 Jun
24.33	3.4	Katherine Livesey	U23	15.12.79	2H1	College Station, USA	16 May
24.37	4.6	Lisa Trotman	U20	(25.08)	2	Exeter	7 Jul
24.41	3.6	Kelly Thomas	U23	(24.58)	2rB	Birmingham	2 Jun
24.42	3.2	Nicole Bowring		(24.60)	4h2	Birmingham	14 Jul
24.49	4.1	Rachel Harris	U20	(24.72)	2	Ipswich	2 Sep
24.67	2.8	Jemma Sims	U17	(24.68)	1	Exeter	7 Jul
24.67	4.1	Victoria Barr	U20	(25.00)	3	Ipswich	2 Sep
24.71	2.6	Syreena Pinel	U23	13.01.79	3	Birmingham	16 Jun
24.71	3.6	Louise Whitehead		(25.26)	2	Cardiff	17 Jun
24.72	3.6	Donna Porazinski	U23	28.01.81	3	Cardiff	17 Jun
24.83	3.6	Carey Easton	U23	(24.88)	3rB	Birmingham	2 Jun
24.84	2.8	Kimberley Velvick	U17	(25.57)	2	Exeter	7 Jul
24.89	2.8	Katie Flaherty	U17	(25.05)	3	Exeter	7 Jul
24.90	2.8	Katherine Jones	U17	(25.18)	4	Exeter	7 Jul
24.96	2.8	Leah Caddick	U17	(25.41)	5	Exeter	7 Jul
24.97	3.6	Vicky Ward		(25.15i)	5B	Birmingham	2 Jun
24.97	3.6	Melanie Pickersgill		(25.16)	4B	Birmingham	2 Jun

24.97	5.2	Nicole Crosby		(24.99)	3	Liverpool	17 Jun
24.98	2.5	Lia Tappin	U15	(25.04)	1	Exeter	7 Jul
25.03	3.6	Alison Thorne		25.09.72	6rB	Birmingham	2 Jun
25.03	4.6	Amanda Applegarth	U20	5.04.84	4	Exeter	7 Jul
25.03	2.2	Sarah Still		(25.13)	1H2	Bedford	14 Jul
25.06	4.6	Cherie Pierre	U20	15.05.84	5	Exeter	7 Jul
Additional Under 17 (1 - 6 above)							
25.24	3.0	Jemma Thake		17.12.85	1	Bedford	28 Jul
25.27	2.3	Jackie Scott		(25.28)	1h2	Sheffield	12 Aug
25.29	2.8	Amanda Shaw		(25.33)	6	Exeter	7 Jul
25.31	2.8	Laura Robinson		11.10.85	7	Exeter	7 Jul
25.37	2.2	Faye Harding		7.09.85	1H	Aberdare	23 Jun
25.37	2.4	Phyllis Agbo		(25.50)	1H2	Sheffield	1 Sep
25.57	3.0	Louise Hazel		6.10.85	2	Bedford	28 Jul
Additional Under 15 (1 above)							
25.28	2.5	Victoria Burgess		(25.67)	2	Exeter	7 Jul
25.58	2.9	Heather Jones		(25.98)	1	Cardiff	17 Jun
25.77	2.5	Michelle Nash		(26.00)	5	Exeter	7 Jul
25.85	2.9	Danielle Barker		19.01.87	2	Cardiff	17 Jun
25.87	3.1	Ella Kempster		15.09.86	2h2	Watford	27 May
26.01	2.5	Venita Akpofure		1.01.87	6	Exeter	7 Jul
hand timing							
23.2	1.7	Shani Anderson		(23.43)	1	Nitra, SVK	25 Aug
23.3 w	3.3	Amy Spencer	U17	(23.45)	1	Bedford	1 Jul
		23.7			1	Stretford	13 May
23.4 w	4.1	Helen Roscoe	U23	(23.80)	1	Bedford	1 Jul
23.6	1.3	James	U20	(22.93)	1	Watford	26 May
23.6 e	0.9	Richardson (estimated)		(23.99)	2	Fullerton CA, USA	26 Apr
		6 performances to 23.7 by 5 athletes including 2 wind assisted					
23.8 w	4.1	Melanie Purkiss	U23	(24.06)	2	Bedford	1 Jul
23.9	0.5	Helen Thieme	U23	(24.37)	1	Loughborough	13 Jun
23.9 w	4.3	Amanda Forrester		29.09.78	1	London (Cr)	3 Jun
24.0	1.3	Lisa Miller	U20	(24.21)	2	Watford	26 May
24.0	1.3	Helen Frost		(24.36)	2h2	Bedford	27 May
24.1		Sabrina Scott	U23	(24.40)	1	Eton	28 Apr
24.1 w	5.1	Nicole Bowring		(24.60)	1	Ashford	12 May
		24.5 -0.4			1	Eton	10 Jun
24.2		Jemma Sims	U17	(24.68)	1	Telford	1 Jul
24.2 w	3.3	Karen Gear	U23	30.09.79	1	Exeter	12 May
		24.9 1.6			3h3	Bedford	27 May
24.3		Eleanor Caney	U20	(24.42)	1	Stourport	12 May
24.3	-1.0	Diane Allahgreen		21.02.75	1	Liverpool	12 May
24.3 w	4.1	Kate Denham	U23	(24.58)	5	Bedford	1 Jul
24.4	-1.0	Melanie Roberts		(24.87i)	2	Liverpool	12 May
24.4 w	3.3	Rachel Harris	U20	(24.72)	2	Bedford	1 Jul
		24.6			1	Wakefield	29 Jul
24.4 w	2.7	Ellena Ruddock		(25.07)	1	Coventry	5 Aug
		24.6 1.1			2	Coventry	29 Apr
24.4 w	3.1	Kim Goodwin		(25.13i)	1	Eton	5 Aug
		24.7 1.5			1	Stafford	7 Jul
24.5	-1.0	Joanne McDougall	U23	23.08.79	3	Liverpool	12 May
24.5 w	3.5	Julie Pratt	U23	(25.14)	1	Southend	13 May
24.5 w	2.7	Sonia Rice	U23	(24.78)	2	Coventry	5 Aug
24.6	1.1	Katherine Livesey	U23	(24.33w)	1H	Lawrence, USA	18 Apr
24.6		Julie Hollman		(24.75)	1	St. Ives	12 May

24.6 w	4.1	Karlene Palmer	U23	(24.88)	6	Bedford	1 Jul
		24.7			1	Bromley	23 Jun
24.6 w	3.3	Sara Whigham	U20	(25.07)	4	Bedford	1 Jul
		25.0 1.2			3h1	Bedford	1 Jul
24.6 w		Janette Niccolls		7.09.76	1	Bournemouth	11 Aug
24.7		Jennifer Culley		(25.11)	2	London (BP)	20 May
24.7		Emma Bryson	U23	(24.80)	1r2	Coatbridge	15 Jul
24.7 w	5.2	Liz Fairs		(24.90)	3	Wigan	10 Jun
24.7 w		Linda Staines	V35	26.12.63	2	Eton	5 Aug
		25.1			3	London (BP)	20 May
24.8	0.4	Katie Flaherty	U17	(25.05)	1	Watford	26 May
24.8	0.6	Felicia Louisy		(24.81)	4h1	Bedford	27 May
24.8		Lisa Trotman	U20	(25.08)	1	Stoke-on-Trent	17 Jun
24.8 mx		Simmone Jacobs		5.09.66	1	Watford	27 Jun
24.8		Victoria Barr	U20	(25.00)	1	York	29 Jul
24.8		Keeley Butler		(25.02)	1	Coatbridge	29 Jul
24.8 w	3.5	Amina Ceesay	U23	(25.24i)	2	Southend	13 May
		25.0			1	Enfield	14 Jul
24.9	2.0	Syreena Pinel	U23	(24.71w)	1rB	Coventry	29 Apr
24.9		Sharon Williams		(25.06i)	1	London (He)	12 May
24.9		Rachael Kay	U23	(25.16i)	1	Stretford	13 May
24.9		Michelle Turner		25.12.77	1	Kingston	23 Jun
24.9		Leah Caddick	U17	(25.41)	1	Bebington	1 Jul
24.9	0.6	Claire Rooney	U20	23.08.83	1rB	Coventry	5 Aug
24.9		Gemma Nicol	U17	(25.57)	1	Grangemouth	16 Sep
25.0		Melinda Cooksey	U20	(24.79i)	3	Stourport	12 May
25.0	-1.0	Louise Whitehead		(25.26)	4	Liverpool	12 May
25.0	1.3	Zoe Wilson		28.08.76	4h2	Bedford	27 May
25.0		Amy Dowsett	U17	30.12.84	2	London (Cr)	23 Jun
25.0		Katherine Jones	U17	(25.18)	2	Telford	1 Jul
25.0		Carley Wenham	U15	(25.95)	1	Eton	1 Jul
25.0		Christine Ohurougu	U20	17.05.84	1	London (Nh)	11 Aug
25.0		Alison Maxwell		13.11.70	1	Portsmouth	1 Sep
25.0		Shereen Charles	U17	27.10.84	2	Portsmouth	1 Sep
25.0 w	3.3	Amy Freeman	U20	23.08.82	6	Bedford	1 Jul
25.0 w	2.1	Montell Douglas	U17	(25.03)	1	London (He)	16 Sep
25.1		Hannah Wood	U23	17.11.81	2	Yate	29 Apr
25.1	-1.0	Danielle Halsall	U23	27.06.81	5	Liverpool	12 May
25.1		Banke Olofinjana		14.05.72	2	London (He)	12 May
25.1		Maria Morganella	U23	(25.12)	4	Dumfries	19 May
25.1	0.9	Vicky Ward		(25.15i)	4	London (He)	10 Jun
25.1		Sarah Blackwell	U17	1.10.84	2	Bebington	1 Jul
25.1		Kelly Massey	U17	11.01.86	3	Telford	1 Jul
25.1		Sharon Wilson		27.10.74	2r2	Coatbridge	15 Jul
25.1		Helen Williams		(25.26)	1	Walton	11 Aug
25.1		Malgorzata Rostek/Waldrop		25.03.77	1	Glasgow (S)	9 Sep

Additional Under 17 (1 - 11 above)

25.2		Jemma Thake	(25.24w)	1	Bury St. Edmunds	1 Jul
25.2 w	5.5	Natasha Cross	13.11.84	1	Exeter	16 Jun
25.2 w		Emily Parker	(25.39)	1	Exeter	1 Sep
25.3		Vicky Griffiths	9.10.84	3	Bebington	1 Jul
25.3		Nichola Nutting	14.09.84	1	Nuneaton	22 Jul
25.3		Katie-Jane Mather	7.01.86	2	Nuneaton	22 Jul
25.3	-2.4	Rebecca Sweeney	(25.59i)	1	Liverpool	12 Aug
25.3		Molly Russell	3.08.86	1	Abingdon	16 Sep
25.3 w	2.2	Victoria Jackson	17.01.86	2	Stoke-on-Trent	16 Jun

25.4		Laura Robinson	(25.31w)	1	Grimsby	6 May
25.4	-0.7	Kimberley Velvick	(25.57)	1	Ashford	13 May
25.4	0.4	Louisa Wells	30.12.84	4	Watford	26 May
25.4		Tamara Doherty	(25.55)	2	Glasgow (S)	3 Jun
25.4		Natalie Plateau	19.10.84	1	Abingdon	22 Jul
25.4 w	2.2	Rowenna Mortimer	4.07.86	3	Stoke-on-Trent	16 Jun
25.5	1.0	Kadi-Ann Thomas	10.02.86	2h2	Watford	26 May
25.5		Gemma Thompson	17.01.86	2	Dublin (S), IRL	23 Jun

Additional Under 15 (1 above)

25.4	-0.1	Victoria Burgess	(25.67)	2	Watford	27 May
25.4	-0.1	Camilla Harkness	(25.95)	1	Watford	27 May
25.5		Jemma Buttler	17.06.87	1	Telford	1 Jul
25.5		Danielle Barker	(25.85w)	1	Newport	14 Jul
25.7		Louise Dickinson	(25.81)	1	Sutton Coldfield	25 Aug
25.8		Heather Jones	(25.98)	2	Brecon	19 Aug
25.8		Amy Harris	14.09.87	1	Banbury	9 Sep
25.9	1.6	Ella Kempster	(25.87w)	1	Colchester	7 May
26.0		Joanna Birch	21.04.87	1	Nuneaton	22 Jul

Under 13

26.72 w	3.8	Felicity James	2.02.89	1	Cardiff	17 Jun
		27.4		2	London (TB)	28 Jul
26.8		Stefanie Knight	4.02.89	1r2	London (TB)	23 Jun
26.9		Cherelle Norriston	29.11.88	2r1	London (TB)	14 Jul
27.0		Nicole Sadler	10.11.88	1	Cambridge	17 Jun
27.0		Annabelle Lewis	20.03.89	1	London (TB)	28 Jul
27.1		Emma Baker	22.09.88	1r2	Portsmouth	1 Sep
27.4		Amy Gibbs	30.03.89	1	London (BP)	26 May
27.4		Laura Hitchman	14.10.88	1r2	Brighton	23 Jun
27.5		Joey Duck	14.04.89	1	Milton Keynes	8 Jul
27.5	1.9	Teresa Andrews		2r1	Kingston	29 Jul
	(10)					
27.6		Carling Meadows	26.09.88	1	Wigan	18 Mar
27.6		Joanne Smith	23.09.88	1h10	East Kilbride	1 Apr
27.61 w	3.8	Zoe Llewelyn	5.10.88	2	Cardiff	17 Jun

Foreign

23.02	*0.3*	*Sarah Reilly (IRL)*	*3.07.73*	*3h3*	*Edmonton, CAN*	*8 Aug*
24.2		*Chioma Ajunwa (NGR) ¶*	*25.12.71*	*1*	*Hemel Hempstead*	*28 Apr*
24.52 i		*Maiteland Marks (USA)*	*19.09.76*	*1*	*Glasgow*	*17 Feb*
		24.60 -1.9		*2*	*Loughborough*	*4 Jul*
24.70 w	*7.8*	*Leanne O'Callaghan (IRL)*	*15.07.74*	*5*	*Bangor*	*2 Jun*
		24.9		*1*	*London (Cr)*	*23 Jun*
		25.02 -1.7		*3h3*	*London (Ha)*	*17 Jun*
24.79 w	*4.7*	*Michelle Carey (IRL) U23*	*20.02.81*	*3rB*	*Bangor*	*2 Jun*
		25.1		*1*	*Loughborough*	*28 Apr*
24.95 i		*Esther Erharuyi (NGR) U20*	*17.04.83*	*3h1*	*Birmingham*	*28 Jan*
25.18mx	*-0.1*	*Margaret Veldman (NED)*	*7.06.74*	*1*	*Stretford*	*19 Jun*

300 Metres

37.08	Sinead Dudgeon	9.07.76	3	Walnut CA, USA	22 Apr
37.27	Donna Fraser	7.11.72	7	Gateshead	19 Aug
37.72	Helen Frost	12.03.74	1r3	Torrevieja, ESP	14 Apr
38.22	Jennifer Culley	4.03.75	1	Claremont, USA	3 Feb
38.66	Vicki Jamison	19.05.77	1	Antrim	21 Aug
38.99	Kerry Jury	19.11.68	1r2	Torrevieja, ESP	14 Apr
39.0	Nicole Bowring	27.01.74	1	Tonbridge	7 Aug

Foreign

37.30	*Sarah Reilly (IRL)*	*3.07.73*	*8*	*Gateshead*	*19 Aug*

Under 17

39.39	Jenny Christie	28.09.85	1	Exeter	7 Jul
39.46	Faye Harding	7.09.85	1	Cardiff	16 Jun
39.71	Liza Parry	24.10.84	2	Exeter	7 Jul
39.84	Jemma Thake	17.12.85	3	Exeter	7 Jul
39.91	Rebecca Sweeney	9.02.85	4	Exeter	7 Jul
39.97 i	Gemma Nicol	27.07.86	1	Birmingham	25 Feb
	40.16		1	Grangemouth	26 Aug
40.0	Laura Finucane	3.08.86	1	Blackpool	12 May
	40.64		2	Nyiregyhaza, HUN	25 Jul
40.05	Vicky Griffiths	9.10.84	5	Exeter	7 Jul
40.28	Lauren Candlish	4.04.86	4	Tullamore, IRL	21 Jul
40.3	Jackie Scott	31.01.85	1	Dunfermline	16 Apr
(10)					
40.4	Rowenna Mortimer	4.07.86	1	Yate	22 Jul
40.5	Leah Caddick	1.06.86	1	Preston	5 Aug
40.54	Marilyn Okoro	23.09.84	1h1	Sheffield	11 Aug
40.6	Alanna Wain	27.04.85	1	Cannock	12 May
40.6	Charlotte Best	7.03.85	1	Crawley	29 Aug
40.63	Emma Kemp	11.10.84	2	Watford	27 May
40.74	Natalie Plateau	19.10.84	3s2	Exeter	6 Jul
40.76	Lucy Sings	9.07.85	4s1	Exeter	6 Jul
40.83	Lauren Webb	17.11.85	1h4	Exeter	6 Jul
40.9	Nicola Lake	28.09.84	2	Cannock	12 May
	41.27		4h1	Exeter	6 Jul
(20)					
40.9	Charli Croll	25.10.84	1rB	Crawley	5 Aug
	41.17		6s1	Exeter	6 Jul
40.9	Lauren Caple	7.03.85	1	Mansfield	26 Aug
	41.03		2	Scunthorpe	19 Aug
40.96	Rebecca Leitch	12.11.84	5	Tullamore, IRL	21 Jul
40.97	Laura Langowski	10.10.84	2h4	Sheffield	11 Aug
41.0	Victoria Webster	24.12.85	2	Wakefield	1 Jul
41.10	Laura Robinson	11.10.85	3	Cudworth	26 May
41.1	Rachael Thompson	15.11.85	1	Bebington	1 Jul
41.24	Rachel Thomas	19.01.85	3	Nyiregyhaza, HUN	25 Jul
41.29	Caroline Wilson	14.09.84	1	Crawley	12 May
41.29	Vicky Lambert	20.11.84	4	Cudworth	26 May
(30)					
41.31 i	Tamara Doherty	15.11.85	1	Glasgow	11 Mar
41.4	Claire Warmington	7.06.85	1	Stretford	12 May
	41.48		5	Cudworth	26 May
41.4	Annabel Hicks	29.09.84	1	Street	9 Jun
41.4	Melanie Canning	19.05.85	1	Hayes	1 Jul
41.44	Christie Hamilton	11.09.84	3h3	Exeter	6 Jul
41.5	Charlotte Beckett	4.01.86	1	Milton Keynes	12 May
41.5	Donna Shorthouse	8.10.84	4	Wakefield	1 Jul

400 Metres

49.59	Katharine Merry	21.09.74	1	Athens, GRE	11 Jun
	50.44		1	Milan, ITA	6 Jun
	50.53 i		1	Birmingham	18 Feb
	50.67		1	London (CP)	22 Jul
	51.03		1	Glasgow (S)	1 Jul
	51.54 i		1	Cardiff	11 Feb
51.77	Donna Fraser	7.11.72	6s3	Edmonton, CAN	6 Aug
	52.02		4h5	Edmonton, CAN	5 Aug
	52.57		2	Birmingham	15 Jul
	52.77		2h2	Birmingham	14 Jul
	53.02		4	Glasgow (S)	1 Jul

51.84	Catherine Murphy		21.09.75	4	Seville, ESP	8 Jun
	51.99 i			2	Birmingham	18 Feb
	52.27			1h2	Birmingham	14 Jul
	52.31 i			1	Birmingham	27 Jan
	52.37			4	Helsinki, FIN	14 Jun
	52.40			4h3	Edmonton, CAN	5 Aug
	52.45 i			4s1	Lisbon, POR	10 Mar
	52.49 i			3	Glasgow	18 Mar
	52.61 i			1h3	Lisbon, POR	9 Mar
	52.65			5	London (CP)	22 Jul
	52.72 i			1	Birmingham	7 Jan
	52.74			2	Birmingham	2 Jun
	52.78			5	Funchal, POR	30 Jun
	53.09			1r3	Irvine CA, USA	6 May
	53.50			5	Birmingham	15 Jul
51.99	Allison Curbishley		3.06.76	5	Bremen, GER	23 Jun
	52.48			1	Birmingham	2 Jun
52.05	Lee McConnell		9.10.78	3s2	Beijing, CHN	28 Aug
	52.31			1r1	Budapest, HUN	1 Jul
	52.41			1	Glasgow (S)	24 Jun
	52.44			6	Beijing, CHN	29 Aug
	52.93			3	Birmingham	15 Jul
	52.99			2h4	Beijing, CHN	27 Aug
	53.04			1	Riga, LAT	2 Jun
	53.28			1	Loughborough	20 May
52.15 i	Lesley Owusu		21.12.78	1h1	Fayetteville, USA	9 Mar
	52.27			1	Birmingham	15 Jul
	52.37 i			1	Lincoln, USA	24 Feb
	52.49 i			2	Fayetteville, USA	10 Mar
	52.49			2	Houston, USA	19 May
	52.66			1h1	Birmingham	14 Jul
	52.72 i			1	Lincoln, USA	3 Feb
	52.74 i			2	Fayetteville, USA	9 Feb
	52.87 i			1h3	Lincoln, USA	23 Feb
	52.88			1	Eton	7 Jul
	52.93			2	Des Moines, USA	28 Apr
	52.93 A			1	Calgary, CAN	30 Jul
	52.98			6	London (CP)	22 Jul
	53.00 i			1r4	Lincoln, USA	17 Feb
	53.02			2h3	Beijing, CHN	27 Aug
	53.20			5s1	Beijing, CHN	28 Aug
52.47 i	Sinead Dudgeon		9.07.76	2	Birmingham	27 Jan
52.68	Helen Frost		12.03.74	5r1	Tula, RUS	9 Jun
	52.79			2r2	Bedford	18 Jul
	52.89			4	Budapest, HUN	1 Jul
	52.91 A			1	Potchefstroom, RSA	12 Feb
	52.99			1	Dublin (S), IRL	29 Jun
	53.08			5	Cork, IRL	7 Jul
	53.18			1	Bedford	21 Jul
	53.19			4	Birmingham	15 Jul
	53.20			3h2	Birmingham	14 Jul
52.75	Helen Thieme	U23	28.09.81	2	Amsterdam, NED	13 Jul
	52.88			2h2	Amsterdam, NED	12 Jul
	53.25			1	Liverpool	23 Jun
	53.27			1	Bedford	30 Jun
53.29	Lisa Miller	U20	13.01.83	2	Grosseto, ITA	20 Jul
	53.46			1r3	Mannheim, GER	16 Jun
(10)						
53.31	Karen Gear	U23	30.09.79	3h1	Amsterdam, NED	12 Jul
53.32	Jenny Meadows	U23	17.04.81	4h1	Amsterdam, NED	12 Jul

70 performances to 53.50 by 12 athletes including 16 indoors

53.52	Kim Wall	U20	21.04.83	3	Grosseto, ITA	20 Jul
54.3	Nicole Bowring		27.01.74	1	London (Elt)	2 Sep
	54.86			3	London (Ha)	17 Jun
54.35	Tanya Blake		16.01.71	3	Claremont, USA	20 Apr
54.38	Melanie Purkiss	U23	11.03.79	6	Gainesville FL, USA	21 Apr
54.39	Jennifer Culley		4.03.75	1	Basel, SUI	4 Jun
54.40	Kim Goodwin		16.05.70	1	Scunthorpe	19 Aug
54.44	Lesley Clarkson	U20	18.07.82	1	Glasgow (S)	7 May
54.58	Carey Easton	U23	16.11.79	2	Glasgow (S)	7 May
(20)						
54.70	Vicki Jamison		19.05.77	1	Belfast	28 Jul
54.79	Dawn Higgins		10.12.75	4h2	Birmingham	14 Jul
54.81 i	Kathryn Sage		27.03.76	2h4	Birmingham	27 Jan
	56.7			1	Coventry	29 Apr
	56.91			3	Cardiff	16 Jun
54.9	Michelle Thomas		16.10.71	1	London (Ha)	10 Jun
	55.05			1	Birmingham	30 Jun
54.97	Olivia Hines	U20	19.10.83	2	Dole, FRA	29 Jul
55.0	Jo Fenn		19.10.74	1	Wigan	4 Aug
	56.96			5r3	Irvine CA, USA	6 May
55.0	Linda Staines	V35	26.12.63	1	Eton	5 Aug
	55.76			1	Portsmouth	12 May
55.04 i	Emma Symonds		5.06.77	2	Birmingham	14 Jan
	55.5			2	Rugby	3 Jun
55.08	Roseline Addo	U23	7.06.80	8	Gainesville FL, USA	31 Mar
55.1	Rebecca Scotcher	U20	2.07.82	1	Rugby	3 Jun
	55.12			1r2	Loughborough	20 May
(30)						
55.16	Vicky Ward		19.06.72	3	Birmingham	2 Jun
55.18	Joanne McDougall	U23	23.08.79	3	Derby	29 Jul
55.27	Alison Thorne		25.09.72	2	Bedford	21 Jul
55.29	Christine Ohuruogu	U20	17.05.84	3	Dole, FRA	29 Jul
55.32	Kelly Sotherton		13.11.76	4	Loughborough	20 May
55.36 i	Heather Brookes	U23	17.07.81	1h2	Birmingham	27 Jan
55.38 mx	Rebecca Lyne	U20	4.07.82	1	Watford	1 Aug
	55.4			1	Leeds	7 Aug
55.39	Katharine Eustace		16.04.75	7h2	Birmingham	14 Jul
55.4	Tracey Duncan	U23	16.05.79	1rB	Wigan	4 Aug
	55.54 i			2h1	Birmingham	27 Jan
	56.32			4rB	Birmingham	2 Jun
55.44	Michelle Pierre		30.09.73	2r2	Loughborough	20 May
(40)						
55.45	Lois Cresswell	U23	12.01.81	4h1	Birmingham	14 Jul
55.46	Liz Williams		2.06.77	1	Bedford	22 Jul
55.54	Louise Whitehead		26.03.75	2	Cardiff	16 Jun
55.58	Sharon Allen		23.10.68	3	Princeton, USA	12 May
55.7	Natalie Smellie	U20	16.01.82	2	London (Ha)	10 Jun
	56.79			2h2	Bedford	29 Jun
55.7	Alex Carter	U23	1.04.80	1	Loughborough	13 Jun
55.7	Mary McClung		19.12.71	1	Coatbridge	29 Jul
	55.84			1h1	Glasgow (S)	24 Jun
55.75	Claire Robinson		18.01.78	4	Glasgow (S)	7 May
55.75	Amy Freeman	U20	23.08.82	3	Scunthorpe	19 Aug
55.79 i	Rachael Kay	U23	8.09.80	1r2	Birmingham	4 Feb
	56.2			1	Wigan	8 Jul
(50)						
55.8	Louretta Thorne		6.05.77	1	Milton Keynes	12 May
	55.89			4	Birmingham	2 Jun
55.8	Jemma Simpson	U20	10.02.84	1	Exeter	16 Jun
55.82	Sally Evans		14.05.75	3	Eton	7 Jul
55.86	Gaby Howell	U20	25.01.82	1	Derby	9 Sep

55.89	Lisa Whigham	U23	14.08.80	5	Glasgow (S)	7 May
55.95 i	Hannah Wood	U23	17.11.81	3h1	Birmingham	27 Jan
	57.0			1	Leamington	12 May
56.09 i	Celia Brown		22.01.77	3h1	Birmingham	13 Jan
	56.69			5	Bedford	21 Jul
56.20	Alison Maxwell		13.11.70	7h1	Birmingham	14 Jul
56.27	Danielle Halsall	U23	27.06.81	3s1	Glasgow (S)	6 May
56.3	Tanya Wilkinson		1.04.70	1	Solihull	24 Jun
	(60)					
56.3	Lisa Vannet		8.11.74	2rB	Wigan	4 Aug
56.4	Gemma Nicol	U17	27.07.86	1	Grangemouth	16 Sep
56.49	Jane McKay		22.04.77	4s1	Glasgow (S)	6 May
56.50	Suzanne McGowan		13.04.78	4h2	Glasgow (S)	24 Jun
56.54	Christine Amede	V35	7.08.63	1	Brisbane, AUS	13 Jul
56.56	Vicky Tunaley	U20	4.06.84	3	Watford	27 May
56.6	Liz Fairs		1.12.77	4rB	Wigan	4 Aug
56.6	Lindsey Singer	U20	4.06.83	1	Liverpool	12 Aug
	57.14			4h2	Exeter	6 Jul
56.6	Lucy Vaughan		20.04.69	1	Stevenage	1 Sep
56.63 i	Vicky Lawrence		9.06.73	2rB	Birmingham	4 Feb
	56.9			1	Rotherham	5 Aug
	(70)					
56.65	Aileen Williams	U23	14.06.81	5s2	Glasgow (S)	6 May
56.7	Jeina Mitchell		21.01.75	1	London (Cr)	23 Jun
56.76	Jo Owbridge	U20	19.01.82	2	Cudworth	27 May
56.8	Lisa Trotman	U20	6.12.82	1	Stretford	1 Apr
56.8	Jennie Mathews	V35	3.07.62	2	Ashford	13 May
	57.44			2	Brisbane, AUS	13 Jul
56.83 i	Emma Davies		9.10.78	2	Cardiff	21 Jan
56.87	Rachel Harris	U20	17.07.82	1	Birmingham	26 May
56.9	Karen Storey		8.11.68	2	Scunthorpe	3 Jun
	56.98			3h1	Glasgow (S)	24 Jun
56.96 mx	Kathryn Evans	U20	1.03.84	1	Inverness	2 Sep
	57.13			1	Inverness	19 Aug
56.97 i	Nicola Sanders	U20	23.06.82	1	Birmingham	4 Feb
	57.07			8r1	Long Beach, USA	21 Apr
	(80)					
56.99 mx	Katie Jones		4.01.77	1	Stretford	31 Jul
	57.4			4	Wigan	10 Jun
57.0	Charlotte Moore	U17	4.01.85	1	Kingston	14 Jul
57.0	Marilyn Okoro	U17	23.09.84	1	Guildford	29 Jul
	57.62			1rB	Derby	9 Sep
57.0	Lorraine Phillips		27.01.75	1rB	Coventry	5 Aug
57.04	Zoe Arnold		10.11.76	1	Antrim	8 Jul
57.07 i	Sarah Smith		18.08.76	3h3	Birmingham	27 Jan
57.1	Charlotte Best	U17	7.03.85	1	Crawley	18 Jul
57.13	Donna Chatting	U20	30.10.83	4	Watford	27 May
57.2	Charmaine Riley	U23	3.10.80	3	Birmingham	24 Jun
57.21	Katherine Livesey	U23	15.12.79	7	Los Angeles CA, USA	14 Apr
	(90)					
57.23 i	Hannah Stares		13.11.78	3h1	Birmingham	13 Jan
	57.3			1	Bath	26 Aug
57.23	Sandra Leigh	V35	26.02.66	1	Watford	13 May
57.26	Kirsten Martin		24.04.76	4	Cardiff	16 Jun
57.3	Laura Seston	U23	9.02.79	1	Ipswich	23 Jun
57.3	Sarah Beale	U20	12.07.82	2	Colchester	23 Jun
57.3	Samantha Adamson	U20	27.03.82	1	Bromley	11 Aug
57.33	Rebecca Martindale	U23	31.12.80	1	Gateshead	25 Aug
57.35	Susan Bovill	U20	6.05.82	3h2	Bedford	29 Jun
57.4	Jessica Cunliffe		25.11.77	4	Birmingham	24 Jun
57.4	Claire Raven		15.06.72	5	Birmingham	24 Jun

57.41	Laura Finucane	U17	3.08.86	1r4	Stretford	19 Jun
57.49	Claire Brason	U20	16.03.83	1	Gateshead	13 May

Additional Under 17 (1 - 5 above)

57.5	Katrina Wootton	2.09.85	1rB	Kingston	14 Jul
57.5	Vicky Griffiths	9.10.84	1	Wakefield	29 Jul
57.5	Rachel Newcombe	25.02.67	2rB	Coventry	5 Aug
57.6	Rebecca Sweeney	9.02.85	1rB	Wakefield	29 Jul
	57.74 i		3	Birmingham	3 Feb
	58.43		3	Derby	9 Sep
57.7	Maria Garavand	30.06.86	1	Bury St. Edmunds	16 Sep
(10)					
57.8	Jenny Christie	28.09.85	1	Sutton Coldfield	17 Jun
57.8	Lauren Webb	17.11.85	1	Carshalton	23 Jun
58.0	Rachael Thompson	15.11.85	1	Wigan	29 Apr
58.04	Laura Langowski	10.10.84	3	Bedford	22 Jul
58.16	Emma Kemp	11.10.84	1	Bedford	28 Jul
58.2	Faye Harding	7.09.85	1	Connah's Quay	26 May
58.5	Lucy Sings	9.07.85	2	Plymouth	19 May
58.5	Claire Burgoyne	9.07.86	1	Cosford	1 Sep
58.66	Elaine McCaffrey	2.11.84	1	Antrim	16 Jun
58.74	Rebecca Leitch	12.11.84	5	Belfast	28 Jul
(20)					
58.90	Natalie Plateau	19.10.84	3	London (He)	26 Aug
58.95	Jemma Thake	17.12.85	3	Bedford	28 Jul

Foreign

53.65	*Maiteland Marks (USA)*		*19.09.76*	*2r1*	*Azusa, USA*	*14 Apr*
54.64	*Sarah Reilly (IRL)*		*3.07.73*	*1h1*	*London (Ha)*	*16 Jun*
55.35	*Michelle Carey (IRL)*	*U23*	*20.02.81*	*3r1*	*Azusa, USA*	*14 Apr*
56.87	*Carolina Nylen (SWE)*	*U23*	*15.09.79*	*1r2*	*Long Beach, USA*	*21 Apr*

600 Yards

1:17.92 i	Lesley Owusu	21.12.78	1	Lincoln	3 Mar

600 Metres

1:27.60 +	Kelly Holmes		19.04.70	m	Gateshead	19 Aug
1:30.68 i	Alex Carter	U23	1.04.80	1	Birmingham	13 Feb
1:33.09	Christa Salt	V35	17.06.64	1	Basel, SUI	1 May

Under 13

1:39.5	Stephanie Lyall	3.02.89	1	Blackpool	23 Sep
1:41.0	Ellie McLoughlin	9.02.89	1	Stretford	27 Aug
1:45.5	Natalie Yates	20.11.88	1	Mansfield	8 Apr
1:46.5	Charlotte Taylor	17.04.89	1	Basildon	9 Jun
1:47.2	Jessica Corrie	22.04.89	1	Liverpool	13 May
1:47.2	Katie Knowles	6.06.90	1	Par	19 Aug
1:47.3	Laura Gillhespy	3.12.88	2	Stretford	16 Apr

800 Metres

1:57.88	Kelly Holmes	19.04.70	2	Zurich, SUI	17 Aug
	1:57.90		2	Brussels, BEL	24 Aug
	1:58.10		1	Gateshead	19 Aug
	1:58.85		2	London (CP)	22 Jul
	1:59.27		2	Brisbane, AUS	5 Sep
	1:59.41		5	Monaco, MON	20 Jul
	1:59.76		6	Edmonton, CAN	12 Aug
	1:59.78		4	Berlin, GER	31 Aug
	2:00.02		2	Melbourne, AUS	9 Sep
	2:00.08		2h1	Edmonton, CAN	9 Aug

(Holmes)	2:00.54			1	Madrid, ESP	7 Jul
	2:01.90			2s1	Edmonton, CAN	10 Aug
	2:02.61			1	Birmingham	14 Jul
2:01.87	Tanya Blake		16.01.71	2	Hengelo, NED	4 Jun
	2:02.30			5	Bremen, GER	23 Jun
	2:02.74			9	London (CP)	22 Jul
	2:04.08			2	Birmingham	14 Jul
2:02.81	Jo Fenn		19.10.74	6	Tula, RUS	9 Jun
	2:02.90 i			3	Birmingham	18 Feb
	2:03.40			1	Eton	7 Jul
	2:04.28			2h1	Birmingham	13 Jul
	2:04.32			2	Braga, POR	4 Jul
	2:04.44 i			3	Glasgow	18 Mar
	2:04.59			1	Loughborough	20 May
	2:04.60			7	Nuremberg, GER	17 Jun
2:03.30	Allison Curbishley		3.06.76	12	London (CP)	22 Jul
	2:04.40			3h1	Birmingham	13 Jul
	2:04.51			2	Budapest, HUN	1 Jul
	2:04.94			1	Watford	9 Jun
2:03.9	Lucy Vaughan		20.04.69	1	Watford	29 Aug
2:03.96	Susan Scott		26.09.77	1h1	Birmingham	13 Jul
	2:04.25			1	Edinburgh	25 Aug
	2:04.88			1	Heverlee, BEL	18 Aug
2:04.04	Jeina Mitchell		21.01.75	2rB	Tula, RUS	9 Jun
2:04.59	Kelly Caffel	U23	10.02.79	2	Liverpool	23 Jun
2:04.67	Hayley Tullett		17.02.73	3	Birmingham	14 Jul
	2:04.97			1	Cardiff	17 Jun
2:04.70	Emma Davies		9.10.78	4	Braga, POR	4 Jul
(10)						
2:04.9	Alex Carter	U23	1.04.80	1	Loughborough	13 Jun
	2:04.94			2	Loughborough	20 May
	2:04.94 mx			1	Stretford	14 Aug
2:04.93 mx	Helen Pattinson		2.01.74	1	Stretford	8 May
	2:05.50			1	Manchester	23 May
2:04.97	Sally Evans		14.05.75	1	Cardiff	4 Jul
2:04.98	Rachel Newcombe		25.02.67	3	Loughborough	20 May
	45 performances to 2:05.0 by 14 athletes including 2 indoors					
2:05.02	Mary McClung		19.12.71	2	Edinburgh	25 Aug
2:05.05	Rebecca Lyne	U20	4.07.82	1	Stretford	31 Jul
2:05.8	Jenny Meadows	U23	17.04.81	2	Loughborough	13 Jun
2:05.86	Charlotte Moore	U17	4.01.85	2	Stretford	31 Jul
2:05.96	Jennifer Ward		22.09.78	4	Loughborough	20 May
2:06.01	Olivia Hines	U20	19.10.83	7	Grosseto, ITA	21 Jul
(20)						
2:06.18	Sarah Knights		25.02.67	5	Loughborough	20 May
2:06.51	Danielle Barnes	U17	8.10.85	4	Debrecen, HUN	15 Jul
2:06.55	Danielle Thornal		9.08.75	2	Waltham, MA, USA	2 Jun
2:06.62	Jemma Simpson	U20	10.02.84	4	Watford	9 Jun
2:06.9	Emma Ward	U20	2.01.82	1	London (Cr)	3 Jun
2:07.24	Ellie Childs	U20	26.05.83	1	Watford	30 May
2:07.25	Morag MacLarty	U17	10.02.86	1	Tullamore, IRL	21 Jul
2:07.3	Lorraine Phillips		27.01.75	2	Rugby	3 Jun
2:07.35	Joanna Ross	U23	18.02.81	2	Glasgow (S)	24 Jun
2:07.5 mx	Vicky Lawrence		9.06.73	2	Stretford	17 Jul
	2:08.98			1	Bedford	27 May
(30)						
2:07.69 mx	Hayley Parkinson-Ovens		5.12.75	1	Grangemouth	1 Aug
	2:08.4			2	Coatbridge	29 Jul
2:07.8	Sarah Bull		4.06.75	3	Loughborough	13 Jun
2:08.02	Hayley Beard	U17	2.12.85	2	Tullamore, IRL	21 Jul
2:08.23	Ellen Leggate		4.02.78	3	Glasgow (S)	24 Jun

2:08.4	Lisa Dobriskey	U20	23.12.83	2	Newport	5 Aug
2:08.49	Kerry Smithson/Gillibrand		13.09.76	3	Eton	7 Jul
2:08.83	Rachel Felton	U23	27.06.79	4	Eton	7 Jul
2:08.54	Natalie Lewis	U20	25.05.82	1	Derby	29 Jul
2:08.57	Sarah Bouchard		23.10.74	1	Stretford	5 Jun
2:08.57	Kate Reed	U20	28.09.82	2	Derby	29 Jul
(40)						
2:08.72 i	Amanda Pritchard	U23	18.03.80	1	Cardiff	10 Mar
2:08.85	Zoe Jelbert	U20	21.01.84	1	Watford	27 May
2:08.85	Donna Riding	U20	28.11.83	1	Stretford	28 Aug
2:08.88	Faye Fullerton	U20	31.05.84	2	Watford	30 May
2:08.88	Katrina Wootton	U17	2.09.85	1	Watford	27 Jun
2:08.9	Bev Blakeman		4.04.74	1	Liverpool	17 Jun
2:09.0	Julie McDevitt/Barnett		15.03.73	4	Coventry	5 Aug
2:09.04	Emma Brady		3.01.74	1rB	Cardiff	4 Jul
2:09.07	Linda Staines	V35	26.12.63	2	Watford	25 Jul
2:09.3	Joy Wright		22.06.75	3rB	Solihull	23 Jun
(50)						
2:09.35 mx	Karen Johns	U23	18.08.80	1	Stretford	28 Aug
	2:09.8			1	Gateshead	1 Aug
2:09.41	Debbie Gunning	V35	31.08.65	3	Watford	30 May
2:09.44	Donna Fraser		7.11.72	4r3	Irvine CA, USA	6 May
2:09.45	Christa Salt	V35	17.06.64	2	Basel, SUI	4 Jun
2:09.45	Michelle Thomas		16.10.71	4h1	Birmingham	13 Jul
2:09.70 i	Celia Brown		22.01.77	3	Glasgow	18 Feb
	2:11.1			4	Wigan	4 Aug
2:09.7	Paula Fryer		14.07.69	3	Liverpool	17 Jun
2:10.00	Barbara Parker	U20	8.11.82	3	Watford	25 Jul
2:10.17	Charlotte Best	U17	7.03.85	2	Sheffield	11 Aug
2:10.26	Rachael Thompson	U17	15.11.85	1	Cudworth	27 May
(60)						
2:10.49	Laura Finucane	U17	3.08.86	2	Cudworth	27 May
2:10.52	Tommy Kemp	U23	5.03.80	2	Philadelphia PA, USA	8 Apr
2:10.70	Kathryn Sage		27.03.76	2rB	Cardiff	4 Jul
2:10.90	Sandra Andreou	V35	24.07.62	2	Watford	27 Jun
2:10.9	Suzanne Hasler	U20	7.04.82	1	Solihull	15 Aug
2:10.92	Claire Raven		15.06.72	10	Solihull	23 Jun
2:10.99	Karen Montador	U23	14.05.79	1	Glasgow (S)	29 Apr
2:11.0	Claire Entwistle		9.12.76	5rB	Solihull	23 Jun
2:11.05	Katie Brennan	U20	27.04.82	2	Stretford	5 Jun
2:11.10	Nisha Desai	U20	5.08.84	4rB	Manchester	23 May
(70)						
2:11.1	Emily Hathaway	U23	22.12.79	1	Leamington	12 May
2:11.1	Emma Hopkins	U15	16.09.86	1	Loughborough	13 May
2:11.1	Nikki Daniels	U20	25.08.82	2	Birmingham	26 May
2:11.1	Lucy Jones	U20	30.11.83	1	Rugby	19 Aug
2:11.19 i	Iona McIntyre	U20	14.03.83	1	Glasgow	14 Jan
2:11.2	Rachel Buller		31.08.76	3	Rugby	3 Jun
2:11.2	Angela Newport		21.10.70	2	Eton	5 Aug
2:11.3	Juliet Potter	U23	24.10.81	1	Nottingham	19 Aug
2:11.44	Freya Murray	U20	20.09.83	1	Derby	9 Sep
2:11.45	Karen McPherson/Hill		6.11.72	3	Stretford	19 Jun
(80)						
2:11.50 i	Lynne Gallagher		21.11.74	3h1	Birmingham	27 Jan
	2:11.5			1	Exeter	1 Sep
2:11.63	Louise Whittaker	U20	29.11.82	3	Stretford	28 Aug
2:11.67	Laurie Cossey	U23	24.11.81	3	Bedford	29 Jun
2:11.7	Adele Bevan	U20	26.03.84	1h1	Watford	26 May
2:11.7	Louisa Wood	U23	31.10.80	1	Bedford	22 Aug
2:11.87	Alice Butler		27.07.73	2	Sheffield	12 May
2:11.9	Jennifer Smith	U20	19.08.83	1	Stretford	14 Aug

2:11.9	Kim Heffernan		20.12.66	1	Brighton	22	Aug
2:11.91	Shirley Griffiths		23.06.72	5	Stretford	31	Jul
2:12.00	Maria Sharp		8.12.73	4	Watford	27	Jun
	(90)						
2:12.20	Tina Wales		2.11.77	1rB	Watford	9	Jun
2:12.26	Vicky Rolfe	U23	27.08.80	2rB	Watford	9	Jun
2:12.39	Danielle Woods	U17	2.10.84	5	Stretford	19	Jun
2:12.4	Ceri Mitchell	U20	9.12.82	6rB	Solihull	23	Jun
2:12.5	Mhairi Walker	U20	20.01.84	1	Livingston	29	Aug
2:12.65	Claire Robson	U20	9.01.84	2	Cudworth	27	May
2:12.7	Jillian Jones		23.12.69	1rB	Coventry	5	Aug
2:12.7	Debbie Sullivan		24.01.72	2	London (Nh)	11	Aug
2:12.7	Sarah Pickering	U20	26.10.83	4	Solihull	15	Aug
2:12.79 i	Kirsty Baird		29.08.71	4h1	Birmingham	27	Jan
	(100)						
2:12.8	Rachael Nathan	U17	27.04.86	1	Leeds	5	Aug
2:12.83	Lois Brooks	U15	10.01.87	1r3	Manchester	23	May
2:12.85	Lisa Whigham	U23	14.08.80	5rB	Glasgow (S)	11	Aug
2:12.90	Dominique Oughton	U23	2.01.81	4rB	Cardiff	4	Jul
2:12.90	Lesley Clarkson	U20	18.07.82	6rB	Glasgow (S)	11	Aug
2:12.92	Sarah Salmon		9.09.74	1	Canberra, AUS	13	Feb

Additional Under 17 (1 - 10 above)

2:13.86	Jenna Hill		16.10.85	3r3	Manchester	23	May
2:14.05	Natalie Fullman		20.05.85	4s1	Exeter	6	Jul
2:14.35	Isabelle Stoate		16.07.86	3r3	Solihull	23	Jun
2:14.37	Emily Adams		27.01.85	5s1	Exeter	6	Jul
2:14.5	Emma Hunt		25.04.86	2	London (He)	23	Jun
2:14.72 i	Gemma Jones		12.11.84	3	Cardiff	11	Feb
	2:16.80			6	Street	7	May
2:14.9	Krystal Palmer		7.09.84	1	Dublin (S), IRL	23	Jun
2:15.1	Hayley Wills		18.01.85	2h2	Watford	26	May
2:15.26	Hollie Smith		9.12.84	2	Watford	25	Jul
2:15.3	Lauren Reynolds		3.10.84	1	St. Ives	12	May
	(20)						
2:15.3	Phillipa Aukett		9.09.84	1h4	Watford	26	May
2:15.38	Nikki Silva		17.08.85	1	London (He)	26	Aug
2:15.6	Helen Glover		17.06.86	1	Exeter	16	Jun
2:15.98	Laura Gilbert		10.06.85	3s2	Exeter	6	Jul
2:16.1	Charlotte Wickham		21.06.85	1	Rotherham	20	May
2:16.3 mx	Laura Nurse		16.07.85	3	Exeter	28	Aug
2:16.4 mx	Katherine Humphries		28.11.85	4	Exeter	28	Aug
2:16.51	Claire Burgoyne		9.07.86	1h1	Sheffield	11	Aug
2:16.52	Sharon Lamont		12.08.86	2	Edinburgh	13	May
2:16.6	Gemma Turtle		15.05.86	1	Watford	23	May
	(30)						
2:16.8	Michelle Jessop		21.09.85	2	Nyiregyhaza, HUN	25	Jul
2:16.90	Claire Wilson		7.11.85	6	Tullamore, IRL	21	Jul
2:17.0	Ruth Chadney		20.04.85	1	Exeter	26	Jun

Additional Under 15 (1 - 2 above)

2:14.32	Nicola Maddick		6.08.87	1	Cudworth	26	May
2:14.32	Elizabeth McWilliams		3.06.87	4	Tullamore, IRL	21	Jul
2:14.52	Sara Luck		18.11.86	2rB	Watford	25	Jul
2:14.67	Linzi Snow		8.06.87	2	Exeter	7	Jul
2:14.81 i	Lynsey Jepson		12.01.87	2	Birmingham	14	Jan
	2:16.1			1	Birmingham	22	Jul
2:15.15	Abby Westley		15.07.87	7r5	Stretford	31	Jul
2:15.3	Nikki Hamblin		20.05.88	1	Bournemouth	22	Jul
2:15.42	Carolyn Plateau		22.08.88	3h2	Exeter	6	Jul
	(10)						
2:15.47	Anna Simmonds		22.09.86	4h2	Exeter	6	Jul

2:16.1	Nicola Bear		14.01.87	2	Stoke-on-Trent	17 Jun
2:16.17	Anna Kirby		16.09.86	2h1	Exeter	6 Jul
2:16.7	Hannah England		6.03.87	1	Worthing	14 Jul
2:17.01	Lisa Lanini		9.10.87	3	Connah's Quay	4 Aug
2:17.30	Lauren Cunningham		22.08.87	4h1	Exeter	6 Jul
2:17.6	Stacey Johnson		15.04.87	2	Telford	1 Jul
2:17.79	Claire Macauley		27.09.86	1	Aberdeen	27 May
2:17.9	Lyndsey Barr		19.01.88	1	Norwich	22 Jul
2:18.1	Megan Foley		14.04.88	1	Ipswich	29 Jul
(20)						
2:18.32	Hannah Bates		8.10.86	5h2	Exeter	6 Jul
2:18.5	Charlotte Browning		8.10.87	3rA	Crawley	18 Jul
2:18.7	Becky Townsend		29.03.87	1	Stretford	8 Jul
2:18.98	Laura Tanner		13.11.86	4r1	Watford	1 Aug
2:19.00	Sarah Davison		4.12.86	6h2	Exeter	6 Jul
Under 13						
2:23.2	Stephanie Lyall		3.02.89	1	Dunfermline	8 Sep
2:23.4	Ellie McLoughlin		9.02.89	2	Rotherham	5 Aug
2:23.77	Natalie Yates		20.11.88		Birmingham	16 Jun
2:25.1	Catriona Witcombe		6.12.88	1r1	Poole	8 Jul
2:25.74	Emma MacAlister-Hall		19.02.89	1	Sheffield	13 May
2:26.09	Jessica Corrie		22.04.89	1r1	Birmingham	2 Sep
2:26.4	Lara Clarke		4.10.88	1	London (He)	23 Jun
2:26.5	Laura Gillhespy		3.12.88	3	Rotherham	5 Aug
2:26.6	Claire Tarplee		22.09.88	1	Nottingham	8 Sep
2:26.69	Emma Pallant		4.06.89		Watford	25 Jul
(10)						
2:26.9	Non Stanford		8.01.89	1	Neath	24 Jun
2:27.2	Emily Pidgeon		1.06.89	1	Cheltenham	13 May
2:27.2	Laura Scougall			1	Birmingham	22 Jul
2:27.2	Lana Taylor		2.10.88	2	Nottingham	8 Sep
2:27.4	Laura Bache		24.10.88	1	Sutton Coldfield	1 Jul
Foreign						
2:08.03	*Carolina Nylen (SWE)*	*U23*	*15.09.79*	*5*	*Ludvika, SWE*	*27 Jun*

1000 Metres

2:43.69 A	Kelly Holmes		19.04.70	1	Rustenberg, RSA	22 Jan
2:45.41 i+	Hayley Tullett		17.02.73	1m	Glasgow	18 Mar
2:48.26	Christa Salt	V35	17.06.64	1	Glarus, SUI	19 May
Under 13						
3:05.9	Natalie Yates		20.11.88	1	Nottingham	27 May
3:08.2	Rhea Fallows		30.01.89	1	Stretford	27 Aug
3:09.9	Emma Pallant		4.06.89	1	Reading	16 Sep
3:10.7	Becky Shore		2.09.88	2	Reading	16 Sep

1200 Metres - Under 13

3:49.6	Non Stanford	8.01.89	1	Yate	22 Jul
3:51.1	Natalie Yates	20.11.88	1	Wakefield	1 Jul
3:52.5	Emily Pidgeon	1.06.89	1r3	Tipton	20 May
3:53.3	Ellie McLoughlin	9.02.89	1	Bury	22 Jul
3:54.54	Claire Tarplee	22.09.88	1r1	Birmingham	2 Sep
3:56.9	Samantha Barber		1	Stretford	13 May
3:57.0	Emma MacAlister-Hall	19.02.89	1	York	20 May
3:59.0	Danielle Walker	17.03.89	2r2	Tipton	20 May
3:59.0	Amanda Bailey	27.11.88	1	Bournemouth	22 Jul
4:00.1	Rhea Fallows	30.01.89	2	Stretford	13 May
4:00.1	Bethan Dainton	12.04.89	1r1	Tipton	20 May
4:00.1	Laura Evans		2	Bury St. Edmunds	22 Jul
4:00.83	Melissa Rowan		2r1	Birmingham	2 Sep

1500 Metres

4:03.54	Hayley Tullett		17.02.73	6	Monaco, MON	20 Jul
	4:04.23			5	Rome, ITA	29 Jun
	4:06.75 i			2	Glasgow	18 Mar
	4:07.83			3	Bremen, GER	24 Jun
	4:09.31			4	Hengelo, NED	4 Jun
	4:13.60			2h3	Edmonton, CAN	4 Aug
	4:13.95			9s2	Edmonton, CAN	5 Aug
4:05.37	Paula Radcliffe		17.12.73	3	Glasgow (S)	1 Jul
4:07.56	Helen Pattinson		2.01.74	11	Rome, ITA	29 Jun
	4:09.22			6	Glasgow (S)	1 Jul
	4:10.86			8	Nice, FRA	9 Jul
	4:11.01			7	Hengelo, NED	4 Jun
	4:13.06			9h2	Edmonton, CAN	4 Aug
	4:13.40			1	Izegem, BEL	9 Jun
	4:14.49			1	Birmingham	14 Jul
	4:16.39			9s1	Edmonton, CAN	5 Aug
4:11.99	Kelly Caffel	U23	10.02.79	1	Watford	25 Jul
	4:12.30			3	Amsterdam, NED	14 Jul
	4:12.34			3	Kiev, UKR	25 May
	4:13.29			3	Lucerne, SUI	27 Jun
	4:13.53			4	Funchal, POR	30 Jun
	4:13.78			1	Loughborough	20 May
	4:17.39			2h2	Amsterdam, NED	12 Jul
	4:18.36			5h3	Beijing, CHN	28 Aug
4:12.08	Kathy Butler		22.10.73	8	Palo Alto, USA	9 Jun
4:13.02	Kerry Smithson/Gillibrand		13.09.76	2	Solihull	23 Jun
	4:16.56			1	Watford	9 Jun
	4:19.08			3	Manchester	23 May
4:13.38	Emma Ward	U20	2.01.82	1	Glasgow (S)	7 May
	4:13.51			2	Grosseto, ITA	22 Jul
	4:15.22			3	Loughborough	20 May
	4:19.75			1	Stoke-on-Trent	18 Aug
	4:19.97			2h2	Grosseto, ITA	20 Jul
4:13.68	Sarah Bull		4.06.75	3	Solihull	23 Jun
	4:17.10			4	Watford	9 Jun
	4:18.32			1	Stretford	31 Jul
	4:19.30			4	Birmingham	14 Jul
4:14.01	Rachel Newcombe		25.02.67	4	Solihull	23 Jun
	4:15.16			2	Cardiff	4 Jul
	4:17.83			1	Glasgow (S)	11 Aug
	4:18.16			6	Watford	9 Jun
	4:18.60			2	Manchester	23 May
4:14.14	Jeina Mitchell		21.01.75	2	Loughborough	20 May
	(10)					
4:14.44	Alex Carter	U23	1.04.80	2	Glasgow (S)	7 May
4:14.46	Ellen Leggate		4.02.78	3	Glasgow (S)	7 May
	4:16.13			3	Birmingham	14 Jul
	4:18.95			7	Cork, IRL	7 Jul
	4:19.29			8	Watford	9 Jun
4:15.01	Liz Yelling		5.12.74	2	Birmingham	14 Jul
4:16.29	Susan Scott		26.09.77	9	Tula, RUS	9 Jun
	4:18.37			3	Budapest, HUN	1 Jul
4:18.68	Angela Newport		21.10.70	2	Watford	25 Jul
	4:19.43			2	Glasgow (S)	11 Aug
4:18.72	Rachel Felton	U23	27.06.79	2	Durham NC, USA	7 Apr
	4:19.49			2h2	Eugene, USA	31 May
4:19.87	Hayley Parkinson-Ovens		5.12.75	1	Glasgow (S)	23 Jun
	56 performances to 4:20.0 by 17 athletes including 1 indoors					
4:20.56	Zoe Jelbert	U20	21.01.84	5	Debrecen, HUN	15 Jul

4:21.37	Sharon Morris		5.07.68	1rB	Watford	9 Jun
4:21.40	Catherine Berry		8.10.75	6	Madrid, ESP	7 Jul
(20)						
4:22.34	Jo Wilkinson		2.05.73	5	Birmingham	14 Jul
4:22.72	Debbie Sullivan		24.01.72	3	Watford	25 Jul
4:22.76	Faye Fullerton	U20	31.05.84	4rB	Watford	9 Jun
4:23.07	Charlotte Moore	U17	4.01.85	1	Bedford	22 Aug
4:23.08	Pauline Thom		2.08.70	9	Arnhem, NED	4 Jul
4:23.13	Ann-Marie Hutchison		21.08.77	4	Glasgow (S)	11 Aug
4:23.8	Hayley Yelling		3.01.74	2	London (Ha)	17 Jun
4:24.41	Debbie Gunning	V35	31.08.65	5rB	Watford	9 Jun
4:24.62	Gillian Palmer	U23	30.12.80	7	Berkeley, USA	20 May
4:24.63 i+	Danielle Thornal		9.08.75	4	New York, USA	20 Jan
(30)						
4:24.69	Natalie Lewis	U20	25.05.82	6	Loughborough	20 May
4:24.70	Katrina Wootton	U17	2.09.85	1	Watford	27 May
4:25.10	Freya Murray	U20	20.09.83	2	Glasgow (S)	23 Jun
4:25.1	Juliet Potter	U23	24.10.81	1	Nottingham	19 Aug
4:25.11	Jo Ankier	U20	5.08.82	8	Loughborough	20 May
4:25.40	Catherine Dugdale		29.11.74	9	Loughborough	20 May
4:25.4 mx	Sarah Bouchard		23.10.74	1	Stretford	17 Jul
	4:25.6			1	Stretford	13 May
4:25.43	Sarah Salmon		9.09.74	1	Canberra, AUS	23 Jan
4:25.53	Tanya Blake		16.01.71	1	Eton	7 Jul
4:25.60 i	Maria Sharp		8.12.73	4	Birmingham	27 Jan
	4:29.53			11rB	Watford	9 Jun
(40)						
4:25.6	Karen Montador	U23	14.05.79	3	Liverpool	23 Jun
4:25.65	Jilly Ingman		17.08.78	14	Watford	9 Jun
4:25.85	Lisa Dobriskey	U20	23.12.83	1	Exeter	7 Jul
4:26.3	Amanda Parkinson		21.07.71	1	Wigan	10 Jun
4:26.3	Tara Krzywicki		9.03.74	2	Nottingham	26 Aug
4:26.47	Penny Thackray		18.08.74	2	Bedford	21 Jul
4:27.17	Louise Whittaker	U20	29.11.82	1rB	Manchester	23 May
4:27.27	Shirley Griffiths		23.06.72	3	Eton	7 Jul
4:27.3	Danielle Barnes	U17	8.10.85	2	Bedford	30 Jun
4:27.45	Katie Brennan	U20	27.04.82	3	Stretford	31 Jul
(50)						
4:27.5	Rachael Nathan	U17	27.04.86	1	Bury St. Edmunds	16 Jun
4:28.56	Jane Potter	U23	24.10.81	2	Street	7 May
4:28.71	Sally Evans		14.05.75	15	Watford	9 Jun
4:28.74	Louise Damen	U20	12.10.82	10rB	Watford	9 Jun
4:28.88	Lynne Gallagher		21.11.74	1	Watford	15 Aug
4:29.04	Jessica Woolley	U23	19.01.80	1rB	Solihull	23 Jun
4:29.06 i	Christa Salt	V35	17.06.64	2	Ludwigshafen, GER	20 Jan
	4:31.90			1	Liestal, SUI	16 May
4:29.13	Susie Rutherford	U23	26.02.79	3	Tempe AZ, USA	5 May
4:29.2	Julie Mitchell		3.10.74	1	Bedford	28 May
4:29.3	Sarah Knights		25.02.67	1	Norwich	13 May
(60)						
4:29.46	Charlotte Dale	U20	23.03.84	1	London (He)	26 Aug
4:29.60	Sophie Alford		5.12.75	2	Bedford	28 May
4:29.74	Danielle Woods	U17	2.10.84	2rB	Solihull	23 Jun
4:29.79	Emma O'Dowd	U23	25.04.80	6	Glasgow (S)	7 May
4:29.8	Bev Blakeman		4.04.74	1	Gateshead	30 May
4:29.82	Ellie Childs	U20	26.05.83	2	London (He)	26 Aug
4:29.93	Sue Lamb		24.03.70	4	Eton	7 Jul
4:30.19	Emma Brady		3.01.74	2rC	Watford	9 Jun
4:30.2	Lucy Vaughan		20.04.69	1	Crawley	18 Jul
4:30.68	Collette Fagan	U20	6.06.82	3	Glasgow (S)	23 Jun
(70)						

4:30.9	Sue Cripsey	U23	8.01.81	2	Norwich	13 May
4:30.9	Kate Reed	U20	28.09.82	1	Yate	9 Jun
4:31.03	Sonia Thomas	U23	16.05.79	6	Eton	7 Jul
4:31.22	Karen Johns	U23	18.08.80	3rC	Watford	9 Jun
4:31.66	Hannah Whitmore	U20	24.02.84	3rB	Solihull	23 Jun
4:31.68 A	Kelly Holmes		19.04.70	7	Roodepoort, RSA	16 Mar
4:31.74	Kathryn Waugh		20.02.73	4rC	Watford	9 Jun
4:31.8	Sandra Andreou	V35	24.07.62	6	London (Ha)	17 Jun
4:31.95	Maria Skelton	U23	18.05.80	1rB	Glasgow (S)	11 Aug
4:32.64 mx	Liz Proctor		31.10.72	2	Stretford	28 Aug
(80)						
4:32.8	Karen Hind	U23	31.07.79	2	Gateshead	30 May
4:33.01	Caroline Pimblett/Johnson		28.01.75	9	Manchester	23 May
4:33.2 i	Jessica Nugent	U20	27.08.84			
	4:33.30			4	Street	7 May
4:33.2	Jo Lodge		6.01.68	1	London (He)	23 Jun
4:33.23	Sarah Herbert	U20	29.08.83	5rB	Solihull	23 Jun
4:33.5	Emily Hathaway	U23	22.12.79	1	Sutton Coldfield	11 Jul
4:33.63	Morag MacLarty	U17	10.02.86	1	Tullamore, IRL	21 Jul
4:33.88	Bernadine Pritchett		25.01.67	8	Eton	7 Jul

Additional Under 17 (1 - 6 above)

4:34.12	Emma Hunt	25.04.86	2	Tullamore, IRL	21 Jul
4:34.49	Jenna Hill	16.10.85	6	Stretford	31 Jul
4:35.78	Gemma Turtle	15.05.86	2	Watford	27 May
4:37.74	Emma Whittaker	31.10.85	1r3	Solihull	23 Jun
(10)					
4:39.26	Isabelle Stoate	16.07.86	4	Watford	27 May
4:40.10	Rosie Smith	28.06.85	1	Sheffield	11 Aug
4:40.14	Vicky Holland	12.01.86	4h1	Exeter	6 Jul
4:40.15	Chloe Wilkinson	16.12.84	5	Watford	27 May
4:40.92	Sharon Lamont	12.08.86	2	Grangemouth	10 Jun
4:40.93	Laura Kenney	27.06.85	2h2	Exeter	6 Jul
4:41.06	Natalie Bass	3.12.85	2	Sheffield	11 Aug
4:41.1	Lauren Reynolds	3.10.84	2	Bury St. Edmunds	16 Jun
4:41.30	Charlotte Best	7.03.85	4	London (He)	26 Aug
4:42.4	Fiona Thompson	15.07.86	1	Coatbridge	15 Jul
(20)					
4:42.61	Stacey Ward	16.01.85	7h1	Exeter	6 Jul
4:43.00	Eloise Pittwood	4.12.85	5h2	Exeter	6 Jul
4:43.8	Charlotte Wickham	21.06.85	1	Jarrow	18 Jul
4:44.1	Jennifer Pereira	8.08.85	1	London (Cr)	22 Jul
4:44.2	Josephine Rhodes	22.03.86	1h2	Watford	26 May
4:44.30	Lorna Vyse	2.12.84	1	Watford	11 Jul
4:44.33	Amanda Jones	7.10.84	10	Street	7 May
4:44.6	Rachel Deegan	10.01.86	3	Stretford	9 Jun
4:44.6	Emily Adams	27.01.85	1	Crawley	18 Jul
4:44.94	Emma Carroll	23.03.86	7h2	Exeter	6 Jul
(30)					
4:45.0	Helen Glover	17.06.86	4h2	Watford	26 May
4:45.5 i	Helen Stevenson	4.12.84	1	Glasgow	25 Jan
4:45.6	Kiera Vogel	31.05.86	3	Stoke-on-Trent	16 Jun
4:45.92 i	Samantha Marshall	26.08.85	3	Birmingham	24 Feb
	4:46.25		2	Edinburgh	13 May
4:46.48	Laura Nurse	16.07.85	5r2	Street	7 May
4:46.8	Cheryl Guiney	24.09.85	1	Belfast	29 Apr
4:46.89	Genevieve Gardener	3.09.84	9	Watford	27 May

Under 15

4:35.85	Charlotte Browning	8.10.87	1	Sheffield	12 Aug
4:37.09	Lynsey Jepson	12.01.87	1	Exeter	7 Jul

4:38.47	Nikki Hamblin		20.05.88	3	Exeter	7 Jul
4:38.70	Leonie Smith		20.12.86	3	Sheffield	12 Aug
4:39.33	Jo Harper		11.05.87	4	Exeter	7 Jul
4:39.37	Hannah England		6.03.87	4	Sheffield	12 Aug
4:39.95	Abby Westley		15.07.87	6	Exeter	7 Jul
4:41.06	Nicola Sykes		30.06.87	7	Exeter	7 Jul
4:44.1	Sara Luck		18.11.86	1	Colchester	7 May
4:44.21	Rebecca Ellis		20.12.86	5h1	Exeter	6 Jul
(10)						
4:44.27	Lyndsey Barr		19.01.88	3	Watford	27 May
4:44.6	Stacey Johnson		15.04.87	1	Rugby	19 Aug
4:45.41	Laura Kirk		20.02.87	6	Sheffield	12 Aug
4:46.03	Becky Townsend		29.03.87	11	Stretford	6 Jun
4:46.31	Sammy Hart		13.04.87	7h1	Exeter	6 Jul
4:46.5	Megan Foley		14.04.88	1	Enfield	1 Jul
4:47.1	Jill Scott		2.02.87	1	Carlisle	20 May
4:48.1	Sarah Drury		30.09.87	2	Stoke-on-Trent	17 Jun
4:48.3	Nicola Maddick		6.08.87	1	Grimsby	13 May
4:48.37	Jennifer Emsley		28.11.86	1	Grangemouth	12 Aug
(20)						
4:48.39	Charlotte Watkins		13.02.88	5	Watford	27 May
4:48.83	Lauren Cunningham		22.08.87	8	Sheffield	12 Aug
4:49.1	Laura Tanner		13.11.86	1	Guildford	23 Jun
4:49.32	Katherine Uphill		19.02.88	4h2	Exeter	6 Jul
4:49.51	Jolene Ennis		17.03.87	9	Sheffield	12 Aug
4:49.7	Louise Durman		23.11.86	2	Exeter	16 Jun
4:49.9 mx	Natalie Real		14.11.87	8r3	Exeter	31 Jul
Under 13						
4:45.7 i	Emily Pidgeon		1.06.89	1	Cardiff	24 Nov
	4:54.51			2r3	Millfield	7 May
4:52.81	Emma Pallant		4.06.89	1r3	Millfield	7 May
4:55.14	Non Stanford		8.01.89	4r3	Millfield	7 May
4:57.9	Natalie Yates		20.11.88	1T	Tamworth	3 Jun
4:58.1	Stacie Preston		12.05.89	1r1	Bromley	1 Sep
4:59.08 mx	Stephanie Lyall		3.02.89	2	Grangemouth	5 Sep
5:00.3	Rhea Fallows		30.01.89	10h2	Stretford	14 Aug
5:01.9	Ellie McLoughlin		9.02.89	1	Wigan	19 Aug
5:02.8	Danielle Walker		17.03.89	1	Blackpool	13 May
5:03.9	Amanda Bailey		27.11.88	1	Banbury	14 Jul
(10)						
5:04.16	Laura Dowsing		17.06.89	8rD	Watford	30 May
5:04.3	Claire Tarplee		22.09.88	1	Birmingham	10 Jun
5:05.2	Dominique Daly		10.01.89	3	Crawley	9 Jun
5:05.8	Jodie Hallett			2r1	Kingston	29 Jul
5:05.8	Catriona Witcombe		6.12.88	1	Southampton	8 Sep
Foreign						
4:32.28	*Kelley Wilder (USA)*		*30.07.71*	*7*	*Glasgow (S)*	*7 May*
4:33.18	*Stephanie Van Graan (RSA)*		*4.02.77*	*7*	*Eton*	*7 Jul*

1 Mile

4:26.52 i	Hayley Tullett		17.02.73	4	Stuttgart, GER	4 Feb
4:38.28	Catherine Berry		8.10.75	4	Princeton, USA	12 May
4:42.67	Danielle Thornal		9.08.75	7	Princeton, USA	12 May
4:45.49 i	Rachel Felton	U23	27.06.79	1h1	Boston, USA	3 Mar

2000 Metres

5:39.3 +e	Paula Radcliffe		17.12.73	2m	Zurich, SUI	17 Aug
5:53.14 +	Joanne Pavey		20.09.73	1m	Rieti, ITA	2 Sep
5:53.8 +	Kathy Butler		22.10.73	2m	Eugene, USA	27 May
5:57.85	Catherine Berry		8.10.75	8	Villeneuve d'Ascq, FRA	17 Jun

3000 Metres

8:26.97	Paula Radcliffe		17.12.73	5	Rome, ITA	29 Jun
	8:28.07			5	Zurich, SUI	17 Aug
	8:32.02			6	Brussels, BEL	24 Aug
	8:42.47			1	Gateshead	19 Aug
	8:44.7 +			2m	Berlin, GER	30 Aug
	8:48.74 +			1m	London (CP)	22 Jul
	8:54.38 +			1m	Bremen, GER	24 Jun
	9:12.90 +			1m	Barakaldo, ESP	7 Apr
8:36.58	Joanne Pavey		20.09.73	9	Brussels, BEL	24 Aug
	8:44.05			2	Rieti, ITA	2 Sep
	8:50.0 +			6m	Berlin, GER	30 Aug
	8:51.14			2	Gateshead	19 Aug
	8:58.97			7	Lausanne, SUI	4 Jul
	9:13.6 +			3m	Birmingham	15 Jul
	9:14.41 +			m	Edmonton, CAN	9 Aug
	9:18 +e			m	Edmonton, CAN	11 Aug
8:40.97	Kathy Butler		22.10.73	10	Brussels, BEL	24 Aug
	8:43.23			10	Saint-Denis, FRA	6 Jul
	8:46.01			2	Eugene, USA	27 May
	8:52.05			3	Gateshead	19 Aug
	8:53.63			13	Rome, ITA	29 Jun
	8:54.96 i			4	Boston, USA	4 Feb
	8:58.60 i			6h2	Lisbon, POR	9 Mar
	9:03.71			1	Bremen, GER	23 Jun
	9:04.81 i			11	Lisbon, POR	10 Mar
	9:13.2 +			2m	Birmingham	15 Jul
8:45.36 i	Hayley Tullett		17.02.73	8	Lisbon, POR	10 Mar
	8:48.25 i			4	Birmingham	18 Feb
	8:51.73			7	Seville, ESP	8 Jun
	8:52.18 i			4	Erfurt,GER	2 Feb
	9:02.23 i			5h1	Lisbon, POR	9 Mar
8:57.3 mx	Liz Yelling		5.12.74	1	Watford	25 Jul
	9:08.13 mx			2	Cardiff	4 Jul
	9:20.23			1	Ashford	11 Aug
8:58.98 mx	Hayley Yelling		3.01.74	1	Cardiff	4 Jul
	9:03.5 +			m	London (CP)	22 Jul
	9:12.80 +			1m	Birmingham	15 Jul
9:03.71	Helen Pattinson		2.01.74	6	Gateshead	19 Aug
	9:05.70			1	Loughborough	20 May
9:04.26 mx	Amanda Parkinson		21.07.71	1	Stretford	6 Jun
	9:25.9 e+			2m	Solihull	23 Jun
9:08.12	Angela Newport		21.10.70	2	Loughborough	20 May
	9:08.91 mx			2	Stretford	6 Jun
9:08.7 mx	Ellen Leggate		4.02.78	1	Watford	27 Jun
(10)						
9:08.90 mx	Bev Jenkins		6.02.70	1	Stretford	8 May
	9:41.63			1	Birmingham	30 Jun
9:09.61 mx	Catherine Berry		8.10.75	3	Cardiff	4 Jul
	9:21.89			1	Knoxville TN, USA	12 Apr
	44 performances to 9:20.0 by 12 athletes including 7 indoors					
9:20.1	Tara Krzywicki		9.03.74	1	Nuneaton	5 Aug
9:20.93 mx	Ann-Marie Hutchison		21.08.77	4	Cardiff	4 Jul
9:21.19	Sheila Fairweather		24.11.77	3	Loughborough	20 May
9:21.36	Juliet Potter	U23	24.10.81	1	Street	7 May
9:21.77	Sarah Bull		4.06.75	4	Loughborough	20 May
9:22.45	Collette Fagan	U20	6.06.82	2	Mannheim, GER	15 Jun
9:23.21	Lucy Elliott	V35	9.03.66	1	Bedford	21 Jul
9:24.49	Dianne Henaghan	V35	6.08.65	1	Glasgow (S)	11 Aug
(20)						

9:25.9 e+	Karen Hind	U23	31.07.79	3m	Solihull	23 Jun
9:28.27 mx	Catherine Dugdale		29.11.74	1	Stretford	28 Aug
	9:36.87			2	Glasgow (S)	11 Aug
9:28.61	Louise Damen	U20	12.10.82	6	Loughborough	20 May
9:30.0	Emma Ward	U20	2.01.82	1	Yate	29 Apr
9:31.06	Hayley Parkinson-Ovens		5.12.75	1	Glasgow (S)	29 Apr
9:31.2	Penny Thackray		18.08.74	1	Sheffield	28 Apr
9:31.69	Rachael Nathan	U17	27.04.86	1	Stoke-on-Trent	18 Aug
9:32.4 mx	Sharon Morris		5.07.68	1	Watford	1 Aug
	9:37.56			1	Bedford	28 Jul
9:32.81	Helen Pearson	U23	8.02.81	7	Loughborough	20 May
9:34.4 +	Birhan Dagne		8.04.78	m	Birmingham	15 Jul
	9:38.74			2	Bedford	21 Jul
(30)						
9:35.3	Debbie Sullivan		24.01.72	1	London (BP)	20 May
9:35.46 +	Danielle Barnes	U17	8.10.85	m	Manchester	23 May
9:35.59	Emma O'Dowd	U23	25.04.80	8	Loughborough	20 May
9:36.01	Amber Gascoigne	U23	5.09.79	9	Loughborough	20 May
9:36.42	Charlotte Dale	U20	23.03.84	3	Stoke-on-Trent	18 Aug
9:37.42	Sharon Hatch	V35	5.09.64	4	Edinburgh	25 Aug
9:39.4	Gillian Palmer	U23	30.12.80	1	Bedford	1 Jul
9:40.93	Sonia Thomas	U23	16.05.79	4	Glasgow (S)	11 Aug
9:41.5	Jo Wilkinson		2.05.73	1	Reading	19 May
9:41.74	Allison Higgins		8.04.72	2	Glasgow (S)	29 Apr
(40)						
9:42.2 mx	Jenny Heath		22.12.77	1	Stretford	24 Apr
9:42.42 i	Emma Ford		16.02.77	2	Birmingham	27 Jan
9:42.9	Lisa Webb	V35	9.10.65	1	London (He)	12 May
9:43.64	Jo Lodge		6.01.68	3	Birmingham	2 Jun
9:44.15 mx	Heather Knight	V35	27.09.63	2	Stretford	28 Aug
9:44.36 i	Jilly Ingman		17.08.78	3	Birmingham	27 Jan
	9:47.7			2	Sheffield	28 Apr
9:44.41 i	Jessica Woolley	U23	19.01.80	1	Cardiff	8 Dec
9:45.1	Kathryn Waugh		20.02.73	1	Gateshead	25 Aug
9:45.50	Clare Martin		18.05.76	10	Loughborough	20 May
9:45.5	Caroline Walsh	U23	29.04.80	1	Loughborough	23 May
(50)						
9:45.8	Faye Fullerton	U20	31.05.84	1	Hayes	29 Apr
9:46.1	Sarah Salmon		9.09.74	1	Canberra, AUS	30 Jan
9:46.2	Christina Radon	U23	12.07.79	3	Wigan	4 Aug
9:47.62	Caroline Pimblett/Johnson		28.01.75	4	Birmingham	2 Jun
9:47.82	Michelle Brooks		6.02.77	2	Lawrence, USA	21 Apr
9:48.55 i	Zoe Jelbert	U20	21.01.84	1	Birmingham	25 Feb
9:48.60	Ruth Brown	U23	9.04.80	5	Glasgow (S)	11 Aug
9:48.6	Kate Reed	U20	28.09.82	1	Yate	3 Sep
9:48.8	Shirley Griffiths		23.06.72	4	Wigan	4 Aug
9:49.1 mx	Sue Cripsey	U23	8.01.81	1	Watford	11 Apr
(60)						
9:49.86	Claire Smallwood		15.03.77	6	Glasgow (S)	11 Aug
9:50.40 i	Pauline Thom		2.08.70	2	Nenagh, IRL	4 Feb
	9:51.22			5	Birmingham	2 Jun
9:50.74	Dorothea Lee		28.07.77	2	Street	7 May
9:52.1	Clare Martin		14.09.74	3	Solihull	24 Jun
9:53.1 mx	Sonia Clark	U20	1.04.84	1	Stretford	17 Jul
	9:56.0			6	Wigan	4 Aug
9:53.42	Helen Zenner	U20	15.08.82	2	Cardiff	8 Dec
9:53.48 i	Charlotte Moore	U17	4.01.85	2	Birmingham	25 Feb
9:53.5	Andrea Whitcombe		8.06.71	1	Bedford	11 Aug
9:53.84	Courtney Birch	U17	5.10.84	4	Street	7 May
9:53.89	Lisa Mawer		22.05.68	1	Sheffield	12 May
(70)						

9:54.1	Freya Murray	U20	20.09.83	5	Wigan	4 Aug
9:54.1	Karen Sindall	U23	17.01.81	2	Basildon	22 Sep
9:54.32 mx	Morag McDonnell		27.08.73	1r2	Stretford	5 Jun
9:54.4	Debra Curley		20.09.71	1	Wigan	21 Apr
9:55.1	Charlotte Coffey	U23	28.07.80	4	Bedford	1 Jul
9:55.54 i	Sarah Davey		13.10.78	5r1	Gainesville FL, USA	13 Jan
9:55.71 i	Emily Pidgeon	U13	1.06.89	3U15	Cardiff	8 Dec
9:55.8 mx	Maria Skelton	U23	18.05.80	1	Antrim	25 Jul
9:56.5	Pauline Powell		17.05.73	1	Stretford	28 May
9:56.8 mx	Jill Shannon	U20	23.04.82	2	Antrim	25 Jul
(80)						
9:56.83 i	Christa Salt	V35	17.06.64	1	Ludwigshafen, GER	14 Jan
9:56.86 i	Susan Miles	U23	1.11.81	5	Glasgow (S)	18 Feb
9:57.31 i	Charlotte Sanderson	U23	18.03.79	13r3	Ames, USA	10 Feb
9:57.75 mx	Alexa Joel	U20	19.09.83	2	Bedford	30 May
9:58.8	Lauren Deadman	U20	27.03.84	1	Guildford	19 May
9:58.86	Louise Whittaker	U20	29.11.82	1	Stretford	14 Aug

Additional Under 17 (1 - 4 above)

9:58.9 mx	Jenna Hill	16.10.85	2	Stretford	17 Jul
	10:06.2		1	Rotherham	20 May
9:59.0 mx	Gemma Turtle	15.05.86	3	Watford	1 Aug
	10:08.50		3	Sheffield	12 Aug
10:00.65	Emma Hunt	25.04.86	1	Sheffield	12 Aug
10:04.51	Chloe Wilkinson	16.12.84	2	Tullamore, IRL	21 Jul
10:07.93	Cheryl Guiney	24.09.85	3	Tullamore, IRL	21 Jul
10:10.52	Charlotte Wickham	21.06.85	3	Exeter	7 Jul
(10)					
10:10.73	Helen Glover	17.06.86	1	London (Ha)	17 Jun
10:11.68	Genevieve Gardener	3.09.84	2	London (Ha)	17 Jun
10:15.16	Stacey Ward	16.01.85	3	London (Ha)	17 Jun
10:15.78	Jennifer Pereira	8.08.85	4	London (Ha)	17 Jun
10:15.86	Sharon Lamont	12.08.86	4	Tullamore, IRL	21 Jul
10:17.0 mx	Laura Burgoine	28.01.85	2	Watford	25 Jul
10:17.65	Juliet Walker	5.10.84	5	London (Ha)	17 Jun
10:18.6	Isabelle Stoate	16.07.86	1	Exeter	27 Mar
10:19.6	Becky Sanders	15.07.85	12	Bedford	1 Jul
10:22.4	Danielle Woods	2.10.84	1	Stretford	6 Mar
(20)					
10:22.7	Kerry Walker	5.08.85	3	Eton	10 Jun
10:24.36	Liz Spencer	25.04.85	5	Sheffield	12 Aug
10:27.83	Josephine Rhodes	22.03.86	6	London (Ha)	17 Jun
10:28.15	Katherine Humphries	28.11.85	12	Street	7 May
10:28.17	Rosie Smith	28.06.85	2	Gateshead	12 May
10:28.4	Charlotte Best	7.03.85	1	Crawley	30 May
10:29.46	Lisa Knight	31.01.85	6	Sheffield	12 Aug
10:31.5	Lucy O'Gorman	11.02.86	1	Sheffield	28 Apr
10:31.90	Laura Kenney	27.06.85	1	Birmingham	27 May
10:35.4	Laura Nurse	16.07.85	1	Exeter	24 Apr
(30)					
10:37.04	Danielle Cross	26.09.84	14	Street	7 May
10:37.2	Elizabeth Muggeridge	11.11.84	5	Reading	19 May
10:39.06mx	Helena Yates	12.09.85	7	Stretford	19 Jun
10:39.24mx	Amie Booth	19.10.84	6	Watford	30 May
10:40.87	Ffiona Harrison	5.10.84	6	Tullamore, IRL	21 Jul

Foreign

9:40.49	*Kelley Wilder (USA)*	*30.07.71*	*3*	*Glasgow (S)*	*11 Aug*
9:50.6	*Stephanie Van Graan (RSA)*	*4.02.77*	*1*	*London (He)*	*23 Jun*

2 Miles

9:27.6 +e	Paula Radcliffe	17.12.73	1	London (CP)	22 Jul

5000 Metres

14:32.44	Paula Radcliffe		17.12.73	3	Berlin, GER	31 Aug
	14:44.21			1	London (CP)	22 Jul
	14:49.84			2	Bremen, GER	24 Jun
	15:22.62 +			1m	Barakaldo, ESP	7 Apr
15:00.56	Joanne Pavey		20.09.73	6	Berlin, GER	31 Aug
	15:10.62			2h2	Edmonton, CAN	9 Aug
	15:15.98			1	Birmingham	15 Jul
	15:16.47			7	London (CP)	22 Jul
	15:28.41			11	Edmonton, CAN	11 Aug
15:14.62	Kathy Butler		22.10.73	1	Madison, USA	12 May
	15:17.96			3	Brisbane, AUS	4 Sep
	15:20.78			7h1	Edmonton, CAN	9 Aug
	15:34.12			3	Birmingham	15 Jul
	16:29.28			2	Madison, USA	5 May
15:19.12	Hayley Yelling		3.01.74	10	London (CP)	22 Jul
	15:23.28			2	Birmingham	15 Jul
	15:50.36			1	Manchester	23 May
	15:59.39			16h1	Edmonton, CAN	9 Aug
15:54.9	Amanda Parkinson		21.07.71	1	Solihull	23 Jun
15:57.32	Angela Newport		21.10.70	2	Manchester	23 May
	16:23.79			7	Cork, IRL	7 Jul
15:57.4	Juliet Potter	U23	24.10.81	2	Solihull	23 Jun
	15:59.88			3	Manchester	23 May
	16:02.99			7	Amsterdam, NED	14 Jul
	16:15.6			1	Bedford	27 May
15:57.61	Catherine Berry		8.10.75	4	Birmingham	15 Jul
	16:05.88			2	Philadelphia PA, USA	27 Apr
16:04.1	Karen Hind	U23	31.07.79	3	Solihull	23 Jun
16:10.26	Bev Jenkins		6.02.70	4	Manchester	23 May
	16:18.55			2	Liverpool	17 Jun
(10)						
16:10.94	Gillian Palmer	U23	30.12.80	8	Eugene, USA	12 May
	16:18.68			12	Amsterdam, NED	14 Jul
	16:22.4			5	Solihull	23 Jun
	16:22.91			2rB	Walnut CA, USA	20 Apr
	16:25.13			1	Des Moines, USA	26 Apr
16:11.78	Jodie Swallow	U23	23.06.81	1	Glasgow (S)	6 May
	16:29.59			6	Manchester	23 May
16:15.94	Sheila Fairweather		24.11.77	2	Glasgow (S)	6 May
16:16.24	Birhan Dagne		8.04.78	5	Birmingham	15 Jul
16:16.39	Collette Fagan	U20	6.06.82	3	Grosseto, ITA	20 Jul
16:18.32	Penny Thackray		18.08.74	1	Liverpool	17 Jun
	16:24.75			5	Manchester	23 May
	16:27.6 +			2m	Watford	9 Jun
16:18.62	Debbie Sullivan		24.01.72	6	Birmingham	15 Jul
16:24.55	Jo Lodge		6.01.68	1	Eton	7 Jul
16:25.44	Lucy Elliott	V35	9.03.66	2	Eton	7 Jul
	46 performances to 16:30.0 by 19 athletes					
16:31.73	Susie Rutherford	U23	26.02.79	5	Walnut CA, USA	20 Apr
(20)						
16:32.60	Lesley Patterson	U23	12.10.80	7	Manchester	23 May
16:35.0	Michelle Brooks		6.02.77	4	Minneapolis/St Paul, USA	14 Jul
16:37.42	Catherine Dugdale		29.11.74	8	Manchester	23 May
16:38.53	Jilly Ingman		17.08.78	9	Manchester	23 May
16:40.04	Pauline Powell		17.05.73	3	Liverpool	17 Jun
16:47.10	Allison Higgins		8.04.72	1	Glasgow (S)	23 Jun
16:47.19	Helen Pearson	U23	8.02.81	2	London (Ha)	16 Jun
16:48.6	Charlotte Sanderson	U23	18.03.79	12	Solihull	23 Jun
16:50.7	Emma O'Dowd	U23	25.04.80	13	Solihull	23 Jun

16:50.74 i	Sarah Davey		13.10.78	4	Boston, USA	10 Mar
(30)						
16:51.69	Jenny Heath		22.12.77	6	Madrid, ESP	27 May
16:52.7	Morag McDonnell		27.08.73	14	Solihull	23 Jun
16:54.06	Sonia Thomas	U23	16.05.79	4	Glasgow (S)	6 May
16:55.99	Louise Damen	U20	12.10.82	3	London (Ha)	16 Jun
17:00.29	Amber Gascoigne	U23	5.09.79	5	Glasgow (S)	6 May
17:00.64	Susan Miles	U23	1.11.81	6	Glasgow (S)	6 May
17:05.03	Lisa Towns	U23	19.04.79	2	Glasgow (S)	23 Jun
17:05.34	Ann-Marie Hutchison		21.08.77	11	Manchester	23 May
17:09.3	Lisa Mawer		22.05.68	15	Solihull	23 Jun
17:12.5	Susan Harrison		6.08.71	3	Bedford	27 May
(40)						
17:16.38	Michelle Sandison	U23	11.04.80	3	Glasgow (S)	23 Jun
17:18.70	Julie O'Mara		11.02.76	12	Manchester	23 May
17:21.70mx	Lindsay MacNeill		29.03.78	1	Edinburgh	13 May
17:23.22	Clare Martin		14.09.74	13	Manchester	23 May
17:24.2	Lucy Hassell		19.03.78	1	Philadelphia PA, USA	8 Apr
17:27.38	Alison Fletcher	V40	8.06.61	2	Brisbane, AUS	6 Jul
17:27.69mx	Emma Fisher		8.01.70	2	Grangemouth	7 Jun
17:28.1	Bronwen Cardy	V45	26.01.52	1	Solihull	10 Jun
17:28.7	Louise Watson		13.12.71	4	Bedford	27 May
17:29.4	Gemma Phillips	U23	27.10.80	16	Solihull	23 Jun

10000 Metres

30:55.80	Paula Radcliffe		17.12.73	1	Barakaldo, ESP	7 Apr
	31:50.06			4	Edmonton, CAN	7 Aug
31:59.27	Kathy Butler		22.10.73	1	Walnut CA, USA	20 Apr
	32:18.36			5	Brisbane, AUS	7 Sep
33:25.74	Penny Thackray		18.08.74	2	Watford	9 Jun
33:29.27	Bev Jenkins		6.02.70	3	Watford	9 Jun
33:45.58	Liz Yelling		5.12.74	17	Barakaldo, ESP	7 Apr
33:59.79	Tara Krzywicki		9.03.74	20	Barakaldo, ESP	7 Apr
34:23.55	Sheila Fairweather		24.11.77	4	Watford	9 Jun
34:25.78	Charlotte Sanderson	U23	18.03.79	4	Palo Alto, USA	4 May
34:29.3 mx	Allison Higgins		8.04.72	1	Poole	22 Aug
34:52.41	Debbie Robinson		31.01.68	5	Watford	9 Jun
(10)						
34:52.46mx	Pauline Powell		17.05.73	1	Stretford	8 May
34:56.01mx	Julie O'Mara		11.02.76	2	Stretford	8 May
35:41.99	Louise Watson		13.12.71	6	Watford	9 Jun
36:04.80	Alison Fletcher	V40	8.06.61	2	Brisbane, AUS	9 Jul
36:20.10	Bronwen Cardy	V45	26.01.52	1	Brisbane, AUS	9 Jul
36:39.08	Alyson Dixon		24.09.78	1	Glasgow (S)	7 May

5 Kilometres Road

14:57	Paula Radcliffe		17.12.73	1	London (HP)	2 Sep
	15:24 +			m	New York, USA	9 Jun
16:10	Karen Hind	U23	31.07.79	1	Marske	4 Sep
16:23	Hayley Yelling		3.01.74	6	London (HP)	2 Sep
16:28	Dianne Henaghan	V35	6.08.65	1	Sunderland	25 Jul
16:32	Debbie Sullivan		24.01.72	7	London (HP)	2 Sep
16:35	Catherine Berry		8.10.75	1	Pigeon Forge, USA	28 Jul
16:35	Lucy Elliott	V35	9.03.66	8	London (HP)	2 Sep
16:37	Sarah Wilkinson		2.01.70	1	Clydebank	24 Mar
16:38	Charlotte Dale	U20	23.03.84	9	London (HP)	2 Sep
16:41	Birhan Dagne		8.04.78	1	Bath	25 Mar
(10)						
16:41	Louise Damen	U20	12.10.82	1	Poole	4 Sep
16:45	Lucy Wright		17.11.69	2	Bath	25 Mar

16:45	Bev Hartigan		10.06.67	1	Birmingham	9 Aug
16:53	Hayley Haining		6.03.72	1	Glasgow	26 Apr
16:56	Debbie Gunning	V35	31.08.65	1	Southampton	11 Mar
16:57	Morag McDonnell		27.08.73	2	Sunderland	25 Jul
16:58	Ann-Marie Hutchison		21.08.77	1	Cardiff	25 Jul
16:59	Sarah Bull		4.06.75	1	Derby	19 Dec

4 Miles Road

20:54	Catherine Berry		8.10.75	6	Peoria, USA	9 Jun

8 Kilometres Road

25:25 +	Kathy Butler		22.10.73	1m	Chicago, USA	1 Apr

5 Miles Road

24:48 +	Paula Radcliffe		17.12.73	m	New York, USA	9 Jun
	25:18			2	Balmoral	14 Apr
25:49	Amanda Allen		14.07.68	1	Wolverhampton	2 Dec
26:31	Lucy Elliott	V35	9.03.66	1	Portsmouth	2 Dec
26:38	Andrea Green		14.12.68	2	Portsmouth	2 Dec
26:44	Sarah Wilkinson		2.01.70	1	Alsager	4 Feb
26:58	Liz Yelling		5.12.74	6	Balmoral	14 Apr
27:10	Penny Thackray		18.08.74	7	Balmoral	14 Apr
27:17	Jane Livings		13.08.70	3	Portsmouth	2 Dec
27:18	Claire Naylor		18.04.71	2	Alsager	4 Feb
27:18 +	Annie Emmerson		10.05.70	m	Bath	18 Mar
(10)						
27:20	Ann-Marie Hutchison		21.08.77	4	Portsmouth	2 Dec
27:27	Bev Jenkins		6.02.70	1	Manchester	28 May
27:34	Hayley Yelling		3.01.74	10	Balmoral	14 Apr
27:36	Amy Stiles		6.02.75	1	Weston, USA	23 Dec
27:37	Bev Hartigan		10.06.67	11	Balmoral	14 Apr
27:40	Vicky Pincombe		19.06.73	5	Portsmouth	2 Dec
27:45	Kerry Smithson/Gillibrand		13.09.76	3	Alsager	4 Feb
27:45	Jenny Heath		22.12.77	1	Hale	16 Dec
27:47	Kath Scales		28.06.77	4	Alsager	4 Feb
27:51	Ann MacPhail		3.05.70	6	Alsager	4 Feb
(20)						
27:52	Marian Sutton	V35	7.10.63	13	Balmoral	14 Apr
27:54	Debbie Percival	V35	22.04.62	1	Rochester	3 Jun

10000 Metres Road

30:47	Paula Radcliffe		17.12.73	1	New York, USA	9 Jun
	32:00 +			m	Bristol	7 Oct
33:07	Penny Thackray		18.08.74	1	Dewsbury	4 Feb
	33:40			1	Wakefield	8 Apr
	33:50			1	Leeds	2 Dec
33:13	Amanda Allen		14.07.68	3	Cheltenham	9 Sep
	33:44			1	Telford	23 Dec
	33:46			1	Belfast	22 Apr
33:20	Liz Yelling		5.12.74	4	Cheltenham	9 Sep
	33:52			1	London (SP)	1 Jul
33:23	Helen Pattinson		2.01.74	1	Liverpool	14 Oct
33:31	Charlotte Dale	U20	23.03.84	1	Ashford	14 Oct
33:38	Birhan Dagne		8.04.78	5	Cheltenham	9 Sep
33:39	Sharon Morris		5.07.68	6	Cheltenham	9 Sep
	33:47			4	Swansea	23 Sep
33:40	Hayley Haining		6.03.72	8	Glasgow	20 May
33:45 +	Annie Emmerson		10.05.70	m	Bristol	7 Oct
	33:48 +			m	Portsmouth	14 Oct

33:46	Bev Hartigan		10.06.67	2	Dewsbury	4 Feb
33:46	Michelle Dillon		24.05.73	4	Swansea	23 Sep
33:53	Lucy Elliott	V35	9.03.66	1	Bishop Auckland	26 Aug
33:55	Bev Jenkins		6.02.70	1	Manchester	24 Jun
	34:00			1	Salford	13 Apr
34:00	Louise Damen	U20	12.10.82	1	Poole	26 Dec
	24 performances to 34:00 by 15 athletes					
34:03	Andrea Green		14.12.68	3	Dewsbury	4 Feb
34:04	Caroline Pimblett/Johnson		28.01.75	2	Salford	13 Apr
34:08	Debbie Robinson		31.01.68	2	Leeds	2 Dec
34:10	Kerry Smithson/Gillibrand		13.09.76	1	Manchester	4 Mar
34:16	Vicky Pincombe		19.06.73	7	Cheltenham	9 Sep
	(20)					
34:17	Beth Allott		9.02.77	6	Swansea	23 Sep
34:18	Pauline Powell		17.05.73	2	Manchester	24 Jun
34:22	Tara Krzywicki		9.03.74	7	Swansea	23 Sep
34:30	Lynne MacDougall	V35	18.02.65	8	Cheltenham	9 Sep
34:34	Allison Higgins		8.04.72	10	Glasgow	20 May
34:38	Melanie Hayward		14.07.71	1	Lincoln	8 Apr
34:52	Ruth Pickvance	V35	29.09.61	1	Bourton	25 Feb
34:55	Katie Skorupska		3.11.78		Lisses, FRA	11 Mar
34:57	Debbie Gunning	V35	31.08.65	2	Bourton	25 Feb
34:58	Julie O'Mara		11.02.76	2	Wakefield	8 Apr

10 Miles Road

54:40	Beth Allott		9.02.77	1	Manchester	5 Aug
55:13	Annie Emmerson		10.05.70	3	Portsmouth	14 Oct
	55:42 +			1m	Bath	18 Mar
55:28	Lynne MacDougall	V35	18.02.65	1	Carlisle	18 Nov
	56:30			7	Portsmouth	14 Oct
55:41	Andrea Green		14.12.68	1	Canterbury	28 Jan
	56:04			6	Portsmouth	14 Oct
56:55	Melanie Hayward		14.07.71	1	Lincoln	29 Apr
57:18	Morag McDonnell		27.08.73	2	Carlisle	18 Nov
57:18	Jane Livings		13.08.70	1	Hayling Island	25 Nov
57:37	Debbie Percival	V35	22.04.62	1	Folkestone	13 Apr
57:39	Julie O'Mara		11.02.76	2	Manchester	5 Aug
57:40	Vicky Pincombe		19.06.73	8	Portsmouth	14 Oct
	(10)					
58:14	Kath Bailey		25.03.68	10	Portsmouth	14 Oct
58:17	Sharon Morris		5.07.68	1	Buntingford	30 Dec
58:27	Debbie Sullivan		24.01.72	11	Portsmouth	14 Oct
58:32	Susan Harrison		6.08.71	3	Manchester	5 Aug
58:32	Andrea Whitcombe		8.06.71	1	Bedford	26 Dec
58:51	Michaela McCallum	V35	2.06.66	12	Portsmouth	14 Oct

Half Marathon

66:47	Paula Radcliffe		17.12.73	1	Bristol	7 Oct
71:29	Liz Yelling		5.12.74	23	Bristol	7 Oct
	72:26			4	Glasgow	19 Aug
72:43	Amanda Allen		14.07.68	1	Llanwddyn	16 Sep
73:00	Annie Emmerson		10.05.70	31	Bristol	7 Oct
	73:01			1	Bath	18 Mar
73:39	Beth Allott		9.02.77	7	Glasgow	19 Aug
73:52	Birhan Dagne		8.04.78	8	Glasgow	19 Aug
73:56	Andrea Green		14.12.68	1	Stroud	28 Oct
	74:56			1r2	Bristol	7 Oct
	74:58			9	Berlin, GER	1 Apr
74:04	Sharon Morris		5.07.68	14	South Shields	16 Sep

74:06	Bev Hartigan		10.06.67	2	Bath	16 Mar
	74:45			10	Glasgow	19 Aug
74:24	Lynne MacDougall	V35	18.02.65	15	South Shields	16 Sep
	74:37			1	Alloa	25 Mar
(10)						
74:59	Vicky Pincombe		19.06.73	11	Glasgow	19 Aug
	17 performances to 75:00 by 11 athletes					
75:01	Jo Wilkinson		2.05.73	16	South Shields	16 Sep
75:07	Debbie Robinson		31.01.68	17	South Shields	16 Sep
75:43	Claire Naylor		18.04.71	1	Enschede, NED	27 May
76:01	Sharon Dixon		22.04.68	2	Bath	7 Oct
76:20	Louise Copp	V35	13.09.63	5	Bath	18 Mar
76:21	Jo Lodge		6.01.68	19	South Shields	16 Sep
76:47	Susan Harrison		6.08.71	20	South Shields	16 Sep
76:56	Louise Watson		13.12.71	22	South Shields	16 Sep
77:03	Jane Livings		13.08.70	3	Bristol	7 Oct
(20)						
77:09	Tara Krzywicki		9.03.74	1	Nottingham	30 Sep
77:17	Melanie Hayward		14.07.71	1	Luton	1 Apr
77:22	Kath Bailey		25.03.68	1	Jersey	20 May
77:23	Debbie Percival	V35	22.04.62	1	Gillingham	6 May
77:24	Jo-Anne Newcombe	V35	20.02.65	2	Enschede, NED	27 May
77:25	Michaela McCallum		2.06.66	4	Turin, ITA	11 Mar
77:31	Sarah Bradbury	V35	25.02.63	1	Wokingham	11 Feb
77:36	Ruth Pickvance	V35	29.09.61	6	Bath	18 Mar
77:40	Trudi Thomson	V40	18.01.59	11	The Hague, NED	25 Mar
77:42	Ellen Leggate		4.02.78	1	Great Barford	9 Dec
(30)						
77:48	Pauline Powell		17.05.73	23	South Shields	16 Sep
77:55	Ann MacPhail		3.05.70	22	Glasgow	19 Aug
78:33	Julie O'Mara		11.02.76	23	Glasgow	19 Aug
Foreign						
72:57	*Teresa Duffy (IRL)*		*6.07.69*	*7*	*Berlin, GER*	*1 Apr*

Marathon

2:34:43	Beth Allott		9.02.77	2	Lisbon, POR	2 Dec
2:35:40	Debbie Robinson		31.01.68	1	Dublin, IRL	29 Oct
	2:42:19			22	London	22 Apr
2:36:02	Bev Hartigan		10.06.67	6	Berlin, GER	30 Sep
	2:37:45			17	London	22 Apr
2:37:20	Lynne MacDougall	V35	18.02.65	16	London	22 Apr
2:41:49	Trudi Thomson	V40	18.01.59	16	P'yongyang, KOR	15 Apr
	2:46:32			6	Dubai, UAE	12 Jan
	2:49:33			1	Elgin	2 Sep
2:43:49	Louise Watson		13.12.71	23	London	22 Apr
	2:44:23			4	Carpi, ITA	14 Oct
2:43:52	Vicky Pincombe		19.06.73	25	London	22 Apr
2:44:35	Clare Pauzers	V35	2.08.62	26	London	22 Apr
2:45:02	Amy Stiles		6.02.75	17	Rotterdam, NED	22 Apr
	2:45:16			7	Amsterdam, NED	21 Oct
2:45:23	Shona Crombie-Hick		1.06.71	1	Copenhagen, DEN	20 May
(10)						
2:45:23	Ruth Pickvance	V40	29.09.61	25	New York, USA	4 Nov
	2:46:14	V35		27	London	22 Apr
2:46:32	Sharon Dixon		22.04.68	28	London	22 Apr
2:47:07	Louise Copp	V35	13.09.63	19	Rotterdam, NED	22 Apr
2:47:24	Megan Clark		31.07.73	29	London	22 Apr
2:48:53	Susan Harrison		6.08.71	3	Odense, DEN	14 Oct
2:49:12	Kerrie Wood	V35	8.01.66	31	London	22 Apr
2:49:18	Alison Fletcher	V35	8.06.61	32	London	22 Apr

2:50:12	Gillian Horovitz	V45	7.06.55	34	New York, USA	16 Apr
2:50:58	Mandy Spink	V35	12.01.65	33	London	22 Apr
2:51:30	Judy Oakley	V35	10.09.65	34	London	22 Apr
	(20)					
2:51:43	Lisa Knights		12.07.71	35	London	22 Apr
2:51:48	Christine Double	V35	10.06.64		Hong Kong, CHN	4 Feb
2:52:06	Sarah Massey		2.07.68	36	London	22 Apr
2:52:18	Emma Latto		16.01.69	37	London	22 Apr
2:54:00	Malindi Myers		3.10.70	6	Dublin, IRL	29 Oct
2:54:27	Juliette Clark	V35	22.04.64	38	London	22 Apr
2:54:35	Mel Ellis	V35	16.04.64	2	Manchester	23 Sep
2:54:39	Anne Kirtley	V35	12.02.66	39	London	22 Apr
2:54:43	Vivienne Conneely		4.01.76	7	Dublin, IRL	29 Oct
2:54:48	Lindsay Gannon	V35	29.08.66	3	Washington, USA	28 Oct
	(30)					
2:54:55	Kathy Charnock	V35	4.07.62	1	Lake Vyrnwy	1 Jul
2:55:40	Jane Laws	V40	11.01.57	1	Abingdon	21 Oct
2:55:58	Beverley Wilson		26.03.67	40	London	22 Apr
2:56:05	Debra Curley		20.09.71	1	Belfast	7 May
2:56:08	Jo Dering		7.02.69	41	London	22 Apr
2:56:27	Zelah Morrall		21.01.69	42	London	22 Apr
2:56:27	Rosalyn Alexander		18.05.73	8	Dublin, IRL	29 Oct
2:56:59	Jane Selby		17.10.72	44	London	22 Apr
2:57:06	Jenny Gray	V40	21.06.60	45	London	22 Apr
2:58:17	Barbara Parker	V40	29.04.58	46	London	22 Apr
	(40)					
2:58:20	Julie Holdsworth	V40	22.07.61	3	Benidorm, ESP	25 Nov
2:58:23	Julia Smith		69	28	Paris, FRA	8 Apr
2:58:29	Jacqueline Massey	V35	24.01.64	47	London	22 Apr
2:58:57	Penny Buckingham		26.04.67	1	New Milton	9 Sep
2:59:00	Vicki Perry	V40	25.11.57	48	London	22 Apr
2:59:05	Deborah Kay	V40	7.11.60	1	Harrow	4 Nov
2:59:15	Andrea Dennison	V35	22.04.63	49	London	22 Apr
2:59:31	Lesley Whiley	V40	14.05.60	50	London	22 Apr
2:59:31	Gillian Jones		2.11.70	33	Chicago, USA	7 Oct
2:59:39	Lisa Hollick/Elmore		1.01.70	51	London	22 Apr
	(50)					
3:00:32	Helen Cawthorne	V40	9.07.61	2	Nottingham	30 Sep
3:00:36	Alice Braham		17.01.76	52	London	22 Apr
3:01:35	Caroline Owen	V35	62	71	New York, USA	4 Nov
3:01:38	Julia Myatt	V35	3.08.63	53	London	22 Apr
3:01:40	Helen Barber/Sly		13.12.67	1	Leeds	20 May
3:01:48	Pippa Major	V35	23.04.65	54	London	22 Apr
3:02:02	Rachel Joyce		16.06.78	55	London	22 Apr
3:02:22	Susanna Harrison	V35	25.01.63	56	London	22 Apr
3:02:30	Lisa Godding-Feltham		24.11.69	57	London	22 Apr
3:02:31	Teresa Scully	V35	1.10.61	58	London	22 Apr
	(60)					
3:03:18	Jane Boulton	V45	2.04.56	60	London	22 Apr
3:03:20	Kate Jenkins		26.03.74	1	Fort William	29 Apr
3:03:22	Judy Brown	V45	27.10.54	61	London	22 Apr
3:03:50	Dorothy Smale	V40	26.05.60	62	London	22 Apr
3:04:07	Marilyn Gradden	V35	26.01.61	8	Lake Buena Vista, USA	7 Jan
3:04:27	Amanda Proctor		25.07.71	64	London	22 Apr
3:04:27	Erica Christie	V45	10.03.56	15	Dublin, IRL	29 Oct
3:04:32	Helen Yule	V35	10.09.65	65	London	22 Apr
3:04:33	Maggie Hughes		16.04.72	66	London	22 Apr
3:04:36	Tracey Curl	V35	8.07.62	1	Kingston	14 Oct
	(70)					
3:04:46	Jackie Howlett	V35	11.05.64	67	London	22 Apr
3:05:09	Alison Vuagniaux	V40	31.05.60	70	London	22 Apr

3:05:18	Sarah Campbell		31.10.74	35	Rotterdam, NED	22 Apr
3:05:23	Elin Engdahl	V35	12.10.62	72	London	22 Apr
3:05:33	Susanne Carson		2.05.67	73	London	22 Apr
3:05:40	Sue Cariss	V50	17.11.49	6	Manchester	23 Sep
3:05:44	Treena Carney	V35	29.08.61	2	Leeds	20 May
3:05:49	Michelle Awuye		5.03.74	2	Abingdon	21 Oct
3:05:51	Shula Sarner		31.05.70	68	Boston, USA	16 Apr
3:05:52	Wendy Davies	V40	13.06.60	75	London	22 Apr
	(80)					
3:06:05	Patricia Matheson	V45	7.01.54	76	London	22 Apr
3:06:22	Sally Pitts	V40	7.03.61	77	London	22 Apr
3:06:24	Nicola Thompson		10.02.68	78	London	22 Apr
3:06:28	Val Swingler		18.12.66	2	Harrow	4 Nov
3:06:47	Ruth Whitehead		14.01.72	1	Sheffield	29 Apr
3:06:57	Wendy Rothenbaugh	V35	30.03.64	79	London	22 Apr
3:07:00	Tracey West	V35	23.05.65	80	London	22 Apr
3:07:25	Sue Martin-Clarke	V45	13.09.55	82	London	22 Apr
3:07:57	Gail Fortes Mayer		2.12.69	84	London	22 Apr
3:07:57	Nicky Hills	V35	23.05.65	85	London	22 Apr
	(90)					
3:08:00	Elaine Calder	V35	26.04.62	2	Fort William	29 Apr
3:08:10	Nicola Aitken		18.12.78	98	New York, USA	4 Nov
3:08:17	Amanda Clarke		28.03.68	87	London	22 Apr
3:08:20	Marlene Pautard	V35	25.10.62	88	London	22 Apr
3:08:27	Kay Leigh	V40	3.12.60	89	London	22 Apr
3:08:30	Grace Wu		10.02.71	90	London	22 Apr
3:08:42	Julie Drake		21.05.69	91	London	22 Apr
3:08:53	Sarah Guest		5.07.69	92	London	22 Apr
3:09:18	Anna Crockett		11.07.69	94	London	22 Apr
3:09:19	Revis Crowle	V35	26.01.62	95	London	22 Apr
	(100)					
3:09:24	Jennie Vartan	V40	7.12.60	3	Abingdon	21 Oct
3:09:30	Judith Bateman	V40	27.02.57	96	London	22 Apr
3:09:32	Barbara Harries	V40	27.02.58	97	London	22 Apr
3:09:33	Dawn Kenwright	V45	30.08.55	98	London	22 Apr
3:09:40	Caroline Hemsworth	V45	8.05.53	99	London	22 Apr
3:09:45	Jeanette Hardwick	V45	26.08.51	100	London	22 Apr
3:09:54	Gail Pryke	V40	1.04.60	101	London	22 Apr
3:09:56	Trish Sloan	V35	22.03.66	18	Dublin, IRL	29 Oct

Foreign

2:35:27	*Teresa Duffy (IRL)*	*6.07.69*	*15*	*London*	*22 Apr*
3:04:46	*Louise Curtis (NZL)*	*29.07.70*	*68*	*London*	*22 Apr*
3:05:25	*Anna McCutcheon (CAN)*	*3.03.68*	*16*	*Dublin, IRL*	*29 Oct*
3:05:39	*Sharon Cooney (NZL)*	*10.06.68*	*74*	*London*	*22 Apr*
3:08:13	*Estle Viljoen (RSA)*	*8.07.70*	*86*	*London*	*22 Apr*
3:08:14	*Swenja Surminski (GER)*	*30.09.75*		*Hamburg, GER*	*22 Apr*

100 Kilometres - Road

7:58:16	Danielle Sanderson	V35	26.10.62	7	Cleder, FRA	26 Aug
	8:17.37			1	Moreton-in-Marsh	20 May
8:50:19	Hilary Walker	V45	9.11.53	13	Winschoten, NED	29 Sep
9:07:19	Victoria Musgrove	V40	6.09.56	2	Moreton-in-Marsh	20 May
9:11:56	Sharon Gayter	V35	30.10.63	37	Cleder, FRA	26 Aug
9:27:15	Kendra White		8.04.68		Edinburgh	15 Jul
10:04:12	Cecilia Petersson			3	Moreton-in-Marsh	20 May

24 Hours - Road (km)

191.414	Sharon Gayter	V35	30.10.63	Cher St Doulchard, FRA	25 Nov
180.703	Sandra Brown	V50	1.04.49	Doncaster	26 May
153.290	Brenda Barnett			Doncaster	26 May

2000 Metres Steeplechase (2'6" barriers)

6:29.79	Tara Krzywicki		9.03.74	2	Loughborough	20 May
6:53.02	Clare Martin		14.09.74	3	Loughborough	20 May
6:55.04	Jo Ankier	U20	5.08.82	8	Grosseto, ITA	22 Jul
7:01.2	Kathryn Frost	U20	21.02.84	1	Woodford	20 Jun
7:01.74	Allison Higgins		8.04.72	1	Glasgow (S)	18 Jul
7:02.54	Sheila Fairweather		24.11.77	2	Glasgow (S)	18 Jul
7:04.39	Paula Gowing		31.05.78	4	Loughborough	20 May
7:12.2	Bryony Frost	U20	21.02.84	2	Woodford	20 Jun
7:17.78	Jane Pidgeon	V35	23.01.64	2	Brisbane, AUS	14 Jul
7:23.5	Alison Hurford	V40	11.10.60	4	Southampton	14 Jun
(10)						
7:24.9	Sarah-Jane Pickett	U17	24.10.84	5	Southampton	14 Jun
7:26.45	Susan McGrenaghan	U20	11.07.83	3	Glasgow (S)	18 Jul
7:30.2	Megan Jones	U17	5.03.86	6	Southampton	14 Jun

Foreign

7:30.16	*Sara Talia (SWE)*	*U23*	*30.05.79*	*1*	*Glasgow (S)*	*5 May*

3000 Metres Steeplechase (2'6" barriers)

9:52.71	Tara Krzywicki		9.03.74	2	Glasgow (S)	1 Jul
	9:55.01			1	Glasgow (S)	11 Aug
10:21.21	Lois Joslin	U23	1.03.79	5	Walnut CA, USA	20 Apr
10:44.69	Clare Martin		14.09.74	1	Stretford	5 Jun
	10:46.01			6	Glasgow (S)	1 Jul
10:49.39	Jayne Spark/Knowles		16.09.70	1	Stretford	3 Jul
10:55.70	Allison Higgins		8.04.72	2	Glasgow (S)	11 Aug
11:26.15	Paula Gowing		31.05.78	3	Glasgow (S)	11 Aug
11:31.37	Jane Pidgeon	V35	23.01.64	2	Stretford	5 Jun
11:38.90	Sara-Jane Cattermole		29.01.77	2	Perth, AUS	9 Feb

60 Metres Hurdles - Indoors

8.15	Melani Wilkins		18.01.73	2	Glasgow	18 Mar
	8.19			4h2	Lisbon, POR	9 Mar
	8.20			1	Birmingham	28 Jan
	8.30			8s2	Lisbon, POR	9 Mar
	8.38			1h2	Birmingham	28 Jan
	8.41			2	Cardiff	11 Feb
	8.51			2h1	Birmingham	14 Jan
8.28	Sarah Claxton	U23	23.09.79	2	Birmingham	28 Jan
	8.36			1	Cardiff	11 Feb
	8.37			2	Birmingham	14 Jan
	8.40			2	Cardiff	18 Feb
	8.54			1h3	Birmingham	14 Jan
	8.54			6h3	Lisbon, POR	9 Mar
	8.55			1h1	Birmingham	28 Jan
8.35	Julie Pratt	U23	20.03.79	1	Birmingham	14 Jan
	8.40			2h2	Birmingham	28 Jan
	8.43			1h2	Birmingham	14 Jan
	8.44			4	Birmingham	28 Jan
8.38	Bianca Liston		28.05.78	3	Birmingham	28 Jan
	8.48			3	Cardiff	11 Feb
	8.51			1h1	Birmingham	14 Jan
	8.51			1h3	Birmingham	28 Jan
	8.51			1h1	Glasgow	18 Feb
8.40	Rachel King		11.05.76	1	Cardiff	18 Feb
	8.48			4	Glasgow	18 Mar
8.55	Clova Court	V40	10.02.60	6	Birmingham	28 Jan
8.55	Lauren McLoughlin	U20	8.09.82	1J	Cardiff	11 Feb
	27 performances to 8.55 by 7 athletes					

8.57	Clare Milborrow		10.01.77	8	Birmingham	28 Jan
8.59	Kerry Jury		19.11.68	1P1	Birmingham	21 Jan
8.65	Fiona Harrison	U23	30.11.81	3h3	Birmingham	28 Jan
(10)						
8.66	Kelly Sotherton		13.11.76	2P1	Birmingham	21 Jan
8.67	Tamsin Stephens	U23	2.08.80	1h2	Glasgow	18 Feb
8.72	Nicola Gautier		21.03.78	3=P1	Birmingham	21 Jan
8.72	Alyssa Fullelove	U23	16.09.81	1h3	Glasgow	18 Feb
8.75	Katy Sketchley		9.07.73	2h2	Birmingham	14 Jan
8.75	Katherine Livesey	U23	15.12.79	1P	Lincoln, USA	23 Feb
8.77	Katherine Porter	U20	19.08.82	2J	Cardiff	11 Feb
8.78	Julie Hollman		16.02.77	3P4	Prague, CZE	28 Jan
8.81	Lorna Silver/Rogers		10.01.74	3h1	Birmingham	28 Jan
8.81	Gemma Fergusson	U20	20.08.84	2	Birmingham	25 Feb
(20)						
8.86	Kate Brewington	U23	15.10.81	4h1	Birmingham	28 Jan
8.88	Kay Reynolds		15.09.67	4h3	Birmingham	14 Jan
8.93	Danielle Freeman	U23	11.02.80	6P1	Birmingham	21 Jan
8.93	Grace Smith	U20	30.01.82	1h4	Glasgow	18 Feb
8.94	Lynne Fairweather	U23	15.01.80	1	Glasgow	13 Jan
8.94	Rebecca Jones	U20	17.01.83	4P2	Nogent-sur-Oise, FRA	24 Feb
8.95	Vicky Williams	U23	11.04.81	2h3	Glasgow	18 Feb
8.96	Catriona Pennet	U20	10.10.83	1	Glasgow	25 Jan
8.99	Claire Pearson		23.09.78	1	Birmingham	11 Feb
8.99	Sarah Porter	U23	11.12.79	2h4	Glasgow	18 Feb

hand timing

8.5	Liston		(8.38i)	1	Glasgow	18 Feb
8.6	Tamsin Stephens	U23	(8.67i)	2	Glasgow	18 Feb
8.6	Alyssa Fullelove	U23	(8.72i)	3	Glasgow	18 Feb
8.9	Symone Belle	U17	12.11.84	1	Eton	9 Dec

60 Metres Hurdles - Indoors - Under 17 (2'6" barriers)

8.56	Symone Belle	12.11.84	1	Birmingham	25 Feb
8.65	Jessica Ennis	28.01.86	2	Birmingham	25 Feb
8.70	Justine Roach	21.12.84	3	Birmingham	25 Feb
8.78	Chanelle Garnett	16.08.85	4	Birmingham	25 Feb
8.80	Phyllis Agbo	16.12.85	2h4	Birmingham	25 Feb
8.88	Heather Jones	10.09.86	1	Cardiff	24 Nov
8.90	Hannah Elwiss	8.12.84	6	Birmingham	28 Feb
8.94	Pamela Paterson	26.10.85	1	Glasgow	4 Feb
8.98	Louise Hazel	6.10.85	2P	Glasgow	8 Dec
9.03	Katey Read	20.03.86	2h2	Birmingham	25 Feb
(10)					
9.09	Joanne Erskine	28.05.85	2	Glasgow	14 Jan
9.11	Amy Beighton	6.03.86	2	Birmingham	10 Feb
9.15	Lisa McManus	3.01.86	3	Birmingham	10 Feb
9.16	Staci Stewart	20.09.85	P	Glasgow	25 Feb
9.21	Elen Evans	14.02.85	1	Cardiff	20 Jan
9.25	Sally Peake	8.02.86	2	Cardiff	20 Jan
9.27	Nadine Simpson	28.02.86	3h3	Birmingham	25 Feb
9.28	Faye Harding	7.09.85	5P	Glasgow	8 Dec
9.29	Catherine Holdsworth	3.01.86	3	Bedford	13 Jan
9.30	Samantha Day	8.02.86	4h1	Birmingham	25 Feb
(20)					
9.30	Emma Downes	21.02.86	3h4	Birmingham	25 Feb

Overage

9.12	Danielle Fawkes	11.08.85	3P	Glasgow	8 Dec
9.23	Sarah Gallaway	14.11.84	4P	Glasgow	8 Dec

60 Metres Hurdles - Under 15 (2'3" barriers)

8.79		Heather Jones	10.09.86	1h4	Birmingham	25 Feb
9.22		Louise Massingham	28.02.87	1h1	Birmingham	25 Feb
9.22		Leah McGuire	30.01.87	1h2	Birmingham	25 Feb
9.34		Kimberley Brown	1.02.87	1	Birmingham	11 Feb
9.36		Amy Long	4.03.87	2	Birmingham	11 Feb
9.40		Samantha Britton	12.09.86	1	Sheffield	22 Jan
9.4		Natasha Clementis	11.09.86	2	Eton	10 Feb
9.42		Claire Jones	8.11.86	2	Cardiff	20 Jan
9.42		Kim Skinner	21.09.87	P	Glasgow	8 Dec

70 Metres Hurdles - Under 13

11.02 w	2.7	Nafalya Francis	21.04.89	1	Tamworth	27 Aug
		11.1		1	Telford	1 Jul
11.4		Lucy Boggis	27.01.89	1	Abingdon	22 Jul
11.5	-0.5	Amy Gibbs	30.03.89	1r1	Kingston	29 Jul
11.6		Sarah Tippett	9.04.89	1	Bury St. Edmunds	1 Jul
11.6		Meliha Tas		1	Enfield	1 Jul
11.6		Vicky Fleetwood	13.04.90	1	Nuneaton	22 Jul
11.6	-0.5	Hannah Frankson	11.01.89	2r1	Kingston	29 Jul
11.66		Natalie Doyle	5.01.89	1	Glasgow (S)	26 Aug
11.7		Hannah Francis-Smithson	10.11.89	1	Clairville	1 Jul
11.73	-0.8	Jade Surman	27.03.89	1r1	Birmingham	1 Sep
	(10)					
11.8		Charlotte Harbottle	25.06.89	2	Nuneaton	22 Jul
11.9		Rebecca Hall	15.09.88	2	Bury St. Edmunds	1 Jul
11.9		Claire Welch	3.09.88	2	Crawley	27 Aug
11.9		Rachael Haigh		1	Scunthorpe	28 Aug

75 Metres Hurdles - Under 15

10.86	1.9	Heather Jones	10.09.86	1	Cardiff	17 Jun
11.00 w	2.3	Leah McGuire	30.01.87	1	Exeter	7 Jul
		11.16 0.0		1h1	Exeter	6 Jul
11.13	1.7	Samantha Britton	12.09.86	2	Sheffield	12 Aug
11.25 w	2.3	Christina Waters	4.06.87	2	Exeter	7 Jul
		11.3		1	Bebington	1 Jul
		11.37 0.2		2h2	Exeter	6 Jul
11.38 w	2.3	Louise Massingham	28.02.87	4	Exeter	7 Jul
		11.47 0.5		1	Watford	27 May
11.42	1.9	Claire Jones	8.11.86	2	Cardiff	17 Jun
11.49	0.5	Gemma Pike	13.07.87	2	Watford	27 May
11.49 w	2.3	Samantha Cook	6.05.87	5	Exeter	7 Jul
		11.64 0.0		3h1	Exeter	6 Jul
11.51	1.9	Kimberley Brown	1.02.87	3	Cardiff	17 Jun
11.53 w	2.3	Natasha Clementis	11.09.86	6	Exeter	7 Jul
		11.62 0.2		3h2	Exeter	6 Jul
	(10)					
11.59 w		Nicola Schofield	13.09.86	1r1	Bedford	9 Sep
		11.69 1.2		1r2	Birmingham	2 Sep
11.6	1.7	Rachel Peckham	14.02.87	2	Kingston	13 May
11.6		Maria Crowe	20.01.87	1	Hayes	1 Jul
		11.85 1.6		3h2	Sheffield	12 Aug
11.70	1.6	Stacy Mullan	15.09.86	2h2	Sheffield	12 Aug
11.7		Janine McCormack	17.09.86	1	Exeter	9 Jun
11.71	0.4	Amy Long	4.03.87	1	Birmingham	27 May
11.78 w	2.2	Clare Rogers	22.05.88	1h2	London (He)	26 Aug
		11.8		1	Cambridge	1 Sep
		11.89 -0.6		1	London (He)	26 Aug
11.79	0.2	Joanne Baker	15.10.87	4h2	Exeter	6 Jul

11.8		Joanna Kirby		26.10.87	1	Bebington	6 May
11.8		Nafalya Francis	U13	21.04.89	3	Cudworth	16 Jun
	(20)						
11.8		Cheryl Cairney		27.03.87	1	Dumfries	30 Jun
		11.83 w 2.4			1	Grangemouth	12 Aug
11.8		Stephanie Madgett		22.02.87	1	Woking	2 Sep
11.83	1.2	Victoria Garrad		22.11.87	3h3	Sheffield	12 Aug
11.88 w	2.4	Eilidh Child		20.02.87	2	Grangemouth	12 Aug

80 Metres Hurdles - Under 17

11.27	1.0	Symone Belle	12.11.84	1	Watford	27 May
11.31	0.7	Chanelle Garnett	16.08.85	1h3	Sheffield	12 Aug
11.36	1.2	Hannah Elwiss	8.12.84	2	Sheffield	12 Aug
11.43		Joanne Erskine	28.05.85	1	Grangemouth	26 Aug
11.44	-2.0	Justine Roach	21.12.84	1	Birmingham	26 May
11.50	1.5	Nicola Robinson	16.04.86	1h1	Sheffield	12 Aug
11.52	1.0	Phyllis Agbo	16.12.85	3	Watford	27 May
11.52	1.5	Jessica Ennis	28.01.86	2h1	Sheffield	12 Aug
11.56	1.2	Danielle Fawkes	11.08.85	3	Sheffield	12 Aug
11.70	0.7	Emily Parker	7.11.84	2H1	Birmingham	29 Sep
	(10)					
11.76	1.0	Louise Hazel	6.10.85	4	Watford	27 May
11.76	0.2	Samantha Day	8.02.86	4h1	Exeter	6 Jul
11.78	1.2	Cathy Crawford	17.12.84	8	Sheffield	12 Aug
11.82	-2.0	Lisa McManus	3.01.86	3	Birmingham	26 May
11.84	0.7	Melanie Canning	19.05.85	3h3	Sheffield	12 Aug
11.87	-1.6	Pamela Paterson	26.10.85	1	Grangemouth	10 Jun
11.95	-1.6	Staci Stewart	20.09.85	2	Grangemouth	10 Jun
11.99	0.0	Sarah Allsopp	13.10.84	3h2	Exeter	6 Jul
12.00	-1.0	Emma Makin	12.10.85	2h2	Cudworth	26 May
12.02	0.5	Rachel Brenton	18.01.85	2h1	Watford	27 May
	(20)					
12.04	0.5	Angie Broadbelt	12.09.85	3h1	Watford	27 May
12.06	0.9	Claire Sargent	11.03.86	2	Birmingham	2 Sep
12.07	1.5	Elen Evans	14.02.85	1	Cardiff	16 Jun
12.07	-1.9	Susan Edwards	17.10.84	1	Cardiff	7 Jul
12.08	1.2	Emma Perkins	4.09.85	3h3	Watford	27 May
12.09	1.3	Stacy Flint	18.10.85	4h2	Sheffield	12 Aug
12.09	0.9	Gemma Werrett	15.03.86	3	Birmingham	2 Sep

wind assisted

11.21 w	4.8	Hannah Elwiss	(11.36)	1	Exeter	7 Jul
11.38 w	4.8	Danielle Fawkes	(11.56)	2	Exeter	7 Jul
11.43 w	4.8	Nicola Robinson	(11.50)	3	Exeter	7 Jul
11.71 w	2.5	Pamela Paterson	(11.87)	3	Tullamore, IRL	21 Jul
11.72 w	4.8	Sarah Allsopp	(11.99)	5	Exeter	7 Jul
11.76 w	4.8	Lisa McManus	(11.82)	7	Exeter	7 Jul
11.85 w	2.4	Elen Evans	(12.07)	1H	Aberdare	23 Jun
11.96 w	2.6	Stacy Flint	(12.09)	3	Cudworth	26 May
11.98 w	2.6	Emma Makin	(12.00)	4	Cudworth	26 May
12.02 w	2.4	Faye Harding	7.09.85	2H	Aberdare	23 Jun
12.08 w	2.6	Penny Boyd	27.10.84	5	Cudworth	26 May

hand timing

11.3	Justine Roach	(11.44)	1	Leicester	9 Jun
11.4	Phyllis Agbo	(11.52)	1H	Woking	23 Jun
11.6	Louise Hazel	(11.76)	1H	Rugby	23 Jun
11.7	Lisa McManus	(11.82)	3	Leicester	9 Jun
11.8	Pamela Paterson	(11.87)	2	Coatbridge	30 Jun
11.8 w	Staci Stewart	(11.95)	1	Glasgow (S)	3 Jun

11.9		Nadine Simpson		28.02.86	2	London (Nh)	19 May
11.9		Catherine Holdsworth		3.01.86	1	St.ves	19 May
11.9		Rachel Brenton		(12.02)	2	Southampton	20 May
11.9		Maria Garavand		30.06.86	1	London (CP)	20 May
11.9		Katey Read		20.03.86	1	Blackpool	3 Jun
11.9		Carly Dean		14.10.85	1	Basingstoke	10 Jun
11.9		Emma Perkins		(12.08)	3H	Woking	24 Jun
11.9		Gemma Werrett		(12.09)	1	Birmingham	24 Jun
11.9		Sarah Allsopp		(11.99)	1	Cardiff	1 Jul
11.9		Sally Peake		8.02.86	1	Bebington	1 Jul
12.0		Anna Conolly		19.04.86	1	Telford	9 Jun
12.0		Emma Downes		21.02.86	2	Exeter	16 Jun
12.0		Lynsey Harley		2.04.85	1	Grangemouth	30 Jun
12.0		Rachel Thomas		19.01.85	1	Leeds	5 Aug
12.0		Anna Clayton		20.03.85	1H	Peterborough	23 Sep

100 Metres Hurdles - Under 17 (2'6" barriers)

14.19	1.8	Cathy Crawford		17.12.84	1	Tullamore, IRL	29 Jul

100 Metres Hurdles

13.08	0.8	Diane Allahgreen		21.02.75	1	Bedford	18 Jul
		13.11 0.8			1	Birmingham	15 Jul
		13.14 0.4			1rB	Walnut CA, USA	22 Apr
		13.16 1.2			1s1	Bedford	27 May
		13.18 -0.1			4	Beijing, CHN	28 Aug
		13.23 0.6			4	Bremen, GER	24 Jun
		13.25 0.2			1	Loughborough	20 May
		13.28 0.3			1h1	Birmingham	15 Jul
		13.29 1.4			2h4	Beijing, CHN	27 Aug
		13.32 -1.2			3s2	Beijing, CHN	27 Aug
		13.35 0.6			2	Bedford	27 May
		13.44 -2.4			2	Cork, IRL	7 Jul
		13.45 -1.4			1C3	Walnut CA, USA	22 Apr
		13.55 -0.2			1	Glasgow (S)	7 May
		13.60 -0.5			1h3	Glasgow (S)	7 May
13.24	0.8	Melani Wilkins		18.01.73	2	Birmingham	15 Jul
		13.27 0.6			1	Bedford	27 May
		13.27 1.6			2	Bedford	21 Jul
		13.28 0.8			2	Bedford	18 Jul
		13.33 -0.6			1	London (Ha)	17 Jun
		13.40 1.7			1	Basel, SUI	4 Jun
		13.40 0.2			2	Eton	7 Jul
		13.43 1.4			4	Tula, RUS	8 Jun
		13.51 0.8			1h3	Birmingham	15 Jul
		13.55 0.2			2	Loughborough	20 May
		13.63 1.4			2	Konigs Wusterhausen, GER	2 Aug
13.24	1.6	Keri Maddox		4.07.72	1	Bedford	21 Jul
		13.35 0.8			3	Birmingham	15 Jul
		13.38 0.2			1	Eton	7 Jul
		13.44 2.0			1	Birmingham	30 Jun
		13.47 1.4			1h2	Birmingham	15 Jul
		13.52 -0.5			4	Madrid, ESP	27 May
13.36	0.6	Sarah Claxton	U23	23.09.79	3	Bedford	27 May
		13.55 2.0			2h3	Bedford	27 May
		13.60 1.2			2s1	Bedford	27 May
13.42	0.8	Denise Lewis		27.08.72	4	Birmingham	15 Jul
		13.52 1.2			2r2	Seville, ESP	8 Jun
		13.56 0.6			7	Lucerne, SUI	27 Jun
		13.62 0.8			2h3	Birmingham	15 Jul

13.46	1.2	Julie Pratt	U23	20.03.79	5	Amsterdam, NED	15	Jul
		13.47 0.6			4	Bedford	27	May
		13.50 2.0			1h3	Bedford	27	May
		13.50 -0.2			1	Geneva, SUI	9	Jun
		13.50 -0.6			2	London (Ha)	17	Jun
		13.51 0.9			1h2	Bedford	1	Jul
		13.52 0.3			2	Alicante, ESP	18	Apr
		13.58 0.3			3	Alfaz del Pi, ESP	21	Apr
		13.60 0.0			1h3	Alfaz del Pi, ESP	21	Apr
		13.60 0.2			3	Loughborough	20	May
		13.63 0.8			3	Bedford	18	Jul
13.51	-2.6	Rachel King		11.05.76	1	Budapest, HUN	1	Jul
		13.52 0.6			5	Bedford	27	May
		13.52 0.8			5	Birmingham	15	Jul
		13.54 1.4			2h2	Birmingham	15	Jul
		13.59 1.7			3	Basel, SUI	4	Jun
13.60	0.6	Clova Court	V40	10.02.60	6	Bedford	27	May
	56 performances to 13.65 by 8 athletes							
13.66	1.8	Helen Worsey	U20	29.08.82	4h2	Grosseto,TA	20	Jul
13.71	1.0	Kerry Jury		19.11.68	1H2	Ried, AUT	30	Jun
	(10)							
13.81	0.6	Liz Fairs		1.12.77	7	Bedford	27	May
13.90	0.8	Clare Milborrow		10.01.77	4	Bedford	18	Jul
13.94	1.3	Sara McGreavy	U20	13.12.82	2h2	Bedford	27	May
13.96	0.2	Tamsin Stephens	U23	2.08.80	2rB	Eton	7	Jul
14.01	0.3	Fiona Harrison	U23	30.11.81	3	Alicante, ESP	18	Apr
14.05	0.8	Nicola Gautier		21.03.78	1H4	Ried, AUT	30	Jun
14.14	1.3	Gemma Fergusson	U20	20.08.84	1h2	Exeter	6	Jul
14.15	0.2	Katy Sketchley		9.07.73	5	Loughborough	20	May
14.17	-2.7	Katherine Livesey	U23	15.12.79	H	Eugene, USA	1	Jun
14.19	0.5	Kelly Sotherton		13.11.76	3H4	Arles, FRA	9	Jun
	(20)							
14.19	0.8	Alyssa Fullelove	U23	16.09.81	1	Glasgow (S)	23	Jun
14.20	0.2	Lauren McLoughlin	U20	8.09.82	7	Loughborough	20	May
14.20	0.9	Kate Brewington	U23	15.10.81	2h2	Bedford	1	Jul
14.20	1.1	Aileen Wilson	U20	30.03.84	2h2	Bedford	1	Jul
14.23	1.7	Leanne Buxton		27.05.78	2	Crawley	12	May
14.25		Lorna Silver/Rogers		10.01.74	1	Grangemouth	26	Aug
14.32	0.9	Caroline Pearce	U23	1.09.80	3h1	Bedford	1	Jul
14.33	0.5	Julie Hollman		16.02.77	6H4	Arles, FRA	9	Jun
14.34	1.8	Stefanie Pullinger	U20	3.04.83	3h1	Bedford	1	Jul
14.47		Grace Smith	U20	30.01.82	2	Rennes, FRA	22	Sep
	(30)							
14.48	0.8	Sarah Porter	U23	11.12.79	4h3	Birmingham	15	Jul
14.50	0.5	Roz Gonse	U20	1.03.82	1	Bamburg, GER	15	Sep
14.51	1.3	Anne Hollman		18.02.74	4h2	Bedford	27	May
14.53	1.5	Jessica Ennis	U17	28.01.86	2H1	Bedford	4	Aug
14.58	1.3	Kay Reynolds		15.09.67	5h2	Bedford	27	May
14.58	0.7	Emily Parker	U17	7.11.84	2h1	London (He)	26	Aug
14.61	0.9	Laura Turner	U20	12.08.82	3	London (He)	26	Aug
14.62	0.8	Claire Lomas	U23	18.04.80	3	Glasgow (S)	23	Jun
14.63	1.2	Donna-Louise Hutt		6.06.72	1	Bedford	28	Jul
14.66	1.1	Jemma Ooi	U20	2.09.82	5h2	Bedford	1	Jul
	(40)							
14.67	1.3	Leyna Hird	U20	4.02.84	3h2	Exeter	6	Jul
14.68	0.8	Claire Pearson		23.09.78	5h3	Birmingham	15	Jul
14.68	-0.5	Vicky Williams	U23	11.04.81	3	Derby	29	Jul
14.69	1.8	Rebecca Jones	U20	17.01.83	4h1	Bedford	1	Jul
14.70	1.4	Julia Bennett		26.03.70	1H2	Bedford	4	Aug
14.81	1.1	Gemma Bennett	U20	4.01.84	6h2	Bedford	1	Jul
14.81	1.3	Holly Ferrier	U20	13.07.84	4h2	Exeter	6	Jul

14.86	0.9	Samantha Adamson	U20	27.03.82	4	London (He)	26	Aug
14.88		Sara Todd	U23	3.11.79	1	Gateshead	12	May
14.90	1.8	Jenni Molloy	U20	23.09.83	7h1	Bedford	1	Jul
	(50)							
14.90	-0.2	Ruth Dales	U23	29.10.80	3rB	Eton	7	Jul
14.92	0.9	Katie Jones		4.01.77	3rB	Birmingham	2	Jun
14.92		Wendy Laing	V35	29.12.62	1	Brisbane, AUS	12	Jul
14.93	0.1	Amy Teale	U20	30.12.82	3h1	Exeter	6	Jul
14.96	0.8	Emma Reid	U23	5.01.81	4	Glasgow (S)	23	Jun
14.97	-1.9	Laura Redmond	U23	19.04.81	3H7	Arles, FRA	9	Jun
15.02	-2.0	Nusrat Ceesay	U23	18.03.81	4rB	Loughborough	4	Jul
15.05	-0.3	Emma Duck	U23	9.02.81	3	Portsmouth	12	May
15.07	1.6	Danielle Parkinson	U23	2.09.81	1H2	Sheffield	1	Sep
15.09	0.1	Lara Carty	U20	7.03.84	4h1	Exeter	6	Jul
	(60)							
15.10	1.7	Hannah Barnes	U20	2.06.84	4H1	Bedford	14	Jul
15.14	0.1	Sian Polhill-Thomas	U20	4.06.83	5h1	Exeter	6	Jul
15.18	-0.3	Charmaine Johnson	V35	4.06.63	4	Portsmouth	12	May
15.18	1.6	Sarah Still		24.09.75	4=H1	Sheffield	1	Sep
15.21	0.9	Allison English	U23	4.03.79	5h2	Bedford	1	Jul
15.24	1.9	Wendy Davidson	U20	14.10.82	1H2	Bedford	14	Jul
15.30	0.2	Catriona Pennet	U20	10.10.83	2	Corinth, GRE	27	May
15.31	1.5	Rebecca Mitchell	U20	10.12.83	2	Tullamore, IRL	28	Jul

wind assisted

12.98	2.1	Diane Allahgreen		(13.08)	4	Glasgow (S)	1	Jul
		13.15 2.8			1h1	Bedford	27	May
		13.23 2.7			3	Lisbon, POR	16	Jun
		13.26 2.3			3	Vasteras, SWE	3	Jul
		13.42 3.9			1	Liverpool	17	Jun
13.08	2.1	Melani Wilkins		(13.24)	6	Glasgow (S)	1	Jul
		13.22 3.2			1s2	Bedford	27	May
		13.28 2.8			2h1	Bedford	27	May
		13.29 2.1			1	Birmingham	2	Jun
13.29	2.1	Denise Lewis		(13.42)	7	Glasgow (S)	1	Jul
		13.41 2.1			2	Birmingham	2	Jun
13.43	2.1	Julie Pratt	U23	(13.46)	3	Birmingham	2	Jun
		13.53 3.2			2s2	Bedford	27	May
13.56	2.8	Maddox		(13.24)	1	Birmingham	16	Jun
13.58	2.3	King		(13.51)	1	Cardiff	17	Jun
		13.63 3.2			2s2	Bedford	27	May
		16 performances to 13.65 by 6 athletes						
13.73	3.9	Liz Fairs		(13.81)	2	Liverpool	17	Jun
13.77	4.6	Sara McGreavy	U20	(13.94)	1	Exeter	7	Jul
13.78	2.8	Tamsin Stephens	U23	(13.96)	1h1	Bedford	1	Jul
13.80	3.6	Katherine Livesey	U23	(14.17)	1H3	College Station, USA	16	May
14.07	4.6	Gemma Fergusson	U20	(14.14)	2	Exeter	7	Jul
14.08	3.2	Kelly Sotherton		(14.19)	5s2	Bedford	27	May
14.13	3.2	Leanne Buxton		(14.23)	6s2	Bedford	27	May
14.17	3.0	Lauren McLoughlin	U20	(14.20)	2	Cardiff	17	Jun
14.19	3.2	Julie Hollman		(14.33)	7s2	Bedford	27	May
14.35	2.2	Laura Turner	U20	(14.61)	1	pswich	2	Sep
14.42	2.8	Vicky Williams	U23	(14.68)	3h1	Bedford	1	Jul
14.42	2.8	Emma Duck	U23	(15.05)	4h1	Bedford	1	Jul
14.50	2.8	Claire Pearson		(14.68)	4	Birmingham	16	Jun
14.52	4.6	Jemma Ooi	U20	(14.66)	4	Exeter	7	Jul
14.54	4.6	Leyna Hird	U20	(14.67)	5	Exeter	7	Jul
14.63	4.6	Amy Teale	U20	(14.93)	6	Exeter	7	Jul
14.67	3.9	Ruth Dales	U23	(14.90)	3	Liverpool	17	Jun

14.69	2.8	Hannah Stares		13.11.78	6h1	Bedford	27 May
14.70	4.6	Holly Ferrier	U20	(14.81)	7	Exeter	7 Jul
14.72	2.8	Samantha Male		11.04.76	7h1	Bedford	27 May
14.77	4.6	Lara Carty	U20	(15.09)	8	Exeter	7 Jul
14.86	2.4	Laura Redmond	U23	(14.97)	3H1	Bedford	14 Jul
14.87	3.9	Allison English	U23	(15.21)	4	Liverpool	17 Jun
14.94	2.3	Michelle Debono		1.05.72	3	Cardiff	17 Jun
14.96	2.4	Charmaine Johnson	V35	(15.18)	4H1	Bedford	14 Jul
14.98	2.4	Sarah Still		(15.18)	5H1	Bedford	14 Jul
15.01	2.8	Alison Keys	U23	11.07.81	6	Birmingham	16 Jun
15.05	3.6	Susan Potter	U23	??.??.??	3	Beveren, BEL	8 Sep
15.09	2.9	Claire Lidster	U23	26.10.81	1	DouglasOM	9 Jul
15.10	3.0	Wendy Davidson	U20	(15.24)	2H3	Bedford	4 Aug
15.39	2.5	Vicky Consterdine		25.04.75	2H2	Bedford	14 Jul

hand timing

13.4 w	3.1	Julie Pratt	U23	(13.46)	1	Southend	12 May
		13.5 w 2.2			1	Bedford	1 Jul
13.5	-1.3	Wilkins		(13.24)	1h1	London (Ha)	17 Jun
		3 performances to 13.5 by 2 athletes including 2 wind assisted					
13.6 w	3.7	Liz Fairs		(13.81)	1	Wigan	10 Jun
13.9	-0.1	Stefanie Pullinger	U20	(14.34)	1	Dole, FRA	29 Jul
14.1		Kay Reynolds		(14.58)	1	Abingdon	14 Jul
14.1		Lorna Silver/Rogers		(14.25)	1	Bedford	11 Aug
14.1 w	3.4	Kate Brewington	U23	(14.20)	1	Stafford	8 Sep
14.2		Julie Hollman		(14.33)	1	St.ves	12 May
14.2		Anne Hollman		(14.51)	2	St.ves	12 May
14.2 w	2.2	Caroline Pearce	U23	(14.32)	3	Bedford	1 Jul
14.2 w		Emily Parker	U17	(14.58)	1=	Exeter	1 Sep
14.4		Jackie Brett	V35	5.07.65	1	Par	12 May
14.5	-0.1	Leyna Hird	U20	(14.67)	5	Dole, FRA	29 Jul
14.5		Laura Turner	U20	(14.61)	1	Ashford	11 Aug
14.6	-0.3	Sara Todd	U23	(14.88)	1H1	Hexham	19 May
14.6		Jemma Ooi	U20	(14.66)	2	Middlesbrough	17 Jun
14.6		Natalie Butler		25.11.78	1	Oxford	21 Jun
14.6	1.7	Katie Jones		(14.92)	1	Liverpool	24 Jun
14.6		Claire Pearson		(14.68)	1	Nuneaton	19 Aug
14.7		Katherine Porter	U20	19.08.82	1	Abingdon	28 Apr
14.7		Emma Duck	U23	(15.05)	1	Braunton	19 May
14.7		Sarah Lane	U23	4.06.81	1	Scunthorpe	3 Jun
14.7 w	3.7	Joanne Suddes		27.01.77	2	Wigan	10 Jun
14.8	1.0	Samantha Male		(14.72w)	2	Kingston	13 May
14.8		Nikki Gilding		16.05.72	1	Portsmouth	19 May
14.8		Natasha Turner/Spence		8.11.74	2	Oxford	21 Jun
14.8		Gemma Bennett	U20	(14.81)	1	Enfield	14 Jul
14.8		Nusrat Ceesay	U23	(15.02)	1	Basildon	1 Sep
14.9		Sharon Price		10.12.75	2	Coventry	29 Apr
14.9		Amy Teale	U20	(14.93)	2	Gateshead	9 Jun
14.9		Sian Polhill-Thomas	U20	(15.14)	3	Stoke-on-Trent	17 Jun
14.9 w	2.5	Charmaine Johnson	V35	(15.18)	2H	Aberdare	23 Jun
14.9 w	2.9	Jay Peet		4.12.71	1	Wigan	8 Jul
		15.2			2	Birmingham	24 Jun
14.9 w	3.4	Alison Keys	U23	(15.01w)	2	Stafford	8 Sep
15.0		Susan Potter	U23	(15.05w)	2	Braunton	19 May
15.0	2.0	Belinda Samuels		29.11.78	6h4	Bedford	27 May
15.0	-0.4	Tracey Duncan	U23	16.05.79	3rB	Wigan	4 Aug
15.1		Allison English	U23	(15.21)	2	Scunthorpe	3 Jun

15.1	1.2	Orla Bermingham		7.10.75	3	London (Ha)	10 Jun
15.1		Catriona Pennet	U20	(15.30)	4	Stoke-on-Trent	17 Jun
15.1		Mary Onianwa	U23	20.01.81	4	London (TB)	28 Jul
15.2		Gowry Hodge	V40	21.06.60	1	St.ves	19 May
15.2	1.4	Laura Curtis	U23	2.05.81	1rB	Eton	5 Aug
15.2		Lisa Williams		11.04.78	2	Nottingham	19 Aug
15.2		Symone Belle	U17	12.11.84	1	King's Lynn	1 Sep
15.2		Kirsty Roger		24.03.78	1	Aberdeen	9 Sep

Additional Under 17 (1 - 2 above)

15.3		Nadine Simpson	28.02.86	1	London (TB)	20 May
15.3		Justine Roach	21.12.84	1rB	Nuneaton	19 Aug
15.6	-0.9	Emily Mason	28.04.85	2	Wigan	29 Apr

Foreign

13.07	*1.9*	*Kimberly Carson (USA)*	*12.03.74*	*4h3*	*Eugene, USA*	*23 Jun*
15.30	*2.0*	*Margaret Veldman (NED)*	*7.06.74*	*7*	*Birmingham*	*30 Jun*

300 Metres Hurdles - Under 17

42.50	Justine Roach	21.12.84	1	Tullamore, IRL	21 Jul
43.20	Faye Harding	7.09.85	1	Nyiregyhaza, HUN	22 Jul
43.65	Maria Garavand	30.06.86	2	Exeter	7 Jul
43.71	Joanne Erskine	28.05.85	1	Sheffield	12 Aug
43.74	Cathy Crawford	17.12.84	2	Tullamore, IRL	21 Jul
43.86	Melanie Canning	19.05.85	3	Exeter	7 Jul
44.1	Emily Parker	7.11.84	1	Crawley	5 Aug
	44.47		4	Sheffield	12 Aug
44.7	Sarah Gallaway	14.11.84	3	Watford	26 May
	45.75		3h1	Exeter	6 Jul
44.7	Sarah-Jane Pickett	24.10.84	4	Watford	26 May
	45.61		3h3	Exeter	6 Jul
44.73	Angela Shearer	18.01.85	1	Aberdeen	27 May
	(10)				
44.9	Nadine Simpson	28.02.86	1	Watford	9 Jun
45.0	Emma Makin	12.10.85	1	Warrington	12 May
	45.35		1	Cudworth	27 May
45.01	Sian Davies	16.02.85	4	Exeter	7 Jul
45.06	Jenny Bliss	6.07.86	5	Exeter	7 Jul
45.2	Carly Dean	14.10.85	1	London (He)	23 Jun
	46.11		1	Birmingham	1 Sep
45.3	Laura Raven	12.03.85	1	Bromley	11 Aug
	45.95		5h1	Exeter	6 Jul
45.36	Katey Read	20.03.86	1h1	Exeter	6 Jul
45.4	Emma Morris	21.02.86	1	Middlesbrough	1 Jul
	46.50		1	Scunthorpe	19 Aug
45.5	Angie Broadbelt	12.09.85	1	London (BP)	9 Jun
	45.76		4h1	Exeter	6 Jul
45.58	Gemma Collier	25.11.85	2h3	Exeter	6 Jul
	(20)				
45.6	Amy Forsyth	16.10.85	2	London (BP)	9 Jun
45.70	Natalie Mills	29.05.85	2	Birmingham	27 May
45.7	Seonaid Murray	16.03.85	3	Warrington	12 May
	46.03		4h3	Exeter	6 Jul
45.8	Chanelle Garnett	16.08.85	2	Eton	1 Jul
46.0	Lulu Cash-Gibson	22.12.84	3	London (BP)	9 Jun
	46.70		7h2	Exeter	6 Jul
46.15	Jenny Christie	28.09.85	3	Birmingham	27 May
46.2	Hayley Goodall	20.09.84	2	Ashford	13 May
46.2	Catherine Holdsworth	3.01.86	2	St.ves	19 May
46.2	Penny Balsdon	5.04.85	3	Exeter	16 Jun

46.3	Lynsey Harley		2.04.85	1	Grangemouth	6 May
	46.52			2	Edinburgh	13 May
(30)						
46.3	Sharon-Louise Walls		9.10.84	1rB	Bebington	1 Jul
	46.33			1	Birmingham	2 Sep
46.38	Penny Boyd		27.10.84	6h2	Exeter	6 Jul
46.56	Jessica Case		29.10.85	5h2	Sheffield	12 Aug
46.6	Lisa McManus		3.01.86	2	Loughborough	12 May
46.7	Samantha Day		8.02.86	1	Corby	20 May
46.8	Kathryn Dunn		11.06.85	1	Liverpool	12 May
46.8	Staci Stewart		20.09.85	1	Dumfries	30 Jun
46.9	Hannah Slade		29.09.84	1	Yeovil	27 Aug
46.91	Ruth Laybourn		5.10.84	3	Cudworth	27 May

400 Metres Hurdles

54.94	Natasha Danvers		19.09.77	1	Beijing, CHN	31 Aug
	55.37			1	Palo Alto, USA	9 Jun
	55.70			1s2	Beijing, CHN	30 Aug
	55.95			1	Walnut CA, USA	22 Apr
	56.08			3	Gateshead	19 Aug
	56.36			4h3	Edmonton, CAN	5 Aug
	56.56			1	Los Angeles CA, USA	2 Jun
	56.84			2	Fort-de-FranceMart, FRA	28 Apr
	57.26			1h3	Beijing, CHN	30 Aug
56.07	Sinead Dudgeon		9.07.76	2h4	Edmonton, CAN	5 Aug
	56.37			1	Birmingham	14 Jul
	56.46			5	London (CP)	22 Jul
	56.53			1	Dortmund, GER	9 Jun
	56.83			1	Loughborough	4 Jul
	56.92			8s2	Edmonton, CAN	6 Aug
	57.1			1	Glasgow (S)	23 Jun
	57.24			2r1	Budapest, HUN	1 Jul
	58.45			1	Birmingham	2 Jun
	59.21			1h2	Birmingham	13 Jul
57.18	Keri Maddox		4.07.72	7	London (CP)	22 Jul
	57.2			1	Eton	7 Jul
	57.48			1	Bedford	21 Jul
	57.55			7h2	Edmonton, CAN	5 Aug
	58.00			2	Birmingham	14 Jul
	58.07			1	Birmingham	30 Jun
	58.44			5	Lucerne, SUI	27 Jun
	59.34			4	Madrid, ESP	26 May
	59.34			1h1	Birmingham	13 Jul
58.15	Tracey Duncan	U23	16.05.79	1	Ashford	11 Aug
	58.4			1	Wigan	4 Aug
	58.48			2rB	Loughborough	4 Jul
	59.29			1	Liverpool	23 Jun
	59.30			4h4	Beijing, CHN	30 Aug
	33 performances to 59.35 by 4 athletes					
59.49	Celia Brown		22.01.77	2	Glasgow (S)	6 May
59.5	Gowry Hodge	V40	21.06.60	1	St.ves	19 May
59.55	Hannah Wood	U23	17.11.81	1	Merksem, BEL	4 Aug
60.06	Faye Harding	U17	7.09.85	3h2	Debrecen, HUN	13 Jul
60.07	Gemma Dooney	U20	12.05.84	2	Stoke-on-Trent	18 Aug
60.28	Hannah Stares		13.11.78	2	Heverlee, BEL	18 Aug
(10)						
60.42	Donna Porazinski	U23	28.01.81	1	Cardiff	17 Jun
60.50	Sian Scott	U20	20.03.84	2	Murcia, ESP	25 Jul
60.53	Samantha Adamson	U20	27.03.82	1rC	Loughborough	4 Jul
60.6	Nusrat Ceesay	U23	18.03.81	1	Loughborough	23 May
	60.79			2rC	Loughborough	4 Jul

60.6	Natalie Kydd	U20	27.06.84	2	Glasgow (S)	23 Jun
	62.51			2	Edinburgh	25 Aug
60.8	Claire Brason	U20	16.03.83	2	Bedford	1 Jul
	61.24			1	Cudworth	26 May
60.8	Tanya Wilkinson		1.04.70	1	Nottingham	19 Aug
60.84	Susie Williams		2.06.77	1	Bedford	22 Jul
61.0	Jennie Mathews	V35	3.07.62	2	Loughborough	23 May
	61.35			3	Bedford	28 May
61.1	Nicola Sanders	U20	23.06.82	2	Loughborough	13 Jun
	61.54			2	Fullerton CA, USA	26 Apr
(20)						
61.19	Joanne Oates		21.02.78	2	Birmingham	30 Jun
61.21	Katie Jones		4.01.77	1	Scunthorpe	19 Aug
61.30	Kim Heffernan		20.12.66	2h2	Birmingham	13 Jul
61.36	Ruth Brereton	U23	26.06.81	2h2	Glasgow (S)	5 May
61.50	Liz Fairs		1.12.77	1	Cudworth	26 Aug
61.51	Shona MacPherson	U23	31.08.80	2h2	Bedford	28 May
61.59	Rachael Kay	U23	8.09.80	4r4	Tarare, FRA	9 Jun
61.7	Leanne Buxton		27.05.78	4	Eton	7 Jul
	62.02			1	Crawley	13 May
61.8	Jennifer Culley		4.03.75	1	Swindon	11 Aug
61.8	Kelly Sotherton		13.11.76	1rB	Rugby	19 Aug
(30)						
61.85	Laura Curtis	U23	2.05.81	2	Scunthorpe	19 Aug
62.0	Emily Parker	U17	7.11.84	1	Exeter	1 Sep
	63.16			3	Bedford	22 Jul
62.1	Cicely Hall		12.10.78	1	Coventry	5 Aug
	65.33			2h1	Glasgow (S)	5 May
62.2	Christine Amede	V35	7.08.63	3	Wigan	4 Aug
62.4	Natalie Christmas	U20	9.04.84	1	Horsham	14 Jul
	63.62			4	Exeter	7 Jul
62.6	Joanne Suddes		27.01.77	4	Glasgow (S)	23 Jun
	62.77			4h1	Birmingham	13 Jul
62.7	Louise Aylwin	U23	8.04.80	1	Guildford	19 May
	62.73			3h3	Bedford	30 Jun
62.81	Sara Todd	U23	3.11.79	1	Gateshead	13 May
62.81	Kate Williams		10.11.77	5rB	Loughborough	20 May
62.85	Jay Peet		4.12.71	5	Birmingham	30 Jun
(40)						
63.14	Susan Potter	U23	11.08.79	5h1	Birmingham	13 Jul
63.20	Claire Lidster	U23	26.10.81	1	DouglasOM	12 Jul
63.36	Tamsin Stephens	U23	2.08.80	4	Grangemouth	25 Aug
63.4	Karen Lowe	U20	3.05.82	6	Bedford	1 Jul
	63.71			2	Cudworth	26 May
63.5	Jana Riedel		1.09.75	2	Exeter	1 Sep
	65.26			6h2	Bedford	28 May
63.6	Jenni Molloy	U20	23.09.83	1rB	London (He)	23 Jun
	64.29			6	Exeter	7 Jul
63.7	Michele Gillham		8.10.74	3	London (Cr)	3 Jun
63.7	Rebecca Wright		20.12.77	1rB	Eton	7 Jul
63.77	Faith Cripps	U20	23.09.83	5	Exeter	7 Jul
63.96	Michelle Debono		1.05.72	3	Cardiff	17 Jun
(50)						
63.96	Alyssa Fullelove	U23	16.09.81	1	Grangemouth	26 Aug
64.0	Judith Owen		20.06.71	2	Kingston	12 May
64.0	Emma Reid	U23	5.01.81	2rB	Eton	7 Jul
	65.12			3	Glasgow (S)	29 Apr
64.1	Niki Pocock	U23	9.05.79	6	London (Ha)	10 Jun
	65.00			1	Portsmouth	13 May
64.20	Elizabeth Waters		19.02.77	2	Bedford	28 Jul
64.2	Lyndsay Fitzgerald	U23	31.01.80	2	London (He)	23 Jun
	65.20			4	Birmingham	2 Jun

64.31	Maria Garavand	U17	30.06.86	1	Derby	9 Sep
64.35	Helen Walker	U23	12.10.80	2h3	Glasgow (S)	5 May
64.40	Hannah Riley	U20	9.07.82	2	DouglasOM	12 Jul
64.4	Charlotte Randall	U23	10.05.80	2	London (TB)	19 May
	65.31			5h3	Glasgow (S)	5 May
(60)						
64.4	Louise Gregory		11.05.74	1	Enfield	19 May
64.4	Lindsey-Ann McDonnell	U23	13.08.79	3	Exeter	1 Sep
64.46	Kerry Mitchell	U23	23.06.81	2	Dublin (S), IRL	21 Apr
64.48	Sarah Newman	U23	7.10.79	4h3	Bedford	30 Jun
64.5	Sandra Leigh	V35	26.02.66	1	London (Nh)	19 May
65.09	Georgina Roberts	U20	9.07.84	4	Cudworth	26 May
65.1	Carly Austin	U20	16.05.83	1	Abingdon	9 Jun
65.20	Jessica Cunliffe		25.11.77	2	Rugby	19 Aug
65.2	Julia Bennett		26.03.70	2	London (BP)	20 May
65.2	Joanne Erskine	U17	28.05.85	1	Coatbridge	29 Jul
(70)						
65.21	Ruth Waller	U20	6.03.84	3	Rennes, FRA	22 Sep
65.3	Lyndsay Yellop		18.08.78	1	Bedford	20 May
65.42	Kelly Brady	U20	3.11.82	5	Cudworth	26 May
65.5	Dyanna Clarke	V40	27.02.58	2	London (TB)	20 May
65.5	Virginia Mitchell	V35	29.01.63	2	Woking	1 Sep
65.6	Sara Elson		8.05.70	3	Scunthorpe	3 Jun
65.64	Aileen Williams	U23	14.06.81	4	Glasgow (S)	29 Apr
65.7	Anastasia Hounslow	U20	13.12.82	2	Kingston	9 Jun
65.7	Sarah-Jane Pickett	U17	24.10.84	1	Watford	12 Aug
65.79	Rhona Blair		27.11.76	1	Aberdeen	27 May
(80)						
65.8	Jackie Noblet	U23	19.04.79	1	DouglasOM	6 May
65.8	Melissa Tremarco	U20	12.10.82	1	Warrington	12 May
65.8	Rebecca Reid	U20	9.11.83	1	Blackpool	9 Jun
65.8	Leyna Hird	U20	4.02.84	2rB	Tidworth	22 Jul
65.81	Ruth Thompson		7.06.76	2	Sheffield	12 May
65.94	Rebecca Deane	U23	9.01.79	5	Birmingham	2 Jun
65.95	Luisa Giles	U20	23.02.82	1	Birmingham	27 May

Additional Under 17 (1 - 5 above)

66.1	Natalie Mills	29.05.85	1	Mansfield	5 Aug
66.5	Emma Makin	12.10.85	1	Connah's Quay	29 Jul
66.6	Seonaid Murray	16.03.85	2	Connah's Quay	29 Jul
67.6	Lucy Aukett	9.09.84	1	Brighton	23 Jun

Foreign

57.81	*Maiteland Marks (USA)*		*19.09.76*	*1rB*	*Namur, BEL*	*17 Aug*
59.64	*Michelle Carey (IRL)*	*U23*	*20.02.81*	*1*	*Derby*	*29 Jul*
60.6	*Esther Erharuyi (NGR)*	*U20*	*17.04.83*	*1*	*London (BP)*	*28 Apr*
63.2	*Vanessa Magnanini (RSA)*		*26.10.81*	*2*	*Coventry*	*5 Aug*
	63.70			*4*	*Bedford*	*21 Jul*
65.5	*Sara Sappinen (FIN)*	*U23*	*16.09.80*	*1*	*London (Ha)*	*7 Apr*

High Jump

1.95	Susan Jones	8.06.78	1	Bremen, GER	24 Jun
	1.94		1	Loughborough	20 May
	1.91		1	Birmingham	15 Jul
	1.90		1	Lisbon, POR	16 Jun
	1.89		2	Eton	7 Jul
	1.89		4=	London (CP)	22 Jul
	1.88 i		5=	Birmingham	18 Feb
	1.88		13=Q	Edmonton, CAN	10 Aug
	1.88		Q	Beijing, CHN	29 Aug

(Jones)	1.88			4=	Beijing, CHN	31 Aug
	1.86 i			1	Sheffield	20 Jan
	1.86			1	Budapest, HUN	1 Jul
	1.85 i			1	Birmingham	27 Jan
	1.85			1	Bedford	27 May
	1.85			1	Birmingham	2 Jun
1.90	Michelle Dunkley		26.01.78	1	Glasgow (S)	24 Jun
	1.89			2	Loughborough	20 May
	1.89			1	Eton	7 Jul
	1.88			4	Tula, RUS	9 Jun
	1.86			2	Birmingham	15 Jul
	1.86			1	Ashford	11 Aug
	1.85 i			1	Cardiff	4 Feb
	1.85 i			1	Cardiff	11 Feb
	1.85			8	London (CP)	22 Jul
	1.85			14Q	Beijing, CHN	29 Aug
1.87	Aileen Wilson	U20	30.03.84	1	Debrecen, HUN	15 Jul
	1.86			8	Grosseto, ITA	22 Jul
	1.84			1	Exeter	7 Jul
	1.83			Q	Grosseto, ITA	20 Jul
1.84	Julia Bennett		26.03.70	1H	Bedford	4 Aug
	1.83			1H1	Arles, FRA	9 Jun
1.83	Julie Hollman		16.02.77	2H1	Arles, FRA	9 Jun
1.83	Stephanie Higham	U20	26.12.83	Q	Grosseto, ITA	20 Jul
	33 performances to 1.83 by 6 athletes including 5 indoors					
1.80	Rebecca Jones	U20	17.01.83	2H2	Arles, FRA	9 Jun
1.80	Lindsey-Ann McDonnell	U23	13.08.79	1	Exeter	10 Jun
1.80	Jo Jennings		20.09.69	1	Bedford	21 Jul
1.80	Lea Haggett		9.05.72	1	London (TB)	28 Jul
	(10)					
1.78	Debbie Marti		14.05.68	1	Zofingen, SUI	27 May
1.78	Kerry Jury		19.11.68	6H	Ried, AUT	30 Jun
1.78	Emma Perkins	U17	4.09.85	1H	Hull	15 Sep
1.76	Gillian Black	U23	27.10.79	4	Loughborough	20 May
1.75 i	Hazel Melvin		19.11.73	4	Glasgow	21 Jan
1.75	Katherine Livesey	U23	15.12.79	2H	Lawrence, USA	18 Apr
1.75	Jennifer Glaysher	U20	3.05.83	1	Stretford	9 Jun
1.75	Gayle O'Connor	U23	24.08.79	1	Liverpool	17 Jun
1.75	Jessica Ennis	U17	28.01.86	1H	Jarrow	23 Jun
1.75	Stephanie Pywell	U15	12.06.87	1	Exeter	6 Jul
	(20)					
1.75	Samantha Adamson	U20	27.03.82	1	Woking	1 Sep
1.74	Claire Wright	U20	9.09.83	1	Stoke-on-Trent	16 Jun
1.74	Ayamba Akim		21.06.72	1	London (Nh)	11 Aug
1.73 i	Maureen Knight		15.11.73	2=P	Birmingham	20 Jan
	1.65			1	London (BP)	28 Apr
1.73 i	Kelly Sotherton		13.11.76	2=P	Birmingham	20 Jan
	1.70			2	Coventry	29 Apr
1.73 i	Judith Payne	U23	7.07.80	1	Glasgow	18 Feb
	1.73			1	New Haven, USA	14 Apr
1.73 i	Ceri Stokoe	U20	19.04.82	1	Cardiff	18 Feb
	1.66			1	Neath	27 Aug
1.73	Denise Gayle	U23	11.09.79	1	Southend	14 Jul
1.73	Rebecka Bell	U17	1.12.85	1	Guildford	29 Jul
1.72	Chloe Cozens	U23	9.04.80	5	Loughborough	20 May
	(30)					
1.72	Emma Morris	U17	21.02.86	2H	Jarrow	23 Jun
1.72	Carly Prangnell	U17	4.03.86	1	Douglas IOM	13 Jul
1.70 i	Natalie Clark	U20	4.09.82	1	Birmingham	13 Jan
	1.70			5	Bedford	1 Jul

1.70 i	Laura Redmond	U23	19.04.81	1	Glasgow	14 Jan
	1.66			8H	Bedford	4 Aug
1.70 i	Rachel Martin		9.09.78	2	Glasgow	18 Feb
	1.70			2	Birmingham	2 Jun
1.70	Fiona Harrison	U23	30.11.81	2	Sheffield	12 May
1.70	Ailsa Wallace		12.03.77	2	Cambridge	19 May
1.70	Natalie Hulse	U20	2.12.82	1	Stafford	20 May
1.70	Alex Selwyn	U20	20.09.83	2	Stafford	20 May
1.70	Julie Peacock		19.08.70	3	Birmingham	2 Jun
	(40)					
1.70	Claire Dewsbury	U20	16.01.84	1	Scunthorpe	3 Jun
1.70	India Hadland	U17	7.01.85	1	Carshalton	23 Jun
1.70	Rebecca Weale		7.02.78	1	Cheltenham	4 Jul
1.70	Catriona Christie	U17	26.04.85	3	Bedford	21 Jul
1.70	Grace Clements	U20	2.05.84	1H	London (He)	11 Aug
1.70	Donna Maylor	U20	20.05.82	2	Rugby	19 Aug
1.69 i	Jenny Brown	V40	21.05.59	1P	Bordeaux, FRA	8 Mar
1.69	Laura Pitts	U17	9.01.86	1	Bath	29 Jul
1.68 i	Becky Mawer	U20	31.01.84	3	Sheffield	20 Jan
	1.66			1	Wakefield	3 Jun
1.68	Vicki Allan	U17	31.12.85	1	Edinburgh	12 May
	(50)					
1.68	Denise Lewis		27.08.72	5	Birmingham	15 Jul
1.68	Helen Smith	U17	9.10.84	3=	Sheffield	12 Aug
1.68	Sharon Woolrich		1.05.76	1	Portsmouth	1 Sep
1.67	Staci Stewart	U17	20.09.85	1	Glasgow (S)	29 Apr
1.67	Natalia Norford	U20	29.09.82	2	London (TB)	23 Jun
1.67	Sarah Humberstone	U23	6.07.81	1	Leeds	5 Aug
1.67	Kate Evans		4.02.74	3	Rugby	19 Aug
1.67 i	Phyllis Agbo	U17	16.12.85	1P	Glasgow	8 Dec
	1.66			1	Walton	22 Apr
1.66 i	Sarah Still		24.09.75	3P	Glasgow	24 Feb
	1.65			2	Edinburgh	12 May
1.66 i	Wendy Laing	V35	29.12.62	1P	Gateshead	10 Mar
	1.65			2	Brisbane, AUS	7 Jul
	(60)					
1.66	Shani Rainford	U15	6.07.87	1	London (TB)	19 May
1.66	Lucy Howes	U17	27.06.86	1	Basildon	9 Jun
1.66	Catherine Howe	U17	12.12.84	2	Basildon	9 Jun
1.66	Danielle Fidge	U17	19.03.85	1	Kingston	9 Jun
1.66	Katherine Silto	U20	12.08.83	1	Salisbury	9 Jun
1.66	Jan Taylor	U20	5.11.83	1	Exeter	16 Jun
1.66	Sarah-Jane Darrington	U17	25.06.85	1	Peterborough	27 Aug
1.65 i	Antonia Bemrose	U23	3.09.79	3	Birmingham	13 Jan
1.65 i	Stephanie Parsons	U20	22.08.83	1	Glasgow	25 Jan
1.65 i	Danielle Halsall	U20	16.12.82	1	London (CP)	10 Feb
	(70)					
1.65 i	Sonia Crawley	U20	7.12.83	2	Cardiff	14 Feb
1.65 i	Laura Curtis	U23	2.05.81	12=P	Nogent-sur-Oise, FRA	25 Feb
1.65	Kathy Pritchett	U20	11.04.84	1	Stretford	16 Apr
1.65	Jana Riedel		1.09.75	1	Harrow	28 Apr
1.65	Anne Hollman		18.02.74	1	King's Lynn	28 Apr
1.65	Helen Brown	U17	27.12.84	1	Harrow	29 Apr
1.65	Laura O'Sullivan	U20	30.07.82	1	Wigan	29 Apr
1.65	Jenny Reader/Dew		23.12.77	1	Southampton	19 May
1.65	Victoria Hawkins	U20	12.06.84	3	Stafford	20 May
1.65	Nadine Simpson	U17	28.02.86	3	Watford	26 May
	(80)					
1.65	Emily Mason	U17	28.04.85	1	Cudworth	27 May
1.65	Louise Gauld	U23	24.08.80	1	Wigan	10 Jun
1.65	Jennie Woods	U20	28.01.84	2	Stoke-on-Trent	16 Jun

1.65	Rachel Brenton	U17	18.01.85	1H	Abingdon	23 Jun
1.65	Rachel Culshaw	U17	11.08.86	1	Bebington	1 Jul
1.65	Sophie Upton	U17	18.09.85	1	Solihull	8 Jul
1.65	Debbie Armstrong	U17	8.02.86	1	York	29 Jul
1.65	Jenny Pacey	U20	5.02.83	1	Grantham	1 Aug
1.65	Sandra Alaneme	U17	7.01.86	2	Crawley	5 Aug
1.65	Kate Brewington	U23	15.10.81	2	London (Nh)	11 Aug
	(90)					
1.65	Siobhan Dennehy	U20	31.08.82	1	Derby	9 Sep

Additional Under 17 (1 - 24 above)

1.64	Montell Douglas	24.01.86	1	Bromley	15 Apr
1.64	Michelle Hammond	26.03.85	1	Par	9 Jun
1.64	Kate Walsh	28.01.85	1	Hoo	11 Aug
1.63 i	Elen Davies	24.04.86	2	King's Lynn	4 Feb
1.63	Hannah Keight	22.06.85	1	Coventry	29 Apr
1.63	Louise Hazel	6.10.85	1	Woodford	1 Sep

Additional Under 15 (1 - 2 above)

1.64	Katie Renouf	3.06.87	1	Exeter	16 Jun
1.64	Lucy Ramsay	2.06.87	1	Brighton	23 Jun
1.64	Sarah Allison	18.11.86	1	Wigan	22 Jul
1.64	Claire Huck	11.10.86	P	Hull	16 Sep
1.63	Dominique Blaize	3.10.87	1	London (TB)	15 Sep
1.62	Samantha Britton	12.09.86	1	Cudworth	5 Aug
1.61	Rosemary Huntriss	9.10.86	1	Macclesfield	20 May
1.61	Celia Dupont		4	Exeter	6 Jul
	(10)				
1.61	Lisa Ferguson	10.09.86	1	Ellon	23 Aug
1.60	Tanya Brook	20.02.87	1	Leeds	17 May
1.60	Sarah Fielding-Smith	19.11.86	2	Watford	27 May
1.60	Elayne Henderson	31.07.87	1	Dunfermline	7 Jun
1.60	Natasha Speight	9.09.87	1	Corby	24 Jun
1.60	Donna Wilson	1.10.86	1	Bath	29 Jul
1.60	Catherine Smy	7.04.87	2	Glasgow (S)	18 Aug
1.60	Wendy Meadows-Smith	15.07.88	1	Peterborough	27 Aug
1.60	Katie Saddler	15.01.88	1	Reading	16 Sep
1.59	Sarah Devoy	12.01.87	P	Preston	24 Jun
	(20)				
1.59	Rachel Howard	5.08.87	1	Derby	15 Jul
1.59	Carly Sharp	7.09.87	2	Connah's Quay	4 Aug

Under 13

1.53	Helen McDonnell	19.02.89	1	Basildon	9 Jun
1.53	Steffi Capper	12.02.89	1	Wrexham	23 Jun
1.52	Ashley Little	19.01.89	1	Wakefield	25 Jul
1.50	Amy Pelling	10.12.88	1	Peterborough	27 Aug
1.48	Georgina Hood	20.11.88	1B	Kingston	29 Jul
1.48	Claire O'Reilly	7.09.88	1	Nuneaton	19 Aug
1.48	Amelia Montagnani	10.03.90	P	Crawley	9 Sep
1.47	Jade Surman	27.03.89		Birmingham	24 Jun
1.46	Lucy Boggis	27.01.89	1	Perivale	18 Aug
1.46	Juliet Fielden	9.10.88	1	Woodford	1 Sep
1.46	Vikki Hubbard	13.07.89	1	Nottingham	8 Sep
1.45	Courtney Williams	8.03.89	1	Kingston	29 Jul
1.45	Rebecca French	29.09.88	2	Bedford	9 Sep
1.44	Jamie Chambers		1	Crawley	27 Aug

Foreign

1.76	*Niina Masalin (FIN)*		*3.01.77*	*3*	*Saarijarvi, FIN*	*23 Jun*
1.65	*Shebana Jalatin (MAS)*	*U23*	*14.01.81*	*5*	*Eton*	*7 Jul*

Pole Vault

4.40	Janine Whitlock	11.08.73	1	Birmingham	14 Jul
	4.36		1	Budapest, HUN	1 Jul
	4.35		5	London (CP)	22 Jul
	4.35		Q	Edmonton, CAN	4 Aug
	4.35		9	Edmonton, CAN	6 Aug
	4.34		2	Bremen, GER	23 Jun
	4.31		1	Aarhus, DEN	7 Jul
	4.30		1	Tula, RUS	9 Jun
	4.25 i		4	Clermont-Ferrand, FRA	16 Mar
	4.24 i		4	Toulouse, FRA	4 Mar
	4.22 i		2	Grenoble, FRA	10 Feb
	4.20		1	Birmingham	2 Jun
	4.20 exh		2	Sopot, POL	13 Jun
	4.15 i		5=	Wuppertal, GER	2 Feb
	4.12 i		5	Birmingham	18 Feb
	4.10		1	Bedford	28 May
	4.10		7	Prague, CZE	18 Jun
	4.05 i		1	Birmingham	28 Jan
	4.05 i		3	Glasgow	18 Mar
	4.00 i		3=	Torcy-le-Grand, FRA	21 Jan
	4.00		1	Loughborough	20 May
4.20 i	Rhian Clarke	19.04.77	4	Fayetteville, USA	10 Mar
	4.10		4	Austin TX, USA	6 Apr
	4.05 i		1	Houston, USA	23 Feb
	4.03 i		3	Fayetteville, USA	9 Feb
	4.00 i		2	Houston, USA	3 Feb
	4.00		1	Austin TX, USA	5 May
	4.00		9	Beijing, CHN	29 Aug
	3.95 i		1	Houston, USA	12 Jan
	3.85		2	Houston, USA	19 May
	3.80		1	Baton Rouge, USA	14 Apr
	3.80		1	Tampa, USA	11 May
4.00	Irie Hill	16.01.69	1=	Melbourne, AUS	10 Mar
	4.00 exh		1	Moomba, AUS	11 Mar
	4.00		3	Birmingham	14 Jul
	3.95		1	Melbourne, AUS	13 Dec
	3.90 i		1	Furth, GER	21 Jan
	3.90		5=	Melbourne, AUS	1 Mar
	3.90		2	Palo Alto, USA	13 May
	3.90		1	Munich, GER	24 Jun
	3.90 exh		6?	Jockgrim, GER	20 Jul
	3.90		1	Nuremberg, GER	22 Jul
	3.90		1	Heverlee, BEL	18 Aug
	3.85		5	Brisbane, AUS	25 Mar
	3.85		1	Birmingham	30 Jun
	3.85		1	Teningen, GER	19 Jul
	3.80		12=	Modesto CA, USA	12 May
	3.80		1	Oberasbach, GER	22 Jun
	3.80		2=	Ashford	11 Aug
	3.80		1	Eton	22 Aug
	3.80		2	Melbourne, AUS	2 Dec
4.00 A	Lucy Webber	5.02.72	1	El Paso TX, USA	14 Apr
	4.00		2	Birmingham	14 Jul
	3.96		1=	Fullerton CA, USA	26 Apr
	3.85		2	Birmingham	30 Jun
	3.85		1	Loughborough	4 Jul
	3.80		2	Bedford	28 May

3.90	Tracey Bloomfield	U23	13.09.79	4	Birmingham	14 Jul
	3.80			1gue	Coventry	5 Aug
	3.80			5gue	Ashford	11 Aug
	3.80			1	London (He)	26 Aug
3.90	Sonia Lawrence	U23	19.01.80	5	Birmingham	14 Jul
	3.90 i			1	Cardiff	9 Dec
	3.85			1	Derby	29 Jul
3.83	Hilary Smith		28.02.76	1	Connah's Quay	10 Jun
3.81	Zoe Brown	U20	15.09.83	1	Derby	9 Sep
3.80	Kate Dennison	U20	7.05.84	1	Grangemouth	26 Aug
	3.80			1	Ipswich	2 Sep
	68 performances to 3.80 by 9 athletes including 15 indoors					
3.75	Emma Hornby		12.12.73	1	Coventry	29 Apr
(10)						
3.75	Liz Hughes		9.06.77	2	Loughborough	20 May
3.75	Gael Davies	U23	5.02.79	3	Loughborough	4 Jul
3.66 i	Lindsay Hodges	U20	21.09.82	1	Birmingham	24 Feb
3.60 i	Allie Murray-Jessee		13.01.67	2	Glasgow	21 Jan
	3.60 A			7	El Paso TX, USA	14 Apr
	3.60			2	Glasgow (S)	24 Jun
3.60 i	Alison Davies	V35	6.04.61	2=	Cardiff	4 Feb
	3.30	V40		2	Eton	28 Apr
3.60 i	Larissa Lowe	V35	19.08.63	2=	Cardiff	4 Feb
	3.60			1	Bedford	21 Jul
3.60 i	Laura Patterson	U23	31.01.81	1	Glasgow	18 Feb
	3.60			1	Cannock	12 May
3.60 i	Rebecca Lumb		3.09.77	3	Eton	7 Jul
	3.60			2=	Wigan	4 Aug
3.60	Kirsty Maguire	U20	5.07.83	1	Glasgow (S)	18 Jul
3.60	Catherine MacRae	U23	1.01.79	1	Eton	11 Aug
(20)						
3.53	Rebekah Telford		4.11.76	2	Connah's Quay	10 Jun
3.51	Hannah Olson	U15	29.01.88	1	Hoo	19 Aug
3.50 i	Louise Gauld	U23	24.08.80	1	Glasgow	27 Jan
	3.40			5	Bedford	30 Jun
3.50 i	Clare Ridgley		11.09.77	2	Birmingham	28 Jan
	3.50			2	Coventry	5 Aug
3.50 i	Helen Roscoe	U23	4.12.79	3	Glasgow	18 Feb
	3.50			4	Birmingham	2 Jun
3.50	Natalie Olson	U17	9.05.86	1	Carshalton	23 Jun
3.50	Caroline Nutt	U20	17.06.83	1	Scunthorpe	19 Aug
3.50 i	Kim Skinner	U15	21.09.87	1	Glasgow	22 Dec
	3.40			3	Sheffield	11 Aug
3.45	Noelle Bradshaw	V35	18.12.63	1	Abingdon	28 Apr
3.45	Ruth Anness		3.10.78	1	Tipton	24 Jun
(30)						
3.40 i	Anna Leyshon	U23	19.01.80	4	Glasgow	18 Feb
	3.30			6=	Loughborough	20 May
3.40	Gillian Cooke	U20	3.10.82	3	Glasgow (S)	5 May
3.40	Kath Callaghan	U23	11.04.80	3	Guildford	19 May
3.40	Linda Stanton		22.06.73	5	Birmingham	30 Jun
3.30 i	Janet Vousden		25.11.68	3	Birmingham	7 Jan
	3.20			1	Leamington	13 May
3.30 i	Nicole Green		28.01.77	4	Bedford	13 Jan
3.30	Jemma Harding	U23	15.02.79	1	Watford	16 Sep
3.20 i	Sundeep Brar	U17	26.02.85	1	Cardiff	4 Feb
	3.00			1	Southend	13 May
3.20	Becky Ridgley	U23	26.02.80	1	Southampton	28 Apr
3.20	Rachel Gibbens	U17	31.01.86	1	Milton Keynes	12 May
(40)						
3.20	Eugenie Lewis		10.10.74	1	London (Cr)	19 May

3.20	Judy Turton	U20	26.05.84	1	High Wycombe	19 May
3.20	Kate Alexander		28.04.74	2	London (He)	23 Jun
3.20	Caroline Smith	U20	31.07.83	8	Bedford	30 Jun
3.20	Claire Holmes	U17	11.08.85	1	Blackpool	23 Sep
3.15	Zoe Parsons	U20	11.02.83	3	Exeter	6 Jul
3.10 i	Helen Carney	U23	27.03.79	6	Bedford	13 Jan
	2.80			1	Luton	28 Apr
3.10 i	Maria Newton		22.07.66	1	London (CP)	10 Feb
	3.10			1	London (TB)	14 Jul
3.10 i	Suzanne Woods		29.12.76	3	Birmingham	11 Feb
3.10 i	Donna Hunter	U23	9.10.81	5=	Glasgow	18 Feb
	3.00			8	Glasgow (S)	5 May
	(50)					
3.10 i	Amy Rennison	U20	15.06.83	5	Birmingham	24 Feb
	3.10			9=	Bedford	30 Jun
3.10	Angie Nichols	U17	22.09.84	1	London (Cr)	23 Jun
3.10	Dawn-Alice Wright		20.01.76	2	Bedford	28 Jul
3.00 i	Helen Webb	U23	14.04.80	15=	Birmingham	28 Jan
	3.00			3	Derby	29 Jul
3.00 i	Anna Watson	U20	30.04.82	3	Glasgow	4 Feb
	2.90			9	Glasgow (S)	5 May
3.00 i	Jacqueline Marshall	U23	20.07.79	1	Glasgow	7 Feb
3.00	Nathalie Warren	U23	28.08.81	1	Perivale	28 Apr
3.00	Leasa Williams	U20	10.05.84	1	Ipswich	28 Apr
3.00	Melissa Stamp	U23	5.07.81	1	Hexham	19 May
3.00 i	Hollie Tinn	U23	14.04.81	2	Cardiff	9 Dec
	2.80			2	Tamworth	27 Aug
	(60)					
3.00 i	Eilidh Dorrian	U17	8.10.85	2	Glasgow	22 Dec
	2.90			1	Grangemouth	26 Aug
2.95	Emily Morris	U20	30.09.82	6=	Exeter	6 Jul
2.90	Jayne Collins	U23	27.03.80	3	Coventry	29 Apr
2.90	Sophie Dewell	U20	18.09.83	1	Gateshead	12 May
2.90	Jo Hughes		7.02.71	14	Birmingham	2 Jun
2.90	Jocelyn Hird	U20	3.12.83	1	Exeter	16 Jun
2.90	Mandy Humble	U23	15.08.79	4	Liverpool	17 Jun
2.90	Lindsay Johnson	U23	3.12.81	1	Stretford	14 Aug
2.90	Debbie Martin	U23	30.11.79	1	Bath	26 Aug
2.90	Jenny Wood	V40	23.02.57	1	Leeds	9 Sep
	(70)					
2.80 i	Kate Williams	U20	10.05.84	4	Bedford	13 Jan
	2.70			3	Ipswich	28 Apr
2.80 i	Tracy Morris		25.12.69	9	Birmingham	14 Jan
	2.80			5	Leamington	12 May
2.80 i	Nikki Witton		30.09.72	5	Cardiff	4 Feb
	2.70			1	Newport	20 May
2.80	Helen Croskell		22.11.72	2	Ipswich	28 Apr
2.80	Rachel Fairless	U20	19.03.82	2	Gateshead	12 May
2.80	Sara Nichols	U20	9.06.83	1	Watford	30 May
2.80	Michelle Ball	U20	9.05.83	1	Blackpool	9 Jun
2.80	Jacqui-Ann Lloyd	U20	16.06.84	1	Cardiff	16 Jun
2.80	Julie Hynan	U23	23.05.80	2	Stretford	19 Jun
2.80	April Harwood	U20	11.09.82	1	Corby	10 Jul
	(80)					
2.80	Carys Holloway	U20	23.07.82	2	Brecon	18 Jul
2.72	Susan Yeomans	V45	16.03.53	3	Welwyn	1 Sep
2.70	Karen Smith		25.12.78	2	Erith	7 May
2.70	Nadine Simpson	U17	28.02.86	1	London (Nh)	19 May
2.70	Tara Mooney	U17	1.10.84	2	Antrim	26 May
2.70	Chissie Head	U23	18.12.79	4	Rugby	3 Jun
2.70	Kim Hobbs		12.12.78	4	London (Cr)	3 Jun

2.70	Ann Wainwright	V45	26.10.54	3	Scunthorpe	3	Jun
2.70	Catryn Grundy	U17	25.05.86	5	Tullamore, IRL	21	Jul
2.70	Julie Page	U20	11.07.84	1	Mansfield	19	Aug
	(90)						
2.70	Chloe Corcoran	U17	29.09.85	2	Basildon	1	Sep
2.70	Helen Leadbetter	U20	24.06.82	1	Portsmouth	1	Sep
2.70	Elizabeth Harris	U23	19.12.80	3	Stevenage	1	Sep
2.70	Louise Hart	U20	27.05.83	4	Stevenage	1	Sep
2.70	Anna Price	U17	18.08.85	5	Ipswich	2	Sep
2.65	Janet Lyon	V35	12.03.62	1	Dunfermline	19	May
2.65	Dawn Jones		16.02.70	1	Bromley	11	Aug
2.60 i	Lorna Bayley	U17	6.07.85	3	Bedford	13	Jan
2.60 i	Alison Lister	U23	18.06.80	7	Birmingham	4	Feb
	2.60			1	Abingdon	13	May
2.60	Lucy Newman	U20	2.03.83	1	Crawley	12	May
	(100)						
2.60	Jenny Cuthbertson	U20	11.06.84	4	Cudworth	26	May
2.60	Nicola Hewitt	U15	11.12.87	2	Cudworth	27	May
2.60	Tracey Hare	U20	9.03.82	5	London (Cr)	3	Jun
2.60	Sarah Friday	U20	14.11.82	2	Cardiff	7	Jul
2.60	Kiera Lacey	U17	13.08.86	1	Leeds	5	Aug
2.60 i	Jennifer Graham	U20	1.07.84	1	Glasgow	15	Aug
2.60	Amie Everitt		1.11.78	2	Basingstoke	1	Sep
2.60	Anne Goad	V40	11.08.58	1	Erith	16	Sep

Additional Under 15 (1 - 3 above)

2.50	Becky Lilley	4.03.88	1	Cheltenham	4	Jul
2.30	Kate Arrandale	3.05.87	1	Salisbury	9	Sep

Under 13

2.02	Sarah Murtagh	18.11.88	1	Bath	26	Jun
1.90	Holly Gadsdon	16.04.89	1	Par	23	Sep
1.85	Jasmin Hicks	1.03.90	2	Par	23	Sep

Foreign

3.85	*Laura Ballotta (ITA)*		*17.08.71*	*2*	*Sulmona, ITA*	*30*	*Sep*
3.50	*Erin Kinnear (IRL)*	*U17*	*26.10.84*	*1*	*Sheffield*	*11*	*Aug*
3.42	*Juliet Claffey (IRL)*		*30.04.78*	*2*	*Newport*	*5*	*Aug*
3.40	*Shirley Buchanan/Austin (IRL)*		*20.01.73*	*1*	*Eton*	*6*	*Jun*

Long Jump

6.68w	2.7	Jade Johnson	U23	7.06.80	1	Bedford	28	May
		6.67 w 2.3			2	Glasgow (S)	1	Jul
		6.60 w 2.5			1	Ashford	11	Aug
		6.59 1.9			*	Ashford	11	Aug
		6.58 0.8			1	Arles, FRA	9	Jun
		6.58 1.6			*	Glasgow (S)	1	Jul
		6.55 w 2.8			1	Bedford	18	Jul
		6.52 1.0			1	Amsterdam, NED	13	Jul
		6.50 -0.2			Q	Amsterdam, NED	12	Jul
		6.49 -0.1			5	Bremen, GER	24	Jun
		6.45 w			1	Kingston	13	May
		6.41 -0.5			2	Loughborough	20	May
		6.37 0.2			6	Thessaloniki, GRE	22	Aug
		6.32 0.3			4	Helsinki, FIN	14	Jun
6.53 w	2.3	Denise Lewis		27.08.72	3	Glasgow (S)	1	Jul
		6.46 1.8			3	Seville, ESP	8	Jun
		6.34 1.4			*	Glasgow (S)	1	Jul
6.46 w	7.5	Jo Wise		15.03.71	1	Stellenbosch, RSA	23	Feb
		6.35 A 0.0			1	Potchefstroom, RSA	12	Feb
		6.34 i			1	Birmingham	3	Feb

6.37 w	2.3	Julie Hollman		16.02.77	3H	Ried, AUT	1 Jul
		6.35 1.4			*	Ried, AUT	1 Jul
		6.31 w 2.8			3	Ashford	11 Aug
		6.27 1.8			2H	Arles, FRA	10 Jun
6.36 w	3.2	Ann Danson		4.05.71	2	Ashford	11 Aug
		6.21 1.3			1	Bedford	21 Jul
6.33	1.8	Ruth Irving		20.07.74	1	Riga, LAT	2 Jun
		6.27 -0.1			3	Loughborough	20 May
6.28 w	6.2	Kelly Sotherton		13.11.76	2	Dublin (S), IRL	29 Jun
		6.23 1.9			4H	Arles, FRA	10 Jun
6.27		Sarah Claxton	U23	23.09.79	1	Biella, ITA	22 Sep
6.24		Joyce Hepher	V35	11.02.64	1	Bedford	20 May
6.22 w	4.0	Donita Benjamin		7.03.72	1	Birmingham	30 Jun
		6.07			2	Eton	7 Jul
		33 performances to 6.20 by 10 athletes including 1 indoors and 12 wind assisted					
6.14 w		Sarah Wellstead	U23	22.10.79	1	Hoo	11 Aug
		6.10			1	Enfield	14 Jul
6.09	-0.2	Symone Belle	U17	12.11.84	5	Loughborough	20 May
6.07 w	2.5	Phyllis Agbo	U17	16.12.85	1	Exeter	7 Jul
		5.91 0.6			2	Stoke-on-Trent	18 Aug
6.05 w?		Jackie Spargo		12.01.71	1	Coventry	29 Apr
6.05	1.6	Julia Bennett		26.03.70	6H	Arles, FRA	10 Jun
6.04	1.9	Kim Rothman	V35	6.09.64	3	Bedford	18 Jul
6.02	1.0	Joanna Trotman	U23	5.10.80	2	Bedford	29 Jun
6.02 w	3.7	Sarah Humphreys	U17	16.10.84	2	Exeter	7 Jul
		5.86 2.0			1	Tullamore, IRL	21 Jul
5.97	0.5	Elaine Smith	U20	16.05.83	2	Dole, FRA	29 Jul
5.95		Janine Whitlock		11.08.73	1	Colchester	27 Aug
	(20)						
5.93		Fiona Westwood	U23	27.02.81	1	Sheffield	12 May
5.91		Tracy Joseph		29.11.69	1	Basingstoke	1 Sep
5.91 w	5.0	Katherine Livesey	U23	15.12.79	11	College Station, USA	18 May
		5.83 1.8			5	Lincoln, USA	5 May
5.90	0.3	Natasha May	U23	21.02.80	1	Derby	29 Jul
5.89 w	2.6	Fiona Harrison	U23	30.11.81	1	Glasgow (S)	6 May
		5.88 1.9			*	Glasgow (S)	6 May
5.88 w	3.3	Kate Brewington	U23	15.10.81	6	Bedford	18 Jul
		5.87 1.2			1H	Bedford	15 Jul
5.86		Syreena Pinel	U23	13.01.79	1	Loughborough	12 May
5.86	1.5	Kerry Jury		19.11.68	17H	Arles, FRA	10 Jun
5.86	1.7	Rebekah Passley	U15	9.03.87	1	Sheffield	12 Aug
5.84		Rebecca White	U23	5.06.80	1	Guernsey	2 Jun
	(30)						
5.84		Nadia Williams	U23	17.11.81	1	Bedford	11 Aug
5.84 w	2.7	Sarah Still		24.09.75	1	Edinburgh	13 May
		5.74 1.6			3H	Bedford	15 Jul
5.84 w		Lucy Atunumuo	U23	4.11.80	5	Kingston	13 May
		5.58 0.4			6	Bedford	29 Jun
5.81		Belinda Samuels		29.11.78	1	Cannock	12 May
5.80 i		Debbie Harrison		13.11.78	4	Birmingham	28 Jan
		5.68 0.4			6	Alicante, ESP	18 Apr
5.80		Danielle Humphreys	U20	16.05.84	1	Mansfield	19 Aug
5.79		Karlene Turner	U17	9.01.85	1	London (He)	16 Sep
5.77		Rosie Curling	U23	5.09.80	1	New Haven, USA	14 Apr
5.77		Nikki Gilding		16.05.72	1	Portsmouth	10 May
5.76		Gemma Holt		20.12.72	1	Ashford	14 Jul
	(40)						
5.76		Emily Parker	U17	7.11.84	1	London (TB)	28 Jul
5.76 w	4.0	Mary Devlin	U23	14.09.79	1	Tullamore, IRL	24 Jun
		5.61			1	Antrim	19 Jun

5.76 w		Anna-Maria Thorpe		15.07.71	1	Bournemouth	11 Aug
		5.62			1	London (He)	12 May
5.74 w	2.7	Nicola Gautier		21.03.78	20H	Arles, FRA	10 Jun
		5.67 i			P	Prague, CZE	28 Jan
		5.56 1.7			*	Arles, FRA	10 Jun
5.74 w	2.9	Caroline Pearce	U23	1.09.80	2H	Bedford	15 Jul
		5.60 1.8			6	Glasgow (S)	6 May
5.73		Sarah Roberts		25.06.78	1	Bath	26 Aug
5.73 w		Sarah Godbeer		10.06.77	2	Bournemouth	11 Aug
		5.58			1	Southampton	28 Apr
5.71 w		Amy Woodman	U17	1.11.84	2	Coventry	29 Apr
		5.67			1	Yate	12 May
5.70		Rachel Brenton	U17	18.01.85	2	Abingdon	28 Apr
5.69		Angela Williams	U23	13.05.81	1	Bromley	15 Apr
	(50)						
5.69	1.9	Zainab Ceesay	U20	27.10.83	3	Bedford	1 Jul
5.69		Chanelle Garnett	U17	16.08.85	1	Stevenage	1 Sep
5.69	1.4	Laura Redmond	U23	19.04.81	2H	Sheffield	2 Sep
5.69 w		Rachel Peacock	U20	18.05.82	3	Bournemouth	11 Aug
5.67 i		Lara Richards	U20	7.03.83	1	Cardiff	18 Feb
		5.59 -0.1			1	Cardiff	12 Jun
5.67		Stephanie Morgan		4.03.75	2	Stafford	8 Sep
5.66 w	4.7	Stephanie Madgett	U15	22.02.87	1	Exeter	7 Jul
		5.52			1	Woking	2 Dec
5.65		Ruth Laybourn	U17	5.10.84	1	Cleckheaton	9 Jun
5.64 w	3.0	Gillian Cooke	U20	3.10.82	1	Wigan	10 Jun
5.63		Katie Richardson	U20	12.09.82	2	Sheffield	12 May
	(60)						
5.63	-0.2	Hannah Barnes	U20	2.06.84	2	Exeter	6 Jul
5.62		Frances Harris		1.06.72	2	Enfield	14 Jul
5.62 w	4.3	Danielle Parkinson	U23	2.09.81	5H	Bedford	15 Jul
5.61		Laura Singleton	U17	6.04.85	1	Cannock	12 May
5.61		Kirsty Corbett	U20	16.05.82	1	Southend	12 May
5.61		Stacy McGivern		14.12.76	1	Enfield	14 Jul
5.61 w	5.2	Lucy Ramsay	U15	2.06.87	3	Exeter	7 Jul
		5.41			1	Brighton	23 Jun
5.60		Faith Cripps	U20	23.09.83	1	Milton Keynes	12 May
5.60		Mandy Crompton	U20	25.03.82	1	Oldham	29 Jul
5.60		Joanne Oates		21.02.78	2	Rotherham	5 Aug
	(70)						
5.60	0.2	Louise Bloor	U17	21.09.85	2	Sheffield	11 Aug
5.60 w	4.4	Vicky Lambert	U17	20.11.84	4	Exeter	7 Jul
		5.55			2	Cleckheaton	9 Jun
5.59		Ellie Darby	U17	20.12.85	2	Cannock	12 May
5.58		Banke Olofinjana		14.05.72	2	London (He)	12 May
5.58		Michala Gee		8.12.75	1	Blackpool	3 Jun
5.58		Henrietta Paxton	U20	19.09.83	1	Wakefield	29 Jul
5.58 w	4.0	Katy Benneworth	U17	5.10.84	5	Exeter	7 Jul
5.57		Anne Hollman		18.02.74	1	St. Ives	12 May
5.57		Rebecca Bates	U20	16.05.82	1	Solihull	24 Jun
5.56 i		Sarah Lane	U23	4.06.81	2	Cardiff	11 Feb
	(80)						
5.56		Cathryn Dale		31.05.77	2	Leamington	12 May
5.56	2.0	Gemma Jones	U23	25.02.79	1	Cardiff	17 Jun
5.56		Denae Matthew	U15	3.04.87	1	Telford	1 Jul
5.56	0.2	Sally Peake	U17	8.02.86	1	Connah's Quay	4 Aug
		5.56 w			1	Wrexham	9 Jun
5.55	1.0	Rebecca Jones	U20	17.01.83	27H	Arles, FRA	10 Jun
5.55		Leah McGuire	U15	30.01.87	1	Great Yarmouth	5 Aug
5.54		Jackie Jenner		25.10.76	1	London (ME)	19 May
5.53		Hayley Goodall	U17	20.09.84	2	London (BP)	20 May

5.53		Louise Hazel	U17	6.10.85	1	Bedford	28 Jul
5.53		Frances Noble	U17	2.05.86	1	Rotherham	5 Aug
	(90)						
5.52	0.0	Kate Evans		4.02.74	3	Coventry	5 Aug
5.52		Liz Patrick		29.08.77	3	Rugby	19 Aug
5.52 w	3.0	Hazel Carwardine	U23	6.11.80	2	Bedford	22 Jul
5.50	1.0	Siobhan McVie	U20	6.07.84	4	Corinth, GRE	27 May
5.50		Kim Wall	U20	21.04.83	2	Guildford	23 Jun

Additional Under 17 (1 - 18 above)

5.48 w	3.7	Laura Reed	6.10.84	8	Exeter	7 Jul
		5.39		3	Birmingham	26 May
5.47		Cara Roberts	24.05.85	1	Bournemouth	9 Jun
	(20)					
5.47 w	4.0	Katia Lannon	14.09.85	9	Exeter	9 Jul
		5.33		1	Horwich	1 Jul
5.47 w	6.3	Anna Clayton	20.03.85	3H	Birmingham	30 Sep
		5.36		1	Ipswich	9 Jun
5.46		Emma Wooff	21.05.85	2	Bebington	1 Jul
5.46		Emma Perkins	4.09.85	3	Crawley	5 Aug
5.45		Natalie Plateau	19.10.84	3	Abingdon	28 Apr
5.45		Tara Murphy	16.05.85	1	Nyiregyhaza, HUN	25 Jul
5.43		Vicky Griffiths	9.10.84	2	Stoke-on-Trent	17 Jun
5.43 w	3.0	Georgina Shaw	13.03.86	13	Exeter	7 Jul
		5.41		1	Stretford	9 Jun
5.40		Ellen Eagles	9.09.84	1	Nuneaton	5 Aug
5.39		Nadine Simpson	28.02.86	1	Luton	3 Jun
	(30)					
5.38		Catherine Holdsworth	3.01.86	1	Chelmsford	1 Sep
5.37		Angela Barrett	25.12.85	1	Kingston	23 Jun
5.37		Rebecka Bell	1.12.85	2	Guildford	29 Jul
5.36		Laura Betts	6.11.84	1	Ipswich	28 Apr
5.36		Sophie Newington	15.09.85	1	Brecon	19 Aug
5.36 w	3.4	Michelle Doherty	24.09.84	3	Connah's Quay	4 Aug
5.35 i		Faye Harding	7.09.85	3P	Glasgow	8 Dec

Additional Under 15 (1 - 5 above)

5.45		Amy Harris	14.09.87	1	Nuneaton	19 Aug
5.41 w	2.8	Aimee Palmer	7.11.86	1	Birmingham	27 May
		5.32		1	Cannock	13 May
5.37 w	3.0	Lauren Taylor	29.10.86	4	Exeter	7 Jul
		5.20		1	Abingdon	14 Jul
5.36		Dominique Blaize	3.10.87	1	London (TB)	18 Aug
5.32		Nike Osifodunrin	21.11.86	1	Coatbridge	15 Jul
	(10)					
5.30	0.5	Claire Linskill	12.01.88	3	London (He)	26 Aug
5.29 i		Naida Bromley	27.09.86	P	Gateshead	10 Mar
		5.21		1	Wakefield	3 Jun
5.28		Abigail Clark	11.01.87	1	Kingston	9 Jun
5.28 w		Ruth Hatch	4.07.87	1	Kingston	9 Sep
5.26		Nuala Curran	11.03.87	1	Tullamore, IRL	2 Jun
5.26 w		Emma Heath	1.10.86	1	Coventry	29 Apr
5.25		Amanda Fletcher	18.11.86	1	King's Lynn	1 Jul
5.23 w	3.6	Layla Hawkins	3.09.86	3B	Exeter	7 Jul
		5.22 0.9		1	Birmingham	1 Sep
5.22		Natalie Jowett	18.09.86	1	Bedford	29 Jul
5.20	0.2	Rachel Abbs	21.12.86	1	Cudworth	27 May
	(20)					
5.20		Kim Skinner	21.09.87	P	Grangemouth	8 Jul
5.20		Emma Bonny	9.09.87	1	Kingston	14 Jul
5.20		Carly Walker	30.08.87	1	Bournemouth	11 Aug
5.20 w	2.6	Laura Willey	22.10.86	8	Exeter	7 Jul

Under 13

5.14		Jade Surman		27.03.89	1	Nuneaton	5 Jul
4.95		Steffi Capper		12.02.89	1	Telford	1 Jul
4.94		Cherelle Norriston		29.11.88	2	London (TB)	14 Jul
4.91		Hannah Frankson		11.01.89	1	Horsham	14 Jul
4.85		Rachel Hermit-Smith		24.09.88	1	Birmingham	22 Jul
4.82		Emma Baker		22.09.88	1	Hayes	23 Jun
4.82		Rebecca Hall		15.09.88	1	Bury St. Edmunds	1 Jul
4.75		Amelia Montagnani		10.03.90	1	London (TB)	18 Aug
4.75		Claire Triggs		3.09.88	1	Banbury	8 Sep
4.71		Courtney Williams		8.03.89	3	Kingston	29 Jul

Foreign

6.65		*Chioma Ajunwa ¶ (NGR)*		*25.12.71*	*1*	*Lagos, NGR*	*21 Jul*
5.80		*Margaret Veldman (NED)*		*7.06.74*	*1*	*Rotherham*	*5 Aug*
5.69	*0.6*	*Taneisha Robinson-Scanlon (IRL)*		*19.11.77*	*4*	*Riga, LAT*	*23 Jun*

Triple Jump

14.51	1.1	Ashia Hansen		5.12.71	Q	Edmonton, CAN	8 Aug
		14.18 w 3.5			1	Visby, SWE	19 Jul
		14.10 -0.6			7	Edmonton, CAN	10 Aug
		14.09 1.5			1	Birmingham	14 Jul
		14.07 -0.3			4	London (CP)	22 Jul
		13.94 0.0			3	Viareggio, ITA	22 Aug
		13.93 0.0			5	Gateshead	19 Aug
		13.89 0.4			5	Rieti, ITA	2 Sep
		13.83 1.1			*	Visby, SWE	19 Jul
		13.23 -0.2			1	Karlstad, SWE	29 Aug
13.39 i		Michelle Griffith		6.10.71	1	Cardiff	11 Feb
		13.25 i			1	Birmingham	27 Jan
13.11	0.0	Jade Johnson	U23	7.06.80	8	Gateshead	19 Aug
		13.02			1	Eton	4 Aug
13.09 w	2.2	Rebecca White	U23	5.06.80	1	Bedford	30 Jun
		12.85 0.7			3	Birmingham	14 Jul
		12.84 0.1			1	Loughborough	20 May
		12.84 -1.1			6	Madrid, ESP	27 May
		12.82 0.3			7	Bremen, GER	23 Jun
		12.70 i			2	Cardiff	10 Mar
12.97 w	2.6	Debbie Rowe		8.09.72	1	Birmingham	2 Jun
		12.96 w 2.3			2	Birmingham	14 Jul
		12.90 -0.3			*	Birmingham	14 Jul
		12.88 1.5			1	Bedford	21 Jul
		12.81 w 3.3			4	Ashford	11 Aug
		12.70 w 2.1			1	Bedford	27 May
12.82 i		Liz Patrick		29.08.77	2	Cardiff	11 Feb
		12.57 w 4.8			6	Ashford	11 Aug
		12.38 1.0			2	Loughborough	20 May
		28 performances to 12.70 by 6 athletes including 4 indoors and 7 wind assisted					
12.63		Kate Evans		4.02.74	1	Rugby	19 Aug
12.43 w	2.5	Caroline Stead		14.09.71	4	Birmingham	14 Jul
		12.11 0.6			1	London (He)	12 May
12.35		Angela Williams	U23	13.05.81	1	Reading	19 May
12.35 w	2.4	Leandra Polius	U23	14.05.80	3	Liverpool	23 Jun
		12.23 -0.4			1	Eton	10 Jun
	(10)						
12.32 i		Jodie Hurst		21.06.77	1	Cardiff	18 Feb
		11.98 1.3			3	Bedford	27 May
12.27 w	2.3	Rachel Brenton	U17	18.01.85	1	Tullamore, IRL	21 Jul
		12.10 1.8			*	Tullamore, IRL	21 Jul

12.23 i		Anna-Maria Thorpe		15.07.71	5	Birmingham	27 Jan
		12.18 w?			1	Bournemouth	11 Aug
		12.17 2.0			1	Bedford	22 Jul
12.17	1.4	Katharine Streatfield	U20	28.07.83	2	Corinth, GRE	26 May
12.11		Marcia Walker		27.05.70	1	Eton	11 Aug
12.10		Hazel Carwardine	U23	6.11.80	1	Scunthorpe	19 Aug
12.10 w	3.1	Rachel Peacock	U20	18.05.82	1	Bedford	30 Jun
		12.04 0.7			1	London (He)	26 Aug
12.05	1.5	Charmaine Turner	U23	5.12.81	2	Coventry	5 Aug
12.05 w	4.0	Emily Parker	U17	7.11.84	1	Ipswich	2 Sep
		12.01 i			1	Birmingham	25 Feb
		11.98			1	Kingston	14 Jul
12.04 w	2.3	Azaria Francis	U20	12.04.83	3	Bedford	30 Jun
		11.80 -0.8			2	Derby	29 Jul
	(20)						
12.03 w		Angela Barrett	U17	25.12.85	1	London (WL)	17 Jun
		11.87 1.3			2	Tullamore, IRL	21 Jul
11.96	1.1	Linsi Robinson	U20	9.01.84	4	Bedford	30 Jun
11.84 w	4.2	Sarah Wellstead	U23	22.10.79	1	Carshalton	23 Sep
		11.41			2	London (TB)	19 May
11.82 w		Nikki Barr/Goddard		26.04.70	3	Wigan	10 Jun
		11.58 -0.4			3	Glasgow (S)	23 Jun
11.80		Natalie Brant	U20	11.12.82	2	Kingston	23 Jun
11.79		Carly Robson	U20	5.12.83	1	Watford	9 Jun
11.77	0.0	Julia Straker	U20	25.11.82	2	Exeter	6 Jul
11.77 w		Julia Bennett		26.03.70	1	Hoo	11 Aug
11.76	1.1	Alison McAllister	U17	26.02.85	1	Birmingham	26 May
11.76	0.6	Kosnatu Abdulai	U17	8.02.85	2	Watford	27 May
	(30)						
11.75 w	2.4	Michelle Doherty	U17	24.09.84	3	Tullamore, IRL	21 Jul
		11.12			1	Brecon	18 Jul
11.67 w		Maurine Okwue		13.05.78	3	Bournemouth	11 Aug
		11.54 0.0			6	London (Ha)	16 Jun
11.66		Aisha Myton	U20	3.01.84	1	London (TB)	19 May
11.66 w	3.7	Joanne Stanley		30.03.77	2	Liverpool	17 Jun
		11.49			1	Gateshead	13 May
11.65	-1.1	Rebecca Bates	U20	16.05.82	3	Tallahassee FL, USA	14 Apr
11.63 w	3.9	Michala Gee		8.12.75	3	Liverpool	17 Jun
		11.54			1	Blackpool	3 Jun
11.60		Sarah Roberts		25.06.78	1	Gloucester	4 Aug
11.59		Nina Ezeogu	U20	11.10.82	1	Abingdon	28 May
11.59	1.6	Natasha Brunning		10.03.73	1	Eton	15 Aug
11.57		Nikki Gilding		16.05.72	1	Portsmouth	19 May
	(40)						
11.55		Stephanie Morgan		4.03.75	1	Stafford	8 Sep
11.49		Stacy McGivern		14.12.76	1	King's Lynn	28 Apr
11.48 w	3.1	Ruth Hatch	U15	4.07.87	1	Carshalton	23 Sep
		11.47 1.8			*	Carshalton	23 Sep
11.47 i		Sian Jones	U20	20.01.83	2	Cardiff	18 Feb
		11.37 0.3			4	Derby	29 Jul
11.47 w	2.8	Mary Devlin	U23	14.09.79	7	Bedford	27 May
		11.46 i			5	Dublin, IRL	4 Feb
		11.44			4	Glasgow (S)	7 May
11.46		Fiona Hutchison		18.01.77	1	Dumfries	19 May
11.44		Sandra Alaneme	U17	7.01.86	1	Erith	9 Jun
11.44 w		Sara Barry	U20	8.06.83	1	Salisbury	12 May
		11.40			5	Exeter	6 Jul
11.43 i		Julia Johnson	U23	21.09.79	2	Glasgow	17 Feb
11.42 i		Emma Wooff	U17	21.05.85	1	Sheffield	21 Jan
		10.98 0.7			1	Cudworth	26 May
	(50)						

11.41 w	3.9	Kelly Brow		24.09.78	4	Liverpool	17 Jun
		11.30			2	Wakefield	24 Jun
11.40 i		Gillian Cooke	U20	3.10.82	1	Glasgow	27 Jan
		11.38			5	Glasgow (S)	7 May
11.40		Gemma Holt		20.12.72	3	Guildford	19 May
11.40	1.4	Nadia Williams	U23	17.11.81	5	Bedford	21 Jul
11.37	0.5	Sally Peake	U17	8.02.86	4	Tullamore, IRL	21 Jul
11.36	0.5	Helen Williams	U20	13.01.83	2	Cudworth	27 May
11.35		Kirsty Corbett	U20	16.05.82	1	Southend	12 May
11.30		Diana Osagede	U17	18.01.85	3	London (BP)	20 May
11.30		Cathryn Dale		31.05.77	4	Coventry	5 Aug
11.29		Phyllis Agbo	U17	16.12.85	2	Harrow	29 Apr
	(60)						
11.27		Laura Betts	U17	6.11.84	2	Erith	9 Jun
11.27		Fiona Davidson		29.01.73	1	Aberdeen	5 Aug
11.26		Rachael Burns	U20	5.08.83	1	Wigan	29 Apr
11.26	1.8	Gemma Hartshorne	U17	19.01.85	7	Sheffield	12 Aug
11.26 w	3.0	Alison Rough	U20	1.06.83	1	Grangemouth	16 Jun
		11.22 1.5			*	Grangemouth	16 Jun
11.25 i		Claire Lomas	U23	18.04.80	2	Glasgow	27 Jan
11.24		Alison Croad	U20	10.06.82	1	Bournemouth	12 May
11.24 w	5.1	Katherine Silto	U20	12.08.83	1	Exeter	16 Jun
		11.18			1	Cheltenham	18 Jul
11.19		Sally Ash	U23	4.11.80	1	Bedford	20 May
11.19		Louise Wood	U20	13.05.83	1	Braintree	11 Aug
	(70)						
11.18	-1.5	Stacey Savage	U17	30.12.84	5	Exeter	6 Jul
11.18		Sarah Strevens	U23	7.10.81	2	London (Nh)	11 Aug
11.16 w	3.1	Rachel Atkinson		26.05.73	7	Birmingham	2 Jun
11.14 i		Janice Pryce	V40	2.09.59	1	Bordeaux, FRA	11 Mar
11.14		Ruth Clements		15.05.74	1	Abingdon	13 May
11.14		Kara Miller	U17	6.04.85	1	Horsham	14 Jul
11.08 i		Sharon Oakes	U20	26.08.82	4	Cardiff	11 Feb
11.08 w	3.3	Abigail Clark	U15	11.01.87	2	Carshalton	23 Sep
11.04		Jennie Wright	U20	21.09.83	1	Walton	22 Apr
11.04		Elizabeth Webb	U20	16.12.83	1	Barry	10 May
	(80)						
11.03		Maureen Knight		15.11.73	1	London (BP)	28 Apr
11.02		Jenny Pacey	U20	5.02.83	1	Bury St. Edmunds	17 Jun
11.01		Laura Ridley	U17	20.03.86	1	Blackpool	12 May
11.00		Catherine Barnes		28.09.77	1	Southampton	19 May

Additional Under 17 (1 - 16 above)

10.98		Catriona Christie	26.04.85	1	Reading	12 May
10.95		Nia Nwidobie	4.01.86	2	Blackpool	9 Jun
10.92		Laura McGawn	13.04.85	1	Ayr	13 Jun
10.91		Michelle Nester	18.02.85	2	Kingston	12 May
	(20)					
10.86 w	3.2	Laura McAuley	11.06.85	10	Sheffield	12 Aug
10.85		Nicola Martell	20.09.85	1	Southend	13 May
10.82		Elen Davies	24.04.86	1	Norwich	13 May
10.80		Vicky Lamb	11.10.84	4	Derby	9 Sep
10.79	-1.4	Frances Noble	2.05.86	11	Exeter	6 Jul
10.75 i		Vicky Lloyd	5.03.86	1	Cardiff	20 Jan
		10.74		1	Neath	12 May
10.73		Jessica Doughty	6.07.85	1	Connah's Quay	26 May
10.71		Julie Chandler	12.02.85	1	Norwich	9 Jun
10.71	0.7	Joanne Nicoll	27.12.84	1	Grangemouth	10 Jun
10.71		Carly Palmer	21.12.84	1	Portsmouth	1 Sep
	(30)					
10.70		Imogen Miles	7.08.86	1	Abingdon	16 Sep

Foreign

12.72	*0.8*	*Taneisha Robinson-Scanlon (IRL)*		*19.11.77*	*3*	*Tula, RUS*	*8*	*Jun*
11.98 w		*Cathriona Hannafin (IRL)*		*19.09.72*	*3*	*Bangor*	*2*	*Jun*
		11.59	*1.6*		*3*	*Dublin (S), IRL*	*22*	*Jul*
11.92		*Lydia Nakagiri Saka (SWE)*	*U23*	*20.01.79*	*1*	*Bromley*	*23*	*Jun*
11.12		*Lisa Antill (AUS)*	*U20*	*14.10.82*	*1*	*High Wycombe*	*19*	*May*

Shot

17.08	Jo Duncan		27.12.66	1	London (WF)	19	Aug
	16.99			1	Loughborough	20	May
	16.84			1	Birmingham	14	Jul
	16.81 i			1	London (Ha)	4	Feb
	16.59			1	Birmingham	2	Jun
	16.56			1	Bedford	28	May
	16.46			1	Southend	12	May
	16.09			1	Varazdin, CRO	5	Jul
	15.88			1	Eton	7	Jul
	15.84			2	Ashford	11	Aug
	15.83			1	London (Ha)	17	Jun
	15.58			1	Birmingham	30	Jun
	15.54 i			1	London (Ha)	14	Jan
	15.36			8	Bremen, GER	24	Jun
	15.17 i			4	Birmingham	28	Jan
16.31	Julie Dunkley	U23	11.09.79	1	Bedford	1	Jul
	16.31			2	Birmingham	14	Jul
	15.97			1	Glasgow (S)	7	May
	15.88			1	Liverpool	23	Jun
	15.86			2	Eton	7	Jul
	15.84			1	Ashford	13	May
	15.79			10	Amsterdam, NED	12	Jul
	15.79			2	London (WF)	19	Aug
	15.74			1	Bedford	21	Jul
	15.71			8	Halle, GER	19	May
	15.66 i			1	Cardiff	11	Feb
	15.52			Q	Amsterdam, NED	12	Jul
	15.50			3	Ashford	11	Aug
	15.47 i			2	Birmingham	28	Jan
15.79 i	Philippa Roles		1.03.78	1	Cardiff	24	Nov
	15.23 i			1	Cardiff	18	Feb
	15.19			2	Varazdin, CRO	5	Jul
	15.18 i			3	Birmingham	28	Jan
	15.13 i			1	Cardiff	20	Jan
	15.12			1	Cardiff	17	Jun
	15.07 i			2	Cardiff	11	Feb
15.45	Denise Lewis		27.08.72	2	Birmingham	2	Jun
15.32	Eva Massey	U23	22.12.80	3	Birmingham	14	Jul
	15.30			1	Belfast	28	Jul
	15.27			1	Wigan	4	Aug
	15.09			3	Liverpool	23	Jun
	15.06			1	Bangor	2	Jun
	15.06			4	Ashford	11	Aug
	15.00			1	Dublin (S), IRL	22	Jul
15.31 i	Maggie Lynes	V35	19.02.63	1	London (CP)	20	Jan
	15.10 i			1	London (CP)	18	Feb
	15.09			1	London (B)	9	Sep
	15.08 i			5	Birmingham	28	Jan
	15.05			3	Eton	7	Jul
	15.04			2	Wigan	4	Aug
15.00	Christina Bennett		27.02.78	1	Kingston	23	Jun

51 performances to 15.00 by 7 athletes including 13 indoors

14.68	Claire Smithson	U20	3.08.83	1	Watford	26 May
14.66	Vickie Foster		1.04.71	2	Bedford	28 May
14.64	Nicola Gautier		21.03.78	1H	Ried, AUT	30 Jun
	(10)					
14.50	Myrtle Augee	V35	4.02.65	1	Bromley	11 Aug
14.34	Rebecca Peake	U20	22.06.83	3	Stoke-on-Trent	18 Aug
14.24 i	Eleanor Gatrell		5.10.76	6	Birmingham	28 Jan
	13.95			1	Bournemouth	20 May
14.09	Tracy Axten	V35	20.07.63	1	London (He)	23 Jun
14.00	Natasha Smith		6.06.77	4	Bedford	28 May
13.99	Charlotte Spelzini	U20	7.01.83	4	Stoke-on-Trent	18 Aug
13.77	Charmaine Johnson	V35	4.06.63	1H	Bedford	14 Jul
13.62	Mhairi Walters	U23	19.06.81	3	Bedford	1 Jul
13.50	Helen Wilding		25.10.76	1	Liverpool	24 Jun
13.38	Carol Parker		22.09.69	3	Birmingham	30 Jun
	(20)					
13.36 i	Carol Marshall		11.01.77	2	Wakefield	13 Jan
	12.89			1	Hull	8 Apr
13.23	Rebecca Roles	U23	14.12.79	2	Rugby	3 Jun
13.08	Joanna Bennett	U20	6.08.83	3	Watford	26 May
12.98 i	Julie Hollman		16.02.77	7P	Prague, CZE	28 Jan
	12.40			11H	Ried, AUT	30 Jun
12.97	Kara Nwidobie	U23	13.04.81	1	Blackpool	3 Jun
12.97	Lesley Brannan		13.09.76	1	Connah's Quay	10 Jun
12.88	Emma Beales		7.12.71	2	Kingston	14 Jul
12.82	Joan Macpherson	U23	18.09.80	1	Basingstoke	1 Sep
12.80 i	Frances Miller	U17	26.12.84	1	Glasgow	25 Jan
	12.63			1	Grangemouth	10 Jun
12.77 i	Alison Rodger	U17	29.10.84	1	Glasgow	9 Dec
	12.67			4	Bedford	1 Jul
	(30)					
12.75	Chloe Cozens	U23	9.04.80	4	Bedford	1 Jul
12.71	Navdeep Dhaliwal		30.11.77	1	Glasgow (S)	29 Apr
12.63	Debbie Woolgar	V35	10.03.65	1	Southampton	19 May
12.56	Shelley McLellan	U20	21.03.83	1	Watford	9 Jun
12.54	Claire Everett	U23	25.06.79	2H	Bedford	14 Jul
12.51	Emma Merry		2.07.74	2	Rugby	19 Aug
12.51	Alana Smith	U17	18.01.85	1	Derby	9 Sep
12.50	Amy Wilson	U23	31.12.80	1	Ipswich	10 Jun
12.49 i	Kate Morris	U20	18.01.83	4	Birmingham	24 Feb
	12.49			4	Watford	26 May
12.43	Belinda Heil	U20	8.03.82	5	Watford	26 May
	(40)					
12.33	Emma Carpenter	U20	16.05.82	1	Exeter	1 Sep
12.27	Paula Hendriks	U20	25.01.83	1	Birmingham	26 May
12.23	Mary Anderson		2.09.67	1	Grangemouth	1 Aug
12.22	Laura Redmond	U23	19.04.81	12H	Arles, FRA	9 Jun
12.19 i	Somma Power	U17	18.08.85	1	London (CP)	20 Jan
	12.13			3	Tullamore, IRL	21 Jul
12.19	Debbie Callaway	V35	15.07.64	2	Guildford	23 Jun
12.18	Shelley Drew/Newman		8.08.73	4	London (Ha)	10 Jun
12.18	Lorraine Shaw		2.04.68	9	Eton	7 Jul
12.07	Anne Hollman		18.02.74	1	Peterborough	19 May
12.07	Nicola Dudman	U20	5.10.83	1	Norwich	17 Jun
	(50)					
11.98 i	Sally Hinds	U17	2.02.86	1	Cardiff	24 Nov
	11.36			1	Neath	27 Aug
11.95	Laura Douglas	U20	4.01.83	1	Wigan	29 Apr
11.94	Jenny Grimstone	U23	30.04.79	1	Ashford	14 Jul
11.91	Emma Higgins	U20	8.09.82	5	Exeter	7 Jul
11.87	Jolene Marshall	U20	22.10.83	8	Bedford	1 Jul

11.87	Natasha Mighty		21.12.70	1	Reading	27 Aug
11.87	Sarah Beer	U20	29.04.84	3	Exeter	1 Sep
11.85	Jenny Kelly		20.06.70	2	Ashford	13 May
11.84	Julia Bennett		26.03.70	16H	Ried, AUT	30 Jun
11.81 i	Joanne Street	U20	30.10.82	1	Birmingham	4 Feb
(60)						
11.81	Karen Smith		25.12.78	2	Ashford	14 Jul
11.76	Glenys Morton	V40	17.06.60	1	Loughborough	12 May
11.76	Katie Halford	U20	4.10.82	1	Exeter	9 Jun
11.71	Cathy-Ann Hill		4.05.77	6	Coventry	5 Aug
11.68	Sharon Wray	U20	8.10.82	6	Exeter	7 Jul
11.68	Louise Kneen		14.08.74	3	Douglas IOM	8 Jul
11.67	Kerry Elliott	U17	17.05.85	1	Gateshead	13 May
11.64	Andrea Jenkins		4.10.75	4	Abingdon	28 Apr
11.63	Clova Court	V40	10.02.60	13	Birmingham	2 Jun
11.61	Catherine Garden		4.09.78	4	Wigan	10 Jun
(70)						
11.61	Lydia Morgan	U20	1.09.83	1	Warrington	26 Aug
11.52 i	Alyson Hourihan	V40	17.10.60	3	Cardiff	20 Jan
	11.35			3	Cardiff	16 Jun
11.52	Kerry Jury		19.11.68	3	Cudworth	26 Aug
11.45	Maureen Knight		15.11.73	1	London (BP)	14 Jul
11.44	Rebecca Chamberlain	U23	7.09.79	2	Bournemouth	20 May
11.44	Louise Finlay	U20	2.10.83	1	Cardiff	16 Jun
11.43	Elaine Cank	U23	5.12.79	1	Telford	12 May
11.42	Lorraine Henry		16.09.67	3	Bedford	28 Jul
11.41	Sharon Gibson	V35	31.12.61	1	Yate	29 Apr
11.37	Donna Maylor	U20	20.05.82	1	Wakefield	29 Jul
(80)						
11.28	Joanne Holloway		10.05.76	5	Eton	28 Apr
11.28	Laura Fox	U17	25.10.84	1	Watford	16 Sep
11.27	Shaunette Richards	U20	15.08.83	2	Wigan	29 Apr
11.26	Kelly Sotherton		13.11.76	3	Coventry	29 Apr
11.26	Kerri Fardoe	U20	22.11.83	2	Birmingham	26 May
11.24	Hayley Bryan	U17	4.03.86	2	Beveren, BEL	8 Sep
11.23	Joan Amaa	U23	15.12.81	2	London (He)	12 May

Additional Under 17 (1 - 8 above)

11.16	Candace Schofield	3.11.84	1	Crawley	12 May
11.04	Dani Wheeler	12.10.85	3	Exeter	7 Jul
(10)					
10.92	Danielle Hall	27.11.84	1	Ashford	13 May
10.91	Ellisha Dee	24.10.84	2	Watford	27 May
10.80	Lucy Sutton	29.08.86	1	Peterborough	22 Apr
10.55	Lauren Therin	19.01.86	1	Basildon	30 Jun
10.54 i	Debbie Collinson	23.10.85	1	Birmingham	3 Feb
	10.50		1	Grimsby	29 Jul
10.47	Nicola Gore	17.11.84	1	Ormskirk	3 Jun
10.46	Candice Francis	7.02.85	1	Birmingham	24 Jun
10.46	Tania Nell	21.05.86	4	Crawley	5 Aug
10.43	Helen Ephgrave	29.10.84	1	Kingston	9 Jun
10.36	Jessica Weir	3.10.84	4	Exeter	7 Jul
(20)					
10.31	Kate Butters	25.07.86	1	Kingston	17 Jun
10.30	Phyllis Agbo	16.12.85	2H	Hull	15 Sep

Foreign

14.35	*Angeline Gbahy (FRA)*		*16.07.76*	*4*	*London (Ha)*	*17 Jun*
13.18	*Laura Ballotta (ITA)*		*17.08.71*	*1*	*Lodi, ITA*	*19 May*
12.13	*Sulueti Tagilala (FIJ)*	*U23*	*24.08.80*	*1*	*Aldershot*	*26 Jul*
11.60	*Yolande Jacobs (RSA)*		*9.11.76*	*2*	*Bath*	*13 May*

Shot - Under 15 - 3.25kg

12.71	Chloe Edwards	12.05.87	1	King's Lynn	29	Apr
12.52	Naomi Magbadelo	16.04.87	1	Erith	9	Jun
12.46	Hayley Thomas	16.12.86	1	Eton	11	Aug
12.18	Candee Rhule	16.09.87	2	London (Elt)	2	Sep
12.08	Stephanie Owen	31.12.86	1	Derby	16	Sep
11.57	Laura Shirley	27.03.87	2	Exeter	6	Jul
11.46	Samantha Manchester	10.12.86	2	Erith	9	Jun
11.44	Ashleigh Palmer-Johnson	19.09.86	1	Reading	16	Sep
11.43	Zenab Farag	21.09.86	1	Crawley	27	Aug
11.36	Nimi Iniekio	25.10.86	5	Exeter	6	Jul
	(10)					
11.29	Emma Shaw	19.09.86	1	Cleckheaton	2	Sep
11.10	Lynette Tucker	18.07.87	1	Middlesbrough	1	Jul
11.03	Rachel Cork	11.10.86	1	Exeter	16	Jun
10.99	Eshere Singh	15.07.87	1	Southampton	28	Apr
10.97	Laura Cooper	23.05.87	5	Sheffield	12	Aug
10.87	Hannah Bowe	6.12.86	1	Tullamore, IRL	2	Jun
10.85	Hazel Robertson	27.07.87	1	Elgin	14	Jul
10.84	Eden Francis	19.10.88	1	Loughborough	16	Sep
10.82	Louise Watton	30.10.86	2	Watford	26	May
10.75	Christina Carding	26.02.87	2	Basingstoke	1	Sep
	(20)					
10.64	Kimberley Jones	11.06.88	1	Colwyn Bay	1	Sep
10.62	Caroline Jones	9.02.87	1	Woking	14	Jul
10.59 i	Kayleigh Southgate	15.01.88	5	Birmingham	24	Feb
	10.58		7	Sheffield	12	Aug
10.57	Gemma Llewelyn	23.04.87	1	Warrington	24	Jun

Shot - Under 13 - 2.72kg

12.07	Rebecca Hall	15.09.88	1	Bury St. Edmunds	14	Aug
11.59	Eden Francis	19.10.88	2	Nottingham	8	Sep
10.83	Nicola Stevenson	8.05.89	1	Crawley	27	Aug
10.04	Isobel Retburg		1	Grantham	29	Jul
9.98	Jenny Dunford		1	Gloucester	25	Aug
9.40	Nicola McSweeney		1	Kingston	29	Jul
9.39	Katy Wilson	1.09.88	1	Middlesbrough	22	Jul
9.34	Bethany Rogers		1	Birmingham	2	Sep
9.22	Denise Unwin	6.01.89	1	Blackpool	9	Sep
9.19	Louise Burton	23.12.88	1	Macclesfield	2	Sep
	(10)					
9.13	Kayleigh Hill	12.12.88	1	Oldham	19	Aug
9.08	F. Cottingham		2	Peterborough	27	Aug
9.07	Terri Beddows	21.07.89	1	Aberdare	15	Jul
9.07	Siobhan Cameron	15.12.88	1	Grangemouth	12	Aug
9.05	Elizabeth Yarnold	31.10.88	1	Hoo	19	Aug

Discus

59.10	Shelley Drew/Newman	8.08.73	1	Ashford	11	Aug
	58.75		1	Bedford	21	Jul
	58.44		1	London (BP)	20	May
	58.35		2	Dublin (S), IRL	29	Jun
	57.69		1	Loughborough	4	Jul
	57.22		1	Birmingham	14	Jul
	57.10		1	London (Ha)	10	Jun
	56.77		6	Halle, GER	19	May
	56.28		1	Bedford	22	Jul
	56.05		1	Eton	7	Jul
	55.92		1	London (WF)	19	Aug
	55.28		1	Bedford	28	May

(Newman)	54.92			1	Cambridge	1	Sep
	54.70			1	London (BP)	28	Apr
	54.24			1	Birmingham	30	Jun
	54.15			1	Loughborough	23	May
	53.32			1	Birmingham (Un)	7	May
	52.85			1	London (Ha)	17	Jun
58.98	Philippa Roles		1.03.78	1	Loughborough	20	May
	56.86			5	Halle, GER	19	May
	56.51			4	Budapest, HUN	1	Jul
	56.28			Q	Beijing, CHN	29	Aug
	55.06			1	Cardiff	17	Jun
	55.02			6	Beijing, CHN	30	Aug
	54.95			3	Ashford	11	Aug
	54.85			3	Varazdin, CRO	5	Jul
	54.18			8	Bremen, GER	23	Jun
	54.17			1	Wigan	10	Jun
	54.01			2	Wigan	4	Aug
	53.95			3	Szombathely, HUN	3	Jul
	53.90			2	Eton	7	Jul
	53.52			2	Birmingham	2	Jun
	53.51			3B	Nice, FRA	18	Mar
	53.45			2	Birmingham	14	Jul
	53.34			7	Madrid, ESP	27	May
	52.97			3	Bedford	21	Jul
	52.70			1	Neath	12	May
	52.52			1	Cardiff	27	Jun
54.81	Claire Smithson	U20	3.08.83	1	Bedford	1	Jul
	53.65			1	Brighton	23	Jun
	53.13			1	Ipswich	2	Sep
	52.80			1	Watford	26	May
	52.74			1	Exeter	6	Jul
53.12	Emma Carpenter	U20	16.05.82	1	Exeter	1	Sep
	53.00			6	Grosseto, ITA	20	Jul
	52.38			2	Ipswich	2	Sep
	46 performances to 52.00 by 4 athletes						
51.79	Rebecca Roles	U23	14.12.79	2	Cardiff	17	Jun
51.25	Emma Merry		2.07.74	1	Rugby	3	Jun
50.33	Jackie McKernan	V35	1.07.65	3	Bangor	2	Jun
47.93	Tracy Axten	V35	20.07.63	2	Rugby	10	Jun
47.79	Nicola Talbot		17.02.72	2	Bedford	28	May
47.26	Lorraine Shaw		2.04.68	3	Birmingham	2	Jun
(10)							
47.23	Eva Massey	U23	22.12.80	1	Dublin (S), IRL	21	Jul
46.97	Debbie Callaway	V35	15.07.64	2	Liverpool	8	Jul
46.94	Vickie Foster		1.04.71	3	Birmingham	14	Jul
46.57	Emma Beales		7.12.71	1	Eton	10	Jun
46.38	Joanna Bradley	U23	23.08.79	2	Bedford	1	Jul
46.08	Joan Macpherson	U23	18.09.80	3	Bedford	1	Jul
46.00	Elaine Cank	U23	5.12.79	2	Merksem, BEL	4	Aug
45.90	Susan Freebairn	V35	22.08.65	1	Glasgow (S)	18	Apr
45.51	Kara Nwidobie	U23	13.04.81	1	Scunthorpe	19	Aug
44.58	Navdeep Dhaliwal		30.11.77	1	Glasgow (S)	23	Jun
(20)							
44.38	Rebecca Hardy		11.11.68	6	Bedford	28	May
43.79	Sarah Henton		4.05.73	2	London (Ha)	10	Jun
42.96	Ellisha Dee	U17	24.10.84	1	London (Ha)	27	Jun
42.85	Hannah Corneby	U23	22.01.81	1	Stafford	7	Jul
42.65	Claire Moore	U20	29.03.82	3	Bedford	1	Jul
42.45	Maggie Lynes	V35	19.02.63	1	London (BP)	20	May
42.13	Carly Burton	U23	14.10.80	5	London (Ha)	17	Jun
42.06	Helen Wilding		25.10.76	2	Liverpool	17	Jun

	41.55	Donna Williams		7.10.78	1	Stretford	13 May
	41.28	Susan Backhouse		6.12.78	2	Loughborough	4 Jul
(30)	41.28	Danielle Hall	U17	27.11.84	1	Sheffield	11 Aug
	41.26	Alyson Hourihan	V40	17.10.60	3	Cardiff	27 Jun
	41.17	Lesley Bryant	V45	12.04.56	1	Grantham	12 May
	41.12	Sharon Andrews		4.07.67	8	Eton	7 Jul
	41.02	Andrea Jenkins		4.10.75	3	London (TB)	23 Jun
	40.92	Myrtle Augee	V35	4.02.65	1	Southampton	1 Sep
	40.81	Belinda Heil	U20	8.03.82	1	Kingston	13 May
	40.78	Jacqui Loney	U23	17.04.79	1	Inverness	2 Sep
	40.78	Laura Fox	U17	25.10.84	1	Derby	9 Sep
	40.63	Angela Mitchell	V35	17.08.65	1	Kingston, JAM	21 Jun
(40)	40.61	Carol Parker		22.09.69	6	Coventry	5 Aug
	40.52	Emma Forrester	U20	2.12.83	1	Telford	9 Jun
	40.43	Lydia Morgan	U20	1.09.83	1	Warrington	26 Aug
	40.14	Tasha Saint-Smith		20.12.75	1	Enfield	14 Jul
	40.09	Laura Wood		31.10.78	1	Stretford	19 Jun
	39.99	Eugenie Lewis		10.10.74	1	London (Cr)	23 Jun
	39.82	Christina Bennett		27.02.78	1	Bedford	22 Jul
	39.81	Joanne John	U23	12.11.80	2	London (He)	12 May
	39.80	Claire Cameron	V40	3.10.58	6	Rugby	3 Jun
	39.79	Angela Lockley	U17	7.10.84	1	Stoke-on-Trent	17 Jun
(50)	39.55	Candie Lintern	U20	5.02.82	1	Crawley	15 Apr
	39.54	Laura Evans		28.09.74	1	Grantham	4 Aug
	39.46	Katie Halford	U20	4.10.82	1	Exeter	1 Sep
	39.32	Alana Smith	U17	18.01.85	2	Derby	9 Sep
	39.19	Laura Douglas	U20	4.01.83	3	Derby	9 Sep
	39.07	Lorraine Henry		16.09.67	2	Bedford	20 May
	38.99	Alison Rodger	U17	29.10.84	4	Bedford	1 Jul
	38.81	Vicci Scott	U23	21.09.80	1	Stretford	5 Jun
	38.68	Mhairi Walters	U23	19.06.81	3	Glasgow (S)	18 Jul
	38.43	Kim Rawling	U20	22.07.83	2	Portsmouth	23 Jun
(60)	38.40	Catherine Lane		18.11.76	1	Abingdon	14 Jul
	38.04	Candice Francis	U17	7.02.85	4	Exeter	6 Jul
	37.85	Julie Robin		16.01.77	1	College Park, USA	7 Apr
	37.79	Catherine Garden		4.09.78	2	Wigan	10 Jun
	37.73	Sue Lawrence		25.11.70	1	Southend	12 May
	37.73	Elizabeth Dwan	U20	16.10.82	4	Scunthorpe	3 Jun
	37.67	Debra Monds		25.02.78	1	Blackpool	16 Jun
	37.60	Fallon Harrison	U17	1.05.85	1	Grimsby	6 May
	37.59	Kate Morris	U20	18.01.83	2	London (He)	23 Jun
	37.59	Ffion Jones	U20	19.07.83	3	Stafford	8 Sep
(70)	37.22	Amanda Sheppard		26.02.68	1	Cleckheaton	24 Jun
	36.81	Jenny Duff	U20	29.07.82	1	Oxford	21 Jun
	36.79	Amie Hill	U23	9.09.80	2	Glasgow (S)	5 May
	36.70	Christina Carding	U15	26.02.87	1	Sheffield	12 Aug
	36.59	Rebecca Chamberlain	U23	7.09.79	5	London (Ha)	10 Jun
	36.55	Donna Calvert	U23	26.06.79	1	Grimsby	6 May
	36.43	Elaine Giles	U20	25.04.83	1	Derby	12 May
	36.39	Paula Griffiths	U20	10.02.82	2	London (Ha)	27 Jun
	36.36	Debbie Woolgar	V35	10.03.65	2	Brighton	23 Jun
	36.31	Laura Chalmers	U17	1.05.86	1	Connah's Quay	4 Aug
(80)	36.27	Lyn Sprules		11.09.75	3	Hemel Hempstead	28 Apr
	36.21	Eleanor Gatrell		5.10.76	1	Bournemouth	20 May
	36.09	Sharon Wray	U20	8.10.82	2	Telford	9 Jun
	36.06	Karen Heweth	V40	29.11.59	2	Leeds	5 Aug
	36.03	Donna Swatheridge	U17	4.03.85	3	Crawley	5 Aug

Additional Under 17 (1 - 10 above)

35.62	Melanie Harrison		27.11.85	4	Derby	9 Sep
35.40	Hollie Redman		12.12.85	1	Milton Keynes	19 May
35.26	Candace Schofield		3.11.84	2	Bromley	11 Aug
35.19	Lauren Therin		19.01.86	4	Watford	27 May
35.07	Hayley Bryan		4.03.86	4	Beveren, BEL	8 Sep
34.70	Coralie Hancock		1.03.85	2	Poole	8 Jul
34.54	Kirsty Billin		24.05.85	1	Carshalton	23 Sep
34.48	Iyesha Tomlinson		19.02.86	1	Hayes	1 Jul
34.27	Lucy Sutton		29.08.86	1	Abingdon	9 Jun
33.73	Hayley Hood		12.09.85	5	Derby	9 Sep
(20)						
33.57	Tara Woodley		25.12.84	8	Sheffield	11 Aug
33.51	Sarah Davies		13.03.86	2	Sandown IOW	9 Sep
33.48	Alex Merrill		12.05.86	1	Blackpool	3 Jun
33.48	Kylie Brown		13.10.84	1	Bedford	9 Sep
33.23	Somma Power		18.08.85	4	Kingston	14 Jul
33.05	Kerry Elliott		17.05.85	1	Jarrow	2 May
32.77	Vicky Cooper		10.10.85	1	Stretford	11 Jun
32.74	Jessica Weir		3.10.84	1	Salisbury	9 Jun
32.67	Leonie Drury		2.07.85	1	Exeter	9 Jun
32.54	Rachael Atkinson		20.12.85	3	Birmingham	2 Sep
(30)						
32.30	Jemima Hall		20.02.85	5	Stoke-on-Trent	17 Jun

Additional Under 15 (1 above)

34.83	Dominique Lord		8.04.87	1	Abingdon	16 Sep
33.82	Kirsty Law		11.10.86	1	Inverness	19 Aug
33.74	Rebecca Saunders		8.02.88	2	Kingston	16 Jun
33.67	Naomi Magbadelo		16.04.87	1	Cambridge	2 Sep
33.53	Emma Shaw		19.09.86	1	Cleckheaton	2 Sep
33.34	Lynsey Clark		2.09.86	2	Exeter	7 Jul
32.83	Samantha Manchester		10.12.86	2	Sheffield	12 Aug
32.82	Amber Spencer		12.01.87	1	London (He)	26 Aug
32.77	Lianne Tucker		18.07.87	1	Scunthorpe	19 Aug
(10)						
32.65	Gemma Llewelyn		23.04.87	1	Bebington	1 Jul
32.30	Amy Howard		3.03.87	1	Stretford	27 Aug
32.13	Sarah Holt		17.04.87	4	Sheffield	12 Aug
30.80	Hayley Thomas		16.12.86	2	Colchester	7 May
30.75	Ruth Hay		4.11.87	1	Loughborough	15 Aug
30.32	Eshere Singh		15.07.87	1	London (TB)	23 Jun
30.22	Louise Watton		30.10.86	1	Southampton	20 May
30.09	Stephanie Owen		31.12.86	2	Blackpool	23 Sep
29.97	Hazel Robertson		27.07.87	2	Grangemouth	12 Aug
29.71	Chloe Edwards		12.05.87	4	London (He)	26 Aug
(20)						
29.55	Jessica Mole		19.03.87	1	Colchester	23 Jun
29.34	Monique Buchanon		27.09.86	1	London (Cr)	22 Jul

Foreign

39.70	*Yolande Jacobs (RSA)*		*9.11.76*	*1*	*Bath*	*12 May*
39.59	*Katharina Heinrich (GER)*		*5.07.72*	*1*	*Grimsby*	*3 Jun*
36.10	*Sulueti Tagilala (FIJ)*	*U23*	*24.08.80*	*1*	*Cosford*	*4 Jul*

Discus - Under 13 - 0.75kg

34.16	Rebecca Hall	15.09.88	1	Peterborough	27 Aug
30.48	Finesse Thompson	30.03.90	1	London (Elt)	2 Sep
27.85	Eden Francis	19.10.88	1	Banbury	2 Sep
26.82	Nicola Stevenson	8.05.89	2	Crawley	27 Aug
26.80	Jenny Dunford		1	Gloucester	25 Aug

26.72	Rachelle Brace	18.03.89	1	Dartford	22 Sep
26.39	Alice Exeter	7.02.89	1	Bromley	16 Jun
26.25	Francesca Harris	25.07.89	1	Carmarthen	8 Jul
24.41	Emma Long		1B	Kingston	29 Jul
24.06	Sarah Collins		1	Walton	7 Jun
(10)					
23.82	Hanna Jaques	8.08.89		Reading	16 Sep
23.77	Louise Yard	21.01.89	1	Basildon	19 Aug
23.62	Lauren Clark	23.06.89	1	Colchester	17 Jun
23.60	Kirsty Bate		2	Walton	7 Jun
23.22	Emma Hart	13.03.90	1	Cambridge	19 Aug

Hammer

68.15	Lorraine Shaw	2.04.68	3	Nice, FRA	17 Mar
	67.98		3	Bremen, GER	24 Jun
	67.94		1	Birmingham	2 Jun
	67.68		1	Szombathely, HUN	3 Jul
	67.62		1	Bellville, RSA	27 Feb
	67.43		1	Halle, GER	19 May
	67.14		3	Clermont-Ferrand, FRA	15 Jun
	66.97		1	Birmingham	15 Jul
	66.37		3	Gateshead	19 Aug
	66.13		2	Madrid, ESP	26 May
	65.98		1	Tula, RUS	9 Jun
	65.91		1	Stellenbosch, RSA	23 Feb
	65.89		6	Edmonton, CAN	7 Aug
	65.52		2	Budapest, HUN	1 Jul
	65.34		1	London (BP)	6 Jun
	64.71		1	Eton	7 Jul
	64.59		1	Port Elizabeth, RSA	16 Feb
	64.50		1B	London (Col)	28 Apr
	64.37		Q	Edmonton, CAN	6 Aug
	64.05		1	London (Col)	28 Apr
	63.84		1	Bedford	21 Jul
	63.35		1	Cheltenham	18 Jul
	58.64 (5kg)		1	Cheltenham	7 May
62.99	Lyn Sprules	11.09.75	1	London (Ha)	16 Jun
	62.26		1	Bedford	18 Jul
	60.92		1	London (He)	23 Jun
	60.41		1	Rugby	10 Jun
	60.32		1	Hemel Hempstead	28 Apr
	59.61		1	Ashford	11 Aug
	59.38		2	Birmingham	15 Jul
	59.05		1	Bedford	27 May
	58.88		1	London (He)	12 May
	58.72		1	Bedford	22 Jul
	58.51		3	Birmingham	2 Jun
	57.28		2	Eton	7 Jul
	57.22		2	Dublin (S), IRL	29 Jun
62.00	Liz Pidgeon	27.04.77	1	Varazdin, CRO	5 Jul
	61.48		4	Budapest, HUN	1 Jul
	60.28		9	Halle, GER	19 May
	60.22		2	London (Ha)	16 Jun
	59.75		2	Birmingham	2 Jun
	59.60		4	Szombathely, HUN	3 Jul
	58.97		4	Birmingham	15 Jul
	58.84		3	Ashford	11 Aug
	58.81		2	Bedford	27 May
	58.59		1	Wigan	4 Aug
	58.58		1	Southend	12 May
	58.32		2	London (Ha)	10 Jun

60.35	Zoe Derham	U23	24.11.80	1	London (Ha)	10 Jun
	59.57			1	Bath	12 May
	59.30			3	Birmingham	15 Jul
	59.27			1	Liverpool	23 Jun
	59.08			2	Ashford	11 Aug
	58.53			2	London (BP)	6 Jun
	58.42			1	Rugby	19 Aug
	58.26			2	Cheltenham	18 Jul
	57.80			1	Derby	29 Jul
	57.59			1C	London (Col)	28 Apr
	57.05			1	Bedford	1 Jul
58.31	Mhairi Walters	U23	19.06.81	1	Edinburgh	25 Aug
57.62	Suzanne Roberts		19.12.78	1	Scunthorpe	19 Aug
	57.51			1	Loughborough	20 May
57.40	Sarah Moore		15.03.73	2	London (Col)	29 Apr
	62 performances to 57.00 by 7 athletes					
56.62	Lesley Brannan		13.09.76	1	Connah's Quay	13 May
56.21	Diana Holden		12.02.75	1	London (Cr)	23 Jun
56.06	Rachael Beverley	U23	23.07.79	3	Loughborough	20 May
(10)						
55.42	Vicci Scott	U23	21.09.80	1	Glasgow (S)	23 Jun
54.54	Nicola Dudman	U20	5.10.83	1	Dole, FRA	29 Jul
54.37	Shirley Webb	U23	28.09.81	1	Cleckheaton	23 Dec
54.12	Carys Parry	U23	24.07.81	2C	London (Col)	28 Apr
53.66	Christina Bennett		27.02.78	1	Kingston	23 Jun
53.53	Catherine Garden		4.09.78	1	Coatbridge	29 Jul
53.13	Katy Lamb	U20	21.08.82	1	London (BP)	14 Jul
52.46	Esther Augee	V35	1.01.64	7	Birmingham	2 Jun
52.41	Sarah Harrison	U23	1.03.79	2	London (He)	23 Jun
52.00	Laura Douglas	U20	4.01.83	1	Derby	9 Sep
(20)						
51.94	Lucy Marshall	U23	28.11.81	5	Palo Alto, USA	4 May
51.34	Helen Taylor	U20	19.07.82	2	Liverpool	12 Aug
51.04	Joanne Holloway		10.05.76	7	Wigan	4 Aug
50.73	Andrea Jenkins		4.10.75	1	Eton	10 Jun
50.27	Helen Wilding		25.10.76	2	Liverpool	17 Jun
50.02	Helen Arnold		5.10.78	1	Portsmouth	13 May
48.94	Frances Miller	U17	26.12.84	15Q	Debrecen, HUN	12 Jul
48.08	Janet Smith	V35	7.10.64	2	London (BP)	10 Jun
47.83	Ann Gardner		11.10.68	1	Mansfield	19 Aug
47.63	Joanne John	U23	12.11.80	8	London (Ha)	16 Jun
(30)						
47.27	Belinda Heil	U20	8.03.82	1	London (Cr)	19 May
46.79	Julie Lavender		9.11.75	1	Sunderland	27 May
46.10	Diane Smith	V40	15.11.60	4	Liverpool	17 Jun
45.56	Suzanne Last		11.01.70	5	La Coruna, ESP	9 Apr
45.34	Jean Clark		5.10.68	2	Watford	13 Jun
45.28	Helen Gilbert	U20	1.03.82	3	Scunthorpe	19 Aug
45.15	Angela Lockley	U17	7.10.84	3	Sheffield	12 Aug
44.86	Laura Chalmers	U17	1.05.86	2	Grangemouth	10 Jun
44.67	Marina Semenova	V35	12.07.64	1	Coventry	29 Apr
44.65	Natasha Forgie	U20	12.05.84	1	Dartford	12 Aug
(40)						
44.53	Faye Blacktin	U23	5.11.81	1	Welwyn	29 Jul
44.45	Joan Macpherson	U23	18.09.80	1	Basingstoke	1 Sep
43.99	Karen Chambers		31.08.68	4	Grendon Hall	7 Oct
43.84	Vickie Foster		1.04.71	4	Rugby	3 Jun
43.82	Philippa Roles		1.03.78	11	Wigan	4 Aug
43.57	Eleanor Gatrell		5.10.76	1	London (Elt)	28 Apr
43.27	Marian Routledge		9.05.71	5	Liverpool	17 Jun
43.18	Cassie Wilson		24.09.77	3	Loughborough	23 May

43.01	Katie Horne	U23	23.05.79	8	Bedford	1 Jul
42.95	Catherine Lane		18.11.76	2	London (TB)	23 Jun
	(50)					
42.80	Sheena Parry		16.11.77	3	Barry	8 Aug
42.74	Jenny Foster		6.09.77	3	Stretford	19 Jun
42.57	Madelaine Robinson	U23	13.10.81	1	Carlisle	12 May
42.48	Lynsey Selbie	U20	9.03.83	3	Corinth, GRE	27 May
42.39	Kelly Roberts		24.01.76	1	Connah's Quay	26 May
42.34	Claire Pardo	U23	9.08.81	1	Guildford	21 Apr
42.29	Sarah Dobriskey	U17	13.08.85	4	Derby	9 Sep
42.26	Verina Horner		15.09.72	1	Gateshead	25 Aug
42.25	Sarah Morgan	U20	9.05.84	3	Exeter	7 Jul
42.21	Laura Allan	U17	11.02.85	1	Middlesbrough	17 Jun
	(60)					
42.06	Laura Wood		31.10.78	4	Stretford	31 Jul
41.67	Sarah Drake	U17	13.08.85	1	Wakefield	3 Jun
41.52	Anna Howard	U20	18.07.83	4	Watford	27 May
41.47	Tracy Rea	U23	19.01.79	2	Leeds	5 Aug
41.40	Maysoon Elkhawad		27.02.77	4	New Haven, USA	14 Apr
41.00	Karen Bell	U20	18.06.82	2	Elgin	1 Jan
40.98	Kim Rawling	U20	22.07.83	1	Carn Brea	5 Aug
40.93	Alex Merrill	U17	12.05.86	1	Stretford	19 Jun
40.84	Karen Ainsley	U23	24.06.80	1	Mansfield	24 Jun
40.80	Natasha Smith		6.06.77	3	London (Ha)	12 May
	(70)					
40.71	Janette Brown		19.02.73	3	London (Cr)	3 Jun
40.43	Susan McKelvie	U17	15.06.85	5	Aberdeen	27 May
40.34	Joanne Harding	V35	12.04.64	1	Stretford	3 Jun
40.13	Sarah Deacon	U20	18.03.83	1	London (Nh)	11 Aug
40.12	Laura Perry		4.06.75	1	Nuneaton	5 Aug
40.01	Tanya Bilous	U17	7.05.86	1	Gloucester	23 Jun
39.94	Jenny Earle	V40	28.11.58	1	Hoo	19 May
39.87	Carly Burton	U23	14.10.80	2	Bromley	10 Jun
39.75	Siobhan Hart		15.06.75	1	Stevenage	1 Sep
39.63	Jennifer Ayero/West	U23	13.09.79	2	Oxford	23 Jun
	(80)					
39.61	Jenny Wood	V40	23.02.57	1	Cleckheaton	3 Jun
39.58	Emma King	U23	25.07.81	2	Portsmouth	12 May
39.23	Anna Bowyer	U20	29.09.82	2	Salisbury	22 Jul
39.22	Gemma Roach	U20	16.02.83	2	Bracknell	19 May
39.19	Sue Lawrence		25.11.70	2	London (Nh)	19 May
39.08	Jacqui Loney	U23	17.04.79	2	Elgin	14 Jul
39.00	Lisa-Marie Shippen	U20	19.10.83	2	Gateshead	25 Aug
38.74	Rebecca Hardy		11.11.68	2	London (PH)	11 Aug
38.71	Eva Massey	U23	22.12.80	1	Belfast	28 Jul
38.62	Lynette Bristow		17.11.77	1	Stourport	24 Jun
	(90)					
38.59	Bolanle Ogun		2.09.77	2	Nuneaton	5 Aug
38.37	Paula Coombs	V35	31.12.61	1	Crawley	13 May
38.26	Bethan Lishman	U20	15.11.83	6	Newport	5 Aug
38.19	Helen Ephgrave	U17	29.10.84	1	Portsmouth	29 Apr
38.15	Melissa Clapham	U20	6.09.82	1	King's Lynn	1 Sep
38.12	Carol Parker		22.09.69	4	Rugby	19 Aug
37.96	Emily Oliver	U20	8.02.84	1	Bromley	25 Jul
37.70	Kirsty Walters	U17	6.09.84	1	Edinburgh	13 May
37.56	Amy Church	U17	22.04.86	1	Sandown IOW	8 May
37.55	Myrtle Augee	V35	4.02.65	2	Bromley	11 Aug
	(100)					
37.48	Karen Moody		20.07.67	3	Stafford	7 Jul
37.47	Debbie Callaway	V35	15.07.64	3	Crawley	5 Aug
37.41	Hannah Lia	U17	15.11.84	1	Aberdare	10 Jun
37.38	Melissa Ashley		17.03.77	4	London (WL)	1 Sep

37.27	Zoe Parsons		15.11.69	3	Rugby	10 Jun
37.20	Vicky Gorton		9.05.77	1	Nelson	2 Sep
37.09	Susan Freebairn	V35	22.08.65	2	Milton Keynes	29 Sep
37.06	Kelly Anderson	U23	17.07.80	2	Perivale	11 Aug

Additional Under 17 (1 - 13 above)

36.17	Sally Hinds		2.02.86	1	Brecon	19 Aug
35.83	Elizabeth Edwards		18.12.84	3	Peterborough	27 Aug
35.74	Jenna Lander		31.08.85	3	Sandown IOW	9 Sep
33.96	Caoimhe Gilroy		24.09.85	1	Antrim	26 May
32.84	Nyree-Claire James		28.12.84	2	Cardiff	16 Jun
32.75	Frances O'Gorman		29.10.84	2	London (BP)	14 Jul
32.48	Chiara Collins		25.03.85	2	Rotherham	5 Aug
	(20)					
32.30	Catherine Newton		25.10.85	1	Grimsby	29 Jul
31.86	Danielle Hall		27.11.84	2	Brighton	23 Jun
31.67	Hollie Redman		12.12.85	1	Great Yarmouth	7 May
31.57	Katie-Jo Halling		13.01.85	6	Tullamore, IRL	21 Jul
31.55	Angela Farmer		27.03.85	2	Scunthorpe	19 Aug
31.44	Sue Frost		27.09.84	4	Portsmouth	1 Sep
30.31	Jemima Hall		20.02.85	6	Bedford	22 Jul
30.17	Amanda Moodie		11.09.85	6	Liverpool	12 Aug

Foreign

47.93	*Olivia Kelleher (IRL)*		*9.10.75*	*1*	*Hastings*	*1 Sep*
40.30	*Sara Nystrom (FIN)*	*U20*	*8.01.84*	*1*	*Sandown IOW*	*19 Mar*
38.33	*Yolande Jacobs (RSA)*		*9.11.76*	*2*	*Coventry*	*29 Apr*

Hammer - Under 15 - 3.25kg

40.70	Catherine Marvin		18.04.87	1	Sandown IOW	9 Sep
34.97	Shaeleen Bruce		3.11.86	1	Grangemouth	12 Aug
33.59	Hazel Robertson		27.07.87	2	Grangemouth	12 Aug
33.16	Lorne Tait		16.01.87	1	Inverness	2 Sep
30.43	Hannah Cameron		3.03.88	3	Grangemouth	12 Aug

Javelin

55.85	Karen Martin		24.11.74	1	Derby	29 Apr
	55.59			4	Halle, GER	19 May
	55.30			1	Derby	12 May
	54.82			1	Birmingham	14 Jul
	53.03			1	Bedford	18 Jul
	52.63			8	Bremen, GER	23 Jun
	51.14			1	Ashford	11 Aug
55.40	Goldie Sayers	U20	16.07.82	2	Grosseto, ITA	22 Jul
	53.97			6	Tampere, FIN	22 Aug
	53.74			1	Bedford	30 Jun
	52.74			1	Stoke-on-Trent	18 Aug
	51.20			1	Liverpool	8 Jul
54.49	Kelly Morgan	U23	17.06.80	2	Birmingham	14 Jul
	53.75			2	Bedford	21 Jul
	53.14			1	Wigan	4 Aug
	51.90			1	Exeter	31 Jul
53.10	Kirsty Morrison		28.10.75	1	Hania, GRE	18 Apr
	51.92			1	Newport	5 Aug
	51.60			2	Loughborough	20 May
	51.43			2	Bangor	2 Jun
	51.25			1	Bedford	27 May
52.86	Linda Gray		23.03.71	1	Eton	10 Jun
	51.74			2	Varazdin, CRO	5 Jul
	51.39			1	Peterborough	27 Aug
52.76	Jenny Kemp	U23	18.02.80	2	Liverpool	23 Jun

52.74	Lorna Jackson		9.01.74	3	Birmingham	14 Jul
51.65	Chloe Cozens	U23	9.04.80	1	Loughborough	20 May
	27 performances to 51.00 by 8 athletes					
49.36	Sharon Gibson	V35	31.12.61	1	Birmingham	30 Jun
49.25	Nicola Gautier		21.03.78	1H	Ried, AUT	1 Jul
	(10)					
47.55	Katie Amos		13.11.78	1	London (Ha)	16 Jun
47.13	Samantha Redd	U20	16.02.84	2	Bedford	30 Jun
46.29	Katy Watts	U23	25.03.81	1	Oxford	23 Jun
45.89	Denise Lewis		27.08.72	7	Birmingham	14 Jul
45.81	Jennifer Ayero/West	U23	13.09.79	4	Bedford	27 May
45.65	Louise Mathews	U20	27.10.83	1	Ipswich	2 Sep
45.18	Noelle Bradshaw	V35	18.12.63	2	London (Ha)	16 Jun
44.31	Melanie Burrows		7.08.76	3	London (Ha)	16 Jun
44.11	Rachel Dunn	U20	14.11.82	1	Exeter	7 Jul
43.75	Paula Blank-Collis		13.12.77	1	Belfast	28 Jul
	(20)					
43.74	Sylveen Monaghan		25.08.72	8	Madrid, ESP	27 May
43.70	Jenny Grimstone	U23	30.04.79	1	Bedford	11 Aug
42.82	Rebecca Bartlett	U17	7.03.85	1	Telford	8 Sep
42.76	Katherine Evans		19.11.77	2	Glasgow (S)	6 May
42.73	Charlotte Rees	U20	14.06.84	1	Carmarthen	28 Apr
42.64	Amy Harvey	U20	23.04.82	1	Southend	13 May
42.37	Jo Chapman	U17	10.01.85	1	Watford	26 May
41.92	Claire Bennett	U20	4.02.83	1	Loughborough	13 Jun
41.71	Chissie Head	U23	18.12.79	2	Liverpool	8 Jul
41.44	Louise Watton	U15	30.10.86	1	Southampton	8 Sep
	(30)					
41.35	Lauren Therin	U17	19.01.86	2	Exeter	6 Jul
41.05	Debbie Collinson	U17	23.10.85	1	Rotherham	17 Jun
40.97	Alison Siggery	U20	14.09.83	1	Aberdare	30 Jun
40.80	Suzanne Finnis	U20	12.08.83	1	Woodford	29 Apr
40.78	Hayley Thomas	U15	16.12.86	1	Eton	11 Aug
40.74	Helen Potter		25.06.74	1	Loughborough	23 May
40.71	Roz Gonse	U20	1.03.82	1H	Hexham	20 May
40.70	Helen Mounteney	U17	24.09.84	1	Leicester	9 Jun
40.63	Laura Smith	U20	21.01.84	2	London (Cr)	3 Jun
40.49	Candace Schofield	U17	3.11.84	2	Watford	26 May
	(40)					
40.32	Emily Skucek	U23	24.09.81	4	Glasgow (S)	6 May
39.86	Liz Pidgeon		27.04.77	4	Wigan	4 Aug
39.75	Georgina Hogsden	U23	23.11.81	1	Crawley	27 Aug
39.56	Lisa Fryer	U20	30.05.84	1	Tullamore, IRL	29 Jul
39.32	Carol Wallbanks	U20	9.12.82	4	Bedford	30 Jun
38.88	Joanne Harding	V35	12.04.64	1	Liverpool	24 Jun
38.83	Julie Hollman		16.02.77	14H	Ried, AUT	1 Jul
38.78	Sarah Ellis	U20	27.10.83	2	Crawley	27 Aug
38.51	Jenny Leng	U20	1.02.84	1	Wigan	29 Apr
38.51	Eloise Manger	U17	6.01.85	1	Blackpool	9 Jun
	(50)					
38.28	Nicola Smith	U20	6.03.82	1	Guildford	29 Jul
38.24	Vicky James	U23	13.05.81	1	Cheltenham	12 May
38.23	Banke Olofinjana		14.05.72	1	London (ME)	23 Jun
38.21	Cathy Edgar	U23	27.02.80	1	Antrim	19 Jun
38.20	Wendy Newman		31.08.71	5	Wigan	4 Aug
38.07	Hayley Boddey	U20	14.02.83	7	Exeter	7 Jul
37.99	Paula Hendriks	U20	25.01.83	2	Cannock	12 May
37.62	Emma Lilley		2.05.76	1	Rotherham	5 Aug
37.55	Joanna Parry		5.03.78	2	Crawley	24 Mar
37.54	Laura Bolton	U23	22.01.79	1	Portsmouth	23 Jun
	(60)					
37.52	Julia Bennett		26.03.70	23H	Arles, FRA	10 Jun

37.44	Vanessa Stennett		3.06.69	1	Southampton	1	Sep
37.37	Aimee Styles	U20	1.05.82	1	Abingdon	14	Jul
37.17	Fiona Harrison	U23	30.11.81	5	Glasgow (S)	6	May
37.16	Caroline Garrett	V35	14.06.63	2	Basingstoke	1	Sep
37.12	Lucy Cook/Budgen		11.09.75	1	London (TB)	14	Jul

Additional Under 17 (1 - 7 above)

36.94	Anna Hoyle		12.02.85	1	Blackpool	12	May
36.88	Christine Lawrence		4.04.86	1	London (CP)	8	Apr
36.60	Joanna Blair		1.03.86	1	Birmingham	24	Jun
(10)							
36.31	Laura Whittingham		6.06.86	1	Wakefield	23	Sep
36.14	Helen Davis		31.01.85	1	Sandown IOW	9	Sep
36.03	Elizabeth Dunn		5.01.85	4	Watford	26	May
34.98	Sara Siggery		30.06.85	1	Cardiff	7	Jul
34.88	Sarah Browne		8.01.85	1	Carlisle	9	Jun
34.67	Venetia Ellis		15.09.85	2	Stevenage	1	Sep
34.39	Allyson France		7.02.85	1	Leeds	22	Jul
34.33	Anna Price		18.08.85	4	Rugby	19	Aug
34.29	Emma Calliste		2.02.85	1	London (He)	9	Jun

Additional Under 15 (1 - 2 above)

36.37	Melissa O'Neil		13.02.87	1	Basingstoke	1	Sep
35.10	Cara Moseley		21.07.87	2	Exeter	16	Jun
34.38	Sarah Devoy		12.01.87	1	Stoke-on-Trent	9	Jun
34.37	Rosie Semenytsh		28.05.87	1	Birmingham	2	Sep
34.24	Lisa Edwards		4.02.87	2	Sheffield	11	Aug
33.01	Janine Mullineux		12.02.87	1	Stretford	27	Aug
32.78	Katie Bennett		5.10.86	1	Nottingham	13	May
32.76	Lianne Clarke		14.01.87	1	Connah's Quay	4	Aug
(10)							
32.64	Josie Jamieson		17.07.87	2	Connah's Quay	4	Aug
32.52	Carrie Williams		9.02.87	1	Carmarthen	9	Jun
32.23	Stephanie Novak		20.09.86	1	Preston	5	Aug
32.11	Kelly-Jane Berry		23.04.87	1	Bath	24	Jun
32.08	Shani Rainford		6.07.87	1	London (TB)	18	Aug
31.74	Lucy Martin		8.11.86	4	Exeter	7	Jul
31.32	Amanda Lyons		12.03.87	1	Aberdeen	27	May
31.31	Lynsey Stephenson		18.11.86	1	Newport	22	Jul
31.16	Laura Carr		18.02.89	1	Southampton	1	Sep
30.70	Victoria Royce		6.06.87	1	Cambridge	19	Aug

Foreign

54.43	*Silvia Cruz (POR)*	*U23*	*29.12.80*	*1*	*Bedford*	*21*	*Jul*
42.74	*Alison Moffitt (IRL)*		*6.10.69*	*2*	*Dublin (S), IRL*	*22*	*Jul*
37.00	*Katrina Campbell (IRL)*		*8.03.72*	*1*	*Belfast*	*18*	*Apr*

Javelin - Under 13 - 400 gm

34.27	Laura Carr		18.02.89	1	Kingston	29	Jul
31.24	Rachelle Brace		18.03.89	1	Dartford	22	Sep
30.80	Lucy Boggis		27.01.89	1	Abingdon	13	May
29.00	Louise Burton		23.12.88	1	Warrington	12	May
28.33	Natazia Fistrovic			1	Crawley	27	Aug
27.73	Rachael Fleary		16.07.90	1	Carlisle	24	Jun
27.04	Holly Gadsdon		16.04.89	1	Par	16	Sep
26.95	Amanda Manchester		27.09.88	4	Kingston	29	Jul
26.78	Samantha Riley		31.10.88	1	Stretford	27	Aug
26.46	Jo Wray		29.07.89	1	Watford	1	Aug
(10)							
25.86	Victoria Buxton		1.06.89	1	Neath	5	May
25.69	Jenny Dunford			1	Gloucester	4	Aug
25.07 600g	Lauren Ellis		22.05.89	1	Wigan	19	Aug

Heptathlon

5933 Julie Hollman 16.02.77 2 Ried, AUT 1 Jul
14.38/0.0 1.78 12.40 24.75/0.4 6.37w/2.3 38.83 2:18.30
5840 3 Arles, FRA 10 Jun
14.33/0.5 1.83 11.29 24.75/0.6 6.27/1.8 37.35 2:20.47
5537 1 Bedford 5 Aug
15.5/2.0 1.81 11.88 25.17/0.9 6.12w/2.2 36.59 2:22.69
5784 Nicola Gautier 21.03.78 8 Ried, AUT 1 Jul
14.05/0.8 1.60 14.64 25.13/1.1 5.53/1.4 49.25 2:21.00
5666 12 Arles, FRA 10 Jun
14.06/-1.1 1.62 14.53 25.42/0.3 5.74w/2.7 40.77 2:21.30
5687 Kerry Jury 19.11.68 10 Ried, AUT 1 Jul
13.71/1.0 1.78 11.42 24.32/0.9 5.66/1.5 33.49 2:17.96
5635 15 Arles, FRA 10 Jun
14.05/-1.1 1.77 11.18 24.52/1.3 5.86/1.5 33.68 2:19.37
5589 1 Sheffield 2 Sep
13.93/1.6 1.75 11.10 24.44/1.5 5.79w/2.8 32.78 2:19.59
5476 2 Bedford 5 Aug
14.1/2.0 1.69 11.41 25.16/0.9 5.75/1.2 34.85 2:16.88
5554 Katherine Livesey U23 15.12.79 3 College Station, USA 17 May
13.80w/3.6 1.75 11.13 24.33w/3.4 5.69w/3.6 31.14 2:19.97
5385 1 Lawrence, USA 19 Apr
14.2w/2.6 1.75 10.33 24.6/1.1 5.69w/3.2 31.28 2:18.67
5375 10 Eugene, USA 2 Jun
14.17/-2.7 1.73 10.14 25.11/-1.2 5.75/0.0 31.56 2:19.22
5534 Julia Bennett 26.03.70 14 Ried, AUT 1 Jul
14.90/-0.1 1.78 11.84 25.73/0.8 6.05w/2.7 36.84 2:23.06
5508 18 Arles, FRA 10 Jun
14.87/-1.8 1.83 11.16 25.92/-0.1 6.05/1.6 37.52 2:26.46
5452 auto (5406hand 14.8Hur) 3 Bedford 5 Aug
14.70/1.4 1.84 11.55 26.59/0.7 6.00/1.7 36.66 2:28.53
5410 Kelly Sotherton 13.11.76 20 Arles, FRA 10 Jun
14.19/0.5 1.65 11.12 24.17/1.3 6.23/1.9 25.76 2:23.41
5208 Fiona Harrison U23 30.11.81 26 Arles, FRA 10 Jun
14.43/-2.1 1.65 9.00 25.50/0.3 5.54/1.5 36.48 2:16.08
5114 Laura Redmond U23 19.04.81 31 Arles, FRA 10 Jun
14.97/-1.9 1.62 12.22 25.68/-0.2 5.53/1.4 35.01 2:27.32
5107 2 Sheffield 2 Sep
15.08/1.6 1.63 12.08 26.05/1.5 5.69/1.4 35.02 2:27.99
5068 1 Bedford 15 Jul
14.86w/2.4 1.61 11.85 25.84w/2.2 5.63w/2.6 32.24 2:26.11
5039 5 Bedford 5 Aug
15.29/1.2 1.66 11.88 26.46/1.9 5.57/1.8 35.49 2:28.04
5053 Roz Gonse U20 1.03.82 4 Bedford 5 Aug
14.60/1.2 1.54 11.05 25.81w/3.2 5.44/1.9 40.41 2:27.70
27 performances to 5000 points by 9 athletes
4969 Kate Brewington U23 15.10.81 2 Bedford 15 Jul
14.29w/2.4 1.61 9.69 25.46w/2.2 5.87/1.2 31.76 2:36.77
(10)
4959 Rebecca Jones U20 17.01.83 32 Arles, FRA 10 Jun
14.99/-1.8 1.80 10.78 26.29/0.6 5.55/1.1 33.54 2:44.15
4908 Charmaine Johnson V35 4.06.63 3 Bedford 15 Jul
14.96w/2.4 1.61 13.77 26.64/1.8 5.23/1.8 36.97 2:41.00
4857 Aileen Wilson U20 30.03.84 33 Arles, FRA 10 Jun
14.62/-1.9 1.80 10.28 25.66/0.9 4.50/0.5 23.16 2:19.08
4825 Sarah Still 24.09.75 4 Bedford 15 Jul
14.98w/2.4 1.61 8.79 25.03w/2.2 5.74/1.6 23.36 2:23.57
4801 Jessica Ennis U17 28.01.86 9 Bedford 5 Aug
14.53/1.5 1.72 8.67 25.55/2.0 5.24/0.8 23.57 2:25.04

4795 Caroline Pearce U23 1.09.80 5 Bedford 15 Jul
14.41w/2.4 1.61 10.27 26.30w/2.2 5.74w/2.9 27.14 2:36.40

4771 Hannah Barnes U20 2.06.84 2 Bedford 15 Jul
15.10/1.7 1.49 9.14 25.53/0.1 5.58/1.9 32.53 2:23.78

4688 w Danielle Parkinson U23 2.09.81 6 Bedford 15 Jul
15.16w/2.5 1.61 9.15 25.41w/2.2 5.62W/4.3 30.79 2:40.36

4626 5 Sheffield 2 Sep
15.07/1.6 1.63 8.85 25.44/1.5 5.48/1.8 28.96 2:40.17

4616 Claire Everett U23 25.06.79 7 Bedford 15 Jul
15.86w/2.5 1.58 12.54 26.84/1.8 5.11w/2.2 26.39 2:25.31

4600 Tamsin Stephens U23 2.08.80 7 Sheffield 2 Sep
14.08/1.6 1.54 9.71 25.72/1.5 5.06/1.2 21.00 2:25.36

(20)

4557 Wendy Laing V35 29.12.62 2 Brisbane, AUS 5 Jul
15.08/-0.6 1.57 10.97 27.60/-0.4 5.06/0.0 32.75 2:30.20

4441 Wendy Davidson U20 14.10.82 16 Bedford 5 Aug
15.10w/3.0 1.57 9.84 25.64/2.0 5.22/1.4 23.74 2:38.92

4419 Natalie Hulse U20 2.12.82 4 Bedford 15 Jul
16.08/1.9 1.64 8.06 26.97/0.1 5.45/1.2 28.53 2:31.06

4372 Vicky Consterdine 25.04.75 8 Bedford 15 Jul
15.39w/2.5 1.49 9.20 26.57/1.8 5.32w/3.6 23.24 2:25.64

4294 Lara Carty U20 7.03.84 1 Hull 16 Sep
15.10 1.62 7.18 27.41 5.12 26.94 2:31.78

4280 Sara Todd U23 3.11.79 2 Hexham 20 May
14.6/-0.3 1.43 8.34 25.3/2.0 5.03/1.4 24.54 2:31.6

4267 Faith Cripps U20 23.09.83 1 Abingdon 24 Jun
15.6 1.53 8.48 26.8 5.28 25.91 2:29.1

4223 Mhairi Walker U20 20.01.84 9 Sheffield 2 Sep
17.02/1.6 1.57 7.75 26.48w/2.4 5.11/1.9 22.27 2:16.68

4215 Katy Taylor U23 18.06.80 1 Blandford 13 Jun
15.5 1.56 9.90 26.2 4.92 22.07 2:34.9

4214 Stephanie Little U23 5.11.81 3 Aberdare 24 Jun
15.7w/2.5 1.52 9.34 27.99/-1.1 5.08/0.1 29.64 2:31.11

(30)

4194 Vicky Williams U23 11.04.81 1 Birmingham 17 Jun
14.76/1.1 1.52 8.40 26.54/-0.1 5.12w/3.4 28.44 2:50.24

4071 Teresa Mainstone U23 13.07.81 1 Crawley 9 Sep
17.3 1.53 9.19 27.4 5.15 33.08 2:37.1

4060 Grace Clements U20 2.05.84 1 London (He) 12 Aug
16.63/-0.7 1.70 7.77 27.44/-1.8 4.71/-2.2 31.05 2:44.21

4055 Judith Butler U23 5.10.79 9 Bedford 15 Jul
16.37w/2.5 1.52 8.37 27.26/1.8 5.21w/2.9 23.24 2:32.49

4055 Alex Hewett U20 10.09.82 2 London (He) 12 Aug
17.51/-2.2 1.55 9.25 28.43/-1.8 4.85/-1.1 35.55 2:32.71

4043 Rebecca Reid U20 9.11.83 1 Preston 24 Jun
16.1 1.48 9.04 26.9 4.69 25.98 2:27.4

4037 Amanda Wale 14.10.70 4 Hexham 20 May
16.1/-0.3 1.43 8.56 27.8/2.0 5.08/1.4 26.70 2:24.7

4019 Jenny Pacey U20 5.02.83 1 King's Lynn 20 May
16.8 1.63 9.92 27.9 5.06 23.83 2:39.7

4017 Sara Barry U20 8.06.83 1 Exeter 24 Jun
16.4 1.53 9.21 27.7 5.33 25.28 2:40.2

4006 Carly Austin U20 16.05.83 2 Abingdon 24 Jun
16.7 1.47 8.38 27.8 4.91 29.97 2:25.4

(40)

4000 Laura Bolton U23 22.01.79 1 Par 23 Sep
16.1 1.45 9.28 27.6 5.01 36.90 2:49.8

3984 Laura Taylor U20 22.04.84 3 Abingdon 24 Jun
15.7 1.53 8.02 27.7 5.21 20.11 2:32.5

3931 Hayley Jasper U20 1.05.84 5 Hull 16 Sep
17.43 1.53 6.81 26.94 4.66 29.18 2:25.01

3871 Jodie Favell U20 4.11.82 3 Rugby 24 Jun
15.7 1.45 8.96 27.8 4.88 30.53 2:48.5
3842 Olivia Ross-Hurst U20 10.12.83 1 Woking 24 Jun
18.3 1.63 8.46 27.5 5.25 20.66 2:35.3
3837 Claire Roddis U20 22.12.83 1 Hexham 20 May
16.0w/2.2 1.49 8.80 27.9w/3.4 4.57/0.3 31.19 2:44.2
3836 Jackie Jenner 25.10.76 1 Erith 16 Sep
15.8 1.45 10.00 28.2 5.35 30.10 3:07.4
3822 Jane Greer U20 19.07.84 4 Abingdon 24 Jun
17.7 1.47 8.43 27.8 5.20 28.24 2:35.4
3801 Abigail Ashby 23.11.77 1 Grangemouth 8 Jul
16.63/-0.6 1.46 9.65 28.0 5.04 28.76 2:51.96

Heptathlon - Under 17

4945 Phyllis Agbo 16.12.85 1 Woking 24 Jun
11.4 1.66 9.69 25.5 5.86/-0.7 32.00 2:37.3
4587 Faye Harding 7.09.85 1 Aberdare 24 Jun
12.2w/2.4 1.62 7.45 25.37w/2.2 5.24/0.3 25.09 2:21.40
4538 Jessica Ennis 28.01.86 2 Hull 16 Sep
12.11 1.75 8.59 26.61 5.22 22.78 2:29.95
4520 Emma Perkins 4.09.85 2 Woking 24 Jun
11.9 1.75 9.61 27.6 5.31 25.68 2:37.3
4510 Louise Hazel 6.10.85 1 Rugby 24 Jun
11.6 1.54 8.92 25.6 5.16 28.53 2:32.1
4436 w Emily Parker 7.11.84 1 Birmingham 30 Sep
11.70/0.7 1.56 7.69 25.39/0.8 5.51W/4.9 17.89 2:27.53
4396 * Birmingham 30 Sep
5.37w/3.9
4388 Chanelle Garnett 16.08.85 2 Birmingham 30 Sep
11.51/0.7 1.50 8.31 26.40/0.8 5.51w/3.1 21.06 2:29.03
4382 Jenny Christie 28.09.85 1 Abingdon 24 Jun
12.3 1.59 7.94 25.6 5.09 29.10 2:33.6
4346 Danielle Fawkes 11.08.85 5 Hull 16 Sep
12.04 1.54 8.71 26.28 4.92 30.15 2:33.43
4339 Sarah Gallaway 14.11.84 3 Woking 24 Jun
12.3 1.57 10.19 26.8 5.15/0.8 26.19 2:35.8
(10)
4248 w Anna Clayton 20.03.85 3 Birmingham 30 Sep
12.18/0.7 1.50 7.97 26.20/0.8 5.47w/6.3 27.43 2:41.48
4194 2 Rugby 24 Jun
12.2 1.51 8.45 26.1 5.14 27.92 2:41.3
4224 Emma Morris 21.02.86 2 Jarrow 24 Jun
12.3 1.72 6.46 26.2 4.83 16.47 2:22.7
4161 Ruth Laybourn 5.10.84 3 Jarrow 24 Jun
12.8 1.57 8.12 26.3 5.39 23.75 2:39.6
4134 Samantha Backwell 4.02.85 1 Street 7 May
13.2 1.61 7.86 27.5 5.08 25.52 2:27.8
4094 Jemma Garrett 21.09.85 4 Jarrow 24 Jun
13.1 1.51 6.95 25.8 5.26 18.70 2:23.5
4077 Penny Boyd 27.10.84 5 Jarrow 24 Jun
12.3 1.51 8.61 27.4 4.44 28.64 2:27.6
4068 Catherine Holdsworth 3.01.86 4 Birmingham 30 Sep
12.11/0.7 1.50 9.11 27.07/1.0 5.17w/3.3 22.42 2:42.35
4053 Rachel Brenton 18.01.85 2 Abingdon 24 Jun
12.1 1.65 7.58 27.2 5.21 23.65 2:51.3
4033 Liza Parry 24.10.84 3 Abingdon 24 Jun
13.1 1.50 8.48 25.6 4.86 23.66 2:35.2
3991 w Nikki Brady 26.07.85 5 Birmingham 30 Sep
13.01/-0.3 1.53 7.55 27.52/1.0 5.13W/4.6 25.38 2:34.36
3828 2 Birmingham 17 Jun
13.26/0.9 1.45 7.88 27.13/1.2 4.91w/2.3 22.24 2:32.86

3951	Hollie Lundgren				10.10.85	5	Woking		24 Jun
	13.2	1.60	9.84	29.3		4.94/0.3	32.90	2:50.9	
3938	Samantha Brough				22.02.85	6	Woking		24 Jun
	13.2	1.54	9.40	28.1		4.71/-1.3	22.54	2:28.8	
3912	Rachel Gibbens				31.01.86	4	Abingdon		24 Jun
	12.3	1.59	7.32	28.5		4.81	19.97	2:29.3	
3879	Sarah Walsh				28.01.85	12	Hull		16 Sep
	13.49	1.51	8.42	27.78		5.02	22.75	2:33.80	
3876	Hayley Goodall				20.09.84	1	Erith		16 Sep
	12.7	1.51	7.19	27.2		5.37	18.10	2:38.2	
3872	Kimberley Miles				4.08.85	12	Sheffield		2 Sep
	14.44w/2.9	1.39	8.55	27.61w/2.4		4.88/1.3	33.09	2:30.62	
3872	Elen Evans				14.02.85	6	Birmingham		30 Sep
	12.35/0.7	1.59	8.29	29.02/1.0		4.57w/3.4	28.45	2:43.76	
3870 w	Juliet Fullwood				1.07.85	7	Birmingham		30 Sep
	12.83/-0.3	1.50	7.55	27.74/1.3		4.89w/4.1	22.55	2:32.11	
3846	Frances Noble				2.05.86	6	Jarrow		24 Jun
	13.1	1.48	8.40	27.0		5.25	17.90	2:38.6	
3829 w	Laura Singleton				6.04.85	9	Birmingham		30 Sep
	13.14/-0.1	1.44	8.75	27.59/1.3		5.38w/5.3	23.11	2:47.42	
(30)									
3826	Jade Weekes				15.11.84	2	Erith		16 Sep
	13.3	1.57	9.02	27.7		4.58	25.68	2:42.9	
3809	Laura Betts				6.11.84	8	Woking		24 Jun
	12.8	1.45	8.36	27.5		5.12/-0.5	25.41	2:47.6	
3807	Kate Marsh				15.05.86	10	Birmingham		30 Sep
	12.54/-0.3	1.41	8.36	27.11/0.8		4.76w/2.7	30.66	2:51.85	

Pentathlon - Under 15

3028	Rebekah Passley				9.03.87	1	Hull	16 Sep
	5.59	12.00	8.21	1.55		2:43.30		
2867	Claire Huck				11.10.86	2	Hull	16 Sep
	4.83	12.70	8.59	1.64		2:43.50		
2861	Cherri Morrison				27.09.86	1	Birmingham	30 Sep
	5.07/1.6	12.28/-1.1	8.07	1.44		2:30.95		
2825	Laura Jones				28.09.86	1	Woking	24 Jun
	4.68	12.4	8.32	1.51		2:31.9		
2806	Samantha Britton				12.09.86	1	Abingdon	24 Jun
	4.82	11.6	6.77	1.52		2:36.9		
2801	Linsey Nash				7.11.86	2	Birmingham	30 Sep
	4.92w/3.0	12.76/-2.9	9.84	1.47		2:40.78		
2794	Kim Skinner				21.09.87	1	Grangemouth	8 Jul
	5.20	12.52w/2.4	8.93	1.46		2:44.21		
2791	Lucy Rodgers				1.07.87	1	London (He)	12 Aug
	4.94/-0.8	12.94/-2.8	7.86	1.48		2:30.66		
2788	Rebecca Long				3.10.86	4	Hull	16 Sep
	4.63	12.83	8.03	1.52		2:29.67		
2785	Natalie Wallis				20.10.86	5	Hull	16 Sep
	4.96	12.43	7.70	1.46		2:33.24		
(10)								
2771	Katie Renouf				3.06.87	1	Exeter	24 Jun
	4.43	13.0	8.74	1.54		2:31.1		
2754	Sarah Fielding-Smith				19.11.86	2	Woking	24 Jun
	4.68	12.9/0.5	7.06	1.60		2:35.4		
2746	Carly Sharp				7.09.87	3	Birmingham	30 Sep
	4.81w/2.9	12.37/-1.1	7.14	1.50		2:34.32		
2730	Dominique Blaize				3.10.87	1	Crawley	9 Sep
	5.02	12.5	7.78	1.60		2:53.9		
2728	Sarah Devoy				12.01.87	2	Preston	24 Jun
	4.87	12.6	10.20	1.59		3:04.1		

2712	Emily Bonnett				22.09.87	8	Hull	16 Sep
	4.59	12.19	7.83	1.43	2:31.33			
2706	Sara Luck				18.11.86	4	Birmingham	30 Sep
	4.21w/3.2	13.06/-2.3	6.57	1.53	2:19.99			
2702	Joanne Grout				17.09.86	1	Hexham	26 Aug
	4.65	12.99	9.40	1.40	2:32.24			
2688	Layla Hawkins				3.09.86	4	Woking	24 Jun
	4.90	12.2	8.69	1.45	2:47.1			
2676	Claire Wait				7.11.86	3	Preston	24 Jun
	4.89	12.7	9.02	1.41	2:41.2			
	(20)							
2673	Caroline Smith				15.09.86	3	Rugby	24 Jun
	4.42	12.5	8.73	1.37	2:28.1			
2672	Hannah Weekes				14.12.87	5	Woking	24 Jun
	4.98	13.0	6.56	1.54	2:39.6			
2663	Rosemary Huntriss				9.10.86	1	Macclesfield	9 Sep
	4.90	12.7	8.05	1.56	2:52.3			
2647	Meghan Waldron				4.09.86	6	Woking	24 Jun
	4.58	12.2	6.62	1.51	2:37.3			
2647	Cheryl Cairney				27.03.87	3	Grangemouth	8 Jul
	4.50	11.94w/2.4	7.18	1.40	2:31.19			
2642	Lucie Shipley				19.10.86	2	Jarrow	24 Jun
	4.55	12.9	8.17	1.51	2:39.3			
2640	Shani Rainford				6.07.87	7	Woking	24 Jun
	4.48	14.5/0.6	9.70	1.63	2:46.7			
2631	Sarah Allison				18.11.86	4	Preston	24 Jun
	4.77	13.7	8.85	1.56	2:47.7			
2621	Vicki Novell				25.02.87	2	Abingdon	24 Jun
	4.89	13.2	6.94	1.46	2:34.8			
2617	Ruth Hatch				4.07.87	6	Birmingham	30 Sep
	5.06w/2.5	12.12/-1.1	8.14	1.47	2:58.02			
	(30)							
2612	Lauren Newman				17.01.87	7	Birmingham	30 Sep
	4.34w/3.8	12.71/-2.9	6.02	1.53	2:29.57			

Under 13

2532 w	Jade Surman				27.03.89	12	Birmingham	30 Sep
	4.55W/5.0	12.70/-2.3	7.22	1.47	2:41.61			

Pentathlon - Under 13

2358	Amelia Montagnani				10.03.90	1	Crawley	9 Sep
	4.73	12.8	8.24	1.48	3:00.6			
2218	Courtney Williams				8.03.89	1	Portsmouth	7 May
	4.57	12.8	6.60	1.36	2:46.9			
2187	Rachel Davidson				29.04.89	1	Grangemouth	8 Jul
	4.18/1.5	11.96/1.7	7.63	1.24	2:42.90			
2169	Ashley Little				19.01.89	1	Rotherham	16 Sep
	3.90	13.4	6.85	1.47	2:52.2			
2119	Sarah Lamb					1	Hexham	26 Aug
	4.25	12.45	7.07	1.33	3:01.8			
2113	Kayleigh Hill				12.12.88	1	Carlisle	15 Jul
	4.17	13.4	8.28	1.27	2:52.3			
2097	Meghan Maslen				19.10.88	2	Grangemouth	8 Jul
	3.90/1.8	12.74/1.2	5.34	1.36	2:36.59			
2090	Stephanie Lamb					2	Hexham	27 Aug
	4.11	13.08	7.47	1.27	2:50.72			
2064	Laura Gillhespy				3.12.88	2	Carlisle	15 Jul
	3.99	13.3	6.10	1.18	2:33.6			
	(10)							
2052	Hayley Kruse				1.01.89	1	Hemel Hempstead	15 Jul
	4.26	13.7	5.41	1.39	2:44.7			

2000 Metres Walk - Track - Under 13

9:59.0	Fiona McGorum	U15	10.11.88		Leicester	18 Oct
	10:19.8	U13		1	Birmingham	29 Sep
10:38.1	Rebecca Mersh		28.01.89	2	Birmingham	29 Sep
11:35.0	Laura Gimson		14.10.90		Leicester	22 Nov

3000 Metres Walk - Track

13:14.73	Niobe Menendez		1.09.66	1	Ashford	11 Aug
	14:04.49 i			3	Birmingham	27 Jan
	14:08.70 +			1m	Birmingham	14 Jul
14:02.55 i	Sharon Tonks		18.04.70	2	Birmingham	27 Jan
	14:11.6			1	Stourport	12 May
	14:19.51			1	Birmingham	30 Jun
14:05.6	Sara-Jane Cattermole		29.01.77	1	Perth, AUS	7 Dec
	14:12.4			1	Tonbridge	16 Apr
	14:16.02 mx			1	Perth, AUS	4 Mar
14:20.70	Sophie Hales	U17	30.03.85	1	Hull	15 Sep
14:21.01	Jane Kennaugh/Gibson		26.01.73	2	Birmingham	30 Jun
14:21.90	Katie Stones	U17	22.11.85	2	Hull	15 Sep
14:22.42	Wendy Bennett	V35	21.12.65	3	Birmingham	30 Jun
14:42.2	Miranda Heathcote		18.09.72	2	Tonbridge	16 Apr
14:47.59 i	Kate Horwill		26.01.75	4	Birmingham	27 Jan
	15:17.6			2	Dudley	14 Oct
14:49.40 i	Nicola Phillips	U20	23.04.83	1	Birmingham	25 Feb
	15:46.1			3	Dudley	14 Oct
(10)						
15:13.41	Jo Hesketh		16.06.69	2	Crawley	12 May
15:17.0	Karen Ratcliffe	V40	1.06.61	2	Coventry	21 Jul
15:28.0	Kim Braznell	V45	28.02.56	1	Eton	23 Jun
15:39.97	Bryna Chrismas	U17	18.06.86	3	Hull	15 Sep
15:45.4	Verity Snook		13.11.70	2	London (WF)	19 Aug
15:45.98	Bridget Kaneen	V35	15.08.65	4	Birmingham	30 Jun
15:46.7	Natalie Geens	U17	27.12.84	4	Dudley	14 Oct
15:48.2	Claire Reeves	U20	31.07.84	5	Dudley	14 Oct
16:02.2	Ann Lewis	V50	29.12.47	1	London (BP)	20 Jun

Additional Juniors

16:03.25	Rebecca Mersh	U13	28.01.89	1	Sheffield	12 Aug
16:04.3	Jenny Gagg	U15	20.02.88	1	Hull	2 Sep
16:17.92	Nicky Reynolds	U17	24.06.85	4	Tullamore, IRL	21 Jul
16:18.92	Fiona McGorum	U13	10.11.88	2	Sheffield	12 Aug

Foreign

14:25.4	*Estle Viljoen (RSA)*	*8.07.70*	*1*	*London (WF)*	*19 Aug*

5000 Metres Walk - Track

23:46.30	Niobe Menendez		1.09.66	1	Birmingham	14 Jul
24:20.46	Sharon Tonks		18.04.70	2	Birmingham	14 Jul
24:24*	Wendy Bennett	V35	21.12.65	1	Tamworth	22 Sep
	24:35.85			3	Birmingham	14 Jul
24:43.9 mx	Sara-Jane Cattermole		29.01.77	2	Perth, AUS	21 Feb
25:16.2	Jane Kennaugh/Gibson		26.01.73	1	Douglas IOM	26 Sep
25:21*	Karen Ratcliffe	V40	1.06.61	2	Tamworth	22 Sep
25:31.5	Sophie Hales	U17	30.03.85	1	Birmingham	29 Sep
25:36.56	Miranda Heathcote		18.09.72	5	Birmingham	14 Jul
26:10.9	Kim Braznell	V45	28.02.56	1	Eton	24 Jun
26:35.5	Bridget Kaneen	V35	15.08.65	2	Douglas IOM	26 Sep
26:47.3	Katie Stones	U17	22.11.85	2	Birmingham	29 Sep

Additional Juniors

27:04.5	Bryna Chrismas	U17	18.06.86	3	Birmingham	29 Sep
27:34.7	Kelly Mann	U20	8.09.83	1	Birmingham	29 Sep
27:38.1	Nicola Phillips	U20	23.04.83	2	Birmingham	29 Sep
27:44.6	Claire Reeves	U20	31.07.84	1	Hull	14 Sep
27:57.3	Nicky Reynolds	U17	24.06.85	4	Birmingham	29 Sep
29:21.85	Natalie Geens	U17	27.12.84	3	Sheffield	12 Aug
29:34.5	Jemma Evans	U17	25.01.86	5	Birmingham	29 Sep
30:06.52	Natasha Fox	U17	21.09.85	4	Sheffield	12 Aug
	* running watch					

Foreign

24:53.02	*Estle Viljoen (RSA)*		*8.07.70*	*4*	*Birmingham*	*14 Jul*

Road

23:54	Sharon Tonks		18.04.70	1	Tamworth	2 Dec
	24:30			1	Birmingham	17 Nov
24:19	Sophie Hales	U17	30.03.85	2	Bexley	8 Dec
24:23	Sara-Jane Cattermole		29.01.77	1	Steyning	10 Jun
24:36	Wendy Bennett	V35	21.12.65	1	Leamington	21 Apr
25:11	Jane Kennaugh/Gibson		26.01.73	1	Douglas IOM	30 May
25:22	Kate Horwill		26.01.75	2	Birmingham	17 Feb
25:35	Jo Hesketh		16.06.69	3	Bexley	8 Dec
25:47	Katie Stones	U17	22.11.85	6	Budapest, HUN	9 Sep
25:52	Liz Corran	V45	23.09.55	1	Castletown IOM	14 Jan
25:59	Nicola Phillips	U20	23.04.83	2	London (VP)	4 Feb
(10)						
26:11	Bryna Chrismas	U17	18.06.86	1	Tamworth	13 Jan
26:15	Melanie Wright	V35	5.04.64	2	Tamworth	2 Dec

Additional Juniors

26:25	Natalie Geens	U17	27.12.84	3	Tamworth	2 Dec
26:32	Nicky Reynolds	U17	24.06.85	2	Birmingham	5 May
26:55	Claire Reeves	U20	31.07.84	5	Steyning	10 Jun

Foreign

24:13	*Estle Viljoen (RSA)*		*8.07.70*	*1*	*Bexley*	*8 Dec*

10000 Metres Walk - Track

49:51.6	Sara-Jane Cattermole		29.01.77	1	Perth, AUS	7 Feb
49:52.1	Niobe Menendez	V35	1.09.66	1	Birmingham	29 Sep
51:13.4	Wendy Bennett	V35	21.12.65	2	Birmingham	29 Sep
52:28.2	Karen Ratcliffe	V40	1.06.61	3	Birmingham	29 Sep
53:58.1	Jane Kennaugh/Gibson		26.01.73	4	Birmingham	29 Sep
54:27.9	Jo Hesketh		16.06.69	1	Crawley	16 Sep

Foreign

52:18.23	*Estle Viljoen (RSA)*		*8.07.70*	*1*	*London (He)*	*12 Aug*

10 Kilometres Walk - Road

47:05	Sara-Jane Cattermole		29.01.77	1	Cambridge, AUS	15 Jul
	48:28			1	Murdoch, AUS	26 Aug
	50:42			3	Birmingham	5 May
48:08	Niobe Menendez	V35	1.09.66	1	Birmingham	17 Nov
	49:19	-		2	Birmingham	5 May
	49:37 +	-		10m	Dublin, IRL	16 Jun
48:16	Lisa Kehler		15.03.67	1	Birmingham	15 Dec
48:58	Wendy Bennett	V35	21.12.65	1	Worcester	20 Oct
	49:36			2	Birmingham	17 Nov
	50:18			1	Tamworth	2 Dec
	50:45			4	Birmingham	5 May

51:45	Karen Ratcliffe	V40	1.06.61	2	Worcester	20	Oct
52:48	Catherine Charnock		3.05.75	6	Birmingham	5	May
53:04	Sharon Tonks		18.04.70	1	Leek Wootton	18	Aug
53:08	Jo Hesketh		16.06.69	15	Lanciano, ITA	11	Mar
53:11	Miranda Heathcote		18.09.72	7	Birmingham	5	May
53:18	Sophie Hales	U17	30.03.85	1	Leamington	21	Apr
(10)							
53:36	Jane Kennaugh/Gibson		26.01.73	1	Castletown IOM	15	Aug
53:46	Liz Corran	V45	23.09.55	1	Douglas IOM	21	Jan
53:55	Kate Horwill		26.01.75	2	Tamworth	2	Dec
54:27	Bridget Kaneen	V35	15.08.65	1	St. Johns IOM	16	Dec
54:35	Sally Warren		29.01.78	3	Molesey	7	Jan
54:40	Katie Stones	U17	22.11.85	2	Leamington	21	Apr
55:08	Claire Reeves	U20	31.07.84	3	Leamington	21	Apr
56:56	Sarah Graves/Chetwynd		4.06.74	3	Tamworth	2	Dec
57:12	Natalie Geens	U17	27.12.84	4	Leamington	21	Apr
57:13	Bryna Chrismas	U17	18.06.86	5	Leamington	21	Apr

Foreign

51:41	*Estle Viljoen (RSA)*		*8.07.70*	*5*	*Birmingham*	*5*	*May*

20 Kilometres Walk Road

1:39:10	Sara-Jane Cattermole		29.01.77	1	Murdoch, AUS	21	Jan
	1:39:41			1	Perth, AUS	29	Jul
	1:40:42			1	Murdoch, AUS	9	Dec
	1:47:35			6	Leamington	21	Apr
	1:49:50			1	Basildon	26	May
1:41:37	Niobe Menendez		1.09.66	8	Dublin, IRL	16	Jun
	1:42:08			3	Mohlin, SUI	9	Sep
	1:45:19			4	Leamington	21	Apr
1:46:15	Sharon Tonks		18.04.70	5	Leamington	21	Apr
	1:46:53			6	Mohlin, SUI	9	Sep
1:47:39	Jane Kennaugh/Gibson		26.01.73	14	Dublin, IRL	16	Jun
	1:48:55			7	Leamington	21	Apr
1:47:46	Wendy Bennett	V35	21.12.65	15	Dublin, IRL	16	Jun
1:50:35	Jo Hesketh		16.06.69	8	Leamington	21	Apr
1:52:54	Liz Corran	V45	23.09.55	4	Douglas IOM	17	Feb
1:54:11	Miranda Heathcote		18.09.72	2	Basildon	26	May
1:55:46	Bridget Kaneen	V35	15.08.65	17	Dublin, IRL	16	Jun

Foreign

1:47:18	*Estle Viljoen (RSA)*		*8.07.70*	*13*	*Dublin, IRL*	*16*	*Jun*

50 Kilometres Walk Road

5:44:24	Marie Latham	V40	18.10.60	1	Isle of Man	29	Apr

100 Miles Walk Road

20:36:45	Sandra Brown	V50	1.04.49	1	Colchester	5	Aug

4 x 100 METRES

42.60	National Team	6	Edmonton, CAN	11 Aug
	(M.Richardson, S.Wilhelmy, V.James, A.Oyepitan)			
43.08	National Team	3h2	Edmonton, CAN	11 Aug
	(M.Richardson, S.Wilhelmy, V.James, A.Oyepitan)			
43.53	National Team	4	Bremen, GER	23 Jun
	(D.Allahgreen, M.Richardson, J.Maduaka, S.Anderson)			
43.77	National Team	1	Arles, FRA	10 Jun
44.18	National Team	2	Glasgow (S)	1 Jul
	(D.Allahgreen, M.Richardson, J.Maduaka, S.Anderson)			
44.31	National Under 23 Team	1	Amsterdam, NED	15 Jul
	(S.Burnside, H.Roscoe, S.Scott, A.Oyepitan)			
44.66	England	1	Loughborough	20 May
	(J.Whitlock, J.Maduaka, S.Scott, S.Anderson)			
44.66	National Junior Team U20	3	Grossetto, ITA	22 Jul
	(D.Norville, E.Caney, A.Spencer, V.James)			
45.24	British Universities	2	Loughborough	20 May
	(D.Allahgreen, R.White, E.Freeman, A.Oyepitan)			
45.25	National Junior Team U20	3	Mannheim, GER	16 Jun
	(A.Spencer, D.Norville, V.James, A.Oyepitan)			
45.30	National Junior Team U20	3	Loughborough	20 May
	(K Oughton, E.Caney, A.Spencer, V.James)			
45.42	National Junior Team U20	1	Liverpool	23 Jun
	(D.Norville, E.Caney, A.Spencer, V.James)			
45.54	National U23 Team	2	Liverpool	23 Jun
	(A.Oyepitan, S.Burnside, S.Scott, H.Roscoe)			
45.73	National Junior Team U20	2	Stoke-on-Trent	18 Aug
	(A.Onuorah, D.Norville, A.Spencer, J.Lucas-Read)			
45.94	National Team U19	2	Dole, FRA	29 Jul
	(Amaia Onuora, D.Norville, E.Caney, Anyika Onuora)			
46.08	UK 'B' Team	2	Ashford	11 Aug
	(K.Thomas, Susan Williams, H.Roscoe, E.Freeman)			
46.22	Sale Harriers Manchester	7	Madrid, ESP	26 May
	(M.Veldman, H.Roscoe, A.Danson, R.White)			
46.32	Loughborough University	4	Loughborough	20 May
	(K.Thomas, H.Roscoe, K.Palmer, M.Purkiss)			

With one non-UK athlete

44.72	Shaftesbury Barnet Harriers	1	Eton	7 Jul
	(*C.Ajunwa NGR*, C.Murphy, N.Campbell, S.Anderson)			

Additional National Teams

46.77	Scotland	5	Loughborough	20 May
	(C.McKenna, C.McRooney, S.Burnside, K.Sketchley)			
48.12	Wales Under 23 Team	3	Derby	29 Jul
49.58	Northern Ireland	2	Barry	2 Jun
49.83	Jersey	2	Douglas	Jul

Additional Club Teams (1- 3 above)

46.42	Windsor Slough E & H AC	2	Eton	7 Jul
46.57	Belgrave Harriers	1	Bedford	21 Jul
47.08	Wakefield Harriers	4	Eton	7 Jul
47.3	Edinburgh Woollen Mill	1	Wigan	4 Aug
47.53	Walton AC	1	Bedford	22 Jul
47.54	Birchfield Harriers	2	Bedford	21 Jul
47.74	Shaftesbury Barnet Harriers	4	Birmingham	2 Jun
48.0	Liverpool Harriers AC	1	Liverpool	May
48.1	Wigan & District H and AC	1	Croydon	3 Jun
48.1	City of Glasgow AC	1	Coventry	5 Aug

48.1	Coventry Godiva Harriers		2	Coventry	5 Aug
48.11	Gateshead Harriers & AC		1	Cudworth	26 Aug
48.15	Trafford AC		5	Birmingham	2 Jun
48.2	Team Solent		1	Rugby	3 Jun
48.57	Liverpool Harriers AC	U17	1	Birmingham	2 Sep
48.72	Woodford Green & Essex Ladies		8	Birmingham	2 Jun
48.8	Basildon AC		1	Guildford	23 Jun
48.8	Newham & Essex Beagles		1	London (Nh)	11 Aug
48.84	UWIC		2	Glasgow (S)	7 May
48.85	Pitreavie AAC	U17	1	Grangemouth	26 Aug
48.9	Rugby & District AC		2	Rugby	3 Jun
49.0	Horsham Blue Star Harriers		1	Colchester	23 Jun
49.0	Cardiff AAC		1	Eton	5 Aug

Additional Under 20 Teams (1 - 6 above)

46.48	Great Britain	U18	2	Murcia, ESP	25 Jul
46.57	Midlands		1	Ipswich	2 Sep
47.52	Midlands		1	Derby	29 Jul
47.53	London Schools	U19	1	Exeter	7 Jul
48.44	Scotland		2	Corinth, GRE	26 May
50.0	AA of Wales		1	Brecon	18 Jul
50.6	Northern Ireland		2	Brecon	18 Jul

Additional Under 20 Club Teams (1 - 2 above)

49.5	Wakefield Harriers	U17	1	Wakefield	1 Jul
49.5	Trafford AC		2	Stoke-on-Trent	17 Jun
49.66	Sale Harriers Manchester		1	Derby	9 Sep
49.7	Birchfield Harriers		1	Wakefield	29 Jul
49.9	Windsor Slough E & H AC	U17	1	Eton	1 Jul
50.0	Edinburgh Woollen Mill		3	Wakefield	29 Jul

Additional Under 17 Teams (1 - 2 above)

47.65	England Schools		1	Tullamore, IRL	21 Jul
47.72	Kent Schools		1	Exeter	7 Jul
47.98	Scotland Schools		3	Tullamore, IRL	21 Jul
48.3	Kent AA		1	Crawley	5 Aug
48.4	Middlesex AA		2	Crawley	5 Aug
48.68	Buckinghamshire Schools		2	Exeter	7 Jul
48.98	Scotland	U16	1	Connah's Quay	4 Aug
49.10	Wales Schools		4	Tullamore, IRL	21 Jul

Additional Under 17 Club Teams (1 - 4 above)

50.06	Edinburgh Woollen Mill		2	Glasgow (S)	24 Jun
50.08	Edinburgh Woollen Mill	U15	1	Edinburgh	25 Aug
50.1	Sale Harriers Manchester		2	Wakefield	1 Jul
50.2	Herne Hill Harriers	U15	1	London (TB)	14 Jul
50.2	Bromley Ladies		1	Tonbridge	9 Sep
50.3	Cannock & Stafford AC		1	Stafford	20 May
50.3	Gateshead Harriers & AC		1	Rotherham	20 May
50.3	Dudley & Stourbridge AC		1	Coventry	20 May

Additional Under 15 Teams (1 - 2 above)

49.45	London Schools	1h3	Exeter	7 Jul
50.11	Surrey Schools	2	Exeter	7 Jul
50.30	Greater Manchester Schools	1	Stoke-on-Trent	17 Jun

Additional Under 15 Club Teams (1 - 2 above)

50.5	Leicester Coritanian AC	1	Tipton	24 Jun
50.6	Blackheath Harriers	1	Tonbridge	9 Sep
50.6	Newham & Essex Beagles	1	Basildon	22 Sep

50.80	West Midlands Schools		2	Stoke-on-Trent	17 Jun
51.00	Merseyside Schools		3	Stoke-on-Trent	17 Jun
51.0	Sale Harriers Manchester		1	Wakefield	1 Jul
51.1	Enfield & Haringey AC		1	Enfield	1 Jul
51.3	Dartford Harriers		h	Tonbridge	9 Sep
51.39	Wigan and District H & AC		3	Birmingham	2 Sep
51.4	Havering Mayesbrook AC		1	Kingston	14 Jul

Under 13 Teams

53.8	Edinburgh Woollen Mill		1	Coatbridge	29 Jul
53.8	Kent AA		1rB	Kingston	29 Jul
54.0	Wolverhampton & Bilston AC		1	Birmingham	22 Jul
54.1	Liverpool Harriers AC		1	Liverpool	May
54.22	Birchfield Harriers		1	Birmingham	1 Sep
54.60	Giffnock North AC		1	Glasgow (S)	24 Jun
54.9	Blackheath Harriers		1	Tonbridge	9 Sep
54.9	Bromley Ladies		2	Tonbridge	9 Sep
55.1	Ipswich Harriers		1	Bury St Edmunds	1 Jul
55.10	City of Edinburgh AC		2	Edinburgh	25 Aug
55.4	Birmingham Rowheath		1	Sutton Coldfield	1 Jul

4 x 200 METRES

1:41.47 i	Loughborough University		1	Glasgow	Feb
1:43.76 i	University College in Cardiff		2	Glasgow	Feb
1:44.23 i	Birmingham University		3	Glasgow	Feb
1:45.19 i	Glasgow University		1	Glasgow	7 Feb
1:46.2	Bromley Ladies	U17	1	Tonbridge	9 Sep
1:46.32 i	Dunfermline & West Fife	U17	1	Glasgow	21 Jan
1:46.48	Inverness H		1	Inverness	5 Aug
1:47.0	Cambridge University		1	Oxford	4 Mar
1:47.6	Medway & Maidstone AC	U17	2	Tonbridge	9 Sep
1:47.62 i	Brunel University		3	Birmingham	13 Feb

Additional Under 17 Teams (1 - 3 above)

1:47.70 i	Pitreavie AAC		2	Glasgow	21 Jan
1:48.9	Blackheath Harriers	U15	1	Tonbridge	9 Sep
1:49.8	Dartford Harriers	U15	h	Tonbridge	9 Sep
1:50.18 i	Giffnock North AC		1	Glasgow	11 Mar
1:50.86 i	Livingston & District AC		3	Glasgow	21 Jan
1:51.7	Blackheath Harriers		3	Tonbridge	9 Sep

Additional Under 15 Teams (1 - 2 above)

1:52.1	Bexley AC		3	Tonbridge	9 Sep
1:54.61 i	Pitreavie AAC		1	Glasgow	21 Jan
1:55.23 i	Falkirk Victoria H		1h3	Glasgow	11 Mar
1:55.64 i	Giffnock North AC		1h1	Glasgow	11 Mar
1:55.71 i	Central Region AC		2h3	Glasgow	11 Mar
1:55.76 i	Ayr Seaforth AAC		2h1	Glasgow	11 Mar
1:56.04	Elgin		1	Inverness	5 Aug
1:56.35 i	Kirkintilloch Olympians		5	Glasgow	11 Mar

Under 13 Teams

2:03.13	Inverness H		1	Inverness	5 Aug
2:11.4	Aberdeen AAC		1	Dundee	8 Jul
2:00.12 i	Giffnock North AC		1	Glasgow	11 Mar
2:04.09 i	Harmeny AC		2	Glasgow	21 Jan
2:04.11 i	Whitemoss AC		1h3	Glasgow	11 Mar
2:04.60 i	West Dunbartonshire		1h2	Glasgow	11 Mar
2:05.24 i	Victoria Park AAC		2	Glasgow	11 Mar
2:05.67 i	Ayr Seaforth AAC		4	Glasgow	11 Mar

4 x 400 METRES

3:26.94	National Team		5	Edmonton, CAN	12 Aug
	(L.McConnell 52.3 H.Frost 51.1 N.Danvers 51.97 C.Murphy 51.65)				
3:27.25	National Team		2h2	Edmonton, CAN	11 Aug
	(L.McConnell 52.5 L.Owusu 51.7 C.Murphy 51.49 D.Fraser 51.57)				
3:28.15	National Team		4	Bremen, GER	24 Jun
	(C.Murphy 52.1 H.Frost 51.9 T.Blake 52.15 L.Owusu 51.96)				
3:30.40	National Students Team		2	Beijing, CHN	1 Sep
	(T Duncan, N Danvers, J.Meadows 52.1 L.McConnell 51.50)				
3:31.74	National Under 23 Team		1	Amsterdam, NED	15 Jul
	(K.Gear, J.Meadows, T.Duncan, H.Thieme)				
3:34.37	England		1	Edinburgh	25 Aug
	(K.Gear, K.Wall, L.Miller, H.Frost)				
3:34.63	National Junior Team	U20	1	Grossetto, ITA	22 Jul
	(K.Wall, O.Hines, V.James, L.Miller)				
3:35.55	Scotland		5	Walnut, USA	22 Apr
	(C.Easton, A.Curbishley, M.McClung, S.Dudgeon)				
3:36.39	National Junior Team	U20	1	Stoke-on-Trent	18 Aug
	(O.Hines, L.Clarkson, L.Miller, K.Wall)				
3:36.66	Birchfield Harriers		1	Birmingham	2 Jun
	(M.Thomas, H.Thieme, K.Sotherton, K.Merry 51.5u)				
3:37.96	Scotland		2	Loughborough	20 May
	(L.Whigham 56.4, M.McClung 54.7 C.Easton 54.7 A.Curbishley 52.2)				
3:38.31	National Junior Team	U20	3	Loughborough	20 May
	(R.Scotcher, K.Wall, L.Miller, G.Howell)				
3:38.70	National Under 23 Team		1	Liverpool	23 Jun
	(K.Gear 53.18 J.Meadows 55.05 T.Duncan 55.96 H.Thieme 54.51)				
3:39.04	National Team	U19	1	Dole, FRA	29 Jul
	(O.Hines, C.Ohurugu, L.Miller, K.Wall)				
3:39.95	England		4	Loughborough	20 May
	(K.Jones, N.Ceesay, J.Mitchell, V.Day)				
3:40.15	Edinburgh Woollen Mill		2	Birmingham	2 Jun
	(L.Vannet, S.Dudgeon, C.Easton, A.Curbishley)				
3:40.25	British Universities		5	Loughborough	20 May
	(H.Wood, J.Meadows, N.Sanders, C.Brown)				
3:40.27	National Team		1	Ashford	11 Aug
	(K.Gear, L.Cresswell, T.Duncan, J.Meadows)				
3:40.51 i	National Team		3	Glasgow	18 Mar
	(H.Thieme 55.76 S.Dudgeon 53.47 C.Murphy 54.84 D.Fraser 56.44)				
3:41.51 i	GB Lions		4	Glasgow	18 Mar
	(E.Symonds, J.Mitchell, K Sage, J.Meadows)				
3:41.55	Scotland		3	Edinburgh	25 Aug
	(L.Whigham, C.Easton, L.Clarkson, M.McClung)				

Additional National Teams

3:43.56 i	National Under 23 Team	1	Cardiff	10 Mar
	(H.Brooks, A.Pritchard, J.Meadows, H.Thieme)			
3:51.26	Northern Ireland	4	Edinburgh	25 Aug
	(V.Jamison, T.Stephens, Z.Arnold, Long)			
3:54.66	Wales	6	Edinburgh	25 Aug
	(D.Porazinski, S.Newman, K.Williams, M.Whitehead)			
3:59.78	Jersey	1	Douglas	Jul
4:04.55	Isle of Man	2	Douglas	Jul

Additional Club Teams (1- 3 above)

3:43.0	Windsor Slough E & H AC	1	Wigan	4 Aug
3:43.92	Belgrave Harriers	2	Bedford	21 Jul
3:43.95	Woodford Green & Essex Ladies	1	Eton	7 Jul
3:46.7	Trafford AC	4	Wigan	4 Aug
3:46.72	Birmingham University	2	Glasgow (S)	7 May

3:47.2	Wigan and District H & AC		1	Croydon	3 Jun
3:47.5	Peterborough AC		1	Rugby	3 Jun
3:48.01	Sale Harriers Manchester		8	Madrid, ESP	27 May
3:48.3	City of Stoke AC		2	Croydon	3 Jun
3:48.5	City of Norwich AC		2	Rugby	3 Jun
3:50.4	Team Solent		3	Rugby	3 Jun
3:51.62	Shaftesbury Barnet Harriers		6	Eton	7 Jul
3:52.9	Bristol AC		1	Rugby	19 Aug
3:53.9	Royal Sutton Coldfield		1	Birmingham	24 Jun
3:54.24	Walton AC		1	Bedford	22 Jul
3:54.4	Dunfermline & West Fife		1	Coatbridge	29 Jul
3:56.6	Kingston-upon-Hull AC		1	Scunthorpe	3 Jun
3:56.7	Crawley AC		1	Oxford	23 Jun
3:56.9	Herne Hill Harriers		1	London (Nh)	11 Aug
3:57.0	Basingstoke & Mid Hants AC		1	Eton	5 Aug

Additional Under 20 Teams (1-4 above)

3:51.31	South of England	1	Ipswich	2 Sep
3:51.82i	Great Britain U20	3	Vittel, FRA	3 Mar

Additional Under 20 National Teams

3:55.94	Scotland	3	Corinth, GRE	27 May
4:05.0	AA of Wales	1	Brecon	18 Jul

Under 20 Club Teams

3:57.28	Sale Harriers Manchester	1	Rennes, FRA	22 Sep
4:00.9	Edinburgh Woollen Mill	2	Wakefield	29 Jul
4:01.0	Hertford & Ware AC	1	Southampton	19 May
4:01.2	Liverpool Hariers AC	3	Wakefield	29 Jul
4:01.7	Trafford AC	1	Stoke-on-Trent	17 Jun
4:01.95	Birchfield Harriers	2	Derby	9 Sep

Under 17 Club Team

4:07.8	Tamworth AC	1	Mansfield	19 Aug

With Foreign athletes

3:37.27	Loughborough Students	1	Loughborough	20 May
	(*M.Marks USA, M.Carey IRL*, L.McConnell, L.Cresswell)			
3:40.39	Loughborough Students	1	Glasgow (S)	7 May
	(*M.Carey IRL, C.Nylen SWE*, L.Creswell, M.Marks USA)			

3 x 800 METRES

Under 17 Club Teams

7:01.65	Central AC		1	Glasgow (S)	24 Jun
7:01.94	Pitreavie AAC	U15	1	Glasgow (S)	24 Jun
7:02.98	Pitreavie AAC		2	Glasgow (S)	24 Jun
7:09.0	Medway & Maidstone AC		1	Tonbridge	9 Sep

Additional Under 15 Club Teams (1 above)

7:10.8	Havering Mayesbrook AC	1	Basildon	22 Sep
7:17.7	Woodford Green & Essex Ladies	2	Basildon	22 Sep
7:18.0	Vale Royal AC	1	Macclesfield	10 Jul

Under 13 Teams

7:43.33	Stewartry	1	Glasgow (S)	24 Jun
7:51.2	Stockport Harriers	1	Macclesfield	19 Jun
7:52.96	Harmeny AC	2	Glasgow (S)	24 Jun

1600 METRES MEDLEY

3:54.77 i	England	1	Cardiff	11 Feb
	(E.Freeman, K.Gear, Mitchell, Ruddock)			
3:59.77 i	Midland Counties	1	Cardiff	17 Feb
	(M.Cooksey, H.Thieme, K.Sotherton, Entwhistle)			

MENS INDEX

AARONS Stephen U13 25.10.88, Bexley :
DTC - 25.01
ABERNETHY David James V45 5.09.55, Barrow & F :
SP - 13.99 (14.59-85), DT - 44.92 (46.70-85)
ABEYIE Timothy U20 7.11.82, Belgrave :
100 - 10.42w/10.6/10.69 (10.63-00),
200 - 21.31w/21.4/21.55 (21.3w/21.40-00)
ABLITT Steven U20 16.11.83, Grantham :
3k - 8:35.25, 5k - 15:04.51
ACHIKE Onochie 'Larry' 31.01.75, Shaftesbury Barn :
TJ - 17.21 (17.31w/17.30-00)
ACHURCH Simon 27.12.74, Bedford & County :
DT - 40.57
ADAMS Allan 11.09.72, Clydesdale :
10MR - 49:51 (47:54dh-96/49:28-98),
HMar - 65:39 (64:05-97), Mar - 2:22:22
ADAMS Christopher U23 18.07.81, City of Stoke :
HT - 51.89
ADAMS Nathan U20 14.04.82, Sheffield RWC :
5kW - 23:44.5 (23:28.0-99)
ADAMS Philip 3.11.71, Charnwood :
SP - 13.92 (15.78-97)
ADAMS Raymond U23 5.11.81, Lagan Valley/Birch :
800 - 1:50.56 (1:49.33-00)
ADEJUWON O. Adedamola 27.11.76, Sheff/Hallam U :
TJ - 14.37i/14.34
ADEMUYEWO Adebowale U20 14.05.83, Sale :
100 - 10.78w/10.90
AFILAKA Michael 16.11.71, N & E B/Coventry Un. :
200 - 22.0/22.02 (21.09w-93/21.2-95/21.22-94)
AGUIRREBURUALDE David U17 29.11.85, Preston :
100 - 11.16w (11.56-00)
AGYEPONG Francis Keita 16.06.65, Shaftesbury B :
TJ - 14.72w/14.19 (17.29wA/17.24w/17.18-95)
AIDOO Richard U17 15.02.85, Croydon :
100HY - 13.50w/13.60
AIREY Martin 28.10.70, Blackheath :
1500 - 3:49.55 (3:48.0-96)
AKEHURST Adam U15 13.09.87, Portsmouth :
JTB - 44.04
AKINSANYA Oluwafemi 29.11.69, Peterborough :
LJ - 7.31 (7.37-96),
TJ - 16.28w/15.96 (16.63A-99/16.58-96)
AKPABIO Charles, Herne Hill :
110H - 15.5
AL-AMEEN Alex U13 2.03.89, Blackheath :
80HC - 13.7, DTC - 28.04
ALERT-KHAN Jamahl U15 12.09.86, Shaftesbury B :
100 - 11.11w/11.17, 200 - 22.28w/22.58
ALEXANDER Stephen U17 6.10.84, Trafford :
100HY - 13.23, HJ - 1.96,
LJ - 6.89w/6.73, OctY - 4757
ALEXANDER Tim U23 6.09.79, Medway/B'mouth U :
800 - 1:50.9
ALEXIS Chris U17 29.12.84, Harrow :
LJ - 6.56, TJ - 13.92
ALEXIS-SMITH Richard U15 13.02.87, Sutton & Dist :
80HB - 10.68w/10.82, 100HY - 14.0
ALFRED Ricky 20.12.77, Bedford & County :
100 - 10.7w/10.91 (10.7w/10.87w/10.88-00),
200 - 21.8/21.92 (21.5/21.63w-00)
ALI Abdi U20 26.12.82, WGreen & Ex L :
2kSt - 6:09.5, 3kSt - 9:36.4
ALI Ahmed U17 31.03.86, Newham & Essex B :
800 - 1:54.29, 1500 - 3:56.6, 3k - 8:44.82
ALIX James U23 24.12.81, Dudley & Stour/Leics U :
HJ - 2.00 (2.06-98)
ALLAN Andrew U15 9.04.88, Giffnock :
HJ - 1.75i (1.55-00)
ALLAN David Neil 17.10.70, Border/Pitreavie :
HT - 62.25 (63.71-99)
ALLAN Graeme S. U23 24.09.80, Shaft B/Arbroath :
SP - 14.41 (15.69-00), DT - 41.65 (45.47-00),
HT - 61.04
ALLAN Sam U13 16.09.88, Leeds :
SPC - 11.26
ALLEN Christopher U13 24.03.89, Ilford :
DTC - 26.35
ALLEN Mark U17, Corby :
PV - 3.60
ALLEN Michael U23 7.03.80, Ballymena & A/Border :
LJ - 6.90i, JT - 59.77 (68.34-00)
ALLERTON Ian U17 18.04.85, Blackheath :
400 - 50.70
ALLEYNE R. U17, WGreen & Ex L :
110HJ - 14.9
ALLISON Matthew 26.02.73, Leeds :
JT - 63.16
AMES Steve U17 2.07.85, Bedford Harriers :
3k - 8:58.9
AMOS Glyn V40 30.03.58, Middlesbro & C :
JT - 58.64 (64.48-88)
AMOS Guy 15.06.63, City of Norwich :
3k - 8:23.04, 5k - 13:56.44,
HMar - 64:50 (64:46-00)
ANDERSON David 2.10.77, Elswick :
800 - 1:52.7, 1500 - 3:46.77, 1M - 4:07.7
ANDERSON Ian 23.03.71, Knavesmire :
100kR - 7:17:18
ANDERSON James U15 11.05.87, Woking :
JTB - 45.92
ANDERSON S., Vale of Aylesbury :
100H - 14.5
ANDREWS Nicholas Temperton U23 3.10.81, S Devon :
800 - 1:52.4 (1:49.08-99)
ANIMASHAUN Alexander U17 23.07.85, Harrow :
100 - 11.1/11.17w (12.16-99)
ANKERS Luke U15 23.10.86, :
HJ - 1.75
ANOMELECHI Enyioma U17 10.03.85, Croydon :
TJ - 14.15w/13.70i/13.64
ANOMELECHI Ugochi U20 29.10.83, Croydon :
100 - 10.8w/10.96w/10.98 (10.88w/10.93-00)
ANTHONY Tristan U20 16.12.82, Verlea :
110HJ - 14.16, 110H - 14.64w/14.8/14.81 (14.8-99)
APLIN Aaron Andrew U20 25.11.83, Notts :
200 - 21.9w/22.08i/22.24 (21.76-00)
APPIAH Joe 26.10.70, Kent :
Dec - 5015
ARAM Martin B. Sheehy U20 2.12.83, Liverpool H :
HJ - 2.10 (2.10-00), SP - 13.00, SPJ - 14.01
ARBUTHNOT Stewart U15 9.09.86, Bournemouth :
HTB - 42.32
ARD Paul Robert U20 14.10.82, Oadby & Wigston :
800 - 1:53.21
ARMSTRONG Daniel U17 16.11.84, Sheffield :
100HY - 13.82, OctY - 4701
ARMSTRONG Ryan U17 11.07.85, Liverpool H :
1.5kSt - 4:31.13
ARMSTRONG Samuel 17.02.74, Border/Law & Dist :
JT - 60.45 (65.31-98)
ARMSTRONG Simon John 29.05.62, Bournemouth :
SP - 13.73 (16.52-90), DT - 40.76 (50.22-92)
ARNOLD James 26.02.66, Matlock :
Mar - 2:34:38
ASH James U15 1.09.86, Cheltenham :
400 - 53.5/53.60
ASHE Richard 5.10.74, Harrow :
800 - 1:50.5 (1:49.38-96),
1500 - 3:42.58 (3:41.2-96)
ASHTON Matthew U17 13.12.84, Witney :
3k - 8:54.90

ASHTON Sean U17 20.09.85, Leics Cor :
100HY - 14.0
ASPDEN Richard William 15.10.76, Belgrave :
HJ - 2.05 (2.17i-99/2.16-95)
ATKINSON Gary U15 7.01.87, Sale :
100 - 11.5/11.59, 200 - 22.8w/23.00
ATKINSON Jason U17 28.10.85, Cwmbran :
800 - 1:57.44
ATTON Karl Ronald 14.09.71, Roadhogs :
10kWR - 47:15 (45:40-89),
20kW - 1:35:03 (1:33:41-99),
50kW - 4:18:59 (4:16:30-97)
ATTWOOD David U15 5.04.87, Bristol :
DTB - 38.16
AUBYN-YAO Sosthene U15 7.08.87, Lewisham :
100 - 11.11w/11.4/11.43, 200 - 23.1,
80HB - 11.9, PenB - 2641
AWANAH Mark U20 23.09.82, Blackheath :
200 - 22.15, LJ - 7.66w/7.25 (7.37-00), TJ - 14.27w
AWDE Christopher U17 14.02.85, WGreen & Ex L :
100HY - 14.0, DTY - 41.03, OctY - 4923

BABB Jacob U17 7.12.85, Wessex & Bath :
SPY - 14.91
BACKLEY Stephen James 12.02.69, Cambridge H :
JT - 90.81 (91.46-92)
BADDELEY Andrew James U20 20.06.82, Wirral/
Cambridge University : 800 - 1:52.6 (1:51.92-00),
1500 - 3:52.15 (3:46.36-00)
BADERIN Richard Adekunmi U20 25.03.83, Liv H :
110HJ - 15.29 (15.0w/15.15w/15.2-00
BAILEY James U20 1.10.82, Sale :
2kSt - 5:58.12, 3kSt - 9:45.56 (9:31.2-00)
BAILEY Stuart 6.08.78, Sale :
800 - 1:50.70 (1:49.46-00), 1500 - 3:49.21 (3:45.6-98)
BAILLIE Christopher U23 21.04.81, Bir/Vict Park AAC :
60H - 7.91i, 110H - 13.70w/13.82
BAIRD Lawrence W. 14.12.77, Kingston u H/Sheff U :
100 - 10.90 (10.62w-98),
200 - 22.10 (21.6w-99/21.64w/21.8-00,
400 - 47.97 (47.56i-98/47.83-97)
BAKER Chris U17 30.09.84, Worthing :
HTY - 48.17
BAKER George 14.08.76, Newham & Essex B :
SP - 14.07 (15.22-97)
BAKER Michael U13 6.04.90, Medway :
75HC - 12.7
BALDOCK Sean Michael 3.12.76, Belgrave :
200 - 21.43w (21.1w-97), 400 - 46.35 (45.20-00)
BALDWIN Stefan Mark 26.04.70, Peterborough :
JT - 64.40 (72.92-93)
BALSDON Wayne U20 14.01.83, Newquay & Par :
DecJ - 5108 (5222-00)
BANGS Neil U23 28.03.80, Thurrock :
800 - 1:52.2, 1500 - 3:48.54, 3k - 8:15.90
BANKS Philip U20 8.03.83, AF&D :
3k - 8:32.5
BANNISTER Dominic 1.04.68, Shaftesbury Barnet :
5k - 14:35.78 (13:52.31-97), 10kR - 29:48 (29:39-99)
BAPTIST Olu 19.10.78, Cambridge Harriers :
LJ - 6.99i (7.01-00)
BAPTISTE Leon U17 23.05.85, Enf & Har :
100 - 10.87, 200 - 21.72
BARBOUR Jonathan U23 3.11.80, Blackheath :
100 - 10.13w/10.28 (10.28-00), 200 - 20.78
BARCIS Thomas U20 30.05.83, Peterborough :
JT - 56.12
BARCLAY Matthew U17 1.11.84, Crawley :
100 - 11.0, 200 - 22.40w/22.4 (24.24-99),
LJ - 6.95w/6.79
BARDEN Spencer Christian 31.03.73, Belgrave :
3k - 8:00.92 (7:53.2-97),
5k - 13:54.26 (13:43.84-97)
BARGH Andrew 21.08.76, Team Solent :
400H - 52.64 (52.4-96/52.47-98)
BARKER Jesse U15 7.03.87, Enf & Har :
800 - 2:04.48
BARNARD Paul 27.07.72, Birchfield/North East SH :
HT - 59.02 (62.70-95)
BARNES-SMITH Matthew U17 5.10.85, Ipswich :
3k - 8:46.0
BARRETT Clint 21.11.77, Chelmsford :
Dec - 5376 (5551-99)
BARRETT Oliver U17 25.12.84, Ipswich :
400 - 50.5, 800 - 1:55.50
BARRETT Simon U15 23.04.87, Harrow :
DTB - 38.06
BARRETT Wayne U15 9.12.86, Wilts Sch :
TJ - 12.28
BARTLETT Andrew U15 17.02.87, Havant :
100 - 11.30w/11.36, 200 - 22.94w/23.04, 400 - 53.3
BARTON Matthew U23 22.05.81, Isle of Wight :
TJ - 14.13
BARTON Neil U23 18.07.80, Verlea/Manchester Un :
LJ - 6.92 (7.07-00)
BARTON SMITH Michael U15 2.05.87, Isle of Wight :
HTB - 45.64
BARTON Tim D. 3.10.70, Charnwood :
60 - 6.94i (6.92i-98),
100 - 10.8/10.84 (10.55w-98/10.67-97)
BATCHELOR Perry 11.12.75, Rugby :
60H - 8.23i, 110H - 14.50w/14.54
BATE Roger U20 16.01.83, Warrington :
DT - 40.46, DTJ - 45.44, HT - 46.39, HTJ - 55.82
BATES Darren U15 22.04.87, Mersey Schools :
TJ - 12.03
BATES Neil U20 5.04.84, Manx :
5kW - 24:15.1
BATES Stephen U17 9.09.84, Croydon :
HTY - 50.15
BATTEN Grant U15 11.12.86, Erme Valley :
TJ - 12.01
BATTEN Richard U13 12.10.88, :
100 - 12.6
BATTEN Ross U13 1.03.89, Erme Valley :
JTC - 35.03
BATY Jonathan U15 1.02.87, Stratford :
400 - 53.2, 80HB - 11.5w/11.77, PenB - 2614
BAUER David 25.03.66, Harlow :
DT - 40.65
BAULCH James Steven 3.05.73, Cardiff :
100 - 10.79 (10.51-95), 400 - 46.15 (44.57-96)
200 - 20.93w/21.02i/21.5 (20.84-94),
BAXTER Joshua Nicholas U13 15.09.88, Reading :
100 - 12.3, 200 - 25.80, LJ - 5.19
BAYLEY Tim U23 4.10.81, Belgrave :
200 - 21.81, 400 - 47.52
BEACOM Greg 26.02.78, Portsmouth :
HJ - 1.95 (1.95-99)
BEARD Gregory U20 10.09.82, Belgrave :
SP - 16.38i/16.32 (16.69-00), SPJ - 18.06,
DT - 47.20 (47.90-00), DTJ - 52.20, HTJ - 52.18
BEARD Keith Alan V40 8.11.61, Leiden :
JT - 68.08 (76.10r-91/73.88-90)
BEARMAN Donald J. 16.04.66, Steyning :
10kWR - 43:23, 20kW - 1:29:56
BEASLEY Graham Alexander 24.10.77, Belgrave :
100 - 10.64w/10.65 (10.54w-99),
200 - 20.83w/21.18 (21.03-99), 400 - 48.4
BEAUCHAMP William Ronald 9.09.70, Thames V H :
HT - 72.60 (72.63-99)
BEAUFORD Adam U23 24.10.81, Yeovil Olympiads :
HT - 53.77
BEAUMONT Paul 27.03.63, Belgrave/Army :
110H - 15.0

BEDFORD Tom U20 12.12.83, Shaftesbury Barnet :
2kSt - 6:02.5
BEECH Alexander 17.04.77, Med & Maid :
110H - 15.4
BEEKEN George U15 4.09.86, Corby :
80HB - 11.49, HJ - 1.75, PenB - 2658
BEHARRELL Mark U23 10.01.81, Sale :
PV - 4.60i/4.40 (4.91-99)
BELL Andrew U17 2.09.84, Milton Keynes :
TJ - 14.12w/13.70
BELL John 10.09.73, Newham & Essex B :
400H - 54.51 (53.70-92)
BELL Matthew 2.06.78, Corby :
HT - 63.83
BELL Matthew 14.07.76, Aberdeen Univ :
3kSt - 9:23.01
BELL Simon 26.12.66, Cambridge Harriers :
Mar - 2:35:25 (2:25:26-97)
BELLO-CANO Manuel 3.01.70, Harrow :
110H - 15.4/15.58
BENJAMIN Ekakier U17 4.12.84, Notts :
HJ - 1.95, PV - 4.15, OctY - 4502
BENJAMIN Timothy U20 2.05.82, Cardiff :
60 - 6.75i (6.75i-00), 100 - 10.36w/10.57 (10.48-00),
200 - 20.6w/20.67 (20.60w-99), 400 - 46.10
BENN Thomas U23 20.04.80, WSE&H :
PV - 4.20 (4.50-00)
BENNETT Andrew U20 30.09.82, Belgrave :
400 - 49.1/49.26, 400H - 53.88
BENNETT Christopher U23 18.10.80, Team Solent :
400 - 48.89 (47.80-99)
BENNETT Jonathan U13 20.09.88, Lewes :
DTC - 27.22
BENNETT Simon 16.10.72, Team Solent :
JT - 59.64 (66.58-96)
BENNETT-JACKSON Wade U15 27.02.87, Brighton :
100 - 11.07w/11.50, 200 - 22.89?/23.03
BENSON Stuart U23 12.02.81, Ayr Seaforth :
100 - 10.8, LJ - 6.81w
BENT Colin 12.04.70, Shaftesbury Barnet/RAF :
HJ - 2.05 (2.20-96)
BENTLEY Robin 17.02.65, Wessex & Bath :
Mar - 2:35:58 (2:28:31-99)
BERGL James U17 23.02.85, Warwicks Sch :
SPY - 14.25, DTY - 41.69
BERNARD Jermaine U17 1.12.84, Ipswich :
LJ - 7.19, TJ - 13.24
BERNARD Martyn U17 15.12.84, Wakefield :
HJ - 2.06
BERNSTEIN Jonathan U15 7.03.87, Southend :
HJ - 1.75
BERRILL Nick 63, Northampton :
Mar - 2:32:54 (2:29:02-93)
BERRIMAN Bob 29.03.73, Rowntrees :
LJ - 6.87i/6.77w (6.92-98)
BERRY Kris U17 13.11.84, Corstorphine :
800 - 1:55.9
BERRY Robert 29.07.69, Southport :
1500 - 3:50.12 (3:48.50-99),
3k - 8:19.86, 3kSt - 8:51.2
BERWICK Christopher V55 1.05.46, Leics WC :
50kW - 4:54:54 (4:23:22-86)
BEST Jonathan U20 9.11.82, Border :
TJ - 13.91i (11.31-97)
BEVAN Nigel Charles 3.01.68, Birchfield :
JT - 63.29 (81.70-92)
BIBBY Anthony U17 12.03.85, Mandale :
100HY - 13.49w/13.83 (13.66-00), TJ - 13.36
BIDWELL Mark U17 4.09.84, Chesterfield :
HJ - 1.95 (1.99i-00/1.95-99)
BIGNALL Douglas 20.10.74, Enf & Har :
50 - 5.71i, 100 - 10.29w/10.30 (10.27wA/10.30A-00,
200 - 21.40
BILLINGHAM John U15 16.10.86, Tipton :
400 - 52.29
BILTON Darren 9.03.72, Kingston u Hull :
Mar - 2:25:47 (2:21:34-99)
BINNS Christopher John U20 7.05.82, Blackpool :
HJ - 1.95 (2.00-00)
BIRCH Shane U15 22.10.87, Med & Maid :
SPB - 14.06, DTB - 41.35
BIRCHALL Chris U23 8.03.79, East Cheshire :
10k - 30:28.67
BIRCHALL Robert 14.06.70, Birchfield :
5k - 14:20.44 (14:10.48-99),
10kR - 29:29 (29:22-97), HMar - 64:30
BISHOP Sam U23 17.08.79, City of Stoke :
Dec - 4998
BISSELL Simon Peter U17 25.12.85, Sale :
SPY - 13.93, DTY - 46.60, HTJ - 49.91, HTY - 58.05
BIVINS Tom U20 18.11.83, Charnwood :
DTJ - 42.19
BLACK Christopher Francis V50 1.01.50, C of Edinb :
HT - 59.05 (75.40-83)
BLACK Iain Russell 18.09.70, City of Edinburgh :
PV - 4.20i (4.51-97)
BLACKETT Daniel U13 4.10.88, Gateshead :
LJ - 5.00
BLACKLEDGE Jonathan Edward U17 15.09.84, I o W :
3k - 8:53.59
BLACKMAN Gary U23 24.09.80, Harrow/Loughbro :
3kSt - 8:56.11
BLACKMAN Graham U17 25.03.85, Rushcliffe :
400 - 50.33i/50.64 (50.4-00)
BLAIR Richard U17 15.09.84, Garscube :
LJ - 6.69w (4.57-97), TJ - 13.68
BLAKE Kevin 29.05.67, Swansea :
10k - 31:34.7
BLIGHT Ross 28.05.77, Cardiff/Univ Wales Inst Card :
HT - 46.71 (50.02-00)
BLISS Anthony 7.03.70, Crawley :
110H - 15.4 (15.1-97/15.37w-98/15.51-97)
BODY Steven 6.01.75, Vauxhall :
1500 - 3:48.06, 1M - 4:09.9 (4:07.97-00),
3k - 8:11.32i/8:14.53, 5MR - 23:50, 10kR - 29:48
BOLT Christopher U23 21.09.80, Shaftesbury Barnet :
800 - 1:49.85, 1500 - 3:45.67 (3:42.36-00),
1M - 4:09.9 (4:04.64-00), 3k - 8:20.98i (8:11.8-00)
BOLTON William U20 7.10.82, Blackheath :
2kSt - 6:14.9
BOMBA Michael U15 10.10.86, Liverpool H :
HTB - 46.76
BONEHAM Ian U20 30.09.82, Grantham :
3k - 8:35.39
BONNETT Stephen 13.07.78, City of Stoke :
HJ - 1.96 (2.05i-99/2.04-97)
BOOTH Chris, :
Mar - 2:35:15
BOREHAM James U15 27.11.86, Preseli :
100 - 11.27w/11.58, 200 - 22.82w/23.40
BORSUMATO Anthony Patrick 13.12.73, Sale :
400H - 49.30
BOTTGER Mikael 24.09.75, Oxford City :
DT - 43.25, Dec - 5545
BOTTJER David U15 24.11.86, Basildon :
3k - 9:24.78
BOUNDY Christopher U23 25.12.79, Gateshead :
PV - 4.60
BOUNDY Patrick U23 19.02.79, WSE&H/Notts Univ :
JT - 58.35
BOURNAT Oliver U17 4.12.84, Tonbridge :
HJ - 1.90i, SPY - 14.48, OctY - 4771
BOURNE Michael U23 18.09.79, City of Stoke :
100 - 10.89w

BOWDEN Adam U20 5.08.82, Harrow :
800 - 1:53.35, 1500 - 3:48.27, 3k - 8:26.7,
2kSt - 5:45.00, 3kSt - 9:08.48 (9:04.43-00)
BOWDITCH Kristen Robert 14.01.75, Newham & E B :
5MR - 23:49
BOWERS Russell U13 21.03.89, Nestle Rowntree :
HJ - 1.52
BOWKER David U15 27.11.86, Mansfield :
800 - 2:04.91
BOWLER James U23 2.09.79, Brom & R/Oxford Univ :
800 - 1:52.4, 1500 - 3:41.75,
3k - 8:09.19, 5KR - 14:23
BOWLES Ian U20 6.01.84, Bolton :
2kSt - 6:04.51, 3kSt - 9:42.32
BOWLEY Ian U23 14.11.81, Bedford & County :
PV - 4.10 (4.10-00)
BOWN Simon Paul 21.11.74, Newham & Essex B :
HT - 65.19 (65.32-99)
BOWRON Lee U17 2.10.85, Ealing,Southall & Mx :
1500 - 4:00.83
BOWSER Matthew U20 3.07.83, Lincoln Well :
1500 - 3:51.09, 3k - 8:29.53
BOYLAN David U15 16.12.86, :
PV - 3.05
BOYLE Michael V40 29.12.60, Herne Hill :
10k - 31:36.55 (30:42.1-93)
BOYLES Steven U15 19.01.87, Carmarthen :
80HB - 11.88
BRACKSTONE David U20 13.03.82, C of S/Lough :
200 - 22.0w (21.7w/22.0-00/23.02-98), 110HJ - 15.2,
400 - 49.33i/49.4 (49.0/49.19i-00), 400H - 52.60
BRADBURY Martin U20 20.10.82, Sheffield :
400 - 48.54 (47.94-00)
BRADLEY Colin V45 2.02.56, Surrey WC :
3kW - 13:41.85i (12:54.8-86),
50kW - 4:54:38 (4:33:42-87)
BRADLEY Dominic 22.12.76, Birchfield :
60 - 6.88i (6.83i-99), 100 - 10.54 (10.52w-98),
200 - 21.76w/21.9 (21.7/21.87-99),
60H - 7.84i, 110H - 13.83
BRADLEY Michael V40 27.05.57, Chiltern :
100kR - 7:54:20 (7:12:58-99)
BRADSHAW Liam U13 4.07.89, Croydon :
80HC - 13.8
BRADY David 5.07.62, North Belfast :
Mar - 2:31:22
BRAMBLE Marvin 10.06.77, Blackheath :
TJ - 14.25w (15.31w-97/15.23-95)
BRANCH Kit U17 5.06.85, Basildon :
PV - 3.90
BRANDWOOD Daniel U20 1.10.82, Kingston u Hull :
200 - 21.74w/22.0/22.23, 400 - 49.5, 110HJ - 15.5,
Dec - 5723, DecJ - 5953
BRAVINGTON Craig U15 9.12.86, Bournemouth :
800 - 1:59.21, 1500 - 4:19.2
BRAY Daniel Paul U20 6.09.83, Havant :
400 - 49.38, TJ - 13.84
BREEZE Jonathon U20 8.04.83, Exeter :
HJ - 1.98
BREND Peter A. 2.02.77, Team Solent :
200 - 21.9/21.94, 400 - 46.8/47.03
BREW Daniel U17 20.11.84, Liverpool H :
DTY - 46.26
BRIDGE James U20 28.11.83, Invicta :
200 - 21.7/21.90w/21.92
BRIDGES Marcus 18.03.71, Birchfield :
800 - 1:52.28
BRIERLEY James Richard 31.07.77, Telford :
HJ - 1.95 (2.26-96)
BRIODY J. U15, Dacorum & Tring :
PV - 2.90
BRITTAN Andrew John 17.01.67, Cannock & Staff :
DT - 49.57 (49.76-88)

BRIZZEL Paul 3.10.76, Liverpool H/IRL :
100 - 10.59 (10.28w/10.35-00),
200 - 20.86 (20.54A/20.65-00)
BROADBENT Andrew U17 2.09.84, Halesowen :
400HY - 56.38
BROADHEAD Daniel U20 19.04.82, Rotherham :
PV - 4.50i/4.30
BROCKLEBANK Robert J. 12.10.76, Sale :
HJ - 2.12 (2.16-95)
BROOKS Jerome T. S. 9.08.73, London Irish :
3k - 8:20.12 (8:16.2-00), 5k - 14:42.66 (14:22.71-00)
BROOKS Steven 8.06.70, Bingley :
5k - 14:23.14 (13:52.54-94), 10MR - 49:17,
HMar - 66:02 (61:28-97)
BROOME Adam U17 5.08.85, Wirral :
JTY - 52.22
BROWN Andrew 17.06.77, WG & Ex L/C of Edinb :
800 - 1:49.74
BROWN Andrew 20.12.77, Nene Valley H/Camb Un :
800 - 1:52.2
BROWN David U20 11.02.83, Cardiff :
TJ - 13.86
BROWN Derry U13 12.03.89, Steyning :
2kW - 10:11.6
BROWN Edward James Kenneth U15 6.10.86, C of S :
800 - 2:05.26
BROWN Gareth James 10.05.68, Steyning :
10kW - 45:25.9 (43:54.25-87)
BROWN Gareth 2.09.73, Swindon :
LJ - 7.14 (7.41w-00)
BROWN John 2.02.69, Salford :
HMar - 65:25
BROWN Jonathan Michael 27.02.71, Sheffield :
10MR - 48:25+ (46:28+e-97),
HMar - 63:52+ (61:49-97), Mar - 2:11:24 (2:09:44-99)
BROWN Kevin Dave 10.09.64, Belgrave/JAM :
SP - 13.57 (14.73-98), DT - 54.33 (62.10-00)
BROWN Mark 3.11.76, Newham & Essex B :
60 - 6.99i, 100 - 10.5w,
200 - 21.5w/21.89i (21.6-99/21.91w-00/21.95-99,
300 - 34.2 (33.81-00), 400 - 47.21i/47.67 (46.37-99)
BROWN Michael 6.05.62, Enf & Har :
TJ - 13.90 (16.15-89)
BROWN Richard 24.05.74, Havering :
TJ - 13.81
BROWN Richard V55 18.11.46, Surrey WC :
100MW - 19:50:39 (16:50:28-93)
BROWNE Curtis 11.09.75, Birchfield :
60 - 6.81i (6.77i-96), 100 - 10.50 (10.38w/10.42-99)
BRUCE Calum 28.02.75, Pitreavie :
HT - 54.33 (54.79-00)
BRUCE Steven U15 19.10.86, Woking :
1500 - 4:19.65
BRUNT Daniel 23.04.76, Sheffield :
SP - 14.02 (14.49-97), DT - 44.27 (47.94-00)
BRUTON Matthew U15 18.10.86, Sale :
JTB - 45.78
BRYAN Justin 16.08.69, Cwmbran :
SP - 14.15 (14.54-99), DT - 44.04 (45.29-98)
BUCHANAN Andrew I. 12.09.70, AF&D :
PV - 4.20 (4.50-94)
BUCHANAN Harold U15 13.10.86, Bury :
100 - 11.57w, 200 - 23.3w/23.55, 400 - 51.77
BUCK Matthew 5.04.74, WGreen & Ex L :
PV - 4.60 (4.60-96)
BUCK Richard Thomas U15 14.11.86, Scarborough :
400 - 52.32
BUCKFIELD Nicholas Jean 5.06.73, Crawley :
PV - 5.75A/5.60 (5.80-98)
BUCKINGHAM Mark John U17 4.05.85, Holmfirth :
3k - 8:58.43, 1.5kSt - 4:29.65
BUCKLEY Adam John U23 6.12.80, Sale/Bath Univ :
200 - 22.0w (21.7-00/23.28-97), 400 - 47.37i/47.55 (47.04-00)

BUCKLEY Alan 25.10.74, Gateshead :
5k - 14:13.29 (14:05.74-00), 10k - 29:45.31
BUDD Alex U17 6.12.84, Portsmouth :
400 - 50.91, 800 - 1:57.92
BUDD David U23 8.12.79, Sheffield :
TJ - 13.93
BUDDEN Nicholas 17.11.75, City of Norwich :
400 - 47.61 (46.34-96)
BULL Gareth U17 3.03.85, Cardiff :
SPY - 14.14, DTY - 48.93, HTY - 47.47,
DecY - 5208, OctY - 4436
BULL Michael P. 6.06.70, Notts :
Dec - 5906 (6051-97)
BULL Nathan U15 3.06.87, Tipton :
PV - 3.10
BULL Simon U20 29.09.82, Cardiff :
Dec - 5298w/5106, DecJ - 5413
BULL Suna 25.01.75, WSE&H :
Dec - 5797
BULLEY David Robert U17 4.06.86, Wirral :
SPY - 13.97
BULLEY Simon John U17 19.09.84, Wirral :
DTY - 44.20, HTY - 47.84
BULMAN James U15 7.11.86, Norfolk Sch :
1500 - 4:20.34
BULMAN Neil Andrew 7.09.77, Northampton :
HT - 47.19 (49.02-98)
BURGESS Alistair, Cambridge University :
400H - 55.6/55.86
BURGESS Louis U20, Epsom & Ewell :
LJ - 6.85
BURKINSHAW Brendan U17 5.04.85, Bradford :
PV - 3.60
BURNETT Grant U17 21.03.85, Inverness :
200 - 22.68, 400 - 50.80
BURNS Daniel U17 6.09.84, Tynedale :
HJ - 1.95
BURNS Ian T. 20.09.77, Gateshead :
JT - 61.91 (63.22-00)
BURNS William 13.12.69, Salford :
HMar - 64:19+ (66:24-98),
Mar - 2:18:29 (2:15:42-00)
BURRELL Jonathan 24.11.75, Chelmsford :
800 - 1:52.7 (1:52.5-98), 1500 - 3:51.11
BURROWS Craig 8.08.74, Ilford :
DT - 41.22 (42.37-00)
BURROWS Matthew U17 27.11.84, City of Plymouth :
HJ - 1.90
BURSLEM Richard U20 4.01.84, Sale :
LJ - 6.96
BUTLER A. U15, Wycombe :
HJ - 1.75
BUTLER David 9.12.78, Charnwood/Chelt & GLos U :
LJ - 7.14
BUTLER Kenny 17.09.63, Army :
Mar - 2:24:45 (2:24:42-00)
BUTLER Matthew Rhys U23 4.04.80, Cardiff/
Univ Wales Inst Card : 60H - 8.39i
BUTT H. U17, Norfolk Sch :
HJ - 1.90
BUTTLER Stephen 20.02.75, City of Stoke :
100 - 10.81 (10.7w/10.81-93),
200 - 21.8w/21.97w/22.0 (21.8-93/22.06-92)

CADMAN Lewis Charles U17 6.07.85, Bed & Co :
1500 - 4:02.49, 3k - 8:44.4
CADWALLADER Lee 17.01.69, Liverpool H :
800 - 1:52.24 (1:47.43-93)
CAINE Andrew 17.06.77, Tynedale :
3k - 8:17.83 (8:16.60-00), 5k - 14:11.42, 10k - 29:33.94
CAINES Daniel Stephen U23 15.05.79, Birchfield :
60 - 6.86i, 200 - 21.05, 300 - 32.8i+,
400 - 45.58 (45.37-00)
CAIRNS Steven Mark 3.11.67, Border/Hunter's BT :
5k - 14:43.3, 3kSt - 8:56.16 (8:55.2-99)
CALDWELL Benjamin Ian U20 3.03.82, Bolton/Lough :
400 - 49.17 (48.45-00), 400H - 54.5/54.77 (54.4/54.67-00)
CAMBON Alessandro U23, Univ Wales Newport :
PV - 4.75
CAMERON George, :
SP - 13.36
CAMERON John U23 27.02.81, :
SP - 13.67
CAMERON Rezlimond V40 18.05.60, Thames Valley :
TJ - 14.39i/14.35 (16.32w-89/16.20-88)
CAMPBELL Christian U17 10.06.85, Ealing,S & Mx :
TJ - 13.49w
CAMPBELL Daniel U17 24.02.86, Croydon :
HJ - 1.90
CAMPBELL Darren Andrew 12.09.73, Belgrave :
100 - 10.16 (10.04-98), 200 - 20.41 (20.13-00)
CAMPBELL Fraser U17 30.05.86, Elgin :
HTY - 53.83
CAMPBELL James U15 1.04.88, Cheltenham :
JTB - 43.31
CAMPBELL Kenneth William 30.09.72, TVH/C of Ed :
100 - 10.5dt/10.93w (10.88-96)
CAMPBELL Malcolm 3.01.71, Cambuslang :
5k - 14:13.30, 10k - 29:53.66 (29:16.47un-96),
10kR - 29:44, HMar - 65:13 (64:48-97), Mar - 2:20:36
CAMPBELL Mark U20 6.07.82, Annadale Striders :
200 - 22.02
CAMPBELL Paul William Alexander U23 26.03.80,
Mandale/Teeside Univ : 200 - 21.63
CAMPBELL Steven U17 10.11.84, Shettleston :
PV - 3.70
CAPELING Kirk U23 27.02.80, Medway :
HT - 45.75
CAPEWELL Jan Paul U13 10.01.89, Halesowen :
JTC - 38.62
CARELESS Robert 7.09.74, Charnwood :
HT - 60.65
CAREY Tom U20 26.02.84, Huntingdon :
400H - 56.5/56.75
CARISS Chris 1.03.75, Bingley :
Mar - 2:25:23
CARLETON Jonathan U23 4.11.79, Ballymena & A :
100 - 10.8w (10.72w/10.8-00/10.89-99),
200 - 21.86 (21.60?/21.66-00)
CARLISLE Nigel 30.12.75, Ballymena & Antrim :
800 - 1:51.81
CARMODY Noel Philip V45 24.12.56, Cambridge H :
3kW - 13:37.40 (12:26.49-91)
CARPENTER Steven U17 30.12.85, Woking :
PV - 3.60
CARR Gary U20 24.09.82, Ashford :
100 - 10.9 (10.93-00)
CARROLL Tom U17 3.05.85, Shildon :
100 - 11.0w
CARRUTHERS Gillen U20 24.09.82, Ballymena & A :
DT - 40.88
CARSON Sean U20 13.04.84, Ayr Seaforth :
JT - 58.98
CARTER Daniel W. U23 15.04.80, WGreen & Ex L/
Brunel Univ : JT - 73.00 (73.56-00)
CARTER Simon 5.03.75, Med & Maid/Reading Un :
JT - 63.81 (66.37-98)
CARTER Thomas U20 20.08.82, Vale Royal/
Loughborough Studnts :
1500 - 3:53.5
CASEY Theo U20 3.06.84, Croydon :
HJ - 2.07
CASSIDY Seamas U15 12.11.86, Harrow :
LJ - 6.28
CASTLE John 68, AF&D/Army :
Mar - 2:34:48

CAUDERY Stuart 19.11.66, Cornwall AC :
PV - 4.20i (4.20-99)
CAWLEY Ian 21.11.78, Team Solent/Loughborough :
60H - 8.29i, 110H - 14.73w/14.86 (14.78-00)
CHALLENGER Benjamin 7.03.78, Belgrave :
HJ - 2.26 (2.30-99)
CHAMBERS Dwain Anthony 5.04.78, Belgrave :
100 - 9.97w/9.99 (9.97-99), 200 - 20.31
CHAMPION Michael 3.01.75, Blackheath :
200 - 21.68w/21.8/21.82 (21.12w/21.3/21.32-00)
CHAPMAN Daniel U13 14.09.88, Southend :
DTC - 31.42
CHAPMAN Frank 17.01.70, RAF :
Dec - 5639
CHAPMAN James U13 23.11.88, Harrow :
SPC - 11.51
CHARLESWORTH Robert U23 25.03.79, Peterbro :
JT - 65.89
CHARLTON Adam U20 11.05.84, Shaftesbury Barnet :
100 - 10.7, 200 - 21.6/21.66w/22.02,
400 - 47.9/48.01
CHASTON Justin Thomas 4.11.68, Belgrave :
3kSt - 8:46.29 (8:23.90-94)
CHATT James U23 11.02.80, Dartford/Loughbro :
60 - 6.90i, 100 - 10.58w/10.7/10.79 (10.7-97/10.74-00),
200 - 21.2w/21.53,
300 - 35.2 (34.22i-99/34.6-98), 400 - 47.1
CHATTINGTON Ryan U17 2.09.84, Sale :
TJ - 13.38
CHEESEMAN Christopher V40 11.12.58, Surrey WC/
Thames H & H : 5kW - 21:05.29,
10kWR - 43:21 (42:11-00), 20kW - 1:30:26 (1:26:53-99),
30kW - 2:35:16+ (2:27:11-94),
50kW - 4:18:00 (4:07:49-99)
CHESTER Karim U17 6.11.84, Blackheath :
HTJ - 52.59, HTY - 60.52
CHEUNG Lewis U20 12.12.83, Liverpool H :
LJ - 6.90w, TJ - 14.60i/14.47w/14.16
CHILDS Naved U23 12.05.81, Brecon/Cambridge Un :
TJ - 13.90
CHILDS Nick U15 17.09.86, Shaftesbury Barnet :
JTB - 44.32
CHILDS Richardo U17 9.10.84, Brecon :
LJ - 6.88
CHIN Darren U23 30.06.81, Belgrave :
60 - 6.80i, 100 - 10.5/10.52 (10.51-99)
CHRISTIE Jeffrey U20 24.09.82, Leamington :
400 - 49.1, 400H - 51.8/52.25
CHRISTIE Mark U17 11.09.84, Gateshead :
PV - 4.70
CLAGUE Samuel U17 26.02.86, Reading :
SPY - 14.60, DTY - 41.24
CLARE Jeffrey Mark 21.03.65, Trafford :
DT - 45.12 (55.60-88)
CLARKE Ian 6.11.72, Enf & Har :
100 - 10.8 (10.6/10.79-00)
CLARKE Jonathan 20.11.67, Swansea :
JT - 61.36 (68.74-86)
CLARKE Matthew 15.11.76, Daventry :
800 - 1:51.62
CLARKE S. Ezra 9.12.74, Belgrave :
TJ - 14.08 (15.75-97)
CLARKE Wayne A. R. 24.12.75, Peterborough :
HT - 60.78
CLAY Alastair 12.09.78, Border :
400H - 55.1/55.95
CLAY Matthew U20 9.06.84, Parkside :
LJ - 6.85i/6.83, DecJ - 5325
CLAY Robert U23 11.05.80, Sheffield/Hallam Un. :
200 - 21.88
CLEMENTS Andrew V40 59, Poole :
Mar - 2:34:44
CLEMENTS Andrew U20 28.11.82, AF&D :
110HJ - 15.25w/15.5, 400H - 54.6/55.11,
DecJ - 6218w/5796
CLEMENTS Christian U20 19.07.83, Bournemouth :
800 - 1:54.60
COATES Peter 21.03.68, Durham City H :
Dec - 5121 (5226DD-00/5184-99)
COATS Edward M. U23 14.06.80, Harrow :
PV - 4.13 (4.35-99), Dec - 6497 (6843-99)
COCKERELL William 74, Belgrave :
Mar - 2:32:27
COLE Brian, Royal Navy :
Mar - 2:32:44 (2:32:43-00)
COLEMAN Andrew 29.09.74, Enf & Har :
5MR - 23:31 (23:31-00)
COLEMAN Michael 14.05.78, Medway :
10k - 30:48.8, Mar - 2:21:47
COLEY Alexander U17 8.02.86, Sheffield :
100 - 11.12w/11.13,
200 - 22.60 (22.59w-00)
COLLARD David U17 25.01.85, City of Edinburgh :
100HY - 14.0, HJ - 1.95
COLLINGS Philip U17 15.02.85, Bridgewater :
HTY - 48.15
COLLINS Aiden U15 18.10.86, Chelmsford :
TJ - 12.76w/12.44
COLLINS Liam James O'Neill 23.10.78, Sale/
Loughborough Studnts :
60H - 8.09i (7.94i-00),
110H - 14.73w/14.9/15.19 (14.05-00)
COLLYMORE Fabian U17 19.10.84, Blackheath :
100 - 11.0 (11.15-00), 200 - 21.9/22.49
COLTHERD Michael U20 28.12.82, Barrow & Furn :
800 - 1:53.53 (1:50.31-00)
COLTON Matthew U20 5.11.82, Basildon :
110HJ - 14.69w/14.77 (14.65-00),
110H - 15.3, 400H - 57.0
COMERFORD Nicholas 23.04.66, Cardiff :
10MR - 49:14 (48:38-00)
COMISSIONG Jason Kyle U20 7.09.83, Thames VH:
TJ - 14.30 (14.46w-00)
CONDON Allyn 24.08.74, Sale :
60 - 6.74i (6.64i-98/6.68-00), 100 - 10.42 (10.21-99),
200 - 20.60i/20.99 (20.53i-98/20.59w-99/20.63-97),
400 - 47.93i (46.23i-99/46.8-98/47.43-94)
CONDON David Jonathan 11.04.72, Newham & E B :
SP - 16.92 (17.16-00)
CONNOLLY Stuart Craig U20 9.02.83, Morpeth :
200 - 21.99
CONNOR Joseph U15 17.12.86, Liverpool H :
DTB - 38.48, HTB - 46.68
CONNOR Tom U17 30.03.85, Eastbourne AC :
LJ - 6.67
CONTEH Jermaine U13 12.05.89, S London :
400 - 62.9
COOK Austin James Gareth 20.02.69, Sutton & Dist :
SP - 13.92 (14.59-90), DT - 43.54 (49.20-90),
HT - 60.43 (67.32-91)
COOK Gavin 30.03.70, Thames Valley :
HT - 51.43 (62.58-88)
COOK Philip 7.05.69, Barry/Les Croupiers :
10k - 31:20.4, Mar - 2:33:07 (2:28:45-99)
COOKE Ben U23 10.04.81, Wirral/Birmingham Univ. :
800 - 1:51.84, 1500 - 3:48.79
COOKE Simon U17 3.10.85, Chichester :
SPY - 14.64, DTY - 45.26
COOMBES James U23 4.10.81, Rhondda :
SP - 13.70
COOPER Paul 30.01.75, Shaftesbury Barnet :
800 - 1:52.48 (1:51.9-94)
COOPER Paul 4.12.76, WGreen & Ex L :
JT - 62.27 (67.03-99)

COOPER Rufus Henry U23 24.02.79, WSE&H :
PV - 4.50i/4.50 (4.90-00)
CORCORAN Fyn 17.03.78, Harrow :
110H - 15.1/15.21 (15.11w-99), LJ - 7.00 (7.01-98), SP - 13.60, Dec - 7050 (7116-99)
CORNELL Ryan U15 10.07.87, Winchester :
PV - 2.90
CORNISH Glen U23 27.10.79, Sale :
3kSt - 9:23.36
CORRIGAN J. Paul 19.01.66, North Shields Poly :
SP - 14.05 (16.04-89)
CORRIGAN Kyle U15 27.09.86, Annadale Striders :
PV - 3.30
CORRIGAN Michael 1.12.77, St. Marys Univ/IRL :
TJ - 14.33
COSSINS Daniel U17 22.12.84, Wessex & Bath :
200 - 21.8/22.15, 400 - 49.6
COSTELLO Scott U15 9.06.87, :
PV - 3.10i/3.10
COTTON Simon 26.07.67, Tipton :
10k - 30:40.52 (29:34.4-97), 3kSt - 9:19.6
COTTON Steven James U23 8.02.79, N Devon :
JT - 58.10 (58.75-00)
COWLISHAW David 17.09.67, London Irish :
1500 - 3:51.23
COX Ben U17 19.03.85, Cheltenham :
1.5kSt - 4:29.9
COX Kelly U17 21.01.85, Herne Hill :
800 - 1:57.5
COX Laurence U15 15.03.88, AF&D :
1500 - 4:17.99, 3k - 9:34.42
COX Michael U17 15.01.86, Harrow :
PV - 3.70
CRAMPTON Ian 28.01.62, Durham City H :
Mar - 2:34:20 (2:31:05-00)
CRANFIELD Peter U17 26.09.84, Liverpool H :
SP - 13.94, SPJ - 14.54, SPY - 16.43, DTY - 45.40, HT - 47.07, HTJ - 51.55, HTY - 57.55
CRANIE Martin U15 26.09.86, Somerset Sch :
200 - 23.4w
CRAWFORD Damien John 22.08.68, London I/Sparta :
JT - 56.63 (70.34r?-91/67.84r-90/67.16-92)
CRAWFORD Jason U20 20.07.83, Kingston u Hull :
SP - 13.28
CRAWLEY Luke U23 5.09.81, Solihull & S Heath/Bath Univ :
HJ - 2.10i (2.15-00)
CRAWSHAW Jonathon U23 28.09.81, Craw/Ox Univ :
110H - 15.57w?
CREAK David U20 30.08.83, Great Yarmouth :
400 - 49.2/49.33
CREIGHTON James U20 15.09.83, Liverpool H :
HJ - 2.01
CRIPPS Damon 9.10.70, Liverpool H :
DT - 40.74, HT - 52.50
CROAD Malcolm 27.10.73, Harrow :
HT - 47.53 (61.22-92)
CRONSHAW Darran 1.02.78, Bath Univ :
HJ - 2.05i/2.00
CROSSLEY Paul U23 30.03.79, Luton/Bath Univ :
60H - 8.12i, 110H - 14.3w/14.37w/14.4/14.42, 400H - 55.3/55.64 (53.62-97)
CROSSMAN Peter, :
24Hr - 185.250km
CROW Tyrone U15 14.09.86, Mandale :
400 - 52.78
CROWE Thomas Francis U17 9.03.85, Kent Sch :
400HY - 58.9
CROWLEY Mark U20 15.11.83, Enf & Har :
HJ - 2.05i/2.05
CRYER Martyn U23 16.10.81, Salford/Loughbro :
1500 - 3:51.43, 3k - 8:20.24, 5k - 14:31.74
CUDDY Grant 6.01.77, Sale :
800 - 1:48.27 (1:47.2-97)
CUFF Jon U23 30.03.80, Gloucester AC :
400H - 53.1/54.95 (53.06-99)
CULLEN Keith John 13.06.72, Chelmsford :
5k - 13:53.4 (13:17.21-97), 5KR - 14:12 (13:31-96)
CURRAN Paul 3.04.77, North Down :
HJ - 1.96, TJ - 14.13 (15.15-97)
CURTIS James U17, Enf & Har :
JTY - 53.82
CURTIS Paul U23 29.05.80, Shaftesbury Barnet :
400 - 49.04 (48.14-97)
CUTTS Luke Arron U15 13.02.88, Barnsley :
PV - 3.30

DACK Christopher U20 28.11.82, Donc & Stain :
DecJ - 5881
DALKINS Mark 9.09.71, Birchfield :
HMar - 66:48
DALMEDO Daniel U23 14.03.80, Hill/Staffs Univ :
5k - 14:43.92
DANCE Nicholas U20 27.09.83, Bracknell :
HJ - 1.95
DARBY Brian Roy Senfuma 14.10.72, Cov Godiva/ Loughborough Studnts : 100 - 10.8 (10.8-00), 200 - 21.7/21.73w (21.5-00), 400 - 47.40
DASHPER Wayne 19.10.74, Telford/Royal Navy :
3kSt - 9:26.80 (9:17.82-00)
DAVENPORT Richard John U17 12.09.85, Glouc AC :
100 - 11.0 (11.27-00), 200 - 22.1, 400 - 48.59, 800 - 1:54.24
DAVEY Ian U20 25.10.82, Shildon :
800 - 1:52.1
DAVID Andrew 9.09.69, WGreen & Ex L :
60H - 8.4i (8.24i-97), 110H - 15.4 (14.83-95)
DAVIDSON Christopher 4.12.75, Newham & Essex B :
LJ - 7.62 (7.94w-97/7.90-99)
DAVIES Adam Christopher U20 27.07.84, Glouc AC :
800 - 1:53.04
DAVIES Christopher 19.10.76, Telford/Staffs Univ :
1500 - 3:50.2 (3:45.2-99), 5k - 14:27.06 (14:01.97-99)
DAVIES James U20 5.12.82, Wakefield :
400 - 48.1/48.25
DAVIES James U15 29.09.86, Surrey WC :
100 - 11.19w/11.49
DAVIES Jonathan U15 2.03.87, R Sutton Coldfield :
3k - 9:38.4
DAVIES Kevin 11.01.78, Telford/RAF :
HT - 58.37 (59.24-00)
DAVIES Kris U23 30.10.81, Cardiff :
LJ - 7.28w/7.09
DAVIES Mark Howard 10.01.71, Tonbridge :
SP - 14.64 (15.56-92), DT - 46.20 (53.06-92)
DAVIES Matthew 23.07.71, WGreen & Ex L :
800 - 1:52.38 (1:49.9-96), 1500 - 3:50.79 (3:44.2-96)
DAVIES Matthew 16.09.78, Swansea/ Univ Wales Inst Card : JT - 55.06 (58.03-99)
DAVIES Stephen U20 16.02.84, Newport :
800 - 1:52.47
DAVIES Tom U15 9.11.86, Telford :
PV - 3.45
DAVIES Tommy U17 3.08.85, Team Solent :
3k - 8:51.00io/9:04.16
DAVIS Adam Gareth 19.11.72, Corby/RAF :
PV - 4.55 (4.70-92), SP - 14.87, DT - 41.57
DAVIS Andrae Dean U17 27.09.85, WGreen & Ex L :
SPY - 15.31, DTY - 41.16, OctY - 5279
DAVIS Daniel U15 12.12.87, Croydon :
80HB - 11.47
DAVIS James U17 10.10.84, Portsmouth :
3kW - 13:25.30 (13:22.96-00), 5kW - 24:21.52 (23:36.76-00)

DAVIS Luke U23 1.01.80, Shaftesbury Barnet :
60 - 6.93i (6.92i-00), 100 - 10.81w (10.40w/10.45-97),
200 - 21.72i/21.8/22.11w (21.70-97)
DAVIS Mark Gavin 1.03.77, Birchfield :
PV - 5.10i/4.60 (5.20-99)
DAVISON Tristan U13 4.04.89, Southend :
DTC - 29.98
DAVOILE Ryan James 29.09.78, Coventry Godiva/
Loughborough Studnts : 800 - 1:52.10 (1:50.6-97)
DAVOREN Patrick 13.03.72, Phoenix :
1500 - 3:46.13 (3:42.3-99), 1M - 4:10.8 (4:02.77-99),
5k - 14:26.84 (14:16.0-95), 3kSt - 8:57.63 (8:55.95-99)
DAWKINGS Alex U13, Horsham BS :
DTC - 28.99
DAWSON David L.U20 3.02.84, Exeter :
SP - 14.26, SPJ - 15.42, DTJ - 41.24
DAWSON Nicholas John 11.05.78, Belgrave :
200 - 21.77w/22.09 (21.43w/21.48-97)
DAY Harold John V40 2.04.59, Cardiff :
Mar - 2:34:55
DAY Stephen U20 10.02.82, Shaftesbury Barnet :
PV - 4.40 (4.50-00)
DE HAAFF Ryan U17 9.11.84, Guernsey :
100 - 11.0
DE JONGE Emil 2.09.72, Shaftesbury Barnet/RSA :
5k - 14:04.28, 10kR - 29:08, 3kSt - 9:13.8
DE NOBRIGGA Charles U17 22.11.84, Derby & Co :
400HY - 56.76
DEACON Mark Jared 15.10.75, Border :
100 - 10.98 (10.8-95/10.92-00), 200 - 21.30 (21.14-96),
400 - 46.56 (45.69-00), 400H - 53.67
DEACON-BROWN James U20 26.05.84, Gateshead :
JT - 56.59
DEAKIN Robert 21.10.66, Staffs Moorlands :
HMar - 66:48, Mar - 2:23:29
DEAKIN Simon 5.10.77, Leeds :
800 - 1:52.08, 1500 - 3:44.55,
3k - 8:11.88, 5k - 14:25.8
DEAN Andrew 30.06.78, Solihull & S Heath/
Loughborough Studnts : 400H - 54.52
DEANE Arthur V45 22.05.54, Liverpool H :
10k - 31:38.0
DEARMAN Geoffrey Clive 4.08.77, Bel/Brunel Univ :
200 - 21.8/21.85w (21.5/22.08i-98), 400 - 47.64 (45.83-00)
DEETH Ian U23 25.06.79, Bel/Falkirk/Brunel Univ :
200 - 21.95 (21.63w/21.94-00),
300 - 34.84i, 400 - 48.10
DEIGHTON Kevin U17 1.01.85, WGreen & Ex L :
400HY - 57.68
DELAFIELD Andrew U23 19.03.80, Sheffield :
400 - 48.92
DEMPSEY Thomas Christopher U20 15.12.83, Hales :
HT - 57.26, HTJ - 61.25
DENMARK Robert Neil 23.11.68, Basildon :
3k - 7:59.57 (7:39.55-93),
5k - 13:36.30 (13:10.24-92), 5KR - 14:15 (13:30-96),
5MR - 23:18 (22:41-95), 10k - 28:46.70 (28:03.31-00),
10kR - 28:53 (28:36-92), HMar - 64:13 (62:37-94),
10MR - 49:44 (46:50+-94/49:10-99)
DENSLEY Martin Richard U23 1.05.81, E, Sl & Mx :
PV - 4.85
DERRIEN Paul 5.08.71, Team Solent :
HT - 45.09 (45.89-99)
DESAILLY Franck 20.01.73, Swansea/FRA :
110H - 15.3w
DEVINE James Russell 24.04.68, Inverness :
HT - 66.53
DEVLIN Gareth 2.06.76, Loughbro/Sale/IRL :
LJ - 7.16w/6.93 (7.55w-00/7.30-96)
DEVONISH Marlon 1.06.76, Coventry Godiva :
100 - 10.29w/10.30 (10.13-98), 200 - 20.29 (20.25-99)
DICKENSON Derek Paul V50 4.12.49, Dac & Tring :
HT - 49.09 (73.20-76)
DICKENSON Joe U15 7.12.86, Birchfield :
80HB - 11.79
DICKINSON John U20 27.01.83, Haslemere :
Dec - 5986w/5976
DICKSON Charles U13 25.11.88, :
75HC - 12.6
DICKSON Marlon 17.11.78, Belgrave :
60 - 6.9i (6.8i/6.82i-00),
100 - 10.7/10.90 (10.46w-99/10.60-00),
200 - 21.9w/21.95 (21.36w-00/21.49-98)
DINGLE Paul U13 4.09.88, Jersey :
80HC - 13.5, LJ - 5.26
DINGLEY Matthew U20 12.01.83, Birchfield :
JT - 56.09 (57.29-00)
DINHAM Ryan U17 19.08.85, Tonbridge :
400HY - 56.62
DIRRANE Sean U17 17.10.85, Leeds :
1500 - 4:04.73, 3k - 8:58.42, 1.5kSt - 4:41.6
DJAN Geoffrey U20 21.07.82, Birchfield :
200 - 21.9/22.42, 400 - 48.08 (47.93-00)
DOBBING Thomas F. 5.02.73, C of Edinburgh/RAF :
JT - 65.01 (65.22-93)
DOBSON Robert William V55 4.11.42, Ilford :
100MW - 19:46:11
DOCHERTY William U17 2.04.85, Kilbarchan :
1.5kSt - 4:27.51, 3kSt - 9:52.3
DOCKING James U15 19.11.86, City of Plymouth :
JTB - 49.95
DODDS Christopher U13 30.01.89, Ashford :
1500 - 4:47.3
DODS Darren 26.12.74, Guildford & G :
110H - 15.6, LJ - 6.88 (6.98-99)
DODSWORTH Ian U17 16.12.84, Peterlee :
PV - 3.90
DOHERTY Brian U20 2.06.83, W DUNB :
SPJ - 13.61i, DT - 41.09, DTJ - 43.22
DOHERTY Ian 12.03.65, Staffs Moorlands :
24Hr - 194.731km
DON Tim 14.01.78, :
1500 - 3:47.71
DONALDSON Alasdair M. 21.06.77, Newham & E B/
Pitreavie : 400 - 48.75 (47.84-00),
800 - 1:49.41 (1:47.32-00)
DONKIN Bradley 6.12.71, Birchfield :
800 - 1:50.62 (1:46.86-98), 1500 - 3:51.83
DONNELLY John U23 11.09.79, B & A/Queen's Univ/
Border : LJ - 6.88i/6.85 (7.04w-00),
TJ - 14.30w/14.12 (14.83-99)
DONOGHUE Mark U20 27.09.83, Liv.Pemb Sefton :
2kSt - 6:10.83
DONOVAN Daniel 8.10.70, Shaftesbury Barnet :
100 - 10.63w/10.64 (10.4wdt-99/10.62w-97),
200 - 21.40 (21.18-97)
DORAN Lee Michael U17 5.03.85, Carlisle/Aspatria :
JT - 55.84, JTY - 67.31
DORRIAN Matthew U20 24.03.84, Giffnock :
PV - 4.40
DOSANJH Nathan Luke U23 13.02.79, Solihull & S H/
Butler Univ, USA : 800 - 1:52.56 (1:51.88-00),
1500 - 3:51.80 (3:47.77-00), 1M - 4:11.27i#
DOUGAL Neil U23 7.03.80, Motherwell :
400 - 49.10, 800 - 1:48.71
DOUGLAS Matthew 26.11.76, Belgrave/Brunel Univ :
400 - 47.7/48.86i (46.65A-00/47.5-98/47.64-97),
110H - 14.63 (14.00-99), 400H - 49.68 (49.26-00)
DOUGLAS Nathan James U20 4.12.82, Oxford City :
100 - 10.96w (12.4-97), LJ - 7.20, TJ - 15.50
DOWNES John Michael 21.07.67, London Irish/IRL:
10k - 30:05.34 (29:32.8-97)
DOWSE Richard U17 3.01.85, Scunthorpe :
800 - 1:53.95
DOWSETT Nicholas J.E. 24.11.78, WG & Ex L/Lond U :
LJ - 6.90i/6.88w (7.15w-96/7.04i/7.02-97)

DOWSON David U23 11.01.81, Middlesbro & C :
SP - 14.42
DOYLE Brian 12.03.77, City of Edinburgh/Cumb :
60 - 6.82i (6.79i-99), 100 - 10.70 (10.59-98),
200 - 21.20 (21.15w-00)
DOYLE-HOWSON Darren U17 23.05.85, Colwyn Bay :
1500 - 4:02.78
DOYLEY Danny U13 28.12.88, Croydon :
200 - 26.0
DRAKE Andrew Paul 6.02.65, Coventry Godiva :
3kW - 12:02.24i (11:31.0-90),
10kW - 43:21.0 (41:18.64-88),
10kWR - 42:49 (41:25+/41:26-00)
DRAPER Mark U20 28.06.84, WSE&H :
1500 - 3:54.4, 3k - 8:29.53
DRAYCOTT Adam U17 7.11.84, Notts :
100HY - 13.7/13.90
DUBLIN Gavin U20 5.10.83, Croydon :
400 - 49.24
DUFFY Anthony P. V45 26.06.56, Bolton :
10k - 31:16.8 (29:51.5-89),
Mar - 2:28:52 (2:17:09-89)
DUMA Ogadina U15 5.09.86, Enf & Har :
80HB - 11.35w/11.5/11.56
DUNFORD Edward James U17 15.09.84, Birchfield :
100 - 11.1, 100HY - 13.15w/13.16, 110HY - 14.58,
110HJ - 15.1/15.49 (15.07-00), HJ - 1.98,
LJ - 6.79w/6.60i/6.55 (6.78-00), SPJ - 13.99,
SPY - 15.98, DTJ - 43.90, DTY - 48.07,
JTY - 54.93, DecY - 6858, OctY - 5741
DUNFORD James Robert U17 14.01.86, Birchfield :
OctY - 4226
DUNFORD William U15 21.04.87, Birchfield :
PV - 2.85, JTB - 45.43
DUNLOP John U20, Edinburgh University :
400 - 49.21
DUNNE Jimmy U13 21.10.88, WSE&H :
HJ - 1.50
DUPUY Jason 31.01.71, Shaftesbury Barnet :
800 - 1:52.81 (1:49.53-99)
DURHAM Peter U20 13.04.84, Cleethorpes :
TJ - 13.81
DYBALL Gareth U23 16.03.81, WGreen & Ex L :
HJ - 1.95 (2.00-98)
DYER Michael U17 27.09.84, Reading :
100HY - 14.10, 400H - 56.8, 400HY - 57.2, OctY - 4896

EARLE Robert Bernard V40 15.09.60, WG & Ex L :
SP - 13.59i/13.51 (14.87i-93/14.80-86),
DT - 41.05 (45.12-90), HT - 58.29 (62.60-95)
EARNSHAW Jonathan 24.08.77, Guildford & G :
1500 - 3:51.60
EAST Michael John 20.01.78, Newham & Essex B :
800 - 1:48.66, 1500 - 3:38.94, 1M - 3:59.61,
3k - 8:12.77 (8:04.27-00),
5k - 14:38.96 (14:28.0-00), 5MR - 23:50
EASTMAN Gavin U23 28.06.80, Enf & Har :
60 - 6.95i (6.9i-99), 100 - 10.43w/10.8/10.81 (10.75-99),
200 - 21.4w/21.7/22.13 (21.7/22.09-00)
EASTON Mark Jonathan 24.05.63, Surrey WC :
3kW - 12:59.7 (11:24.4-89),
5kW - 21:42.4 (20:01.65i-90/20:36.59+-89),
10kWR - 44:38 (40:53-89), 20kW - 1:29:40 (1:24:04-89),
35kW - 2:55:00 (2:42:13-93)
EASTWOOD Simon 18.04.65, Bedford & County :
PV - 4.21
EDGAR Tyrone U20 29.03.82, WGreen & Ex L :
60 - 6.86i, 100 - 10.17w/10.4/10.49 (10.39-00),
200 - 20.8w/20.96
EDLIN Darren U20 10.04.82, Goole :
400 - 48.9/48.96
EDMONDS Stephen 15.05.69, Birchfield :
10k - 31:58.5
EDMUNDS Cypren 20.06.70, Thames Valley :
200 - 21.72 (20.97-97)
EDMUNDS Gregor 25.04.77, Shettleston :
SP - 15.85un/14.37
EDMUNDS Thomas U15 12.12.86, Sussex Sch :
SPB - 13.06
EDNEY Simon V40, Bideford :
Mar - 2:30:22
EDSALL Charles K. 2.05.74, Havant :
110H - 15.2 (15.1-94/15.20-95)
EDWARDS Jonathan David 10.05.66, Gateshead :
TJ - 17.92 (18.43w/18.29-95)
EDWARDS Jonathan 6.11.78, Peterbro/Loughbro :
300 - 34.06, 400 - 47.46
EDWARDS Levi U23 23.11.80, Blackheath :
LJ - 7.20 (7.35w/7.27-00)
EDWARDS Mark Simon 2.12.74, Charnwood :
SP - 19.64 (19.72-00), DT - 46.97
EDWARDS Marvin 28.04.69, Newham & Essex B :
HT - 49.58 (53.72-88)
EDWARDS Michael 19.10.68, Belgrave :
PV - 4.90 (5.64un-99/5.52-93)
EDWARDS Neil U23 28.06.79, Wrexham/Leeds Univ :
Dec - 4973
EDWARDS Nicholas U23 22.03.81, Glouc AC/
Royal Navy : 110H - 15.6
EDWARDS Noel 16.12.72, Leamington :
800 - 1:51.29 (1:48.58-99)
EDWARDS-PALMER Daniel U13 19.09.88, :
100 - 12.6
EFOBI Nnamdi U15 14.09.86, Enf & Har :
DTB - 46.15, HTB - 53.76
EKOKU Abi 13.04.66, Belgrave :
DT - 54.47 (60.08-90)
EL SHEIKH Khaled 26.07.78, S & S H/London Univ :
HJ - 1.95i/1.95 (2.00i/2.00-00)
ELDER Craig U20 22.05.82, Sale/Strathclyde Univ :
LJ - 6.82 (6.98-00)
ELIAS Matthew U23 25.04.79, Cardiff :
400 - 46.88i/46.9 (47.25-00), 400H - 49.57
ELLAMS Craig 24.11.72, City of Stoke :
HT - 62.69 (64.39-00)
ELLERSHAW Philip 9.02.76, Blackpool :
100 - 10.8/10.89w/10.99 (10.6w/10.7/10.83-99),
200 - 21.99w/22.0 (21.6w-99/21.8-00/22.06-95
ELLINGTON James U17 6.09.85, Belgrave :
100 - 10.85, 200 - 21.94w/22.6/22.61
ELLIOTT Kenny U20 5.07.83, Regent House :
400H - 56.8
ELLIOTT Mark U23 12.08.80, C of Edinb/Glas Univ :
HJ - 1.95i (2.00i/2.00-99)
ELLIOTT Mensah Abraham 29.08.76, Blackheath :
100 - 10.97, 60H - 7.91i,
110H - 13.88 (13.69w/13.7/13.82-00), 400H - 54.37
ELLIOTT Neil 10.04.71, Border/City of Edinburgh :
SP - 15.86 (16.22-00), DT - 51.97
ELLIS Benjamin John U23 16.11.81, Winchester :
100 - 10.6w/10.94w, 200 - 21.5w/21.7/21.90 (21.85-00)
ELLIS Ieuan T. V40 11.05.60, Elswick :
Mar - 2:27:52 (2:13:21-86)
ELLIS Kevin 18.06.76, Peterborough :
60 - 6.8i/6.85i, 100 - 10.6w/10.65 (10.49w-00/10.6w-99),
200 - 21.7w/21.73, 300 - 35.0
ELLIS Samuel U20 23.06.82, Barnsley :
200 - 22.21 (22.0/22.20-00), 400 - 47.7/47.92
ELLWOOD Wayne 26.09.74, Blackpool :
400 - 49.07i (47.50-97)
ELSWORTHY Jake U20 9.03.83, Croydon :
DecJ - 5119
EMANUEL David 27.12.66, Birchfield :
TJ - 14.22 (15.91-91)
EMANUEL Lee U17 24.01.85, Hastings :
1500 - 4:00.20

EMEZIE Michael U15, :
PenB - 2569
EMMETT Peter U17 24.04.85, Salisbury :
3k - 8:56.58
ENIH-SNELL Chuka U20 2.03.84, Swansea :
HJ - 2.18
ENRIGHT Stephen U17 5.09.84, Halifax :
1500 - 4:04.8, 3k - 8:52.02
EROGBOGBO Temitayo Faruq 8.03.75, Birchfield :
TJ - 15.56w (16.44w-97/16.32-95)
ETHERINGTON G. U15, Exeter :
80HB - 11.5/11.57w/11.61
EVANS David 23.01.76, Birchfield :
JT - 56.90
EVANS Gareth 28.05.77, RAF/Sheffield :
110H - 15.54 (15.3-99/15.37-98), Dec - 5231
EVANS Jake U17 26.07.86, Carmarthen :
SPY - 14.04
EVANS James U15 7.11.86, :
JTB - 48.28
EVANS Matthew U13 9.09.88, Carmarthen :
SPC - 14.47, DTC - 35.35
EVANS Paul William V40 13.04.61, Belgrave :
10kR - 29:25 (28:13-95), Mar - 2:18:35 (2:08:52-96),
HMar - 63:15 (60:09un-95/61:18-97),
EVLING-JONES Louis U20 20.06.83, Peterborough :
110HJ - 15.3/15.37 (15.2-00), 110H - 15.6w,
DecJ - 6247
EVLING-WHITE Joseph U15 3.12.86, Corby :
TJ - 12.46w/12.43, PenB - 2585
EWULO Ezekiel U17 29.01.86, Herne Hill :
LJ - 6.65
EXLEY Scott 9.02.78, Belgrave :
100 - 10.78w/10.87 (10.7-00), Dec - 6759
EYONG Onen U17 18.02.85, Belgrave :
LJ - 7.47w/7.46

FABEN Stuart 28.02.75, Belgrave :
JT - 73.15 (76.66i-96/75.37-00)
FAHEY Thomas U17 27.09.84, Dartford :
3k - 8:50.82, 5k - 15:29.2
FAIRLAMB Neil 13.03.76, City of Stoke :
Dec - 5568 (5875-98)
FALCONER William 20.12.78, C of Edinb/Strathcl U :
SP - 14.81, DT - 41.36
FANNING Robert 31.10.78, Sale/IRL :
300 - 34.83, 400 - 48.3/48.46i/48.93 (47.9-97/48.05-98)
FARAH Mohamed U20 23.03.83, WSE&H :
800 - 1:53.1, 1500 - 3:46.1, 3k - 8:09.24,
5k - 13:56.31
FARENDEN Simon U17 6.10.85, Chesterfield :
100 - 11.0 (11.47-00), 200 - 21.46, 400 - 50.5
FARLEY Paul Ivor U17 1.12.84, Isle of Wight :
DTY - 41.09, HTJ - 49.13, HTY - 59.50
FARMER Paul 23.11.77, Luton :
5k - 14:46.6, 3kSt - 9:09.05 (8:59.01mb/9:01.64-99)
FARNHAM Carlton U15, Devon Sch :
200 - 23.34
FARQUHARSON Billy 14.04.75, Mansfield :
3kSt - 9:12.23
FARQUHARSON Ruddy Anthony V40 26.03.61,
Telford/RAF : TJ - 14.53 (15.59w/15.57-85)
FARROW Kevin 8.09.75, Derby & Co :
1500 - 3:50.59 (3:47.94-00),
3k - 8:21.16i (8:08.8-00), 5KR - 14:19
FASINRO Ibrahim 'Tosi' 28.03.72, Enf & Har :
TJ - 15.50 (17.30w/17.21-93)
FAULKNER Stewart 19.02.69, Birchfield :
LJ - 7.14w/7.12 (8.15-90)
FAVELL Peter U20 16.03.82, Chesterfield :
DTJ - 41.55 (43.93-99)
FEASEY Stephen U13 12.09.88, Kingston u Hull :
800 - 2:16.0
FEASEY Terry 5.08.77, Bas & MH/Loughbro :
800 - 1:50.32
FEIGHAN Mike 5.11.65, Bideford :
100kR - 7:43:14
FEIL Dirk 9.03.65, Morpeth/GER :
PV - 4.30i (4.40-97)
FELCE Alex U15 11.09.86, Gloucester L :
800 - 1:58.79io/2:00.1, 1500 - 4:05.48, 3k - 9:09.3
FELL Adam U17 20.04.85, Holmfirth :
400HY - 56.70
FENNEMORE Dennis U20 19.06.84, Harrow :
TJ - 13.86
FENTON Malcolm Leonard V45 12.02.56, Ipswich :
SP - 13.66i (14.62-96), HT - 59.90 (62.42-82)
FERDINAND Philip U20 18.11.82, Birchfield :
TJ - 15.34w/14.72 (14.98-00)
FERGUS Jason Robert 11.10.73, Shaftesbury Barn :
100 - 10.4w/10.43w/10.7 (10.34w-94/10.4-93/10.44-92),
200 - 21.2w/21.67 (20.85w-99/20.91-97)
FERGUSON Martin M. 17.09.64, City of Edinburgh :
10k - 31:45.1 (30:43.6-89),
Mar - 2:32:40 (2:26:45-95)
FERNANDEZ Andre U23 2.03.80, Thames Valley :
200 - 22.0w (22.12w-00), 300 - 34.8, 400 - 48.03,
LJ - 7.34w/7.18 (7.31-00)
FEWTRELL James U23 22.12.80, Bedford & County :
1500 - 3:47.94, 1M - 4:09.23, 3k - 8:08.04
FIELD Matthew U13 13.12.88, Kingston & Poly :
TJ - 10.52
FIELD Peter U20 21.05.82, City of Stoke :
HT - 57.16, HTJ - 62.53 (62.65-00)
FIFTON Rikki U17 17.06.85, Tower Hamlets :
100 - 10.56, 200 - 21.4w/21.48w/21.5/21.67
FINCH Lloyd U20 26.10.83, Leics WC :
3kW - 12:26.0i (12:34.98-99), 5kW - 20:47.23,
10kW - 44:29.4, 10kWR - 43:49 (43:38-99)
FINCH Luke U17 21.09.85, Leics WC :
3kW - 12:56.52, 5kW - 21:58.8,
10kW - 47:10.4, 10kWR - 46:00
FINCH Rodney 5.08.67, Southampton City/Army :
1500 - 3:45.92 (3:37.97-93),
3k - 8:14.03i/8:15.39 (7:53.99i-94/7:56.93-99),
5MR - 23:28, 10kR - 29:26
FINDEL-HAWKINS David, Milton Keynes :
24Hr - 188.529km
FINDLATER Joshua U15, Croydon :
LJ - 6.08
FINILL Chris V40 31.12.58, Harrow :
100kR - 7:24:20 (7:22:50-00)
FISH Benjamin U20 21.05.82, Blackburn :
3k - 8:26.53, 5k - 14:38.15, 10k - 31:09.3
FISHER Gavin 18.11.77, West Suffolk/Loughbro :
HJ - 1.95 (2.00-96)
FISHER Ian 15.09.70, Otley :
Mar - 2:21:52 (2:20:26-00)
FITZPATRICK Nicholas U13 29.10.88, Corby :
HJ - 1.55
FITZSIMMONS James 20.04.74, Shaftesbury Barnet :
10k - 31:01.35, Mar - 2:24:24, 3kSt - 8:57.93
FLANNERY Tim, Border :
110H - 14.89
FLEMING Peter Ross V40 5.01.61, Leslie Deans RC :
HMar - 64:53 (62:52-93)
FLETCHER Mark U15 4.11.86, Preston :
LJ - 6.08
FLINT Andrew 9.11.76, Thames Valley :
DT - 45.08
FLINT Benjamin 16.09.78, Belgrave :
PV - 5.05A/5.00 (5.40-99)
FLINT Christopher V55 6.12.44, London Vidarians :
100MW - 21:32:39 (20:17:28-89)
FLOYD Michael Anthony 26.09.76, Sale :
HT - 66.49 (69.38-00)

FLYNN Julian T. 3.07.72, Belgrave :
LJ - 7.51w/7.25 (7.76w/7.70-99),
TJ - 14.17w/14.00 (15.32-93)
FOGG Nicholas 24.03.78, Shaftesbury Barnet :
HT - 50.12 (52.56?-00)
FOLEY Dan U17 11.09.84, Wolverhampton & B :
800 - 1:56.2
FOOKS Andrew 26.04.75, Thames Valley :
3kSt - 9:13.0 (8:56.83-95)
FORBES James U15 1.11.86, Edinburgh Acad :
PV - 3.00
FORD Antony U20 26.05.83, Blackpool :
3k - 8:25.0, 5k - 15:01.20
FORDE James U17 10.04.85, Sparkhill :
HTY - 58.53
FORDE Karl U20 15.04.83, Rowheath :
60 - 6.97i, 100 - 10.71w (10.66w/10.70-99),
200 - 21.97i (21.9w-00/21.92w-99/22.0-00
FORDHAM Gavin James U23 1.02.79, Bed & C/Birm U :
HJ - 2.00i/1.96 (1.99-00), PV - 4.13, Dec - 6590
FORREST Anthony 22.12.76, AF&D/Milton Keynes :
3kSt - 9:16.8
FORREST Oliver U13 11.09.88, Hertford & Ware :
DTC - 29.62
FORSTER Tom U15 27.09.86, Cornwall Sch :
80HB - 11.9
FOSTER William Randolph Garnet V40 9.08.58,
Blackheath : 10k - 31:10.6 (29:14.34-96)
FOWLES Steven James U17 16.05.85, Thurrock :
100 - 10.78w/10.82
FOX Morris 30.04.63, City of Stoke :
SP - 16.10, DT - 45.25 (46.40-95)
FOX Richard U13 20.09.88, Fleet & Crookham :
80HC - 13.6
FOXWORTHY Nicholas U20 20.05.83, Exeter :
DecJ - 5098
FRAMPTON Matthew U20 10.04.84, Bournemouth :
HT - 47.66, HTJ - 54.20
FRANCE Chris U20 29.01.84, Telford :
HJ - 1.98 (1.98-00)
FRANCE Craig U15 11.01.87, W Cheshire :
80HB - 11.87, PenB - 2592
FRANCIS Nick 29.08.71, Shaftesbury Barnet :
Mar - 2:20:00
FRANCIS Ricardo U13 26.11.88, Hallamshire :
100 - 12.5, 200 - 25.7
FRANKLIN Andrew U23 13.09.80, Trafford :
1500 - 3:49.12, 5k - 14:38.4,
2kSt - 5:41.12, 3kSt - 8:42.82
FRASER Peter 28.01.78, Aberdeen :
JT - 56.14 (58.95-98)
FREARY Paul 3.04.68, Belgrave :
1500 - 3:51.00 (3:43.3-91), 5k - 14:40.01 (13:55.34-96)
FREMPONG Kenneth U20 17.07.84, Kingston u Hull :
100H - 14.61, 110HJ - 14.44
FRENCH Jon 11.12.75, City of Norwich :
LJ - 7.20w/6.88 (7.38w/7.22-99),
TJ - 13.87 (14.69-99)
FRICKER Simon David 14.07.75, Team Solent :
SP - 15.34, DT - 49.94 (49.96-97)
FRIEND Andrew U15 2.08.87, AF&D :
3k - 9:13.7
FRIMPONG James U20 17.09.82, Worcester AC :
DTJ - 42.29
FROST Andrew Derek U23 17.04.81, Isle of Wight/
St. Marys Univ : SP - 13.83, HT - 61.30
FROST Howard U23 9.12.81, Kent :
100 - 10.7w, 300 - 35.6, 400H - 52.9/54.13
FROST Russell U23 23.06.80, Kent :
100 - 10.8w (10.8w-99), 300 - 35.6, 400 - 48.1 (48.89-00)
FRY Jason U20 6.01.83, Southend :
PV - 4.45
FUGALLO Alexander 28.01.70, Shaftesbury Barnet :
200 - 21.74w (21.20w-89/21.2/21.26-90)
FULFORD Andrew U20 23.06.82, Swindon :
800 - 1:50.82, 1500 - 3:53.0
FULLER Peter John 30.04.78, Epsom & Ewell :
HT - 53.23
FULLER William 19.10.76, Epsom & Ewell :
SP - 15.70 (16.36-97), HT - 54.00 (54.20-97)
FURBER Matthew U17 28.10.84, Worthing :
800 - 1:58.4
FURLONG Kevin M. 19.05.70, Manx H :
110H - 15.5 (14.9-98/15.10-95)

GALLAGHER Andrew U20 15.02.83, Border :
JT - 66.95
GALLAGHER Anthony U17 16.10.84, Liv.Pem Sefton :
SPY - 13.84 (14.39i/13.98-00), DTY - 43.27
GALLIE Adam U17 5.11.84, Derby & Co :
HJ - 2.01
GARDEN Michael U15 27.10.86, WGreen & Ex L :
PV - 2.90
GARDENER Jason John 18.09.75, Wessex & Bath :
100 - 10.23 (9.98-99), 200 - 21.6 (20.65-99)
GARDINER Richard 11.06.73, Cardiff :
5k - 14:31.21, 10k - 30:55.5 (30:43.04-00)
GARDINER Stephen U15 21.09.86, Regent House :
HJ - 1.83
GARDINER Timothy U15 20.11.86, Stroud :
JTB - 46.53
GARDNER Rupert Arthur John U17 9.10.84, Milt K :
400 - 50.39i/50.6, 100HY - 14.10, 400H - 55.18,
400HY - 54.53, OctY - 4728
*GARENAMOTSE Gable U23 30.06.79, Cardiff/UWIC/
BOT : LJ - 8.26w/7.99, TJ - 15.92i (16.05-98)*
GARLAND Dale U23 13.10.80, Guernsey/Bath Univ :
400H - 53.22, LJ - 7.25,
TJ - 14.48w/13.92i (14.32-98), Dec - 6294
GARLAND Lee 18.12.74, Guernsey :
3kSt - 9:29.04, 400H - 55.43 (55.23-99)
GARNER Mark U20 2.11.83, Mansfield :
DecJ - 5183
GASCOIGNE Robert 5.10.74, Sale :
400H - 55.85 (55.21-97)
GATE Simon U20 21.09.82, Border :
HT - 46.27 (48.17-00), HTJ - 50.95 (52.46-00)
GAWTHORPE Richard James U23 28.01.81, Der & C/
Oxford Univ : 400H - 55.3 (56.00-00)
GAYLE Nicholas U17 4.01.85, City of Stoke :
100HY - 13.68
GEARING Chris U15 30.09.86, Medway :
SPB - 16.14, DTB - 42.43, HTB - 53.87
GEORGE Christopher U17 27.09.84, V of Aylesbury :
OctY - 4300
GHENT Brendon 7.09.76, Rugby :
60 - 6.77i, 100 - 10.53 (10.36w/10.4-00/10.51-99),
200 - 21.14w/21.30 (21.0/21.01-99)
GIBBINS Joe U13 12.11.88, :
TJ - 11.33
GIBLIN Christopher U23 20.06.81, Liverpool H :
HJ - 2.10 (2.12-99)
GIBSON Alex 3.11.77, Chelmsford :
SP - 13.53, JT - 57.28 (60.48-98), Dec - 6360
GILBERT James U17 19.11.85, Lincoln Well :
HJ - 1.90
GILDING Paul 2.10.75, Worthing :
60H - 8.4i, 110H - 15.0/15.15w/15.41 (15.28-00),
HJ - 1.95i/1.95 (2.03i/2.01-93), Dec - 5387 (5639-00)
GILHOOLY Anthony 26.03.76, Newham & Essex B :
HJ - 1.95 (2.18i-97/2.18-99)
GILL Andrew Robert 19.02.70, Bedford & County :
110H - 15.4 (14.41w-89/14.8-96/14.91-91),
400H - 55.46 (52.78-91)

GILL Anthony 19.09.77, Border/Staffs Univ :
300 - 35.47i, 60H - 8.24i (8.21i-99),
110H - 15.0/15.02 (14.22w/14.29-99), 400H - 54.97
GILL Jamie U17 29.10.85, Cannock & Stafford :
100 - 11.0/11.11w/11.19, 200 - 22.3/22.35w/22.65
GILL Stephen U17 25.09.84, Middlesbro & C :
400 - 49.6/50.00
GILLESPIE Ian 18.05.70, Birchfield :
3k - 7:59.58i (7:48.28-97),
5k - 14:24.39 (13:18.06-97), 5MR - 23:50
GIRDLER Dominic Paul U20 6.03.82, Charnwood :
100 - 10.95 (10.8w-00), 200 - 22.08w (25.0-96),
60H - 7.92i, 60HJ - 7.90i,
110HJ - 13.97 (13.96w-00), 110H - 14.07w/14.16
GIRVAN Richard Thomas 26.07.76, Anna Str/ Border :
800 - 1:49.78 (1:49.13-97), 1500 - 3:46.44
GITTENS Luke U23 4.01.81, Cardiff :
110H - 14.87 (14.86w-00)
GLANVILLE Craig U15 21.09.86, Gateshead :
200 - 23.4 (23.64-00), 400 - 50.72, 800 - 2:03.6,
80HB - 11.78, LJ - 6.16i, PenB - 2962
GLEDHILL Peter, Barnsley :
100kR - 8:15:18
GLENNIE Mark U20 19.02.82, Team Solent :
800 - 1:53.01
GODDARD Samuel John U20 4.01.83, Paddock Wd :
JT - 59.37
GOLDING Julian Antonio 17.02.75, Blackheath :
100 - 10.77 (10.28-97), 200 - 20.81 (20.18-98)
GOLLEY Julian Quintin Patrick 12.09.71, Thames VH :
LJ - 7.34w/7.18 (7.24-00), TJ - 16.93w/16.30 (17.06-94)
GOODGER Mark 17.12.78, Newport/Bath Univ :
800 - 1:51.51
GOODLIFFE Nicholas U20 12.05.82, Holm/Staffs Un :
1500 - 3:48.29, 3k - 8:23.25, 5k - 14:41.42
GOODREM Greg U20 14.09.83, Southend :
HJ - 2.00
GOODWIN Jon 22.09.76, Team Solent :
400H - 55.5 (52.5/53.14-97)
GORDON Alastair 16.04.78, Worthing :
100 - 10.8/10.92 (10.8-98), 200 - 21.73,
400 - 48.48 (47.98-00/48.2-98)
GORDON Peter V50 2.07.51, Gateshead :
DT - 54.68 (61.62-91)
GORDON Stephen U20 14.02.83, :
100 - 10.9
GORE Thomas U15 15.01.87, Oxford City :
200 - 23.11
GOUDIE Andrew 4.10.78, Belgrave :
3kW - 12:37.8, 5kW - 21:49.63,
10kWR - 44:57, 20kW - 1:34:40
GOULD Daniel U17 9.11.84, Leighton Buzzard :
100 - 11.1 (12.36-99)
GOULD Robert John 16.01.76, Trafford/Chester Un :
3k - 8:14.46i/8:21.76 (8:16.4-99),
5k - 14:12.56, 10k - 29:34.10, HMar - 64:46
GOULDBOURNE Marcus U23 12.06.81, Pud & Bram :
SP - 14.57, DT - 48.03
GOW David Allan U23 9.02.79, Shettleston :
800 - 1:51.78 (1:49.18-99)
GRAFFIN Allen Gordon 20.12.77, Tonbridge/Belgrave :
3k - 8:05.16A (8:03.22-98), 5k - 13:40.07, 5MR - 23:34
GRAFFIN Andrew Neill 20.12.77, Tonbridge/Belgrave :
800 - 1:47.5, 1500 - 3:35.97, 1M - 3:55.42,
3k - 8:20.94i (8:04.63i-00/8:07.58-99)
GRAHAM Andrew U17 14.11.84, Gosforth :
800 - 1:58.48
GRAHAM Andrew U13 19.12.89, Belgrave :
2kW - 11:01.6 (10:48.0-99)
GRAHAM Anthony 15.10.63, Tipton :
HMar - 66:00 (64:48-94)
GRAHAM Daniel Alexander U23 3.08.79, Liverpool H :
HJ - 2.21 (2.22-00)
GRAHAM Douglas 1.01.77, City of Edinburgh :
PV - 4.20i (4.26-96)
GRANT Dalton 8.04.66, WGreen & Ex L :
HJ - 2.26i/2.23 (2.37i-94/2.36-91)
GRANT Dwayne U20 17.07.82, Blackheath :
60 - 6.79i, 100 - 10.22w/10.3w/10.4/10.47,
200 - 20.4w/20.64
GRANT Mark 17.05.71, Luton :
PV - 5.11
GRAY Paul 25.05.69, Cardiff :
60H - 7.97i (7.78i-95), 110H - 13.63 (13.53-94)
GREAVES Damien David 19.09.77, Newham & E B :
110H - 13.68 (13.62-00)
GREAVES Daniel U20 4.10.82, Charnwood :
DT - 43.66, DTJ - 47.16
GREEN Clifton Paul U23 10.10.79, Belgrave :
JT - 66.73
GREEN Joseph U13 1.11.88, Cambridge Harriers :
HJ - 1.57
GREEN Michael Stephen 12.10.76, Blackb/Troy St U :
1500 - 3:49.27 (3:48.14-00), 3k - 8:10.06,
5k - 14:14.38 (14:12.56-99), Mar - 2:26:05
GREEN Paul 7.04.72, Sale :
3k - 8:24.24 (8:03.56-99),
5k - 14:20.12 (13:56.27-97),
10k - 30:40.93 (29:51.2-96), HMar - 64:57
GREEN Royston U20 4.01.82, Exeter :
800 - 1:51.6, 1500 - 3:52.58
GREEN Stephen Harold 18.02.71, Trafford :
800 - 1:52.97 (1:48.9-95), 1500 - 3:47.65 (3:39.19-94)
GREEN Steven Christopher U20 15.01.83, Cornwall/
Cambridge U : 110HJ - 14.7/14.71, 400H - 52.29
GREENE Richard U17 11.10.84, Enf & Har :
DTY - 43.64, HTJ - 49.08, HTY - 56.55
GREENFIELD Luke U23 6.05.81, Thames VH /NZL :
HT - 58.57
GREENLAND Philip U17 10.10.84, Croydon :
LJ - 7.10w/6.96
GREENWOOD Luke U13 31.10.88, Bridport R :
400 - 59.9
GREGG Steven U15 27.06.87, Chesterfield :
800 - 2:04.8
GREGORY Michael 5.11.76, Winchester :
1500 - 3:48.97
GREY Edwin U23 23.03.81, Brom & R/Loughbro :
100 - 10.94w (11.8-97), 110H - 15.26w/15.6 (15.77-99)
GRIERSON Andrew U23 23.11.79, WSE&H :
HT - 57.34 (59.12-98)
GRIERSON Gordon U17 12.10.85, WSE&H :
HTY - 53.65
GRIEVES David U17 17.11.84, Jarrow & Hebburn :
100 - 11.02
GRIFFIN Neil V50 28.05.48, WSE&H :
SP - 13.51 (16.06-77), DT - 42.99 (51.66-80)
GRIFFITH Mark U23 25.11.81, WGreen & Ex L/
St. Marys Univ : 3kSt - 9:23.84 (9:22.44-99)
GRIFFITHS Kyle U15 10.10.86, London Schools :
LJ - 6.09
GRIFFITHS Thomas U13 18.09.88, Swansea :
75HC - 12.9
GRIME Ian Stuart 29.09.70, Newham & Essex B :
1500 - 3:46.49 (3:40.1-96), 3k - 8:17.46i (7:55.4-96),
5k - 14:28.81 (13:37.00-97), 10kR - 29:46 (29:21-00)
GRIME Peter John 8.11.69, Durham Univ :
5k - 14:31.72, 10k - 30:52.69
GROVES Michael U20 21.03.84, Cwmbran :
200 - 21.90
GUEST Craig U20 25.10.82, Charnwood :
JT - 55.00 (55.17-99)
GUNN Alistair U23, Falkirk :
SP - 13.81
GUNN Chris U20 13.09.82, Birchfield :
Dec - 5461

GUNN Luke U17 22.03.85, Derby & Co :
1500 - 4:01.75, 1.5kSt - 4:20.43

HAGAN Garry U17 21.11.84, Shaft B/Clydesdale :
SP - 13.31, SPJ - 13.75, SPY - 15.60,
DT - 42.26, DTJ - 45.82, DTY - 52.44
HAINES Gareth U17 21.11.84, Carmarthen :
HJ - 1.90
HALE Darren V40 2.10.59, Salford :
Mar - 2:30:17 (2:22:09-97)
HALE Steven 20.04.77, Birchfield :
DT - 41.62 (44.53-00)
HALES Matthew John MacKenzie U23 6.10.79, Stey :
3kW - 12:08.57i/12:51.96 (12:07.54-00),
10kWR - 44:00+ (45:00-99), 20kW - 1:28:40
HALEY Stuart U17 9.12.84, Gateshead :
100 - 11.0 (11.07w-00), 200 - 22.35
HALL Alex U20 2.02.82, Cambridge Harriers :
LJ - 7.22 (7.29-99)
HALL Brendan Russell U15 5.09.87, Cannock & St :
SPB - 13.64
HALL Brian Nigel U20 17.11.82, Bolton :
HJ - 2.11
HALL Calvin U20 15.11.83, Birchfield :
HJ - 2.01
HALL Dominic 21.02.71, Highgate Harriers :
800 - 1:52.37 (1:49.1-98)
HALL Jason U17, Lincoln Well :
1.5kSt - 4:34.77
HALL Max U15 29.12.86, Dartford :
PV - 3.00
HALL Samuel Thomas U17 15.10.85, Shaftesbury B :
1.5kSt - 4:30.04
HALL Stuart 21.12.64, Tipton :
10MR - 49:08, HMar - 65:42, Mar - 2:18:46
HALLETT Jason U20 29.03.82, Cardiff :
JT - 60.15
HALLIGAN John U20 4.05.83, Manx :
3kSt - 9:34.53
HAMBRIDGE Simon U13 18.02.89, Nuneaton :
2kW - 11:17.1o (11:08.4-00)
HAMILTON Carl U13 30.06.89, :
75HC - 12.4
HAMILTON Christopher 4.11.78, Rotherham :
100 - 10.8w/10.95
HANN Michael, WSE&H :
SP - 14.62, DT - 40.21
HANSARD Richard U15 5.11.86, Watford :
80HB - 11.45
HANSFORD Matthew U17 20.02.86, Exeter :
100HY - 13.7/14.01, OctY - 4543
HANSON Mark U23 13.05.81, Enf & Har/Brunel Univ :
60 - 6.90i, 100 - 10.60w/10.76, 200 - 21.7w/22.0
HARDIE James U20 16.04.82, Belgrave :
HJ - 2.06i/2.02 (2.05-00)
HARDING Ben U15 12.12.86, City of Portsmouth :
800 - 2:01.38, 1500 - 4:15.8, 3k - 9:19.4
HARDING Jason U20 24.09.82, Coventry Godiva :
100 - 10.90w
HARDING Nick U15 15.12.86, Crawley :
HTB - 46.27
HARGREAVES Kyle U15 11.07.87, :
HJ - 1.75
HARLAND Andrew U17 23.08.85, West Suffolk :
JTY - 52.67
HARLAND Kim U20 21.02.82, Carmarthen :
HJ - 1.98 (2.01-00)
HARLE Robert Keith U23 1.06.79, St Albans St/CuAC :
100 - 10.8/10.92w (10.8/10.97-00),
200 - 22.0/22.20w (21.8/22.07-00)
HARPER Ben U20 7.09.82, Cannock & Stafford :
HTJ - 48.02
HARPHAM Peter U17 2.11.84, Sheffield :
100 - 11.06w/11.18
HARRIES Kirk 7.08.74, Thames Valley :
110H - 15.25 (14.45w-97/14.65-98)
HARRIS Adam U15 7.09.86, Pembroke :
DTB - 39.29
HARRIS Ashley U13 18.03.89, Croydon :
LJ - 5.13
HARRIS Daniel U15 1.10.86, City of Plymouth :
80HB - 11.9/11.91, LJ - 6.46, PenB - 2608
HARRIS Richard 16.08.71, Rotherham :
3kSt - 9:21.73
HARRISON David U13 17.10.88, Blackheath :
JTC - 35.46
HARRISON Edward U15 10.12.86, Med & Maid :
80HB - 11.3/11.31w/11.46
HARRISON Julian 4.08.76, Sheffield :
HJ - 2.05
HARRISON Nsa U20 27.11.83, Worcester AC :
SPJ - 14.78, DTJ - 41.21
HART Andrew 13.09.69, Coventry Godiva :
800 - 1:50.10i (1:45.71-98),
1k - 2:24.88i (2:18.78-96)
HART Tom 7.12.77, WSE&H :
5k - 14:35.26, 10k - 31:06.3
HARTLAND Ben U13 14.06.89, Barry :
LJ - 5.11
HARTLEY John V45 21.11.56, Clayton-Le-Moors :
Mar - 2:35:14
HARVEY Lawrence U23 26.08.81, Ashford :
TJ - 13.97
HARVEY Mark U20 2.07.84, Neath :
PV - 4.10
HARVEY Steven U17 24.01.85, Notts :
100 - 11.1
HARWOOD Laurence U17 9.03.85, Isle of Wight :
HTY - 57.31
HARWOOD Paul 19.07.71, AF&D :
Mar - 2:30:45 (2:28:44-99)
HARWOOD Scott U15 1.10.86, Rotherham :
PenB - 2687
HARWOOD William U15 25.09.86, Cleethorpes :
TJ - 13.20
HASLETT Matthew U17 16.09.84, Border :
HJ - 1.90
HASSAN Malcolm Mark U20 27.11.82, Sunderland :
800 - 1:50.7, 1500 - 3:53.99
HASSELL Alan U15 24.06.87, Cannock & Stafford :
HJ - 1.90
HATTON Darren U23 21.03.79, Ashford :
PV - 4.30, LJ - 6.84 (7.01w-97/6.97-98),Dec - 7020,
SP - 13.89i/13.50, DT - 42.30, JT - 61.86
HATTON Felix U17 9.10.84, Kingston & Poly :
JTY - 58.32
HAUGHIAN Samuel U23 9.07.79, WSE&H :
1500 - 3:47.13 (3:45.23-99),
3k - 8:03.94 (7:57.24-99),
5k - 13:46.35, 10k - 29:10.5, 10MR - 49:30
HAUGHIAN Tim U15 29.11.86, WSE&H :
1500 - 4:16.75, 3k - 9:26.2
HAWKINS Malcolm U20 17.12.83, Stratford :
400H - 56.4
HAY Alistair U17 7.09.85, Central :
800 - 1:57.8
HAY John David U20 4.06.83, Corby :
HTJ - 50.86 (51.88-00)
HAY Wayne U23 25.09.80, WSE&H :
LJ - 6.88i (6.79-96)
HAYDEN Lewis U13 10.08.89, Nuneaton :
2kW - 10:00.0o/10:14.7
HAYES Kevin 10.11.70, Nuneaton :
1500 - 3:50.6 (3:48.95-96)

HAYES Martin U23 31.08.79, Sheffield :
HT - 46.03 (48.12-97)
HAYES Scott 4.01.73, Thames Valley :
SP - 15.42 (16.15i-98/15.62-95),
DT - 50.24 (54.16-97)
HAYHURST Ross U13 15.10.88, Liverpool H :
SPC - 11.39
HAYMAN Nigel 25.09.74, Bournemouth :
110H - 15.3 (15.2-97/15.33w-99/15.39-97)
HAYNES Alex U17 6.09.84, North Shields Poly :
1.5kSt - 4:35.33
HAYWARD Andrew 26.10.74, Rowntrees :
JT - 60.09 (60.96-99)
HAYWARD Robert U17 22.09.84, Invicta :
1500 - 4:04.7
HAYWARD Stephen William Moore 30.07.74, Sale/ Scottish Borders/IRL : SP - 16.58 (18.79-00)
HAZELL Ben U17 1.10.84, Basingstoke & MH :
400HY - 56.42, OctY - 4533
HEAD Paul 1.07.65, Newham & Essex B :
DT - 42.73 (44.40-00), HT - 70.33 (74.02-90)
HEAD Stephen V40 21.10.58, Newham & Essex B :
SP - 13.38 (14.44-89)
HEALEY Richard V45 17.11.54, Portsmouth :
DT - 42.45 (45.50-81)
HEALY Mark 4.04.70, Lliswerry :
Mar - 2:33:31
HEANEY Robert U13 10.02.89, Bedford & County :
1500 - 4:47.4
HEANLEY James U17 1.04.85, WSE&H :
JTY - 52.48
HEANLEY John U23 25.09.80, WSE&H/London Univ. :
110H - 14.93w/15.0/15.28, PV - 4.62,
LJ - 7.23i/7.04, TJ - 14.42, Dec - 7129
HEAP John 8.11.70, Hallamshire :
Mar - 2:27:40
HEATH Brett 6.01.75, Havering :
DT - 41.93 (44.50-00)
HEATON Robert U23 6.05.81, Preston/Oxford Univ :
TJ - 13.98
HEDMAN Graham U23 6.02.79, WGreen & Ex L :
100 - 10.85 (10.7w-98/10.8-99/10.83w-98,
200 - 21.3w/21.56, 400 - 47.63
HEMERY Adrian U20 6.08.82, Swindon/Cambridge U :
110H - 15.5/15.56, Dec - 6788
HENDERSON Adam U13 18.02.89, Arbroath :
75HC - 12.99w
HENDRY Martyn John 10.04.75, City of Edinburgh :
60H - 8.23i (8.00i-98), 110H - 15.0/15.13 (14.16-97)
HENNESSY Andrew D. 24.08.77, TVH /London Univ. :
1500 - 3:51.77 (3:46.32-99),
3k - 8:18.82i (8:16.8-00), 3kSt - 8:45.4 (8:39.71-99)
HENRY Cori 9.12.76, Notts :
100 - 10.8 (10.5w/10.8-96/10.96-00),
200 - 21.4/21.59 (20.8w-96/20.9-99/21.34-96),
400 - 47.2/47.41 (46.50-96)
HENRY James U20 31.07.84, Spenborough :
2kSt - 6:13.02
HENRY Robert U17 22.10.84, Kingston u Hull :
100HY - 13.60, OctY - 4615
HENTHORN James 20.02.77, Team Solent/UWIC :
60 - 6.92i (6.71i-00),
100 - 10.50w/10.68 (10.22w-97/10.39-99),
200 - 21.37i/21.5/21.51 (20.93-99)
HEPPLES Stephen David U23 6.01.80, Loftus/ Teeside Univ : 3k - 8:10.53, 5k - 14:09.41
HEPPLEWHITE Daniel U15 2.09.86, Bournemouth :
SPB - 16.12, DTB - 39.84
HERBERT Scott 12.02.74, Milton Keynes :
200 - 22.0 (21.20-96)
HERMANN Daniel John U23 3.03.81, Pudsey & Bram/ Leeds Poly : 800 - 1:51.87
HERMANN Derek U23 7.04.79, Carmarthen :
JT - 57.77 (61.85-00)
HERRING Christopher U23 3.03.81, Mandale/ Edge Hill Univ : 400H - 55.60 (54.02-99)
HERRINGTON Gary Hugh V40 31.03.61, Rugby :
SP - 13.67 (14.88-98), DT - 51.09 (56.66-96),
HT - 45.91 (50.91-98)
HERRINGTON Samuel Edward U15 2.10.86, Corby :
SPB - 15.32, DTB - 52.43
HEWITSON Dale U17 11.09.84, Elswick :
SPY - 15.46
HIBBARD William U15 24.03.87, Wilts Sch :
PV - 3.00
HIBBERT Paul N. 31.03.65, Birchfield :
400 - 49.1 (47.38-96), 110H - 15.53 (14.89-00),
400H - 51.31 (50.52-96)
HICKS Mark U15 12.07.87, Cwmbran :
80HB - 11.8/11.84w/11.92
HICKS Maurice 1.01.70, Team Solent/Junction 10 :
HT - 52.32 (56.14-96)
HIGBEE Tony U20 21.09.83, :
DecJ - 5326
HIGGINS Ben U15 27.09.86, Ipswich :
200 - 23.5
HIGGINS Marcus U13 3.11.88, Solihull & S Heath :
SPC - 12.11
HIGHAM Keith Robert U17 7.11.85, Border :
PV - 4.40i/4.10
HILL Gavin U15 22.12.86, Middlesbro & C :
DTB - 40.23, HTB - 51.03
HILL Michael Christopher 22.10.64, Leeds :
JT - 84.88 (86.94-93)
HILL Mick 2.09.75, Tipton :
5k - 14:43.50 (14:34.8-97), 10k - 30:35.16
HILLIER Chris U17 23.02.85, Wimborne :
800 - 1:56.60
HILLIER James 3.04.78, Birchfield/Birmingham Univ. :
60H - 8.36i, 400H - 50.40
HILSTON James U23 25.02.79, Belgrave :
HJ - 1.95 (2.00-96)
HILTON Jonathan 11.01.74, Sale :
TJ - 15.23w/14.97i/14.82 (15.59w/15.42-00)
HILTON Martin 9.05.75, Leeds :
1500 - 3:51.42, 3k - 8:16.17
HINTON Michael U13 22.02.89, Wolverhampton & B :
200 - 26.0
HINZE Alistair U17 25.09.85, Herne Hill :
LJ - 6.72w (6.21i/6.20-00)
HIORNS Jonathan U15 2.10.86, Basingstoke & MH :
400 - 51.34
HISCOX Darren 21.03.72, Bridgend :
HMar - 66:01 (64:56-96)
HISLOP Matthew U15 31.01.87, Shaftesbury Barnet :
200 - 23.43w (25.58-99)
HITCHENS Alex U15 12.12.86, Cornwall AC :
DTB - 40.42
HLIOUAT Najib 28.08.77, Belgrave :
800 - 1:52.33
HO Darren U17 20.03.85, Shettleston :
100HY - 13.80w/13.8/14.01
HOAD James U15 1.02.88, Enf & Har :
PV - 3.00
HODGKINSON Alex U17 1.12.84, Shaftesbury B :
1500 - 4:02.49
HODGSON Gavin Andrew 1.02.78, Border :
400H - 54.71 (53.7-00)
HOGAN James U17 2.12.84, :
3k - 8:56.37
HOGAN Nicholas U23 15.10.80, WSE&H/IRL :
100 - 10.5w/10.55w/10.7
HOLDEN Oliver U17 30.05.86, Halesowen :
3k - 8:56.36

HOLDEN Tom U20 2.02.84, Tipton :
800 - 1:54.5
HOLDER Graham Paul 16.01.72, Shaftesbury Barnet :
DT - 40.40 (41.46-99), HT - 61.50 (61.91-99)
HOLDER James 12.10.76, Birchfield/CAN :
110H - 15.12w, Dec - 6999
HOLGATE Martin C. 2.11.65, WGreen & Ex L :
400H - 55.5 (54.2/54.51-95)
HOLLADAY Robert 10.01.75, Morpeth :
Mar - 2:19:26
HOLLAND Daniel U17 7.11.84, Liv.Pembroke Sefton :
100 - 11.18w (12.37-99)
HOLLAND James U17 1.04.85, Thurrock :
SPY - 14.36, DTY - 42.51
HOLLIDAY Adrian U15 17.01.87, Border :
1500 - 4:17.8, 3k - 9:27.5
HOLLIDAY Ian 9.12.73, Sale :
HJ - 2.10 (2.16-98)
HOLLIER Steven 27.02.76, Wolverhampton & B :
3kW - 12:41.0 (12:10.0-96), 5kW - 21:04.36,
10kWR - 44:00+ (42:18+-00/42:29-95),
20kW - 1:29:26 (1:27:04t-00/1:28:34-99),
30kW - 2:18:31, 50kW - 4:09:27 (4:07:18-00)
HOLLINGSWORTH Ivan 20.05.75, Wallsend :
1500 - 3:48.89 (3:48.32-96)
HOLMES Andrew U15 20.04.87, Norfolk Sch :
LJ - 6.04
HOLMES Mike V45 13.03.53, Salford :
Mar - 2:35:44
HOLMES Ryan U17 31.10.84, Basildon :
HTY - 47.56
HOLSGROVE Tim U20 11.12.82, Wirral :
PV - 4.40i/4.40
HOLTBY John U20 27.03.82, Kingston u Hull :
110HJ - 15.17 (14.46w/14.88-00),
SPJ - 14.27 (14.29-00)
HOMMA Takayuki U15 19.02.87, Belgrave/JPN :
100 - 11.55, LJ - 6.28
HONOUR Nathan 15.11.77, Woking :
100 - 10.7/10.87, 200 - 21.7/21.84 (21.7-99),
300 - 35.8, 400 - 49.1 (48.3/48.45-99)
HOOD Keith 13.09.72, Corstorphine :
3kSt - 9:24.18 (9:15.0-00)
HOOTON Robin David 5.05.73, City of Edinburgh :
800 - 1:51.7 (1:47.7-96)
HOPKINS Joel 24.11.77, Enf & Har :
400H - 54.0/54.83
HOPKINSON Andrew U20 20.09.83, Sale :
110HJ - 14.9w/15.17, 110H - 15.6, 400H - 55.03
HOPLEY James Edward U15 28.01.87, Telford :
JTB - 45.39
HOUGH Robert S.D. 3.06.72, Sheffield :
3kSt - 8:56.64 (8:26.33-96)
HOUGHTON Ben U23 6.08.80, B & A/Gateshead/IRL :
JT - 63.75 (64.34-97)
HOUSLIN Livon V40 2.11.60, Thames Valley :
JT - 61.05 (63.92-92)
HOWARD Paul 19.10.66, WGreen & Ex L :
JT - 61.41 (65.10-91)
HOWARTH Paul 30.10.77, Wirral :
3k - 8:19.53i, 5k - 14:39.42i# (14:39.64-00),
3kSt - 9:20.78
HOWE Christopher William 17.11.67, WGrn & Ex L :
DT - 41.17 (44.84-90), HT - 63.40 (66.97-98)
HOWELL Tim U20 6.12.82, City of Stoke :
110HJ - 15.40, Dec - 5462, DecJ - 5398
HOWES Matthew U15 6.01.87, Northampton :
3k - 9:38.5
HOWES Michael U15 6.11.86, Leeds :
SPB - 13.21
HOYTE Justin U17 20.11.84, Wigan :
100 - 11.01w

HUDSPITH Ian 23.09.70, Morpeth :
1500 - 3:51.3 (3:47.6-94), 3k - 8:11.79 (8:03.9-95),
5k - 14:03.50 (13:52.8-97),
10k - 28:40.63 (28:35.11-97),
HMar - 65:42 (62:53-96)
HUDSPITH Mark E. 19.01.69, Morpeth :
5k - 14:12.50 (13:49.37-00), 5MR - 23:34 (23:22-99),
HMar - 65:40+ (62:50dh-95/63:19-97),
Mar - 2:13:13 (2:11:58-95)
HUGHES Brian C. 6.01.70, Trafford :
PV - 4.32, Dec - 6025 (6105-00)
HUGHES David U20 31.05.84, Scunthorpe :
110HJ - 14.7w/14.85w/15.06,
Dec - 5623, DecJ - 6308
HUGHES Ioan 8.10.78, Trafford :
LJ - 7.22w/7.14
HUGHES Kevin Michael 30.04.73, Newham & E B :
PV - 5.20 (5.61-99)
HUGHES Peter U20 12.12.83, Ynys Mon :
DT - 40.21, DTJ - 41.50
HUGHES Steven U20 25.02.82, Scun/Loughbro :
Dec - 6151
HULSE G.Ewart W. 21.01.62, Colwyn Bay :
HT - 47.92 (54.62-91)
HUMPHRIES Tom U17 24.09.84, Cannock & Stafford :
1500 - 4:03.80, 3k - 8:53.61
HUNT Iain U17 24.11.84, Cwmbran :
200 - 22.4/22.41w/22.67, LJ - 6.59
HUNT Simon U23 27.08.79, Solihull & S Heath :
HJ - 1.95
HUNT Toby U15 28.12.86, WSE&H :
SPB - 13.89, DTB - 37.97, PenB - 2682
HUNTER Christopher U23 3.03.81, Jarrow & Heb :
Dec - 5028 (5770-99)
HUNTER Richard Andrew 12.01.71, Morpeth :
110H - 15.53w (14.79w-89/14.8/14.99-95),
LJ - 6.80, Dec - 5689 (6092-92)
HUNTER Roger 10.03.76, Skyrac :
110H - 15.1/15.14 (15.0-96), DT - 41.31,
Dec - 6749 (7159-97)
HUNTER Stephen Carl U15 22.12.86, Hallamshire :
100 - 11.24w/11.40, 200 - 23.09w/23.47, HJ - 1.79
HUNTINGDON Stuart U13 2.12.88, City of Norwich :
1500 - 4:47.9
HUNTLEY Matthew U17 29.10.84, Cambridge H :
JTY - 53.38
HURREN Richard U20 24.09.83, Harrow/Falkirk :
PV - 4.60
HURST Lee 29.07.72, Belgrave :
3kSt - 9:07.38 (8:48.34-96)
HUSSEY Andrew 17.05.73, Birchfield :
Mar - 2:35:41
HUTCHESON Peter U15 18.11.86, Crawley :
80HB - 11.59, JTB - 51.34
HUTCHINSON Michael Innes 5.10.65, Trafford :
3kSt - 9:21.4 (8:50.61-92)
HYLTON Mark David 24.09.76, WSE&H :
100 - 10.68 (10.60-98), 400 - 46.09 (45.24-98),
200 - 21.10 (21.04i-97/21.09-95)

IDDON Christopher U20 8.10.82, Bolton :
800 - 1:53.84
IDOWU Phillips Olaosebikan 30.12.78, Belgrave :
100 - 10.81, LJ - 7.23 (7.83-00), TJ - 17.38w/17.33
IGI Abdi U15 12.12.87, Ealing,Southall & Mx :
800 - 2:04.96, 1500 - 4:20.71, 3k - 9:24.61
ILIFFE Niklas U23 6.03.81, Team Solent :
DT - 44.08
INGRAM Geoff 31.01.68, RAF/City of Norwich :
LJ - 6.88, Dec - 5686 (6148-98)
IRELAND Adam 5.10.78, Copeland/Oxford Univ :
TJ - 13.99 (13.99-00)

IRVING Jan 4.03.77, Sale :
LJ - 6.86 (7.20w/7.18-98)
IRVING Peter U20 28.01.83, Jersey :
110H - 15.31, 400H - 54.41
IVE Joe U15 12.05.87, Kingston & Poly :
PV - 3.10
IVEMY Craig U17 28.03.86, Hailsham :
3k - 8:50.87

JACKSON Ben U17 22.11.84, Dacorum & T :
PV - 3.65
JACKSON Colin Ray 18.02.67, Brecon :
110H - 13.32 (12.8w-90/12.91-93)
JACKSON Edward U20 4.01.82, Swindon/AF&D :
800 - 1:53.3, 1500 - 3:54.4
JACKSON Graham U17 12.11.85, Gateshead :
TJ - 13.70
JACOBS Matthew U17 28.02.85, Carmarthen :
TJ - 13.63w/13.46
JACOBS Sam U17 19.09.84, Ipswich :
3k - 8:55.8
JAMES Alan 26.03.62, WSE&H :
HT - 50.87
JAMES Christopher U20 9.12.82, Milton Keynes :
HTJ - 52.59
JAMES Robert U15 1.04.87, Birchfield :
80HB - 11.44w/11.62
JAMES Ryan U17 10.05.85, Stratford :
100 - 11.08, LJ - 6.77w/6.51
JANVIER Nick 9.08.70, :
Mar - 2:29:54
JARRETT Anthony Alexander 13.08.68, Enf & Har :
110H - 13.45 (13.00-93)
JARRETT Philip U15 18.03.87, Sheffield :
80HB - 11.96, LJ - 6.07, PenB - 2718
JEFFERSON Chris U15, Durham Sch :
TJ - 12.33
JEGEDE J. U15, Newham & Essex B :
LJ - 6.01
JEMI-ALADE Michael 13.10.64, City of Edinburgh :
DT - 46.97 (52.38-87)
JENNINGS Gary 21.02.72, Newham & Essex B :
400H - 53.94 (49.82-95)
JENNINGS Neil A. 18.09.77, Mandale/Newcastle Un :
200 - 22.13w (22.1-95), 400 - 46.91
JENNINGS Thomas U17 27.01.85, Holmfirth :
OctY - 4319
JENNS Scott U23 13.12.80, Tipton :
DT - 42.02
JERVIS Alan Peter U20 27.07.84, City of Stoke :
PV - 4.50i/4.20 (4.25-00)
JILLONS Daniel U20 3.04.83, Suffolk Sch :
TJ - 14.10w/13.94
JOHNSON Andrew U17 13.05.86, Blackheath :
100HY - 13.97
JOHNSON Michael U15 28.09.86, Bournemouth :
200 - 23.3w, 80HB - 11.6/11.78
JOHNSON Peter V45 54, City of Norwich :
Mar - 2:34:23
JOHNSON Tyson U15 24.06.87, Halesowen :
JTB - 49.04
JOHNSTON Cameron B. U20 22.10.82, Croydon :
PV - 4.60 (4.70-00)
JOHNSTON Mark U17 18.10.84, Livingston :
800 - 1:57.0, 1500 - 3:59.79
JOLLEY Roberts U17 26.04.85, Southend :
SPY - 13.89
JONES Andres 3.02.77, Cardiff :
5MR - 23:26, 10k - 30:20.7 (28:00.50-00)
JONES Andrew U17 13.02.85, Bolton :
PV - 3.60
JONES Ben U20 6.11.82, Milton Keynes :
HTJ - 50.36
JONES Ben U17 14.01.86, Wirral :
3k - 8:52.51
JONES Chris U17 17.07.85, Basingstoke & MH :
400HY - 58.61
JONES David U20 19.02.84, Carmarthen :
2kSt - 6:07.85
JONES Egryn 1.11.71, Cardiff :
PV - 4.70 (4.90-95)
JONES Gareth U20 1.07.82, Sale :
200 - 21.9
JONES Gary 6.01.72, WSE&H :
100 - 10.60w/10.7/10.77 (10.7-97),
200 - 21.59w/21.76 (21.6-00)
JONES Jamie 8.12.71, Overton :
10k - 31:22.5, Mar - 2:32:31
JONES Kris U20 7.03.83, Newport :
110HJ - 15.1/15.44w
JONES Matthew U20 12.02.82, Wrexham :
5k - 15:28.2
JONES Matthew U20 10.10.82, City of Stoke :
800 - 1:54.32, 1500 - 3:47.97,
5k - 14:54.98 (14:40.2-00)
JONES Michael David 23.07.63, Belgrave :
HT - 76.43
JONES Michael U17 12.12.84, Hereford :
HTY - 48.12 (51.19-00)
JONES Nick 10.07.74, Tipton :
10kR - 29:39 (29:27-99), 10MR - 49:13 (48:40-97),
HMar - 64:00 (63:12-00), Mar - 2:20:32 (2:20:22-98)
JONES Paul 11.04.78, Stoke :
110H - 15.53 (15.19w/15.27-99),
PV - 4.76i/4.55 (4.75-99), LJ - 7.03
JONES Rhodri 14.08.66, Westbury/Yate :
Mar - 2:19:27 (2:18:34-00)
JONES Robin Evans Hugh V45 1.11.55, Ranelagh :
Mar - 2:32:35 (2:09:24-82)
JORDAN John U23 18.01.81, Basildon/Leeds Univ :
100 - 10.84w/10.90, 200 - 21.8w (22.4/22.43w/22.60-97)
JOSEPH J., Army :
100 - 10.6w?/10.71, 200 - 22.05
JOSEPH Jason U17 27.11.85, Enf & Har :
HTY - 56.70
JOSEPH Rafer Ernest Lewis 21.07.68, Bas & MH :
DT - 47.08 (52.00-96)
JOUSIFFE Warren 27.05.77, WSE&H :
PV - 4.60i/4.60 (4.70-96)
JUDSON Paul U17 20.06.86, Cannock & Stafford :
100 - 11.18w
JUKES Robert U20 18.09.83, Basingstoke & MH :
DTJ - 41.83
JULIEN Chris U15 14.09.87, Enf & Har :
100 - 11.52, 200 - 23.5 (24.28w-00)

KACOU Alain U13 25.10.88, Herne Hill :
200 - 25.7, HJ - 1.50, LJ - 5.16,
TJ - 11.75, SPC - 11.97
KAIGHAN Glen U15 14.11.86, Barrow & Furness :
200 - 23.10w/23.45
KAMOGA Eddie U13 25.12.88, WGreen & Ex L :
200 - 26.0, SPC - 11.35
KANEEN Peter V40 12.07.61, Manx H :
3kW - 13:16.9 (13:14.2-99), 5kW - 22:51.1,
10kWR - 47:12, 50kW - 4:40:00
KARAGIOUNIS Leon 15.10.75, Notts/Notts U/GRE :
JT - 61.75
KEAN Alasdair V50 5.11.47, Derby & Co :
Mar - 2:35:23 (2:16:51-83)
KEATING Scott U15 24.10.86, Havering :
HJ - 1.80, LJ - 6.11
KEENAN Scott U23 31.07.81, Ayr Seaforth :
400 - 48.82 (48.58-98)
KEETON Michael 14.12.76, Notts :
TJ - 14.85 (15.06-99)

KELLEY John U20 6.08.84, Newark :
200 - 21.8w/21.89w/22.22
KELLIE Peter U20 2.01.84, Gloucester AC :
3k - 8:30.9, 2kSt - 5:51.61, 3kSt - 9:22.7
KELLY Bryan 29.12.73, Liverpool H :
SP - 16.18, DT - 50.95
KELLY Sean 8.11.72, Rowntrees/Kingston & Poly :
800 - 1:52.7 (1:49.9-95)
KELSEY Ben U17 23.09.84, Oxford City :
DTY - 43.75
KELVEY Sam U17 12.07.86, Notts :
JTY - 53.39
KERR Darren 6.10.69, Bedford & County :
HT - 48.58
KERR Eric 9.12.64, Luton :
HT - 47.81 (54.58-95)
KERR Glen 27.10.74, Bedford & County :
HT - 61.48
KERR Hugh 4.01.76, Ayr Seaforth :
400 - 48.9 (47.69i/47.75-95), 800 - 1:52.2
KERRY Philip U20 19.03.83, Coventry Godiva :
100 - 10.8w/10.95w (11.1-99/11.91-97)
KESKA Karl 7.05.72, Birchfield :
5k - 13:24.63 (13:23.07-99), 5MR - 22:59 (22:57-00),
10k - 28:06.29 (27:44.09-00), 10kR - 28:56 (28:39-99)
KETT Andrew 1.09.77, City of Norwich :
800 - 1:52.21i (2:01.7-96)
KEYWOOD Stephen J. V40 28.09.61, Tonbridge :
Mar - 2:34:03 (2:28:50-93)
KHAN Kamran U20 2.10.83, Sale :
HT - 51.20, HTJ - 52.46 (52.57-00)
KIDGER Joel U23 16.03.80, Crawley :
800 - 1:50.9
KILKO N. U20, Sale :
SPJ - 14.19
KING Daniel U20 30.05.83, Colchester H :
3kW - 12:40.8, 5kW - 22:49.4
KING Dominic U20 30.05.83, Colchester H :
3kW - 12:37.64 (12:33.31-00),
5kW - 21:50.48 (21:25.17i-00),
10kW - 47:08.54 (45:36.3-00), 10kWR - 44:06
KING Edward 26.11.75, Sale/Brighton :
800 - 1:49.98i/1:50.87 (1:48.00-99)
KING Shane 8.02.74, Bolton :
200 - 22.0w (21.6w-99)
KING Thomas U15 3.04.87, Bournemouth :
HJ - 1.80
KINGMAN Robert 21.02.73, Newham & Essex B/RAF :
PV - 4.90 (5.02-94)
KINGWELL Jason 8.10.70, Verlea :
HT - 47.54 (48.38-97)
KINSEY Nicholas V40 10.11.59, Blackheath :
Mar - 2:36:03
KIRK Chris U17 6.09.85, Wakefield :
LJ - 6.68
KIRK George 15.10.70, Sale/Shettleston :
10k - 31:59.6
KIRK Neil 14.09.78, Med & Maid/Michigan Univ :
800 - 1:52.11 (1:49.57-98), 1500 - 3:46.89, 1M - 4:02.83i#
KIRKWOOD Craig 8.10.74, Tipton/NZL :
5k - 13:58.88 (13:57.58-00),
HMar - 64:57 (63:43-00), Mar - 2:13:18
KITE Lewis U23 23.11.79, Cheltenham :
100 - 10.6w/10.97
KITNEY Timothy J. U23 26.04.80, Belgrave :
JT - 60.76 (68.08-98)
KNIGHT Andrew G. 26.10.68, Cambridge Harriers :
800 - 1:51.8 (1:48.38-94)
KNIGHTS Christopher U17 17.10.85, Peterborough :
3k - 8:59.5
KNOWLES Richard Jonathan 12.11.75, Birchfield :
100 - 10.74, 200 - 21.26 (21.1-97/21.16w-00/21.24-99),
400 - 47.3/47.82 (45.84-97)
KNOX Chris U17 27.03.85, West Suffolk :
HJ - 1.90
KNOX Steven U13, :
LJ - 5.19
KRUGER Alexander Eaton 18.11.63, Sheffield :
DT - 40.60 (45.46-96), JT - 56.06 (60.98-95)
KRUSZEWSKI Andrew P. V40 7.04.59, Cambridge H :
DT - 46.57 (51.26-92)
KYEREME Kojo 23.12.74, Shaftesbury Barnet :
1500 - 3:49.90

LACY Dean U17 29.12.84, Cambridge Harriers :
1.5kSt - 4:38.2
LADROWSKI Marc U23 13.07.79, C of Plym'th/RAF :
HJ - 1.95 (1.96-00)
LAGAN Andrew U13 15.12.88, Richmond & Zetland :
800 - 2:16.1
LAKE Stephen 10.03.73, Med & Maid :
LJ - 6.88
LAM Gary U13 24.02.89, Halesowen :
80HC - 13.3
LAMB Chris U17 11.05.85, Chester le Street :
1M - 4:27.0, 3k - 8:47.08
LAMBERT Christopher Patrick U23 6.04.81, Bel/Harv :
55 - 6.0i (6.42i-00), 60 - 6.65i, 100 - 10.24,
200 - 20.84 (20.63-99)
LAMBERT Daniel U17 2.07.85, Belgrave :
400 - 50.6i/51.0, 400HY - 58.6
LAMBLEY Matthew U15 18.09.87, Sheffield :
HTB - 50.92
LANCASHIRE Thomas U17 2.07.85, Bolton :
800 - 1:58.20, 1500 - 3:55.77
LAPSINS Gareth U15 5.07.87, Blackpool :
PV - 3.20
LASHORE Akinola 28.03.73, Blackheath :
60 - 6.82i (6.77i-98),
100 - 10.54 (10.35A-99/10.38r-00/10.4-98/10.44-97),
200 - 21.66w/21.94 (20.99-97)
LASLETT Paul U23 12.05.80, AF&D/Un Wales Newp :
400 - 48.9, 800 - 1:52.0
LATHAM Mark 13.01.76, City of Stoke :
HJ - 1.95 (2.12i-98/2.11-94)
LATHAM Mark U17 13.05.85, Liverpool H :
HJ - 1.95
LAU Jordon U20 23.09.83, Chelmsford :
LJ - 7.18 (7.21-00)
LAVENDER Ben U15 25.12.86, Morpeth :
100 - 11.5w, 200 - 23.30w/23.33
LAWRENCE Ben U17 13.04.86, Cannock & Stafford :
SPY - 14.43
LAWRENCE Mark 26.01.71, Notts :
LJ - 7.25w/6.91 (7.33-93), TJ - 14.76w/14.67
LAWS Mark U17 29.09.85, Gateshead :
PV - 3.60
LAWS Oliver U23 18.03.80, Telford/Loughbro :
5k - 14:27.7, 10k - 31:30.91
LAWTON Nathan U15 3.11.86, City of Stoke :
PV - 3.50
LEACH Rod 29.05.72, City of Edinburgh/Army :
10k - 31:04.8, 3kSt - 9:20.4
LEADER Steven 24.11.66, Enf & Har :
PV - 4.20 (4.90-90)
LEAMAN Ian 14.10.78, Exeter :
200 - 21.9w (21.5w/21.80w/21.8-97/22.10-96
LEASE Gareth 14.11.77, Cardiff :
PV - 4.20i (4.40i/4.35-98)
LEE Ben U15 22.10.86, Woking :
JTB - 48.18
LEE James U23 6.02.79, Gateshead :
400H - 55.11
LEES Joseph U17 12.09.84, Arbroath :
DecY - 5569, OctY - 4775

LEES Simon U23 19.11.79, S & S H/Loughbro :
400 - 48.87i (49.08-00), 800 - 1:47.35, 1500 - 3:42.77
LEGGATE Daniel Richard 5.10.74, Harrow/Fife AC :
5k - 14:39.80 (14:26.2-96), 10k - 30:39.00
LEITCH Ian U20 12.07.84, Pitreavie :
HJ - 1.95
LEITCH Mark 17.11.68, Army/Shaftesbury Barnet :
SP - 14.40i/13.85 (15.57i-00/14.72-99)
LEMONCELLO Andrew U20 12.10.82, Dunf & W Fife :
5k - 14:58.6, 3kSt - 9:04.41
LEONARD Daniel Jason U20 3.01.84, Milton Keynes :
HJ - 1.95i (2.01i/2.01-00)
LERWILL Thomas 17.05.77, Belgrave/Bath Univ :
800 - 1:51.11i (1:47.27-96)
LETHBRIDGE Daniel U23 1.04.81, Crawley :
DT - 40.40
LEVETT William 6.09.75, Vauxhall :
10k - 31:16.80 (30:16.89-00)
LEVY Noel 22.06.75, Belgrave :
400 - 48.93 (47.8-92/47.82-93)
LEWIS Andrew 9.03.68, Harrow :
100 - 10.88w (10.7-91/10.80w/10.89-94),
60H - 8.28i (8.23i-93), 110H - 14.87 (14.67w/14.8-94),
LJ - 7.35i/7.21w/7.00 (7.54-97),
SP - 14.21i (14.10-98), Dec - 6476 (7221-94)
LEWIS Benjamin U23 6.03.81, Birchfield :
100 - 10.58, 200 - 21.1w/21.13w/21.48 (20.80w/21.32-99)
LEWIS Daniel U20 16.10.83, Shaftesbury Barnet :
2kSt - 5:59.78, 3kSt - 9:28.0
LEWIS Darren U17 12.04.86, Tipton :
100HY - 14.14w, 400HY - 57.69
LEWIS Marlon U20 7.09.83, Rowheath :
LJ - 6.94 (7.02w/6.99-00)
LEWIS Robert 2.09.78, Bedford & County :
200 - 21.8w/22.0 (22.0-99/22.72-97),
400 - 48.20 (47.72-00), 400H - 51.69 (51.29-00)
LEWIS Sean U15 10.09.87, City of Stoke :
HTB - 46.64
LEWIS Simon U20 14.01.83, City of Stoke :
PV - 4.30i/4.20 (4.20-00)
LEWIS Steven U17 20.05.86, City of Stoke :
PV - 4.20
LEWIS-FRANCIS Mark U20 4.09.82, Birchfield :
60 - 6.51i, 100 - 9.97w/10.12 (10.10-00)
LINDLEY Ian V45 3.12.55, Bingley :
SP - 13.81i/13.47 (17.87i/17.58-81)
LINDSAY Mark Stephen U17 5.11.84, Wakefield :
JTY - 63.89
LINSELL Steven W. 13.10.63, Leeds :
HJ - 1.95 (2.00-97)
LINSKEY Christian U23 14.06.80, Shaftesbury Barn :
PV - 5.20 (5.21i-99/5.20-98)
LISHMAN Mark U17 24.11.84, Crawley :
110HJ - 14.7
LITTLE David Andrew U23 28.02.81, Border :
HT - 59.15
LITTLE John M. V45 14.04.53, Border :
DT - 42.51 (43.70-95)
LITTLE Matthew U20 22.07.83, Bedford & County :
HJ - 2.00 (2.05i-00)
LITTLER Stephen 20.09.73, N Fylde AC :
Mar - 2:30:54
LIVESEY Christopher James U23 8.08.80, Preston :
800 - 1:51.90 (1:51.89-00),
1500 - 3:45.82 (3:45.3-99), 3k - 8:13.29 (8:12.6-99)
LIVINGSTON Jason Christopher¶ 17.03.71, Shaft B :
60 - 6.65i (6.51i-92)
LIVINGSTONE Andrew U15 3.05.88, Thurrock :
3k - 9:30.9
LIVINGSTONE Stuart U23 29.08.79, C of Edinburgh :
HJ - 2.00i/2.00 (2.08i-97/2.06-98)
LLOYD Ben U23 1.04.79, Oxford Univ/Manx :
JT - 57.90
LLOYD Joseph 9.04.73, Swansea :
400H - 54.1/54.68 (54.37-97)
LLOYD Martin Andrew U23 18.06.80, Bexley :
HJ - 2.05 (2.15i/2.15-98), Dec - 6030
LLOYD Steven J. 20.03.74, Seaton :
SP - 13.68, DT - 43.07 (43.94-94)
LLOYD-HARVEY Charles U17 21.10.84, Carmarthen :
1.5kSt - 4:40.38
LLOYD-JONES Peter John 28.09.76, City of Norwich/
Loughborough Studnts : 300 - 35.29, 400 - 48.6
LOADER Joe 21.07.73, Bristol Univ./Highgate H :
Mar - 2:27:37 (2:26:07-95)
LOBB Huw 29.08.76, Bedford & County :
5k - 14:45.3, 3kSt - 9:05.77
LOBO Jason 18.09.69, Belgrave :
800 - 1:50.83 (1:45.82-99), 1500 - 3:48.37 (3:44.06-99),
3k - 8:14.62A (8:12.88i-96)
LOCKLEY James U17 25.06.85, Cheltenham :
3k - 8:55.49
LOCKWOOD Bobby U17 1.02.86, Cambridge H :
SPY - 14.17, DTY - 46.23
LOLE Matthew U20 23.01.83, Coventry Godiva :
2kSt - 6:05.75, 3kSt - 9:41.5
LOMAX Matthew U15 19.09.86, Shildon :
1500 - 4:18.3, 3k - 9:28.89
LONG Jonathan U15 4.10.86, WGreen & Ex L :
800 - 2:03.0, PenB - 2633
LOUGHRAN Garth U13 16.04.89, :
JTC - 34.05
LOUGHRAN Stuart 19.02.76, Swansea :
JT - 66.29 (68.91-98)
LOVE Matthew U17 28.12.84, WSE&H :
100HY - 14.1/14.13
LOVETT Anthony U20 20.09.82, Enf & Har :
JT - 59.81 (60.54-00)
LOVETT David 13.09.78, Portsmouth/St. Marys Univ :
SP - 15.02i/14.85 (15.06-00), DT - 52.97
LOW Charles 9.10.74, Shaftesbury Barnet :
3kSt - 8:40.85 (8:37.63-00)
LOWE Andrew 6.03.76, Trafford :
HJ - 2.00 (2.08-00)
LOWERY James U23 17.10.80, WG & Ex L/Lond U :
Dec - 6070
LOWNDES William U15 10.10.86, Vale Royal :
SPB - 14.90, DTB - 38.49
LOWTHIAN Ian U23 10.10.80, Liverpool H :
300 - 35.40, 400 - 47.92 (47.11-99)
LUCAS David U15 11.01.87, Medway :
80HB - 11.83
LUCAS Liam U20 15.12.82, Dartford :
110HJ - 14.93w/14.94, 110H - 15.3
LUMSDEN Graham U17 7.05.85, Lancaster & Mor :
HJ - 1.90
LUND Simon N. 22.12.65, Wigan Phoenix :
Mar - 2:34:33 (2:27:39-94)
LUNDMAN Jonathan U23 7.12.81, Newham & E B :
JT - 63.95 (65.18-00)
LUTTON Kevin U17 26.11.84, Aberdeen :
HJ - 1.91
LYNAS Paul 15.09.76, Annadale Striders/Queen's U :
110H - 15.6
LYNCH Lawrence 1.11.67, Enf & Har :
400H - 53.8 (50.05-96)

MACDONALD Stewart 10.12.65, Bingley :
Mar - 2:28:24
MACEY Dean 12.12.77, Harrow :
100 - 10.72 (10.65w/10.69-99), 400 - 46.21,
110H - 14.34, HJ - 2.15, PV - 4.70 (4.80-00),
LJ - 7.59 (7.77-00), SP - 15.77,
DT - 47.41 (47.77-99), Dec - 8603
MACGEE William 9.06.68, WSE&H/Falkirk :
100 - 10.8 (10.92-98)

MACINTOSH Robin U17 2.03.85, City of Edinburgh :
800 - 1:56.7, 1500 - 4:04.92
MACKAY Craig U17 30.10.84, Perth :
400HY - 57.87
MACKAY Graeme D. U23 4.10.80, Chiltern/Oxford U :
HT - 51.94
MACKIE Ian 27.02.75, Pitreavie :
100 - 10.19w/10.30 (10.00w-98/10.17-96),
200 - 20.85 (20.68w-00)
MACLEAN Angus U23 20.09.80, T Solent/Soton Univ :
800 - 1:49.39, 1500 - 3:39.88,
3k - 8:14.04i/8:14.54, 5KR - 14:25
MADDEN Michael J. 13.09.65, Newquay & Par :
HT - 48.63 (55.92-93)
MADDY Emeka U17 19.12.84, Herne Hill :
HJ - 1.95
MADEIRA-COLE Charles H. 29.11.77, Newham & E B :
TJ - 15.86w/15.59 (15.82i/15.79-98)
MAHONEY Oliver U20 21.10.83, Wirral :
PV - 4.45
MAITLAND Peter 21.01.73, Swansea :
SP - 14.20
MAITLAND Tim U15 5.12.86, Harrow :
HJ - 1.81
MAJEKODUNMI Semi U20 29.06.83, Belgrave :
TJ - 14.52
MAJOR Adam U23 2.11.81, Elgin/S B/Edinburgh Un :
SP - 15.38i/15.00 (15.44-00), DT - 51.61
MAJOR Stuart 5.05.70, S London :
5k - 14:38.15, 10k - 30:51.12
MAKAO Sakchai U20 10.12.82, Shetland :
TJ - 14.15w (13.60-99)
MAKASI Michael U15 6.12.86, Kent :
800 - 2:05.25
MALCOLM Anthony 15.02.76, Cardiff/Loughbro :
LJ - 6.83 (7.55-00)
MALCOLM Christian Sean U23 3.06.79, Cardiff :
50 - 5.83i+, 60 - 6.64i, 100 - 10.09w/10.11, 200 - 20.08
MALEY Gavin 19.05.78, Havering :
800 - 1:52.63 (1:52.5-98)
MALIN Darren U17 19.06.85, Annadale Striders :
800 - 1:56.71, 1500 - 4:00.91, 3k - 8:53.27
MALINS Duncan 12.06.78, Newham & Essex B :
60H - 7.93i, 110H - 14.19 (14.08w/14.10-00)
MALLOCH Ewan 4.08.76, Lanc & Mor/Cambridge Un :
3kSt - 9:28.58 (8:54.70-99)
MALONE Daniel U15 4.11.86, Liverpool H :
800 - 2:05.27
MALONE Ian 17.03.64, :
Mar - 2:27:22
MALONEY Matthew U15 16.10.86, Liverpool H :
80HB - 11.79
MANCHESTER Benjamin U17 1.04.85, Bingley :
400HY - 53.3?/56.55
MANDY Mark 19.11.72, Birchfield/IRL :
HJ - 2.10 (2.26i-97/2.25-95)
MANNION John U15 7.07.87, Liverpool H :
800 - 2:04.46
MANSBRIDGE David C. 4.06.64, Telford :
Mar - 2:35:31 (2:22:23-94)
MANVELL Lee U23 11.12.80, Weymouth :
Dec - 5333
MANVILLE Gerald 21.12.78, Crawley/Army :
PV - 4.15 (4.21-00), Dec - 5369 (5599-99)
MARAR Leith A. 7.11.68, Belgrave :
DT - 46.97 (55.68-96)
MARCHANT Billy U13 27.08.89, Brighton :
80HC - 13.7
MARCHMENT Carl U20 30.12.82, Basingstoke & MH :
Dec - 6048, DecJ - 6058
MARKHAM Gregory 28.11.78, Rotherham :
JT - 56.54 (60.86-98)
MARLAND Chris U23 9.11.80, Deeside :
DT 41.43
MARSH Brett 20.01.76, Newquay & Par :
SP - 13.55, HT - 47.95 (47.98-99)
MARSH M. U20, Dorset :
LJ - 6.83
MARSHALL Guy Richard ¶ 24.09.71, Kingston u Hull :
SP - 15.95 (16.65-98)
MARSHALL James U23 6.02.81, Dudley & Stourb :
200 - 22.07i (22.0/22.20-00)
MARSHALL Stuart U23 2.12.80, Coventry Godiva :
200 - 22.0, 400 - 48.6/48.98
MARTIN Ben U15 1.05.87, Exeter :
JTB - 44.73
MARTIN Daniel U20 9.03.82, Southampton City :
HTJ - 49.21 (54.34dh/52.40-00)
MARTIN Nathan U17 16.11.84, Shaftesbury Barnet :
200 - 22.0 (22.98age?-00)
MARTIN Wayne Daniel 12.08.76, WGreen & Ex L :
200 - 22.0 (21.9-97/22.17i-00/22.44-97),
400 - 48.32i (48.07-99)
MARVIN Richard U13 29.01.89, Isle of Wight :
JTC - 38.70
MASON Brett U20 21.03.82, Sheffield :
HJ - 2.00
MASON Duncan 8.12.68, Salford :
HMar - 66:04 (65:17-00), Mar - 2:23:08 (2:21:10-00)
MASON Lee Karl U20 23.01.83, Swindon :
400 - 49.33
MASON Richard 25.09.69, Nuneaton :
Mar - 2:22:32
MASSEY Martyn U15, Cannock & Stafford :
JTB - 44.19
MASSINGHAM Gavin U20 4.10.82, Sunderland :
800 - 1:52.2
MASTERS Scott U15 29.11.86, Sparkhill :
100 - 11.4, 200 - 23.6
MATAKAINEN Petri 3.04.75, Sale/FIN :
JT - 66.80 (72.29-00)
MATTHEWS Andrew U17 26.10.84, WSE&H :
100 - 10.93
MATTHEWS Lawrence 11.08.65, Salford/Oxford Un :
HMar - 65:08 (63:45-93), Mar - 2:27:36 (2:19:10-93)
MATTOCK Richard U13 1.10.88, Telford :
1500 - 4:40.1
MAY Curtis U20 28.01.84, Herne Hill :
TJ - 14.25w/13.79
MAYNARD Daniel U15 4.12.87, Charnwood :
80HB - 11.37
MAYNARD Joseph U17 25.07.85, Torfaen :
400HY - 57.75
MAYO Anthony 8.07.74, Swansea :
100 - 10.7wdt
MAYO James 24.02.75, Cannock & Stafford/Army :
800 - 1:50.10 (1:48.2-96)
MAYO Thomas 2.05.77, Cannock & Stafford :
800 - 1:49.47 (1:49.1-99), 1500 - 3:38.3+/3:38.34,
1M - 3:55.57, 3k - 8:00.62, 5k - 14:03.20
MAYOCK John Paul 26.10.70, Barnsley :
1500 - 3:34.43 (3:31.86-97),
1M - 3:54.05 (3:50.32-96), 2k - 4:57.09i (4:56.75-99),
3k - 7:44.08i/7:56.06 (7:43.31i-97/7:47.28-95),
5MR - 23:32, 10kR - 28:59
MAYS Jermaine U20 23.12.82, Kent :
800 - 1:52.2, 1500 - 3:52.7, 5k - 15:18.0,
2kSt - 5:47.29, 3kSt - 9:10.8
MBANEFO Chuma U15 25.02.87, Middlesex Sch :
DTB - 37.76
MBIRH G., Thames Valley :
100 - 10.7, 200 - 21.7
MCADOREY John 16.09.74, Border/B & Antrim/IRL :
60 - 6.89i (6.87i-96),
100 - 10.36w/10.46 (10.28w-00)

MCALLISTER Joe U23 23.12.80, Loughbro/ St Malachy's/IRL : 5k - 14:19.31
MCBURNEY Craig 8.09.68, Morpeth/Army : 10k - 31:16.11
MCBURNEY Paul 14.03.72, N & E B/Lisburn/IRL : 400 - 48.77 (45.85-97)
MCCALLA Isacc U20 28.03.82, Harrow : 110HJ - 14.65, 110H - 15.2w (15.34w-00)
MCCALLUM Jonathan 19.11.75, Croydon : 1500 - 3:42.16 (3:37.75-00), 3k - 8:07.27i# (8:22.3-98)
MCCASH Lee U23 22.10.81, Sale : 3k - 8:15.90, 5k - 14:23.42
MCCLOSKEY Paul U17 9.05.85, Pitreavie : 1.5kSt - 4:37.36
MCCONKEY Michael U17 5.12.84, North Down : DTY - 42.25, JTY - 54.32, DecY - 5070
MCCONVILLE Brendan U23 3.01.79, North Down : 110H - 15.47, HJ - 2.00 (2.02-98), PV - 4.50, Dec - 6911
MCCORKELL George Michael U13 16.01.89, Harm : JTC - 37.07
MCCORMICK Nicholas U23 11.09.81, Tynedale : 1500 - 3:46.84 (3:45.19-00), 1M - 4:07.45
MCCOURT Colin U17 11.12.84, Bournemouth : 1500 - 3:54.54, 3k - 8:38.94
MCCRACKEN Gary 23.01.78, Border/Kirkintillock : 110H - 15.32 (14.8w/15.14-98)
MCCULLOUGH Alan 9.08.63, North Belfast : Mar - 2:31:05 (2:29:18-00)
MCDADE Jason U23 3.04.80, WGreen & Ex L : 110H - 14.8w/14.90w/15.01, HJ - 2.00 (2.16i-99/2.15-98), Dec - 6547 (6774-99)
MCDERMID Liam U17 23.11.84, Victoria Park H/IRL : 200 - 21.87, 400 - 48.78, 100HY - 13.4/13.68, 400HY - 55.11
MCDIARMID Alistair U17 16.10.85, Harrogate : SPY - 14.17i/14.05, DTY - 48.60, HTY - 53.70
MCDONALD A. U20, Gloucester Sch : 110HJ - 15.5
MCDONALD Ben U15 9.11.86, Telford : 1500 - 4:20.50
MCDONALD Denzil 11.10.65, Newham & Essex B : SP - 14.71 (16.10-94), DT - 47.47 (55.04-95)
MCDONALD Iain U15, R Sutton Coldfield : HJ - 1.75
MCDONALD Michael John Joseph 24.08.65, B & A/ Border/Queen's Univ/IRL : TJ - 14.29i (15.78-94)
MCDONALD Richard U23 11.01.80, S B/Loughbro/ Perth : 400 - 47.67, 110H - 15.60w, 400H - 50.70
MCDONNELL Stephen U23 24.07.80, Liverpool H/IRL : 400H - 51.97
MCDOWELL Tom U17 11.02.85, Wessex & Bath : PV - 4.05
MCEVOY Stephen 23.05.63, Met. Police : HT - 49.11 (57.14-96)
MCEWAN Greg U23 9.04.81, Shaft B/Dunf& W Fife : 800 - 1:51.7 (1:51.48-00)
MCFALL David U23 15.10.80, Brecon/UWIC : PV - 4.20
MCFARLANE Andrew U20 28.02.83, Leeds/Loughbro : HJ - 2.01
MCFARLANE Jim U23 16.06.79, Cambridge Un : JT - 58.68
MCFARLANE John 9.06.72, Thames H & H : Mar - 2:30:14 (2:29:43-00)
MCGEOCH Michael I. V45 15.08.55, Les Croupiers : Mar - 2:34:12 (2:17:58-83)
MCGINLEY Cathal U23 16.08.79, Dundee Univ/IRL : Dec - 6148
MCGLORY Philip U20 2.09.83, Liverpool H : 5k - 15:18.69
MCGONIGLE Dermot 62, Shettleston : Mar - 2:35:51
MCGOUGH Jamie U17 20.05.85, Yeovil Olympiads : DTY - 41.90
MCHUGH Paul U15 5.06.87, Liverpool H : 1500 - 4:15.43, 3k - 9:32.6
MCILROY Benjamin U20 2.09.83, : Dec - 5316, DecJ - 5314
MCILROY James 30.12.76, Abbey/St. Marys Univ : 400 - 48.93, 800 - 1:47.42 (1:45.32-98)
MCILWHAM John 29.02.72, Blackpool : 400H - 53.7/54.50 (52.7/52.80-99)
MCINNES Duncan 1.05.78, Law & Dist/Pitreavie : HJ - 2.00i (2.05i/2.05-97)
MCINTOSH Leslie U23 25.02.81, Liverpool H : HT - 46.29 (52.09-00)
MCINTOSH Mark U20 8.08.82, Harrow : 1500 - 3:51.4, 3k - 8:28.4
MCINTYRE Mark 14.10.70, Shaftesbury Barnet : 60 - 6.93i (6.79i-97)
MCKAY Callum U17 17.02.85, AF&D : 100HY - 13.8, 400HY - 55.24, OctY - 4217
MCKEE Paul 15.10.77, Liverpool H/IRL : 200 - 21.42 (20.87w/21.1/21.20-00), 400 - 46.42 (45.92-00)
MCKENZIE Ian U23 3.07.81, Inverclyde/Bel/Glas Un : PV - 4.41
MCKERNAN Michael 28.11.78, Coventry Godiva : TJ - 15.49
MCKINLAY Scott U20 11.04.83, Pitreavie : 400H - 56.68 (56.4-00), DecJ - 5375
MCKOWN Paul U15 12.06.87, Liverpool H : JTB - 43.37
MCLEAN Colm U23 7.06.80, St Malachy's/Loughbro/ IRL : 1500 - 3:44.26 (3:40.42-00)
MCLEAN-FOREMAN Alasdair James U23 10.11.81, Belgrave/Harvard : 800 - 1:49.84
MCLELLAN Neil 10.09.78, Stevenage & NH : JT - 68.78
MCLENNAN Stephen 17.11.78, WSE&H : PV - 4.40 (4.70-96)
MCLEOD Ryan U17 7.06.85, Elswick : 1500 - 4:03.76, 1M - 4:30.3, 3k - 8:54.9
MCMASTER Colin U23 15.01.80, Shaft B/Law & Dist : HJ - 2.13i/2.10 (2.15-97)
MCMEEKEN James U15 25.09.86, Basingstoke & MH : DTB - 37.15
MCMULLAN Iain George 15.06.78, Lisburn/Ulster U/ Trafford : SP - 16.56
MCNIEL Jamie U17 23.11.84, Sparkhill : 100 - 10.76w/10.83, 200 - 22.4 (23.20w-99)
MCRAE Leon U23 3.11.80, WGreen & Ex L/Bath Un : 60 - 6.9i, 100 - 10.82w (11.1-96/11.66-97), 200 - 21.59w/22.12, 400 - 48.38, 400H - 51.8/51.96
MCWILLIAMS Ron 20.08.68, Deeside/RAF : 3kSt - 9:27.87
MEE James U13 1.07.89, Mansfield : 400 - 59.6
MEEPANDY Farel U23 27.12.79, Bel/Loughbro/CGO : TJ - 15.26 (15.73w/15.54i/15.45-00)
MELBER Stephen L. U23 26.02.79, Oxford Univ : JT - 59.34 (61.27-00)
MELIA Adam U15 26.10.86, Kingston & Poly : DTB - 39.15
MELLOR Dean Ashley 25.11.71, Sale : PV - 5.00 (5.30-95)
MELLUISH Christopher Jeremy V55 15.07.44, Camb H : HT - 48.29? (62.10-74)
MERRICK Olvin Essop 24.05.74, WGreen & Ex L : 100 - 10.88, LJ - 7.15 (7.59w-98/7.58-00)

MERTINS Michael U15 31.01.87, :
SPB - 13.63
MIAH Monu U20 10.01.84, WGreen & Ex L :
100 - 10.64w/10.96 (10.7/10.79-00),
200 - 22.14i (21.31w/21.45-00)
MICHAELSON Thomas U15 3.01.87, Liverpool H :
800 - 2:02.62, 1500 - 4:13.2, 3k - 9:14.8
MIDDLETON Barry 10.03.75, Sale/Aberdeen :
400 - 48.54i (47.44i-97/48.1-00/48.48-97)
MILES Mark Thomas 24.03.77, Belgrave :
1500 - 3:46.46, 3k - 8:05.90 (7:57.21-99),
5k - 13:53.74, 10k - 30:03.82
MILES Paul U23 14.09.80, Birchfield/Wolvs Univ :
PV - 4.30
MILL Thomas U17 21.12.85, R Sutton Coldfield :
HJ - 1.90
MILLAR Stuart U20 9.03.83, Cheltenham :
SPJ - 14.16, JT - 58.05
MILLER Ian U15 9.01.87, Birchfield :
200 - 23.6, TJ - 12.81
MILLER Mark 10.11.71, Enf & Har :
HT - 56.31 (59.72-00)
MILLER Robert U20 20.01.84, Aberdeen :
Dec - 5275, DecJ - 5257
MILLS Christopher Leslie 12.11.75, Winchester :
PV - 4.60
MILLWARD Stephen U23 29.06.79, Wirral :
3kSt - 9:30.75
MINNIKIN Stephen 4.01.72, Sheffield :
HT - 58.76 (62.20-96)
MITCHELL Andrew U23 30.07.80, N & E B/Loughbro :
3kSt - 9:01.28
MITCHELL Andrew 30.07.76, Kilbarchan/Border :
400 - 47.55 (47.51-98)
MITCHELL James U15 11.10.86, Peterborough :
1500 - 4:09.4, 3k - 8:59.6
MITCHELL John U23 13.05.81, St Andrews Univ :
JT - 55.36 (56.07-00)
MITCHELL Neil U17, R Sutton Coldfield :
200 - 22.3
MITCHELL Robert U23 14.09.80, Shaftesbury Barnet :
HJ - 2.25
MITCHELL Terrence V40 23.08.59, Dunf & W Fife :
Mar - 2:34:28 (2:17:56-92)
MITCHINSON David 4.09.78, Newham & Essex B :
1500 - 3:50.74 (3:50.51-00), 5k - 14:19.14,
10k - 30:00.4, 2kSt - 5:45.65, 3kSt - 8:45.9 (8:45.06-00)
MKANDWIRE Wanangma U23 4.10.80, Rugby/Sheff U :
HJ - 1.95
MOIR Gareth U23 17.12.80, Ipswich/Bath Univ :
HJ - 1.98 (2.00-00), Dec - 5356
MONAGHAN Ian U23 6.11.81, Harrow/Brunel Univ :
400H - 54.2/55.74
MONEY Daniel James 17.10.76, Sale :
60 - 6.73i (6.72i-98),
100 - 10.33w/10.46 (10.16w/10.32-97),
200 - 20.92w/20.99 (20.75w/20.92-97)
MONTAGUE Michael U15 30.05.87, Shettleston :
400 - 53.5
MONYE Ndubuisi U17 10.05.85, WSE&H :
SPY - 15.97, OctY - 4393
MOORE Colin V40 25.11.60, Bingley :
10k - 30:43.54 (28:13.13-90)
MOORE James U20 18.11.83, Kingston u Hull :
100 - 10.88w
MOORE Jonathan U20 31.05.84, Birchfield :
LJ - 7.98, TJ - 16.43
MOORE Louis Calvin U17 8.09.85, City of Stoke :
HJ - 1.90i, LJ - 6.63, OctY - 4760
MOORE Rudi U23 25.03.81, Sparta :
Dec - 5011
MOORES Paul U20 3.08.84, Tamworth :
2kSt - 5:59.19, 3kSt - 9:53.1
MOORHOUSE Julian 13.11.71, Birchfield :
1500 - 3:46.04 (3:43.41-00),
3k - 8:07.57 (7:53.11-00),
5k - 13:51.75 (13:42.35-00)
MORAN Anthony U17 8.01.86, Trafford :
1500 - 4:00.59, 3k - 8:42.11
MORBY Paul James U23 15.01.79, Solihull & S H :
800 - 1:52.02 (1:50.39-99)
MORELAND John R. V40 13.09.58, Rugby :
DT - 46.49 (51.76-95)
MOREY Andrew 16.01.72, London Heathside :
100 - 10.8
MORGAN Derek N. 4.04.69, Bristol :
200 - 22.0 (21.2-93/21.55-91)
MORGAN Mark 19.08.72, Swansea :
5k - 14:37.2 (13:57.91-99), 5MR - 23:33
MORGAN Michael U15 22.11.86, Beechmount/
St Malachy's : 800 - 2:05.1
MORGAN Nathan 30.06.78, Birchfield :
60 - 6.79i (6.77i-99), 100 - 10.38, LJ - 7.97 (8.11-98)
MORGAN-LEE Andrew 1.03.69, Salford :
5k - 14:30.10 (14:02.43-99), 10kR - 29:52 (29:41-95),
HMar - 64:51, 3kSt - 9:04.3 (8:43.95-00)
MORGANELLA Alessandro 28.05.77, Border :
DT - 42.03 (44.64-00)
MORLAND Stuart U17 16.05.86, Liverpool H :
800 - 1:58.40
MORLEY Roger 20.09.77, Bedford & County :
800 - 1:51.02
MORRIS Carl U23 5.05.80, Yeovil Oly/Exeter Univ :
10k - 31:02.15
MORRIS James U23 2.12.79, Swansea :
LJ - 6.96 (6.98-00)
MORRIS Michael 16.07.74, Morpeth :
1500 - 3:47.91 (3:43.52-00)
MORRISON Peter, Fife AC :
100kR - 7:39:45
MORTER Robert U15 25.10.86, Cwmbran :
1500 - 4:20.32
MORTON Dominik U15 13.12.86, Halesowen :
3k - 9:26.70
MOSCROP Howard Wilson V40 16.12.57, Swindon :
400H - 54.1 (51.4-84/51.57-82)
MOSES Alister William 5.07.78, Reigate :
800 - 1:52.10, 1500 - 3:44.62,
3k - 8:17.3, 5MR - 23:48
MOSS Christopher Robert U23 17.06.79, Bel/Lough :
800 - 1:48.95 (1:47.75-00), 1500 - 3:44.33
MOSS Damien U20 2.09.82, Northampton :
800 - 1:53.13 (1:52.64-00)
MOULTON David U23 7.09.81, Blackheath/Bath Univ :
800 - 1:50.8
MOUNTFORD David U20 23.06.82, City of Stoke :
LJ - 7.32w/7.29 (7.33-00), TJ - 14.32w
MOWBRAY Philip 19.03.73, C of Edinb/Hunter's BT :
3k - 8:07.11 (7:59.5-97), 5k - 13:58.48 (13:49.44-97)
MUDD Paul U15 6.09.86, Basildon :
80HB - 11.60, PenB - 2764
MUIR Andrew C. 20.06.73, Kilbarchan/Edinburgh Un :
10k - 31:23.18 (31:07.33-00)
MULVANEY Christopher Shaun U23 25.05.81, Border/
Michigan Univ : 800 - 1:49.69i (1:49.86-00),
1500 - 3:49.01 (3:46.84-99), 1M - 4:02.95i# (4:10.93-00)
MUNGHAM Robert U17 1.12.84, Bracknell :
HTY - 53.08
MUNRO Ian U20 5.09.83, Cambuslang :
800 - 1:52.1
MUNROE Gary 12.04.69, Shaftesbury B/RAF/CAN :
LJ - 7.09w/6.98 (7.52w?-99/7.27-96)
MURCH Kevin I. V40 11.11.58, Rugby :
JT - 61.23 (69.02-89)

MURDOCH Iain U23 10.07.80, Avonside/Loughbro :
1500 - 3:45.70, 1M - 4:05.4 (4:04.00-99),
3k - 8:20.06i (8:27.0-99), 2kSt - 5:37.32,
3kSt - 8:49.55 (8:42.79-00)
MURDOCH Steven V40 16.04.61, Border :
10k - 31:48 (30:19.1-95)
MURPHY Denis U23 14.09.79, N & E B/Loughbro :
800 - 1:52.25
MURPHY James U15, :
SPB - 13.75
MURPHY Kevin 6.04.74, WGreen & Ex L :
3kSt - 9:21.56
MURPHY Stephen James U20 6.01.83, Shaft Barnet :
1500 - 3:51.37, 3k - 8:29.15 (8:21.69-00),
2kSt - 5:55.26 (5:50.6-00)
MURPHY Stephen U20 10.02.82, City of Edinb/Bel :
400H - 56.36 (53.2/53.37-00)
MURRAY Gary U23 31.01.80, Finn Valley/IRL :
1500 - 3:47.57, 1M - 4:06.70
MURRAY Keiron James 18.06.75, Manx :
400 - 48.45
MURRAY Thomas V40 18.05.61, Inverclyde :
10kR - 29:51 (29:09-97), HMar - 66:46 (65:34-92)
MUSA Christopher U15 5.12.86, Tower Hamlets :
100 - 11.18w/11.26, 200 - 23.0, 80HB - 10.73w/10.95
MUSCHAMP Gandolph U17 6.12.84, Highgate H :
LJ - 6.74
MUTAI John 26.05.66, Bromsgrove & R/KEN :
10kR - 29:41 (29:21-99), 10MR - 48:17,
HMar - 62:49 (60:52-99), Mar - 2:14:13 (2:13:20-00)
MYERS Richard U20 21.12.83, Gateshead :
110HJ - 15.40
MYLES Gary 3.02.63, Cannock & Stafford :
110H - 15.6 (14.55-83)

N'GORAN Frank U15 22.07.87, Essex Sch :
100 - 11.09w/11.33
NAISMITH David U23 15.12.79, N & E B/Loughbro :
200 - 21.64 (21.6-99), 400 - 46.82 (46.27-99)
NANCI Pepi U15 7.10.86, Milton Keynes :
80HB - 11.63w/11.7, HJ - 1.80, SPB - 15.05,
HTB - 43.08, JTB - 51.77, PenB - 2974
NASH Kevin 6.02.77, Belgrave :
3k - 8:18.44i (8:28.6-94), 3kSt - 8:57.63 (8:43.21-96)
NASH Samuel 22.10.71, Thames Valley :
LJ - 7.00 (7.41wA-00/7.01-97)
NASRAT James Thomas U20 10.01.83, Newport :
800 - 1:50.05
NAUGHTON Joe 17.10.74, Havering/IRL :
110H - 15.3w (15.34-99), PV - 4.20 (4.40-99)
NAYLOR Donald E. 5.09.71, Swansea/Hunter's BT :
1500 - 3:46.90, 3k - 8:11.92,
5k - 14:19.90 (13:58.88-00), 3kSt - 8:39.2
NEBLETT Gavin U23 27.12.79, Blackheath :
100 - 10.97 (10.95-97)
NEELY Ian 29.12.74, Border/Ballymena & Antrim :
400H - 53.3/53.86 (52.34-98)
NEILL Dave V45 56, Staffs Moorlands :
Mar - 2:34:18
NEILL Steven 11.08.66, Telford/RAF :
1500 - 3:49.71 (3:46.1-98)
NELSON Alex U15 21.03.88, City of Stoke :
100 - 11.16w/11.4, 200 - 23.3
NELSON Anthony U17 14.09.84, Croydon :
TJ - 14.12w/13.94
NESBETH Michael U23 1.03.79, Croydon :
LJ - 6.96 (7.35i-99/7.30-00), TJ - 15.47w?/15.34
NEWARK Paul U17 3.10.84, Med & Maid :
100 - 11.0w/11.1 (12.04-99)
NEWBURY Ian U15 17.09.86, Cardiff :
HJ - 1.75
NEWMAN Lee Jon 1.05.73, Belgrave :
SP - 18.37 (18.85-96), DT - 57.38 (60.48-97)
NEWTON Keith 12.12.68, WGreen & Ex L :
TJ - 14.83w/14.79
NEWTON Keith 14.03.63, Brighton :
10k - 31:55.0
NEWTON Richard U15 10.02.87, Preston :
1500 - 4:16.59
NEWTON Robert U23 10.05.81, Sale/Bath Univ :
60H - 7.98ir?, 60HJ - 7.93i,
110H - 14.0w/14.09 (13.93w-99/13.95-00)
NEZIRAJ Yiber U15, Croydon :
JTB - 44.99
NICELY Jeavon U15 27.11.86, Birchfield :
TJ - 12.69w/12.60
NICHOL Ross U13, :
JTC - 35.43
NICHOLL David 16.09.69, City of Edinburgh :
HT - 53.20 (57.06-97)
NICHOLLS Dexter U15 28.05.87, Herne Hill :
TJ - 12.06
NICHOLLS John S. 1.09.65, Sale :
SP - 15.32i/15.12 (15.98-99)
NICHOLLS Philip U20 29.09.83, Tipton :
3k - 8:31.74, 5k - 14:54.5, 2kSt - 6:06.8
NICHOLLS Russell U20 8.03.83, Enf & Har :
400 - 47.80
NICHOLSON Andrew U17 25.03.86, Sussex Sch :
TJ - 13.24
NICKLESS James U17 27.10.84, Halesowen :
1.5kSt - 4:28.30
NICOLSON Christian 19.09.73, Team Solent :
3k - 8:04.57, 5k - 13:54.50 (13:45.26-00)
NIELAND Nicholas 31.01.72, Shaftesbury Barnet :
JT - 82.93 (85.09-00)
NIMMO Thomas 9.05.71, City of Edinburgh :
400 - 48.70 (47.99-92), 800 - 1:50.32 (1:49.0-92)
NITSCH Mark 3.03.78, Peterborough :
400H - 55.3 (53.4-00/53.93-99)
NOAD Ben 6.05.76, Bristol :
3k - 8:10.45 (8:06.69i-99), 5KR - 14:13,
5k - 14:03.23i/14:11.40 (13:48.98i/13:57.93-00),
5MR - 23:20, 10kR - 29:10, 10MR - 48:49
NOBLE Ian 2.04.77, Trafford :
PV - 4.50 (4.80-99)
NOEL Anthony J. 8.09.63, Cambridge Harriers :
100 - 10.7/10.89 (10.5w-99/10.6-98/10.64-99),
200 - 22.0/22.07 (21.7-98/21.86-99)
NORMAN Andrew U23 19.08.80, Altrincham :
10k - 31:39.23 (31:08.76-00)
NORMAN Anthony Josephus 5.07.63, Woking :
SP - 13.35 (14.94-88), JT - 55.29 (68.74-87)
NORMAN Dave 4.11.78, Altrincham :
10k - 31:40.80
NORRIS Chris U20 8.10.82, Enf & Har :
2kSt - 6:06.52
NORRIS Stephen 21.06.68, Salisbury :
3kSt - 9:28.6 (9:19.05-96)
NORRISS Paris U17 27.02.85, AF&D :
DTY - 44.13, OctY - 4478
NORTH Christian I.R. 2.02.74, Bristol :
PV - 5.15i/5.00 (5.30-99/5.10dhex-98)
NORTH Ewen 13.07.78, Hallamshire/Hallam Un. :
1500 - 3:50.91, 3k - 8:20.80
NORTHALL Luke U17 30.11.84, Wrexham :
3k - 8:39.00, 1.5kSt - 4:40.8
NOTMAN Lee 14.10.75, Border :
400 - 48.57
NOYCE Michael 31.10.77, Winchester :
3kSt - 9:22.0
NUNAN James U20 16.09.83, Gloucester AC :
HT - 46.82, HTJ - 52.73
NWOKORO Chin 13.03.77, Harrow/Cambridge Un :
110H - 15.5 (15.65-00)

NYAMANYO Suote U17 3.10.84, Mandale :
100HY - 13.45, LJ - 6.87
NZELU Udobi Onyedika U15 11.10.86, Sale :
800 - 2:02.41

O'BRIEN Anthony 14.11.70, Morpeth :
1500 - 3:50.38, 3k - 8:20.18 (8:19.7-99),
5k - 14:01.86, 5KR - 14:16, 10k - 29:28.70,
HMar - 65:40+ (64:46-96)
O'BRIEN Barry 3.07.76, Gateshead :
400 - 49.02 (48.0/48.33-99)
O'DONOVAN Ross U17 12.03.86, Thames Valley :
100 - 10.87w/11.01
O'DOWD Matthew 15.04.76, Swindon :
1500 - 3:47.21 (3:45.10-99), 3k - 7:55.75,
5k - 13:30.56, 5MR - 23:08, 10k - 28:52.97,
10kR - 28:48, HMar - 62:40 (62:38-99)
O'HARA Jason 28.10.76, Shaftesbury Barnet :
PV - 4.40
O'KEEFE Kieran U17 19.03.86, Charnwood :
DTY - 44.39, HTY - 47.76
O'LEARY David U23 3.08.80, Liverpool H :
400H - 53.3/54.40 (54.03-99)
O'LEARY Terry U15 23.01.87, Havering :
JTB - 44.87
O'RAWE Andrew 8.09.63, Roadhogs :
20kW - 1:35:45 (1:34:05-96)
O'RAWE James 3.02.73, Roadhogs :
10kW - 47:53.0 (43:25.2-96), 10kWR - 44:11 (43:12-00),
20kW - 1:38:25 (1:28:46-99)
OAKES Christopher 19.10.70, Army :
Dec - 5649 (5951-97)
OBOH Laurence U20 14.05.84, Belgrave :
60 - 6.91i, 100 - 10.66w/10.70, 200 - 21.30
OCTAVE Philip 12.06.78, WG & Ex L/Reading Un :
400 - 48.96i/49.1 (47.8/47.85-99)
ODOUZA Uche U15, Exeter :
100 - 11.5
ODUDU Okeoghene 24.10.76, Blackburn/Oxford Un :
110H - 15.2/15.31 (15.11-00)
ODUNDO-MENDEZ Marimba U15 30.09.86, AF&D :
100 - 11.38, 200 - 22.50w/22.79i/22.80
ODUOZA Uche Francis U15 15.10.86, Exeter :
80HB - 11.5, HJ - 1.81
OGUNYEMI Akeem 4.06.74, Enf & Har :
100 - 10.63 (10.6-97)
OHRLAND Martin U23 19.11.79, Chelmsford :
HJ - 1.96, Dec - 5160
OHRLAND Stuart 6.09.75, Newham & Essex B :
HJ - 2.05i/2.00 (2.20i-97/2.18-99)
OJO Sayo U23 9.05.80, WGreen & Ex L :
TJ - 14.45w/14.26 (14.62-99)
OKE Tosin U23 1.10.80, Cambridge Harriers/
Manchester Univ :
TJ - 16.08i/15.72 (16.57-99)
OKOIGUN Mike U15 1.02.87, Middlesex Sch :
TJ - 12.22
OKOROAFU Lee 12.09.76, WGrn & Ex L/Army/NGR :
200 - 21.73, 110H - 15.1, 400H - 54.67, LJ - 7.20
OLSEN Scott U23 19.12.79, Cardiff/UWIC :
3kSt - 9:30.67
OMAR Shugri U17 20.12.84, Ealing,Southall & Mx :
800 - 1:55.8, 1500 - 4:01.28, 3k - 8:46.12
OMONUA Samson 16.06.76, Enf & Har :
100 - 10.8 (10.5/10.59-96),
200 - 22.0w (21.8-98/22.11-96)
ONI Samson U23 25.06.81, Belgrave :
HJ - 2.20i/2.18
ONIBIJE Fola U17 25.09.84, Ealing,Southall & Mx :
200 - 22.09 (21.98-00)
ONUOHA Chinedum U15 12.11.86, Trafford :
100 - 11.09w/11.3/11.35,
LJ - 6.25w, PenB - 2606
ONWUBALILI David U20 5.12.82, Belgrave :
DTJ - 50.94
OPARKA Jonathon U23 27.01.80, Arb/Bord/Dundee U :
60 - 6.74i, 100 - 10.43w/10.6/10.61 (10.6-00),
TJ - 13.95w (14.08-96)
OPARKA Richard U20 28.07.82, Arbroath :
SP - 13.58, SPJ - 14.12 (14.21-00)
OPENSHAW Michael 8.04.72, Birchfield :
3k - 7:54.10, 5k - 13:24.44,
10kR - 29:52 (29:05-00)
ORFORD Karl Vincent U17 28.12.84, Basildon :
HJ - 1.90
ORLONISHE Fola U17 14.07.86, Tower Hamlets :
100HY - 13.78w/14.0
ORMESHER Andrew J. U17 29.05.85, Wigan :
JTY - 53.18
ORR Christopher James U20 20.06.83, Border :
SPJ - 14.14, DT - 42.89, DTJ - 45.06 (45.27-00)
OSANO Curtis U15 8.03.87, Hants S :
TJ - 12.63
OSAZUWA John U23 4.05.81, Belgrave/NGR :
HT - 61.94 (62.87-00)
OSHO Set U15 28.09.86, Brighton :
100 - 11.5, 200 - 23.04w/23.10
OSTRIDGE Matthew U20 23.02.83, Telford :
HJ - 2.10
OSUIDE Stanley 30.11.74, Thames Valley :
HJ - 2.10 (2.15-91)
OUCHE Matthew U17 6.03.85, Newham & Essex B :
60 - 6.99i, 100 - 10.60w/10.8/10.81, 200 - 21.7/21.76
OUDNEY Graeme U17 11.04.85, Dundee HH :
800 - 1:56.19
OVERALL Scott U20 9.02.83, WSE&H :
800 - 1:53.89, 1500 - 3:51.48, 3k - 8:28.0
OWEN John N. 28.10.64, Swansea :
HT - 52.52 (52.96-95)
OWEN Neil James 18.10.73, Belgrave :
60H - 7.97i (7.72i-96), 110H - 13.87 (13.5w-96/13.60-95)
OWEN Nicholas U23 17.07.80, K & P/Brunel Univ :
SP - 15.49 (15.59-00), DT - 41.80 (43.40-00),
Dec - 6005
OYEDIRAN Akinbode Ademola V40 27.11.59, H Hill :
TJ - 14.15 (15.91i/15.78-84)

PAGE Adam 17.10.78, Guernsey :
LJ - 6.85
PAGE Christopher U23 13.11.80, Cardiff :
400 - 48.94i (47.51-00)
PAIN Ashleigh U15 16.10.87, Tipton :
3k - 9:39.3
PAISLEY Derek 1.12.73, Pitreavie/Bath Univ :
400H - 53.46 (52.83-94)
PALLISTER Jack U15 22.02.87, Cannock & Stafford :
HTB - 46.84
PALMER Adrian Mark 10.08.69, Cardiff :
HT - 60.56 (62.56-94)
PALMER Andrew 13.04.77, Team Solent :
HJ - 1.95 (2.00-95)
PALMER Ian U23 22.11.81, Bournemouth :
400H - 54.3 (56.62-00)
PALMER Martin 5.04.77, Yate/Chelt & GLos Un :
10kR - 29:17
PALMER Nathan U20 16.06.82, Cardiff :
60H - 8.03i, 110H - 14.06
PALMER Ryan U20 21.06.83, Sale :
200 - 21.80w/22.0, 400 - 48.3/48.55
PAPRELL Mark U13 25.11.88, :
75HC - 12.6
PAPURA Dominic U23 12.02.81, Cardiff :
100 - 10.70w/10.8/10.98 (10.8-00),
200 - 21.5w/21.6/21.61w/21.67
PARK Iain Ross 16.07.74, Harrow/Falkirk :
DT - 40.21 (44.96-98), HT - 63.54 (64.64-98)

PARKER Adam U15 25.09.86, Verlea :
400 - 52.1/52.77?
PARKER Andrew U23 1.08.80, Swansea :
100 - 10.6wdt/10.8w (10.72w/10.78-00)
PARKER Andrew U20 10.12.83, Wolverhampton & B :
3kW - 12:47.86 (12:29.90-00), 5kW - 22:36.98,
10kW - 47:24.5, 10kWR - 46:17
PARKER David U23 28.02.80, Shafte Ba/Loughbro :
JT - 78.33
PARKER James U23 29.09.80, Epsom & Ewell :
110H - 15.1/15.15, 400H - 55.1, Dec - 5495
PARKER Jonathon 1.05.76, Blackheath/Oxford Univ :
400H - 55.9 (53.80-95)
PARKER Richard U15 21.11.86, Cannock & Stafford :
SPB - 14.79
PARKER Richard U17 22.02.85, Sale :
3k - 8:41.13
PARKER Steven U15 6.10.86, Hereford & Worcs Sch :
SPB - 13.05
PARKIN John U23 23.02.79, Colwyn Bay :
HT - 50.10 (51.18-98)
PARKINSON Ian Philip U23 17.02.79, Wycombe/
Loughborough Studnts : PV - 4.10 (4.30-97)
PARPER Michael 20.05.78, Belgrave :
400 - 48.82i (46.54-97)
PARR Christopher Daniel U17 13.11.84, Gateshead :
800 - 1:55.68, 1500 - 4:01.21, 3k - 8:37.3
PARRY Philip John 4.10.65, Harrow :
JT - 62.16 (70.00-94)
PARSONS Gary 17.05.71, Cambridge & Colr'dge :
DT - 40.28 (42.95-98)
PARSONS Thomas Martin U20 5.05.84, S & S Heath :
HJ - 2.01
PARTINGTON Stephen Wyand 17.09.65, Manx H :
3kW - 12:09.8 (11:33.4-95), 5kW - 21:07.5 (20:09.0-92),
10kWR - 43:38 (40:40hc-92/40:49-94),
20kW - 1:29:52 (1:24:09sh-94/1:24:18-90)
PATERSON Martin U15, Staffs Moorlands :
1500 - 4:20.9
PATON Colin, Ballydrain :
100kR - 8:06:30
PATTON Andrew U23 23.01.81, Middlesbro & C :
LJ - 6.85 (6.95w-97)
PAUL Robert U23 12.11.80, E & E/St. Marys Univ :
HJ - 2.10i/2.06 (2.10-00)
PAYNE Russell H. V40 11.09.60, Birchfield :
HT - 51.06 (56.62-86)
PAYNE Stephen J. V45 1.12.55, Royal Navy :
Mar - 2:31:27 (2:29:36-00)
PAYNE Tim U15 23.09.86, Solihull & S Heath :
HJ - 1.80
PEACOCK Shane 5.03.63, Birchfield :
HT - 63.98 (71.60-90)
PEARCE Jamie U15 23.09.86, Croydon :
LJ - 6.11
PEARSON John Terry 30.04.66, Charnwood :
HT - 65.90 (70.33-00)
PEARSON Kenneth W.G. 9.07.72, City of Edinburgh :
Dec - 4902 (5864-95)
PEDLEY Will U15 22.09.86, Gloucester L :
200 - 23.4w
PEEL Matthew U17 7.01.85, Crawley :
400 - 51.0
PEERLESS Matthew U20 3.12.82, Corst/C of Edinb :
PV - 4.10i (4.10i-00/4.01-99), Dec - 4910 (5034-00)
PEET James U20 2.12.82, Rowheath :
110HJ - 14.82w/14.85, 110H - 15.6
PENK Andrew 19.09.78, Cardiff :
PV - 5.01
PENN Andrew Shaun 31.03.67, Nuneaton :
3kW - 12:16.0 (11:35.5-97), 20kW - 1:28:18 (1:23:34-92)
5kW - 21:18.02 (20:16.0-88),
10kWR - 43:23 (41:47+-92/42:00-93),
PERRYMAN Guy St. Denis Mansfield V40 2.11.58,
Reading : SP - 13.81 (16.58-89)
PETROS Daniel U17 8.08.85, Ealing,Southall & Mx :
400 - 50.67
PETTIGREW Adrian U15 12.11.86, Tower Hamlets :
80HB - 11.56, HJ - 1.81, PenB - 2768
PETTS Chris U23 22.01.80, Ashford :
HJ - 1.95 (2.07-00)
PHILIP Colin U23 8.06.79, City of Edinburgh :
400 - 48.52i/48.98 (48.35-00)
PHILIPSON James U15 18.03.87, Sale :
3k - 9:34.01
PHILLIPS Adrian Martin 29.07.75, Ealing,S & Mx :
LJ - 7.10
PHILLIPS Craig U17 29.09.85, Deeside :
TJ - 13.63w (12.00-00)
PHILLIPS James U13 13.12.88, Ashford :
400 - 58.3, 800 - 2:17.8
PHILLIPS Jonathan U23 8.05.80, Cardiff/UWIC :
5k - 14:43.73
PHILLIPS Steven 17.03.72, Rugby :
LJ - 7.60 (8.07w-99/8.03-98)
PICKERING Craig U15 16.10.86, Milton Keynes :
100 - 11.00w/11.12, 200 - 23.23w/23.29
PICKERING Robert U15 3.11.87, Bridlington :
3k - 9:37.08
PICKERING Shaun Desforges V40 14.11.61,
ACC Amsterdam : SP - 16.01 (20.45-97)
PICKERING Shaun U17 3.02.85, Bridlington :
3k - 8:55.74
PICKETT Andrew U20 11.05.82, Dartford :
3k - 8:37.5, 5k - 15:15.58
PICKUP Bradley U13 4.04.89, Bournemouth :
LJ - 5.15
*PILBOROUGH Matt U23 10.07.79, Halesowen/
Birmingham Univ./USA : PV - 4.40i (4.10-00)*
PISANO Ed U15 22.11.86, Shaftesbury Barnet :
800 - 2:05.04
PITT David U13 1.09.88, Halesowen :
100 - 12.2, 200 - 25.4
PITT Roderick U23 4.03.81, City of Edinburgh :
200 - 21.9w/22.16
PLANO Matthew 8.10.76, Trafford :
3k - 8:21.13i, 5k - 14:32.22i (14:31.5-99),
3kSt - 9:21.92 (8:54.66-99)
PLANT Raymond 13.05.68, City of Stoke :
Mar - 2:27:44 (2:20:23-97)
PLASKETT Simon U23 9.04.79, Wycombe/Loughbro :
300 - 34.14, 400 - 47.18
PLATTS Stephen James 12.03.66, Morpeth :
10k - 31:32.84 (31:01.18-00)
PLUMMER Daniel U23 4.01.81, Blackheath :
100 - 10.7/10.74 (10.67w-96), 200 - 21.66w/22.03
PLUNKETT Gerard Peter U23 30.06.80, Hallamshire :
JT - 64.20, Dec - 6511 (6587-99)
POBIE William 6.12.78, Herne Hill :
100 - 10.70w/10.8/10.94, 200 - 22.0w
POORE Brad 24.07.78, Belgrave :
10k - 30:54.32
POPE Daniel U15 24.12.86, Gateshead :
HJ - 1.75
POTTER Adam Charles U23 12.04.80, Ox C/Bath Un :
100 - 10.7, 200 - 21.4/21.95, 300 - 34.7,
400 - 46.75, LJ - 7.39w?/7.07 (7.17-00),
TJ - 14.13 (14.63-99)
POWELL Graham U17 7.03.85, Skyrac :
800 - 1:58.02, 400HY - 57.7
*POWER Garry 1.09.62, Herne Hill/IRL :
DT - 48.43 (48.98-86)*
PRADY Steven U17 19.02.85, Havering :
HJ - 1.95
PRATT David 23.11.75, Bedford & County :
100 - 10.98, 400 - 48.32

PREDDY Ryan U20 30.01.84, Gloucester AC :
200 - 22.08, 400 - 47.80, 800 - 1:54.54
PREVOST Ricardo U17 31.10.85, Harrow :
HJ - 1.90 (1.90-00)
PRICE David U15 12.01.87, Newport :
SPB - 14.26, DTB - 44.58
PRICE Gareth U23 27.11.79, Shaftesbury Barnet :
1500 - 3:47.27
PRICE Glyn A. 12.09.65, Swansea :
PV - 4.20 (4.80-90)
PRICKETT Edward U20 28.01.83, Crawley :
1500 - 3:48.15, 3k - 8:19.9, 5k - 14:33.99
PRIDE Simon 20.07.67, Swansea/Keith :
Mar - 2:16:27
PRINCE Warren U17 18.03.85, Luton :
100 - 11.0w, 200 - 22.33
PRITCHARD Ashley U23 14.07.79, Macclesfield :
Dec - 5620
PRITCHARD Nicholas 5.12.72, Newport :
PV - 4.20 (4.60-95)
PRITCHARD Nick U15 19.01.87, Crawley :
80HB - 11.89w/12.0/12.01
PRITCHARD Simon 10.09.68, Banbury :
Mar - 2:35:38
PRITCHARD Tim U20 7.10.82, Grimsby :
SPJ - 13.51
PROCTER David U17 11.11.84, Carmarthen :
HTY - 50.48
PROCTOR David U17 22.10.85, Rochdale :
800 - 1:58.10
PROCTOR Mark Anthony 15.01.63, N & E B/RAF :
SP - 19.30 (20.85i-98/20.40-99),
DT - 50.48 (57.14-00), HT - 46.98 (53.70-93)
PROUDLOVE Michael 26.01.70, City of Stoke :
Mar - 2:23:17
PROWSE Barrie U17 2.03.85, Cornwall AC :
OctY - 4480
PURCELL Ian U17 20.12.84, Ballymena & Antrim :
400HY - 57.63
PURSGLOVE Lee U15 14.10.87, Chorley :
HJ - 1.84

QUARRY Jamie Stephen 15.11.72, Harrow/Falk :
60H - 8.07i, 110H - 14.42 (14.10-94),
PV - 4.60 (4.65-98), LJ - 7.29 (7.42w-00),
SP - 14.25 (14.43-97), DT - 41.57 (43.18-95),
Dec - 7625 (7739-99)
QUINN David Joseph U17 7.09.84, Annadale Str :
DTY - 42.75
QUINN Robert 10.12.65, Kilbarchan :
5k - 14:35.0 (14:00.91-95)

RADZIUS Robert U17 26.02.85, Hercules Wimb :
400HY - 58.6
RAESIDE Bruce U23 2.12.81, Notts :
3kSt - 9:14.6
RAGAN David James U20 26.03.83, Bas & MH :
800 - 1:54.5
RALPH Paul 16.12.67, Trafford :
LJ - 7.29w? (7.38w-00), TJ - 15.13 (15.76w-97/15.67-95)
RAMOS Jonathan U23 29.06.80, Ports/Brunel Univ :
LJ - 6.88
RAMSEY Chris U17 2.11.84, Sphinx :
1.5kSt - 4:33.10
RANCE Stuart, Portsmouth/Coventry University :
HJ - 1.95 (1.95-98)
RANDALL Matthew 28.04.70, WGreen & Ex L :
TJ - 14.38 (15.37-95)
SINGH RANDHAWA Manjit U23 19.10.80, Can & Staf/
DMU Leicester : SP - 13.50 (13.73-00)
RANGER Tom 20.11.77, Peterborough :
800 - 1:51.2, 1500 - 3:45.30

RATCLIFFE Trevor 9.03.64, Dacorum & Tring :
JT - 61.42 (66.78-96)
RAVEN Gareth 9.05.74, East Cheshire :
3k - 8:21.27 (8:14.06-00),
5k - 14:16.24, HMar - 66:05
RAWLINSON Christopher 19.05.72, Belgrave :
200 - 21.67w/22.09 (21.53-00),
400H - 48.27 (48.14-99)
RAYNER Andrew U20 16.01.82, Blackheath :
3k - 8:35.83i (9:13.3-97)
READLE David U23 10.02.80, Belgrave/Southern Ill :
SP - 17.69i/15.47 (17.50-00), DT - 43.01 (45.72-00)
RECORD Chris U15 12.09.86, WSE&H :
JTB - 49.93
REDMOND John V40 15.10.57, Kingston u Hull :
Mar - 2:29:49 (2:27:50-94)
REECE Ashley U13 8.09.88, Havering :
1500 - 4:44.7
REED Paul 2.06.62, Border :
SP - 16.43 (17.04-88), DT - 53.24 (58.36-99)
REES Andrew 1.02.71, :
Mar - 2:30:41
REES Ben U20 25.03.82, Peterborough :
800 - 1:54.24
REES Gareth U20 15.01.82, Sale/Loughborough :
400H - 55.2/55.83 (54.02-00)
REES Jason U17, Cardiff :
PV - 3.60
REES Martin V45 28.02.53, Swansea :
HMar - 66:29
REES Thomas U17 9.03.86, Swansea :
JTY - 54.75
REES-JONES Steve 24.12.74, Sheffield :
800 - 1:51.03 (1:49.92-97),
1500 - 3:44.09, 3k - 8:24.81i
REEVES Matthew U15 9.10.86, Sale :
800 - 2:02.4
REID Alan 19.04.66, Peterhead :
Mar - 2:34:07, 100kR - 7:13:30
REID Edward U23 22.07.81, Charnwood :
DT - 45.93
REID Graeme U23 14.04.79, Clydes/Iona Coll, USA :
3k - 8:19.43i (8:19.08i-00), 5k - 14:04.46
REID James 1.01.75, Law & Dist :
Mar - 2:29:02 (2:21:15-00)
REID Stewart 15.11.73, Border/Pitreavie :
800 - 1:51.78 (1:50.26-99)
REILLY Brendan Anthony John 23.12.72, Bel/IRL :
HJ - 2.00i (2.32i-94/2.31-92)
REINA Eduardo Enrique 9.12.68, Kent/Ox Univ/HON :
HT - 49.61 (50.96-98)
REISS Michael 17.06.63, Highgate Harriers :
HT - 46.00 (50.60-94)
RENFREE Andrew James 18.05.75, Shaftesbury B :
1500 - 3:50.86 (3:44.88-00), 1M - 4:06.74 (4:05.9-96)
REVELL Paul U23 18.11.80, Scar/Loughborough :
TJ - 14.55w/14.08 (14.55w/14.25-99)
REYNOLDS Christopher U17 23.01.85, WGrn & Ex L :
800 - 1:53.64, 1500 - 3:57.62
REYNOLDS Luke U15 4.09.86, North Down/Lagan V :
80HB - 11.90
REYNOLDS Tomas James U17 20.12.84, N Down :
100HY - 14.0/14.19w, DecY - 5359
RHODES Peter U13 20.09.88, Kendal :
HJ 1.50
RICE Lloyd U17 13.02.85, Bristol :
100 - 10.9/10.97w/10.99
RICHARDS Dominique U23 12.09.79, Harrow :
100 - 10.67w/10.7/10.96 (10.60w/10.69-99),
200 - 21.6w/21.64 (21.3-99/21.40-00),
400 - 48.5 (49.34-97), LJ - 7.27 (7.66w-00/7.52i-99/7.35-00)
RICHARDS Gary U20 22.04.82, Salford :
800 - 1:52.89

RICHARDS Gregory Roy V45 25.04.56, N Lond & MH :
DT - 41.94 (50.66-91)
RICHARDS Henry U23 15.05.81, Charnwood :
60 - 6.90i (6.89i-99),
100 - 10.70w/10.85 (10.69w/10.75-98),
200 - 21.92i/22.04 (21.61w-00)
RICHARDS Leslie U17 29.03.85, Middlesbro & C :
DT - 40.06, DTJ - 46.07, DTY - 50.61
RICHARDS Paul 13.02.65, Neath :
Mar - 2:30:34
RICHARDS Thomas Austin 13.11.78, Newham & E B/
Cambridge University : PV - 5.00 (5.25-99)
RICHARDSON Alan Matthew U23 15.01.81, Border/
Leeds Univ : PV - 4.70
RICHARDSON Mark Austin ¶ 26.07.72, WSE&H :
100 - 10.60 (10.35-98), 400 - 45.14 (44.37-98),
200 - 21.31 (20.6w-96/20.62-97)
RICHARDSON Paul U20 11.02.82, Charnwood :
800 - 1:53.1
RICKETTS David U23 2.12.79, Kingston u H/Birm U :
10k - 30:54.39
RIDDELSDELL Tim U15 26.01.87, Isle of Wight :
JTB - 45.05
RIDER Scott Frederick 22.09.77, Enf & Har :
SP - 16.86 (17.04i/17.04-00),
DT - 51.17 (52.81-00), HT - 45.67
RILEY Alex U20 17.09.83, Leics Cor :
100 - 10.9w (11.1-00), 200 - 22.05w/22.36
RILEY David U17 25.10.84, Morpeth :
100 - 10.9w, 200 - 21.67
RILEY Martin J. V40 6.04.60, Massey Ferguson :
Mar - 2:34:32 (2:25:43-89)
RIMMER Michael U17 3.02.86, Liv.Pembroke Sefton :
400 - 49.7, 800 - 1:52.36, 1500 - 4:00.3
RITCHIE Darren 14.02.75, Sale/Scottish Borders :
LJ - 7.69w/7.00 (7.92w-99/7.90-00)
ROBB Bruce 27.07.77, Pitreavie :
SP - 16.67, DT - 54.25
ROBBIN-COCKER Olubunmi 27.11.75, Trafford/SLE :
HJ - 2.05 (2.05-98), TJ - 14.29 (14.94-95)
ROBERSON Mark W. 13.03.67, Newham & Essex B :
JT - 80.80 (85.67-98)
ROBERTS Barry U15 24.09.86, :
SPB - 14.30, DTB - 40.87
ROBERTS Ben U23 15.01.80, City of Stoke :
60H - 8.42i (8.39i-99),
110H - 15.4/15.56 (14.98w-98/15.1/15.19-99),
PV - 4.12i, SP - 14.05i/13.98, DT - 40.12, Dec - 6475
ROBERTS Colin U23 20.01.81, City of Norwich/
Loughborough Studnts : 110H - 14.58w/14.7/14.95
ROBERTS Euron Lloyd U17 18.11.85, Eryri :
100HY - 14.12
ROBERTS Mark 1.09.69, Kingston & Poly :
110H - 15.5 (15.3-98/15.65-92), Dec - 5866
ROBERTS Mark Stuart V40 12.02.59, Potteries Mar :
Mar - 2:30:59 (2:19:19-92)
ROBERTS Martin V40 1.03.60, Cannock & Stafford :
HT - 45.59 (53.08-88)
ROBERTS Martin U20 20.09.83, Scunthorpe :
100 - 10.98w (11.11-00), 200 - 21.66w/22.06
ROBERTS Matthew U20 8.07.84, Crawley :
400H - 56.2/56.94
ROBERTS Peter 19.09.71, Swansea :
DT - 40.06 (44.52-90)
ROBERTSON David U17 17.12.84, Jarrow & Hebburn :
100HY - 13.9/13.96, DecY - 5054, OctY - 4235
ROBERTSON Hamish U15 1.11.86, Grantham :
800 - 2:05.25, 1500 - 4:16.41, 3k - 9:26.3, HJ - 1.75
ROBERTSON Kenneth U15 6.04.88, Falkirk :
JTB - 43.41
ROBERTSON-ADAMS Charles Lyndon 5.12.77, N & EB :
400H - 50.24
ROBINSON Daniel 4.08.73, Tipton :
5k - 14:34.5, 10k - 29:31.98
ROBINSON Daniel U17 23.10.84, AF&D :
1500 - 4:01.46
ROBINSON Daniel 13.01.75, Tipton :
10kR - 29:42, HMar - 64:23, Mar - 2:16:51
ROBINSON James 27.08.76, Tipton :
PV - 4.12i (4.30i/4.30-94)
ROBINSON Keith V45 9.02.52, Havering :
HT - 46.50 (53.38-81)
ROBINSON Tom U17 14.06.85, Blackheath :
PV - 3.80
ROBINSON Tom U17, Blackheath :
400HY - 58.5
ROBSON Adam U17 6.11.85, Hartlepool :
100 - 11.1
ROBSON Lewis U15 9.01.88, Gateshead :
400 - 53.15, PenB - 2778
RODEN James U23 24.11.81, Chorley/Manchester U :
Dec - 5063
RODGERS David 16.06.67, Lochaber :
Mar - 2:32:20 (2:28:53-00)
ROE Thomas U20 25.06.82, City of Norwich :
LJ - 7.19
ROGERS Adam U20 10.04.83, Jarrow & Hebburn :
400 - 48.11i (48.8-00/48.85-99)
ROGERS Craig 14.02.76, Birchfield :
SP - 15.09 (15.88-97)
ROGERS Duncan U17 10.10.84, Horsham BS :
100HY - 13.56
ROGERS Stephen A. 1.09.71, Liv.Pembroke Sefton :
PV - 4.20 (4.60-95)
ROLLINS Andrew 20.03.78, Trafford :
SP - 14.13 (15.34-99), DT - 48.49 (48.56-00)
ROPER Peter 66, Poole :
Mar - 2:33:56
ROPER Simon U23 20.09.79, Derby & Co :
LJ - 6.85 (7.25w/7.21-00)
ROSENBERG Luke U23 29.06.80, Harrow :
SP - 14.26, DT - 52.81
ROSS Stephen 65, Mansfield :
Mar - 2:34:15
ROSSITER Martin R. 4.09.69, Peterborough :
TJ - 15.11 (15.53w-99/15.20-97)
ROWE Alex V40 10.04.57, Wesham :
Mar - 2:34:08 (2:28:16-99)
ROYDEN Barry Mark 15.12.66, Medway :
10k - 30:41.9 (28:47.17-94),
Mar - 2:19:32 (2:18:54-00)
ROYE Jordan Peter U15 3.11.87, Croydon :
80HB - 11.50
RUBEN Alan V40 9.03.57, :
Mar - 2:34:31 (2:29:54-98)
RUBENIS Richard 10.11.73, Telford :
100 - 10.97 (10.5w/10.7-94/10.75-00)
RUDKIN Alan 5.11.78, Peterborough :
DT - 41.47 (43.84-99)
RUMBOLD James Lee U23 4.11.81, Bournemouth :
DT - 42.25 (43.62-00)
RUSBRIDGE Simon U20 13.05.82, Exeter :
800 - 1:53.4
RUSSELL Alaister 17.06.68, Border/Law & Dist :
5k - 14:45.0 (14:17.1-96)
RUSSELL Daniel U15 2.04.87, Shaftesbury Barnet :
3k - 9:24.5
RUSSELL Jamie U23 1.10.81, Sheffield :
HJ - 2.16i/2.15, LJ - 6.85 (6.90-00)
RUSSELL Patrick U17 17.03.85, Bridgewater :
HTY - 48.68
RUSSELL Robert U20 13.07.82, Thames Valley :
5k - 15:18.0 (15:12.20-00)
RUTHERFORD Greg U15 17.11.86, Milton Keynes :
LJ - 6.16

RUTTERFORD J. 1.09.78, Army :
HJ - 1.95
RUTTERFORD Neil 3.06.68, Army :
Dec - 5562
RYAN Charles Peter V45 9.04.54, Sheffield RWC :
50kW - 4:52:22 (4:18:30-82)

SACHA James U17 10.02.86, Guildford & G :
DTY - 40.67
SAGGERS Carl Peter Maurice U20 20.09.83, E & H :
SP - 14.07, SPJ - 15.46, DT - 43.70,
DTJ - 49.61, HT - 58.12, HTJ - 65.75
SALAMI Raymond 11.04.75, Newham & Essex B :
100 - 10.8w (10.2w/10.59w-99/10.6-96/10.66-99
SALMON Sean U15 29.11.86, Herne Hill :
HJ - 1.75, LJ - 6.03
SALT BERRYMAN Jacob U15 27.10.86, S London :
SPB - 13.41
SALTER Thomas U20 7.01.83, Cannock & Stafford :
HJ - 1.98 (1.98-00)
SALVADOR-AYLOTT Livio 18.07.73, Harrow :
JT - 58.17
SAMMUT Steven 3.05.67, Team Solent :
HT - 59.58 (60.90dh/60.61-00)
SAMPSON Christopher 30.09.75, Morpeth :
3kSt - 9:15.5 (9:13.54-00)
SAMUEL Joseph U17 27.12.84, Kilbarchan :
100 - 11.1
SAMUYIWA David 4.08.72, Thames Valley :
100 - 10.6/10.70 (10.2wdt-98/10.4-97/10.53w-00/10.66-97,
200 - 21.8 (21.2-97/21.43w-00/21.46-97)
SANDERSON David 6.05.71, Sale :
TJ - 15.01 (15.72w-93/15.29-92)
SANFORD Mark 19.04.78, Chelmsford :
1500 - 3:49.87
SANKOFA Moyo U15 12.12.86, Herne Hill :
400 - 53.0/53.82
SAULTERS Alan U20 29.01.83, Abbeydale :
LJ - 6.95, TJ - 14.56w
SAVAGE David 13.11.72, Sale :
110H - 15.50 (15.1w-96/15.34-95),
400H - 52.9/53.34 (50.97-96)
SAVILLE Ben 10.11.77, Cleethorpes/Hull Univ :
JT - 57.52 (60.60-99)
SAVILLE Chris U17 9.10.84, Hertford & Ware :
800 - 1:57.34
SAWHNEY Simon U20 10.06.83, Lagan Valley :
LJ - 6.91, TJ - 14.26w/14.15
SAWYER Anthony J. U23 29.04.80, WGreen & Ex L :
60H - 8.49i, 110H - 14.80w/15.03, HJ - 1.99i,
PV - 4.12, Dec - 6983
SCANLON Robert 13.04.74, Coventry Godiva :
1500 - 3:47.29 (3:41.3-96)
SCHMITT Vincent, Oadby & Wigston :
Mar - 2:34:40
SCOTT Allan U20 27.12.82, S B/Glas U/Whitemoss :
60H - 8.03i, 110HJ - 13.9/14.83 (14.20-00),
110H - 14.26, LJ - 6.94 (7.07w/6.96i-98)
SCOTT Darren 7.03.69, Trafford :
100 - 10.87 (10.5w?-99/10.61w-98/10.74-95),
200 - 21.57 (21.0w?-99/21.19w-98/21.3/21.35-95
SCOTT Paul U20 3.01.82, WSE&H :
SPJ - 13.82
SCOTT Richard 14.09.73, WGreen & Ex L :
110H - 15.03w/15.2, 400H - 52.7/53.27 (52.39-99)
SCOTT Ryan U15 20.02.87, Yate :
100 - 11.2w/11.35w/11.5, 200 - 22.91w/23.0/23.11
SCOTT Sandy 1.09.76, Shett/Glasgow Univ/Border :
300 - 35.60i
SCRAGG Jem U17 30.12.84, Swindon :
3k - 8:48.36

SEAR Richard A. U23 21.08.79, Bel/London Univ :
60H - 8.25i/8.3i, HJ - 1.95 (2.01-97)
110H - 14.3w/14.34w/14.4/14.51 (14.37-97),
SEAWARD Joe U13 22.10.88, :
JTC - 40.05
SEMPERS Kevin U17 24.11.85, Scunthorpe :
OctY - 4353
SEMPLE Stuart U20 3.11.83, Basingstoke & MH :
DTJ - 41.84
SENBANJO Oladipo U20 20.03.82, Notts/Oxford Un :
TJ - 13.98 (14.21w-98)
SESAY Mark Gavin 13.12.72, Trafford :
400 - 47.51 (46.22-97), 800 - 1:49.90 (1:45.68-99)
SHALDERS Steven U23 24.12.81, Cardiff :
60 - 6.98i, LJ - 7.28w/7.20i (7.29-99),
TJ - 16.28
SHANKEY Mark U17 19.12.84, Serpentine :
800 - 1:57.86, 1500 - 3:56.94, 3k - 8:31.22
SHARLAND Tom U20 5.10.83, Ipswich :
3k - 8:24.85, 5k - 15:00.21
SHARMAN William U17 12.09.84, Corby :
100HY - 13.88, HJ - 1.95, OctY - 4444
SHARP Stephen 31.12.75, Belgrave :
1500 - 3:45.33 (3:43.42-99),
5k - 14:18.53, 5MR - 23:40
SHARPE Phill U23 6.03.81, Border :
JT - 68.49 (71.79-00)
SHAW Ryan U15 30.12.86, WGreen & Ex L :
80HB - 11.7/11.76, LJ - 6.33, PenB - 2786
SHEERAN Richard U17 27.11.85, Sale :
400 - 49.73, 800 - 1:56.6
SHEPHERD Andrew 9.11.78, Exeter/Loughbro :
HJ - 1.95 (2.00-99)
SHEPHERD Bruce David 20.03.67, Aberdeen :
HT - 47.79 (53.18-96)
SHEPHERD Dominic 11.12.76, Trafford :
60 - 6.85i, 60H - 8.39i, PV - 4.72i (4.90-94)
SHEPLEY Sebastian 23.11.67, Westbury :
Mar - 2:31:40 (2:27:01-98)
SHEPPARD Kevin U23 21.01.79, Army/Tipton :
800 - 1:52.69, 1500 - 3:48.91
SHERIDAN Mark D. 17.06.70, Crawley :
HT - 50.09 (56.02-91)
SHERMAN Andrew U23 28.09.81, Swindon/Loughbro :
800 - 1:52.6 (1:52.23-00), 1500 - 3:48.31
SHERRATT Jonathan U15 18.10.86, :
100 - 11.5
SHIELDS David U15 18.02.88, Omagh :
HJ - 1.75
SHOKER Mardeep U15 9.02.87, Medway :
80HB - 11.4w/11.47
SHONE Matthew 10.07.75, WGreen & Ex L :
800 - 1:48.67 (1:47.99-99), 1500 - 3:46.19
SHORROCK Alexander U17 28.09.84, Wigan :
SPY - 14.78
SHORTMAN Luke U15 14.10.87, Cambridge & Col :
HTB - 44.53
SHOWELL Gavin 29.09.72, Tamworth :
PV - 4.40 (4.75-00)
SHRUBB Nathan U15 11.10.86, Morpeth :
800 - 2:03.20, 1500 - 4:20.29
SHUBOTHAM Carl U15 10.04.87, Stoke :
1500 - 4:17.88, 3k - 9:29.17
SHUTE Russell U17 21.05.85, Oadby & Wigston :
800 - 1:58.2, 1500 - 4:02.26
SICHEL William Morley V45 1.10.53, Moray RR :
24Hr - 200.599km (246.704km-00)
SIDOLI Alex U17 29.05.85, Middlesex Sch :
400HY - 58.9
SILLAH-FRECKLETON Mohammed U23 11.09.80,
Blackheath : 60H - 8.10i (8.09i-00),
110H - 14.2/14.34w/14.42

SIMON Delroy 27.11.78, Harrow :
3kSt - 9:08.6 (9:00.81-00)
SIMPKINS Matthew U20 9.05.82, S & S H/Bristol Un :
800 - 1:54.32, 1500 - 3:54.0 (3:53.82-00)
SIMPSON Jason, S London :
5k - 14:42.4
SIMPSON Jonathan U20 27.05.82, Falkirk/Belgrave :
400 - 48.09
SIMPSON Michael 6.01.70, WSE&H :
HMar - 66:45
SIMPSON Scott E. U23 21.07.79, Wx & Bath/UWIC :
PV - 5.20
SIMS Andrew U20 9.09.82, Newport :
3kSt - 9:49.8
SINGH D. U17, Basildon :
1.5kSt - 4:40.2
SKEETE John ¶ 8.09.78, Harrow/Falkirk :
60 - 6.59idrg/6.7i/6.72i!
SKETCHLEY David 25.02.76, Team Solent :
JT - 61.77 (62.01-00)
SKINNER Michael U23 21.11.79, Blackhth/Brunel U :
800 - 1:51.2 (1:50.79-00), 1500 - 3:45.28
SLADE Russell U20 25.04.83, Med & Maid :
800 - 1:54.01
SLEEMAN Christopher J. U23 20.03.80, Tonb/Oxf U :
400 - 48.5, 400H - 52.6/52.97
SLOMAN Thomas U13, :
JTC - 36.00
SLUE Leroy U23 11.12.81, Croydon :
100 - 10.8/10.97 (10.92-99)
SLYTHE Paul J. 5.09.74, Newham & Essex B :
100 - 10.7w/10.8 (10.4w-97/10.58w/10.7/10.73-96),
200 - 21.92 (21.22-96), 400 - 47.14 (45.94-98),
Dec - 5116
SMALL Michael V45 31.03.54, Belgrave :
SP - 13.76, DT - 43.34 (45.40-85),
HT - 47.46 (49.98-86)
SMALL Vernon U20 1.01.82, Enf & Har :
400 - 48.82
SMALLWOOD Luke U13 11.09.88, Med & Maid :
400 - 61.9
SMART Michael U17 18.11.85, Harrow :
800 - 1:58.21, 1500 - 3:58.7
SMITH Alistair U20 22.02.84, AF&D :
3kSt - 9:56.1
SMITH Andrew U17 2.10.84, Middlesbro & C :
HTY - 56.17
SMITH Anthony U20 11.01.83, Thurrock :
DTJ - 43.27 (44.42-00)
SMITH Ben U20 12.06.82, Shaftesbury Barnet :
HJ - 2.00 (2.00-98)
SMITH Ben U15 6.06.87, Worthing :
HJ - 1.75
SMITH Blake U15 16.02.87, Guernsey :
80HB - 11.5w/12.1
SMITH Carl Anthony V40 17.05.58, Shaftesbury B :
JT - 60.87 (69.94r-91)
SMITH Cameron U20 17.01.84, Cardiff :
3kW - 12:46.13i/13:07.0 (13:05.18-00),
5kW - 23:31.82i (23:48.30-00),
10kW - 47:42.76, 10kWR - 46:21
SMITH Christopher James 27.11.75, Arbroath :
JT - 59.20 (62.30-96)
SMITH Christopher U23 26.04.79, Liverpool H :
400 - 48.90 (48.16-00)
SMITH Colin P. V40 11.09.57, Portsmouth :
SP - 14.29 (15.54-89), HT - 46.99 (48.98-89)
SMITH David 21.06.62, North East SH :
HT - 48.70 (77.30-85)
SMITH David W. 2.11.74, Belgrave :
HT - 73.30 (75.10-96)
SMITH Francis U23 2.10.81, Pitreavie :
110H - 15.05
SMITH Gary 20.02.71, Luton :
LJ - 6.86 (7.58w-00/7.49-97)
SMITH Gavin U17 15.02.85, AF&D :
3k - 8:56.7, 1.5kSt - 4:37.4
SMITH Glen Ernest 21.05.72, Birchfield :
SP - 13.81 (14.71-96), DT - 61.29 (65.11-99)
SMITH Gregory U20 29.01.84, Bournemouth :
110HJ - 15.0/15.25, 400H - 56.7
SMITH Jonathan U17 26.10.84, Peterborough :
JTY - 52.63
SMITH Leigh Matthew U20 24.09.82, Birchfield :
LJ - 7.21 (7.29-00)
SMITH Mark 14.09.74, Harrow :
HJ - 2.00 (2.07-91)
SMITH Matthew 26.12.74, Tipton :
1500 - 3:46.10 (3:45.59-97), 5MR - 23:32,
3k - 8:05.64 (7:58.15i-98/7:59.23-99),
5k - 14:03.16 (14:01.53-99), 10k - 28:43.45
SMITH Michael U23 3.06.79, Bolton :
100 - 10.50w/10.8/10.88 (10.8/10.85-00),
200 - 21.9w/22.0/22.10
SMITH Michael John 20.04.63, Coventry RWC :
20kW - 1:38:51 (1:30:52-87),
30kW - 2:37:11 (2:24:14+-89/2:26:01.0t+-86),
35kW - 2:58:35 (2:40:37-89),
50kW - 4:32:55 (4:09:22-89)
SMITH Nicholas U20 6.12.82, Dunf & W Fife/S B :
100 - 10.51w/10.65, 200 - 21.5w/21.58
SMITH R. U17, Staffs Sch :
100HY - 14.1
SMITH Richard William U23 17.01.81, Peterborough :
PV - 4.70 (4.90-99)
SMITH Richard Blake U20 12.10.82, Middlesbro & C :
400H - 52.3/52.36
SMITH Robert U17 3.03.85, Colchester & T :
200 - 22.6, 400 - 49.19, 400HY - 58.4, OctY - 4316
SMITH Robert U20 3.12.82, Basildon :
800 - 1:54.13, 1500 - 3:49.79
SMITH Robert U15 6.12.86, Carmarthen :
JTB - 45.70
SMITH Robin Alistair U20 11.09.83, City of Stoke :
110HJ - 14.7w/14.89w/14.99,
Dec - 5997, DecJ - 6264
SMITH Rory U17 12.12.84, Wirral :
800 - 1:56.26 (1:55.90-00),
1500 - 4:02.41 (4:01.28-00), 3k - 8:51.92
SMITH Ruan U17 6.03.86, City of Norwich :
DTY - 41.60
SMITH Shane U17 13.05.85, North Shields Poly :
400 - 50.12
SMITH Sullivan 23.10.74, Swansea :
10k - 31:58.9, 3kSt - 9:25.6
SMITH Wesley U23 26.02.79, Belgrave :
JT - 59.02 (60.86-00)
SMYTH Jeremy 11.08.78, City of Edinburgh/Shett :
JT - 58.98 (59.95-00)
SMYTH Paul U13, Ballymena & Antrim :
HJ - 1.50
SNOW Michael U20 5.09.82, Northampton :
400 - 49.33i (48.69-99)
SNOW Tom U17 7.09.85, WGreen & Ex L :
800 - 1:54.84, 1500 - 4:02.4, 3k - 8:53.6
SOALLA-BELL Anthony 3.10.76, Shaftesbury B/SLE :
SP - 15.39i/14.77 (15.89-99), DT - 42.11
SOLLITT Gary 13.01.72, Team Solent :
SP - 16.58 (17.29i-99/17.14-97)
SOOS Ricky Istvan U20 28.06.83, Mansfield :
800 - 1:48.43, 1500 - 3:46.70, 2kSt - 5:43.23
SOUGRIN Neil 14.05.71, Enf & Har :
DT - 43.24 (47.82-94)
SOUTH James 4.01.75, Southend :
SP - 14.42, DT - 48.46

SOUTHWARD Anthony 31.01.71, Trafford :
110H - 14.96 (14.6w-98/14.69-96), PV - 4.45,
SP - 13.37 (13.82-96), DT - 40.28 (43.46-98),
Dec - 7133 (7425-96)
SPEAIGHT Neil Anthony 9.09.78, Bel/Brunel Univ :
800 - 1:47.16
SPEAKE William J. 24.01.71, Notts :
Mar - 2:27:50 (2:26:49-94)
SPEIGHT Christian U13 2.12.88, Mansfield :
HJ - 1.50
SPICER Matthew William 18.05.71, Bristol :
HT - 51.37 (60.26jr?-90/59.68-96)
SPILLER Kyle U15 17.01.87, Rhondda :
SPB - 13.09, DTB - 38.00
SPRINGINGS Grant U20 26.02.82, :
SPJ - 14.14
SPURLING Christopher 27.11.75, Sale :
TJ - 13.93 (14.20-96)
SQUIRE Derrick John Preston U20 7.12.83, Can & St :
SP - 14.56, SPJ - 15.73, HT - 51.67, HTJ - 52.98
SQUIRRELL John 16.12.75, Belgrave :
400H - 55.21
ST.CLAIR Darren U17 6.04.85, Enf & Har :
400 - 50.4, 800 - 1:54.6
STAMP Terence 18.02.70, Newham & Essex B :
60 - 6.85i (6.70i-98),
100 - 10.6w/10.72 (10.4-97/10.47-95)
STANILAND Andrew William U15 21.01.87, Skyrac :
PenB - 2601
STANLEY Tom U15 11.04.87, Crawley :
400 - 52.94
STANYARD Chris U15, Hants S :
LJ - 6.00
STAPELY Stephen U20 19.05.84, Dartford :
DecJ - 5452
STASAITIS Reginaldas 6.04.67, N Lond & M H/LTU :
HJ - 2.00 (2.08-84), TJ - 14.88 (15.62w/15.53-99)
STEADMAN Darren U15 26.01.87, Colchester H :
HJ - 1.85, LJ - 6.07, PenB - 2719
STEELE Andrew U17 19.09.84, Trafford :
200 - 22.1/22.21, 400 - 48.62
STEINLE Mark 22.11.74, Blackheath :
10MR - 49:02+ (48:25-98),
HMar - 64:05+ (62:23-99), Mar - 2:10:46
STEPHENS Gavin James 12.09.77, Wort/Brunel Un :
200 - 22.0/22.18 (21.57w/22.00-00), 400 - 48.63
STEPHENSON Barry, Loughborough Studnts :
10k - 31:52.18
STEPHENSON Christian 22.07.74, Cardiff :
1500 - 3:41.94, 3k - 8:15.01 (7:53.23-00),
3kSt - 8:38.46 (8:25.37-00)
STERLING Scott 6.12.78, Basildon :
1500 - 3:51.4
STEVENS Kyle U17 3.06.85, Sutton & District :
SP - 13.32, SPY - 15.41, DTY - 41.84
STEVENS Paul U20 15.11.83, Kingston u Hull :
PV - 4.70
STEVENTON David U17 6.12.84, City of Stoke :
HTY - 48.61
STEWART Alan U17 9.12.84, Liv.Pembroke Sefton :
3k - 8:57.39
STEWART Alaster 5.10.72, Belgrave :
5k - 14:45.76
STEWART Calvin U17 17.02.85, Wessex & Bath :
HJ - 1.90, LJ - 6.57w (4.17-97)
STEWART Camara U20 11.09.83, Notts :
HJ - 1.95i (1.95-00)
STEWART Glen 7.12.70, RRC :
1500 - 3:43.79 (3:38.66-96),
3k - 8:04.82i (7:55.15-99),
5k - 13:37.17, 10k - 28:40.14, HMar - 65:34
STEWART John U23 30.12.79, Sale/Loughbro :
60 - 6.82i (6.82i-00),
100 - 10.79 (10.36w-99/10.40-00),
200 - 21.48i/21.60 (20.83-00)
STEWART Jonathan U23 22.05.80, Halifax/Fife AC :
800 - 1:49.94 (1:49.53-00)
STEWART Kris George U23 11.04.80, S B/Stirling U/
Scot Border : 200 - 21.29, 400 - 47.53 (47.31-97)
STEWART Mark 15.05.71, Manx H :
3kW - 13:06.84
STIMPSON Alan 25.04.68, New Marske :
10k - 31:55.6
STIMSON Bradley U15 1.09.86, Nene Valley H :
200 - 23.2/23.44w/23.52
STIMSON Tom U15 2.09.86, Nene Valley H :
80HB - 10.99w/11.27
STODDART Dwayne U23 29.12.80, WSE&H :
60H - 8.4i (8.3i/8.33i-00),
110H - 14.5/14.54w/14.66 (14.51w/14.59-00)
STOKES Stuart 15.12.76, Sale :
1500 - 3:46.32, 2kSt - 5:39.13 (5:38.4-99),
3kSt - 8:33.15
STONE Darrell Richard 2.02.68, Steyning :
10kWR - 43:05+/43:44 (40:45-89),
20kW - 1:28:51 (1:23:27un-93/1:23:58-96),
30kW - 2:28:00+ (2:11:30-94),
35kW - 2:58:19 (2:40:49-95),
50kW - 4:21:55 (4:10:23-90)
STONE Darryl Frank U20 6.06.83, Basildon :
HJ - 2.10 (2.10-00)
STONE Kairnil 21.10.76, Newham & Essex B :
5k - 14:29.96, 10k - 31:03.76
STONES Alex U17 17.09.84, Telford :
100 - 11.10, 200 - 22.2
STOREY Rikki U15 25.09.86, Birchfield :
100 - 11.4w
STOVES Christopher U20 20.02.84, Sale :
800 - 1:50.13, 1500 - 3:50.01
STRACHAN Richard U15 18.11.86, Leeds :
400 - 52.96
STRANGE Alasdair U20 5.04.83, Shettleston :
PV - 4.10
STRONACH Paul A.G. 18.05.68, Severn :
SP - 13.37 (13.96-89)
STURROCK Craig U17 7.01.85, Gateshead :
SPY - 13.86i
STYLES Iain Bruce 2.10.75, Cheltenham/Birm Univ. :
SP - 15.47
SUMMERS James Alexander Edward 7.10.65,
Royal Navy : HT - 46.02 (58.86un-87/55.78-88)
SUMNER Ben U20 16.08.83, St Albans Striders :
400H - 56.46
SURETY Steven Christopher U23 18.02.80, Basildon/
Brunel Univ : 100 - 10.8w (10.7w/10.95-98),
300 - 35.29i, 400 - 48.36i/48.7, 400H - 51.8/51.82
SUTCLIFFE Christopher U23 9.01.79, Telford :
HJ - 1.95
SUTTON Adam C. U23 22.03.81, Prest/Prov Un :
3k - 8:12.77i (8:26.16-99),
5k - 14:03.61, 10k - 29:10.98
SUTTON Matthew U23 8.09.81, Birchfield :
HT - 54.20 (57.64-00)
SUTTON Robert U17, Walton :
400HY - 58.5
SWAIN Anthony Michael 17.01.75, Wake/Hudd Univ. :
HT - 55.46 (62.88-97)
SWAIN Ashley U23 3.10.80, Team Solent/Staffs Un :
60H - 8.36i, PV - 5.20, LJ - 6.96
SWARAY Tyrone 7.11.77, Blackheath :
60 - 6.88i
SWEARMAN Andrew 1.02.74, Kingston u Hull :
5k - 14:40.80

SWEENEY Conor U23 28.12.81, St Malachy's/ Loughbro/IRL : 800 - 1:49.35, 1500 - 3:43.85
SWEENEY Gary U15 31.01.87, Moray RR/Elgin : PenB - 2611
SWEENEY Mark 26.02.77, Birchfield/Birmingham U : HJ - 2.00i (2.00i/2.00-97)
SWEETMAN David 27.01.71, Charnwood : 110H - 15.5 (14.22w/14.43-98)
SWEETMAN Ryan U15 4.11.86, Harrogate : PV - 3.05
SWIFT-SMITH Justin 28.08.74, Shaftesbury Barnet : 800 - 1:49.4 (1:47.9-97), 1500 - 3:46.24 (3:42.59-00), 3k - 8:18.61 (8:13.32-00)
SYERS Aidan U20 29.06.83, Croydon : 100 - 10.31w/10.52, 200 - 22.0
SYMONDS Chris 21.11.73, Enf & Har : 3kSt - 9:28.4
SYMONS Dave V40 21.10.58, Thames H & H : Mar - 2:29:33

TADESSE Kassa 21.08.74, Belgrave : 10k - 30:57.96 (29:42.93-93), 10kR - 29:16 (28:15sh-96/29:05-94), 10MR - 48:32 (47:43-93), HMar - 64:04 (62:51-97)
TALBOT Nicholas P. 14.12.77, Notts/Oxford Univ : 5k - 14:46.51, 3kSt - 8:59.27 (8:55.59-99)
TANSER Toby 21.07.68, Sparvagens : Mar - 2:33:53 (2:18:02-97)
TATTERSHALL James U23 25.11.81, Kingston u H : 110H - 15.6 (15.58w-00)
TAYLOR David William 9.01.64, Blackheath : 3k - 8:24.5 (7:57.64-99), 5k - 14:08.14 (13:44.71-99), 5KR - 14:16, 5MR - 23:42 (23:30-99), 10k - 29:22.22 (29:00.04-99)
TAYLOR David U17 21.11.84, South Devon : TJ - 13.41
TAYLOR Greg U13 5.01.89, Montrose : 75HC - 12.94w
TAYLOR Gregg 1.08.77, Trafford/Chester University : 800 - 1:49.85, 1500 - 3:42.73, 1M - 4:09.24, 3k - 8:10.68
TAYLOR Ian J. 2.07.67, Telford : DT - 42.86 (49.44-93)
TAYLOR Jack U15 5.06.87, Thames Valley : 3k - 9:36.9
TAYLOR James U20 24.04.82, Hallamshire : DT - 40.37, DTJ - 42.58 (43.95-00)
TAYLOR James U15, Horsham BS : LJ - 6.14
TAYLOR Philip U17 20.03.85, Liv.Pembroke Sefton : 400 - 49.89
TAYLOR Robert Wesley James U23 9.06.80, Wake : HT - 46.61 (49.65-00)
TAYLOR Shaun 19.01.76, Hereford : PV - 4.10
TAYLOR Wayne Richard U15 17.10.87, Grimsby : 80HB - 11.9
TEAGUE Christopher 11.03.69, : Mar - 2:26:38 (2:24:36-99)
TEAR Adam 12.08.75, Cleethorpes : DT - 42.03
TEATE Andy U17 6.09.84, Mandale : 800 - 1:57.36
TEDD Phil J.A. 7.11.76, Bingley : 800 - 1:51.16, 1500 - 3:44.82 (3:43.54-00)
TEJAN COLE Kamil U17 21.01.85, Herne Hill : 200 - 22.48i (22.51-00)
TELFORD Craig U23 1.06.79, Wallsend : 100 - 10.84w
TENNY Joe U15 9.06.87, Watford : 80HB - 11.57w/11.61
TESSEN Francois U23 80, Univ W Inst Card/FRA : TJ - 14.74w/14.44i/14.31
THACKERY Carl Edward 14.10.62, Hallamshire : 10MR - 49:48 (46:21+/46:26-91)
THICKPENNY Robert 17.07.76, Peterborough : PV - 4.20 (4.80-99)
THIE James 27.06.78, Cardiff/Univ Wales Inst Card : 800 - 1:51.76 (1:50.52-00), 1500 - 3:44.51 (3:42.85-00), 3k - 8:14.19i (8:16.12-98)
THOMAS Andrew U23 29.01.81, Invicta : 3kSt - 9:27.6 (9:27.03-00)
THOMAS Andrew U17 14.06.86, Birchfield : DTY - 42.51
THOMAS Barry V.S. 28.04.72, Sheffield : 110H - 15.04 (14.62w-95/14.81-92), HJ - 1.96 (2.05-92), PV - 4.85 (5.00-92), LJ - 7.25w/6.98 (7.44-92), SP - 14.15i/13.77 (14.06-96), DT - 42.92, JT - 56.75 (62.40-97), Dec - 7410 (7766-95)
THOMAS Iwan Gwyn 5.01.74, Newham & Essex B : 100 - 10.67w (10.90+-97), 400 - 45.70 (44.36-97), 200 - 21.14A/21.25w (20.87-97),
THOMAS Joselyn 11.07.71, WGrn & Ex L/Army/SLE : 100 - 10.76 (10.3w/10.36w-98/10.51-97)
THOMAS Julian U15 28.12.86, Birchfield : 100 - 11.09w/11.1/11.23, 200 - 22.03w/22.3/22.74i/22.76, HJ - 1.75
THOMAS Keston U23 17.04.81, Serpentine/GRN : LJ - 7.07, TJ - 14.01
THOMAS Luke U13 27.03.89, Enf & Har : LJ - 5.15
THOMAS Matthew 27.04.76, Newham & Essex B : 100 - 10.87, 200 - 22.09
THOMAS Nicholas U23 4.04.79, Newham & Essex B : 100 - 10.6w/10.69 (10.61-00), 200 - 21.53w/22.09 (21.9-00), TJ - 15.87i/15.54 (16.31-00)
THOMAS Paul U23 1.10.80, Team Solent : PV - 4.60
THOMAS Philip U17 21.10.84, Swansea : 400HY - 57.51, OctY - 4227
THOMAS Ryan U15 21.03.87, Epsom & Ewell : 100 - 11.51w/11.71, HJ - 1.75, LJ - 6.46, PenB - 2866
THOMAS Simon David U23 4.03.81, Southend/ Cambridge University : HJ - 2.00i (2.10-99)
THOMAS Timothy Paul 18.11.73, Cardiff : PV - 5.40i/5.40 (5.40-97)
THOMASSEN Olau U23 19.02.80, Newham & Ex B/ Loughborough Studnts/DEN : 400H - 53.35
THOMPSON Adam U13 8.11.88, Grimsby : DTC - 26.69
THOMPSON Christopher U23 17.04.81, AF&D/ Loughborough Studnts : 1500 - 3:43.55, 3k - 8:04.01, 5k - 13:45.27, 5KR - 14:13
THOMPSON Daniel U17 27.12.84, City of Stoke : OctY - 4351
THOMPSON Darren U23 6.11.79, Belgrave : 100 - 10.93, LJ - 7.84w/7.53 (7.56-98)
THOMPSON Gavin U23 9.04.80, Crawley : 800 - 1:52.14, 1500 - 3:48.56 (3:47.20-99)
THOMPSON Kevin U20 24.10.83, Liverpool H : TJ - 14.80w/14.68
THOMPSON Mark U20 7.07.82, Lisburn : SPJ - 13.59
THOMPSON Matthew U17 29.12.84, Black Isle/NSP : 100HY - 13.72w/13.9 (14.11-00), OctY - 4253
THOMPSON Neville Leigh V45 28.03.55, Shaft B : DT - 51.84 (55.68-93)
THOMPSON Ross U23 7.12.81, Gateshead : HT - 56.91 (57.38-99)
THOMPSON Scot William U23 10.08.81, Pitr/Bel/ Bath Univ : SP - 14.77 (15.00-00), DT - 51.42
THOMPSON Stephen U15 5.09.86, : 100 - 11.43w/11.48, 200 - 22.99w/23.42
THORNE-LADEJO Du'aine 14.02.71, Birchfield : 200 - 21.58i+ (20.96-93), 400 - 46.31i (44.66-96), 400H - 49.29

THURGOOD Matthew U20 29.12.83, Verlea :
TJ - 14.08, DecJ - 5340
THURGOOD Stuart Dennis 17.05.76, Harlow :
HT - 54.87 (56.91-00)
TICKNER Ben U23 13.07.81, Wells/Exeter Univ :
1500 - 3:49.22, 5k - 14:34.52
TICKNER Frank U20 12.10.83, Wells :
2kSt - 6:02.6
TILLEY Kevin 67, S London :
Mar - 2:35:36
TINDAL Lee U23 19.02.80, Team Solent :
60H - 8.4i, 110H - 14.7/14.77w/14.82
TIPPER James 16.05.72, Cannock & Stafford :
200 - 21.9/22.13w (21.6w-90/21.68-92)
TIPTON Carl 4.02.77, Telford/Manchester Univ :
800 - 1:51.86, 1500 - 3:51.05
TITMAN Carl U15 9.09.86, Peterborough :
PV - 3.35
TOAL Thomas U15 23.12.86, Charnwood :
JTB - 43.85
TOBIN Robert John U20 20.12.83, Basingstoke & MH :
100 - 10.9, 200 - 21.7, 400 - 47.10, 800 - 1:53.6
TOBIN Shaun 13.10.62, Swansea :
10k - 31:17.5 (30:23.37-96)
TOHILL Paul U20 9.10.82, Border/Mid Ulster :
110HJ - 15.26 (15.0/15.08-00), 110H - 15.16w/15.37,
HJ - 1.98 (2.01-00), Dec - 6250, DecJ - 6114
TOMLINSON Christopher U23 15.09.81, Mandale :
100 - 10.6w/10.61w/10.83,
LJ - 8.19w/7.87, TJ - 15.35
TOMLINSON Gavin U23 2.02.80, Hull Ach/Hull Univ :
10k - 31:48.69
TOMS Robert U23 7.08.80, WSE&H/UWIC :
HJ - 2.00i (2.05-97)
TONNER James 3.06.75, Kilmarnock/Border :
1500 - 3:45.98
TOOLE Ross U15 8.10.86, Kilbarchan :
1500 - 4:15.61, 3k - 9:28.2
TORRY Paul U20 17.10.82, Ellon :
Dec - 5405
TOWERS Jamie U15, Tonbridge :
SPB - 13.50
TOWNSEND Matthew U13, WSE&H :
DTC - 26.16
TOYE Simon U17 24.09.85, Thurrock :
400 - 50.18
TRAVIS Martin U15 10.07.88, Bristol :
JTY - 54.59
TREMAYNE Christopher James U17 11.11.84,
Cannock & Stafford : PV - 4.71
TREMBLE Darren Robert U13 6.04.89, Crawley :
800 - 2:17.7mx
TRESSIDER Ross U20 8.01.83, Thurrock :
110HJ - 14.81w/14.88, 400H - 57.0, DecJ - 5372
TREZONA Rob 6.03.75, City of Norwich :
400H - 56.0
TRIBBLE Matthew U23 17.10.79, Eastbourne GS :
Dec - 5229
TROCEY U. U17, Newham & Essex B :
100 - 11.1
TROMANS Glynn 17.03.69, Coventry Godiva :
3k - 8:07.60 (7:58.31-99), 5k - 13:43.40, 5KR - 14:25,
5MR - 23:40 (23:38-99), 10k - 28:31.33 (28:21.07-99),
HMar - 65:39 (63:31-99)
TULBA Phillip William 20.09.73, Bas & MH/Loughbro :
800 - 1:50.31 (1:48.31-98), 1500 - 3:46.55 (3:42.3-98),
3k - 8:09.11i (8:06.51i-99/8:14.8-00)
TULLETT Ian Roger 15.08.69, Belgrave :
PV - 5.20 (5.35-98)
TURNBULL Gareth U23 14.05.79, St Malachy's/
Loughborough Studnts/IRL : 1500 - 3:38.28,
5k - 14:05.27
TURNER Andrew 29.08.63, Bournemouth :
SP - 14.52 (14.86i-96/14.74-94),
DT - 46.01 (47.40-95), HT - 48.61 (51.76-96)
TURNER Andrew D. U23 19.09.80, Notts/Brunel Univ :
100 - 10.8w, 60H - 8.22i, 110H - 14.22w/14.29,
LJ - 6.93 (7.23w-97/7.16-00)
TURNER Clive U17 24.11.84, Enf & Har :
100 - 10.69w/10.78, 200 - 22.14
TURNER Daniel 27.11.78, Team Solent :
HJ - 2.20
TURNER David V40 20.10.57, York CIU :
50kW - 4:55:53 (4:45:56-91)
TURNER Douglas 2.12.66, Cardiff :
60 - 6.76i (6.74i-96), 100 - 10.26w/10.37 (10.26w-96),
200 - 20.54 (20.36w-97/20.43-96)
TURNER James U20 12.08.83, Nuneaton :
JT - 58.37 (58.81-00)
TURNER Keiran U15 8.02.87, Wigan :
200 - 22.8w/23.6, 400 - 52.57
TURNER Lee U20 30.06.82, City of Stoke :
1500 - 3:54.46
TURNER Mark 9.11.72, Birchfield/Coventry Univ :
800 - 1:52.46
TURNER Richard U17 23.09.84, Shildon :
400 - 50.71
TWIDALE Paul U15 30.09.86, Cleethorpes :
400 - 52.23i/52.59, LJ - 6.00i (6.05-00),
PenB - 2669
TWIGG Matthew 18.07.69, Rugby :
SP - 14.78 (15.05-98), DT - 51.63
TYE-WALKER Christopher U20 20.09.82, WSE&H :
60H - 8.41i, 110HJ - 14.49w/14.6/14.64, 110H - 15.0
TYLER Geoffrey Alan V50 30.09.48, Sale :
SP - 13.34 (16.30-77), DT - 45.33 (55.42-80)
TYPE Christopher U23 5.10.81, Cardiff/UWIC :
PV - 4.75 (4.80i-00)

UDECHUKU Emeka U23 10.07.79, WG EL/Lough:
SP - 18.29i/18.23, DT - 59.97 (62.07-00)
UGONO Uvie 8.03.78, WGreen & Ex L :
100 - 10.68w/10.7/10.76 (10.32w-98/10.36-00)
URSELL Nangeloum U23 1.10.81, Blackheath :
200 - 22.15 (21.9w-99), 400H - 53.3/54.31 (52.87-99)

VALE Owen U15 1.06.87, Wessex & Bath :
800 - 2:05.43
VAN CLEEF Ivan, Aberdeen/Aberdeen Univ :
110H - 15.39
VAN DER MERWE Alex U20 5.01.84, Exeter :
JT - 64.04
VAN RENSBURG Francois 2.08.70, Shaft Barn/RSA :
3k - 8:28.35
VAN ZYL Anton 20.01.75, Shaftesbury Barnet/RSA :
5k - 14:49.2
VANDENBERG Adam Philip U20 2.06.84, AF&D :
800 - 1:53.7
VANHINSBERGH Thomas 28.12.78, Crawley :
HJ - 1.95 (2.07-97)
VASS David U17 31.12.85, West Norfolk :
400 - 50.91
VAUX-HARVEY Matthew 30.03.76, Stourport :
10MR - 49:34 (49:32-00)
VENGDASALAM Natham 11.03.64, Liv.Pemb Sefton :
Mar - 2:23:46
VERNON Steven U23 17.10.80, Stockport :
1500 - 3:50.01
VICKERS Gary 26.02.71, Telford :
800 - 1:48.85
VICKERS Peter U20 11.06.84, Mandale :
100 - 10.95w (11.04-00)
VINCE Andrew Ivor V40 9.05.59, Falkirk :
SP - 13.59i (18.04-83)

VINCE Nicholas U20 29.01.82, Falkirk/Sale :
SP - 13.36i (13.55-00),
SPJ - 14.17i/13.66 (14.50-00), DTJ - 41.30
VINCENT Martin U17 12.04.86, Rugby :
PV - 3.80

WADE Christopher U20 22.09.82, Halifax :
SPJ - 13.76
WAIN Andrew 2.06.65, Nene Valley H :
SP - 14.13 (14.86-99), DT - 40.82 (42.08-00)
WAINE Mike V45 17.02.56, Woking :
Mar - 2:32:51 (2:29:53-97)
WAKE Andrew 14.09.68, Morpeth :
PV - 4.85et/4.66i/4.60
WALCOTT Andrew 11.01.75, Belgrave :
100 - 10.94w (10.58-97)
WALDEN Matthew U20 30.11.83, Scunthorpe :
DecJ - 5798
WALES Alan U17 7.08.85, Aberdeen :
800 - 1:56.7, 1500 - 4:04.11, 3k - 8:56.09
WALKER Adam U23 16.11.79, Crawley/Loughro :
PV - 4.60
WALKER Douglas ¶ 28.07.73, N & E B/C of Edinb :
200 - 21.09 (20.35-98)
WALKER Graeme U23 20.02.79, Fife AC :
800 - 1:51.4
WALKER John U17 4.03.85, Greenock Glenpark :
1.5kSt - 4:29.92
WALKER Leigh 17.08.77, Crawley :
PV - 4.80 (4.90-00)
WALKER Paul James U17 15.08.85, Cardiff :
PV - 4.40
WALL Terry 12.06.70, Morpeth :
Mar - 2:33:30 (2:26:13-99)
WALLACE Lewis U17 27.01.85, Enf & Har :
JTY - 61.02
WALLACE Robert U15 5.01.87, Bromley :
TJ - 12.07
WALMSLEY Dennis 5.09.62, Bourton RR :
Mar - 2:28:24 (2:21:19-95), 100kR - 7:46:37
WALMSLEY Kevin 6.09.67, Manx H :
10kWR - 46:01
WALPOLE Ben U15 1.11.86, Elswick :
400 - 52.93
WALSH Christopher 1.10.78, Shaft B/Teeside Univ :
HT - 58.74 (60.53-00)
WALSH Edward U17 21.10.85, Belgrave :
100HY - 13.7
WALSH Peter U23 5.05.80, Liverpool H :
800 - 1:50.01
WALTER Bill U17 11.10.85, Bournemouth :
SPY - 15.25
WALTERS Chris U17 23.09.84, Guildford & G :
100HY - 13.51w/13.86
WARBURTON Christopher William U20 23.08.83,
Notts : 2kSt - 6:00.26
WARD Ashley Keith 1.08.64, Crawley :
DT - 41.77 (47.70-82)
WARD Jonathan 25.11.65, Ashford :
DT - 41.07 (44.55-00)
WARD Ray 22.08.75, Sheffield :
1500 - 3:50.53 (3:50.51-00)
WARD Richard James Stephen U20 5.05.82, Bel/
Manchester Univ : 800 - 1:50.9,
1500 - 3:44.96, 3k - 8:27.07i/8:39.1 (8:24.73-00)
WARD Tim U20 27.05.82, Border :
100 - 10.63w/10.8/10.83, 200 - 21.8/21.91
WARKE Peter U17 22.05.86, Lagan Valley :
200 - 22.4/22.69, 400 - 50.3, 400HY - 58.41
WARLEY Matthew James U17 1.08.85, Cheltenham :
800 - 1:57.7
WARREN Carl 28.09.69, Birchfield :
10MR - 48:51, Mar - 2:18:38

WATKINS Andrew U15 8.12.87, Pontypridd :
100 - 11.19w/11.29, 200 - 22.61w/22.68,
400 - 53.27?/53.3
WATKINS Ben 12.11.78, City of Norwich :
200 - 21.9w (21.75-98)
WATKINS James U20 30.10.82, Somerset Sch :
400 - 49.14
WATKINSON Robert 10.03.74, Roth/Teeside Univ :
800 - 1:49.62, 1500 - 3:48.35
WATSON Andrew U20 9.03.83, Woking :
400H - 57.0
WATSON Christopher U20 22.05.83, Bel/Vict PAC :
800 - 1:50.89
WATSON David U20 29.06.83, Kilbarchan :
TJ - 13.96w
WATSON Derek U20 22.05.83, Bel/Vict PAC :
1500 - 3:50.1
WATSON Garth 20.04.73, Newham & Essex B :
800 - 1:52.03 (1:49.05-00)
WATT Adam U17 29.10.84, Aberdeen :
800 - 1:56.4, 1500 - 4:04.3,
3k - 8:55.31, 1.5kSt - 4:27.90
WATT Timothy James 19.09.66, Steyning :
5kW - 23:34.10
WATTS Andy U17, Notts :
400HY - 58.3
WAYMAN Joseph U15 18.02.87, Rushcliffe :
400 - 53.4
WEAVER Matthew 14.11.73, Harrow :
PV - 4.90 (5.00-99)
WEBB Anthony 75, Ashford :
Mar - 2:35:52
WEBB David U20 17.03.82, Leeds/Birmingham Univ. :
5k - 15:23.51
WEBB Philip Stephen 17.07.78, Peterborough :
200 - 21.82w (21.01w-97/21.31i/21.4-98/21.44-97,
400 - 48.7/48.94 (48.0-99)
WEBB Steven U17, Medway :
1.5kSt - 4:32.4
WEDDERBURN Theo U15 1.01.88, Cambridge & Col :
100 - 11.17w/11.29
WEIR Andrew 22.08.67, Thames H & H/Herne Hill :
10k - 31:53.89
WEIR Richard U20 7.08.84, Derby & Co :
800 - 1:54.22
WEIR Robert Boyd V40 4.02.61, Birchfield :
DT - 63.03 (65.08-00)
WEKWETE Garai U13 9.10.88, Abingdon :
200 - 25.9
WELFORD Anthony U15 5.10.87, Gosforth :
800 - 2:03.1, 1500 - 4:19.2?
WELLS Louis 6.02.78, Enf & Har :
800 - 1:52.2 (1:51.7-99)
WELLS Stuart U23 26.07.79, WGreen & Ex L :
LJ - 7.18 (7.68w-99/7.56-97)
WELLSTEAD David U20 17.12.82, Sutton & District :
TJ - 14.16
WESTAWAY Ryan U20 2.03.83, Yeovil Olympiads :
HJ - 1.96, Dec - 5738, DecJ - 5994
WESTLAKE Sam U20 14.09.83, N Devon :
SP - 13.31, SPJ - 14.82, DT - 41.18, DTJ - 44.21
WESTMEIJER Jeroen 5.07.70, Epsom & Ewell/NED :
SP - 13.69 (14.10-00)
WESTON Paul 6.10.67, Cardiff :
TJ - 14.71w/14.65 (15.64w-98/15.46-92)
WESTON Robert 16.03.77, Royal Navy :
Dec - 5076
WETHERIDGE Nicholas 11.10.72, Basildon :
1500 - 3:49.70, 5k - 13:53.77, HMar - 64:03
WETHERILL Andrew V40 6.12.57, Sutton-in-Ashfield :
Mar - 2:28:42 (2:24:31-00)
WHALLEY Robert Simon 11.02.68, City of Stoke :
3k - 7:58.30i (7:51.4-97), 5MR - 23:22

WHEELER Craig 14.06.76, Trafford :
2kSt - 5:42.95, 3kSt - 8:55.38 (8:34.67-99)
WHITBY Benedict 6.01.77, WSE&H :
1500 - 3:46.10, 5KR - 14:22, 3kSt - 8:32.68
WHITE Gary U17 16.06.85, Rugby :
TJ - 14.41
WHITE Paul U17, Mandale :
1.5kSt - 4:37.0
WHITE Steffan David 21.12.72, Coventry Godiva :
3k - 8:05.08 (8:01.90i-94/8:03.20-96), 5k - 13:56.56
WHITEHEAD Timmon U20 20.04.82, Guildford & G :
HTJ - 54.73 (59.39dh/56.52-00)
WHITEHOUSE Paul U20 10.03.83, Birchfield :
100 - 10.9 (11.93-97)
WHITEMAN Anthony William 13.11.71, Shaft Barnet :
800 - 1:49.00 (1:45.81-00), 1500 - 3:34.88 (3:32.34-97),
1M - 3:55.16 (3:51.90-98)
WHITMORE Andrew U17 8.02.85, Peterborough :
100 - 10.82w/10.99
WHITTAKER D. U17, Trafford :
100 - 11.08
WHITTINGHAM Simon 18.09.78, Watford :
HJ - 1.95 (2.00-00)
WHITTLE Robert U23 14.06.81, Bas & MH/Loughro :
800 - 1:52.09 (1:51.76-00), 1500 - 3:49.50
WHYTE Stephen Anthony 14.03.64, Luton/Falkirk :
SP - 16.71i/16.45 (17.78-89),
DT - 46.50 (50.40-94), HT - 60.61 (67.82-89)
WIBBERLEY Stephen U15 4.01.87, Bolton :
400 - 52.15, 800 - 2:04.3
WIFFEN Ben U17 30.10.84, Tonbridge :
800 - 1:57.6, 1500 - 3:57.04
WILD James Gary U20 1.10.82, Birchfield :
HJ - 2.05
WILD Jonathan D. 30.08.73, Sale :
1500 - 3:47.70 (3:40.02-97), 5KR - 14:15,
3k - 8:02.78 (7:53.10i-96/7:55.16-95),
5k - 13:52.72 (13:45.1-96), 10k - 28:39.33
WILKIN Mitchell U17 6.12.85, Southend :
LJ - 6.83
WILKINS Perriss 12.12.69, Sale :
SP - 15.16 (15.29lg-00), DT - 61.68 (66.64-98)
WILKINSON Jonathon 17.02.62, Telford :
JT - 57.61 (63.88-00)
WILKINSON Neil 12.03.69, Cambuslang/Salford :
3k - 8:21.3, 5k - 14:31.8,
10k - 30:04.5 (29:56.52-96)
WILLIAMS Allan Peter V45 30.05.53, Cambridge H :
PV - 4.33i/4.20 (5.25-77)
WILLIAMS Alun 22.06.62, City of Norwich/RAF :
DT - 40.06 (43.78-96)
WILLIAMS Barrington Chester V45 11.09.55, Rugby :
LJ - 7.03 (8.05i/8.01-89)
WILLIAMS Bradley U15 22.06.87, Harrogate :
SPB - 13.13
WILLIAMS D., Wolverhampton & B :
LJ - 6.81
WILLIAMS Edward 1.10.70, Thames Valley :
400 - 48.1 (46.84-94), 800 - 1:51.64 (1:49.41-96)
WILLIAMS Gareth J. 16.08.66, Medway :
Mar - 2:29:02
WILLIAMS Glenn David U17 24.03.85, Cardiff :
SPY - 15.51, DTY - 48.38, HTY - 56.43
WILLIAMS James John U20 17.07.82, Cardiff/UWIC :
3k - 8:30.7i, 3kSt - 9:26.9
WILLIAMS Kevin S. 15.12.71, Cardiff :
60 - 6.79i (6.63i-97), 200 - 21.90 (21.30-97),
100 - 10.61w/10.70 (10.30w/10.34-97)
WILLIAMS Lucien U17 13.08.85, Notts :
LJ - 6.90
WILLIAMS Mark 7.09.64, Tamworth :
3kW - 13:12.0, 5kW - 23:13.4, 20kW - 1:38:48
WILLIAMS Matthew U20 31.01.84, Wolves & B :
400H - 55.73
WILLIAMS Nathan U13 12.05.89, Enf & Har :
200 - 26.0
WILLIAMS Nicholas U20 2.02.82, Traff/Crewe & A :
HT - 55.37, HTJ - 56.88 (63.20-00)
WILLIAMS Philip J. U17 28.09.84, Rochdale :
1500 - 4:03.16, 3k - 8:58.34
WILLIAMS Rhys U20 27.02.84, Bridgend :
400 - 49.45, 400H - 53.0/53.42
WILLIAMS Rhys U23 4.10.81, Swansea :
JT - 58.72
WILLIAMS Richard U23 22.10.81, Shaftesbury B :
3kSt - 9:35.9 (9:15.72-00)
WILLIAMS Simon David U23 5.10.80, Bas & MH :
SP - 13.52, DT - 46.10 (46.38-00)
WILLIAMSON Lewis U17 7.09.85, Leeds :
DTY - 44.14
WILLIAMSON Paul Lee 16.06.74, Thames Valley :
PV - 5.30A/5.30 (5.55-00)
WILLS Christopher 18.05.76, Birchfield :
PV - 4.20 (4.80-98)
WILSON Alan U15 12.10.86, Ayr Seaforth :
100 - 11.5
WILSON Alloy U23 25.01.80, Blackheath :
60 - 6.9i (6.9i-00/6.93i-98),
400 - 48.49i/48.5/49.17 (46.64-98)
WILSON Colin 30.10.77, WGn & Ex L/Soton City :
60 - 6.8i/6.91i, 100 - 10.77w/10.8
WILSON Gary U17 18.09.85, Belgrave :
LJ - 7.09w/6.87, TJ - 13.50
WILSON Kevin U20 28.09.82, Chichester :
HJ - 2.03
WILSON Kirk U17 21.12.85, Morpeth :
1.5kSt - 4:35.5
WILSON Simon 30.04.74, Med & Maid :
400H - 55.0 (54.9-98/55.03-99), Dec - 5402
WILSON Vincent 1.04.73, Morpeth :
800 - 1:49.03 (1:48.68-98),
1500 - 3:42.81, 1M - 4:09.2 (4:03.3-98)
WINCHCOMBE Nigel Christopher V40 10.12.59, Linc W :
DT - 40.32 (48.88-85), HT - 52.19 (59.18-88)
WINSHIP Mark U20 29.09.83, Enf & Har :
110HJ - 15.5, 400H - 54.1
WISCOMBE Lee U23 12.07.80, Jarrow & Hebburn :
400H - 53.68
WISEMAN Mark 9.02.69, Army/WSE&H :
SP - 15.65, DT - 51.07
WITTY Jon U15 1.10.86, Cannock & Stafford :
400 - 53.58
WOOD Ben U15, Isle of Wight :
HJ - 1.75
WOOD Joshua 19.04.74, Harlow :
60 - 6.99i (6.9i-99/6.98i-00)
WOOD Matt U15 14.12.86, Blackburn :
800 - 2:00.49, 1500 - 4:20.9
WOODHALL Richard U23 9.07.80, Dudley & Stourb :
JT - 55.75
WOODS Alan Peter V50 27.03.51, Birchfield :
HT - 46.96 (57.24-78)
WOODWARD Lyndon U23 22.11.80, Cannock & St :
SP - 16.48
WOODWARD Nathan U13 17.10.89, Tamworth :
800 - 2:18.5
WOOLCOTT Nicholas David V40 7.04.61, Enf & Har :
DT - 48.41 (55.34-88)
WOOLER D., RAF :
TJ - 14.12
WORKMAN Richard J. 31.05.71, Trafford :
400 - 48.7/48.93 (47.81-98)
WRAY Alan 6.01.71, Harrow :
3kSt - 9:13.14

WRAY Iain U15 13.09.86, Carmarthen :
HJ - 1.75
WRIGHT Finlay F.H. U23 7.02.81, WSE&H/Oxford U :
100 - 10.8w/10.84w?, 200 - 21.8/21.89
WRIGHT James U20 2.04.82, WGreen & Ex L :
110H - 15.29, Dec - 6176
WRIGHT Joseph U15 16.12.86, Kettering :
200 - 23.49
WRIGHT Lewis U15, Cardiff :
80HB - 11.8/11.95
WURR Timothy U23 1.03.79, Leamington/Birm Univ. :
HT - 55.64
WYLLIE William 12.07.73, Trafford :
HJ - 1.95 (2.11-91)
WYNNE Neil U20 14.04.82, Deeside :
400 - 49.5
WYSS Mark U17 12.07.85, Cheltenham :
DTY - 43.10

YAMBASU Aiah 10.11.73, Thames Valley :
60 - 6.82i, 100 - 10.8/10.81 (10.7-96)
YATES Daniel U23 7.06.81, Matlock/Crewe & A :
3kSt - 9:32.06 (9:17.77-00)
YATES Peter Derek V40 15.06.57, Dacorum & Tring :
JT - 66.86 (77.84-87)
YEBOAH Bernard U17 7.01.86, Croydon :
LJ - 7.10w/7.03
YELLING Martin 7.02.72, Bedford & County :
3k - 8:23.21i (8:07.0-96), 10kR - 29:51,
HMar - 66:48 (66:00-00)
YEWER Bradley U23 10.02.79, Newbury :
1500 - 3:51.18 (3:51.17-00)
YIEND Bradley U23 25.10.80, Birchfield/Loughbro :
400 - 48.06, 400H - 52.62
YOUNG Andrew 20.06.77, Victoria Park H :
800 - 1:50.00 (1:49.13-98), 1M - 4:10.12
YOUNG Jason 18.07.69, SGA (Prof) :
SP - 15.05
YOUNG Martin 11.07.72, Roadhogs :
10kW - 48:01.1 (43:39.0-96)
YOUNG Matthew U13 6.07.89, Milton Keynes :
400 - 60.2, 1500 - 4:46.2

ZAIDMAN Antony Adam 18.03.62, Enf & Har :
SP - 14.12 (17.87i-83/17.22-81)
ZAMANI Ani U13 17.09.88, Enf & Har :
100 - 12.5, 200 - 25.6
ZAWADSKI Adam 19.12.74, Belgrave :
800 - 1:52.3 (1:50.7-97), 1500 - 3:42.90
ZERAFFA Ross U17 2.11.85, Chelmsford :
SPY - 14.10
ZISKA Heri 12.10.67, Belgrave/DEN :
DT - 44.23
ZISSLER Nick U15 12.09.86, Richmond & Zetland :
1500 - 4:15.67
ZULEWSKI Alex U20 6.06.82, Thames VH/Bath Univ :
110HJ - 14.4w/14.60, 110H - 15.2/15.47,
400H - 54.0/54.45

For brevity in the index the previous age descriptions of the events have been kept. This should not cause any confusion since the age group of each athlete is clearly shown in the new form eg U15 but some examples will clarify this.

A **J** after an event is an Under 20 event eg 110HJ - 110 metres hurdles with 3'3" hurdles

A **Y** or an **I** is an Under 17 event (men and women)
eg 100HY - 100 metres hurdles with 3' 0" hurdles Heptl - Heptathlon with Under 17 implements

A **B** or a **G** is an Under 15 event (men and women) eg JTB - 600 gram Javelin SPG - 3.25kg Shot

A **C** or an **M** is an Under 13 event (men and women) eg SPC - 3.25kg Shot SPM - 2.72kg Shot

WOMENS INDEX

ABBS Rachel U15 21.12.86, Durham City H :
LJ - 5.20
ABDULAI Kosnatu U17 8.02.85, Stevenage & NH :
TJ - 11.76
ADAMS Emily U17 27.01.85, AF&D :
800 - 2:14.37, 1500 - 4:44.6
ADAMSON Samantha U20 27.03.82, Hertford & Ware :
400 - 57.3, 100H - 14.86, 400H - 60.53,
HJ - 1.75 (1.75-97)
ADDO Roseline Emefa Ama U23 7.06.80, Newbury/
East Tennessee Univ : 200 - 24.81, 400 - 55.08
AGBO Phyllis U17 16.12.85, Thames Valley :
200 - 25.37w/25.50, 60HI - 8.80i, 80HI - 11.4/11.52,
HJ - 1.67i/1.66, LJ - 6.07w/5.91, TJ - 11.29,
SP - 10.30, Hepl - 4945
AINSLEY Karen U23 24.06.80, Rowheath/Birm Univ. :
HT - 40.84
AITKEN Nicola 18.12.78, WSE&H :
Mar - 3:08:10
AJUNWA Chioma ¶ 25.12.71, Shaftesbury Barn/NGR :
100 - 11.60 (10.84-92), 200 - 24.2, LJ - 6.65 (7.12-96)
AKIM Ayamba 21.06.72, Herne Hill :
HJ - 1.74 (1.74-99)
AKPOFURE Venita U15 1.01.87, Blackheath :
100 - 12.5, 200 - 26.01w
ALANEME Sandra U17 7.01.86, Blackheath :
HJ - 1.65 (1.65-00), TJ - 11.44
ALEXANDER Katherine 28.04.74, Shaftesbury Barnet :
PV - 3.20 (3.30-96)
ALEXANDER Rosalyn 18.05.73, :
Mar - 2:56:27
ALFORD Sophie 5.12.75, Ealing,Southall & Mx/Army :
1500 - 4:29.60
ALLAHGREEN Diane 21.02.75, Liverpool H/Liv Univ :
60 - 7.27i, 100 - 11.38w/11.50,
200 - 24.3 (24.0w-99/24.26w-00/24.81-94,
100H - 12.98w/13.08 (12.99-99)
ALLAN Laura U17 11.02.85, Pitreavie :
HT - 42.21
ALLAN Vicki U17 31.12.85, Giffnock :
HJ - 1.68
ALLEN Amanda 14.07.68, Birchfield :
5MR - 25:49, 10kR - 33:13 (32:46un-96/33:05-92),
HMar - 72:43
ALLEN Lisa 7.04.78, Colchester & T :
100 - 12.1w/12.25
ALLEN Sharon 23.10.68, WGreen & Ex L :
200 - 25.03 (23.63un-00/24.20i-97/24.5/24.51-99,
400 - 55.58 (54.62i-97/54.85un-00)
ALLISON Sarah U15 18.11.86, Border :
HJ - 1.64, PenG - 2631
ALLOTT Elizabeth 9.02.77, Salford :
10kR - 34:17, 10MR - 54:40, HMar - 73:39,
Mar - 2:34:43
ALLSOPP Sarah U17 13.10.84, Dudley & Stourbridge :
80HI - 11.72w/11.9/11.99 (11.67w/11.82-00)
AMAA Joan U23 15.12.81, Barnet/Brunel Univ :
SP - 11.23 (11.58-99)
AMEDE Christine F. V35 7.08.63, WSE&H :
400 - 56.54 (55.35-90), 400H - 62.2 (59.43-98)
AMEOBI Titi U17 20.11.84, Gateshead :
60 - 7.9i (7.9i-00), 100 - 12.07w/12.2/12.27
AMOS Katie 13.11.78, Thurrock :
JT - 47.55
ANDERSON Kelly U23 17.07.80, Havant :
HT - 37.06
ANDERSON Mary Caroline 2.09.67, City of Edinburgh :
SP - 12.23 (15.48-85)
ANDERSON Shani 7.08.75, Shaftesbury Barnet :
60 - 7.5i (7.48i-99), 100 - 11.40 (11.3w/11.34-00),
200 - 23.12w/23.2/23.43 (23.20-00)
ANDREOU Sandra Agnola V35 24.07.62, WG & Ex L :
800 - 2:10.90 (2:05.9-79),
1500 - 4:31.8 (4:14.0-84)
ANDREWS Sharon Nivan 4.07.67, WGreen & Ex L :
DT - 41.12 (56.24-94)
ANDREWS Teresa U13, Radley :
100 - 13.2, 200 - 27.5
ANKIER Joanna U20 5.08.82, Shaft Barn/Notts Univ :
1500 - 4:25.11, 2KSTW - 6:55.04
ANNESS Ruth Evelyn 3.10.78, WG & EL/Luton Univ :
PV - 3.45
ANTILL Lisa U20 14.10.82, Belgrave/AUS :
TJ - 11.12
APPLEGARTH Amanda U20 5.04.84, South Devon :
200 - 25.03w (25.3/25.53-99)
ARMSTRONG Debbie U17 8.02.86, Gateshead :
HJ - 1.65
ARNOLD Helen Louise 5.10.78, Team Solent :
HT - 50.02 (54.72-97)
ARNOLD Zoe 10.11.76, Lagan Valley :
400 - 57.04 (55.98-99)
ARRANDALE Kate U15 3.05.87, Salisbury :
PV - 2.30
ASH Sally U23 4.11.80, City of Norwich/Loughbro :
TJ - 11.19 (11.34-99)
ASHBY Abigail 23.11.77, Rowntrees :
Hep - 3801 (4613-97)
ASHLEY Melissa 17.03.77, Thames Valley :
HT - 37.38 (38.64-00)
ASTARITA Sabina U15 15.10.86, Kirkintillock :
100 - 12.6
ATIJOSAN Lanre U15 17.10.86, Cambridge Harriers :
100 - 12.1/12.18w/12.25
ATKINSON Rachael U17 20.12.85, Wigan :
DT - 32.54
ATKINSON Rachel 26.05.73, Sale :
TJ - 11.16w (12.20w-96/11.88-98)
ATUNUMUO Lucy U23 4.11.80, Sutton & District :
LJ - 5.84w/5.58 (5.88-00)
AUGEE Esther M. V35 1.01.64, WGreen & Ex L :
HT - 52.46 (56.76-93)
AUGEE Myrtle Sharon Mary V35 4.02.65, Bromley :
SP - 14.50 (19.03-90), DT - 40.92 (49.44-95),
HT - 37.55 (46.64-95)
AUKETT Lucy U17 9.09.84, Worthing :
400H - 67.6
AUKETT Phillipa U17 9.09.84, Worthing :
800 - 2:15.3
AUSTIN Carly U20 16.05.83, Oxford City :
400H - 65.1, Hep - 4006
AUSTIN Shirley 20.01.73, AF&D/IRL :
(nee BUCHANAN) PV - 3.40
AWUYE Michelle 5.03.74, :
Mar - 3:05:49
AXTEN Tracy V35 20.07.63, Shaftesbury Barnet :
SP - 14.09 (15.81-98), DT - 47.93 (58.18-97)
AYERO Jennifer U23 13.09.79, Ealing,Southall & Mx :
(see WEST)
AYLWIN Louise U23 8.04.80, Exeter/Exeter Univ :
400H - 62.7/62.73

BACHE Laura U13 24.10.88, Tipton :
800 - 2:27.4
BACKHOUSE Susan 6.12.78, Wakefield/Loughbro :
DT - 41.28 (45.29-00)
BACKWELL Samantha U17 4.02.85, Yeovil Olympiads :
Hepl - 4134 (4254-00)
BAILEY Amanda U13 27.11.88, Wimborne :
1200 - 3:59.0, 1500 - 5:03.9
BAILEY Emma Louise U20 25.07.84, Northampton :
60 - 7.73i

BAILEY Kathryn 25.03.68, Havant :
10MR - 58:14 (55:48-93), HMar - 77:22 (74:07-95)
BAIRD Kirsty 29.08.71, City of Glasgow/Glasgow Un :
800 - 2:12.79i (2:12.62-96)
BAKER Emma U13 22.09.88, City of Plymouth :
100 - 13.0, 150 - 19.9, 200 - 27.1, LJ - 4.82
BAKER Joanne U15 15.10.87, Wigan :
75HG - 11.79
BALL Michelle U20 9.05.83, Blackpool :
PV - 2.80 (2.80-00)
BALLOTTA Laura 17.08.71, Edinburgh WM/ITA :
PV - 3.85, SP - 13.18
BALSDON Penny U17 5.04.85, Newquay & Par :
300H - 46.2
BARBER Helen 13.12.67, Horsforth :
(see SLY)
BARBER Samantha U13, East Cheshire :
1200 - 3:56.9
BARKER Danielle U15 19.01.87, Neath :
60 - 8.09i, 100 - 12.47w (13.18-99),
200 - 25.5/25.85w
BARNES Catherine 28.09.77, Winchester :
TJ - 11.00 (11.49-95)
BARNES Danielle U17 8.10.85, Newquay & Par :
800 - 2:06.51, 1500 - 4:27.3, 3k - 9:35.46+
BARNES Hannah U20 2.06.84, Sheffield :
100H - 15.10, LJ - 5.63, Hep - 4771
BARNETT Brenda, Buxton :
24Hr - 153.290km
BARNETT Julie 15.03.73, City of Glasgow :
(nee MCDEVITT) 800 - 2:09.0
BARR Lyndsey U15 19.01.88, Shaftesbury Barnet :
800 - 2:17.9, 1500 - 4:44.27
BARR Nicola 26.04.70, Edinburgh WM :
(see GODDARD)
BARR Victoria U20 14.04.82, Gateshead :
200 - 24.67w/24.8/25.00 (24.34-00)
BARRETT Angela U17 25.12.85, Parkside :
LJ - 5.37, TJ - 12.03w/11.87
BARRY Sara U20 8.06.83, Yate :
TJ - 11.44w/11.40, Hep - 4017 (4019-00)
BARTLETT Rebecca U17 7.03.85, Telford :
JT - 42.82
BASS Natalie U17 3.12.85, Leamington :
1500 - 4:41.06
BATE Kirsty U13, Sutton & District :
DTM - 23.60
BATEMAN Judith V40 27.02.57, Brighton :
Mar - 3:09:30
BATES Hannah U15 8.10.86, Phoenix :
800 - 2:18.32
BATES Rebecca U20 16.05.82, City of Stoke :
LJ - 5.57 (5.60-97), TJ - 11.65 (11.86-00)
BAYLEY Lorna U17 6.07.85, Sutton :
PV - 2.60i (2.70-00)
BEALE Sarah U20 12.07.82, Horsham BS :
400 - 57.3
BEALES Emma Jay 7.12.71, Bedford & County :
SP - 12.88 (14.53-92), DT - 46.57 (54.68-95)
BEAR Nicola U15 14.01.87, Liv.Pembroke Sefton :
800 - 2:16.1
BEARD Hayley U17 2.12.85, Stevenage & NH :
800 - 2:08.02
BEATTIE Natalie 30.01.78, Pitreavie :
100 - 11.91 (11.82w/11.89-99),
200 - 24.51 (24.49-99)
BECKETT Charlotte U17 4.01.86, Milton Keynes :
300 - 41.5
BEDDOWS Terri U13 21.07.89, Swansea :
SPM - 9.07
BEER Sarah U20 29.04.84, Exeter :
SP - 11.87
BEIGHTON Amy U17 6.03.86, Leics Cor :
60HI - 9.11i
BELL Karen U20 18.06.82, Edinburgh WM :
HT - 41.00 (46.39-00)
BELL Rebecka U17 1.12.85, City of Norwich :
HJ - 1.73, LJ - 5.37
BELLE Symone U17 12.11.84, Tower Hamlets :
100 - 12.4 (12.18w/12.3-99), 60H - 8.9i,
60HI - 8.56i, 80HI - 11.27 (11.18w/11.20-00),
100H - 15.2, LJ - 6.09 (6.11-00)
BEMROSE Antonia Marie U23 3.09.79, AF&D :
HJ - 1.65i (1.76-96)
BENJAMIN Dawn Donita 7.03.72, WSE&H/Army :
60 - 7.40i, 100 - 11.63 (11.4w/11.43-00),
LJ - 6.22w/6.07 (6.45w/6.26-00)
BENNETT Christina Jayne 27.02.78, Epsom & Ewell :
SP - 15.00 (15.55-99), DT - 39.82 (42.88-99),
HT - 53.66 (53.74-00)
BENNETT Claire U20 4.02.83, Cannock & Stafford :
JT - 41.92
BENNETT Gemma U20 4.01.84, Newham & Essex B :
100H - 14.8/14.81
BENNETT Joanna U20 6.08.83, Epsom & Ewell :
SP - 13.08
BENNETT Julia Margaret 26.03.70, Epsom & Ewell :
100H - 14.70 (14.43w-96/14.67-00),
400H - 65.2 (61.7/61.84-97),
HJ - 1.84 (1.92i-90/1.89-94),
LJ - 6.05 (6.13i-98/6.12-94), TJ - 11.77w,
SP - 11.84 (12.15i-99/12.07-98), JT - 37.52,
Hep - 5534 (5747w-96/5538-00)
BENNETT Katie U15 5.10.86, Notts :
JT - 32.78
BENNETT Wendy V35 21.12.65, Worcester AC :
3kW - 14:22.42, 5kW - 24:24, 10kW - 51:13.4,
10kWR - 48:58, 20kW - 1:47:46
BENNEWORTH Katy U17 5.10.84, Blackheath :
100 - 12.4w/12.57w (12.6-99), LJ - 5.58w/5.46
BERMINGHAM Orla 7.10.75, WGreen & Ex L :
100H - 15.1 (13.8w-95/13.87w-94/13.93-95)
BERRY Catherine Ann 8.10.75, Kingston & Poly :
1500 - 4:21.40, 1M - 4:38.28, 2k - 5:57.85,
3k - 9:09.61mx/9:21.89, 5k - 15:57.61,
5KR - 16:35 (16:26-00), 4MR - 20:54
BERRY Kelly-Jane U15 23.04.87, Wessex & Bath :
JT - 32.11 (36.03-00)
BEST Charlotte U17 7.03.85, Crawley :
300 - 40.6, 400 - 57.1, 800 - 2:10.17,
1500 - 4:41.30, 3k - 10:28.4
BETTS Laura Nadine U17 6.11.84, Tonbridge :
LJ - 5.36 (5.53-00), TJ - 11.27, Hepl - 3809
BEVAN Adele U20 26.03.84, Crawley :
800 - 2:11.7
BEVERLEY Rachael Ann U23 23.07.79, Sale :
HT - 56.06 (60.88-99)
BILLIN Kirsty U17 24.05.85, Sutton :
DT - 34.54
BILOUS Tanya U17 7.05.86, Gloucester L :
HT - 40.01
BIRCH Courtney U17 5.10.84, Liv.Pembroke Sefton :
3k - 9:53.84 (9:35.52-00)
BIRCH Joanna H. U15 21.04.87, Rushcliffe :
100 - 12.58w, 200 - 26.0
BIRKIN Kelly U17 27.04.86, Cwmbran :
100 - 12.46w/12.49, 200 - 25.47
BLACK Gillian Elizabeth U23 27.10.79, C of Glasgow :
HJ - 1.76 (1.83-99)
BLACKTIN Faye U23 5.11.81, Hertford & Ware :
HT - 44.53
BLACKWELL Sarah U17 1.10.84, Liv.Pemb Sefton :
100 - 12.1/12.31, 200 - 25.1
BLAIR Joanna U17 1.03.86, Coventry Godiva :
JT - 36.60

BLAIR Rhona 27.11.76, City of Edinburgh :
400H - 65.79
BLAIZE Dominique U15 3.10.87, Kingston & Poly :
HJ - 1.63, LJ - 5.36, PenG - 2730
BLAKE Tanya-Gee 16.01.71, Trafford :
400 - 54.35, 800 - 2:01.87 (2:00.10-98), 1500 - 4:25.53
BLAKEMAN Beverley 4.04.74, Sunderland :
800 - 2:08.9 (2:05.33-98), 1500 - 4:29.8 (4:28.56-99)
BLISS Jennifer Anne U17 6.07.86, Brighton :
300H - 45.06
BLOOMFIELD Christine Beverley 12.02.68, Belgrave :
60 - 7.38i (7.32i-99), 100 - 11.50w/11.67 (11.32-99),
200 - 23.77 (22.85-99)
BLOOMFIELD Tracey U23 13.09.79, Guildford & G :
PV - 3.90 (3.90-00)
BLOOR Louise U17 21.09.85, Rotherham :
LJ - 5.60
BODDEY Hayley U20 14.02.83, Derby LAC :
JT - 38.07
BOGGIS Lucy I. U13 27.01.89, Radley :
70HM - 11.4, HJ - 1.46, JTM - 30.80
BOLTON Laura Clare U23 22.01.79, Newquay & Par :
JT - 37.54 (38.15-99), Hep - 4000
BONNETT Emily U15 22.09.87, Yeovil Olympiads :
PenG - 2712
BONNY Emma U15 9.09.87, Havering :
LJ - 5.20
BOOTH Amie U17 19.10.84, Bedford & County :
3k - 10:39.24mx (10:23.6-00)
BOUCHARD Sarah 23.10.74, Salford :
800 - 2:08.57, 1500 - 4:25.4mx/4:25.6 (4:23.74mx-00)
BOULTON Jane V45 2.04.56, Crowborough :
Mar - 3:03:18 (2:52:36-97)
BOVILL Susan U20 6.05.82, Sutton & District :
400 - 57.35 (56.46-99)
BOWE Hannah U15 6.12.86, N I Schools :
SPG - 10.87
BOWRING Nicole 27.01.74, WSE&H :
200 - 24.1w/24.42w/24.5/24.60,
300 - 39.0, 400 - 54.3/54.86
BOWYER Anna U20 29.09.82, Exeter :
HT - 39.23
BOYD Penny U17 27.10.84, Mandale :
80HI - 12.08w, 300H - 46.38, Hepl - 4077
BOYLE Anna U20 29.03.83, Ballymena & Antrim :
100 - 12.14w (12.0/12.15-99)
BRACE Rachelle U13 18.03.89, Dartford :
DTM - 26.72, JTM - 31.24
BRADBURY Sarah V35 25.02.63, AF&D :
HMar - 77:31
BRADLEY Joanna U23 23.08.79, Ashford :
DT - 46.38 (49.10-00)
BRADSHAW Noelle Elizabeth V35 18.12.63, AF&D :
PV - 3.45 (3.50-98), JT - 45.18 (46.81-00)
BRADY Emma Elizabeth 3.01.74, Trafford :
800 - 2:09.04, 1500 - 4:30.19 (4:26.86-00)
BRADY Kelly U20 3.11.82, Trafford :
400H - 65.42
BRADY Nicola U17 26.07.85, Stoke :
Hepl - 3991w/3828
BRAHAM Alice 17.01.76, Parkside :
Mar - 3:00:36
BRANNAN Lesley 13.09.76, Birchfield :
SP - 12.97,
HT - 56.62
BRANT Natalie V. U20 11.12.82, Epsom & Ewell :
TJ - 11.80 (11.94w-00)
BRAR Sundeep U17 26.02.85, Basildon :
PV - 3.20i/3.00
BRASON Claire U20 16.03.83, North Shields Poly :
400 - 57.49, 400H - 60.8/61.24
BRAZNELL Kimberley V45 28.02.56, Dudley & Stourb :
3kW - 15:28.0 (14:17.74-95), 5kW - 26:10.9 (24:16.4-95)
BRENNAN Katie U20 27.04.82, Warrington :
800 - 2:11.05, 1500 - 4:27.45
BRENTON Rachel U17 18.01.85, Radley :
80HI - 11.9/12.02, HJ - 1.65 (1.66-00), LJ - 5.70,
TJ - 12.27w/12.10, Hepl - 4053
BRERETON Ruth U23 26.06.81, Herne Hill/London U :
400H - 61.36
BRETT Jacquelyn Charis V35 5.07.65, Newquay & P :
100H - 14.4 (13.86-87)
BREWINGTON Katherine Ann U23 15.10.81, Havering :
100 - 12.1w, 60H - 8.86i, 100H - 14.1w/14.20,
HJ - 1.65, LJ - 5.88w/5.87, Hep - 4969
BRISTOW Lynette 17.11.77, Worcester AC :
HT - 38.62
BRITTON Samantha U15 12.09.86, Chesterfield :
60HG - 9.40i, 75HG - 11.13, HJ - 1.62, PenG - 2806
BROADBELT Angie U17 12.09.85, Thames Valley :
80HI - 12.04, 300H - 45.5/45.76
BROMLEY Naida U15 27.09.86, Wakefield :
LJ - 5.29i/5.21
BROOK Tanya U15 20.02.87, Parkside :
HJ - 1.60 (1.60-00)
BROOKES Heather U23 17.07.81, Sale :
200 - 25.19i (24.41w/24.8/25.11-00),
400 - 55.36i (54.00-00)
BROOKS Lois U15 10.01.87, Stockport :
800 - 2:12.83
BROOKS Michelle Louise 6.02.77, Sale :
3k - 9:47.82 (9:24.81-00), 5k - 16:35.0
BROUGH Samantha U17 22.02.85, Stevenage & NH :
Hepl - 3938
BROW Kelly 24.09.78, Wakefield :
TJ - 11.41w/11.30 (11.64-00)
BROWN Celia 22.01.77, Shaftesbury Barnet/Birm Un :
400 - 56.09i/56.69, 400H - 59.49,
800 - 2:09.70i/2:11.1 (2:09.71-00)
BROWN Helen U17 27.12.84, Thames Valley :
HJ - 1.65 (1.65-00)
BROWN Janette 19.02.73, Middlesbro & C :
HT - 40.71 (46.01-00)
BROWN Jennifer A. V40 21.05.59, Ashford :
HJ - 1.69i (1.73-89)
BROWN Judy V45 27.10.54, St Albans Striders :
Mar - 3:03:22
BROWN Kimberley U15 1.02.87, Oadby & Wigston :
60HG - 9.34i, 75HG - 11.51
BROWN Kylie U17 13.10.84, Hertford & Ware :
DT - 33.48
BROWN Ruth U23 9.04.80, Darl/Northumbria Univ :
3k - 9:48.60
BROWN Sandra V50 1.04.49, Surrey WC :
24Hr - 180.703km (194.032km-98),
100MW - 20:36:45 (18:50:29-92)
BROWN Zoe U20 15.09.83, Shaftesbury Barnet/B & A :
PV - 3.81
BROWNE Sarah U17 8.01.85, Barrow & Furness :
JT - 34.88
BROWNING Charlotte Lucy U15 8.10.87, AF&D :
800 - 2:18.5, 1500 - 4:35.85
BRUCE Shaeleen U15 3.11.86, Pitreavie :
HTG - 34.97 (39.75-00)
BRUNNING Natasha Rosina 10.03.73, AF&D :
TJ - 11.59
BRYAN Hayley U17 4.03.86, Exeter :
SP - 11.24, DT - 35.07
BRYANT Lesley Karen V45 12.04.56, :
DT - 41.17 (55.42-80)
BRYSON Emma U23 5.04.81, C of Glasgow/Glas U :
100 - 12.19, 200 - 24.7/24.80
BUCHANAN Shirley 20.01.73, AF&D/IRL :
(see AUSTIN)
BUCHANON Monique U15 27.09.86, WGreen & Ex L :
DT - 29.34

BUCKINGHAM Hollie U15 3.12.86, Exeter :
100 - 12.5w
BUCKINGHAM Penny 26.04.67, Guernsey :
Mar - 2:58:57
BUDGEN Lucy 11.09.75, Medway :
(nee COOK) JT - 37.12
BULL Sarah 4.06.75, Derby LAC/Loughborough :
800 - 2:07.8, 1500 - 4:13.68, 3k - 9:21.77,
5KR - 16:59
BULLER Rachel L. 31.08.76, City of Norwich :
800 - 2:11.2 (2:07.56-98)
BURBIDGE Kiri U17 2.10.85, Bournemouth :
100 - 12.4
BURGESS Victoria A. U15 4.10.86, Southampton City :
100 - 12.2, 200 - 25.28w/25.4/25.67
BURGOINE Laura U17 28.01.85, Bedford & County :
3k - 10:17.0mx (10:15.68-00)
BURGOYNE Claire U17 9.07.86, Shrewsbury :
400 - 58.5, 800 - 2:16.51
BURNS Rachael U20 5.08.83, Wigan :
TJ - 11.26
BURNSIDE Susan U23 3.02.80, EWM/Edinburgh Un :
60 - 7.45i, 100 - 11.6w/11.61w/11.74, 200 - 23.88
BURROWS Melanie 7.08.76, Ashford :
JT - 44.31
BURTON Carly U23 14.10.80, Ashford :
DT - 42.13 (44.37-99), HT - 39.87 (41.16-99)
BURTON Louise U13 23.12.88, Macclesfield :
SPM - 9.19, JTM - 29.00
BUTLER Alice 27.07.73, Wakefield :
800 - 2:11.87 (2:04.9mx-97/2:06.8-98)
BUTLER Judith U23 5.10.79, Oadby & Wigston :
Hep - 4055
BUTLER Kathy 22.10.73, WSE&H :
1500 - 4:12.08 (4:07.68CAN-97), 2k - 5:53.8+,
3k - 8:40.97, 5k - 15:14.62 (15:10.69-98),
8KR - 25:25+, 10k - 31:59.27
BUTLER Keeley 24.03.75, Coventry G/City of Edinb :
100 - 12.1/12.18 (12.01-96),
200 - 24.8/25.02 (24.4w/24.45-93)
BUTLER Natalie 25.11.78, WSE&H :
100H - 14.6 (14.78w/14.89-98)
BUTTERS Kate U17 25.07.86, Hastings :
SP - 10.31
BUTTLER Jemma U15 17.06.87, Birchfield :
60 - 7.97i, 100 - 12.21w/12.3/12.52, 200 - 25.5
BUXTON Leanne 27.05.78, Birch/DMU (Beds) Univ :
100H - 14.13w/14.23 (13.96w-00/13.97-99),
400H - 61.7/62.02
BUXTON Victoria U13 1.06.89, Carmarthen :
JTM - 25.86

CADDICK Leah U17 1.06.86, Southport :
100 - 12.4, 200 - 24.9/24.96w/25.41, 300 - 40.5
CAFFEL Kelly U23 10.02.79, Oxford City :
800 - 2:04.59 (2:03.48mp/2:04.35-00),
1500 - 4:11.99 (4:10.22-00)
CAIRNEY Cheryl U15 27.03.87, Glasgow SOS :
75HG - 11.8/11.83w, PenG - 2647
CALDER Elaine V35 26.04.62, :
Mar - 3:08:00
CALLAGHAN Katherine Jane U23 11.04.80, WSE&H :
PV - 3.40
CALLAWAY Deborah Ann V35 15.07.64, AF&D :
SP - 12.19 (14.88-93), DT - 46.97 (58.56-96),
HT - 37.47 (44.64-96)
CALLISTE Emma U17 2.02.85, Thames Valley :
JT - 34.29
CALVERT Donna U23 26.06.79, Wakefield :
DT - 36.55 (37.53-98)
CAMERON Claire V40 3.10.58, City of Glasgow :
DT - 39.80 (46.34-85)
CAMERON Hannah U15 3.03.88, Edinburgh WM :
HTG - 30.43
CAMERON Siobhan U13 15.12.88, W DUNB :
SPM - 9.07
CAMPBELL Katrina 8.03.72, Lisburn/Queen's U/IRL :
JT - 37.00 (42.13-99)
CAMPBELL Sarah 31.10.74, Glasgow Univ :
Mar - 3:05:18 (2:59:31-00)
CANDLISH Lauren U17 4.04.86, Pitreavie :
300 - 40.28
CANEY Eleanor U20 28.05.84, Solihull & S Heath :
100 - 11.92w/12.0/12.09,
200 - 24.15w/24.3/24.42 (24.29-00)
CANK Elaine U23 5.12.79, Telford :
SP - 11.43 (12.57-99), DT - 46.00 (46.40-99)
CANNING Melanie U17 19.05.85, Ealing,S & Mx :
300 - 41.4, 80HI - 11.84 (11.7/11.74w/11.80-00),
300H - 43.86
CAPLE Lauren Emma U17 7.03.85, Derby LAC :
300 - 40.9/41.03
CAPPER Steffi J. U13 12.02.89, Telford :
HJ - 1.53, LJ - 4.95
CARDING Christina U15 26.02.87, Basingstoke & MH :
SPG - 10.75 (10.80-00), DT - 36.70
CARDY Bronwen G. V45 26.01.52, Bromsgrove & R :
5k - 17:28.1 (16:44.94-89), 10k - 36:20.10 (34:37.3-00)
CAREY Michelle U23 20.02.81, Loughborough/IRL :
200 - 24.79w/25.1, 400 - 55.35, 400H - 59.64
CARISS Susan V50 17.11.49, Bingley :
Mar - 3:05:40 (3:04:33-00)
CARNEY Helen U23 27.03.79, Luton/St. Marys Univ :
PV - 3.10i/2.80 (2.80-00)
CARNEY Treena V40 29.08.61, Dewsbury :
Mar - 3:05:44
CARPENTER Emma U20 16.05.82, Exeter :
SP - 12.33 (12.53-00), DT - 53.12
CARR Laura U13 18.02.89, Dorchester :
JT - 31.16, JTM - 34.27
CARROLL Emma U17 23.03.86, Liverpool H :
1500 - 4:44.94
CARSON Kimberly 12.03.74, Belgrave/USA :
100H - 13.07 (12.72-96)
CARSON Susanne 2.05.67, Gala :
Mar - 3:05:33
CARTER Alexandra U23 1.04.80, Vale RI/Loughbro :
400 - 55.7, 600 - 1:30.68i,
800 - 2:04.9 (2:03.78mp-00), 1500 - 4:14.44
CARTY Lara U20 7.03.84, Basildon :
100H - 14.77w/15.09 (14.83-00), Hep - 4294 (4538-00)
CARWARDINE Hazel U23 6.11.80, Bolton :
LJ - 5.52w (5.31-97), TJ - 12.10
CASE Jessica U17 29.10.85, S London :
300H - 46.56
CASH-GIBSON Lulu U17 22.12.84, Highgate Harriers :
300H - 46.0/46.70
CATTERMOLE Sara-Jane 29.01.77, Dartford :
3KSTW - 11:38.90, 3kW - 14:05.6,
5kW - 24:43.9mx (24:16.0-97),
5kWR - 24:23 (23:32+-00),
10kW - 49:51.6 (49:05.0-99), 10kWR - 47:05,
20kW - 1:39:10 (1:35:52sh/1:36:40-00)
CAWTHORNE Helen V40 9.07.61, Redhill :
Mar - 3:00:32
CEESAY Amina U23 19.11.79, Newham & Essex B :
100 - 11.86w/12.14 (12.1-00),
200 - 24.8w/25.0/25.24i (24.79-99)
CEESAY Nusrat U23 18.03.81, N & E B/Loughbro :
100H - 14.8/15.02 (14.8-99),
400H - 60.6/60.79 (60.53-98)
CEESAY Zainab U20 27.10.83, Newham & Essex B :
LJ - 5.69 (6.15-00)
CHADNEY Ruth U17 20.04.85, Bournemouth :
800 - 2:17.0 (2:15.5-00)

CHALMERS Laura U17 1.05.86, Elgin :
DT - 36.31, HT - 44.86
CHAMBERLAIN Rebecca U23 7.09.79, Bournemouth :
SP - 11.44 (11.46i-98), DT - 36.59
CHAMBERS Jamie L. U13, Crawley :
HJ - 1.44
CHAMBERS Karen Louise 31.08.68, Border :
HT - 43.99 (48.66-00)
CHANDLER Julie U17 12.02.85, City of Norwich :
TJ - 10.71
CHAPMAN Joanna U17 10.01.85, West Suffolk :
JT - 42.37
CHARLES Shereen U17 27.10.84, Ealing,S & Mx :
60 - 7.90i, 100 - 12.1/12.23w/12.30 (12.27-00),
200 - 25.0
CHARNOCK Catherine 3.05.75, Dudley & Stourbridge :
10kWR - 52:48 (47:51-99)
CHARNOCK Kathryn V35 4.07.62, Wigan Phoenix :
Mar - 2:54:55 (2:47:28-99)
CHATTING Donna U20 30.10.83, Southampton City :
400 - 57.13
CHETWYND Sarah 4.06.74, Tamworth :
(nee GRAVES) 10kWR - 56:56
CHILD Eilidh U15 20.02.87, Pitreavie :
75HG - 11.88w
CHILDS Ellie Joanne U20 26.05.83, Basildon :
800 - 2:07.24, 1500 - 4:29.82
CHRISMAS Bryna U17 18.06.86, Kingston u Hull :
3kW - 15:39.97, 5kW - 27:04.5,
5kWR - 26:11 (26:11-00), 10kWR - 57:13
CHRISTIE Catriona Rosanna U17 26.04.85, WSE&H :
HJ - 1.70, TJ - 10.98 (11.10-00)
CHRISTIE Erica M. V45 10.03.56, Victoria Park AAC :
Mar - 3:04:27 (2:54:24-86)
CHRISTIE Jenny U17 28.09.85, Leamington :
300 - 39.39, 400 - 57.8, 300H - 46.15, HepI - 4382
CHRISTMAS Natalie U20 9.04.84, Crawley :
400H - 62.4/63.62
CHURCH Amy U17 22.04.86, Isle of Wight :
HT - 37.56
CLAFFEY Juliet 30.04.78, Border/IRL :
PV - 3.42
CLAPHAM Melissa U20 6.09.82, Colchester & T :
HT - 38.15
CLARK Abigail U15 11.01.87, Sutton & District :
LJ - 5.28, TJ - 11.08w
CLARK Jean 5.10.68, Edinburgh WM :
HT - 45.34 (50.34-97)
CLARK Juliette V35 22.04.64, Belgrave :
Mar - 2:54:27
CLARK Lauren U13 23.06.89, Havering :
DTM - 23.62
CLARK Lynsey U15 2.09.86, Havering :
DT - 33.34
CLARK Megan 31.07.73, Thames H & H :
Mar - 2:47:24
CLARK Natalie U20 4.09.82, Kingston u Hull :
HJ - 1.70i/1.70 (1.76-99)
CLARK Sonia U20 1.04.84, Sale :
3k - 9:53.1mx/9:56.0
CLARKE Amanda 28.03.68, Sutton-in-Ashfield :
Mar - 3:08:17
CLARKE Dianne Olivia V40 27.02.58, Thames Valley :
400H - 65.5 (62.9-94/65.33-98)
CLARKE Lara U13 4.10.88, Shaftesbury Barnet :
800 - 2:26.4
CLARKE Lianne Theresa U15 14.01.87, Neath :
JT - 32.76
CLARKE Rhian Clare 19.04.77, WGreen & Ex L/
Houston University : PV - 4.20i/4.10 (4.15-00)
CLARKSON Lesley U20 18.07.82, Inv/Glasgow Univ :
200 - 24.96 (24.87w-99), 400 - 54.44, 800 - 2:12.90
CLAXTON Sarah U23 23.09.79, Colchester & T :
60H - 8.28i, 100H - 13.36 (13.28w-98),
LJ - 6.27 (6.56-99)
CLAYTON Anna U17 20.03.85, West Suffolk :
80HI - 12.0, LJ - 5.47w/5.36, HepI - 4248w/4194
CLEMENTIS Natasha U15 11.09.86, Epsom & Ewell :
60HG - 9.4i, 75HG - 11.53w/11.62
CLEMENTS Grace U20 2.05.84, Dartford :
HJ - 1.70, Hep - 4060
CLEMENTS Ruth 15.05.74, Radley :
TJ - 11.14
CLUBLEY Christina U17 4.11.85, Kingston u Hull :
100 - 12.19w/12.25, 200 - 25.34
COFFEY Charlotte U23 28.07.80, Bristol/Bristol Un :
3k - 9:55.1 (9:52.4-99)
COLLIER Gemma U17 25.11.85, Exeter :
300H - 45.58
COLLINS Chiara U17 25.03.85, Sale :
HT - 32.48
COLLINS Jayne U23 27.03.80, Birchfield :
PV - 2.90 (3.10-99)
COLLINS Sarah U13, Fleet & Crookham :
DTM - 24.06
COLLINSON Deborah Joy U17 23.10.85, Kingston u H :
SP - 10.54i/10.50, JT - 41.05
BLANK-COLLIS Paula 13.12.77, Verlea :
JT - 43.75
CONNEELY Vivienne 4.01.76, Neath :
Mar - 2:54:43
CONOLLY Anna R. U17 19.04.86, Telford :
80HI - 12.0
CONSTERDINE Victoria 25.04.75, Stockport :
100H - 15.39w, Hep - 4372
COOK Lucy 11.09.75, Medway :
(see BUDGEN)
COOK Samantha U15 6.05.87, Verlea :
75HG - 11.49w/11.64
COOKE Gillian U20 3.10.82, EWM/Glasgow Univ :
PV - 3.40, LJ - 5.64w, TJ - 11.40i/11.38 (11.66-00)
COOKSEY Melinda U20 19.05.84, Tipton :
200 - 24.79i/25.0 (24.85-00)
COOMBS Paula V40 31.12.61, Hastings :
HT - 38.37 (38.50-00)
COONEY Sharon 10.06.68, Highgate Harriers/NZL :
Mar - 3:05:39 (2:55:51-99)
COOPER Laura U15 23.05.87, Telford :
SPG - 10.97
COOPER Vicky U17 10.10.85, City of Stoke :
DT - 32.77
COPP Louise V35 13.09.63, Cardiff :
HMar - 76:20, Mar - 2:47:07
CORBETT Kirsty U20 16.05.82, Ilford/Loughbro :
LJ - 5.61, TJ - 11.35 (11.71w-99)
CORCORAN Chloe U17 29.09.85, Parkside :
PV - 2.70
CORK Rachel U15 11.10.86, Wimborne :
SPG - 11.03
CORNEBY Hannah E. U23 22.01.81, Cannock & St :
DT - 42.85
CORRAN Elizabeth M. V45 23.09.55, Manx H :
5kWR - 25:52 (24:51-95),
10kWR - 53:46 (51:37hc-96/51:38-95),
20kW - 1:52:54 (1:47:10-96)
CORRIE Jessica U13 22.04.89, Liverpool H :
600 - 1:47.2, 800 - 2:26.09
COSSEY Laurie U23 24.11.81, Havering :
800 - 2:11.67
COTTINGHAM F. U13, :
SPM - 9.08
COURT Clova V40 10.02.60, WSE&H :
100 - 12.13w/12.29 (11.43w-97/11.6-87/11.68-97),
60H - 8.55i (8.12i-94), 100H - 13.60 (13.04-94),
SP - 11.63 (14.44-97)

COX Laura Elizabeth U15 21.01.88, Tipton :
200 - 25.98i (26.8-00)
COZENS Chloe U23 9.04.80, Bed & C/Loughbro :
HJ - 1.72 (1.80-98), SP - 12.75,
JT - 51.65 (51.79-00)
CRAWFORD Catherine Marie U17 17.12.84, Regent H :
80HI - 11.78, 100HI - 14.19, 300H - 43.74
CRAWLEY Sonia U20 7.12.83, Solihull & S Heath :
HJ - 1.65i (1.70i/1.68-99)
CRESSWELL Lois U23 12.01.81, R S Coldfield/Lough :
400 - 55.45
CRIPPS Faith U20 23.09.83, Milton Keynes :
400H - 63.77, LJ - 5.60, Hep - 4267
CRIPSEY Susan U23 8.01.81, Bed & C/E Anglia Un :
1500 - 4:30.9, 3k - 9:49.1mx
CROAD Alison U20 10.06.82, Poole/UWIC :
TJ - 11.24
CROCKETT Anna 11.07.69, Bridgend :
Mar - 3:09:18
CROLL Charli U17 25.10.84, Herne Hill :
60 - 7.9i/7.94i, 100 - 12.57 (12.27-00),
200 - 25.19i (25.01w/25.23-99), 300 - 40.9/41.17
CROMBIE-HICK Shona 1.06.71, Mornington :
Mar - 2:45:23 (2:42:44-00)
CROMPTON Mandy U20 25.03.82, Oldham & Royton :
LJ - 5.60
CROSBY Nicole 23.10.76, Wakefield :
100 - 12.06w/12.25 (11.80w/11.93-00),
200 - 24.97w/24.99 (24.3w/24.35-98)
CROSKELL Helen 22.11.72, Tonbridge :
PV - 2.80
CROSS Danielle U17 26.09.84, Newquay & Par :
3k - 10:37.04
CROSS Natasha U17 13.11.84, Swansea :
100 - 12.4 (12.54w-00), 200 - 25.2w (25.08-00)
CROWE Maria U15 20.01.87, Medway :
75HG - 11.6/11.85
CROWLE Revis V35 26.01.62, East Cornwall :
Mar - 3:09:19
CRUZ Silvia U23 29.12.80, Belgrave/POR :
JT - 54.43
CULLEY Jennifer 4.03.75, Belgrave :
200 - 24.7/25.11, 300 - 38.22,
400 - 54.39 (54.11-98), 400H - 61.8
CULSHAW Rachel U17 11.08.86, Wigan :
HJ - 1.65
CUNLIFFE Jessica 25.11.77, Rugby :
400 - 57.4, 400H - 65.20
CUNNINGHAM Laura U17 14.02.85, Avonside :
60 - 7.90i (7.86i-00)
CUNNINGHAM Lauren Kerry U15 22.08.87,
Stevenage & NH :
800 - 2:17.30 (2:16.46-00), 1500 - 4:48.83
CURBISHLEY Allison 3.06.76, Edinburgh WM :
400 - 51.99 (50.71-98), 800 - 2:03.30
CURL Tracey V35 8.07.62, Norwich RR :
Mar - 3:04:36
CURLEY Debra 20.09.71, Wigan :
3k - 9:54.4, Mar - 2:56:05
CURLING Roseanne U23 5.09.80, Bristol/Camb Un :
LJ - 5.77
CURRAN Nuala U15 11.03.87, N I Schools :
LJ - 5.26
CURTIS Laura U23 2.05.81, Kingston u Hull/Birm Un :
100H - 15.2, 400H - 61.85, HJ - 1.65i (1.65-96)
CURTIS Louise 29.07.70, Highgate Harriers/NZL :
Mar - 3:04:46
CUTHBERTSON Jenny U20 11.06.84, Rotherham :
PV - 2.60 (2.65-00)

DAGNE Birhan 8.04.78, Belgrave :
3k - 9:34.4+/9:38.74 (9:10.47-94),
5k - 16:16.24 (15:36.35-00),
5KR - 16:41 (16:18-99), 10kR - 33:38 (33:19-99),
HMar - 73:52 (72:53-99)
DAINTON Bethan U13 12.04.89, Cwmbran :
1200 - 4:00.1
DALE Cathryn 31.05.77, Rugby :
LJ - 5.56 (5.69w/5.66-00), TJ - 11.30 (11.78-00)
DALE Charlotte U20 23.03.84, Invicta :
1500 - 4:29.46, 3k - 9:36.42 (9:34.9mx/9:35.25-00),
5KR - 16:38, 10kR - 33:31
DALES Ruth Marie U23 29.10.80, Wake/Bradford Un :
100H - 14.67w/14.90
DALY Dominique U13 10.01.89, Crawley :
1500 - 5:05.2
DAMEN Louise U20 12.10.82, Bournemouth :
1500 - 4:28.74 (4:23.38-00), 3k - 9:28.61,
5k - 16:55.99, 5KR - 16:41, 10kR - 34:00
DANBY Joy U17 5.09.84, Kingston u Hull :
100 - 12.4
DANIELS Nikki U20 25.08.82, City of Stoke :
800 - 2:11.1 (2:11.1-00)
DANSON Ann Elizabeth 4.05.71, Sale :
100 - 11.86w/12.1/12.14 (11.8w-94/11.91-95),
LJ - 6.36w/6.21 (6.38w-94/6.21i/6.21-00)
DANVERS Natasha 19.09.77, Shaftesbury Barnet :
400H - 54.94
DARBY Ellie U17 20.12.85, Birchfield :
LJ - 5.59 (5.71w-00)
DARRINGTON Sarah-Jane U17 25.06.85, Bed & Co :
HJ - 1.66
DATE Natasha U15 18.11.86, Swansea :
60 - 8.06i, 100 - 12.5w
DAVEY Sarah 13.10.78, Worthing/Un N Florida :
3k - 9:55.54i (9:58.17-00),
5k - 16:50.74i (16:52.67-00)
DAVIDSON Fiona 29.01.73, Aberdeen :
TJ - 11.27 (12.15i-95/12.06w/11.91-96)
DAVIDSON Lucy U17 19.11.85, Solihull & S Heath :
100 - 12.3w
DAVIDSON Rachel U13 29.04.89, Stewartry :
PenM - 2187
DAVIDSON Wendy U20 14.10.82, City of Stoke :
100H - 15.10w/15.24 (15.11-00), Hep - 4441
DAVIES Alison V40 6.04.61, WSE&H :
PV - 3.60i/3.30 (4.00-00)
DAVIES Elizabeth Sian U17 16.02.85, Dudley & St :
300H - 45.01
DAVIES Elen U17 24.04.86, City of Norwich :
HJ - 1.63i (1.61-99), TJ - 10.82
DAVIES Emma J. 9.10.78, Belgrave/Soton Univ :
400 - 56.83i (55.19-00), 800 - 2:04.70 (2:02.39-98)
DAVIES Gael Iona U23 5.02.79, Chelt/Loughbro :
PV - 3.75
DAVIES Samantha U23 20.09.79, Birchfield :
60 - 7.44i, 100 - 11.59w/11.77 (11.4w/11.44-00),
200 - 23.81i/24.57 (23.06-00)
DAVIES Sarah U17 13.03.86, Bournemouth :
DT - 33.51
DAVIES Wendy V40 13.06.60, Windle Valley :
Mar - 3:05:52
DAVIS Helen Marie U17 31.01.85, Isle of Wight :
JT - 36.14 (38.47-00)
DAVISON Sarah J. U15 4.12.86, Durham City H :
800 - 2:19.00
DAY Samantha U17 8.02.86, Tamworth :
60HI - 9.30i, 80HI - 11.76, 300H - 46.7
DEACON Sarah U20 18.03.83, Havering :
HT - 40.13
DEADMAN Lauren U20 27.03.84, Havering :
3k - 9:58.8
DEAN Carly U17 14.10.85, Bournemouth :
80HI - 11.9, 300H - 45.2/46.11
DEANE Rebecca U23 9.01.79, WGreen & Ex L :
400H - 65.94

DEBONO Michelle 1.05.72, Herne Hill :
100H - 14.94w (15.15-00), 400H - 63.96
DEE Ellisha U17 24.10.84, Thames Valley :
SP - 10.91, DT - 42.96
DEEGAN Rachel Sarah U17 10.01.86, Sale :
1500 - 4:44.6
DENHAM Kate U23 18.03.80, Team Solent :
100 - 12.1/12.27 (12.09-00),
200 - 24.3w/24.58 (24.34w/24.51-97)
DENNEHY Siobhan U20 31.08.82, Chelm/Camb Univ :
HJ - 1.65 (1.65-99)
DENNISON Andrea M. V35 22.04.63, Bradford :
Mar - 2:59:15
DENNISON Kate U20 7.05.84, Stoke :
PV - 3.80
DERHAM Zoe U23 24.11.80, Birchfield :
HT - 60.35
DERING Joanne 7.02.69, WSE&H :
Mar - 2:56:08
DESAI Nisha U20 5.08.84, Morpeth :
800 - 2:11.10
DEVLIN Mary U23 14.09.79, B & A/Ulster Univ. :
LJ - 5.76w/5.61,
TJ - 11.47w/11.46i/11.44 (11.78-00)
DEVOY Sarah U15 12.01.87, Liverpool H :
HJ - 1.59, JT - 34.38, PenG - 2728
DEW Jennifer 23.12.77, Southampton City :
(nee READER) HJ - 1.65 (1.73-98)
DEWELL Sophie U20 18.09.83, Middlesbro & C :
PV - 2.90
DEWSBURY Claire U20 16.01.84, Bournemouth :
HJ - 1.70 (1.70-00)
DHALIWAL Navdeep 30.11.77, S Barnet/Vict PAAC :
SP - 12.71 (13.35-98), DT - 44.58
DICKINSON Louise U15 5.11.86, Park Hill HS :
60 - 7.88i, 100 - 12.5, 200 - 25.64i/25.7/25.81
DICKSON Lauren U17 2.04.86, Ayr Seaforth :
60 - 7.95i, 100 - 12.4w/12.49w (12.59-00)
DICKSON Louise U15 4.09.86, Edinburgh WM :
60 - 7.80i, 100 - 12.3/12.37w/12.47 (12.46-00),
200 - 25.30
DILLON Michelle 24.05.73, Bristol :
10kR - 33:46
DIXON Alyson 24.09.78, Sunderland/Sunderland Un :
10k - 36:39.08
DIXON Sharon Jane 22.04.68, Parkside :
HMar - 76:01, Mar - 2:46:32 (2:46:30-00)
DOBRISKEY Lisa U20 23.12.83, Ashford :
800 - 2:08.4, 1500 - 4:25.85
DOBRISKEY Sarah U17 13.08.85, Ashford :
HT - 42.29
DOHERTY Michelle U17 24.09.84, Sparta :
LJ - 5.36w, TJ - 11.75w/11.12
DOHERTY Tamara U17 15.11.85, W DUNB :
60 - 7.95i, 100 - 12.2w/12.45w (12.5/12.51-00),
200 - 25.20i/25.4/25.55, 300 - 41.31i
DOONEY Gemma U20 12.05.84, Wigan :
400H - 60.07
DORRIAN Eilidh U17 8.10.85, Giffnock :
PV - 3.00i/2.90
DOUBLE Christine V35 10.06.64, :
Mar - 2:51:48
DOUGHTY Jessica U17 6.07.85, Brecon :
TJ - 10.73
DOUGLAS Laura U20 4.01.83, Sale :
SP - 11.95, DT - 39.19 (39.62-00), HT - 52.00
DOUGLAS Montell U17 24.01.86, Bromley :
100 - 11.87w/11.90, 200 - 25.0w/25.03, HJ - 1.64
DOWNES Emma U17 21.02.86, Swansea :
60HI - 9.30i, 80HI - 12.0
DOWSETT Amy U17 30.12.84, Croydon :
100 - 12.28, 200 - 25.0
DOWSING Laura U13 17.06.89, West Suffolk :
1500 - 5:04.16
DOYLE Natalie U13 5.01.89, Falkirk :
75 - 10.1, 70HM - 11.66
DRAKE Julie Elizabeth 21.05.69, Brighton :
Mar - 3:08:42 (2:58:22-92)
DRAKE Sarah U17 13.08.85, Wakefield :
HT - 41.67
DREW Shelley Jean 8.08.73, Belgrave :
(see NEWMAN)
DRURY Leonie U17 2.07.85, Exeter :
DT - 32.67
DRURY Sarah U15 30.09.87, Vale Royal :
1500 - 4:48.1
DUCK Emma U23 9.02.81, Team Solent :
100H - 14.42w/14.7/15.05
DUCK Joey S. U13 14.04.89, Milton Keynes :
75 - 10.0, 100 - 13.0/13.04w,
150 - 19.2, 200 - 27.5
DUDGEON Sinead Marie 9.07.76, Edinburgh WM :
60 - 7.63i,
100 - 11.96 (11.72w-99/11.8-94/11.93-95),
200 - 24.18 (23.23w-00/23.59-99), 300 - 37.08,
400 - 52.47i (52.05-99), 400H - 56.07 (55.24-99)
DUDMAN Nicola Pauline U20 5.10.83, Verlea :
SP - 12.07, HT - 54.54
DUFF Jennifer U20 29.07.82, Rugby/Oxford Univ :
DT - 36.81
DUFFY Teresa 6.07.69, WGreen & Ex L/IRL :
HMar - 72:57, Mar - 2:35:27
DUGDALE Catherine 29.11.74, Swansea :
1500 - 4:25.40, 3k - 9:28.27mx/9:36.87,
5k - 16:37.42
DUNCAN Joanne V35 27.12.66, WGreen & Ex L :
SP - 17.08
DUNCAN Lauren U15 21.03.88, WSE&H :
100 - 12.62
DUNCAN Tracey Andrea U23 16.05.79, WGn & Ex L :
400 - 55.4/55.54i/56.32 (55.2/56.18-00),
100H - 15.0 (14.79-97), 400H - 58.15 (57.92-00)
DUNFORD Jenny U13, Birchfield :
SPM - 9.98, DTM - 26.80, JTM - 25.69
DUNKLEY Julie U23 11.09.79, S B/Greenwich Univ :
SP - 16.31 (16.40-00)
DUNKLEY Michelle Lisa 26.01.78, WGreen & Ex L :
HJ - 1.90 (1.93-00)
DUNN Elizabeth U17 5.01.85, Huntingdon :
JT - 36.03
DUNN Kara U17 12.10.84, Ealing,Southall & Mx :
60 - 7.89i (7.89i-99),
100 - 12.3/12.56 (12.02w/12.2-99/12.21-00)
DUNN Kathryn U17 11.06.85, Liverpool H :
300H - 46.8
DUNN Rachel U20 14.11.82, Huntingdon :
JT - 44.11
DUPONT Celia U15, Norfolk Sch :
HJ - 1.61
DURMAN Louise U15 23.11.86, Dursley :
1500 - 4:49.7
DWAN Elizabeth U20 16.10.82, Gateshead :
DT - 37.73

EAGLES Ellen U17 9.09.84, Tipton :
LJ - 5.40
EARLE Jennifer S. V40 28.11.58, Guildford & G :
HT - 39.94 (42.49-98)
EASTON Carey U23 16.11.79, EWM/Edinburgh Univ :
200 - 24.83w/24.88 (24.56-99),
400 - 54.58 (54.28-98)
EDGAR Catherine U23 27.02.80, Lagan Valley :
JT - 38.21 (41.48-00)
EDWARDS Chloe U15 12.05.87, Huntingdon :
SPG - 12.71, DT - 29.71

EDWARDS Elizabeth U17 18.12.84, Huntingdon :
HT - 35.83
EDWARDS Lisa U15 4.02.87, Exeter :
JT - 34.24
EDWARDS Susan U17 17.10.84, Oswestry :
80HI - 12.07
ELKHAWAD Maysoon 27.02.77, Chelm/Camb Univ :
HT - 41.40 (41.78-00)
ELLIOTT Kerry U17 17.05.85, Gateshead :
SP - 11.67, DT - 33.05
ELLIOTT Lucy Helen V35 9.03.66, Shaftesbury Barnet :
3k - 9:23.21 (9:19.2-97), 5k - 16:25.44 (15:34.40-97),
5KR - 16:35 (15:54-95), 5MR - 26:31 (25:54sh-97),
10kR - 33:53 (33:02-98)
ELLIS Lauren A. U13 22.05.89, Wigan :
JTM - 25.07600g
ELLIS Lucy U15 5.02.88, Brecon :
100 - 12.6
ELLIS Melanie V35 16.04.64, Shaftesbury Barnet :
Mar - 2:54:35 (2:46:55-99)
ELLIS Rebecca U15 20.12.86, Vale Royal :
1500 - 4:44.21
ELLIS Sarah U20 27.10.83, Havant :
JT - 38.78 (41.99-00)
ELLIS Venetia U17 15.09.85, Herne Hill :
JT - 34.67
ELMORE Lisa 1.01.70, Shaftesbury Barnet :
(nee HOLLICK) Mar - 2:59:39 (2:51:16-98)
ELSON Sara Jo-Anne 8.05.70, Gateshead :
400H - 65.6 (58.19-92)
ELWISS Hannah U17 8.12.84, Preston :
100 - 12.4, 60HI - 8.90i, 80HI - 11.21w/11.36
EMMERSON Annaleah 10.05.70, Bath Univ :
5MR - 27:18+, 10kR - 33:45+,
10MR - 55:13, HMar - 73:00
EMSLEY Jennifer U15 28.11.86, City of Glasgow :
1500 - 4:48.37
ENDACOTT Katherine U23 29.01.80, City of Plymouth :
60 - 7.52i, 100 - 11.76w/11.9/11.94 (11.89-99),
200 - 24.74 (24.57-99)
ENGDAHL Elin V35 12.10.62, Thurrock :
Mar - 3:05:23
ENGLAND Hannah U15 6.03.87, Oxford City :
800 - 2:16.7, 1500 - 4:39.37
ENGLISH Allison U23 4.03.79, Kingston u Hull :
100H - 14.87w/15.1/15.21 (14.64w/14.76-97)
ENNIS Jessica U17 28.01.86, Sheffield :
100 - 12.3, 200 - 25.25, 60HI - 8.65i, 80HI - 11.52,
100H - 14.53, HJ - 1.75, Hep - 4801, Hepl - 4538
ENNIS Jolene U15 17.03.87, Clydesdale :
1500 - 4:49.51
ENTWISTLE Claire 9.12.76, Wigan :
800 - 2:11.0 (2:09.73-97)
EPHGRAVE Helen U17 29.10.84, Guildford & G :
SP - 10.43, HT - 38.19
ERHARUYI Esther U20 17.04.83, Belgrave/NGR :
200 - 24.95i, 400H - 60.6
ERSKINE Joanne U17 28.05.85, Dunfermline & W Fife :
60HI - 9.09i, 80HI - 11.43, 300H - 43.71, 400H - 65.2
EUSTACE Katharine 16.04.75, Bristol :
400 - 55.39 (54.91-97)
EVANS Elen U17 14.02.85, Carmarthen :
60HI - 9.21i, 80HI - 11.85w/12.07, Hepl - 3872
EVANS Jemma U17 25.01.86, Wirral :
5kW - 29:34.5
EVANS Kate Victoria 4.02.74, Rugby :
HJ - 1.67 (1.78-90), LJ - 5.52 (5.60-90),
TJ - 12.63 (13.04w-00/13.03-97)
EVANS Katherine 19.11.77, Coventry Godiva/Birm Un :
JT - 42.76 (45.37-99)
EVANS Kathryn U20 1.03.84, Elgin :
60 - 7.65i, 100 - 12.07w/12.15, 200 - 24.81,
400 - 56.96mx/57.13
EVANS Laura Mair 28.09.74, Grantham :
DT - 39.54
EVANS Laura U13, Bury :
1200 - 4:00.1
EVANS Sally 14.05.75, Sale :
400 - 55.82 (55.32-98), 800 - 2:04.97, 1500 - 4:28.71
EVERETT Claire U23 25.06.79, C of Norwich/Brunel U :
SP - 12.54, Hep - 4616 (4759-96)
EVERITT Amie 1.11.78, Huntingdon :
PV - 2.60 (2.80-98)
EXETER Alice U13 7.02.89, Dartford :
DTM - 26.39
EZEOGU Nina U20 11.10.82, Newham & Essex B :
TJ - 11.59

FAGAN Collette U20 6.06.82, City of Glasgow :
1500 - 4:30.68, 3k - 9:22.45, 5k - 16:16.39
FAIRLESS Rachel U20 19.03.82, Middlesbro & C :
PV - 2.80
FAIRS Elizabeth 1.12.77, Trafford :
200 - 24.7w/24.90 (24.65w/24.76-00), 400 - 56.6,
100H - 13.6w/13.73w/13.81 (13.49-00), 400H - 61.50
FAIRWEATHER Lynne U23 15.01.80, Edinburgh WM :
60H - 8.94i (8.75i-96)
FAIRWEATHER Sheila 24.11.77, C of Glas/Glas Un :
3k - 9:21.19, 5k - 16:15.94 (16:07.34-98),
10k - 34:23.55, 2KSTW - 7:02.54
FALLOWS Rhea Joanne U13 30.01.89, Stockport :
1k - 3:08.2, 1200 - 4:00.1, 1500 - 5:00.3
FARAG Zenab H. U15 21.09.86, Dartford :
SPG - 11.43
FARDOE Kerri U20 22.11.83, Shrewsbury :
SP - 11.26
FARMER Angela U17 27.03.85, Liverpool H :
HT - 31.55
FAVELL Jodie U20 4.11.82, Holbeach :
Hep - 3871
FAWKES Danielle U17 11.08.85, Barrow & Furness :
200 - 25.27, 60HI - 9.12io,
80HI - 11.38w/11.56, Hepl - 4346
FELTON Rachel U23 27.06.79, Shaft B/Boston Un :
800 - 2:08.83, 1500 - 4:18.72, 1M - 4:45.49i
FENN Joanne 19.10.74, WGreen & Ex L :
400 - 55.0/56.96 (55.72-00), 800 - 2:02.81
FERGUSON Lisa U15 10.09.86, Ellon :
HJ - 1.61
FERGUSSON Gemma U20 20.08.84, N Shields Poly :
60H - 8.81i, 100H - 14.07w/14.14
FERRIER Holly U20 13.07.84, Peterborough :
100H - 14.70w/14.81
FIDGE Danielle U17 19.03.85, Croydon :
HJ - 1.66
FIELDEN Juliet L. U13 9.10.88, Tonbridge :
HJ - 1.46
FIELDING-SMITH Sarah U15 19.11.86, Brighton :
HJ - 1.60, PenG - 2754
FINLAY Louise U20 2.10.83, Rhondda :
SP - 11.44 (12.05-00)
FINNIS Suzanne U20 12.08.83, WGreen & Ex L :
JT - 40.80 (45.84-00)
FINUCANE Laura U17 3.08.86, Pendle :
300 - 40.0/40.64, 400 - 57.41, 800 - 2:10.49
FISHER Emma 8.01.70, Shaftesbury Barnet :
5k - 17:27.69mx
FISTROVIC Natazia U13, Epsom & Ewell :
JTM - 28.33
FITZGERALD Lyndsay U23 31.01.80, WSE&H/
St. Marys Univ : 400H - 64.2/65.20 (63.6/64.06-99)
FLAHERTY Katie U17 1.10.85, Basildon :
100 - 12.3w/12.4/12.49,
200 - 24.8/24.89w/25.05 (24.98-00)
FLEARY Rachael V. U13 16.07.90, Carlisle/Aspatria :
JTM - 27.73

FLEETWOOD Vicky U13 13.04.90, Charnwood :
70HM - 11.6
FLETCHER Alison Kay V40 8.06.61, Camb H/Dulwich R :
5k - 17:27.38 (17:10.54-97),
10k - 36:04.80 (35:18.59-93), Mar - 2:49:18
FLETCHER Amanda U15 18.11.86, Rugby :
LJ - 5.25
FLINT Stacy U17 18.10.85, Kingston u Hull :
80HI - 11.96w/12.09
FOLEY Megan Elizabeth U15 14.04.88, Havering :
800 - 2:18.1, 1500 - 4:46.5
FOLLOS Rachel U15 15.10.86, Tipton :
100 - 12.6 (12.5w-99)
FORD Emma 16.02.77, Liverpool H :
3k - 9:42.42i (9:27.01i-98/9:30.83-99)
FORGIE Natasha U20 12.05.84, Dartford :
HT - 44.65
FORRESTER Amanda 29.09.78, City of Stoke :
60 - 7.45i, 100 - 11.37,
200 - 23.9w (23.9-00/25.02-97)
FORRESTER Emma U20 2.12.83, Telford :
DT - 40.52
FORSYTH Amy U17 16.10.85, Belgrave :
300H - 45.6
FORTES MAYER Gail 2.12.69, Sneyd :
Mar - 3:07:57
FOSTER Jenny 6.09.77, Trafford :
HT - 42.74
FOSTER Vickie 1.04.71, AF&D :
SP - 14.66 (15.44-00), DT - 46.94 (49.25-00),
HT - 43.84 (45.46-97)
FOX Laura Elizabeth U17 25.10.84, Ashford :
SP - 11.28, DT - 40.78
FOX Natasha U17 21.09.85, Dartford :
5kW - 30:06.52
FRANCE Allyson U17 7.02.85, Scarborough :
JT - 34.39
FRANCIS Azaria U20 12.04.83, Croydon :
TJ - 12.04w/11.80
FRANCIS Candice U17 7.02.85, Birchfield :
SP - 10.46, DT - 38.04
FRANCIS Eden C. U13 19.10.88, Leics Cor :
SPG - 10.84, SPM - 11.59, DTM - 27.85
FRANCIS Nafalya LeKeziah U13 21.04.89, Leics Cor :
70HM - 11.02w (11.50-00), 75HG - 11.8
FRANCIS-SMITHSON Hannah U13 10.11.89, Leeds :
70HM - 11.7
FRANKSON Hannah U13 11.01.89, Ilford :
75 - 9.9, 100 - 13.21, 70HM - 11.6, LJ - 4.91
FRASER Donna Karen 7.11.72, Croydon :
100 - 12.05 (11.2wA-98/11.32w-97/11.57-00),
200 - 23.61i/23.97 (22.90w/22.96i-97/23.08-00),
300 - 37.27 (35.71-00), 400 - 51.77 (49.79-00),
800 - 2:09.44
FREEBAIRN Susan V35 22.08.65, City of Glasgow :
DT - 45.90 (46.70-94), HT - 37.09 (37.30-95)
FREEMAN Amy U20 23.08.82, Spenborough :
200 - 25.0w, 400 - 55.75
FREEMAN Danielle U23 11.02.80, Leeds :
60H - 8.93i (8.50i-00)
FREEMAN Emily U23 24.11.80, Wakefield :
60 - 7.64i, 100 - 11.66w/11.8/11.92 (11.83-99),
200 - 23.67i/23.72
FRENCH Rebecca U13 29.09.88, Chelmsford :
HJ - 1.45
FRIDAY Sarah U20 14.11.82, Prestatyn :
PV - 2.60
FROST Bryony U20 21.02.84, Isle of Wight :
2KSTW - 7:12.2
FROST Helen Paula 12.03.74, Birchfield :
200 - 24.0/24.36 (24.11w/24.14-00),
300 - 37.72 (37.55-00), 400 - 52.68 (52.40-00)
FROST Kathryn U20 21.02.84, Isle of Wight :
2KSTW - 7:01.2
FROST Suzanne Lynette U17 27.09.84, C of Plymth :
HT - 31.44
FRYER Lisa U20 30.05.84, Lagan Valley :
JT - 39.56 (40.98-00)
FRYER Paula Tracy 14.07.69, Sale :
800 - 2:09.7 (1:59.76-91)
FULLELOVE Alyssa U23 16.09.81, Kilbarchan/Glas U :
60H - 8.6i/8.72i, 100H - 14.19 (14.07w-00),
400H - 63.96
FULLERTON Faye Alexis U20 31.05.84, Havering :
800 - 2:08.88, 1500 - 4:22.76,
3k - 9:45.8 (9:42.3-00)
FULLMAN Natalie U17 20.05.85, Medway :
800 - 2:14.05
FULLWOOD Juliet U17 1.07.85, Grantham :
Hepl - 3870w

GADSDON Holly C. U13 16.04.89, Newquay & P :
PV - 1.90, JTM - 27.04
GAGG Jenny U15 20.02.88, Kingston u Hull :
3kW - 16:04.3
GALLAGHER Lynne 21.11.74, Shaftesbury Barnet :
800 - 2:11.50i/2:11.5 (2:11.21-98), 1500 - 4:28.88
GALLAWAY Sarah U17 14.11.84, Harrow :
60HI - 9.23io (8.99i-00),
300H - 44.7/45.75 (43.73-00), Hepl - 4339
GANNON Lindsay C. V35 29.08.66, Royal Navy/Alton :
Mar - 2:54:48
GARAVAND Maria U17 30.06.86, City of Norwich :
400 - 57.7, 80HI - 11.9, 300H - 43.65, 400H - 64.31
GARDEN Catherine 4.09.78, Edinburgh WM :
SP - 11.61 (12.50-97), DT - 37.79 (42.72-94),
HT - 53.53 (54.03-99)
GARDENER Genevieve U17 3.09.84, Guildford & G :
1500 - 4:46.89, 3k - 10:11.68
GARDNER Ann 11.10.68, Corby :
HT - 47.83 (55.60-98)
GARNETT Chanelle U17 16.08.85, Herne Hill :
60HI - 8.78i, 80HI - 11.31, 300H - 45.8 (45.6-00),
LJ - 5.69 (5.74-99), Hepl - 4388
GARRAD Victoria U15 22.11.87, Wirral :
75HG - 11.83
GARRETT Caroline Jane V35 14.06.63, Worthing :
JT - 37.16
GARRETT Jemma U17 21.09.85, Jarrow & Hebburn :
Hepl - 4094
GASCOIGNE Amber U23 5.09.79, Wells/Loughbro :
3k - 9:36.01 (9:25.95-98), 5k - 17:00.29
GATRELL Eleanor 5.10.76, Woking :
SP - 14.24i/13.95 (14.68-98), DT - 36.21 (39.57-00),
HT - 43.57
GAULD Louise U23 24.08.80, EWM/C of Edinburgh :
HJ - 1.65 (1.65i-96), PV - 3.50i/3.40
GAUTIER Nicola Louise 21.03.78, Trafford :
200 - 25.13 (24.81-97), 60H - 8.72i (8.65i-98),
100H - 14.05 (13.92w-99),
LJ - 5.74w/5.67i/5.56 (5.70-00),
SP - 14.64 (15.09-00), JT - 49.25, Hep - 5784
GAYLE Denise U23 11.09.79, Barnet :
HJ - 1.73
GAYTER Sharon M. V35 30.10.63, New Marske :
100kR - 9:11:56, 24Hr - 191.414km (212.606km-98)
GBAHY Angeline 16.07.76, Newham & Essex B/FRA :
SP - 14.35
GEAR Karen U23 30.09.79, N Devon :
100 - 12.20, 200 - 24.2w/24.9 (24.87-99),
400 - 53.31
GEE Michala 8.12.75, Rotherham :
LJ - 5.58 (5.74w/5.64-00),
TJ - 11.63w/11.54 (11.80w-00)

GEENS Natalie U17 27.12.84, Solihull & S Heath :
3kW - 15:46.7, 5kW - 29:21.85 (27:38.4-00),
5kWR - 26:25, 10kWR - 57:12
GEORGE Lianne U15 25.11.86, Phoenix :
200 - 25.51
GIBBENS Rachel U17 31.01.86, Milton Keynes :
PV - 3.20, Hepl - 3912
GIBBS Amy U13 30.03.89, Bromley :
75 - 10.0, 100 - 13.2, 150 - 20.2,
200 - 27.4, 70HM - 11.5
GIBSON Jane 26.01.73, Manx H :
(nee KENNAUGH) 3kW - 14:21.01,
5kW - 25:16.2, 5kWR - 25:11 (24:44-99),
10kW - 53:58.1, 10kWR - 53:36 (51:34-99), 20kW - 1:47:39
GIBSON Sharon Angelia V40 31.12.61, Notts :
SP - 11.41 (13.50-82), JT - 49.36 (50.85-99)
GILBERT Helen U20 1.03.82, Birchfield :
HT - 45.28
GILBERT Laura U17 10.06.85, City of Norwich :
800 - 2:15.98
GILDING Nicola 16.05.72, Brighton :
100H - 14.8, LJ - 5.77 (5.84-89), TJ - 11.57
GILES Elaine Marian U20 25.04.83, Derby LAC :
DT - 36.43
GILES Luisa U20 23.02.82, City of Stoke :
400H - 65.95
GILLIBRAND Kerry 13.09.76, Sale :
(nee SMITHSON) 800 - 2:08.49 (2:08.4-98),
1500 - 4:13.02, 5MR - 27:45, 10kR - 34:10
GILLHAM Michele 8.10.74, Ashford :
400H - 63.7 (60.18-97)
GILLHESPY Laura Kate U13 3.12.88, Blackpool :
600 - 1:47.3, 800 - 2:26.5, PenM - 2064
GILROY Caoimhe U17 24.09.85, Rathfarnham :
HT - 33.96
GIMSON Laura U13 14.10.90, Leics Cor :
2kW - 11:35.0
GLAYSHER Jennifer U20 3.05.83, Preston :
HJ - 1.75
GLOVER Helen U17 17.06.86, Cornwall AC :
800 - 2:15.6, 1500 - 4:45.0, 3k - 10:10.73
GOAD Anne V40 11.08.58, Dartford :
PV - 2.60
GODBEER Sarah 10.06.77, Exeter :
LJ - 5.73w/5.58
GODDARD Nicola 26.04.70, Edinburgh WM :
(nee BARR) TJ - 11.82w/11.58 (12.42w-97/12.27-98)
GODDING-FELTHAM Lisa 24.11.69, White Horse :
Mar - 3:02:30 (2:56:50-99)
GONSE Rosalyn U20 1.03.82, Bed & Co/E Anglia Un :
100H - 14.50, JT - 40.71, Hep - 5053
GOODALL Hayley Jane U17 20.09.84, Ashford :
300H - 46.2, LJ - 5.53, Hepl - 3876 (3928-00)
GOODWIN Kim Louise 16.05.70, Kingston u Hull :
100 - 12.1w (12.0-88/12.06-87), 400 - 54.40
200 - 24.4w/24.7/25.13i (24.25w-96/24.3-99/24.49-96)
GORE Nicola U17 17.11.84, W Cheshire :
SP - 10.47 (10.56-00)
GORTON Victoria 9.05.77, Pendle :
HT - 37.20
GOSSMAN Nicola U15 4.11.86, City of Glasgow :
60 - 7.74i, 100 - 12.0w/12.09w/12.13,
200 - 24.81i/24.85
GOWING Paula 31.05.78, Bristol :
2KSTW - 7:04.39, 3KSTW - 11:26.15
GRADDEN Marilyn J. V40 26.01.61, Epsom & Ewell :
Mar - 3:04:07 (2:55:59-95)
GRAHAM Jennifer U20 1.07.84, Larkhall :
PV - 2.60i
GRAVES Sarah 4.06.74, Tamworth :
(see CHETWYND)
GRAY Jenny V40 21.06.60, Vauxhall :
Mar - 2:57:06
GRAY Linda 23.03.71, Peterborough :
JT - 52.86
GREEN Andrea 14.12.68, Dartford :
5MR - 26:38, 10kR - 34:03 (33:41-00),
10MR - 55:41, HMar - 73:56 (73:28-00)
GREEN Nicole 28.01.77, Enf & Har :
PV - 3.30i (3.60-99)
GREER Jane U20 19.07.84, Oxford City :
Hep - 3822
GREGORY Louise 11.05.74, Ipswich :
400H - 64.4 (62.2-95/64.16-92)
GRIFFITH Michelle Amanda 6.10.71, WSE&H :
TJ - 13.39i (14.14w-00/14.08-94)
GRIFFITHS Paula U20 10.02.82, Parkside :
DT - 36.39 (37.30-99)
GRIFFITHS Shirley 23.06.72, Wakefield :
800 - 2:11.91 (2:07.3-96),
1500 - 4:27.27 (4:14.41i-97/4:15.68-96),
3k - 9:48.8 (9:23.8-93)
GRIFFITHS Victoria U17 9.10.84, Liverpool H :
200 - 25.3 (25.49-00), 300 - 40.05,
400 - 57.5, LJ - 5.43 (5.55-00)
GRIMSTONE Jenny U23 30.04.79, Shaftesbury Barn :
SP - 11.94 (11.95-00), JT - 43.70
GROUT Joanne U15 17.09.86, Solihull & S Heath :
PenG - 2702
GRUNDY Catryn U17 25.05.86, Pontypridd :
PV - 2.70
GUEST Sarah 5.07.69, St Albans Striders :
Mar - 3:08:53
GUINEY Cheryl U17 24.09.85, Lagan Valley :
1500 - 4:46.8 (4:45.75-00), 3k - 10:07.93
GUNNING Deborah V35 31.08.65, WGreen & Ex L :
800 - 2:09.41 (2:05.65-93),
1500 - 4:24.41 (4:12.69-90),
5KR - 16:56 (16:08-95), 10kR - 34:57 (34:17-92)

HADLAND India U17 7.01.85, N Devon :
HJ - 1.70 (1.70-00)
HAGGETT Lea Maureen 9.05.72, Belgrave :
HJ - 1.80 (1.92-96)
HAIGH Rachael U13, Scunthorpe :
70HM - 11.9
HAINING Hayley 6.03.72, City of Glasgow :
5KR - 16:53 (15:49-98), 10kR - 33:40 (33:25-96)
HALES Sophie Rebecca U17 30.03.85, Steyning :
3kW - 14:20.70, 5kW - 25:31.5, 5kWR - 24:19,
10kWR - 53:18
HALFORD Katie U20 4.10.82, Exeter :
SP - 11.76, DT - 39.46
HALL Cicely Jane 12.10.78, C of Norwich/Newc Univ :
400H - 62.1/65.33 (60.83-97)
HALL Danielle U17 27.11.84, Cambridge Harriers :
SP - 10.92, DT - 41.28, HT - 31.86
HALL Jemima U17 20.02.85, Bolton :
DT - 32.30, HT - 30.31
HALL Rebecca A. U13 15.09.88, Boston TC :
70HM - 11.9, LJ - 4.82, SPM - 12.07, DTM - 34.16
HALLETT Jodie U13, Sussex Sch :
1500 - 5:05.8
HALLING Katie-Jo U17 13.01.85, Rhondda :
HT - 31.57
HALSALL Danielle U23 27.06.81, Liv H/Edge Hill Un :
200 - 25.1, 400 - 56.27
HALSALL Danielle U20 16.12.82, Southend :
HJ - 1.65i
HAMBLIN Nikki U15 20.05.88, Dorchester :
800 - 2:15.3, 1500 - 4:38.47
HAMILTON Christie U17 11.09.84, Cheltenham :
300 - 41.44
HAMILTON Louise U13 19.09.88, City of Edinburgh :
100 - 13.2

HAMMOND Michelle U17 26.03.85, Kernou :
HJ - 1.64
HANCOCK Coralie U17 1.03.85, Southampton City :
DT - 34.70
HANNAFIN Cathriona 19.09.72, Border/IRL :
TJ - 11.98w/11.59 (12.08-99)
HANSEN Ashia Nana 5.12.71, Shaftesbury Barnet :
TJ - 14.51 (15.16i-98/15.15-97)
HARBOTTLE Charlotte U13 25.06.89, Nuneaton :
70HM - 11.8
HARDING Faye Marie U17 7.09.85, Wrexham :
200 - 25.37w (25.6-00), 300 - 39.46, 400 - 58.2,
60HI - 9.28i, 80HI - 12.02w, 300H - 43.20,
400H - 60.06, LJ - 5.35i (5.13-00), Hepl - 4587
HARDING Jemma U23 15.02.79, Bedford & County :
PV - 3.30
HARDING Joanne V35 12.04.64, Trafford :
HT - 40.34 (40.99-00), JT - 38.88 (39.39-99)
HARDWICK Jeanette V50 26.08.51, Hastings :
Mar - 3:09:45
HARDY Rebecca Jana 11.11.68, Highgate Harriers :
DT - 44.38 (45.20-97), HT - 38.74 (40.93-98)
HARE Tracey U20 9.03.82, Ashford :
PV - 2.60 (2.80-00)
HARKNESS Camilla U15 10.01.87, Guildford & G :
100 - 12.5w/12.6, 200 - 25.4/25.95
HARLEY Lynsey U17 2.04.85, Pitreavie :
80HI - 12.0, 300H - 46.3/46.52 (46.1-00)
HARPER Jo U15 11.05.87, Cannock & Stafford :
1500 - 4:39.33
HARRIES Barbara V40 27.02.58, Cardiff :
Mar - 3:09:32 (3:02:27-94)
HARRIS Amy M. U15 14.09.87, Halesowen :
200 - 25.8, LJ - 5.45
HARRIS Elizabeth U23 19.12.80, Stevenage & NH :
PV - 2.70
HARRIS Frances 1.06.72, Newham & Essex B :
LJ - 5.62
HARRIS Francesca U13 25.07.89, Pembroke :
DTM - 26.25
HARRIS Rachel U20 17.07.82, Birchfield :
100 - 12.26w, 200 - 24.4w/24.49w/24.6/24.72, 400 - 56.87
HARRISON Deborah 13.11.78, Birchfield/Birm Univ. :
LJ - 5.80i/5.68 (6.02w-00/5.89-99)
HARRISON Fallon U17 1.05.85, Chesterfield :
DT - 37.60
HARRISON Ffiona U17 5.10.84, Pembroke :
3k - 10:40.87
HARRISON Fiona Jane U23 30.11.81, Barn/Leeds U :
60H - 8.65i, 100H - 14.01, HJ - 1.70 (1.71-99),
LJ - 5.89w/5.88 (5.91w-99), JT - 37.17,
Hep - 5208 (5279-00)
HARRISON Melanie U17 27.11.85, Havering :
DT - 35.62
HARRISON Sarah U23 1.03.79, Shaftesbury Barnet :
HT - 52.41 (54.15-99)
HARRISON Susan 6.08.71, Leamington :
5k - 17:12.5 (16:32.73-00), 10MR - 58:32 (57:24-00),
HMar - 76:47, Mar - 2:48:53
HARRISON Susanna J. V35 25.01.63, Woking :
Mar - 3:02:22
HART Emma U13 13.03.90, Southend :
DTM - 23.22
HART Louise U20 27.05.83, Stevenage & NH :
PV - 2.70
HART Sammy U15 13.04.87, Middlesbro & C :
1500 - 4:46.31
HART Siobhan 15.06.75, Enf & Har :
HT - 39.75
HARTIGAN Beverley Marie 10.06.67, Birchfield :
5KR - 16:45 (15:49-95), 5MR - 27:37 (27:09-00),
10kR - 33:46 (33:02-95), HMar - 74:06, Mar - 2:36:02
HARTSHORNE Gemma U17 19.01.85, Telford :
TJ - 11.26
HARVEY Amy Charlotte Elizabeth U20 23.04.82, Braint :
JT - 42.64 (47.57-00)
HARWOOD April U20 11.09.82, Rugby/Loughbro :
PV - 2.80
HASLER Suzanne U20 7.04.82, R Sutton Coldfield :
800 - 2:10.9 (2:10.6-99)
HASSELL Lucy 19.03.78, Oxford Univ :
5k - 17:24.2
HATCH Ruth L. U15 4.07.87, Epsom & Ewell :
LJ - 5.28w, TJ - 11.48w/11.47, PenG - 2617
HATCH Sharon V35 5.09.64, Sparta :
3k - 9:37.42
HATHAWAY Emily U23 22.12.79, R Sutton Coldfield :
800 - 2:11.1 (2:09.06-99), 1500 - 4:33.5
HAWKINS Layla U15 3.09.86, Bromley :
LJ - 5.23w/5.22, PenG - 2688 (2890-00)
HAWKINS Victoria U20 12.06.84, Halesowen :
HJ - 1.65
HAY Ruth Marion U15 4.11.87, Corby :
DT - 30.75
HAYWARD Melanie 14.07.71, East Hull :
10kR - 34:38, 10MR - 56:55, HMar - 77:17
HAZEL Louise U17 6.10.85, Peterborough :
100 - 12.01w/12.20, 200 - 25.57w (25.6-00),
60HI - 8.98i, 80HI - 11.6/11.76, 100H - 15.73,
HJ - 1.63, LJ - 5.53, Hepl - 4510
HEAD Christine U23 18.12.79, City of Norwich :
PV - 2.70 (2.70-00), JT - 41.71 (43.70-00)
HEATH Emma U15 1.10.86, Bristol :
60 - 8.05i, LJ - 5.26w
HEATH Jennifer 22.12.77, Sale :
3k - 9:42.2mx (9:41.83mx-00/9:58.1-99),
5k - 16:51.69, 5MR - 27:45
HEATHCOTE Miranda 18.09.72, Tonbridge :
3kW - 14:42.2, 5kW - 25:36.56,
10kWR - 53:11, 20kW - 1:54:11
HEFFERNAN Kim S. V35 20.12.66, Medway :
800 - 2:11.9 (2:07.1-87), 400H - 61.30
HEIL Belinda U20 8.03.82, Croydon :
SP - 12.43 (12.52-00), DT - 40.81,
HT - 47.27 (47.38-00)
HEINRICH Katharina 5.07.72, Rowntrees/GER :
DT - 39.59
HEMSWORTH Caroline V45 8.05.53, Falmouth RR :
Mar - 3:09:40
HENAGHAN Dianne V35 6.08.65, Morpeth :
3k - 9:24.49 (9:22.68-00), 5KR - 16:28
HENDERSON Elayne U15 31.07.87, Central :
HJ - 1.60
HENDRIKS Paula U20 25.01.83, Wolverhampton & B :
SP - 12.27, JT - 37.99 (38.32-99)
HENRY Lorraine 16.09.67, City of Norwich :
SP - 11.42 (13.09-88), DT - 39.07 (43.88-90)
HENTON Sarah 4.05.73, Birchfield :
DT - 43.79 (50.98-97)
HEPHER Joyce Elena V35 11.02.64, Bromley :
LJ - 6.24 (6.80w/6.75-85)
HERBERT Sarah U20 29.08.83, Bristol :
1500 - 4:33.23
HERMIT-SMITH Rachel U13 24.09.88, Halesowen :
LJ - 4.85
HESKETH Joanne 16.06.69, Steyning :
3kW - 15:13.41, 5kWR - 25:35, 10kW - 54:27.9,
10kWR - 53:08, 20kW - 1:50:35
HEWETH Karen V40 29.11.59, Hull Achilles :
DT - 36.06 (38.82-93)
HEWETT Alexandra U20 10.09.82, Hillingdon :
Hep - 4055
HEWITT Nicola Faye U15 11.12.87, Scunthorpe :
PV - 2.60

HICKS Annabel U17 29.09.84, Somerset Sch :
300 - 41.4
HICKS Jasmin U13 1.03.90, Newquay & Par :
PV - 1.85
HIGGINS Allison 8.04.72, Kilmarnock :
3k - 9:41.74, 5k - 16:47.10, 10k - 34:29.3mx,
10kR - 34:34, 2KSTW - 7:01.74,
3KSTW - 10:55.70
HIGGINS Dawn 10.12.75, Belgrave :
400 - 54.79 (53.24-00)
HIGGINS Emma U20 8.09.82, WSE&H :
SP - 11.91
HIGHAM Stephanie Anne U20 26.12.83, Border :
HJ - 1.83
HILL Amie U23 9.09.80, Oxford City/Birmingham Un :
DT - 36.79 (40.72-96)
HILL Cathy-Ann 4.05.77, Team Solent :
SP - 11.71 (13.10-96)
HILL Irie Heidi Alexa 16.01.69, WSE&H :
PV - 4.00 (4.20-00)
HILL Jenna U17 16.10.85, Sale :
800 - 2:13.86, 1500 - 4:34.49,
3k - 9:58.9mx/10:06.2
MCPHERSON/HILL Karen 6.11.72, Trafford :
800 - 2:11.45 (2:06.3-91)
HILL Kayleigh U13 12.12.88, Wigan :
100 - 13.1, SPM - 9.13, PenM - 2113
HILLS Nicky V35 23.05.65, Deal Triathlon :
Mar - 3:07:57
HIND Karen U23 31.07.79, Gateshead :
1500 - 4:32.8 (4:31.12-00), 5k - 16:04.1,
3k - 9:25.9e+ (9:18.59-00), 5KR - 16:10
HINDS Sally U17 2.02.86, Swansea :
SP - 11.98i/11.36, HT - 36.17
HINDS Tanya U15 19.05.88, Leics Cor :
100 - 12.5/12.57w/12.60
HINES Olivia U20 19.10.83, Herne Hill :
400 - 54.97, 800 - 2:06.01
HIRD Jocelyn U20 3.12.83, Wimborne :
PV - 2.90
HIRD Leyna U20 4.02.84, Exeter :
100H - 14.5/14.54w/14.67, 400H - 65.8
HITCHMAN Laura A. U13 14.10.88, Brighton :
100 - 13.1, 200 - 27.4
HOBBS Kim 12.12.78, Middlesbro & C :
PV - 2.70 (3.00-00)
HODGE Gowry P. V40 21.06.60, Highgate Harriers :
100H - 15.2 (14.0-92/14.52w-89/14.65-82),
400H - 59.5 (54.63-92)
HODGES Lindsay U20 21.09.82, Yeovil Oly/UWIC :
PV - 3.66i (3.55-99)
HOGSDEN Georgina U23 23.11.81, Sutton & District :
JT - 39.75 (41.62-00)
HOLDEN Diana 12.02.75, Belgrave :
HT - 56.21 (57.95-98)
HOLDSWORTH Catherine U17 3.01.86, Colchester H :
60HI - 9.29i, 80HI - 11.9, 300H - 46.2,
LJ - 5.38, Hepl - 4068
HOLDSWORTH Julie M. V40 22.07.61, Baildon :
Mar - 2:58:20
HOLLAND Vicky U17 12.01.86, Cheltenham :
1500 - 4:40.14
HOLLICK Lisa 1.01.70, Shaftesbury Barnet :
(see ELMORE)
HOLLMAN Anne Marie 18.02.74, Peterborough :
100H - 14.2/14.51 (13.98w-99/14.1-96/14.19-00),
HJ - 1.65 (1.70-99), LJ - 5.57 (5.67-96), SP - 12.07
HOLLMAN Julie Caroline 16.02.77, Peterborough :
200 - 24.6/24.75 (24.47w-98/24.72-00), 60H - 8.78i,
100H - 14.19w/14.2/14.33 (14.1w-99/14.14w/14.24-98,
HJ - 1.83, LJ - 6.37w/6.35 (6.51-00),
SP - 12.98i/12.40 (12.64-00), JT - 38.83,
Hep - 5933
HOLLOWAY Carys U20 23.07.82, Brecon :
PV - 2.80 (2.90-00)
HOLLOWAY Joanne 10.05.76, WSE&H :
SP - 11.28 (12.02i-96/12.00-98), HT - 51.04
HOLMES Claire U17 11.08.85, Wigan :
PV - 3.20
HOLMES Kelly 19.04.70, Ealing,Southall & Mx :
600 - 1:27.60+ (1:26e-00/1:26.0+-95),
800 - 1:57.88 (1:56.21-95),
1k - 2:43.69A (2:32.55-97),
1500 - 4:31.68A (3:58.07-97)
HOLMES Sarah U17 21.11.85, Woking :
100 - 12.59
HOLT Gemma 20.12.72, AF&D :
LJ - 5.76 (6.03A-99/5.99-98), TJ - 11.40
HOLT Sarah Joanne U15 17.04.87, Spenborough :
DT - 32.13
HOOD Georgina U13 20.11.88, Oxford City :
HJ - 1.48
HOOD Hayley Marie U17 12.09.85, Sale :
DT - 33.73 (33.96-00)
HOPKINS Emma U15 16.09.86, Leics Cor :
800 - 2:11.1
HORNBY Emma 12.12.73, Birchfield :
PV - 3.75 (3.91-98)
HORNE Katherine Ann U23 23.05.79, City of Glasgow/
Loughbro : HT - 43.01
HORNER Verina 15.09.72, Middlesbro & C :
HT - 42.26
HOROVITZ Gillian P. V45 7.06.55, AF&D :
Mar - 2:50:12 (2:36:52-92)
HORWILL Katherine 26.01.75, Dudley & Stourbridge :
3kW - 14:47.59i/15:17.6 (13:59.89-99),
5kWR - 25:22 (24:37-99), 10kWR - 53:55 (49:38-99)
HOSKINS Lorraine U13, Rowheath :
75 - 10.1, 100 - 13.1, 150 - 19.6
HOUNSLOW Anastasia U20 13.12.82, Guildford & G :
400H - 65.7
HOURIHAN Alyson J. V40 17.10.60, Cardiff :
SP - 11.52i/11.35 (12.41-92),
DT - 41.26 (43.58-92)
HOWARD Amy U15 3.03.87, Skyrac :
SPG - 10.55, DT - 32.30
HOWARD Anna U20 18.07.83, Oxford City :
HT - 41.52
HOWARD Rachel U15 5.08.87, Chesterfield :
HJ - 1.59
HOWE Catherine U17 12.12.84, Chelmsford :
HJ - 1.66
HOWELL Gabrielle U20 25.01.82, Shaft B/Birm Univ. :
400 - 55.86 (54.7-98/54.98-99)
HOWES Lucy U17 27.06.86, Thurrock :
HJ - 1.66
HOWLETT Jackie V35 11.05.64, Hallamshire :
Mar - 3:04:46
HOYLE Anna U17 12.02.85, Preston :
JT - 36.94
HUBBARD Vikki U13 13.07.89, Grantham :
HJ - 1.46
HUCK Claire U15 11.10.86, Kendal :
HJ - 1.64, PenG - 2867
HUGHES Elizabeth 9.06.77, Bromley :
PV - 3.75
HUGHES Johanne 7.02.71, Shaftesbury Barnet :
PV - 2.90 (3.13-99)
HUGHES Maggie 16.04.72, Eastleigh RC :
Mar - 3:04:33
HULSE Natalie U20 2.12.82, City of Stoke :
HJ - 1.70 (1.70-98), Hep - 4419
HUMBERSTONE Sarah U23 6.07.81, Clee/Hull Univ :
HJ - 1.67 (1.68-98)
HUMBLE Amanda U23 15.08.79, Liverpool H :
PV - 2.90

HUMPHREYS Danielle U20 16.05.84, Mansfield :
LJ - 5.80
HUMPHREYS Sarah U17 16.10.84, Border :
LJ - 6.02w/5.86
HUMPHRIES Katherine U17 28.11.85, Exeter :
800 - 2:16.4mx, 3k - 10:28.15
HUNT Emma U17 25.04.86, Shaftesbury Barnet :
800 - 2:14.5, 1500 - 4:34.12, 3k - 10:00.65
HUNTER Donna U23 9.10.81, Pitreavie/Stirling Univ :
PV - 3.10i/3.00 (3.10-00)
HUNTRISS Rosemary U15 9.10.86, Warrington :
HJ - 1.61, PenG - 2663
HURFORD Alison J. V40 11.10.60, Bristol :
2KSTW - 7:23.5
HURST Jodie 21.06.77, Sale :
TJ - 12.32i/11.98 (12.64-00)
HUTCHISON Ann-Marie 21.08.77, Neath :
1500 - 4:23.13, 3k - 9:20.93mx (9:42.52-00),
5k - 17:05.34, 5KR - 16:58, 5MR - 27:20
HUTCHISON Fiona 18.01.77, City of Glasgow :
TJ - 11.46
HUTT Donna-Louise 6.06.72, Northampton :
100H - 14.63 (14.4-91)
HYNAN Julie U23 23.05.80, Trafford :
PV - 2.80 (3.00-99)

INGMAN Jilly 17.08.78, Barnsley :
1500 - 4:25.65 (4:19.3-99),
3k - 9:44.36i/9:47.7 (9:12.37mx-99/9:16.42-00),
5k - 16:38.53 (15:59.00-99)
INIEKIO Nimi U15 25.10.86, Brighton :
SPG - 11.36
IRVING Ruth 20.07.74, Edinburgh WM :
LJ - 6.33

JACKSON Lorna J. 9.01.74, Edinburgh WM :
JT - 52.74 (57.19-00)
JACKSON Victoria U17 17.01.86, Wigan :
200 - 25.3w
JACOBS Kim Simone Geraldine V35 5.09.66, Shaft B :
100 - 11.85 (11.18w-97/11.31-88), 200 - 24.8mx (22.95-96)
JACOBS Yolande 9.11.76, Bristol/RSA :
SP - 11.60 (12.07-99), DT - 39.70 (42.93-99),
HT - 38.33 (40.91-99)
JALATIN Shebana U23 14.01.81, WGreen & EL/MAS :
HJ - 1.65
JAMES Angharad U23 7.04.79, Swansea/UWIC :
60 - 7.67i (7.61i-00),
100 - 12.0w/12.06 (11.87w/11.90-00), 200 - 24.37
JAMES Felicity U13 2.02.89, Cardiff :
75 - 9.8, 100 - 12.7db/12.93,
150 - 19.4, 200 - 26.72w/27.4
JAMES Nyree-Claire U17 28.12.84, Cardiff :
HT - 32.84
JAMES Vernicha U20 6.06.84, Belgrave :
60 - 7.60i (7.5i/7.52i-00),
100 - 11.43w/12.05 (11.85-00), 200 - 22.93
JAMES Vicky U23 13.05.81, Cheltenham :
JT - 38.24 (40.37-00)
JAMIESON Josie U15 17.07.87, Shetland :
JT - 32.64
JAMISON Victoria Anne 19.05.77, Lagan Valley :
100 - 12.20 (11.93-97), 200 - 24.70 (24.06-98),
300 - 38.66, 400 - 54.70 (52.87R/52.97-98)
JAQUES Hanna U13 8.08.89, WSE&H :
DTM - 23.82
JASPER Hayley Laurette U20 1.05.84, Huntingdon :
Hep - 3931
JELBERT Zoe U20 21.01.84, Newquay & Par :
800 - 2:08.85 (2:08.80-00), 1500 - 4:20.56,
3k - 9:48.55i (9:37.54i-00/10:11.9-99)
JENKINS Andrea Louise 4.10.75, Bedford & County :
SP - 11.64, DT - 41.02, HT - 50.73
JENKINS Beverley 6.02.70, Salford :
3k - 9:08.90mx/9:41.63 (9:16.02-00),
5k - 16:10.26 (16:08.96-99), 5MR - 27:27,
10k - 33:29.27, 10kR - 33:55
JENKINS Kate 26.03.74, Carnethy :
Mar - 3:03:20 (2:56:09-99)
JENNER Jackie 25.10.76, Tonbridge :
LJ - 5.54 (5.62-99), Hep - 3836
JENNINGS Joanne Loraine 20.09.69, Rugby :
HJ - 1.80 (1.94i-93/1.91-98)
JEPSON Lynsey Rebecca U15 12.01.87, Leics Cor :
800 - 2:14.81i/2:16.1 (2:13.18-00), 1500 - 4:37.09
JESSOP Michelle U17 21.09.85, Milton Keynes :
800 - 2:16.8
JOEL Alexa U20 19.09.83, Basildon :
3k - 9:57.75mx
JOHN Joanne E. U23 12.11.80, Eal,S & M/St. Marys U :
DT - 39.81 (40.92-00), HT - 47.63
JOHNS Karen Lesley U23 18.08.80, Shild/N'thumbria U :
800 - 2:09.35mx/2:09.8, 1500 - 4:31.22
JOHNSON Caroline 28.01.75, Sale :
(nee PIMBLETT) 1500 - 4:33.01 (4:21.3-96),
3k - 9:47.62 (9:18.6mx-98/9:25.8-97), 10kR - 34:04
JOHNSON Charmaine Rachael V35 4.06.63, E & E :
100H - 14.9w/14.96w/15.18 (14.36-94),
SP - 13.77 (14.29-93), Hep - 4908 (5495-92)
JOHNSON Jade U23 7.06.80, Herne Hill :
100 - 12.0 (11.72w/12.0-98/12.09-00),
LJ - 6.68w/6.59, TJ - 13.11
JOHNSON Julia U23 21.09.79, Invicta/Warwick Univ. :
TJ - 11.43i (12.50-98)
JOHNSON Lindsay U23 3.12.81, Trafford/Sheff UN :
PV - 2.90
JOHNSON Sinead U15 24.12.86, Telford :
60 - 7.74i, 100 - 11.92w/12.12, 200 - 25.13
JOHNSON Stacey U15 15.04.87, Cannock & Stafford :
800 - 2:17.6, 1500 - 4:44.6
JONES Amanda U17 7.10.84, Swansea :
1500 - 4:44.33
JONES Carly U15 24.12.86, Gateshead :
60 - 8.0i/8.20i
JONES Caroline U15 9.02.87, Chelmsford :
SPG - 10.62
JONES Claire U15 8.11.86, Pembroke :
100 - 12.4, 60HG - 9.42i, 75HG - 11.42
JONES Dawn 16.02.70, Hertford & Ware :
PV - 2.65
JONES Ffion U20 19.07.83, Deeside :
DT - 37.59
JONES Gemma U23 25.02.79, Cwmbran :
LJ - 5.56 (5.73-97)
JONES Gemma U17 12.11.84, Cardiff :
800 - 2:14.72i/2:16.80
JONES Gillian 2.11.70, St Helens :
Mar - 2:59:31
JONES Heather U15 10.09.86, Carmarthen :
200 - 25.58w/25.8/25.98 (25.88i-00),
60HI - 8.88i, 60HG - 8.79i, 75HG - 10.86
JONES Jillian Avril 23.12.69, AF&D :
800 - 2:12.7 (2:04.97-93)
JONES Katherine U17 21.01.85, Cannock & Stafford :
100 - 12.3/12.59w (12.38w/12.49-99),
200 - 24.90w/25.0/25.18
JONES Katie 4.01.77, Trafford :
400 - 56.99mx/57.4 (55.78-00),
100H - 14.6/14.92 (14.2w-00/14.56w/14.72-98,
400H - 61.21 (58.75-00)
JONES Kimberley U15 11.06.88, Newtown :
SPG - 10.64
JONES Laura U15 28.09.86, Hertford & Ware :
PenG - 2825
JONES Lowri U20 22.07.83, Cardiff :
100 - 12.21 (11.95w/12.05-99)

JONES Lucy U20 30.11.83, Bristol :
800 - 2:11.1
JONES Megan U17 5.03.86, AF&D :
2KSTW - 7:30.2
JONES Rebecca U20 17.01.83, Wrexham :
60H - 8.94i, 100H - 14.69 (14.65w-00),
HJ - 1.80 (1.83i/1.83-00), LJ - 5.55 (5.66w/5.65-00),
Hep - 4959 (5186-00)
JONES Sian U20 20.01.83, Swansea :
TJ - 11.47i/11.37
JONES Susan Eva 8.06.78, Trafford :
HJ - 1.95
JOSEPH Tracy Carol 29.11.69, Basingstoke & MH :
LJ - 5.91 (6.44w-97/6.39-98)
JOSLIN Lois U23 1.03.79, Enf & Har/Butler Un, USA :
3KSTW - 10:21.21
JOWETT Natalie U15 18.09.86, Milton Keynes :
100 - 12.4/12.49w, LJ - 5.22
JOYCE Rachel 16.06.78, :
Mar - 3:02:02
JURY Kerry 19.11.68, Wakefield :
200 - 24.32 (23.80w-98/24.12-99), 300 - 38.99,
60H - 8.59i (8.51i-00), 100H - 13.71,
HJ - 1.78 (1.81-97), LJ - 5.86 (6.08w-98/5.97-99),
SP - 11.52 (12.00-98),
Hep - 5687 (6005w-98/5908-99)

KANEEN Bridget V35 15.08.65, Manx H :
3kW - 15:45.98 (15:18.1-99),10kWR - 54:27,
5kW - 26:35.5 (26:33.5-00), 20kW - 1:55:46 (1:54:21-00)
KAY Deborah V40 7.11.60, Parkside :
Mar - 2:59:05 (2:47:36-93)
KAY Rachael U23 8.09.80, Wigan :
200 - 24.9/25.16i (24.44-95), 400 - 55.79i/56.2,
400H - 61.59 (58.91-99)
KEHLER Lisa Martine 15.03.67, Wolverhampton & B :
10kWR - 48:16 (45:03-98)
KEIGHT Hannah U17 22.06.85, R Sutton Coldfield :
HJ - 1.63 (1.65i/1.65-00)
KELLEHER Olivia Maria 9.10.75, WSE&H/IRL :
HT - 47.93 (57.53-99)
KELLY Jennifer Angela 20.06.70, Peterborough :
SP - 11.85 (14.88i-90/14.73-91)
KEMP Emma U17 11.10.84, Stevenage & NH :
300 - 40.63, 400 - 58.16
KEMP Jennifer U23 18.02.80, Liverpool H :
JT - 52.76
KEMP Thomasin U23 5.03.80, Oxford Univ :
800 - 2:10.52
KEMPSTER Ella U15 15.09.86, Newham & Essex B :
200 - 25.87w/25.9
KENNAUGH Jane 26.01.73, Manx H :
(see GIBSON)
KENNEY Laura U17 27.06.85, R Sutton Coldfield :
1500 - 4:40.93, 3k - 10:31.90
KENWRIGHT Dawn L. V45 30.08.55, Sarn Helen :
Mar - 3:09:33 (3:03:36-89)
KEYS Alison U23 11.07.81, Cannock & Stafford :
100H - 14.9w/15.01w (15.0-99)
KING Emma U23 25.07.81, Guernsey :
HT - 39.58 (42.02-00)
KING Rachel 11.05.76, Belgrave :
100 - 12.04 (11.8w-97/11.88-00),
60H - 8.40i (8.39i-99),
100H - 13.51 (13.44w-98/13.46-99)
KINNEAR Erin U17 26.10.84, Lagan Valley/IRL :
PV - 3.50
KIRBY Anna S. U15 16.09.86, Mandale :
800 - 2:16.17
KIRBY Joanna U15 26.10.87, Wirral :
75HG - 11.8
KIRK Laura U15 20.02.87, Skyrac :
1500 - 4:45.41
KIRTLEY Anne V35 12.02.66, Hallamshire :
Mar - 2:54:39
KNEEN Louise S. 14.08.74, Western (I.O.M.) :
SP - 11.68
KNIGHT Heather V35 27.09.63, Altrincham :
3k - 9:44.15mx (9:16.5mx-98/9:31.93-00)
KNIGHT Lisa U17 31.01.85, Cannock & Stafford :
3k - 10:29.46 (10:26.3-00)
KNIGHT Maureen 15.11.73, Belgrave :
HJ - 1.73i/1.65, TJ - 11.03, SP - 11.45
KNIGHT Stefanie U13 4.02.89, Herne Hill :
75 - 10.1, 100 - 13.0, 150 - 19.7, 200 - 26.8
KNIGHTS Lisa 12.07.71, Sutton-in-Ashfield :
Mar - 2:51:43 (2:48:59-00)
KNIGHTS Sarah 25.02.67, C of Norwich/E Anglia Un :
800 - 2:06.18, 1500 - 4:29.3 (4:26.74-00)
KNOWLES Jayne Clare 16.09.70, Altrincham :
(nee SPARK) 3KSTW - 10:49.39
KNOWLES Katie Rebecca U13 6.06.90, Cornwall AC :
600 - 1:47.2
KRUSE Hayley U13 1.01.89, Verlea :
PenM - 2052
KRZYWICKI Tara 9.03.74, Charnwood :
1500 - 4:26.3 (4:21.67-00),
3k - 9:20.1 (9:19.10-00),
10k - 33:59.79 (33:04.55-99), 10kR - 34:22,
HMar - 77:09, 2KSTW - 6:29.79, 3KSTW - 9:52.71
KWAKYE Jeanette U20 20.03.83, WGreen & Ex L :
60 - 7.66i, 100 - 11.88w/12.03 (11.8w-98)
KYDD Natalie U20 27.06.84, Motherwell :
400H - 60.6/62.51

LACEY Kiera U17 13.08.86, Cleethorpes :
PV - 2.60
LAING Wendy Jean V35 29.12.62, Liverpool H :
100H - 14.92 (14.14w-93/14.2-81/14.35-86),
HJ - 1.66i/1.65 (1.75-93), Hep - 4557 (5351-93)
LAKE Nicola U17 28.09.84, Cannock & Stafford :
300 - 40.9/41.27
LAMB Katy U20 21.08.82, Dartford :
HT - 53.13
LAMB Sarah U13, Solihull & S Heath :
PenM - 2119
LAMB Stephanie U13, Solihull & S Heath :
PenM - 2090
LAMB Susan 24.03.70, Sale :
1500 - 4:29.93 (4:11.57-96)
LAMB Vicky U17 11.10.84, Sale :
TJ - 10.80
LAMBERT Vicky U17 20.11.84, Wakefield :
300 - 41.29, LJ - 5.60w/5.55
LAMONT Sharon U17 12.08.86, Pitreavie :
800 - 2:16.52, 1500 - 4:40.92, 3k - 10:15.86
LANDER Jenna U17 31.08.85, Tamworth :
HT - 35.74
LANE Catherine 18.11.76, Dacorum & T/Glas Univ :
DT - 38.40 (40.72-98), HT - 42.95
LANE Sarah U23 4.06.81, Cardiff :
100H - 14.7, LJ - 5.56i/5.27 (5.56-96)
LANGOWSKI Laura U17 10.10.84, Tamworth :
300 - 40.97, 400 - 58.04
LANINI Lisa Mair U15 9.10.87, Wrexham :
800 - 2:17.01 (2:16.1-00)
LANNON Katia U17 14.09.85, Manchester :
LJ - 5.47w/5.33
LASHLEY Charlene U17 1.09.85, WSE&H :
60 - 7.91i
LAST Suzanne F. 11.01.70, Medway :
HT - 45.56 (49.68-00)
LATHAM Marie V40 18.10.60, Manx H :
50kW - 5:44:24
LATTO Emma J. 16.01.69, Herne Hill :
Mar - 2:52:18

LAUER Veronique 27.02.74, Belgrave/FRA :
3kW - 15:06.0
LAVENDER Julie 9.11.75, Sunderland :
HT - 46.79 (51.62-94)
LAW Kirsty U15 11.10.86, Inverness :
DT - 33.82
LAWRENCE Christine U17 4.04.86, Invicta :
JT - 36.88
LAWRENCE Sonia U23 19.01.80, Cardiff/UWIC :
PV - 3.90
LAWRENCE Susan 25.11.70, Thurrock :
DT - 37.73, HT - 39.19 (40.58-99)
LAWRENCE Victoria 9.06.73, Blackpool :
400 - 56.63i/56.9,
800 - 2:07.5mx/2:08.98 (2:03.52-96)
LAWS Jane V40 11.01.57, London Heathside :
Mar - 2:55:40
LAYBOURN Ruth U17 5.10.84, Wakefield :
300H - 46.91, LJ - 5.65, Hepl - 4161
LEADBETTER Helen U20 24.06.82, Ealing,S & Mx :
PV - 2.70
LEE Dorothea 28.07.77, Bristol :
3k - 9:50.74
LEES Tamsin U20 24.04.84, Newton Abbot :
100 - 12.26w (12.2/12.39-99)
LEGGATE Ellen Jane 4.02.78, Cirencester/Fife AC/
Camb Un : 800 - 2:08.23 (2:06.59-96),
1500 - 4:14.46, 3k - 9:08.7mx (9:45.2-98),
HMar - 77:42
LEIGH Kay V40 3.12.60, Todmorden :
Mar - 3:08:27 (3:03:51-98)
LEIGH Sandra Christine V35 26.02.66, Steve & NH :
400 - 57.23 (52.75-91), 400H - 64.5 (61.8-93/63.04-86)
LEITCH Rebecca U17 12.11.84, Lagan Valley :
300 - 40.96 (40.9-00), 400 - 58.74 (57.69-00)
LENG Jennifer U20 1.02.84, Sale :
JT - 38.51
LEWIS Ann V50 29.12.47, AF&D :
3kW - 16:02.2 (15:52.71i/15:55.0-96)
LEWIS Annabelle U13 20.03.89, Kingston u Hull :
100 - 13.0, 150 - 20.0, 200 - 27.0
LEWIS Denise 27.08.72, Birchfield :
200 - 24.60 (24.01w-00/24.10-97),
100H - 13.29w/13.42 (13.13-00),
HJ - 1.68 (1.87-99),
LJ - 6.53w/6.46 (6.77w-97/6.69-00),
SP - 15.45 (16.12-99), JT - 45.89 (51.13-00)
LEWIS Eugenie 10.10.74, Croydon :
PV - 3.20 (3.30-00), DT - 39.99
LEWIS Natalie U20 25.05.82, Cardiff/UWIC :
800 - 2:08.54 (2:08.15-00), 1500 - 4:24.69
LEYSHON Anna U23 19.01.80, Swansea/UWIC :
PV - 3.40i/3.30
LIA Hannah U17 15.11.84, Cardiff :
HT - 37.41 (38.04-00)
LIDSTER Claire U23 26.10.81, Team Solent :
100H - 15.09w, 400H - 63.20
LILLEY Emma 2.05.76, Bingley :
JT - 37.62
LILLEY Rebecca Anne Louise U15 4.03.88, Hales :
PV - 2.50
LINSKILL Claire U15 12.01.88, N Devon :
LJ - 5.30
LINTERN Candie U20 5.02.82, Crawley :
DT - 39.55 (44.49-99)
LISHMAN Bethan U20 15.11.83, Border :
HT - 38.26
LISTER Alison Claire U23 18.06.80, Oxford Univ :
PV - 2.60i/2.60 (2.80-00)
LISTON Bianca 28.05.78, WSE&H :
60H - 8.38i
LITTLE Ashley Louise U13 19.01.89, Leeds :
HJ - 1.52, PenM - 2169
LITTLE Stephanie U23 5.11.81, Newport :
Hep - 4214
LIVESEY Katherine Dawn U23 15.12.79, Blackpool/
Univ of Nebraska : 100 - 12.21,
200 - 24.33w/24.6 (24.78-97), 400 - 57.21,
60H - 8.75i, 100H - 13.80w/14.17 (14.15-00),
HJ - 1.75 (1.75-96), LJ - 5.91w/5.83, Hep - 5554
LIVINGS Jane 13.08.70, Wells :
5MR - 27:17, 10MR - 57:18, HMar - 77:03
LLEWELYN Gemma U15 23.04.87, Wigan :
SPG - 10.57, DT - 32.65
LLEWELYN Zoe U13 5.10.88, Newport :
100 - 13.2/13.28, 200 - 27.61w
LLOYD Jacqui-Ann U20 16.06.84, Carmarthen :
PV - 2.80
LLOYD Vicky U17 5.03.86, Pembroke :
TJ - 10.75i/10.74
LOCKLEY Angela U17 7.10.84, Trafford :
DT - 39.79, HT - 45.15
LODGE Joanna 6.01.68, WSE&H :
1500 - 4:33.2, 3k - 9:43.64,
5k - 16:24.55, HMar - 76:21 (75:21-99)
LOGAN Sharifa U13, Wolverhampton & B :
150 - 19.9
LOMAS Claire U23 18.04.80, C of Edinburgh/Edinb U :
100 - 11.76w, 100H - 14.62, TJ - 11.25i (11.02-97)
LONEY Jacqui U23 17.04.79, Elgin/Aberdeen Univ :
DT - 40.78, HT - 39.08
LONG Amy U15 4.03.87, Northampton :
60HG - 9.36i, 75HG - 11.71
LONG Emma U13, Poole :
DTM - 24.41
LONG Rebecca U15 3.10.86, Bingley :
PenG - 2788
LORD Dominique U15 8.04.87, Radley :
DT - 34.83
LOUISY Felicia 17.05.74, Luton :
60 - 7.67i, 100 - 12.16 (11.74-00),
200 - 24.78i/24.8/24.81 (24.06w/24.37-00)
LOWE Karen U20 3.05.82, Blackpool/Birmingham Un :
400H - 63.4/63.71 (62.20-99)
LOWE Larissa V35 19.08.63, WSE&H :
PV - 3.60i/3.60
LUCAS-READ Jade U20 17.01.84, Hercules Wimb :
100 - 11.64w/11.82
LUCK Sara U15 18.11.86, Havering :
800 - 2:14.52, 1500 - 4:44.1, PenG - 2706
LUMB Rebecca 3.09.77, Trafford :
PV - 3.60i/3.60
LUNDGREN Hollie U17 10.10.85, WSE&H :
Hepl - 3951
LYALL Stephanie Anne U13 3.02.89, Harmeny :
600 - 1:39.5, 800 - 2:23.2, 1500 - 4:59.08mx
LYNE Rebecca Louise U20 4.07.82, Hallam/Loughro :
400 - 55.38mx/55.4 (55.41-00), 800 - 2:05.05
LYNES Margaret Tracey V35 19.02.63, WGrn & Ex L :
SP - 15.31i/15.09 (16.57-94),
DT - 42.45 (44.76-93)
LYON Janet A. V35 12.03.62, Aberdeen :
PV - 2.65 (2.70-00)
LYONS Amanda U15 12.03.87, Edinburgh WM :
JT - 31.32

MACALISTER-HALL Emma U13 19.02.89, Rown :
800 - 2:25.74, 1200 - 3:57.0
MACAULEY Claire U15 27.09.86, Pitreavie :
800 - 2:17.79
MACDERMOTT Nicole U17 15.08.86, WSE&H :
100 - 12.34w/12.41
MACDOUGALL Lynne V35 18.02.65, City of Glasgow :
10kR - 34:30 (33:22-00), 10MR - 55:28,
HMar - 74:24, Mar - 2:37:20

MACLARTY Morag U17 10.02.86, Central :
800 - 2:07.25, 1500 - 4:33.63
MACNEILL Lindsay 29.03.78, Shettleston :
5k - 17:21.70mx
MACPHAIL Ann 3.05.70, City of Glasgow :
5MR - 27:51, HMar - 77:55 (76:26-00)
MACPHERSON Joan U23 18.09.80, Bas & MH/Brun U :
SP - 12.82, DT - 46.08, HT - 44.45
MACPHERSON Shona U23 31.08.80, C of Glasgow :
400H - 61.51 (61.47-99)
MACRAE Catherine U23 1.01.79, WSE&H :
PV - 3.60
MADDICK Nicola U15 6.08.87, Kingston u Hull :
800 - 2:14.32, 1500 - 4:48.3
MADDOX Keri 4.07.72, Sale :
100H - 13.24 (12.95-99),
400H - 57.18 (55.22-00)
MADGETT Stephanie U15 22.02.87, Bracknell :
75HG - 11.8 (11.73-00), LJ - 5.66w/5.52
MADUAKA Joice 30.09.73, WGreen & Ex L :
100 - 11.38w/11.42 (11.24-99),
200 - 23.04w/23.14A/23.31 (22.83-99)
MAGBADELO Naomi U15 16.04.87, Cambridge H :
SPG - 12.52, DT - 33.67
MAGNANINI Vanessa 26.10.81 U23, Rugby/RSA :
400H 63.2/63.70
MAGUIRE Kirsty U20 5.07.83, Edinburgh WM :
PV - 3.60
MAINSTONE Teresa U23 13.07.81, Horsham BS :
Hep - 4071
MAJOR Pippa V35 23.04.65, S London :
Mar - 3:01:48
MAKIN Emma U17 12.10.85, Warrington :
80HI - 11.98w/12.00, 300H - 45.0/45.35,
400H - 66.5
MALE Samantha Kate 11.04.76, AF&D :
100H - 14.72w/14.8 (14.25w/14.38-99)
MANCHESTER Amanda J. U13 27.09.88, Med & Maid :
JTM - 26.95
MANCHESTER Samantha U15 10.12.86, Med & Maid :
SPG - 11.46, DT - 32.83
MANGER Eloise U17 6.01.85, Chorley :
JT - 38.51
MANN Kelly U20 8.09.83, Birchfield :
5kW - 27:34.7 (27:15.4-99)
MARDLE Eleanor 27.07.78, Cardiff :
100 - 12.0w (12.1-96/12.20w/12.29-97)
MARKS Maiteland 19.09.76, Belgrave/Loughbro/USA :
60 - 7.5i/7.54i, 100 - 12.0,
200 - 24.52i/24.60, 400 - 53.65, 400H - 57.81
MARS Shaliena U13, Enf & Har :
150 - 20.1
MARSH Kate U17 15.05.86, City of Stoke :
Hepl - 3807
MARSHALL Carol Jane 11.01.77, Kingston u Hull :
SP - 13.36i/12.89 (14.24-97)
MARSHALL Jacqueline U23 20.07.79, Edinburgh WM :
PV - 3.00i (3.10-00)
MARSHALL Jolene U20 22.10.83, Ashford :
SP - 11.87
MARSHALL Lucy A. U23 28.11.81, Rugby :
HT - 51.94
MARSHALL Samantha U17 26.08.85, Pitreavie :
1500 - 4:45.92i/4:46.25
MARTELL Nicola U17 20.09.85, Harwich :
TJ - 10.85
MARTI Debora Jane 14.05.68, Bromley :
HJ - 1.78 (1.95i-97/1.94-96)
MARTIN Clare 14.09.74, Telford :
3k - 9:52.1, 5k - 17:23.22,
2KSTW - 6:53.02, 3KSTW - 10:44.69
MARTIN Clare 18.05.76, Newport :
3k - 9:45.50
MARTIN Debbie U23 30.11.79, Bristol :
PV - 2.90
MARTIN Karen Lesley 24.11.74, Derby LAC/WRAF :
JT - 55.85 (59.50-99)
MARTIN Kirsten 24.04.76, Newport :
400 - 57.26
MARTIN Lucy U15 8.11.86, Preston :
JT - 31.74
MARTIN Rachel 9.09.78, Sale/Crewe & Alsager :
HJ - 1.70i/1.70 (1.76-97)
MARTIN-CLARKE Susan J. V45 13.09.55, Dartford :
Mar - 3:07:25 (2:42:32-89)
MARTINDALE Rebecca U23 31.12.80, Border :
400 - 57.33
MARVIN Catherine Price U15 18.04.87, Isle of Wight :
HTG - 40.70
MASALIN Niina 3.01.77, Sale/FIN :
HJ - 1.76
MASLEN Meghan U13 19.10.88, Aberdeen :
PenM - 2097
MASON Emily U17 28.04.85, Wakefield :
100H - 15.6, HJ - 1.65
MASSEY Eva Maria U23 22.12.80, WSE&H :
SP - 15.32, DT - 47.23 (47.72-00), HT - 38.71
MASSEY Jacqueline Ann V35 24.01.64, Mansfield :
Mar - 2:58:29
MASSEY Kelly U17 11.01.86, Wolverhampton & B :
100 - 12.2/12.43, 200 - 25.1
MASSEY Sarah 2.07.68, Altrincham :
Mar - 2:52:06
MASSINGHAM Louise U15 28.02.87, Walton :
60HG - 9.22i, 75HG - 11.38w/11.47 (11.46-00)
MATHER Katie-Jane U17 7.01.86, Derby LAC :
100 - 12.3/12.58w, 200 - 25.3
MATHESON Patricia V45 7.01.54, Stourbridge RC :
Mar - 3:06:05
MATHEWS Jennifer Ann V35 3.07.62, Ashford :
400 - 56.8/57.44 (54.6-88/55.36-84),
400H - 61.0/61.35 (57.41-88)
MATHEWS Louise U20 27.10.83, Thurrock :
JT - 45.65
MATTHEW Denae U15 3.04.87, Leics Cor :
100 - 12.29w/12.31, 200 - 25.50, LJ - 5.56
MAWER Lisa 22.05.68, Bingley :
3k - 9:53.89 (9:44.36-94), 5k - 17:09.3 (17:02.84-94)
MAWER Rebecca U20 31.01.84, Grimsby :
HJ - 1.68i/1.66 (1.73-99)
MAXWELL Alison 13.11.70, Milton Keynes :
200 - 25.0 (25.00-00), 400 - 56.20 (55.0-00)
MAY Natasha U23 21.02.80, Sale/Sheff UN :
LJ - 5.90
MAYLOR Donna U20 20.05.82, Birchfield :
HJ - 1.70, SP - 11.37 (11.69-00)
MCALLISTER Alison U17 26.02.85, Sale :
TJ - 11.76
MCAULEY Laura U17 11.06.85, Mid Ulster :
TJ - 10.86w
MCCAFFREY Elaine U17 2.11.84, Abbeydale :
400 - 58.66
MCCALLA Michaela U13, Birchfield :
75 - 10.05, 150 - 20.16
MCCALLUM Michaela Jane V35 2.06.66, Winchester :
10MR - 58:51, HMar - 77:25 (76:07-00)
MCCLUNG Mary 19.12.71, Edinburgh WM :
400 - 55.7/55.84 (54.06-00),
800 - 2:05.02 (2:03.92-00)
MCCONNELL Lee 9.10.78, Shaftesbury Barnet :
200 - 23.66, 400 - 52.05
MCCORMACK Janine U15 17.09.86, Exeter :
75HG - 11.7
MCCUTCHEON Anna 3.03.68, Highgate H/CAN :
Mar - 3:05:25

MCDEVITT Julie 15.03.73, City of Glasgow :
(see BARNETT)
MCDIARMID Kirsteen U17 28.04.86, Pitreavie :
100 - 12.0w/12.15, 200 - 25.16
MCDONNELL Helen U13 19.02.89, Havering :
150 - 20.0, HJ - 1.53
MCDONNELL Lindsey-Ann U23 13.08.79, N Devon :
400H - 64.4, HJ - 1.80
MCDONNELL Morag 27.08.73, Saltwell :
3k - 9:54.32mx, 5k - 16:52.7,
5KR - 16:57, 10MR - 57:18
MCDOUGALL Joanne U23 23.08.79, Southport :
200 - 24.5, 400 - 55.18
MCGAWN Laura U17 13.04.85, Ayr Seaforth :
TJ - 10.92
MCGIVERN Stacy 14.12.76, Peterborough :
LJ - 5.61 (5.62-00), TJ - 11.49 (11.82w-00/11.64-95)
MCGORUM Fiona U13 10.11.88, Leics Cor :
2kW - 9:59.0, 3kW - 16:18.90
MCGOWAN Suzanne 13.04.78, Motherwell :
200 - 25.24 (24.79w-95/24.9/24.99-93), 400 - 56.50
MCGREAVY Sara U20 13.12.82, Leamington :
100H - 13.77w/13.94
MCGRENAGHAN Susan U20 11.07.83, Kilbarchan :
2KSTW - 7:26.45
MCGUIRE Leah Christine U15 30.01.87, Gt Yarmouth :
60HG - 9.22i, 75HG - 11.00w/11.16, LJ - 5.55
MCINTYRE Iona-Eilidh U20 14.03.83, Dunf & W Fife :
800 - 2:11.19i (2:11.00i-00/2:11.2-97)
MCKAY Jane 22.04.77, C of Glasgow/Strathclyde Un :
400 - 56.49 (55.8/55.82-00)
MCKELVIE Susan U17 15.06.85, Edinburgh WM :
HT - 40.43
MCKENNA Carolyn U20 4.05.84, Avonside :
100 - 12.29
MCKERNAN Jacqueline Lena V35 1.07.65, Lisburn :
DT - 50.33 (60.72-93)
MCLELLAN Shelley U20 21.03.83, Stevenage & NH :
SP - 12.56
MCLOUGHLIN Eleanor Rachel U13 9.02.89, Stockport :
600 - 1:41.0, 800 - 2:23.4, 1200 - 3:53.3,
1500 - 5:01.9
MCLOUGHLIN Lauren U20 8.09.82, Cardiff :
60H - 8.55i, 100H - 14.17w/14.20 (14.14w-00)
MCMANUS Lisa U17 3.01.86, Oadby & Wigston :
60HI - 9.15i, 80HI - 11.7/11.76w/11.82, 300H - 46.6
MCSWEENEY Nicola U13, Bucks Sch :
SPM - 9.40
MCVIE Siobhan U20 6.07.84, City of Glasgow :
LJ - 5.50 (5.76w/5.67-00)
MCWILLIAMS Elizabeth U15 3.06.87, Ballymena & A :
800 - 2:14.32
MEADOWS Carling U13 26.09.88, Wigan :
150 - 20.1, 200 - 27.6
MEADOWS Jennifer U23 17.04.81, Wigan :
100 - 11.8w/11.94, 200 - 23.90w (24.32-00),
400 - 53.32, 800 - 2:05.8
MEADOWS-SMITH Wendy U15 15.07.88, W Suffolk :
HJ - 1.60
MEITE Yasmine U17 6.09.84, Shildon :
60 - 7.93i (7.9i-00)
MELVIN Hazel 19.11.73, City of Glasgow :
HJ - 1.75i (1.85-97)
MENENDEZ Niobe J. V35 1.09.66, Steyning :
3kW - 13:14.73, 5kW - 23:46.30, 10kW - 49:52.1,
10kWR - 48:08, 20kW - 1:41:37 (1:40:12-99)
MERRILL Alexandra U17 12.05.86, Skyrac :
DT - 33.48, HT - 40.93
MERRY Emma Louise 2.07.74, Rugby :
SP - 12.51 (13.77-00), DT - 51.25 (57.75-99)
MERRY Katharine 21.09.74, Birchfield :
200 - 23.12 (22.76-00), 400 - 49.59
MERSH Rebecca U13 28.01.89, Sheffield RWC :
2kW - 10:38.1, 3kW - 16:03.25
MIGHTY A. D. Natasha 21.12.70, Radley/Wolvs Univ :
SP - 11.87
MILBORROW Clare 10.01.77, Horsham BS :
100 - 12.18 (12.16w-00), 60H - 8.57i (8.57i-00),
100H - 13.90 (13.61w-00/13.89-99)
MILES Imogen U17 7.08.86, Radley :
TJ - 10.70
MILES Kimberley U17 4.08.85, Aberdeen :
Hepl - 3872
MILES Susan U23 1.11.81, Hillingdon/UWIC :
3k - 9:56.86i (9:49.1mx/9:56.80-00), 5k - 17:00.64
MILLER Frances U17 26.12.84, Elgin :
SP - 12.80i/12.63, HT - 48.94
MILLER Kara U17 6.04.85, S London :
TJ - 11.14
MILLER Lisa U20 13.01.83, Cambridge Harriers :
60 - 7.7i, 100 - 11.94w,
200 - 24.0/24.09i/24.21, 400 - 53.29
MILLS Natalie U17 29.05.85, Mansfield :
300H - 45.70 (44.28-00), 400H - 66.1
MITCHELL Angela V35 17.08.65, Parkside :
DT - 40.63 (42.05-98)
MITCHELL Ceri U20 9.12.82, Southampton City :
800 - 2:12.4
MITCHELL Jeina Sophia 21.01.75, Croydon :
400 - 56.7 (55.9-97), 800 - 2:04.04 (2:03.36-97),
1500 - 4:14.14
MITCHELL Julie 3.10.74, Jarrow & Hebburn :
1500 - 4:29.2 (4:22.52-97)
MITCHELL Kerry U23 23.06.81, Lisburn :
400H - 64.46
MITCHELL Rebecca U20 10.12.83, Regent House :
100H - 15.31 (15.24-00)
MITCHELL Virginia C. V35 29.01.63, Woking :
400H - 65.5 (61.85-99)
MOFFITT Alison J. 6.10.69, WSE&H/N Down/IRL :
JT - 42.74 (47.72-99)
MOLE Jessica U15 19.03.87, Colchester H :
DT - 29.55
MOLLOY Jennifer U20 23.09.83, Bournemouth :
100H - 14.90, 400H - 63.6/64.29
MONAGHAN Sylveen 25.08.72, Sale :
JT - 43.74
MONDS Debra 25.02.78, Wigan :
DT - 37.67
MONTADOR Karen U23 14.05.79, Edinburgh WM :
800 - 2:10.99, 1500 - 4:25.6
MONTAGNANI Amelia U13 10.03.90, Herne Hill :
HJ - 1.48, LJ - 4.75, PenM - 2358
MOODIE Amanda U17 11.09.85, Edinburgh WM :
HT - 30.17
MOODY Karen 20.07.67, Cannock & Stafford :
HT - 37.48 (39.02-00)
MOONEY Tara U17 1.10.84, Lagan Valley :
PV - 2.70
MOORE Charlotte U17 4.01.85, Bournemouth :
400 - 57.0, 800 - 2:05.86,
1500 - 4:23.07, 3k - 9:53.48i (9:50.1-00)
MOORE Claire U20 29.03.82, Gateshead :
DT - 42.65
MOORE Sarah Louise 15.03.73, Bristol :
HT - 57.40
MORGAN Kelly U23 17.06.80, WSE&H :
JT - 54.49 (58.45-00)
MORGAN Lydia U20 1.09.83, Vale Royal :
SP - 11.61, DT - 40.43
MORGAN Sarah U20 9.05.84, Mandale :
HT - 42.25
MORGAN Stephanie 4.03.75, Cannock & Stafford :
LJ - 5.67 (5.97-93), TJ - 11.55 (11.76-94)

MORGANELLA Maria U23 2.10.79, Border :
100 - 12.28w, 200 - 25.1/25.12
MORRALL Zelah 21.01.69, Serpentine :
Mar - 2:56:27
MORRIS Emily U20 30.09.82, Kingston u Hull :
PV - 2.95 (3.00-99)
MORRIS Emma U17 21.02.86, South Shields :
300H - 45.4/46.50, HJ - 1.72, Hepl - 4224
MORRIS Kate U20 18.01.83, Medway :
SP - 12.49i/12.49, DT - 37.59
MORRIS Sharon 5.07.68, Bedford & County :
1500 - 4:21.37 (4:20.35-00),
3k - 9:32.4mx/9:37.56 (9:26.6mx-99/9:28.68-00),
10kR - 33:39, 10MR - 58:17, HMar - 74:04
MORRIS Tracy 25.12.69, Coventry Godiva :
PV - 2.80i/2.80 (2.90-99)
MORRISON Anastasia U15 4.09.86, Enf & Har :
100 - 12.58w
MORRISON Cherri A. U15 27.09.86, Sale :
PenG - 2861
MORRISON Kirsty 28.10.75, Medway :
JT - 53.10 (55.91-99)
MORTIMER Rowenna U17 4.07.86, Bristol :
200 - 25.4w, 300 - 40.4
MORTON Glenys V40 17.06.60, Leics Cor :
SP - 11.76 (11.84-84)
MOSELEY Cara L. U15 21.07.87, Cornwall Sch :
JT - 35.10
MOUNTENEY Helen U17 24.09.84, Birchfield :
JT - 40.70
MUGGERIDGE Elizabeth U17 11.11.84, Enf & Har :
3k - 10:37.2
MULLAN Stacy U15 15.09.86, Regent House :
75HG - 11.70
MULLINEUX Janine U15 12.02.87, Horwich :
JT - 33.01
MURPHY Catherine Ann 21.09.75, Shaftesbury Barn :
60 - 7.5imx (7.39i-00), 100 - 11.48,
200 - 23.35i/23.35w/23.74 (23.28-99), 400 - 51.84
MURPHY Tara U17 16.05.85, Team Solent :
LJ - 5.45
MURRAY Freya U20 20.09.83, Edinburgh WM :
800 - 2:11.44, 1500 - 4:25.10, 3k - 9:54.1
MURRAY Seonaid U17 16.03.85, Macclesfield :
300H - 45.7/46.03, 400H - 66.6
MURRAY-JESSEE Alison 13.01.67, City of Glasgow :
PV - 3.60i/3.60A/3.60 (3.95A-99/3.60-98)
MURTAGH Sarah U13 18.11.88, AVON S :
PV - 2.02
MUSGROVE Victoria V45 6.09.56, Wrexham :
100kR - 9:07:19
MYATT Julia V35 3.08.63, North Staffs RRA :
Mar - 3:01:38
MYERS Malindi 3.10.70, Headington :
Mar - 2:54:00
MYTON Aisha U20 3.01.84, Herne Hill :
TJ - 11.66

NAKAGIRI SAKA Lydia U23 20.01.79, WSE&H/SWE : TJ - 11.92
NASH Linsey U15 7.11.86, Basildon :
PenG - 2801
NASH Michelle U15 19.03.87, Herne Hill :
60 - 8.00i, 200 - 25.66i/25.77w/26.00
NATHAN Rachael U17 27.04.86, Lincoln Well :
800 - 2:12.8, 1500 - 4:27.5, 3k - 9:31.69
NAYLOR Claire 18.04.71, Sutton-in-Ashfield :
5MR - 27:18, HMar - 75:43
NELL Tania U17 21.05.86, Herne Hill :
SP - 10.46
NELSON Tatum L. 17.12.78, Sale :
60 - 7.57i (7.50i-96), 100 - 11.81w (11.63-97),
200 - 24.07
NESTER Michelle U17 18.02.85, Belgrave :
TJ - 10.91
NEWCOMBE Jo-Anne V35 20.02.65, Shaftesbury B :
HMar - 77:24 (74:54-97)
NEWCOMBE Rachel 25.02.67, Liverpool H :
400 - 57.5 (55.19-92),
800 - 2:04.98 (2:03.28-98), 1500 - 4:14.01
NEWINGTON Sophie U17 15.09.85, Swansea :
100 - 12.59 (12.56w-99), LJ - 5.36
NEWMAN Lauren U15 17.01.87, WGreen & Ex L :
PenG - 2612
NEWMAN Lucy U20 2.03.83, Horsham BS :
PV - 2.60 (2.80-99)
NEWMAN Sarah U23 7.10.79, Pembroke/UWIC :
400H - 64.48
NEWMAN Shelley Jean 8.08.73, Belgrave :
(nee DREW) SP - 12.18 (12.34-96),
DT - 59.10 (60.82-98)
NEWMAN Wendy 31.08.71, WGreen & Ex L :
JT - 38.20 (43.17-99)
NEWPORT Angela 21.10.70, Basingstoke & MH :
800 - 2:11.2 (2:03.67-94),
1500 - 4:18.68 (4:09.29-94),
3k - 9:08.12 (9:05.86mx-00),
5k - 15:57.32 (15:43.99-99)
NEWTON Catherine U17 25.10.85, Chesterfield :
HT - 32.30
NEWTON Maria Angela V35 22.07.66, Medway :
PV - 3.10i/3.10 (3.40-98)
NICCOLLS Janette 7.09.76, Thames Valley :
100 - 11.9w/12.20w (11.84w/12.0-96/12.04-99),
200 - 24.6w (24.6/24.79w/24.84-00)
NICHOLS Angela U17 22.09.84, Wycombe :
PV - 3.10
NICHOLS Sara U20 9.06.83, Wycombe :
PV - 2.80
NICOL Gemma U17 27.07.86, Dunfermline & W Fife :
200 - 24.9/25.57, 300 - 39.97i/40.16, 400 - 56.4
NICOLL Joanne U17 27.12.84, Motherwell :
TJ - 10.71
NOBLE Frances U17 2.05.86, Bingley :
LJ - 5.53, TJ - 10.79, Hepl - 3846
NOBLET Jackie U23 19.04.79, Preston :
400H - 65.8 (65.0/65.42-00)
NORFORD Natalia U20 29.09.82, Bedford & County :
HJ - 1.67 (1.73-99)
NORRISTON Cherelle U13 29.11.88, Thames Valley :
100 - 12.9/13.06, 200 - 26.9, LJ - 4.94
NORVILLE Danielle U20 18.01.83, Telford :
60 - 7.52i, 100 - 11.69w/11.75, 200 - 23.61
NOVAK Stephanie U15 20.09.86, Preston :
JT - 32.23
NOVELL Vicki U15 25.02.87, Hereford & Worcs Sch :
PenG - 2621
NUGENT Jessica Natalie Rosemary U20 27.08.84,
Shaftesbury B : 1500 - 4:33.2i/4:33.30 (4:29.37-00)
NURSE Laura U17 16.07.85, N Devon :
800 - 2:16.3mx, 1500 - 4:46.48, 3k - 10:35.4
NUTT Caroline U20 17.06.83, Scunthorpe :
PV - 3.50
NUTTING Nichola Kate U17 14.09.84, Oadby & Wig :
100 - 12.2/12.33w/12.35, 200 - 25.3
NWIDOBIE Kara U23 13.04.81, Blackpool :
SP - 12.97 (13.38-00), DT - 45.51
NWIDOBIE Nia U17 4.01.86, Blackpool :
TJ - 10.95
NYLEN Carolina U23 15.09.79, Loughbros/SWE :
400 - 56.87, 800 - 2:08.03
NYSTROM Sara U20 8.01.84, Isle of Wight/FIN :
HT - 40.30

O'CALLAGHAN Leanne 15.07.74, Wycombe/IRL :
60 - 7.69i (7.60i-00),
100 - 11.88w/12.1/12.26 (11.96-00),
200 - 24.70w/24.9/25.02 (24.50w/24.8/24.87i-00)
O'CONNOR Gayle U23 24.08.79, Liverpool H :
HJ - 1.75 (1.75-99)
O'DOWD Emma U23 25.04.80, Swindon/Loughbro :
1500 - 4:29.79, 3k - 9:35.59, 5k - 16:50.7
O'GORMAN Frances U17 29.10.84, Hastings :
HT - 32.75
O'GORMAN Lucy U17 11.02.86, Penistone Footpath R :
3k - 10:31.5
O'HALLORAN Charlotte U13, Cheltenham :
150 - 20.1
O'MARA Julie 11.02.76, Wakefield :
5k - 17:18.70, 10k - 34:56.01mx, 10kR - 34:58,
10MR - 57:39, HMar - 78:33 (78:04-00)
O'NEIL Melissa U15 13.02.87, Worthing :
JT - 36.37
O'REILLY Claire U13 7.09.88, Derby LAC :
HJ - 1.48
O'SULLIVAN Laura U20 30.07.82, Liverpool H :
HJ - 1.65 (1.69-99)
OAKES Sharon Elizabeth U20 26.08.82, Medway :
TJ - 11.08i (11.93-00/11.60?w-99)
OAKLEY Judy V35 10.09.65, Portsmouth :
Mar - 2:51:30
OATES Joanne 21.02.78, Bingley :
400H - 61.19, LJ - 5.60
ODUNSI Sola U15 22.08.87, Bedford & County :
100 - 12.6w
OGUN Bolanle 2.09.77, Birchfield/Wolvs Univ :
HT - 38.59
OHUROUGU Christine U20 17.05.84, Newham & E B :
200 - 25.0, 400 - 55.29
OKORO Marilyn U17 23.09.84, Shaftesbury Barnet :
300 - 40.54, 400 - 57.0/57.62
OKWUE Maurine Inkeira 13.05.78, Thames Valley :
TJ - 11.67w/11.54 (11.58-99)
OLIVER Emily U20 8.02.84, Blackheath :
HT - 37.96
OLOFINJANA Banke 14.05.72, Tower Hamlets :
200 - 25.1, LJ - 5.58 (5.70-97), JT - 38.23
OLSON Hannah Astrid U15 29.01.88, Ashford :
PV - 3.51
OLSON Natalie Victoria U17 9.05.86, Ashford :
PV - 3.50
ONIANWA Mary U23 20.01.81, Sutton & District :
100H - 15.1
ONUORA Amalachukwu U17 16.03.86, Belgrave :
100 - 11.97w/12.01, 200 - 24.96
ONUORA Anyika U17 28.10.84, Liverpool H :
100 - 11.86, 200 - 24.62
OOI Jemma U20 2.09.82, Middlesbro & C :
100H - 14.52w/14.6/14.66
OSAGEDE Diana U17 18.01.85, WGreen & Ex L :
TJ - 11.30
OSIFODUNRIN Nike U15 21.11.86, Edinburgh WM :
LJ - 5.32
OUGHTON Dominique U23 2.01.81, Team S/Birm Un :
800 - 2:12.90
OUGHTON Karen U20 26.01.83, Coventry Godiva :
60 - 7.64i, 100 - 11.96w/12.0/12.05, 200 - 25.09
OWBRIDGE Joanne U20 19.01.82, Kingston u Hull :
400 - 56.76
OWEN Caroline V35 62, :
Mar - 3:01:35
OWEN Charlotte U13 27.12.88, Colwyn Bay :
100 - 13.2w/13.24
OWEN Judith 20.06.71, S London :
400H - 64.0 (63.14-00)
OWEN Stephanie U15 31.12.86, Cannock & Stafford :
SPG - 12.08, DT - 30.09
OWUSU Lesley D. 21.12.78, WSE&H/U of Nebraska :
60 - 7.55i, 100 - 11.93w/11.99 (11.7w-98),
200 - 23.73i/23.75w/23.86, 400 - 52.15i/52.27,
600Y - 1:17.92i
OYEPITAN Abiodun U23 30.12.79, S B/Brunel Univ :
60 - 7.40i, 100 - 11.17w/11.29, 200 - 23.71

PACEY Jenny U20 5.02.83, Lincoln Well :
HJ - 1.65, TJ - 11.02, Hep - 4019 (4019-00)
PAGE Julie U20 11.07.84, Tamworth :
PV - 2.70
PALLANT Emma U13 4.06.89, AF&D :
800 - 2:26.69, 1k - 3:09.9, 1500 - 4:52.81
PALMER Aimee U15 7.11.86, Cannock & Stafford :
LJ - 5.41w/5.32
PALMER Carly U17 21.12.84, Milton Keynes :
TJ - 10.71
PALMER Gillian U23 30.12.80, EWM/Univ of Wash'ton :
1500 - 4:24.62 (4:22.93-00),
3k - 9:39.4 (9:16.12-00), 5k - 16:10.94 (15:56.58-00)
PALMER Karlene J. U23 23.10.80, WSE&H/Loughbro :
200 - 24.6w/24.7/24.88 (24.41w/24.42-97)
PALMER Krystal U17 7.09.84, Enniskillen :
800 - 2:14.9
PALMER-JOHNSON Ashleigh U15 19.09.86, WSE&H :
SPG - 11.44
PARDO Claire Anne U23 9.08.81, Guildford & G/
London U : HT - 42.34 (43.32-00)
PARKER Barbara A. V40 29.04.58, Jersey :
Mar - 2:58:17 (2:54:56-87)
PARKER Barbara U20 8.11.82, City of Norwich :
800 - 2:10.00
PARKER Carol Ann 22.09.69, Coventry Godiva :
SP - 13.38 (14.76i-91/14.71-90),
DT - 40.61 (44.70-89), HT - 38.12 (39.08-95)
PARKER Emily U17 7.11.84, Epsom & Ewell :
200 - 25.2w/25.39, 80HI - 11.70,
100H - 14.2w/14.58, 300H - 44.1/44.47,
400H - 62.0/63.16, LJ - 5.76,
TJ - 12.05w/12.01i/11.98, HepI - 4436w/4396
PARKINSON Amanda 21.07.71, Sale :
1500 - 4:26.3 (4:12.9unmx-95/4:14.19-98),5k - 15:54.9,
3k - 9:04.26mx/9:25.9e+/9:27.59 (9:02.67mx-00/9:19.6-96)
PARKINSON Danielle U23 2.09.81, Sale/Leeds Univ :
100H - 15.07, LJ - 5.62w (5.51-00),
Hep - 4688w/4626
PARKINSON-OVENS Hayley 5.12.75, Edinburgh WM :
800 - 2:07.69mx/2:08.4, 1500 - 4:19.87,
3k - 9:31.06
PARRY Carys L. U23 24.07.81, Rhondda/Loughbro :
HT - 54.12
PARRY Joanna 5.03.78, Southampton City :
JT - 37.55
PARRY Liza Marie U17 24.10.84, Dudley & Stourb :
300 - 39.71 (38.90-00), HepI - 4033 (4104-00)
PARRY Sheena 16.11.77, Rhondda :
HT - 42.80 (43.52-99)
PARSONS Stephanie U20 22.08.83, Fife AC :
HJ - 1.65i
PARSONS Zoe Marie U20 11.02.83, Ashford :
PV - 3.15
PARSONS Zoe 15.11.69, Rugby :
HT - 37.27 (38.29-00)
PASSLEY Rebekah U15 9.03.87, Herne Hill :
LJ - 5.86,
PenG - 3028
PATERSON Pamela U17 26.10.85, Edinburgh WM :
60 - 7.75i, 100 - 12.46w/12.55, 60HI - 8.94i,
80HI - 11.71w/11.8/11.87
PATRICK Elizabeth Sian 29.08.77, Birchfield :
LJ - 5.52 (5.65-00),
TJ - 12.82i/12.57w/12.38 (12.92-00)

PATTERSON Laura Joanne U23 31.01.81, Wycombe/ Staffs Univ : PV - 3.60i/3.60
PATTERSON Lesley U23 12.10.80, Loughborough C : 5k - 16:32.60
PATTINSON Helen Teresa 2.01.74, Preston : 800 - 2:04.93mx/2:05.50 (2:03.75-00), 1500 - 4:07.56 (4:04.82-00), 3k - 9:03.71, 10kR - 33:23
PAUTARD Marlene V35 25.10.62, Ranelagh : Mar - 3:08:20 (3:01:33-98)
PAUZERS Clare V35 2.08.62, Herne Hill : Mar - 2:44:35 (2:43:27-97)
PAVEY Joanne 20.09.73, Bristol : 2k - 5:53.14+ (5:44.4+e-00), 3k - 8:36.58, 5k - 15:00.56 (14:58.27-00)
PAXTON Henrietta U20 19.09.83, Birchfield : LJ - 5.58 (5.75-99)
PAYNE Judith A. U23 7.07.80, Wakefield/Camb Un : HJ - 1.73i/1.73 (1.76-98)
PEACOCK Julie 19.08.70, Shaftesbury Barnet : HJ - 1.70 (1.85-94)
PEACOCK Rachel U20 18.05.82, Bournem'th/Bath U : LJ - 5.69w (5.66-97), TJ - 12.10w/12.04
PEAKE Rebecca U20 22.06.83, Derby LAC : SP - 14.34
PEAKE Sally U17 8.02.86, Wirral : 60HI - 9.25i, 80HI - 11.9, LJ - 5.56/5.56w, TJ - 11.37
PEARCE Caroline U23 1.09.80, Huntingdon/Lough : 100H - 14.2w/14.32, LJ - 5.74w/5.60 (5.83-99), Hep - 4795
PEARSON Claire 23.09.78, Leics Cor/Loughbro : 60H - 8.99i (8.82i-00), 100H - 14.50w/14.6/14.68 (14.18w/14.56-00)
PEARSON Helen U23 8.02.81, Cornwall AC/Birm Un : 3k - 9:32.81, 5k - 16:47.19
PECKHAM Rachel U15 14.02.87, Epsom & Ewell : 75HG - 11.6
PEET Josephine 4.12.71, Bristol : 100H - 14.9w/15.2 (14.59-93), 400H - 62.85 (61.00-99)
PELLING Amy U13 10.12.88, Kettering : HJ - 1.50
PENNET Catriona U20 10.10.83, Edinburgh WM : 60H - 8.96i, 100H - 15.1/15.30
PERCIVAL Deborah J. V35 22.04.62, Medway : 5MR - 27:54, 10MR - 57:37 (57:06-00), HMar - 77:23 (74:13-97)
PEREIRA Jennifer U17 8.08.85, Medway : 1500 - 4:44.1 (4:32.86-00), 3k - 10:15.78 (10:04.4-00)
PERKINS Emma U17 4.09.85, Worthing : 80HI - 11.9/12.08, HJ - 1.78, LJ - 5.46, HepI - 4520
PERRY Laura Helen Susan 4.06.75, Dudley & Stour : HT - 40.12 (42.62-00)
PERRY Victoria A. V40 25.11.57, Altrincham : Mar - 2:59:00
PETERSSON Cecilia, : 100kR - 10:04:12
PHILLIPS Gemma U23 27.10.80, Kendal/Birm Univ. : 5k - 17:29.4
PHILLIPS Lorraine 27.01.75, Team Solent : 400 - 57.0 (56.3-00/56.35-99), 800 - 2:07.3 (2:05.75mp-00)
PHILLIPS Nicola U20 23.04.83, Dartford : 3kW - 14:49.40i/15:46.1 (14:29.37i-00/14:49.59-99), 5kW - 27:38.1 (25:11.46-99), 5kWR - 25:59 (25:33-00)
PICKERING Sarah U20 26.10.83, Cannock & Stafford : 800 - 2:12.7 (2:12.02-00)
PICKERSGILL Melanie Jane 20.04.73, Trafford : 100 - 12.23w (12.06-99), 200 - 24.97w/25.16 (25.0-99/25.08-98)
PICKETT Sarah-Jane U17 24.10.84, AF&D : 2KSTW - 7:24.9, 300H - 44.7/45.61, 400H - 65.7
PICKVANCE Ruth V40 29.09.61, Swansea : 10kR - 34:52, HMar - 77:36, Mar - 2:45:23
PIDGEON Elizabeth Sarah 27.04.77, WGreen & Ex L : HT - 62.00 (63.61-00), JT - 39.86 (42.94-99)
PIDGEON Emily Claire U13 1.06.89, Gloucester L : 800 - 2:27.2, 1200 - 3:52.5, 1500 - 4:45.7i/4:54.51, 3k - 9:55.71i
PIDGEON Jane V35 23.01.64, Notts : 2KSTW - 7:17.78 (7:15.48-00), 3KSTW - 11:31.37
PIERRE Cherie U20 15.05.84, Shaftesbury Barnet : 200 - 25.06w (24.99-98)
PIERRE Michelle 30.09.73, Shaftesbury Barnet : 400 - 55.44 (52.77-97)
PIKE Gemma U15 13.07.87, City of Norwich : 75HG - 11.49
PIMBLETT Caroline 28.01.75, Sale : (see JOHNSON)
PINCOMBE Victoria 19.06.73, Bideford : 5MR - 27:40 (26:43-99), 10kR - 34:16 (34:04-99), 10MR - 57:40, HMar - 74:59, Mar - 2:43:52
PINEL Syreena U23 13.01.79, Birchfield : 100 - 12.24w (12.0w-99/12.1-00/12.12w-99/12.41-95), 200 - 24.71w/24.9 (24.32w/24.46-00), LJ - 5.86 (6.11-99)
PITTS Laura U17 9.01.86, Exeter : HJ - 1.69
PITTS Sally V40 7.03.61, Witney : Mar - 3:06:22 (3:06:07-96)
PITTWOOD Eloise U17 4.12.85, N Devon : 1500 - 4:43.00
PLATEAU Carolyn U15 22.08.88, Radley : 800 - 2:15.42
PLATEAU Natalie U17 19.10.84, Radley : 200 - 25.4 (25.56w), 300 - 40.74, 400 - 58.90, LJ - 5.45
POCOCK Nicola U23 9.05.79, AF&D : 400H - 64.1/65.00 (63.6-99/64.09-98)
POLHILL-THOMAS Sian U20 4.06.83, Liverpool H : 100H - 14.9/15.14 (14.9/14.99-00)
POLIUS Leandra U23 14.05.80, Newham & Essex B : TJ - 12.35w/12.23 (12.52-00)
PORAZINSKI Donna-Marie U23 28.01.81, Newport : 200 - 24.72w (25.24-98), 400H - 60.42
PORTER Katherine U20 19.08.82, Blackheath : 60H - 8.77i, 100H - 14.7 (14.4/14.41-99)
PORTER Sarah U23 11.12.79, Sutton & D/Birm Un : 60H - 8.99i (8.77i-99), 100H - 14.48 (14.1-99/14.12w-98/14.30-99)
POTTER Helen 25.06.74, Trafford : JT - 40.74
POTTER Jane U23 24.10.81, Charnwood : 1500 - 4:28.56 (4:26.63-00)
POTTER Juliet U23 24.10.81, Charnwood : 800 - 2:11.3, 1500 - 4:25.1, 3k - 9:21.36, 5k - 15:57.4
POTTER Susan U23 11.08.79, Bournemouth : 100H - 15.0/15.05w, 400H - 63.14
POWELL Pauline 17.05.73, Blackburn : 3k - 9:56.5 (9:41.5-98), 5k - 16:40.04, 10k - 34:52.46mx, 10kR - 34:18, HMar - 77:48
POWELL Xanine U23 21.05.79, Cambridge Harriers : 60 - 7.7i/7.74i, 100 - 11.96w/12.1, 200 - 24.74i/24.76 (24.61w?-00)
POWER Somma U17 18.08.85, Basildon : SP - 12.19i/12.13, DT - 33.23
PRANGNELL Carly U17 4.03.86, Isle of Wight : HJ - 1.72
PRATT Julie U23 20.03.79, WGreen & Ex L : 100 - 12.19 (12.1-00), 200 - 24.5w/25.14 (24.8-99), 60H - 8.35i, 100H - 13.4w/13.43w/13.46 (13.28w/13.40-99)
PRESTON Stacie U13 12.05.89, AF&D : 1500 - 4:58.1

PRICE Anna U17 18.08.85, R Sutton Coldfield :
PV - 2.70, JT - 34.33
PRICE Danielle U15 8.11.86, Cwmbran :
100 - 12.59w
PRICE Sharon 10.12.75, R Sutton Coldfield :
100H - 14.9 (14.4w-95/14.43w-93/14.61-95)
PRITCHARD Amanda U23 18.03.80, Cardiff :
800 - 2:08.72i (2:07.32-96)
PRITCHETT Bernadine 25.01.67, WGreen & Ex L :
1500 - 4:33.88
PRITCHETT Kathy U20 11.04.84, Wrexham :
HJ - 1.65 (1.70-00)
PROCTOR Amanda 25.07.71, Basingstoke & MH :
Mar - 3:04:27
PROCTOR Elizabeth 31.10.72, Bolton :
1500 - 4:32.64mx (4:28.28mx-00/4:29.1-99)
PRYCE Janice V40 2.09.59, Notts :
TJ - 11.14i (11.18-00)
PRYKE Gail V40 1.04.60, Ipswich Jaffa :
Mar - 3:09:54
PULLINGER Stefanie U20 3.04.83, Bracknell :
100H - 13.9/14.34
PURKISS Melanie U23 11.03.79, Team Solent :
100 - 11.74w/12.0/12.05 (11.55w/11.76-99),
200 - 23.8w/24.06 (23.64w/23.80-99), 400 - 54.38
PYWELL Stephanie U15 12.06.87, Mansfield :
HJ - 1.75

RADCLIFFE Paula Jane 17.12.73, Bedford & Co :
1500 - 4:05.37, 2k - 5:39.3+e (5:39.20-93),
3k - 8:26.97, 2M - 9:27.6+e (9:27.5e-97/9:32.07-99),
5k - 14:32.44, 5KR - 14:57,
5MR - 24:48+/25:18 (24:47-99),
10k - 30:55.80 (30:26.97-00),
10kR - 30:47, HMar - 66:47
RADON Christina U23 12.07.79, Shaft B/Birm U :
3k - 9:46.2
RAINFORD Shani U15 6.07.87, Herne Hill :
HJ - 1.66, JT - 32.08, PenG - 2640
RAMSAY Lucy U15 2.06.87, Brighton :
HJ - 1.64, LJ - 5.61w/5.41
RANDALL Charlotte U23 10.05.80, Sutt & D/London U :
400H - 64.4/65.31 (63.18-00)
RATCLIFFE Karen V40 1.06.61, Coventry RWC :
3kW - 15:17.0 (14:02.29-93),
5kW - 25:21 (24:12.11-93),
10kW - 52:28.2 (49:39.0-91),
10kWR - 51:45 (48:30-94)
RAVEN Claire Heather 15.06.72, Coventry Godiva :
400 - 57.4 (53.99-92), 800 - 2:10.92 (2:03.15-97)
RAVEN Laura U17 12.03.85, Cambridge Harriers :
300H - 45.3/45.95 (45.30-00)
RAWLING Kimberley U20 22.07.83, Newquay & Par :
DT - 38.43, HT - 40.98
REA Tracy U23 19.01.79, Rowntrees :
HT - 41.47
READ Katey U17 20.03.86, Stockport :
60HI - 9.03i, 80HI - 11.9, 300H - 45.36
READER Jennifer 23.12.77, Southampton City :
(see DEW)
REAL Natalie U15 14.11.87, Bournemouth :
1500 - 4:49.9mx (4:58.7-00)
REDD Samantha U20 16.02.84, Brighton :
JT - 47.13
REDMAN Hollie U17 12.12.85, Braintree :
DT - 35.40, HT - 31.67
REDMOND Laura A. U23 19.04.81, Edinburgh WM :
100H - 14.86w/14.97, HJ - 1.70i/1.66 (1.70-00),
LJ - 5.69, SP - 12.22, Hep - 5114
REED Kate U20 28.09.82, Bristol :
800 - 2:08.57, 1500 - 4:30.9, 3k - 9:48.6
REED Laura U17 6.10.84, Bristol :
LJ - 5.48w/5.39

REES Charlotte U20 14.06.84, Swansea :
JT - 42.73 (43.11-00)
REEVES Claire U20 31.07.84, Dartford :
3kW - 15:48.2, 5kW - 27:44.6,
5kWR - 26:55 (26:47-00),
10kWR - 55:08 (54:51-00)
REID Emma U23 5.01.81, Edinburgh WM :
100H - 14.96 (14.9-00),
400H - 64.0/65.12 (62.60-00)
REID Rebecca U20 9.11.83, Barrow & Furness :
400H - 65.8, Hep - 4043
REILLY Sarah E. 3.07.73, Birchfield/IRL :
60 - 7.58i (7.46i-00),
100 - 11.53w/11.63 (11.45wIRE/11.49IRE-00),
200 - 23.02, 300 - 37.30, 400 - 54.64
RENNISON Amy U20 15.06.83, Sale :
PV - 3.10i/3.10 (3.10-99)
RENOUF Katie U15 3.06.87, Exeter :
HJ - 1.64, PenG - 2771
RETBURG Isobel U13, Grantham :
SPM - 10.04
REYNOLDS Kay Suzzanne 15.09.67, Radley :
100 - 12.1, 60H - 8.88i (8.58i-99),
100H - 14.1/14.58 (13.9-99/13.96w-00/14.03-99)
REYNOLDS Lauren U17 3.10.84, Huntingdon :
800 - 2:15.3, 1500 - 4:41.1
REYNOLDS Nicky U17 24.06.85, Birchfield :
3kW - 16:17.92 (16:01.9-00),
5kW - 27:57.3, 5kWR - 26:32
RHODES Josephine U17 22.03.86, Swindon :
1500 - 4:44.2, 3k - 10:27.83
RHULE Candee U15 16.09.87, Southwark :
SPG - 12.18
RICE Sonia U23 8.01.81, Coventry Godiva :
200 - 24.5w/24.78 (24.7-00)
RICHARDS Lara Elesia U20 7.03.83, Newport :
LJ - 5.67i/5.59 (5.82w-99/5.80w?/5.75i/5.75-00
RICHARDS Shaunette U20 15.08.83, Birchfield :
SP - 11.27 (12.98lg/12.48-99)
RICHARDSON Eleanor U17 1.07.86, Inverness :
100 - 12.58
RICHARDSON Katie U20 12.09.82, Wakefield :
LJ - 5.63 (5.69-00)
RICHARDSON Marcia Maureen 10.02.72, WSE&H :
60 - 7.28i (7.24i-00),
100 - 11.42w/11.43 (11.29w/11.35-00),
200 - 23.6e/23.99 (23.4-93/23.53-95)
RIDGLEY Clare Louise 11.09.77, Team Solent :
PV - 3.50i/3.50 (3.60-98)
RIDGLEY Rebecca Jane U23 26.02.80, Team Solent/
Loughbro : PV - 3.20 (3.50-99)
RIDING Donna U20 28.11.83, Sale :
800 - 2:08.85
RIDLEY Laura U17 20.03.86, Preston :
100 - 12.2, TJ - 11.01
RIEDEL Jana 1.09.75, Reading :
400H - 63.5/65.26, HJ - 1.65
RILEY Charmaine U23 3.10.80, R Sutton Coldfield/
Cov Univ : 400 - 57.2
RILEY Hannah U20 9.07.82, Manx :
400H - 64.40
RILEY Samantha U13 31.10.88, Stockport :
JTM - 26.78
ROACH Gemma U20 16.02.83, WSE&H :
HT - 39.22
ROACH Justine U17 21.12.84, Leics Cor :
60HI - 8.70i, 80HI - 11.3/11.44,
100H - 15.3 (15.1-00), 300H - 42.50
ROBERTS Cara U17 24.05.85, Bournemouth :
60 - 7.94i, LJ - 5.47 (5.56-00)
ROBERTS Georgina U20 9.07.84, Bingley :
400H - 65.09

ROBERTS Kelly 24.01.76, Deeside :
HT - 42.39
ROBERTS Melanie 2.03.78, Liverpool H :
60 - 7.60i, 100 - 11.74w/11.92 (11.9-00),
200 - 24.4/24.87i (24.90-98)
ROBERTS Sarah 25.06.78, Forrest of Dean :
LJ - 5.73, TJ - 11.60
ROBERTS Susan Elizabeth U13 22.11.88, Team Sol :
75 - 10.1, 150 - 20.2
ROBERTS Suzanne 19.12.78, Wakefield/Loughbro :
HT - 57.62 (58.83-00)
ROBERTSON Hazel U15 27.07.87, Falkirk :
SPG - 10.85, DT - 29.97, HTG - 33.59
ROBIN Julie 16.01.77, Edinburgh WM/Royal Navy :
DT - 37.85 (45.10-94)
ROBINSON Claire 18.01.78, Basingst & MH/Birm Un :
400 - 55.75
ROBINSON Debra 31.01.68, Sutton-in-Ashfield :
10k - 34:52.41, 10kR - 34:08,
HMar - 75:07, Mar - 2:35:40
ROBINSON Laura U17 11.10.85, Wakefield :
200 - 25.31w/25.4, 300 - 41.10
ROBINSON Linsi U20 9.01.84, Nuneaton :
TJ - 11.96
ROBINSON Madeleine U23 13.10.81, Border/Glas Un:
HT - 42.57
ROBINSON Nicola Jane U17 16.04.86, Nuneaton :
100 - 12.2, 200 - 25.36, 80HI - 11.43w/11.50
ROBINSON Sian Louise U20 31.03.82, Nuneaton :
100 - 11.83w/12.00, 200 - 24.95
ROBINSON-SCANLON Taneisha 19.11.77, S B/IRL:
LJ - 5.69 (5.93-98), TJ - 12.72
ROBSON Carly U20 5.12.83, WSE&H :
TJ - 11.79 (11.83-00)
ROBSON Claire U20 9.01.84, Teesdale :
800 - 2:12.65
RODDIS Claire U20 22.12.83, Trafford :
Hep - 3837
RODGER Alison U17 29.10.84, Victoria Park AAC :
SP - 12.77i/12.67, DT - 38.99
RODGERS Lucy U15 1.07.87, Thurrock :
PenG - 2791
ROGER Kirsty 24.03.78, Inverness :
100H - 15.2 (14.6w-97/14.76-00)
ROGERS Bethany U13, Cannock & Stafford :
SPM - 9.34
ROGERS Clare U15 22.05.88, Cambridge & Colr'dge :
75HG - 11.78w/11.8/11.89
ROGERS Lorna Jane 10.01.74, Shaft B/Dundee HH :
(nee SILVER) 60H - 8.81i,
100H - 14.1/14.25 (14.13-00)
ROLES Philippa 1.03.78, Sale :
SP - 15.79i/15.19 (15.95i-99),
DT - 58.98 (60.00-99), HT - 43.82 (55.09-99)
ROLES Rebecca U23 14.12.79, Rugby :
SP - 13.23, DT - 51.79 (51.79-99)
ROLFE Vicky U23 27.08.80, Bristol :
800 - 2:12.26 (2:11.05-99)
RONEY Sarah U13 27.03.89, Giffnock :
100 - 13.1
ROONEY Claire U20 23.08.83, C of Glas/Strathcl Un :
100 - 12.02, 200 - 24.9
ROSCOE Helen U23 4.12.79, Sale/Loughborough :
60 - 7.59i, 100 - 11.73 (11.66w-00),
200 - 23.4w/23.80, PV - 3.50i/3.50 (3.50-00)
ROSS Joanna U23 18.02.81, Victoria Park AAC/
Glasgow Univ Cal : 800 - 2:07.35 (2:06.38-00)
ROSS-HURST Olivia U20 10.12.83, Hertford & Ware :
Hep - 3842
ROSTEK Malgorzata 25.03.77, City of Glasgow :
(see WALDROP)
ROTHENBAUGH Wendy V35 30.03.64, Derby LAC :
Mar - 3:06:57 (3:06:04-00)
ROTHMAN Kimberly V35 6.09.64, WSE&H :
LJ - 6.04 (6.19-00)
ROUGH Alison U20 1.06.83, City of Glasgow :
TJ - 11.26w/11.22 (11.31w-99/11.27i-00)
ROUTLEDGE Marian 9.05.71, Kingston u Hull :
HT - 43.27
ROWAN Melissa U13, Liverpool H :
1200 - 4:00.83
ROWE Deborah 8.09.72, Birchfield :
TJ - 12.97w/12.90 (13.14w/12.97-00)
ROYCE Victoria U15 6.06.87, Cambridge & Colr'dge :
JT - 30.70
RUDDOCK Ellena 23.02.76, Rugby :
60 - 7.67i (7.54i-98),
100 - 11.90w/11.9/12.12 (11.49w-00/11.63A-99/11.67-98),
200 - 24.11i/24.4w/24.6/25.07 (23.71-97)
RUSSELL Molly U17 3.08.86, Radley :
100 - 12.30, 200 - 25.3
RUTHERFORD Susannah Rose U23 26.02.79, Darl/Az U :
1500 - 4:29.13, 5k - 16:31.73

SADDLER Katie U15 15.01.88, Reading :
HJ - 1.60
SADLER Nicole U13 10.11.88, Ipswich :
200 - 27.0
SAGE Kathryn 27.03.76, Newport :
400 - 54.81i/56.7/56.91 (55.58-00), 800 - 2:10.70
SAINT-SMITH Tasha 20.12.75, Enf & Har :
DT - 40.14 (44.68-94)
SALMON Sarah 9.09.74, Newquay & Par :
800 - 2:12.92 (2:10.8-96),
1500 - 4:25.43 (4:24.00-96),
3k - 9:46.1 (9:27.75i-00/9:40.87-96)
SALT Christa V35 17.06.64, Basel :
600 - 1:33.09 (1:31.58i-00),
800 - 2:09.45 (2:06.15-99),
1k - 2:48.26 (2:45.83-00),
1500 - 4:29.06i (4:22.96-97),
3k - 9:56.83i (9:46.25i-95)
SAMUELS Belinda 29.11.78, Birchfield :
100H - 15.0 (14.50w-00/14.98-99), LJ - 5.81
SANDERS Nicola U20 23.06.82, Wycombe :
400 - 56.97i/57.07 (55.66-99),
400H - 61.1/61.54 (58.96-99)
SANDERS Rebecca U17 15.07.85, Saracens :
3k - 10:19.6
SANDERSON Charlotte Elizabeth U23 18.03.79, Bing/
University of Tulsa : 3k - 9:57.31i,
5k - 16:48.6, 10k - 34:25.78
SANDERSON Danielle V35 26.10.62, Watford :
100kR - 7:58:16
SANDISON Michelle U23 11.04.80, Stirling Univ :
5k - 17:16.38
SAPPINEN Sara U23 16.09.80, Havering/FIN :
400H - 65.5
SARGENT Claire U17 11.03.86, Havering :
80HI - 12.06
SARNER Shula 31.05.70, :
Mar - 3:05:51
SAUNDERS Rebecca U15 8.02.88, Dartford :
DT - 33.74
SAVAGE Stacey U17 30.12.84, Shaftesbury Barnet :
TJ - 11.18
SAYERS Goldie Katherine D. U20 16.07.82, Peterbro :
JT - 55.40
SCALES Kath 28.06.77, Tipton :
5MR - 27:47
SCHOFIELD Candace U17 3.11.84, Horsham BS :
SP - 11.16, DT - 35.26 (35.72-00), JT - 40.49
SCHOFIELD Nicola U15 13.09.86, Havering :
75HG - 11.59w/11.69
SCHOFIELD Sarah U13 8.10.88, Liverpool H :
150 - 20.0 (19.3un-00)

SCOTCHER Rebecca U20 2.07.82, Peterborough :
400 - 55.1/55.12 (54.28-99)
SCOTT Jackie U17 31.01.85, Pitreavie :
100 - 12.57, 200 - 25.27w/25.28, 300 - 40.3
SCOTT Jill U15 2.02.87, Sunderland :
1500 - 4:47.1
SCOTT Sabrina U23 2.06.79, Herne Hill :
100 - 11.50w/11.68, 200 - 24.1/24.40 (24.37-00)
SCOTT Sian U20 20.03.84, Bournemouth :
400H - 60.50
SCOTT Susan 26.09.77, City of Glasgow :
800 - 2:03.96, 1500 - 4:16.29 (4:16.16-99)
SCOTT Victoria Rosemary U23 21.09.80, Traff/Liv U :
DT - 38.81, HT - 55.42
SCOUGALL Laura U13, Birchfield :
800 - 2:27.2
SCULLY Teresa V40 1.10.61, :
Mar - 3:02:31 (2:55:37-99)
SELBIE Lynsey U20 9.03.83, Border/Nithsdale :
HT - 42.48 (42.97-00)
SELBY Jane 17.10.72, :
Mar - 2:56:59
SELWYN Alex U20 20.09.83, Coventry Godiva :
HJ - 1.70 (1.71-00)
SEMENOVA Marina V35 12.07.64, Birchfield :
HT - 44.67 (50.04-99)
SEMENYTSH Rosanna Marie U15 28.05.87, WSE&H :
JT - 34.37
SESTON Laura U23 9.02.79, Ipswich :
400 - 57.3 (55.16-99)
SHANNON Jill U20 23.04.82, Lagan Valley :
3k - 9:56.8mx
SHARP Carly U15 7.09.87, Edinburgh WM :
HJ - 1.59, PenG - 2746
SHARP Maria 8.12.73, Belgrave :
800 - 2:12.00 (2:08.73-95),
1500 - 4:25.60i/4:29.53 (4:22.30-00)
SHAW Amanda U17 28.09.84, Barnsley :
100 - 12.2/12.54, 200 - 25.29w/25.33
SHAW Emma U15 19.09.86, Skipton :
SPG - 11.29 (11.34-00), DT - 33.53
SHAW Georgina U17 13.03.86, Sale :
LJ - 5.43w/5.41
SHAW Lorraine A. 2.04.68, Sale :
SP - 12.18 (14.21-94), DT - 47.26 (55.04-94), HT - 68.15
SHEARER Angela U17 18.01.85, Aberdeen :
300H - 44.73
SHEPPARD Amanda 26.02.68, Wakefield :
DT - 37.22 (42.81-98)
SHERLIKER Kessia U17 9.11.85, Southampton City :
200 - 25.27 (25.01w/25.10-00)
SHIPLEY Lucie U15 19.10.86, Scunthorpe :
PenG - 2642
SHIPPEN Lisa-Marie U20 19.10.83, Morpeth :
HT - 39.00
SHIRLEY Laura U15 27.03.87, Basildon :
SPG - 11.57
SHORE Becky U13 2.09.88, WSE&H :
1k - 3:10.7
SHORTHOUSE Donna U17 8.10.84, Mansfield :
300 - 41.5
SIGGERY Alison U20 14.09.83, Carmarthen :
JT - 40.97 (41.11-00)
SIGGERY Sara U17 30.06.85, Carmarthen :
JT - 34.98
SILTO Katherine U20 12.08.83, Swindon :
HJ - 1.66, TJ - 11.24w/11.18 (11.25w/11.19-00)
SILVA Nikki U17 17.08.85, Hertford & Ware :
800 - 2:15.38
SILVER Lorna Jane 10.01.74, Shaft B/Dundee HH :
(see ROGERS)
SIMMONDS Anna U15 22.09.86, Worcester AC :
800 - 2:15.47
SIMPSON Jemma Louise U20 10.02.84, Newquay & P :
400 - 55.8, 800 - 2:06.62
SIMPSON Nadine U17 28.02.86, Stevenage & NH :
60HI - 9.27i, 80HI - 11.9, 100H - 15.3, 300H - 44.9,
HJ - 1.65, PV - 2.70, LJ - 5.39
SIMPSON Stacey Louise U15 25.01.88, Ayr Sch :
60 - 8.08i
SIMS Jemma U17 2.05.85, Notts :
60 - 7.83i (7.68i-00),
100 - 12.0/12.04w/12.15 (11.99w/12.15-00),
200 - 24.2/24.67w/24.68 (24.63-00)
SINDALL Karen U23 17.01.81, Ilford :
3k - 9:54.1
SINGER Lindsey U20 4.06.83, Birchfield :
400 - 56.6/57.14
SINGH Eshere U15 15.07.87, Exeter :
SPG - 10.99, DT - 30.32 (30.74-00)
SINGLETON Laura U17 6.04.85, Wolverhampton & B :
LJ - 5.61, Hepl - 3829w
SINGS Lucy U17 9.07.85, City of Plymouth :
300 - 40.76, 400 - 58.5
SKELTON Maria U23 18.05.80, Lagan Valley :
1500 - 4:31.95, 3k - 9:55.8mx
SKETCHLEY Katy 9.07.73, Team Solent :
60H - 8.75i (8.44i-97),
100H - 14.15 (13.57w/13.78-98)
SKINNER Kimberly U15 21.09.87, Falkirk :
100 - 12.5/12.62, 200 - 25.81, 60H - 9.42i,
PV - 3.50i/3.40, LJ - 5.20, PenG - 2794
SKORUPSKA Katharine Wanda Taylor 3.11.78, EWM :
10kR - 34:55
SKUCEK Emily U23 24.09.81, Newport/Birm Un :
JT - 40.32 (40.89-00)
SLADE Hannah U17 29.09.84, Yeovil Olympiads :
300H - 46.9
SLOAN Patricia A. V35 22.03.66, Salford :
Mar - 3:09:56 (2:54:41-98)
SLY Helen 13.12.67, Horsforth :
(nee BARBER) Mar - 3:01:40 (2:58:40-00)
SMALE Dorothy V40 26.05.60, WSE&H :
Mar - 3:03:50 (2:59:59-97)
SMALLWOOD Claire 15.03.77, Jarrow & Hebburn :
3k - 9:49.86
SMELLIE Natalie U20 16.01.82, WGreen & Ex L :
400 - 55.7/56.79 (56.72-00)
SMITH Alana U17 18.01.85, Edinburgh WM :
SP - 12.51, DT - 39.32
SMITH Caroline Jane U20 31.07.83, Radley :
PV - 3.20
SMITH Caroline A.L. U15 15.09.86, Havering :
PenG - 2673
SMITH Deandra U15 3.12.86, Stevenage & NH :
100 - 12.4/12.49, 200 - 25.64
SMITH Diane V40 15.11.60, Hull Achilles :
HT - 46.10
SMITH Elaine U20 16.05.83, Mandale :
LJ - 5.97
SMITH Grace U20 30.01.82, Sale/Bath Univ :
60H - 8.93i (8.93i-00), 100H - 14.47 (14.39w-00)
SMITH Helen Nicola U17 9.10.84, Basildon :
HJ - 1.68
SMITH Hilary 28.02.76, Birchfield :
PV - 3.83
SMITH Hollie U17 9.12.84, Chelmsford :
800 - 2:15.26
SMITH Janet Carole V35 7.10.64, WSE&H :
HT - 48.08 (50.62-97)
SMITH Jennifer U20 19.08.83, Warrington :
800 - 2:11.9
SMITH Joanne U13 23.09.88, Whitemoss :
100 - 13.1, 200 - 27.6
SMITH Julia Francis 69, Ixelles :
Mar - 2:58:23

SMITH Karen 25.12.78, Ashford :
PV - 2.70, SP - 11.81 (11.92-97)
SMITH Laura U20 21.01.84, Border :
JT - 40.63
SMITH Leonie M.E. U15 20.12.86, AF&D :
1500 - 4:38.70
SMITH Natasha 6.06.77, WSE&H :
SP - 14.00 (14.12-97), HT - 40.80 (44.00-98)
SMITH Nicola U20 6.03.82, AF&D :
JT - 38.28 (38.55-99)
SMITH Rosie U17 28.06.85, Durham City H :
1500 - 4:40.10, 3k - 10:28.17
SMITH Sarah 18.08.76, Peterborough :
400 - 57.07i (57.5-00)
SMITHSON Claire U20 3.08.83, Brighton :
SP - 14.68, DT - 54.81
SMITHSON Kerry 13.09.76, Sale :
(SEE GILLIBRAND)
SMY Catherine U15 7.04.87, Banchory :
HJ - 1.60
SNOOK Verity Beatrice 13.11.70, AF&D :
3kW - 15:45.4 (13:16.23-96)
SNOW Linzi U15 8.06.87, WGreen & Ex L :
800 - 2:14.67
SOTHERTON Kelly Jade 13.11.76, Birchfield :
60 - 7.75i (7.74i-98), 100 - 12.00 (11.80w/11.85-97),
200 - 24.01w/24.17 (24.03-97),
400 - 55.32 (54.17-97), 60H - 8.66i,
100H - 14.08w/14.19 (14.15-00), LJ - 6.28w/6.23,
400H - 61.8 (61.8-97), HJ - 1.73i/1.70 (1.75-97),
SP - 11.26 (11.84-98), Hep - 5410 (5585-97)
SOUTHGATE Kayleigh U15 15.01.88, C of Norwich :
SPG - 10.59i/10.58
SPARGO Jacqueline 12.01.71, Coventry Godiva :
LJ - 6.05? (6.11w-95/6.08-96)
SPEIGHT Natasha U15 9.09.87, Mansfield :
HJ - 1.60
SPELZINI Charlotte U20 7.01.83, Cambridge & Col :
SP - 13.99
SPENCE Natasha 8.11.74, Oxford City :
(nee TURNER) 100H - 14.8 (14.23w/14.4-93/15.28-92)
SPARK Jayne Clare 16.09.70, Altrincham :
(see KNOWLES)
SPENCER Amber U15 12.01.87, Southampton City :
DT - 32.82
SPENCER Amy U17 19.09.85, Belgrave :
60 - 7.54i, 100 - 11.66, 200 - 23.3w/23.45
SPENCER Elizabeth U17 25.04.85, Holmfirth :
3k - 10:24.36
SPINK Mandy V35 12.01.65, Long Eaton :
Mar - 2:50:58 (2:45:10-00)
SPRULES Lyn 11.09.75, Shaftesbury Barnet :
DT - 36.27 (40.72-93),
HT - 62.99 (63.96-00)
SQUIRES Stephanie U20 3.11.82, Rugby :
100 - 12.28w (12.3/12.43-99)
STAINES Linda V35 26.12.63, Basingstoke & MH :
200 - 24.7w/25.1 (23.1/23.51-89),
400 - 55.0/55.76 (50.98-91),
800 - 2:09.07 (2:01.82-93)
STAMP Melissa U23 5.07.81, Gateshead/Sund Univ :
PV - 3.00
STANFORD Non R. U13 8.01.89, Swansea :
800 - 2:26.9, 1200 - 3:49.6, 1500 - 4:55.14
STANLEY Joanne Marie 30.03.77, Middlesbro & C :
TJ - 11.66w/11.49 (11.90i/11.82w?-99/11.81-00)
STANTON Linda Mary 22.06.73, Sale :
PV - 3.40 (3.72-95)
STARES Hannah 13.11.78, Belgrave :
400 - 57.23i/57.3, 100H - 14.69w (14.9/14.93-00),
400H - 60.28
STEAD Caroline 14.09.71, Belgrave :
TJ - 12.43w/12.11 (12.67-96)
STENNETT Vanessa 3.06.69, Walton :
JT - 37.44 (37.82-00)
STEPHENS Tamsin Anne U23 2.08.80, Bir/Loughbro :
60H - 8.6i/8.67i (8.65i-00),
100H - 13.78w/13.96 (13.93-00),
400H - 63.36 (62.40-00), Hep - 4600
STEPHENSON Lynsey U15 18.11.86, Tipton :
JT - 31.31
STEVENSON Helen U17 4.12.84, Giffnock :
1500 - 4:45.5i
STEVENSON Nicola J. U13 8.05.89, Bridgend :
SPM - 10.83, DTM - 26.82
STEWART Staci U17 20.09.85, City of Glasgow :
60HI - 9.16i, 80HI - 11.8w/11.95,
300H - 46.8, HJ - 1.67
STILES Amy 6.02.75, Westbury :
5MR - 27:36, Mar - 2:45:02
STILL Sarah 24.09.75, Aberdeen :
200 - 25.03w/25.13 (24.4-99/24.48-00),
100H - 14.98w/15.18 (14.61-99),
HJ - 1.66i/1.65 (1.68-99), LJ - 5.84w/5.74 (5.85-99),
Hep - 4825 (5014-00)
STOATE Isabelle U17 16.07.86, N Devon :
800 - 2:14.35, 1500 - 4:39.26, 3k - 10:18.6
STOCKBRIDGE Lucy U23 1.07.79, Cambridge Un :
100 - 12.08w/12.21
STOKOE Ceri U20 19.04.82, Swansea :
HJ - 1.73i/1.66 (1.73-00)
STONES Katie U17 22.11.85, Kingston u Hull :
3kW - 14:21.90, 5kW - 26:47.3,
5kWR - 25:47, 10kWR - 54:40
STOREY Karen 8.11.68, Gateshead :
400 - 56.9/56.98
STRACHAN Emma U15 10.04.87, Leamington :
100 - 12.43w/12.50
STRAKER Julia U20 25.11.82, Morpeth :
TJ - 11.77
STREATFIELD Katharine U20 28.07.83, Soton City :
TJ - 12.17
STREET Joanne U20 30.10.82, Tamworth :
SP - 11.81i (12.55-00)
STREVENS Sarah U23 7.10.81, Newham & Essex B :
TJ - 11.18 (11.26-00)
STYLES Aimee U20 1.05.82, Dacorum & Tring :
JT - 37.37 (38.00-99)
SUDDES Joanne 27.01.77, Edinburgh WM :
100H - 14.7w (14.29w/14.4/14.53-99),
400H - 62.6/62.77
SULLIVAN Deborah 24.01.72, Havering :
800 - 2:12.7 (2:09.8-00), 1500 - 4:22.72 (4:21.12-99),
3k - 9:35.3 (9:34.30-97), 5KR - 16:32,
5k - 16:18.62 (16:07.51-00), 10MR - 58:27
SURMAN Jade U13 27.03.89, Birchfield :
70HM - 11.73, HJ - 1.47, LJ - 5.14, PenM - 2532w
SURMINSKI Swenja 30.09.75, Serpentine/GER :
Mar - 3:08:14
SUTTON Lucy U17 29.08.86, Oxford City :
SP - 10.80, DT - 34.27
SUTTON Marian R. V35 7.10.63, Westbury :
5MR - 27:52 (25:56+-97/26:48-99)
SWALLOW Jodie U23 23.06.81, Loughborough :
5k - 16:11.78
SWATHERIDGE Donna U17 4.03.85, Basingst & MH :
DT - 36.03
SWEENEY Rebecca U17 9.02.85, Sale :
200 - 25.3/25.59i (25.40-00),
300 - 39.91 (39.48-00), 400 - 57.6/57.74i/58.43
SWINGLER Val V35 18.12.66, :
Mar - 3:06:28
SYKES Nicola U15 30.06.87, Leighton Buzzard :
1500 - 4:41.06
SYMONDS Emma 5.06.77, City of Norwich :
400 - 55.04i/55.5 (54.6/54.86-96)

TAGILALA Sulueti U23 24.08.80, Army/FIJ :
SP - 12.13, DT - 36.10
TAIT Lorne U15 16.01.87, Elgin :
HTG - 33.16
TALBOT Nicola 17.02.72, Birchfield :
DT - 47.79 (54.24-93)
TALIA Sara U23 30.05.79, Loughborough Coll/SWE :
2KSTW - 7:30.16
TANNER Laura S. U15 13.11.86, AF&D :
800 - 2:18.98, 1500 - 4:49.1
TAPPIN Lia Adina U15 9.01.87, Enf & Har :
60 - 7.87i, 100 - 12.4, 200 - 24.98w/25.04
TARPLEE Claire U13 22.09.88, Solihull & S Heath :
800 - 2:26.6, 1200 - 3:54.54, 1500 - 5:04.3
TAS Meliha U13, Enf & Har :
70HM - 11.6
TAYLOR Charlotte U13 17.04.89, Colchester & T :
600 - 1:46.5
TAYLOR Helen U20 19.07.82, Wakefield :
HT - 51.34
TAYLOR Jan U20 5.11.83, Cheltenham :
HJ - 1.66
TAYLOR Katy U23 18.06.80, Cambridge University :
Hep - 4215
TAYLOR Lana U13 2.10.88, Derby LAC :
800 - 2:27.2
TAYLOR Laura U20 22.04.84, Radley :
Hep - 3984
TAYLOR Lauren U15 29.10.86, Radley :
LJ - 5.37w/5.20
TEALE Amy U20 30.12.82, North Shields Poly :
100H - 14.63w/14.9/14.93
TELFORD Rebekah 4.11.76, Trafford :
PV - 3.53
THACKRAY Penny D. 18.08.74, Wakefield :
1500 - 4:26.47 (4:22.4-97),
3k - 9:31.2 (9:23.5mx-96), 5k - 16:18.32 (16:16.01-97),
5MR - 27:10, 10k - 33:25.74, 10kR - 33:07
THAKE Jemma U17 17.12.85, West Suffolk :
200 - 25.2/25.24w (25.06-00), 300 - 39.84,
400 - 58.95
THERIN Lauren U17 19.01.86, Jersey :
SP - 10.55, DT - 35.19 (36.38-00), JT - 41.35
THIEME Helen U23 28.09.81, Birchfield :
100 - 12.22w, 200 - 23.9/24.32w/24.37, 400 - 52.75
THOM Pauline 2.08.70, Edinburgh WM :
1500 - 4:23.08 (4:22.31-98),
3k - 9:50.40i/9:51.22 (9:36.7-98)
THOMAS Hayley U15 16.12.86, Thurrock :
SPG - 12.46, DT - 30.80, JT - 40.78
THOMAS Kadi-Ann U17 10.02.86, Milton Keynes :
100 - 12.05w/12.11, 200 - 25.5
THOMAS Kelly U23 9.01.81, Sale/Loughborough :
100 - 11.71w/11.87 (11.83-00),
200 - 24.41w/24.58 (24.32-00)
THOMAS Michelle 16.10.71, Birchfield :
400 - 54.9/55.05 (52.47-99), 800 - 2:09.45
THOMAS Rachel U17 19.01.85, Leeds :
300 - 41.24 (40.81-00), 80HI - 12.0
THOMAS Sonia U23 16.05.79, Sale/Loughborough :
1500 - 4:31.03 (4:28.60-99),
3k - 9:40.93, 5k - 16:54.06 (16:52.00-99)
THOMPSON Finesse U13 30.03.90, WGreen & Ex L :
DTM - 30.48
THOMPSON Fiona U17 15.07.86, Central :
1500 - 4:42.4
THOMPSON Gemma U17 17.01.86, Sparta :
100 - 12.2/12.52, 200 - 25.5
THOMPSON Nicola 10.02.68, Charnwood :
Mar - 3:06:24
THOMPSON Rachael U17 15.11.85, Liverpool H :
300 - 41.1, 400 - 58.0, 800 - 2:10.26
THOMPSON Ruth 7.06.76, Pendle :
400H - 65.81 (64.4-00/65.52-97)
THOMSON Trudi V40 18.01.59, Pitreavie :
HMar - 77:40 (74:34-96), Mar - 2:41:49 (2:38:23-95)
THORNAL Danielle 9.08.75, :
800 - 2:06.55, 1500 - 4:24.63i+, 1M - 4:42.67
THORNE Alison 25.09.72, WSE&H :
200 - 25.03w (24.3-98/24.97-93),
400 - 55.27 (55.11-98)
THORNE Louretta 6.05.77, WSE&H :
400 - 55.8/55.89 (54.23-99)
THORPE Anna-Maria 15.07.71, Thames Valley :
LJ - 5.76w/5.62 (5.96w/5.94-00),
TJ - 12.23i/12.18w?/12.17 (12.84-99)
TINN Hollie U23 14.04.81, Rugby/UWIC :
PV - 3.00i/2.80
TIPPETT Sarah U13 9.04.89, Ipswich :
70HM - 11.6
TODD Sara L. U23 3.11.79, Jarrow & Hebburn :
100H - 14.6/14.88 (14.55-00),
400H - 62.81 (61.57-99), Hep - 4280
TOMLINSON Iyesha U17 19.02.86, WGreen & Ex L :
DT - 34.48
TONKS Sharon Jayne 18.04.70, Bromsgrove & R :
3kW - 14:02.55i/14:11.6 (14:07.8-00),
5kW - 24:20.46 (24:20.07-98), 5kWR - 23:54,
10kWR - 53:04 (49:46-00),
20kW - 1:46:15 (1:42:10sh-00)
TOWNS Lisa U23 19.04.79, WSE&H/Brunel Univ :
5k - 17:05.03
TOWNSEND Becky U15 29.03.87, Leeds :
800 - 2:18.7,
1500 - 4:46.03
TREMARCO Melissa U20 12.10.82, Wirral :
400H - 65.8
TRIGGS Claire E. U13 3.09.88, Witney :
LJ - 4.75
TROTMAN Joanna U23 5.10.80, Croy/Greenwich Un :
LJ - 6.02 (6.02?-00)
TROTMAN Lisa-Deane U20 6.12.82, Trafford :
200 - 24.37w/24.8/25.08, 400 - 56.8
TUCKER Jessica U15 3.06.87, Brecon :
60 - 8.05i, 100 - 12.49w
TUCKER Lianne U15 18.07.87, Blaydon :
DT - 32.77
TUCKER Lynette U15 18.07.87, Blaydon :
SPG - 11.10
TULLETT Hayley 17.02.73, Swansea :
800 - 2:04.67 (2:01.25-00),
1k - 2:45.41i+, 1500 - 4:03.54 (4:01.23-00),
1M - 4:26.52i (4:26.50i-00/4:48.88-95),
3k - 8:45.36i/8:51.73 (8:45.39-00)
TUNALEY Victoria U20 4.06.84, Ipswich :
400 - 56.56
TURNER Charmaine U23 5.12.81, Team Sol/Brunel U :
TJ - 12.05
TURNER Karlene U17 9.01.85, WSE&H :
LJ - 5.79 (5.83-00)
TURNER Laura Kate U20 12.08.82, Parkside/Brunel U :
100H - 14.35w/14.5/14.61
TURNER Michelle 25.12.77, Parkside :
100 - 12.1 (11.9w-99/11.92-00), 200 - 24.9
TURNER Natasha 8.11.74, Oxford City :
(see SPENCE)
TURTLE Gemma Anne U17 15.05.86, Chiltern :
800 - 2:16.6, 1500 - 4:35.78,
3k - 9:59.0mx/10:08.50
TURTON Judy U20 26.05.84, Wycombe :
PV - 3.20

UNWIN Denise U13 6.01.89, Stockport :
SPM - 9.22
UPHILL Katherine U15 19.02.88, Bristol :
1500 - 4:49.32
UPTON Sophie L. U17 18.09.85, Solihull & S Heath :
HJ - 1.65

VAN GRAAN Stephanie 4.02.77, Shaft B/RSA :
1500 - 4:33.18, 3k - 9:50.6 (9:31.9-00)
VANNET Lisa 8.11.74, Edinburgh WM :
100 - 12.28w, 200 - 24.88 (24.53w-00),
400 - 56.3 (54.54-96)
VARTAN Jennie V40 7.12.60, Bishops Stortford :
Mar - 3:09:24
VAUGHAN Lucy 20.04.69, AF&D :
400 - 56.6, 800 - 2:03.9,
1500 - 4:30.2
VELDMAN Margaret 7.06.74, Sale/NED :
100 - 12.09w, 200 - 25.18mx (25.15-98), 100H - 15.30,
LJ - 5.80 (6.03w-00/5.94i-98/5.94-00)
VELVICK Kimberley U17 3.01.85, Ashford :
60 - 7.8i/7.85i (7.8i-00),
100 - 12.3w/12.4/12.50 (12.27-00),
200 - 24.84w/25.32i/25.4/25.57 (24.98-00)
VILJOEN Estle 8.07.70, Hercules Wimbledon/RSA :
Mar - 3:08:13, 3kW - 14:25.4, 5kW - 24:53.02,
5kWR - 24:13, 10kW - 52:18.23,
10kWR - 51:41, 20kW - 1:47:18
VOGEL Kiera U17 31.05.86, Liv.Pembroke Sefton :
1500 - 4:45.6 (4:42.42-00)
VOUSDEN Janet 25.11.68, Coventry Godiva :
PV - 3.30i/3.20 (3.20-00)
VUAGNIAUX Alison V40 31.05.60, City of Bath :
Mar - 3:05:09 (3:01:24-00)
VYSE Lorna U17 2.12.84, Woking :
1500 - 4:44.30

WAIN Alanna U17 27.04.85, City of Stoke :
300 - 40.6 (39.58-00)
WAINWRIGHT Ann V45 26.10.54, Cannock & Staff :
PV - 2.70
WAIT Claire U15 7.11.86, Shrewsbury :
PenG - 2676
WALCOTT Chloe U15 29.01.88, Sutton :
100 - 12.6
WALDRON Meghan U15 4.09.86, Horsham BS :
PenG - 2647
WALDROP Malgorzata 25.03.77, City of Glasgow :
(nee ROSTEK) 200 - 25.1 (24.17-99)
WALE Amanda 14.10.70, Wrexham :
Hep - 4037 (4546-98)
WALES Tina 2.11.77, Swindon :
800 - 2:12.20
WALKER Carly U15 30.08.87, Bournemouth :
LJ - 5.20
WALKER Danielle U13 17.03.89, Burnley :
1200 - 3:59.0, 1500 - 5:02.8
WALKER Helen Charlotte U23 12.10.80, Middlesb & C/
Sussex University : 400H - 64.35 (62.92-98)
WALKER Hilary C. V45 9.11.53, Serpentine :
100kR - 8:50:19 (7:50:09-93)
WALKER Juliet U17 5.10.84, WGreen & Ex L :
3k - 10:17.65
WALKER Kerry U17 5.08.85, Bedford & County :
3k - 10:22.7
WALKER Marcia 27.05.70, WSE&H :
TJ - 12.11
WALKER Mhairi U20 20.01.84, Livingston :
800 - 2:12.5, Hep - 4223
WALL Kimberly Jaclyn U20 21.04.83, Basildon :
100 - 11.9 (11.8-00/12.13-98),
200 - 24.28w/24.33 (24.04-00),
400 - 53.52, LJ - 5.50
WALLACE Ailsa 12.03.77, Cardiff/Oxford Univ :
HJ - 1.70 (1.73i/1.70-94)
WALLBANKS Carol U20 9.12.82, Border :
JT - 39.32 (42.73-00)
WALLER Ruth U20 6.03.84, Sale :
400H - 65.21
WALLIS Natalie U15 20.10.86, Newham & Essex B :
PenG - 2785
WALLS Sharon-Louise U17 9.10.84, Wigan :
300H - 46.3/46.33
WALSH Caroline Elizabeth U23 29.04.80, S B/Loughbro :
3k - 9:45.5 (9:13.4mx/9:20.38-99)
WALSH Kate U17 28.01.85, Dacorum & Tring :
HJ - 1.64
WALSH Sarah U17 28.01.85, Dacorum & Tring :
Hepl - 3879 (3972-00)
WALTERS Kirsty Lynn U17 6.09.84, City of Glasgow :
HT - 37.70 (40.72-00)
WALTERS Mhairi Lee U23 19.06.81, City of Glasgow :
SP - 13.62, DT - 38.68, HT - 58.31
WARD Emma U20 2.01.82, City of Stoke/Staffs Univ :
800 - 2:06.9 (2:06.02-00), 1500 - 4:13.38,
3k - 9:30.0 (9:27.63-00)
WARD Jennifer 22.09.78, City of Glasgow :
800 - 2:05.96 (2:05.10-00)
WARD Stacey U17 16.01.85, Basildon :
1500 - 4:42.61 (4:39.6-00), 3k - 10:15.16
WARD Victoria 19.06.72, WGreen & Ex L :
200 - 24.97w/25.1/25.15i (23.84w/24.07-98),
400 - 55.16 (53.58-00)
WARMINGTON Claire U17 7.06.85, Trafford :
100 - 12.4, 300 - 41.4/41.48
WARREN Nathalie U23 28.08.81, Walton/London Un :
PV - 3.00
WARREN Sally 29.01.78, Steyning :
10kWR - 54:35 (51:20-98)
WATERS Christina U15 4.06.87, Wirral :
75HG - 11.25w/11.3/11.37
WATERS Elizabeth 19.02.77, Coventry Godiva :
400H - 64.20 (62.69-98)
WATKINS Charlotte U15 13.02.88, Havering :
1500 - 4:48.39
WATSON Anna U20 30.04.82, City of Glas/Glas Univ :
PV - 3.00i/2.90 (3.03-98)
WATSON Louise Carole 13.12.71, Med & Maid :
5k - 17:28.7 (15:57.06-95),
10k - 35:41.99 (33:21.46-96),
HMar - 76:56 (75:45-00), Mar - 2:43:49
WATTON Louise U15 30.10.86, Wimborne :
SPG - 10.82, DT - 30.22, JT - 41.44
WATTS Katy Louise U23 25.03.81, Basingst & MH/
Brunel Univ : JT - 46.29
WAUGH Kathryn 20.02.73, Liverpool H :
1500 - 4:31.74 (4:31.2-96), 3k - 9:45.1
WEALE Rebecca 7.02.78, Yeovil Olympiads :
HJ - 1.70
WEBB Elizabeth U20 16.12.83, Cardiff :
TJ - 11.04
WEBB Helen Julie U23 14.04.80, Halesowen :
PV - 3.00i/3.00 (3.20-00)
WEBB Lauren U17 17.11.85, Sutton & District :
300 - 40.83, 400 - 57.8
WEBB Lisa Jane V35 9.10.65, Shaftesbury Barnet :
3k - 9:42.9 (9:11.45-88)
WEBB Shirley Catherine U23 28.09.81, NSP/C of Ed/
Edinburgh U : HT - 54.37
WEBBER Lucy Kate 5.02.72, Belgrave :
PV - 4.00A/4.00 (4.04-00)
WEBSTER Michelle U17 18.04.85, Bedford & County :
100 - 12.49
WEBSTER Victoria U17 24.12.85, Gateshead :
300 - 41.0

WEEKES Hannah U15 14.12.87, Stevenage & NH :
PenG - 2672
WEEKES Jade U17 15.11.84, Dartford :
Hepl - 3822 (3846-00)
WEIR Jessica U17 3.10.84, Wilts Sch :
SP - 10.36 (10.48-00), DT - 32.74 (33.48-99)
WELCH Claire U13 3.09.88, Med & Maid :
70HM - 11.9
WELLS Louisa U17 30.12.84, West Suffolk :
100 - 12.2/12.40, 200 - 25.4
WELLSTEAD Sarah U23 22.10.79, Sutton & District :
LJ - 6.14w/6.10, TJ - 11.84w/11.41 (11.63-97)
WENHAM Carley Ann U15 14.03.88, Crawley :
60 - 8.00i, 100 - 12.03w/12.1/12.29,
200 - 25.0/25.95
WERRETT Gemma Elizabeth Harvie U17 15.03.86,
Cannock & Stafford : 80HI - 11.9/12.09
WEST Jennifer U23 13.09.79, Ealing,Southall & Mx :
(nee AYERO) HT - 39.63, JT - 45.81
WEST Tracey V35 23.05.65, Worksop :
Mar - 3:07:00
WESTLEY Abby U15 15.07.87, Hallamshire :
800 - 2:15.15, 1500 - 4:39.95
WESTWOOD Fiona U23 27.02.81, Wakefield :
100 - 12.18w (13.3-97), LJ - 5.93 (6.02-00)
WHEELER Dani U17 12.10.85, Dacorum & Tring :
SP - 11.04
WHIGHAM Lisa U23 14.08.80, Vict PAAC/Strathcl U :
400 - 55.89, 800 - 2:12.85
WHIGHAM Sara U20 7.10.83, Victoria Park AAC :
100 - 12.04w/12.09, 200 - 24.6w/25.0/25.07
WHILEY Lesley V40 14.05.60, Reading RR :
Mar - 2:59:31 (2:58:21-00)
WHITCOMBE Andrea 8.06.71, Parkside :
3k - 9:53.5 (8:58.59-91), 10MR - 58:32 (57:05-00)
WHITE Kendra 8.04.68, Quakers :
100kR - 9:27:15
WHITE Rebecca U23 5.06.80, Sale/Bath Univ :
60 - 7.64i (7.55i-98),
100 - 11.82w/11.9/11.98 (11.45w-98),
LJ - 5.84 (5.87w/5.85-00), TJ - 13.09w/12.85
WHITEHEAD Margaret Louise 26.03.75, Swansea :
200 - 24.71w/25.0/25.26 (24.03w-98/24.1-93/24.24-97),
400 - 55.54 (53.34-99)
WHITEHEAD Ruth 14.01.72, Bingley :
Mar - 3:06:47 (3:04:59-99)
WHITLOCK Janine 11.08.73, Trafford :
100 - 11.75w/12.14 (11.56-99), PV - 4.40, LJ - 5.95
WHITMORE Hannah U20 24.02.84, Charnwood :
1500 - 4:31.66
WHITTAKER Emma U17 31.10.85, Frome :
1500 - 4:37.74
WHITTAKER Louise U20 29.11.82, Sale :
800 - 2:11.63 (2:10.89-00), 1500 - 4:27.17,
3k - 9:58.86
WHITTER Emma U23 20.07.80, Herne Hill :
60 - 7.62i (7.56i-00), 200 - 24.22i (23.73w/24.08-99)
WHITTINGHAM Laura U17 6.06.86, Wakefield :
JT - 36.31
WICKHAM Charlotte U17 21.06.85, Gateshead :
800 - 2:16.1, 1500 - 4:43.8 (4:43.1-00), 3k - 10:10.52
WILDER Kelley E. 30.07.71, City of Glas/Oxf U/USA :
1500 - 4:32.28, 3k - 9:40.49 (9:36.51-00)
WILDING Helen 25.10.76, Trafford :
SP - 13.50 (13.88-95), DT - 42.06 (42.90-95),
HT - 50.27
WILHELMY Sarah U23 2.02.80, Southend :
100 - 11.24w/11.44, 200 - 22.84w/23.27 (23.23-98)
WILKINS Melani Dawn 18.01.73, WSE&H :
60H - 8.15i, 100H - 13.08w/13.24 (13.17-00)
WILKINSON Chloe U17 16.12.84, Shaftesbury Barn :
1500 - 4:40.15 (4:39.56-00),
3k - 10:04.51 (9:58.6mx/10:04.5-00)
WILKINSON Jo 2.05.73, Bedford & County :
1500 - 4:22.34, 3k - 9:41.5 (9:37.0mx-00),
HMar - 75:01
WILKINSON Sarah 2.01.70, Salford :
5KR - 16:37 (15:53-00), 5MR - 26:44 (26:29-00)
WILKINSON Tanya 1.04.70, City of Stoke :
400 - 56.3, 400H - 60.8 (60.2/60.32-98)
WILLEY Laura U15 22.10.86, Wigan :
100 - 12.6, LJ - 5.20w
WILLIAMS Aileen U23 14.06.81, Ayr S/Glasgow Univ :
400 - 56.65, 400H - 65.64
WILLIAMS Angela U23 13.05.81, Medway :
LJ - 5.69, TJ - 12.35
WILLIAMS Carrie U15 9.02.87, Carmarthen :
JT - 32.52
WILLIAMS Courtney U13 8.03.89, Jersey :
HJ - 1.45, LJ - 4.71, PenM - 2218
WILLIAMS Donna Maria 7.10.78, Sale :
DT - 41.55 (48.08-96)
WILLIAMS Elizabeth 2.06.77, Walton :
200 - 24.19w/24.78 (24.1-99),
400 - 55.46 (54.53-99)
WILLIAMS Helen 2.06.77, Walton :
100 - 12.0/12.10 (11.99w-98),
200 - 25.1/25.26 (24.49w/24.8-98/25.07-95)
WILLIAMS Helen U20 13.01.83, Vale Royal :
TJ - 11.36
WILLIAMS Kate U20 10.05.84, Southend :
PV - 2.80i/2.70 (2.80-00)
WILLIAMS Kathryn S. 10.11.77, Swansea :
400H - 62.81 (60.21-96)
WILLIAMS Leasa U20 10.05.84, Southend :
PV - 3.00
WILLIAMS Lisa S. 11.04.78, Telford :
100H - 15.2 (14.81-96)
WILLIAMS Nadia U23 17.11.81, Shaft B/Luton Univ :
LJ - 5.84, TJ - 11.40
WILLIAMS Rebecca U13 18.03.89, Newport :
100 - 13.1
WILLIAMS Sharon Bernadette 20.05.70, Thames VH :
60 - 7.72i (7.42i-96), 100 - 12.1/12.17w (11.53-95),
200 - 24.9/25.06i (23.80w/23.9/23.91-95)
WILLIAMS Susan 2.06.77, Walton :
100 - 11.83 (11.61w-98/11.79-00),
200 - 23.76w/23.79 (23.59-99), 400H - 60.84
WILLIAMS Victoria U23 11.04.81, Yate/UWIC :
60H - 8.95i, 100H - 14.42w/14.68,
Hep - 4194 (4289-98)
WILLS Hayley U17 18.01.85, Hertford & Ware :
800 - 2:15.1
WILSON Aileen J. U20 30.03.84, Peterborough :
100H - 14.20, HJ - 1.87, Hep - 4857
WILSON Amy U23 31.12.80, Ipswich :
SP - 12.50 (13.03-99)
WILSON Beverley 26.03.67, Cleethorpes :
Mar - 2:55:58
WILSON Caroline U17 14.09.84, East Grinstead :
300 - 41.29
WILSON Cassie 24.09.77, Bingley/Loughbro :
HT - 43.18
WILSON Claire U17 7.11.85, Shetland :
800 - 2:16.90
WILSON Donna U15 1.10.86, Erme Valley :
HJ - 1.60
WILSON Katy U13 1.09.88, Birtley :
SPM - 9.39
WILSON Sharon 27.10.74, Dunfermline & W Fife :
100 - 11.96, 200 - 25.1 (25.0-00/25.77w-96)
WILSON Zoe 28.08.76, Birchfield :
100 - 11.98 (11.52w/11.66-00),
200 - 25.0 (23.74w-00/23.91-99)
WISE Joanne 15.03.71, Coventry Godiva :
LJ - 6.46w/6.35A (6.76-99)

WITCOMBE Catriona E. M. U13 6.12.88, Winchester :
800 - 2:25.1, 1500 - 5:05.8
WITTON Nikki 30.09.72, Newport :
PV - 2.80i/2.70 (2.85-00)
WOOD Hannah U23 17.11.81, Solihull & S H/Sheff U :
200 - 25.1, 400 - 55.95i/57.0 (55.6/56.06-00),
400H - 59.55
WOOD Jennifer V40 23.02.57, Spenborough :
PV - 2.90 (3.20-97), HT - 39.61 (44.93-98)
WOOD Kerrie V35 8.01.66, Stockport :
Mar - 2:49:12
WOOD Laura 31.10.78, Trafford :
DT - 40.09 (41.28-98), HT - 42.06
WOOD Louisa U23 31.10.80, Bedford & County :
800 - 2:11.7
WOOD Louise U20 13.05.83, Braintree :
TJ - 11.19
WOODLEY Tara U17 25.12.84, City of Norwich :
DT - 33.57
WOODMAN Amy U17 1.11.84, Bristol :
100 - 12.4w (12.5/12.53w-99/12.56-00),
LJ - 5.71w/5.67
WOODS Danielle U17 2.10.84, Liverpool H :
800 - 2:12.39, 1500 - 4:29.74, 3k - 10:22.4
WOODS Jennie U20 28.01.84, Liverpool H :
HJ - 1.65 (1.66-98)
WOODS Suzanne 29.12.76, Basildon :
PV - 3.10i (3.20i/3.20-98)
WOOFF Emma U17 21.05.85, Wigan :
LJ - 5.46, TJ - 11.42i/10.98
WOOLGAR Deborah Caroline V35 10.03.65, Worthing :
SP - 12.63 (14.18-89), DT - 36.36 (40.92-91)
WOOLLEY Jessica U23 19.01.80, Bristol :
1500 - 4:29.04, 3k - 9:44.41i
WOOLRICH Sharon 1.05.76, City of Portsmouth :
HJ - 1.68 (1.70-94)
WOOTTON Katrina U17 2.09.85, Bedford & County :
400 - 57.5, 800 - 2:08.88, 1500 - 4:24.70
WORSEY Helen U20 29.08.82, Birchfield/Loughbro :
100H - 13.66
WRAY Josephine Anne U13 29.07.89, West Suffolk :
JTM - 26.46
WRAY Sharon U20 8.10.82, Oswestry :
SP - 11.68 (11.71-00), DT - 36.09
WRIGHT Claire U20 9.09.83, Liverpool H :
HJ - 1.74 (1.77-00)
WRIGHT Dawn-Alice 20.01.76, Coventry G/Brunel U :
PV - 3.10 (3.10-94)
WRIGHT Jennifer U20 21.09.83, Bracknell :
TJ - 11.04
WRIGHT Joy 22.06.75, Herne Hill :
800 - 2:09.3
WRIGHT Lucy 17.11.69, Leeds :
5KR - 16:45 (16:33-00)
WRIGHT Melanie V35 5.04.64, Nuneaton :
5kWR - 26:15 (23:24-95)
WRIGHT Rebecca 20.12.77, WSE&H/Cambridge Un :
400H - 63.7 (61.38-00)
WU Grace 10.02.71, Serpentine :
Mar - 3:08:30

YARD Louise U13 21.01.89, Havering :
DTM - 23.77
YARNOLD Elizabeth U13 31.10.88, Tonbridge :
SPM - 9.05
YATES Helena U17 12.09.85, Holmfirth :
3k - 10:39.06mx
YATES Natalie U13 20.11.88, Mansfield :
600 - 1:45.5, 800 - 2:23.77, 1k - 3:05.9,
1200 - 3:51.1, 1500 - 4:57.9
YELLING Elizabeth 5.12.74, Bedford & County :
1500 - 4:15.01, 3k - 8:57.3mx/9:20.23 (9:15.25-98),
5MR - 26:58 (26:09-00), 10k - 33:45.58 (33:07.9-00),
10kR - 33:20 (33:10-00), HMar - 71:29
YELLING Hayley 3.01.74, WSE&H :
1500 - 4:23.8, 3k - 8:58.98mx/9:03.5+,
5k - 15:19.12, 5KR - 16:23 (16:20-99),
5MR - 27:34 (26:42-99)
YELLOP Lyndsay Victoria 18.08.78, City of Norwich :
400H - 65.3
YEOMANS Susan V45 16.03.53, Watford :
PV - 2.72
YULE Helen V35 10.09.65, Lliswerry :
Mar - 3:04:32

ZAWADA Sarah U20 9.04.82, AF&D :
100 - 12.1 (11.87w-97/12.0-98/12.25-95)
ZENNER Helen U20 15.08.82, Team Sol/Oxford Univ :
3k - 9:53.42

Obituary 2000

The deaths were recorded in 2000 of the following notable figures in British Athletics:

George Bailey (b. 29 Apr 1906). 1st Empire Games steeplechase 1930. 5th 1932 Olympics steeplechase (after UK record 9:16.0 in heats). AAA 10 miles champion 1933.

Lyn Bevan (b. 31 Aug 1932) on 1 September. Welsh cross-country champion 1954-5.

Ken Brookman (b. 1926) on 8 September. Notable coach.

Madge Carruthers (b.1913) in December. President of the Scottish Women's AAA 1973-6. Scottish women's team manager Commonwealth Games 1970.

Cecil Dale. GB team manager for many years.

Margaret Elgie (b.5 Apr 1935) on 21 November. Secretary of Welsh Women's AAA. Welsh Commonwealth Games team manager 1986 and 1990 and administrator for many British teams.

John Hedgethorne (b. 25 Sep 1931) on 21 January. Editor of *Race walking record*. Set a 50km walk best of 4:52:29 in 1973.

Edgar Mellor on 1 September. 1st in AAA 4x440y 1937.

Percy Price 4th RWA 50km walk 1950.

John Wilson **'Paddy' Proctor** (b. 3 Sep 1923) on 26 October. 5th European 50km walk 1950. RWA champion at 50km walk 1950, 20 miles 1952.

Mike Rawson (b. 26 May 1934) on 26 October. 1958 European champion at 800m and Empire Games bronze at 880y. AAA champion 880y 1958, indoor 440y 1965.

Dr **Alan Richardson** MBE in December. Secretary Northern Counties Division 1 (North Esat) for 20 years.

Phil Romaine (b.23 Sep 1946) in April. National Youths cross-country champion 1963 (and 2nd 1964).

Norman Stang a leading official, died as a result of being hit by a hammer at the U20s.

Obituary 2001

Colin Andrews (b. 1 Sep 1931 Cleckheaton) in Clevedon on 27 January. AAA decathlon champion 1958-60, in the last of these he set a British record of 6176 (1950 tables, 6481 on the 1985 tables). Five internationals 1959-62.

Gerry Batty

Simon Brooks (b. 17 Dec 1929) at Ampleforth Abbey in September. He set a British record for 220y hurdles with 24.2 for Oxford/Cambridge v AAA in June 1950 and ran 24.0 for a course measured at 219.5y at the Cambridge Cupper's meeting in February 1951 on a track that may have been downhill.

Ruth Christmas (b. 12 Nov 1904) in April. One of the pioneers of women's middle distance running. A member of London Olympiades, she set her first British record in 1929, clocking 2:23.8 for 800m and in 1930 was second to Gladys Lunn in the WAAA 880y, the winner establishing a world record of 2:18.2 and Christmas running an estimated 2:21.8. In 1932 she set a highly unofficial world best for the mile of 5:27.5 from scratch in a handicap race in London, timed by coaches and journalists. She won the WAAA 800m title (2.23.0) in 1933. Later she married a Frenchman, becoming known as Ruth Christmas-Paysant, won French titles at 800 in 1935 and cross country in 1936 and represented France against Italy. She was the aunt of novelist Simon Raven.

Jerry Cornes (b. 23 Mar 1910 Darjeeling, India) on 19 June. He was third in the Empire Games mile in 1930 and in 1934 when he ran his pb of 4:13.6e. He ran the third leg for the British team which set a world 4x1500m relay record of 15:55.6 in Cologne in 1931 and the following year took the Olympic silver medal at 1500 in a British record of 3:52.6. In Berlin 1936 he finished sixth in his fastest ever time of 3:51.4, another UK record. He was AAA mile champion in 1932.

Ron Goodman on 6 July at the age of 89. A member of Herne Hill Harriers, he was a leading official in Britain for many years and was president of the AAA 1984-7.

Norman Horrell on 2 December. Welsh champion at 880y 1958 and cross-country 1959 and 1961-2.

John Jewell on 18 August at the age of 89. A founder member of the Road Runners Club and former president of South London Harriers, he was for many years editor of the RRC's informative newsletter and he was a pioneer of accurate course measurement for road races.

John Legge on 18 February at the age of 70. Chairman of the AAA Road Running Committee, team manager, and a hugely enthusiastic proponent of ultra-distance running.

Kim McDonald (b. 27 Sep 1956) was found dead from a suspected heart attack on 7 November while on holiday in Brisbane. He was founder and chief executive of Kim McDonald International Management (KIM) and one of the world's foremost athletes' agents. He had personal bests of 4:02.1 for the mile (1983), 7:56.01 for 3000 (1979), 13:49.1 for 5000 (1979), 28:58.1 for 10,000 (1982) and 2:19:34 for the marathon (1981).

Bill Marlow a former AAA National Coach for the Midlands, at the age of 82. His most successful protegé was Peter Radford, who he coached from a schoolboy of 16 to a world record setter at 200m/220y and Olympic 100m bronze medallist in 1960.

Ernie Pomfret (b. 18 Apr 1941 Haswell, Co Durham,) of cancer on 1 May. A member of Houghton Harriers, he made 19 international appearances for Britain at the steeplechase 1963-7 and, after 3rd in 1962, was 2nd at the AAAs each year 1963-7. He was 10th in the 1964 Olympics, 6th in the 1966 Commonwealth Games and 12th in the 1966 Europeans. pbs: 3000m 8:10.4 (1967), 2M 8:48.8 (1967), 5000m 14:05.4 (1970), 2000mSt 5:33.6 (1967, UK best), 3000mSt 8:37.0 (1967).

Bill Roberts (b. 5 April 1912 Salford) on 5 December. He won an Olympic gold medal at 4x400m in 1936 after a pb 46.87 for fourth in the individual 400m. He competed at a second Olympics in 1948, when he was the British team captain; at 36 he remains Britain's oldest ever 400m international. His international career began at the 1934 Empire Games, with silver at 440y. He did not run in the relay then, but took a silver in 1938 when he was the 440y individual champion and also 6th at 220y (pb 21.5 in heat). He missed the 1938 Europeans but returned after War service in the RAF to earn a relay silver in 1946. He was AAA champion at 440y in 1935 and 1937 and won six of his eight individual races in international matches 1935-46.

Louise Schramm (b. 18 Dec 1971) was killed in a car accident on 20 February. An international pole vaulter with a best of 3.75 in 1998, she was a member of Epsom & Ewell AC and was a doctor.

Jack Stubbs (b. 19 Dec 1904) on 27 November. Well-known as a chief timekeeper, he had been a notable cross-country and road runner in a long career for South London Harriers 1926-48. He was 5th at 5000m at the World Student Games at Darmstadt in 1930.

Stan West (b. 13 Feb 1913) on 13 August. He represented Britain seven times at high jump between 1933 and 1945, including at the 1936 Olympic Games, and was AAA champion indoors and out (in a pb of 1.90) in 1935.

Dave Williams Welsh team manager at two Commonwealth Games, and coach to a great many Welsh MD stars inc Plain, Hayward, Fowles, Maplestone, and more recently advisor to Tanni Grey.

Information provided by Peter Matthews

AMENDMENTS TO BRITISH ATHLETICS 2001

From Peter Matthews & Martin Rix and others

INTERNATIONAL RESULTS

p.113 European Cup: women's HT: Melinte was disqualified, so move 2-8 up to 1-7. And amend women's score to: 1. RUS 124, 2. GER 111, 3. FRA 87, 4. ITA 79, 5. GBR 78, 6. ROM 72, 7. UKR 71, 8. GRE 56.

p.117 It was not France v GB 'B' but v ENGLAND 'A'.

p.124 RWA 20k at Holme Pierrepont (not Nottingham)

Add AAA Road 10km at Bradford, 10 Sep: Men: 1. Julius Kimtai KEN 29:06, 2. Mike Openshaw 29:13, 3. Matt Vaux-Harvey 29:31; Women: 1. Liz Yelling 33:10, 2. Sarah Wilkinson 33:20, 3. Birhan Dagne 34:08

CHAMPIONSHIP RESULTS

p.124 RWA 35k/Women's 10k on 6 May

p.126 Men: WAL 5000 - Adam Jones (different athlete to Andres),
Women: 5000 Ruth Schofield 19:12.0, w3000W - Philippa Reilly; NIR w400H - Finnegan

p.127 South women Hept - Stares, 5000W Sangvik NOR; Midland LJ -Timothy Sercombe

p.128 U20 3000 Richard Ward 8:24.73, JT Phill Sharpe, Women 5000W O'Keeffe
U17 100H Harmse RSA, Women TJ 11.70/legal (+1.2) Parker

MERIT RANKINGS

WMar Dixon prev. pb 2:50:45 '99 W400H Brown prev. pb 62.2 '99

WSP Massey confirmed as UK – and ranked 8th, rest move down WHJ Shaw 4th ECp

MEN 2000

100m: 10.85 Fifton +1.0 1s2 30 Jul; U15: add 11.1 Farenden 1 Bingham 28 Jul
200m: 20.76 Benjamin 20 Oct, 20.77 19 Oct, 20.88 Grant 20 Oct; U17: 22.4 Farenden 1 Bingham 28 Jul ; U15 add 23.02/+0.5 David Vass 2r2 Watford 26 Jul; U13: 25.5 hand timed Ferriby
400m: 48.99 Davolls 8 Jul, 49.0 Notman 14.10.75
800m: 1:54.20 Rusbridge 13.05.82, 1:58.65i Davenport - position 2nd
3000m: 8:53.66 Snow 7 Jun (position in race unknown), 9:03.54 Humphries 6 Sep, 9:50.7 McCulloch 3r2
3000mSt: Foreign: 9:12.48 Von Grot
70mH: 11.98w Douglas 1P 2 Sep
80mH (U13): add 13.22/-0.6 Douglas 3 Grangemouth 17 Jun
HJ: Foreign: Tyron Peacock 16.12.76 3= Stellenbosch, RSA 4 Mar
PV: 4.81 Penk - at Connah's Quay
LJ: 7.01 Baptist (no e) 19.10.78
TJ: U15: 12.16 Grant Clements 27.1.86 1 Barking 10 Sep (Hertford & Ware)
SP (U13): 12.47i overage was Hall not Birch
HT: 65.31 Bown 2 Loughborough 12 Sep
Dec: 6470 Taylor – LJ 6.50
3000mW: 14:46.81 Davis 30.8.87
5000mW: 22:48.91 Parker etc. 30 Jul
20kmW: venue Holme Pierrepont (and in women's 20kmW)
30kW: add 2:33:49(20M) Mark Easton 1 Colchester 2 Apr
50kW: 3:57:10 Maddocks etc. Sint-Oedenrode is HOL not BEL
4x400: U20 Club teams: 3:18.76 Shaftesbury Barnet (B Gibb, J Collins, C Erskine, G McEwan) 1 Ljubljana, SLO 23 Sep

WOMEN 2000

100m: 11.98 –0.2 Stephanie Douglas
150m: 19.2 Simpson also 1 Ayr 21 May
200m: 25.08i Court V35 at time
1500m: 4:50.22 Isabelle Stoate
3000m: 9:18.59 Hind b. 31.7.79 (& 1500, 5000, 10k)
2000mSt: 6:36.49 Krzywicki 2'6"?
400mH Foreign: Michelle Carey b. 20.2.81 (also 400m)
PV: 3.85A Murray-Jessee 1 El Paso, USA 9 Dec; 3.20 Leyshon 2nd. 3.10 Hunter 2nd
LJ: 5.29 Barrett
TJ: add 10.77 Angela Barratt 25.12.85 1 London (TB) 16 Sep
DT: 49.69 Jacqui McKernan 1.7.65 1 Belfast – May, 45.58 Macpherson
HT: 67.44 Shaw 4th at Gateshead; 42.02 King 2 Jul, 41.55 Gilbert 1 Corby 27 Jun (from 40.83), 38.50 Coombs V35 31.12.61
HT(U15): Chalmers 42.18 1 Elgin 22 Aug
JT: 41.34 King - position 5th, 39.55 Mathews, 38.67 Redd 7 Jul, 34.84 Lawrence 26 Aug
3000W: 12:59.0mx Kehler, 14:08.52 Menendez (and in other walks lists), 14:10.9 Cattermole 1 Perth 22 Oct
5000W: 25:11.33 Warren
10000W: add 50:08.0+ (no judges) Menendez m Plymouth 9 Jan (listed as road)
20kW: 1:39:28 Kehler etc. 12 Mar

2nd IAAF WORLD YOUTH CHAMPIONSHIPS

Debrecen, HUN 11 - 15 July 2001

These championships are now established as a true World Championships for young athletes, the age group is Under 18 in the year of competition. Britain did well with a relatively small team. All medallists are included to show the very high level required at every event.

MEN

100 Metres wind –0.2 (13 Jul)

1.	Darrel Brown	TRI	10.31
2.	Willie Hodge	USA	10.41
3.	Jonathan Wade	USA	10.53
6s2	**Rikki Fifton**		**10.89**

200 Metres wind –1.1 (15 Jul)

1.	Jonathan Wade	USA	20.95
2.	Michael Grant	USA	21.30
3.	Dion Rodriguez	TRI	21.36
5.	**Lawrence Oboh**		**21.66**

400 Metres (14 Jul)

1.	Karol Grzegorczyk	POL	46.90
2.	Piotr Kedzia	POL	47.12
3.	Jermaine Gonzales	JAM	47.51
4.	**Ryan Preddy**		**47.80**

800 Metres (15 Jul)

1.	Salam Al-Badri	QAT	1:50.15
2.	Cosmas Rono	KEN	1:50.35
3.	Liao Fu-Pin	TPE	1:51.35
8.	**Christopher Stoves**		**1:52.73**
6s1	**Michael Rimmer**		**1:52.38**

1500 Metres (15 Jul)

1.	Isaac Songok	KEN	3:36.78
2.	Sameuel Dadi	ETH	3:39.78
3.	Abdul R. Suleiman	QAT	3:42.03

3000 Metres (14 Jul)

1.	Markos Geneti	ETH	7:55.82
2.	David Kilel	KEN	7:56.95
3.	James Kwalia	KEN	7:57.71

2000 Metres Steeplechase (15 Jul)

1.	David Kirwa	KEN	5:33.40
2.	Brimin Kipruto	KEN	5:36.81
3.	Abrham Kebeto	ETH	5:37.76
9h1	**Peter Kellie**		**6:00.52**
11h2	**Paul Moores**		**6:13.33**

110 Metres Hurdles 3' wind 0.2 (14 Jul)

1.	Nassim Messjian	QAT	13.27
2.	Marthinus v d Vyer	RSA	13.35
3.	Eddy Delepine	FRA	13.39

400 Metres Hurdles (14 Jul)

1.	Amine Alozen	SYR	50.25
2.	Jonathan Walker	USA	51.32
3.	Kenji Narisako	JPN	52.09

High Jump (14 Jul)

1.	Aleksey Dmitrik	RUS	2.23
2.	James Watson	AUS	2.21
3.	Aliaksandr Plisko	BLR	2.19
12.	**Chuka Enih-Snell**		**2.05**

Pole Vault (15 Jul)

1.	Artyom Kuptsov	RUS	5.15
2.	Vincent Favretto	FRA	5.15
3.	Go Kishita	JPN	5.00

Long Jump (13 Jul)

1.	Thiago Carahyba Dias	BRA	7.72
2.	Abdulla Al-Walid	QAT	7.62
3.	Andrew Howe-Besozzi	ITA	7.61

Triple Jump (15 Jul)

1.	**Jonathan Moore**		**16.36**
2.	David Girard	CUB	16.33
3.	Osniel Tosca	CUB	15.67

Shot 5 kg (13 Jul)

1.	Georgi Ivanov	BUL	19.73
2.	Yasser Ibrahim	EGY	19.58
3.	Lee Min-Won	KOR	19.57

Discus 1.5 kg (14 Jul)

1.	Khaled Al-Suwaidi	QAT	62.67
2.	Robert Harting	GER	62.04
3.	Omad El Ghafaly	EGY	61.06

Hammer 5 kg (15 Jul)

1.	Juzsef Horvath	HUN	80.11
2.	Werner Smit	RSA	79.48
3.	Kirill Ikonnikov	RUS	77.75

Javelin 700 g (15 Jul)

1.	Teemu Wirkkala	FIN	76.18
2.	Hamad Khalifa	QAT	73.56
3.	Tero Jarvenpaa	FIN	68.85

Octathlon (12/13 Jul)

1.	Rene Oruman	EST	6219
2.	Essa Mufarrah	KSA	6024
3.	Jason Dudley	AUS	5997

10000 Metres Walk (14 Jul)

1.	Vladimir Kanaykin	RUS	42:55.75
2.	Mikalai Seredovich	BLR	43:44.32
3.	Francisco Flores	MEX	43:53.13
23.	**Cameron Smith**		**47:42.76**
dnf	**Luke Finch**		

Relay 100, 200, 300, 400 Metres (15 Jul)

1.	Poland	1:50.46
2.	United States	1:50.90
3.	South Africa	1:51.35

WOMEN

100 Metres wind 0.5 (13 Jul)

1.	Allyson Felix	USA	11.57
2.	Kerron Stewart	JAM	11.72
3.	Zuzana Kosov	CZE	11.83

200 Metres wind 0.3 (15 Jul)

1.	Angel Perkins	USA	23.07
2.	**Amy Spencer**		**23.45**
3.	Zuzana Kosov	CZE	23.98
6s2	**Eleanor Caney**		**24.66**

400 Metres (14 Jul)

1.	Stephanie Smith	USA	52.19
2.	Jerrika Chapple	USA	52.80
3.	Anneisha McLaughlin	JAM	53.35

800 Metres (15 Jul)

1.	Cherotich Kipkorir Ruto	KEN	2:05.50
2.	Veronika Plesarov	CZE	2:06.01
3.	Carlene Robinson	JAM	2:06.18
4.	**Danielle Barnes**		**2:06.51**
8.	**Jemma Simpson**		**2:11.38**

1500 Metres (15 Jul)

1.	Georgie Clarke	AUS	4:14.08
2.	Florence Kyalo	KEN	4:15.71
3.	Sentayehu Ejigu	ETH	4:17.51
5.	**Zoe Jelbert**		**4:20.56**
4h2	**Faye Fullerton**		**4:27.45**

3000 Metres (14 Jul)

1.	Sally Chepyego	KEN	9:09.05
2.	Mestawat Tufa	ETH	9:11.60
3.	Fridah Domongole	KEN	9:12.70

100 Metres Hurdles 2'6" wind 0.4 (13 Jul)

1.	Kathrin Geissler	GER	13.49
2.	Ashley Lodree	USA	13.75
3.	Carla Fick	RSA	13.75

400 Metres Hurdles (14 Jul)

1.	Camille Robinson	JAM	58.72
2.	Kimberly Crow	AUS	59.28
3.	Olga Nikolayeva	RUS	59.41
5.	**Faye Harding**		**60.21**
6h1	**Natalie Kydd**		**63.59**

High Jump (14 Jul)

1.	**Aileen Wilson**		**1.87**
2.	Petrina Price	AUS	1.81
3.	Lavern Spencer	LCA	1.81

Pole Vault (14 Jul)

1.	Silke Spiegelburg	GER	4.00
2.	Aleksandra Kiryashova	RUS	4.00
3.	Anna Olko	POL	3.95

Long Jump (13 Jul)

1.	Shermin Oksuz	AUS	6.41
2.	Elena Anghelescu	ROM	6.32
3.	Angela Dies	GER	6.03
17Q	**Symone Belle**		**5.62**

Triple Jump (13 Jul)

1.	Alina Popescu	ROM	13.76
2.	Svetlana Bolshakova	RUS	13.32
3.	Michelle Sanford	USA	13.22

Shot (14 Jul)

1.	Valerie Adams	NZL	16.87
2.	Michelle Carter	USA	15.23
3.	Yullia Leantsiuk	BLR	15.08
19Q	**Frances Miller**		**11.88**

Discus (13 Jul)

1.	Ma Xuejun	CHN	54.93
2.	Darya Pishchalnikova	RUS	49.37
3.	Amarachi Ukabam	USA	46.13

Hammer (14 Jul)

1.	Andrea Keri	HUN	59.86
2.	Berta Castells	ESP	59.65
3.	Maria Smaliachkova	BLR	59.16
15Q	**Frances Miller**		**48.94**

Javelin (14 Jul)

1.	Kimberley Mickle	AUS	51.83
2.	Justine Robbeson	RSA	51.54
3.	Andrea Kvetova	CZE	51.49
20Q	**Samantha Redd**		**41.36**

Heptathlon (14/15 Jul)

1.	Annett Wichmann	GER	5470
2.	Christine Schulz	GER	5346
3.	Amandine Constantin	FRA	5296

5000 Metres Walk (13 Jul)

1.	Jiang Kun	CHN	22:49.21
2.	Ksenia Ischeykina	RUS	22:58.43
3.	Snaizhana Yurchanka	BLR	23:28.51
15.	**Sophie Hales**		**26:35.46**

Relay 100, 200, 300, 400 Metres (15 Jul)

1.	United States	2:03.83
2.	Jamaica	2:07.45
3.	Romania	2:09.70

Data from Mark Butler

Late Information

A 'new' British athlete has appeared at university in the USA. Add to 2001 women's lists.

Shot

14.84	Ade Oshinowo	U23	12.02.80	1	Champaign, USA	11 May

Discus

47.98	Ade Oshinowo	U23	12.02.80	1	Indiana, USA	21 Apr

Hammer

47.86	Ade Oshinowo	U23	12.02.80		Bloomington, USA	18 May

Other Publications

Commonwealth Games

Umbra will publish in June the most comprehensive book ever on athletics at the Commonwealth Games. Every single known performance will be recorded together with an index of every athlete to have competed at the Games. This book will be unique in its coverage of the Games.

To order use the contacts listed previously or follow the links from www.umbra.co.uk